BRITAIN AND THE GREAT WAR, 1914-1918

BRITAIN AND THE GREAT WAR, 1914-1918

A Subject Bibliography of Some Selected Aspects

Second Edition

Compiled by
Barry Wintour

Greenengle
Publishing

Published by Greenengle Publishing

Copyright © 2014 by Barry J. C. Wintour
All rights reserved.

ISBN 978-0-9928081-0-5

CONTENTS

INTRODUCTION .... **VIII**

PART 1: GENERAL BACKGROUND WORKS 9

1. Broad Perspectives 9
   1.1 General 9
   1.2 Britain 11

2. Histories and Studies of the Great War 13
   2.1 General Aspects 13
   2.2 Particular Aspects 15

PART 2: PRELUDE TO WAR 21

1. Global Aspects 21

2. British Aspects 29
   2.1 General 30
   2.2 Foreign Policy and Diplomacy 33
   2.3 Anglo-German Relations 37
   2.4 Strategy 39
   2.5 Imperialism 41
   2.6 The Army 42
   2.7 Militarism 43
   2.8 The Anti-War Lobby 45

PART 3: THE WAR YEARS 46

1. General 46

2. The Civilian Scene 51
   2.1 General 51
   2.2 Responses to the War 52
   2.3 Intellectuals 58
   2.4 Labour, Industrial Relations 71
   2.5 Socialism 78

	2.6	Politicians and Political Parties 84
	2.7	The Press 93
	2.8	Church and Religion 99
	2.9	Ireland 103
	2.10	Women 110
	2.11	Doubts and Dissent 122
	2.12	War Hysteria 146
	2.13	Air and Naval Raids 151

3. The Cultural Scene 153
- 3.1 General 153
- 3.2 Art (see also Appendix 3) 155
- 3.3 Literature 162
- 3.4 Music 184
- 3.5 Leisure 193

4. Waging War 206
- 4.1 War and the State 206
- 4.2 Propaganda 223
- 4.3 War Aims and Strategy 292
- 4.4 Intelligence, Espionage 304
- 4.5 The Armed Forces 310
- 4.6 Science and Technology 351

5. Legacies 365
- 5.1 General 365
- 5.2 Social Conditions, Social Structure 368
- 5.3 The State 373
- 5.4 Politics 377
- 5.5 Gender, Sex and Sexuality 380

PART 4: REMEMBERING THE WAR 387

1. General 387

2. Memorialisation and Commemoration 392
- 2.1 General 392
- 2.2 Britain and Ireland 394

3. The Military Post-Mortem 402

4. Cultural Impacts 412

4.1	General	412
4.2	Literature	413
4.3	Film Making	460
4.4	Art	474
4.5	Music	486

PART 5: APPENDICES 490

1. Research Aids 490
  1.1 Bibliographical Tools 490
  1.2 Archives and Special Collections 500
  1.3 Research Centres 503
  1.4 Reference Tools 504
  1.5 Great War Websites 507

2. Propaganda Materials Sent to the USA 510

3. Artists Active during the Great War 522

4. Sassoon's Public Protest (1917) 524

INDEX 525

Introduction

Apart from the inclusion of a number of general background works, this bibliography primarily aims to list records in the English language which cover selected aspects of the impact of the First World War on Great Britain, with some coverage as well of its impact on Ireland.

The number of works published on the First World War, even if confined to 'Britain' and to the English language, is enormous. This bibliography constitutes a fraction of the published output from the early 20th century up to recent times. The arrangement is by subjects intended to encompass a selection of publications representative of the social, political, cultural, and military aspects of the First World War in relation to the years when the war was being fought and also to the years after the war had ended. Some general works and works of relevance specifically to the pre-war years are included in prefatory sections of the bibliography as background material.

An introductory preamble is included in many of the subject sections and sub-sections of this bibliography for the purpose of providing an historical context relevant to the works listed within them. In addition, some of the individual works within the sections are provided with an explanatory note or indication of their contents where this might prove useful to a reader.

As well as the original date of publication a number of the books listed are also provided with information about the date a publisher has reprinted them. Such is the continued interest in the First World War that publishers may well decide in the future to produce reprints of other books recorded here because of their importance or popularity.

For those who like to purchase works on the First World War many of the books listed can be obtained online from large or specialised bookshops or from an organisation like *Amazon*. A considerable number of them are also borrowable by students from their academic libraries, or by members of the public from public libraries which have a substantial non-fiction stock. Many of the periodical articles listed can be downloaded online as printed texts; members of some organisations can do this without cost via the electronic resources provided by their libraries, while members of the general public will normally only be able to do this via a library (such as, for example the British Library) which provides a printed text download service to the public for a fee.

For those who want to delve further into a study of the First World War the bibliography includes an appendix (Appendix 1) which provides a guide to a variety of general and specialised research resources which might be of some assistance.

The index which concludes the bibliography provides a list of keywords on which the bibliography can be searched. This list is not comprehensive; it is representative of a selection of the people and organizations referred to in the bibliography, interspersed with a number of the subjects covered that are included for the purpose of providing a supplement to the list of subjects contained in the **Contents** pages.

Barry Wintour

September 2018

PART 1: GENERAL BACKGROUND WORKS

1. Broad Perspectives

The works selected here provide a broad background - in a general context in **Part 1, section 1.1** and in the specific context of Britain in **Part 1, section 1.2**. Background works specifically related to the Great War are recorded in **Part 1, section 2: Histories and Studies of the Great War**

1.1 General

Abbenhuis, M.M. 'A Most Useful Tool for Diplomacy and Statecraft: Neutrality and Europe in the "Long" Nineteenth Century, 1815-1914', *International History Review*, 35 (2013), 1-22

— *An Age of Neutrals: Great Power Politics, 1815-1914* (Cambridge: Cambridge University Press, 2014)

Andrzejewski, S. *Military Organization and Society*, 2nd edn (London: Routledge & Kegan Paul,1968)

Baker, G. W. and D. W. Chapman, eds. *Man and Society in Disaster* (New York, Basic Books, 1962)

Black, J. *The Age of Total War, 1860-1945* (Westport, Conn.: Praeger Security International, 2006; repr. Plymouth: Rowman & Littlefield, 2010)

— *Avoiding Armageddon: From the Great War to the Fall of France, 1918-40* (London: Bloomsbury, 2012)

— *A Century of Conflict : War 1914-2014* (Oxford: Oxford University Press, 2015)

Blom.P. *The Vertigo Years: Change and Culture in the West, 1900-1914* (London: Weidenfeld & Nicolson 2008)

Bond, B. *War and Society in Europe, 1870-1970*, rev. edn (Montreal: McGill-Queen's University Press, 1998)
First published by Leicester University Press in association with Fontana Paperbacks, 1983.

Bond, B., and I. Roy, eds. *War and Society: A Yearbook of Military History*, 2 vols (London, Croom Helm, 1975-77)

Cahm, E. and V. Fisera, eds. *Socialism and Nationalism in Contemporary Europe* (1848-1945), 3 vols (Nottingham: Spokesman, 1979-1980)
Edited version of the proceedings of a conference held at Portsmouth Polytechnic, 16-18 September 1977

Coker, C. *War and the Twentieth Century: The Impact of War on Modern Consciousness* (London: Brassey's, 1994)

Ferguson, N. *The War of the World: History's Age of Hatred* (London : Penguin, 2007)
Originally published London: Allen Lane, 2006, under the title *The War of the World: 1914-1989*

Falls, C. *The Nature of Modern Warfare* (London: Methuen, 1941)

Fieldhouse, D. K. *Economics and Empire, 1830-1914*, rev. edn (London: Macmillan, 1984)

Gildea, R. *Barricades and Borders, Europe 1800-1914*, 3rd edn (Oxford: Oxford University Press, 2002)

Goebel, S and D. Keene, eds. *Cities into Battlefields: Metropolitan Scenarios, Experiences, and Commemorations of Total War* (Farnham: Ashgate, 2011)
In an analysis of the global impact of military conflict on metropolises in the era of the First and Second World Wars this work explores the way in which cities were transformed into battlefields as a result of the blurring of the the boundaries between home and front.

Gollwitzer, H. *Europe in the Age of Imperialism.1880-1914* (translated from the German by David Adam and

General Background Works

Stanley Baron) (London: Thames & Hudson, 1969)

Halévy, E. *The Era of Tyrannies: Essays on Socialism and War*, translated by R. K. Webb (London: Allen Lane, The Penguin Press, 1967)

Harari, Y. N. *The Ultimate Experience: Battlefield Revelations and the Making of Modern War Culture, 1450-2000* (Basingstoke: Palgrave Macmillan, 2008)

Higham, R. and M. Parillo, eds. *The Influence of Airpower upon History: Statesmanship, Diplomacy, and Foreign Policy since 1903* (Lexington, Kentucky: University Press of Kentucky, 2013

Howard, M *Empires, Nations, and Wars* (Stroud: Spellmount, 2007)
Originally published as *The Lessons of History*: Oxford: Oxford University Press, 1991.
Brings together the major articles and lectures of Sir Michael Howard during his time at the University of Oxford between 1980 and 1989. Among them are included 'Empire Race and War in pre 1914 Britain', 'Europe on the Eve of the First World War', and 'The Edwardian Arms Race'.

— *War and the Liberal Conscience* (London: Temple Smith, 1978; repr. London: Hurst, 2008)

Howard, M. and W. R. Louis, eds. *The Oxford History of the Twentieth Century* (Oxford: Oxford University Press, 1998)

Hobsbawm, E. J. *The Age of Empire* (London: Weidenfeld & Nicolson, 1987; repr. London: Phoenix, 2000)

— *Age of Extremes: The Short Twentieth Century, 1914-1991* (London: Michael Joseph, 1995)

Hodgson, G. *People's Century*, 2 vols (London: BBC Books, 1995-1996), I: *From the Dawn of the Century to the Start of the Cold War, 1995*
Published to accompany the BBC TV documentary series.

Joll, J. *Europe Since 1870: An International History*, 4th edn (London: Penguin, 1990)

Kennedy, P. *The Rise and Fall of the Great Powers: Economic Change and Military Conflict from 1500 to 2000* (London: Random House, 1987)

Kershaw, I. *To Hell and Back: Europe, 1914-1949*, Penguin History of Europe, 8 (London: Allen Lane, 2015)

Kornhauser, W. *The Politics of Mass Society* (London: Routledge & Kegan Paul, 1960)

Marwick, A. *War and Social Change in the Twentieth Century: A Comparative Study of Britain, France, Germany, Russia and the United States* (London: Macmillan, 1974)

Murray, N. *The Rocky Road to the Great War: The Evolution of Trench Warfare to 1914* (Washington, D.C.: Potomac Books, 2013)

Murray, W. and others, eds. *The Shaping of Grand Strategy: Policy, Diplomacy and War*, edited by Williamson Murray, Richard Hart Sinnreich and James Lacey (Cambridge: Cambridge University Press, 2011)

Nef, J. U. *War and Human Progress* (London: Routledge & Kegan Paul 1950)

The New Cambridge History of American Foreign Relations, 4 vols (Cambridge: Cambridge University Press, 2013) III: *The Globalizing of America, 1913-1945*, by Akira Iriye

Rich, N. *Great Power Diplomacy*, 2 vols (Boston: McGraw-Hill, 1992-2002)
Vol 1. *1814-1914* (1992); Vol 2. *1914-Present* (2002)

Schumpeter, A. *Capitalism, Socialism and Democracy*, [5th edn] (London: Routledge, 1994)
This edition originally published: London: Allen & Unwin, 1976. Previous ed.: London: Allen and Unwin, 1954.

Sorokin, P. A. *Man and Society in Calamity: The Effects of War, Revolution, Famine, Pestilence upon Human Mind, Behavior, Social Organization and Cultural Life* (New York: E. P. Dutton, 1942; repr. Greenwood Press, 1968)

Spiegel, H. W. *The Economics of Total War* (New York: Appleton-Century, 1942)

Stone, N. *Europe Transformed, 1878-1918*, 2nd edn (Oxford: Blackwell, 1999)

Toynbee, A. *War and Civilisation*, selected by Albert Vann Fowler from 'A Study of History' (London: Oxford University Press, 1951)

Travers, T. and C. Archer, eds. *Men at War: Politics, Technology, and Innovation in the Twentieth Century* (Chicago: Precedent, 1982; repr. New Brunswick (U.S.A.): Transaction Publishers, 2011)

Traverso, E. *Fire and Blood: The European Civil War 1914-1945* (London: Verso, 2016)

Waller, W., ed. *War in the Twentieth Century* (New York: Dryden Press, 1940; repr. Whitefish, MT: Kessinger, 2008)

Watson, A. 'Culture and Combat in the Western World, 1900-1945', *Historical Journal*, 51 (2008), 529-546

Welch, D. and J. Fox, eds. *Justifying War: Propaganda, Politics and the Modern Age* (Basingstoke : Palgrave Macmillan, c2012)
Based on papers presented at the conference on 'Justifying war: propaganda, politics and the modern age' held in Kent, 2007

Winter, J. M, ed. *War and Economic Development: Essays in Memory of David Joslin* (Cambridge: Cambridge University Press, 1975)

Wright, Q. *A Study of War*, 2 vols. (Chicago: University of Chicago Press, 1942)
An abridgment by Louise Leonard Wright was published in 1964 by the University of Chicago Press which also published a 2nd edn in 1983

1.2 Britain

Bell, C. M. *Churchill and Sea Power* (Oxford: Oxford University Press, 2013)

Brooks, D. *The Age of Upheaval: Edwardian Politics, 1899-1914* (Manchester: Manchester University Press, 1995)

Conley, M. *From Jack Tar to Union Jack: Representing Naval Manhood in the British Empire* (Manchester: Manchester University Press, 2009)

Dangerfield, G. *The Strange Death of Liberal England* (New York: H. Smith and R. Haas, 1935; repr. London: Serif, 1997)

Floud, R. and P. A. Johnson, eds. *The Cambridge Economic History of Modern Britain*, 3 vols (Cambridge: Cambridge University Press, 2004)

Ford, B., ed. *The Cambridge Cultural History of Britain*, 9 vols (Cambridge: Cambridge University Press, 1988: repr. 1992), IX: *Modern Britain*
Previously published as: *The Cambridge Guide to the Arts in Britain*. 1988-1991

Friedberg, G. L. *Weary Titan: Britain and the Experience of Relative Decline, 1895-1905* (Princeton: Princeton University Press, 1988)

Gilbert, B. *British Social Policy, 1914-1939* (London: Batsford 1970)

Goodlad, G. 'Britain and the Challenge of War', *History Review*, 54 (2006), 3-8

General Background Works

—— 'British Governments, War & Society, 1793-1918', *History Review*, 55 (2006), 9-14

Gough, B. *Pax Britannica: Ruling the Waves and Keeping the Peace before Armageddon* (Basingstoke: Palgrave Macmillan, 2014)

James, L. *Warrior Race: A History of the British at War from Roman Times to the Present* (London: Abacus, 2002)

Johnson, G. *The Foreign Office and British Diplomacy in the Twentieth Century* (London: Routledge, 2005)
This book was previously published as a special issue of the journal, *Contemporary British History*

Kennedy, P. M. *The Realities Behind Diplomacy: Background Influences on British External Policy, 1865-1980*, new edn (London: Fontana, 1985)

King, L. *Family Men: Fatherhood and Masculinity in Britain, c.1914–1960* (Oxford: Oxford University Press 2015)

Marwick, A. *Britain in the Century of Total War: War, Peace and Social Change 1900-1967* (London: Bodley Head, 1968)

Morris, A. J. A., ed. *Edwardian Radicalism, 1900-1914: Some Aspects of British Radicalism* (London: Routledge & Kegan Paul, 1974)

Peden, G. C. *Arms, Economics, and British Strategy: From Dreadnoughts to Hydrogen Bombs* (Cambridge Cambridge University Press, 2007; repr, 2009)

Pois, R. A. and P. Langer. *Command Failure in War: Psychology and Leadership* (Bloomington, Ind.: Indiana University Pres, 2004)

Pollard, S. *The Development of the British Economy, 1914-1990*, 4th rev. edn (London: Arnold, 1992)

Pope. R. *War and Society in Britain, 1899-1948* (London: Longman, 1991)

Pugh, M. *The Making of British Politics, 1867-1939*, 2nd edn (Oxford: Blackwell, 1993; repr. 1996)

Ramsden, J. *The Age of Balfour and Baldwin, 1902–1940* (London: Longman, 1978)

Read, D. *Edwardian England, 1901-1915: Society and Politics* (London: Harrap, 1972)

Searle, G. R. *A New England: Peace and War 1886-1918* (Oxford: Oxford University Press, 2004)

Shannon, R. *The Age of Salisbury, 1881–1902: Unionism and Empire* (London: Longman, 1996)

Stevenson, J. *British Society 1914-45* (London: Penguin, 1984)

Strachan, H. 'Merging Past with Present: A History of the Military Historian', *Despatches* (The Magazine of the Friends of the Imperial War Museum), 2, no. 13 (2011), 26-30
A reflection on the changing role of the military historian

Strange, J-M. *Fatherhood and the British Working Class, 1865-1914* (Cambridge: Cambridge University Press, 2015)

Struk, J. *Private Pictures: Soldiers' Inside View of War* (London: I. B. Tauris 2011)
The author looks at war in relation to the pictures soldiers have taken from the origins of popular photography in the Boer War through to the present day.

Suonp, M. 'Britain, Balkan Conflicts and the Evolving Conceptions of Militarism, 1875-1913', *History*, 99 (2014), 632-651

Taylor, A. J. P. *English History, 1914-1945*, new edn (Oxford: Oxford University Press, 1992)

Towle, P. *Going to War: British Debates from Wilberforce to Blair* (Basingstoke: Palgrave Macmillan, 2009)

Wrigley, C. J. ed. *A Companion to Early Twentieth-Century Britain* (Oxford: Blackwell Pub., 2003)

— *A History of British Industrial Relations*, 2 vols (Brighton: Harvester, 1982-1987)

2. Histories and Studies of the Great War

2.1 General Aspects

Barnett, C. *The Great War* (London: BBC, 2003)
This edition, text first published by the Park Lane Press in 1979, was published to accompany the re-transmission in 2003 on BBC2 of the television series 'The Great War', first broadcast in 1964.

Beckett, I. F. W. *The Great War, 1914-1918* (Harlow: Longman, 2001)

The Cambridge History of the First World War, edited by Jay Winter and the editorial committee of the International Research Centre of the Historial de la Grande Guerre, 3 vols (Cambridge: Cambridge University Press, 2014)
Vol. 1. *Global War*; Vol..2. *The State*; Vol.3. *Civil Society*

Chickering, R. and S. Forster, eds. *Great War, Total War: Combat and Mobilization on the Western Front, 1914-1918* (Cambridge: Cambridge University, 2000)
Co-published with German Historical Institute, Washington

Churchill, Sir W. S. *The World Crisis*, 3rd edn, 6 vols (London: Butterworth, 1931)
Vol 1, 1911-1914; Vol 2, 1915: Vols 3-4, 1916-1918; Vol 5, The Aftermath; Vol 6, The Eastern Front

Cowley, R., ed. *The Great War: Perspectives on the First World War* (London: Pimlico, 2004)

Cruttwell, C. R. M. F. *A History of the Great War, 1914-1918* (Oxford: Clarendon Press, 1934)

Ellis, J. and M. Cox. *The World War I Databook: The Essential Facts and Figures for all the Combatants* (London: Aurum Press, 1993; repr. 2001)

Falls, C. *The First World War* (London: Longmans, 1960)

Ferro, M. *The Great War 1914-1918*, trans. by Nicole Stone (London, Routledge, 1973; repr. 2002)

Frantzen, A. J. *Bloody Good. Chivalry, Sacrifice, and the Great War* (Chicago, Ill: University of Chicago Press, 2004)

Gilbert, M. *The First World War* (London: Weidenfeld & Nicolson, 1994)

Hardach, G. *The First World War, 1914-18* (London: Allen Lane, 1977)

Horne, J., ed. *A Companion to World War I* (Oxford: Wiley-Blackwell, 2010; repr. in paperback: 2012)

Howard, M *The First World War* (Oxford: Oxford University Press, 2002)

Keegan, J. *The First World War* (London: Hutchinson, 1998)

Keene, J. D. and M. S. Neiberg, eds. *Finding Common Ground: New Directions in First World War Studies* (Leiden: Brill, 2011)
4th Conference of the International Society for First World War Studies held in Washington D.C. in 2007

Krause, J., ed. *The Greater War: Other Combatants and Other Fronts, 1914-1918* (Basingstoke: Palgrave Macmillan, 2014)

Liddell-Hart, B. H.. *History of the First World War*, enlarged edn (London: Cassell 1970)

General Background Works

Liddle P. H., and others, eds. *The Great World War 1914-45*, edited by P. Liddle, J. Bourne, and I. Whitehead, 2 vols (London: HarperCollins, 2000-2001)
Contents: Vol 1. Lightning Strikes Twice; Vol 2. The People's Experience

Meyer, G. J. *A World Undone: The Story of the Great War, 1914-1918* (New York, N.Y.: Bantam Dell, 2007)

Neiberg, M. S. *Fighting the Great War: A Global History* (Cambridge, Mass.: Harvard University Press, 2005)

— *The World War I Reader* (New York: New York University Press, 2007)

Purnell's History of the First World War, 8 vols (London: Purnell for BPC Publishing Co., 1969-70)

Robbins, K. *The First World War* (Oxford: Oxford University Press, 1984; repr. 1993)

Sheffield, G. *The First World War Remembered* (London: Andre Deutsch in association with IWM, 2014)
The book also contains a film on DVD entitled *Our Empire's Fight for Freedom* alongside a series of vertans' first-hand accounts called *We Fought on the Western Front*

Söondhaus, L. *World War One: The Global Revolution* (Cambridge: Cambridge University Press, 2011)

Stevenson, D. *1914-1918: The History of the First World War* (London: Allen Lane 2004)

Stone, N. *World War One: A Short History* (London: Allen Lane 2007)

Storey, W. K. *The First World War: A Concise Global History* (Lanham: Rowman & Littlefield, 2009)

Strachan, H.. *The First World War*, 3 vols (Oxford: Oxford University Press, 2001-), I: *To Arms* (2001)

— *The First World War: A New Illustrated History* (London: Simon & Schuster, 2003)
Based on the television series, 'The First World War', produced by Work Clements & Company and broadcast in the UK on Channel 4 in ten parts in 2003

— *The Oxford Illustrated History of the First World War*, ed. by H. Strachan (Oxford: Oxford University Press, 1998)

— *World War 1: A History*, ed. by H. Strachan (Oxford: Oxford University Press, 1998)

Ströhn, M., ed. *World War I Companion* (Oxford: Osprey Publishing, 2013)

Taylor, A. J. P. *The First World War: An Illustrated History.* (Harmondsworth: Penguin, 1963; repr. 1981)

Terraine, J. *The First World War* (London: Hutchinson, 1965)

The Times History of the War, 22 vols (London, The Times, 1914-1921)
Also published under the title, *The Times History and Enyclopaedia of the War*

Toland, J. *No Man's Land: 1918, the Last Year of the Great War* (Garden City, N.Y: Doubleday, 1980; repr. Lincoln: University of Nebraska Press, 2002)

Tucker, S. C. *The Great War, 1914-18* (London: Routledge,1998)

Willmott, H. P. *World War* I, 2nd edn (London: Dorling Kindersley 2008)
Previous edn published as *First World War* in 2003 to coincide with the 90th anniversary of the armistice.

Wilson, H. W. and J. A. Hammerton. *The Great War: The Standard History of the All-Europe Conflict*, Millenium edn, 6 Vols (London: Trident Press International, 1999)
Originally published in 13 vols, London: Amalgamated Press, 1914-1919

Winter, J. and B. Baggett. *1914-1918: The Great War and the Shaping of the 20th Century* (London: BBC Books,

1996)
The book published to accompany the television series of the same title

Wrenn, A. *The First World War* (Cambridge: Cambridge University Press, 1997)

2.2 Particular Aspects

Books

Barnett, C. *The Swordbearers: Supreme Command in the First World War* (London: Eyre & Spottiswoode, 1963; repr. London: Cassell, 2001)

Beatty, J. *The Lost History of 1914: How the Great War was Not Inevitable* (London: Bloomsbury 2012)

Beckett, I. F. W. *The Making of the First World War* (New Haven, Conn.; London: Yale University Press 2012)

Beckett, I. F. W., ed. *1917: Beyond the Western Front* (Leiden; Boston: Brill, 2009)

Bennett, S. H. and C. F. Howlett, eds. *Antiwar Dissent and Peace Activism in World War I America: A Documentary Reader* (Lincoln: University of Nebraska Press, 2014)

Ben-Yehuda, N. *Atrocity, Deviance, and Submarine Warfare: Norms and Practices during the World Wars* (Ann Arbor: The University of Michigan Press, 2013)

Bergen, L. van. *Before My Helpless Sight: Suffering, Dying and Military Medicine on the Western Front* (Farnham: Ashgate, 2009)

Black, J. *The Great War and the Making of the Modern World* (London: Continuum, 2011)

Braybon, G., ed. *Evidence, History and the Great War: Historians and the Impact of 1914-18* (Oxford: Berghahn, 2004)

Broadberry, S. and M. Harrison, eds. *The Economics of World War I* (Cambridge: Cambridge University Press 2005)

Bürgschwentner, J., and others, eds. *Other Fronts, Other Wars?: First World War Studies on the Eve of the Centennial*, edited by Joachim Bürgschwentner, Matthias Egger, Gunda Barth-Scalmani (Leiden; Boston: Brill 2014)

Cassar G. H. *Trial by Gas: The British Army at the Second Battle of Ypres* (Washington, D.C.: Potomac Books 2014)

Caglioti, D. L. 'Subjects, Citizens, and Aliens in a Time of Upheaval: Naturalizing and Denaturalizing in Europe during the First World War", *Journal of Modern History*, 89 (2017), 495-530

Cecil, H. and P. H. Liddle, eds. *At the Eleventh Hour: Reflections, Hopes and Anxieties at the Closing of the Great War, 1918* (Barnsley: Leo Cooper, 1998)

— *Facing Armageddon: The First World War Experienced* (London: Leo Cooper, 1996)

Chambers, F. P. *The War Behind the War, 1914-18: A History of the Political and Civilian Fronts* (London: Faber & Faber, 1939; repr. New York: Arno Press, 1972)

Chapman, and others. *Comics and the World Wars: A Cultural Record*, by Jane Chapman, Anna Hoyles, Andrew Kerr and Adam Sherif (Houndmills, Basingstoke: Palgrave Macmillan, 2015)

Coetzee, F and M. Shevin-Coetzee. *Authority, Identity and the Social History of the Great War* (Oxford: Berghahn Books, 1995)

Controvich, J. T. *The United States in World War I: A Bibliographic Guide* (Lanham, Md.: Scarecrow Press, 2012)

Cowper, H., and others. *World War I and its Consequences* (Buckingham: Open University Press, 1989)

General Background Works

Cross, T., ed. *The Lost Voices of World War I: An International Anthology of Writers, Poets, and Playwrights*, [compiled and edited] by T. Cross, new edn (London: Bloomsbury, 1998)
Published to coincide with the Armistice Festival mounted by Tim Cross on the 80th anniversary of the end of the First World War. Rupert Brooke, Wilfred Owen, and Edward Thomas are included among the British writers rrepreseentative of the 800 writers around the world listed in an appendix as killed during the war.

Das, S. *Touch and Intimacy in First World War Literature* (Cambridge: Cambridge University Press, 2005)

Dedio, G. and F. Dedio. *The Great War Diaries* (London: BBC Books 2014)
Published to accompany the television series entitled *The Great War Diaries*

Dehne, P. A. *On the Far Western Front: Britain's First World War in South America* (Manchester: Manchester University Press, 2009)

Duffett, R. *The Stomach for Fighting: Food and the Soldiers of the Great War* (Manchester: Manchester University Press 2012)

Eksteins, M. *Rites of Spring: The Great War and the Birth of the Modern Age* (London: Papermac, 2000)

Emden, R van. *Meeting the Enemy: The Human Face of the Great War* (London: Bloomsbury 2014)

Englund, P. *The Beauty and the Sorrow: An Intimate History of the First World War*, translated by Peter Graves (London: Profile 2012)

Ferguson, N. *The Pity of War: Explaining War* (London: Allen Lane, 1998)

Feltman, B. K. *The Stigma of Surrender: German Prisoners, British Captors, and Manhood in the Great War and Beyond* (Chapel Hill: University of North Carolina Press, 2015)

Floyd, R. *Abandoning American Neutrality: Woodrow Wilson and the Beginning of the Great War, August 1914-December 1915* (Basingstoke: Palgrave Macmillan, 2013)

Ford, R. *Eden to Armageddon: World War I in the Middle East* (London: Weidenfeld & Nicolson, 2009)

Friedman, N. *Fighting the Great War at Sea: Strategy, Tactics, and Technology* (Barnsley: Seaforth Publishing, 2014)

Fussell, P. *The Great War and Modern Memory*, [new edn] (New York; Oxford: Oxford University Press, 2000)
Originally published in 1975

Greenhalgh, E. *Victory Through Coalition: Britain and France during the First World War* (Cambridge: Cambridge University Press, 2005)

Haimson, L. and G. Sapelli, ed. *Strikes, Social Conflicts and the First World War: An International Perspective* (Milan: Feltrini, 1992)

Harrison, R. 'Writing History on the Page and Screen: Mediating Conflict through Britain's First World War Ambulance Trains', *Historical Journal of Film, Radio and Television*, 35 (2015), 559-578

Hertog, J. den and S. Kruizinga, eds. *Caught in the Middle: Neutrals, Neutrality and the First World War* (Amsterdam: Aksant, 2011)

Horne, J. N., ed. *State, Society, and Mobilisation in Europe during the First World War* (Cambridge: Cambridge University Press, 1997, repr. 2002)

'How Total Was the Great War? Germany, France, Great Britain, and the United States, 1914-1918', Conference at Schloß Münchenwiler, Bern, October 9-12, 1996.
Cosponsored by the German Historical Institutes in Washington, London, and Paris; the Swiss National Foundation; and

the Max and Elsa Beer-Brawand Foundation. Conveners: Roger Chickering and Stig Förster. The third conference in the series "Germany and the United States on the Road to Total War, 1860-1945"

Hughes-Wilson, J. *A History of the First World War in 100 Objects* (London: Cassell Illustrated in association with the Imperial War Museum, 2014)
Provides a history of the First World War via the stories behind 100 items of material evidence such as weapons, letters home, items of trench decoration, and the paintings of official war artists.

Hull, I. V. *A Scrap of Paper: Breaking and Making International Law during the Great War* (Ithaca: Cornell University Press, 2014)

Hutchinson, H. *The War That Used Up Words: American Writers and the First World War* (New Haven; London: Yale University Press, 2015)
"In this provocative study, Hazel Hutchison takes a fresh look at the roles of American writers in helping to shape national opinion and policy during the First World War. From the war's opening salvos in Europe, American writers recognized the impact the war would have on their society and sought out new strategies to express their horror, support, or resignation. By focusing on the writings of Henry James, Edith Wharton, Grace Fallow Norton, Mary Borden, Ellen La Motte, E. E. Cummings, and John Dos Passos, Hutchison examines what it means to be a writer in wartime, particularly in the midst of a conflict characterized by censorship and propaganda. Drawing on original letters and manuscripts, some never before seen by researchers, this book explores how the essays, poetry, and novels of these seven literary figures influenced America's public view of events, from August 1914 through the Paris Peace Conference of 1919, and ultimately set the literary agenda for later, more celebrated texts about the war". [Summary of book provided by the publisher]

Jarboe, A. T. 'Healing the Empire: Indian Hospitals in Britain and France during the First World War', *Twentieth Century British History*, 26:3 (2015), 347-369

Jeffery, K. *1916: A Global History* (London: Bloomsbury, 2015)

Jones, H. *Violence against Prisoners of War in the First World War: Britain, France and Germany, 1914–1920* (Cambridge: Cambridge University Press, 2011)

Kimber, A. C. *An American on the Western Front: The First World War Letters of Arthur Clifford Kimber, 1917—18*, edited by Patrick Gregory and Elizabeth Nurser, (Stroud: The History Press, 2016)

Kramer, A. *Dynamic of Destruction: Culture and Mass Killing in the First World War* (Oxford: Oxford University Press, 2007)

Krause, J., ed. *The Greater War: Other Combatants and Other Fronts, 1914-1918* (Basingstoke: Palgrave Macmillan, 2014)

Macleod, J. and P. Purseigle, eds. *Uncovered Fields: Perspectives in First World War Studies* (Leiden: Brill 2004)
Includes among the chapters the following: *A Community at War: British Civilian Internees at the Ruhleben Camp in Germany, 1914-1918* by Matthew Stibbe; *Stereotypical Bedfellows: The Combination of Anti-Semitism with Germanophobia in Great Britain, 1914-1918* by Susanne Terwey; *'Gladder to be Going out than Afraid": Shellshock and Heroic Masculinity in Britain, 1914-1919'* by Jessica Meyer

Mayhew, E. *Wounded: A New History of the Western Front in World War I* (Oxford: Oxford University Press 2013)

Mills, B. *Treacherous Passage: Germany's Secret Plot against the United States in Mexico during World War I* (Lincoln: Potomac Books, an imprint of the University of Nebraska Press, 2017)

Milne, L. *Laughter and War: Humorous-Satirical Magazines in Britain, France, Germany and Russia 1914-1918* (Newcastle upon Tyne: Cambridge Scholars Publishing, 2016)

Morrow, J. H. *The Great War: An Imperial History* (London: Routledge, 2003)

Mosse, G. L. 'Two World Wars and the Myth of the War Experience', *Journal of Contemporary History*, 21 (1986), 491-513

Mulligan, W. *The Great War for Peace* (New Haven, CT: Yale University Press, 2014)

General Background Works

In this book the author refutes the view that the Great War and its immediate aftermath had a disastrous effect on the rest of the 20th century and takes the unconventional line that the first two decades of the century - and the Great War in particular - played an important role in assisting the development of a peaceful new order on a global scale.

O'Hara, V., and others, eds. *To Crown the Waves: The Great Navies of the First World War* {Annapolis, Maryland: Naval Institute Press 2013)

Offer, A. *The First World War: An Agrarian Interpretation* (Oxford: Clarendon Press, 1989; repr. 1991)

Panichas, G. A, ed. *Promise of Greatness: The War of 1914-1918*: [A Memorial Volume for the Fiftieth Anniversary of the Armistice] (London: Cassell, 1968)
This book consists of 48 separate essays written in 1967-1968 especially for this book, most of them by persons who lived through World War One (e.g. Robert Graves, Edmund Blunden, Basil Liddell Hart, Vera Brittain, Charles Edmund Carrington, Alec Waugh, Compton Mackenzie, R. H. Mottram, Cyril Falls, R. C. Sherriff)

Pound, R. *The Lost Generation* (London: Constable, 1964)

Proctor, T. M. *Civilians in a World at War, 1914-1918* (New York: New York University Press, 2010)

— *Female Intelligence: Women and Espionage in the First World* War (New York: New York University Press, 2003)

Pugsley, C. *The Anzac Experience: New Zealand, Australia, and Empire in the First World* (War Auckland [N.Z.]: Reed Pub, 2004)

Purseigle, P., ed. *Warfare and Belligerence: Perspectives in First World War Studies* (Leiden: Brill, 2005)
Includes among the chapters the following: "It all goes wrong!": German, French and British approaches to mastering the Western front by Dennis Showalter; New Jerusalems: Sacrifice and redemption in the war experiences of English and German military chaplains by Patrick Porter; From Liberalism to Labour: Josiah C. Wedgwood and English Liberalism during the First World War by Paul Mulvey; Huts, demobilization, and the quest for an associational life in rural communities in England after the Great War by Keith Grieves

Roshwald, A. and R. Stites, ed. *European Culture in the Great War: The Arts, Entertainment and Propaganda, 1914-18* (Cambridge: Cambridge University Press, 1999; repr. 2002)

Saunders, N. J., ed. *Matters of Conflict: Material Culture, Memory and the First World War* (London: Routledge, 2004)
In its multidisciplinary approach and wide-ranging contributions this book examines the significance of the material legacy (e.g. trench art, postcards, war memorials, museums, etc) of the First World War.

Schmitt, B. E. and H. C. Vedeler. *The World in the Crucible, 1914-1919* (New York: Harper and Row, 1984)

Shevin-Coetzee, M. and F. Coetzee, eds. *World War I and European Society: A Sourcebook* (Lexington: D.C. Heath, 1995)

Sondhaus, L. *The Great War at Sea: A Naval History of the First World War* (Cambridge University Press, 2014)

Spiering, M. and M. Wintle, eds. *Ideas of Europe since 1914: The Legacy of the First World War* (Basingstoke: Palgrave Macmillan 2002)

Stevenson, D. *Cataclysm: The First World War as Political Tragedy* (New York: Basic Books, 2004)

— *The First World War and International Politics* (Oxford: Oxford University Press, 1988)

Stibbe, M. *German Anglophobia and the Great War, 1914-1918*, Studies in the Social and Cultural History of Modern Warfare, 11 (Cambridge: Cambridge University Press, 2001)

Still, W. N. *Crisis at Sea: The United States Navy in European Waters in World War 1* (Gainesville: University Press of Florida, 2006)

Striner, R. *Woodrow Wilson and World War I: A Burden Too Great to Bear* (Lanham: Rowman & Littlefield 2014)

Terraine, J. *Impacts of War 1914 and 1918* (London: Hutchinson, 1970; repr. London: Cooper, 1993)

Tombs, R. and E. Chabal. *Britain and France in Two World Wars: Truth, Myth and Memory* (London: Bloomsbury Publishing, 2013)

Tooze, A. *The Deluge: The Great War, America, and the Remaking of the Global Order, 1916-1931* (New York: Viking, 2014)

Wall, R. and J. M. Winter, eds. *The Upheaval of War: Family, Work and Welfare in Europe, 1914-18* (Cambridge: Cambridge University Press, 1988; repr. 2005)

Watson, A. *Ring of Steel: Germany and Austria-Hungary, 1914-1918* (London: Allen Lane, 2014; repr. London: Penguin Books 2015)

Wawro G. *A Mad Catastrophe: The Outbreak of World War I and the Collapse of the Habsburg Empire* (New York: Basic Books, 2014)

Williams, J. *The Other Battleground: The Home Fronts, Britain, France and Germany, 1914-1918* (Chicago: Henry Regnery, 1972)

Winter, J. M. *The Experience of World War I* (London, Oxford University Press, 1989)

— *Sites of Memory, Sites of Mourning: The Great War in European Cultural History* (Cambridge: Cambridge University Press, 1995)

Winter, J. M. and J-L. Robert, eds. *Capital Cities: London, Paris, Berlin, 1914-18*, 2 vols (Cambridge: Cambridge University Press, 1997-2007)

Wohl, R. *The Generation of 1914* (London: Weidenfeld & Nicolson, 1980)

Woodward, D. R. *America and World War I: A Selected Annotated Bibliography of English-Language Sources* (London: Routledge, 2007

Zeman, Z A B. *A Diplomatic History of the First World War* (London: Weidenfeld & Nicolson, 1971)

Articles

Barrett, M. and P. Stallybrass. 'Printing, Writing and a Family Archive: Recording the First World War', *History Workshop Journal*, 75 (2013), 1-32

Chickering, R. 'Imperial Germany's Peculiar War, 1914-1918', *Journal of Modern History*, 88 (2016), 856-894
Review Article: World War I Centennial Series

Das, S. 'Indian Sepoy Experience in Europe, 1914-18: Archive, Language, and Feeling', *Twentieth Century British History*, 25 (2014), 391-417

DiNardo, R. L. 'The Limits of Technology: The Invasion of Serbia, 1915', *Journal of Military History*, 79 (2015), 981-996

'The Editors New Perspectives on the Cultural History of Britain and the Great War', *Twentieth Century British History*, 25 (2014), 345-346
This review of 4 articles (assembled under the editorial guidance of Martin Francis), offering a number of new perspectives on the cultural history of Britain during the war of 1914–8, "constitutes the first of a number of engagements in the pages of *Twentieth Century British History*, with the centenary of the First World War, between now and 2018". The 4 articles are:
Francis, M. 'Attending to Ghosts: Some Reflections on the Disavowals of British Great War Historiography', *Twentieth Century British History*, 25 (2014), 347-367; **Rose**, S. O. 'The Politics of Service and Sacrifice in WWI Ireland and India', *Twentieth Century British History*, 25 (2014), 368-390; **Grayzel**, S. R. 'Defence Against the Indefensible: The Gas Mask, the State and British Culture during and after the First World War', *Twentieth Century British History*, 25 (2014), 418-434; **Das**, S.

General Background Works

'Indian Sepoy Experience in Europe, 1914-18: Archive, Language, and Feeling', *Twentieth Century British History*, 25 (2014), 391-417

Feltman, B. K. 'Prisoners of Britain: German Civilian and Combatant Internees during the First World War', *Social History*, 39:1 (2014), 128-130

— 'Tolerance As a Crime? The British Treatment of German Prisoners of War on the Western Front, 1914-1918', *War In History*, 17 (2010), 435-458

Hughes, M. 'Searching for the Soul of Russia: British Perceptions of Russia during the First World War, *Twentieth Century British History*, 20 (2009), 198-226

Kempshall, C. 'Pixel Lions – The Image of the Soldier in First World War Computer Games', *Historical Journal of Film, Radio and Television*, 35 (2015), 656-672

Lambert, N.A. 'Righting The Scholarship: The Battle-Cruiser in History and Historiography', *Historical Journal*, 58, (2015), 275-307

Maguire, A. 'Colonial Encounters', *History Today*, 65:12 (2015), 39-45
The First World War tore Europe apart, but it also created chance meetings between different cultures.

Mihăilescu, D. 'Comics from the World Wars as Palimpsest-Laden Tools for Historical Analysis', *Rethinking History*, 20 (2016), 586-593

Pourcher, Y. 'Trains in World War I', *Historical Reflections*, 38:1 (2012), 87-104

Prior, R. 'The Heroic Image of the Warrior in the First World War', *War and Society* (Duntroon Australia), 23 (2005), 43-52

Rose, S. O. 'The Politics of Service and Sacrifice in WWI Ireland and India', *Twentieth Century British History*, 25 (2014), 368-390

Rüger, J. 'Sovereignty and Empire in the North Sea, 1807-1918', *American Historical Review*, 119, (2014), 313-338

Saunders, N. J. *Trench Art*, 2nd edn (Barnsley: Pen & Sword Military, 2011)

Smith, J. 'Brazil and the Two World Wars', *Historian* (Historical Association), 84 (2004), 16-21

Smith, L. 'The Wounds of War', *Despatches* (The Magazine of the Friends of the Imperial War Museum), no. 19 (2014), 26-28
An article about The Friends Ambulance Unit during the first World War

Stevenson, D. 'The First World War and European Integration', *International History Review*, 34, (2012), 841-863

Stibbe, M. 'The Internment of Civilians by Belligerent States during the First World War and the Response of the International Committee of the Red Cross', *Journal of Contemporary History*, 41 (2006), 5-20

Winkler, J. R. 'Information Warfare in World War I', *Journal of Military History*, 73 (2009), 845-868

PART 2: PRELUDE TO WAR

1. Global Aspects

Europe entered the 20th century with a legacy of tensions central to which was the military defeat of France by Germany in 1870-71. Since then France had sought not only to secure its frontiers but also to obtain revenge and the restoration of the provinces of Alsace and Lorraine which she had lost to Germany; it was in large part because of the threat that this presented that Bismarck engineered the secret defensive agreement with Austria-Hungary and Italy, known as the Triple Alliance, in 1882. A further threat to Germany was the alliance between France and Russia that was finalised in 1894. This alliance became even more of a danger when Britain established the 'Entente Cordiale' with France in 1904 and settled disputes with Russia over Persia in 1907, a combination of initial understandings which solidified eventually into the Triple Entente. By July 1914, therefore, there were the two major power blocs of the Triple Alliance (Germany, Italy, and Austria-Hungary with their associate Romania) and the Triple Entente (France, Britain, and Russia, with their protégé Serbia) confronting each other.

During this period of developing agreements between the Great Powers (mostly originally signed for defensive purpose) Europe was becoming increasingly unstable. The territorial ambitions of the Great Powers, manifested in their fierce competition for economic, regional, and colonial expansion[1], steadily developed into intense rivalry. At the same time smaller independent states were seeking to counter the ambitions of the Great Powers or to realize their own ambitions to expand at the expense of their neighbours. Austria-Hungary (the 'Dual Monarchy') was becoming increasingly volatile and insecure with its explosive mixture of races and religious groups and hostile neighbours on its frontiers. Nationalist movements were developing in many areas, not least among the multi-racial empires of Eastern Europe where the mounting tide of national self awareness was especially strong. The multi-ethnic Balkan peninsula was a particularly troublesome area where the territorial ambitions of independent Balkan states and the competing interests not only of the Austro-Hungarian and Ottoman Empires but also of Russia, Italy and France were among the problems which were producing a dangerous clash of local rivalries. Internally the German and Russian empires were in danger of political breakdown from the escalating challenge from liberal and socialist quarters.

The dangers arising out of the turbulence of Europe were exacerbated by the desire of nations, great and small to develop their armed forces with the object of achieving military superiority over their local, regional or global rivals. This was particularly exemplified by the naval arms races that developed between a number of nations - between Turkey and Greece in the Aegean, between Turkey and Russia in the Black Sea, between Austria-Hungary, Italy and France in the Mediterranean but, above all between Britain and Germany for control of the Baltic and supremacy in general, the naval rivalry of the latter nations particularly contributing to the deterioration of the diplomatic status quo in Europe. Europe steadily became divided into armed camps prepared to engage in war which, if it materialised, would, in the belief of many contemporaries, have global as well as European dimensions in view of the international scramble all over the world for colonial territories and the trade routes they afforded.

War was in the air. This atmosphere was reflected in debate and in the works of writers, painters and sculptors. Some quarters in European society, especially in the area of the arts and journalism, were inclined to view war in national terms as a means of relieving popular unrest and creating stronger social bonds. Such approval of war was not shared by those who attended the Second International (1912), the influential medium of international socialism at the time. Their clear condemnation of war caused European regimes generally to fear the possibility of a pacifist rebellion against any war in which they might become engaged (a fear which proved groundless, patriotism proving triumphant over the pacifism of the Second International when the critical point was reached in 1914).

---

[1] There were also non-European players in the scramble to acquire colonial territories or to achieve influence over them. For example, Japan had an interest in China and, isolationist as it was, the United States had a lobby of capitalists keen to acquire economic control of Latin America and the Pacific Rim.

Prelude to War

Documents

Dugdale, E. T. S., ed. *German Diplomatic Documents, 1871-1914*, selected and translated by E. T. S. Dugdale; with a preface by the Rt. Hon. Sir Rennell Rodd and an introduction by J. W. Headlam-Morley, 4 vols (London: Methuen, 1928-1931; repr. 1969)
The volumes have the following titles: 1. Bismarck's Relations with England, 1871-1890; 2. From Bismarck's Fall to 1898, with a preface by the Rt. Hon. Sir Charles Eliot; .3. The Growing Antagonism, 1898-1910 ; with a preface by the Rt. Hon. Sir Maurice Bunsen; 4. The Descent to the Abyss, 1911-1914, with introductions by the Rt. Hon Sir Malcolm Robertson and Admiral Sir Herbert Richmond
This selection (based on *Die Grosse Politik der europäischen Kabinette 1871-1914: Sammlung der diplomatischen Akten des Auswärtigen Amtes*, edited by Johannes Lepsius, Albrecht Mendelssohn Bartholdy and Friedrich Thimme 1922-27) contains those documents of particular relevance to Great Britain.

Geiss, I. *July 1914: The Outbreak of the First World War. Selected Documents* (London: Batsford, 1967)

Germany. Nationalversammlung (1919-1920). *Official German Documents Relating to the World War*, translated under the supervision of the Carnegie Endowment for International Peace, Division of International Law, 2 vols (New York; London: Oxford University Press, 1923)
This 2 volume set contains the reports of the committees established by the German National Constituent Assembly to inquire into the responsibility for the war

Gooch, G. P. and H. W. Temperley. *British Documents on the Origins of the War, 1898-1914*, 11 vols [in 13] (London: HMSO, 1926-1929)

Great Britain. Parliament. *Collected Diplomatic Documents Relating to the Outbreak of The European War*, Cd. 7860 (London: HMSO, 1915)

— *Documents Respecting the Negotiations Preceding the War Published by the Russian Government, Miscellaneous*, 11, Cd 7626 (London: HMSO, 1914).

Oman, Sir C. W. C. *The Outbreak of the War of 1914-18: A Narrative Based Mainly on British Official Documents* (London: HMSO, 1919)

Williamson, S. R. and R. van Wyk. *July 1914: Soldiers, Statesmen, and the Coming of the Great War* (Basingstoke: Palgrave Macmillan, 2003)
A documentary history which focuses on the role played by key civilian and military leaders of the major powers and Serbia in the crisis leading to the Great War.

Books

Abbenhuis, M. *An Age of Neutrals: Great Power Politics, 1815–1914* (Cambridge: Cambridge University Press, 2014)

Adams, M. C. C. *The Great Adventure: Male Desire and the Coming of World War I* (Bloomington, Ind: Indiana University Press, 1990)

Albertini, L. *The Origins of the War of 1914*, translated and edited by I. M. Massey, 3 vols, new and updated edn (New York: Enigma Books, 2004)
This translation was originally published: Oxford: Oxford University Press, 1952-1957. The volumes have the following titles: 1. European relations from the Congress of Berlin to the eve of the Sarajevo murder; 2. The crisis of July 1914 from the Sarajevo outrage to the Austro-Hungarian general mobilization; 3. The epilogue of the crisis of July 1914. The declarations of war and of neutrality

Alexander, R. S. *Europe's Uncertain Path, 1814-1914* (Oxford: Wiley-Blackwell 2012)

Allan, T. *The Causes of World War I* (Oxford: Heinemann, 2003)
Includes titles of useful websites

Angell, N. *The Great Illusion: A Study of the Relation of Military Power in Nations to their Economic and Social Advantage*

(London: Heinemann, 1913)
First published London: Simpkin, Marshall, Hamilton, Kent, 1909 under the title *Europe's Optical Illusion*.

Barraclough, G. *From Agadir to Armageddon: Anatomy of a Crisis* (London: Weidenfeld & Nicolson, 1982)

Beatty, J. *The Lost History of 1914: How the Great War was Not Inevitable* (London: Bloomsbury 2012)

Benson, E. F. *The Outbreak of War 1914* (London: P. Davies, 1933)

Boemeke, M. F. and others., eds. *Anticipating Total War: The German and American Experiences, 1871-1914*; edited by Manfred F. Boemeke, Roger Chickering and Stig Föster, new edn (Cambridge: German Historical Institute and Cambridge University Press, 2006)

Blom.P. *The Vertigo Years: Change and Culture in the West, 1900-1914* (London: Weidenfeld & Nicolson 2008)

Bönker, D. *Militarism in a Global Age: Naval Ambitions in Germany and the United States before World War I* (Ithaca: Cornell University Press, 2012)

Braunthal, J. *History of the International*, 2 vols (London: Nelson, 1966-1967), I: *1864-1914*, translated by H. Collins and K. Mitchell (1966)

Bridge, F.R. *1914: The Coming of the First World War* (London: The Historical Association, 1983)

Bridge, F. R. and R. Bullen. *The Great Powers and the European States System, 1815-1914*, 2nd edn (Harlow: Longman, 2005)

Chatfield, C. and P. van den Dungen, eds. *Peace Movements and Political Cultures* (Knoxville: University of Tennessee Press, 1988)
Papers of a conference held at Bad Tatzmannsdorf and Stadtschlaining, Austria, in Aug. 1986; sponsored by the Council on Peace Research in History (United States)

Chrastil, R. *Organizing for War: France, 1870-1914* (Baton Rouge: Louisiana State University Press, 2010)

Churchill, Sir W. S. *The World Crisis*, 3rd edn, 6 vols (London: Butterworth, 1931), I: *1911-1914*

Clark, C. M. *The Sleepwalkers: How Europe Went To War In 1914* (London: Penguin Books, 2013

Clark, I. F. *Voices Prophesying War: Future Wars, 1763-3749*, 2nd edn (Oxford: Oxford University Press, 1992)
This revised edition of: *Voices Prophesying War, 1763-1984*, (London: Oxford University Press, 1966) is an updating of a comprehensive study of all branches of the fiction of future warfare, a genre that has enjoyed a wide readership since the late 18th century.

Clark, I. F., ed. *The Tale of the Next Great War, 1871-1914: Fictions of Future Warfare and of Battles Still-To-Come* (Liverpool: Liverpool University Press, 1995)

Darby, G. *The Origins of the First World War* (London: Longman, 1998)

Echevarria, A. J. *Imagining Future War: The West's Technological Revolution and Visions of Wars to Come, 1880-1914* (Oxford: Harcourt Education, 2007)

Evans, R. J. W. and H. Pogge von Strandemann, eds. *The Coming of the First World War* (Oxford: Clarendon Press, 1988; repr. 1990)

Farrar, L. L. *The Short-War Illusion: German Policy, Strategy and Domestic Affairs, August-December 1914* (Oxford: ACB-Clio, 1973)

Fromkin, D. *Europe's Last Summer: Why the World Went to War in 1914* (London: William Heinemann, 2004)

Gardner, H. *The Failure to Prevent World War I: The Unexpected Armageddon* (Burlington, VT: Ashgate, 2014)

Geppert, D., and others, eds. *The Wars before the Great War: Conflict and International Politics before the Outbreak of the First World War*, edited by Dominik Geppert, William Mulligan, and Andreas Rose (Cambridge: Cambridge University Press 2015)

Hale, O. J. *The Great Illusion, 1900-1914* (London: Harper & Row, 1971)

— *Publicity and Diplomacy, With Special Reference to England and Germany, 1890-1914* (New York: D. Appleton Century, for the Institute for Research in the Social Sciences, University of Virginia, 1940; repr. Gloucester, Mass.: Peter Smith, 1964)

Halpern, P. *The Mediterranean Situation, 1908-1914* (Cambridge, Mass.: Harvard University Press, 1971)

Hamilton, R. F. and H. H. Herwig, eds. *The Origins of World War I* (Cambridge: Cambridge University Press, 2003)

— *Decisions for War, 1914-17* (Cambridge: Cambridge University Press, 2004)
Revised and abridged paperback version of *The Origins of World War I* (see above)

— *War Planning 1914* (Cambridge: Cambridge University Press, 2010)

Hastings, M. *Catastrophe 1914: Europe Goes to War* (London: William Collins, 2013)

Haupt, G. *Socialism and the Great War: The Collapse of the Second International* (Oxford: Clarendon Press, 1972)
Originally published in French, 1965

Hendrickson, J. K. *Crisis in the Mediterranean: Naval Competition and Great Power Politics, 1904-1914* (Annapolis, Maryland: Naval Institute Press, 2014)

Henig, R. *The Origins of the First World War* (London: Routledge, 1989)

Hermann, D. G. *The Arming of Europe and the Making of the First World War* (Princeton, N.J: Princeton University Press, 1996)
The book has the following chapters: The European armies in 1904; The European armies and the first Moroccan crisis, 1905-1906; Military effectiveness and modern technology, 1906-1908; The Bosnia-Herzegovina annexation crisis and the recovery of Russian power, 1908-1911; The second Moroccan crisis and the beginning of German panic, 1911-1912; The Balkan Wars and the spiral of armaments, 1912-1913; The European armies and the outbreak of the First World War

Herwig, H. H. 'Industry, Empire, and the First World War', in *Modern Germany Reconsidered, 1870-1945*, edited by G. Martel (London: Routledge, 1992)

Herwig, H. H., ed. *The Outbreak of World War I: Causes and Responsibilities* (Boston: Houghton Mifflin, 1997)

Hobson, R. *Imperialism at Sea: Naval Strategic Thought, the Ideology of Sea Power and the Tirpitz Plan, 1875-1914* (Boston: Brill Academic Publishers, 2002)

Howard, M *Empires, Nations, and Wars* (Stroud: Spellmount, 2007)
A collection of the major articles and lectures of Sir Michael Howard during his time as Regius Professor of Modern History in the University of Oxford between 1980 and 1989. Includes chapters on 'Prussia in European History', 'The Doctrine of the Offensive in 1914', and 'Europe on the Eve of the First World War'. Originally published as The Lessons of History, Oxford: Oxford University Press, 1991.

Jannen, W. *The Lions of July: Prelude to War, 1914* (Novato, Calif.: Presidio, 1996)

Jemnitz, J. *The Danger of War and the Second International (1911)*, [translated by P. Félix] (Budapest: Akadémiai Kiadó, 1972)

Joll, J. *The Origins of the First World War*, [revised by] G. Martel, 3rd edn (Harlow: Longman, 2007)

Global Aspects

— 'Politicians and the Freedom to Choose: The Case of July 1914', in *The Idea of Freedom, Essays in Honour of Isaiah Berlin*, edited by A. Ryan (Oxford: Oxford University Press, 1979)

Kennedy, P. M., ed. *The War Plans of the Great Powers, 1880-1914* (London: Allen & Unwin, 1979; repr. 1985)

Kennedy, P. M. and A. Nicholls, eds. *Nationalist and Racialist Movements in Britain and Germany before 1914* (London: Macmillan in association with St Antony's College, Oxford, 1981)

Koch, H., ed. *The Origins of the First World War: Great Power Rivalry and German War Aims*, 2nd edn (London: Macmillan, 1984)

Lafore, L. D. *The Long Fuse: An Interpretation of the Origins of World War I*, 2nd edn (Prospect Heights, Ill: Waveland Press, 1997)

Langdon, J. W. *July 1914: The Long Debate, 1918-1990* (Oxford: Berg, 1991)

Langer, W. L. *Diplomacy of Imperialism, 1890-1902*, 2nd edn (New York; Knopf, 1951; repr. 1968)

— *European Alliances and Alignments 1871-1890*, 2nd edn (New York: Knopf, 1950; repr. Westport, Conn: Greenwood Press, 1977)

Langhorne, R. *The Collapse of the Concert of Europe: International Politics, 1890-1914* (London: Macmillan, 1981)

Le Bon, G. *Psychology of the Great War: The First World War and Its Origins*, with a new introduction by Martha Hanna and a new foreword by Irving Louis Horowitz (New Brunswick, N.J.: Transaction Publishers, 1999) Originally published: London : T. Fisher Unwin, 1916

Lebow, R. N. 'Contingency, Catalysts and Nonlinear Change: The Origins of World War I', in *Explaining War and Peace: Case Studies and Necessary Condition Counterfactuals*, edited by Gary Goertz and Jack S. Levy (London: Routledge, 2007)

Lee, D. E. *Europe's Crucial Years: The Diplomatic Background of World War I, 1902-1914* (Hanover, N.H.: University Press of New England for Clark University Press, 1974)

Levy, J. S. 'The Role of Crisis Management in the Origins of World War I', in *Avoiding War: Problems of Crisis Management*, edited by Alexander L. George (Boulder, CO.: Westview Press, 1991)

— 'The Role of Necessary Conditions in the Outbreak of World War 1', in *Explaining War and Peace: Case Studies and Necessary Condition Counterfactuals*, edited by Gary Goertz and Jack S. Levy (London: Routledge, 2007)

Levy, J. S. and J. A. Vasquez., eds. *The Outbreak of the First World War: Structure, Politics, and Decision-Making* (Cambridge: Cambridge University Press, 2014)

Lyon, J. B. *Serbia and the Balkan Front, 1914: The Outbreak of the Great War* (New York: Bloomsbury Academic, 2015)

MacMillan, M. *The War that Ended Peace: The Road to 1914* (New York: Random House, 2013)

Martel, G. *The Month that Changed the World: July 1914* (Oxford: Oxford University Press, 2014; repr. 2017)

— *The Origins of the First World War*, Seminar Studies in History, 3rd edn (Harlow: Pearson Longman, 2003)

Massie, R. K. *Dreadnought: Britain, Germany and the Coming of the Great War* (London: Cape, 1992)

Maurer, J. H. *The Outbreak of the First World War: Strategic Planning, Crisis Decision Making, and Deterrent Failure* (Westport, CT.: Greenwood Press, 1995)

May, E. R. *Knowing One's Enemies: Intelligence Assessment before the Two World Wars* (Princeton, N.J.: Princeton

University Press, 1984; repr. 1986)

Mayer, A. J. 'Domestic Origins of the First World War', in *The Responsibility of Power, Historical Essays in Honor of Hajo Holborn*, edited by Leonard Krieger and Fritz Stern (London: Macmillan, 1968)
Originally published, New York: Doubleday, 1967

—— *The Persistence of the Old Regime: Europe to the Great War* (London: Croom Helm, 1981)

McCullough, E. *How the First World War Began: The Triple Entente and the Coming of the Great War, 1914-18* (Montreal: Black Rose Books, 1999)

McDonough, F. *The Origins of the First and Second World Wars* (Cambridge: Cambridge University Press, 1997)

McKercher, B., ed. *Arms Limitation and Disarmament: Restraints on War, 1899-1939* (Westport, Conn.: Praeger, 1992)

McMeekin, S. *The Russian Origins of the First World War* (Cambridge, Mass.: Belknap Press of Harvard University Press, 2011)

Miller, G. D. *The Shadow of the Past: Reputation and Military Alliances before the First World War* (Ithaca: Cornell University Press, 2012)

Miller, J. B. D. *Norman Angell and the Futility of War: Peace and the Public Mind* (London: Palgrave Macmillan, 1986)

Miller, S. E., and others, ed. *Military Strategy and the Origins of the First World War*, revised and expanded edn (Princeton: Princeton University Press, 1991)

Milward, A. S. and S. B. Saul. *The Development of the Economies of Continental Europe, 1850-1914* (London: George Allen & Unwin, 1977)

Mombauer, A. Helmuth von Moltke and the Origins of the First World War (Cambridge: Cambridge University Press, 2001)

Mombauer, A., ed. *The Origins of the First World War: Controversies and Consensus* (London: Longman, 2002)

Mulligan, W. *The Origins of the First World War* (Cambridge: Cambridge University Press, 2010)

Neiberg. M. S. *Dance of the Furies: Europe and the Outbreak of World War* I (Cambridge, Mass.: Belknap Press of Harvard University Press, 2011)

Nolan, M. E. The Inverted Mirror: Mythologizing the Enemy in France and Germany, 1898-1914. (New York: Berghahn Books, 2005)

Otte, T. G. July Crisis: The World's Descent Into War, Summer 1914 (Cambridge: Cambridge University Press 2014)

Pettifer, J. and T. Buchanan, eds. *War in the Balkans: Conflict and Diplomacy before World War I* (London: I.B. Tauris, 2016)

Pick, D. *Faces of Degeneration: A European Disorder*, new edn (Cambridge: Cambridge University Press, 1989; repr. 1993)

—— *War Machine: The Rationalisation of Slaughter in the Modern Age* (New Haven, Conn.: Yale University Press, 1993; repr. 1996)

Ponting, C. *Thirteen Days: The Road to the First World War* (London: Chatto & Windus, 2002)

Global Aspects

Pope, G. *History: The Origins of the First World War: Sources, Skills, Concepts* (Victoria, Australia: IBID Press, 2002)

Remak, J., ed. *The Origins of World War I, 1870-1914* (Fort Worth: Harcourt Brace College Publishers, 1995)

Rich, N. *Great Power Diplomacy*, 2 vols (Boston: McGraw-Hill, 1992-2002), I: *1814-1914* (1992)

Schmitt, B. *The Origins of the First World War* (London: The Historical Association, 1972)

Schroeder, P. W. 'Necessary Conditions and World War 1 as an Unavoidable War', in *Explaining War and Peace: Case Studies and Necessary Condition Counterfactuals*, edited by Gary Goertz and Jack S. Levy (London: Routledge, 2007)

Scott, J. F. *Five Weeks: The Surge of Public Opinion on the Eve of the Great War* (New York: John Day, 1927)

Seton-Watson, R. W. *Sarajevo: A Study in the Origins of the Great War* (London: Hutchinson, 1926; repr. New York: Howard Fertig, 1988)

Snyder, J. *The Ideology of the Offensive: Military Decision-Making and the Disasters of 1914* (Ithaca, N.Y.: Cornell University Press, 1984)

Sondhaus, L. *World War One: The Global Revolution* (Cambridge: Cambridge University Press, 2011)

Soroka, M. *Britain, Russia and the Road to the First World War: The Fateful Embassy of Count Aleksandr Benckendorff (1903-16)*, Birmingham Studies in First World War History (Farnham: Ashgate, 2010)

Steinberg, J. *Yesterday's Deterrent: Tirpitz and the Birth of the German Battlefleet*, new edn (Aldershot: Gregg Revivals, 1993)

Stevenson, D. *Armaments and the Coming of War: Europe, 1904-1914* (Oxford: Clarendon Press, 1996; repr. 2000)

— *The Outbreak of the First World War: 1914 in Perspective* (Basingstoke: Macmillan, 1997)

Strachan, H. *The Outbreak of the First World War* (Oxford: Oxford University Press, 2004)

Stromberg, R. N. *Redemption by War: The Intellectuals and 1914* (Lawrence: The Regent's Press of Kansas, 1982)

Taylor, A. J. P. *The Struggle for Mastery in Europe, 1848-1914*, 2 vols (London: Folio Society, 1998)
The volumes have the following titles: 1. Balancing the Powers 1848-1878; 2. From Peace to War 1878-1914. Originally published in one vol, Oxford: Clarendon Press, 1954

— *War by Time-Table: How the First World War Began* (London: Macdonald, 1969)

Thomson, G. M. *The Twelve Days: 24 July to 4 August 1914* (London: Hutchinson, 1964; repr. London: Secker and Warburg, 1975)

Thompson, W. R. 'Powderkeg, Sparks and World War 1', in *Explaining War and Peace: Case Studies and Necessary Condition Counterfactuals*, edited by Gary Goertz and Jack S. Levy (London: Routledge, 2007)

Tuchman, B. W. *The Guns of August* (London: Robinson, 2000)
Originally published as: *August 1914* London: Constable, 1962

— *The Proud Tower: A Portrait of the World before the War, 1890-1914* (London: Hamish Hamilton, 1966; repr. London: Papermac, 1997)

Tunstall, G. A. *Planning for War against Russia and Serbia: Austro-Hungarian and German Military Strategies, 1871-1914* (New York: Columbia University Press, 1993)

Turner, L. C. F. *Origins of the First World War* (London: Edward Arnold, 1970; repr, 1983)

Wawro G. *A Mad Catastrophe: The Outbreak of World War I and the Collapse of the Habsburg Empire* (New York: Basic Books, 2014)

White, J. *Transition to Global Rivalry: Alliance Diplomacy and the Quadruple Entente, 1895-1907* (Cambridge: Cambridge University Press, 1995)

Williamson, S. R., ed. *The Origins of a Tragedy: July 1914* (St. Louis, Mo: Forum Press, 1981)

Williamson, S. R., and R. van Wyk, eds. *July 1914: Soldiers, Statesmen, and the Coming of the Great War* (Basingstoke: Palgrave Macmillan, 2003)

Wilson, K. M., ed. *Decisions for War, 1914* (London: UCL Press, 1995)

Zeman, Z.A.B. 'The Balkans and the Coming of War', in T*he Coming of the First World War*, edited by R. J. W. Evans and Hartmut Pogge von Strandmann (Oxford: Clarendon Press, 1990)

Zuber, T. *Inventing the Schlieffen Plan German War Planning, 1871-1914* (Oxford: Oxford University Press 2002; repr. 2014)
In this work Zuber challenges the traditional assumptions about the existence of a 'Schlieffen Plan' and, presenting a radically different picture of German war planning between 1871 and 1914, comes to the conclusion that, in fact, a 'Schlieffen Plan' never really existed.

Articles

Abbenhuis, M.M. 'A Most Useful Tool for Diplomacy and Statecraft: Neutrality and Europe in the "Long" Nineteenth Century, 1815-1914', *International History Review*, 35 (2013), 1-22
In this article the author draws attention to the existence of a nineteenth-century international system in whch Eurpean states endeavoured to pursue a policy of avoidng war as a way of benefitting their political, economic, and imperial interests.

Adamthwaite, A. 'Organizing for War: France, 1870-1914', *International History Review*, 34 (2012), 918-919

Bowler, P. J. 'Malthus, Darwin and the Concept of Struggle', *Journal of the History of Ideas*, 37 (1976), 631-50

Crook, D. P. 'Darwin on War and Aggression', *Australian Journal of Politics and History*, 29 (1983), 344-53

Dickinson, F.R. 'Toward a Global Perspective of the Great War: Japan and the Foundations of a Twentieth-Century World', *American Historical Review*, 119 (2014), 1154-1183

Dutton, D. 'The War That Ended Peace: How Europe Abandoned Peace for the First World War/Catastrophe: Europe Goes to War 1914', *International History Review*, 36 (2014), 815-817

Fairbanks, C. H. 'The Origins of the Dreadnought Revolution: A Historiographical Essay', *International History Review*, 13 (1991), 246-72

Ferguson, N. 'Public Finance and National Security: The Domestic Origins of the First World War Revisited', *Past and Present*, (1994), 141-68

Gale, B. 'Darwin and the Concept of a Struggle for Existence', *Isis*, 63 (1972), 321-44

Imlay, T. C. 'The Origins of the First World War', *Historical Journal*, 49 (2006), 1253-1272
Review articles.

Lammers, D. 'Arno Mayer and the British Decision for War: 1914', *Journal of British Studies*, 12.2 (1973), 137-165

Levy, J. S. 'Preferences, Constraints, and Choices in July 1914', *International Security*, 15.3 (1990-91), 151-86

Levy, J. S. and others. 'Mobilization and Inadvertence in the July Crisis' *International Security*, 16.1 (1991), 189–203

Loewenberg, P. 'Arno Mayer's "Internal Causes and Purposes of War in Europe", an Inadequate Model of Human Behavior, National Conflict and Historical Change', *Journal of Modern History*, 42 (1970), 628-36

Lynn-Jones, S. M. 'Detente and Deterrence: Anglo-German Relations, 1911-1914', *International Security*, 11 (1986), 121–150

Maehl, W. H. 'Bebel's Fight against the "Schlachtflotte", Nemesis to the Primacy of Foreign Policy', *Proceedings of the American Philosophical Society*, 121:3 (1977), 209-226

Mayer, A. J. 'Internal Causes and Purposes of War in Europe, 1870-1956', *Journal of Modern History*, 41 (1969), 291-303

Offer, A. 'Going to War in 1914: A Matter of Honour?', *Politics and Society*, 23 (1995), 213-41

Otte, T. G. 'The Great Carnage', *New Statesman*, 13 December 2012
T. G. Otte offers a revisionist reading of the First World War

Reynolds, D. 'The Origins of the Two "World Wars": Historical Discourse and International Politics', *Journal of Contemporary History*, 38 (2003), 29-44

Ruger, J. Revisiting the Anglo-German Antagonism', *Journal of Modern History*, 83 (2011), 579-617
Review article

Sagan, S. D. '1914 Revisited: Allies, Offense, and Instability', *International Security*, 11(1986), 15-175

Stevenson, D. 'Militarization and Democracy in Europe before 1914', *International Security*, 22 (1997), 125-61

Strachan, H. 'Review Article: The First World War: Causes and Course', *Historical Journal*, 29 (1986), 227-55

Stromberg, R. 'The Intellectuals and the Coming of War in 1914', *Journal of European Studies*, 3 (1973), 109-22

Trachtenberg, M. 'The Meaning of Mobilization in 1914', *International Security*, 15.3 (1990-91), 120-150

Turner, L. C. F. 'The Role of the General Staffs in July 1914', *Australian Journal of Politics and History*, 11 (1965), 305-23

Van Evera, S. 'The Cult of the Offensive and the Origins of the First World War' *International Security*, 9.1 (1984), 58–107

Weinroth, H. 'Norman Angell and The Great Illusion: An Episode in pre-1914 Pacifism', *Historical Journal*, 17 (1974), 551-74

Williamson, S. R. 'The Origins of World War I', *Journal of Interdisciplinary History*, 18 (1988), 795-818

Young, H. 'The Misunderstanding of August 1, 1914', *Journal of Modern History*, 48 (1976), 644-65

Zuber, T. 'The Schlieffen Plan: Fantasy or Catastrophe?', *History Today*, 52, Issue 9 (2002), 40-46
In this article the author argues that the German army's plan for a quick victory in France in 1914 was a fabrication concocted after the war.

2. British Aspects

In the pre-war years there was a significant element of pacifism in British society. Prophecies of war, ideas such as war as a panacea for the ills of the age or as fact of life related to the Darwinian concept of the survival of the fittest, the literature of apocalypse, and jingoism were all evident in the pre-war decade but they were by no means dominant. In this period Norman Angell had published his book, *The Great Illusion,* "which sought to show that not even the victor could profit economically from war". This book was widely read and provided an influential contrast to the writings of the warmongers. 'Angellism' fitted in well with the strong tendencies towards pacifism which existed at that time in Britain, particularly in the labour movement and among those of liberal opinion. The latter tendencies developed into an active peace movement but the peace groups and societies involved in it failed to achieve unity in their activities in spite of the efforts by bodies like the British National Peace Council and the British Council of Associated Churches for Fostering Friendly Relations between the British and German Peoples (masterminded by two Liberal MPs, J. Allen Baker, a Quaker, and Willoughby Dickinson, an Anglican) to co-ordinate them. In spite of a number of newspapers using every opportunity to stir up anti-German feelings among its readers, there were also some newspapers and periodicals in which pacifist views could be read as, for example, newspapers like the *Daily News* (edited by A. G. Gardiner) and the *Manchester Guardian* (edited by C. P. Scott), a weekly magazine like *The Nation* (edited by H. W. Massingham), and pacifist publications like *The Peacemaker*, *The Herald of Peace*, and *War and Peace*. Above all, the pre-war years from 1906 constituted a period of dominance (in a Liberal-Labour coalition) of the Edwardian Liberal Party which, in spite of continuous pressure from the warmongers, among whom could be counted the hawkish members of the Unionist Party, refused to budge from its ideological commitment to 'peace', to which it steadfastly adhered right up to the beginning of the Great War.

When the British people finally realized in the summer of 1914 how serious the international crisis in Europe had become their attitude was characterized by neither an immediate nor a united desire for war. Until Belgium was invaded in the first days of August the idea of getting embroiled in an European conflict was subject to considerable differences of opinion and was met in many quarters with positive opposition. Opposition to a war was the purpose behind the formation of the British Neutrality League and the British Neutrality Committee in July 1914, and both these groups maintained a vigorous campaign for neutrality right up to the time of the Government's declaration of war. At the end of July the feeling that Britain should adopt a neutral stance was very strong, especially in the City, the north of England and in the Liberal and Labour parties. Academics joined in the outcry for neutrality with the *Scholars' Protest Against War with Germany* which was published in *The Times* on 1st August. There were frequent anti-war demonstrations and rallies. Judging by Keir Hardie's anti-war 'Appeal to the Working Class' (co-authored by Arthur Henderson) and the huge 'Stop the War' rallies held throughout the country on August 1 and 2 1914 (particularly the rally on August 2 in Trafalgar Square where Keir Hardie, H. M. Hyndman, George Lansbury, and Arthur Henderson addressed an assembly of 15,000 people) those members of the working-class who were aware of what was going on were disposed towards peace on the eve of the war.

When it came to the crunch in 1914 the Government itself was split right down the middle, with Lloyd George prominent among the neutralists. This is hardly surprising in view of the fact that the British government had been dominated since 1906 by a party committed to 'peace' and was therefore never likely to have wanted to cross swords with Germany; nor was it at all likely, as it has sometimes been argued, that it was looking to war as a way of extricating itself from its internal troubles (the Irish question, industrial strife and suffragette demonstrations). The strenuous diplomatic efforts made between 1912 and 1914 to effect a compromise and conciliation with Germany were hardly the work of a government determined to engage in a war with Germany.

It was not until the invasion of Belgium that a decisive shift in British opinion occurred.. At that point there developed a distinct erosion of the opposition to a war. Many neutralists and doubters felt obliged, albeit reluctantly in many cases, to acquiesce in Britain becoming embroiled in a war and, although an important group of socialists, liberals, and pacifists remained implacably opposed to this, the change in the overall national mood ultimately helped the Government to make the decision to declare war on Germany, a declaration to which the British people in general responded enthusiastically.

2.1 General

Biographies

Gilbert, B. B. *David Lloyd George: A Political Life*, 2 vols (London: Batsford: 1987-92), II: *The Organizer of Victory, 1912–1916* (1992)

Grigg, J. *Lloyd George*, 4 vols (London: Penguin, 2002-03), III: *From Peace To War, 1912–1916* (2002)
The 4 vols were originally published: London : Eyre Methuen, 1973-1985

Books

British Aspects

Brock, M. 'Britain Enters the War', in *The Coming of the First World War*, edited by R. J. W. Evans and H. P. von Standemann (Oxford: Clarendon Press, 1988; repr. 1990)

Charmley, J. *Splendid Isolation?: Britain, the Balance of Power and the Origins of the First World War* (London: Hodder & Stoughton, 1999)

Chlders, E. *Riddle of the Sands* (London: Smith, Elder & Co., 1903)
There are numerous modern reprints of this work of which one of the latest is London: Atlantic Books, 2009. Set in the years of European tension leading up to the First World War this immensely popular spy novel of the time sensationally captured the public imagination with its plot of the discovery, and eventual foiling, of Germany's plan to invade England.

Eby, C. D. *The Road to Armageddon: The Martial Spirit in English Popular Literature, 1870-1914* (Durham: Duke University Press, 1987)

Fest, W. 'Jingoism and Xenophobia in the Electioneering Strategies of British Ruling Elites Before 1914', in *Nationalist and Racialist Movements in Britain and Germany before 1914*, edited by P. M. Kennedy and A. J. Nicholls (London: Macmillan in association with St Antony's College, Oxford, 1981)

Friedberg, G. L. *Weary Titan: Britain and the Experience of Relative Decline, 1895-1905* (Princeton: Princeton University Press, 1988)

Gooch, J. 'Attitudes to War in late Victorian and Edwardian England', in *War and Society: A Yearbook of Military History*, edited by B. Bond and I. Roy, Vol 1 (London: Croom Helm, 1975)

Grayzel, S. R. '"A promise of Terror to Come": Air Power and the Destruction of Cities in British Imagination and Experience, 1908-39', in *Cities into Battlefields: Metropolitan Scenarios, Experiences and Commemorations of Total War*, edited by S. Goebel, and D. Keene (Farnham: Ashgate, 2011)

Hazlehurst, C. *Politicians at War, July 1914 to May 1915: A Prologue to the Triumph of Lloyd George* (London: Jonathan Cape, 1971)
Early chapters show how the British Cabinet moved towards intervention in the war

Howard, M *Empires, Nations, and Wars* (Stroud: Spellmount, 2007)
A collection of the major articles and lectures of Sir Michael Howard during his time as Regius Professor of Modern History in the University of Oxford between 1980 and 1989. Includes chapters on 'Empire, Race and War in pre-1914 Britain', and 'The Edwardian Arms Race'. Originally published as *The Lessons of History*, Oxford : Oxford University Press, 1991.

Hutcheson, J. A. *Leopold Maxse and The National Review, 1893-1914: Right-Wing Politics and Journalism in the Edwardian Era (*New York: Garland, 1989)

Kennedy, P. M. *The Rise of the Anglo-German Antagonism, 1860-1914* (London: Ashfield Press, 1987)

— 'The Pre-War Right in Britain and Germany', in *Nationalist and Racialist Movements in Britain and Germany before 1914*, edited by P. M. Kennedy and A. Nicholls (London: Macmillan in association with St Antony's College, Oxford, 1981)

Kohe, K. 'The British Imperialist Intelligentsia and the Kaiserreich', in *Nationalist and Racialist Movements in Britain and Germany before 1914*, edited by P. M. Kennedy and A. Nicholls (London: Macmillan in association with St Antony's College, Oxford, 1981)

Laity, P. *The British Peace Movement 1870-1914* (Oxford: Oxford University Press, 2001)

Morris, A. J. A.. *The Scaremongers: The Advocacy of War and Rearmament, 1896-1914* (London: Routledge & Kegan Paul, 1984)

Newton, D. *The Darkest Days: The Truth behind Britain's Rush to War, 1914* (London: Verso , 2014)

Nicolson, C. 'Edwardian England and the Coming of the First World War', in *The Edwardian Age: Conflict and Stability, 1900-1914*, ed. by A. O'Day (London: Macmillan, 1979)

Playne, C. *The Pre-War Mind in Britain: An Historical Review* (London: Allen & Unwin, 1928: repr. 1948)

Ramsden, J. *Don't Mention the War: The British and Germans Since 1890* (London: Little, Brown, 2006)

Searle, G. 'The Revolt from the Right in Edwardian Britain', in *Nationalist and Racialist Movements in Britain and Germany before 1914*, edited by P. M. Kennedy and A. Nicholls (London: Macmillan in association with St Antony's College, Oxford, 1981)

Sidorowicz, A. T. 'The British Government, the Hague Peace Conference of 1907, and the Armaments Question', in *Arms Limitation and Disarmament: Restraints on War, 1899-1939*, edited by B. McKercher (Westport, Conn.: Praeger, 1992)

Summers, A. 'The Character of Edwardian Nationalism', in *Nationalist and Racialist Movements in Britain and Germany before 1914*, edited by P. M. Kennedy and A. Nicholls (London: Macmillan in association with St Antony's College, Oxford, 1981)

Wells, H. G. *The War in the Air* (London: Nelson, 1908)
A novel prophetic of the use of the aircraft for the purpose of warfare, a phenomenon of total war which emerged in the First World War and was fully realized in the Second World War. There have been a number of reprints of this novel of which one of the most recent was publsied by Penguin in 2005.

Wilkinson, G. R. *Depictions and Images of War in Edwardian Newspapers, 1899-1914* (Basingstoke: Palgrave Macmillan, 2003)

Winzen, P. 'Treitschke's Influence on the Rise of Imperialist and Anti-British Nationalism in Germany', in *Nationalist and Racialist Movements in Britain and Germany before 1914*, edited by P. M. Kennedy and A. Nicholls (London: Macmillan in association with St Antony's College, Oxford, 1981)

Articles

Bell, C. M. 'Sir John Fisher's Naval Revolution Reconsidered: Winston Churchill at the Admiralty, 1911-1914', *War In History*, 18 (2011), 333-356

Bones, A. J. 'British National Dailies and the Outbreak of War in 1914', *International History Review*, 35 (2013), 975-992

Fletcher, A. 'Patriotism, the Great War and the Decline of Victorian Manliness', *History*, 99, (2014), 40-72

French, D. 'The Edwardian Crisis and the Origins of the First World War', *International History Review*, 4 (1982), 207-21

Gordon, M. 'Domestic Conflict and the Origins of the First World War: The British and German Cases', *Journal of Modern History*, 46 (1974), 191-226

Hampshire, J. '"Spy fever" in Britain, 1900 to 1914', *Historian* (Historical Association), 72 (2001), 22-27

Johnson, M. 'The Liberal Party and the Navy League in Britain before the Great War', *Twentieth Century British History*, 22 (2011), 137-163

Lammers, D. 'Arno Mayer and the British Decision for War', *Journal of British Studies*, 12 (1973), 137-65

Martel, G. 'The Meaning of Power: Rethinking the Decline and Fall of Great Britain', *International History Review*, 13 (1991), 695-725

Meacham, S. 'The Sense of an Impending Clash: English Working-Class Unrest before the First World War', *American Historical Review*, 77 (1972), 1343-64

Morgan-Owen, D.G. '"History is a Record of Exploded Ideas": Sir John Fisher and Home Defence, 1904-10', *International History Review*, 36 (2014), 550-572

Neilson, K. '"Greatly Exaggerated": The Myth of the Decline of Britain before 1914', *International History Review*, 13 (1991), 695-725

Paris, M. 'Fear of Flying: The Fiction of War 1886-1916', *History Today*, 43 (1993) 29

Reynolds, P. 'The Man Who Predicted the Great War', *History Today*, 63:5 (2013)
About the financier Jan Bloch who in 1901, in a lecture delivered at the Royal United Service Institution (now the Royal United Services Institute), warned Britain's military establishment of the disastrous consequences that would result from engaging in offensive operations in a major conflict in Europe.

Stearn, T. 'The Case For Conscription', *History Today*, 58, Issue 4 (2008), 16-22
In this article the author points out that among the supporters of the campaign for compulsory military service in Edwardian Britain were those who saw this service as a necessary measure against the threat of invasion and the menace of German militarism.

2.2 Foreign Policy and Diplomacy

An undercurrent of acute anxiety and tension was a persistent feature of the international scene in the decade preceding the outbreak of war. In this dangerous climate international disputes frequently tended to upset the stability of a Europe in which relations between the Great Powers had deteriorated into rivalry between two distinct groups (the Triple Alliance of Germany, Italy, and Austria-Hungary with their associate Romania, and the Triple Entente of France, Britain, and Russia, with their protégé Serbia), with the countries within these groups all, except Britain, operating conscript armies. It was the volatility of the European situation, within which the threat to the balance of power arising from Germany's aggressive ambitions was a major concern, that influenced the British government's decision to develop a policy involving a rapprochement with France and Russia and, in support of this, an improvement in Britain's ability to respond militarily if this became necessary.

Autobiographies, Biographies, Memoirs

Buchanan, Sir G. W. *My Mission to Russia and other Diplomatic Memories*, 2 vols (London: Cassell, 1923; repr. in one vol, New York: Arno Press, 1970)

Burton, D. H. *Cecil Spring Rice: A Diplomat's Life* (London: Associated University Presses, 1990)

Busch, B. C. *Hardinge of Penshurst: A Study in the Old Diplomacy* (Hamden, Conn.: Archon Books, 1980)

Conwell-Evans, T. P. *Foreign Policy from a Back Bench, 1904-1918: A Study based on the Papers of Lord Noel-Buxton*; with introductory notes by the Rt. Hon. Lord Noel-Buxton and G. P. Gooch. (London: Oxford University Press, 1932)

Crowe, S. and E. Corp. *Our Ablest Public Servant: Sir Eyre Crowe 1864-1925* (Braunton: Merlin, 1993)

Goschen, Sir W. E. *The Diary of Edward Goschen, 1900-1914*, edited by C. H. D. Howard (London: Royal Historical Society, 1980)

Grey, E., 1st Viscount Grey of Fallodon. *Twenty-Five Years 1892-1916*, 2 vols (London: Hodder & Stoughton, 1925)

Haldane, R. B., Viscount Haldane. *Before the War* (London: Cassell, 1920)
Introduction: "The purpose of the pages which follow is ... to explain the policy pursued towards Germany by Great Britain through the eight years which ... preceded the Great War of 1914."

Hamilton, K. *Bertie of Thame: Edwardian Ambassador* (Woodbridge: Royal Historical Society, 1990)
This biography mainly covers the period between 1905 and 1918 during which years Sir Francis Bertie (from 1915 Lord Bertie of Thame), a senior British diplomat of the late Victorian and Edwardian eras, was Britain's ambassador in Paris, and,

with his influence on Sir Edward Grey and other British statesmen, helping to foster the development and maintenance of the entente cordiale.

Hardinge, Sir A. H. *A Diplomatist in Europe* (London: J. Cape, 1927)

— *A Diplomatist in the East* (London: J. Cape, 1928)

Hardinge, C., Baron Hardinge of Penshurst. *Old Diplomacy: The Reminiscences of Lord Hardinge of Penshurst* (London: John Murray, 1947)

Robbins, K. *Sir Edward Grey: A Biography of Lord Grey of Fallodon* (London: Cassell, 1971)

Waterhouse, M. *Edwardian Requiem: A Life of Sir Edward Grey* (London: Biteback Publishing, 2013)

Books

Andrews, C. 'The Entente Cordiale from its Origins to 1914', in *Troubled Neighbours: Franco-British Relations in the Twentieth Century*, edited by N. Waites (London: Weidenfeld and Nicolson, 1971)

Bourne, K. *The Foreign Policy of Victorian England 1830-1902* (Oxford: Clarendon Press, 1970)

Bridge, F. R. *Great Britain and Austria-Hungary, 1906-14: A Diplomatic History* (London: Weidenfeld and Nicolson, 1972)

Charmley, J. *Splendid Isolation? Britain and the Balance of Power, 1874-1914* (London: Hodder & Stoughton, 1999)

Churchill, R. P. *The Anglo-Russian Convention of 1907* (Cedar Rapids, Ia: Torch Press, 1939; facsim repr. Freeport: Books for Libraries, 1972)

Crampton, R. J. *The Hollow Détente: Anglo-German Relations in the Balkans, 1911-1914* (London: Prior, 1980)

Greaves, R. L. *Persia and the Defence of India 1884-1892: A Study of the Foreign Policy of the Third Marquis of Salisbury* (London: University of London, Athlone Press, 1959)

Grenville, J. A. S. *Lord Salisbury and Foreign Policy: The Close of the Nineteenth Century*, new edn, with corrections (London: Athlone Press, 1970)

Hamilton, K. A. 'Great Britain, France, and the Origins of the Mediterranean Agreements of 16 May 1907', in *Shadow and Substance in British Foreign Policy 1895-1939*, edited by B. J. C. McKercher and D. J. Moss (Edmonton: University of Alberta Press, 1984)

Heller, J. *British Policy Towards the Ottoman Empire, 1908-1914* (London: Cass, 1983)

Hinsley, F. H., ed. *British Foreign Policy under Sir Edward Grey* (Cambridge: Cambridge University Press, 1977)

Howard, C. *Splendid Isolation: A Study of Ideas Concerning Britain's International Position and Foreign Policy during the Later Years of the Third Marquis of Salisbury* (London: Macmillan, 1967)

Johnson, G. *The Foreign Office and British Diplomacy in the Twentieth Century* (London: Routledge, 2005)
This book was previously published as a special issue of the journal, *Contemporary British History*

Jones, R. A. *The British Diplomatic Service, 1815-1914* (Waterloo, Ont., Canada: Wilfrid Laurier University Press, 1983)

Kennedy, P. M. *The Realities Behind Diplomacy: Background Influences on British External Policy, 1865-1980*, new edn (London: Fontana, 1985)

Lowe, C. J. *Salisbury and the Mediterranean, 1886-1896* (London: Routledge & Kegan Paul, 1965)

British Aspects

Lowe, C. J. and M. C. Dockrill. *The Mirage of Power*, 3 vols (London: Routledge, 1972), I: *British Foreign Policy, 1902-1914*

Lowe, P. *Great Britain and Japan, 1911-1915: A Study of British Far Eastern Policy* (London: Macmillan, 1969)

Martel, G. *Imperial Diplomacy: Rosebery and the Failure of Foreign Policy under Sir Edward Grey* (London: Mansell, 1986)

Miller, G. *The Millstone: British Naval Policy in the Mediterranean, 1900-1914, the Commitment to France and British Intervention in the War* (Hull: University of Hull Press, 1999)
This book, together with the following two books by Geoffrey Miller, provide a comprehensive account of British naval and diplomatic policy in the two decades prior to the Great War, focusing in particular on the escape of the German ships Goeben and Breslau (*Superior Force*), the origins of the Dardanelles Campaign (*Straits*), and the political and diplomatic pressures involved in the British decision to enter the war in August 1914

— *Straits: British Policy towards the Ottoman Empire and the Origins of the Dardanelles Campaign* (Hull: University of Hull Press, 1997)

— *Superior Force: The Conspiracy behind the Escape of Goeben and Breslau* (Hull: University of Hull Press, 1996)

Monger, G. W. *The End of Isolation: British Foreign Policy, 1900-1907* (London: Nelson, 1963)

Nish, I. *The Anglo-Japanese Alliance: The Diplomacy of Two Island Empires, 1894-1907*, 2nd edn (London: Athlone, 1985)

Otte, T. G. *The Foreign Office Mind: The Making of British Foreign Policy, 1865–1914* (Cambridge: Cambridge University Press, 2011)

Owen, D. *The Hidden Perspective: The Military Conversations 1906-1914* (London: Haus 2014)

Rolo, P. J. V. *Entente Cordiale: The Origins and Negotiations of the the Anglo-French Agreements of 8 April 1904* (London: Macmillan, 1969)

Soroka, M. *Britain, Russia and the Road to the First World War: The Fateful Embassy of Count Aleksandr Benckendorff (1903-16)*, Birmingham Studies in First World War History (Farnham: Ashgate, 2010)

Steiner, Z. S. *The Foreign Office and Foreign Policy, 1898-1914* (London: Cambridge University Press, 1969; repr. London: Ashfield, 1986)

Steiner, Z. S. and K. Neilson. *Britain and the Origins of the First World War*, 2nd edn (Basingstoke: Palgrave Macmillan, 2003)

White, J. A. *Transition to Global Rivalry: Alliance Diplomacy and the Quadruple Entente, 1895-1907* (Cambridge: Cambridge University Press, 1995)
By using the term 'Quadruple Entente', which relates to the agreements concluded in 1904 and 1907 between Britain, France, Russia and Japan, the author is intent on drawing attention to the emergence of Japan as an important world power and, thereby, providing a wider global view of the pre-war years than can be achieved through the use of the more familiar term, 'Triple Entente' (which, of course, omits Japan).

Wilson, K. M. 'Great Britain', in *Decisions for War 1914*, edited by Keith Wilson (London: UCL Press, 1994)

— 'The New Foreign Office and The "Education" of Public Opinion Before the First World War, 1906-1914', in *Empire and Continent: Studies In British Foreign Policy from the 1880's to the First World War*, ed. by K. M. Wilson (London: Mansell, 1987)

— *Policy of the Entente: Essays on the Determinants of British Foreign Policy, 1904-1914* (Cambridge: Cambridge University Press, 1985)

Articles

Abbenhuis, M.M. 'A Most Useful Tool for Diplomacy and Statecraft: Neutrality and Europe in the "Long" Nineteenth Century, 1815-1914', *International History Review*, 35 (2013), 1-22
In this article the author draws attention to the existence of a nineteenth-century international system in whch Eurpean states, particularly Great Britain, endeavoured to pursue a policy of avoidng war as a way of benefitting their political, economic, and imperial interests.

Bogdanor, V. 'August 1914: The Shadows Lengthen', *History Today*, 64, Issue 8 (2014), 19-25
In this article Bogdanor takes the view that, because Britain's efforts to preserve the Concert of Europe in the run up to the First World War were in vain as a result of the actions of other countries, Britain could not avoid being dragged into the conflict.

Butterfield, H. 'Sir Edward Grey in July 1914', *Historical Studies*, 5 (1965), 7-8

Coogan, J. W. and R. F. Coogan, 'The British Cabinet and the Anglo-French Staff Talks, 1905–14: Who Knew What and When Did He Know It?', *Journal of British Studies*, 24 (1985), 110-31

Corp, E. T. 'Sir Eyre Crowe and the Administration of the Foreign Office, 1906-1914', *Historical Journal*, 22 (1979), 443-54

— 'Sir Willam Tyrrell: The Eminence Grise of the British Foreign Office, 1912-1915', *Historical Journal*, 25 (1982), 697-708

Cosgrove, R. A. 'The Career of Sir Eyre Crowe: A Reassessment', *Albion*, 4 (1972), 193-205

Edwards, E. W. 'The Japanese Alliance and the Anglo-French Agreement of 1904', *History*, 42 (1957), 19-27

Ekstein, M. 'Sir Edward Grey and Imperial Germany in 1914', *Journal of Contemporary History*, 6 (1971), 121-31

Gilbert, B. 'Pacifist to Interventionist: David Lloyd George in 1911 and 1914. Was Belgium an Issue?', *Historical Journal*, 28 (1985), 863-885

Gowen, R. J. 'British Legerdemain at the 1911 Imperial Conference: The Dominions, Defense Planning, and the Renewal of the Anglo-Japanese Agreement', *Journal of Modern History*, 52 (1980) 385-413

Hatton, P. H. S. 'The First World War: Britain and Germany in 1914, the July Crisis and War Aims', *Past and Present*, 36 (1967), 138-43

Heindel, R. H. 'British Diplomats and the Press', *Public Opinion Quarterly*, 2 (1938), 435-41

Koch, H. W. 'The Anglo-German Alliance Negotiations: Missed Opportunity or Myth?', *History*, 54 (1969), 378-392

McKercher, B. J. C. 'Diplomatic Equipoise: The Lansdowne Foreign Office, the Russo-Japanese War of 1904-5, and the Global Balance of Power', *Canadian Journal of History*, 24 (1989), 299-339

Martel, G. 'The Limits of Commitment: Rosebery and the Definition of the Anglo-Understanding', *Historical Journal*, 26 (1983), 387-404

Neilson, K. '"A Dangerous Game of American Poker": Britain and the Russo-Japanese War', *Journal of Strategic Studies*, 12 (1989), 63-87

— '"My Beloved Russians": Sir Arthur Nicolson and Russia, 1906-1916', *International History Review*, 9 (1987), 521-54

Otte, T.G. 'Detente 1914: Sir William Tyrrell's Secret Mission to Germany', *Historical Journal*, 56 (2013), 175-204

Steiner, Z. S. Great Britain and the Creation of the Anglo-Japanese Agreement,' *Journal of Modern History*, 31 (1959), 27-36

—— 'Grey, Hardinge and the Foreign Office, 1906-1910', *Historical Journal*, 10 (1967), 415-39

—— 'The Last Years of the Old Foreign Office, 1898-1905', *Historical Journal*, 6 (1963), 59-90

Temperley, H. 'British Secret Diplomacy from Canning to Grey', *Cambridge Historical Journal*, 6 (1938), 1-32

Valone, S. J. '"There Must Be Some Misunderstanding": Sir Edward Grey's Diplomacy of August 1, 1914', *Journal of British Studies*, 27 (1988), 405-24

Williams, B. J. 'The Strategic Background to the Anglo-Russian Entente of August 1907', *Historical Journal*, 9 (1966), 360-73

Wilson, K. M. 'The Anglo-Japanese Agreement of August 1905 and the Defending of India: A Case of the Worst Scenario', *Journal of Imperial and Commonwealth History*, 21 (1993), 334-56

—— 'The British Cabinet's Decision for War', *British Journal of International Studies*, 1 (1975), 148-59

—— 'British War Plans and the Military Entente with France before the First World War', *British Journal of International Studies*, (1977)

—— 'The Foreign Office and "Education" of Public Opinion Before the First World War', *Historical Journal*, 26 (1983), 403-11

—— 'Imperial Interests in the British Decision for War, 1914: The Defence of India in Central Asia,', *Review of International Studies*, 10 (1984), 189-203

—— 'The Question of Anti-Germanism at the British Foreign Office before the First World War', *Canadian Journal of History*, 18 (1983), 23-42

Wilson, T. 'Britain's "Moral Commitment" to France in August 1914', *History*, 64 (1979), 380-90

2.3 Anglo-German Relations

Books

Anderson, P. R. *The Background of Anti-English Feeling in Germany, 1890-1902* (New York: Octagon, 1969)

Bridgham, F., ed. *The First World War as a Clash of Cultures* (Rochester, NY: Camden House, 2006)

Crampton, R. J. *The Hollow Détente: Anglo-German Relations in the Balkans, 1911-1914* (London: George Prior Publishers, 1980)

Hayes, P. 'Britain, Germany, and the Admiralty's Plans for Attacking German Territory, 1906-1915', in *War, Strategy, and International Politics: Essays in Honour of Sir Michael Howard*, edited by L. Freedman, P. Hayes and R. O'Neill (Oxford: Clarendon Press, 1992)

Hoffman, R. J. S. *Great Britain and the German Trade Rivalry, 1875-1914* (Philadelphia: University of Pennsylvania Press, 1933; repr. New York: Garland, 1983)

Kennedy, P. M. *The Rise of the Anglo-German Antagonism, 1860-1914* (London: Ashfield Press, 1987)

Massie, R. *Dreadnought: Britain, Germany and the Coming of the Great War*, new edn (London: Jonathan Cape, 1992; repr. London: Pimlico, 2004)

Mayer, S. L. 'Anglo-German Rivalry at the Algeciras Conference', in *Britain and Germany in Africa,: Imperial*

Rivalry and Colonial Rule, edited by P. Gifford and W. R. Louis (New Haven: Yale University Press, 1967; repr. Ann Arbor, Mich.: Books on Demand, 1997)
Essays presented at a conference on imperial rivalry and colonial rule held at Yale University in the Spring of 1965

Padfield, P. *The Great Naval Race: The Anglo-German Naval Rivalry, 1900-1914* (London: Hart-Davis, MacGibbon, 1974; repr. Edinburgh: Birlinn, 2005)

Rose, L. A. *Power at Sea*, 3 vols (Columbia, MO: University of Missouri Press, 2007), III: *The Age of Navalism, 1890-1918*
Among the topics covered in this book is the naval race between Britain and Germany in the years before the war.

Rüger, J. *The Great Naval Game: Britain and Germany in the Age of Empire* (Cambridge: Cambridge University Press, 2007)
A new, highly original perspective on the flourishing of the Anglo-German antagonism before the First World War.

Scully, R. *British Images of Germany: Admiration, Antagonism, and Ambivalence, 1860-1914* (Houndmills, Basingstoke: Palgrave Macmillan 2012

Seligmann, M. S. *Rivalry in Southern Africa, 1893-99: The Transformation of German Colonial Policy* (Basingstoke: Macmillan, 1998)

— *Spies in Uniform: British Military and Naval Intelligence on the Eve of the First World War* (Oxford: Oxford University Press, 2006)
The focus of the book is on the military and naval attachés located in Berlin within the period 1900 and 1914. A useful insight into Anglo-German relations, pre-World War I intelligence, and the role of service attachés in the intelligence gathering process.

Seligmann, M. S., ed. *Naval Intelligence from Germany: The Reports of the British Naval Attachés in Berlin, 1906-1914* (Aldershot: Ashgate for the Navy Records Society, 2007)
Useful collection of primary documents, designed to afford insight into British thinking about Germany and its navy during the Anglo-German naval arms race before the First Wortld War by examining reports (on matters such as German naval expansion, the objectives of Admiral von Tirpitz and the development of German equipment) provided by the last four naval attachés in post in Berlin before the outbreak of war in 1914.

Seligmann, M. S, and others, eds. *The Naval Route to the Abyss: The Anglo-German Naval Race 1895-1914*, edited by Matthew S. Seligmann, Frank Nägler and Michael Epkenhans (Farnham: Ashgate 2014)

Articles

Hatton, P. H. S. 'Harcourt and Solf: The Search for an Anglo-German Understanding through Africa, 1912-14', *European Studies Review*, 1 (1971), 123-46

Kennedy, P. M. 'The Development of German Naval Operations Plans Against England, 1896-1914', *English Historical Review*, 89 (1974), 48-76

Lambert, N.A. 'Righting The Scholarship: The Battle-Cruiser in History and Historiography', *Historical Journal*, 58, (2015), 275-307

Langhorne, R. T. B. 'Anglo-German Negotiations Concerning the Future of the Portuguese Colonies, 1911-14', *Historical Journal*, (1973), 361-87

— 'The Naval Question in Anglo-German Relations, 1912-1914', *Historical Journal*, 14 (1971), 359-70

Louis, W. R. 'Sir Percy Anderson's Grand African Strategy, 1883-1896', *English Historical Review*, 81 (1966), 292-314

Mackay, R. F. 'The Admiralty, the German Navy, and the Redistribution of the British Fleet, 1904-1905, *Mariner's Mirror*, 56 (1970), 341-6

Otte, T.G. 'Detente 1914: Sir William Tyrrell's Secret Mission to Germany', *Historical Journal*, 56 (2013), 175-204

Rüger, J. Revisiting the Anglo-German Antagonism', *Journal of Modern History*, 83 (2011), 579-617
Review article

Steinberg, J. 'The Copenhagen Complex', *Journal of Contemporary History*, 1 (1966), 23-46

— 'The Novella of 1908: Necessities and Choices in the Anglo-German Arms Race', *Transaction of the Royal Historical Society*, 5th series, 21 (1971), 25-43

Wilkinson, R. 'Germany, Britain and the Coming of War in 1914', *History Review*, 42 (2002), 21-26
An explanation of what went wrong in Anglo-German relations before the Great War.

2.4 Strategy

Diaries, Letters

Esher, R. B. B., 2nd Viscount. *Journals and Letters of Reginald, Viscount Esher*, edited by M. V. Brett, 4 vols (London: I. Nicholson & Watson, 1934-1938), III: *1910-1915* (1934) edited by Oliver S. B. Brett, Viscount Esher.
"On the CID [Committee of Imperial Defence] and its subcommittees he [i.e. Esher] had an active role in defence planning. In 1909, for example, he unsuccessfully proposed, contrary to the rival War Office and Admiralty strategies for possible war with Germany, a strategy of naval blockades and raids, with a token land force to assist the French" [extract from William M. Kuhn, 'Brett, Reginald Baliol, second Viscount Esher (1852–1930)', *Oxford Dictionary of National Biography*, Oxford University Press, 2004; online edn, Jan 2008].

Books

Blyth, R. J. and others, eds. *The Dreadnought and the Edwardian Age*, edited by Robert Blyth, Andrew Lambert and Jan Rueger (Farnham: Ashgate, 2011)

Cobb, S. *Preparing for Blockade, 1885-1914: Naval Contingency for Economic Warfare* (Farnham: Ashgate, 2013)

D'Ombrain, N. *War Machinery and High Policy: Defence Administration in Peacetime Britain, 1902–1914* (London: Oxford University Press, 1973)

Fergusson, T. G. *British Military Intelligence, 1870-1914: The Development of a Modern Intelligence Organization* (London: Arms and Armour, 1984)

French, D. *British Economic and Strategic Planning, 1905-15* (London: Allen & Unwin, 1982)

Gooch, J. *The Plans of War: The General Staff and British Military Strategy c. 1900-1916* (London: Routledge, 1974)

Grimes, S. T. *Strategy and War Planning in the British Navy, 1887-1918* (Woodbridge: Boydell, 2012)

Haggie, P. 'The Royal Navy and War Planning in the Fisher Era', in *The War Plans of the Great Powers, 1880-1914*, edited by P. Kennedy (London: Allen & Unwin, 1979; repr. 1985)

Hayes, P. 'Britain, Germany, and the Admiralty's Plans for Attacking German Territory, 1906-1915', in *War, Strategy, and International Politics: Essays in Honour of Sir Michael Howard*, edited by L Freedman, P. Hayes and R. O'Neill (Oxford: Clarendon Press, 1992)

Howard, M. *The Continental Commitment: The Dilemma of British Defence Policy in the Era of Two World Wars*, The Ford Lectures in the University of Oxford, 1971 (London: Maurice Temple Smith Ltd., 1972; repr. London Ashfield Press, 1989)

Jackson, J. *The Committee of Imperial Defence, the Foreign Office and the Drift to a Continental Commitment: A Study in British Policy Making, 1902-1914* (Ilfracombe: Arthur H. Stockwell, 2002)

Jones, M. 'About Turn: British Strategic Transformation from Salisbury to Grey', in *The Shaping of Grand Strategy: Policy, Diplomacy and War*, edited by Williamson Murray, Richard Hart Sinnreich and James Lacey (Cambridge: Cambridge University Press, 2011)

Lambert, N. A. *Planning Armageddon: British Economic Warfare and the First World War* (Cambridge, Mass.: Harvard University Press, 2012)

McDermott, J. 'The Revolution in British Military Thinking from the Boer War to The Moroccan Crisis', in *The War Plans of the Great Powers*, ed. by P. Kennedy (London: Allen & Unwin, 1979; repr. 1985)

Marder, A. J. *British Naval Policy, 1880-1905: The Anatomy of British Sea Power* (London: Putnam, 1940)
Reprinted London: Cass, 1964 under the title *The Anatomy of British Sea Power: A History of British Naval Policy in the Pre-Dreadnought Era, 1880-1905*

— *From the Dreadnought to Scapa Flow: The Royal Navy in the Fisher Era, 1904-1919*, 5 vols (London: Oxford University Press, 1961-1970), I: *The Road to War, 1904-1914* (1961)

Massie, R. *Dreadnought: Britain, Germany and the Coming of the Great War*, new edn (London: Jonathan Cape, 1992; repr. London: Pimlico, 2004)

Miller, G. *The Millstone: British Naval Policy in the Mediterranean, 1900-1914, the Commitment to France and British Intervention in the War* (Hull: University of Hull Press, 1999)
This book, together with the following two books by Geoffrey Miller, provide a comprehensive account of British naval and diplomatic policy in the two decades prior to the Great War, focusing in particular on the escape of the German ships Goeben and Breslau (Superior Force), the origins of the Dardanelles Campaign (Straits), and the political and diplomatic imperatives behind the British decision to enter the war in August 1914

— *Straits: British Policy towards the Ottoman Empire and the Origins of the Dardanelles Campaign* (Hull: University of Hull Press, 1997)

— *Superior Force: The Conspiracy behind the Escape of Goeben and Breslau* (Hull: University of Hull Press, 1996)

Neilson, K. "The British Empire Floats on the British Navy": British Naval Policy, Belligerent Rights, and Disarmament, 1902-1909, in *Arms Limitation and Disarmament: Restraints on War, 1899-1939*, edited by B. McKercher (Westport, Conn.: Praeger, 1992)

Padfield, P. *The Great Naval Race: The Anglo-German Naval Rivalry, 1900-1914* (London Hart-Davis, MacGibbon, 1974; repr. Edinburgh: Birlinn, 2005)

Parkinson, R. *The Late Victorian Navy: The Pre-Dreadnought Era and the Origins of the First World War* (Woodbridge: Boydell Press, 2008)

Prete, R. A. *Strategy and Command: The Anglo-French Coalition on the Western Front, 1914* (Montreal: McGill-Queen's University Press, 2009)

Seligmann, M. S. *The Royal Navy and the German Threat 1901-1914: Admiralty Plans to Protect British Trade in a War Against Germany* (Oxford: Oxford University Press, 2012)

Williams, R. *Defending the Empire: The Conservative Party and British Defence Policy, 1899–1915* (New Haven: Yale University Press, 1991)

Williamson, S. R. *The Politics of Grand Strategy: Britain and France Prepare for War, 1904-1914* (Cambridge, Mass.: Harvard University Press, 1969; repr. London: Ashfeld, 1989)

Articles

Coogan, J. W. and P. F. Coogan. 'The British Cabinet and Anglo-French Staff Talks, 1905-1914: Who Knew What and When Did He Know It?', *Journal of British Studies*, 24 (1985), 110-131

Gordon, D. C. 'The Admiralty and Dominion Navies, 1902-1914', *Journal of Modern History*, 33 (1961), 407-22

Haggie, P. 'The Royal Navy and War Planning in the Fisher Era', *Journal of Contemporary History*, 8 (1973), 113-32

Hargreaves, J. D. 'The Origins of the Anglo-French Military Conversations in 1905', *History*, 36 (1951), 244-8

McDermott, J. 'The Revolution in British Military Thinking from the Boer War to the Moroccan Crisis' *Canadian Journal of History*, 21 (1986), 159-78

Mackay, R. F. 'The Admiralty, the German Navy, and the Redistribution of the British Fleet, 1904-1905', *Mariner's Mirror*, 56 (1970), 341-6

Mackintosh, J. P. 'The Role of the Committee of Imperial Defence before 1914', *English Historical Review*, 77 (1962), 490-503

Martin, C. 'The Complexity of Strategy: '"Jackie"' Fisher and the Trouble with Submarines', *Journal of Military History*, 75 (2011), 441-470

Offer, A. 'The Working Classes, British Naval Plans and the Coming of the Great War', *Past and Present*, 107 (1985), 204-26

Steinberg, J. 'The Novella of 1908: Necessities and Choices in the Anglo-German Arms Race', *Transactions of the Royal Historical Society*, 5th series, 21 (1971), 25-43

Wilson, K. M. 'To the Western Front: British War Plans and the "military entente" with France before the First World War', *British Journal of International Studies*, 3 (1977), 151-68

Weinroth, H. 'Left-Wing Opposition to Naval Armaments in Britain before 1914', *Journal of Contemporary History*, 6 (1971), 93-120

2.5 Imperialism

Books

Baumgart, W. *Imperialism: The Idea and Reality of British and French Colonial Expansion, 1880-1914* (Oxford: Oxford University Press)
Revised translation of the author's *Der Imperialismus*, published Wiesbaden: Steiner, 1975.

Busch, B. C. *Britain and the Persian Gulf, 1894-1914* (Berkeley: University of California Press, 1967)

Cain, P. J. and A. G. Hopkins. *British Imperialism, 1688-2000*, 2nd edn (New York: Longman, 2001)
First edition published London: Longman, 1993 in 2 volumes. Vol. 1. *British Imperialism: Innovation and Expansion*. Vol. 2. *British Imperialism: Crisis and Deconstruction*

Gifford, P. and W. R. Louis, eds. *Britain and Germany in Africa: Imperial Rivalry and Colonial Rule* (New Haven: Yale University Press, 1967; repr. Ann Arbor, Mich.: Books on Demand, 1997)

Gillard, D. *The Struggle for Asia: A Study in British and Russian Imperialism* (London: Methuen, 1977; repr. 1980)

Kennedy, P. *The Realities Behind Diplomacy: Background Influences on British External Policy, 1865-1980* (London: Fontana, 1981; repr 1985)

MacKenzie, J. M. *Imperialism and Popular Culture* (Manchester: Manchester University Press, 1986)
Although several chapters cover the period after the Great War, this book focuses on a variety of media (e.g. the theatre, juvenile literature, education, popular art, etc) by means of which nationalist and imperialist ideas were conveyed in late-Victorian and Edwardian times.

— *Propaganda and Empire: The Manipulation of British Public Opinion, 1880-1960*, new edn (Manchester: Manchester University Press, 1984)

Mangan, J. A. *Images of Empire in the Late Victorian Public School* (Leeds: University of Leeds, 1980)
Reprinted from the *Journal of Educational Administration and History*, Vol.12, no.1, January 1980, 31-39.

Matthew, H. C. G. *The Liberal Imperialists: The Idea and Politics of a Post-Gladstonian Élite* (London: Oxford University Press, 1973)

Porter, A. N. *The Origins of the South African War: Joseph Chamberlain and the Diplomacy of Imperialism, 1895-1899* (Manchester: Manchester University Press, 1980)

Porter, B. *The Lion's Share*, 4th edn (Harlow; Pearson Longman, 2004)
A leading general history of British imperialism, from its Victorian heyday to present times.

Robinson, R. and J. Gallagher. *Africa and the Victorians: The Official Mind of Imperialism*, 2nd edn (London: Macmillan, 1981)

Sanderson, G. N. *England, Europe and the Upper Nile* (Edinburgh: Edinburgh University Press, 1965)

— 'The European Partition of Africa: Origins and Dynamics', in *Cambridge History of Africa*, edited by R. Oliver and G. N. Sanderson, vol 6 (Cambridge: Cambridge University Press, 1985)
Volume 6 of The Cambridge History of Africa covers the period 1870--1905, when the European powers (Britain, France, Germany, Portugal and Italy) divided the continent into colonial territories and competed with each other for control over vast tracts of land and valuable mineral resources.

Schreuder, D. M. *The Scramble for Southern Africa, 1877-1895: The Politics of Partition Reappraised* (Cambridge: Cambridge University Press, 1980)

Seligmann, M. S. *Rivalry in Southern Africa, 1893-99: The Transformation of German Colonial Policy* (Basingstoke: Macmillan, 1998)

Articles

Hatton, P. H. S. 'Harcourt and Solf: The Search for an Anglo-German Understanding through Africa, 1912-14', *European Studies Review*, 1 (1971),123-46

Langhorne, R. T. B. 'Anglo-German Negotiations Concerning the Future of the Portuguese Colonies, 1911-14', *Historical Journal*, (1973), 361-87

Louis, W. R. 'Sir Percy Anderson's Grand African Strategy, 1883-1896', *English Historical Review*, 81 (1966), 292-314

O'Brien, P. K. 'The Cost and Benefits of British Imperialism, 1846-1914', *Past and Present*, 120 (1988), 163-200

Wilson, K. M. 'Imperial Interests in the British Decision for War, 1914: The Defence of India in Central Asia,', *Review of International Studies*, 10 (1984), 189-203

2.6 The Army

Books

Beckett, I. F. W. *The Amateur Military Tradition, 1558-1945* (Manchester: Manchester University Press, 1991)

Bond, B. *The Victorian Army and the Staff College* (London: Eyre Methuen Ltd, 1972)

French, D.. *Military Identities: The Regimental System, the British Army, and the British People, c. 1870-2000* (Oxford: Oxford University Press, 2005)

Harries-Jenkins, G. *The Army in Victorian Society* (London: Routledge and Kegan Paul, 1977)

Jones, S. *From Boer War to World War: Tactical Reform of the British Army, 1902-1914* (Norman: University of Oklahoma Press, 2012)

Mallinson. A. *1914: Fight the Good Fight: Britain, the Army and the Coming of the First World War* (London: Bantam Press, 2013)

Prete, R.A. *Strategy and Command: The Anglo-French Coalition on the Western Front, 1914* (Montreal: McGill-Queen's University Press, 2009)

Spiers, E. M. *Haldane: An Army Reformer* (Edinburgh: Edinburgh University Press, 1980)

— 'The Regular Army in 1914', in *A Nation in Arms: A Social Study of the British Army in the First World War*, edited by Ian F. W. Beckett and Keith Simpson (Manchester: Manchester University Press, 1985; repr. London: Donovan, 1990)

Travers, T. *The Killing Ground: The British Army, the Western Front and the Emergence of War, 1900–1918* (London, Allen and Unwin, 1987)

Articles

Bond, B. 'The Late Victorian Army', *History Today*, 11 (1961), 616-24

Brodick, G. 'A Nation of Amateurs', *The Nineteenth Century*, 48 (1900), 526-527

Connelly, M. L. 'The Army, the Press and the Curragh Incident, March 1914', *Historical Research*, (Oxford), 84; (2011), 535-557

Evans, N. 'The British Army and Technology before 1914', *Journal of the Society for Army Historical Research*, 90 (2012), 113-122

Hall, B. N. 'The "Life-Blood" of Command? The British Army, Communications and the Telephone, 1877-1914', *War and Society* (Duntroon Australia), 27, Issue 2 (2008), 43-66

Low, S. 'The Future of the Great Armies', *The Nineteenth Century*, 47 (1899), 390-2

Mallinson, A. 'The British Army: The New Contemptibles?', *History Today*, 64, Issue 8 (2014), 4-5
The author sees a parallel between the neglect of the British Army in recent years to the state of affairs in August 1914.

Maxwell, H. 'Are We Really a Nation of Amateurs?', *The Nineteenth Century*, 48 (1900), 1051-1063

Travers, T. 'The Hidden Army: Structural Problems in the British Officer Corps, 1900-1918', *Journal of Contemporary History*, 17 (1982), 537

— 'The Offensive and the Problem of Innovation in British Military Thought, 1870-1915', *Journal of Contemporary History*, 13 (1978), 546

— 'Technology, Tactics, and Morale: Jean de Bloch, the Boer War, and British Military Theory. 1900-1914', *Journal of Modern History*, 51 (1979), 264-286

Wilkinson, G. '"Soldiers by Instinct, Slayers by Training": The *Daily Mail* and the Image of the Warrior, 1899-1914', *Journal of Newspaper and Periodical History*, 8 (1992)

2.7 Militarism

With a background of aggressive colonization and empire building and a people brought up over the years on nationalistic and patriotic music, poetry, and art, there could be some justification for discerning a distinctly militaristic streak in the character of the British nation as it entered the 20th century. This might well also seem to be reflected in aspects of British society such as the 'muscular Christianity' of the public schools, the establishment of officer corps in schools and universities, and the emulation of 'muscular Christianity' among the lower social orders (as exemplified by the popularity of the Boy's Brigade, the Boy Scouts and other similar youth organisations). Yet, this apparent militaristic tendency is not borne out by the negative reaction to the National Service League's vigorous campaign to introduce compulsory military service in the pre-war decade. The notion of conscript armies as espoused in other parts of Europe found no favour in Britain and, traditionally, the soldier tended to be looked down on by the British people.

Books

Best, G. 'Militarism and the Victorian Public School', in *The Victorian Public School: Studies in the Development of an Educational Institution*, a symposium edited by B. Simon and I. Bradley (Dublin: Gill and Macmillan, 1975)

Boyd, K. *Manliness and the Boy's Story Paper in Britain: A Cultural History, 1855-1940* (Basingstoke : Palgrave Macmillan, 2002)

Deslandes, P. R. *Oxbridge Men: British Masculinity and the Undergraduate Experience, 1850-1920* (Bloomington, IN: Indiana University Press, 2005)

Jeal, T. *Baden-Powell: Founder of the Boy Scouts* (New Haven: Yale University Press, 2007)
Previous ed.: London: Hutchinson, 1989

Johnson, M. *Militarism and the British Left, 1902-1914* (Houndmills, Basingstoke: Palgrave Macmillan, 2013)
This work challenges the view that early twentieth century British militarism was identified with the Radical Right.

Mcgaughey, J. G. V. *Ulster's Men: Protestant Unionist Masculinities and Militarization in the North of Ireland, 1912-1923* (Montreal; Ithaca: McGill-Queen's University Press, 2012)

Newsome, D. *Godliness and Good Learning: Four Studies on a Victorian Ideal* (London: Murray, 1961; repr. London: Cassell, 1988)

Mackenzie, J. M. 'The Imperial Pioneer and Hunter and the British Masculine Stereotype in late Victorian and Edwardian Times, in *Manliness and Morality: Middle-Class Masculinity in Britain and America, 1800-1940*, edited by J. A. Mangan and J. Walvin (Manchester: Manchester University Press, 1987)

Mangan, J. A. 'Athleticism: A Case Study of the Evolution of an Educational Ideology', in *The Victorian Public School: Studies in the Development of an Educational Institution*, a symposium edited by B. Simon and I. Bradley (Dublin: Gill and Macmillan, 1975)

Springhall, J. 'Building Character in the British Boy', in *Manliness and Morality: Middle-Class Masculinity in Britain and America, 1800-1940*, edited by J. A. Mangan and J. Walvin (Manchester: Manchester University Press, 1987)

— *Youth, Empire, and Society: British Youth Movements, 1883-1940* (London: Croom Helm, 1977)

Vance, N. 'The Ideal of Manliness', in *The Victorian Public School: Studies in the Development of an Educational Institution*, a symposium edited by B. Simon and I. Bradley (Dublin: Gill and Macmillan, 1975)

Articles

Adams, R. J. Q. 'The National Service League and Mandatory Service in Edwardian Britain', *Armed Forces and Society*, 12 (1985), 53-74

Anderson, O. 'The Growth of Christian Militarism in Mid-Victorian Britain', *English Historical Review*, 86 (1971), 46-72

Summers, A. 'Militarism in Britain before the Great War' *History Workshop Journal*, 2 (1976), 104-23

2.8 The Anti-War Lobby

Biographies, Memoirs

Baker, E. B. and P. J. N. Baker, Baron Noel-Baker. *J. Allen Baker, M.P.: A Memoir* (London: Swarthmore Press, 1927)

Marrin, A. *Sir Norman Angell* (Boston: Twayne Publishers, 1979)

White, H. C. *Willoughby Hyett Dickinson, 1859-1943: A Memoir* (Gloucester: Privately printed by J. Bellows, 1956)

Books

Morris, A. J. A. *Radicalism Against War, 1906-1914: The Advocacy of Peace and Retrenchment* (London: Longman, 1972)
The unpublished Oxford thesis, 'Radical liberal criticism of British foreign policy 1906-1914' (1964) by A. J. Dorey, is employed to a large extent as the basis of Chapters 2 and 6, and parts of other chapters.

Newton, D. J. *British Labour, European Socialism and the Struggle for Peace, 1889-1914* (Oxford: Oxford University Press, 1985)

Sidorowicz, A. 'The British Government, the Hague Peace Conference 1907 and the Armaments Question', in *Arms Limitation and Disarmament: Restraints on War, 1899-1939*, edited by B. McKercher (Westport, Conn.: Praeger, 1992)

Swartz, M. 'A Study In Futility; The British Radicals at the Outbreak of the First World War', in *Edwardian Radicalism*, ed. by A. J. A. Morris (London: Routledge and Kegan Paul, 1974)

Articles

Howard, C. 'MacDonald, Henderson, and the Outbreak of War, 1914', *Historical Journal*, 20 (1977), 871-91

Morris, A. J. A. 'The English Radicals' Campaign for Disarmament and the Hague Conference of 1907', *Journal of Modern History*, 43 (1971), 367-93

Weinroth, H. S. 'British Radicals and the Balance of Power, 1902-1914', *Historical Journal*, 13 (1970), 653-82

— 'Left-Wing Opposition to Naval Armaments in Britain before 1914', *Journal of Contemporary History*, 6 (1971), 93-12

PART 3: THE WAR YEARS

1. General

The records listed in this general section represent a selection of works which cover aspects of the history of Britain during the war years in a broad overview (**Part 3, section 1.1**) and also in relation to specific localities and regions (**Part 3, section 1.2**). Works covering more specialized aspects are listed within **sections 2 to 5 of Part 3**.

Books

Best, G. F. A. *Churchill and War* (London: Hambledon and London, 2005)

Best, N. *The Greatest Day in History: How The Great War Really Ended* (London: Weidenfeld & Nicolson, 2008)

Brown, M. *The Imperial War Museum [IWM] Book of 1914: The Men Who Went to War* (London: Sidgwick and Jackson, 2004

— *The Imperial War Museum [IWM] Book of the First World War: A Great Conflict Recalled in Previously Unpublished Letters, Diaries, Documents and Memoirs* (London: Sidgwick & Jackson in association with the Imperial War Museum, 1991; repr. London: Pan Books 2002)

Bourne, J. M. *Britain and the Great War, 1914-1918* (London: Edward Arnold, 1989)

Charman, I. *The Great War: The People's Story* (London: Random House, 2014)
A reconstruction of the experiences of indivduals through their diaries and letters published to accompany the ITV series of the same title transmitted in August 2014

Constantine, S., and others, ed. *The First World War in British History* (London: Edward Arnold, 1995)

Hynes, S. *A War Imagined: The First World War and English Culture* (London: Bodley Head, 1990)

Liddle, P. H. *The Worst Ordeal: Britons at Home and Abroad, 1914-1918* (London: Leo Cooper, 1994)

Liddle, P. H., ed., *Home Fires and Foreign Fields: British Social and Military Experience in the First World War* (London: Brasseys Defence Publishers, 1985)

Lloyd George, D. *War Memoirs*. 2nd edn, 2 vols (London: Odhams, 1942)
Originally published in 6 vols: London: Nicholson & Watson, 1933-36

Meyer, J., ed. *British Popular Culture and the First World War* (Leiden; Boston: Brill, 2008)

Moynihan, M, ed. *People at War, 1914-1918* (Newton Abbot: David & Charles, 1973)

Robb, G. *British Culture and the First World War* (Basingstoke: Palgrave, 2002)

Roper, M. *The Secret Battle: Emotional Survival in the Great War* (Manchester: Manchester University Press, 2010)

Turner, J., ed. *Britain and the First World War* (London: Routledge, 1988)

Wilson, T. *The Myriad Faces of War: Britain and the Great War, 1914-1918* (Cambridge: Polity Press, 1986)

Winegard, T. C. *Indigenous Peoples of the British Dominions and the First World War* (New York: Cambridge University Press, 2011)

General

Winter, J. M. *The Great War and the British People* (London: Macmillan, 1985)

Woodward, Sir L. *Great Britain and the War of 1914-1918* (London: Methuen, 1967)

Local and Regional Studies (see also Part 3, section 2.9 on Ireland)

Armitage, F. P. *Leicester, 1914-1918: The War-Time Story of a Midland Town* (Leicester: Edgar Backus, 1933)

Ashley-Smith, G. *Kineton in the Great War 1914-1921* (Studley: Brewin Books, 1998)

Barlow, R. *Wales and the First World War* (Cardiff: University of Wales Press, 2006)

Bavin, W.D. *Swindon's War Record* (Swindon: John Drew Ltd., 1922)

Blackmore, J. P. *A Richer Dust: The Marlingford Men Who Died in the Great War* (Wymondham: John N. Nickalls Publications, 2004)

Brazier, R. H. and E. Sandford. *Birmingham and the Great War, 1914-1919* (Birmingham: Cornish, 1921)

British Association For Local History. *Local History and the First World War* [http://www.balh.org.uk/education/local-history-and-the-first-world-war]

Buckell, J. 'The Conscientious Objectors of Northampton during the First World War', *Local Historian*, 46:3 (2016), 180-193

Bullock, R. *Salford 1914-1920: The County Borough and the First World War* (Manchester: Neil Richardson, 2001)

Bush, J. *Behind the Lines; East London Labour, 1914-1919* (London: Merlin Press, 1984)

Campbell, A. *Crieff in the Great War* (Edinburgh: University Press, 1925)

Carlile, J. C., ed. *Folkestone during the Great War: A Record of the Town's Life and Work* (Folkestone: F. J. Parsons, 1920)

Clark, A. *Echoes of the Great War: The Diary of the Reverend Andrew Clark, 1914-1919*, edited with an introduction by J. Munson (Oxford: Oxford University Press, 1985)
This book is a condensation of the Reverend Andrew Clark's 92 volume diary in which he recounts the effects of the First World War on English life, with particular reference to Great Leighs, in Essex where he was rector at the time.

Clayton, J. T., ed. *Craven's Part in the Great War* (Bradford: Percy Lund, Humphries and Co., 1919)

Cookstown's War Dead, 1914-1918; 1939-1945, compiled and edited by Cookstown District Council in conjunction with The Friends of the Somme Mid Ulster Branch (Cookstown: Cookstown District Council, 2007)

Cross, D. *Bromsgrove School at War, 1914-1918* (Kidderminster: D. Cross, 1997)

Dayus, K. *Where There's Life*, 2nd rev. edn (London: Virago Press, 1991)
This autobiography includes Kathleen Dayus's years in Birmingham during the Great War when she worked in a small munitions shop. It is one of a series of books she wrote about her life from Edwardian times onwards that have been collected in *The Girl from Hockley* edited by Joanna Goldsworthy (London: Virago, 2006)

Devereux, J. and G. Sacker. *Leaving All That Was Dear: Cheltenham and the Great War* (Cheltenham: Promenade Publications, 1997)

Elliston, R. A. *Eastbourne's Great War* (Seaford: S.B. Publications, 1999)

Englander, D. 'Tenants and Politics: The Birmingham Tenants' Federation During and after the First World War', *Midland History*, 6 (1981), pp. 124-41

Firth, J. B. *Dover and the Great War* (Dover: Alfred Leney & Co. Ltd., 1919)

Foynes, J. P. *Brightlingsea and the Great War 1914-1918* (J. P. Foynes, 1993)

Gates, W. G. *Portsmouth and the Great War* (Portsmouth: Portsmouth Evening News, 1919)

Gilder, A. *A Widow with Five Children to Support: Memories of a Great War Victim in Long Eaton* (Newport: Gildertext, 1995)

Gillam, G. *Enfield at War 1914-1918: Events in Edmonton, Enfield and Southgate during the First World War* (London: Enfield Archaeological Society, 1982)

Grieves, K. 'St Albans: Life on the Home Front, 1914–1918', *Social History*, 42:4 (2017), 560-562

Grimsby's War Work: An Account of the Borough's Effort during the Great War, 1914-1919 (Grimsby: Humberside County Council Archive Service, 1994)
Facsimile edition with a new index of the work originally published Grimsby: W. H. Jackson, 1919

Hall, D. *The Unreturned Army: County Louth Dead in the Great War, 1914-1918* (Dublin: County Louth Archaeological and Historical Society, 2005)

— *World War 1 and Nationalist Politics in County Louth, 1914 - 1920* (Dublin: Four Courts Press, 2005)

Harding, A. W. *On Flows the Tay: Perth and the First World War* (Dunfermline: Cualann Press, 2004)

Haxby Local History Group. *Haxby in Wartime 1914-1918 and 1939-1945*, researched and compiled by Pauline Briggs ... [et al.]. Editor: Tom Smith (Malton: Bestprint & Design, 2004)

Haynes, D. *Malpas and the Great War* (Malpas: D. Haynes, 1993)

History of Birmingham, 3 vols (London: Oxford University Press, 1952-1974), II: *Borough and City, 1865-1938*, by Asa Briggs (1952)

Holford, J. *Reshaping Labour: Organisation, Work, and Politics; Edinburgh in the Great War and After* (London: Croom Helm, 1988)

Hopkins, E. 'The Great War 1914-1918', in *The Making of the Second City: Birmingham 1850-1939* (Stroud: Tempus, 2002)

Howell, C. *No Thankful Village: The Impact of the Great War on a Group of Somerset Villages* (Bath: Fickle Hill, 2002)

Hunt, W. M. *A Town Remembers Those Commemorated on the Boston War Memorial* (Boston: Richard Kay Publications, 2002)

Kimberley, S. *Humberside in the First World War* (Hull: Local History Archives Unit, 1988)

Lee, J. A. *Todmorden and the Great War* (Todmorden: Waddington & Sons, 1922)

Lethbridge, J. P. *Birmingham in the First World War* (Birmingham: Newgate Press, 1993)

— *More about Birmingham in the First World War* (Birmingham: Newgate Press, 1994)

Longbottom, F. W. *Chester in the Great War* (Chester: Phillipson & Golder, 1920)

Luck, K. 'The Growing Pains of the 'Women on the Land Movement' in Wiltshire 1914-1917: Recruitment and Training Women Before the Formation of the Women's Land Army', *Local Historian*, 47:3 (2017), 193-207

General

MacDonagh, M. *In London during the Great War* (London: Eyre & Spottiswoode, 1935)

Macdonald, C. M. M. and E. W. McFarland, eds. *Scotland and the Great War* (East Linton: Tuckwell, 1998)

MacKie, D. M. *Forfar and District in the War: A Record of Service in the Great Struggle, 1914-1919* (Forfar: Forfar War Memorial Committee, 1921)

Markham, J., ed. *Keep the Home Fires Burning: The Hull Area in the First World War* (Beverley: Highgate, 1988)

Markwick, W. F. *Stamford and the Great War: An Authentic Record of the War Work of the Mayor and Mayoress and other Inhabitants of the Ancient and Royal Borough of Stamford, with Some Account of the Local Conditions during the War Period, 1914-1919* (Stamford: Dolby Brothers, 1920)

Martin, J. and R. King. 'Civil Defence Activities during the First World War: A Case-Study of Hinckley, Leicestershire', *Local Historian*, 47:2 (2017), 127-137

Meeres, F. *Norfolk in the First World War* (Chichester: Phillimore, 2004)

Middlebrook, M. *Boston in Time of War* (Boston: Richard Kay Publications, 1974)

Miller, F. *The Hartlepools and the Great War* (West Hartlepool: Charles A. Sage, 1920)

Mitchinson, K. W. *Saddleworth 1914-1919: The Experience of a Pennine Community during the Great War* (Oldham: Saddleworth Historical Society, 1995)

Moorhouse, G. *Hell's Foundations: A Town* [Bury]*, Its Myths and Gallipoli* (London: Hodder & Stoughton, 1992)

Moore, H. K. and W. C. B. Sayers. *Croydon and the Great War* (Croydon: Corporation of Croydon, 1920)

Nunn, D. *Britannia Calls: Nottingham Schools and the Push for Great War Victory* (Nottingham: Knowle Hill Publishing, 2010)
In this wider perspective of British social history during the Great War the author provides an account of the contributions of elementary education to the British war effort in Nottingham and of the effect of the war upon those who delivered and received education in that city. *Britannia Calls* "was a play performed by Nottingham elementary school children on Empire day 1915 and 1916"--T.p. verso.

Oakley, W. H. *Guildford in the Great War* (Guildford: Billing & Sons Ltd., 1934)

Owain, G. *Ruthin and the Great War 1914-19: An Account of Ruthin's Involvement in the First World War* (Invisus Publications, 2005)

Peacock, A. J. *York in the Great War 1914-1918* (York: York Settlement Trust, 1993)

'Publications about Aspects of the First World War: A Compilation of Reviews', *Local Historian*, 47:3 (2017), 244-249

The Record of Haddenham (Bucks) in the Great War (Haddenham: B. W. Soper, 1922)

Reynolds, B. and C. Reynolds. *The London Gunners Come to Town: Life and Death in Hemel Hempstead in the Great War* (Tring: CODIL Language Systems Ltd., 1995)

Roberts, M. A., ed. *Rochford Great War Memories*, compiled and edited by M. A. Roberts (Hockley: Rochford Historical Society, 1995)

Roberts, R. *A Ragged Schooling: Growing up in the Classic Slum* (Manchester: Manchester University Press, 1976; repr. Manchester: Mandolin, 1997)
Relates to Salford

Robertson, W. *Middlesbrough's Effort in the Great War* (Middlesborough: Jordisan & Co. Ltd., 1922)

Rowson, J. W. *Bridport and the Great War: Its Record of Work at Home and in the Field* (London: T. Werner Laurie Ltd., 1923)

Rudkin, D. J. *Emsworth during the First World War* (Rowlands Castle: Castle Communications Centre, 1994)

Scott, W. H. *Leeds in the Great War 1914-1918* (Leeds: Leeds Libraries & Arts Committee, 1923)

Sheldon, C. W. *Roll of Honour: The Story of the Hundreds of Leek Men Who Fell in the First World War* (Leek: Three Counties Publishing Ltd., 2004)

Senior, M. *No Finer Courage: A Village in the Great War* (Stroud: Sutton Publishing, 2004)
Relates to Lee (Buckinghamshire)

Skirrey, T. *Brave Sons of Shirebrook* (Matlock: Derbyshire County Council, Libraries & Heritage Department, 2000)

Slater, G., ed. *My Warrior Sons: The Borton Family Diary 1914-1918* (London: P. Davies, 1973)
An abridgement of a 9 vol diary kept by A. C. Borton, which includes transcriptions of letters written by various members of the Borton family and friends.

Slocombe, I. *The First World War Tribunals in Swindon* (Devizes: Wiltshire Family History Society, 1997)

— *First World War Tribunals in Wiltshire* (Devizes: Wiltshire Family History Society, 1997)

Sokoloff, S. 'From the Heartland: Letters, Memoirs and Local Histories of 1914-1918 and 1939-1945', *Local Historian*, 46:2 (2016), 151-156

— 'Military Service Tribunals in the First World War: A Northamptonshire Study', *Local Historian*, 47:3 (2017), 208-226

— 'Review Article: Books on Local Aspects of the First World War', *Local Historian*, 45:1 (2015), 71-73

Stone, G. F. and C. Wells, eds. *Bristol and the Great War 1914-1919* (Bristol: J. W. Arrowsmith, 1920)

Tall, S. and B. Sunley. *Kenilworth and the Great War – A Tribute to the Fallen* (Kenilworth: Clock Tower Publications, 2004)

Tattersfield, D. *A Village Goes to War: A History of the Men of Ravensthorpe Who Fell in the Great War* (Coventry?: Barkers Trident, 2000)

Taylor, K. and T. Brown. *A Derbyshire Parish at War: South Darely and the Great War, 1914-1919* (Bakewell: Country Books, 2001)

Walker, J. *West Wickham and the Great War* (West Wickham: Hollies Publications, 1988)

Warner, P. *Nine Nightingales* (Studley: Brewin Books, 1997)
Relates to Tardebigge and Bromsgrove

Wasley, G. *Devon in the Great War, 1914-1918* (Tiverton: Devon Books, 2000)

Weiner, M.-F. and Silver, J. R.. 'Pierpont Morgan and the Wall Hall Estate during two World Wars', *Local Historian*, 46:4 (2016), 315-326
In February 1915 John Pierpont Morgan Jr (d 1942), an American banker who bought Wall Hall (an estate in the parish of Aldenham) in 1910, offered the use of his garage as a Voluntary Aid Detachment Hospital. The hospital opened on 23 March 1915 with 20 beds for wounded and convalescent soldiers. By 1917 the number of beds had increased to fifty. Upon Morgan's death Hertfordshire County Council acquired the property, which became the residence of the United States of America's Ambassador, Joseph Kennedy, for the duration of the Second World War.

White, B. 'Sowing the Seeds of Patriotism? The Women's Land Army in Devon, 1916-1918', *Local Historian*, 41:1

(2011), 13-27

Williams, D. W. *Heroic Circumstances: An Account of the Sacrifices of the Men and Women of Ruthin and District during the Great War, 1914-18* (Ruthin: Coelion Trust, 1997)

2. The Civilian Scene

2.1 General

Books

Addison, P. *Churchill on the Home Front, 1900-1955* (London: Cape, 1992) Andrews, M. and J. Lomas, eds. *The Home Front in Britain: Images, Myths and Forgotten Experiences since 1914* (Basingstoke: Palgrave Macmillan, 2014)

Beckett, I. F. W. *Home Front 1914-1918: How Britain Survived the Great War* (London: The National Archives, 2006)

Bilton, D. *The Home Front in the Great War: Aspects of the Conflict 1914-1918* (Barnsley: Leo Cooper, 2003)

Cahalan, P. *Belgian Refugee Relief Work in England during the Great War* (New York: Garland 1982)

Chandler, M. *The Home Front, 1914-18* (Oxford: Heinemann Educational, 2001)

Charman, T. *The First World War on the Home Front* (London: Andre Deutsch in association with IWM, 2014)
In this book Terry Charman (Senior IWM Historian) draws on the archives of the Imperial War Museum to feature previously unpublished excerpts from diaries, letters, and newspaper reports that illustrate the wide-ranging social and economic changes that took place in Britain during the war years.

Cooksley, P. *The Home Front* (Stroud: Tempus, 2006)
Civilian life in World War One

Dakers, C. *The Countryside at War* (London: Constable, 1987)

De Groot, G. J. *Back in Blighty: The British at Home in World War One* (London: Vintage, 2014)

— *Blighty: British Society in the Era of the Great War* (London: Longman, 1996)

Duncan, R. *Pubs and Patriots: The Drink Crisis During World War One* (Liverpool: Liverpool University Press 2013)

Gregory, A. *The Last Great War: British Society and the First World War* (Cambridge: Cambridge University Press, 2008)

Horn, P. *Rural Life in England in the First World War.* (Dublin: Gill and Macmillan, 1984)

Kennedy, R. *The Children's War: Britain, 1914-1918* (Basingstoke: Palgrave Macmillan, 2014)

Liddle, P. H., ed., *Home Fires and Foreign Fields: British Social and Military Experience in the First World War* (London: Brasseys Defence Publishers, 1985)

Marwick, A. *The Deluge: British Society and the First World War*, 2nd edn (Basingstoke: Macmillan Education, 1991)

Martin, C. *English Life in the First World War* (London: Wayland 1974; repr 1988)

Pankhurst, E. S. *Home Front: A Mirror to Life in England during the First World War* (London: Heinemann, 1932; repr. London: Cresset Library, 1987)

Peel, D. C. ["Mrs. C. S. Peel"]. *How We Lived Then 1914-1918: A Sketch of Social and Domestic Life in England*

During the War (London: John Lane, 1929)

Playne, C E. *Britain Holds On, 1917-1918* (London: Allen & Unwin, 1933)

—— *Society at War 1914-1916.* (London: Allen & Unwin, 1931)

Proctor, T. M. *Civilians in a World at War, 1914-1918* (New York: New York University Press, 2010)

Roper, M. *The Secret Battle: Emotional Survival in the Great War* (Manchester: Manchester University Press, 2010)

Turner, E. S. *Dear old Blighty* (London: Michael Joseph, 1980)

Ugolini, L. *Civvies: Middle-Class Men on the English Home Front, 1914–18* (Manchester: Manchester University Press, 2013)

Van Emden, R. and S. Humphries. *All Quiet on the Home Front: An Oral History of Life in Britain during the First World War* (London: Headline 2003)

Waites, B. *A Class Society at War: England 1914-1918* (Leamington Spa: Berg, 1987)

Articles

Doyle, J. 'The Nation on its Honour, *History Today*, 67:2 (2017), 3
About food shortages and rationing in the First World War.

Feltman, B.K. 'Prisoners of Britain: German Civilian and Combatant Internees during the First World War', *Social History*, 39 (2014), 128-130

Elliot, R. 'An Early Experiment in National Identity Cards: The Battle Over Registration in the First World War', *Twentieth Century British History*, 17 (2006), 145-176

Fisher, J. 'The Impact of Military Service on the British Foreign Office and Diplomatic and Consular Services, 1914-8', *International History Review*, 34, (2012), 431-448

Grant, P. '"An Infinity of Personal Sacrifice": The Scale and Nature of Charitable Work in Britain during the First World War', *War And Society* (Duntroon Australia), 27, Issue 2 (2008), 67-88

Grayzel, S. R. 'Defence Against the Indefensible: The Gas Mask, the State and British Culture during and after the First World War', *Twentieth Century British History*, 25 (2014), 418-434

Panayi, P. 'Today's History: Forgotten Prisoners of the Great War', *History Today*, 62, (2012), 34-35

Pourcher, Y. 'Trains in World War I', *Historical Reflections*, 38, Issue 1 (2012), 87-104

Sykes, A. 'Which War? The English Radical Right and the First World War', *War and Society* (Duntroon Australia), 23 (2005), 59-74

White, J. 'London's Wartime Housing Crisis', *History Today*, 63, Issue 11 (2013), 43
About the housing crisis in London preccipitated by the Great War and its profound effect on all classes and on the capital.

2.2 Responses to the War

There was a remarkable degree of support for the war, once it had been declared, among a wide range of people – members of the professional, commercial and working classes, churchmen, intellectuals, academics, university students, scientists, composers, painters, dramatists, poets, novelists, even some suffragettes and Irish nationalists – and an overwhelming response to the call for volunteers to join the armed forces. Even members of the Labour Party and the trade unions, against war right up to the last moment, dropped their opposition and gave the government its support.

The Civilian Scene

Nevertheless, to describe this reaction to the outbreak of the war as one of mass enthusiasm would be to overstate the case. There were considerable numbers of people who were not at all enthusiastic. The City (including influential figures like Lord Rothschild), which had previously made strenuous use of its influence to prevent a war, was certainly not enthusiastic, fearing that the war would result in financial chaos. Among socialists, liberals, pacifists, and intellectuals there were some individuals who immediately adopted an anti-war stance or, alternatively, supported the war with considerable misgivings. Although most of the press, hitherto largely anti-war, came round to supporting the decision to go to war there were some newspapers, particularly in the North, which were highly critical of it and may well have influenced the views of some of their readers. Crowd demonstrations of enthusiasm for the war primarily occurred in urban areas. The response was less demonstrative in the rural communities where many farmers were far from happy to have their labour force denuded by recruitment of their workers to the armed forces and their horses commandeered for military purposes.

The attitudes of individuals towards the war, as well as their wartime experiences, were very much shaped by their class identities. The working-class shared in the national enthusiasm to volunteer for military service, but this attitude was by no means so nearly universal and immediate as it was among the middle and upper classes. Robert Roberts in his book *The Classic Slum* (listed below) recalled that the declaration of war 'caused no great outburst of patriotic fervour' in the slums of Salford, and that propaganda had been necessary to stir it up. Among the most impoverished it is understandable that there could be an indifference to the war that reflected their disillusion with society (see, for instance, the note below appended to H. Anstey's article, 'The Home Side of War Time' under the heading **Contemporary Material**). In neither urban nor rural areas is it likely that those members of the population on the poverty line, preoccupied with the ever present task of making ends meet, would be particularly enthusiastic about the war unless they believed it could improve their lot. Nevertheless, large numbers of the working-class voluntarily joined up at the beginning of the war, their motives ranging from the mundane to the patriotic but underlying them all was an assumption, almost universally held in the country, that the war would be neither long nor horrific.

The eagerness to join up was even greater among professionals and white-collar workers than among the manual workers. As Trevor Wilson put it, "the former, with generally middle-class aspirations that caused them to marry later and breed less and to identify passionately with mother country and Empire, had both stronger incentives to enlist and fewer domestic responsibilities to restrain them". The enlistment rate for these middle class workers was twice as great as for manual workers but this has to be seen in relation to the fact that the latter included those who were the poorest and least nourished in the country and, even if eager to enlist, were most likely to be declared medically unfit. The patriotism of the middle class men who rushed to the colours was emulated by their wives and daughters who enthusiastically joined in the war effort in many ways, such as rolling bandages for the Red Cross, knitting socks for soldiers, generally busying themselves in war-related charities, and even leaving the shelter of their homes to enter the wartime workforce.

The upper classes, traditionally of a martial disposition and closely identified with the state, had little difficulty greeting the war with enthusiasm. No social group was more enthusiastic than the aristocracy. The sons flocked spontaneously to the colours; their fathers offered their great houses as makeshift hospitals and vigorously aided the government in its recruitment drives, and their mothers threw themselves wholeheartedly into the war effort by organizing charity bazaars, and even, in the case of the Duchess of Westminster, establishing a Red Cross hospital in France, and, in the case of the Duchess of Sutherland, organizing an ambulance unit to serve in Belgium.

More than any other social group, the upper classes tended to see the war through rose coloured spectacles viewing it in unrealistically chivalric terms, as the diaries, letters and descriptions of the war emanating from aristocratic soldiers and their families frequently show. In his novel, *The Pretty Lady* (1918), however, Arnold Bennett takes a somewhat jaundiced view of upper class attitudes, painting a critical picture of frivolity in high society during the war and taking a cynical view of what passed for 'war work' among some members of the upper classes. Although this novel represents a somewhat biased middle class view of the upper classes in the war it does contain an element of truth in that some members of the upper classes no doubt continued their usual round of parties and extravagant entertaining, oblivious to the idea of wartime austerity. This attitude, however, may simply have been a form of escapism which was no different to the attitude of people of other classes who sought amusement and entertainment as an antidote to the harsh realities of war.

Autobiographies, Biographies, Memoirs

The War Years

The brief selection of biographical material here and of the records listed below under **Contemporary Material** are representative of a cross-section of a nation – soldiers, statesman, politicians, poets, intellectuals, literary figures, newspapermen, and the various classes of which British society was constituted – confronted by a war which few originally thought would be of such long duration and savagery. Many other works in this bibliography contain some allusion to the British people's responses to the war but in this respect the works recorded in **Part 3, section 2.11** on **Doubts and Dissent** are especially pertinent in that they provide an insight into the deviations from the British public's generally supportive attitude to the war.

Cassar, G. H. *Kitchener: Architect of Victory* (London: Kimber, 1977)
When war broke out, the government's initial 'Business as Usual' plans for the management of the war economy were based on the idea of a war lasting no more than nine months. Kitchener, however, forecast a war of far longer duration and called for the formation of a mass army that would need to be maintained in the field for several years.

Coppard, G. *With a Machine Gun to Cambrai: The Tale of a Young Tommy in Kitchener's Army, 1914-1918*, revised and enlarged edn (London: Imperial War Museum, 1980; repr. London Cassell, 1999)
"Glossing over my childhood, I merely state that in 1914 I was just an ordinary boy of elementary education and slender prospects. Rumours of war broke out and I began to be interested in the Territorials tramping the street in their strong boots. Although I seldom saw a newspaper, I knew about the assassination of the Archduke Ferdinand at Sarajevo. News placards screamed out at every corner, and military bands blared out their martial music in the main street of Croydon. This was too much for me to resist, and as if drawn by a magnet, I knew I had to enlist straightaway." [Extract (on p. 1) from the book]

Davenport-Hines, R. P. T. *Ettie: The Intimate Life and Dauntless Spirit of Lady Desborough* (London: Weidenfeld & Nicolson, 2008)
In 1915 Julian [Lady Desborough's eldest son] and her second son Billy were killed fighting on the Western Front. Her brave public reaction to these tragedies was typical of her courageous spirit (see also below, under **Contemporary Material**, Lady Desborough's *Pages from a Family Journal 1888-1915*)

Gilbert, M. *Winston S. Churchill*, vol 3, 1914-1916 (London, Heinemann, 1971)
"Winston dashed into the room radiant, his face bright, his manner keen, one word pouring out on another how he was going to send telegrams to the med., to the North Sea, and God knows where. You could see he was a really happy man" (p. 31). [The scene when the Cabinet convened at 10 Downing Street 15 minutes after the ultimatum to Germany expired, unanswered, as later described by David Lloyd George in a private letter to Mrs Asquith]. A reprint of this work entitled *The Challenge of War: Winston Churchill, 1914-1916,* by Martin Gilbert was published by Minerva (London) in 1990.

Gollin, A. M. *Proconsul in Politics: A Study of Lord Milner in Opposition and in Power* (London: A. Blond, 1964)
"Lord Milner hoped that the war would force into being stronger government, leading in turn to a strengthened empire, a more formidable military and disciplined society" (De Groot, *Blighty*, 1996, p.13). "War would 'ring out the feud of rich and poor'. The imperial ideal would replace the class prejudice and 'ancient forms of party strife'" (Bourne, *Britain and the Great War*, 1989, p.230, on the attitude of Milnerite radicals)

Grey, E., 1st Viscount Grey of Fallodon. *Twenty-Five years 1892-1916*, 2 vols. (London: Hodder & Stoughton, 1925)
If the words attributed to Grey by a friend about 'the lamps … going out all over Europe' and not seeing 'them lit again in our lifetime' (Grey, vol. 2, p. 20) really were his words, it appears that he was not very enthusiastic about the coming war even though he had made the case for entering into it.

Hardy, G. H. *Bertrand Russell and Trinity: A College Controversy of the Last War 1914-18* (Cambridge: printed for the author at the University Press, 1942)
Reproduced in facsimile with a foreword by C. D. Broad, Cambridge: Cambridge University Press, 1970. Although not initially the unwavering opponent of the war that he subsequently became Russell was by September 1914 totally put off by the frenzied nature of war propaganda, especially in relation to what he considered to be the extreme prejudice against Germany, which outraged his sense of justice.

Leventhal, F. M. *Arthur Henderson* (Manchester: Manchester University Press, 1989)
Henderson assumed the chairmanship of the Labour party at the beginning of the war and subsequently became a cabinet minister in successive Coalition Governments. While he believed in the need to defeat Germany he was also intent on ensuring that working class interests were not neglected in time of war. He personified the level-headed patriotism which characterised the majority of the Labour Party.

Lloyd George, D. *War Memoirs.* 2nd edn, 2 vols (London: Odhams, 1942)

The Civilian Scene

Originally published in 6 vols: London: Nicholson & Watson, 1933-36. Lloyd George's eve of the war arguments for non-intervention ceased when Germany invaded Belgium. After that he supported Britain's entry into the war and subsequently prosecuted the war with great vigour when he became Prime Minister

Mackenzie, J *The Children of the Souls* (London: Chatto & Windus, 1986)
Portrays the lives and attitudes of an elite group of English intellectuals who died fighting in World War I.

Marquand, D. *Ramsay MacDonald* (London: Cape, 1977; repr. London: Richard Cohen, 1997)
Macdonald was opposed to Britain's involvement in the war and relinquished his chairmanship of the Labour Party because of its broad support of the war.

Montague, C. E. *Disenchantment* (London: Chatto & Windus, 1922; repr. London: Macgibbon & Kee, 1968)
"A sour, soiled, crooked old world [was] to be rid of bullies and crooks and reclaimed for straightness, decency, good-nature". [Montague's view of the initial public reaction to the war on p. 3 of *Disenchantment*]

Morley, J., Viscount. *Memorandum on Resignation, August 1914* (London: Macmillan, 1928)
Pro-German sympathies and antipathy to Russia, allied to a concern that the defeat of Germany would result in Russia gaining predominance in Europe, led to Morley opposing entry into a war against Germany and resigning from the cabinet on the outbreak of the war in August 1914. Even Germany's invasion of Belgium failed to change his attitude. His *Memorandum on Resignation*, describing the events of July-August 1914, was not published until 1928 - after his death.

Richards, F. *Old Soldiers Never Die* (London: Faber, 1933)
"Look here, Dick, there is only one way to treat foreigners from Hong Kong to France and that is to knock hell out of them". [This extract from the book (on p. 12) of advice given to Richards by one of his mates illustrates the racially arrogant reaction of some people to the outbreak of war – a not entirely surprising reaction from a member of a country long used to being regaled with news of decisive imperial victories over native troops.]

Roynon, G. *Home Fires Burning: The Great War Diaries of Georgina Lee, 1914-1919* (Stroud: Sutton, 2006)
In a work that provides a vivid insight into the manner in which British society coped with the pressures and crises of the First World War the reader is able to detect that the mood of the diarist changes from one of optimism initially to one eventually of having to face the fact that the war was going to be of a long and drawn out duration.

Scott, C. P. *The Political Diaries of C. P. Scott, 1911-28*, edited with an introduction and commentary by T. Wilson (London: Collins, 1970)
Scott edited the *Manchester Guardian*, which he purchased in 1905, from 1872 to 1929. Prior to the war he had tended to discount the threat from Germany but once Britain was committed to war he took the view that it must be conducted wholeheartedly. For this reason he believed that Asquith should be replaced by Lloyd George who he considered to have the passionate commitment to the struggle which Asquith lacked.

Spender, J. A. and C. Asquith. *Life of Herbert Henry Asquith, Lord Oxford and Asquith*, 2 vols (London: Hutchinson, 1932)
"'So it's all up?' she said. 'Yes, it's all up.' Henry sat at his writing tables, leaning back, pen in hand. I got up and leant my head against his. We could not speak for tears'. [Extract from the book describing the scene when Asquith was visited by his wife in the Prime Minister's room in the Commons on the outbreak of the war]

Vansittart, P., ed. *Voices from the Great War* (London: Cape, 1981; repr. London: Pimlico, 1998)
In his response to the call for volunteers to J. B. Priestley was not motivated by anything 'that was rational and conscious … I went at a signal from the unknown ... there out of the unclouded blue of that summer, a challenge that was almost like a conscription of the spirit, little to do really with King and Country and flag-waving and hip-hip-hurrah, a challenge to what we felt was our untested manhood. Other men, who had lived as easily as we had, had drilled and marched and borne arms - Couldn't we?' [Quotation (on pp. 261-2) extracted from the book]

Books

Bourne, S. *Black Poppies: Britain's Black Community and the Great War* (Stroud: The History Press, 2014)

Dewhirst, I. *The Story of a Nobody: A Working Class Life, 1880-1939* (London: Mills and Boon, 1980)
This book gives the impression that in 1914 many ordinary working class people were little aware of what was going on in the outside world and that they were quite surprised when they heard that the country was at war.

Girouard, M. *The Return to Camelot: Chivalry and the English Gentleman* (New Haven: Yale University Press, 1981)

Hendley, M. C. *Organized Patriotism and the Crucible of War: Popular Imperialism in Britain, 1914-1932* (Montréal, Québec: McGill-Queen's University Press, 2012)
In this book's comparison of how three major patriotic organizations founded between 1901 and 1902 (the National Service League, the League of the Empire, and the Victoria League) fared during the war the author shows that the National Service League, with its strongly masculinist and militaristic character, failed to flourish in wartime whereas the League of the Empire and the Victoria League, strongly female in their membership and with aims and concepts related to education and hospitality, family, home and kinship, prospered not only during the war but beyond into the 1920's. The author sees this as an indication of how the traumatic nature of the Great War produced a fundamental reshaping of popular patriotism and imperialism that is evident to the author in his comparison of the post-war histories of the above organizations.

Hochschild, A. *To End All Wars: A Story of Loyalty and Rebellion, 1914-1918* (Boston: Houghton Mifflin Harcourt, 2011)

Lambert, A. *Unquiet Souls: The Indian Summer of the British Aristocracy, 1880-1918* (London: Macmillan, 1984)
The 1st United States edition (New York: Harper & Row, 1984) was entitled *Unquiet Souls: A Social History of the Illustrious, Irreverent, Intimate Group of British Aristocrats known as "the Souls"*

Osborne, J. M. *The Voluntary Recruiting Movement in Britain, 1914-1916* (London: Garland, 1982)

Parker, P. *The Old Lie: The Great War and the Public School Ethos* (London: Constable, 1987)
As well as exploring the evolution of the codes of patriotism, chivalry and sportsmanship of the public schools and their percolation through lower levels of the society of the time the author also utilises appropriate poetry, plays, and prose of the period to reflect the different responses to the war - varying from glorifying in it to deploring it, from greeting it patriotically to rebelling against it.

Pennell, C. *A Kingdom United: Popular Responses to the Outbreak of the First World War in Britain and Ireland* (Oxford: Oxford University Press, 2012)

Reader, W. J. *At Duty's Call: A Study in Obsolete Patriotism* (Manchester: Manchester University Press, 1988)

Roberts, R. *The Classic Slum: Salford Life in the First Quarter of the Century* (London: Penguin, 1971)
The author recalled that the declaration of war "caused no great outburst of patriotic fervour" in the slums of Salford, and that such a reaction had to be stirred up by propaganda.

Sheriff, R. C. 'The English Public Schools in the War', in *Promise of Greatness: The War of 1914-1918*: [A Memorial Volume for the Fiftieth Anniversary of the Armistice], edited by G. A. Panichas (London: Cassell, 1968)

Turner, E.S. *Dear Old Blighty* (London: Michael Joseph, 1980)

Whiteside, N. 'The British Population at War', in *Britain and the First World War*, ed. by J. Turner (London: Routledge, 1988)

Winter, J. 'The Army and Society; The Demographic Context', in *A Nation In Arms: A Social Study of the British Army In The First World War*, ed. by I. Beckett and K. Simpson (Manchester: Manchester University Press, 1985; repr. London: Donovan, 1990)
"Unemployment did not fill the ranks of Kitchener's Army, popular sentiment did. The protection of 'little Belgium', the defence of the empire, the need to be seen to be doing one's military duty alongside the men of one's district or village: these may sound like outworn clichés today, but in 1914 they had force and substance in the minds of ordinary people". [Quotation from Jay Winter's chapter in the book]

Articles

Bourne, S. 'Black Poppies: The Experiences of Black Citizens of Britain and the Empire, who answered the call to serve the Mother Country during the First World War', *History Today*, 63, (2013), 51-71

Collins, T. 'English Rugby Union and the First World War', *Historical Journal*, 45 (2002), 797-818
"The idea that war was a football match writ large was commonly expressed in Britain during the First World War. This article looks at the attitudes and actions of the English Rugby Football Union and its supporters before, during, and after

the First World War to examine how such beliefs were utilized by sports organizations and the impact they had on the military and on society as a whole. Rugby union football was viewed both by its supporters and general observers alike as the most enthusiastic and committed sporting supporter of the war effort; the article explores rugby's overtly ideological stance as a means of shedding light on broader discussions about the cultural impact of the war, such as in the works of Paul Fussell and Jay Winter, and about the continued survival of traditional and Edwardian ideas of patriotism among the English middle classes in the immediate post-war period." [Abstract from the internet]

Douglas, R. 'Voluntary Enlistment in the First World War and the Work of the Parliamentary Recruiting Committee [PRC]', *Journal of Modern History*, 42 (1970), 564-85

Fletcher, A. 'Patriotism, the Great War and the Decline of Victorian Manliness', *History*, 99, (2014), 40-72

— 'A New Moral Order: Britain at the Start of the Great War', *History Today*, 64, Issue 8 (2014), 26-33
In this article the author explores the response of ordinary people in Britain to the declaration of war during August 1914.

Fowler, S. 'War Charity Begins at Home', *History Today*, 49 (1999), 17-23
In this article Simon Fowler describes a response to war that was represented by the great increase in voluntary charity work which in his view was an important influence in helping to unite the British people in support of the war effort.

Pennell, C. 'Community Responses to the Outbreak of War, August 1914', *Local History News*, Number 104 (Summer 2012)

Veitch, C. '"Play Up! Play Up! And Win the War!": Football, The Nation and the First World War 1914-1915', *Journal of Contemporary History*, 20 (1985), 363-78

Winter, J. 'Britain's Lost Generation of the First World War', *Population Studies*, 31 (1977), 449-66
Includes some interesting statistics about enlistment. Men in commercial and clerical occupations represented the highest enlistment rates in the early months of the war, a trend which continued throughout 1915 and 1916 as is evident from the fact that throughout 1915 and 1916 29 percent of industrial workers had volunteered by February 1916 whereas, in comparison, there was a voluntary enlistment of 40 per cent of the men employed in banking, finance, or commerce, in the professions (accountants, architects, solicitors, advertising agents, estate agents), and men working in the entertainment trades (hotels, pubs, theatres, musical halls, cinemas, and restaurants)

Contemporary Material

Anstey, H. 'The Home Side of War Time', *Contemporary Review*, 108 (1915), 237-243
In this article Anstey refers to a woman at a working-women's meeting saying: "She did not see what difference it would make if the Germans did come and rule England. She had always been poor, and didn't suppose she would be worse off with them than without them".

Bishop, A. and M. Bostridge, eds. *Letters from a Lost Generation: First World War Letters of Vera Brittain and Four Friends - Roland Leighton, Edward Brittain, Victor Richardson, Geoffrey Thurlow* (London: Little, Brown, 1998)
A selection of letters, written between 1913 and 1918, between Vera Brittain and her fiancé (Roland Leighton), her brother Edward, and their close friends, Victor Richardson and Geoffrey Thurlow, that provide a portrayal of the impact of the war on five young people of a particular class and their response to it.

Brooke, R. *"1914": Five Sonnets* (London : Sidgwick & Jackson, 1915)
Some people may well find this verse excessively romantic. Nevertheless, it does epitomise the feelings of many of Brooke's social class in 1914.

Desborough, E. A. P., Baroness Grenfell, comp. *Pages from a Family Journal 1888-1915* (Eton: Eton College, privately printed by Spottiswoode, Ballantyne & Co., 1916)
Lady Desborough suffered the loss of her two elder sons, Julian and Billy, both killed fighting in France in 1915. In this work, which, as her husband wrote in its preface, was "compiled by my wife from the journal which she kept for our children from their earliest years", she recounts the story of their lives as a memorial to her sons and as a way of alleviating her grief. In this work can be detected the stoicism of an aristocrat confronted with the loss of two sons in the war.

'Famous British Authors Defend England's War', *New York Times*, Sunday Supplement, 18 October 1914
Sub-titled 'Fifty-three of the Best-Known Writers of the Empire Sign a Vigorous Document Saying that Great Britain Could Not Have Refused to Join the War Without Dishonour'. This was a reprint of the manifesto (dated September 1914

with the authors' signatures in facsimile) which had resulted from a meeting of British authors at Wellington House on 4 September 1914 that Charles Masterman had arranged for propaganda purposes. The manifesto's signatories were William Archer, H. Granville Barker, J. M. Barrie, Arnold Bennett, A. C. Benson, Robert Hugh Benson, Laurence Binyon, Robert Bridges (the Poet Laureate), Hall Caine, R. C. Carton, C. Haddon Chambers, G. K. Chesterton, Hubert Henry Davies, Arthur Conan Doyle, H. A. L. Fisher, John Galsworthy, F. Anstey, H. Rider Haggard, Thomas Hardy, Anthony H. Hawkins, Maurice Hewlett, Robert Hichens, Jerome K. Jerome, Henry Arthur Jones, Rudyard Kipling, W. J. Locke, John Masefield, A. E. W. Mason, Henry Newbolt, Barry Pain, Gilbert Parker, Eden Phillpotts, Arthur Pinero, Arthur Quiller-Couch, Owen Seaman, May Sinclair, Flora Annie Steel, George M. Trevelyan, George Otto Trevelyan, H. G. Wells, Israel Zangwill

Harrison, J. E. *Alpha and Omega* (London: Sidgwick & Jackson, 1915)
A reprint of this work was published by AMS Press in 1973. Consists of a collection of essays, one of which was entitled *Epilogue on the War: Peace with Patriotism* (see below)

— *Peace With Patriotism*, 2nd edn (Cambridge: G. Bell,1915)
In this work Jane Harrison, a Cambridge lecturer, expressing astonishment at the reaction of students and dons to the call to join up, wrote: 'it came to me as something of a shock to find that many of them ... went, not reluctantly, but with positive alacrity'. In her opinion, they rushed into the war thoughtlessly and uncritically 'driven by a thirst for primary sensations'. During the war Jane Harrison was a lecturer in classical archaeology at Newnham College, Cambridge

Jacks, L.P. 'The Peacefulness of Being At War', *Hibbert Journal*, (1915), 99-102
"I doubt if there ever was a time when in general the minds of Englishmen were so agitated as they were in the few years preceding the war. Rest for our souls was hardly to be found anywhere. In religion, in philosophy, in politics, we were all at sixes and sevens, fighting one another in the name of our ideals, or striving to rouse the lethargic masses who cared not a button for any of our idealism; and often, it must be confessed, we were in a chronic state of irritation; and to make matters worse, a school of writers had arisen, represented by Mr. Bernard Shaw, who made it their business to irritate and, incidentally, to confuse us still further. Compared to this aimlessness and confusion the war had brought a sense of 'mission' and 'peace of mind'" [extract from the article].

Owen, H. *Common Sense about the Shaw: Being a Candid Criticism of "Common Sense about the War" by Bernard Shaw* (London Allen & Unwin, 1915)

Russell, B. A. W., 3rd Earl Russell. *Justice in War-Time* (London: Allen and Unwin, 1916)
Although not initially the unwavering opponent of the war that he subsequently became he was by September 1914 reacting strongly, like Shaw, not so much against the war (a grim necessity) as against the frenzied nature of war propaganda, especially in relation to what he considered to be the extreme prejudice against Germany, which outraged his sense of justice.

— 'War: The Cause and the Cure', *The Labour Leader*, 11, no. 39 (Sep 24 1914), 2

— 'Will This War End War?', *The Labour Leader*, 11, no. 37 (Sep 10 1914), 2

— 'Why Nations Love War', *War and Peace*, 2, no. 14 (Nov 1914), 20-1

Shaw, G. B. *Common Sense about the War* (London: The Statesman Publishing Co., 1914)
The New Statesman, vol. 4, no. 84, November 14, 1914. Special War Supplement

Wells, H. G. *The War that Will End War* (London: Palmer, 1914)
This work sets out Wells's case for supporting the allies.

2.3 Intellectuals

2.3.1 Academia

'Academia' is interpreted here as meaning the teachers and students at universities and other higher education institutions in existence during the war years. Almost half of this academic population were in the Universities of Cambridge and Oxford.

On the eve of the war some academics were uneasy about the prospect of being involved in a conflict with Germany. At Cambridge a manifesto against war with Germany that attracted 81 signatories reflected this uneasiness which was also expressed by a considerable number of other academics in the *Scholars' Protest Against War with Germany* which was published in *The Times* on 1st August 1914 [2]. Most of this opposition to British intervention subsided after Britain declared war, particularly after Germany's invasion of Belgium that caused many early academic opponents of the war to change their minds. A change of mind was also influenced at the beginning of the First World War by a manifesto[3] in which 93 prominent German scientists, scholars and artists declared their unequivocal support of German military actions. This provoked a response in *The Times* of 21 October, 1914, headed 'Reply to German Professors' and signed by 150 British academics, that, in its concluding paragraph, declared that Germany "stands revealed as the common enemy of Europe and of all peoples which respect the Law of Nations".

Once war had broken out the nation's campuses mostly came out in support of Britain's entry into the war. Undergraduates readily responded to the call to arms and universities were rapidly denuded of their male students. Younger able-bodied dons also joined in the eagerness to serve in the armed forces. H.G. Moseley, a brilliant young physicist who died at Gallipoli in 1915, was an example of the not unusual case of a science don who joined up immediately without any hesitation (it has been calculated that 35 Fellows of the Royal Society and 55 members of the Royal Institute of Chemistry were killed in combat and, no doubt, many other promising scientists destined to reach that level of excellence suffered the same fate).

The war undoubtedly took a tragic toll of Britain's graduate population. In an article, 'Battle of the Dons of War' in the *Times Higher Education Supplement* of 30 October 1998 (see below under **Articles**) that was critical of the part played by some dons in lending their active public support to the prosecution of the war, Niall Ferguson highlights the war's devastating effects with the following statistics: "Twelve per cent of all men mobilised in Britain between 1914 and 1918 were killed; but for graduates of the ancient English universities, the figure was far higher. Nearly a fifth of Oxford graduates who served did not return from the war; the figure for Cambridge was 18 per cent. Colleges such as King's, Cambridge, and Balliol, Oxford, suffered mortality rates twice the national average. Among those who matriculated at Oxford in the years 1910 to 1914, a staggering 29.3 per cent were killed. Nor was the phenomenon of a "lost generation" peculiar to Oxbridge. The mortality rates were just as high at the Royal Technological College, Glasgow, the London City and Guilds and the Royal School of Mines".

Most of those dons who were left on the campuses, if not always totally committed to the war, decided to give it their support[4], albeit sometimes reluctantly, particularly in the case of those who admired German scholarship or who before the war had enjoyed ties of friendship and common intellectual endeavour with German colleagues and regretted the adverse effect the war was having on traditional academic objectivity. An impressive group of humanities academics chose to serve their country in government departments[5], and a number of eminent scientists and engineers[6] willingly applied their knowledge and expertise on government bodies for the benefit of the war effort Most of the academics who expressed their attitudes publicly were motivated by what they saw as their duty to support the war in positive ways such as helping to sustain morale and to counteract talk of peace without total victory. They frequently did this by writing propagandistic material for circulation in the press and in pamphlets (e.g the famous series of patriotic pamphlets produced by the History Faculty of Oxford University, a selection of which are listed below in the section **Contemporary Writings of Academics on the**

---

[2] But for a different, and after the war had begun, more common view of an academic see below under H. Stuart Jones's letter 'A Scholar's Protest' to *The Times* of 4 August 1914 in the section **Contemporary Writings of Academics on the War.**

[3] *Der Aufruf "An die Kulturwelt!": Das Manifest der 93 und die Anfange der Kriegspropaganda im Ersten Weltkrieg* (4 October 1914). A translation of this manifesto by Jeffrey Verhey and Roger Chickering can be found on the internet at http://germanhistorydocs.ghi-dc.org/pdf/eng/817_Bernhard vom Brocke_156.pdf

[4] Arnold Toynbee in a passage of his autobiography, *Experiences* (1969), took the view that "in the First World War, almost all of us, in both camps, were not only wholeheartedly belligerent but were also naively sure that our cause - whichever of the two it happened to be - was one hundred percent righteous ...".

[5] e.g. John Maynard Keynes joined the Treasury in 1915; Ernest Barker worked temporarily for the Ministry of Labour; Arnold Toynbee and Lewis Namier both worked in intelligence departments of the Foreign Office; Herbert Fisher served as President of the Board of Education in the coalition government; Sir C. W. C. Oman worked for the Press Bureau and the Foreign Office; H. W. C. Davis helped to run a department that was a constituent part of the Ministry of Blockade.

[6] e.g. J. J. Thomson, Ernest Rutherford, Sir Charles Parsons and a number of other university science professors contributed their expertise to the Admiralty's Board of Invention and Research, and John Scott Haldane did valuable work for the War Office.

War). Against the prevailing attitude, the *Cambridge Magazine*[7], an unofficial student publication edited by C. K. Ogden, became notorious for its willingness to print viewpoints which did not toe the official patriotic line (as exemplified by its acceptance of controversial pieces from writers like Russell and Sassoon and excerpts from German and Austrian papers). In contrast at Oxford the student magazine *Varsity* became so anti-German that many people became alienated by its stance as, for example, when a hundred people felt impelled to sign a letter of protest against the magazine's harassment of the German professor H.G. Fiedler.

Although there continued to be misgivings about the war among some academics (Goldsworthy Lowes Dickinson is a particularly noteworthy example) only a minority, of whom Bertrand Russell especially stands out for his categorical and unwavering opposition to the war[8], were involved in public expressions of anti-war sentiment or the need for a compromise peace. As the war ground on, however, the enthusiasm of some of those academics who had hitherto been staunch supporters of the war began to wane and increasingly towards the end of the war found an outlet in their support of the idea of a League of Nations, to which some of those members of the academic community who had been less committed to the war, especially those associated with the Union of Democratic Control (UDC), had already given their approval.

The war soured relations between British and German scholars as was exemplified from the outset by the publication by two of Germany's most distinguished scholars, Ernest Hackel and Rudolph Eucken, of a protest on August 20, 1914 in the *Vossiche Zeitung* against England's case for being involved in the war[9], and by the publication in October 1914 of the German manifesto of the 93. This was the beginning of a slanging match between British and German academics and intellectuals as is evident in publications such as the British response to the German Manifesto of the 93, Gilbert Murray's 'German Scholarship', John Cowper Powys's *The German Menace of German Culture*, Ford Madox Hueffer's *When Blood is Their Argument*, and Sir Arthur Quiller-Couch's 'Right and Left Among the Professors: Sir Arthur Quiller-Couch on Huns and Historians'. There were writers like W. P. Paterson (*German Culture: The Contributions of the Germans to Knowledge, Literature, Art and Life*, 1915), James Moulton (*British and German Scholarship*, 1915), and Ernest Belfort Bax (*German Culture Past and Present*, 1915) who made a serious effort to treat German scholarship objectively but their efforts were against the prevailing trend for British scholars to denigrate German scholarship. Although British scientists were among the signatories of the response to the German Manifesto of the 93 at the beginning of the war and sometimes engaged in petty hostility towards their German counterparts (by, for instance, calling for a boycott of German scientists and scientific publications) they did not get engaged in the war of words between Britain and Germany to the extent of their humanities colleagues, particularly the historians.

Autobiographies, Biographies, Memoirs

Appleyard, R. *Charles Parsons: His Life and Work* (London: Constable, 1933)
When the Admiralty set up its own Board of Invention and Research during the war Sir Charles Parsons was among the number of eminent scientists it recruited

Barker, Sir. E. *Age and Youth* (London: Oxford University Press, 1953)
Fellow and tutor, New College, Oxford, 1913-20. Although mostly teaching at Oxford during the First World War, Ernest Barker worked temporarily for the Ministry of Labour. Positive supporter of the war, writing in defence of Britain's role in the war for popular audiences.

Bliss, M. *William Osler: A Life in Medicine* (Oxford: Oxford University Press, 1999; repr. 2007)
This biography is not only about the evolution of modern medicine, the training of doctors, holism in medical thought, and the doctor-patient relationship, but also about humanism, Victorianism, the Great War, and much else. Osler devoted a good deal of time to war work, both as a consultant to military hospitals and as a participant in relief agencies. Osler was Regius Professor of Medicine at Oxford, 1904-19

Cannadine, D. *G. M. Trevelyan: A Life In History* (London: HarperCollins, 1992; repr. London: Penguin, 1997)
Trevelyan was a Fellow of Trinity College, Cambridge, later Regius Professor of Modern History, 1927-40, and Master, 1940-51 at that College. Supported Britain's declaration of war. Raised and commanded British Red Cross ambulance unit

---

[7] The *Cambridge Magazine* reached a circulation 25,000 during the war.

[8] Russell was not immediately totally opposed to the war in its first few weeks but he was soon disgusted by the hysterical and unfair nature of the war propaganda directed against Germany.

[9] This was quoted in 'Germany and the Neutrals' in *The Times* for 25 August, 1914.

The Civilian Scene

on Italian front, 1914-18

Caroe, G. M. *William Henry Bragg, 1862-1942: Man and Scientist* (Cambridge: Cambridge University Press, 1978)
Bragg became a member of the Admiralty Board of Invention and Research as a result of which he spent a period of time at the Naval Experiment Station at Hawkcraig and at Harwich working on submarine detection.

Clark, R. W. The *Life of Bertrand Russell* (London: Cape, 1975; repr. Harmondsworth: Penguin, 1978)
Russell was a Fellow and lecturer at Trinity College at the beginning of the war. Throughout the war he was, unlike most of his academic contemporaries, involved in public expressions of opposition to the war through his political publications and his membership of the No-Conscription Fellowship and the Union of Democratic Control. He was removed from his lectureship in 1916 after being found guilty on a charge relating to a leaflet he had written in support of the No-Conscription Fellowship (he was reinstated in 1919). In 1918 he was imprisoned for an article he wrote in *The Tribune* that resulted in his being charged and found guilty of sedition on the grounds that the article was prejudicial to Britain's relations with its American ally.

Dickinson, G. L. *The Autobiography of G. Lowes Dickinson and Other Unpublished Writings*, edited by D. Proctor (London: Duckworth, 1973)
Lecturer in political science at Kings College, Cambridge, 1896-1920. Regarding international anarchy as the root cause of the war, he called soon after its outbreak for the establishment of a league of nations. He was prominent in the Bryce Group but his critical attitude to the war found its most positive expression in his involvement in the Union of Democratic Control. He was unhappy with the patriotic and propagandistic stance displayed by many British historians.

Douglas, C. G. 'John Scott Haldane', *Obituary Notices of Fellows of the Royal Society*, 2 (1936–8), 115–39
Haldane, Reader in physiology at Oxford, 1907-13, was Director of the Mining Research Laboratory (founded at Bentley Colliery near Doncaster) from 1912-36. Advised the War Office on the development of defensive and retaliatory measures against the use of chemical weapons by the Germans, working on the design of respirators and the medical aspects of war-gas poisoning.

Eve, A. S. *Rutherford: Being The Life and Letters of the Rt Hon. Lord Rutherford, O.M.* (Cambridge: Cambridge University Press, 1939)
Rutherford was Professor of Physics at Manchester in 1907. During the war Rutherford acted as consultant to the Admiralty Board of Invention and Research on anti-submarine warfare, leading the way in submarine detection, in which W. H. Bragg and A.S. Eve were also notably engaged during the war. Cavendish professor of experimental physics, Cambridge, 1919-37.

Fisher, H. A. L. *An Unfinished Autobiography* (London: Oxford University Press, 1940)
Fisher's vice-chancellorship of Sheffield University was interrupted in December 1916 by an invitation from Lloyd George to join his newly formed coalition government as President of the Board of Education where he remained employed for the rest of the war.

—— *James Bryce*, 2 vols (London: Macmillan, 1927; repr. Westport, Conn.: Greenwood Press, 1973)
Bryce was a jurist, historian and statesman. Presided over the commission to consider alleged German atrocities. A supporter of a league of nations, a project he enthusiastically sought to foster during the war. The Bryce Group, a loosely organised committee of Liberals whose object (under the nominal chairmanship of Lord Bryce) was to discuss ways of preventing wars in the future, particularly by means of a league of nations, was named after him

Forster, E M. *Goldsworthy Lowes Dickinson* (London: Arnold, 1962)
Dickinson was a lecturer in political science at Kings College, Cambridge, 1896-1920. Regarding international anarchy as the root cause of the war, he called soon after its outbreak for the establishment of a league of nations He was prominent in the Bryce Group but his critical attitude to the war found its most positive expression in his involvement in the Union of Democratic Control. He was unhappy with the patriotic and propagandistic stance displayed by many British historians.

Gooch, G. P. *Under Six Reigns* (London: Longman, 1958)
While critical of Sir Edward Grey's policy in the events leading to the war, Gooch supported Britain's entry into that war once Germany had invaded Belgium. Although he unreservedly condemned the latter invasion he maintained throughout the war as joint editor (1911-60) of the *Contemporary Review* a moderate voice, opposing hostility directed at the German people as a whole and appealing for a quick end to the war.

Hardy, G. H. *Bertrand Russell and Trinity: A College Controversy of the Last War 1914-18* (Cambridge: printed for the author at the University Press, 1942)
Reproduced in facsimile with a foreword by C. D. Broad, Cambridge: Cambridge University Press, 1970

The War Years

Harrod, Sir R. F. *The Life of John Maynard Keynes* (Houndmills: Palgrave Macmillan, 2003)
Facsimile of edition published London: Macmillan, 1951. Keynes was a lecturer in economics at Cambridge when war began. In January 1915 Keynes was recruited to the Treasury and in May 1915 he joined the finance division, where he took a prominent part in the organization of inter-allied finance.

Heilbron, J. L. *H. G. J. Moseley: The Life and Letters of an English Physicist, 1887-1915* (Berkeley: University of California Press, 1974)
Moseley was a physics lecturer at Manchester University, 1910-14. His motivation to join up, typical of many other young academics who volunteered to fight, was an overwhelming sense of duty. He was killed in action at Gallipoli.

Hobson, J. A. and M. Ginsberg. *L. T. Hobhouse: His Life and Work* (London: Allen & Unwin,1931; repr. London: Routledge/Thoemmes, 1996)
When the First World War broke out Hobhouse initially joined the British Neutrality Committee, but the growing German threat made him change his mind. First Professor of Sociology, London University, 1907-29.

McNeill, W. H. *Arnold Toynbee: A Life* (Oxford,: Oxford University Press, 1989)
Toynbee, who began his teaching career as a fellow of Balliol College in 1912, was involved in government propaganda work from 1915 onwards and in May 1917 was formally appointed to the foreign intelligence department of the Foreign Office.

Murray, G. *An Unfinished Autobiography*, with contributions by his friends (London: Allen & Unwin, 1960)
Murray was Regius professor of Greek at Oxford when war broke out. During the war he became increasingly involved in government activities after overcoming his initial doubts about Britain's declaration of war. Throughout the war Murray was involved in discussions about international peace, some of them within the League of Nations Society (1915), to the vice-presidency of which he was appointed in 1916.

Namier, J., Lady. *Lewis Namier: A Biography* (London: Oxford University Press, 1971)
Lewis Namier gained a first in modern history at Balliol, Oxford, in 1911, but was rejected for a fellowship at All Souls in November of that year. During the war he served briefly with the Royal Fusiliers but after five months with them he was transferred to the Foreign Office where, in the political intelligence department, he favoured the aspirations of the subject nations of the Austro-Hungarian empire.

Ogg, D. *Herbert Fisher, 1865–1940: A Short Biography* (London: Arnold, 1947)
Fisher's vice-chancellorship of Sheffield University was interrupted in December 1916 by an invitation from Lloyd George to join his newly formed coalition government as President of the Board of Education where he remained employed for the rest of the war.

Oman, Sir C. W. C. *Things I Have Seen* (London: Methuen, 1933)
Charles Oman was Chichele Professor of Modern History at Oxford , 1905-46. Worked for the Press Bureau and the Foreign Office during the war. The latter work was recognised with a knighthood (KBE) in 1920

Russell, B. A. W., 3rd Earl Russell. *Autobiography* (London: Routledge, 2000)
Originally published in 3 Vols [Vol 1, 1872-1914; Vol 2, 1914-1944; Vol 3, 1944-1967], London: Allen & Unwin, 1967-1969. Russell was a Fellow and lecturer at Trinity College at the beginning of the war. Throughout the war he was, unlike most of his academic contemporaries, involved in public expressions of opposition to the war through his political publications and his membership of the No-Conscription Fellowship and the Union of Democratic Control. He was removed from his lectureship in 1916 after being found guilty on a charge relating to a leaflet he had written in support of the No-Conscription Fellowship (he was reinstated in 1919). In 1918 he was imprisoned for an article he wrote in *The Tribune* that resulted in his being charged and found guilty of sedition on the grounds that the article was prejudicial to Britain's relations with its American ally.

Sadleir, M. *Michael Ernest Sadler (Sir Michael Sadler K.C.S.I.), 1861-1943: A Memoir* (London: Constable, 1949)
Sir Michael Sadler was Vice-Chancellor, Leeds University, 1911-1923. He distanced himself from the crude propaganda that was directed against Germany during the First World War. "Something of Sadler's stature is revealed by his public behaviour during the war years. With his background knowledge of Germany he was much in demand for talks, and more than one recruiting committee must have experienced some embarrassment at finding that it had staged a critical lecture on German education rather than a propagandist address" [extract from Higgins, J. H. 'Michael Sadler and the German Connection', *Oxford Review of Education*, Vol. 16 (1990), 245-253)]

Scaife, W. G. *The Hon. Sir Charles Algernon Parsons (1854-1931): Scientific Engineer* (Dublin: Irish Academy, 2002)
When the Admiralty set up its own Board of Invention and Research during the war Sir Charles Parsons was among the number of eminent scientists it recruited

Skidelsky, R. *John Maynard Keynes*, 3 vols (London: Macmillan, 1983-2000), I: *Hopes Betrayed 1883-1920*, new edn (1992)
Keynes was a lecturer in economics at Cambridge when war began. In January 1915 Keynes was recruited to the Treasury and in May 1915 he joined the finance division, where he took a prominent part in the organization of inter-allied finance.

Smith, M. F. *Arthur Lionel Smith, Master of Balliol College, 1916–1924: Biography and Some Reminiscences* (London: John Murray, 1928)
A. L. Smith was a firm supporter of Britain's involvement in the war. Aided the war effort with lectures at workers' meetings and at public schools. From 1917 to 1919 served as chairman of the Ministry of Reconstruction's committee on adult education.

Strutt, R. J., Baron Rayleigh. *The Life of Sir J. J. Thomson* (Cambridge: Cambridge University Press, 1942)
Thomson was Cavendish professor of Experimental Physics at Cambridge at beginning of the war. One of the members of the Board for Invention and Research during the First World War. Presided over the government commission of 1916 to inquire into the position of science in education.

Terrill, R. *R. H. Tawney and His Times* (London: Deutsch, 1974)
Tawney was a lecturer in political economy at Glasgow University, 1906-8 before becoming involved as a teacher in WEA classes in Rochdale and Manchester, 1908-14. Lecturer in economic history, London School of Economics, 1917 and 1920-1949. Enlisted as a private in 1915 and was wounded in 1916.

Thomson, Sir J. J. *Recollections and Reflections* (London: G. Bell, 1936)
Thomson was Cavendish professor of Experimental Physics at Cambridge at beginning of the war. One of the members of the Board for Invention and Research during the First World War. Presided over the government commission of 1916 to inquire into the position of science in education

Toynbee, A. *Experiences* (London: Oxford University Press, 1969)
Toynbee was involved in government propaganda work from 1915 onwards and in May 1917 was formally appointed to the foreign intelligence department of the Foreign Office.

Trevelyan, G. M. *An Autobiography and other Essays* (London: Longmans, 1949)
Trevelyan was a Fellow of Trinity College, Cambridge, later Regius Professor of Modern History, 1927-40, and Master, 1940-51 at that College. Supported Britain's declaration of war. Raised and commanded British Red Cross ambulance unit on Italian front, 1914-18

Weaver, J. R. H. and A. L. Poole. *Henry William Carless Davis: A Memoir, and a Selection of his Historical Papers* (London: Constable, 1933)
Davis held fellowships and lectured at Oxford in the pre-war years. During the war he helped to organise a 'trade clearing house' which expanded into a war trade intelligence department of which he became vice-chairman. The latter department was a constituent part of the Ministry of Blockade. Awarded the CBE in 1919.

Wilson, D. *Rutherford: Simple Genius* (London: Hodder & Stoughton, 1983)
Rutherford was Professor of Physics at Manchester in 1907. During the war Rutherford acted as consultant to the Admiralty Board of Invention and Research on anti-submarine warfare, leading the way in submarine detection, in which W. H. Bragg and A.S. Eve were also notably engaged during the war. Cavendish professor of experimental physics, Cambridge, 1919-37

Wood, A. *Bertrand Russell: The Passionate Sceptic* (London: Allen & Unwin, 1957; repr. 1963)
Russell was a Fellow and lecturer at Trinity College at the beginning of the war. Throughout the war he was, unlike most of his academic contemporaries, involved in public expressions of opposition to the war through his political publications and his membership of the No-Conscription Fellowship and the Union of Democratic Control. He was removed from his lectureship in 1916 after being found guilty on a charge relating to a leaflet he had written in support of the No-Conscription Fellowship (he was reinstated in 1919). In 1918 he was imprisoned for an article he wrote in *The Tribune* that resulted in his being charged and found guilty of sedition on the grounds that the article was prejudicial to Britain's relations with its American ally.

Books

Deslandes, P. R. *Oxbridge Men: British Masculinity and the Undergraduate Experience, 1850-1920* (Bloomington, IN: Indiana University Press, 2005)

'Manifesto of the Intellectuals of Germany', in *Thus Spake Germany*, ed. by W. W. Coole and M. F. Potter (London: Routledge, 1941)
This refers to the publication at the beginning of the First World War of the manifesto of 93 prominent German scientists, scholars and artists, declaring their unequivocal support of German military actions.

Stromberg, R. N. *Redemption by War: The Intellectuals and 1914* (Lawrence: The Regent's Press of Kansas, 1982)

Wallace, S. *War and the Image of Germany: British Academics, 1914-1918* (Edinburgh: Donald, 1988)

Wallas, G. *Men and Ideas*, essays edited by May Wallas, with a preface by Gilbert Murray (London: Allen & Unwin, 1940)
Includes an essay, *Comment on Dr. Jack's Article 'The Peacefulness of Being at War'* [see latter article below in the section headed **Contemporary Writings of Academics on the War.** Graham Wallas was Professor of Political Science at London School of Economics, 1914-23

Winter, J. M. 'Oxford and the First World War', in *The History of the University of Oxford*, general editor, T. H. Aston, 8 vols (Oxford: Oxford University Press, 1984-2000), VIII: *The Twentieth Century*, ed. by B. Harrison, 1994

Articles

'Academic Peril', *Blackwood's Magazine*, 197 (1915), 663-671

Badash, L. 'British and American Views of the German Menace in World War I', *Notes and Records of the Royal Society of London*, 34:1 (1979), 91-121

Barnard-Cogno, C. 'Jane Harrison (1850-1928), between German and English Scholarship', *European Review of History*, 13 (2006), 661-676

Crawley, C. W. 'Sir George Prothero and His Circle', *Transactions of the Royal Historical Society*, Ser. 5, 20 (1970), 101-27
Prothero was Professor of Modern History, Edinburgh, 1894-99, editor of *Quarterly Review*, 1899-1922, and co-editor, *Cambridge Modern History*, 1901-12. Served as historical adviser to the Foreign Office between 1917 and 1919. Out of this work emerged the handbooks under his general editorship that were supplied to British delegates at the Peace Conference at Versailles in 1919.

Ferguson, N. 'Battle of the Dons of War', *Times Higher Education Supplement*, 30 October 1998

Higgins, J. H. 'Michael Sadler and the German Connection', *Oxford Review of Education*, 16 (1990), 245-253
See note above under Sadleir's work on *Michael Ernest Sadler (Sir Michael Sadler K.C.S.I.), 1861-1943: A Memoir* (1949)

Hirsch, F. E. 'Biographical Article: George Peabody Gooch', *Journal of Modern History*, 26 (1954), 260-71

Flaig, H. 'The Historian as Pedagogue of the Nation', *History*, 59 (1974), 18

Hearnshaw, F. J. C. 'History as a Means of Propaganda', *Fortnightly Review*, n.s.114 (1923), 330

Irish, T. 'Fractured Families: Educated Elites In Britain and France and the Challenge of the Great War', *Historical Journal*, 57, (2014), 509-530

Johnson, E. 'Keynes' Attitude to Compulsory Military Service', *Economic Journal*, 70 (1960),

'Oxford and the War', *Times Literary Supplement*, 20 (1921), 114

Peacock, S. 'From "Epilogue" to *Epilegomena*: Jane Ellen Harrison, World War I, and Asceticism', *History of European Ideas*, 28:3 (2002), 189-203

Powicke, F. M. 'H. W. C. Davis', *English Historical Review*, 43 (1928), 578–84

Prochaska, F. 'Somerville College and the Great War', *History Today*, 65:5 (2015)
"The First World War transformed women-only Somerville College. It became a hospital for convalescing soldiers, housed poets and writers and changed forever the fortunes of female students" [quotation extracted from article].

Wang, Z. 'The First World War, Academic Science, and the "Two Cultures": Educational Reforms at the University of Cambridge', *Minerva*, 33 (1995), 107-127

Theses

Pogge von Strandmann, H. 'Historians, Nationalism and War: The Mobilisation of Public Opinion in Britain and Germany' (unpublished doctoral thesis, University of Oxford, 1998)

Contemporary Writings of Academics on the War

Listed below is a selection of works by academics on the subject of the war. Some of them are clearly propagandistic in their intent (particularly the examples below of some of the series of **'Oxford Pamphlets'** produced by the History Faculty of Oxford University). A number of the propagandistic works were the result of Masterman calling on the writers of England for help when he set about the task of developing propaganda at Wellington House. This call was readily answered by an army of writers who either became workers in the government service or wrote propaganda pieces. Among the latter were a number of well known academics (e.g. Gilbet Murray, Ernest Barker, Henry Davis, John Rose, Ramsay Muir, John Muirhead, Arnold Toynbee). Bertrand Russell was not one of this number (his thoughts on the war stand out as an exception to the generally supportive attitude of academics to the involvement of Britain in the war) and there were academics, like Michael Sadler, who distanced themselves from the sort of crude propaganda that was sometimes directed against Germany during the First World War.

Barker, Sir E. *Nietzsche and Treitschke: The Worship of Power in Modern Germany*, Oxford Pamphlets, 20 (London: Oxford University Press, 1914)

Bryce, J. W., Viscount Bryce of Dechmont. *Essays and Addresses in Wartime* (London: Macmillan, 1918)
This work contains the following chapters: Neutral nations and the war; The attitude of Great Britain in the present war; The war state: its mind and its methods; War and human progress; Presidential address delivered to the British Academy, June 30, 1915; Presidential address delivered to the British academy, July 14, 1916; The principle of nationality and its applications; A league of nations to preserve peace

Coulton, G. G. *The Main Illusions of Pacifism: A Criticism of Mr. N. Angell and of the Union of Democratic Control* (Cambridge: Bowes and Bowes, 1916)
Coulton was Birkbeck lecturer in ecclesiastical history at Trinity College, Cambridge during the war. A strong supporter of the National Service League, advocating compulsory national service for home defence, and campaigned energetically for it; his book *The Case for Compulsory Military Service* was published in 1917

— *Pacifist Illusions: A Criticism of the Union of Democratic Control* (Cambridge: Bowes & Bowes, 1915)

Davis, H. W. C. *What Europe Owes to Belgium*, Oxford Pamphlets, 36 (London: Oxford University Press, 1914)

Dicey, A. V. *How We Ought to Feel About the War*, Oxford Pamphlets, 55 (Oxford: Oxford University Press, 1914)
Professor of English law and fellow of All Souls, Oxford, 1882-1909

Fisher, H. A. L. *The British Share in the War* (London: Nelson, 1915)

Gooch, G. P. *The Project of a League of Nations* (London: 1917)

Harrison, J. E. *Alpha and Omega* (London: Sidgwick & Jackson, 1915)
A reprint of this work was published by AMS Press in 1973. Consists of a collection of essays, one of which was entitled *Epilogue on the War: Peace with Patriotism*.

— *Peace With Patriotism*, 2nd edn (Cambridge: G. Bell,1915)

In this work Jane Harrison, a Cambridge lecturer, expressing astonishment at the reaction of students and dons to the call to join up, wrote: 'it came to me as something of a shock to find that many of them ... went, not reluctantly, but with positive alacrity'. In her opinion, they rushed into the war thoughtlessly and uncritically 'driven by a thirst for primary sensations'. During the war Jane Harrison was a lecturer in classical archaeology at Newnham College, Cambridge

Jacks, L.P. 'The Peacefulness of Being At War', *Hibbert Journal*, (1915), 99-102
"I doubt if there ever was a time when in general the minds of Englishmen were so agitated as they were in the few years preceding the war. Rest for our souls was hardly to be found anywhere. In religion, in philosophy, in politics, we were all at sixes and sevens, fighting one another in the name of our ideals, or striving to rouse the lethargic masses who cared not a button for any of our idealism; and often, it must be confessed, we were in a chronic state of irritation; and to make matters worse, a school of writers had arisen, represented by Mr. Bernard Shaw, who made it their business to irritate and, incidentally, to confuse us still further. Compared to this aimlessness and confusion the war had brought a sense of 'mission' and 'peace of mind'" [extract]. Jacks was Principal, Manchester College, Oxford (originally located in London), 1915-31, and editor of the *Hibbert Journal*, 1902-47.

Jones, H. S. A Scholar's Protest, *The Times*, 4 August 1914
Letter to the Editor of *The Times* by H. Stuart Jones, Fellow of Trinity College, Oxford, criticising the Cambridge Manifesto (which called attention to the intellectual services rendered by Germany to the world) for its failure to recognise the manifestations of Germany's threatening and aggressive attitude.

Lindsay, A. D. 1st Baron Lindsay. *War Against War*, Oxford Pamphlets, 16 (Oxford: Oxford University Press, 1914)
Lindsay was a fellow and classical tutor, Balliol College, Oxford, 1906-22. Served as deputy controller of labour in France and Lieutenant-Colonel, 1917-19

Muir, R. *Britain's Case Against Germany: An Examination of the Historical Background of the German Action of 1914* (Manchester: Manchester University Press, 1914)
Ramsay Muir was Professor of Modern History at Manchester, 1914-21

Muirhead, J. H. *German Philosophy and the War*, Oxford Pamphlets, 62 (Oxford: Oxford University Press, 1915)
Professor of Philosophy, Birmingham, 1896-22

Murray, G. *Faith, War and Policy: Addresses and Essays on the European War* (Boston: Houghton Mifflin Company; London: Oxford University Press, 1918)
This work contains the following chapters: First thoughts on the war (August, 1914); How can war ever be right? (September, 1914); Herd instinct and the war (February, 1915); India and the war (March, 1915); The evil and the good of the war (October, 1915); Democratic control of foreign policy; How we stand now (March, 1916); Ireland; America and the war (August, 1916); America and England (November, 1916); The sea policy of Great Britain (October, 1916); Oxford and the war: a memoir of Arthur George Heath (September, 1916); The turmoil of war (March, 1917)

— *The Foreign Policy of Sir Edward Grey, 1906-15* (Oxford: Clarendon Press, 1914)

— 'German scholarship', *Quarterly Review*, 223 (April 1915), 330–339

— 'Herd Instinct and the War', *Atlantic Monthly*, (1915)
In this article Gilbert Murray admires "the quickened pulse, the new strength and courage, the sense of brotherhood, the spirit of discipline and self-sacrifice".

— *How Can War Ever Be Right?*, Oxford Pamphlets, 1914-1915, 18 (London: Oxford University Press, 1914)
A former neutralist, yet in the above pamphlet, which he wrote for the Oxford pamphlet series, Murray supports Britain's entry into the war because in spite of the fact that he was able to "sympathize with every step" of the pacifist argument he was not able to acquiesce in what seemed to be the acceptance of evil. It was "a cardinal fact that in some cases it was better to fight and be broken than to yield peacefully". The "mere act of resisting to death" could be "in itself a victory".

— 'Thoughts on the War', *Hibbert Journal*, 13 (1914), 68-81

Namier, L. B. *The Case of Bohemia* (London: Czech National Alliance of Great Britain, 1917)

Osler, Sir W. *Science and War*, An Address Delivered at the University of Leeds Medical School in October, 1915 (Oxford: Clarendon Press, 1915)

The Civilian Scene

Although Osler indicates in this address that he is able to see the beneficial effects of science at the service of war, as exemplified by the advances made in the care of the wounded and sick and in the prevention of epidemics among soldiers, he is emotionally horrified by the fact that science has increased man's capacity to wreak mass destruction of human beings by air, land, and sea to a horrific level.

Pollard, A. F. *The War: Its History and Morals, A Lecture* (London: Longmans, 1915)
Pollard was Professor, Constitutional History, University College, London, 1903-31

Raleigh, W. A. *England and the War: Being Sundry Addresses Delivered During the War and Now First Collected* (Oxford: Clarendon Press, 1918)
This work contains the following chapters: Might is right; The war of ideas; The faith of England; Some gains of the war; The war and the press; Shakespeare and England. Raleigh was a Professor of English Literature and Fellow of Merton, Oxford, in 1914.

'Reply to German Professors. Reasoned Statement by British Scholars', *The Times*, 21 Ocrtober 1914
Letter, signed by 150 British academics, in response to *Der Aufruf "An die Kulturwelt!": Das Manifest der 93 und die Anfange der Kriegspropaganda im Ersten Weltkrieg*, the manifesto (published on 4 October 1914) in which 93 prominent German scientists, scholars and artists declared their unequivocal support of German military actions

Right and Left Among the Professors: Sir Arthur Quiller-Couch on Huns and Historians', *Cambridge Magazine*, 4 (1914), 119

Rose, J. H. *Why Are We At War?* (Cambridge: Heffer, 1914)
Rose, a Reader in Modern History, 1911-1919, was one of the eighty-one signatories of the Cambridge manifesto against war with Germany, but Germany's invasion of Belgium led to a change in his attitude and he became one of the most zealous supporters of Britain's involvement in the war, engaging wholeheartedly in propaganda work by means of the publications he produced and the lectures he gave to popular audiences and troops on the western front.

— *Why We Carry On* (London: T. Fisher Unwin, 1918)
Contents (from t.-p.): I. What if the central empires win?; II. Could Great Britain have averted the war?; III. How did the Anglo-French entente come about?; IV. Did Great Britain "encircle" Germany?; V. Why shield Austria?; VI. Why should France recover Alsace-Lorraine?; VII. Conclusion. [Nos. II. and V. are reprinted from the *Daily Chronicle*, no.III. from *Land and Water*, no. IV. from the *New Europe*]

Russell, B. A. W., 3rd Earl Russell. 'Christianity and the War', *The Labour Leader* 11, no. 52 (Dec 24 1914), 7

— *Justice in War-Time* (London: Allen and Unwin, 1916)

— 'War: The Cause and the Cure', *The Labour Leader* 11, no. 39 (Sep 24 1914), 2

— 'Will This War End War?', *The Labour Leader* (London), 11, no. 37 (Sep 10 1914), 2

— 'Why Nations Love War', *War and Peace* (London), 2, no. 14 (Nov 1914), 20-1

Sadler, Sir M. E. 'The Universities and the War', in *The Empire and the Future*: a series of imperial studies lectures delivered in the University of London, King's College, with pref. note by A.P. Newton, and introduction by A.D. Steel-Maitland (London: Macmillan 1916)

— Sadler, Sir M. E. *Modern Germany and the Modern World* (London: Macmillan, 1914)
Written for the Victoria League but see note above under Sadleir's work on *Michael Ernest Sadler (Sir Michael Sadler K.C.S.I.), 1861-1943: A Memoir* (1949)

'Scholars' Protest Against War with Germany', *The Times*, 1 August 1914
A protest by a number of university professors and others against being drawn into a war "with a nation so near akin to our own, and with whom we have so much in common" and an appeal to English scholars to support this protest. The signatories of the protest were C. G. Browne, Professor of Arabic, Cambridge; F. C. Burkitt, Norrisian Professor of Divinity, Cambridge; J. F. Carpenter, Principal, Manchester College, Oxford; F. J. Foakes-Jackson, Fellow of Jesus College, Cambridge; H. Latimer Jackson, Rector of Little Canfield, Essex; Kirsopp Lake, Professor, Leiden and Harvard; W. M. Ramsay, Professor Emeritus, Aberdeen University; W. B. Selbie, Principal, Mansfield College, Oxford; J. J. Thomson, Cavendish Professor of Experimental Physics, Cambridge. This opposition to war largely evaporated after Germany's invasion of Belgium and the publication of the manifesto in which 93 prominent German scientists, scholars and artists

declared their unequivocal support of German military actions.

Selbie, W. B. *The War and Theology*, Oxford Pamphlets, 53 (London: Oxford University Press, 1915)
Selbie was Principal Mansfield College, Oxford, 1909-32

Smith, A. L. *The Christian Attitude to War*, Oxford Pamphlets, 52 (London: Oxford University Press, 1915)

To the Christian Scholars of Europe, Oxford Pamphlets, 2 (Oxford: Oxford University Press, 1914)
A reply from Oxford to the German Address to Evangelical Christians.

Toynbee, A. J. *The German Terror in France* (London: Hodder and Stoughton, 1917)

Trevelyan, G. M. *The Servians and Austria* (London: The Victoria League, 1915)

Why We Are At War: Great Britain's Case, by members of the Oxford Faculty of Modern History (Oxford: Clarendon Press, 1914)
"The sole responsibility for the book rests ... with those who sign this preface" [i.e. E. Barker, H.W.C. Davis, C.R.L. Fletcher, Arthur Hassall, L.G. Wickham Legg, and F. Morgan]. Has "An Appendix of Original Documents including the Authorized English Translation of the White Book issued by the German Government".

2.3.2 Bloomsbury Group

'Bloomsbury' was the name given to a group of writers, artists, and intellectuals whose meetings in the early years of the twentieth century were originally centred on 46, Gordon Square after it had become in 1904 the Bloomsbury residence of the Stephen sisters, Vanessa (later married to Clive Bell) and Virginia (later married to Leonard Woolf). This informal group of friends was bound together by "a similarity - but not an identity - of taste and outlook and a shared rejection of conventional prejudices" (Gadd, D. *The Loving Friends: A Portrait of Bloomsbury*). Amongst others who moved in the Bloomsbury circle during the years of the Great War, were Maynard Keynes, David Garnett, Duncan Grant, E. M. Forster, Lytton Strachey, Clive and Vanessa Bell, Virginia and Leonard Woolf, Roger Fry, and Bertrand Russell. In the words of Gadd in his book., *The Loving Friends*, "Lady Ottoline Morell, though never in the true sense a member of the Bloomsbury circle, knew them all, was on terms of intimacy with a number of them, and was their hostess for many years in her houses in London and Oxfordshire".

Most of those associated with the Bloomsbury group were opposed to the war but only Bertrand Russell was a really active campaigner against it. Apart also from Clive Bell, who wrote a pacifist pamphlet in 1915, and Lytton Strachey, who for a while took part in the anti-conscription campaign, the group's opposition was largely passive. Nearly all the Bloomsbury men were conscientious objectors, with the notable exception of Leonard Woolf who was ready to serve as a soldier but was rejected on medical grounds.

While the civilian population was on the whole committed to winning the war, the members of the Bloomsbury group represented a small minority of intellectuals who mostly chose to distance themselves from the war and avoid getting personally involved. The main exceptions were Maynard Keynes, the Treasury official, Bertrand Russell, the anti-war campaigner, and Leonard Woolf, the left-wing journalist and League of Nations advocate, all of whom in their different ways became actively involved in the war.

Autobiographies, Biographies, Memoirs, Diaries

Garnett, D. *The Golden Echo*, 3 vols (London: Chatto & Windus, 1955-1982)

Gathorne-Hardy, R., ed. *Ottoline at Garsington: Memoirs of Lady Ottoline Morrell, 1915-18* (London: Faber, 1963; repr. 1974)

Harrod, Sir R. F. *The Life of John Maynard Keynes* (Houndmills: Palgrave Macmillan, 2003)
Facsimile of edition published London: Macmillan, 1951.

Holroyd, M. *Lytton Strachey: A Critical Biography* (London: Chatto & Windus, 1994; repr. London: Vintage, 1995)
Originally published London: Heinemann, 1967-1968 in 2 vols.

Huxley, J., ed. *Aldous Huxley, 1884-1963: A Memorial Volume* (London: Chatto & Windus, 1965)

Jarrett, J. L., ed. 'D. H. Lawrence and Bertrand Russell', in *A D.H. Lawrence Miscellany*, ed. by H. T. Moore (Carbondale: Southern Illinois Press, 1959; repr. London: Heinemann, 1961)

Lee, H. *Virginia Woolf* (London: Chatto & Windus, 1996)

Skidelsky, R. *John Maynard Keynes*, 3 vols (London: Macmillan, 1983-2000), I: *Hopes Betrayed 1883-1920*, new edn (1992)

Tomalin, C. *Katherine Mansfield: A Secret Life* (London: Viking, 1987)

Weintraub, S. *Bernard Shaw, 1914-1916: Journey to Heartbreak* (London: Routledge, 1973)
Originally published under the title of *Journey to Heartbreak: The Crucible Years*, New York: Weybright and Talley, 1971.

Woolf, L. *Beginning Again; An Autobiography of the Years 1911-1918* (London: Hogarth, 1965)

Woolf, V. *Letters of Virginia Woolf*, editor Nigel Nicolson; assistant editor Joanne Trautmann, 6 vols. (London: Hogarth Press, 1975-1980), II: *The Question of Things Happening (1912-1922)*, (1976)

Books

Atkin, J. *A War of Individuals: Bloomsbury Attitudes to the Great War* (Manchester: Manchester University Press, 2002)
Provides examples of the sort of pacifism assumed by the Bloomsbury Group in relation to a portrayal of its less well-known members who espoused the Group's attitude to the Great War

Bell, C. *Old Friends* (London: Chatto & Windus, 1956; repr. London: Cassell, 1988)

— *Peace at Once* (Manchester: National Labour Press, 1915)

Bell, J., ed. *We Did Not Fight: 1914-1918 Experiences of War Resisters* (London: Cobden-Sanderson, 1935)

Bell, Q. *Bloomsbury* (London: Phoenix, 1986, repr. 1997)
Originally published London: Weidenfeld & Nicolson, 1968.

Delany, P. *D. H. Lawrence's Nightmare: The Writer and His Circle during the Years of the Great War* (Hassocks: Harvester Press, 1979)

Edel, L. *Bloomsbury: A House of Lions* (London: Hogarth Press, 1979; repr. Harmondsworth: Penguin, 1981)

Gadd, D. *The Loving Friends; A Portrait of Bloomsbury* (London: Hogarth Press, 1974)

Jarrett, J. L. 'D. H. Lawrence and Bertrand Russell', in *A D. H. Lawrence Miscellany*, [Essays by Various Authors] edited by H.T. Moore (London: Heinemann, 1961)

Huxley, A. *Crome Yellow* (London: Vintage, 2004)
Originally published London: Chatto, 1921. A novel in which some of the characters are based on members of the Bloomsbury circle

Johnstone, J. K. *The Bloomsbury Group: A Study of E. M. Forster, Lytton Strachey, Virginia Woolf and their Circle* (London: Secker & Warburg, 1954)

Levenback, K. L. *Virginian Woolf and the Great War* (Syracuse, N.Y.: Syracuse University Press, 1999)

Rosenbaum, S. P. *The Bloomsbury Group: A Collection of Memoirs, Commentary and Criticism*, 2nd rev. edn (Toronto: Toronto University Press, 1995)

Potts, G. and L. Shahriari, eds. *Virginia Woolf's Bloomsbury*, 2 vols (Basingstoke: Palgrave Macmillan in association

with the Institute of English Studies, School of Advanced Study, University of London, 2010)
The origins of the papers presented in both volumes of *Virginia Woolf's Bloomsbury* lie in the Fourteenth Annual International Conference on Virginia Woolf which was hosted by the Institute of English Studies at the University of London in June 2004.

2.3.3 The Souls

'The Souls' were a small social set who in the late Victorian era, rebelling against the philistinism of contemporary aristocratic society, began making use of their house parties for philosophical and intellectual discussion rather than ostentatious display and typical aristocratic pursuits (although they also indulged in less serious activities such as charades and word games, lawn tennis, golf and bicycling). The core of this group, of which Arthur Balfour was the central figure, was initially based on the friendship between four families - the Balfours, Lyttletons, Tennants, and Wyndhams – and, later, on the intermarriages of the families of the Asquiths, Tennants, Charteris, and Manners. Among the group were some of the most distinguished English politicians and intellectuals of the time; many of its male members belonged to the Crabbe Club, founded by Wilfrid Scawen Blunt. The name of the group was mockingly coined by Admiral Lord Charles Beresford, who is quoted as having said at a dinner party: "You all sit and talk about each others' souls — I shall call you the 'Souls'". Although of a predominantly aristocratic flavour (including as it did men such as Arthur Balfour, George Curzon, and William Grenfell and women such as Ettie Desborough, Margot Asquith, Mary Elcho and Violet Granby) the group was not limited to a particular class of society as it embraced a wide range of friends such as the Pre-Raphaelite artists William Morris and Edward Burne Jones, the writers Henry James, Edith Wharton, H.G. Wells and Oscar Wilde, and actors such as Mrs Patrick Campbell, Herbert Beerbohm Tree and Tree's wife Maud. The original group of 'Souls' had faded out by the end of the first decade of the 20th century but their values were perpetuated in a new generation by some of their children in a group called the 'Corrupt Coterie', a clique of English aristocrats and intellectuals of the 1910's that included among its members Lady Diana Manners (later Lady Diana Cooper after her marriage to Duff Cooper), Raymond Asquith, Maurice Baring, Patrick Shaw-Stewart, Edward Horner, Duff Cooper and Sir Denis Anson. A number of the Souls' children were killed fighting in the First World War

Autobiographies, Biographies, Diaries, Letters

Abdy, J. and C. Gere. *The Souls* (London: Sidgwick & Jackson, 1984)

Asquith, M., Countess of Oxford and Asquith. *The Autobiography of Margot Asquith*, edited by Mark Bonham-Carter (London: Eyre & Spottiswoode, 1962; repr. London: Weidenfeld & Nicolson, 1995)
Originally published in 2 vols, London: Thornton Butterworth, 1920-1922

— *Off the Record* (London: Muller, 1843)

Balfour, A. J., 1st Earl of Balfour. *Chapters of Autobiography*, edited by Mrs. Edgar Dugdale (London: Cassell and Company, 1930)

Blow, S. *Broken Blood: The Rise and Fall of the Tennant Family* (London: Faber, 1987)

Davenport-Hines, R. P. T. *Ettie: The Intimate Life and Dauntless Spirit of Lady Desborough* (London: Weidenfeld & Nicolson, 2008)

Longford, E. *A Pilgrimage of Passion: The Life of Wilfrid Scawen Blunt* (London: Weidenfeld & Nicolson, 1979; repr. London: Tauris Parke, 2007)

Mackenzie, J *The Children of the Souls: A Tragedy of the First World War* (London: Chatto & Windus, 1986)
The 'Children' referred to in the title included Raymond Asquith, Julian and Billy Grenfell, Edward Horner, Charles Lister, Ego and Yvo Charteris, and Patrick Shaw Stewart.

Mosley, N. *Julian Grenfell: His Life and the Times of his Death, 1888-1915* (London: Weidenfeld & Nicolson, 1976; repr. with a new preface by the author, London: Persephone, 2000)

Ridley, J. and C. Percy, eds. *The Letters of Arthur Balfour and Lady Elcho, 1885–1917* (London: Hamish Hamilton,

1992)

Skidelsky, R. *John Maynard Keynes*, 3 vols (London: Macmillan, 1983-2000), I: *Hopes Betrayed 1883-1920*, new edn (1992)

Webb, B. P. *The Diary of Beatrice Webb*, edited by N. and J. Mackenzie, 4 vols (Cambridge, Mass.: Belknap Press of Harvard University Press, 1982-1985)

Books

Cannadine, D. *The Decline and Fall of the British Aristocracy* (London: Penguin Books, 2005)

Jalland, P. *Women, Marriage and Politics, 1860–1914* (Oxford: Oxford University Press, 1986)

Lambert, A. *Unquiet Souls: The Indian Summer of the British Aristocracy, 1880-1918* (London: Macmillan, 1984)
The US edition (New York: Harper & Row, 1984) was published under the title, *Unquiet Souls: A Social History of the Illustrious, Irreverent, Intimate Group of British Aristocrats known as "the Souls"*.

Articles

Anon. 'The "Souls", A Brilliant Group: Steadfast Loyalty of Friendship', *The Times* (21 Jan 1929), 13
Letters to the editor.

Ellenberger, N. W. 'The Souls and London "Society" at the End of the Nineteenth Century', *Victorian Studies*, 25 (1982), 133–160

2.4 Labour, Industrial Relations

To the surprise of many contemporaries, in view of the industrial unrest and incessant strikes since 1910, the labour force of workers who remained behind on the Home Front demonstrated, through their trade union leadership, their willingness to cooperate with the war effort by agreeing to suspend restrictive trade practices (e.g. the Shell and Fuses Agreement and the Treasury Agreement), and acquiescing in their officials joining government advisory committees, working in Whitehall departments, and serving in the Coalition Government. This co-operation and relinquishment of labour's most effective industrial weapons were not solely inspired by patriotism; it also contained within it a belief on the part of organised labour that the war provided opportunities to improve its position within the political structure and as a result of this to achieve long term post-war benefits for labour.

In spite of the willingness of labour to allow its industrial power to be weakened it was not without other means of exerting extra-parliamentary pressure. In August 1914 the War Emergency Workers' National Committee, a federal group of representatives of the Labour Party and the wider labour movement was formed to protect workers from the adverse effects of wartime industrial dislocation. It developed campaigns, masterminded by Sydney Webb, on a comprehensive range of issues affecting living standards and working conditions on which it lobbied the government. For the first two years of the war it was this body rather than the parliamentary Labour Party which provided the main focus for dealing with wartime distress and the grievances of the working-class that arose from it.

The underlying patriotism of the British working class generally as a group, bolstered by anticipation of the rewards it hoped to receive for its industrial sacrifices when peace came, continued to exist as a powerful influence throughout the war. Nevertheless industrial unrest and strikes did occur, arising in varying degrees and at various times over matters such as pay, working conditions, dilution, manpower controls and a wide variety of associated grievances related, for instance, to food and fuel shortages, taxes, escalating prices, profiteering, industrial fatigue, restrictions on drink, and distrust of the Government's post-war intentions. The number of strikes, however, was significantly less in comparison with the years immediately preceding the war.

The war witnessed a significant development of the power of shop stewards who saw the opportunity to step into the gap opened up as a result of the willingness of the official trade union leadership to collaborate with the government and allow its industrial muscle to be weakened. The shop stewards used this opportunity to exert considerable influence in the areas of unrest among the working class but this did not result in labour taking a revolutionary path. When the Leeds Conference, attended by an enthusiastic variety of delegates (from trades councils, local Labour Parties, socialist organizations, women's industrial and political groups, and leaders of the Labour Party), met in early June 1917 and, welcoming the Russian revolution, called for the formation of 'Workers and Soldiers' Councils along Russian lines, the reaction by the rank and file was lukewarm. The proceedings of the Conference, as an indicator of working-class opinion, were much less significant than the participation of workers in the frequent outbursts of anti-German feeling, the support given to the war by right wing groups like the British Workers League, and the harassment of pacifist demonstrators. Even the worst periods of industrial unrest in 1917 and 1918 were ultimately followed by a resurgence of patriotism and a chauvinistic determination to defeat the Germans and make them pay for the cost of the war.

Monitoring labour became an important element in the government's industrial strategy and, following a decision in April 1917 to institute a system of systematic surveillance, arrangements were made for the production of weekly reports, covering stoppages, disputes and settlements and providing a general overview of the labour situation, and in the same year the Government also appointed a number of Commissions of Enquiry into Industrial Unrest for different regions of the country (see below in this section under **Contemporary Official Papers**). The task of summarizing the reports was given to one of the Labour ministers, George Barnes, who was of the opinion that the root of unrest was not derived from 'feelings of a revolutionary nature' but from grievances such as those related to the high price of food and its unequal distribution, and the effects of the Munitions of War and Military Service Act (especially those restricting the mobility of labour by compelling workers to obtain leaving certificates from their employers before they could change jobs). Among the 'psychological conditions' making for unrest Barnes included 'the feeling that there has been inequality of sacrifice, that the government has broken solemn pledges, that the trade union officials are no longer to be relied upon, and that there is a woeful uncertainty as to the industrial future'.

Proposals for institutional reform of industrial bargaining had been made before the war but it was during the war that the public debate on such matters was accelerated as a result of the specific labour problems arising out of the wartime economy and the wish to utilise wartime experience in the reconstruction of post-war society. From mid-1916, there began to appear what became a huge wartime corpus of literature on reconstruction, the largest part of which was written by those whom P. B. Johnson in his *Land Fit for Heroes* has termed the 'reconstructionists', a group of radical thinkers imbued with a strong belief in the imminence of a great era of reform. They provided much of the intellectual force for the large programme of reconstruction planned by Addison and his colleagues in the Ministry of Reconstruction after that was set up in July 1917. One of the most important products of its work on the industrial front was an interim Report of the Reconstruction Committee on Joint Standing Industrial Councils, based on the work of the committee appointed under the chairmanship of J. H. Whitley on October 1916 to report on 'the Relations of Employers and Employees' (see below in this section under **Contemporary Official Papers**). Out of these reports emerged the 'Whitley Councils', a system of regular formal consultative meetings between workers and employers, vested also with the power to cover any issue related to pay and conditions of service, and to take matters through to arbitration if necessary. The principle of joint consultation met with the approval of many people, including trade union leaders like J. R. Clynes, but within the Labour movement generally considerable numbers viewed it sceptically because they were doubtful about the actual reality of the existence of an industrial consensus which was claimed to have been achieved during the war (as was exemplified by the scepticism from their different standpoints of an influential trade unionist like Ernest Bevin and of a prominent member of the shop stewards movement like J. T. Murphy).

Autobiographies, Biographies. Memoirs

Barnes, G. N. *From Workshop to War Cabinet* (London: H. Jenkins, 1923)
Barnes was a trade unionist and politician (MP, 1906-22). Minister of Pensions, 1916-17. In August 1917 he entered the war cabinet (replacing Arthur Henderson) as minister without portfolio representing the interests of organized labour; in the latter role he headed a major government inquiry into industrial unrest in 1917. Resigned from the Labour Party in 1918 but remained in government.

Brown, G. *Maxton*, new edn (Edinburgh: Mainstream, 2002)
James Maxton , one of the leading figures of the Independent Labour Party (ILP) in Glasgow and a key player during the Red Clydeside period, was a pacifist and totally opposed to Britain's involvement in the war and to the introduction of conscription. He was imprisoned in 1916 for making speeches supporting strike action at a demonstration to oppose the Munitions Act.

Bullock, A. *The Life and Times of Ernest Bevin*, 3 vols (London: Heinemann, 1960-1983), I: *Trade Union Leader, 1881-1940* (1960)
Bevin was a trade unionist leader during the war. National organizer of the Dockers' Union in 1914; delegate to the Trades Union Congress in 1915; on executive of the Transport Workers' Federation in 1916.

Clynes, J. R. *Memoirs*, 2 vols (London: Hutchinson, 1937), I: *1869-1924*
Clynes was a Labour leader and politician (MP 1906-31). President of the National Union of Gas Workers and and General Labourers (later of General and Municipal Workers), 1912-37; Parliamentary Secretary to Food Controller, 1917; Food Controller and Privy Councillor, 1918.

Gallacher, W. *Revolt on the Clyde: An Autobiography*, 4th edn (London: Lawrence & Wishart, 1978)
Gallacher was a working-class agitator and politician. Joined Social Democratic Federation, 1906; Chairman of Clyde Workers' Committee in 1916 in which year he was imprisoned for sedition. Supported Russian Revolution and Soviet Union, 1917.

Hodge, J. *From Workman's Cottage to Windsor Castle* (London: Sampson Low, 1931)
Hodge was a trade unionist and politician. Became the first Minister of Labour in December 1916. Involved in the writing of the *Weekly Reports of the Labour Situation* that were instituted in 1917.

Murphy, J. T. *New Horizons* (London: John Lane, 1941)
The Marxist theorist of the Shop Stewards' Movement.

Weiler, P. *Ernest Bevin* (Manchester: Manchester University Press,1993)

Bibliographies

Chamberlin, W. *Industrial Relations in Wartime: Great Britain, 1914-18*; An Annotated Bibliography of Materials in the Hoover Library on War, Revolution and Peace (Stanford, CA: Stanford University Press, 1940)

Books

Askwith, G. R., Baron. *Industrial Problems and Disputes* (London: John Murray, 1920)
Askwith was Britain's chief industrial commissioner, 1911-19. Notable arbitrator

Briggs, A. and J. Saville, eds. *Essays in Labour History:* [vol 2] *1886-1923*, (London: Macmillan, 1971)
Contains the following chapters: 1. Introduction, by A. Briggs; 2. Keir Hardie's conversion to socialism, by F. Reid; 3. The Marxism of the Social Democratic Federation, by H. Collins; 4. The Leeds Corporation strike in 1913, by J. E. Williams; 5. The triple industrial alliance, 1913-1922, by P. S. Bagwell; 6. Ramsay MacDonald and the Labour Party, by C. L. Mowat; 7. The Clyde Workers' Committee and the dilution struggle, by J. Hinton.; 8. The foundation of the Co-operative Party, by S. Pollard; 9. The War Emergency Workers' National Committee, 1914-1920, by R. Harrison; 10. Guild socialism and the Labour Research Department, by M. Cole; 11. The Building Guilds, by F. Matthews; 12. Guild socialism: the Storrington Document

Bush, J. *Behind the Lines; East London Labour, 1914-1919* (London: Merlin Press, 1984)

Charles, R. *The Development of Industrial Relations in Britain, 1911-1939: Studies in the Evolution of Collective Bargaining at a National and Industry Level* (London: Hutchinson, 1973)

— *Trade Unionism and Munitions* (Oxford: Clarendon Press, 1923)

Clegg, H. A., and others. *A History of British Trade Unions Since 1889*, by H. A. Clegg, A. Fox and A. F. Thompson, 3 vols (Oxford: Clarendon Press, 1964-1994), II: *1910-1933*, by H. A. Clegg (1985)

Clynes, J. R. 'Unity Between Classes', in *The War and Unity*, being lectures delivered at the Local Lectures Summer Meeting of the University of Cambridge, 1918, edited by D. H. S. Cranage (Cambridge: Cambridge University Press, 1919)

The War Years

In this lecture Clynes suggests that 'the manner in which [the workman] is to be treated, hours, wages, conditions of employment, relations between section and section, and working division and working division , all those things which were regarded previously as the private monopoly of the foreman or manager must in future become the common concern of the workmen collectively, and they must have some voice in how these things are to be settled'.

Coates, K and T. Topham. *The History of the Transport and General Workers' Union* (Oxford: Blackwell, 1991-), I: *The Making of the Transport and General Workers' Union: The Emergence of the Labour Movement 1870-1922*. Pt 2: *1912-1922: From Federation to Amalgamation* (1991)

Cole, G. D. H. *A Short History of the British Working Class Movement*, 3rd edn, 3 vols (London: Allen & Unwin, 1937; repr. in facsimile London: Routledge, 2002), III: *1900-1937*

—— *Trade Unionism and Munitions* (Oxford: Clarendon Press, 1923)

Cronin, J. E. 'Strikes and Power in Britain, 1870-1920', in *Strikes, Wars and Revolutions in an International Perspective: Strike Waves in the Late Nineteenth and Early Twentieth Centuries*, edited by L. H. Haimson and C. Tilly (Cambridge: Cambridge University Press, 1989)

Fox, A. *History and Heritage: The Social Origins of the British Industrial Relations System* (London: George Allen & Unwin, 1985)

Garton Foundation. *Memorandum on the Industrial Situation after the War ...* Privately circulated among employers, representatives of labour, and public men of all parties, May-September, 1916. Now published as revised in the light of criticisms and suggestions received, October, 1916 (London: Harrison, 1916)

Graubard, S. *British Labour and Russian Revolution, 1917-1924* (Cambridge, Mass.: Harvard University Press, 1956)

Great Britain. Labour Party. *Labour and the New Social Order: A Report on Reconstruction* (revised in accordance with the resolutions of the Labour Party Conference, June 1918) (London: Labour Party, 1918)

Great Britain. Ministry of Munitions. *History of the Ministry of Munitions*, 12 vols (London, HMSO, 1918-1922)
The volumes have the following titles: 1. Industrial mobilisation, 1914-1915; 2. General organisation for munitions supply; 3. Finance and contracts; 4. The supply and control of labour, 1915-1916; 5. Wages and welfare; 6. Man power and dilution; 7. The control of materials; 8. Control of industrial capacity and equipment; 9. Review of munitions supply; 10-12. The supply of munitions

Great Britain. War Emergency Workers' National Committee. *General Correspondence and Political Records of the British Labour Party. Part 3, War Emergency Workers' National Committee 1914-1918*, Archives of the British Labour Party, series 3 (Brighton: Harvester Press Microform, 1981)
Twelve 35mm microfilm reels.

Harrison, R. 'The War Emergency Workers' National Committee', in *Essays in Labour History*, 1886-1923, ed. by A. Briggs and J. Saville (London: Macmillan, 1971)

Hatton, T. J. 'Unemployment and the Labour Market, 1870-1939', in *The Cambridge Economic History of Modern Britain*, edited by R. Floud and P. Johnson, 3 vols (Cambridge: Cambridge University Press, 2004), II: *Economic Maturity, 1860-1939*

Henderson, A. *The Aims of Labour* (London: Headley, 1917)

Hinton, J. 'The Clyde Workers' Committee and the Dilution Struggle', in *Essays in Labour History*, 1886-1923, ed. by A. Briggs and J. Saville (London: Macmillan, 1971)

—— *The First Shop Stewards' Movement* (London: Allen & Unwin, 1973, repr. 1977)

—— *Labour and Socialism* (Brighton: Wheatsheaf Books, 1983)

Holford, J. *Reshaping Labour: Organisation, Work, and Politics; Edinburgh in the Great War and After* (London: Croom Helm, 1988)

Horne, J. N. *Labour at War: France and Britain, 1914-18* (Oxford: Clarendon, 1991)

Johnson, P. B. *Land Fit for Heroes: The Planning of British Reconstruction, 1916-1919* (Chicago: University of Chicago Press, 1968)

Kellogg, P. U. and A. Gleason. *British Labor and the War* (New York: Boni and Liveright, 1919)

Kirkaldy, A. W. *Labour, Finance and the War: Being the Results of Inquiries Arranged by the Section of Economic Science and Statistics of the British Association ... During the Years 1915 and 1916* (London: Pitman, 1916)

Laybourn, K., and D. Murphy. *Under the Red Flag: A History of Communism in Britain, c.1849-1991* (Stroud: Sutton, 1999)

Lowe, R. *Adjusting to Democracy: The Role of the Ministry of Labour in British Politics, 1916-1939* (Oxford: Clarendon Press, 1986)

— 'The Demand for a Ministry of Labour: Its Establishment and Initial Role' (unpublished doctoral thesis, University of London, 1975)

— 'The Ministry of Labour, 1916-19: A Still Small Voice?', in *War and the State: The Transformation of British Government, 1914-1919*, ed. by K. Burk (London: Allen & Unwin, 1982)

McCurdy, C. A., ed. *A Clean Peace: The War Aims of British Labour*, Complete Text of the War Aims Memorandum of the Inter-Allied Labour and Socialist Conference held in London, February 23, 1918 (London: Smith, 1918)

McLean, F. *The Legend of Red Clydeside* (Edinburgh: John Donald, 1983, repr. 1999)

— 'Red Clydeside 1915-19', in *Popular Protest and Public Order*, ed. by J. Stevenson and R. Quinault (London: Allen & Unwin, 1976)

Middlemass, K. *The Clydesiders: A Left Wing Struggle for Parliamentary Power* (London: Hutchinson, 1965)

Murphy, J. T. *Compromise or Independence: An Examination of the Whitley Report with a Plea for the Rejection of the Proposals for Joint Standing Industrial Councils* (Sheffield: Sheffield Workers' Committee, 1918)

Orton, W. A. *Labour in Transition: A Survey of British Industrial History Since 1914* (London: P. Allen, 1921)

Pearce, R. *Britain: Economy, Society and Industrial Relations, 1900-39*, 2nd edn (London: Hodder & Stoughton, 2002)

Pelling, H. *History of British Trade Unionism*, 5th edn (London: Macmillan, 1992)

Pimlott, B. and C. Cook., eds. *Trade Unions in British Politics: The First 250 Years*, 2nd edn (London: Longman, 1991)

Pollard, S.A. *A History of Labour in Sheffield* (Liverpool: Liverpool University Press, 1959; repr. Aldershot: Gregg Revivals, 1993)

Pribicevic, B. *The Shop Stewards' Movement and Workers' Control, 1910-1922* (Oxford: Blackwell, 1950)

Price, R. *Labour in British Society: An Interpretive History* (London: Croom Helm, 1986; repr. London: Routledge, 1990)

Reid, A. 'The Impact of the First World War Upon British Workers', in *The Upheaval of War: Work and Welfare in Europe, 1914-18*, edited by Richard Wall and Jay Winter (Cambridge: Cambridge University Press, 1988)

— 'Dilution, Trade Unionism and the State In Britain During The First World War', in *Shop floor Bargaining and the State: Historical and Comparative Perspectives*, edited by S. Tolliday and J. Zeitlin (Cambridge: Cambridge University Press,1985)

— 'World War I and the Working Class in Britain', in *Total War and Social Change*, edited by Arthur Marwick (Basingstoke: Macmillan, 1988)

Roberts, B. C. *The Trades Union Congress, 1868-1921* (London: George Allen & Unwin, 1958)

Rubin, G. R. *War, Law and Labour: The Munitions Acts, State Regulation and the Unions, 1915-1921* (Oxford: Clarendon Press, 1987)

Rubinstein, D. 'Trade Unions, Politicians and Public Opinion, 1906-1914', in *Trade Unions in British Politics: The First 250 Years*, ed. by B. Pimlott and C. Cook, 2nd edn (London: Longman, 1991)

Silbey, D. *The British Working Class and Enthusiasm for War, 1914-1916* (London: Frank Cass, 2004)

Waites, B. *A Class Society at War: England 1914-1918* (Leamington Spa: Berg, 1987)

— 'The Government of the Home Front and the "Moral Economy" of the Working Class', in *Home Fires and Foreign Fields, British Social and Military Experience in the Great War*, ed. by P. H. Liddle (Manchester: Manchester University Press, 1985)

Whetham, W. C. D. *The War and the Nation: A Study in Constructive Politics* (London: Murray, 1917)

Wrigley, C. J. *David Lloyd George and the British Labour Movement: Peace and War* (Hassocks: Harvester, 1976; repr. London: Gregg Revivals, 1992)

— 'The First World War and the State Intervention in Industrial Relations', in *A History of British Industrial Relations*, edited by Chris Wrigley, 2 vols (Brighton: Harvester, 1982-1987), II: *1914-1939* (Brighton: Harvester, 1987; repr. Aldershot: Gregg Revivals, 1993)

— *A History of British Industrial Relations, 1914-1939* (Aldershot: Gregg Revivals, 1993)
Facsimile reprint of edn originally published as *A History of British Industrial Relations, Vol 2: 1914-1939*, Brighton: Harvester, 1987

— 'The Impact of the First World War on the British Labour Movement', in *Strategy and Intelligence: British Policy During the First World War*, ed. by M. Dockrill and D. French (London: Hambledon, 1986)

— 'The State and the Challenge of Labour in Britain, 1917-20', in *Challenges of Labour: Central and Western Europe, 1917-20*, edited by Chris Wrigley (London: Routledge, 1993)

— 'Trade Unionists, Employers and the Cause of Industrial Unity and Peace, 1916-1921', in *On the Move: Essays in Labour and Transport History Presented to Philip Bagwell*, ed. by C. Wrigley and J. Shepherd (London: Hambledon Press, 1991)

— 'Trade Unions and Politics in World War I', in *Trade Unions in British Politics: The First 250 Years*, ed. by B. Pimlott and C. Cook, 2nd edn (London: Longman, 1991)

Wrigley, C. J. and J. Shepherd, eds. *On the Move: Essays in Labour and Transport History presented to Philip Bagwell* (London: Hambledon Press, 1991)

Articles

Bevin, E. 'The Reconstruction of Industry', *Athenaeum*, May 1917

Clinton, A. 'Trades Councils during the First World War', *International Review of Social History*, 15 (1970), 202-234

Coles, A. J. 'The Moral Economy of the Crowd: Some Twentieth Century Food Riots', *Journal of British Studies*, 18 (1978), 157-76

Douglas, R. 'The National Democratic Party and the British Workers' League', *Historical Journal*, 15 (1972), 533-52

Doyle, B. 'Who Paid the Price of Patriotism? The Funding of Charles Stanton During the Merthyr Boroughs By-Election of 1915', *English Historical Review*, 109 (1994), 1215-1222

Englander, D. and J. Osborne. 'Jack, Tommy, and Henry Dubb; The Armed Forces and the Working Class', *Historical Journal*, 21 (1978), 593–621

Foster, J. 'Strike Action and Working-Class Politics on Clydeside, 1914-1919', *International Review of Social History*, 35 (1990), 33-70

Gardiner, A. G. 'Mr Henderson and the Labor Movement', *Atlantic Monthly*, 122 (1918), 221-30

Harley, J. H. 'The Conscription of Industry', *Contemporary Review*, May (1916)

Henderson, A. 'The Outlook for Labour', *Contemporary Review*, 113 (1918)

Howkins, A. 'Edwardian Liberalism and Industrial Unrest: A Class View of the Decline of Liberalism', *History Workshop Journal*, 4 (1977), 143-61

Klarman, M. 'Osborne: A Judgement Gone Too Far?', *English Historical Review*, 103 (1988), 21-39

Melling, J. 'Whatever Happened to Red Clydeside? Industrial Conflict and the Politics of Skill in the First World War', *International Review of Social History*, 35 (1990), 3-32

Mór-O'Brien, A. 'Patriotism on Trial: the Strike of the South Wales Miners, July 1915', *Welsh History Review*, 12 (1984/85), 76–105

Pelling, H. 'The Politics of the Osborne Judgement', *Historical Journal*, 25 (1982), 889-909

Rubin, G. B 'Explanations for Law Reform: The Case of Wartime Labour Legislation, 1915-1916', *History*, 72 (1987), 250-70

Sires, R. V. 'Labor Unrest in England, 1910-1914', *Journal of Economic History*, 15 (1955), 246-266

Swift, D. 'Labour and the War Emergency: The Workers' National Committee' during the First World War', *History Workshop Journal*, 81 (2016), 84-105

Stubbs, J. O. 'Lord Milner and Patriotic Labour, 1914-18', *English Historical Review*, 87 (1972), 717-54

Weinroth, H. S. 'Labour Unrest and the Food Question in Great Britain, 1914-1918', *Europa* 1.2 (1978), 140-6

Whiteside, N. 'Industrial Welfare and Labour Regulation in Britain at the Time of the First World War', *International Review of Social History*, 25 (1980), 307-331

— 'Welfare Legislation and the Unions during the First World War', *Historical Journal*, 23 (1980), 857-74

Whiting, R. 'Taxation and the Working Class, 1915-24', *Historical Journal*, 33 (1990), 895-916

Contemporary Official Papers

Commission of Enquiry into Industrial Unrest. *Reports, 1917-18*

— *North Eastern Area*, Cd 8662

— *North Western Area*, Cd 8663

— *Yorkshire and Midlands Area*, Cd 8664

— *West Midlands Area*, Cd 8665

— *London and South Eastern Area*, Cd 8666

— *South Western Area*, Cd 8667

— *Wales and Monmouthshire*, Cd 8668

— *Summary by G. N. Barnes*, Cd 8696

Great Britain. Ministry of Reconstruction. Committee on Relations between Employers and Employed. *Final Report*, Cd. 9153 (London: H.M.S.O., 1918)

— *Report on Works Committees*, Cd 9001 (London: H.M.S.O., 1918)

Great Britain. Ministry of Reconstruction. Reconstruction Committee. Sub-Committee on Relations Between Employers and Employed. *Interim Report on Joint Standing Industrial Councils*, Cd. 8606 (London: H.M.S.O., 1918)

Weekly Reports on Labour Situation, with Indexes to Reports for 29 November 1917 to 30 June 1918, and 1 July to 31 December 1918 (National Archives, under Ministry of Munitions, Munitions Council: Historical Records Branch MUN 5/55/300/47)

Website

Glasgow Digital Library. *Red Clydeside: A History of the Labour Movement in Glasgow 1910-1932* [http://gdl.cdlr.strath.ac.uk/redclyde/]
Provides images and information on the history of Red Clydeside and the Scottish Labour movement of the early 20th century. This collection is part of the Glasgow Digital Library and is maintained by the Centre for Digital Library Research at the University of Strathclyde

2.5 Socialism

Although the Labour Representation Committee (established in 1900 when a combination of representatives of all the socialist groups in Britain - the Independent Labour Party, the Social Democratic Federation and the Fabian Society – joined forces with trade union leaders) won 29 seats in the election of 1906, the Labour Party which emerged continued to be a loose alliance of unions and socialist groups (with an uneasy association with the Liberal Party) that was unable to achieve a coherent and coordinated expression of their socialism. The trade unionists, dominant in this emergent Labour Party and disinterested for the most part in the philosophy of socialism and sceptical about its adoption by middle class intellectuals, narrowly viewed the Party simply as a means of promoting union interests. At the outbreak of war, therefore, the Labour Party as an entity had failed to commit itself to a completely socialistic programme, and socialists were having to find the means to express their socialism primarily through their membership of the number of different organisations of which the Labour party was loosely composed - the Independent Labour Party (ILP), the Fabian Society, the British Socialist Party[10] and the National Socialist Party[11]. Most of the members of the ILP were against the war and focused their attention on the need to bring about a peace by negotiation (although there were differences of opinion as to whether an Allied victory was a necessary prerequisite of peace) and to defend the conditions of workers and soldiers' dependents. Although against the war the leaders of the ILP - MacDonald, Snowden, Keir

---

[10] Formed in 1911 when representatives of the Social Democratic Foundation, the left wing of the ILP, the network of clubs associated with *The Clarion* newspaper, and various local socialist societies joined together to found this new Marxist organisation.

[11] Established in 1916 by Hyndman and his followers as a result of their secession from the British Socialist Party over differences of opinion, particularly on the war.

Hardie and Jowett - were not extremists and were not in favour either of militant anti-war activity or a break with the Labour Party which, together with most trade unionists, largely supported the war. Ramsay MacDonald (chairman of the Labour Party at the outbreak of war) and Philip Snowden, two of the most prominent figures in the ILP, were among the members who subsequently sought to work for a negotiated peace through the Union of Democratic Control. For his attitude to the war MacDonald was ousted from the chairmanship of the Labour Party which voted to support the Government.

Unlike the ILP, which mostly concentrated on campaigning for peace by negotiation along the lines advocated by the UDC, the British Socialist Party took the more militant line of members like E. C. Fairchild and John Maclean as it had no difficulty in doing once its opponents within the party - a group led by Henry Hyndman that had adopted a patriotic stance by supporting the government - had defected and formed the National Socialist Party. The militancy of the BSP (British Socialist Party), and John Maclean in particular, was especially evident on Clydeside where it became (together with the Socialist Labour Party[12] and some left wing members of the Independent Labour Party) strongly associated with the Clyde Workers' Committee which, led by Willie Gallacher, became the revolutionary focus of shop steward power and working-class unrest in Glasgow during 1915 to 1916. As elsewhere in Britain, however, the shop stewards movement failed to direct working class unrest into a serious socialistic channel. Unrest was to do with traditional grievances about the rights of skilled workers, piece rates and free collective bargaining. There was nothing distinctly socialist about these concerns. Few of the rank and file were willing to be led by shop stewards along the road to revolution. Ultimately socialists like John Maclean and Willie Gallacher had to seek revolutionary change through communism.

Although the ILP continued to work within the Labour Party, it was hampered by the hostility of the moderate centre and right wing of the latter party and had little chance for most of the war of getting the Labour Party to abandon its pro-Government view of the war. The Labour Party remained committed to a patriotic support of the prosecution of the war until 1917 when Arthur Henderson, its leader, resigned from the Coalition. After this Henderson and his party engaged in formal defiance of government policy for the first time, making a determined effort to function as a national party with a potential to form an alternative government. In this period of opposition Henderson joined forces with Ramsay MacDonald and Sidney Webb and in 1917, a new Party Constitution was drafted by Sidney Webb and Arthur Henderson and later adopted by the Party Conference in February 1918. This document propounded in explicit terms a socialist view of society and together with *Labour and The New Social Order*, the programme which accompanied it, launched the formal acceptance by the Labour Party of a socialist ideology.

The Webbs, R. H. Tawney, and G. D. H. Cole were among the most prominent socialist intellectuals during the Great War. Their wartime activities reflected their different attitudes to the war. The Webbs worked constructively on the home front, with Sydney Webb becoming Labour's intellectual leader through his work on the War Emergency Workers' National Committee and his influential involvement in the drafting of the Labour Party's constitution and accompanying programme, *Labour and The New Social Order*, at the end of the war. Tawney felt impelled to participate in the war as a soldier. Cole opposed the war, campaigning against conscription and involving himself in the pacifist movement.

Almost all the Fabian Socialists supported the war on the grounds of their opposition to Germany's aggressive militarism. C. E. Chesterton, an elected member of the Fabian Society's executive committee, was particularly enthusiastic in his support of the war and uncompromisingly hostile to Germany (as is exemplified in his *The Perils of Peace* [q.v.])

In the literary world there were some socialists like H. G. Wells and Arnold Bennett who were sufficiently enthusiastic in their support of the war to work for the government in propaganda departments. Bernard Shaw on the other hand was an example of a literary figure who did not share this enthusiasm and was criticised for the controversial views he expressed in his *Common Sense about the War*.

Among socialists generally there were some who, regarding all war as contrary to socialist principles, refused compulsory military service and were, like the Guild Socialists William Mellor and Robin Page Arnot (secretary of the Fabian Research Department) prepared to risk imprisonment in their adherence to their principles for opposing the war.

---

[12] During the first year of the war several of the SLP's members became shop stewards in the engineering industry and were closely involved in Clydeside strikes from 1915-1917.

Bibliographies

Winter, J. M. 'A Bibliography of the Published Writings of R. H. Tawney', *Economic History Review*, n.s. 25 (1972), 137-153

Autobiographies, Biographies, Memoirs, Diaries

Brockway, A. F., Baron Brockway. *Socialism Over Sixty Years: The Life of Jowett of Bradford, 1864-1944* (London: Allen and Unwin, 1946)

Broom, J. *John Maclean* (Loanhead: Macdonald, 1973)

Brown, G. *Maxton*, new edn (Edinburgh: Mainstream, 2002)
James Maxton, one of the leading figures of the Independent Labour Party (ILP) in Glasgow and a key player during the Red Clydeside period, was a pacifist and totally opposed to Britain's involvement in the war and to the introduction of conscription. He was imprisoned in 1916 for making speeches supporting strike action at a demonstration to oppose the Munitions Act.

Canning, A. 'Barbour, Mary (1875–1958)', *Oxford Dictionary of National Biography*, Oxford University Press, 2004; online edn, May 2006 [http://www.oxforddnb.com/view/article/54393, accessed 6 Nov 2013]
Mary Barbour first became politically active in the Kinning Park Co-operative Guild, later joining the Independent Labour Party and the Socialist Sunday School movement. She became seriously politically active during the Glasgow rent strike of 1915, when she was involved in organising tenant committees and in organising local women to drive out sheriff's officers and resist evictions. [Information extracted from above item in online Oxford DNB]

Carpenter, L. P. *G. D. H. Cole: An Intellectual Biography* (London: Cambridge University Press, 1973)

Cole, M. I. *Beatrice Webb* (London: Longmans, 1945)

— *Growing Up into Revolution* (London: Longmans, 1949)

— *The Life of G. D. H. Cole* (London: Macmillan, 1971)

— *The Webbs and their Work* (London: Muller, 1949; repr. Brighton: Harvester, 1974))

Corr, H. 'Crawfurd, Helen (1877–1954)', *Oxford Dictionary of National Biography*, Oxford University Press, 2004; online edn, Sept 2010 [http://www.oxforddnb.com/view/article/40301, accessed 6 Nov 2013]
" … Her political activism and involvement in radical politics entered an intense phase in 1914 when she joined the Independent Labour Party (ILP) and then began to organise Scottish women in a campaign to oppose Britain's involvement in the First World War …" [Quotation extracted from above item in online Oxford DNB]

Gallacher, W. *Revolt on the Clyde: An Autobiography*, 4th edn (London: Lawrence & Wishart, 1978)

Hamilton, M. A. *Arthur Henderson: A Biography* (London: William Heinemann, 1938)

Hannan, J. *The Life of John Wheatley* (Nottingham: Spokesman, 1988)
Through his active opposition to Britain's involvement in the war and to its introduction of conscription, and as a leading light in the rent strikes which took place in Glasgow in 1915, John Wheatley exerted considerable influence on the labour movement during the Red Clydeside period

Hughes, E. *Keir Hardie* (London: George Allen & Unwin, 1956)

Hyndman, R. T. *Last Years of H. M. Hyndman* (London: Grant Richards, 1923)

Kirkwood, D. *My Life of Revolt* (London: G. G. Harrap, 1935)
"Kirkwood, a shop steward during the Red Clydeside period, became involved in Labour politics in Glasgow, joining the Independent Labour Party around 1909 where he worked closely with John Wheatley, James Maxton and Emanuel Shinwell. Kirkwood became one of the leaders of the Clyde Workers' Committee". [Glasgow Digital Library. *Red Clydeside: A History of the Labour Movement in Glasgow 1910-1932* [http://gdl.cdlr.strath.ac.uk/redclyde/]

Knox, W. *James Maxton* (Manchester: Manchester University Press, 1987)

McNair, J. *James Maxton: The Beloved Rebel* (London: Allen & Unwin, 1955)

Marquand, D. *Ramsay MacDonald* (London: Cape, 1977; repr. London: Richard Cohen, 1997)

Milton, N. *John Maclean* (London: Pluto Press, 1973)

Morgan, K. O. *Keir Hardie: Radical and Socialist* (London: Weidenfeld & Nicolson, 1975; repr. London Phoenix Giants, 1997)

Muggeridge, K and R. Adams.. *Beatrice Webb* (London: Secker & Warburg, 1967)

Postgate, R. *The Life of George Lansbury* (London: Longmans, 1951)

Ripley, B. J. and J. McHugh. *John Maclean* (Manchester: Manchester University Press, 1989)

Sewell, B. *Cecil Chesterton* (Faversham: Saint Albert's Press, 1975)
Chesterton joined the Fabian Society in 1901 and became an elected member of the executive committee. A strong supporter of Britain's involvement in the war, he visited the United States in 1915 to lecture and debate in favour of the allied cause. From 1916 to 1918 he served in the army, dying of nephritis in a French military hospital on 6 December 1918.

Shinwell, E. *Conflict without Malice* (London: Oldhams, 1955)
Emanuel Shinwell, chairman of Glasgow Trades Council between 1916-1919, was actively involved in the political life of Glasgow during the Red Clydeside period.

Smillie, R. *My Life for Labour* (London: Mills and Boon, 1924)
A founder member of the Scottish Labour Party in 1888 and of the Independent Labour Party in 1893. President of the National Council Against Conscription when it was formed in 1915. He also presided over the Leeds Convention of June 1917 which welcomed the Russian revolution of February 1917 and called for the creation across the country of councils of workmen and soldiers' delegates. Smillie combined these activities with committee work aimed at defending the interests of the miners and working people generally. He served on the War Emergency Workers' National Committee, acting as its chairman from September 1915 until the end of the war.

Snowden, P., Viscount Snowden. *An Autobiography*, 2 vols. (London: Ivor Nicholson & Watson, 1934), I: *1864-1919*

Terrill, R. *R. H. Tawney and his Times: Socialism as Fellowship* (London: Deutsch, 1974)
Bibliography of the published writings of R. H. Tawney on pp. 287-313.

Webb, B. P. *Diaries, 1912-1924*, edited by M. I. Cole (London: Longmans, 1952)

—*The Diary of Beatrice Webb*, edited by N. and J. Mackenzie, 4 vols (Cambridge, Mass.: Belknap Press of Harvard University Press, 1982-1985)
An abridged version by Lynn Knight, entitled *The Diaries of Beatrice Webb*, was published in 2000 by Virago in association with the London School of Economics and Political Science.

Williams, J. R., and others. *R. H. Tawney: A Portrait by Several Hands* [J. R. Williams, R. Titmuss and F. J. Fisher] (London: Workers' Educational Association, 1960)

Wrigley, C. J. *Arthur Henderson* (Cardiff: University of Wales Press, 1990)

Books

Archives of the Independent Labour Party, 1856-1975: A detailed guide to the Microform Collections, [compiled and edited by David Tyler] (Reading: Research Publications, 1990)

Beer, M. *A History of British Socialism*, edited [and written] by M. Beer. 2 vols, Routledge Library of British Political History, vol 5: Labour and Radical Politics 1762-1937 (London: Routledge, 2002)
Facsimile of edn published: London : George Allen & Unwin, 1953.

Bevir, M. *The Making of British Socialism* (Princeton, N.J.: Princeton University Press, 2011)

Callaghan, J. T. *Socialism in Britain since 1884* (Oxford: Blackwell, 1990)

Chesterton, C. E. *The Perils of Peace*, with an introduction by Hilaire Belloc (London: Werner Laurie, 1917)
In this work Chesterton's hostile attitude to Germany leads him to believe that the only satisfactory outcome of the war would be Germany's unconditional surrender without any concessions.

Clayton, J. *The Rise and Decline of Socialism in Great Britain, 1884-1924* (London: Faber & Gwyer, 1926)

Cole, M. *The Story of Fabian Socialism* (London: Mercury, 1961; repr. 1963)

Dowse, R. E. *Left in the Centre: The Independent Labour Party, 1893-1940* (London: Longmans, 1966)

Duncan, R. and A. McIvor, eds. *Militant Workers: Labour and Class Conflict on the Clyde 1900-1950*, essays in honour of Harry McShane (Edinburgh: John Donald, 1992)

Fainsod, M. *International Socialism and the World War* (Cambridge, Mass.: Harvard University Press, 1935; repr. New York: Octagon, 1973)

Great Britain. Independent Labour Party. *The War in Europe: Manifesto of the Independent Labour Party* (London: Independent Labour Party, 1916?)

Great Britain. Labour Party. *Labour and the New Social Order: A Report on Reconstruction* (revised in accordance with the resolutions of the Labour Party Conference, June 1918) (London: Labour Party, 1918)

Hannam, J. and K. Hunt. *Socialist Women, Britain, 1880's to 1920's* (London: Routledge, 2002)

Harrison, R. 'The War Emergency Workers' National Committee', in *Essays in Labour History, 1886-1923*, ed. by A. Briggs and J. Saville (London: Macmillan, 1971)

Hinton, R. *Labour and Socialism: A History of the British Labour Movement, 1867-1974* (Brighton: Wheatsheaf, 1983)

James, D., and others, eds. *The Centennial History of the Independent Labour Party*, a collection of essays edited by David James, Tony Jowitt and Keith Laybourn (Halifax: Ryburn, 1992)

Kendall, W. *The Revolutionary Movement in Britain, 1900-21: The Origins of British Communism* (London: Weidenfeld & Nicolson, 1969)

Laybourn, K., and D. Murphy. *Under the Red Flag: A History of Communism in Britain, c.1849-1991* (Stroud: Sutton, 1999)

McBriar, A. M. *Fabian Socialism and English Politics, 1884-1918* (Cambridge: Cambridge University Press, 1962; repr. 1966)

McCurdy, C. A., ed. *A Clean Peace: The War Aims of British Labour*, Complete Text of the War Aims Memorandum of the Inter-Allied Labour and Socialist Conference held in London, February 23, 1918 (London: Smith, 1918)

MacDonald, J. R. *Patriots and Politics* (London: National Labour Press: 1917)
A lecture delivered on Sunday, April 15, 1917, at the Metropole Theatre, Glasgow, under the auspices of the Glasgow I.L.P. Federation.

— *Socialism after the War* (Manchester: National Labour Press, 1917)

McKinlay, A. and R. J. Morris, eds. *The ILP [Independent Labour Party] on Clydeside, 1893-1932: From Foundation to Disintegration* (Manchester: Manchester University Press, 1991)

Martin, D. E. and D. Rubinstein, eds. *Ideology and the Labour Movement* (London: Croom Helm, 1979)

Pease, E. R. *The History of the Fabian Society*, 3rd edn (London: Cass, 1963)

Pelling, H. *The Challenge of Socialism*, 2nd edn (London: A. & C. Black, 1968)
Selections from writers of the 18th - 20th centuries.

Postgate, R. W. *The International (Socialist Bureau) during the War* (London: The Herald, 1918)

Sacks, B. F. *The Independent Labour Party and International Socialism during the World War*, University of New Mexico Bulletin. Sociological Series, vol.2, no.4. (Albuquerque: The University of New Mexico, 1936)

— *The Independent Labour Party and Social Amelioration in Great Britain during the World War*, University of New Mexico Bulletin. Sociological Series, vol.2, no.6. (Albuquerque: The University of New Mexico, 1940)

— *Relations between the Independent Labour Party and the British Labour Party during the World War*, The University of New Mexico Bulletin. Sociological series, vol. 2, no. 5 (Albuquerque: University of New Mexico, 1938)

Smyth, J. J. *Labour in Glasgow 1896-1936: Socialism, Suffrage and Sectarianism* (East Linton: Tuckwell Press, 2000)

Tsuzuki, C. *H. M. Hyndman and British Socialism*, edited by H. Pelling (London: Oxford University Press, 1961)

Ulam, A. B. *Philosophical Foundations of English Socialism* (Cambridge, Mass.: Harvard University Press, 1951

Walling, W. E., ed. *The Socialists and the War: A Documentary Statement of the Position of the Socialists of all Countries, with reference to their Peace Policy*, including a summary of the revolutionary state socialist measures adopted by the Governments at war (New York: Holt, 1915; repr. New York, Garland, 1972)

Winter, B. *The ILP [Independent Labour Party]: Past and Present* (Leeds: Independent Labour Publications, 1993)
Revised and updated version of *The ILP: A Brief History* (1982)

Winter, J. M. *Socialism and the Challenge of War: Ideas and Politics in Britain, 1912-18* (London: Routledge & Kegan Paul, 1974; repr. Aldershot; Gregg Revivals, 1993)

Articles

Brand, C. F. 'British Labour and The International during the Great War', *The Journal of Modern History*, 8 (1936), 40-63

Cox, J. 'Skinning a Live Tiger Paw by Paw: Reform, Revolution and Labour', *International Socialism*, Issue 87 (Summer 2000)

Foster, J. 'Strike Action and Working-Class Politics on Clydeside, 1914-1919', *International Review of Social History*, 35 (1990), 33-70

Harrison, A. 'The Stockholm Curtain-Raiser', *English Review*, 25 (1917), 262-71

Henderson, A. 'The New Labour Party Constitution', *Fabian News*, 29 (1918)

MacDonald, J. R. 'Is Democracy Possible', *Socialist Review*, 13 (1916)

— 'Socialism during War', *Socialist Review*, 12 (1914)

McKibbin, R. 'Why Was There No Marxism in Great Britain?' *English Historical Review*, 99 (1984), 297-331

Meynell, H. 'The Stockholm Conference of 1917', *International Review of Social History*, 5 (1960), 1-25; 202-25

Ryan, M. 'Britain's Biggest Left Party, 1893-1945, and What Became of It: The History of the ILP ', *Solidarity*, 3/85, 8 December 2005

Sacks, B. F. 'The Independent Labour Party and World War Peace Objectives', *Pacific Historical Review*, 5:2 (1936), 161-73

Winter, J. M. 'Arthur Henderson, the Russian Revolution, and the Reconstruction of the Labour Party', *Historical Journal*, 15 (1972), 753-773

Archival Material

Archives of the Independent Labour Party
Housed in the British Library of Political and Economic Science. Information about accessing the annual conference reports can be found at http://library-2.lse.ac.uk/archives/handlists/ILP/ILP.html. See also *Archives of the Independent Labour Party, 1856-1975: A Detailed Guide to the Microform Collections*, [compiled and edited by David Tyler] (Reading: Research Publications, 1990)

Website

Glasgow Digital Library. *Red Clydeside: A History of the Labour Movement in Glasgow 1910-1932*
[http://gdl.cdlr.strath.ac.uk/redclyde/]
Provides images and information on the history of Red Clydeside and the Scottish Labour movement of the early 20th century. This collection is part of the Glasgow Digital Library and is maintained by the Centre for Digital Library Research at the University of Strathclyde

2.6 Politicians and Political Parties

The war produced a period of electoral stagnation. An electoral truce declared at the beginning of the war provided for the filling of any future vacancies in parliamentary seats by the sitting party in the constituency without bye-election, and no general election was held until the end of 1918.

The Liberal Government under Asquith, with its majority dependent on the support of the Labour Party and the Irish Nationalist Party, managed to carry the country with it when war was declared on 4 August 1914 in spite of considerable misgivings within the Liberal Party and the resignation of two of its cabinet members who opposed the war (John Burns and Lord Morley). The Government continued to receive support from the Irish Nationalist Party and the Labour Party, the latter participating in the generally patriotic mood of the country at this time and the former seeing the opportunity to foster the cause of Home Rule by a demonstration of Irish loyalty at a time of English crisis. After the Easter Rebellion of 1916 and the Government's failure to settle the matter of Home Rule satisfactorily the members of the Irish Nationalist Party virtually seceded from Westminster, and anti-parliamentary forces with no interest in supporting the war began to achieve a dominant position in Ireland.

The Conservative Party, hawkish in its attitude and long given to pre-war warnings of the German threat, was enthusiastic in support of the war when it came and was happy not only to acquiesce in a 'party truce' but also, from may 1915, to participate in a coalition government first led by Asquith (until December 1916) and then by Lloyd George. Although the party was never in power it was able to press strongly throughout the war for a vigorous and effective prosecution of the war by exerting considerable influence, under the astute leadership of Bonar Law, both on the Liberal Government and on successive Coalition Governments in the area of matters related to the running of the war and the ways to achieve victory.

Many members of the Liberal Party, aware of the hawkish nature of the influence which the Conservatives might have on the government, were unhappy with Asquith bringing the Conservative leader, Andrew Bonar Law and his colleagues into a coalition. The relations of Liberals and their leadership became increasingly strained and the majority of their party became deeply divided between lukewarm support of the war effort and reluctant opposition to war measures that often seemed contrary to Liberal principles. This situation ultimately culminated in a split of the party caused by the formation of a new Coalition Government under Lloyd George in December 1916 and by Asquith, who refused to serve in it, leading a group of his supporters on to the opposition benches. From then on Liberals had a dual leadership, with on the one hand Lloyd George, the Prime Minister, supported by Liberals who were prepared to accept his total commitment to achieving complete victory by whatever means necessary (including the policy of the 'knock out blow' as opposed to a negotiated peace), and on the other hand Asquith, the Leader of the Opposition supported by Liberals who wished to run the war on Liberal principles and looked to him to be in the forefront of their opposition to Government's policies which violated those principles.

With the notable exception of the Independent Labour Party and the British Socialist Party, the Labour movement in both parliament and the country generally backed the government's war effort and approved the participation of Labour party members in successive Coalition governments. Significantly, however, Ramsay MacDonald and Philip Snowden refused to take this line, deciding instead to work for a negotiated peace through organisations such as the Union of Democratic Control and the Independent Labour Party. For his attitude to the war MacDonald was ousted from the Labour Party's chairmanship which was taken over by Arthur Henderson who subsequently became a cabinet minister in successive Coalition Governments. Henderson was motivated by a belief in the need not only to defeat Germany but also to ensure that working class interests were not neglected in time of war. Labour's loyalty to the Coalition persisted until 1917 when in the situation following the Russian Revolution, Henderson (by then a member of Lloyd George's War Cabinet) broke with the Coalition on the issue of sending delegates to a conference of all socialist parties - allied, neutral, and enemy - which was being promoted at Stockholm. Although George Barnes, another Labour MP, replaced him in the War Cabinet Henderson remained leader of the Labour Party which joined him in engaging in formal defiance of government policy for the first time in the war. From this moment the Labour Party began launching its bid for independence as a party with not only its own statement of 'Peace and War Aims' and a new party constitution (together with a programme entitled 'Labour and the New Social Order'), but also with its creation of a party machinery designed to enable it to compete effectively by itself in a general election.

There were a number of other political parties active during the war. These included the British Socialist Party, the National Socialist Party, and the Socialist Labour Party (all noted in the preamble to **Part 3, section 2.5** on **Socialism**). Apart from the National Socialist Party, which was an offshoot of the British Socialist Party, there were two other parties, the National Democratic Party (NDP) and the National Party, which were inaugurated during the war. The NDP was derived from Lord Milner's British Workers League (BWL)[13] which was established with a view to providing working men with an alternative (Conservative) leadership to that of socialist or trade unionist. The National Party[14] was established in August 1917 by Henry Page Croft for the purpose of opposing the 'corrupt compromises' of the coalition and realising the principles of 'National Production and Imperial Unity'.

Autobiographies, Biographies, Diaries, Memoirs

Amery, L. S. *My Political Life*, 3 vols (London: Hutchinson, 1953-1955), II: *War and Peace, 1914-29* (1953)

Armstrong, H. C. *Grey Steel (J. C. Smuts): A Study in Arrogance* (Harmondsworth: Penguin 1939)

Asquith, H. H., 1st Earl of Oxford and Asquith. *Memories and Reflections, 1852-1927*, [edited by A. Mackintosh], 2 vols (London: Cassell, 1928)

Blake, R. *The Unknown Prime Minister: The Life and Times of Andrew Bonar Law, 1858-1923* (London: Eyre and Spottiswoode, 1955)

---

[13] 10 of the 18 candidates who the BWL sponsored in 1918 in industrial seats where the Conservatives were not likely to win were elected as the 'National Democratic Party'.

[14] "In addition to tariffs, the National Party advocated neo-corporatist ideas (for example trade associations and a 'standard comfort wage') to deal with unemployment and poverty; a strict peace treaty with Germany; stiff restrictions on alien immigration; and publication of the details of party funds. It briefly claimed seven MPs and eighteen peers, as well as press support from *The Morning Post*, *The Globe*, and its own monthly journal, *National Opinion* (published from October 1917 to November 1922). Twenty-five candidates were fielded at the 1918 election, but only two (Croft and Sir Richard Ashmole Cooper) were returned. None the less, the National Party received just over 94,000 votes - one of the highest polls (in percentage terms) achieved by any minor party in the twentieth century". [Extracted from Andrew S. Thompson, 'Croft, Henry Page, first Baron Croft (1881–1947)', *Oxford Dictionary of National Biography*, Oxford University Press, 2004; online edn, Jan 2008]

The War Years

Brock, M., and others.ed. *Margot Asquith's Great War Diary 1914-1916: The View from Downing Street*, selected and edited by Michael and Eleanor Brock; with the assistance of Mark Pottle (Oxford: Oxford University Press, 2014)
Margot Asquith's diary of this period, as selected and presented in this work, is an interesting evocation of the British politicis of this period, providing a fascinating insight into the wartime scene as viewed from 10 Downing Street, revealing the political skirmishing that lay behind the warfare on the Western Front, and including character sketches of many important figures such as Lloyd George, Churchill, and Kitchener.

Campbell, J. *F. E. Smith: First Earl of Birkenhead* (London: Cape, 1983)
F. E. Smith was Head of Press Bureau in 1914; Solicitor-General in first coalition government, May 1915; Attorney-General, November 1915; member of the Cabinet until end of the war. Among the cases in which he was engaged in court were the trial of Sir Roger Casement (1916) and the trial of the Wheeldons (1917)

Carter, V. B., Baroness Asquith of Yarnbury. *Champion Redoubtable: The Diaries and Letters of Lady Violet Bonham Carter, 1914-1945*, edited by Mark Pottle (London: Weidenfeld and Nicolson, 1998)
Violet Bonham Carter, the only daughter of H. H. Asquith, kept a diary from the age of 18. Supported her father on political platforms, 1905-1918. Her close proximity to British politics and upper class social life from the outbreak of the first world war to the end of the second enabled her to write with revealing insight about the milieu in which she lived.

Cassar, G. H. *Lloyd George at War 1916-1918* (London: Anthem Press, 2009; repr. 2011)

Cregier, D. M. 'McKenna, Reginald (1863–1943)', *Oxford Dictionary of National Biography*, Oxford University Press, 2004; online edn, Jan 2011 [http://www.oxforddnb.com/view/article/34744, accessed 16 Nov 2013]
McKenna was the Liberal MP, North Monmouthshire, 1895-1918; Home Secretary 1911-15; Chancellor of the Exchequer, May 1915 to December 1916. In late 1915 McKenna and most of his Liberal cabinet colleagues fought a strenuous but vain battle to stop Lloyd George and the Conservative ministers bringing in military conscription. After the split of the Liberal party, caused by the formation of a new Coalition Government under Lloyd George in December 1916, McKenna went over with Asquith and other Liberal former ministers to the front opposition bench where he remained for the rest of the war. [Information extracted from the above item in the online Oxford DNB].

Chamberlain, Sir A. *Down the Years* (London: Cassell, 1935)

Chisholm, A. and M. Davie. *Beaverbrook: A Life* (London: Hutchinson, 1992)

Colvin, I. *The Life of Lord Carson*, 3 vols (London: Victor Gollancz, 1932-1936)
Vol 1 is by E. Marjoribanks

Croft, H. P., 1st Baron Croft of Bournemouth. *My Life of Strife* (London: Hutchinson, 1948)
See also biography by A. S. Thompson below

Driberg, T. E. N., Baron Bradwell. *Beaverbrook: A Study in Power and Frustration* (London: Weidenfeld & Nicholson, 1956)

Dugdale, B. E. C. *Arthur James Balfour, First Earl of Balfour*, 2 vols (London: Hutchinson, 1936), II: *1906-1930*

Dutton, D. *Austen Chamberlain: Gentleman in Politics* (Bolton: Ross Anderson, 1985)

Egremont, M. *Balfour* (London: Collins, 1980)

Elton, G., Baron Elton. *Life of James Ramsay MacDonald, 1866-1919* (London: Collins, 1939)

Farr, M. *Reginald McKenna, 1863-1943: A Life* (London: Frank Cass, 2004)

— *Reginald McKenna: Financier among Statesmen* (London: Routledge, 2008)

Gilbert, B. B. *David Lloyd George: A Political life*, 2 vols (London: Batsford: 1987-92), II: *The Organizer of Victory, 1912–1916* (1992)

Gilbert, M. *The Challenge of War: Winston Churchill, 1914-1916* (London: Minerva, 1990)
Originally published as *Winston S. Churchill*, by R. S. Churchill and M. Gilbert, vol 3, 1914-1916, London, Heinemann, 1971.

The Civilian Scene

— *World in Torment: Winston S. Churchill, 1916-1922* (London: Minerva, 1995)
Originally published as *Winston S. Churchill*, by R. S. Churchill and M. Gilbert, vol 4, 1916-1922, London, Heinemann, 1975.

Gollin, A. M. *Proconsul in Politics: A Study of Lord Milner in Opposition and in Power* (London: A. Blond, 1964)

Grey, E., 1st Viscount Grey of Fallodon. *Twenty-Five years 1892-1916*, 2 vols. (London: Hodder & Stoughton, 1925)

Grigg, J. *Lloyd George*, 4 vols (London: Penguin, 2002-03)
Vol. 3. From peace to war, 1912-1916 . Vol. 4. War leader, 1916-1918. This work was originally published: London: Eyre Methuen, 1973-1985

Haldane, R. B., Viscount Haldane. *An Autobiography* (London: Hodder & Stoughton, 1929)

Hamilton, M. A. *Arthur Henderson: A Biography* (London: William Heinemann, 1938)

Kent, W. *John Burns: Labour's Lost Leader* (London: William & Norgate, 1950)

James, L. *Churchill and Empire* (London: Weidenfeld & Nicolson, 2013; repr. London: Phoenix, 2014)

Jenkins, R. *Asquith: Portrait of a Man and an Era* (London: Collins, 1964; repr. London: Papermac, 1994)

Jones, T. *Lloyd George* (London: Oxford University Press, 1951)

Koss, S. E. *Asquith* (London: Hamilton, 1976; repr. 1985)

— *Lord Haldane: Scapegoat For Liberalism* (New York: Columbia University Press, 1969)

Leventhal, F. M. *Arthur Henderson* (Manchester: Manchester University Press, 1989)

Lloyd George, F. L., Countess. *Lloyd George: A Diary*, by Frances Stevenson [i.e. Frances Louise Lloyd George]; edited by A. J. P. Taylor (London: Hutchinson, 1971)

Lloyd George, D., 1st Earl. *War Memoirs*, 2nd edn, 2 vols (London: Odhams, 1942)

Mallet, C. *Lord Cave: A Memoir* (London: John Murray, 1931)

McKenna, S. *Reginald McKenna, 1863–1943: A Memoir* (London: Eyre & Spottiswoode, 1948)
The author, Stephen McKenna, a popular novelist in his time, was the nephew of Reginal McKenna.

Marquand, D. *Ramsay MacDonald* (London: Cape, 1977; repr. London: Richard Cohen, 1997)

Morgan, K. O. *Lloyd George* (London: Weidenfeld and Nicolson, 1974)

Morley, J., Viscount. *Memorandum on Resignation, August 1914* (London: Macmillan, 1928)

— *Recollections*, 2 vols (London: Macmillan, 1917; repr. 1924)

Hamer, D. A. *John Morley: Liberal Intellectual in Politics* (Oxford: Clarendon Press, 1968)

Morris, A. J. A. *C. P. Trevelyan: Portrait of a Radical* (Belfast: Blackstaff Press, 1977)

Newton, T. W. L., 2nd Baron. *Lord Lansdowne: A Biography* (London: Macmillan , 1929)

— *Retrospection* (London: Murray, 1941)

O'Brien, T. H. *Milner: Viscount Milner of St James and Cape Town, 1854-1925* (London: Constable, 1979)

Owen, F. *Tempestuous Journey: Lloyd George, his Life and Times* (London: Hutchinson, 1954)

Pugh, M. 'Runciman, Walter, first Viscount Runciman of Doxford (1870–1949)', *Oxford Dictionary of National Biography*, Oxford University Press, 2004; online edn, Jan 2011[http://www.oxforddnb.com/view/article/35868, accessed 6 Nov 2013]
"Wartime experience made Runciman acutely aware of Britain's reliance on imports, and in the long run this began to undermine his free trade convictions. At the time, however, he appeared to be a highly orthodox Liberal. He was among the ministers who believed in running the war by voluntary recruiting rather than conscription, on the grounds that the loss of manpower to the army would eventually be so damaging to industrial output as to be counter-productive. Consequently, when Asquith was displaced as prime minister in a coup by Lloyd George in December 1916, Runciman joined the majority of his Liberal colleagues in refusing to serve in the new coalition". [Quotation extracted from the above item in the online Oxford DNB]. Runciman was Liberal MP for Dewsbury, 1902-1918; President of Board of Trade, 1914-1916.

Robbins, K. *Sir Edward Grey* (London: Cassell, 1971)

Rowland, P. *Lloyd George* (London: Barrie & Jenkins, 1975)

Scott, C. P. *The Political Diaries of C. P. Scott, 1911-28*, edited with an introduction and commentary by T. Wilson (London: Collins, 1970)
Scott edited the *Manchester Guardian*, which he purchased in 1905, from 1872 to 1929

Snowden, P., Viscount Snowden. *An Autobiography*, 2 vols. (London: Ivor Nicholson & Watson, 1934), I: *1864-1919* (1934)

Spender, J. A. and C. Asquith. *Life of Herbert Henry Asquith, Lord Oxford and Asquith*, 2 vols (London: Hutchinson, 1932)

Taylor, A. J. P *Beaverbrook* (London: Hamilton, 1972)

— *Lloyd George: Twelve Essays* (London: Hamilton, 1971; repr. Aldershot: Gregg Revivals, 1994)

Thompson A. S., 'Croft, Henry Page, first Baron Croft (1881–1947)', *Oxford Dictionary of National Biography*, Oxford University Press, 2004; online edn, Jan 2008 [http://www.oxforddnb.com/view/article/32633, accessed 6 Nov 2013]
" In November 1914 Croft went to France with the 1st volunteer battalion of the Hertfordshire regiment, which he had joined as an undergraduate, and which he was to command within a year … He fought on the Somme in 1916 as commander of the 68th infantry brigade and was twice mentioned in dispatches. After spending twenty-two months at the front—longer than any other MP—he returned to Britain to take up his seat in the House of Commons". [Quotation extracted from above item in the online Oxford DNB]

Thompson, J. L. *Forgotten Patriot: A Life of Alfred, Viscount Milner of St. James's and Cape Town, 1854-1925* (Madison, N.J.: Fairleigh Dickinson University Press, 2007)

Toye, R. *Churchill's Empire: The World that Made Him and the World He Made* (London: Macmillan, 2010; repr. 1915

Trevelyan, Sir C. P. *From Liberalism to Labour* (London: Allen and Unwin, 1921)

Trevelyan, G. M. *Grey of Fallodon: Being the Life of Sir Edward Grey, Afterwards Viscount Grey of Fallodon* (London: Longmans, Green, 1937; repr. 1948)

Wallace, J. 'The Political Career of Walter Runciman, first Viscount Runciman of Doxford (1870–1949) ' (unpublished doctoral thesis, University of Newcastle, 1994)

Waterhouse, M. *Edwardian Requiem: A Life of Sir Edward Grey* (London: Biteback Publishing, 2013)

Williamson, P. *Stanley Baldwin: Conservative Leadership and National Values* (Cambridge: Cambridge University Press, 1999)

The Civilian Scene

Wrigley, C. J. *Arthur Henderson* (Cardiff: University of Wales Press, 1990)
Arthur Henderson was Labour MP Barnard Castle, 1903-18. Secretary of Labour Party, 1911-34. Opposed to Britain entering the European war in early August 1914 but subsequently supported the war effort as the Labour leader in the House of Commons. Joined the Union of Democratic Control, but resigned from it when he took cabinet office as President of the Board of Education in 1915 (he was also made a Privy Councillor in that year). Acted as adviser on labour in the cabinet, 1915-1917 (including also in the small war cabinet formed in December 1916). Also held office in the coalition government in 1916 as Paymaster General and Minister without Portfolio. Resigned in August 1917 after clashing with the government on the matter of his recommending Labour Party participation in an International Socialist conference planned to take place in Stockholm. During the remaining years of the war he focussed his efforts on the reorganization of the Labour Party getting heavily involved in the revision of the party constitution and playing a major role in the drafting of its new policy statement, *Labour and the New Social Order*, which was approved at the June 1918 conference.

Zebel, S. H. *Balfour: A Political Biography* (Cambridge: Cambridge University Press, 1973)

Books

Archives of the Independent Labour Party, 1856-1975: A detailed guide to the Microform Collections, [compiled and edited by David Tyler] (Reading: Research Publications, 1990)

Ball, S. *The Conservative Party and British Politics, 1902-1951* (London: Longman, 1995)

Ball, S. and I. Holliday, eds.. *Mass Conservatism: The Conservatives and the Public since the 1880's* (London: Frank Cass, 2002)

Beaverbrook, W. M. A., 1st Baron. *Men and Power 1917-1918* (London: Hutchinson, 1956; repr. London: Collins, 1966)

— *Politicians and the Press* (London: Hutchinson, 1926)

— *Politicians and the War, 1914-1916*, new edn (London: Collins, 1966)

Beers, L. *Your Britain: Media and the Making of the Labour Party* (Cambridge, MA: Harvard University Press, 2010)

Bentley, M. *The Liberal Mind, 1914–1929* (Cambridge: Cambridge University Press, 1977)

Blake, R. *The Conservative Party from Peel to Thatcher* (London: Fontana, 1985)

Brand, C. F. *British Labour's Rise to Power: Eight Studies* (London: Oxford University Press, 1941)

— *The British Labour Party: A Short History*, rev. edn (Stanford, Calif.: Hoover Institution Press, 1974)

Bridgen, P. *The Labour Party and the Politics of War and Peace 1900-1924* (Woodbridge; Rochester, NY: Boydell Press, 2009)

Bullock, A. L. C., Baron, and M. Shock, ed. *The Liberal Tradition from Fox to Keynes* [Letters and Speeches] (London, A. and C. Black, 1956; repr. Oxford: Clarendon Press, 1967)

Cawood, I. *The Liberal Unionist Party: A History* (London; New York: I.B. Tauris, 2012)

Charmley, J. *A History of Conservative Politics Since 1830*, 2nd edn (Basingstoke: Palgrave Macmillan, 2008)
Previous edition has title: *A History of Conservative Politics 1900-1996*

Clarke, P. F. *Liberals and Social Democrats* (Cambridge: Cambridge University Press, 1978; repr. Aldershot: Gregg Revivals, 1993)

Cline, C. A. *Recruits to Labour: The British Labour Party, 1914-1931* (Syracuse: Syracuse University Press, 1963)

Dangerfield, G. *The Strange Death of Liberal England* (New York: H. Smith and R. Haas, 1935; repr. London:

Serif, 1997)

David, E. I., ed. *Inside Asquith's Cabinet: From the Diaries of Sir Charles Hobhouse* (London: Murray, 1977)

Davies, A. J. *We, the Nation: The Conservative Party and the Pursuit of Power* (London: Little Brown, 1995)

Dowse, R. E. *Left in the Centre: The Independent Labour Party, 1893-1940* (London: Longmans, 1966)

Dutton, D. *His Majesty's Loyal Opposition: The Unionist Party in Opposition, 1905-1915* (Liverpool: Liverpool University Press, 1992)

Francis, M. and I. Zweiniger-Bargielowska, eds. *The Conservatives and British Society, 1880-1990* (Cardiff: University of Wales Press, 1996)

Fry, M. G. *And Fortune Fled: David Lloyd George, the First Democratic Statesman, 1916-1922* (New York; Oxford: Peter Lang, 2011)

Gash, N, and others. *The Conservatives: A History from their Origins to 1965*, edited with an introduction and epilogue by Lord Butler (London: Allen & Unwin, 1977)

Fyfe, H. *The British Liberal Party* (London: Allen & Unwin, 1928)

Hazlehurst, C. *Politicians at War, July 1914 to May 1915: A Prologue to the Triumph of Lloyd George* (London: Jonathan Cape, 1971)

A History of the Conservative Party. Editorial board John Barnes and others. 4 vols (London: Longman, 1978), III: *The Age of Balfour and Baldwin 1902-1940*, by John Ramsden

Howard, M. *War and the Liberal Conscience*, George Macaulay Trevelyan Lecture, 1977, [Updated edn] with a New Postscript (Oxford: Oxford University Press, 1989)

Kellogg, P. U. and A. Gleason. *British Labor and the War* (New York: Boni and Liveright, 1919)

Keohane, N. *The Party of Patriotism: The Conservative Party and the First World War* (Farnham: Ashgate, 2010)

Laybourn, K., and D. Murphy. *Under the Red Flag: A History of Communism in Britain, c.1849-1991* (Stroud: Sutton, 1999)

Lloyd George, D. *The Truth About the Peace Treaties*, 2 vols (London: Victor Gollancz, 1938)

McKibbin, R.I. *The Evolution of the Labour Party, 1910-1924* (Oxford: Clarendon Press, 1974; repr.1991)

— *Parties and People, England 1914-1951* (Oxford: Oxford University Press, 2010)

Martin, L. W. *Peace Without Victory: Woodrow Wilson and the British Liberals* (New Haven: Yale University Press, 1958; repr. London: Kennikat Press, 1973)

Matthew, H. C. G. *The Liberal Imperialists: The Ideas and Politics of a Post-Gladstonian Élite* (London: Oxford University Press, 1973)

Morgan, K. O. *The Age of Lloyd George: The Liberal Party and British Politics, 1890-1929*, 2nd edn (London: Allen and Unwin, 1978)

Nineteen Sixteen-Nineteen Twenty: The Lloyd George Coalition in War and Peace, with an introduction by Sir William Sutherland (London: L. J. Gooding, 1920)

Poirier, P. P. *The Advent of the Labour Party* (London: Allen & Unwin, 1958)

Pugh, M. *The Making of British Politics, 1867-1939*, 2nd edn (Oxford: Blackwell, 1993; repr. 1996)

— *The Tories and the People, 1880-1935* (Oxford: Blackwell, 1985)

Ramsden, J. *The Relations between the Independent Labour Party and the British Labour Party during the World War*, The University of New Mexico Bulletin. Sociological series, vol. 2, no. 5 (Albuquerque: University of New Mexico, 1938)

Searle, G. R. *The Liberal Party; Triumph and Disintegration, 1869-1929*, 2nd edn (Basingstoke: Palgrave, 2001)

Selden, A. and S. Ball, eds. *Conservative Century: The Conservative Party since 1900* (Oxford: Oxford University Press, 1994)

Smith J. *The Taming of Democracy: The Conservative Party, 1880-1924* (Cardiff: University of Wales Press, 1997)

Spender, J. A. *The Public Life: [Politics in Great Britain during the Nineteenth and Early Twentieth Centuries]*, 2 vols (London: Cassell, 1925)

Stansky, P., ed. *The Left and War: The British Labour Party and World War 1, 1914-1918* (London: Oxford University Press, 1969)

Stubbs, J. O. 'The Impact of the Great War on the Conservative Party', in *The Politics of Reappraisal*, edited by G. Peele and C. Cook (London: Macmillan, 1975)

Sweet, D. 'The Domestic Scene: Parliament and People', in *Home Fires and Foreign Fields, British Social and Military Experience in the Great War*, ed. by P. H. Liddle (Manchester: Manchester University Press, 1985)

Tanner, D. *Political Change and the Labour Party, 1900-1918* (Cambridge: Cambridge University Press, 1990)

Taylor, A. J. P. *Politics in Wartime and Other Essays* (London: Hamilton, 1964)

Thorpe, A. *A History of the Labour Party*, 4th edn (London: Palgrave, 2015)

Turner, J. *British Politics and the Great War: Coalition and Conflict, 1915-1918* (New Haven, Conn.: Yale University Press, 1992)
Wartime debates on post-war economic policy are summarised in this work, pp 336-53

Wyburn-Powell, A. *Defectors and the Liberal Party 1910 to 2010: A Study of Inter-Party Relations* (Manchester: Manchester University Press, 2012)

Willis, I. C. *England's Holy War: A Study of English Liberal Idealism during the Great War* (New York: Knopf, 1928)
"The three little books making up this volume were originally published in England in 1919, 1920, and 1921, under the respective titles of *How We Went Into the War, How We Got On With the War, And How We Came Out of The War*.--Pref." Based on in depth research into the files of the English, especially the liberal, press of the period of the Great War

Wilson, T. *The Downfall of the Liberal Party, 1914-1935* (London: Collins, 1966)

Articles

Ball, S. 'Parliament and Politics in Britain, 1900-1951', *Parliamentary History*, 10 (1991), 243-76

Barker, R. 'Political Myth: Ramsay MacDonald and the Labour Party', *History*, 61 (1976), 46-56

Bernstein, G. L. 'Yorkshire Liberalism During the First World War', *Historical Journal*, 32 (1989), 102-29

Cronin, J. 'The British State and the Structure of Political Opportunity', *Journal of British Studies*, 27 (1988), 199-231

David, E. I. 'The Liberal Party Divided, 1916-18', *Historical Journal*, 13 (1970), 509-32

Dowse, R.E. 'The Entry of Liberals into the Labour Party, 1910-20', *Yorkshire Bulletin of Economic and Social Research*, 13 (1961)

Fraser, P. 'Lord Beaverbrook's Fabrications in "Politicians and the War, 1914-1916"', *Historical Journal*, 25 (1982), 147-166

Gardiner, A. G. 'Mr Henderson and the Labour Movement', *Atlantic Monthly*, 122 (1918)

Gilbert, B. 'Pacifist To Interventionist: David Lloyd George in 1911 and 1914. Was Belgium an Issue?', *Historical Journal*, 28 (1985), 863-885

Ehrman, J. 'Lloyd George and Churchill as War Ministers', *Transactions of the Royal Historical Society*, 5th series, 11 (1961), 101-115

Gooch, J. 'The Maurice Debate, 1918', *Journal of Contemporary History*, 3 (1968), 211-228

Howard, C. 'Macdonald, Henderson, and the Outbreak of War, 1914', *Historical Journal*, 20 (1977), 871-91

Johnson, M. 'The Liberal War Committee and the Liberal Advocacy of Conscription in Britain, 1914-1916', *Historical Journal*, 51 (2008), 399-420

Lockwood, P. A. 'Milner's Entry into the War Cabinet, December 1916', *Historical Journal*, 7 (1964), 120-134

McGill, B. 'Asquith's Predicament, 1914-18', *Journal of Modern History*, 3 (1967), 283-303

McKibbin, R. I. 'Arthur Henderson as Labour Leader', *International Review of Social History*, 23 (1978), 79–101

— 'James Ramsay MacDonald and the Problem of the Independence of the Labour Party, 1910-1914', *Journal of Modern History*, 42 (1970), 216-235

McEwen, J. M. 'The Liberal Party and the Irish Question During the First World War', *Journal of British Studies*, 12 (1972), 109-131

— 'The Struggle for Mastery in Britain', *Journal of British Studies*, 18 (1978), 131-156

Morgan, K. O. 'Lloyd George's Premiership', *Historical Journal*, 13 (1970), 130-157

Murphy, R. 'Walter Long, the Unionist Ministers, and the formation of Lloyd George's Government in December 1916', *Historical Journal*, 29 (1986), 735-45

Pugh, M. 'Asquith, Bonar Law and the First Coalition', *Historical Journal*, 17 (1974), 813-36

— 'The Great War and the Decline of the Liberal Party', *History Sixth*, 5 (1989)

— 'Politicians and the Women's Vote, 1914-1918', *History*, 69 (1974), 358-74

— 'Popular Conservatism in Britain: Continuity and Change, 1880-1987', *Journal of British Studies*, 27 (1988), 254-82

Quinault, R. 'Asquith: A Prime Minister at War, *History Today*, 64, Issue 5 (2014), 40-46
Roland Quinault re-evaluates the wartime reputation of Herbert Asquith, who resigned as premier in late 1916.

Rubinstein, D. 'Henry Page-Croft and the National Party, 1917-22', *Journal of Contemporary History*, 9 (1974), 129-48

Sacks, B. F. 'The Independent Labour Party and World War Peace Objectives', *Pacific Historical Review*, 5 (1936), 161-73

Stubbs, J. 'The Unionists and Ireland, 1914-1918', *Historical Journal*, 33 (1990), 867-93

Thorpe, A. , 'Labour Leaders and the Liberals, 1906-1924', *Cercles* 21 (2011), 39-54

Winter, J. M. 'Arthur Henderson, the Russian Revolution, and the Reconstruction of the Labour Party', *Historical Journal*, 15 (1972), 753-773

Annual reports

Archives of the British Conservative and Unionist Party [microform]: the Conservative Party Annual Conference Reports, 1867-1946 (Brighton: Harvester, 1982)

Archives of the British Liberal Party [microform]: National Liberal Federation Annual Reports and Council Proceedings, 1877-1936 (Brighton: Harvester, 1975)

Archives of the Independent Labour Party
Held at the British Library of Political and Economic Science. Information about accessing the annual conference reports can be found at http://library-2.lse.ac.uk/archives/handlists/ILP/ILP.html. See also *Archives of the Independent Labour Party, 1856-1975: A Detailed Guide to the Microform Collections*, [compiled and edited by David Tyler] (Reading: Research Publications, 1990)

Labour Party Annual Reports, 1900-1949 (reports of the annual conference)
5 reels of microfilm held in The British Library's Microform Research Collections at Boston Spa

Speeches

Speeches made in Parliament during the war can be found in the relevant sections of the following reports:

Official Report, House of Commons (5th Series), Jan 1909 to March 1981

Official Report, House of Lords (5th Series) Jan 1909 to 2004

Some speeches made by politicians, both inside and outside Parliament, were also published as pamphlets as, for example, the following:

Asquith, H. H., 1st Earl of Oxford and Asquith. *The War: Its Causes and Its Message: Speeches Delivered by the Prime Minister August-October 1914* (London: Methuen, 1914)
Speeches made in the House of Commons, at the Guildhall, and in Edinburgh, Dublin and Cardiff.

Lloyd George, D. *The Great War; Speech Delivered by the Rt. Hon. David Lloyd George at the Queen's Hall London on September 19th, 1914* (London: Harrison, 1914)
"We have been living in a sheltered valley for generations. We have been too comfortable and too indulgent ... and the stern hand of Fate has scourged us to an elevation where we can see the great everlasting things that matter for a nation - the great peaks we had forgotten, of Honour, Duty, patriotism, and clad in glittering white, the great pinnacle of Sacrifice pointing like a rugged finger to Heaven" [quotation from the above pamphlet].

2.7 The Press

On the eve of the outbreak of war most of the British press, with the notable exception of *The Times*, had either been unenthusiastic about involvement in a war or completely opposed to it, and Liberal papers such as the *Manchester Guardian* and the *Daily News* and Liberal writers such as A. G. Gardiner, H. W. Massingham, and C. P. Scott had been strenuously arguing that there was no reason for Britain to be embroiled in it. As soon as Germany had invaded Belgium, however, the press generally approved Britain's entry into the war, enthusiastically for the most part, albeit painfully on the part of the liberal papers.

Once this change of attitude had taken place the press in general, and the mass circulation dailies in particular, took the line that their columns should be used to help maintain civilian morale at home and support for the army abroad. Most newspapers not only did this but also frequently denied individuals and groups who were against the war access to their columns, and attacked aliens, pacifists, conscientious objectors, socialists, strikers, and all the others they lumped together as 'shirkers'. The effect of this hostility was to help create the situation where in the second half of the war dissenters not only found it extremely difficult to rent premises for their public meetings but were also fearful of violent disruption if they were successful in holding them. Although there were times when newspapers criticised the government, most notably on the matter of the shell shortage in 1915 and of troop undermanning on the western front in 1918[15], they were on these occasions motivated by the patriotic concern that the government was not prosecuting the war as effectively and vigorously as it should. In contrast, the press barely ever criticised the conduct of the war by the armed forces.

Most of the press were a willing party to the collective efforts that were made to obscure the truth from the public and, in the case sometimes of some unscrupulous correspondents, even to fabricate tales of heroism when there was a lack of such news to report. The rarity of a newspaper being prosecuted for flouting the censorship of the Press Bureau exemplifies the willingness of the press to cooperate. It was because of this acquiescence and the jingoistic propaganda in which most newspapers indulged (particularly scurrilously in the case of Gordon Bottomley and *John Bull*) that Arthur Ponsonby felt impelled to write after the war in his book, *Falsehood in Wartime*, that there was 'no more discreditable period in the history of journalism'.

In a national press world dominated by patriotic and jingoistic newspapers (although one newspaper, *The Daily News*, became increasingly anti-war as the conflict wore on), anti-war and pro-peace views had little scope for their expression. The presence of such views in the press was due mainly to their publication in a small number of papers with a far more limited circulation such as *Common Sense*, *The Labour Leader*, *The Daily Herald* (which became *The Herald*, a weekly, after the outbreak of war), *Forward*, *The Bradford Pioneer*, *The UDC*, *Tribunal* and *The Worker* (the last three of which were established during the war). Apart from their publication in the latter newspapers, dissenting views were sometimes aired in periodicals like *The Nation* and *The New Statesman* but neither of these had anywhere near the size of circulation and popularity of the mainstream national newspapers.

Bibliographies, Encyclopaedias

Griffiths, D., ed.. *The Encyclopedia of the British Press, 1422–1992* (London: Macmillan, 1992)

Linton, D. *The Twentieth-Century Newspaper Press in Britain: An Annotated Bibliography* (London: Mansell, 1994)
This bibliography deals with the 20th-century British newspaper press and the individuals concerned with it - proprietors, journalists and illustrators. Its 3500 entries include: books, theses, articles commemorative issues, a chronology and a detailed subject index.

Autobiographies, Biographies, Diaries, Letters

Ayerst, D. *Garvin of The Observer* (London: Croom Helm, 1985)
Garvin edited the *Pall Mall Gazette* from 1912 to 1915 and *The Observer* from 1908 to 1942.

Brockway, A. F., Baron Brockway. *Inside the Left: Thirty Years of Platform, Press, Prison and Parliament* (London: Allen and Unwin, 1942; repr. 1947)
Brockway was editor of the *Labour Leader*, 1912-17.

Chisholm, A. and M. Davie. *Beaverbrook: A Life* (London: Hutchinson, 1992)
Beaverbrook purchased *Daily Express*, 1916; launched *Sunday Express*, 1918.

Felstead, S. T. *Horatio Bottomley: A Biography of an Outstanding Personality* (London: J. Murray, 1936)
Bottomley founded *John Bull* in 1906

Ferris, P. *The House of Northcliffe: The Harmsworths of Fleet Street* (London: Weidenfeld & Nicolson, 1971)

F. W. Hirst by his Friends (London: Oxford University Press, 1958)
Hirst was editor of the *Economist* 1907-16. After being forced to resign from the editorship of *The Economist* in 1916 because

---

[15] On 7 May 1918 a letter by Major-General Sir Frederick Maurice appeared in the press, claiming among other issues that, contrary to its public statements, the Government had left Haig's forces short of troops. This was followed by a debate in the House of Commons on 9 May 1918.

of his anti-war views he set up his own paper, *Common Sense* (financed by anti-Lloyd George Liberals) which he particularly employed to campaign for a negotiated peace.

Fyfe, H. *My Seven Selves* (London: Allen & Unwin, 1935)
The author was special correspondent for the *Daily Mail* from 1907 to 1918. In July 1918 he replaced H. G. Wells at Crewe House, where he made his contribution to the British propaganda campaign in enemy territories.

— *Northcliffe: An Intimate Biography* (London: Allen & Unwin, 1930)

— *Sixty Years of Fleet Street* (London: Allen & Unwin, 1949)

Gwynne, H. A. *The Rasp of War: The Letters of H. A. Gwynne to the Countess Bathurst, 1914–1918*, selected and edited by K. Wilson (London: Sidgwick & Jackson, 1988)
H. A. Gwynne was editor of the *Morning Post* and Lady Bathurst the owner during the war.

Hammond, J. L. *C. P. Scott of the Manchester Guardian* (London: G. Bell, 1934)

Harris, H. W. *J. A. Spender* (London: Cassell, 1946)
Spender edited the *Westminster Gazette* from 1896 to 1922

Havighurst, A. F. *Radical Journalist: H. W. Massingham, 1860-1924* (Cambridge: Cambridge University Press, 1974)

Hirst, F. W. *In the Golden Days* (London: Frederick Muller, 1947)
Hirst was editor of the *Economist* 1907-16. After being forced to resign from the editorship of the *Economist* in 1916 because of his anti-war views he set up his own paper, *Common Sense* (financed by anti-Lloyd George Liberals) which he particularly employed to campaign for a negotiated peace.

Jones, Sir R., *A Life In Reuters* (London: Hodder & Stoughton, 1951)
Jones became managing director of Reuters during the war. When the Ministry of Information was formed in Britain in 1918, with Beaverbrook as its Minister, Jones became its full-time director of propaganda.

Massingham, H. J. *Remembrance: An Autobiography* (London: Batsford, 1942)
Harold John Massingham was the eldest of the six children of the radical Liberal journalist Henry William Massingham (1860–1924).

Nevinson, H. W. 'Massingham, Henry William (1860–1924)', rev. A. J. A. Morris, *Oxford Dictionary of National Biography*, Oxford University Press, 2004; online edn, Oct 2008
[http://www.oxforddnb.com/view/article/34923, accessed 7 Nov 2013]
"Before the First World War he [Massingham] constantly challenged the Liberal Imperialist-inspired foreign policy pursued by Edward Grey … During the war he made certain that his paper was a primary forum for the discussion of … designs to prevent future wars. He supported Lord Lansdowne's plea for a peace settlement in November 1917. President Woodrow Wilson's fourteen points and League of Nations were, Massingham believed, 'the best means of achieving peace for ever' (The Nation, 16 Nov 1918)". [Quotation extracted from above item in the online Oxford DNB]. Massingham was editor of *The Nation* from 1907 to 1923.

Pound, R. and G. Harmsworth. *Northcliffe* (London: Cassell, 1959)

Repington, C. à Court. *The First World War*, 2 *vols* (Aldershot: Gregg Revivals, 1991)
Facsimile of edn published London: Constable, 1920 under the title, *First World War, 1914-1918: Personal Experiences*. The author was military correspondent first of the *Morning Post* and, then of *The Times*, 1904-1918

— *The Letters of Lieutenant-Colonel Charles à Court Repington CMG: Military Correspondent of The Times, 1903-1918*, selected and edited by A. J. A. Morris (Stroud: Sutton for the Army Records Society, 1999)

Riddell, G. A., Baron Riddell. *Lord Riddell's War Diary, 1914-1918* (London: Nicholson and Watson, 1933)
The author was chairman of the *News of the World* from 1903-1934

— *The Riddell Diaries, 1908-1923*, edited and with an introduction by J. M. McEwen (London: Athlone Press, 1986)

Ryan, A. P. *Lord Northcliffe* (London: Collins, 1953)

Scott, C. P. *The Political Diaries of C. P. Scott, 1911-28*, edited with an introduction and commentary by T. Wilson (London: Collins, 1970)
Scott edited the *Manchester Guardian*, which he purchased in 1905, from 1872 to 1929.

Spender, J. A. *Life, Journalism and Politics*, 2 vols (London: Cassell, 1927)
The author edited the *Westminster Gazette* from 1896 to 1922.

Steed, H. W. *Through Thirty Years 1892-1922: A Personal Narrative*, 2 vols. (London: Heinemann, 1924)
The author was head of the foreign department of *The Times* from 1914-1919.

Strachey, A. *St Loe Strachey: His Life and His Paper* (London: V. Gollancz, 1930)
St Loe Strachey was editor and proprietor of the *Spectator*, 1898-1925.

Taylor, A. J. P. *Beaverbrook* (London: Hamilton, 1972)
Beaverbrook purchased *Daily Express*, 1916; launched *Sunday Express*, 1918.

Thomas, Sir W. B. *A Traveller in News* (London: Chapman and Hall, 1925)
"The chief object of these reminiscences was a desire to give some sketch of the character of Lord Northcliffe."—Pref. Thomas spent most of the war as a well-regarded correspondent in France for the *Daily Mail*. Wrote *With the British on the Somme* (1917).

— *The Way of a Countryman* (London: Michael Joseph, 1944)

Wrench, Sir J. E. L. *Geoffrey Dawson and our Times* (London: Hutchinson, 1955)
Geoffrey Dawson was editor of *The Times* 1912-1919, 1923-1941

Books

Ayerst, D. *Guardian: Biography of a Newspaper* (London: Collins, 1971)

Beaverbrook, W. M A., 1st Baron. *Politicians and the Press* (London:: Hutchinson, 1926)
The author purchased the *Daily Express* in 1916 and launched the *Sunday Express* in 1918

Bingham, A. and M. Conboy. *Tabloid Century: The Popular Press in Britain, 1896 to the Present* (Oxford: Peter Lang, 2015)

Blumenfeld, R. D. *The Press in My Time* (London: Rich & Cowan, 1933)
The author was editor of the *Daily Express* from 1904-1932

Boyce, D. G. 'Crusaders Without Chains: Power and the Press Barons 1896-1951', in *Impacts and Influences: Essays on Media Power in the Twentieth Century*, edited by J. Curran, A. Smith and P. Wingate (London: Methuen, 1987)

Catterall, P. and others, ed. *Northcliffe's Legacy: Aspects of the British Popular Press, 1896-1996*, edited by P. Catterall, C. Seymour-Ure, A. Smith (Basingstoke: Macmillan in association with the Institute of Contemporary British History, 2000)
This work originated in papers for a conference at the Institute of Historical Research organised by the Institute of Contemporary British History and the University of Kent in 1996.

C. P. Scott, 1846–1932: The Making of the Manchester Guardian [Essays by various authors] (London: Muller, 1946)

Engel, M. *Tickle the Public: One Hundred Years of the Popular Press* (London: Gollancz, 1996)

Esposito, P. 'Public Opinion and the Outbreak of the First World War: Germany, Austria-Hungary and the War in the Newspapers of Northern England' (unpublished master's thesis, University of Oxford, 1997)

Farrar, M. J. *News From the Front: War Correspondents on the Western Front, 1914-18* (Stroud: Sutton, 1998)

The Civilian Scene

Front Page: Celebrating 100 Years of the British Newspaper 1906-2006: I Read the News Today, 2 vols (London: British Library, 2006)
Published on the occasion of an exhibition held at the British Library, London, May-Oct. 2006. Produced in the format of a tabloid newspaper. The second volume consists entirely of facsimile pages from historic newspapers. "Jointly presented by the British Library and the Newspaper Publishers Association" -- v. [1], p. 2. "All the newspapers displayed in the ... exhibition are from the ... collection of John Frost" -- v. [1], p. 37. See also *Online Gallery: Front Page; The British Newspaper, 1906-2006* at http://www.bl.uk/onlinegallery/features/frontpage/memorable.html

Gibbs, Sir P. *Adventures In Journalism* (London: Heinemann, 1923)
The author was a war correspondent in the Great War.

— *Realities of War*, new and revised edn (London: Hutchinson, 1929)

— *The War Dispatches*, edited by Catherine Prigg (London: A. Gibbs & Phillips Ltd., 1964)

Gollin, A. M. *The Observer and J. L. Garvin, 1908-1914: A Study in Great Editorship* (Oxford: Oxford University Press, 1960)
Garvin edited the *Pall Mall Gazette* from 1912 to 1915 and *the Observer* from 1908 to 1942.

Griffiths, D. *Fleet Street: Five Hundred Years of the Press* (London: British Library, 2006)
Published to accompany the exhibition *The Front Page* held at the British Library in Spring 2006 (see record above.)

Hampton, M. *Visions of the Press in Britain, 1850-1950* (Urbana: University of Illinois Press, 2004)

Herd, H. *The March of Journalism: The Story of the British Press from 1622 to the Present Day* (London: Allen & Unwin, 1952)

Hindle, W. *The Morning Post, 1772-1937: Portrait of a Newspaper* (London: Routledge, 1937)

Hyams, E. S. *The New Statesman: The History of the First Fifty Years, 1913-1936* (London: Longmans, 1963)

Inwood, S. 'The Role of the Press in English Politics during the First World War, With Special Reference to the Period 1914-1916' (unpublished doctoral thesis, University of Oxford, 1971)

Jones, K.. *Fleet Street and Downing Street* (London: Hutchinson, 1920)

Knightley, P. *The First Casualty: The War Correspondent as Hero, Propagandist and Myth Maker from the Crimea to Iraq* (London: Deutsch, 2003)

Koss, S. *Fleet Street Radical: A. G. Gardiner and the Daily News* (London: Allen Lane, 1973)
Gardiner was editor of the *Daily News* from 1902-1919

— *The Rise and Fall of the Political Press in Britain*, 2 vols (London: Hamilton, 1981-1984), II: *The Twentieth Century*, 1984

Lee, A. J. *The Origins of the Popular Press, 1855–1914* (London: Croom Helm, 1976)

Lytton, N. *The Press and the General Staff* (London: Collins, 1920)

Matthews, J. J. *Reporting the Wars* (Minneapolis: University of Minnesota Press, 1957)
The history of war reporting from the time of the Napoleonic Wars until the end of World War II.

Mills, W. H. *The Manchester Guardian: A Century of History* (London: Chatto & Windus, 1921)

Morris, A. J. L. 'A study of John St Loe Strachey's editorship of the *Spectator*', (unpublished doctoral thesis., University of Cambridge, 1986)

Pierce, R. N. *Lord Northcliffe: Trans-Atlantic Influences*, Journalism Monographs, 40 (Lexington, Kentucky:

Association for Education in Journalism, 1975)

Rappaport, A. *The British Press and Wilsonian Neutrality* (Stanford, California: Stanford University Press, 1951)

Robbins, K. 'The Freedom of the Press: Journalists, Editors, Owners and Politicians in Edwardian Britain', in *Too Mighty to be Free: Censorship and the Press in Britain and the Netherlands* [Papers delivered to the ninth Anglo-Dutch Historical Conference at University College, London, in 1987], edited by A.C. Duke and C.A. Tamse (Zutphen: De Walburg, 1987)

Stephens, M. *A History of News*, new edn (Forth Worth: Harcourt Brace, 1997)
Originally published as *A History of News from the Drum to the Satellite*, New York: Viking, 1988

Storey, G. *Reuters' Century, 1851-1951* (London: Parrish, 1951)

Stubbs, J. 'Appearance and Reality: A Case Study of the *Observer* and J. L. Garvin, 1914–1942', in *Newspaper History: From The Seventeenth Century to the Present Day*, edited by G. Boyce, J. Curran, and P. Wingate (London: Constable, 1978)

Taylor, S. J. *The Great Outsiders: Northcliffe, Rothermere and the 'Daily Mail'* (London: Weidnefeld & Nicolson, 1996)

Thompson, J. L. *Northcliffe: Press Baron in Politics, 1865-1922* (London: Murray, 2000)

— *Politicians, the Press and Propaganda: Lord Northcliffe and the Great War, 1914-1919* (Kent, OH: Kent State University Press, 1999)

The Times. *The History of The Times*, 4 vols (London: The Times, 1935-52), IV: *The 150th Anniversary and Beyond 1912-1948;* Pt.1: *1912-1920* (1952)

Willis, I. C. *England's Holy War: A Study of English Liberal Idealism during the Great War* (New York: Knopf, 1928)
"The three little books making up this volume were originally published in England in 1919, 1920, and 1921, under the respective titles of *How We Went Into the War, How We Got On With the War, And How We Came Out of The War.*--Pref." Based on an in depth research into the files of the English, especially the liberal, press of the period of the Great War

Wilson, K. M. *A Study in the History and Politics of the Morning Post, 1905–1926* (Lampeter: Edwin Mellen, 1990)

Articles

Bazley, A. W. 'C. E. W. Bean', *Historical Studies*, 14 (1969–71), 147–54

Bones, A.J. 'British National Dailies and the Outbreak of War in 1914', *International History Review*, 35 (2013), 975-992

Drisceoil, D. O. 'Keeping Disloyalty within Bounds? British Media Control in Ireland, 1914-19', *Irish Historical Studies*, 149 (2012), 52-69

Finn, M. 'Local Heroes: War News and the Construction of "Community" in Britain, 1914-18', *Historical Research* (Oxford) 83 (2010), 520-538
Focusing on the city of Liverpool and its environs as a case study this article argues that a view of the trench experience, fostered both by soldiers' correspondence and the local press, helped to provide community-oriented narratives of combat that contributed to making bereavement bearable, war better understood and mobilization sutainable.

Heindel, R. H. 'British Diplomats and the Press', *Public Opinion Quarterly*, 2 (1938), 435-41

Gardiner, A. G. 'Two Journalists, C. P. Scott and Lord Northcliffe: A Contrast', *Nineteenth Century and After*, 111 (1932), 247–56

Gollin, A. M. Review: *The Rasp of War: The Letters of H. A. Gwynne to the Countess Bathurst, 1914–1918*, edited by K. Wilson (London: Sidgwick & Jackson, 1988), *English Historical Review*, 107, (1992), 760

McEwen, J. M 'The National Press during the First World War: Ownership and Circulation', *Journal of Contemporary History*, 17 (1982), 459-486

— 'The Press and the Fall of Asquith', *Historical Journal*, 21 (1978), 863-83

— 'Northcliffe and Lloyd George At War, 1914-18', *Historical Journal*, 24 (1981), 651-72

Neander, J. and R. Martin. 'Media and Propaganda: The Northcliffe Press and the Corpse Factory Story of World War I', *Global Media Journal*, 3 (2010), 67-82

Simons, J. 'The Times Broadsheets: A Canon for the Front', *Literature and History*, 11:2 (2002) 39-51
A critical analysis of contents of *The Times* broadsheets issued in 1915, and 1943-1946. An offprint of this paper is held at http://www.iwm.org.uk/collections/item/publication/121012

Riddell, G. A., Baron Riddell. 'The Relations of the Press with the Army in the Field', *Royal United Service Institution Journal*, 66 (1921), 385-397

Wadsworth, A. P. 'Newspaper Circulation 1800-1954', *Transactions of the Manchester Statistical Society*, 4 (1955)

Contemporary Material

Cowley, J. 'Newspaper Circulation and the War', in *Sell's World's Press: The Handbook of the Fourth Estate* (London: Sells, 1915)

'The Duty of a Newspaper', *Spectator*, 113 (1915), 649

Hughes, S. L. *Press, Platform and Parliament* (London: Nisbet, 1918)

Northcliffe, A. H., Viscount. *At the War: (Letters, Telegrams, Cablegrams, and Other Writings About the War, and Kindred Matters)*, new and enlarged edn (London: Hodder & Stoughton, 1917)
Published for the Joint War Committee of the British Red Cross Society, and the order of St. John of Jerusalem in England.

'The Press and the Public', *Economist*, 81 (1915), 926-7

Raleigh, Sir W. *The War and the Press*. A Paper Read Mar. 14, 1918 to the Essay Society, Eton College (Oxford: Clarendon Press, 1918)

Simonis, H. *The Street of Ink: An Intimate History of Journalism* (London: Cassell, 1917)

Walker, J. *Newspapers and War and Other Essays in Wartime* (Bradford: Reformers' Bookshop, 1917)

2.8 Church and Religion

Most churchmen accepted the justice of the arguments made for Britain going to war. This was to be expected in the case of the Church of England because it was the national established church with a close association with the state. It was perhaps surprising, however, that the majority of the Free Churches, with their radical past and no links to the state to inhibit them, and most Catholics, in spite of the Pope's opposition to the war, also acquiesced in Britain's involvement in the war. All churches, however, had some pacifists among their ranks[16].

On the outbreak of war there soon developed a religious atmosphere which became imbued with the idea that the British people were fighting in a just cause with God alongside to support them. Many ministers and priests embraced this idea of a holy war, preaching in support of it, assisting in the recruiting campaign, and generally encouraging patriotism in their congregations. It is for this general willingness to support the war effort that in the aftermath of the war the churches were criticised for their un-Christian stance during the war years. Such criticism, however, was not entirely justified. Some members of the clergy were prepared to expose themselves to public hostility and unpopularity by, for example, involving themselves in the peace movement, speaking out

---

[16] Comparatively, the ratio of pacifists to total numbers was greater in the Free Churches.

against those who wanted Zeppelin bombing attacks to be revenged with blood-thirsty reprisals, or campaigning for the rights of conscientious objectors. There were also a substantial number of ministers and priests who joined up as chaplains and, although their work has sometimes been viewed unsympathetically, it cannot be denied that for some soldiers they fulfilled a need for spiritual care and comfort, particularly for the wounded and dying, often at the risk of their own lives.

British soldiers on the Western Front, who were predominantly Christian and most likely to have been brought up on the Bible and 'The Pilgrim's Progress', would not have found it difficult to respond to notions of the struggle between good and evil, and to phrases like the 'great Sacrifice', and the 'Christian Soldier', as is evident in a great deal of the literature and letters they wrote. The influence of religion at the front was also evident in the story of the crucified soldier, and the apparition of angels (the Angels of Mons). Some soldiers may have derived considerable solace from this influence but others came to terms with their suffering in the trenches by adopting a fatalistic and stoic approach to it.

Spiritualism began to have an increased influence on the lives of some people as a result of the effects of the war. With the huge losses of life experienced by bereaving households and by soldiers in the front line spiritualism became a powerful means for fulfilling the need of people who wanted in some way to communicate with the dead as a way of achieving solace for the loss of relatives and friends. Spiritualism spread rapidly on the civilian front as the death toll mounted and more and more people were confronted with the trauma of bereavement. Sir Arthur Conan Doyle, who lost both a son and a brother in the war, was one prominent figure seeking such spiritualist solace; another was the physicist Sir Oliver Lodge, who had also lost a son. Some British soldiers also turned to spiritualist phenomena as a means of coming to terms with the trauma of losing so many of their comrades in battle.

Bibliographies

Field, C. D. *British Religion and the First World War: A Select Bibliography of Modern Literature* (2017)
https://clivedfield.files.wordpress.com/2017/02/first-world-war-religion-bibliography-edn-1.pdf

Biographies

Lockhart, J. G. *Cosmo Gordon Lang* (London: Hodder & Stoughton, 1949)

Marchant, Sir J. *Dr. John Clifford, C. H: Life, Letters and Reminiscences* (London: Cassell, 1924)
Clifford was an influential Baptist leader (former President of the National Free Church Council) Although an opponent of the South African War, he played an important part in securing Free Church support for the First World War in 1914.

Wilkinson, A. 'Lang, (William) Cosmo Gordon, Baron Lang of Lambeth (1864–1945)', *Oxford Dictionary of National Biography*, Oxford University Press, 2004; online edn, Jan 2011
[http://www.oxforddnb.com/view/article/34398, accessed   22 Feb 2014]
Although Lang had come to accept Britain's participation in the war after considerable misgivings about whether the church should support it, his uneasiness about the role of the church led him to play "a leading part in the national mission of repentance and hope mounted by the church in 1916 to dispel misconceptions and to call for social and personal penitence" [quotation extracted from above article].

Books

Bainton, R. H. *Christian Attitudes to War and Peace: A Historical Survey and Critical Re-Evaluation* (Nashville, Abingdon Press, 1960; repr. 1996)

Bergen, D. L., ed. *The Sword of the Lord: Military Chaplains from the First to the Twenty-First Century* (Notre Dame, Ind.: University of Notre Dame Press, 2004)

Best, K. A *Chaplain at Gallipoli, the Great War Diaries of Kenneth Best*, edited by G. Roynon, War Diaries (London: Simon & Schuster in association with the Imperial War Museum, 2011)

Brandon, R. *The Spiritualists: The Passion for the Occult in the Nineteenth and Twentieth Centuries* (London: Weidenfeld & Nicholson, 1983)

The Civilian Scene

Doyle, Sir A. C. *The History of Spiritualism*, 2 vols (London: Cassell, 1926)
Vol.2 contains a chapter with the title 'Spiritualism and the War'. Vol.1 was reprinted, London: Spiritual Truth, 2001: vol. 2 was reprinted, Oxshott, Surrey: Spiritual Truth, 2002.

Hoover, A. I. *God, Germany, and Britain in the Great War: A Study in Clerical Nationalism* (New York: Praeger, 1989)
Many ministers and priests fostered the idea that the war was a holy war. Although these sentiments were condemned by some in the church, others had no difficulty approving them.

Jones, K. J. *Conan Doyle and the Spirits: The Spiritualist Career of Sir Arthur Conan* Doyle (Wellinborough: Aquarium, 1989)

Lloyd, R. B. *The Church of England, 1900-65* (London: SCM Press, 1966)

Madigan, E. *Faith under Fire: Anglican Army Chaplains and the Great War* (Basingstoke: Palgrave Macmillan 2011)

Marrin, A. *The Last Crusade: The Church of England in the First World War* (Durham, North Carolina: Duke University Press, 1974)

Mews, S. 'Neo-Orthodoxy, Liberalism and War: Karl Barth, P. T. Forsyth and John Oman, 1914-18', in *Renaissance and Renewal in Christian History*, Papers Read at the Fifteenth Summer Meeting and the Sixteenth Winter Meeting of the Ecclesiastical History Society, edited by Derek Baker (Oxford: Blackwell, 1977)

Mews, S. P. 'The Effect of the First World War on English Religious Life and Thought (unpublished masters thesis, Leeds University, 1967)

— 'Religion and Society in the First World War' (unpublished doctoral thesis, Cambridge University, 1975)

Moynihan, M., ed. *God on Our Side: The British Padres in World War One* (London: Secker & Warburg, 1983)

Schweitzer, R. *The Cross and the Trenches: Religious Faith and Doubt among British and American Great War Soldiers* (Westport, CN: Praeger, 2003)

Snape, M. *God and the British Soldier: Religion and the British Army in the First and Second World Wars* (London: Routledge, 2005)

Tucker, I. R. 'The English Quakers in World War 1 (unpublished doctoral thesis, University of North Carolina, 1972)

Wiel. J. A. de. *The Catholic Church in Ireland, 1914-1918. War and Politics* (Dublin: Irish Academic Press, 2003)

Wilkinson. A. *The Church of England and the First World War*, 2nd edn (London: SCM Press, 1978)

— *Dissent or Conform: War, Peace, and the English Churches, 1900-1945* (London: SCM Press, 1986)

Wolffe, J. *God and Greater Britain: Religion and National Life in Britain and Ireland, 1850-1950* (London: Routledge, 1994)

Yoder, J. H. *Christian Attitudes to War, Peace, and Revolution: A Companion to Bainton* (Elkhart, Ind.: [Mennonite Biblical Seminaries], 1983)
Companion to: *Christian Attitudes to War and Peace: A Historical Survey and Critical Re-Evaluation*, by Roland Herbert Bainton (see record above)

— *Christian Attitudes to War, Peace, and Revolution*, [a collection of Yoder's lectures and writings] edited by Theodore J. Koontz, and Andy Alexis-Baker (Grand Rapids, Mich.: Brazos Press, 2009)

Articles

Callan, P. 'Ambivalence towards the Saxon Shilling: The Attitudes of the Catholic Church in Ireland towards Enlistment during the First World War', *Archivum Hibernicum*, 41 (1986), 99-111

Clements, K. W. 'Baptists and the Outbreak of the First World War', *Baptist Quarterly*, 26 (1975), 74-92

Field, C. 'Keeping the Spiritual Home Fires Burning: Religious Belonging in Britain during the First World War', *War And Society* (Duntroon Australia),33, 2014), 244-268

Mews, S. 'Spiritual Mobilization in the First World War', *Theology*, 74 (1971), 258-264

Morgan, S. 'A "Feminist Conspiracy": Maude Royden, Women's Ministry and the British Press, 1916-1921', *Womens History Review*, 22 (2013), 777-800
In arguing that Royden's rise to fame has a bearing on the connections between feminism, suffrage and women's ordination this article examines the way in which the latter controversial issues were handled by individual churchmen through the religious and popular press.

Robinson, A. 'Eton's Great War Scandal', *History To--Day*, 43 (1993), 16-20
"Andrew Robinson looks at the 1915 uproar about a speech on 'Christian Charity' towards Germany which cost the headmaster of Britain's most famous public school his job." Sub-title.

Schweitzer, R. 'The Cross and Trenches: Religious Faith and Doubt among Some British Soldiers on the Western Front', *War and Society*, 16 (1998), 33-58

Contemporary Material

Begbie, H. *On the Side of the Angels: An Answer to 'The Bowmen'* (London: Hodder & Stoughton, 1915)

Bevan, E. *Brothers All: The War and the Race Question* (London: Oxford University Press, 1914)
The imperial war effort a is seen as symbolizing Christian unity.

Burn, P. *On Forgiving our Enemies*, SPCK Wartime Tracts, 15 (London: SPCK, 1915)

Carrington, H. *Psychical Phenomena and the War* (London: Laurie, 1918)

A Catholic. *Is Germany Anti-Catholic ?* (London: Burns & Oates, 1915?)

Clifford, J. *The War and the Churches* (London: Clarke, 1914)
For John Clifford it was a question of Kaiser or Christ. In one of his sermons he declared that the war was one 'of principles, central and fundamental to man's existence, development and progress and well-being in all the coming ages'. The struggle was 'for the right of the human soul to freedom, independence and self-control against an arrogant, autocratic, swaggering and cruel military caste'.

Cranage, D. H. S., ed. *The War and Unity*, being lectures delivered at the Local Lectures Summer Meeting of the University of Cambridge, 1918 (Cambridge: Cambridge University Press, 1919)

Doyle, Sir A. C. *The New Revelation* (London: Hodder & Stoughton, 1918)

Goddard, G. 'Orthodoxy and the War, *Occult Review*, 27 (1918), 84

Graham, J. W. 'War: A Quaker Apologises', *Hibbert Journal*, 14 (1915), 123-134

Halifax, C. L. W., Viscount. *'Raymond': Some Criticisms* (London: A. R. Mowbray, 1917)

Henson, H. 'The Paradox of Christianity', *Challenge*, (1915)

Jones, H. 'The War and Morality', in *Ethical and Religious Problems of the War*, edited by J. Estlin Carpenter (London: Lindsey, 1916)

Lodge, O. J. *Raymond, or, Life and Death: With Examples of the Evidence for Survival of Memory and Affection after Death* (London: Methuen, 1916)

Mathews, B, ed. *Christ and the World War: Sermons Preached in War-Time* (London: J. Clarke & Co., 1917)

Machen, A. *The Bowmen and other Legends of the War* (London: Simpkin, 1915)

Mercier, C. A. *Spiritualism and Sir Oliver Lodge* (London: Mental Culture Enterprise, 1917)

Pym, T. W. and G. Gordon. *Papers from Picardy by two Chaplains* (London: Constable, 1917)

Selbie, W. B. *The War and Theology*, Oxford Pamphlets, 53 (London: Oxford University Press, 1915)

'Society of Friends and this War', *Spectator*, 114 (1915), 844-5

Ward, J. S. M. *Gone West: Three Narratives of After-Death Experiences*, communicated through the mediumship of J. S. M. Ward (London: Rider, 1918)

Wedgewood, J. I. *Spiritualism and the Great War* (London: Theosophical Publishing House, 1919)

2.9 Ireland

On the eve of war Irish unrest over the question of the Home Rule bill had reached crisis proportions. Nationalists, especially the Irish Volunteers (a newly formed body in the south of Ireland dedicated to the achievement of full Home Rule) and an emerging revived Irish Republican Brotherhood (a small group of republican extremists opposed to any form of British rule) wanted the bill to apply to the whole of Ireland; on the other hand an Ulster Volunteer Force was threatening armed revolt unless Ulster counties in the north were excluded from it.

This crisis was temporarily defused as a result of the war. A few weeks after its outbreak a bill encompassing Home Rule for all Ireland was passed but on the agreed understanding that it should not be implemented for twelve months or until the war ended, and that the question of the bill being amended to exclude Ulster from the Home Rule arrangements should be shelved until then. Although, therefore, the conflict between nationalists and unionists over the position of Ulster remained unsettled both sides felt that they had achieved some progress towards achieving their objectives. It was in these circumstances that Carson, the unionist leader, and John Redmond, the leader of constitutional nationalism, saw political advantages to be gained from assisting the war effort and felt willing, therefore, to call on those they represented to enlist. There was an enthusiastic response. Large numbers of nationalist Irishmen and Irishmen from Ulster volunteered to join the British army.

Not all nationalists responded to the call to arms. Although tens of thousands of Redmond's Irish Volunteers joined up a small minority[17] did not do so because they were strongly opposed to becoming involved in a British war, and solely interested in the promotion of the cause of Irish nationalism (an attitude, shared by other dissentient nationalist groups[18]). Revolutionary action, however, was only favoured by a minority of extremists[19]. Yet by the end of the war the Home Rule truce was in total disarray. The combination of the British Government's mishandling of the Easter Rising, its failure to implement Home Rule, and its abortive attempt to introduce conscription in Ireland had the effect of seriously weakening the constitutional nationalist party and enabling Sinn Féin, which steadily gained ground during the war, to take over from it as the dominant political force in the south of Ireland.

---

[17] Some 13,000 out of 180,000 seceded from the main body of Irish Volunteers.

[18] Dissentient nationalist groups, other than the dissident Irish Volunteers, included the clandestine Irish Republican Brotherhood, the Irish Citizen Army, the *Fianna* (a youth organization), and *Cumann na Mban* (a women's organization).

[19] These minority extremists consisted of a group of conspirators (including Patrick Pearse, etc) who were intent on the Irish Republican Brotherhood and those with like sympathies taking revolutionary action against the British government before the war was over. An eccentric supporter of this group was Sir Roger Casement who had hoped to bolster the Irish cause with the backing of German arms.

The attempt to introduce conscription in Ireland aroused such deep resentment, particularly among nationalists, that the Government completely abandoned the idea of extending conscription to Ireland This reaction in Ireland to conscription should not, however, be allowed to obscure the fact that Irishmen in their tens of thousands from North and South volunteered for service in the British Army. In the first six months of the war 50,000 men joined up, and although the number of recruits dwindled from 1916 (as happened similarly on the British mainland) they picked up again in 1918 (as was also the case on the British mainland). Irishmen joined up at a rate which was broadly comparable to that of Great Britain as a whole. The number of recruits to the British Army which Ireland contributed during the war amounted to a total of 200,000, of whom about sixty percent were Catholic.

Autobiographies, Biographies

Arthur, Sir G. *General Sir John Maxwell* (London: Murray, 1932)
Maxwell was commander-in-chief of British troops in Ireland in 1916.

Boyne, S. *Emmet Dalton: Somme Soldier, Irish General, Film Pioneer* (Sallins, Co. Kildare: Merrion Press, 2015)
From 1923 he worked in Ireland and the U.S. in film production. In 1958 he founded Irish Ardmore Studios in Bray. His company helped produce films such as *The Blue Max*, *The Spy Who Came in from the Cold* and *The Lion in Winter*, all of which were filmed in Ireland.

Brennan, R. *Allegiance* (Dublin: Brown & Nolan, 1950)
An account of the author's connection with the struggle for Irish independence, including his activities during the First World War.

Coogan, T. P *Michael Collins: A Biography* (London: Hutchinson, 1990; repr. New York: Palgrave, 2002)
Irish revolutionary leader. Prominent as organiser in the Volunteer and Sinn Féin movement. Took part in the Easter rebellion of 1916.

Colvin, I.. *The Life of Lord Carson*, 3 vols (London: Gollancz, 1932-1936)
Vol 1 is by E. Marjoribanks. On the outbreak of war Carson was the accepted leader of the Protestant Ulster camp (encompassing the counties of Ulster) which was opposed to Home Rule and which was prepared to back this militantly on the eve of the war via the Ulster Volunteer Force previously created by Carson and Sir James Craig.

Curtayne, A. *Francis Ledwige: A Life of the Poet* (London: Martin Brian & O'Keefe Ltd., 1972; repr. Dublin, New Island Books, 1998)
Although a strong nationalist Ledwige joined, after much heart-searching, the British Army (Royal Inniskilling Fusiliers) in 1914 and died on the Western front in 1917.

Denman, T. *A Lonely Grave: The Life and Death of William Redmond* (Dublin: Irish Academic Press, 1995)
William Hoey Kearney Redmond, an Irish nationalist politician in the House of Commons like his brother John Redmond, was one of the first to volunteer for the British Army as a member of the Irish Volunteers. He was killed in Flanders in 1917.

Edwards, R. D. *James Connolly* (Dublin: Gill & Macmillan, 1981; repr. 1998)
Connolly, a revolutionary socialist whose activities eventually became linked to the campaign for an Ireland free from British rule, played a leading part in the Easter Uprising of 1916 for which he was executed.

— *Patrick Pearse: The Triumph of Failure* (London: Gollancz, 1977; repr. Swords: Poolbag, 1990)
Pearse was an Irish writer, educationalist, and nationalist who became an iconic figure in Irish republican history. In 1915 he joined the Irish Republican Brotherhood and in the 1916 Easter Rising was involved as Commander-in-Chief of the insurgents and President of the provisional government, roles for which he was subsequently executed.

Gwynn, S. *John Redmond's Last Years* (London : Arnold, 1919)
John Redmond, leader of the Home Rule Party at Westminster since 1900, had the life-long ambition to achieve Irish self-government and a reconciliation between unionists and nationalists and between Ireland and England by statesmanlike methods.

Mitchell, A. *Casement* (London: Haus, 2003)

The Civilian Scene

After a consular career Casement became an Irish revolutionary and in 1913 was on the committee of the Irish National Volunteers. During the war he was hanged by the British for his part in working with Germany and Irish nationalists in the planning of the Easter Rising of 1916.

Morgan, A. *James Connolly: A Political Biography* (Manchester: Manchester University Press, 1988)

Ó Broin, L. *Dublin Castle and the 1916 Rising: The Story of Sir Matthew Nathan*, rev. edn (London: Sidgwick & Jackson, 1970)
Nathan was under-secretary for Ireland, 1914-1916.

— *W. E. Wylie and the Irish Revolution*, 1916-1921 (Dublin: Gill & Macmillan, 1989)
William Wylie was a KC who was selected as prosecutor at the Courts Martial following the Easter Rising of 1916.

O'Connor, U. *Oliver St John Gogarty: A Poet and His Times* (London: Cape, 1964; repr. Dublin: O'Brien Press, 2000)
Gogarty was a surgeon who moved into literary and political circles and published novels, poems, and volumes of reminiscences.

Sawyer, R. *Casement: The Flawed Hero* (London: Routledge, 1984)

Books

Bartlett, T. and K. Jeffery, eds. *A Military History of Ireland* (Cambridge: Cambridge University Press, 1996)

Bew, P. *Ideology and the Irish Question: Ulster Unionism and Irish Nationalism*, 1912-1916 (Oxford: Clarendon Press, 1994; repr 1998)

Bowman, T. *Irish Regiments in the Great War: Discipline and Morale* (Manchester: Manchester University Press, 2003)

Boyce, D. G. *The Sure Confusing Drum: Ireland and the First World War*. Inaugural lecture delivered at the College on 8 February 1993 (Swansea: University College of Swansea, 1993)

Casement, Sir R. D. *The Crime Against Europe*, introduced by B. Clifford, with *Casement as Traitor-Patriot*, by W. J. Maloney (Belfast: Athol Books, 2002)
Casement's pamphlet was originally published in 1915 by the Celtic Press, Philadelphia, as *The Crime Against Europe: A Possible Outcome of the War of 1914*.

Codd, P. 'Recruiting and Responses to the War in Wexford', in *Ireland and the First World War*, edited by D. Fitzpatrick (Dublin: Trinity History Workshop, 1986; repr. Mullingar: Lilliput Press and Trinity History Workshop, 1988)

Doerries, R. R. *Prelude to the Easter Rising: Sir Roger Casement in Imperial Germany* (London: Frank Cass, 2000)

Dooley, T. P. *Irishmen or English Soldiers?: The Times and World of a Southern Catholic Irish Man (1876-1916) Enlisting in the British Army During the First World War* (Liverpool: Liverpool University Press, 1995)

Downes, M. 'The Civilian Voluntary Aid Effort', in *Ireland and the First World War*, edited by D. Fitzptrick (Dublin: Trinity History Workshop, 1986, repr. Mullingar: Lilliput Press and Trinity History Workshop, 1988)

Dungan, M. *Irish Voices from the Great War* (Dublin: Irish Academic Press, 1995)
Through the diaries, letters, literary works and oral accounts of soldiers this work brings together some of the personal experiences of the Irishmen - Unionist and Nationalist – who fought in the war, covering a selection of the most important battles and campaigns in which the Irish Divisions and Regiments were engaged

— *They Shall Not Grow Old: Irish Soldiers and the Great War* (Dublin: Four Courts Press, 1997)

Fitzpatrick, D. *Harry Boland's Irish Revolution* (Cork: Cork University Press, 1999; repr. 2003)

— 'Militarism in Ireland, 1900-1922', in *A Military History of Ireland*, ed. by T. Bartlett and K. Jeffery (Cambridge: Cambridge University Press, 1996)

— 'The Overflow of the Deluge: Anglo-Irish Relationships, 1914-1922', in *Irish and Irish-Australia: Studies in Cultural and Political History*, ed. by O. MacDonagh and F. W. Mandle (London: Croom Helm, 1986)

— *Politics and Irish Life, 1913-1921: Provincial Experience of War and Revolution* (Dublin: Gill & Macmillan, 1977; repr. Cork: Cork University Press, 1998)

Fitzpatrick, D., ed. *Ireland and the First World War* (Dublin: Trinity History Workshop, 1986, repr. Mullingar: Lilliput Press and Trinity History Workshop, 1988)

— *Revolution?: Ireland 1917-1923* (Dublin: Trinity History Workshop, 1990)

Foster, R. F. *Vivid Faces: The Revolutionary Generation in Ireland, 1890-1923* (London: Allen Lane, 2014)

Foster, R. H. 'Irish Methodism and War', in *Irish Methodism in the Twentieth Century*, ed. by A. McCrea (Belfast: Irsish Methodist Publishing Co., 1931)

Gibbon, M. *Inglorious Soldier* (London: Hutchinson, 1968)

Grayson, R. S. *Belfast Boys: How Unionists and Nationalists Fought and Died Together in the First World War* (London: Continuum, 2010)

Grayson, R. S. and F. McGarry, eds. *Remembering 1916: The Easter Rising, the Somme and the Politics of Ireland* (Cambridge: Cambridge University Press 2016)

Gregory, A. and S. Pašeta. *Ireland and the Great War: 'A War to Unite Us All'?* (Manchester: Manchester University Press, 2002)

Griffith, K. and T. E. O'Grady. *Curious Journey: An Oral History of Ireland's Unfinished Revolution* (London: Hutchinson, 1982; repr. Dublin: Mercier Press, 1998)
This work views recent Irish history through the eyes of avowed republicans by means of the authors interviewing nine Irish veterans who had lived through the dramatic period in which a Gaelic reawakening, the Easter Rising, the guerrilla warfare against the British (followed by the civil war) had all taken place.

Harris, H. *The Irish Regiments in the First World War* (Cork: Mercier Press, 1968)

— 'The other half million', in *1916: The Easter Rising*, edited by O. D. Edwards and F. Pyle (London: MacGibbon & Kee, 1968)

Hart, P. *The IRA at War, 1916-1923* (Oxford: Oxford University Press, 2003)

Hennessey, D. *Dividing Ireland: World War 1 and Partition* (London: Routledge, 1998)

Howie, D. and J. Howie. 'Irish Recruiting and the Home Rule Crisis of August-September 1914', in *Strategy and Intelligence: British Policy During the First World War*, ed. M. Dockrill and D. French (London: Hambledon, 1986)

Jeffery, K. *Ireland and the Great War* (Cambridge: Cambridge University Press, 2000)
Based on the Lees Knowles lectures of 1998, given at Trinity College, Cambridge.

— 'The Great War in Modern Irish Memory', in *Men, Women and War*, Papers Read Before The XXth Irish Conference of Historians, Held at Magee College, University of Ulster, 6-8 June 1991, ed. by T. G. Fraser and K. Jeffery (Dublin: Lilliput Press, 1993)

Johnson, N. C. *Ireland, the Great War, and the Geography of Remembrance* (Cambridge: Cambridge University Press, 2003)

Johnstone, T. *Orange, Green, and Khaki: The Story of the Irish Regiments in the Great War, 1914-1918* (Dublin: Gill and Macmillan, 1992)

Kipling, R. *The Irish Guards in the Great War*. Edited and compiled from their diaries and papers by Rudyard Kipling, 2 vols, new edn (Staplehurst: Spellmount, 1997)
Originally published London: Macmillan, 1923.

Leonard, J. 'The Catholic Chaplaincy', in *Ireland and the First World War*, edited by D. Fitzpatrick (Dublin: Trinity History Workshop, 1986; repr. Mullingar: Lilliput Press and Trinity History Workshop, 1988)

— 'The Reaction of Irish Officers in the British Army to the Easter Rising of 1916', in *Facing Armageddon: The First World War Experienced*, edited by H. Cecil and P. H. Liddle (London: Leo Cooper, 1996)

Lucey, D. J. 'Cork Public Opinion and the First World War' (unpublished master's thesis, University College, Cork, 1972)

Lyons, J. B. *The Enigma of Tom Kettle: Irish Patriot, Essayist, Poet, British Soldier, 1880-1916* (Dublin: Glendale Press, 1983)

Maloney, W. J. *The Forged Casement Diaries* (Dublin: Talbot Press, 1936)

Martin, F. X., ed. *The Easter Rising, 1916 and University College Dublin*, general editor, F. X. Martin (Dublin: Browne & Nolan, 1966)
Lectures delivered in February and March 1966 by five participants in the rising.

— *The Irish Volunteers, 1913-1915*; recollections and documents edited by F. X. Martin (Dublin: Duffy, 1963)

— *Leaders and Men of the Easter Rising: Dublin 1916* (London: Methuen, 1967)

McGarry, F. *The Rising: Ireland, Easter 1916* (Oxford: Oxford University Press 2011)

Mcgaughey, J. G. V. *Ulster's Men: Protestant Unionist Masculinities and Militarization in the North of Ireland, 1912-1923* (Montreal; Ithaca: McGill-Queen's University Press, 2012)

McMahon, P. *British Spies and Irish Rebels: British Intelligence and Ireland, 1916-1945* (Woodbridge: Boydell Press, 2008)

Nic Dhiarmada, B. *The 1916 Irish Rebellion* (Cork: Cork University Press, 2016)
This is the companion book to a three-part documentary series broadcast worldwide in 2016. Narrated by Liam Neeson, the documentary, entitled *1916 The Irish Rebellion*, and its related seventy-minute version are initiatives of the Keough-Naughton Institute for Irish Studies at the University of Notre Dame. It was broadcast on BBC 4 on 28 March 2016.

Norway, M. L., and A. H. Norway. *The Sinn Fein Rebellion As They Saw It*, by Mary Louisa and Arthur Hamilton Norway, edited and with an introduction by Keith Jeffery (Dublin: Irish Academic Press, 1999)
Includes *The Sinn Fein Rebellion As I Saw It*, by Mrs. Hamilton Norway [i.e. Mary Louisa Hamilton] (London: Smith, Elder, 1916) and Arthur Hamilton Norway's *Irish Experiences In War*. The text of the latter memoir is taken from a photocopy in the papers of Dr. Leon Ó Broin in the National Library of Ireland (MS 24,894).

Nowlan, B., ed. *The Making of 1916: Studies in the History of the Rising* (Dublin: Stationery Office, 1969)
Essays by various authors issued in commemoration in 1966 of the fiftieth anniversary of the Rising of Easter Week 1916.

O'Halpin, E. *The Decline of the Union: British Government in Ireland, 1892-1920* (Dublin: Gill & Macmillan, 1987)

Orr, P. *The Road to the Somme: Men of the Ulster Division Tell Their Story* (Belfast: Blackstaff Press, 1987)

Paseta, S. *Irish Nationalist Women 1900-1918* (Cambridge: Cambridge University Press, 2013)

Pearse, P. H. *Political Writings and Speeches* (Dublin: Talbot Press, 1952; repr. 1962)

Pennell, C. 'Presenting the War in Ireland, 1914-1918', in *World War I and Propaganda*, edited by T. R. E.

Paddock (Leiden; Boston: Brill, 2014)

Phillips, W. A. *The Revolution in Ireland, 1906-1923*, 2nd edn (London : Longmans, 1926)

Ryan, D. *The Rising: The Complete Story of Easter Week*, 4th edn (Dublin: Golden Eagle Books, 1966)

Stephens, J. *The Insurrection in Dublin* (Dublin: Maunsel, 1916; repr. Gerrards Cross: Colin Smyth, 1992)

Stokes, R. *Death in the Irish Sea: The Sinking of RMS Leinster* (Cork: Collins, 1998)

Sweeney, J. A. 'In the GPO: The Fighting Men', in *The Easter Rising, 1916 and University College Dublin*, general editor, F. X. Martin (Dublin: Browne & Nolan, 1966)

Taillon, R. *When History Was Made ... The Women of 1916*, 2nd edn (Belfast: Beyond the Pale Publications, 1999)

Townshend, C. *Easter 1916: The Irish Rebellion* (London: Allen Lane, 2005; repr. London: Penguin, 2006)

— *Political Violence in Ireland: Government and Resistance Since 1848* (Oxford: Clarendon, 1983; repr. 2001)

Urquhart, D. '"The Female of the Species Is More Deadlier Than the Male"?: The Ulster Women's Unionist Council, 1911-1940', in *Coming Into Light: The Work, Politics and Religion of Women in Ulster, 1840-1940*, edited by J. Holmes and D. Urquhart (Belfast: Institute of Irish Studies, Queen's University of Belfast, 1994)

Ward, M. *Unmanageable Revolutionaries: Women and Irish Nationalism*, new edn (London: Pluto Press, 1995)

Wheatley, M. *Nationalism and the Irish Party: Provincial Ireland, 1910-1916* (Oxford: Oxford University Press, 2005)

Wiel, J van de. *The Catholic Church in Ireland, 1914-1918: War and Politics* (Dublin: Irish Academic Press, 2003)

Articles

Bourke, J. 'Irish Tommies: The Construction of a Martial Manhood, 1914-1918', *Bullan*, 3/2 (1998), 13-30

Bowman, T. 'Composing Divisions: The recruitment of Ulster and National Volunteers into the British Army in 1914', *Causeway*, 2/1 (1995), 24-29

— 'The Ulster Volunteer Force and the Formation of the 36th (Ulster) Division', *Irish Historical Studies*, 32 (2001), 498-518

Boyce, D. G. 'British Opinion, Ireland and the War, 1916-1918', *Historical Journal*, 17 (1974), 575-594

— 'Ireland and the First World War', *History Ireland*, 2/3 (1994), 48-53

Bull, P. 'Sacrifice, Liberalism and the Great War: The Case of Ireland', *War And Society* (Duntroon Australia), 23 (2005), 13-22

Callan, P. 'Ambivalence towards the Saxon Shilling: The Attitudes of the Catholic Church in Ireland towards Enlistment during the First World War', *Archivum Hibernicum*, 41 (1986), 99-111

Callan, P. 'British Recruitment in Ireland, 1914-1918', *Revue Internationale d'Histoire Militaire*, 63 (1985), 41-50

— 'Recruiting for the British Army in Ireland during the First World War', *Irish Sword*, 17 (1987), 42-56

Denman, T. 'The Catholic Irish Soldier in the First World War: The "Racial environment"', *Irish Historical Studies*, 27 (1991), 352-65

Dooley, T. A. M. 'County Monaghan, 1914-1918: Recruitment, the Rise of Sinn Féin and the Partition Crisis', *Clogher Record*, 16 (1998), 144-158

Drisceoil, D. O. 'Keeping Disloyalty within Bounds? British Media Control in Ireland, 1914-19', *Irish Historical Studies*, 149 (2012), 52-69

Fitzpatrick, D. 'The Logic of Collective Sacrifice: Ireland and the British Army, 1914-1918', *Historical Journal*, 38 (1995), 1017-30

Gibney, J. 'Ireland: Easter Rising or Great War?', *History Today*, 65, Issue 4 (2015), 7

Graham, C. C. and R. van Dopperen. 'Roger Casement on Screen: The Background Story on an Historical Film Opportunity, 1915–1916', *Historical Journal of Film, Radio and Television*, 36 (2016), 493-508

Grigg, J. 'Nobility and the Unselfish Commitment', *Encounter*, March (1990), 21-7

Martin, F. X. '1916 - Myth, Fact and Mystery', *Studia Hibernica*, 7 (1967), 7-124

McConnel, J. 'Recruiting Sergeants for John Bull? Irish Nationalist MPs and Enlistment during the Early Months of the Great War', *War In History*, 14 (2007), 408-428

McEwen, J. M. 'The Liberal Party and the Irish Question during the First World War', *Journal of British Studies*, 12 (1972), 109-31

Perry, N. 'Maintaining Regimental Identity in the Great War: The Case of the Irish Infantry Regiments', *Stand To!: The Journal of the Western Front Association*, 52 (1998)

— 'Nationality in the Irish Infantry Regiments in the First World War, *War and Society*, (1994), 65-95

Rose, S. O. 'The Politics of Service and Sacrifice in WWI Ireland and India', *Twentieth Century British History*, 25 (2014), 368-390

Townshend, C. The Suppression of the Easter Rising', *Bullan*, 1/1 (1994), 27-47

Ward, A. J. 'Lloyd George and the 1918 Conscription Crisis', *Historical Journal*, 17 (1974), 107-29

Contemporary Material

Connolly, J. *A Socialist and War, 1914-1916*, [reprints of articles by James Connolly published during the Great War] edited by P. J. Musgrove (London: Lawrence & Wishart, 1941)
Two of the articles appeared in *Forward*, the remaining articles were originally published in two papers, now no longer in existence, *The Irish Worker*, edited by James Larkin, and the *Workers' Republic*, edited by James Connolly.

Ervine, St. John. *Changing Winds* (Dublin: Maunsel, 1917)
This semi-autobiographical novel revolves around the experiences of Henry Quinn during the Great War and much of it is set in Dublin, where the story includes the Easter Rebellion of 1916.

—'The Story of the Irish Rebellion', *Century Magazine*, (1917), 22-39

Kerr, S. P. *What The Irish Regiments Have Done*, with a diary of a visit to the front by John E. Redmond, M.P. (London: T. Fisher Unwin, 1916)

Lavery, F., comp. *Irish Heroes in War*, foreword by John E. Redmond, M.P; *The Irish in Great Britain*, by T. P. O'Connor M.P.; *The Tyneside Irish Brigade*, by Joseph Keating (London: Everett, 1917)

Law, H. A. *Why is Ireland at War?* (London: Maunsel, 1915)
A 2nd edition was published in Dublin by Maunsel in 1916.

Macdonagh, M. *The Irish at the Front 1916*, with an introduction by John Redmond (London: Hodder & Stoughton, 1916)

— *The Irish on the Somme*; being the Second Series of "The Irish at the Front", by Michael MacDonagh, with an introduction by John Redmond (London: Hodder & Stoughton, 1917)

Norway, M. L. [Mrs. Hamilton Norway]. *The Sinn Fein Rebellion As I Saw It* (London: Smith, Elder, 1916)
See also above in the **Books** sub-section: Norway, M. L., and A. H. Norway. *The Sinn Fein Rebellion As They Saw It*, by Mary Louisa and Arthur Hamilton Norway, edited and with an introduction by Keith Jeffery (Dublin: Irish Academic Press, 1999)

Redmond, J. E. *Ireland and the War.* Extracts from speeches made in the House of Commons and in Ireland since the outbreak of the War, by J. E. Redmond, M.P., Chairman, Irish Parliamentary Party (Dublin: Sealy, Bryers & Walker, 1915)

— *The Voice of Ireland*: Being An Interview with John Redmond, M.P., and Some Messages From Representative Irishmen Regarding the Sinn Fein Rebellion (London: Nelson, 1916)

2.10 Women

At the start of the war many women joining in the national surge of patriotism could initially only see their war role in domestic and supportive terms by engaging in such activities as gathering up parcels for war refugees, rolling bandages for the Red Cross, knitting scarves and socks for soldiers, establishing charitable organisations to assist the families of soldiers or Belgian refugees (an activity embraced by a number of upper-class women), and generally helping to 'keep the home fires burning'.

There were also, however, women who, wanting to be involved in a more dynamic and satisfying role, soon grasped the opportunity to fill the gaps in a great range of occupations occasioned by the labour shortages resulting from the huge numbers of men joining the armed forces By the war's end, huge numbers of women had entered the workforce, many of them traditionally 'masculine' occupations such as engineering, munitions, public transport (buses and trains), business, and agriculture. A substantial number of women also enrolled as nurses and orderlies of the Voluntary Aid Detachment (V.A.D.) of the Red Cross or joined the First Aid Nursing Yeomanry (acting as ambulance drivers and mechanics near the frontline). Eventually women were also serving with the military forces in non-combatant roles (for example as cooks, waitresses, mechanics, drivers, clerks, telephonists, and shorthand typists). The war produced an increase in women's employment from 26% in 1914 to 36% by 1918. One million women worked in munitions industries, 40,000 served as nurses, 20,000 joined the Women's Land Army as agricultural workers, and 80,000 served in women's military auxiliary corps. The numbers of female clerical workers had been growing before the war but expanded significantly during the war because of the increase of paperwork in all areas of everyday life. The greatest numerical increase of women workers during the war was in the areas of banking, finance, and commerce, which took on an extra 429,000 women, and unlike other areas, such as industry and transport, most of these women kept their jobs after the war.

These dramatic contributions by women to the war effort (encouraged by the government's appeal in March 1915 for women to join a Register of Women for War Service) were not solely motivated by patriotism. Women who left domestic service to work in factories and workshops, for example, may well have been motivated by the attraction of better wages and conditions as by feelings of patriotism Many women, whether already working or not, and married women as well, found that the war opened up a whole new range of opportunities to get involved in jobs which had the potential to provide independence, companionship, excitement, or adventure. Even middle- and upper-class women grasped the opportunities available to them serving, for example, as doctors, nurses and orderlies in hospitals, as office workers, as policewomen in areas suffering from social dislocation because of the war, as workers in munitions factories (normally in a managerial or welfare role) and even, surprisingly in view of the physical nature of the work, as agricultural workers. The prospect of a different sort of life which the new job options opened up for all classes may well have been as powerful a reason as patriotism for women's willingness to embrace a wartime role.

During the war women received a great deal of praise and distinct attention in the press and wartime literature for their work as nurses, munitions workers, and military auxiliaries. The work of women in the munitions factories was particularly acclaimed in wartime propaganda (e.g. Hall Caine's government sponsored *Our Girls: Their Work for the War*, 1916) and idealized in romantic fiction (e.g. Bessi Marchant's *A Girl Munition Worker*, 1916), and the dedication and devotion of nurses was a constant theme in much wartime literature (e.g. Wilfred Meynell's novel, *Who Goes There?*, 1916). Nevertheless women in war work also encountered considerable prejudice. Male workers and trade unions were initially hostile to the escalation of the employment of women in factories. For some people the independence that good wages in factory work gave to young women was a cause for concern especially when it was felt that these wages were being spent on fine clothes, going to pubs and cinemas, and dining out in restaurants.. The latter behaviour was seen by some as inappropriate in a time of austerity and self-sacrifice, but it was also perhaps a reflection of middle class resentment of how upwardly mobile the working class had become. Eulogistic as the press and much war time literature were in their treatment of women involved in the war effort such women could still be subject to gossip and censure whenever their behaviour seemed unconventional. In comparison with other forms of women's war work, nursing was unique in meeting with almost universal approval.

No realm of women's war work met with greater resistance or aroused more controversy than military service. In spite of this a dedicated group of middle- and upper-class women began in the early years of the war to establish unofficial female auxiliary para-military units (initially confined to the propertied classes but eventually developed into units recruiting from a much broader section of the population). By 1916 the success of this para-military activity was beginning to command some official recognition and by 1917 had so convinced the authorities of the viability of an official military unit for women (which had the additional attraction of freeing more men for combat service) that in March of that year the Army created the Women's Army Auxiliary Corps (WAAC). The other armed services soon followed suit. In November 1917 the Navy created its own auxiliary, the Women's Royal Naval Service (WRNS) and in April 1918 the Royal Air Force did likewise with the creation of the Women's Royal Air Force (WRAF).

Many women joined in the extreme jingoistic mood of the nation in the early years of the war. Some of them displayed a total disregard for the dangers to which their sons (or other's sons) would be exposed by encouraging them to join up, by handing out white feathers to young men who had not joined up (or by shunning them) and by engaging vigorously in the recruitment campaigns. A considerable number of women novelists and poets wrote insensitively and jingoistically about the war. These responses to the war have occasionally contributed to an image of women passionately patriotic, even militaristic, but oblivious to the reality and horrors of war. This image is unfair to the considerable number of women whose attitudes to the war were quite different. While some leading suffragettes (e.g. Millicent Fawcett and Emmeline and Christabel Pankhurst[20]) and their organisations came out in support of the war, a number of prominent feminists like Olive Schreiner and Sylvia Pankhurst refused to support the war and condemned those suffragettes who, in their view, had become part of the machinery of war. Sylvia Pankhurst and other women of like mind also concerned themselves with the plight and conditions of women workers and the welfare of soldiers' dependents. Some women played a significant part, through their activities in a variety of groups, in the agitation for peace (see **Part 3, section 2.11.3** on **Pacifism and the Peace Movement**) and in the opposition to conscription (see section **Part 3, 2.11.2** on **Conscription and Conscience**). Not all women novelists and poets glossed over the horrors of war or wrote with the insensitivity characteristic of much of Jesse Pope's poetry. Account should also be taken of the large numbers of women who suffered bereavement as a result of the war. It can well be imagined that their feelings were akin to those expressed in a collection of women's poetry, gathered together under the heading of *Scars Upon My Heart*, which 'shows the agonies women went through to reconcile themselves with the death of those they loved, and how much they yearned to feel that their death had not been in vain'. As the war dragged on and the trauma of bereavement entered more and more households it is difficult to believe that women any longer retained the sort of patriotic enthusiasm of the early years of the war that led some of them to encourage, even pressurise, men to go off to fight.

Autobiographies, Biographies, Memoirs, Diaries, Letters

Appleton, E. *A Nurse at the Front: The Great War Diaries of Sister Edith Appleton*, edited by Ruth Cowen, War Diaries (London: Simon & Schuster in association with the Imperial War Museum, 2013)

Asquith, Lady C. *Diaries, 1915-1918*, with a foreword by L.P. Hartley (London: Hutchinson, 1968; repr. London: Century, 1987)
Lady Cynthia Asquith, daughter of the 11th Earl of Wemyss, was the wife of Herbert ('Beb') Asquith, the second son of Herbert Henry Asquith (Prime Minister from 1908-1916) by the latter's first wife Helen (died 1891). [**See also** note about

---

[20] Suffragettes like Millicent Fawcett (President of the NUWSS [National Union of Women's Suffrage Societies]), Emmeline Pankhurst (leader of the Women's Social and Political Union (WSPU) and Christabel Pankhurst, lent their wholehearted support to the war through their organisations, lobbying the government to utilise women's labour, publicly assisting the recruitment campaign, and embracing anti-Germanism as ways of promoting the rights of women.

the diaries under MacKenzie below].

Asquith, M., Countess of Oxford and Asquith. *The Autobiography of Margot Asquith*, edited by Mark Bonham-Carter (London: Eyre & Spottiswoode, 1962; repr. London: Weidenfeld & Nicolson, 1995)
Originally published in 2 vols, London: Thornton Butterworth, 1920-1922. Margot Asquith, the sixth daughter of Sir Charles Tennant, married Herbert Henry Asquith (Prime Minister from 1908-1916) as his second wife in 1894. A legend in her time as a social hostess and wit.

Asquith, M., Countess of Oxford and Asquith, ed. *Myself When Young: By Famous Women of To-Day* (London: Frederick Muller, 1918; repr. 1938)
Contents: The Countess of Oxford and Asquith; Margaret Campbell ("Marjorie Bowen"); Gabrielle Chanel; Elizabeth Sloan Chesser; Caroline Haslett; The Baroness von Hutten; Amy Johnson; Ethel Levey; The Marchioness of Londonderry; Mary, Countess of Minto; Sylvia Pankhurst; Edith Picton-Tubervill; A. Maude Royden; Irene Vanbrugh; Ellen Wilkinson.

Badeni, J *The Slender Tree: A Life of Alice Meynell* (Padstow: Tabb House, 1981)
Alice Meynell was a poet, essayist, and journalist.

Bagnold, E. *A Diary without Dates* (London: W. Heinemann, 1918)
In this work the author wrote of her hospital experiences in the Great War as a nurse (a job from which she was dismissed for writing critically of the hospital administration, resulting in her subsequently becoming a driver in France for the remainder of the war years). She wrote of her driving experiences in her novel *The Happy Foreigner* (q.v.)

Banks, O. *The Biographical Dictionary of British Feminists*, 2 vols (Brighton: Wheatsheaf, 1985-1990)
Vol 1: 1800-1930 (1985): Vol 2: A Supplement, 1900-1945 (1990)

Bartley, P. *Emmeline Pankhurst* (London: Routledge, 2002)
"Emmeline Pankhurst assisted by her daughter Christabel established the Women's Social and Political Union (WSPU) in 1903. On the outbreak of war she called for a temporary suspension of the WPSU's militant activities and asked her followers to support the war effort, arguing that there would be no point in fighting for the vote if Britain was conquered. In line with this argument WPSU's organ, *The Suffragette* was renamed *Britannia* with 'For King, For Country, For Freedom' as its motto. She supported conscription and campaigned for the employment of women in war work. In 1915 she and others involved in the WSPU, such as Annie Kenney and Flora Drummond, organised, at the request of Lloyd George, a Women's Right to Serve demonstration designed to help overcome trade union opposition to the employment of female labour. In 1916 and 1918 she toured the USA, her first tour to help raise money for Serbia and her second tour (which also included Canada) to support women's war work and campaign against Bolshevism (which she also advised Kerensky to deal firmly with when she met him while staying in Russia in 1917). In November 1917 the WSPU was renamed the Women's Party of which she became the treasurer. Her ambition that Christabel should become the first woman MP by standing as a Women's Party candidate for the constituency of Smethwick in the general election of December 1918 was not realized". [Quotation extracted from June Purvis, 'Pankhurst, Emmeline (1858–1928)', *Oxford Dictionary of National Biography*, Oxford University Press, 2004; [http://www.oxforddnb.com/view/article/35376, accessed 31 Dec 2013]

Beauman, N. *Cynthia Asquith* (London: Hamish Hamilton, 1987)

Bennett, D. *Margot: A Life of the Countess of Oxford and Asquith* (London: Arena, 1984; repr. 1986)

Berry, P and M. Bostridge. *Vera Brittain: A Life* (London: Chatto & Windus, 1995; repr. London: Virago, 2001)

Bilbrough, E. *My War Diary 1914-1918* (London: Ebury Press in association with IWM, 2014)
Snapshot of what life was like on the home front during the First World War

Bondfield, M. G. *A Life's Work* (London: Hutchinson, 1949)
As an ILP [Independent Labour Party] administrative committee member (1913–21) Bondfield criticized the government's war policies. Helped Mary Macarthur (with whom she established the National Federation of Women Workers in 1906) to organize and protect women involved in war work. In 1915 she resumed full-time union work as the NFWW's organizing secretary.

Borden, M. *The Forbidden Zone: A Nurse's Impressions of the First World War* (London: Hesperus Press, 2008)
A paperback reprint of the author's *The Forbidden Zone* published London: Heinemann, 1929.

Brittain, V. *Chronicle of Youth: War Diary 1913-1917*, ed. by Alan Bishop and Terry Smart (London: Gollancz, 1981; repr. London: Phoenix, 2002)
This work is a publication of the diaries on which Vera Brittain's *Testament of Youth* was based.

— *Testament of Youth: An Autobiographical Study of the Years 1900-1925*, with a new introduction by Mark Bostridge and a preface by Shirley Williams (London: Virago Press, 2004)
Originally published: London: Victor Gollancz, 1933. First published by Virago Press in 1978.

Brock, M., and others.ed. *Margot Asquith's Great War Diary 1914-1916: The View from Downing Street*, selected and edited by Michael and Eleanor Brock; with the assistance of Mark Pottle. (Oxford: Oxford University Press, 2014)

Bullock, I. and R. Pankhurst, eds. *Sylvia Pankhurst: From Artist to Anti-fascist* (Basingstoke: Macmillan, 1992

Burnett, J., ed. *Useful Toil: Autobiographies of Working People from the 1820's to the 1920's*, new edn (London: Routledge, 1994)

Carter, V. B., Baroness Asquith of Yarnbury. *Champion Redoubtable: The Diaries and Letters of Lady Violet Bonham Carter, 1914-1945*, edited by Mark Pottle (London: Weidenfeld and Nicolson, 1998)
Violet Bonham Carter, the only daughter of H. H. Asquith, kept a diary from the age of 18. Supported her father on political platforms, 1905-1918. Inside British politics and upper class social life from the outbreak of the first world war to the end of the second, she wrote revealingly about what she saw in her diaries and letters.

Clifford, C. *The Asquiths* (London: John Murray, 2002)

Cooper, Lady D., Viscountess Norwich. *Autobiography* (Wilton, Salisbury: M. Russell, 1979)
Contents: *The Rainbow Comes and Goes*. Originally published: London : Hart Davis, 1958; *The Light of Common Day*. Originally published: London: Hart Davis, 1959; *Trumpets from the Steep*. Originally published: London: Hart Davis, 1960.
A glittering debutant as Diana Manners (later Lady Diana Cooper after her marriage to Duff Cooper), she joined in 1910 the circle of the 'Corrupt Coterie', a clique of English aristocrats and intellectuals of the 1910's (which included Duff Cooper who she married in 1919). During the war she worked as a nurse at Guy's and at the hospital established by her parents in their London house in Arlington Street.

Courtney, C., Baroness Courtney of Penwith. *Extracts from a Diary during the War* (London: Printed for private circulation, 1927)
Kate Courtney, a suffragist and peace campaigner, became Lady Courtney of Penwith on the elevation of her husband Leonard Courtney, Liberal MP and woman's suffrage campaigner, to the peerage in 1906. She persisted with her pacifism throughout the war. She was honorary secretary of the National Union of Women's Suffrage Societies (NUWSS) from 1911-1915

Crewdson, R., ed. *Dorothea's War: The Diary of a First World War Nurse* (London: Weidenfeld & Nicolson 2013)

Davies, M. L., ed. *Life as We Have Known It*, by co-operative working women ... with an introductory letter by Virginia Woolf (London: Hogarth, 1931; repr. London: Virago Press, 1977)
Account of working women's lives - impoverished childhoods, humdrum work, harsh family life - by members of the Women's Co-operative Guild. Margaret Llewelyn Davies (1861-1944) was secretary of the latter Guild.

Fawcett, M.G. *What I Remember* (London: T. Fisher Unwin, 1924; repr. Bristol: Thoemmes Press, 1995)
Millicent Fawcett was a leading light in the women's suffrage movement. President of the National Union of Women's Suffrage Societies (NUWSS) during the war. Fiercely anti-pacifist and a wholehearted supporter of Britain's war effort.

— *The Women's Victory – And After: Personal Reminiscences, 1911-1918* (London: Sidgwick & Jackson, 1920; repr. London: British Library, 1987)

Fletcher, S. *Maude Royden: A Life* (Oxford: Blackwell, 1989)
Maude Royden was a suffragist, socialist, pacifist, lay preacher and campaigner for the ordination of women. See also autobiography in *Myself When Young*, edited by Margot Asquith (see record above).

Forbes, Lady A. S. B.. *Memories and Base Details* (London: Hutchinson, 1921)
Lady Forbes carried out a great deal of humanitarian work for British soldiers on the Western Front, including establishing

The War Years

British Soldiers' Buffets (canteens commonly known as Angelinas) and using canteen profits to build recreation huts.

Furse, Dame K. S. *Hearts and Pomegranates: The Story of Forty-Five years, 1875-1920* (London: Peter Davies, 1940)
Dame Katherine Furse organized the VAD Department in London 1914-17 and became Commandant-in-Chief in 1916 when a joint committee was set up to co-ordinate the VAD work of the British Red Cross Society and the order of St John of Jerusalem. From 1917-19 she was director, with the equivalent rank of rear-admiral, of a new organization, the Women's Royal Naval Service (WRNS).

Gore, E. *The Better Fight: The Story of Dame Lilian Barker* (London; Geoffrey Bles, 1965)
Dame Lilian Barker made a major contribution to Britain's war effort first as the commandant of the Women's Legion cookery section (where she provided valuable training of cooks for the army) and later as lady superintendent at the Royal Arsenal, Woolwich overseeing the welfare of some 30,000 women. She was honoured with a CBE in 1917.

Gorham, D. *Vera Brittain: A Feminist Life* (Cambridge, MA: Blackwell, 1996; repr. Toronto: Toronto University Press, 2000)

Hallam, A. and N. Hallam, eds. *Lady under Fire on the Western Front; The Great War Letters of Lady Dorothie Fielding, MM* (London: Pen & Sword, 2010)
Lady Dorothie Mary Evelyn Feilding was almost three years on the Western Front in Belgium driving ambulances for the Munro Motor Ambulance Corps, an all-volunteer unit. For her bravery she received the Belgian Order of Leopold, the French Croix de Guerre and the British Military Medal (the first woman to be awarded this medal). The letters she wrote home reflect her varied experiences as a woman at the front coping with shell bombardment, gossip, funding work, lice, vehicle maintenance and even marriage proposals.

Hamilton, M. A. *Margaret Bondfield* (London: Leonard Parsons, 1924)
As an ILP [Independent Labour Party] administrative committee member (1913–21) Bondfield criticized the government's war policies. Helped Mary Macarthur (with whom she established the National Federation of Women Workers in 1906) to organize and protect women involved in war work. In 1915 she resumed full-time union work as the NFWW's organizing secretary.

Hamilton, P. *Three Years or the Duration: The Memoirs of a Munitions Worker, 1914-1918* (London: Peter Owen, 1978)

Hannam, J. 'Pankhurst, (Estelle) Sylvia (1882–1960)', *Oxford Dictionary of National Biography*, Oxford University Press, 2004; online edn, Jan 2011

Izzard, M. P. *A Heroine in Her Time: A Life of Dame Helen Gwynne-Vaughan, 1879-1967* (London: Macmillan, 1969)
In early 1917 Helen Gwynne-Vaughan was appointed chief controller of the Women's Army Auxiliary Corps (renamed Queen Mary's Army Auxiliary Corps in April 1918) at a time when this organization was being established as a means of alleviating the problem posed by shortages of military manpower in areas ranging from catering to machine maintenance. In September 1918 she was appointed head of the Women's Royal Air Force (WRAF).

Lawrence, M. *Shadow of Swords: A Biography of Elsie Inglis* (London: Michael Joseph, 1971)
Elsie Inglis was famous particularly for her foundation of the Scottish Women's Hospitals for the Foreign Service, on the basis of which she realized her vision in the Great War for creating all-women medical units of doctors, nurses, orderlies and drivers and sending them to the Western and Serbian fronts. She herself ran the medical services in Serbia from 1915 to 1917.

Leneman, L. *Elsie Inglis: Founder of Battlefront Hospitals Run Entirely by Women* (Edinburgh: National Museums of Scotland, 1998)

— *In the Service of Life: The Story of Elsie Inglis and the Scottish Women's Hospitals* (Edinburgh: Mercat Press, 1994)

Liddington, J. *The Life and Times of a Respectable Rebel: Selina Cooper, 1864–1946* (London: Virago, 1984)
A radical suffragist operating in 1914 as a member of the ILP and the National Union of Women's Suffrage Societies (NUWSS), Selina Cooper opposed the war, supported local conscientious objectors, and in 1917 led a Women's Peace Crusade procession through Nelson. In spite of her internationalist and anti-war stance which was directly contrary to that of the NUWSS which, under the influence of Millicent Fawcett, supported the war she did not, unlike other internationalist suffragists, resign from her membership of that organisation.

The Civilian Scene

MacKenzie, R. N. 'Asquith, Lady Cynthia Mary Evelyn (1887–1960)', *Oxford Dictionary of National Biography*, Oxford University Press, 2004; online edn, Jan 2011
[http://www.oxforddnb.com/view/article/30480, accessed 7 Nov 2013]
" … Her diaries provide a dynamic portrait of aristocratic life during the war; side by side with trivia about hair-styles and dinner parties are simple and moving entries about the deaths of many of the young men with whom she had grown up, including two of her brothers …". [Quotation extracted from above item in online Oxford DNB]

Mitchell, D. *Queen Christabel: A Biography of Christabel Pankhurst* (London: Macdonald and Jane's, 1977)
Christable Pankhurst assisted her mother Emmeline to form the Women's Social and Political Union (WSPU) in 1903 and in the pre-war years was involved in militant suffragette activities and the editing of *The Suffragette* (1912-14). Shortly after the outbreak of the First World War, following the suspension of militant activities by the WSPU, she returned from the continent (where she had fled before the war to avoid imprisonment) and embarked on a six-month tour of the USA with the backing of the British government and the principle object of persuading the Americans to enter the war in support of Britain and the allies. She was, however, frequently critical of government policy or government figures during the war, sometimes voicing this criticism in *Britannia* (the new name for *The Suffragette*) which she edited. It was in large part because of this that the WPSU sometimes incurred the hostility of the government and that its offices were on occasions raided. Towards the end of 1917 the WPSU was reconstituted as the Women's Party[21] and in the general election of December 1918 she stood (with the support of the coalition government) unsuccessfully as this Party's candidate for the constituency of Smethwick.

Mitchell, G., ed. *The Hard Way Up: The Autobiography of Hannah Mitchell, Suffragette and Rebel* (London: Faber, 1968; repr. London: Virago, 1977)
Hannah Mitchell was a socialist and suffragette. In the pre-war yeas she was a part-time paid organizer of the Women's Social and Political Union (WSPU) from which she resigned to join a breakaway group, the Women's Freedom League, headed by Mrs Charlotte Despard. During the war she became a pacifist supporting such anti-war organizations as the ILP, No Conscription Fellowship (NCF) and the Women's International League for Peace and Freedom.

Mulvihill, M. *Charlotte Despard: A Biography*, new edn (London: Pandora, 1994)
A feminist and socialist reformer, Charotte Despard was for a time a member of the Women's Social and Political Union (WSPU) and suffered imprisonment before the war for her suffragette activities. After the split in the suffragette movement in 1907 she left the WSPU and eventually became president of the Women's Freedom League, an office she held until the spring of 1918. During the war she joined Sylvia Pankhurst in the socialist pacifist movement. She campaigned unsuccessfully as a pacifist Labour parliamentary candidate for Battersea in the general election of 1918. Her only brother was Sir John French, commander-in-chief of the British expeditionary force in the early part of the war.

Peel, D. C. ["Mrs. C. S. Peel"]. *Life's Enchanted Cup: An Autobiography (1872-1933)* (London: John Lane, 1933)
Constance Peel was involved in a number of activities in aid of the war effort, organizing a Soldiers' and Sailors' Wives Club in Lambeth, working as a speaker for the United Workers' Association and the National War Savings Association, co-directing the women's service for the Ministry of Food during the period of voluntary food rationing (March 1917–March 1918) and touring the country to address meetings on the promotion of the economical use of food.

Pethick-Lawrence, E., Baronesss Pethick-Lawrence. *My Part in a Changing World* (London: Gollancz, 1938; repr. Westport, Conn : Hyperion Press, 1976)
Emmeline Pethick-Lawrence was a women's rights activist and pacifist. Treasurer of the Women's International League for Peace and Freedom, 1915-22. Co-editor of *Votes for Women* (London: The Reformer's Press, 1907-1918). Attended the international women's peace conference at The Hague in 1915. Highly critical of the terms of the Versailles peace settlement.

Pope-Hennessy, J. *Queen Mary, 1867-1953* (London: Allen & Unwin, 1959; repr. London: Phoenix Press, 2000)

Romero, P. W. E. *Sylvia Pankhurst: Portrait of a Radical* (New Haven: Yale University Press, 1987)
See also autobiography in *Myself When Young*, edited by Margot Asquith (see record above)

Rubinstein, D. *A Different World for Women: The Life of Millicent Garrett Fawcett* (London : Harvester-Wheatsheaf, 1991)
Millicent Fawcett was a leading light in the women's suffrage movement. President of the National Union of Women's

---

[21] This Party was designed to serve the interests of women voters by embracing policies such as those of a feminist nature (e.g. equal opportunity of employment, equal pay, equal marriage laws, and equality of parental rights) and those of an anti-socialist nature such as the abolition of trade unions. Emmeline Pankhurst was the honorary treasurer of the Party, Annie Kenney its honorary secretary, Flora Drummond its chief organizer, while Christabel continued as editor of *Britannia*, its official newspaper.

Suffrage Societies (NUWSS) during the war

Smith, L. N. *Four Years out of Life* (London: Philip Alan, 1931)
Nursing experiences on the Western Front, illustrated by the author's own atmospheric woodcuts

Swanwick, H. M. *I Have Been Young* (London: Victor Gollancz, 1935)
Helena Swanwick was editor (1909-14) of the suffragist newspaper, *The Common Cause* from which she resigned in 1914 because of differences with her colleagues over the issue of war. Served as a member of the executive committee of the Union of Democratic Control and as chairman of the Women's International League for Peace and Freedom (1915-22). Throughout the war she lent her support to the campaign for a negotiated peace and the future creation of an organization devoted to maintaining international peace. She was unhappy with the terms both of the Versailles settlement and of the League of Nations as it was set up in 1919.

Vellacott, J. 'Marshall, Catherine Elizabeth (1880–1961)', *Oxford Dictionary of National Biography*, Oxford University Press, 2004 (online edn). See also note 23

Webb, B. P. *Diaries, 1912-1924*, edited by M. I. Cole (London: Longmans, 1952)

—*The Diary of Beatrice Webb*, edited by N. and J. Mackenzie, 4 vols (London : Virago in association with the London School of Economics and Political Science, 1982-1984), III: 1905-1924: *The Power to Alter Things* (1984)
An abridged version by Lynn Knight, entitled *The Diaries of Beatrice Webb*, was published in 2000 by Virago in association with the London School of Economics and Political Science. With her husband Sydney, Beatrice Webb held a central possition in British left-wing intellectual and political life for almost 70 years. Vol. 3 provides a fund of insights and anecdotes about the people and politics of early modern Britain.

Winslow, B. *Sylvia Pankhurst: Sexual Politics and Political Activism* (London: UCL Press, 1996)
This study highlights Sylvia Pankhurst's political involvement in the suffrage, working class and socialist movements. It is intended for undergraduate courses in women's studies. See also autobiography in *Myself When Young*, edited by Margot Asquith (q.v.)

Anthologies

Marlow, J., ed. *The Virago Book of Women and the Great War 1914-1918* (London: Virago, 1998)
This anthology provides a broad collection of women's writings on the First World War from Britain, the USA, France, Germany, and Russia. It includes extracts from diaries (published and unpublished), autobiographies, letters, newspapers, and memoirs representative of a very diverse range of women of all ages, classes, and creeds engaged in a variety of occupations (as, for example, wartime surgeons, nurses, foresters, train drivers, bus conductors, bank clerks, censors, munitions workers, policewomen).

Books

Alberti, J. *Beyond Suffrage: Feminists in War and Peace, 1914-1928* (London: Macmillan, 1989)
In this book, the author explores the experience of 14 women over the period 1914 to 1928, the year when the enfranchisement of women in Britain was completed.

Bland, L. 'In the Name of Protection: The Policing of Women in the First World War', in *Women in Law: Explorations in Law Family and Sexuality*, edited by Julia Brophy and Carol Smart (London: Routledge, 1985)

Brock, C. *British Women Surgeons and Their Patients, 1860–1918* (Cambridge: Cambridge University Press, 2017)

Bruley, S. *Women in Britain Since 1900* (Basingstoke: Macmillan, 1999)

Bussy, G. and M. Tims. *Pioneers for Peace: Women's International League for Peace and Freedom 1915-1965*, 2nd edn (London: Women's International League for Peace and Freedom, 1980)

Carr, K. *Women Who Dared: Heroines of the Great War* (London: S.W. Partridge, 1920)

Condell, D. and J. Liddiard, comps. *Working for Victory? Images of Women in the First World War, 1914-18* (London: Routledge, 1987; repr. 1991)
Includes a selection of contemporary photos which, with extended captions and accompanying text illustrations,

demonstrate the roles played by women during the Great War.

Crofton, E. *The Women of Royaumont: A Scottish Women's Hospital on the Western Front* (East Linton, East Lothian : Tuckwell Press, 1997)

Dent, O. *A V.A.D. in France* (Burgess Hill: Diggory Press, 2005)

Fell, A. S. and C. E. Hallett, eds. *First World War Nursing: New Perspectives* (London: Routledge, 2013)
A collection of works by scholars in a collaborative approach to Allied wartime nursing in a wide range of interdisciplinary aspects such as the history of the profession, recruitment, teaching, differing national socio-political backgrounds, and traditional cultural and gender notions of women and nursing.

Gold, M. *Wartime Is Your Time. Women's Lives in World War: Women's Image in Magazines Compared with the Reality of their Wartime Lives* (Edgeware: Hytheway, 1996)

Goldman, D, ed. *Women and World War I: The Written Response* (Basingstoke: Macmillan, 1993)
Brings the letters, poetry, novels, short stories and memoirs that women from Britain, America, France, Germany, Australia and Russia wrote about the war into literary focus.

Gould, J. 'Women's Military Service in First World War Britain', in *Behind The Lines: Gender and the Two World Wars*, edited by M. Higonnet and others (New Haven: Yale University Press, 1987)

Griffin, B. *The Politics of Gender in Victorian Britain: Masculinity, Political Culture, and the Struggle for Women's Rights* (Cambridge: Cambridge University Press, 2012)

Hallett, C. E. *Nurse Writers of the Great War* (Manchester: Manchester University Press 2016)

Hannam, J. and K. Hunt. *Socialist Women: Britain, 1880s to 1920s* (London: Routledge 2002)

Griffiths, G. *Women's Factory Work in World War I* (Stroud: Alan Sutton, 1991)

Haslam, B. *From Suffrage to Internationalism: The Political Evolution of Three British Feminists, 1908-1939* (New York: P. Lang, 1999)
Focuses on the careers of Helena Swanwick, Catherine Marshall, and Kathleen Courtney

Hendley, M. C. Organized Patriotism and the Crucible of War: *Popular Imperialism in Britain, 1914-1932* (Montréal, Québec: McGill-Queen's University Press, 2012)
In this book's comparison of how three major patriotic organizations founded between 1901 and 1902 (the National Service League, the League of the Empire, and the Victoria League) fared during the war the author shows that the National Service League, with its strongly masculinist and militaristic character, failed to flourish in wartime whereas the League of the Empire and the Victoria League, strongly female in their membership and with aims and concepts related to education and hospitality, family, home and kinship, prospered not only during the war but beyond into the 1920's. The author sees this as an indication of how the traumatic nature of the Great War produced a fundamental reshaping of popular patriotism and imperialism that is evident to the author in his comparison of the post-war histories of the above organizations. This book affords an insight into women's roles in Britain during the height of popular imperialism.

Holton, S. S. *Feminism and Democracy: Women's Suffrage and Reform Politics in Britain, 1900-1918* (Cambridge: Cambridge University Press, 1986; repr 2002)

Jackson. L. A. *Women Police: Gender, Welfare and Surveillance in the Twentieth Century* (Manchester: Manchester University Press, 2006)

King, S. *Women, Welfare, and Local Politics, 1880-1920: "We might be trusted"* (Brighton: Sussex Academic Press, 2006)

Lamm, D. 'Emily Goes to War: Explaining the Recruitment to the Women's Army Auxiliary Corps in World War I', in *Borderlines: Gender and Identities in War and Peace, 1870-1930*, edited by Billie Melman (London: Routledge, 1998)

Lee, J. *War Girls: The First Aid Nursing Yeomanry in the First World War* (Manchester: Manchester University Press,

2005)
Includes personal testimonies e.g. diaries, letters and memoirs from the women themselves.

Mackenzie, M. *Shoulder to Shoulder: A Documentary* (London: Allen Lane, 1975)
"'The material in this book represents the basis of my [the compiler's] story outline for the television series "Shoulder to Shoulder" ...' [Acknowledgements]. The series televised by the BBC in 1974 depicted the struggle fought between 1895 and 1918 by British women to gain the right to vote, focusing in particular on the determining role played by the Pankhurst family.

McEwen, Y. *It's a Long Way to Tipperary: British and Irish Nurses in the Great War* (Dunfermline: Cualann Press, 2006)

Marwick, A. *Women at War, 1914-1918* (London: Fontana, 1977)

Mitchell, D. J. *Women on the Warpath: The Story of the Women of the First World War* (London: Jonathan Cape, 1966)
First published in 1965 under the title of *The Monstrous Regiment*

Noakes, L. *Women in the British Army: War and the Gentle Sex, 1907-1948* (London: Routledge, 2006)

Pankhurst, E. S. *The Home Front: A Mirror to Life in England during the World War* (London: Hutchinson, 1932; repr. London: Cresset Library, 1987)

Paseta, S. *Irish Nationalist Women 1900-1918* (Cambridge: Cambridge University Press, 2013)

Patterson, D. S. *The Search for Negotiated Peace: Women's Activism and Citizen Diplomacy in World War I* (London: Routledge, 2007)

Pierson, R. R., and others, ed. *Women and Peace: Theoretical, Historical and Practical Perspectives* (London: Croom Helm, 1987)

Potter, J. *Boys in Khaki, Girls in Print: Women's Literary Responses to the Great War 1914—1918* (Oxford: Clarendon, 2005)

Powell, A. *Women in the War Zone: Hospital Service in the First World War* (Gloucestershire: History Press 2009)

Proctor, T. *Female Intelligence: Women and Espionage in the First World War* (New York: New York University Press, 2003)
A history of the female spies who served Britain during the First World War

Pugh, M. *Women and the Women's Movement in Britain, 1914-1999*, 2nd edn (Basingstoke: Macmillan, 2000)
Rev. edn of *Women and the Women's Movement in Britain*, 1914-1959.

Purvis, J. 'Christabel Pankhurst and the Women's Social and Political Union [WSPU]', in *The Women's Suffrage Movement, New Feminist Perspectives*, edited by M. Joannou and J. Purvis (Manchester: Manchester University Press, 1998)

Rendel, M. 'The Contribution of the Women's Labour League to the Winning of the Franchise', in *Women in the Labour Movement: The British Experience*, ed. by J. Middleton (London: Croom Helm, 1977)

Smyth, J. J. 'Rents, Peace, Votes: Working-Class Women and Political Activity in the First World War', in *Out of Bounds: Women in Scottish Society, 1800-1945*, ed. by E. Breitenbach and E. Gordon (Edinburgh, Edinburgh University Press, 1992)

Strachey, R. C. *The Cause: A Short History of the Women's Movement in Great Britain* (London: G. Bell, 1928; repr. London: Virago, 1978)
The author, best known as Ray Strachey, was a strong and patriotic supporter of the British war effort. She was closely associated with Millicent Fawcett in the expulsion of pacifist colleagues from the National Union of Women's Suffrage Societies (NUWSS). Became parliamentary secretary of the NUWSS (1915) and chairman of the Women's Service Employment Committee during the war.

Thom, D. *Nice Girls and Rude Girls: Women Workers in World War 1* (London: Tauris, 1997; repr. 2000)

— 'Women and Work in Wartime Britain', in *The Upheaval of War: Work and Welfare in Europe, 1914-18*, edited by Richard Wall and Jay Winter (Cambridge: Cambridge University Press, 1988)

Thomas, G. *Life on all Fronts: Women in the First World War* (Cambridge: Cambridge University Press, 1989)

Twinch, C. *Women of the Land: Their Story during two World Wars* (Cambridge: Lutterworth Press, 1990)

Vellacott, J. *Pacifists, Patriots and the Vote: The Erosion of Democratic Suffragism in Britain During the First World War* (Basingstoke: Palgrave Macmillan, 2007)

Wheelwright, J. *Amazons and Military Maids: Women Who Dressed as Men in the Pursuit of Life, Liberty and Happiness*, new edn (London: Pandora, 1994)
Through an examination of memoirs and diaries, military records, journalistic reports, and anecdotal sources this book reveals the story of British and American women (and also some women of other nationalities) who fought in American and European wars of the eighteenth, nineteenth and twentieth centuries, masquerading as men (as, for example, was the case in one of the book's biographies of individuals, of an Englishwoman, Flora Sandes, who during the First World War went to Serbia as a nurse, but eventually fought as a man in the Serbian army).

Wiltsher, A. *Most Dangerous Women: Feminist Peace Campaigners of the Great War* (London: Pandora, 1985)

Woollacott, A. *On Her Their Lives Depend: Munition Workers in the Great War* (Berkeley: University of California Press, 1994)
An analysis of oral histories, workers' journals, newspapers and official reports which presents a portrait of women munitions workers in Britain during the Great War.

Zweiniger-Bargielowska, I., ed. *Women in Twentieth-Century Britain* (Harlow: Longman, 2001)

Articles

Benton, S. 'Women, War and Citizenship', *History Workshop Journal*, 58 (2004), 326-334
Review of Nicoletta Gullace's, *The Blood of Our Sons: Men, Women and the Renegotiation of British Citizenship during the Great War* (New York: Palgrave Macmillan, 2002) and Sonya Rose's, *Which People's War? National Identity and Citizenship in Wartime Britain 1939-1945* (Oxford: Oxford University Press, 2003)

Cowper, J. M. 'Women on Active Service Forty Years Ago', *Army Quarterly*, 74 (1957), 115-25

Creighton, M. 'The Women Police', *Fortnightly Review*, 114 (1920)

Culleton, C. 'Gender-Charged Munitions: The Language of World War One Munitions Reports', *Women's Studies International Forum*, 11 (1988), 109-116

— 'Working-Class Women's Services Newspapers and The First World War', *Imperial War Museum Review*, 10 (1995)

Gullace, N. 'White Feathers, and Wounded Men: Female Patriotism and the Memory of the Great War', *Journal of British Studies*, 36 (April 1997), 178-206

Hallett, C. E. 'Saving Lives on the Front Line', *History Today*, 67:7 (2017), 24
The significance of the work of military nurses at Passchendaele.

Heald, H. 'For England's Sake: Women Engineers in the First World War', *History Today*, 64:10 (2014), 28-35
The author discusses the opportunities the First World War presented to women interested in engineering.

Kitching, P. 'Four Faces of nursing and the First World War', *Historian* (Historical Association), 119 (2013), 30-35

Lammasniemi, L. 'Regulation 40D: Punishing Promiscuity on the Home Front during the First World War', *Women's History Review*, 26 (2017), 584-596

Levine, P. '"Walking the Streets in a Way No Decent Woman Should": Women Police in World War I', *Journal of Modern History*, 66(1994), 44

Luck, K. 'The Growing Pains of the 'Women on the Land Movement' in Wiltshire 1914-1917: Recruitment and Training Women Before the Formation of the Women's Land Army', *Local Historian*, 47:3 (2017), 193-207

McCarthy, H. 'Pacifism and Feminism in the Great War', *History Today*, 65, Issue 4 (2015), 4

McDermid, J. 'Women at Work, 1860-1939: How Different Industries Shaped Women's Experiences', *Social History*, 39 (2014), 279-281

McEnroe, N. 'The Duchess and the Soldier', *History Today*, 64 (2014), 4-5
This article is about the ten oil paintings by Victor Tardieu (1870-1937) which depict the tented field hospital established and run by Millicent, Duchess of Sutherland at Bourbourg, twelve miles south-west of Dunkirk, during the summer of 1915. Tardieu served there as an auxiliary with the Duchess of Sutherland for several months and subsequently joined the American Ambulance Field Service, during which time he was commissioned to produce war posters used to generate funds from the American public. The ten paintings were given to the Duchess by the artist and have descended through the Sutherland family. They have now been acquired by the Florence Nightingale Museum, which exhibited them to honour the work of the Duchess of Sutherland and her nurses in the First World War from March 14th to October 26th, 2014 [http://www.florence-nightingale.co.uk/]. The image accompanying McEnroe's article [Oil on panel. 8.5 x 10.75 inches. Signed, inscribed and dated, 'Bourbourg Aout 1915'. Dedicated to Millicent, Duchess of Sutherland (1867-1955)] is one of the ten paintings exhibited.

Monger, D. 'Nothing Special?: Propaganda and Women's Roles in Late First World War Britain, *Women's History Review*, 23 (2014), 518-542
"This article explores women's roles as subjects, objects and producers of National War Aims Committee propaganda in Britain during 1917–18" (extract from an abstract on the internet)

Morgan, S. 'A "Feminist Conspiracy": Maude Royden, Women's Ministry and the British Press, 1916-1921', *Womens History Review*, 22 (2013), 777-800
In arguing that Royden's rise to fame has a bearing on the connections between feminism, suffrage and women's ordination this article examines the way in which the latter controversial issues were handled by individual churchmen through the religious and popular press.

Newberry, J. V. 'Anti-War Suffragists', *History*, 62 (1977), 411-425

Reeves, J. 'The Liverpool Women's War Service Bureau and its Work 1914-1918', *Local Historian*, 44:4 (2014), 312-324

Robert, K. 'Gender, Class and Patriotism: Women's Paramilitary Units in First World War Britain', *International History Review*, 19 (1997), 52-3

Roberts, H. 'A Woman's Eye: British Women and Photography during the First World War', *Despatches* (The Magazine of the Friends of the Imperial War Museum), no. 18 (2014), 40-44
An article by Hilary Roberts, IWM Curator of Photography, about the role of women photographers in the First World War

Scollan, M. 'Gladys Lilian King and the Work of the Women Police in London's Strand 1918-19: A Memoir', *Womens History Review*, 23 (2014), 256-271
This edited transcription of a previously unpublished memoir, written by Gladys Lilian King, describes the work of the Women Police Service in London's Strand during the last years of the First World War when she was stationed at the Beaver Hut (opened by the Canadian Young Men's Christian Association in 1918). Based on her experience there she provides an insight into the supervision of Commonwealth soldiers by women police.

Smith, A. 'The Pankhursts and the War: Suffrage Magazines and First World War Propaganda', *Women's History Review*, 12 (2003), 103-118

Tylee, C. M. 'Maleness Run Riot - The Great War and Women's Resistance to Militarism', *Women Studies*

International Forum, 2 (1988), 199-210

Vellacott, J. 'Feminist Consciousness and the First World War', *History Workshop Journal*, 23 (1987), 81-101

— 'A Place for Pacifism and Transnationalism in Feminist Theory: The Early Work of the WILPF [Women's International League for Peace and Freedom], *Women's History Review*, 2 (1993), 23–56

Ward, P. 'Women of Britain Say Go: Women's Patriotism in the First World War', *Twentieth Century British History*, 12 (2001), 23-45
The author examines the patriotic activities of some aristocratic and middle-class women in Great War and notes that these had repercussions on postwar politics.

White, B. 'Sowing the Seeds of Patriotism? The Women's Land Army in Devon, 1916-1918', *Local Historian*, 41:1 (2011), 13-27

Woollacott, A. 'Khaki Fever and its Control: Gender, Class, Age and Sexual Morality on the British Homefront in the First World War', *Journal of Contemporary History*, 29 (1994), 325-347

— 'Maternalism, Professionalism and Industrial Welfare Supervisors in World War I Britain', *Women's History Review*, 3 (1994), 29-56

Contemporary Material

Alec-Tweedie, E. B.. *Women and Soldiers* (London: John Lane, The Bodley Head, 1918)

Billington, M. F. *The Roll Call of Serving Women; A Record of Women's Work for Combatants and Sufferers in the Great War* (London: Religious Tract Society, 1915)

Bowser, T. *The Story of British V.A.D. Work In The Great War* (London: Andrew Melrose, 1917)

Caine, Sir T. H. H. *Our Girls: Their Work for the War* (London: Hutchinson, 1916)

Cosens, M. *Lloyd George's Munition Girls* (London: Hutchinson, 1916)

Davies, M. L., ed. *Maternity: Letters from Working Women* (London: Bell, 1915; repr. London: Virago, 1989)

George, W. L. *The Intelligence of Women* (London: Herbert Jenkins, 1917)

McLaren, B. *Women of the War*, with an introduction by the Right Honourable H. H. Asquith (London: Hodder and Stoughton, 1917)

Marshall, C., and others. *Militarism versus Feminism: Writings on Women and War*, by Catherine Marshall, C. K. Ogden and Mary Sargant Florence (London Allen & Unwin, 1915)
A reprint of this work, edited by Margaret Kamester and Jo Vellacott has been published: London: Virago, 1987.

Pankhurst, C. *The War: A Speech Delivered at the London Opera House, on September 8th, 1914* (London: Women's Social & Political Union, 1914)

Sinclair, M. *A Journal of Impressions in Belgium* (London: Hutchinson, 1915)

Stone, G. *Women War Workers: Accounts Contributed by Representative Workers of the Work done by Women in the More Important Branches of War Employment* (London: Harrap, 1917)
Reprinted under the title of *Women War Workers of World War I*, London: Mansion Field, 2007

Swan, A. S. *Letters to a Bride* (London: Hodder & Stoughton, 1915)

Taylor, J. T. 'The Mill Girl', *Millgate Monthly*, (1914), 14-15

Yates, L. K. *The Women's Part: A Record of Munitions Work* (London: Hodder and Stoughton, 1918)

2.11 Doubts and Dissent

2.11.1 General

While the majority of the British people generally remained committed to the war throughout its duration, although not with the same patriotic fervour as evinced in its early months, anti-war dissent did manifest itself in various ways, chiefly among a small minority of pacifists, socialists, feminists, and intellectuals.

Dissent was characterised by a diversity of views, sometimes of a contradictory nature (e.g. deploring the war yet believing that the war had to be fought to a victorious conclusion rather than that it should be ended as quickly as possible by means of a negotiated peace). The views of many dissenters found expression in bodies such as the Union of Democratic Control (UDC) and the League of Nations Society; some expressed their views directly in conscientious objection.

The government reacted to the potential dangers of dissent by ensuring that the Defence of the Realm Act (DORA) contained clauses which would enable it to stifle dissent whenever it was considered necessary. Some dissenters, including Morel and Russell, were imprisoned under DORA, but in general the government adopted a low key approach in relation to the application of DORA, tending to rely, for example, on private groups and newspapers attacking pacifist group with propaganda campaigns.

While there was dissent in Ireland arising for similar reasons to those on the British mainland, it became entangled there in the controversy over Home Rule. This aspect is treated in **Part 3, section 2.9 on Ireland**.

Literature Review

Pearce, C. 'Writing about Britain's 1914-18 War Resisters - Literature Review', *Reviews in History* (Institute of Historical Research), review no. 1779 (18 June 2015)

Books

Barrett, C. *Subversive Peacemakers, War Resistance 1914–1918: An Anglican Perspective* (Cambridge: Lutterworth Press, 2014)

Binfield, C. *So Down to Prayers: Studies in English Nonconformity, 1780-1920* (London: Dent, 1977)

Carsten, F. L. *War Against War: British and German Radical Movements in the First World War* (London: Batsford, 1982)

Hinton, J. *Protests and Visions: Peace Politics in Twentieth Century Britain* (London: Hutchinson Radius, 1989)

Koss, S. E. *Nonconformity in British Politics* (London: Batsford, 1975)

Millman, B. *Managing Domestic Dissent in First World War Britain* (London: Frank Cass, 2000)

Rose, T. *Aspects of Political Censorship, 1914-1918* (Hull: Hull University Press, 1995)

Russell, B. A. W., 3rd Earl Russell. *Prophecy and Dissent, 1914-1916*, edited by Richard A. Rempel, The Collected Papers of Bertrand Russell, 13 (London: Unwin Hyman, 1988; repr. London: Routledge, 2000)
This collection, which covers some of Russell's publications opposing Britain's involvement in the war during the period August 1914 to December 1916, encompasses his attitude to the Liberal Party, his move towards the Independent Labour Party, his role in the Union of Democratic Control, his active involvement with the No-Conscription Fellowship, his belief in the need for a swift and fair peace, and the persistent attempts on the part of the government to harry Russell.

Swartz, M. 'A Study in Futility: The British Radicals at the Outbreak of the First World War', in *Edwardian Radicalism*, ed. by A. J. A. Morris (London: Routledge, 1974)

Taylor, A. J. P. *The Trouble Makers: Dissent Over Foreign Policy, 1792-1939*, The Ford Lectures Delivered in the University of Oxford in Hilary Term, 1956 (London: Hamish Hamilton, 1957; repr. London: Pimlico, 1993)

Wlkinson, A. *Dissent or Conform: War, Peace, and the English Churches, 1900-1945* (London: SCM Press, 1986)

Articles

Crook, D. P. 'Peter Chalmers Mitchell and Antiwar Evolutionism in Britain during the Great War', *Journal of the History of Biology*, 22: 2 (1989), 325-356

Millman, B. 'HMG and the War against Dissent, 1914-18', *Journal of Contemporary History*, 40 (2005), 413-440

Newberry, J. V. 'Anti-War Suffragists', *History*, 62 (1977), 411-425

Weinroth, H. 'Peace by Negotiation and the British Anti-War Movement, 1914-1918', *Canadian Journal of History*, 10 (1975), 369-92

2.11.2 Conscription and Conscience

Throughout the war there were a number of 'conscientious objectors', so named because of their objection to taking up arms on religious or political grounds. Soon after the war began they received almost immediate support from the No Conscription Fellowship (NCF), a body (chaired by Clifford Allen and including Bertrand Russell among its most active members) which owed its establishment in the autumn of 1914 to the impetus given by Fenner Brockway, editor of the strongly anti-war Independent Labour Party newspaper, *Labour Leader*. Brockway, Allen and Russell all subsequently suffered a period of imprisonment for their militant activities as did many other members of the NCF which consisted mainly of young men eligible for call-up; it has been estimated that half of the approximately 12,000 members served prison sentences during the war The NCF, working with two other organisations (the Friends Service Committee and the Fellowship of Reconciliation) focused on a campaign against the Military Service Acts of 1915 and 1916 which introduced compulsory conscription but provided for the exemption of pacifists of military age from military service on grounds of conscience (the decisions about exemption being left to a system of tribunals). In their campaign against these Acts the NCF brought to bear every possible means to get its message across, holding protest meetings, publishing leaflets and pamphlets, inaugurating from March 1915 a weekly newspaper, *The Tribunal*, briefing MPs and drafting questions to Ministers. After conscription became law the NCF concentrated on aiding men who had defied the call to join up.

A number of women played their part in the activities of the NCF not only in a supportive and sympathetic role but also as active members and workers of the organisation itself. Prominent in the latter category were Catherine E. Marshall, Sylvia Pankhurst, Lydia Smith (who edited the NCF journal *The Tribunal*) and Violet Tillard (who acted as General Secretary for a period and was sentenced to 61 days imprisonment for refusing to tell the police who the NCF printers were), but there were numerous other women who helped to keep the NCF going as it dwindled in numbers as a result of male members being imprisoned. Some women members suffered imprisonment as, for example, Joan Beauchamp who was jailed twice, Edith Smith who served 6 months for printing a leaflet without submitting it for censorship, and, notoriously, Alice Wheeldon who was convicted of plotting to kill Lloyd George and Arthur Henderson with poison darts.

Another body which was formed during the war to campaign against conscription was the National Council against Conscription which later continued its activities with a broader remit under the name of the National Council for Civil Liberties. With an executive which included people like Clifford Allen, Charles Ammon, Margaret Bondfield, John Clifford, Alex Gossip, Henry Hodkin, George Lansbury, F. W. Pethick-Lawrence, Robert Williams and H. W. Massingham, this group sought to work for the repeal of the Military Service Act, to prevent conscription from becoming a permanent feature of British life, and generally to safeguard all civil liberties which seemed to be at risk. It was, however, too small a group to have a major impact. Most of its members were more active in other dissenting bodies.

It is estimated that there were in the region of 16,500 conscientious objectors, about 90 per cent of whom ultimately accepted the decisions of the tribunals and performed alternative non-combatant war service at home (e.g. roadmaking) or at the front (e.g. in ambulance units and as stretcher bearers), although before doing so some 6261 of them suffered a spell in prison at least once. A small hard core of some 1300 'absolutists' rejected all compulsory service - some from religious conviction, some as upholders of personal liberty, a few as socialists opposed to participation in a capitalist war - and in consequence faced arrest, trial, and imprisonment. Of these 'absolutists' about 64 per cent spent two or more years in prison, 142 were given life sentences, and 17 received death sentences (later commuted to life imprisonment); 10 died in prison. In many cases imprisoned 'absolutists' received brutal treatment.

Conscientious objectors ('conchies' as they were labelled) suffered widespread hostility and persecution – from the government, the police, the army's High Command, most churches and the jingoist press – added to which were the immense personal pressures they had to endure from communities, neighbours, friends, even families. Their disenfranchisement in the Representation of the People Act of 1918 is an indication of the strength of popular disapproval of them on the home front throughout the war. In the front-line, however, the attitude of grass-roots soldiers towards 'conchies' was more moderate.

Autobiographies, Biographies

Brockway, A. F., Baron Brockway. *Inside the Left: Thirty Years of Platform, Press, Prison and Parliament* (London: Allen and Unwin, 1942; repr. 1947)
By 1912 Brockway was editor of the Independent Labour Party newspaper, the *Labour Leader*. Prominent in the ILP's opposition to the war, as a journalist, and then through the No-Conscription Fellowship as an opponent of military conscription. On four occasions he was sentenced to gaol - the last time, in July 1917, to two years hard labour.

Gilbert, M. *Plough My Own Furrow: The Story of Lord Allen of Hurtwood as Told Through His Writings and Correspondence* (London: Longmans, 1965)

Howell, D. 'Allen, (Reginald) Clifford, Baron Allen of Hurtwood (1889–1939)', *Oxford Dictionary of National Biography*, Oxford University Press, 2004; online edn, May 2011
[http://www.oxforddnb.com/view/article/30390, accessed 8 Nov 2013]
Clifford Allen was inflexibly anti-war. A central figure in the formation of the No-Conscription Fellowship (NCF) and later its chairman, his activities in 1916 after the introduction of military conscription (on which he adopted the absolutist position) and his refusal to accept the option of non-combatant work involved him in clashes with the authorities that ultimately led to his being arrested, court-martialled, and jailed in August 1916. After being released twice and rearrested, he was eventually sentenced to two years hard labour but finally released in December 1917. [Information extracted from above item in online Oxford DNB]

Lansbury, G. *My Life* (London: Constable, 1928)
Labour leader, politician, and uncompromising pacifist. From 1912 to 1922 he was editor–proprietor of the *Daily Herald*. Between 1914 and 1918 the paper was published as a pacifist and anti-war weekly, campaigning against conscription and supporting conscientious objectors.

Marwick, A. J. B. *Clifford Allen: The Open Conspirator* (Edinburgh: Oliver & Boyd, 1964)

Russell, B. A. W., 3rd Earl Russell. *Autobiography* (London: Routledge, 2000)
Originally published in 3 Vols [Vol 1, 1872-1914; Vol 2, 1914-1944; Vol 3, 1944-1967], London: Allen & Unwin, 1967-1969
Throughout the war Russell was, unlike most of his academic contemporaries, involved in public expressions of opposition to the war through his political publications and his membership of the No-Conscription Fellowship and the Union of Democratic Control.

Vellacott, J. 'Marshall, Catherine Elizabeth (1880–1961)', *Oxford Dictionary of National Biography*, Oxford University Press, 2004 (online edn). See also note 23

Books

Adams, R. J. Q. and P. P. Poirier. *The Conscription Controversy in Great Britain, 1900-1918* (Basingstoke: Macmillan, 1987)

Bell, J., ed. *We Did Not Fight: 1914-1918 Experiences of War Resisters* (London: Cobden-Sanderson, 1935)

Boulton, D. *Objection Overruled* (London: MacGibbon & Kee, 1967)
A study of groups and movements in England that were opposed to World War I

Ellsworth-Jones, W. *We Will Not Fight: The Untold Story of the First World War's Conscientious Objectors* (London: Aurum Press, 2008)

Graham, J. W. *Conscription and Conscience; a History, 1916-1919* (London: Allen and Unwin, 1922; repr. New York, Augustus M. Kelley, 1969)

Goodall, F. *A Question of Conscience: Conscientious Objection in Two World Wars* (Phoenix Mill, Stroud: Sutton Publishing Ltd., 1997)

Jones, H. 'The War and Morality', in *Ethical and Religious Problems of the War*, edited by J. Estlin Carpenter (London: Lindsey, 1916)

Kennedy, T. C. *The Hound of Conscience: History of the No-Conscription Fellowship 1914-1918* (Fayetteville, Arkansas: University of Arkansas Press, 1981)

Mcdermott, J. *British Military Service Tribunals, 1916-1918: 'A Very Much Abused Body of Men'* (Manchester: Manchester University Press, 2011)

Meyer, F. B. *The Majesty of Conscience* (London: National Labour Press, 1917)

Rae, John *Conscience and Politics: The British Government and the Conscientious Objector to Military Service, 1916-1919* (London: Oxford University Press, 1970)

Robbins, K. 'The British Experience of Conscientious Objection', *in Facing Armageddon: The First World War Experienced*, ed. by H. Cecil and P. H. Liddle (London: Leo Cooper, 1996)

Rogerson, S. *Twelve Days*, with a foreword by B. H. Liddell Hart (London: Arthur Baker, 1933)
A personal record of twelve days on the Somme in 1916 while Rogerson was serving as a subaltern with the 2nd Battalion of the West Yorkshire Regiment. Reprinted London: Greenhill, 2006 under the title, *Twelve Days on the Somme: A Memoir of the Trenches, 1916*, with a new preface and introduction. On the matter of conscientious objectors Rogerson provides us with a front-line attitude to them which reveals a tolerance that is in contrast with the contempt with which they were mostly treated on the home front (see pp 161-163 of the book)

Rowbotham, S. *Friends of Alice Wheeldon* (New York: Monthly Review Press, 1987)
Contents: Friends of Alice Wheeldon; Rebel networks in the First World War. *Friends of Alice Wheeldon* was also published, (London: Pluto, 1986), with the text of the author's play of the same name first performed at the Rotherham Arts Centre in March 1980. Alice Wheeldon, like all the Wheeldon family, was involved in anti-war campaigning and sheltering conscientious objectors. For this reason the Wheeldons were subjected to close surveillance by the intelligence services that led, in early 1917, to the authorities finding a pretext to charge Alice, along with others (including her sisters Harriet and Winifred) with conspiring to assassinate the prime minister, David Lloyd George, together with Arthur Henderson (the Labour Party leader in the Coalition). Sentenced for this to ten years' penal servitude, she only served a short period of her sentence (until December 1918) and subsequently died in the post-war influenza epidemic, on 21 February 1919.

Articles

Buckell, J. 'The Conscientious Objectors of Northampton during the First World War', *Local Historian*, 46:3 (2016), 180-193

Cain, E. R. 'Conscientious Objection in France, Britain, and the United States', *Comparative Politics*, 2 (1970) 274-307

Dekar, P. R. 'Twentieth-Century British Baptist Conscientious Objectors', *Baptist Quarterly*, 35 (1994), 35-44

Dicey, A. V. 'The Conscientious Objector', *Nineteenth Century*, 83 (1918), 357-73

Hughes, M. 'A Patchwork of Dissent: Conscientious Objectors in Lancashire during the First World War', *Local Historian*, 47:4 (2017), 283-297

Johnson, E. 'Keynes' Attitude to Compulsory Military Service', *Economic Journal*, 70 (1960), 160-165

Kennedy, T. C. Public Opinion and the Conscientious Objector, 1915- 1919', *Journal of British Studies*, 12 (1972-73), 105-19

McDermott, J. 'Conscience and the Military Service Tribunals during the First World War: Experiences in Northamptonshire', *War in History*, 17 (2010), 60-85

O'Brien, M. '"Conchie": Emrys Hughes and the First World War', *Welsh History Review*, 13 (1987), 328-352

Peacock, A.J. 'History of Conscientious Objection and its Opposition in the City of York', *York Historian*, 5 (1984), 39-40

Smith, L. 'The Wounds of War', *Despatches* (The Magazine of the Friends of the Imperial War Museum), no. 19 (2014), 26-28
An article about The Friends Ambulance Unit during the First World War

Sokoloff, S. 'Military Service Tribunals in the First World War: A Northamptonshire Study', *Local Historian*, 47:3 (2017), 208-226

Spinks, P. '"The War Courts": The Stratford-upon-Avon Borough Tribunal 1916-1918', *Local Historian*, 32:4 (2002), 210-217

Thomis, M. I. 'Conscription and Consent: British Labour and the Resignation Threat, 1916', *Australian Journal of Politics and History*, 23 (1977), 10-18

Wilson, H. W. 'Conscience and the Conscientious Objector', *National Review*, 410 (1917), 189-197

2.11.3 Pacifism and the Peace Movement

The British declaration of war on August 4 1914 created a dilemma for the broad group of radicals (political and religious) who in the preceding years had opposed war and who might loosely be considered to represent a peace movement. They were faced with a situation where they had to decide between joining in the almost universally patriotic support for the war or opposing it. For many of them the decision presented real difficulties. Some of them had enthusiastically joined in the 'pacifist' rallies and demonstrations on the eve of the war but once war had been declared felt unable to maintain their pacifist stance. There were, however, a number who remained true to their pacifist principles and persisted in maintaining their opposition to the war right up to its end; they exerted an important influence in a peace movement which gathered momentum as the war progressed in political groups (Union of Democratic Control, National Council of Civil Liberties. Independent Labour Party, and the No Conscription Fellowship (NCF), religious groups (Peace Society, Quakers, Fellowship of Reconciliation), and women's groups (Women's International League for Peace and Freedom, Women's Peace Crusade). Working for an early negotiated peace became one of the chief aims of the peace movement as was clearly evident, for example, when the Independent Labour Party set up the Peace Negotiations Committee in the Autumn of 1916. This was greatly aided in 1917 (at a time when the hitherto solid public opposition to anything suggestive of pacifism was being undermined by war weariness) by the publication in *The Daily Telegraph* of proposals for a negotiated peace by Lord Lansdowne, a respected Tory elder statesman.

Women played an important part in the agitation for peace, particularly through two organisations, the Women's Peace Crusade and the Women's International League for Peace and Freedom[22] (of which Helena Swanwick

---

[22] The WILPF was formed at an International Women's Congress for Peace and Freedom held at the Hague in 1915. The Congress was attended by a number of women from Britain (e.g. Helena Swanwick, Emily Hobhouse, Emmeline Pethick-Lawrence) in spite of the efforts of pro-war suffragists like Millicent Fawcett of the NUWSS to prevent British attendance at it. Among the main objectives of the League were those of getting governments to produce a list of war aims and to accept the idea of a negotiated peace.

became the chairperson and Catherine Marshall[23], Maude Royden and Emmeline Pethwick-Lawrence were other prominent British members). Although women who supported the pacifist cause were in a minority and faced fierce opposition from those who believed that their activities undermined the efforts of the armed forces, the women's peace movement they represented remained one of the most effective voices of opposition during the war. As war weariness mounted, the Women's Peace Crusade gained significant support in certain parts of the nation. One of its rallies in Glasgow, for example, attracted over 10,000 people in July 1917.

The peace movement had little effect on changing public and governmental attitudes to the war. This was to a large extent due to the differing ideologies, jealousies between new and existing peace societies, and power struggles between groups, a combination of difficulties that prevented the development of concerted and effective co-operation. As a result the peace movement never became strong enough to convince the public that it was preferable to seek a negotiated peace rather than continue the war to a military conclusion.

Pacifist men of military age who were opposed to the war from religious or political conviction and unwilling to join the armed services were likely to be brought into potential conflict with the state once the Military Service Acts of 1915 and 1916 which introduced compulsory conscription were passed. For these aspects of pacifism see **Part 3, section 2.11.2** on **Conscription and Conscience**.

Autobiographies, Biographies

Anderson, N. *Noel-Buxton: A Life* (London: Allen & Unwin, 1952)
During the First World War Noel Buxton worked for the Admiralty, and promoted the Armenian cause on a visit to the United States in 1916. The entry of the US into the conflict seemed to end any hope of the negotiated peace which he had been promoting. As well as being disillusioned by this he became increasingly disenchanted by the attitude of the Liberal Party and its leadership to the war.

Angell, N. *After All: An Autobiography* (London: Hamish Hamilton, 1951)

Balme, J. H. *To Love One's Enemies: The Work and Life of Emily Hobhouse*. Compiled from letters and writings, newspaper cuttings and official documents (Cobble Hill: Hobhouse Trust, 1994)

Bunsen, V. de. *Charles Roden Buxton: A Memoir* (London: Allen and Unwin, 1947)
Throughout the First World War Charles Buxton was consistently in favourr of a peace by negotiation. He was a founder member of the Union of Democratic Control. In 1917 he left the Liberals and joined the Independent Labour Party.

Ceadel, M. *Living the Great Illusion: Sir Norman Angell, 1872-1967* (Oxford: Oxford University Press, 2009)
In the pre-war years Norman Angell had become an influential figure with the publication of his world-wide best-seller, *The Great Illusion*, and the establishment of the Garton Foundation which aimed "to promote the study of international polity" (in effect, the promotion of Angellism) and provided the funds for Norman Angell's monthly pacifist journal, *War and Peace* (absorbed during the war by the *Contemporary Review*). On 28 July 1914 he organised the Neutrality League in a fruitless attempt to keep Britain out of a European war. After war was declared he helped to launch the Union of Democratic Control (UDC) with a group of like-minded radicals. In the spring of 1915, after a brief spell in late 1914 serving with an ambulance corps at Dunkirk, he visited the USA where he campaigned for American neutrality in the war. Later in 1915 he returned to Britain to volunteer for military service and after being rejected returned to the USA where he remained for the rest of the war. During the latter period he advocated the creation of an international organization (influencing President Wilson's thoughts on these lines, it has been claimed) but not actually at this time taking a leading role in the movement for a league of nations.

Courtney, C., Baroness Courtney of Penwith. *Extracts from a Diary during the War* (London: Printed for private circulation, 1927)

---

[23] Catherine Marshall was a leading figure in the National Union of Women's Suffrage Societies (NUWSS), the political work of which was developed under her leadership as parliamentary secretary and under Kathleen Courtney's leadership as honorary secretary in the pre-war period to 1914. After the outbreak of war she resigned from office as a result of the stance taken by the NUSS on the issue of the war that was opposed to her desire for the suffrage movement to be involved in the peace campaign. Her activities during the war included involvement in the planning of the Women's International Congress at The Hague in April 1915 and helping to develop the British section of the International Committee of Women for Permanent Peace, later the Women's International League for Peace and Freedom (WILPF). She also worked for the No-Conscription Fellowship, where, with Bertrand Russell, she became particularly involved in the political aspects.

The War Years

Kate Courtney, a suffragist and peace campaigner, became Lady Courtney of Penwith on the elevation of her husband Leonard Courtney, Liberal MP and woman's suffrage campaigner, to the peerage in 1906. She persisted with her pacifism throughout the war. In the pre-war period to 1914 she was honorary secretary of the National Union of Women's Suffrage Societies (NUWSS).

Davies, G. M. L. *Pilgrimage of Peace*, with a Memoir by C. E. Raven (London: Fellowship of Reconciliation, 1950)
At the end of 1913 the author took up full-time work, without pay, with the Fellowship of Reconciliation. As a conscientious objector he was imprisoned more than once during the years 1917-19.

Fletcher, S. *Maude Royden: A Life* (Oxford: Blackwell, 1989)
Maude Royden was a suffragist, socialist, pacifist, lay preacher and campaigner for the ordination of women.

Gilbert, M. *Plough My Own Furrow: The Story of Lord Allen of Hurtwood as Told Through His Writings and Correspondence* (London: Longmans, 1965)
Clifford Allen was inflexibly anti-war. A central figure in the formation of the No-Conscription Fellowship (NCF) and later its chairman, his activities in 1916 after the introduction of military conscription (on which he adopted the absolutist position) and his refusal to accept the option of non-combatant work involved him in clashes with the authorities that ultimately led to his being arrested, court-martialled, and jailed in August 1916. After being released twice and rearrested, he was eventually sentenced to two years hard labour but finally released in December 1917.

Gunn, P. *Vernon Lee: Violet Paget, 1856–1935* (London: Oxford University Press, 1964)
In the years just before the First World War, Vernon Lee, pseudonym of Violet Paget, employed her talents as an author to raise in a wide range of publications numerous political issues such as women's equality, economic justice, international co-operation, and anti-militarism. During the war, she joined the ranks of the Union of Democratic Control and supported the women's peace crusade. In 1915 she wrote, the anti-war morality play *The Ballet of the Nations* (republishing it in 1920 within a philosophical commentary under the title of *Satan the Waster*).

Hamilton, M. A. *Remembering My Good Friends* (London: Jonathan Cape, 1944)
In 1914 Mary Agnes Hamilton joined the Independent Labour Party (the constitution of which she helped to draw up) and was one of the original members of the Union of Democratic Control. She was an assistant editor of *Common Sense* in 1916, and also wrote for the monthly *War and Peace*. Her activities included membership of the *1917 Club* (a mixture of radical Liberals and the Labour left, founded by Ramsay Macdonald to promote world peace) and association with such intellectual circles as Lady Ottoline Morell's gatherings and a literary group which included the Woolfs, the Huxleys, D. H. Lawrence, and Lytton Strachey. By 1918 she she had become well-known as a journalist and speaker.

Hirst, F. W. *In the Golden Days* (London: Muller, 1947)
Hirst was editor of the *Economist* 1907-16. After being forced to resign from the editorship of the *Economist* in 1916 because of his anti-war views he set up his own paper, *Common Sense* (financed by anti-Lloyd George Liberals) which he particularly employed to campaign for a negotiated peace. In 1917 he was actively involved with Lord Lansdowne's negotiated peace initiative, and when advice was being sought in the drafting of Woodrow Wilson's Fourteen Points he was among the leading British radicals to be consulted by Colonel House.

Lansbury, G. *My Life* (London: Constable, 1928)
George Lansbury was a labour leader, politician, and uncompromising pacifist. Supported women's suffrage and defended conscientious objectors. From 1912 to 1922 he was editor–proprietor of the *Daily Herald*. Between 1914 and 1918 the paper was published as a pacifist and anti-war weekly, campaigning against conscription, supporting conscientious objectors, and welcoming the Russian revolutions of February and October 1917.

Marrin, A. *Sir Norman Angell* (Boston: Twayne Publishers, 1979)

Marwick, A. J. B. *Clifford Allen: The Open Conspirator* (Edinburgh: Oliver & Boyd, 1964)

Morris, A. J. A. 'C. P. Trevelyan', in *Biographical Dictionary of Modern Peace Leaders*, editor in-chief, H. Josephson (Westport, Conn: Greenwood Press, 1985)
Sir Charles Philips Trevelyan was liberal MP, Elland Division of Yorkshire, 1899-1918. Advocated peace by negotiation throughout the war.

— 'The Odyssey of an Anti-War Liberal [C. P. Trevelyan]', in *Doves and Diplomats: Foreign Offices and Peace Movements in Europe and America in the Twentieth Century*, edited by S. Wank (Westport, Conn: Greenwood Press, 1978)

The Civilian Scene

Newton, T. W. L., 2nd Baron. *Lord Lansdowne: A Biography* (London: Macmillan, 1929)
Although Lansdowne strongly supported the decision for war in August 1914 and was happy in May 1915 to take office as minister without portfolio in the inner war committee of Asquith's coalition he became doubtful about the possibility of a decisive allied victory and, increasingly attracted to the idea of a negotiated peace as the losses on the Western Front mounted, he submitted his views on these lines in a memorandum to Asquith on 13 November 1916. It was on this memorandum that his famous peace letter printed in *The Daily Telegraph* on 29 November 1917 was based.

Pethick-Lawrence, E., Baronesss Pethick-Lawrence. *My Part in a Changing World* (London: Gollancz, 1938; repr. Westport, Conn : Hyperion Press, 1976)
Emmeline Pethick Lawrence was a women's rights activist and pacifist. Treasurer of the Women's International League for Peace and Freedom, 1915-22. Co-editor of *Votes for Women* (London The Reformer's Press, 1907-1918). Attended the international women's peace conference at The Hague in 1915. Highly critical of the terms of the Versailles peace settlement.

Russell, B. A. W., 3rd Earl Russell. *Autobiography* (London: Routledge, 2000)
Originally published in 3 Vols [Vol 1, 1872-1914; Vol 2, 1914-1944; Vol 3, 1944-1967], London: Allen & Unwin, 1967-1969
Russell was a Fellow and lecturer at Trinity College at the beginning of the war. Throughout the war he was, unlike most of his academic contemporaries, involved in public expressions of opposition to the war through his political publications and his membership of the No-Conscription Fellowship and the Union of Democratic Control. He was removed from his lectureship in 1916 after being found guilty on a charge relating to a leaflet he had written in support of the No-Conscription Fellowship (he was reinstated in 1919). In 1918 he was imprisoned for an article he wrote in *The Tribune* that resulted in his being charged and found guilty of sedition on the grounds that the article was prejudicial to Britain's relations with its American ally.

Shepherd, J. *George Lansbury: At the Heart of Old Labour* (Oxford: Oxford University Press, 2002)

Swanwick, H. M. *I Have Been Young* (London: Victor Gollancz, 1935)
Helena Swanwick was the editor (1909-14) of the suffragist newspaper, *The Common Cause*, from which she resigned in 1914 because of differences with her colleagues over the issue of war. Served as a member of the executive committee of the Union of Democratic Control and as chairman of the Women's International League for Peace and Freedom (1915-22). Throughout the war she lent her support to the campaign for a negotiated peace and the future creation of an organization devoted to maintaining international peace. She was unhappy with the terms both of the Versailles settlement and of the League of Nations as it was set up in 1919

Vellacott, J. 'Marshall, Catherine Elizabeth (1880–1961)', *Oxford Dictionary of National Biography*, Oxford University Press, 2004 (online edn) See also note 23

Vipont, E., pseud. [i.e. Elfrida Vipont Foulds]. *Arnold Rowntree: A Life* (London: Bannisdale Press, 1955)
Arnold Rowntree (part of the family Rowntree Cocoa business) was a member of the Liberal Party and elected the MP for York in the 1910 General Election. Strongly critical of the foreign policy of Herbert Asquith and Sir Edward Grey and opposed to Britain's involvement in the First World War, he joined the joined the Union of Democratic Control (UDC) at the beginning of the war although he severed his connection with it shortly afterwards

Books

Addams, J. *Women at the Hague: The International Congress of Women and its Results* (Urbana: University of Illinois Press, 2003)
Originally published New York : Macmillan, 1915

Barrett, C. *Subversive Peacemakers, War Resistance 1914–1918: An Anglican Perspective* (Cambridge: Lutterworth Press, 2014)

Bussy, G, and M. Tims. *Pioneers for Peace: Women's International League for Peace and Freedom 1915-1965*, 2nd ed (London: Women's International League for Peace and Freedom, 1980)

Ceadel, M. *Pacifism in Britain 1914-1945: The Defining of a Faith* (Oxford: Clarendon Press, 1980)

— *Semi-Detached Idealists: The British Peace Movement and International Relations, 1854–1945* (Oxford: Oxford University Press, 2000)

Crosby, G. R. *Disarmament and Peace in British Politics, 1914-1919* (Cambridge, Mass: Harvard University Press, 1957)

Forster, K. *The Failures of Peace: The Search for a Negotiated Peace during the First World War* (Washington: American Council on Public Affairs, 1941)

Laity, P. *The British Peace Movement 1870-1914* (Oxford: Oxford University Press, 2001)

McCallum, R B. *Public Opinion and the Last Peace* (London: Oxford University Press, 1944)

Martin, L. W. *Peace Without Victory: Woodrow Wilson and the British Liberals* (New Haven: Yale University Press; repr. London: Kennikat Press, 1973)

Newberry, J. V. 'Russell and the Pacifists in World War 1', in *Russell in Review: The Bertrand Russell Centenary Celebrations at McMaster University, October 12-14, 1972*, edited by J. E. Thomas and Kenneth Blackwell (Toronto: Stevens, Hakkert, 1976)

Patterson, D. S. *The Search for Negotiated Peace: Women's Activism and Citizen Diplomacy in World War I* (London: Routledge, 2007)

Pierson, R. R., ed. *Women And Peace: Theoretical, Historical and Practical Perspectives* (London: Croom Helm, 1987)

Robbins, K. *The Abolition of War, 1914-1919: The Peace Movement in Britain 1914-1919* (Cardiff: University of Wales Press, 1976)

Russell, B. A. W., 3rd Earl Russell. *Pacifism and Revolution, 1916-18*, edited by Richard Rempel [and others], Collected papers of Bertrand Russell, 14 (London: Routledge, 1995)
This volume includes papers from the period when Bertrand Russell was writing for *The Tribunal*, the official weekly publication of the No-Conscription Fellowship, of which Russell was Acting Chairman. These papers reveal Russell's reactions to the manner in which the war had developed, and reflect his growing dedication to pacifism and the sort of political and philosophical issues which were to become characteristic of his future work.

Swanwick, H M. *Builders of Peace: Being Ten Years' History of the Union of Democratic Control* (London: Swarthmore Press, 1924)

Vellacott, J. *Bertrand Russell and the Pacifists in the First World War* (Brighton: Harvester, 1980)

Wallis, J. *Valiant For Peace: A History of The Fellowship of Reconciliation, 1914-1989* (London: Fellowship of Reconciliation, 1991)
The Fellowship of Reconciliation was inaugurated in Cambridge in 1914, on the brink of the Great War, and has been involved in campaigning, peace and reconciliation in conflicts around the world ever since

Wiltsher, A. *Most Dangerous Women: Feminist Peace Campaigners of the Great War* (London: Pandora, 1985)

Theses

Hafer, P. C. 'The Paths to Peace: The Efforts of Norman Angell, 1914–1918' (unpublished doctoral thesis, Ball State University, 1972)

Hines, P. D. 'Norman Angell: Peace Movement, 1911-1915' (unpublished doctoral thesis, Ball State University, 1964)

Articles

Alexander, H. G. 'A Nearly Forgotten Chapter in British Peace Activity – 1915', *Journal of the Friends' Historical Society*, 55 (1987), 139-43

Bisceglia, L. 'The Politics of a Peace Prize' *Journal of Contemporary History*, 7 (1972), 263-273

Bowen, E. J. 'Attitudes to Peace And War - Sussex Peace Groups, 1914-1945', *Southern History*, 9 (1987), 141-59

Crangle, J. V and J. O. Baylen. 'Emily Hobhouse's Peace Mission, 1916', *Journal of Contemporary History*, 14 (1979), 731-44

Larsen, D. 'War Pessimism in Britain and an American Peace in Early 1916', *International History Review*, 34 (2012), 795-817

Martin, L. W. 'Woodrow Wilson's Appeals to the People of Europe: British Radical Influence on the President's Strategy', *Political Science Quarterly*, 74 (1959), 498-516

Morgan, K. O. 'Peace Movements in Wales, 1899-1945', *Welsh History Review*, 10 (1980-81), 398-430

Newberry, J. V. 'Anti-War Suffragists', *History*, 62 (1977), 411-425

Sacks, B. F. 'The Independent Labour Party and World War Peace Objectives', *Pacific Historical Review*, 5 (1936), 161-73

Stevenson, D. 'The Failure of Peace by Negotiation in 1917', *Historical Journal*, 34, (1991), 65-86

Vellacott, J. 'A Place for Pacifism and Transnationalism in Feminist Theory: The Early Work of the WILPF [Women's International League for Peace and Freedom]', *Women's History Review*, 2 (1993), 23–56

Weinroth, H. 'Peace by Negotiation and the British Anti-War Movement, 1914-1918', *Canadian Journal of History*, 10 (1975), 369-92

Winters, F. 'Exaggerating the Efficacy of Diplomacy: The Marquis of Lansdowne's 'Peace Letter' of November 1917', *International History Review*, 32 (2010), 25-46

Contemporary Material

The works selected below that were published during the war years provide an idea of some contemporary attitudes and philosophising on the question of achieving peace or adopting a pacifist stance (and in some case the dangers of such a stance) in the circumstances of the war in which Britain was engaged.

Angell, Sir N. *Modern Wars and the Peace Ideal* (London: National Labour Press, 1915)

Ballard, F. *The Mistakes of Pacifism, or, Why a Christian Can Have Anything To Do With War* (London: Charles H. Kelly, 1915)

Buxton, C. R., ed. *Towards a Lasting Settlement*, by G. L. Dickinson [and others] (London: Allen & Unwin, 1915)
This work contains the following chapters: The basis of permanent peace, by G. L. Dickinson; Nationality, by C. R. Buxton; The freedom of the seas, by H. Sidebotham; The open door, by J. A. Hobson; The parallel of the great French war, by Irene C. Willis; War and the woman's movement, by A. Maude Royden.; The organization of peace, by H. N. Brailsford; Democracy and publicity in foreign affairs, by P. Snowden; The democratic principle and international relations, by Vernon Lee [pseud.]

Chesterton, C. E. *The Perils of Peace*, with an introduction by Hilaire Belloc (London: Werner Laurie, 1917)

Coulton, G. G. *The Main Illusions of Pacifism: A Criticism of Mr. N. Angell and of the Union Of Democratic Control* (Cambridge: Bowes and Bowes, 1916)
Coulton was a strong supporter of the National Service League, advocating compulsory national service for home defence, and an energetic campaigner for it; his book *The Case for Compulsory Military Service* (1917) ran to nearly 400 pages.

— *Pacifist Illusions: A Criticism of the Union of Democratic Control* (Cambridge: Bowes & Bowes, 1915)

Dickinson, G. L. *The War and the Way Out* (London: Chancery Lane Press, 1915)

Gosling, H. *Peace: How to Get and Keep It* (London: Cassell, 1917)

Hart, H. L. *The Bulwarks of Peace* (London: Methuen, 1918)

Hayward, C. W. *The Abolition of War: The British Empire's Terrible Responsibility - and Glorious Opportunity* (London: Daniel, 1916)

Heath, C. *Pacifism in Time of War* (London: Headley, 1915)

Lansdowne, H. C. K. Petty-Fitzmaurice., 5th Marquis of Lansdowne. '[Letter Calling for Belligerents to Present their War Aims and Consider the Possibilities of a Negotiated Peace]', *Daily Telegraph*, 29 November, 1917

MacClure, S. S. *Obstacles to Peace* (London: Paul, 1917)

Marshall, C., and others *Militarism versus Feminism: Writings on Women and War*, by Catherine Marshall, C. K. Ogden and Mary Sargant Florence (London Allen & Unwin, 1915)
These essays written during the early months of the First World War provide an insight into the beginnings of pacifism and feminism in the twentieth century. A reprint of this work, edited by Margaret Kamester and Jo Vellacott has been published: London: Virago, 1987.

Martin, H.., ed. *The Ministry of Reconciliation; Christian Pacifism: Its Grounds and Implications* (London: Headley, 1917)

Nordentoft, S. *Practical Pacifism and its Adversaries* ... with an introduction by G. K. Chesterton (London: Allen & Unwin, 1917)

Peace Overtures and their Rejection, UDC Pamphlets, 27 (London: Union of Democratic Control, 1918)

Owen, H. *Disloyalty: The Blight of Pacifism* (London: Hurst & Blackett, 1918)

Preston, Sir J. *Peace and Victory* (London: Nisbet, 1917)

Prothero, Sir G. W. *A Lasting Peace: A Conversation Between X. (a Neutral) and Y. (an Englishman)* (London: Hodder & Stoughton, 1917)

Russell, B. A. W., 3rd Earl Russell. *The Philosophy of Pacifism*, Peace and Freedom Pamphlets, 1 (London: Headley, 1915)

Solano, E. J. *The Pacifist Lie: A Book for Sailors and Soldiers* (London: Murray, 1918)

Wellock, W. *Pacifism: What It Is and What It Is Capable of Doing: An Appeal to the Churches and to the Democracy* (Manchester: Blackfriars Press, 1916)

Between 1914 and 1918 the Union of Democratic Control produced a number of leaflets on the cause of peace and ways of achieving it. Some examples are listed below (the asterisked items were rejected by the Censor):

America and a Permanent Peace, Leaflet 31

How to Get a Permanent Peace, Leaflet 44

Labour and a Permanent Peace, Leaflet 24

President Wilson's Message to the World, Leaflet 33

President Wilson's Peace Terms (The Fourteen Points), Leaflet 47

Some People Are Asking: Is This the Time to Talk about Terms of Settlement?, Leaflet 7

Suggestions for Terms of a Peace Settlement, Leaflet 39

Terms of Peace, by C. R Buxton, Leaflet 18

Then Why Go On?, Leaflet 38 *

Trevelyan, C. *The Case for Negotiations*, Leaflet 27 *

Why Must the War Go on?, by A Ponsonby, Leaflet 29 *

Why We Should Think about Peace, by A. Ponsonby, Leaflet 10

2.11.4 League of Nations Ideas

Early in the war, at a time when the phrase, "the war to end war" began to circulate and H. G. Wells had published his book, *The War that Will End War* (October 1914) and George Bernard Shaw had written "in the future we must fight, not alone for England, but for the welfare of the world" (in 'The Last Spring of the Old Lion', *New Statesman*, Dec. 12, 1914), it was evident that there had begun to develop a concern, felt not only by pacifists but also by some supporters of the war, for the need to prevent war in the future by some form of post-war league of nations. This concern gathered momentum as the war progressed and grew into a campaign which began to have a significant impact as the British people became increasingly aware, particularly in 1917 and 1918, of the devastating effects of the war in which they were engaged.

One of the central figures in this campaign was Goldsworthy Lowes Dickinson. From the very beginning of the war he endeavoured, as a member of the Cambridge section of the UDC, to promote a debate on the idea of a league of nations (a phrase which may have originated with him) as a means of preventing war and soon found support from a wide range of liberal opinion. In this debate the Bryce Group which he inaugurated played an important part. This Group, so named after Lord Bryce who was its nominal chairman, was a loosely organised committee of Liberals and some UDC participants like J. A. Hobson, Norman Angell and Arthur Ponsonby. As the views of this Group, and all the other individuals and bodies who joined in the debate, developed it became evident that they contained considerable differences of detail but, nevertheless, aided by the publications of intellectuals like Dickinson, Bryce, Brailsford, Angell, Woolf, and Hobson, a broad acceptance in progressive Liberal circles of the idea of some kind of new international league had emerged by mid-1915, and this proved to be sufficiently influential to inspire the establishment of a League of Nations Society (May 1915). The latter society, formed by Dickinson and numbering among its ranks J. A. Hobson and H. N. Brailsford, was in agreement with the UDC's focus on the problem of preventing future wars but, whereas the UDC initially concentrated on the idea of solving it by means of a democratic control over foreign policy, the society took the view that it could best be solved by developing the idea of a league of nations based on a proactive system of mutual defence against aggression ('collective security' as termed by J. A. Hobson). The UDC also in due course embraced the league of nations approach.

Ideas about a post-war league of nations were taking shape throughout the war but it was not until the last two years of the war that they began to have a major impact. In those years war weariness and industrial unrest reached a peak and the public were more willing to listen to ideas about peace and the prevention of wars. In this changing atmosphere people and groups who supported the idea of a league of nations became more active in publicising and promoting it. In 1917 the UDC set out its proposals, among which were a comprehensive peace programme which included the foundation of an International Council or League of Nations, and in the same year the League of Nations Society[24] held an influential first mass meeting (League of Nations Society. *Proceedings of the First Annual Meeting held at the Caxton Hall, July 20th 1917*, see below under **Contemporary Material**). In government circles Lord Robert Cecil became convinced by the horrific nature of the war that some form of league of nations must be formed at the end of the war, and the Labour Party embraced the views of the Independent Labour Party and the UDC about a post-war league in its Memorandum on War Aims (December 1917). In 1918 H. G. Wells was recruited by Lord Northcliffe's ministry of propaganda at Crewe House, to work on a statement of war aims, a task which was to include the matter of the setting up of a league

---

[24] In the following year (24 June 1918) another body, the League of Free Nations Association, was established under the Chairmanship of Gilbert Murray but soon after its establishment it was merged with the League of Nations Society to form the League of Nations Union (on October 13th 1918), describing itself as a British organization founded to promote the formation of a World league of free peoples for the securing of international justice, mutual defence and permanent peace.

of nations[25]; even Lloyd George himself, hitherto wedded entirely to the concept of the 'knock-out' blow, felt obliged to refer to the league idea in his address on war aims to an audience of trades unionists at Caxton Hall on 5 January 1918, and subsequently to highlight it by giving 'A League of Nations' a separate subheading, in the published version of the address.

President Wilson's championship of the League idea also began to have an influence on opinion in Britain, especially after the American entry into the war. By the close of the war many people in Britain were beginning to feel that the best hope for lasting peace in the future lay in a league of nations as encapsulated in Wilson's 'Fourteen Points'. As Bertrand Russell put it in his *Portraits from Memory*, "during the last weeks [of the war], in common with most other people, I based my hopes on Wilson with his Fourteen Points and his league of nations".

The development of the League idea owed a great deal to the dilemma with which many liberal intellectuals were confronted when faced with the prospect of the war, namely, having to make a choice between supporting or opposing their country's involvement in it. For those intellectuals who, like Bryce and Wells, fully supported the war, or who like Dickinson and Leonard Woolf, reluctantly accepted it because they could see no practical way to oppose it, promoting the concept of a league of nations was the means by which they could ease their troubled consciences; they felt that by helping to develop a radical and constructive new deal in international relations for a lasting peace in the future the huge sacrifice of life would not ultimately be in vain. Not all liberal intellectuals, however were convinced by this argument. L. P Jacks, the editor of the *The Hibbert Journal*, for example, felt that the likely persistence of international hatreds and ambitions did not bode well for the success of such a league, and made it clear in his article, 'Human Nature and the War' (*Current History*, vol 5, 1916) that in his view "the federation of the world would be a cockpit of civil war". He was not alone in this sceptical attitude, but the views of those who shared it did not prevent the League idea from growing in popularity towards the end of the war.

Autobiographies, Biographies

Ceadel, M. *Living the Great Illusion: Sir Norman Angell, 1872-1967* (Oxford: Oxford University Press, 2009)

Cecil, R., 1st Viscount Cecil of Chelwood. *A Great Experiment: An Autobiography* (London: Cape, 1941)
Robert Cecil (1864-1958) was parliamentary under-secretary, foreign affairs, 1915-18; Minister of Blockade, 1916-18; assistant secretary of state, foreign affairs, 1918-19 He became the first ministerial convert to the league of nations idea, circulating a memorandum on the subject in September 1916 and, thereafter, continuing to exert pressure on the government to commit itself to the idea. In January 1919 he was appointed as adviser on league issues to Britain's delegation at the Paris peace conference, where he played an important part in establishing the League of Nations and helping to shape its covenant.

Dickinson, G. L. *The Autobiography of G. Lowes Dickinson and other Unpublished Writings*, edited by D. Proctor (London: Duckworth, 1973)
Dickinson was a lecturer in political science at Kings College, Cambridge, 1896-1920. Because of his belief that international anarchy was the root cause of the war he became an advocate soon after its outbreak for the establishment of a league of nations (a term of which he may have been the inventor). He was the inaugurator of the Bryce Group, a loosely organised committee of Liberals whose object (under the nominal chairmanship of Lord Bryce) was to discuss ways of preventing wars in the future, particularly by means of a league of nations. His critical attitude to the war found its most positive expression in his involvement with the Union of Democratic Control.

Fisher, H. A. L. *James Bryce*, 2 vols (London: Macmillan, 1927; repr. Westport, Conn.: Greenwood Press, 1973)
Bryce was a jurist, historian and statesman. Served 1907-13 as ambassador to the United States. Presided over the commission to consider alleged German atrocities. An enthusiastic supporter during the war of the idea of a league of nations. The Bryce Group, a loosely organised committee of Liberals whose object (under the nominal chairmanship of Lord Bryce) was to discuss ways of preventing wars in the future, particularly by means of a league of nations, was named after him.

Forster, E. M. *Goldsworthy Lowes Dickinson* (London: Edward Arnold, 1934; repr. 1962)

Leventhal, F. M. *The Last Dissenter: H. N. Brailsford and His World* (Oxford: Clarendon, 1985)

---

[25] H.G. Wells expanded his ideas about a league of nations in his book, *In the Fourth Year: Anticipations of a World Peace*, published in 1918.

As a journalist Brailsford wrote successively for the *Manchester Guardian*, *Daily News*, and the *Nation* from 1907-23. He joined the Independent Labour Party in 1907. Served on the Executive Committee of the Union of Democratic Control and on the Labour Party Advisory Committee on International Questions in both of which committees he was an advocate of a negotiated peace and a settlement that did not aim to be punitive. He was also an advocate of a league of nations, proposals for which he outlined in his work of that name (see below under **Contemporary Material**). His ideas were well known not only in Britain but also in the USA where they came to the notice of President Woodrow Wilson's advisers.

Townshend, J. *J. A. Hobson* (Manchester: Manchester University Press, 1990)
Hobson, an economist and frequent contributor to *The Nation* (1906-20), was an active member of the International Arbitration League and among the founders of the British Neutrality Committee (inaugurated just before the outbreak of the war). During the war he was a member of the Bryce Group, a loosely organised committee of Liberals whose object (under the nominal chairmanship of Lord Bryce) was to discuss ways of preventing wars in the future, particularly by means of a league of nations) He also served on the executive committee of the Union of Democratic Control, where he was an advocate of a negotiated peace settlement and open diplomacy.

Wilson, D. *Leonard Woolf: A Political Biography* (London: Hogarth Press, 1978)

Woolf, L. S. *An Autobiography*, with an introduction by Quentin Bell, 2 vols (Oxford: Oxford University Press, 1980)
First published as a 5 vol work between 1960 and 1969 under titles: *Sowing* (1880-1904); *Growing* (1904-1911); *Beginning Again* (1911-1918); *Downhill All the Way* (1919-1939); and, *The Journey not the Arrival Matters* (1939-1969).

Books

Bartlett, R. J. *The League to Enforce Peace* (Chapel Hill: University of North Carolina Press, 1944)

Cecil, H. 'Lord Robert Cecil and the League of Nations during the First World War', in *Home Fires and Foreign Fields, British Social and Military Experience in The Great War*, edited by P. H. Liddle (Manchester: Manchester University Press, 1985)

Egerton, G. W. *Great Britain and the Creation of the League of Nations: Strategy, Politics, and International Organisation, 1914–1919* (London: Scolar Press, 1979)

Manson, J. M. 'Leonard Woolf as an Architect of the League of Nations', in *Voyages Out, Voyages Home*. Selected Papers from the Eleventh Annual Conference on Virginia Woolf, edited by Jane de Gay and Marion Dell (Clemson, SC: Clemson University Digital Press, 2010)

Marburg, T. *The Development of the League of Nations Idea: Documents and Correspondence of Theodore Marburg*, edited by John H. Latané, 2 vols (New York: Macmillan, 1932)

Mason, C. M. 'British Policy on the Establishment of a League of Nations, 1914-1919' (unpublished doctoral thesis, University of Cambridge, 1970)

Pedersen, S. *The Guardians: The League of Nations and the Crisis of Empire* (Oxford: Oxford University Press, 2015)

Winkler, H. R. *The League of Nations Movement in Great Britain, 1914-1919* (New Brunswick, N.J.: Rutgers University Press, 1952)

Theses

Cecil, H. P. 'The Development of Lord Robert Cecil's Views on the Securing of a Lasting Peace, 1915-19' (unpublished doctoral thesis, University of Oxford, 1971)

McCarthy, H. *The British People and the League of Nations: Democracy, Citizenship and Internationalism, c. 1918-45* (Manchester: Manchester University Press, 2011)

Raffo, P. S. 'Lord Robert Cecil and the League of Nations' (unpublished doctoral dissertation, University of Liverpool, 1967)

Articles

Robbins. K. G. 'Lord Bryce and the First World War, *Historical Journal*, 10 (1967), 255-78

Yearwood, P. J. Guarantee of Peace: The League of Nations in British Policy, 1914-1925 (Oxford: Oxford University Press, 2009)

— '"On the Safe and Right Lines": The Lloyd George Government and the Origins of the League of Nations, 1916–1918', *Historical Journal*, 32 (1989), 131-155
This article covers such matters as the coalition government's attitude to the concept of establishing a league of nations, the incorporation of ideas for a 'league of nations to insure peace and justice' as an important plank in President Wilson's peace initiative, the joint endorsement of the creation of such a body by the *Entente* in response to Wilson's initiative, and the explanation by A. J. Balfour, the foreign secretary, that, as a condition of durable peace, 'behind international law, and behind all treaty arrangements for preventing or limiting hostilities, some form of international sanction should be devised which would give pause to the hardiest aggressor'.

Contemporary Material

Angell. Sir N. *The Political Conditions of Allied Success: A Plea for the Protective Union of the Democracies* (New York and London: Putnam's, 1918)

— *War Aims: The Need for a Parliament of the Allies* (London: Headley, 1917)

Barker, Sir E. *A Confederation of Nations: Its Powers and Constitution* (Oxford: Clarendon Press, 1918)

Brailsford, H. N. *The Covenant of Peace: An Essay on the League of Nations* (London: Headley, 1918)

— *A League of Nations* (London: Headley, 1917)

Bryce, J. W., Viscount Bryce of Dechmont, and others. *Proposals for The Prevention of Future Wars* (London: Allen & Unwin, 1917)

Cock, R. *Counsel of European Nations* (London: Elliot Stock, 1918)

Dickinson, G. L. *Foundations of a League of Peace* (Boston, Mass.: World Peace Foundation, 1915)

— *Problems of International Settlement*, [by] the Central Organization for a Durable Peace, the Hague, [With and Introduction by G. Lowes Dickinson] (London: Allen & Unwin for the National Peace Council, 1918)

Gore, C. *The League of Nations: The Opportunity of the Church.* (London: Hodder & Stoughton, 1918)

Henderson, A. *The League of Nations and Labour* (London: Oxford University Press, 1918)

Hobson, J. A. *A League of Nations*, UDC Pamphlets, 15a (London: Union of Democratic Control, 1915)

— *Towards International Government* (London: Allen & Unwin, 1915)

Houston, H. S. *Blocking New Wars* (London: Allen & Unwin, 1918)

Jacks, L. P. 'Human Nature and The War', *Current History*, 5 (1916)

Keen, F. N. *A League of Nations with Large Powers* (London: Allen & Unwin, 1918)

Lloyd George, D. *British War Aims: Statement by the Prime Minister ... on January 5, 1918* (London: H.M.S.O., 1918)
"This statement was delivered to a meeting of the Representatives of Labour called to consider the question of further efforts for the prosecution of the war." – verso of title page. Lloyd George referred to a League of Nations in this statement.

Murray, G. *The League of Nations and the Democratic Idea* (Oxford: Oxford University Press, 1918)

Paish, G.. *A Permanent League of Nations* (London: T. Fisher Unwin, 1918)

Pollard, A. F. *The League of Nations; An Historical Argument* (Oxford: Clarendon, 1918)

Smuts, J. C. *The League of Nations: A Practical Suggestion* (London: Hodder and Stoughton, 1918)

Wells, H. G. *In the Fourth Year: Anticipations of a World Peace* (London : Chatto & Windus, 1918)
Caption title: *In The Fourth Year: The League of Free Nations*. In 1918 Wells was recruited by Lord Northcliffe's propaganda ministry at Crewe House, where his task was to work on a statement of war aims, chief among which was the setting up of the League of Nations.

Woolf, L. S. *The Framework of a Lasting Peace* (London: Allen & Unwin, 1917)

— *International Government*: Two Reports by L. S. Woolf prepared for the Fabian Research Department, Together with a Project, by a Fabian Committee, for a Supernational Authority that Will Prevent War (London: Fabian Society, 1916)
"This volume is the outcome of a Committee of the Fabian Research Department ... To Mr. L. S. Woolf was committed the task of preparing two reports (which appear as Parts I and II of this volume); and upon this investigation the Committee drafted what now stands as Part III". Another issue of this work was published by Allen & Unwin in 1916 'with an introduction by Bernard Shaw'.
"Part 1, the first of Woolf's two reports, and pt. 3, the Fabian International Agreements Committee's project (Articles suggested for adoption by an international conference ...) appeared first in London in 1915 as supplements to the July 10 and July 17 issues of the *New Statesman*, with collective title, 'Suggestions for the prevention of war'."
[Information provided in the catalogue record of the online print of *International Government* at: https://archive.org/details/internationalgo00commgoog]
Woolf's reports became part of the basis for the League of Nations and then the United Nations.

A substantial amount of material was published by the **League of Nations Society** during the war. Some examples are listed below.

Brodie, J., ed. *The Demand of Labour for a League of Nations* (1918)

— *The Demand of the Churches for a League of Nations* (1918)

Dickinson, W. H., 1st Baron Dickinson. *Disarmament and a League of Nations* (1918)

— *A League of Nations and its Critics* (1917)

Gooch, G. P. *The Project of a League of Nations* (1917)

Grey, E., 1st Viscount Grey of Fallodon. *A League of Nations* (1918)

— *Viscount Grey on a League of Nations, at a meeting held at Central Hall, Westminster, October 10, 1918* (1918)

League of Nations Society. *Explanations and Objects of the Society* (1916)

— *How to Prevent War* (1917)

— *League of Nations: Scheme of Organisation*, prepared by a sub-committee of the League of Nations Society; with a foreword by Sir W. H. Dickinson, Chairman of the sub-committee (1918)

— *The League of Nations Society* (1915)

— *Proceedings of the First Annual Meeting held at the Caxton Hall, July 20th 1917*: including the report of the Executive Committee from the beginning of the Society to March 31st 1917 (1917)

— *Report of Meeting, May 14th, 1917*: Speeches delivered by Viscount Bryce, General Smuts ... [and others] (1917)

Shaw, T., 1st Baron Craigmyle. *An Address Delivered by Lord Shaw of Dunfermline at a General Meeting of the [League Of Nations] Society, 15th December, 1916*, League of Nations Society Publications, 7 (1917)

— *The League of Nations: Speech by Lord Shaw of Dunfermline, House of Lords, June 26th, 1918* (1917)

Stephen, K. *Arbitration in History* (1918)

Spalding, H. N. *What a League of Nations Means* (1918)

Unwin, Sir R. *Functions of a League of Nations* (1917)

Williams, A. *A League of Nations: How to Begin It* (1917)

— *The Minimum of Machinery* (1917)

Wilson, W. *The League of Nations: "The Final Triumph of Justice and Fair Dealing"*, latest speech by President Wilson, New York, September 27, 1918 (1918)

Woolf, L. S. *A Durable Settlement after the War by means of a League of Nations* (1917)

Although **The League of Free Nations Association** (founded 24 June 1918) had only a brief existence before it was merged with the League of Nations Society to form the League of Nations Union (on October 13th 1918), it published under its name a number of pamphlets, examples of which are listed below:

Bennett, A. *Independence and Sovereignty* (1918)

Bourgeois, L. *A Great French Statesman Explains Why We Must Form the League of Nations Now* (1918)

Davies, D. *The Church and the League of Nations* (1918)

League of Free Nations Association. *The League of Free Nations Association* (1918)

McCurdy, C. A. *The League of Free Nations* (1918)

Stead, F. H. *The Case for an International Police Force* (1918)

2.11.5 Union of Democratic Control

The Union of Democratic Control was founded in the month after the outbreak of war by Charles P. Trevelyan (the main promoter), E. D. Morel, Ramsay MacDonald, Arthur Ponsonby, and Norman Angell with the object of organizing a group of opponents of the war and committing them to the task of, firstly, establishing parliamentary control over foreign policy and ending secret diplomacy; secondly, ensuring that the post-war negotiations were such as 'to form an international understanding depending on popular parties rather than on governments'; and, thirdly, achieving peace terms that treated the defeated nations fairly and did not artificially rearrange frontiers in a way liable to cause future wars[26]. Derived from these three objectives but with the addition of the objective of armament control, the UDC's manifesto of four cardinal points[27] for a durable peace settlement was drawn up in September 1914 and remained the focus of the organisation's major objectives until

---

[26] These three objectives were the basis of a private circular drawn up by Trevelyan with the participation of MacDonald, Angell, and Morel in the second week of the war.

[27] **1**. No Province shall be transferred from one Government to another without the consent by plebiscite or otherwise of the population of such Province. **2**. No Treaty, Arrangement, or Undertaking shall be entered upon in the name of Great Britain without the sanction of Parliament. Adequate machinery for ensuring democratic control of foreign policy shall be created. **3**. The Foreign Policy of Great Britain shall not be aimed at creating alliances for the purpose of maintaining the 'Balance of Power', but shall be directed to concerted action between the Powers, and the setting up of an International Council, whose deliberations and decisions shall be public, with such machinery for securing international agreement as shall be the guarantee of an abiding peace. **4**. Great Britain shall propose, as part of the Peace Settlement, a plan for the drastic reduction, by consent, of the armaments of all the belligerent Powers, and to facilitate that policy shall attempt to secure the general nationalisation of the manufacture of armaments and the control of the export of armaments by one country to another [MacDonald, Trevelyan, Angell, and Morel, Circular Letter, Sept. 1914, and Manifesto: U.D.C., G.C. 1, Annex, 'Second Letter'].

the end of the war. The five founders quickly established the organization on a solid footing and comprised its first Executive Committee. The UDC was also set up with a General Council which in theory was its governing body but in practice it was the Executive Committee which managed affairs and developed policy. E. D. Morel, serving at first as both secretary and treasurer, rapidly became the dominant and driving force of the organisation, working full-time for it assisted by a small staff of secretaries and regional organizers.

Support for the organization came not only from radical Liberals but also from Labour, (increasingly large sections of which embraced the UDC's views as the war progressed) and a growing contingent of socialist members, especially from the Independent Labour Party. Some Quakers and other Christians (dismayed by the mostly jingoistic attitude of the established churches), and a number of those who had previously collaborated in anti-imperial, anti-South African War, and pro-women's suffrage campaigns, also joined the ranks of UDC membership. Among the politically active women who joined the organisation were Kate Courtney, Vernon Lee, Ethel Snowden, Mary Agnes Hamilton, Helena Swanwick, and Irene Cooper Willis. The many other intellectuals, publicists, and politicians who subsequently either became members of the organization or closely associated with it included Bertrand Russell, Henry N. Brailsford, J. A. Hobson, M. Phillips Price, Fenner Brockway, F. W. Pethick-Lawrence, G. P. Gooch, Lord Courtney of Penwith, G. Lowes Dickinson, Leonard Woolf, J. M. Keynes, Charles Roden Buxton, C. P. Scott, Graham Wallas, Israel Zangwill and MPs such as Arthur Henderson, F. W. Jowett, Philip Morrell, Philip Snowden, H. B. Lees-Smith, and Arnold Rowntree.

Within a year of its foundation, the UDC had established 50 local branches; at its peak in late 1917 it had reached its maximum membership of some 10,000 individuals in 100 branches. Apart from granting membership to individuals the UDC also accepted affiliated membership from societies, clubs, trade councils and local branches of the Independent Labour Party. Affiliation had a significant effect on UDC's membership. Affiliated organizations, mainly Labour, rose from about 50 in June 1915 to 107 (with a membership of over 300,000) in November of that year; by the end of the war the number of affiliated bodies had risen to 300 with a membership totalling 650,000.

The UDC did not subscribe to the popular and official view which attributed all guilt for the war to Germany, and joined the Independent Labour Party and peace organizations in calling for an early negotiated peace as opposed to a 'fight to the finish'. By 1917, encouraged by a climate of public opinion which was beginning to favour the idea of a post-war league of nations and by President Woodrow Wilson's interest in this and the idea of peace without victory, the UDC published in July of that year a comprehensive peace programme. This programme[28] was based on a number of principles which included no annexations or indemnities, the restoration of sovereignty to invaded countries, the internationalisation of colonial territories, the foundation of an International Council to keep the peace, disarmament, and the creation of machinery for the democratic control of foreign policy. By this time a strong alliance between the UDC and Labour had become well established and most of the UDC's members had become identified politically with Labour. In 1917 one-third of the Labour Party's national executive were members of the UDC and it is, therefore, not surprising that its memorandum on war aims of December 1917 followed the principles of the UDC peace manifesto so closely.

Initially the UDC relied heavily on the distribution of pamphlets to spread its propaganda, selling 500,000 in the first year of its foundation. After that, and for the duration of the war, the publication of pamphlets was reduced to a trickle as they were expensive and time-consuming to produce and not effective enough to gain mass support for the UDC's campaign. To achieve the latter goal the UDC began in 1915 to concentrate on holding public meetings and to publish its own journal. Public meetings, which the UDC actively mounted for the rest of the war, made a great contribution to the effectiveness of its propaganda campaign, commanding much wider public attention, particularly among workers, than could be achieved by the printed word alone.

The UDC and it members suffered a considerable amount of persecution and ill-treatment both from the government and the public. Meetings of the organisation were frequently subject to violent disruption and their speakers were sometimes assaulted. Some daily newspapers adopted an intensely hostile attitude to the organisation and maintained it throughout the war. It was by no means uncommon for raids to be made on the homes of its members; and Morel suffered a spell of 6 months in prison in 1917 for violating a DORA regulation. The strength of the public and governmental hostility that the activities of the UDC provoked is perhaps an indication of how effective and significant it was in the eyes of contemporaries.

---

[28] The UDC's peace programme appeared in the *Manchester Guardian*, 2 July 1917. It is also contained in Swanwick's *Builders of Peace* (1924), pp. 81-5. The *Manchester Guardian* published a criticism of the programme on 2 July and Charles Trevelyan's rebuttal on 11 July 1917; a criticism from a Fabian angle was published in the *New Statesman*, 7 July 1917.

One of the reasons why the UDC was able to make a significant impact was that it possessed among its members and supporters a number of distinguished and well-connected leaders who could bring to bear their considerable influence on the task of winning party and public support. The latter task was assisted by newspapers and journals which either supported the UDC (e.g. *War and Peace*, the *Daily Herald*, the *Labour Leader*, and the *Cambridge Magazine*), or were sympathetic to some of its views (e.g. the *Daily News*, the *Nation*, the *Manchester Guardian* and the *Westminster Gazette*), or held an attitude to the war close to that of the UDC (e.g. the weekly *Common Sense*).

Autobiographies, Biographies

Angell, N. *After All: An Autobiography* (London: Hamish Hamilton, 1951)

Brockway, A. F., Baron Brockway. *Inside the Left: Thirty Years of Platform, Press, Prison and Parliament* (London: Allen and Unwin, 1942; repr. 1947)

— *Socialism Over Sixty Years: The Life of Jowett of Bradford, 1864-1944* (London: Allen and Unwin, 1946)
Frederick Jowett was a socialist and politician consistently opposed to war throughout his life although he could not be considered a pacifist as he believed nations had a right to defend themselves. A member of the executive of the Union of Democratic Control, he aligned himself with those who wanted a clear definition of British war aims and peace by negotiation.

Brittain, V. *Pethick-Lawrence: A Portrait* (London: Allen & Unwin, 1963)
A biography of Baron Frederick William Pethick-Lawrence (1871-1961)

Bunsen, V. de. *Charles Roden Buxton: A Memoir* (London: Allen and Unwin, 1947)
Throughout the First World War Charles Buxton was consistently in favour of a peace by negotiation. He was a founder member of the Union of Democratic Control. In 1917 he left the Liberals and joined the Independent Labour Party.

Cline, C. *E. D. Morel, 1873–1924: The Strategies of Protest* (Dundonald, Belfast: Blackstaff, 1980)

Cocks, F. S. *E. D. Morel: The Man and His Work* (London: Allen and Unwin, 1920)
E. D. Morel joined the campaign for neutrality on the eve of war and when this failed helped to launch the Union of Democratic Control (UDC) of which he became secretary, an office he held until his death. During the war he was imprisoned for six months for a technical breach of the Defence of the Realm Act (DORA).

Dickinson, G. L. *The Autobiography of G. Lowes Dickinson and other Unpublished Writings*, edited by D. Proctor (London: Duckworth, 1973)
Dickinson was a lecturer in political science at Kings College, Cambridge, 1896-1920. Regarding international anarchy as the root cause of the war, he called soon after its outbreak for the establishment of a league of nations. He was prominent in the Bryce Group but his critical attitude to the war found its most positive expression in his involvement with the Union of Democratic Control.

Elton, G. E., Baron. *Life of James Ramsay MacDonald, 1866-1919* (London: Collins, 1939)

Fisher, H. A. L. *James Bryce*, 2 vols (London: Macmillan, 1927; repr. Westport, Conn.: Greenwood Press, 1973)

Forster, E. M. *Goldsworthy Lowes Dickinson* (London: Edward Arnold, 1934; repr. 1962)

Gooch, G. P. *Life of Lord Courtney* (London: Macmillan, 1920)
A biography of Leonard Henry Courtney, Baron Courtney of Penwith (1832-1918).

— *Under Six Reigns* (London: Longmans, 1958)

Gunn, P. *Vernon Lee: Violet Paget, 1856–1935* (London: Oxford University Press, 1964)
In the years just before the First World War, Vernon Lee, pseudonym of Violet Paget, employed her talents as an author to raise in a wide range of publications numerous political issues such as women's equality, economic justice, international co-operation, and anti-militarism. During the war, she joined the ranks of the Union of Democratic Control and supported the women's peace crusade. In 1915 she wrote the anti-war morality play, *The Ballet of the Nations* (republishing it in 1920 within

a philosophical commentary under the title of *Satan the Waste*).

Hamilton, M. A. *Arthur Henderson: A Biography* (London: William Heinemann, 1938)

— *Remembering My Good Friends* (London: Jonathan Cape, 1944)
In 1914 Mary Agnes Hamilton joined the Independent Labour Party (the constitution of which she helped to draw up) and was one of the original members of the Union of Democratic Control. She was an assistant editor of *Common Sense* in 1916, and also wrote for the monthly *War and Peace*. Her activities included membership of the *1917 Club* (a mixture of radical Liberals and the Labour left, founded by Ramsay Macdonald to promote world peace) and association with such intellectual circles as Lady Ottoline Morell's gatherings and a literary group which included the Woolfs, the Huxleys, D. H. Lawrence, and Lytton Strachey. By 1918 she had become well-known as a journalist and speaker.

Hammond, J. L. *C. P. Scott of the Manchester Guardian* (London: Bell & Sons, 1934)
Although initially supporting and encouraging the UDC he soon found that he could not continue to do this because of his differences with the UDC, not in relation to its basic objectives, but on the matter of prosecuting the war, the winning of which he believed should be the foremost priority.

Hobson, J. A. *Confessions of an Economic Heretic: The Autobiography of J. A. Hobson*, edited and introduced by Michael Freeden (London: Allen & Unwin, 1938; repr. Hassocks: Harvester, 1976)
Hobson served on the executive committee of the Union of Democratic Control

Jarrett, J. L., ed. 'D. H. Lawrence and Bertrand Russell', in *A D. H. Lawrence Miscellany*, ed. by H.T. Moore (Carbondale: Southern Illinois Press, 1959; repr. London: Heinemann, 1961)

Jones, R. A. *Arthur Ponsonby: The Politics of Life* (Bromley: Helm, 1989)
A critic of Grey's foreign policy, Arthur Ponsonby was one of the MPs against war in the debate of 3 August 1914. Helped to create a focus for those who disapproved of the war in the Union of Democratic Control, the organisation of which he was one of the founders. A member of the Bryce Group, the realization of the idea of a league of nations became an overriding objective for him.

Marquand, D. *Ramsay MacDonald* (London: Cape, 1977; repr. London: Richard Cohen, 1997)
In the pre-war years Ramsay Macdonald was an influential member of the Independent Labour Party (ILP) and played an important role in the formation of the Labour Party of which he became the chairman in 1911. In August 1914 he resigned from the chairmanship because of his opposition to the declaration of war and the Labour Party's support of it and, in collaboration with a group of other anti-war radicals, helped to found the Union of Democratic Control (UDC) [see notes 26 and 27 for the main objectives of this organization]. Throughout the war he maintained this anti-war stance both through the ILP (for which, after the death of Keir Hardie, he became the leading figure) and the Union of Democratic Control. The important link between the ILP and the UDC in their opposition to the war was very much due to Ramsay MacDonald's influential presence in both organisations.

Morris, A. J. A. *C. P. Trevelyan: Portrait of a Radical* (Belfast: Blackstaff Press, 1977)
Sir Charles Philips Trevelyan was liberal MP, Elland Division of Yorkshire, 1899-1918. Advocated peace by negotiation throughout the war. One of the founder members of the Union of Democratic Control. Became Union's principal advocate in the Commons.

Pethick-Lawrence, F. W., Baron Courtney of Penwith. *Fate Has Been Kind* (London: Hutchinson, 1943)
Baron Courtney was a pre-war women's suffrage campaigner. Became treasurer of the Union of Democratic Control. Stood unsuccessfully in 1917 at the by-election for South Aberdeen as a 'peace by negotiation' candidate. He was a conscientious objector, refusing to join up when he became liable for conscription in 1918 (he was assigned to work on the land).

Russell, B. A. W., 3rd Earl Russell. *Autobiography* (London: Routledge, 2000)
Originally published in 3 Vols [Vol 1, 1872-1914; Vol 2, 1914-1944; Vol 3, 1944-1967], London: Allen & Unwin, 1967-1969

Snowden, P., Viscount Snowden. *An Autobiography*, 2 vols. (London: Ivor Nicholson & Watson, 1934), I: *1864-1919*
Philip Snowden was the national chairman of the Independent Labour Party (ILP), 1903-06 and 1917-20. Labour MP for Blackburn, 1906-18. Supporter of conscientious objectors, taking a strong stand against conscription through the No Conscription Fellowship (NCF) (for whom, as the fellowship's chief spokesman in parliament, he subjected the government to continual harassment). Member of the Union of Democratic Control's General Council and Executive Committee but gave little time to his UDC activities. During the war he was, after Macdonald, the most influential leader of the ILP.

Swanwick, H. M. *I Have Been Young* (London: Victor Gollancz, 1935)
Helena Swanwick was the editor (1909-14) of the suffragist newspaper, *The Common Cause* from which she resigned in 1914 because of differences with her colleagues over the issue of war. Served as a member of the executive committee of the Union of Democratic Control and as chairman of the Women's International League for Peace and Freedom (1915-22). Throughout the war she lent her support to the campaign for a negotiated peace and the future creation of an organization devoted to maintaining international peace. She was unhappy with the terms both of the Versailles settlement and of the League of Nations as it was set up in 1919.

Trevelyan, C. P. *From Liberalism to Labour* (London: Allen and Unwin, 1921)
Sir Charles Philips Trevelyan was liberal MP, Elland Division of Yorkshire, 1899-1918. Advocated peace by negotiation throughout the war. Primary promoter, and founder member, of the Union of Democratic Control.

Vipont, E., pseud. [i.e. Elfrida Vipont Foulds]. *Arnold Rowntree: A Life* (London: Bannisdale Press, 1955)
Arnold Rowntree (part of the family Rowntree Cocoa business) was a member of the Liberal Party and elected the MP for York in the 1910 General Election. Strongly critical of the foreign policy of Herbert Asquith and Sir Edward Grey and opposed to Britain's involvement in the First World War, he joined the Union of Democratic Control (UDC) at the beginning of the war although he severed his connection with it shortly afterwards.

Woolf, L. *An Autobiography*, with an introduction by Quentin Bell, 2 vols (Oxford: Oxford University Press, 1980)
First published as a 5 vol work between 1960 and 1969 under titles: *Sowing* (1880-1904); *Growing* (1904-1911); *Beginning Again* (1911-1918); *Downhill All the Way* (1919-1939); and, *The Journey not the Arrival Matters* (1939-1969).
Leonard Woolf, the Fabian Society's foremost researcher in international affairs, was in frequent contact with leaders of the UDC

Wrigley, C. J. *Arthur Henderson* (Cardiff: University of Wales Press, 1990)
Arthur Henderson took over the chairmanship of the Labour party at the beginning of the war and briefly served as a member of the UDC's General Council, from which he resigned when he took cabinet office in the Coalition Government in 1915. After his resignation from the cabinet in 1917 he again became associated with the UDC, helping the Labour Party to implement UDC ideas by participating with Ramsay Macdonald and Sidney Webb in the formulation of a statement of war aims (later in December 1917 approved by the Labour movement as the *Memorandum on War Aims*) and playing a major role in the drafting of its new policy statement, *Labour and the New Social Order*, which was approved at the June 1918 conference.

Books

Ceadel, M. *Semi-Detached Idealists: The British Peace Movement and International Relations, 1854–1945* (Oxford: Oxford University Press, 2000)

Coulton, G. G. *The Main Illusions of Pacifism: A Criticism of Mr. N. Angell and of the Union of Democratic Control* (Cambridge: Bowes and Bowes, 1916)

— *Pacifist Illusions: A Criticism of the Union of Democratic Control* (Cambridge: Bowes & Bowes, 1915)

Fieldhouse, H. N. 'Noel-Buxton and A. J. P. Taylor's "The Trouble Makers"', in *A Century of Conflict, 1850-1950: Essays for A. J. P. Taylor*, edited by M. Gilbert (London: H. Hamilton, 1966)

Harris, S. *Out of Control: British Foreign Policy and the Union of Democratic Control, 1914–1918* (Hull: University of Hull Press, 1996)

Swartz, M. *The Union of Democratic Control in British Politics during the First World War* (Oxford: Clarendon Press, 1971)

Taylor, A. J. P. *The Trouble Makers: Dissent Over Foreign Policy, 1792-1939*, The Ford Lectures Delivered in the University of Oxford in Hilary Term, 1956 (London: Hamish Hamilton, 1957; repr. London: Pimlico, 1993)

Swanwick, H. M. *Builders of Peace: Being Ten Years' History of The Union of Democratic Control* (London: Swarthmore, 1924)

Trevelyan, C. P. *Union of Democratic Control: Its History and Its Policy* (London: U.D.C, 1919)

Wuliger, R. 'Idea of Economic Imperialism with Special Reference to the Life and work of E. D. Morel' (unpublished doctoral thesis, London School of Economics, 1953)

Articles

Hanak, H. 'The Union of Democratic Control during the First World War', *Bulletin of the Institute of Historical Research*, 36 (1963), 168-180

'[First public meeting of the UDC held in Cambridge on 4 March 1915]', *Cambridge Magazine*, 4, no.16 (6 March 1915)

Temperley, H. 'British Secret Diplomacy from Canning to Grey', *Cambridge Historical Journal*, 6 (1938), 1-32

Contemporary Material

Books, pamphlets and leaflets produced by the UDC in the Great War are listed below. The UDC also began publishing a monthly journal, *The U.D.C.* in November 1915 (from July 1919 it was *Foreign Affairs: A Journal of International Understanding*).

Pamphlets

A Misrepresentation Exposed (1918)

A Pole. *The Polish Problem* (1915)

Angell, N. *America and the Cause of the Allies* (1916)

— *The Prussian in Our Midst* (1915)

— *Shall This War End German Militarism?* (1914)

Brailsford, H. N. *The Origins of the Great War* (1914)

— *Turkey and the Roads of the East* (1916)

Dickinson, G. L. *Economic War after the War* (1916)

Gooch, G. P. *The Races of Austria-Hungary* (1917)

Hobson, J. A. *Labour and the Costs of War* (1916)

— *A League of Nations* (1915)

King, J. *The Russian Revolution: The First Year* (1918)

Lambert, R. C. *Alsace and Lorraine* (1918)

MacDonald, J. R. *War and the Workers* (1915)

Morel, E. D. *The African Problem and the Peace Settlement* (1917)

Morel, E. D., and others. *The Morrow of the War* (1914)

The National Policy (1915)

Newbold, J. T. W., and others. *The International Industry of War* (1915)

Peace Overtures and Their Rejection (1918)

Ponsonby, A. *Parliament and Foreign Policy* (1915)

Rex v. E. D. Morel: Trial at Bow Street (1917)

Russell, B. A. W., 3rd Earl Russell. *War - the Offspring of Fear* (1914)

Swanwick, H. M. *Women and War* (1915)

The Peace Debate in the House of Commons (May 23, 1916)

Tawney, R. L. *The War to End War: A Plea to Soldiers by a Soldier* (1917)

Towards an International Understanding: Being the Opinions of Some Allied and Neutral Writers (1915)

Why We Should State Terms of Settlement (1915)

Leaflets

The leaflets listed below were produced between 1914 and 1918 (the asterisked items were rejected by the Censor):

America and a Permanent Peace (Leaflet 31)

The Attack upon Freedom of Speech: Astounding Official Defence. House of Commons Sequel to the Broken-Up Meeting at the Memorial Hall, 29th November, 1915 (Leaflet 21)

The Attack upon Freedom of Speech: The Broken-Up Meeting at the Memorial Hall, 29th November, 1915 (Leaflet 20)

British Working-men - Observe! (Leaflet 34)

The Case for Negotiations, by C. Trevelyan (Leaflet 27) *

Crushing Germany (Leaflet 5)

Do Nations Want to Fight? (Leaflet 9)

Free Russia and the Union of Democratic Control, by E. D. Morel (Leaflet 37)

French Members of Parliament and the "Knock-out Blow" (Leaflet 35) *

General Smuts on Victory (Leaflet 45)

How to Get a Permanent Peace (Leaflet 44)

How to Obtain Popular Control over Foreign Policy (Leaflet 46)

Labour and a Permanent Peace (Leaflet 24)

Lord Loreburn and Lord Courtney of Penwith in the House of Lords, November 8th, 1915 (Leaflet 16)

Manifesto of Russian Workers and Soldiers (Leaflet 36)

Mr. Ponsonby and Mr. Trevelyan in the House of Commons, November 11th, 1915 (Leaflet 15)

Must the War Go on till Russia Gets Constantinople? (Leaflet 32) *

The Civilian Scene

Our Soldiers and the Union of Democratic Control (Leaflet 8)

Our Ultimate Objects in This War, by E. D. Morel (Leaflet 22)

A Patched-up Peace (Leaflet 12)

The Prime Minister's Declaration, February 23rd 1916 (Leaflet 26)

President Wilson's Message to the World (Leaflet 33)

President Wilson's Peace Terms (The Fourteen Points) (Leaflet 47)

Resolutions Passed at the Second Annual Meeting of the General Council of the Union of Democratic Control, October 10th 1916 (Leaflet 30)

Russia's Real Aims (Leaflet 39)

Secret Diplomacy, No. 1 (Leaflet 40)

Secret Diplomacy, No. 2 (Leaflet 41)

Secret Diplomacy, No. 3 (Leaflet 43)

Secret Diplomacy a Menace to the Security of the State, by E. D. Morel (Leaflet 19)

A Soldier's View (Corporal Lees Smith) (Leaflet 39)

Some People Are Asking: Is This the Time to Talk about Terms of Settlement? (Leaflet 7)

Suggestions for Terms of a Peace Settlement (Leaflet 39)

Terms of Peace, by C. R. Buxton (Leaflet 18)

The Union of Democratic Control, by E. D. Morel (Leaflet 13)

The Union of Democratic Control: Its Motives, Objects and Policy (Leaflet 23)

The Union of Democratic Control: What It Is and What It Is Not (Leaflet 14)

Then Why Go On? (Leaflet 38) *

Vindication of Mr. Morel in the House of Commons (Leaflet 42)

War and Diplomacy, by E.D. Morel (Leaflet 11)

What Is a Treaty? (Leaflet 6)

What Is the Balance of Power? (Leaflet 4)

What Our Allies Think about Economic War (Leaflet 28)

What the Press Now Say: More Support for the U.D.C. (Leaflet 17)

Why Have the People Taken No Interest in Foreign Affairs? (Leaflet 3)

Why Must the War Go on?, by A Ponsonby (Leaflet 29) *

Why Should Democracy Control Foreign Policy? (Leaflet 1)

Why We Should Think about Peace, by A. Ponsonby (Leaflet 10)

Why You Should Join the Union of Democratic Control (Leaflet 2)

Whither?, by E. D. Morel (Leaflet 25) *

Books

Brailsford, H. N. *A League of Nations* (London: Headley Bros., 1917)

— *The War of Steel and Gold*, 3rd edn (London: Bell & Sons, 1915)

Buxton, C. R. *Towards a Lasting Settlement* (London: Allen & Unwin, 1915)

Cocks, F. S. *The Secret Treaties and Understandings* (London: U.D.C., 1918)

Dickinson, G. L. *The European Anarchy* (London: Allen and Unwin, 1916)

Hobson, J. A. *Democracy After the War* (London: Allen and Unwin, 1917)

— *The New Protectionism* (London: Cobden Club, 1916)

— *Towards International Government* (London: Allen and Unwin, 1915)

Langdon Davies, B. N. *The A.B.C. of the U.D.C.* (London: U.D.C., 1915)

MacDonald, J. R. *National Defence: A Study In Militarism* (London: Allen and Unwin, 1917)

Morel, E. D. *Africa and the Peace of Europe* (London: National Labour Press, 1917)

— *Red Rubber*, rev. edn (London: National Labour Press, 1918)

— *Ten Years of Secret Diplomacy* (London: National Labour Press, 1915)

— *Truth and The War* (London: National Labour Press, 1916)

Pethick-Lawrence, F. W. *A Levy on Capital* (London: Allen and Unwin, 1918)

Ponsonby, A. *Democracy and Diplomacy* (London: Methuen, 1915)

— *Wars and Treaties, 1815-1914* (London: Allen and Unwin, 1918)

Woolf, L. S. *The Future of Constantinople* (London: Allen and Unwin, 1917)

2.12 War Hysteria

The war roused most of the population to a display of fierce nationalism which was inflamed by propaganda (conducted in its most base and obscene form by Horatio Bottomley and hardly less despicably by the British Empire Union[29]) and by the introduction of racism into parliamentary politics by Henry Page Croft's establishment of the National Party. This situation lent itself to outbreaks of mass hysteria which at times during the war manifested itself in acts of persecution, even of violence, against aliens and anti-war dissenters. This was compounded by the attitude of those in authority, including the police, who increasingly saw all forms of protest, whether principled political opposition, conscientious objection, or agitation arising from discontent

---

[29] The Anti-German League which became the British Empire Union after 1915 included among its ranks, Admiral Beresford, Havelock Wilson, Ellis Powell and William Joynson-Hicks. The BEU produced the 1918 film *Once a Hun, Always a Hun*, which advocated a ban on trading with Germany after the war.

with conditions in wartime industry, as unpatriotic, even subversive, and necessary to eradicate. Attempts by those in authority to stifle such protest whether it was expressed in the press, in pamphlet literature, in public meetings, or in the workplace were the direct result of this attitude.

Spy mania[30], the paranoia about an "Unseen Hand" [see below in the section on **Contemporary Material** under Women's Imperial Defence Council, *The "Unseen Hand" Meeting (1917)*], the shelling of coastal towns, Germany's use of gas on the Western front, the sinking of the Lusitania, the publication of the Bryce report on German atrocities, the Zeppelin raids, the threat posed by the successful German offensive in July 1918, and the generally jingoistic stance of the popular press and of much that was written about the war all contributed powerfully to anti German attitudes and to outbursts of mass hysteria, developing on occasions into mob violence, against aliens and dissenters.

It is not altogether surprising that in this atmosphere meetings took place at which speakers with particularly extreme anti-German views often found a ready platform for ranting about internal treason and treachery, the pernicious nature of German influences, and the horrors that would result from a German victory[31]. Admiral Charles Beresford called for full internment of enemy aliens and advocated the establishment of vigilante teams to search out foreign traitors. A particularly bigoted Conservative MP, William Joynson-Hicks, was also hostile to aliens and used the opportunity of sharing the platform with Dr Powell at a meeting on 8 February 1917 to voice his hostility to aliens, particularly, Germans resident in Britain. Dr Ellis Powell, editor of the *Financial News*, attracted huge crowds in his speeches about the German-inspired 'unseen hand' ('a magnetic and dexterous personality ... at work permeating every department of our public life, rewarding subservience, and penalising independence'). Speeches like these were readily echoed in extremist literature in which homosexuality and all other things thought to be perverse were attributed to Germany's malign influence[32]. In a wartime article, *Efficiency and Vice*, Arnold White accused Germany of attempting 'to abolish civilisation as we know it, to substitute Sodom and Gomorrah for the New Jerusalem, and to infect clean nations with Hunnish erotomania'. Some spy novels also expressed this popular race hatred and national paranoia[33], helping the spread of spy mania and xenophobia among the British people - one of the war's most unpleasant aspects. Spy novels often alleged German infiltration of the highest levels of British society, stimulating the 'hidden hand' belief held by some that British military defeats were the work of traitors (e.g. Dorothea Flatau's *Yellow English*, 1918). Perhaps the most infamous example of the depths to which the mood of public hysteria could descend can be found in the publication in January 1918 of an article in the newspaper, *The Vigilante* (owned and edited by the MP Noel Pemberton Billing). This article claimed that the German Secret Service held a book containing the names of 47,000 British establishment members (including cabinet ministers and privy councillors) who were sexual perverts and that Britain was losing the war because these people were being blackmailed by the Germans to reveal secrets. In April 1918 this article was followed by a short paragraph in *The Vigilante* entitled 'The Cult of the Clitoris' which condemned a private performance of Oscar Wlilde's *Salome* (starring the dancer Maud Allen), suggesting that the list of the subscribers to this performance might contain many names of the aforementioned 47000[34].

---

[30] There was a strong tendency to regard every alien as a potential spy. This was a matter with which the authorities became obsessed as was demonstrated by the huge expansion during the war of the security services dealing with counter-espionage (i.e. MI5) and aliens (i.e. MI9), and by the establishment when war began of a special constabulary for London which within 3 weeks of the outbreak of the war employed 20,000 amateur guards to patrol strategic points like bridges, tunnels, waterworks, gasworks and canals.

[31] Some sections of the community may well have been receptive to the extreme views expressed at these sort of meetings but much public speaking, although often fiercely patriotic and supportive of the war, was of a more moderate tone and not likely to degenerate into hysterical ravings. Nor should it be forgotten that public meetings advocating peace did occasionally take place, particularly towards the end of the war, in spite of all the efforts to suppress them.

[32] It is hardly surprising that in this atmosphere Rose Allatini's *Despised and Rejected* (1917), which featured a hero who was not only a pacifist but a homosexual, was suppressed under DORA as a threat to the war effort.

[33] e.g. F. E. Eddis's *"That Goldheim"*, 1918, which emphasised the need to restrict immigration and ensure a Britain for Britons; John Buchan's novel *Greenmantle*, in which the villain is portrayed as a German officer who is not only sadistic but also homosexual.

[34] As a result of this article Noel Pemberton Billing was sued by Maud Allen (although he was not in fact the author of either this article or the one published in January 1918, both of which were actually written by Capt Harold Spencer). In the sensational libel trial that followed Wilde's devoted "friend" Robbie Ross and his one time lover, Lord Alfred Douglas, both became embroiled in a bitter battle over Wilde's reputation and this helped to raise interest in the newspapers and among the public to a hysterical level (see also below under Barker's *The Eye in the Door* and Hoare's *Wilde's Last Stand*).

Public hostility to everything German, exacerbated by the vitriolic assaults of writers like Bottomley in his journal, *John Bull*, even extended to politicians and public servants with German sounding names[35] or alleged pro-German sympathies[36]. Nor were the royal family immune from this climate of anti-German prejudice among the British people. Aware of the embarrassing nature of the royal family's strong German links George V decided in 1917 to dilute these links by changing its name to Windsor and allowing for future members of the royal family to be permitted to marry into British families. Prince Louis taking the name Mountbatten and being ennobled as the Marquess of Milford Haven, and the Duke of Teck, the Queen's brother, being made the Marquess of Cambridge represented further efforts to distance the royal family from its German links and to identify it in far closer fashion with the British nation and its history.

The war years proved to be a miserable time for foreigners. Extreme nationalism and wartime paranoia (inflamed by organisations like the British Empire Union and the British Empire League sponsoring rallies around the country calling for concerted actions against aliens) created an extremely hostile climate for all foreigners, including friendly aliens. October 1914 witnessed the beginning of the process of arresting all male Germans, Austrians and Hungarians of military age who were not naturalised. They were either interned or repatriated. In the execution of these actions the distinction between friendly and enemy aliens became increasingly blurred. By August 1918, the government, succumbing to huge pressure from the right, became even more repressive by assuming powers to revoke the citizenship of naturalised Germans and Austrians. In some areas of the country anti-German attitudes sometimes developed into an irrational hatred of all foreigners. Mobs not only destroyed German shops but often went further than this as, for example, when they went on to loot businesses owned by Italians and Russians or to attack blacks and Chinese, many of whom lived in port cities working as seamen and dockers. Anti-Semitic attacks also occurred, encouraged no doubt by public hostility whipped up, for example, by press articles scathingly critical of Jews who had not joined up, or, by some MPs and public officials expressing their opinion that Jews were guilty of 'profiteering' and 'job snatching'. Violent outbursts of anti-Semitism were directed with particular vehemence against the tens of thousands of Russian Jews who lived in London as resident aliens; one of particular violence, involving a pitched battle between 2000 and 3000 Jews and gentiles, occurred in September 1917 in the streets of Bethnal Green.

Autobiographies, Biographies

Bennett, G. M.   *Charlie B: A Biography of Admiral Lord Beresford of Metemmeh and Curraghmore* (London : Dawnay, 1968)

Billing, N. P.   *P-B.* [i.e. Noel Pemberton Billing]: *The Story of His Life* (Hertford: Imperialist Press, 1917)
During the war Billing ran his own 'purity' candidates at by-elections, under cover of an organization called The Society of Vigilantes, which he had founded in his later teens to promote 'purity of life' in Britain. See also note 34.

Freeman, R.   *Admiral Insubordinate: The Life and Times of Lord Beresford* (Self published via Lulu.com, 2008)

Hyman, A.   *The Rise and Fall of Horatio Bottomley: The Biography of a Swindler* (London: Cassell, 1972)

Koss, S. E.   *Lord Haldane: Scapegoat For Liberalism* (New York: Columbia University Press, 1969)
A biography of Richard Burdon Haldane, 1st Viscount Haldane, 1856-1928.
http://copac.ac.uk/search?sub=Haldane, Richard Burdon, Viscount Haldane of Cloan, 1856-1928.

Symons, J.   *Horatio Bottomley: A Biography* (London: Cresset Press, 1955; repr. London: House of Stratus, 2001)
Bottomley used his journalistic and rhetorical talents throughout the war in a gross display of aggressive chauvinistic patriotism which he expressed via his editorship of *John Bull* (founded by him in 1906) and his speeches at the numerous meetings he addressed as an unofficial recruiter.

Taylor, H. A.   *Jix, Viscount Brentford*: being the official biography of the Rt. Hon. William Joynson-Hicks, first Viscount Brentford of Newick (London: Stanley Paul, 1933)

---

[35] Prince Louis of Battenerg, born in Austria to a German prince, felt obliged to resign his office as First Sea Lord and de-germanise his name to Mountbatten.

[36] Among the people who suffered attacks in this respect were R. B. Haldane and Sir Edgar Speyer. As a result of these attacks Haldane offered his resignation on two occasions, each rejected by Asquith, but ultimately Asquith succumbed to public pressure by dropping Haldane when he formed his coalition government in May 1915; similarly Speyer offered on 17 May 1915 to resign his baronetcy and membership of the privy council, but neither the King nor Asquith was willing to accept the offer.

The Civilian Scene

Thomson, Sir B. H. *My Experiences at Scotland Yard* (Garden City, New York: Doubleday, 1923)
Thomson was appointed assistant commissioner of the Metropolitan Police and head of the CID at New Scotland Yard in 1913. During the war he performed a number of roles one of which involved arresting and interrogating spies (one of whom was the famous Mata Hari); twelve of them were executed between 1914 and 1918.

— *Queer People* (London: Hodder & Stoughton, 1922)

— *The Scene Changes* (London: Collins, 1939)

Books

Barker, P. *The Eye in the Door* (London: Plume, 1993)
One of the aspects of the Great War featured in this novel is the hysterical attitude in Britain to homosexuals at the time. This is brought out in the character of Charles Manning who because of his homosexuality is terrorised via the infamous article "The Cult of the Clitoris" which triggered the sensational court case that created such a public stir in 1918 (see also note 34 and the annotation below under Hoare's *Wilde's Last Stand*)

Dowling, C. 'The Campaign of Hate', in *Purnell's History of the First World War*, 8 vols (London: Purnell for BPC Publishing Co., 1969-70)

Cresarani, D. 'An Embattled Minority: The Jews in Britain during the First World War', in *The Politics of Marginality: Race, The Radical Right and Minorities in Twentieth Century* Britain, edited by Tony Kushner and Kenneth Lunn (London: Frank Cass, 1990)

Epperson, A. R. *Unseen Hand: Introduction to the Conspiratorial View of History* (Tucson, Ariz.: Publius, 1985)

Hoare, P. *Wilde's Last Stand: Decadence, Conspiracy and the First World War* (London: Duckworth, 1997)
As well as portraying the darker side of wartime society, (e.g. transvestites in the trenches, drug clubs in London, and what the author discerns as the seeds of post-war British fascism) the author also uses original documents and archives to provide a history of the sensational libel trial that followed the publication of the article, 'The Cult of the Clitoris' which was published in *The Vigilante* in April 1918.

Knightley, P. *The Second Oldest Profession: Spies and Spying in the Twentieth Century*, rev. edn (London: Pimlico, 2003)

Macdonald, C. M. M. 'May, 1915: Race, Riots, and Representations of War', in *Scotland and the Great War*, edited by Catriona M. M. Macdonald and Elaine W. McFarland (East Lothian: Tuckwell, 1998)

Panayi, P. 'Anti-German Riots in Britain during the First World War', in *Racial Violence in Britain in the Nineteenth and Twentieth Centuries*, edited by P. Panayi, rev. edn (Leicester: Leicester University Press, 1993)

— 'The British Empire Union in the First World War', in *The Politics of Marginality: Race The Radical Right, and Minorities in Twentieth Century Britain*, edited by T. Kushner and K. Lunn (London: Cass, 1990)

— *The Enemy in our Midst: Germans in Britain during the First World War* (New York: Berg, 1990)

— 'An Intolerant Act by an Intolerant Society: The Internment of Germans in Britain during the First World War', in *The Internment of Aliens in Twentieth Century Britain*, edited by David Cesarani and Tony Kushner (London: Frank Cass, 1993)

Panayi, P., ed. *Racial Violence in Britain in the Nineteenth and Twentieth Centuries*, rev. edn (Leicester: Leicester University Press, 1993)
Previous edn published as: *Racial Violence in Britain, 1840-1950* (1993)

Sellers, L. *Shot in the Tower: The Story of the Spies Executed in the Tower of London during the First World War* (London: Leo Cooper, 1997)

West, N. *MI6: British Secret Intelligence Operations, 1909-45* (London: Weidenfeld & Nicolson, 1983)

Wrigley, C. J. '"In The Excess of their Patriotism", The National Party and Threats of Subversion', in *Warfare, Diplomacy and Politics, Essays in Honour of A .J. P. Taylor* edited by C. Wrigley (London: Hamilton, 1986)

Articles

Bush, J. 'East London Jews and the First World War', *London Journal*, 6 (1980), 147-61

Cesarani, D. 'An Embattled Minority: The Jews in Britain during the First World War', *Immigrants and Minorities*, 8 (1989), 61-81

French, D. 'Spy Fever In Britain, 1900-15', *Historical Journal*, 21 (1978), 355-70

Hiley, N. P. 'Counter-Espionage and Security in Britain During the First World War', *English Historical Review*, 101 (1986), 635-70

— 'The Failure of British Counter-Espionage against Germany, 1907-1914', *Historical Journal*, 28 (1985),

— 'Internal Security in Wartime; The Rise and Fall of PMS 2', *British Security in Wartime*, 1 (1986)

Panayi, P. 'Anti-German Riots in London during the First World War', *German History*, 7 (1989), 184-203

— 'Germans in Britain during the First World War, *Historical Research*, 64 (1991), 63-76

Rubin, G. 'Race, Retailing and Wartime Regulation', *Immigrants and Minorities*, 7 (1988), 184-205

Contemporary Material

British Empire Union. *Close the German Banks.* Report of a Meeting (London: Financial News, 1917)
Reprinted from the *Financial News*

Colvin, I. D. *The Unseen Hand in English History* (London: The National Review Office, 1917)
"It is the purpose of this book to show, by examining a segment of our history [from the reign of Elizabeth to the end of the eighteenth century] that England is most happy when the national interest and the government work together, and least happy when our government is controlled by the unseen hand of the foreigner." – p. 10 of Introduction to the work (the whole of which is available on the internet at https://archive.org/details/unseenhandinengl00colvuoft). A paperback reprint of this work was published by Forgotten Books in 2012.

Eddis, F. E. *"That Goldheim": A Spy Story, Exposing a Special Danger resulting from Alien Immigration* (London: Selwyn & Blount, 1918)
Published under the auspices of the British Empire Union.

Lequeux, W. T. *Britian's Deadly Peril. Are We Told the Truth?* (London: S. Paul & Co.,1915)
Includes material on spies and their danger.

Oppenheim, L. 'On War Treason', *Law Quarterly Review*, 33 (1917), 266

Powell, E. T. *King or Republic?: A Tract for the Times, Being The Plain Truth About the Latest Device of the Unseen Hand, together with a Study of the Constitutional and Spiritual Evolution of the Kingship* (London: Financial News 1916)

'The treatment of enemy aliens', *Quarterly Review*, 445 (1915), 415-425

Varley, K. *The Unseen Hand in Britain: The Camorra, the Navy and the New State* (London: Generation Press, 1916)

Women's Imperial Defence Council. *Huge "Unseen Hand" Meeting: Lord Kitchener's Sister Occupies The Chair* (London: Financial News, 1915)
Reprinted from the *Financial News*

— *The "Unseen Hand" Meeting: Special Royal Commission Demanded* (London: Financial News, 1917)
The Meeting was arranged by the Women's Imperial Defence Council "to protest against the influence of the "Unseen

Unhand" ('the Treacherous and Devilish Influence which is at work to bring about a British Defeat and a German Victory'). An account of the meeting appeared in the *Financial News*, 9 February, 1917 and was reprinted as a pamphlet with the above title.

2.13 Air and Naval Raids

During the war Britain was subjected to bombardment from both the air and the sea. While the shelling of an enemy coastline by naval craft had happened in the past, dropping bombs from the air on civilian populations and industrial targets represented a new phenomenon in which both the Allies and the Triple Entente were involved. The first air raids on civilian targets were carried out by Zeppelins on French and Belgian Channel ports on 21 August 1914; this was followed by a raid on Paris on 30 August. The first British town to be attacked from the air was Great Yarmouth (on 19 January 1915) and five months later (on 31 May 1915) London was bombed for the first time. These early aerial raids were by dirigibles but later in the war conventional aircraft were used, starting with the attack on Folkestone by Gotha bombers on 25 May 1917 and extending to similar attacks on London by day and night, the earliest of which were carried out on 13 June and 7 July 1917. The bulk of the 1,570 wartime civilian deaths in Britain were the result of the German air raids which accounted for 1,413 of them. Defence against aerial raids and air raid precautions gradually evolved in the course of the war. 'Blackouts' of designated areas and an official air raid warning system were introduced. Protection was provided by searchlights and anti-aircraft guns and, additionally, by aeroplanes but in spite of this the Germans only lost 24 Gotha bombers in 397 sorties over England, a remarkably small loss when it is taken into consideration that over 300 British aeroplanes were engaged in air defence and that hundreds of thousands of shells were fired from anti-aircraft guns[37]. Comparatively, Zeppelins, used mostly in the early years of the war without inflicting any significant damage, suffered greater losses than the Gotha bombers, being more vulnerable in combat and liable to accidents.

The German air raids were designed to demoralise the British public by destroying homes, crippling means of supply and inflicting heavy casualties but in this respect they failed to have a significant impact. The air raids carried out by Gotha bombers towards the end of the war were the most effective and on a couple of occasions caused near-panic in London yet the casualty rate and damage inflicted from the air over the whole period of the war was negligible. In areas least affected by air raids people seemed to be more irritated by the discomfort and inconvenience resulting from the lighting restrictions introduced as an air raid precautionary measure than demoralised by the bombing itself. Among the general public there was also, allied to the distress and anger resulting from being bombed, a feeling of indignation derived from a conviction that defenceless civilians, especially women and children, should not be exposed to death and destruction like the members of the armed forces who are specially equipped and trained to cope with such trauma.

As well as bombardment from the air the British civilian population had to endure shelling from German naval craft which in the course of the war raided a number of fishing villages and North Sea ports, including Yarmouth, West Hartlepool, Whitby, Scarborough, and Lowestoft. These raids were not designed simply to create havoc and destruction; they were primarily intended to have the effect of forcing Britain's Grand Fleet to divert, for the purpose of coastal defence, some of its ships which could then be attacked in isolation from the main fleet[38].

Books

Bushby, J. R. *The Air Defence of Britain* (London: Allan, 1973)

Castle, H. G. *Fire Over England: The German Air Raids of World War I* (London: Secker & Warburg, 1982)

Charlton, L. E. O. 'The New Factor in Warfare', in *The Air Defence of Britain*, by John R. Bushby (London:

---

[37] It has been calculated that 14,540 rounds of anti-aircraft fire were needed to bring down one aircraft.

[38] Britain's navy would like to have engaged the German High Seas Fleet in a major battle but Germany had no intention of coming into direct collision with the whole might of Britain's Grand Fleet while its main battle fleet remained inferior in numbers (which would always have been the case if the British navy stuck to its strategy of keeping the greater part of the Grand Fleet always together in the area of the North Sea and English Channel). Germany's naval strategy was to try to engage with the Grand Fleet piecemeal by luring elements of it away and destroying them in isolation from their main fleet until the point was reached when the High Seas Fleet could engage in a major battle with its adversary on level terms in respect of numbers.

Allan, 1973)

Cole, C. and E. F. Cheesman. *The Air Defence of Britain, 1914-1918* (London: Putnam, 1984)

Faulkner, N. and N. Durrani. *In Search of the Zeppelin War: The Archaeology of the First Blitz* (Stroud: Tempus, 2008)

Fegan, T. *The "Baby Killers": German Air Raids on Britain in the First World War* (Barnsley: Leo Cooper, 2002)

Grayzel, S. R. *At Home and Under Fire. Air Raids and Culture in Britain from the Great War to the Blitz* (Cambridge: Cambridge University Press, 2012)
Gendered approach to the history of the air peril in interwar Britain

— '"A promise of Terror to Come": Air Power and the Destruction of Cties in British Imagination and Experience, 1908-39', in *Cities into Battlefields: Metropolitan Scenarios, Experiences and Commemorations of Total War*, edited by S. Goebel, and D. Keene (Farnham: Ashgate, 2011)

Hanson, N. *First Blitz: The Secret Plan to Raze London to the Ground in 1918* (London: Doubleday, 2008; repr. London: Corgi Books, 2009)

Hyde, A. *The First Blitz: The German Bomber Campaign against Britain in the First World War* (Barnsley: Leo Cooper, 2002)

McKenna, M. 'The Development of Air Raid Precautions in Britain during the First World War', in *Men at War: Politics, Technology, and Innovation in the Twentieth Century*, edited by Timothy Travers and Christon Archer (Chicago: Precedent, 1982)

Marsay, M. *Bombardment: The Day the East Coast Bled* (Scarborough: Great Northern Publishing, 1999)
"Accounts of the German Naval raids on Scarborough and Whitby on Wednesday, 16th December 1914, (with details of the raid on the Hartlepools), and the German submarine attack on Scarborough on Tuesday, 4th September 1917"--T.p.

Mason, F. K. *Battle over Britain: A History of the German Air Assaults on Great Britain, 1917-18 and July-December 1940 and of the Development of Britain's Air Defences between the World Wars*, 2nd edn (Bourne End: Aston, 1990)

Massie, R. K. *Castles of Steel: Britain, Germany and the Winning of the Great War at Sea* (New York: Random House, 2003; repr. London: Pimlico, 2005)

Morris, J. *The German Air Raids on Great Britain 1914-1918*, [new edn] (Stroud: Nonsuch, 2007)
First published: London: S. Low, Marston & Co, 1925. When it was originally published in 1925 Morris's *The German Air Raids on Great Britain 1914-1918* was the first complete account of the German bombardment of Britain during the First World War, in which 280 tons of bombs were dropped. Morris outlines how the menace presented by airship and aeroplane bombing began, escalated and was countered.

Rimmell, R. L. *Air War over Great Britain, 1914-1918* (London: Arms & Armour, 1987)

— *Zeppelin!: A Battle for Air Supremacy in World War I* (London: Conway Maritime Press, 1984)

White, C. M. *The Gotha Summer: The German Daytime Air Raids on England, May to August 1917* (London: Hale, 1986)

Wyatt, R. J. *Death from the Skies: The Zeppelin Raids over Norfolk, 19 January 1915* (Norwich: Gliddon, 1990)

Theses

Barthram, A. 'How did London Civilians Respond to the German Airship Raids of 1915?' (dissertation submitted by Adrienne Barthram in her final year in relation to the BA (Hons) Modern History degree, University of Westminster, that she was awarded in 2007)
Online version at http://www.londonairshipraids1915.co.uk/index.htm

Platt, B. '"Terrorizing the Fortress of London"? German Bombings, Public Pressure, and the Creation of the British Home Defense System in World War I', A thesis presented in partial fulfilment of the requirements for the degree Master of Arts in History (unpublished masters thesis, Terre Haute, Indiana State University, 2010) [http://hdl.handle.net/10484/959]

Articles

'Air Raids', *Spectator*, 119 (1917), 348-9

Bewsher, P., 'The First Raid', *Blackwoods*, 205 (1919), 257-73

Edwards, F. A. 'The Air Raids on London', *Quarterly Review* (1921), 270-91

Fredette, R. H., 'First Gothas over London: The Story of a Daring Raid and its Aftermath', *Air Power Historian*, 8 (1961), 194-206
Relates to the raid of 13 June 1917

Grey, C. G. 'The Defence of London', *London Magazine*, 39 (1918), 451-8

'The New Phase of Air Raids on England', *Current History*, 6 (1917), 76-8

Sadler, J. 'On British Soil: Hartlepool, 16 December, 1914', *Historian* (Historical Association), 123 (2014), 28-31
About the bombardment of Hartlepool by the German Navy.

Stevenson, W. C. 'Raiding England from the Sky', *Outlook*, 114 (1916), 445-54

Stienon, C. 'Zeppelin Raids and their Effects on England', *Current History*, 6 (1917), 333-8

Wiggam, M. 'At Home and under Fire: Air Raids and Culture in Britain from the Great War to the Blitz', *Contemporary British History*, 27 (2013), 118-120

Woodward, D. R., 'Zeppelins over London', *British History Illustrated*, 2 (1975), 40-51

Wyatt, H. R. 'Air Raids and the New War', in *Nineteenth Century*, 82 (1917), 31-8

'The Zeppelin Raid on London, May 1915', *Spectator*, 114 (1915), 769-71 'Zeppelins in a New Raid Meet Disaster', *Current History*, 7 (1917), 458-60

3. The Cultural Scene

3.1 General

The war provided the inspiration for many of the works produced by the composers, painters, dramatists, poets and novelists of the time. Establishment figures tended to depict the war in a straightforward patriotic manner as a just and heroic crusade. This was not, however, a universal tendency and, as the war dragged on and the reality of it began to sink in, some artists, especially those poets and painters who had first hand experience of the battle front, began presenting the war in a far less sanguine manner.

The response of the British people to the war was in general reflected in the patriotic nature of the was exhibitions mounted by museums and art galleries. On occasion exhibitors manifested extreme levels of intolerance and xenophobia (as, for instance, in the case of one London gallery owner not allowing his galleries to be used for exhibitions by 'enemy aliens, conscientious objectors, or sympathizers with the enemy'). In spite of their generally patriotic stance and the fact that this had the effect of attracting greatly increased attendances, museums and art galleries were not immune from the criticism that they were an expensive luxury in time of war. Cost savings no doubt represented the ostensible reason for the Government Committee on Public Retrenchment deciding to close many public museums and art galleries in 1916 but it also seems evident that the decision was also motivated by the government's desire to demonstrate to the world how seriously Britain was involved in its war efforts. Following a strong protest about this action from newspapers, particularly from the *Observer*, the *New Statesman*, the *Nation* and the *Manchester Guardian*, the Government reversed its decision but not only because of pressure from the press but also because it became increasingly aware that the visual arts could perform a propagandistic role.

At first the war had the effect of producing a climate of opinion which encouraged artistic conservatism and attacked modernism, which was equated with alien, foreign influences. Nevertheless there were in Britain modernists who had hopes that the war would produce a change away from an establishment culture. The desire for such a change had already been foreshadowed in the radical movement of vorticism[39] that emerged in London immediately before the First World War. Vorticism, a short-lived literary and artistic movement influenced by the Futurists and the Cubists, was launched with the first issue of the journal *Blast* which was co-founded by Ezra Pound, the American poet, and Percy Wyndham Lewis, the abstract painter and writer. This issue included among other material two manifestos by Lewis (the 'Blast' and 'Bless' manifestos) 'blasting' the current state of British art and culture and extolling the virtues of vorticism. The harsh, geometrical, semi-abstract style of Lewis's painting reflected the vorticist view of a modern world of machinery and industry in a state of complexity and rapid change. Vorticists like Lewis hoped that the war would open up a new artistic era and act as the catalyst to the ending of the stifling effect of tradition and of the reluctance of British art to embrace radical change.

Books

Cork, R. *Vorticism and Abstract Art in the First Machine Age*, 2 vols (London: G. Fraser, 1976)
Contents: Vol 1. Origins and Development; Vol. 2. Synthesis and Decline

Ferguson, J. *The Arts in Britain in World War I* (London: Stainer and Bell, 1980)

Ford, B., ed. *The Cambridge Cultural History of Britain*, 9 vols (Cambridge: Cambridge University Press, 1992), VIII: *Early Twentieth Century Britain* (1992)

Gough, P. *A Terrible Beauty: British Artists in the First World War* (Bristol: Sansom & Co., 2010)
In-depth survey of artists of the Great War, including Paul Nash, Muirhead Bone, Nevinson, Orpen, Stanley Spencer and Wyndham Lewis. Also published under the title *A Terrible Beauty: War, Art and Imagination 1914-1918*. A reprint of the work was published by Sansom in 2014.

Jones, B. and B. Howell. *Popular Arts of the First World War* (London: Studio Vista, 1972)

Kavanagh, G. *Museums and the First World War: A Social History* (London: Leicester University Press, 1994)
This work covers the period from just prior to the beginning of the war in August 1914 up to 1920, set in the context of museum developments before and after this period of time.

Robb, G. *British Culture and the First World War* (Basingstoke: Palgrave, 2002)

Thacker, T. *British Culture and the First World War: Experience, Representation and Memory* (London: Bloomsbury Academic, 2014)

Tholas-Disset, C. and K. A. Ritzenhoff, eds. *Humor, Entertainment, and Popular Culture during World War I* (London: Palgrave Macmillan, 2015)

Wees, W. C. *Vorticism and the English Avant-Garde* (Manchester: Manchester University Press, 1972)

Wilcox, D. J. *The London Group, The Artists and their Works* (London: Scolar Press, 1995)[40]

---

[39] A number of distinguished artists had some association with the movement, including Henri Gaudier Brzeska, William Roberts, Edward Wadsworth, and David Bomberg. The First World War brought Vorticism to an end (although in 1920 Lewis made a brief attempt to revive it with Group X), but a number of Lewis's associates were later prominent in the London Group (see note 40).

[40] The London Group was an art society formed in London, England, in 1915 when the Camden Town Group, the vorticists, and several smaller groups came together to provide an opportunity for young avant-garde artists to exhibit. At the time of the Great War the

Contemporary Material

Adcock, A. St. John. 'British Authors and the War', *Bookman*, 49 (December 1915), 87

'Art after Armageddon', *Athenaeum*, (September 12 1914)

Baker, C. H. C. 'Art and War', *Saturday Review*, 118 (August 22 1914)

Bell, C. 'Art and War', *International Journal of Ethics*, 26 (October 1915)

'Chronicles', *Blast*, no. 2 (July 1915)

Colton, W. R. 'The Effects of War on Art', *The Architect*, 45 (March 17 1916)

Galsworthy, J. 'Art and War', *Fortnightly*, 98 (November 1915)

Image, S. *Art, Morals and the War*. A Lecture delivered in the Ashmolean Museum, Oxford on Thursday, November 12, 1914 (London: Oxford University Press, 1916)

'Manifesto', *Blast*, no. 1 (June 20, 1914)

'Miss Asquith on Art and War', *Morning Post*, (October 10, 1916)

Randall, A. W. G. 'Poetry and Patriotism', *Egoist*, 3 (February 1, 1916)

'The Theatrical Year. Playwrights in War-Time', *The Times* (January 1, 1917)

Scott, C. 'The Connection of the War with Art and Music', *The Monthly Musical Record*, 46 (March 1 1916)

3.2 Art (see also Appendix 3)

Many of the works of the artists of this period were directly related to the war, especially those of the artists officially appointed to depict it. Until the latter artists were recruited by the government most paintings related to the war were produced on an artist's own initiative, or commissioned for illustrated magazines, or private charities. The works of the latter sort that achieved the greatest popularity and the widest circulation portrayed soldiers in heroic, sentimental or inspirational scenes, painted by conventional artists (like John Charlton, Christopher Clark, Fred Roe, Fortunino Matania, and R. Caton Woodville) who had no first-hand experience of the battlefield and relied purely on their imagination and traditional ways of depicting war. Often disseminated via illustrated magazines and postcards, these paintings, evoking little of the reality of war, had a widespread and influential impact. Some artists, however, were not prepared to depict the war in an idealised and romantic fashion and by 1916 some artists (like Charles Sims and Mark Gertler, in their completely differing styles) were producing paintings which expressed a far more realistic view of the war.

The pictures commissioned by the government during the war[41] involved over ninety artists, a number of whom had initially been serving in the forces but had later been recruited as official war artists. The first recruits to be sent abroad as official war artists were Muirhead Bone and Francis Dodd (this was in 1916); later recruits in 1917 included Eric Kennington, William Orpen, Paul Nash, C. R. W. Nevinson and William Rothenstein, and the numbers in 1918 (and some in 1919) were expanded under the British War Memorials Committee's

---

London Group included the abstract sculptor Jacob Epstein, the vorticists Wyndham Lewis and Edward Wadsworth and the Cubist painter David Bomberg.

[41] This official war artists scheme, originally instituted at Wellington House in 1916 for propaganda purposes, eventually changed its aim via the War Artists Advisory Committee (set up by the Ministry of Information under the British War Memorials Committee programme in 1918) to one primarily of creating a record and a memorial to the Great War rather than as an aid to propaganda. A number of British artists were also given official commissions via the Canadian War Memorials Fund which was established in November 1916 to provide 'suitable memorials in the form of Tablets, Oil-Paintings, etc to the Canadian heroes and heroines in the war.'.

programme established by Lord Beaverbrook and Arnold Bennett for the commissioning of many more artists (among whom were John Sargent, Augustus John, John Nash, Henry Lamb, Henry Tonks, Colin Gill, William Roberts, Wyndham Lewis, Stanley Spencer, Philip Wilson Steer, George Clausen, Bernard Meninsky, Charles Pears, Sydney Carline, David Bomberg, Austin Osman Spare, and the sculptors, Gilbert Ledward and Charles Jagger).

The reality of war was missing in the paintings of the first official war artists (Muirhead Bone and Francis Dodd) recruited and sent to the Front in 1916 by Wellington House, the Government's Propaganda Bureau. Dodd was simply commissioned to paint portraits of Britain's leading military and naval figures, and a considerable proportion of Bone's work was devoted to drawings of soldiers playing football or at rest, and of men and equipment being moved to and from the front lines. Their works were devoid of the tragedy and chaos of war, an effect which fitted well with the original purely propagandistic motivation for recruiting official war artists[42]. Later, among the artists the government recruited in 1917 and 1918, were a number, like Henry Lamb, Wyndham Lewis, William Roberts, Paul and John Nash, Stanley Spencer, Eric Kennington and Christopher Nevinson, who utilised their first-hand experience of military service to break away from the prevailing idealised and romantic approach and to depict the scenes of war in starkly modernist terms. Many of the war paintings of these artists (and of other artists recruited by the Government in the last two years of the war) bore the distinct influence of the modernist avant garde movement in which a number of them had participated in the years preceding the Great War. Not surprisingly, the modernist depiction of the war that characterized the works of the new generation of war artists was not always blessed with official approval, sometimes running into trouble with the censors[43]. Apart from problems with the censors, some exhibits in 1918 of official war art also resulted in attacks from the popular press, primarily aimed at the modernist works of Wyndham Lewis, William Roberts, and David Bomberg. To many members of the public the anti-heroic nature of avant garde war paintings was repugnant. This attitude was also evident in parliament where concern was expressed about the showing of such paintings in public galleries and the amount of government expenditure on them.

The items listed below consist of a selection of the works of individual artists and of the exhibitions of war art which were produced while the war was in progress.. Selections of the work of individual artists and of exhibitions produced after the war are listed within **section 4.4** (**Art**) of **Part 4** (**Remembering the War**) which also includes catalogues, books, articles, and other material related to war art produced both during the war and after it.

Contemporary Artists and their Work

Although art during the years 1914-1918 was not devoid of works which bore no relation to the war (see some examples in **Appendix 3: Artists Active during the Great War**) it was the war which had the dominant impact on many of the British artists who were living in this period.

Listed below are a selection of the works of contemporary artists chosen as examples of the different approaches to depicting the war (e.g. idealised and romantic in the case of Lady Butler, Fortunino Matania, Lucy Kemp-Welch and Richard Jack; sentimental in the case of James Clark and John Hassall; inspired by the courageous resistance of the Belgians in the case of Walter Sickert; personally emotional in the case of Charles Sims and George Clausen; macabre and desolate in the case of James Pryde; virulently anti-German in the case of Charles E. Butler; chivalric in the case of George Frampton; and in the case of Duncan Grant, John Fergusson, David Bomberg, Christopher Nevinson, Paul Nash, Jacob Epstein, Mark Gertler, William Roberts, and Wyndham Lewis mainly expressed unheroically or in a starkly modernist style).

---

[42] Although the decision to commission war paintings was initially motivated by their potential value as propaganda war artists seemed to be pretty free to choose what they wanted to paint or sketch (except in the case of Dodd being specifically commissioned to paint portraits of Britain's leading military and naval figures) without any real pressure on them to produce works of an overtly propagandist nature; there were, however, occasions when their works could be made to serve the purpose of propaganda by accompanying them with a commentary of a propagandist nature (as happened, for example, in the case of the edition of drawings of Muirhead Bone published in June 1917) or were censored because they contained aspects considered to be too distressing for public viewing. An interesting direct effort to influence an artist was made by David Lloyd George who asked John Singer Sargent to paint a propagandist picture showing collaboration between British and American troops. The artist rejected the commission and instead painted *Gassed*, graphically showing a group of soldiers suffering from the effects of a gas attack.

[43] For example, Nevinson's painting *Paths of Glory* was considered to be unacceptable and was subjected to a ban. Nevinson, however, went ahead and exhibited it, covering it with a paper banner marked "CENSORED".

The Cultural Scene

Although the battle front was the theme of much of the work produced, aspects of the situation on the home front were also recorded, such as the conversion of industry to war production (e.g. Anna Airy, *Shop for Machining 15-inch Shells: Singer Manufacturing Company, Clydebank, Glasgow*); women working in factories (e.g. Flora Lion, *Women's Canteen at Phoenix Works, Bradford*); air raids (e.g. Walter Bayes, *The Underworld: Taking Cover in a Tube Station during a London Air Raid*; William Nicholson, *The Ballroom of the Piccadilly Hotel during an Air Raid*); censorship (e.g. Alexander Bryce, *The Censorship: Strand House, Portugal Street, London*); rehabilitation of servicemen (e.g. John Lobley, *The Queen's Hospital for Facial Injuries, Frognal, Sidcup: The Toy-Makers' Shop*); profiteering (e.g. morally satirised in Christopher Nevinson's *He Gained a Fortune But He Gave a Son*)

A considerable number of the works were by officially appointed war artists. Muirhead Bone and Francis Dodd[44], were the first two of these appointments in 1916, the former producing bland scenes of the battlefront and the latter painting conventional portraits of leading army and naval figures. The work of the later official war artists (e.g. John Singer Sargent, Eric Kennington, William Orpen, Augustus John, etc) tended to possess greater realism and a compassionate sensitivity to the human aspects and tragedies of warfare, characteristics that in the case of the style of painting in which they were expressed by some of these war artists (e.g. Christopher Nevinson, Paul Nash, Wyndham Lewis, William Roberts and David Bomberg) sometimes met with the disapproval of the censors or the popular press.

The war also lent itself to portraiture of military leaders by a number of artists (e.g. John Lavery, William Orpen, Francis Dodd, Jacob Epstein).

Listed below is a brief selection of the works of contemporary artists that are related to the war. Asterisked items are held in the Imperial War Museum (IWM); items indicated with a + sign were officially commissioned.

Airy, A. *Shop for Machining 15-inch Shells: Singer Manufacturing Company, Clydebank, Glasgow* (1918)*+
Oil painting on canvas

Bayes, W. *The Underworld: Taking Cover in a Tube Station during a London Air Raid* (1918)*
Oil painting on canvas

Bomberg, D. *Billet* (1915) [Victoria and Albert Museum]

— *Sappers at Work: A Canadian Tunneling Company*, first version (1918) [Tate Collection]+
Oil on canvas. In 1917 the Canadian authorities commissioned Bomberg to paint a picture to celebrate an operation in which sappers successfully blew up a salient of the German defences at Saint-Eloi near Arras. The resulting painting, *Sappers at Work* was rejected in its first version because of its abstract nature. To reverse this rejection, Bomberg in 1919 produced a second more conventional version (see Bomberg under the heading of **Paintings in section 4.4 (Remembering the War: Art)** which was accepted.

Bone, Sir M. *From the After Deck of a Battleship (HMS Tiger from HMS Repulse)* (1917) [Tate Collection]
Drawing and watercolour on paper

— *In the War Zone 1916* (1916) [Tate Collection]
Drawing and watercolour on paper

— *Tanks* (1916) [Cheltenham Art Gallery and Museum]
Charcoal on paper

— *A View in Flanders behind the Lines, Showing Locre and the Tops of Dug-Outs on the Scherpenber* (1916) [Tate Collection]
Drawing and watercolour on paper

---

[44] In 1916 Charles Masterman, the head of the War Propaganda Bureau recruited Dodd to replace Muirhead Bone, as Britain's official war artist on the Western Front. While in France Dodd produced more than thirty portraits of senior military officers. There was a mixed response to his portraits of military leaders. While some of the sitters were pleased with the result, Haig included, many found that the portraits made them appear arrogant, and others ridiculous. However, two special edition volumes were issued, one for the admirals, and one for the generals, which both sold well. The portraits were also included in a very popular joint exhibition of Bone and Dodd's work in mid-1918.

The War Years

Bryce, A. J. C. *The Censorship: Strand House, Portugal Street, London* (1918-1919)*
Oil painting on canvas

Butler, C. E. *Blood and Iron* (1916)*
Oil painting on canvas

Butler, Lady E. (née Thompson) *The Dorset Yeoman at Agagia, 26th Feb. 1916* (1917) [Dorset County Council)]

Clark, J. *The Great Sacrifice* (1914)* [St Mildred's Church, Battenberg Chapel, Isle of Wight]
Oil painting, a print of which first appeared in *The Graphic* at Christmas 1914. This painting, featuring a British serviceman lying dead at the foot of the Cross, was donated by Clark to a war relief charity and purchased by Queen Mary to give to Princess Beatrice in memory of her son, Prince Maurice of Battenburg, who died at Ypres. The original now hangs as a memorial in St Mildred's Church, Battenberg Chapel, Isle of Wight.

Clausen, Sir G. *Youth Mourning* (1916)*
Oil painting on canvas. Probably inspired by the distress of Clausen's daughter when her fiancé was killed on the battlefield

Dodd, F. *Admiral Sir John Rushworth Jellicoe, GCB, OM, GCVO* (1917)*+
Charcoal drawing

— *Field-Marshal Sir Douglas Haig, GCB, GCVO, KCIE* (1917)*+
Charcoal drawing

— *General Sir Edmund H H Allenby, KCB* (1917)*+
Charcoal drawing

Epstein, Sir. J. *Admiral Lord Fisher* (1916) *
Sculpture in bronze

— *The Tin Hat* (1916) *
Sculpture in bronze

— *The Risen Christ* (1917-1919)[45] [National Galleries of Scotland. Gallery of Modern Art]
Sculpture, bronze

— *Torso in Metal from the 'Rock Drill'* (1913-1916) (Tate Gallery, London]

Fergusson, J. D. *Dockyard, Portsmouth* (1918)*
Oil painting on canvas

Frampton, Sir G. *Saint George: Memorial to Lieutenant Francis Mond, RFA RAF* (1918)*
Sculpture in bronze

Gertler, M. *Merry-Go-Round* (1916) [Tate Collection]
Oil painting on canvas. This painting, considered by some critics as the most important British painting of the First World War, was exhibited in the Mansard Gallery in May 1917 after a refusal by one gallery to display it because Gertler was a conscientious objector.

Ginner, I. C. *The Shell Filling Factory* (1918) [National Gallery of Canada, Ottawa]+
Oil on canvas. Commissioned by the Canadian War Memorials Fund.

Grant, D. *In Memoriam: Rupert Brooke* (1915) [Yale Center for British Art, Paul Mellon Collection, New Haven]
Oil and collage on panel

---

[45] "*The Risen Christ* began as a portrait of Epstein's friend, the composer Bernard van Dieren. It was begun in 1917 when van Dieren was ill, and Epstein wanted to make a mask of him looking 'spiritual and worn with suffering.' After making a mask from clay, the piece then developed into the figure of Christ. Work was temporarily put on hold when Epstein was enlisted in 1917 but continued a year later. The artist considered the figure to be an anti-war statement and declared that he would ideally like it to be remodelled and made hundreds of feet high as a 'mighty symbolic warning to all lands'" [caption accompanying the image of *The Risen Christ* in the National Galleries of Scotland Online Collection].

The Cultural Scene

Hassall, J. *The Vision of St George over the Battlefield* (1915) *
Oil on canvas

Hayward, A. R. *The Soldier's Buffet, Charing Cross Station* (1918)*
Oil painting on canvas

Jack, R. *The Second Battle of Ypres, 22 April to 25 May 1915* (1918) [Beaverbrook Collection of War Art, Canadian War Museum, Ottawa]
This painting, portraying the Canadian stand during the Second Battle of Ypres, was the first of well nigh a thousand works, by over one hundred artists, commissioned by the Canadian War Memorials Fund (CWMF), an organization established by Lord Beaverbrook to document Canada's war effort.

John, A. E. *The Canadians Opposite Lens* (1918) [National Gallery of Canada, Ottawa]+
Charcoal on paper. This miniature cartoon of the mining district of Lens, crowded with troops, stretcher-bearers and refugees was meant to be the basis for a large-scale oil painting which Augustus John had been commissioned to produce by the Canadian War Memorials Fund. The forty-foot canvas which was to emerge from this cartoon was never executed.

Kemp-Welch, L. *Forward the Guns!* (1917) [Tate Collection]
Oil painting on canvas

Kennington, E. *The Kensingtons at Lavente* (1915)*
Oil painting on glass. When exhibited in the spring of 1916 its portrayal of exhausted soldiers created a sensation.

Lavery, J. *Admiral Sir Cecil Burney, GCMG, KCB, Commander-in-Chief, Coast of Scotland (1859-1929)* (1917)*
Oil painting on canvas. In 1917 Charles Masterman, head of the government's War Propaganda Bureau (WPB) recruited Britain's two leading portrait painters, Lavery and William Orpen to paint pictures of British military leaders in France. Soon after receiving the invitation, however, Lavery was involved in a serious car-crash during a Zeppelin bombing raid and, being unfit to travel to France, agreed to paint pictures of the Home Front.

— *Kite Balloons, Roehampton* (1915)*
Oil painting on canvas

— *Munitions, Newcastle* (1917) *
Oil painting on canvas

Lewis, P. W. *A Canadian Gun Pit* (1918) [National Gallery of Canada, Ottawa]
Oil painting on canvas

— *Officer and Signallers* (1918)*
Pen, ink, crayon and watercolour on paper

Lion, F. *Women's Canteen at Phoenix Works, Bradford* (1918)*
Oil painting on canvas

Lobley, J. H. *The Queen's Hospital for Facial Injuries, Frognal, Sidcup: The Toy-Makers' Shop* (1918)*
Oil painting on canvas

Matania, F. *The Last Message* (1917)*
Oil painting on canvas

Nash, P. *After the Battle* (1918)*+
Pen and watercolour on paper

— *Void (Néant)* (1918) [National Gallery of Canada. Ottawa]
Oil painting on canvas

— *We are Making a New World* (1918)*
Oil painting on canvas

— *The Ypres Salient at Night* (1918)*
Oil painting on panel

Nevinson, C. R. W. *After a Push* (1917)*
Oil painting on canvas

— *A Taube* (1916)*
Oil painting on canvas

— *The Doctor* (1916)*+
Oil painting on canvas

— *French Troops Resting* (1916)*
Oil painting on canvas

— *He Gained a Fortune But He Gave a Son* (1918) [University Art Gallery, Hull]
Oil painting on canvas

— *La Mitrailleuse* (1915) [Tate Collection]
Oil painting on canvas

— *La Patrie* (1916) [Birmingham Museums and Art Gallery]
Nevinson joined the Red Cross in 1914 working with the Quaker Friends Ambulance Unit near Dunkirk and his earliest paintings depict French troops. *La Patrie* portrays an horrific incident he experienced when his unit came upon a goods yard full of dead and dying French and German soldiers.

— *Paths of Glory* (1917)*+
Oil painting on canvas. Regarded by the censors as too controversial to be exhibited (it depicted the taboo subject of dead British soldiers) but in spite of the ban on it Nevinson went ahead and exhibited it, covering it with a paper banner marked "CENSORED".

Nicholson, W. *The Ballroom of the Piccadilly Hotel during an Air Raid* (1918) [Mr. And Mrs. C. Ch. Mout Collection]

Orpen, Sir W. *The Big Crater* (1917)*

— *Dead Germans in a Trench* (1918)*
Oil painting on canvas

— *Death Among the Wounded in the Snow* (1918) *
Pencil and watercolour on paper

— *Field Marshall Sir Douglas Haig (1861-1928), KT, GCB, GCVO, KCIE, Commander-in-Chief, France, from 15 December 1915* (1917)*
Oil painting on canvas

Pryde, J. *The Monument* (1916-17) [Government Art Collection, London]
Oil on canvas

Roberts, W. P. *The Gas Chamber* (1918)*
Ink, pencil and watercolour on paper

Sargent, J. S. *The Interior of a Hospital Tent* (1918)*
Watercolour. Late in September 1918, while gathering material for *Gassed* near Peronne, Sargent was struck down with influenza and taken to a hospital near Roisel. Here, he spent a week in a hospital bed next to the war-wounded, the source of inspiration for this work.

— *Gassed* (1918-1919)*+
Oil on canvas (seven feet high by twenty feet long) In mid 1918 Singer was commissioned to produce a painting for memorial purposes. This was arranged through both a formal invitation by the British War Memorials Committee, and a personal letter sent by Lloyd George. Following a visit to the Western Front with Henry Tonks in July 1918 he composed several studies for the subject he had chosen (i.e. soldiers blinded by gas being led in lines back to the hospital tents and the dressing stations) in preparation for the large canvas *Gassed* which was completed in 1919.

The Cultural Scene

Sickert, W. R. *The Integrity of Belgium* (1914) [Government Art Collection, UK]
Oil on canvas
Although born in Munich, Sickert was appalled by Germany's aggression and much regretted being too old to enlist.

— *The Soldiers of King Albert the Ready* (1914) [Graves Art Gallery, Sheffield]
Oil on canvas.

Sims, C. *Clio and the Children* (1913-1915) [Royal Academy of Arts]
Oil painting on canvas. Clio, the Muse of history is depicted, reading from a scroll to a group of nine children in a meadow. The painting was initially designed, when first painted in 1913, as a serene and idyllic image. However, grief-stricken, following the death of his eldest son in World War I, Sims returned to the painting in 1915 and added red paint to Clio's scroll to represent blood and symbolise his belief that the war had forever violated the innocence of youth and that History's lessons were brutal rather than noble ones.

Williamson, H. S. *A German Attack on a Wet Morning,* April 1918 (1918)*+
Oil painting on canvas

Contemporary Exhibitions and Collections

Bone, Sir M. *Catalogue of Drawings of the Western Front by Muirhead Bone*, chosen from the collection presented by H.M. Government to the British Museum (London: T. & R. Annan & Sons, 1917)
Catalogue of an exhibition held at the Gallery of T. & R. Annan & Sons, London, 7th-31st March, 1917.

— *Drawings of the Western Front by Muirhead Bone*; exhibited with the permission of H.M. government by P. & D. Colnaghi & Obach in their galleries (London: P. & D. Colnaghi & Obach, 1917)
Catalogue of an exhibition held at P. & D. Colnaghi & Obach, London, January-February 1917.

— *The Western Front: Drawings by Muirhead Bone*, with text by C. E. Montague and an introduction by Sir Douglas Haig, 2 vols (London: Published by authority of the War Office from the offices of "Country Life", Ltd, 1917)
Masterman was aware that the right sort of pictures would help the war effort. In May 1916 Masterman recruited Bone as Britain's first official war artist. Commissioned as an honorary second lieutenant, Bone arrived in France during the Battle of the Somme. After completing 150 drawings of the war, Bone returned to England in October, 1916. Bone was then replaced by his brother-in-law, Francis Dodd. Over the next few months Bone drew pictures of shipyards and battleships. He visited France again in 1917 where he took particular interest in the ruined towns and villages.

British Artists at the Front, with introductions by Campbell Dodgson and C. E. Montague, 4 pts (London: Country Life and George Newnes, Ltd., 1918)
Contents: pt. 1. C.R.W. Nevinson; pt. 2. Sir John Lavery; pt. 3. Paul Nash; pt. 4. Eric Kennington. Continuation of *The Western Front: Drawings by Muirhead Bone*, London: Country Life, 1917-1918.

Epstein, J. *Catalogue of an Exhibition of the Sculpture of Jacob Epstein* (London: Ernest Brown & Phillips, 1917)
Dealer's catalogue to accompany an exhibition held at Ernest Brown & Phillips, The Leicester Galleries, London Feb.-Mar. 1917.

Fine Art Society. *Britain's Efforts and Ideals in the Great War*. Illustrated in sixty-six lithographs by eighteen artists; exhibited at The Fine Arts Society, London, July, 1917 (London: Fine Art Society, 1917)

— *[Catalogues 1915]* (London: Fine Art Society, 1915)
Catalogues of exhibitions held at the Fine Art Society, London, 1915. Includes Portraits of British commanders taking part in the war on sea & land; Designs for war memorials and rolls of honour; Records of an artist's summer in the Trentino & the Italian war zone by Hugh de T. Glazebrook; Colour sketches in Gallipoli & the Dardanelles by Norman Wilkinson; War cartoons by Louis Raemaekers.

— *[Catalogues 1916]* (London: Fine Art Society, 1916)
Catalogues of 11 exhibitions held at the Fine Art Society, London, 1916. Includes colour reproductions of the war cartoons of Louis Raemaekers; Exhibition of war pictures & photographs; New series of war cartoons by Louis Raemaekers & of the colour reproductions for the edition de luxe; Anzac April 25th 1915 by Charles Dixon; Drawings of Belgium & of war lithographs by Frank Brangwyn.

— *[Catalogues 1917]* (London: Fine Art Society, 1917)
Catalogues of 16 exhibitions held at the Fine Art Society, London, 1917. Includes Second exhibition of war cartoons by

Louis Raemaekers; Drawings & lithographs of munitions works by Joseph Pennell; Britain's efforts & ideals in the Great War illustrated in 66 lithographs by 18 artists; Impressions of the Western Front by Lieut. Keith Henderson; Sketches of the Western Front: Vimy Ridge to the Somme by Lt. R. Borlase Smart; War pictures in various lands by Matteo Lovatti.

— *[Catalogues 1918]* (London: Fine Art Society, 1918)
Catalogues of 9 exhibitions held at the Fine Art Society, London. Includes War cartoons & studies at the front by Louis Raemaekers.

Orpen, Sir W. *War Paintings and Drawings Executed on the Western Front by Major Sir William Orpen*, with an introductory note by Arnold Bennett and a portrait of the artist (London: Edinburgh Press, 1918)
Catalogue of an exhibition in the Spring of 1918 at Agnews, London, under the auspices of the Ministry of Information

Rochdale Art Gallery. *War Sketches and Portraits [of Muirhead Bone and Francis Dodd]* (Rochdale: Art Gallery, 1918)
Catalogue of an exhibition held at the Art Gallery, County Borough of Rochdale, May 1918.

Whitechapel Art Gallery. Exhibition of War Drawings by Lieut. Muirhead Bone, and Lithographs by Kennington, Brangwyn, Clausen … Also a Memorial Exhibition of the Works of Lieut. H. Samuel Teed (London: Whitechapel Art Gallery, 1917)

3.3 Literature

There were few voices of dissent in Britain's literary world. George Bernard Shaw and Thomas Hardy were almost alone among the literary heavyweights in their lack of enthusiasm for the war, and while there were literary members of the Bloomsbury Group and some younger writers like Francis Meynell and D. H. Lawrence opposed to the war, members of the literary world as a whole joined in the patriotic response of the British people. The disillusionment and disenchantment which characterised much of the literary output on the war after it had ended, particularly in the 1930's, were not characteristic of the attitude of most authors writing about the war when it was actually in progress. During the course of the war authors were generally supportive. Quite a number (e.g. some academics and novelists) took time off from the sort of writing for which they were commonly known in order to publish propagandistic material in direct support of the war. A considerable number joined the armed services, or, in the case of some women authors, saw active service at the Front as nurses or were otherwise engaged in war work of some description.

Novels were read by an audience that showed no signs of dwindling during the war years, and an audience for poetry expanded. Over half of what was sold in Smith's, Mudie's and Boot's and of what was sold in bookshops, was fiction in one form or another and dominated by the theme of war. Nevertheless books of travel, scholarship, criticism, politics and sociology also continued to find an audience and polemical works dealing with the war and carrying titles like *J'Accuse*, *My Adventures as a Spy*, *The German Spy System in France*, *Germany's Swelled Head*, *How Belgium Saved Europe*, *The Hero of Liege*, *Secrets of the German War Office*, *On the Side of the Angels*, and *Remember Louvain* commanded a ready sale in W. H. Smith shops at an early stage in the war.

Women contributed a considerable proportion of the novels, poetry, and memoirs written during the First World War. Most of these authors are unknown to us to-day. Few of their works are considered to have any particular literary merit but they are of historical interest for what they reveal about the attitude of women to the war and the part they played in it.

Critical studies, bibliographies, and other material relating generally to the literature of the First World War and dealing not only with authors who published works while the war was in progress but also with authors who wrote in the decades after the war had ended, are listed within section **4.2** (**Literature**) of **Part 4** (**Remembering the War**)

3.3.1 Memoirs

While popular fiction had the greatest appeal for readers during the war years, biographies of war heroes and memoirs of war experiences also sold well. Much of the latter material was written by officers (only, therefore, representative of a particular group of enlisted men) and characterised by a belief in the righteousness and ultimate triumph of Britain's cause. Memoirs of war experiences were by no means exclusive to male authors.

A considerable number of women who had seen frontline service in the medical corps or military services also produced them (e.g. Sister Martin-Nicholson's *My Experiences on Three Fronts*; Flora Sandes's *An English Woman Sergeant in the Serbian Army*; May Sinclair's *A Journal of Impressions in Belgium*)

Alexander, H. M. *On Two Fronts: Being the Adventures of an Indian Mule Corps in France and Gallipoli* (London: W. Heinemann, 1917)

Corbett-Smith, A. *Retreat from Mons*, by one who shared in it (London: Cassell, 1917)

Durand, Sir M. *A Life of Field-Marshall Sir George White V.C.*, 2 vols (Edinburgh: William Blackwood & Sons, 1915)

Gilliland, H. G. *My German Prisons: Being the Experience of an Officer during Two-and-a-Half Years as a Prisoner of War* (London: Hodder and Stoughton, 1918)

Kernahan, C. *The Experience of a Recruiting Officer* (London: Hodder & Sotughton, 1915)

Martin-Nicholson, M. E. L. G. *My Experiences on Three Fronts* (London: Allen & Unwin, 1916)

Redmond, W. *Trench Pictures From France* (London: Melrose, 1917)

Rosher, H. *In the Royal Naval Air Service: Being the Letters of the late Harold Rosher to his Family*, with an introduction by Arnold Bennett (London: Chatto & Windus, 1916)
A facsimile of this work was published, London: Greenhill, 1986

Sandes, F. *An English Woman-Sergeant in the Serbian Army* (London: Hodder and Stoughton, 1916)

Sinclair, M. *A Journal of Impressions in Belgium* (London: Hutchinson, 1915)

3.3.2 Fiction

Critical studies, bibliographies, and biographical and other material relevant to First World War fiction are included within the section **4.2.3 (Fiction)** of **Part 4 (Remembering the War)** where they relate both to novelists who produced fiction bearing directly or obliquely on the Great War during the war (and in some cases after it as well) and also to novelists whose fiction was similarly influenced by the First World War theme in the inter-war and post Second World War years.

Contemporary Fiction

Novels in which authors ignored, or were oblivious to, the reality of wartime conditions (books of humour, tales of espionage and adventure, colourful romances, and historical swashbucklers) and which could be described as escapist fiction were written throughout the war years. Also published were a great number of sentimental 'home front novels' motivated by the desire of the authors to reflect the quiet fortitude and perseverance, or the uplifting effects which can arise from war, rather than to dwell on its atrocities and horrors. The war's popular sentimental and generally escapist fiction, including a considerable proportion written by women who sentimentalised the war in terms of compassion, domesticity, self-sacrifice, and romance[46] (see asterisked examples of women writers in the sections below), constituted the majority of the novels that were published. Although some contemporary critics were contemptuous of these novels, publishers, reviewers, and booksellers generally took the view that this was what the general reading public wanted - as an antidote to the misery of war and the human problems generated by it - and judging by the ready market for this type of fiction they would appear to have been right. Most of the novels listed below are representative examples of this type of fiction and with a few exceptions (e.g. John Buchan, Ian Hay) are largely forgotten today, but listed also (under the sub-heading of **Novels Outside the Mainstream**) are some examples of novels which did not conform to the prevailing fashion.. A few of the latter novels could even be labelled 'anti-war'. 'Anti-war' novels, however, were rare (the heyday of the publication of this type of novel did not occur until some ten years after the war

---

[46] Surprisingly, Marie Corelli, who for more than thirty years dominated the world of popular fiction, commanding phenomenal sales of her books, avoided the theme of war in her novels of this period.

had ended) but the fact that they were published at all shows that some authors had the courage to write novels against the generally patriotic trend and that some publishers were prepared to publish them in spite of the risk of prosecution under the censorship laws (DORA). In general, however, publishers were cautious about releasing anything too controversial not only because of the fear of prosecution but also because they were probably aware that many bookstores and libraries refused to have anti-war novels on their shelves.

- **'Home Front' Novels**

Most of these novels have been forgotten by critics and readers alike. These novelists offered few profound insights about the war, preferring to depict it in predictable and patriotic ways although, unusually among these writers, there were some, like Rudyard Kipling in *Mary Postgate* and Mrs Humphrey Ward in *Missing* who were not afraid to portray the bleaker side of war, some, like Stella Benson, Violet Hunt and Rebecca West who resisted simplistic 'keep the home fires burning' representations of women's roles, and two writers, Ford Madox Ford and Violet Hunt, who jointly produced a curiously atypical novel, *Zeppelin Nights*, in which a group of intellectuals pass the time away while sitting out the nightly Zeppelin raids on London during the early part of the war by listening to historical readings by their artist friend, Serapion Hunter.

Benson, S. *This is the End* (London: Macmillan, 1917)

Castle, A. *Little House in Wartime* (London: Constable, 1915) *

Buckrose, J. E., pseud. [i.e. Annie Jameson]. *The Silent Legion* (London: Hodder & Stoughton, 1918) *

— *Wartime in Our Street: The Story of Some Companies Behind the Firing-Line* (London: Hodder & Stoughton, 1917)*
Short stories

Chartres, A. *Vae Victis* (London: Edward Arnold, 1917)*

Delafield, E. M., pseud. *The War-Workers* (London: Heinemann, 1918) *

Hope, L. *Behold and See!* (London: Hurst & Blackett, 1917)*

Howard, K.., pseud. [i.e. John Keble Bell]. *The Smiths in War Time* (London: John Lane, 1917)

Hunt, V. *Their Lives* (London: Stanley Paul & Co., 1916)

Hunt, V. and F. M. Ford (Joseph Leopold Ford Hermann Madox Hueffer). *Zeppelin Nights: A London Entertainment* (London: John Lane, 1916)

Kaye-Smith, S. *Little England* (London: Nisbet, 1918) *

Kipling, R. 'Mary Postgate', *Nash's and Pall Mall Magazine*, (September 1915)
Short Story. Also published in Kipling's *A Diversity of Creatures*, London: Macmillan, 1917; reprinted London: Penguin, 1987 in an edition edited by Paul Driver

Meynell, W. *Aunt Sarah and the War: A Tale of Transformations* (London: Burns & Oates, 1914)

— *Who Goes There?* (London: Burns & Oates, 1916)

Sherwood, M. *The Worn Doorstep* (London: Hodder & Stoughton, 1917) *

Ward, Mrs Humphrey. *'Missing'* (London: W. Collins, 1917) *

West, R. *Return of the Soldier* (London: Nisbet & Co., 1918)
A paperback edition of the is work was published, New York: Modern Library, 2004.

- **Adventure and Spy Novels**

The Cultural Scene

The adventure genre was particularly suited to adopting the war as a literary theme and the thousands of books produced in this mode were the most frequently requested in shops and libraries. These books were staunchly patriotic. Their authors were at pains to emphasise that Britain's cause was clearly moral whereas Germany's was manifestly evil.

Bell, J. J. *Cupid in Oilskins* (London: Hodder & Stoughton, 1916)

Buchan, J., 1st Baron Tweedsmuir. *Greenmantle* (London: Thomas Nelson, 1916)

— *The Thirty-Nine Steps* (Edinburgh: Blackwood, 1915)

Doyle, Sir A. *The Last Bow: Some Reminiscences of Sherlock Holmes* (London: J. Murray, 1917)

Eddis, F. E. *"That Goldheim": A Spy Story, Exposing a Special Danger Resulting From Alien Immigration* (London: Selwyn & Blount, 1918)

Ferguson., A. *Stealthy Terror* (London: John Lane, 1917)

Flateau, D. *Yellow English* (London: Hutchinson, 1918)

Girvin, B. *Munition Mary* (London: Humphrey Milford, 1918)

Gould, N. *The Rider in Khaki* (London: John Long, 1917)

LeQueux, W. *The German Spy* (London: Newnes, 1914)

Lynn, E. *In Khaki for the King: A Tale of the Great War* (London: W. & R. Chambers, 1915)

— *Knights of the Air* (London: W. & R. Chambers, 1918)

Oppenheim, E. P. *The Double Traitor* (London: Hodder & Stoughton, 1915)

Sapper, pseud. [i.e. Herman Cyril MacNeile.] *The Human Touch* (London: Hodder & Stoughton, 1918)

— *Men, Women, and Guns* (London: Hodder & Stoughton, 1916)

— *No Man's Land* (London: Hodder & Stoughton, 1917)

Trent, M. *Alice Blythe Somewhere in England* (Cleveland: Goldsmith Publishing co., 1918)
A paperback reprint of this book was published, Milton Keynes: Lighting Source UK Ltd., 2010)

- **Romance Genre**

Writers in the romantic vein, like the writers of adventure stories, were equally zealous in the utilisation of the war theme and in their books, a selection of which are provided below, deliberately adapted their literary conventions and formulaic plotlines to the war scene.

Ayres, R. *The Long Lane to Happiness* (London: Hodder & Stoughton, 1915) *

— *Invalided Out* (London: Hodder & Stoughton, 1918) *

Black, D. *Her Lonely Soldier* (London: Hodder & Stoughton, 1916) *

Haggard, Sir H. R. *Love Eternal* (London: Cassell, 1918)

The Love of an Unknown Soldier: Found in a Dug-Out (London: John Lane, 1918)
This work, although a series of letters from a British officer to a nurse and found in a trench after his death, can be considered as a sort of novel because of the literary form in which it was written. The letters are written in the chivalric terms of a soldier seen as a mediaeval knight in love with the woman of his desire. The anonymous author has been

identified as Coningsby Dawson. A best-seller during the Great War. Various reprints of it (including a paperback published by BiblioLife) were published in 2009. A study of this work is included in Bruley, S. '"The Love of an Unknown Soldier": A Story of Mystery, Myth and Masculinity in World War I', *Contemporary British History*, 19 (2005), 459-479

Marchant, B. *A Girl Munition Worker* (Glasgow: Blackie & Son, 1916)

Ruck, A. R. *The Lad with the Wings* (London: Hutchinson, 1915) *

— *The Bridge of Kisses* (London: Hutchinson, 1917)

— *The Girls at His Billet* (London: Hutchinson, 1916) *

— *The Land-Girl's Love Story* (London: Hodder & Stoughton, 1918) *

Sélincourt, H. de. *A Soldier of Life* (London; Constable, 1916) *

Tweedale, V. C. *The Heart of a Woman* (London: Hurst & Blackett, 1917) *

- **'True Life' Stories**

Innumerable writers took the opportunity to meet the popular demand for 'true life' stories illustrative of bravery and endurance in the face of hardship and danger by producing books such as:

Deeds that Thrill the Empire: True Stories of the Most Glorious Acts of Heroism of the Empire's Soldiers and Sailors during the Great War, written by well-known authors, 2 vols (London: Hutchinson, 1917)

Foster, S. N. *Plain Tales from the War* (London: Collins, 1914)

Westerman, P. F. *Deeds of Pluck and Daring in the Great War* (London: Blackie & Son, 1917)

In similar vein was the sort of book which sought to dramatize a soldier's life for the reading public on the home front. Of these Ian Hay's *The First Hundred Thousand* was one of the most successful and a best-seller throughout the war. Hay's 'true life' stories, like those of his many imitators, as for example those cited below, were mixtures of patriotism and light-hearted optimism which sought to reassure those at home by not painting too gloomy a picture of the front.

Cable, B., pseud. [i.e. Ernest Andrew Ewart] *Between the Lines* (London: Smith, Elder & Co., 1917)

Hay, I., pseud. [i.e. John Hay Beith]. *Carrying On - After the First Hundred Thousand* (Edinburgh: Blackwood, 1917)

— *The First Hundred Thousand: Being the Official Chronicle of a Unit of "K(1)"* (Edinburgh: Blackwood, 1915)

Lyons, A. N. *Kitchener Chaps* (London: John Lane, 1915)

Sapper, pseud. [i.e. Herman Cyril MacNeile.] *Sergeant Michael Cassidy, R.E.* (London: Hodder & Stoughton, 1916)

- **Novels Outside the Mainstream**

Although fiction written between 1914 and 1918 was dominated by authors who wrote in the vein of the categories indicated above there were some who produced novels which did not follow the mainstream, as can be seen in the selections listed below:

There were some novels which did not utilise the war as a theme or background, such as those by authors in the following selection:

Douglas, N. *South Wind* (London: Secker, 1917; repr. Harmondsworth Penguin, 1976)

Lawrence, D. H. *The Rainbow* (London: Methuen, 1915; repr. Oxford: Oxford University Press, 1997)

Mackenzie, Sir C. *The Early Life and Adventures of Sylvia Scarlett* (London: Secker, 1918; repr. London: Hamilton & Co., 1963)

Moore, G. *The Brook Kerith* (London: T. Werner Laurie, 1916; repr. London: Kaye & Ward, 1971)

Swinnerton, F. *Nocturne* (London: Secker, 1917; repr. Oxford: Oxford University Press, 1986.)

Some novels touched on the war only in an oblique fashion as was the case, for example, with the following authors:

Conrad, J. *Victory* (London: Methuen, 1915; repr London: David Campbell, 1998)

Ford, F. M. (Joseph Leopold Ford Hermann Madox Hueffer). *The Good Soldier* (London: John Lane, The Bodley Head, 1915; repr. Oxford: Oxford University Press, 2012)

Lewis, W. *Tarr* (London, Egoist, 1918; repr. Harmondsworth: Penguin, 1982)

Waugh, A. K. The *Loom of Youth* (London: Methuen, 1917; repr. 1984)

Webb, M. *The Golden Arrow* (London: Constable, 1916; repr. London: Virago, 1983)

Among the many authors who responded to the war in a direct way there were a few who did not adopt the purely patriotic and sentimental approach of the time but tackled the theme of war with a profounder insight and a greater sense of reality as was exemplified by works such as:

Bennett, A. *The Pretty Lady* (London: Cassell, 1918; repr. Leek, Staffordshire: Churnet Valley Books, 2009)

Galsworthy, J. *Saint's Progress* (London: Heinemann, 1919)
Written during the war

Sinclair, M. *The Tree of Heaven* (London: Cassell, 1917)
A study of this work is included in Mumford, L. S. 'May Sinclair's The Tree of Heaven: The Vortex of Feminism, The Community of War', in *Arms and the Woman: War, Gender, and Literary Representation*, edited by H. M. Cooper and others (Chapel Hill: University of North Carolina Press, 1989)

Walpole, Sir H. *The Dark Forest* (London: Martin Secker, 1916; repr. London: Hart-Davis, 1949)
Walpole spent his three month's of active service with a Red Cross unit in Russia and employed this experience in his book not only to depict day-to-day life on the Russian front but to use it as a background to explore the complex psychological aspects of war.

Wells, H. G. *Mr. Britling Sees it Through* (London, Cassell, 1916; repr. London: Hogarth, 1985)
Wells' initial enthusiasm for 'a war to end war' had become more difficult to sustain by 1916, when he wrote this book, one of the most popular and critically acclaimed novels of the war.

There were also some novelists who even went so far as to produce works, such as those selected below, that could be classed as 'anti-war' because of the way they challenged the legitimacy of the war or were otherwise critical of it in various other ways.

Fitzroy, A. T., pseud. [i.e. Rose Laure Allatini, afterwards Scott] *Despised and Rejected* (London: Daniel, 1918)
DORA (the Defence of the Realm Act) was employed to suppress this work on the grounds that it was a threat to the war effort. A reprint of this work was published, London: GMP, 1988.

Hamilton, M. A. *Dead Yesterday* (London: Duckworth, 1916)

Machen, A. *The Terror* (London: Duckworth, 1917)

Macaulay, R. *Non-combatants and Others* (London : Hodder and Stoughton, 1916; repr. London: Methuen: 1986)

— *What Not: A Prophetic Comedy* (London : Constable, 1919)
In this novel the author ridiculed the wartime bureaucracy and as a result the censors stopped her book (due out in the Autumn of 1918) from being published until after the Armistice.

Snaith, J. *The Coming* (London: Chatto & Windus, 1917)

Wilson, T. W. *The Last Weapon* (London: Daniel, 1916)

3.3.3 Drama (see also 3.5.2. The Theatre)

In the pre-war decade the system of independent actor management which had dominated the theatre in Victorian times was in decline. After the death in 1905 of Henry Irving (the most famous of the actor-managers) the system (carried on by traditional actor mangers like Herbert Beerbohm Tree, Frank Benson, George Alexander, John Hare, Charles Wyndham, Lewis Waller, the Bancrofts, and the Kendals) became increasingly vulnerable to economic pressures and competition from the musical stage with its attraction for managers and actors of more likely box office profits. The individualistic nature of the actor, 'star'-focused characteristics and financing of the actor manager system was able to survive until the First World War and intermittently beyond but, ultimately, it was not able to withstand the increased demand in the war years for escapist entertainment and to compete with the commercial acumen of speculative managers who could see the profit in providing such entertainment. With the deaths in the war years of Waller, Tree, Alexander, and Wyndham the traditional actor-management system virtually came to an end, lingering on only in the person of Frank Benson who continued to mount productions of Shakespeare until the end of the war.

The art and local theatre movement[47] (which had begun to flourish in the Edwardian era as the actor-management theatre system declined) and ideas for a national theatre were also badly hit by the war. Art theatres disappeared, many repertory theatres closed down and the national theatre-movement came to a halt during the years of 1914-1918. The established West End theatres, however, continued to operate in spite of the loss of many of its young actors to the armed forces[48]. A number of revivals of classics were staged and the Old Vic Theatre, under the control of Lilian Baylis, continued to produce Shakespeare[49] throughout the conflict, but no new plays were staged that have survived the passage of time and Harley Granville Barker, one of the most illustrious figures of the Edwardian era, soon ceased to be active in the theatre. Most of the new plays, including melodramas and farce, and some of the revivals (such as *Henry V* and *The Dynasts* (in which Thomas Hardy extols Nelson's victories) were related in some way to the war, frequently with a clearly patriotic and propagandistic content, and leading actors as, for example, Sir John Martin Harvey, Frank Benson, and Herbert Beerbohm Tree were happy to lend their dramatic talents (the latter two as directors as well) to the recruiting drive.

The theatre was in general patriotic in its stance and in any case had little opportunity to engage in dissent as it was subjected to heavier censorship than any other of the other arts. A licence had to be obtained from the Lord Chamberlain's Office before any play could be performed and the vetting to which this Office subjected drama productions could often border on the extreme. Virtually anything in a play considered hurtful to morale on the home front or critical of the armed forces was likely to be subject to excision. Curiously, George Bernard Shaw's *Augustus Does his Bit*, a satirical dig at the British establishment and possibly the most subversive play of the war, escaped censorship and was performed in 1917. Shaw's *Heartbreak House*, his indictment of the war and the British establishment in a much more serious vein, would almost certainly have failed to pass the censor, but it escaped this possible fate because, although written during the war, it was not performed until after the war

---

[47] This was an alternative theatre movement which grew out of the societies, clubs, repertory theatres and individual theatrical projects which were launched in the 1880's and developed in the succeeding decades up to 1914 ; it was representative of the innovative ideas and experimentation in theatre's basics that were fermenting in the period up to the Great War.

[48] "By 1915 Tree estimated that 1500 actors had joined the forces, and by 1918 nearly every able-bodied young actor and many hundreds of young actresses had been conscripted or directed into war work" [*The Revels History of Drama in English*, vol. 7, p.31].

[49] In 1916 there were many productions of Shakespeare in celebration of his tercentenary.

was over [50].

Autobiographies, Biographies

Listed below is a brief selection of biographical material related to some of the figures in the world of drama living during the period of the Great War

Bairnsfather, B. *From Mud to Mufti: With Old Bill on all Fronts* (London: Richards, 1919)

Beerbohm, M. *Herbert Beerbohm Tree: Some Memories of Him and of His Art* (London: Hutchinson, 1917)

Benson, Sir F. R. *My Memories* (London: Ernest Benn, 1930)

Dawick, J. *Pinero: A Theatrical Life* (Niwot: University Press of Colorado, 1993)

Drinkwater, J. *Inheritance: Being the First Book of an Autobiography* (London: Benn, 1931)

Dunkel, W. D. *Sir Arthur Pinero: A Critical Biography with Letters* (Chicago: Chicago University Press, 1941; repr. Port Washington, N.Y: Kennikat Press, 1967)

Harvey, J. M. *The Autobiography* (London: Sampson Low, 1933)

Holroyd, M. *Bernard Shaw*, 5 vols (London: Chatto & Windus, 1988-1992), II: The *Pursuit of Power, 1889-1918* (1989)

Isaac, W. F. E. C. *Ben Greet and the Old Vic* (London: privately printed, 1964)

Knoblauch, E. [afterwards Knoblock, Edward]. *Round the Room: An Autobiography* (London: Chapman & Hall, 1939)

Mackail, D. *The Story of J. M. B.* (London: Davies, 1941)
Biography of James Barrie.

Pogson, R. *Miss Horniman and the Gaiety Theatre, Manchester* (London: Rockliff, 1952)

Purdom, C. B. *Harley Granville Barker: Man of the Theatre, Dramatist and Scholar* (London: Rockliff, 1955)

Thorndike, Dame Sybil and R. Thorndike. *Lilian Baylis* (London: Chapman & Hall, 1938)

Trewin, J. C. *Benson and the Bensonians* (London: Barrie & Rockcliff, 1960)
The Benson referred to in the title is Frank Robert Benson (1858-1939).

Walbrook H. M. *J. M. Barrie and the Theatre* (London: White, 1922)

Weintraub, S. *Bernard Shaw, 1914-1918: Journey to Heartbreak* (London: Routledge, 1973)
Originally published as, *Journey To Heartbreak: The Crucible Years of Bernard Shaw*, New York, Weybright and Talley, 1971

Wilson, K. *Thomas Hardy on Stage* (Basingstoke: Macmillan, 1995)

Books

With the exception of the books by Kosok and Nicholson the books listed below relate specifically to the years of the Great War. Books on drama in the 20th century generally and books which deal specifically with the influence of the Great War on drama up to recent times are listed in the **section 4.2.5 (Drama)** of **Part 4**

---

[50] Shaw seems to have been well aware that this play was not suitable for performance during the war when he wrote in 1919 in his preface to *Heartbreak House*: 'When men are heroically dying for their country, it is not the time to show their lovers and wives and fathers and mothers how they are being sacrificed to the blunders of boobies, the cupidity of capitalists, the ambition of conquerors, the electioneering of demagogues ... ' [Shaw, G. B. *Heartbreak House; Great Catherine; and, Playlets of the War.* London: Constable, 1919, preface liv; repr. Shaw, G. B. *Prefaces*, London: Constable, 1934, preface xv, p.397]

(Remembering the War)

Barker, C. and M. B. Gale, eds *British Theatre between the Wars, 1918–1939*, Cambridge Studies in Modern Theatre (Cambridge: Cambridge University Press 2000)
Includes a chapter entitled 'Theatre and Society: The Edwardian Legacy, the First World War and the Inter-War Years', by Clive Barker.

Collins, L. J. *Theatre at War, 1914-18* (Basingstoke: Macmillan Press Ltd., 1998)

Kosok, H. *The Theatre of War: The First World War in British and Irish Drama* (London: Palgrave Macmillan, 2007)
This work surveys over 200 British and Irish plays, ranging from West End successes to the productions of small amateur companies, that deal in a variety of different ways with the experience of the war – from a foreshadowing of the war before 1914, through a direct association with it during the years of 1914-1918, to the reactions to it in the inter–war years and the years following the 2nd World War.

Nicholson, S. *The Censorship of British Drama, 1900-1968*, 4 vols (Exeter: Exeter University Press, 2003-2005), I: *1900-1932* (2003)
This first volume of an analysis of British theatre censorship covering the years from 1900 until 1968, based on previously undocumented material in the Lord Chamberlain's Correspondence archives, deals with the period before 1932 and provides an insight into the day-to-day operation of the system of theatre censorship together with the principles, policies and practice associated with it in the paticular period under examination.

Williams, G. *British Theatre in the Great War: A Revaluation* (London: Continuum, 2005)

Articles

Engler, B. 'Shakespeare in the Trenches', in *Shakespeare Survey; An Annual Survey of Shakespeare Studies and Production*, edited by S. Wells, 44 (1992), 105-11

H. F. 'Our Theatre in War-Time', *The Athenaeum*, no. 4618 (June 1917)

P. P. H. 'The Drama and the War', *The Outlook*, 35 (27 March 1915)

Walkley, A. B. 'The Theatre and the War', *Cornhill Magazine*, series 3, 47 (1919), 425-34

Zangwill, I. 'Poetic Drama and War', *Poetry Review*, 7 (1916), 29-35

Contemporary Plays

War and war-related plays accounted for a very large proportion of the new plays that were staged during the war. The spate of new plays staged in London and provincial theatres in the early stages of the war (such as *England Expects*, *Call to Arms*, *The Way to Win*, *Your Country Needs You*, and *The King's Men*) were clearly designed to encourage recruiting and help with fund-raising, often including interludes of military music and recitations of patriotic poems, but after this initial emphasis the treatment of the war theme by playwrights became more varied. Plays involving espionage (such as *In Time of War*, *Inside the Lines*, *In the Hands of the Hun*) were by far the most numerous and popular. With their portrayal of Germans as brutal and violent, in common with most of the jingoistic melodrama of the time, they provided ideal support for the propagandists' campaign to whip up hatred of the enemy. Playwrights were chary about exploiting the war for comic purposes. In only a handful of plays did they do this; these included comedies about wartime situations such as Chamber's *The Saving Grace*, *Billeted* by Jesse and Harwood, Barrie's *A Kiss for Cinderella* and Bairnsfather and Eliot's *The Better 'Ole*; plays utlising some of the mechanisms of farce for didactic purpose such as Knoblauch's *A War Committee* and Shaw's *Augustus Does His Bit*; and plays adopting a comic approach through satirical means as in, for example, Galsworthy's *Foundations* and Terry's *General Post* or through ironical means in the case of Shaw's *The Inca of Perusalem*, and *Anajanska, the Bolshevik Princess*. Standing apart as a type of play employing drama as a means of engaging primarily in intellectual debates about the war were plays like Barrie's *Der Tag*, and Jones's *The Pacifists*.

A few of the plays that were staged were of a more serious nature, attempting to deal realistically with war-related social and political issues. In these plays were tackled, for instance, labour problems such as the question of war bonuses (*John Feeney – Socialist*) and strikes (*War Mates* and *Boys of the Old Brigade*), the plight of the maimed

The Cultural Scene

and the crippled (*British to the Backbone*, *Black Widows*, and *The Grousers*), food shortages (*Mrs Pusheen: The Hoarder*, and *Rations*), and profiteering (*When Our Lads Come Marching Home*). The attempt to deal with the realities of war manifested in the latter plays was weakened by the rigour of the severe censorship restrictions imposed by the Lord Chamberlain's Office. Playwrights knew that any play which had anything in it which could be interpreted as detrimental to the war effort or to the morale of the nation would almost inevitably be subject to excision by the censors, even in the later stages of the war when there were signs of some relaxation of the severity of the censorship. This is no doubt part of the reason why few playwrights attempted to portray life in the trenches realistically. While the censors gradually permitted a greater degree of realism on the stage they continued to sanitize realistic elements in a play and if these elements seemed too 'real' to them they cut them out altogether. This is exemplified, for instance, by their modification of Zeppelin air-raid scenes and bomb attacks in *Britain's Guests*, *When Joy Bells are Ringing*, and *Over the Lines* and their dilution of the horrific effect of the bomb explosion in *Home Service* by insisting on it being reproduced innocuously on a big drum. Nevertheless, John Drinkwater's $X = O: A$ *Night of the Trojan War*[51] (1917) and *Abraham Lincoln* (1918), which were both (albeit obliquely) critical of aspects of the war (particularly in the case of the latter play), did manage to reach the stage.

Apart from J. M. Barrie, most of the established playwrights of the pre-war years, such as Jones, Pinero, Shaw and Galsworthy, produced few new plays during the war, although a number of revivals of their plays were staged. Bernard Shaw wrote *Heartbreak House* in 1916 and was at work on *Back to Methuselah* but they were not staged until after the war, as was also the case with *O'Flaherty V.C.* (plans for a production of which at the Abbey Theatre in Dublin during the war fell through[52]); the only new plays of his performed in the war were *Augustus Does His Bit*, *The Inca of Perusalem*, and *Anajanska, the Bolshevik Princess*. Most of the new plays of these playwrights (as for example those among the selection listed below) bore some relation to the war, directly or obliquely expressed.

An alphabetical listing by playwright of the selection of plays mentioned above are provided below. Information about a play's first production is given in parentheses. For a number of the records below an additional bibliographical note is given about the publication of the play:

Anonymous. *Mrs Pusheen: The Hoarder* (Stoke Newington: Alexandra Theatre, 1918)

Anonymous. *Over the Lines*, (Barking: Baths Hall, 1918)

Armstrong, C. F. *Home Service* (Eastbourne: Devonshire Park Theatre, 1918)

Bairnsfather, B. and A. Eliot. *The Better 'Ole* (London: Oxford Theatre, 1917)

Barrie, J. M. *Der Tag* (London: Coliseum Theatre, 1914)
J. M. Barrie, *Der Tag: A Play* (London: Hodder & Stoughton, 1914); also in *Daily Telegraph* (22 Dec. 1914)

— *A Kiss for Cinderella* (London: Empire Theatre, 1916)
The play opened at the Empire Theatre on December 25, 1916 and ran for 152 performances.
J. M. Barrie, *A Kiss for Cinderella*, in: *The Plays of J. M. Barrie* (London: Hodder & Stoughton, rev. ed. 1942), 875-943

— *The New Word* (London: Duke of York Theatre, 1915)
J. M. Barrie, *The New Word*, in: *The Plays of J. M. Barrie* (London: Hodder & Stoughton, rev. ed. 1942), 853-73

— *The Old Lady Shows Her Medals* (London: New Theatre, 1917)
J. M. Barrie, *The Old Lady Shows Her Medals*, in: *The Plays of M. Barrie* (London: Hodder & Stoughton, rev. ed. 1942), 963-92

— *A Well-Remembered Voice* (London: Wyndham's, 1918)
J. M. Barrie, *A Well-Remembered Voice*, in: *The Plays of J. M. Barrie* (London: Hodder & Stoughton, rev. edn. 1942), 1061-82

Bigger, E. D. *Inside the Lines* (London: Apollo Theatre, 1917)

Boyd, D. *John Feeney – Socialist* (Glasgow: Pavilion Theatre, 1915)

---

[51] John Drinkwater was best known in pre-war years for his poems and his work as an actor and director in the Birmingham Repertory Theatre.

[52] Although O'Flaherty V.C. was produced by officers of the 40th Squadron R.F.C. at Treizennes, Belgium, in 1917.

The War Years

Chambers, C. H. *The Saving Grace* (Manchester: Gaiety Theatre, 1917; London: Garrick Theatre, 1917)
C. Haddon Chambers, *The Saving Grace: A Comedy in Three Acts* (London: Heinemann, 1918)

Dande, D. *Your Country Needs You* (Manchester: Tivoli Theatre, September 1914)

Davis, B. *A Call to Arms* (London: Golder's Green Hippodrome Theatre, September, 1914)

Drinkwater, J. *Abraham Lincoln* (London: Birmingham Repertory Theatre, 1918)

— *X = O: A Night of the Trojan War* (Birmingham: Birmingham Repertory Theatre, 1917)
John Drinkwater, *X=0: A Night of the Trojan War*, in: *The Collected Plays of John Drinkwater*, vol. 1 (London: Sidgwick & Jackson, 1925), 139-55

Fraser, Sir J. F. *The Grousers* [adapted for stage by Hugh C. Buckler] (Manchester: Ardwick Empire, November 1917)

Galsworthy, J. *The Foundations* (London: Royalty: 1917)
John Galsworthy, *The Foundations*, in: *The Plays of John Galsworthy* (London: Duckworth, 1929), 461-512

Hicks, S. and E. Knoblauch [afterwards Knoblock, Edward]. *England Expects* (London: London Opera House, 1914)

Jennings, G. E. *The King's Men* (London: Royalty Theatre, 1914)

Jesse, F. T. and H. M. Harwood. *Billeted* (London: Royalty Theatre, 1917)
F. Tennyson Jesse and H.M. Harwood, *Billeted: A Comedy in Three Acts* (London: French, 1920)

Jones, H. A. *The Pacifists* (Southport: Opera House, 1917: London: St James, 1917)
Henry Arthur Jones, *The Pacifists: A Parable in a Farce* (London: Blackie, 1955)

Knoblauch, E. [afterwards Knoblock, Edward]. *The Way to Win* (London: Coliseum Theatre, 1915)

— *A War Committee* ((London: Haymarket Theatre, 1915)
Edward Knoblauch, *A War Committee and The Little Silver Ring* (New York, London: French, 1915)

Lee, B. and R. P. Weston. *Rations* (Colchester: Hippodrome Theatre, 1918)

Mill, C. W. *In Time of War* (South Shields: Theatre Royal, September, 1914)

Mulford. D. *In the Hands of the Hun* (London: Hippodrome Theatre, Willsden, 1915)

Norwood, E. *War Mates* (London: Victoria Palace, 1915)

Phillips, S. *Armageddon* (London: New Theatre, 1915)
Stephen Phillips, *Armageddon: A Modern Epic Drama in a Prologue Series of Scenes and an Epilogue Written Partly in Prose and Partly in Verse* (London, New York: John Lane, 1915)

Pinero, Sir A. W. *Mr. Livermore's Dream: A Lesson in Thrift* (London: Coliseum, 1916)

— *Monica's Blue Boy* (London: New Theatre, 1918)

Rean, C. *When Joy Bells are Ringing* (London: Elephant & Castle Theatre, 1918)

Saville, A. D. *Britain's Guests* (London: Mile End Empire Theatre, 1917)

Sexton, J. *Boys of the Old Brigade* (Liverpool: Lyric Theatre, 1916)

Shaw, G. B. *Annajanska, the Bolshevik Princess* (London: Coliseum Theatre, 1918)

— *Augustus Does his Bit* (London: Court Theatre, 1917)
Bernard Shaw, *Augustus Does His Bit: A True-to-Life Farce*, in: *The Complete Plays of Bernard Shaw* (London: Hamlyn, 1965), 839-48

— *The Inca of Perusalem* (London: Criterion Theatre, 1917)

— *O'Flaherty V.C.* (Treizennes, Belgium: Officers of the 40th Squadron R.F.C., 1917)
Bernard Shaw, *O'Flaherty V.C.: A Recruiting Pamphlet*, in: *The Complete Plays of Bernard Shaw* (London: Hamlyn, 1965) and also in *Heartbreak House, Great Catherine, and Playlets of the War* (London: Constable, 1925). Contents of the latter work include *O'Flaherty VC, The Inca of Perusalem, Augustus Does His Bit, Annajanska*

Shirley, A. *British to the Backbone* (Richmond: Hippodrome, 1917)

Teherine, O. *Black Widows* (London: Savoy Theatre, 1918)

Terry, J. E. H. *General Post* (London: Haymarket Theatre, 1917)
J. E. Harold Terry, *General Post: A Comedy in Three Acts* (London: Methuen, 1917)

Walsh, S. *When Our Lads Come Marching Home* (South Shields; Theatre Royal, 1918)

A number of revivals were staged, including re-runs of Shakespearian drama and Restoration comedies as well as of plays of more recent times. Among these revivals in the early stages of the war were a number that reflected the patriotic enthusiasm of the nation and helped to encourage men to join up. Examples of the latter were:

Hardy, T. *The Dynasts* (London: Kingsway Theatre, November 1914)
Produced by the stage's most famous director, Granville Barker

Parker, L. N. *Drake* (London: His Majesty's Theatre, August 1914)
Revived and presented by Herbert Beerbohm Tree, who was also the lead player in it.

Shakespeare, W. *Henry V*, (London: Shaftesbury Theatre, 28 December, 1914)
Put on by Frank Benson who played the leading role in a production which was clearly desiged to assist the recruiting drive at an early stage of the war

3.3.4 Poetry

Poetry as a medium of expression reached unprecedented levels of popularity during the Great War. The output of poems was immense. Catherine Reilly identified 2225 poets who were published between 1914 and 1918, of whom 552 were women. A large proportion of this huge output was related to the theme of the war. Much of this war-related verse is now largely unknown to the public[53], partly owing to a tendency in anthologies and critical studies published after the 2nd World War to cover the Great War in terms of the poetry of a fairly narrow group of poets like Wilfred Owen, Siegfried Sassoon, Rupert Brooke, Edmund Blunden, Isaac Rosenberg, Edward Thomas, Charles Sorley, Richard Aldington, Robert Graves, Herbert Read, and Ivor Gurney. It was, however, only after the war was over that Edmund Blunden's poems and the bulk of Ivor Gurney's were written, and that the poems which Herbert Read wrote during the war were published. It has also to be remembered that Rosenberg and Owen, who were both killed in 1918, were virtually unknown during the war, their vogue only emerging in recent times.

Poetry about the war was being written during the war years by a multiplicity of people and achieving publication in a number of different ways. As well as the small group of well-educated middle and upper class soldiers, like Sassoon, who subsequently became famous as war poets, there were a large number of other soldiers of all classes who wrote about the war while it was actually in progress in poetry of little or no literary merit (much of it likely to be styled doggerel nowadays) but which is, nevertheless, interesting for the light it throws on their attitudes to the war. Some of the latter poetry was written for the trench magazines which were published by soldiers during the war. A large amount of poetry from all sorts of people (including soldiers) was

---

[53] Although some recent anthologists, like Hibberd, Stephen, and Reilly have resurrected a considerable amount of it in their anthologies, see **section 4.2.4 (Poetry)** of **Part 4 (Remembering the War)** in the sub-section **Anthologies.**

printed in daily newspapers (including *The Times*) and magazines and periodicals of the time, such as *Punch*, *The New Witness*, *The English Review*, *To-Day*, *Poetry Review*, *Graphic*, and *Contemporary Review* or in 'slim volumes'. Eminent writers of the time like John Masefield, Walter de la Mare, John Drinkwater, James Barrie, Conan Doyle, G. K Chesterton, Ford Maddox Ford, establishment figures like Robert Bridges, Thomas Hardy and Rudyard Kipling, relatively well known literary figures like J. C. Squire and Harold Monro, popular writers like John Oxenham, and authors who later achieved fame in other fields, like A. P Herbert, Gilbert Frankau and A. A. Milne, all joined in the urge to write poetry which touched on the war in one way or another.

In the early years of the war poets, both civilians and soldiers, expressed their attitudes to the war in generally patriotic verse dominated by the themes of 'heroism', 'the just war', and 'sacrifice'. Attitudes like this persisted in the works of many poets, mostly civilian poets, throughout the war and its immediate aftermath and were undoubtedly what most publishers and editors wished to select as is clearly exemplified in the anthologies of poetry which were published during the war years. It was not until July 1918, with the publication of Bertram Lloyd's *Poems during the Great War*, which contained pieces by Sassoon, Sitwell, Sackville, and Gibson as well as translations of German poems, that there appeared an anthology which gave the impression that an unequivocal commitment to the war was not shared by all poets. In the publishing world of newspapers and periodicals it was rare for poetry of a controversial or provocative nature to be published. Exceptional in this respect was *The Nation* which was prepared to publish some poems of this nature by Gibson, Sackville, Sassoon, Graves, Sitwell, and Owen during the course of the war. Most publishers and editors, however, chose verse that was likely to bolster the national morale.

As the misery, chaos, and slaughter involved in the attritional trench warfare on the Western Front developed the poetry written by soldiers moved increasingly away from the idealistic and patriotic character of the poetry (as famously exemplified in Rupert Brooke's sonnet cycle, *1914*) written at the beginning of the war. This departure from the model of Brooke's poetry has tended to be seen primarily in relation to the now best known soldier-poets like Sassoon, Graves, and Owen who began to write in graphic and bitter fashion of the conditions at the front (the cold, the mud, the rats and lice) and of a war they had come to visualise in terms of young men dying tragically and wastefully in a cause which no longer seemed obviously justified. This group of poets did not, however, reflect the whole range of attitudes characteristic of the majority of the other soldiers who wrote poetry during the war[54]. The latter poets certainly moved away from a romantic, idealised presentation of the war but their verse was more likely to be expressive of their concern with matters such as mundane essentials (drill, food tobacco, rum, the price of beer, simple pleasures) and their personal feelings (coping with fear, comradeship, homesickness, irritation with the army's hierarchy) rather than a preoccupation with deeper thoughts related to the pity of war and the justice or injustice of the cause for which they were fighting. What they did have in common with poets like Sassoon was a dislike of the romantic and jingoistic attitudes to the war that were characteristic of the verse of many civilian poets. This dislike was voiced with particular severity by Owen. In *Dulce et Decorum* Owen launched a savage attack on the jingoistic sentiments expressed in the poetry of Jesse Pope. Many male civilian poets were just as guilty of the latter type of poetry and by the end of the war a distinct difference in sentiment and style between soldier and civilian poets had developed. Yet, in contrast to the poems of Jesse Pope which so incensed Owen, there were a number of other women poets like Sybil Bristowe, Vera Brittain, May Cannan, Charlotte Mew, Eleanor Farjeon, Rose Macaulay and Mary Borden who displayed sensitivity and compassion, or like Margaret Sackville, Helen Hamilton, Margaret Postgate Cole, Alice Meynell, Winifred Letts, Edith Sitwell, and Gertrude Ford who expressed attitudes implicitly or explicitly critical of the war and warmongering. All the latter women poets wrote war verse which was in striking contrast to the romantic and jingoistic nature of the bulk of the civilian war poetry (of both men and women) written during the war.

In recent times, especially since the 1960's there has been a strong tendency to remember the war in terms of a retreat from idealism into realism and disillusionment represented by the anti-war poetry of Wilfred Owen, Siegfried Sassoon, Edmund Blunden, Isaac Rosenberg, Edward Thomas, Charles Sorley, Richard Aldington, Robert Graves, Herbert Read, and Ivor Gurney. The anti-war sentiments expressed in their poems (a large number of which were not published, in some cases not written, until after the Armistice) can hardly be regarded as a reflection of what was being expressed in the bulk of the poetry published during the years of the Great War. 'Protest', to the extent that it emerged in some of the poetry published in the Great War was mostly from the soldier-poets and seemed to be a reflection not so much of an 'anti-war' attitude but rather of a revulsion against romantic and overly jingoistic attitudes to the war, and of a desire that the war should be written about in

---

[54] All the soldier-poets, however, shared the generally stoical determination to fight on.

a more realistic and unsentimental way. When 'protest' received overt expression in the soldier-poetry of 1917-18 it was most commonly in the form of 'grousing' (sometimes humorously about such topics as lice and plum-and-apple-jam, sometimes seriously against profiteering, the lack of reinforcements, or the inefficiency of the General Staff), and often it was directed against civilians such as strikers, pacifists and 'shirkers' who they felt were hindering the prosecution of the war. Whatever attitudes the soldier-poets expressed in their verse and whatever reservations they had about the war, it is evident that there was generally among them (even in the case of Sassoon, the most famous public 'protester'[55] of them all) a commitment to stick to the task of seeing the war through to its end.

Archives (e.g *The First World War Poetry Digital Archive*), bibliographies, critical studies, autobiographies, biographies, letters, and post-war collections and anthologies relevant to Great War poetry are included in the **section 4.2.4** (**Poetry**) of **Part 4** (**Remembering the War**) where they relate both to poets who wrote about the Great War during the war (and in a number of cases after it as well) and also to poets who produced verse on the subject in the inter-war and post Second World War years. Anthologies and a selection of individual poetical works produced while the Great War was in progress are listed in the sections below.

Contemporary Anthologies

Many of the anthologies of poetry published during the war reflect the stance generally taken by poets and publishers on the home front in relation to the war. In this respect the sort of anthologies that could be read by the public is exemplified by morale-boosting collections like *Poems of the Great War* and *Sonnets for England in War Time* published in 1914 and *Pro Patria: A Book of Patriotic Verse*, a publication in 1915 of reprintings of existing patriotic verse as well as new poems in similar vein by members of the literary establishment. The years 1915 to 1917 witnessed a vogue for work by the 'fighting men' that was reflected in collections like Kyle's *Soldier Poets* (1916, second series, 1917) and Osborne's *The Muse in Arms* (1917), both of which anthologies encapsulated the tone of heroic resistance in a just cause. *Pro Patria* and the *Muse in Arms* show some development in realism but it was not until Bertram Lloyd's *Poems Written During the Great War* was published that an anthology (which included contributions from some of the more controversial poets such as Sassoon, Osbert Sitwell, Margaret S

ackville and Wilfred Gibson) gave the impression that a total commitment to the war was not shared by all those who wrote verse about it.

An Annual of New Poetry: 1917 (London: Constable, 1917)

Bean, C. E. W. ed. *The Anzac Book*, written and illustrated in Gallipoli by the men of Anzac (London: Cassell, 1916)

Blue Cross Fund. London. *A Book of Poems for The Blue Cross Fund* (to help horses in war time) (London: Jarrolds, 1917)
Lady Smith-Dorrien (wife of General Sir Horace Smith-Dorrien) was at that time the President of the Blue Cross Fund

Bridges, R., comp. *The Spirit of Man: An Anthology in English and French from the Philosophers and Poets made by the Poet Laureate in 1915* (London: Longmans Green, 1916)

Clarke, G. H., ed. *A Treasury of War Poetry: British and American Poems of The World War, 1914-1917*, First Series, (Boston: Houghton Mifflin, 1917)

Forshaw, C. F., ed. *One Hundred of the Best Poems on the European War*, by poets of the Empire, vol 1 (London: Elliot Stock, 1915)

Georgian Poetry, edited by Sir Edward H. Marsh, 5 vols (London: The Poetry Bookshop, 1915-1922)
Vol 2. 1913-1915; Vol 3. 1916-1917

Gibbons, H. A. ed. *Songs from the Trenches: The Soul of the A.E.F.*, a collection of verses by American soldiers in France, brought together by Herbert Adams Gibbons from poems submitted in the prize competition of the *New York Herald* (New York & London: Harper Bros, 1918)

---

[55] In 1917 Sassoon famously publicly expressed his feelings about the war in a protest statement, *A Soldier's Declaration*, the full text of which and the events surrounding its publication are included in **Appendix 4: Sassoon's Public Protest.**

Graham, P. A. *The 'Country Life' Anthology of Verse* (London: Country Life, 1915)

Kyle, G. ed. *Soldier Poets: Songs of the Fighting Men* (London: E. Macdonald, 1916)

— *Soldier Poets: More Songs of the Fighting Men* (London: E. Macdonald, 1917)

Halliday, W. J., comp. *Pro Patria: A Book of Patriotic Verse* (London: Dent, 1915)

Lest We forget: A War Anthology (London: Jarrolds, 1915)

Lloyd, B. ed. *Poems Written during the Great War, 1914-1918: An Anthology* (London: Allen and Unwin, 1918)

Macklin, A. E. *The Lyceum Book of War Verse* (London: Erskine Macdonald, 1918)

Monroe, H. and A. C. Henderson, eds. *The New Poetry: An Anthology* (New York: Macmillan, 1917)

Nettleingham, F. T. *Tommy's Tunes: A Comprehensive Collection of Soldiers' Songs, Marching Melodies, Rude Rhymes, and Popular Parodies*, composed, collected and arranged on active service with the B.E.F. (London: Erskine Macdonald, 1917)

Nichols, R. *Ardours and Endurances; Also A Faun's Holiday, and Poems and Fantasies* (London: Chatto & Windus, 1917)

Osborn, E. B., ed. *The Muse in Arms: A Collection of War Poems*, by seamen, soldiers, and flying men who are serving, or who have served, in the Great War (London: Murray, 1917)

Oxford Poetry 1914-1916 (Oxford: Basil Blackwell, 1916)

Poems of the Great War (London: Chatto & Windus on behalf of the Prince of Wales's National Relief Fund, 1914)
"Most of the poems have appeared recently in the Press". Preface.

Some Imagist Poets: An Anthology, 3 vols (London: Constable, 1915-16; Cambridge: Riverside Press, 1917)
Reprinted in part from various periodicals. Includes poems by Richard Aldington, H. D., John Gould Fletcher, F. S. Flint, D. H. Lawrence and Amy Lowell. Vol. 2 has title: *Some Imagist Poets ... An Annual Anthology*.

Songs and Sonnets for England in War Time, being a collection of lyrics by various authors inspired by the Great War (London: John Lane, The Bodley Head, 1914)
45 poems mostly reprinted from periodicals and newspapers. Published for the benefit of the Prince of Wales's National Relief Fund.

Thomas, E. *This England: An Anthology from her Writers* (London: Oxford University Press, 1915)

Told in the Huts: The YMCA Gift Book (London: Jarrolds, 1916)

Wheels: An Anthology of Verse, Cycle [1]-6 (Oxford: Blackwell, 1916-1921)
Includes contributions by O. Sitwell, A. Huxley, S. Sitwell, A. James, I. Tree, S. Vines, E. Sitwell, E. W. Tennant, H. Rootham, A. V. L. de Guevara, N. Cunard. 3rd-6th cycles edited by Edith Sitwell. Cycle 5 published: London: Leonard Parsons, 1920; Cycle 6 published: London: C.W. Daniel, 1921.

Contemporary War Poets

The works selected below were published during the war and represent a response to the war during the conflict by writers who can be considered as 'war poets' in the broad sense that some or all of their verse addressed aspects of the war, whether they were soldiers in the trenches, non-combatants, civilians or whatever. The selection does not include war poems that were written during the war but not published until after it was over (e.g. Richard Aldington wrote a number of war poems on active service as a soldier but they were not published until they were collected in *Images of War* in 1919 [see **section 4.2.4 (Poetry)** of **Part 4 (Remembering the War)** in the sub-section **Works of Individual Poets** for post-war publications of this sort]).

The Cultural Scene

This selection (divided by categories of writer) is illustrative of the wide range of war poetry being written between 1914 and 1918, encompassing the work not only of the now well-known 'war-poets' regarded as worth serious academic study (like Wilfred Owen, Siegfried Sassoon, Rupert Brooke, Isaac Rosenberg, Edward Thomas, Charles Sorley, Richard Aldington, Robert Graves, and Ivor Gurney) but also examples of a number of people, including women, who have mostly been forgotten by the general public but have been rescued from obscurity by being included in some modern post Second World War anthologies [see **section 4.2.4** (**Poetry**) of **Part 4** (**Remembering the War**) in the sub-section **Anthologies**]. Also selected below are examples of the publications of war poems by eminent writers of the time like John Masefield, Walter de la Mare, John Drinkwater, Conan Doyle, G. K Chesterton, Ford Maddox Ford; by contemporary literary establishment establishment figures like Robert Bridges, Thomas Hardy and Rudyard Kipling, and by authors who became well known or better known in fields other than poetry like A. P Herbert, Gilbert Frankau, A. A. Milne, Alec Waugh, and Francis Brett Young.

- **Combatants**

Alchin, G. *Oxford and Flanders* (Oxford: B.H. Blackwell, 1916)

Asquith, H. *The Volunteer and Other Poems* (London: Sidgwick & Jackson, 1915)
Some of the verses were reprinted from *The Pall Mall Gazette* and *The Spectator*. *The Volunteer* was apparently written in 1912 but it did not get published until Britain was at war presumably because it then became topical.

Barnes, R. G., Baron Gorell. *Days of Destiny: War Poems at Home and Abroad* (London: Longmans, 1917)
This sold well. Gorell's poetry frequently appeared in the *Contemporary Review* during the war

Bendall, F. W. D. *Front Line Lyrics* (London: Elkin Matthews, 1918)

Bewsher, P. *The Dawn Patrol and other Poems of an Aviator* (Londobn: Hodder & Stoughton, 1917)

Bower, J. *Songs of the Submarine* (London: McBride Nast, 1917)

Bowman, A. A. *Sonnets from a Prison Camp* (London: John Lane The Bodley Head, 1919)

Brooke, Rupert. *1914 and Other Poems*, edited by Edward Marsh (London: Sidgwick & Jackson, 1915)

— *The Collected Poems of Rupert Brooke*. With a memoir [by Edward Marsh] (London: Sidgwick & Jackson, 1918)

Brown, J. L. C. *Dies Heroica. The War Poems: 1914-1918* (London: Hodder & Stoughton, 1918)

Corbett, N. M .F. *A Naval Motley: Verses Written at Sea during the War and Before it* (London: Methuen, 1916)

Coulson, L. *From an Outpost and Other Poems* (London: E. Macdonald, 1917)
This was so popular that ten thousand copies sold in less than twelve months

Dearmer, G. *Poems* (London: William Heinemann, 1918)
Includes the poem, 'The Turkish Trench Dog'

Ford, F. M. (Joseph Leopold Ford Hermann Madox Hueffer) *On Heaven, and Poems Written On Active Service* (London: John Lane, 1918)

Frankau, G. *The City of Fear and Other Poems* (London: Chatto & Windus, 1917)

— *The Guns* (London: Chatto & Windus, 1916)
Poems reprinted from *Land and Water*, where they appeared under the title, *A Song of the Gun*

— *The Judgement of Valhalla* (London: Chatto & Windus, 1918)

Freston, H. R. *The Quest of Truth and Other Poems* (Oxford: B. H. Blackwell, 1916)

Gibson, W. W. *Battle* (London: Elkin Matthews, 1915)

The War Years

Gibson only spent a short time at the Front

Graves, R. *Fairies and Fusiliers* (London: Heinemann, 1917)

— *Over the Brazier* (London: The Poetry Bookshop, 1916)

Grenfell, J. H. F. *Into Battle: Flanders, April 1915* (London: [Privately printed by the Medici Society], 1915)
Verses, signed J. G., i.e. Julian Henry Francis Grenfell.

Gurney, I. *Severn and Somme* (London: Sidgwick & Jackson, 1917)

Harvey, F. W. *Gloucestershire Friends: Poems from a German Prison Camp* (London: Sidgwick & Jackson, 1917)

— *A Gloucestershire Lad at Home and Abroad* (London: Sidgwick & Jackson, 1916)

Hennesley, E. *Love Songs of a Soldier* (Oxford: B. H. Blackwell, 1916)

Herbert, A. P. *The Bomber Gypsy, and other Poems* (London: Methuen, 1918)

— *Half-Hours at Helles* (Oxford: Blackwell, 1916)
Most of these verses previously appeared in *Punch*.

Hill, B. *Youth's Heritage* (London: Erskine Macdonald, 1917)

Hodgson, W. N. *Verse and Prose in Peace and War* (London: Smith, Elder & Co., 1916)

Holmes, W. K. *Ballads of Field and Billet* (Paisley: Alexander Gardner, 1915)

Ledwige, F. *Last Songs* (London: Herbert Jenkins, 1918)

— *Songs of Peace*, with an introduction by Lord Dunsany (London: Herbert Jenkins Ltd., 1917)

Lee, J. *Ballads of Battle* (London: John Murray, 1916)

Levey, S. *Flanders to Fowey ("Ypres" and "Après"): Verses of Active Service, Hospital, and Convalescence by a Wounded Warrior* (London: The Sivori Levey Publications, 1917)

— *Roehampton Rhymes: Selections for a Dover House Revue, Words Written and Music Composed by Lieutenant Sivori Levey* (London: The Sivori Levey Publications, [1918])

Lyon, P. H. B. *Songs of Youth and War* (London: Erskine MacDonald, 1918)

Lyon, W. S. S. *Easter at Ypres, 1915, and other Poems* (Glasgow: James Maclehose, 1916)

McCrae, J. *In Flanders Fields and other Poems* (London: Hodder & Stoughton, 1919)
'In Flanders Fields' appeared anonymously in *Punch* on 8 December, 1915.

MacGill, P. *Soldier Songs* (London: Herbert Jenkins, 1917)

Mackintosh, E. A. *A Highland Regiment* (London: John Lane, 1917)

— *War the Liberator and Other Pieces* (London: John Lane, 1918)

Mann, H. *A Subaltern's Musings* (London: John Long, 1918)

Manning, F. *Eidola* (London: John Murray, 1917)

Milne, A. A. 'Gold Braid', *Punch*, 1917

The Cultural Scene

— 'From a Full Heart', *Punch*, 1917

Mitchell, C. *Trampled Clay* (London: Erskine Macdonald, 1917)

Monro, H. 'Youth in Arms', in *The New Poetry: An Anthology*, edited by H. Monro and A. C. Henderson (New York: Macmillan, 1917)

Nichols, R. *Ardours and Endurances: Also, a Faun's Holiday and Poems and Phantasies* (London: Chatto & Windus, 1917)

— *Invocation: War Poems and Others* (London: Elkin Mathews, 1915)

Plowman, M. *A Lap Full of Seed* (Oxford: Blackwell, 1917)

Robertson, A. *Comrades* (London: Elkin Mathews, 1916)

Rosenberg, I. 'Break of Day in the Trenches', *Poetry Magazine*, December 1916

— 'Marching (As Seen from the Left File)', *Poetry Magazine*, 1916

Sarson, H. S. *From Field and Hospital* (London: Erskine Macdonald, 1916)

Sassoon, S. *Counter-Attack and Other Poems* (London: Heinemann, 1918)

— *The Old Huntsman and Other Poems* (London: Heinemann, 1917)

Scott, F. G. *In the Battle Silences: Poems Written at the Front* (London: Constable, 1916)

Service, R. *Rhymes of a Red-Cross Man* (London: Fisher Unwin, 1916)

Shakespeare, W. G. *Ypres and Other Poems* (London: Sidgwick & Jackson, 1916)

Sitwell, Sir O. 'The Modern Abraham', *Nation*, 2 February, 1918

Sorley, C. H. *Marlborough: And Other Poems* (Cambridge: Cambridge University Press, 1916)

Stein, E. de. 'Chloe', *Punch* (1918)

— 'Elegy on the Death of Bingo, Our Trench Dog', *Punch* (1918)

Stewart, J. E. *Grapes of Thorns* (London: Erskine Macdonald, 1917)

Streets, J. W. *The Undying Splendour* (London: Erskine Macdonald, 1917)

Tennant, E. W. *Worple Flit and Other Poems* (Oxford: Blackwell, 1916)

Thomas, E. *Last Poems* (London: Selwyn & Blount, 1918)

— *Poems* (London: Selwyn & Blount, 1917)

Vernède, R. E. *War Poems and Other Verses* (London: Heinemann, 1917)

Waterhouse, G. *Rail-Head and Other Poems* (London: Erskine Macdonald, 1916)

Waugh, A. *Resentment* (London: Grant Richards, 1918)

Weaving, W. *The Star Fields and Other Poems* (Oxford: Blackwell, 1916)

Williams, E. C. *The Gutter and the Stars* (London: Erskine Macdonald, 1918)

Wodehouse, E. A. *On Leave: Poems and Sonnets* (London: Elkin Matthews, 1917)[56]

- **Civilians and Non-Combatants**

Binyon, L. *For the Fallen* (London: Hodder & Stoughton, 1917)
Binyon joined the Red Cross in 1914.

— *The Cause: Poems of the War* (London: E. Matthews, 1917)

— *The Four Years: War Poems Collected and Newly Augmented* (London: E. Matthews, 1919)
Contents: Preludes; The winnowing fan; The anvil; Before the dawn; The new world; Into peace

Bridges, R. 'Wake Up England', *The Times* (8th August, 1914)

Chesterton, G. K. 'The Wife of Flanders', in *A Treasury of War Poetry: British And American Poems of the World War, 1914-1917*. First Series, edited by G. H. Clarke (Boston: Houghton Mifflin, 1917)

De La Mare, W. 'Happy England', *Times Literary Supplement*, (27 August, 1914)

Doyle, Sir A. C. 'The Guards Came Through', in *A Treasury of War Poetry: British and American Poems of the World War, 1914-1917*. First Series, edited by G. H. Clarke (Boston: Houghton Mifflin, 1917)

Drinkwater, J. *Swords and Ploughshares* (London: Sidgwick & Jackson, 1915)

— 'We Willed It Not', in *A Treasury of War Poetry: British and American Poems of the World War, 1914-1917*. First Series, edited by G. H. Clarke (Boston: Houghton Mifflin, 1917)

Ewer, W. N. *Five Souls and other Wartime Verses* (London: The Herald, 1917)

— *Satire and Sentiment* (London: The Herald, 1918)

Foxcroft, C. T. *The Night Sister and Other Poems* (London: Methuen, 1918)

Galsworthy, J. 'England to Free Men', in *A Treasury of War Poetry: British and American Poems of the World War, 1914-1917*. First Series, edited by G. H. Clarke (Boston: Houghton Mifflin, 1917)

Gordon, H. *Our Girls in Wartime* (London: John Lane The Bodley Head, 1917)

— *Rhymes of the Red Triangle* (London: John Lane The Bodley Head, 1917)

Hardy, T. 'Men Who March Away', *The Times* (5 September, 1914)

Kennedy, G. A. S.[57] *Rough Rhymes of a Padre* (London: Hodder & Stoughton, [1918])

Kipling, R. '"For All We Have and Are"', in *A Treasury of War Poetry: British and American Poems of the World War, 1914-1917*. First Series, edited by G. H. Clarke (Boston: Houghton Mifflin, 1917)

Laing, A. M. *Carols of a Convict* [i.e. of a conscientious objector] (London: Headley, 1918)

Masefield, J. 'The Island of Skyros', in *A Treasury of War Poetry: British and American Poems of the World War, 1914-1917*. First Series, edited by G. H. Clarke (Boston: Houghton Mifflin, 1917)

Newbolt, Sir H. *St. George's Day and Other Poems* (London: John Murray, 1918)

---

[56] Wodehouse was the elder brother of P.G. Wodehouse.

[57] 'Woodbine Willie'.

— 'The Vigil', in *A Treasury of War Poetry: British and American Poems of the World War, 1914-1917*. First Series, edited by G. H. Clarke (Boston: Houghton Mifflin, 1917)

Oxenham, J., pseud [i.e. William Arthur Dunkerley]. *All's Well: Some Helpful Verse for these Dark Days of War* (London: Methuen, 1915)

— *Be of Good Cheer!* (London: Methuen, 1918)

— *The Fiery Cross: Some Verse for To-day and To-morrow* (London: Methuen, 1917)

— *Hearts Courageous* (London: Methuen, 1918)

— *The Vision Splendid: Some Verse for the Times and the Times To Come* (London: Methuen, 1917)

Rhys, E. *The Leaf Burners and Other Poems* (London: J.M. Dent, 1918)

Seaman, Sir O. *From the Home Front* (London: Constable, 1918)

— *Made in England* (London: Constable, 1916)

— *War Time* (London: Constable, 1915)

Squire, J. C. *Survival of the Fittest* (London: Allen & Unwin, 1916)

Watson, Sir W. *The Man Who Saw: and other Poems arising out of the War* (London: John Murray, 1917)

Young, F. B. *Five Degrees South* (London: Secker, 1917)
Verses written on active service (RAMC) in German East Africa.

- **Women**

Almost all the women war poets maintained their support for the war in varying degrees, and quite frequently adopted a chivalric or bellicose stance which went to the extremes as was particularly exemplified in the verse of Jessie Pope, one of the most popular poets of the time. A number of women wrote poems which were a great deal more sensitive and compassionate than those of Jessie Pope (e.g. Sybil Bristowe, Vera Brittain, May Cannan, Charlotte Mew, Eleanor Farjeon) and there were a few whose poetry included attitudes implicitly or explicitly critical of the war and warmongering (e.g. Margaret Sackville, Helen Hamilton, Margaret Postgate Cole, Alice Meynell, Winifred Letts, Edith Sitwell, Gertrude Ford). Practically all the women war poets encouraged men to enlist, exhorted soldiers to continue fighting despite the heavy loss of life and praised women and non-combatants for their share in the sacrifice.

Poems from most of the poetical works selected below can be found in the anthology, *Scars Upon My Heart* edited and introduced by Catherine Reilly (London: Virago, 1981). Of the 532 women Reilly estimated as writing poetry during the war years she picked out 79 of them for her anthology of 123 poems.

Bristowe, S. 'Over the Top', in *The Lyceum Book of War Verse*, edited by A. E. Macklin (London: Erskine Macdonald, 1918)

Brittain, V. *Verses of a VAD* (London: Erskine Macdonald, 1918)

Cannan, M. W. *In War Time: Poems* (Oxford: Blackwell, 1917)

Cole, Dame M. I. (née Postgate). *Margaret Postgate's Poems* (London: Allen & Unwin, 1918)
Includes the poems, 'Fallen Leaves', 'Afterwards'

Farjeon, E. *Sonnets and Poems* (Oxford: Blackwell, 1918)
Includes the poems, 'Peace', 'Now That You Too'

Ford, S. G. *A Fight to a Finish* (London: Daniel, 1917)

Hamilton, H. *Napoo! A Book of War Bêtes-Noires* (Oxford: Blackwell, 1918)

Jenkins, E. *Poems* (London: Sidgwick & Jackson, 1915)

Letts, W. M. *Hallow-e'en, and Poems of the War* (London: Smith, Elder & Co., 1916)

— *The Spires of Oxford and other Poems* (New York: E.P. Dutton, 1917)
The majority of these poems were published in 1916 under title: "Hallow-e'en and poems of the war." [Publishers' note]

Mackay, H. *London, One November* (London: Andrew Melrose, 1917)
Includes, 'The Train'

Meynell, A. C. [née Thompson]. *Poems on the War*, edited by C. Shorter (London: Privately Printed, 1915)
20 copies of this work were printed for private circulation. A complete edition of her poems was published by Burns, Oates & Washbourne in 1923 and reprinted by them in 1940. A recent reprint of the complete edition was published in 2010 by Kessinger Publishing in the series Kessinger Legacy reprints

Pope, J. *More War Poems* (London: Grant Richards, 1915)

— *Simple Rhymes for Stirring Times* (London : C. A. Pearson, 1916)

— *War Poems* (London: Grant Richards, 1915)

Sackville, Lady M. *The Pageant of War* (London: Simpkin, Marshall, 1916)

Sinclair, M. 'Field Ambulance in Retreat', in *King Albert's Book: A Tribute to the Belgian King and People from Representative Men and Women throughout the World.*, edited by Hall Caine (London: Hodder & Stoughton, 1914)

Sitwell, Dame. E. 'The Dancers (During a Great Battle, 1916)', in *Clowns' Houses*, [poems] by Edith Sitwell (Oxford: Blackwell, 1918)

Smith, C. F. *Fighting Men* (London: Elkin Mathews, 1916)

Stopes, M. C. 'Night on the Shore', in *The Lyceum Book of War Verse*, edited by A. E. Macklin (London: Erskine Macdonald, 1918)

Tynan, K. *Flower of Youth: Poems in War Time* (London: Sidgwick & Jackson, 1915)

3.3.5 Propaganda

In general well known British literary figures (with the notable exception of George Bernard Shaw and D. H. Lawrence) supported the decision to go to war and were prepared to justify and romanticize the Allied cause in works of a clearly propagandistic nature. They continued to produce such works throughout the war although, as the war progressed into a long-drawn-out and costly affair, some deterioration of their support for it can be detected, for instance, in the ironic fiction of H. G. Wells (*Mr Britling Sees It Through*), Arnold Bennett (*The Pretty Lady*), John Galsworthy (*Saint's Progress*), and Ford Madox Ford (*Zeppelin Nights*).

Critical Studies

Buitenhuis, P. *The Great War of Words: British, American, and Canadian Propaganda and Fiction, 1914-1933* (Vancouver: University of British Columbia Press, 1987; repr. London: Batsford, 1989)
The 1989 reprint published in London was entitled, *The Great War of Words: Literature as Propaganda 1914-18 and After*

— 'Writers at War: Propaganda and Fiction in the Great War', *University of Toronto Quarterly*, 45 (1976), 277-94

Small, H. 'Mrs Humphrey Ward and the First Casualty of War', in *Women's Fiction and the Great War*, edited by S. Raitt and T. Tate (Oxford: Clarendon Press, 1997)

Wright, D. G. 'The Great War, Government Propaganda and English "Men of Letters", 1914-16', *Literature and History*, 7 (1978), 70-100

Contemporary Propaganda

When Masterman embarked on the task of developing propaganda at Wellington House one of his first ideas was to call on the writers of England for help. The meeting he set up for this purpose was attended by writers in a variety of fields and included a number of well known literary figures – William Archer, Sir James Barrie, Arnold Bennett, A. C. Benson, R.H. Benson, Robert Bridges, Hall Caine, G. K. Chesterton, W. J. Locke, Sir Arthur Conan Doyle, John Galsworthy, Thomas Hardy, Anthony Hope Hawkins, Maurice Hewlett, W. J. Locke, E. V. Lucas, John Masefield, A. E. W. Mason, Sir Henry Newbolt, Sir Owen Seaman, H. G. Wells, and Israel Zangwill. Some of the latter writers subsequently became workers in the government's propaganda service[58] or wrote propaganda pieces, such as the examples selected below. There were also other literary figures like Hilaire Belloc, Laurence Binyon, John Buchan, Edmund Gosse, Rudyard Kipling, Alfred Noyes, and Mrs Humphrey Ward who produced works of a propagandistic nature such as those below.

After the war some of these writers regretted their willingness to be involved in propaganda as a departure from their integrity as writers.

Archer, W. *The Pirate's Progress: A Short History of the U-Boat* (London: Chatto & Windus, 1918)

Barrie, J. M. *Der Tag* (London: Coliseum Theatre, 1914)

Belloc, H. *The Two Maps of Europe* (London: Pearson, 1915)

Bennett, A. *Liberty; A Statement of the British Case* (London: London: Hodder & Stoughton, 1914)

Binyon, L. 'Now in thy Splendour', *The Times* (11 August 1914)

Bridges, R. 'Wake Up England', *The Times* (8 August, 1914)

Buchan, J., 1st Baron Tweedsmuir. *The Future of the War* (London: Hodder and Stoughton, 1916)
An address reprinted from the *Bookseller*.

Caine, H. *Our Girls: Their Work for the War* (London: Hutchinson, 1916)

Chesterton, G. K. *Letters to an Old Garibaldian* (London: Methuen, 1914)

Doyle, Sir A. C. *To Arms!* (London: Hodder and Stoughton, 1914)

— *The British Campaign in France and Flanders 1914-1918*, 6 vols (London: Hodder & Stoughton, 1916-20)

— *A Visit to Three Fronts* (London: Hodder & Stoughton, 1916)

Ford, F. M. (Joseph Leopold Ford Hermann Madox Hueffer). *Between St. Dennis and St George* (London: Hodder & Stoughton, 1915)

— *When Blood is Their Argument: An Analysis of German Culture* (London: Hodder & Stoughton, 1915)

Galsworthy, J. *A Sheaf* (London: Heinemann, 1916)

---

[58] For example, Kipling was Director of Propaganda to the British Colonies; John Masefield was sent on a pro-war lecture tour of America and paid to write *Gallipoli* with the main aim of influencing American readers; Conan Doyle was commissioned to write *The British Campaign in France and Flanders 1914-1918*; Arnold Bennett became Director of British Propaganda to France; John Buchan was for a time head of the Department of Information (the successor to the War Propaganda Bureau at Wellington House); H. G. Wells worked in the Department of Information and in its successor, the Ministry of Information

Gosse, Sir E. *Inter Arma: Being Essays Written in Time of War* (London: Heinemann, 1916)

Hardy, T. 'Men Who March Away', *The Times* (5 September, 1914)

Hope, A., pseud. [i.e. Anthony Hope Hawkins] *The New (German) Testament*, Some Texts and a Commentary (London: Methuen, 1915)

Kipling, R. 'For All we Have and Are', in *A Treasury of War Poetry: British and American Poems of the World War, 1914-1917*. First Series, edited by G. H. Clarke (Boston: Houghton Mifflin, 1917)
This poem was printed in the *New York Times* (2 September 1914) in an article headed 'Rudyard Kipling Calls To Britons To Stand Up And Meet The War'.

— *France At War* (London: Macmillan, 1915)

Lucas, E. V. *In Gentlest Germany*, by Hun Svedend. Translated from the Svengalese by E. V. Lucas. With 45 illustrations and 1 map by George Morrow (London: Lane, 1915)
A skit on *With the German Armies in the West* by Sven Hedin.

Masefield, J. *Gallipoli* (London: Heinemann, 1916)

— *The Old Front Line, or, The Beginning of the Battle of the Somme* (London: Heinemann, 1917)

Newbolt, Sir H. *St. George's Day and Other Poems* (London: John Murray, 1918)

Noyes, A. *What is England Doing?* (London: Burrup, Mathieson & Sprague, 1916)

Parker, Sir G. *Is England Apathetic?: A Reply* (London: Darling, 1915)
Originally published in the *New York Times* on the first anniversary of the declaration of war.

Seaman, Sir O. 'Pro Patria', *Punch* (12 August 1914)

Ward, Mrs Humphrey [i.e. Mary Augusta Ward] *England's Effort; Six Letters to an American Friend* (London: Smith, Elder, 1914)

— *Towards the Goal* (London: Murray, 1917)

3.4 Music

By 1914 access to music of some sort had become widespread among all classes. Pianos which could be purchased on a hire-purchase basis for as little as a shilling a week, had become a prominent feature in the parlour of many a household and sheet music could be bought for a few pence A piano was commonly to be found in church halls and boy's clubs, and practically every saloon bar would have its piano for providing sing-songs which could be enjoyed by even the poorest. Gramophones had long been available for those who could afford them and gramophone records could be purchased quite cheaply[59]. Music could be heard in music halls, cinemas, concert halls and theatres. Because of cheaper prices a member of the working-class tended to frequent the musical hall and the cinema rather than the concert-hall and the theatre, but as his overall standard of living rose in the course of the war he was increasingly likely to find all forms of musical entertainment affordable.

The cinema was a source of music for everyone. Films were silent and usually accompanied with music which was provided by a small orchestral group, often as little as a dozen players, performing on stringed instruments, piano, harmonium and percussion. It became the tendency for the musical accompaniment to be composed to match particular cinematic scenes but it was also the practice to play classical music in overtures and intervals, and pieces of such music during performances. Cinema audiences were, therefore, able to enjoy the performance of a variety of music and, for the large numbers among them who would not normally have entered a concert hall, the rare experience of hearing the performance of some music of a classical nature.

---

[59] Aided by their extensive advertisement in the press gramophone records sold extremely well and brought music into many households. Popular patriotic songs, or songs like the nostalgic 'Tipperary' (written just before the war and a favourite with the British troops), were typical of the bulk of the records produced during the war.

The Cultural Scene

It was feared by many people that the outbreak of war would result in a serious diminution of the musical life of the country but this did not happen and in fact music flourished throughout the war. Concern about the effect the war might have on the musical profession resulted in the creation of the Music in Wartime Committee to protect the interests of British musicians. There was, however, no protection for German musicians; they and the music of their home country were for a time subjected to a boycott as result of anti-German hostility. This restriction of the classical repertoire, added to all the other problems that had developed in the musical life of the country as a result of the demands of war (such as less music being printed, fewer instruments being made, fewer people entering the music profession, concert-halls being taken over for military purposes, and private funding disappearing), created a musical recession which was, however, short-lived. The war soon had the beneficial effect of producing an increased demand for entertainment and this triggered a musical revival. The loss of younger musicians to the services with the introduction of conscription in 1916 might have produced a crisis but this was avoided as the effect of their disappearance from the theatre pits, the concert platform, the cinemas and the cafés was mitigated by the employment of women to fill the gaps.. Civilians and soldiers flocked to the musical halls, theatres, and cinemas and, thanks to Sir Thomas Beecham, opera flourished. The concert-hall suffered from some setbacks but, through the efforts of such bodies as the Royal Philharmonic Society and the London Symphony Orchestra and the continuation of the Henry Wood's Promenade Concerts, audiences could enjoy listening to orchestral music throughout the war (even prejudice against the performance of the music of Germany eventually subsided). It was, however, light music that the British people particularly wanted to hear; as an antidote to the gloom and weariness of war they wanted to listen to the popular music of composers like Paul Rubens and Ivor Novello.

The outbreak of war was met with patriotic enthusiasm in the nation's concert and music halls and theatres and audiences were served with a variety of music in some way related to the war. In the musical halls recruiting songs were sung and publishers responded with the printing of large quantities of the sheet music of patriotic songs. For patriotic purposes concerts of classical music of the allied countries (i.e. Britain, France and Russia) were arranged and for a time German music was excluded. Britain's leading classical composers joined in the enthusiastic response to the war by producing music of a patriotic nature. Sir Edward Elgar led the way with *Carillon*, his setting to music of a Belgian war poem by Emile Cammaerts, and later composed works incorporating patriotic verse by Laurence Binyon and Rudyard Kipling[60]. Sir Charles Stanford and the poet Sir Henry Newbolt collaborated on *Song of the Sea*, and William Blake's 'Jerusalem' was set to music by Sir Hubert Parry as an inspirational hymn to boost the nation's resolve.

3.4.1 General

Books

Blackwell History of Music in Britain, general editor in chief, I. Spink, 6 vols (Oxford: Blackwell, 1995), VI: *The Twentieth Century*, edited by S. Banfield (1995)

Cooper, M., ed. *New Oxford History of Music*, 10 vols (Oxford: Oxford University Press, 1963-2001), X: *The Modern Age, 1890-1960* (1974)

Ford, B., ed. *The Cambridge Cultural History of Britain*, 9 vols (Cambridge: Cambridge University Press, 1992), VIII: *Early Twentieth Century Britain* (1992)

Fuller, J. G. *Troop Morale and Popular Culture in the British and Dominion Armies, 1914-1918* (Oxford: Clarendon Press, 1990)

Laurence, D. H., ed. *Shaw's Music: The Complete Musical Criticism of Bernard Shaw*, 2nd edn, 3 vols (London: The Bodley Head, 1989), III, *1893-1950*

---

[60] Although the music of Elgar in the Great War tends perhaps to be remembered in terms of his patriotic compositions and the popularity of 'Land of Hope and Glory' (composed long before the war), the exuberant mood of patriotism they reflect is completely absent in the *Cello Concerto* which he composed a year after the war had ended; through the sombre nature of the latter work Elgar seems to be evoking a sense of the tragedy of the war years that he might well have been feeling by the end of the war.

Mackerness, E. D. *A Social History of English Music* (London: Routledge, 1964)

Scholes, P. A., ed. *The Mirror of Music 1844-1944: A Century of Musical Life in Britain as Reflected in the Pages of the Musical Times*, 2 vols (London: Novello, 1947))

Watkins, G. *Proof through the Night: Music and the Great War* (Berkeley: University of California Press, 2002)

Articles

Hiley, N. 'Ploughboys and Soldiers: The Folk Song and the Gramophone in the British Expeditionary Force, 1914-1918', *Media History*, 4 (1998), 61-76

Hullah, A. 'Record of the Music in War Time Committee 1914-20, *Musical News*, (August/September 1920)

Scott, C. 'The Connection of the War with Art and Music', *The Monthly Musical Record*, 46 (1 March 1916)

3.4.2 Popular Music (see also 3.5.2 The Theatre)

Books

Arthur, M. *When This Bloody War is Over: Soldiers Songs of the First World War*. Introduction by Lyn Macdonald (London: Judy Piatkus Ltd., 2001)

Ashwell, L. *Modern Troubadours: A Record of the Concerts at the Front* (London: Glydendal, 1922)

Brophy, J. and E. Partridge. *The Long Trail: What the British Soldier Sang and Said in the Great War of 1914-18*, revised edn (London: Sphere, 1969)
Previous edition published as *Songs and Slang of the British Soldier, 1914-18*, London: Deutsch, 1931.

Gänzll, K. *The British Musical Theatre*, 2 vols (Basingstoke : Macmillan Press, 1987)
Contents: Vol.1. 1865-1914; Vol.2. 1915-1984.

— *The Encyclopedia of the Musical Theatre*, 2 vols (Oxford: Blackwell, 1994)

Girard, S. L., ed. *Songs that Won the War*, collected and edited by S. Louis Giraud, Daily Express Community Song Book, 3 (London: Lane, 1930)

MacQueen-Pope, W. J. *The Melody Lingers On* (London: W. H. Allen, 1950)

Morley, S. *Spread a Little Happiness: The First Hundred Years of the British Musical* (London: Thames and Hudson, 1987)

Murdoch, B. *Fighting Songs and Warring Words: Popular Lyrics of two World Wars* (London: Routledge, 1990)

Nettleinghame, F. T. *Tommy's Tunes: A Collection of Soldier's Songs, Marching Melodies, Rude Rhymes and Popular Parodies*, composed, collected, and arranged by F. T. Nettleingham, new and rev. edn (London: Erskine Macdonald, 1917)

— *More Tommy's Tunes: An Additional Collection of Soldiers' Songs, Marching Melodies, Rude Rhymes and Popular Parodies*, composed, collected, and arranged on active service with the B.E.F by F. T. Nettleinghame (London: Erskine Macdonald, 1918)

Noble, P. *Ivor Novello; Man of the Theatre* (London: Falcon, 1951; repr. London: White Lion Publishers, 1975)

Palmer, R. *What a Lovely War: British Soldiers' Songs from the Boer War to the Present Day*. Foreword by Lyn Macdonald (London: M. Joseph, 1990)

Platt, L. *Musical Comedy on the West End Stage, 1890–1939* (Basingstoke: Palgrave Macmillan, 2004)

Pulling, C. *They Were Singing, and What They Sang About* (London: Harrap, 1952)

Russell, D. *Popular Music in England, 1840-1914*, 2nd edn (Manchester: Manchester University Press, 1997)

Singleton, B. *Oscar Asche, Orientalism, and British Musical Comedy* (Westport, Conn.: Praeger, 2004)

Walsh, C. *Mud, Songs and Blighty: A Scrapbook of the First World War* (London: Hutchinson, 1975)

Whitehouse, E., comp. *London Lights: A History of West End Musicals* (Cheltenham: This England Books, 2005)

Yorke, D., ed. *Mud and Stars: An Anthology of World War Songs and Poetry* (New York: Holt, 1931)

Articles

Burns, R. G. H. 'British Folk Songs of the Great War - Then and Now', *Journal of Military History*, 79 (2015), 1059-1077

Charman, T. ' "… And my heart's right there" ', *Despatches* (The Magazine of the Friends of the Imperial War Museum), No. 14 (2012), 20-22
A reflection by IWM historian, Terry Chapman, on the popular songs of the Firsst World War.

Contemporary Musicals

During the gloomy days of the Great War, audiences wanted light and uplifting entertainment, and they flocked to theatres to see light-hearted revues and musical plays. A number of them (see selection listed below) were highly successful. The music of composers like Paul Rubens (*Betty*; *The Happy Day*; *Tina*), Frederick Norton (*Chu Chin Chow*), Nat Ayer (*The Bing Boys Are Here*; *Houp-La!*), Ivor Novello (*Theodore and Co*), Lionel Monkton (*The Boy*), and Max Darewksi (*Hanky Panky*) and the syncopated rhythms of such American shows as *Houp-La!* (1916) and *Hanky Panky* (1917) played an important part in helping civilians and servicemen to escape the weariness of the war.

Betty. Daly's Theatre (24 April, 1915)
Music composed by Paul Rubens

The Bing Boys Are Here. Alhambra Theatre (April 19, 1916)
The Bing Boys Are Here starring George Robey and Violet Lorraine (famous for their introduction of the song *If You Were the Only Girl in the World*) was the first of a series of revues which played at the Alhambra Theatre during the last two years of World War I. The series included *The Bing Boys on Broadway* and *The Bing Boys are There*. The music for them was written by Nat D. Ayer. The total number of performances for all three reviews was well over 1,000, lasting beyond the Armistice in November 1918. *The Bing Boys Are Here* was one of the three most important musical hits of the London stage during World War I (the other two being *The Maid of the Mountains* and *Chu Chin Chow*); music or scenes from all of these have been included as background in many films set in this period, and they remain intensely evocative of the Great War years.

The Boy. Alhambra Theatre (14 September, 1917)
A musical comedy with music by Lionel Monckton and Howard Talbot, based on Arthur Wing Pinero's 1885 play, *The Magistrate*. It ran for 801 performances - one of the longest runs of any musical theatre piece up to that time.

Chu Chin Chow. His Majesty's Theatre. (3 August 1916)
A musical extravaganza written, produced and directed by Oscar Asche, with music by Frederic Norton, based (with minor embellishments) on the story of *Ali Baba and the 40 Thieves*. It ran for five years and a total of 2,238 performances (more than twice as many as any previous musical).

Hanky Panky. The Empire Theatre (1915)
An Ernest C. Rolls production, by Hartley Carrick, Worton David, and Max Darewski. Music by Max Darewski

The Happy Day. Daly's Theatre (13 May, 1916)
Music composed by Paul Rubens.

Houp La! St. Martin's Theatre (23 November, 1916)
Music by Nat D. Ayer and Howard Talbot. It was produced by Charles B. Cochran at the St. Martin's Theatre on 23

The War Years

November 1916.

The Maid of the Mountains. Daly's Theatre (10 February, 1917)
Light opera or musical play in three acts which, after an initial try out at the Prince's Theatre in Manchester on 23 February 1916, was rewritten and then opened at Daly's Theatre in London on February 10, 1917. Music by Harold Fraser-Simson, with additional music by James W. Tate Directed by Oscar Asche (who had directed the record-setting hit *Chu Chin Chow*). *The Maid of the Mountains* ran for 1,352 performances in its initial London run.

Theodore and Co. Gaiety Theatre (19 September 1916)
Musical comedy in two acts with music by Ivor Novello and Jerome Kern. This show established Ivor Novello as a theatrical composer. Novello's songs from the show include "What A Duke Sould Be" and "Oh, How I Want To Marry".

Tina. Adelphi Theatre (2 November, 1915)
Music composed by Paul Rubens

Yes, Uncle! Prince of Wales Theatre (16 December, 1917)
A musical comedy with music by Nat D. Ayer. It ran for a very successful 626 performances.

Contemporary Songs

The war inspired a flood of popular songs many of which have ever since been evocative of this period of history. This flood ranged from commercially written war-songs, through musical-hall choruses, popular songs from stage musicals and sentimental ballads, to the bawdy, ironic parodies that were enjoyed by servicemen.

In the early days of the war recruiting songs predominated (e.g. *We Don't Want To Lose You But We Think You Ought To Go*) but as the war progressed the songs being sung at home and in the trenches reflected a far wider range of content, giving expression, for instance, to jingoism (e.g. *When Belgium Put the Kibosh on the Kaiser*), patriotism (e.g. *Keep the Home Fires Burning*), humour (*Take me Back to Dear Old Blighty*), sentimentality (e.g. *The Roses of Picardy*), nostalgia (e.g. *It's a Long Way to Tipperary*), and satire (*Oh! It's a Lovely War*). One of the most popular songs of the war, *If You Were the Only Girl In the World*, was from the revue, *The Bing Boys Are Here*. Quite a number of the songs which became favourites with the wartime public were in circulation before the war as was the case with, for instance, *Annie Laurie, Roamin' in the Gloamin', Hello! Hello! Who's your Lady Friend, It's a Long Way to Tipperary, Goodbye Dolly Gray,* and *Who Were You With last Night?*

As well as enjoying the popular songs and ballads of the day and rousing marching songs like *Pick up Your Troubles in your Old Kit Bag* the soldiers in the front line took delight in making parodies of many of them. These parodies were mostly humorous and satirical (e.g. *My Little Wet Hole in the Trench*, an adaptation of the ballad *My Little Grey Home in the West*), but sometimes sardonic (e.g. *I Don't Want to be a Soldier*, an adaptation of the recruiting song, *Come, My Lad, and be A Soldier*), and occasionally bitter (e.g. *I Wore a Tunic*). Even hymns (no doubt rendered familiar to many in peacetime by the Salvation Army playing them on street corners) were parodied (e.g. *When this Bloody War is Over*, an adaptation of *What a Friend We Have in Jesus*). Soldiers also made up their own irreverent lyrics and composed humorous and often obscene marching songs (e.g. *Mademoiselle from Armenteers*).

An alphabetical listing of the selection of songs mentioned above are provided below:

Annie Laurie
The song to "Annie Laurie" was originally written by Anne Laurie's sweetheart, William Douglas, and amended by Lady John Scott (1810-1900) who altered the second verse and composed the third. This song was a favourite with Scottish soldiers during the Crimean War.

Goodbye Dolly Gray
Written in 1898 by Will D. Cobb, with music by Paul Barnes. Sung by troops who went off to the Boer War as well as the B.E.F. which left for France in 1914.

Hello! Hello! Who's your Lady Friend
Written in 1913 by David Worton and Bert Lee and composed by Harry Fragson.

I Don't Want to be A Soldier
A parody of the recruiting song, *Come, My Lad, and be a Soldier*. An example of the sardonic attitude of soldiers to recruiting

songs.

If You Were the Only Girl in the World
Written by Clifford Grey, with music by Nat. D. Ayer. First made famous by George Robey and Violet Lorraine when they sang it in the revue, *The Bing Boys Are Here*, in 1916. *If You Were the Only Boche in the Trench* was the soldiers' parody of this song.

It's a Long Way to Tipperary
Written by Jack Judge in 1912, with music by Harry Williams. One of the hit songs of the Great War.

I Wore A Tunic
One of the few British war songs expressing bitter feelings of veteran soldiers towards those who had escaped military service until conscripted in the later years of the war. Adapted from the drawing-room song, *I Wore a Tulip*.

Keep the Home Fires Burning
Written in 1914, with music by Ivor Novello and lyrics by Lena Guilbert Ford.

My Little Wet Hole in the Trench
An adaptation written in 1915 by Tom Skeyhill of *My Little Grey Home in the West*.

Oh! It's a Lovely War
Written by J. P. Long, with music by M. Scott in 1917. It was the inspiration for Joan Littlewood's production of *Oh! What a Lovely War*, first staged at the Theatre Royal, Stratford in 1963, and subsequently filmed under the direction of Richard Attenborough in 1969.

Pack Up Your Troubles in Your Old Kit-Bag
Written in 1915 by George Asat, with music by Felix Powell.

Roamin' in the Gloamin'
Composed by Harry Lauder before the Great War.

The Roses of Picardy
Written in 1916, with words by Fred. E. Weatherly and music by Haydn Wood.

Take me Back to Dear Old Blighty
Written in 1916 by A. J. Mills, Fred Godfrey and Bennet Scott.

We Don't Want to Lose You, but We Think You Ought to Go
Written and composed by Paul. A. Rubens in 1914. The words of this song were adapted by soldiers in sardonic and witty fashion indicative of their disenchantment with recruiting songs.

When Belgium Put the Kibosh on the Kaiser
Written and composed in 1914 by Alf Ellerton.

When This Bloody War Is Over
An adaptation of the hymn *What a Friend We Have in Jesus*.

Who Were You With last Night?
Written in 1912 by Fred Godfrey, with music by Mark Sheridan. The chorus of this song was especially popular with soldiers.

3.4.3 'Serious' Music

Although it is the light music with which the Great War is predominantly associated 'serious' music continued to be composed and the works of a wide variety of classical composers to be enjoyed by many people. Particularly deserving to be mentioned in the latter respect was Sir Thomas Beecham who through his revitalisation of the Hallé Concerts Society stimulated the enthusiasm of audiences for concert works by French, Russian and above all English composers, and by means of the opera company (the Beecham Opera Company) he founded in 1915 brought a wide repertoire of opera to the provinces as well as London. The public were also able to continue attending the Promenade Concerts which Henry Wood kept going throughout the war. Anti-German feeling led for a time to a decline in performances of German music. Even Henry Wood early in the war felt pressurised by prevailing opinion into substituting a Russian night for the traditional Wagner night at his Promenade Concerts (although later in the war he brought Wagner back). As the popularity of German music declined audiences became familiar as never before with the classical music of other nations (e.g. France and Russia), and the works of British composers received a better hearing. Compositions which reflected the martial mood of the nation (like Tschaikovsy's *1812 Overture* and Elgar's *Carillon*) tended to be especially popular..

Active service in the armed forces interrupted the musical careers of a number of composers and restricted their musical output. Among them were Ralph Vaughan Williams, Arthur Bliss and Ivor Gurney, none of whom produced very much during the war years. Ralph Vaughan Williams began working on some drafts of his *Pastoral Symphony* but this work was not completed until after the war; Arthur Bliss wrote his Piano Quartet in A Minor in 1915 during the Battle of the Somme; and Ivor Gurney composed some songs (i.e. *By a Bierside* and *In Flanders*) but he was mainly interested in writing poetry at this stage in his life. Ernest Moeran was also in the armed forces at this time but his career as a composer did not take off until after the war was over. Some of Britain's most promising composers did not survive the war. George Butterworth, Ernest Farrar, W. D. Browne and Frederick Kelly were all killed in the front line. The bulk of the works composed during the war were by non-combatants (Bax, Bridge, Delius, Elgar, Holst, Ireland, Parry, Stanford). Bax in particular was remarkably prolific producing, in addition to various piano music, his piano quintet, his second violin sonata, songs, and orchestral tone poems such as *The Garden of Fand, November Woods, Tintagel*, and the *Symphonic Variations for piano and orchestra.*

Most British composers active during the war years produced some music related in some sort of manner to the war. It is, however, the patriotic works of composers like Elgar (e.g. *The Spirit of England*) and Parry (e.g. *Jerusalem*) that tend to be remembered among the contemporary hymns, anthems, cantatas and symphonic poems written expressly to voice feelings about the war. Many of Elgar's compositions were of a distinctly propagandistic nature but only one of them, the song *Big Steamers* (a setting of Kipling composed for the Ministry of Food), was actually commissioned by the Government. At no time during the war did the Government have a policy to promote music as a national asset to aid the cause of victory. Elgar also tried to help public morale with several 'lighter' works such as his incidental music to *The Starlight Express* (1915; an adaptation for the stage of Algernon Blackwood's fantasy novel, *A Prisoner in Fairyland*) and his score for the ballet *The Sanguine Fan* (1917).

Autobiographies, Biographies

Anderson, R. *Elgar* (London: Dent, 1993)

Beecham, Sir. T. *Frederick Delius*, rev. edn (London: Severn House, 1975)

— *A Mingled Chime: Leaves from an Autobiography*, new edn (London: Columbus, 1987)
Originally published London: Hutchinson, 1944.

Bliss, Sir A. E. D. *As I Remember*, rev. and enlarged edn (London: Thames Publishing, 1989)

Cardus, N. *Autobiography* (London: Collins, 1947)

— *Second Innings* (London: Collins, 1950)

Day, J. *Vaughan Williams*, rev. 3rd edn (Oxford: Oxford University Press, 1998)

Eastaugh, E. *Havergal Brian: The Making of a Composer* (London: Harrap, 1976)

Foreman, L. *Bax: A Composer and His Times*, rev. edn (Woodbridge: Boydell Press, 2007)

Greene, H. P. *Sir Charles Villiers Stanford* (London: Arnold, 1935)

Holst, I. *Gustav Holst: A Biography*, 2nd edn (Oxford: Oxford University Press, 1969)

McVeagh, D. *Edward Elgar, His Life and Music* (London: J. M. Dent, 1955)

Moore, J. N. *Edward Elgar: A Creative Life* (Oxford: Oxford University Press, 1984; reissued 1999)

Payne, A. *Frank Bridge: Radical and Conservative*, rev. edn (London: Thames Publishing 1999)[61]

Reid, C. *Thomas Beecham: An Independent Biography* (London: Gollancz, 1962)

Searle, M. V. *John Ireland: The Man and His Music* (Tunbridge Well: Midas Books, 1979)

Short, M. *Gustav Holst: The Man and His Music* (Oxford: Oxford University Press, 1990)

Wood, Sir H. J. *My Life of Music* (London: Gollancz, 1938: repr., 1949)

Books

Cox, D. *The Henry Wood Proms* (London: BBC, 1980)

Doctor, J. and D. Wright. *The Proms: A New History*, edited by Jenny Doctor and David Wright; consultant editor, Nicholas Kenyon (London: Thames & Hudson, 2007)

Foreman, L., ed. *Oh My Horses!: Elgar and the Great War*, The Music of Elgar, 2 (Rickmansworth: Elgar Enterprises, 2001)
"With a compact disc of historical recordings."--T.p.

Gollancz, V. *Journey Towards Music* (London: Gollancz, 1964)

Grew, S. *Favourite Musical Performers* (Edinburgh: Foulis, 1923)
Contents: Sir Henry J. Wood; Sir Thomas Beecham; Julius Harrison; Rosina Buckman; Frank Mullings; Robert Radford.; John Coates; Sir Richard Runciman Terry; T. W. North; Albert Sammons; Sir Landon Ronald.

Hughes, M. and R. A. Stradling. *The English Musical Renaissance, 1860-1940: Constructing a National Music*, 2nd edn (Manchester: Manchester University Press, 2001)

Shaw, G. B. *Shaw's Music: The Complete Musical Criticism of Bernard Shaw*, edited by D. H. Laurence, 2nd edn, 3 vols (London: The Bodley Head, 1989), III, 1893-1950

Contemporary Articles

Colles, H. C. 'Music in War-Time' *Proceedings of the Musical Association*, 41st Session, 1914-15 (1915)

Duncan, E. 'Music and War', *Musical Times*, 55 (September 1 1914)

Newman, E. 'The War and the Future of Music', *Musical Times*, 55 (September 1 1914)

Stanford, C. V. 'Music and the War', *Quarterly Review*, (1915)
Reprinted in Stanford's *Interludes: Records and Reflections* (London: Murray, 1922).

Contemporary Compositions

Bax, A. *Elegiac Trio for Flute, Viola, and Harp* (1916)

— *The Garden of Fand* (1916)

— *In Memoriam* (1916)
The Easter Rising of 1916 was reflected in a variety of Bax's music, most notably in the orchestral *In Memoriam* ('In

---

[61] Bridge, a pacifist (and in any case too old to fight) was disturbed by the jingoism of the nation and the loss of friends on the battlefield after the outbreak of war. His reaction was to produce music which reflects his aversion to war, as is evident if one listens to compositions like *Lament* (1915), *Two Poems of Richard Jefferies* (1915), and *A Prayer* (1916-18).

The War Years

memoriam Padraig Pearse'), which remained largely unknown until recorded by Vernon Handley in 1998.

— *November Woods* (1917)

— *Piano Quintet* (1915)

— *Second Violin Sonata* (1915)

— *Symphonic Variations for Piano and Orchestra* (1918)

— *Tintagel* (1917)

Bliss, Sir A. E. D. *Piano Quartet in A* Minor (1915)

Bridge, F. *Lament* (1915)
Bridge composed *Lament* for string orchestra in 1915 in memory of a young friend who, with her family, drowned when the Lusitania was sunk.

— *A Prayer* (1916-18)
This work, a setting of *A Prayer* by the fourteenth-century German mystic Thomas à Kempis, was Bridge's plea for peace.

— *Two Poems of Richard Jefferies* (1915)
" ... In the second of his *Two Poems* for orchestra, Bridge's message was one of hope in a world torn by violence: 'How beautiful a delight to make the world joyous! The song should never be silent, the dancer never still, the laugh should sound like water that runs for ever' (from *The Story of My Heart by Richard Jefferies*, quoted at the top of the score) ... " [Quotation from Paul Hindmarsh, 'Bridge, Frank (1879–1941)', *Oxford Dictionary of National Biography*, Oxford University Press, 2004 [http://www.oxforddnb.com/view/article/32059, accessed 11 Nov 2013]

Delius, F. *Cello Concerto* (1916)

— *Double Concerto* (1916)

— *Requiem* (1916)
Between 1913 and 1916 Delius composed his Requiem, dedicated 'to the memory of all young Artists fallen in the war'. It was not performed until 1922.

— *String Quartet* (1916)

— *Violin Concerto* (1916)

Elgar, Sir E. *Carillon* (1914)
Dramatic recitation with orchestral accompaniment.

— *Piano Quintet* (1918)

— *Polonia* (1916)

—*The Spirit of England* (1917)
Elgar's setting to music of three poems by Laurence Binyon (*The Fourth of August, To Women, For the Fallen*). First performed in its entirety in 1917.

— *String Quartet* (1918)

— *Violin Sonata* (1918)

Holst, G. *Hymn of Jesus* (1917)

— *The Planets* (1917)

Gurney, I. *By a Bierside* (1917)

— *In Flanders* (1917)

Ireland, J. *Chelsea Reach* (London Pieces, no. 1) (1917)

— *An Island Hymn* (1915)

— *Piano Trio* no. 2 (1917)
Good example of the use of march rhythms and 'military' motifs that colour the composer's 'war' music.

— *Rhapsody* (1915)

— *Violin Sonata no. 2* (1917)

Parry, Sir H. *From Death to Life* (1914)
Symphonic poems written as a response to the outbreak of hostilities.

— *Hymn for Aviators* (1915)

— *Jerusalem (1916)*
Choral song to William Blake's words.

— *Songs of Farewell* (1917)

Stanford, C. V. *Irish Rhapsody*, No. 5 (1917)
Dedicated to the Irish Guards.

— *Eroica* (1917)
Intended as a tribute to the allied armies on the Western Front. Second of his Organ Sonatas (1917-1918).

3.5 Leisure

3.5.1 General

The war produced a considerable curtailment of leisure activities. On the home front a number of popular spectator pastimes in the area of sport suffered. Boxing championships were suspended in 1914[62]. By the second year of the war professional football, cricket, horse racing[63], and the Oxford-Cambridge Boat Race had all been abandoned[64]. Pubs also suffered as a result of the restriction of opening hours, the increased price of drink, the regulation of liquor sales in areas important to the war effort, and the dilution of beers and spirits.

For a considerable number of people the theatre, the musical hall and the cinema provided a welcome antidote to the contraction of some of their leisure activities judging by the way they flocked to these forms of entertainment throughout the war. The theatre, formerly largely the preserve of the middle and upper classes, began to be popular with the better-off members of the working class and, in a similar mixing of the classes, members of the middle and upper class were for the first time to be found among the audiences in the cinema. Music halls, which derived much of their support from the lower classes, remained immensely popular but were likely to be out of the reach of the means of the very poor except for the occasional visit. It was the presence of the 3000 cinemas which existed in Britain by 1914 and the relatively cheap admission to them which were mostly responsible for bringing dramatic and musical entertainment of a sort within the reach of the poorer members of the community. For them going to the cinema became an attractive alternative to going to the pub

---

[62] Amateur, professional and carnival bouts, however, were staged in London throughout the war.

[63] Organized meetings ceased in May 1915, though there were occasional events, such as the Racehorse Association Steeple in March 1916, substituting for the cancelled Grand National.

[64] Sport, however, flourished in the trenches where football, rugby, cricket, and boxing experienced a boom with the aid of the various amateur organizers (e.g. officers, chaplains, and sportsmen who had joined up or been conscripted) who took on the responsibility for arranging these sports for the troops in their leisure hours.

at a time when the latter form of leisure was being severely restricted by wartime liquor legislation.

Some people were able to find additional ways of combating wartime austerity. The nightclub and the dance hall became popular venues and although the former was only affordable by the wealthy the latter was frequented by a wider cross-section of the population. It was in general, however, the most prosperous people who had the best opportunities to escape the austerity of war. Those who could afford it and who were not serving in the armed forces could continue to enjoy the pre-war luxuries accessible to the wealthy classes such as dining out in the best restaurants and being diverted by a wide range of fashionable entertainment, including in some cases escaping to their country retreats to throw house parties and indulge in the sporting pastimes of the countryside[65].

For a brief period in 1916 activities involving visits to museum and art galleries became severely restricted when the Government decided to close down all those in London. This decision was soon rescinded not only because of angry public protests, particularly from *The Observer*, *The New Statesman*, *The Nation* and *The Manchester Guardian*, but also because the Government had gradually come round to the view that exhibits in museums and art galleries related to the theme of war could have a propagandistic value. By the end of the war attendances at museums and art galleries had increased significantly.

Amid the worries engendered by war most people seeking an escape from them found it in the light-hearted entertainment that was on offer, particularly in the 'variety' entertainment of revue and musical comedy and the humour provided by the cinema with films like those of the immensely popular Charlie Chaplin. Some no doubt sought diversion from the war by reading, visiting art galleries and museums, going to concerts of classical music, listening to the gramophone, or getting away from it all by taking a holiday[66].

Leisure habits during the war were very much conditioned by the class to which a person belonged. The books and papers people read, the music they liked, their interest in higher culture (art, etc), and all the other aspects of their leisure activities were dependant on many factors, such as their class in society, sex, age, level of education, political preferences and whether they were soldiers or civilians. Members of the middle and upper classes were far more likely than the lower classes to read *The Times* or *The Nation*, the novels of H. G. Wells or John Galsworthy and to attend classical concerts or visit art galleries and museums; members of the lower classes were more likely than the upper and middle classes to read the *Daily Mail* or *John Bull*, the novels of Nat Gould or Berta Ruck, and to attend musical halls and mass spectator sporting events.

Books

Blumenfeld, R. D. *All in a Lifetime* (London: Ernest Benn, 1931)

Beckett, I. F. W. *Home Front, 1914-1918: How Britain Survived the Great War* (Kew: National Archives, 2006)

Bishop, J. *The Illustrated London News Social History of the First World* War (London: Angus and Robertson, 1982; repr. London: Sidgwick & Jackson, 1993)

Ferguson, J. *The Arts in Britain in World War I* (London: Stainer and Bell, 1980)

Fuller, J. G. *Troop Morale and Popular Culture in the British and Dominion Armies, 1914-1918* (Oxford: Clarendon Press, 1990)

Holt, T. *Sport and the British: A Modern History* (Oxford: Clarendon Press, 1989; repr 1992)

Horrall, A. *Popular Culture in London c.1890-1918: The Transformation of Entertainment* (Manchester: Manchester University Press, 2001)

---

[65] In the case of the Bloomsbury Group escaping to a country retreat also involved the gathering together of artists and writers and other celebrities of the day for intellectual conversation as well as other entertainment.

[66] The holiday trade fared surprisingly well throughout the war. Even though beaches were cluttered with barbed wire and some piers cut in half as a protection against invasion many people still wanted, and managed, to go on holiday.

The Cultural Scene

Kavanagh, G. *Museums and the First World War: A Social History* (London: Leicester University Press, 1994)

Mason, A. *Association Football and English Society, 1863-1915* (Brighton: Harvester, 1980)

Mason, T. and E. Riedi. *Sport and the Military: The British Armed Forces, 1880–1960* (Cambridge: Cambridge University Press, 2010)

Meech, T. C. *This Generation: A History of Great Britain and Ireland from 1900 to 1926*, 2 vols (London: Chatto & Windus, 1927-28), II: *1914-1926*

Meyer, J., ed. *British Popular Culture and the First World War* (Leiden; Boston: Brill, 2008)

National Gallery (Great Britain). *Report of the Director of the National Gallery for 1913* (London: HMSO, 1914)

National Gallery (Great Britain). *Report of the Director of the National Gallery for 1919*, (London: HMSO, 1919)

Peel, D. C. ["Mrs. C. S. Peel"]. *How We Lived Then: A Sketch of Social and Domestic Life in England during the War* (London: John Lane, 1929)

Rickards, M. and M. Moody. *The First World War: Ephemera, Mementoes, Documents* (London: Jupiter, 1975)
Based on an exhibition of the collection of the Imperial War Museum [IWM], London, 1970

Robb, G. *British Culture and the First World War* (Basingstoke: Palgrave, 2002)

Tholas-Disset, C. and K. A. Ritzenhoff, eds. *Humor, Entertainment, and Popular Culture during World War I* (London: Palgrave Macmillan, 2015)

Vamplew, W. *Pay Up and Play the Game: Professional Sport in Britain, 1875-1914* (Cambridge: Cambridge University Press, 1988)

Walton, J. K. *The British Seaside Holiday: Holidays and Resorts in the Twentieth Century* (Manchester: Manchester University Press, 2000)

Walvin, J. *Leisure and Society, 1830-1950* (London: Longman, 1978)

Articles

Hiley, N. 'Ploughboys and Soldiers: The Folk Song and the Gramophone in the British Expeditionary Force, 1914-1918', *Media History*, 4 (1998), 61-76

Osborne, J. M. '"To keep the Life of the Nation on the Old Lines", *The Athletic News* and the First World War Journal of Sport History', 14:2 (1987), 137-50

Veitch, C. '"Play Up! Play Up! And Win the War!": Football, The Nation and the First World War 1914-1915', *Journal of Contemporary History*, 20 (1985), 375

3.5.2 The Theatre

During the course of the war the distinctions between the 'legitimate' and 'variety' theatre were blurring; it was not unusual for the 'legitimate' theatre to include revues in its repertoire and for the music halls of the 'variety' theatre to include full-length plays among its presentations with notable figures of both types of theatre moving freely between the two.

In a time of the stresses and strains of war people sought refuge in diversionary entertainment and in the theatre they found it more in the lighter 'variety' entertainment of revue and musical comedy than in the flood of war and war-related plays which were produced throughout the war. While the jingoism and exuberantly patriotic flavour of many of the latter plays were by no means absent from the 'variety' type of entertainment[67] its lighter, more satirical, approach to the war, particularly as represented by the revue, went down well with audiences and had greater popular appeal. Audiences, however, found their best escape from the miseries of war in musicals like *Ch Chin Chow* and the *Maid of the Mountains*, and musical revues such as *The Bing Boys are Here* (with George Robey singing the hit song 'If you Were the Only Girl In the World') [see **Part 3, 3.4.2 (Popular Music**) in the sub-section **Contemporary Musicals**]. No theatrical production and certainly no war or war-related plays could compete with *Chu Chin Chow*, a musical extravaganza set in the Orient, featuring harem girls and comic songs, that had an enormously long run and was undoubtedly the most popular show of the war.

The armed forces derived a great deal of morale-boosting benefit from members of the theatrical profession (actors, artistes and musicians) who had joined up voluntarily or been conscripted and were able with the assistance of talented amateur performers to set up concert parties, affording servicemen both at home and abroad with a variety of different forms of theatrical and musical entertainment[68]. This was aided in 1916 when an Entertainments Department was set up under the auspices of the Navy and Army Canteen Board to provide facilities for theatrical companies to perform in camps and depots. It was further aided by the efforts of Lena Ashwell who early in the war began organising theatrical tours to the Western front. Stimulated by these sort of efforts entertainments for the armed forces by the military, and especially the civilian, concert parties became well organised. By 1917 there were 25 civilian concert parties, composed of both salaried and unpaid actors, touring the war zones in Europe. Permanent theatres had also begun appearing in 1915 at hospitals and bases throughout France. By all these means servicemen abroad, behind the lines, in rest areas, depots and towns, could enjoy all the different sorts of theatrical entertainment available on the home front - plays (including those of Shakespeare and Shaw), shows, pantomimes, revues, and the popular songs of the day, albeit often adapted to suit the environment and humour of the trenches.

As well as being one of the means by which entertainment for the armed forces became successfully organised the theatre made other contributions to the war effort. As well as unofficially helping the government with its recruiting and propaganda campaigns via the recruiting songs sung in the musical halls and the patriotic and jingoistic nature of many of the plays that were staged, it also assisted the government by encouraging people to purchase War Savings Bonds. In the area of charity work the theatre did sterling work, helping to raise millions of pounds for those charities which were involved in the care of soldiers, sailors and their dependants and for those providing funding support of the civilian concert parties that toured the hospitals to give comfort to the wounded.

Although some writers have been contemptuous about the quality of theatrical productions during the Great War, it seems undeniable, judging by the size of some of the audiences, that the theatre provided the various forms of light entertainment that almost everyone, irrespective of class, wanted as a temporary escape from the anxieties of war; in the latter respect the 'theatre' during this period could be said to have flourished. It seems remarkable that the theatre proved so durable in the face of all the problems with which it was confronted in a time of war[69], including a generally unsympathetic government (its implementation of the Amusement Tax was probably the greatest burden the theatre had to bear).

Autobiographies, Biographies

Asche, O. *Oscar Asche: His Life* (London: Hurst & Blackett, 1929)

Ashwell, L. *Myself a Player* (London: Michael Joseph, 1936)

Baker, R. A. *Marie Lloyd: Queen of the Music-Hall* (London: Robert Hale, 1990)
Throughout the First World War Marie Lloyd toured factories and gave special concerts for soldiers.

Cardus, N. *Autobiography* (London: Collins, 1947)

---

[67] The sentimental songs and farcical sketches of the revue tended to be interspersed with patriotic songs and propagandistic one-act plays, and even the dialogue and songs of pantomimes were given a propagandistic and patriotic slant.

[68] Their impact on Sigefried Sassoon was described in his poem, 'Concert party' (included in Sassoon, S. *The War Poems*, arranged by Rupert Hart-Davis (London: Faber & Faber, 1983).

[69] For example, transport restrictions, printing and paper restrictions, loss of personnel due to military conscription, rising prices, disruptions, including lighting restrictions, caused by air raids, and the imposition of the Amusement Tax.

— *Second Innings* (London: Collins, 1950)

Coborn, C. B. *'The Man Who Broke the Bank': Memories of the Stage and Music Hall* (London: Hutchinson, 1929)

Cochran, C. *The Secrets of a Showman* (London: 1925, repr. Heinemann, 1929)

— *I Had Almost Forgotten* (London: Hutchinson, 1932)

— *Cock-a-Doodle-Do* (London: Dent, 1941)

Dean, B. *Seven Ages: An Autobiography, 1888-1927* (London: Hutchinson, 1970)

Gollancz, V. *Journey Towards Music* (London: Gollancz, 1964)

Graves, C. *The Cochran Story* (London: Alien, 1951)

Henson, L. *Yours Faithfully: An Autobiography* (London: Long, 1948)

Hibbert, H. G. *A Playgoer's Memories* (London: Richards, 1920)

Lauder, H. *A Minstrel in France* (Charleston, SC; BiblioBazaar, 2009)
Originally published, (London: Melrose, 1918)

— *Roamin' in the Gloamin'* (London: Hutchinson, 1928)

Loraine, W. *Robert Loraine: Actor, Soldier, Airman* (London: Collins, 1938)

Lupino, S. *From the Stocks to the Stars* (London: Hutchinson, 1934)

May, H. A. *Memories of the Artists' Rifles* (London: Howlett, 1929)

Noble, P. *Ivor Novello: Man of the Theatre* (London: Falcon, 1951; repr. London: White Lion Publishers, 1975)

Randall, H. *Harry Randall: Old Time Comedian* (London: Sampson Low, 1930)

Robey, Sir G. *Looking Back on Life* (London: Constable, 1933)

Walbrook H. M. *J. M. Barrie and the Theatre* (London: White, 1922)

White, J. D. *Born to Star: The Lupino Lane Story* (London: Heinemann, 1957)

Wilson, A. E. *Prime Minister of Mirth: The Biography of Sir George Robey, C.B.E.* (London: Odhams, 1956)

Books

Ashwell, L. *Modern Troubadours: A Record of the Concerts at the Front* (London: Gyldendal, 1922)

Barker, C. and M. B. Gale, eds *British Theatre between the Wars, 1918–1939*, Cambridge Studies in Modern Theatre (Cambridge: Cambridge University Press 2000)
Includes a chapter entitled 'Theatre and Society: The Edwardian Legacy, the First World War and the Inter-War Years', by Clive Barker.

Baylis, L. and C. Hamilton. *The Old Vic* (London: Cape, 1926)

Busby, R. *British Music Hall: An Illustrated Who's Who From 1850 to the Present Day* (London: Elek, 1976)

Carter, H. *The New Spirit in the European Theatre 1914-1924* (London: Benn, 1925)

Collins, L. J. 'The Function of Theatre Entertainment in the First World War, 1914-1918' (unpublished doctoral thesis, University of London, 1994)

— *Theatre at War, 1914-18* (Basingstoke: Macmillan Press Ltd., 1998)

Dean, B. *The Theatre at War* (London: Harrap, 1956)

Fergusson, L. *Old Time Music Hall Comedians* (London: privately printed, 1949)

Fitzsimmons, L. and S. Street, eds. *Moving Performance: British Stage and Screen 1890's-1920's* (Trowbridge: Flicks Books, 2000)

Fuller, J. G. *Troop Morale and Popular Culture in the British and Dominion Armies, 1914-1918* (Oxford: Clarendon Press, 1990)

Klein, H. *Musicians and Mummers* (London: Cassell, 1925)

MacQueen-Pope, W. J. *Gaiety: Theatre of Enchantment* (London: Allen, 1949)

— *Ghosts and Greasepaint* (London: Hale, 1951)

Potton, Edward, ed. *A Record of the United Arts Rifles* (London: Moring, 1920)

Rowell, G. *The Old Vic Theatre: A History* (Cambridge: Cambridge University Press, 1993)

Short, E. and A. Compton-Rickett. *Ring Up the Curtain: Being a Pageant of English Entertainment Covering Half a Century* (London: Jenkins, 1938)

Williams, G. *British Theatre in the Great War: A Revaluation* (London: Continuum, 2005)

Wilson, A. E. *Christmas Pantomime: The Story of an English Institution* (London: Allen & Unwin, 1934)

Articles

Archer, W. 'The Music-Hall, Past and Future', *Fortnightly Review*, 100 (1916), 253-62

Ashwell, L. 'The Theatre and Ruhleben', *Fortnightly Review*, 104 (1918), 574-579

'Concerts and Plays at the Front', in *Stage Year Book*, (1919)

Findon, B. ''War-Time Music and Drama at the Front', *Play Pictorial*, 33 (1919), Supplement no. 200

Weller, B. 'The War-Time Stage', in *Stage Year Book*, (1919)

Contemporary Arts and Theatrical Press

News, reviews of performances, and critical articles related to the theatre and stage appeared in *Era, The Play Pictorial, The Review of Reviews, Stage*, and *Stage Year Book* as well as in the national and provincial newspapers and magazines.

3.5.3 The Cinema

The cinema industry had been in existence long enough for there to be a large number of picture houses by 1914. By 1917 some 20 million tickets were being sold weekly in more than 4000 British cinemas, a three-fold increase in the sale of tickets since 1914. Frontline troops were also able to enjoy films in the cinemas maintained by the military authorities; as an example of this, the 25 cinemas operating in the 11 divisions of the 4th Army were attracting audiences of 40,000 soldiers a week by 1917.

The Cultural Scene

On the outbreak of war fully active, feature length film production was taking place in Britain in some thirty studios up and down the country, with Cecil Hepworth, Will Barker, G. B. Samuelson, Maurice Elvey and George Pearson among the leading British film makers of the time. Domestic fictional film production, however, was hit not only by the economic constraints arising from the war but also from the flow of films arriving from America. The British film industry was unable to compete successfully with the expansion of an American film industry which was not only technologically superior but also able to produce films with better stars and more adventurous stories. It was American rather than British fictional films that dominated the British cinema during the war.

Cinema audiences were also able to see animated film cartoons, a comparatively new form of film which had appeared abroad earlier in the 20th century and was first produced in Britain during the war years. These film cartoons were mostly concerned with the war and often of a propagandistic nature [see **Part 3, 4.2.5.3 (Visual Propaganda)** in the sub-section **The Illustrative Arts: Cartoons** for examples of some of the titles of the film cartoons that were produced].

It was in the area of official war propaganda films that the British film industry did much of its most interesting work [see **Part 3, 4.2.5.3 (Visual Propaganda)** in the sub-section **Cinema: Official and Government Sponsored Films**]

Autobiographies, Biographies, Diaries, Memoirs

The list below is of film-makers who were active during the Great War. Some biographical material of a more general nature is provided within **section 4.3.1 (Film-Making: General) of Part 4: (Remembering the War)**

Brown, S. 'Barker, Will (1867-1951)', in *Reference Guide to British and Irish Film Directors* (British Film Institute) [http://www.screenonline.org.uk/people/id/519480/]

Gifford, D. 'The Early Memoirs of Maurice Elvey', *Griffithiana*, 60–61 (Oct 1997), 77–124

Hepworth, C. *Came the Dawn: Memories of a Film Pioneer* (London: Phoenix House, 1951)

McKernan, L. 'Samuelson, George Berthold (1889–1947)', *Oxford Dictionary of National Biography*, 2004; online edn, Jan 2011 [http://www.oxforddnb.com/view/article/56982, accessed 3 Jan 2014]

Pearson, G. *Flashback: The Autobiography of a British Film-Maker* (London: Allen & Unwin, 1957)

Schickel, R. *D. W. Griffith: An American Life* (London: Simon & Schuster,1984; repr. New York: Limelight Editions, 1996)

Books

The selection of books listed below mostly relate to the years of the Great War. Books dealing generally with film-making and cinematic history are listed within **sections 4.3.1 Film-Making: General)** and **4.3.2.1 (The Cinema: General) of Part 4 (Remembering the War)**

Bryan, J. 'From Film Stories to Film Stars: The Beginnings of the Fan Magazine in Britain, 1911-16', in *Scene-Stealing: Sources for British Cinema Before 1930*, edited by Alan Burton and Laraine Porter (Trowbridge: Flicks Books, 2003)

Burrows., J. *Legitimate Cinema: Theatre Stars in Silent British Films, 1908-1918*, Exeter Studies in Film History (Exeter: University of Exeter Press, 2003)

Fitzsimmons, L. and S. Street, eds. *Moving Performance: British Stage and Screen 1890's-1920's* (Trowbridge: Flicks Books, 2000)

Gifford, D. *British Animated Films, 1895-1985: A Filmography* (Jefferson, North Carolina: McFarland, 1987)

Hammond, M. *The Big Show: British Cinema Culture in the Great War 1914-1918*, Exeter Studies in Film History (Exeter: University of Exeter Press, 2006)

— '"Cultivating Pimple": Performance Traditions and the Film Comedy of Fred and Joe Evans', in *Pimple, Pranks and Pratfalls: British Film Comedy Before 1930*, edited by Alan Burton and Laraine Porter (Trowbridge: Flicks Books, 2000)

— '"A Great American Sensation": Thomas Ince's *Civilization* at The Palladium, Southampton, 1917', in *Hollywood Abroad: Audiences and Cultural Exchange*, edited by Richard Maltby and Melvyn Stokes (London: BFI, 2004)

— 'Letters to America: A Case Study in the Exhibition and Reception of American Films in Britain, 1914-18', in *Young and Innocent?: The Cinema in Britain 1896-1930*, edited by A. Higson (Exeter: University of Exeter Press, 2002)

Hammond, M and M. Williams, eds. *British Silent Cinema and the Great* War (Houndmills, Basingstoke: Palgrave Macmillan, 2011)

Higson, A, ed. *Young and Innocent?: The Cinema in Britain 1896-1930*, Exeter Studies in Film History (Exeter: University of Exeter Press, 2002)

Low, R. *The History of the British Film*, 7 vols (London: Allen & Unwin, 1948-1985; repr. London: Routledge, 1997), III: 1914-1918

McKernan, L. 'The American Invasion and the British Film Industry, 1894-1903', in *Crossing the Pond: Anglo-American Film Relations Before 1930*, edited by Alan Burton and Laraine Porter (Trowbridge: Flicks Books, 2002)

National Council of Public Morals. Cinema Commission of Inquiry. *The Cinema: Its Present Position and Future Possibilities*, being the report of and chief evidence taken by the Cinema Commission of Inquiry instituted by the National Council of Public Morals (London: Williams & Norgate, 1917)[70]
This report examines the cinema in Britain and the effects it might have on the viewing public, providing in the process a great deal of useful statistical information about film distribution and cinema-going in Britain. In the introduction to the report it is stated that the National Council on Public Morals was "deeply concerned with the influence of the cinematograph, especially upon young people, with the possibilities of its development and with its adaptation to national educational purposes", an indication of contemporary concern about the potential danger which the popularity of cinema posed for those members of society considered to be most vulnerable to its influence. *The Bioscope* describes the report as " … an unmatched treasure trove not only of opinions, fears, hopes and prejudices regarding the cinema and its audience, but of evidence relating to the production and exhibition of films in Britain at this time" [quotation extracted from http://thebioscope.net/2007/05/31/the-cinema-its-present-position-and-future-possibilities/). Among those providing evidence for the report were important figurers in the film industry (Cecil Hepworth, J. Brooke Wilkinson, A. E. Newbould, Gavazzi King and F.R. Goodwin), teachers, policemen, magistrates, social workers, and school children.

Robinson, D. *Chaplin: His Life and Art*, new edn (London: Penguin, 2001)

Terpstra, M. *Girls from the Sky: A Critical Catalogue of Women in the Production of Silent British Cinema 1914-1918* (London: British Film Institute, 2006)

Articles

Gledhill, C. 'The Big Show: British Cinema Culture in the Great War 1914–1918', *Screen*, 48 (2007), 125-129
Review of book , *The Big Show*, by M. Hammond published Exeter: University of Exeter Press, 2006.

Hammond, M. 'Laughter During Wartime: The Comedy and the Language of Trauma in British Cinema Regulation 1917', *Screen*, 44.2 (Summer 2003)

— '"A Soul-Stirring Appeal to Every Briton": The Reception of *The Birth of a Nation* in Britain (1915-1916)', *Film

---

[70] The report is also available for download at http://www.archive.org/details/cinemaitspresent00natirich

History, 11.3 (1999), 353-70.

Laugesen, A. 'Forgetting Their Troubles for a While: Australian Soldiers' Experiences of Cinema during the First World War', *Historical Journal of Film, Radio and Television*, 35 (2015), 596-614

Lyons, T. J 'Hollywood and World War 1 1914-1918', *Journal of Popular Film*, 1 (1972), 15-301

Merritt, R. 'D. W. Griffith Directs the Great War: The Making of *Hearts of the World*', *Quarterly Review of Film Studies*, 6 (1981), 45-65

Seton, M. 'The British Cinema, 1914', *Sight and Sound*, Autumn (1937), 136-8

Taylor, P. M. 'Introduction - Britain and the Cinema In World War I', *Historical Journal of Film, Radio and Television*, 13 (1993), 115-116

Ward, P. 'British Animated Propaganda Cartoons of the First World War: Issues of Topicality', *Animation Journal*, 11 (2003), 64-83

— 'Distribution and Trade Press Strategies for British Animated Propaganda Cartoons of the First World War Era', *Historical Journal of Film, Radio and Television*, 25, (2005), 189-201

Theses

Bryan, J. 'The Cinema Looking Glass: The British Film Fan Magazine 1911-1918' (unpublished doctoral thesis, University of East Anglia, 2006)

Contemporary Fiction Films

Commercial film companies capitalised on the war by employing it in blatantly patriotic films (e.g. *Boys of the Old Brigade and Bulldog Grit*), and melodramatic and romantic films which utilised such themes as the spy menace[71] (e.g. *The Crimson Triangle; The Man Who Stayed at Home*), battlefield redemption and the heroism of the British soldier (e.g. *Saving the Colours*), the beastliness of the Germans (e.g. *In the Clutches of the Huns*), women as heroines (e.g. *A Munition Girl's Romance*) and by descending occasionally into pure sentimentality (e.g. *Christmas Without Daddy*). These examples represent the most typical and numerous of the war films that were produced at the time. There were a few exceptions such as films like *The Outrage* (in which the war is integrated into the personal drama as a backdrop); *Democracy* (which brings out the social and political impact of the war); and *The Better 'Ole* and *Kiddies in the Ruins* (the former based on Bruce Bairnsfather's cartoons of "Old Bill" and the latter on French artist Poulbot's newspaper drawings of children in the devastated parts of France).

While war became a popular subject for films (although its vogue waned after 1916) films which had nothing to do with the war continued to be produced throughout the war years. Among the numerous categories of film in which the war theme was absent were adaptations of adventure stories (e.g. *She; The Four Feathers*), crime thrillers, the most notable of which were the "Ultus" films (*Ultus: The Man from the Dead; Ultus and the Grey Lady; Ultus and the Secret of the Night; Ultus and the Three Button Mystery*); sporting films about boxing and horse racing (e.g. *The White Hope; By the Shortest of Heads*), costume drama based on classic novels (e.g. *Adam Bede; The Vicar of Wakefield; Tom Jones; Barnaby Rudge*) or historical figures (e.g. *Jane Shore*); drama based on the novels of contemporary authors (e.g. *The Christian; Traffic; Sally Bishop; Paula*); adaptations of plays (e.g. *The Second Mrs Tanqueray; Caste; Hindle Wakes*); "social problem" films (e.g. *The Bottle; For Her People; The Sweater; The Woman Who Did*); films based on song (e.g. *Annie Laurie*), films with a moral theme (e.g. *Whoso is Without Sin; Profit – and the Loss*); and macabre films as, for instance, those making use of the supernatural (e.g. *The Basilisk; The Avenging Hand; The Monkey's Paw; Flames; The Picture of Dorian Gray; The Sorrows of Satan*).

Humour played its part in helping cinema audiences to forget the weariness of war. Films providing various types of humour progressed in the course of the war from comedies that were little more than short mock melodramas of the "Pimple" skit and music-hall sketch type to those attempting to provide genuine plot-

---

[71] The market was bombarded with spy films until about six months after the beginning of the war, when they abruptly died out. *The Man Who Stayed at Home* was one of the few spy films which appeared after the fashion for them had faded away.

comedy "feature" films (e.g. Hepworth's *The American Heiress*, Samuelson's *In Another Girls Shoes*). The latter, more sophisticated, type of comedy film sometimes featured well-known music-hall comedians (e.g. Billy Merson in *The Man in Possession*; George Robey in *The Anti-Frivolity League*; Lupino Lane in *Nipper and the Curate*) or comic actors of the legitimate stage (e.g. Charles Hawtrey in *Honeymoon for Three*; James Welch in *When Knights Were Bold*). There were also adaptations of classic stage comedies (e.g. Barries's *The Admirable Crichton*; Wilde's *Lady Windemere's Fan*). The most famous British comedy films of the time were the productions featuring Billy Merson, George Robey, and Lupino Lane but the American films starring Charlie Chaplin were by far the most popular in Britain. There was no British comedian to compare with Chaplin. Billy Merson, the most successful British comedian on the screen, was the only person in Britain who came anywhere near to achieving the appeal of Chaplin.

American films gained great popularity with British cinema audiences. The most successful films of the time from the United States were the Chaplin comedies and a number of spectacular films, including D. W. Griffith's *Birth of a Nation* (staring Lillian Gish), Cecil B. DeMille's *The Little American* (starring Mary Pickford), and *The Great Love* and *Hearts of the World* (the latter two films both directed by D. W. Griffith under British auspices).

More details of the films mentioned above are provided in the list below.

A fairly comprehensive list of British fiction films of 1000ft. or more released between August 1914 and December 1918 and shown to the British public in that period can be found in Appendix 4 of *The History of the British Film, 1914-1918*, by Rachel Low, published by Allen & Unwin in 1950.

Adam Bede (International Exclusives, April 9 1918)
Producer: Maurice Elvey. From the novel by George Eliot, adapted by Kenelm Foss

The Admirable Crichton (Samuelson, 1918)
Producer: G. B. Samuelson, from the play by J. M. Barrie

The American Heiress (Hepworth, 1917)
Producer: C. M. Hepworth, from the story by Blanche McIntosh

Annie Laurie (Hepworth, 1916)
Producer: C. M. Hepworth, based on the song

The Anti-Frivolity League (Ideal, 1916)
With George Robey

The Avenging Hand (Cricks, 1915)
Producer: Charles Calvert. Written by W. J. Eliott

Barnaby Rudge (Hepworth, 1915)
Produced and adapted by C. M. Pearson, from the novel by Charles Dickens

The Basilisk (Hepworth, November 1914)
Produced, photographed and written by C. M. Pearson

The Better 'Ole (Welsh-Pearson, July 1918)
Produced and adapted by George Pearson from the play by Bruce Bairnsfather and Arthur Eliot

Birth of a Nation (David W. Griffith Corporation, 3 March 1915)
Directed by D. W. Griffith

The Bottle (Hepworth, 1915)
Producer: C. M. Hepworth. Written by Arthur Shirley

Boys of the Old Brigade (British Oak, 1916)
Produced and written by Mr and Mrs E. G. Batley

Bulldog Grit (Burlingham Standard, 1915)
Directed bt Ethyle Batley

The Cultural Scene

By the Shortest of Heads (Barker, 1915)
With George Formby

Caste (Turner, 1916)
Producer: Larry Trimble, from the play by Tom Robertson

The Christian (London Film Company 1915)
Producer: G. L. Tucker, from the novel by Hall Caine

Christmas Without Daddy (B & C [British and Colonial Kinematograph Co.], 1914)

The Crimson Triangle (Martin, 1915)
Directed by David Aylott

Democracy (Progress, 1918)
Produced and written by Sidney Morgan

Flames (Butchers, February, 1918)
Producer: Maurice Elvey. Adapted by Eliot Stannard from the novel by Robert Hitchens

For Her People (Turner, 1914)
Produced and written by Larry Trimble

The Four Feathers (Lucoque, 1915)
Adapted from A. E. W. Mason's novel

The Great Love (Paramount Pictures, 1918)
Directed by D. W. Griffith

Hearts of the World (D. W. Griffith Productions, 1917)
Directed by D. W. Griffith. Made in 1917 by agreement with the War Office Committee who made over £13,000 out of it. Shown in London on June 24, 1918

Hindle Wakes (Samuelson, May 1918)
Producer: Maurice Elvey. Adapted by Eliot Stannard from the play by Stanley Houghton

Honeymoon for Three (B & C, 1915)
Producer: Maurice Elvey. Written by Eliot Stannard

In Another Girls Shoes (Samuelson, 1917)
Producer: G. B. Samuelson

In the Clutches of the Huns (Phoenix, 1915)
Directed by Joe Evans

Kiddies in the Ruins (Welsh-Pearson, November, 1918)
Producer; George Pearson, from the play by Poulbot and Paul Gull

Lady Windemere's Fan (Ideal, 1916)
From the play by Oscar Wilde

The Little American (Mary Pickford Company, 1917)
Directed by Cecil B. DeMille. Recreated the sinking of the *Lusitania*

The Man in Possession (Homeland, 1915)
Producer: W. Kellino. Billy Merson and Lupino Lane in the cast

The Man Who Stayed at Home (Hepworth, 1915)
Producer: C. M. Hepworth, from the play by Lechmere Worrall

The Monkey's Paw (Magnet, 1915)
From the story by W. W. Jacobs

A Munition Girl's Romance (Broadwest, 1917)
Producer: Walter West. Written by Charles Barrett

Nipper and the Curate (John Bull, 1916)
Writer: Reginald Crompton. Lupino Lane cast as Nipper

The Outrage (Hepworth, 1915)
Producer: C. M. Pearson, from a story by by Albert Chevalier

Paula (Bamforth, 1916)
From the novel by Victoria Cross

The Picture of Dorian Gray (Neptune, 1916)
Producer: Fred W. Durrant. From the play by Oscar Wilde

Pimple Has One (Phoenix 1915)
Directors: Fred and Joe Evans

Pimple Enlists (Phoenix, 1914)
Directors: Fred and Joe Evans

Profit – and the Loss (Ideal, 1917)
Produced and adapted by Eliot Stannard from the play by H. F. Maltby

Sally Bishop (Gaumont-British, 1917)
Producer: George Pearson, from the novel by E. Temple Thurston

Saving the Colours (B & C [British and Colonial Kinematograph Co.], 1914)

The Second Mrs Tanqueray (Ideal, 1916)
Producer: Fred Paul. Adapted by Benedict James from the play by Sir Arthur Pinero

She (Barker, 1916)
Producer: Will Barker. Adapted by Nellie E. Lucoque from the novel by H. Rider Haggard

The Sorrrows of Satan (Samuelson, 1917)
Producer: Alkexander Butler, from the novel by Marie Corelli

The Sweater (Hepworth, 1915)
Producer: Frank Wilson. Written by W. J. Elliott

Tom Jones (Ideal, May 1918)
Producer: Edwin J. Collins. Adapted by Eliot Stannard from the novel by Henry Fielding

Traffic (I. B. Davidson, 1915)
Produced and adapted by Charles Raymond from the story by E. Temple Thurston

Ultus and the Grey Lady (Gaumont, October 1916)
Produced and written by George Pearson

Ultus and the Secret of the Night (Gaumont, January 1917)
Produced and written by George Pearson

Ultus and the Three Button Mystery (Gaumont, August, 1917)
Produced and written by George Pearson

Ultus: The Man from the Dead (Gaumont, March 1916)

The Cultural Scene

Produced and written by George Pearson

The Vicar of Wakefield (Ideal, 1916)
Producer: Fred Paul. Adapted by Benedict James from the novel by Oliver Goldsmith

When Knights Were Bold (London Film Company, 1916)
Producer: Maurice Elvey, from the play by Charles Marlowe

The White Hope (Hepworth, 1915)
Producer: Frank Wilson. Adapted by Victor Montefiore from the novel by W. R. H. Trowbridge

Whoso is Without Sin (Ideal, 1916)
Produced by Fred Paul. Adapted by Fred Paul and Bendict James from the scenario by May Sherman

The Woman Who Did (Broadwest, 1915)
Producer: Walter West, from the novel by Grant Allen

Chaplin Films

With the exception of the asterisked items all the films selected below were directed by Chaplin.

*Making a Living (USA, Keystone, 1914)
Directed by Henry Lehrman

*Kid's Auto Races (USA, Keystone, 1914)
Directed by Henry Lehrman

*A Film Johnny (USA, Keystone, 1914)
Directed by George Nichols

A Busy Day (USA, Keystone, 1914)

Dough and Dynamite (USA, Keystone, 1914)

Twenty Minutes of Love (USA, Keystone, 1914)

Those Love Pangs (USA, Keystone, 1914)

In The Park (USA, Essanay, 1915)

Champion Charlie (USA, Essanay, 1915)

The Tramp (USA, Essanay, 1915)
Charlie's Elopement (USA, Essanay, 1915)

By the Sea (USA, Essanay, 1915)

The Bank (USA, Essanay, 1915)

One A.M. (USA, Mutual, 1916)

The Vagabond, Mutual, 1916)

Police (USA, Mutual, 1916)

Easy Street (USA, Mutual, 1916)

The Immigrant (USA, Mutual, 1916)

The Floorwalker (USA, Mutual, 1916)

The Cure (USA, Mutual, 1916)

The Pawnshop (USA, Mutual, 1916)

Chase Me Charlie (USA, Mutual, 1917)

A Dogs Life (USA, First National, 1918)

The Bond (USA, First National, 1918)

Shoulder Arms (USA, First National, 1918)

4. Waging War

4.1 War and the State

It had long been the belief in government circles that the conduct of war could be left to Britain's soldiers and sailors without encroaching to any real degree on the lives of civilians. It was not surprising, therefore, that on the outbreak of war the Government saw its role as one of ensuring that the war disturbed the domestic economy as little as possible rather than one of organising the nation's economy for total war. The Government's initial attitude, stemming from the general expectation in August 1914 that the war would be of short duration, was encapsulated in the slogan 'Business as Usual' and dominated by a desire to make this idea work with only minimal interference from the state (i.e. minimal sacrificing of laissez-faire liberal principles). This attitude was soon revealed as impractical as Britain's preponderant reliance on a strategy of naval blockade ceased to be feasible when it proved necessary for Britain to recruit masses of soldiers for the purpose of helping its allies to fight a major continental land battle that seemed likely to be of far longer duration than was originally expected.

Inevitably, the Government's strategy for prosecuting the war had to undergo fundamental changes. From an initial belief that war could be waged on the basis of a policy of 'business as usual' with minimal disruption of normal peacetime activity the Government had shifted its position by the end of the war to an acceptance of the fact that the war could only be waged successfully by the state involving itself in practically everything affecting the lives of its citizens. Censoring news, suppressing publications, engaging in close surveillance of civilians, directing 'home' propaganda (in the last years of the war), interning aliens, introducing military conscription, participating in industrial relations, regulating industry and agriculture, rationing food, involving itself in military strategy, and even restricting the use of drink are examples of the increasingly interventionist attitude of the Government as it gradually came to a full realization of the nature of total war. This attitude has been seen as a reflection not of the development of a coherently worked out strategy but rather of a series of improvised and ad hoc measures to meet particular circumstances.

4.1.1 General

Books

Burk, K., ed. *War and the State: The Transformation of British Government, 1914-1919* (London: George Allen & Unwin, 1982)

Cronin, J. E. 'The Crisis of State and Society in Britain, 1917-22', in *Strikes, Wars and Revolutions in an International Perspective: Strike Waves in the Late Nineteenth and Early Twentieth Centuries*, edited by L. H. Haimson and C. Tilly (Cambridge: Cambridge University Press, 1989)

— *The Politics of State Expansion: War, State, and Society in Twentieth-Century Britain* (London: Routledge, 1991)

Dreisziger, N. F, ed. *Mobilization for Total War: The Canadian, American and British Experience, 1914-1918, 1939-45*

(Waterloo, Ont.: Wilfrid Laurier University Press, 1981

Duncan, R. *Pubs and Patriots: The Drink Crisis During World War One* (Liverpool: Liverpool University Press 2013)

Ewing, K. D. and C. A. Gearty. *The Struggle for Civil Liberties: Political Freedom and the Rule of Law in Britain 1914-1945* (Oxford: Oxford University Press, 2000)

Horne, J. N. 'Introduction: Mobilising for "Total War", 1914-1918', in *State, Society, and Mobilisation in Europe during the First World War*, edited by J. Horne (Cambridge: Cambridge University Press, 1997, repr. 2002)

— 'Remobilising for "Total War": France and Britain, 1917-18', in *State, Society, and Mobilisation in Europe during the First World War*, edited by J. Horne (Cambridge: Cambridge University Press, 1997, repr. 2002)

Jones, G. and M. W. Kirby. *Competitiveness and the State: Government and Business in Twentieth Century Britain* (Manchester: Manchester University Press, 1991)

Langan, M. and B. Schwarz, eds. *Crises in the British State, 1880-1930* (London: Hutchinson in association with the Centre for Contemporary Cultural Studies, University of Birmingham, 1985)

Lloyd, E. M. H. *Experiments in State Control* (Oxford: Clarendon Press, 1924)

Messinger, G. S. *British Propaganda and the State in the First World War* (Manchester: Manchester University Press, 1992)

Middlemass, K. *Politics in Industrial Society: The Experience of the British System since 1911* (London: Deutsch, 1980)

Millman, B. *Managing Domestic Dissent in First World War Britain* (London: Cass, 2000)

Turner, J. 'Cabinets, Committees and Secretariats: The Higher Direction of the War', in *War and the State: The Transformation of British Government, 1914-1919*, ed. by K. Burk (London: Allen & Unwin, 1982)

— *Lloyd George's Secretariat* (Cambridge: Cambridge University Press, 1980; repr. 2008)

— 'The Politics of Organized Business in the First World War' in *Businessmen and Politics: Studies of Business Activity In British Politics, 1900-1945*, edited by John Turner (London: Heinemann, 1984)

Wigham, E. *Strikes and the Government, 1893-1981*, 2nd edn (London: Macmillan, 1982)

Articles

Grayzel, S. R. 'Defence Against the Indefensible: The Gas Mask, the State and British Culture during and after the First World War', *Twentieth Century British History*, 25 (2014), 418-434

Johnson, M. 'The Liberal War Committee and the Liberal Advocacy of Conscription in Britain, 1914-1916', *Historical Journal*, 51 (2008), 399-420

4.1.2 The War Economy

After the 'Great Shell Scandal' of 1915 (arising from scarcity of ordnance at the Front) had revealed the flaws in its prosecution of the war the government began to adopt an actively interventionist approach in the industrial field by assuming the wide-ranging powers needed to achieve the volume and efficiency of production required for an effective war effort[72]. This approach was motivated by the government's realization that the key to effective wartime production would lie in the maintenance of harmonious labour relations and the inauguration of workshop procedures designed to improve efficiency. Out of this realization emerged a new level of consultation with employers and unions and a growing involvement in matters of industrial efficiency as is

---

[72] R. H. Tawney estimated that 'not less than two-thirds of the gainfully employed workers in the country were by 1918 engaged in industries subject to one form or another of war-time regulation'.

exemplified by the Munitions of War Act, the Treasury Act, the establishment of the Ministry of Labour, and the participation of businessmen and leading trade unionists in the direction of the war economy. The government's approach to the development of ideas on economic reconstruction was similar and taken on board by the Ministry of Reconstruction (established in 1917) whose members, in addition to tackling the social remit given to them by Lloyd George's undertaking to create a 'land fit for heroes', had an ambitious economic agenda which encompassed a desire to see the improvements in business organization and industrial efficiency, achieved as a result of government intervention, perpetuated after the war as an integral part of peacetime reconstruction.

The use of businessmen in the Government's interventionist approach (epitomised by the employment of Sir Eric Geddes) extended to other areas of the war economy such as agriculture and food supply. Viscount Rhondda, a coal magnate, was, for instance, appointed in 1917 to head the Ministry of Food at a time when the problems of food supply and distribution had reached an acute stage of crisis. It was as a result of his efforts (not only through rationing but also by implementing a policy of price controls and ensuring that the bulk of the food consumed in Britain was purchased and sold through government agency) that these problems were successfully tackled.

Biographies, Memoirs, Diaries

Addison, C. A., Viscount. *Four and a Half Years: A Personal Diary from June 1914 to January 1919*, 2 vols (London: Hutchinson, 1934)

Davenport-Hines, R. P. T. *Dudley Docker: The Life and Times of a Trade Warrior* (Cambridge: Cambridge University Press, 1984)

Grieves, K. *Sir Eric Geddes: Business and Government in War and Peace* (Manchester: Manchester University Press,1989)

Lloyd George, D. *War Memoirs.* 2nd edn, 2 vols (London: Odhams, 1942)
Originally published in 6 vols: London: Nicholson & Watson, 1933-36.

Rhondda, M. H. M., Viscountess. *D. A. Thomas, Viscount Rhondda*, by his daughter and others (London : Longmans, Green and Co., 1921)

Books

Adams, R. J. Q. *Arms and the Wizard: Lloyd George and the Ministry of Munitions, 1915-1916* (London: Cassell, 1978)

Barnett, L. M. *British Food Policy in the First World War* (London: Allen & Unwin, 1985)

Beveridge, W. H., Baron Beveridge. *British Food Control* (Oxford: Humphrey Milford, Oxford University Press, 1928)

Burk, K. 'Wheat and the State during the First World War, in *Strategy and Intelligence: British Policy During the First World War*, ed. by M. Dockrill and D. French (London: Hambledon, 1986)

Cassar, G. H. *Lloyd George at War 1916-1918* (London: Anthem Press, 2009; repr. 2011)

Cline, P. K. 'Eric Geddes and the "Experiment" with Businessmen in Government, 1915-22', in *Essays in Anti-Labour History: Responses to the Rise of Labour in Britain*, edited by K. D. Brown (London: Macmillan, 1974)

Corley, T. A. B. 'The State and Agriculture, 1914-72', in *Competitiveness and the State: Government and Business in Twentieth Century Britain*, edited by Geoffrey Jones and Maurice Kirby (Manchester: Manchester University Press, 1991)

Dewey, P. E. *British Agriculture in the First World War* (London: Routledge, 1989)

— 'The New Warfare and Economic Mobilisation', in *Britain and the First World War*, ed. by J. Turner (London: Routledge, 1988)

French, D. 'The Rise and Fall of Business as Usual', in *War and the State: The Transformation of British Government, 1914-1919*, ed. by K. Burk (London: Allen & Unwin, 1982)

Great Britain. Ministry of Munitions. *History of the Ministry of Munitions*, 12 vols (London: HMSO, 1920-22)
The titles of the vols. are as follows 1. Industrial mobilisation, 1914-1915; 2. General organisation for munitions supply; 3. Finance and contracts; 4. The supply and control of labour, 1915-1916; 5. Wages and welfare; 6. Man power and dilution; 7. The control of materials; 8. Control of industrial capacity and equipment; 9. Review of munitions supply; 10-12. The supply of munitions.

Grieves, K. *The Politics of Manpower, 1914-1918* (Manchester: Manchester University Press, 1988)

— 'The "Recruiting Margin" in Britain: Debates on Manpower during the Third Battle of Ypres', in *Passchendaele in Perspective: The Third Battle of Ypres*, edited by P. H. Liddle (London: Leo Cooper, 1997)

Grigg, J. 'Lloyd George and Ministerial Leadership in the Great War', in *Home Fires and Foreign Fields, British Social and Military Experience in the Great War*, ed. by P. H. Liddle (Manchester: Manchester University Press, 1985)

Harris, J. 'Bureaucrats and Businessmen in British Food Control, 1916-19', in *War and the State: The Transformation of British Government, 1914-1919*, ed. by K. Burk (London: Allen & Unwin, 1982)

Horn, M. *Britain, France and the Financing of the First World War* (Montreal: McGill-Queen's University Press, 2002)

Hurwitz, S. J. *State Intervention in Great Britain: A Study of Economic Control and Social Response, 1914-1919* (New York: Columbia University Press, 1949; repr. London: Cass, 1968)

Kirby, M. W. 'Industry, Agriculture and Trade Unions', in *The First World War in British History*, edited by S. Constantine, M. W. Kirby and M. B. Rose (London: Edward Arnold, 1995)

Kirby, M. W. and M. B. Rose. 'Productivity and Competitive Failure: British Government Policy and Industry, 1914-19', in *Competitiveness and the State: Government and Business in Twentieth Century Britain*, edited by G. Jones and M. W. Kirby (Manchester: Manchester University Press, 1991)

MacLeod, R. M. and K. MacLeod. 'War and Economic Development: Government and the Optical Glass Industry in Britain, 1914-1918', in *War and Economic Development: Essays in Memory of David Joslin*, edited by J. M. Winter (Cambridge: Cambridge University Press, 1975)

Middleton, Sir T. H. *Food Production in War* (Oxford: Clarendon Press, 1923)

Morgan, E. V. *Studies in British Financial Policy, 1914-25* (London: Macmillan, 1952)

Neilson, K. 'Managing the War: Britain, Russia, and ad hoc Government', in *Strategy and Intelligence: British Policy during the First World War*, ed. by M. Dockrill and D. French (London: Hambledon, 1986)

Pollard, S. *The Development of the British Economy, 1914-1990*, 4th edn (London: Edward Arnold, 1992)

Reid, A. 'Dilution, Trade Unionism and the State In Britain During The First World War', in *Shop Floor Bargaining and the State: Historical and Comparative Perspectives*, edited by S. Tolliday and J. Zeitlin (Cambridge: Cambridge University Press, 1985)

Rubin, G. R. *War, Law and Labour: The Munitions Acts, State Regulation and the Unions, 1915-1921* (Oxford: Clarendon Press, 1987)

Trebilock, C. 'War and the Failure of Industrial Mobilisation: 1899 and 1914', in *War and Economic Development: Essays in Memory of David Joslin*, edited by J. M. Winter (Cambridge: Cambridge University Press, 1975)

Turner, J. 'The Politics of Organized Business in the First World War' in *Businessmen and Politics: Studies of Business Activity in British Politics, 1900-1945*, edited by John Turner (London: Heinemann, 1984)

Wrigley, C. J. 'The First World War and the State Intervention in Industrial Relations', in *A History of British Industrial Relations*, edited by Chris Wrigley, 2 vols (Brighton: Harvester, 1982-1987), II: *1914-1939* (Brighton: Harvester, 1987; repr. Aldershot: Gregg Revivals, 1993)

— 'The Ministry of Munitions: An Innovatory Department', in *War and the State: The Transformation of British Government, 1914-1919*, ed. by K. Burk (London: Allen & Unwin, 1982).

Articles

Boswell, J. and J. Bruce. 'Patriots or Profiteers'?: British Businessmen and The First World War', *Journal of European Economic History*, 11 (1982), 423-45

Bryden, L. 'The First World War: Healthy or Hungry?', *History Workshop Journal*, 24 (1987)

Davidson, R. 'The Myth of the "Servile State"', *Bulletin of the Society for the Study of Labour History*, 29 (1974)

Dewey, P. E. 'Agricultural Labour Supply in England and Wales during the First World War', *Economic History Review*, 28 (1975), 100-12

— 'British Farming Profits and Government Policy During the First World War', *Economic History Review*, n.s. 37 (1984), 373-90

— 'Food Production and Policy in the United Kingdom, 1914-18', *Transactions the Royal Historical Society*, 30 (1980), 71-89

— 'Government Provision of Farm Labour in England and Wales, 1914-18', *Agricultural History Review*, 27 (1979), 110-21

Grieves, K. 'Improvising the British War Effort: Eric Geddes and Lloyd George, 1915-18', *War and Society*, 7 (1989), 40-55

Griffin, N. J. 'Scientific Management and the Direction of Britain's Military Labour Establishment during World War I', *Military Affairs*, 42 (1978), 197-201

Manton, K. 'Sir William Beveridge, The British Government and Plans for Food Control in Time of War, c. 1916-1941., *Contemporary British History*, 23 (2009), 363-385

McDermott, J. '"A Needless Sacrifice": British Businessmen and Business as Usual in the First World War', *Albion*, 21 (1989), 263-82

— 'Trading with the Enemy: British Business and the Law during the First World War', *Canadian Journal of History* (1997)

— 'Total War and the Merchant State: Aspects of British Economic Warfare against Germany, 1914-16', *Canadian Journal of History*, 21 (1986), 61-76

Turner, J. 'State Purchase of the Liquor Trade in the First World War', *History Journal*, 23 (1980), 589-615

'The War Profiteers', *The Nation*, 9 February (1918)

Whiting, R. C. 'Taxation and the Working Class, 1915-24', *Historical Journal*, 33 (1990), 895-916

4.1.3 Defence of The Realm

The British government had long been aware of the important part that the various forms of censorship could play in controlling public opinion in time of war. It had already established the apparatus of wartime censorship on a firm basis before the outbreak of hostilities in 1914. Elements of the apparatus already in place before the war were, for example, the creation of the Special (Secret) Branch of the Metropolitan Police's Criminal Investigation Department in 1887, the extension of intelligence gathering with the creation of a military Secret Service Bureau and a new Directorate of Military Intelligence in 1909[73], the passing of the second Official Secrets Act in 1910, the formal establishment in 1912 of a Joint Committee of Admiralty, War Office and Press Representatives for the Informal Censorship of Naval and Military Information, and plans around 1912 for controlling the flow and content of cable communications. On the outbreak of war this basis for wartime censorship was further significantly supplemented by the establishment of a Press Bureau and the passing of the Defence of the Realm Act (DORA)[74], and given immediate practical assistance through the action of restricting the flow of information by the cutting of appropriate communication cables and the creation of routine monitoring of radio telegraph, cable and postal communications[75].

The Defence of the Realm Act (DORA) was passed on 8 August 1914 and extended between 1914 and 1916 with a number of additions and modifications to meet particular circumstances. The total corpus of Defence of the Realm Regulations which grew out of this legislation eventually gave the executive huge powers which in potential effect were virtually tantamount to a suspension of civil rights, the imposition of martial law, and the provision of the police with the authority to take actions which ignored traditional rights and liberties.

Although the Government had through DORA provided itself with such wide-ranging powers it mainly confined its employment of them in the early stages of the war to spy catching, internal security, home defence, and monitoring and censorship of the press, but not, at this stage, to the suppression of anti-war dissent. When war broke out anti-war dissent emerged primarily from the two distinct sources of the conscientious objector, who opposed violence of every kind, and the political objector, who opposed this particular war because they believed it could have been avoided, but both groups, refraining from blatant obstruction of the war effort, concentrated on mounting an opposition to the war in speech and writing, arguing the case for peace being sought by negotiation at the earliest opportunity. Both groups established their own, or joined existing, support organizations; many conscientious objectors on religious grounds also joined political anti-war groups in spite of the differences in their approach. The main anti-war organisations were the No Conscription Fellowship (NCF)[76], the Fellowship of Reconciliation (FoR), the Union of Democratic Control (UDC), the Independent Labour Party (ILP), the National Council Against Conscription (NCAC)[77] and the Women's International League for Peace and Freedom. These were by no means the only anti-war organisations operating actively during the war, but they represented the principal targets both of the government's efforts to stifle opposition to the war and also of the vitriolic attacks mounted in the jingo press. By the summer of 1915 most of them were producing an output of literature which was of sufficient concern to the government to prompt it to mount its first systematic campaign against anti-war organisations and their literature. Police raids on anti-war organisations began to take place as, for example, when the police on 18 August 1915 invaded the offices of the Independent Labour Party and the National Labour Press (which printed for both the ILP and the UDC) and seized 7,000 copies of 19 different pamphlets.

It was not, however, until anti-war dissent reached its peak towards the end of the war that the government felt

---

[73] The new Directorate of Military Intelligence consisted of six sections, one of which, MO5, was given the task of formulating 'policy regarding submarine cables and wireless telegraphy; press correspondents and control of the press in war.'

[74] The original Act consisted of only three clauses, enabling the King in Council to make regulations designed to prevent communication with or assistance to the enemy; to take whatever measures were needed to secure the safety of troops, ships and military installations; and to prevent any activity likely to cause disaffection or to prejudice His Majesty's relations with foreign powers. Regulations continued to be added to the Act throughout the war, and consolidated versions of them produced at intervals. By 28 February 1917 there were 400 pages of Consolidated Regulations and they covered most aspects of public activity. Those by which the press were chiefly affected were Regulations 18, 27, 27C, 51, 51A and 56 (13).

[75] Early in the war the Admiralty cut all cables in the North Sea and the Straits of Dover, except those which were British-owned, and severely restricted Germany's communications with the USA by cutting the German trans-Atlantic cables. Agents of the War Office took possession of every British cable company. The Admiralty controlled all incoming and outgoing material conveyed by radio telegraph (wireless) and the War Office controlled the entire flow of cabled and postal information from overseas.

[76] Founded by Fenner Brockway, editor of the ILP's *Labour Leader*.

[77] The NCAC was founded in January 1916 initially to rally the opposition to the Military Service Bill. After the introduction of conscription it turned its attention to civil liberties, notably to the treatment of conscientious objectors by tribunals and in prisons, and the DORA regulations that threatened freedom of speech. In July 1917 the NCAC changed its name to the National Council for Civil Liberties (NCCL).

the need to employ more use of DORA to combat it. In the last two years of the war, the regulations related to censorship under DORA (extended to cover types of literature - leaflets, broadsheets, and billboards - hitherto exempt) were implemented with greater severity with the result that convictions for writing and distributing seditious literature began to become much more commonplace, and dissenting leaders like Morel and Russell ended up in prison. The government, however, wary of their actions resulting in the creation of public martyrs and a potential backlash, in general proceeded with caution and a preference for leaving dissenting and pacifist groups to be harassed by private groups and newspapers.

Surveillance was also employed as a means of preventing actions likely to be inimical to the government's authority or its ability to maintain public confidence in its conduct of the war. In this respect the Special Branch played an increasingly significant part as the war wore on and domestic unrest became more apparent. There was particularly an awareness of the possible political ramifications of industrial unrest since 1915 and this lay behind the development of an intelligence service within industry which was run initially by the Ministry of Munitions but taken over from December 1916 by the Special Branch. This intelligence service became based on the use of local police informers recruited for the purpose of infiltrating political and union meetings and reporting regularly to their local Authorised Competent Military Authorities (ACMAs) on the whole range of human activities subject to DORA regulations. Infiltration, which even extended to individual households (see Pat Barker's *The Eye in the Door*, listed below) was carried out by agents provocateurs, usually posing as conscientious objectors fleeing from the police. Their reports, forwarded to London, were digested into intelligence summaries for circulation to GHQ, to the Cabinet, and to relevant government departments. These summaries were necessarily a reflection of the attitudes, and prejudices of the informers and, furthermore, were liable to be subject to further misinterpretation[78] by the officials who examined them.

Official Publications

Manual of Emergency Legislation: Comprising All the Acts of Parliament, Proclamations, Orders, etc, Passed and Made in Consequence of the War, edited by A. Pulling, Supplement 2 to December 5th, 1914, Incorporating and Superseding Supplement 1 (London: H. M. S. O., 1914)

Autobiographies, Memoirs

Brockway, A. F., Baron Brockway. *Inside the Left: Thirty Years of Platform, Press, Prison and Parliament* (London: Allen and Unwin, 1942; repr. 1947)

Thomson, Sir B. H. *My Experiences at Scotland Yard* (Garden City, New York: Doubleday, 1923)

— *The Scene Changes* (London: Collins, 1939)

Books

Andrew, C. M. *The Defence of the Realm: The Authorized History of MI5* (London: Allen Lane, 2009)

— *Secret Service: The Making of the British Intelligence Community* (London: Heinemann, 1985)

Barker, P. *The Eye in the Door* (London: Plume, 1993)
The persecution of pacifists, conscientious objectors, and homosexuals and the erosion of freedom arising from the state's constant surveillance of its citizens are among the aspects of the war which Pat Barker includes in this novel.

Boghardt, T. *Spies of the Kaiser: German Covert Operations in Great Britain during the First World War Era* (London: Palgrave Macmillan in conjunction with St. Anthony's College, Oxford, 2004)

Bunyan, T. *The History and Practices of the Political Police in Britain*, 2nd edn (London: Friedmann, 1971)

Defence of the Realm Act (DORA) August 1914 (4 and Geo. V c.29)
The Bill, drafting of which had taken place before the war, was introduced in the House of Commons on 7 August 1914

---

[78] No account was liable to be taken of the differences between the activities of the various bodies; pacifists and suspect shop stewards were likely to be lumped together in the same category as any other groupings, such as the ILP and the UDC, which held views opposed to those of the government.

and passed through all its stages without discussion. The original Act consisted of only three clauses, enabling the King in Council to make regulations designed to prevent communication with or assistance to the enemy; to take whatever measures were needed to secure the safety of troops, ships and military installations; and to prevent any activity likely to cause disaffection or to prejudice His Majesty's relations with foreign powers. Regulations continued to be added to the Act throughout the war, and consolidated versions of them appeared at intervals. By 28 February 1917 there were 400 pages of Consolidated Regulations, and they covered most aspects of public activity.

Ewing, K. D. and C. A. Gearty. *The Struggle for Civil Liberties: Political Freedom and the Rule of Law in Britain 1914-1945* (Oxford: Oxford University Press, 2000)

Felstead, S. T. *German Spies at Bay: Being an Actual Record of the German Espionage in Great Britain During the Years 1914-1918*, compiled from Official Sources (London: Hutchinson, 1920)

Ferris, J. R. '"Airbandit": C³I and Strategic Air Defence during the First Battle of Britain, 1915-1918', in *Strategy and Intelligence: British Policy during the First World War*, edited by Michael Dockrill and David French (London: Hambledon, 1996)

Geary, R. *Policing Industrial Disputes: 1883-1985* (Cambridge: Cambridge University Press, 1985)

Great Britain. War Office *The Inadvertent Disclosure of Military Information* (London: HMSO?, 1916)

Hooper, D. *Official Secrets: The Use and Abuse of the Act* (London: Secker & Warburg, 1987)

Millman, B. *Managing Domestic Dissent in First World War Britain* (London: Frank Cass, 2000)

Morgan, J. *Conflict and Order: The Police and Labour Disputes in England and Wales 1900-1939* (Oxford: Clarendon, 1987)

Morton, J. *Spies of the First World War: Under Cover for King and Kaiser* (London: National Archives, 2010)
The titles of the chapters of this work are as follows: Part One: 1. The early spy novels and Germans in England. 2. The formation of MI5 and MI6. 3. Pre-First World War German spies in England and abroad. 4. Pre-First World War British and other spies abroad. Part Two: 5. German spies. 6. The spy-masters, English, French and German. 7. Codes and codebreakers. Part Three: 8. Shot in the tower 1914-1916. 9. The spy survivors. 10. Women spies. 11. German spies in Europe, America and India during the war. 12. After the war was over.

Occleshaw, M. E. *Armour Against Fate: British Military Intelligence in the First World War* (London: Columbus, 1988)

Porter, B. J. *The Origins of the Vigilant State: The London Metropolitan Police Special Branch before the First World War* (London: Weidenfeld & Nicolson, 1987)

Rowbotham, S. *Friends of Alice Wheeldon* (New York: Monthly Review Press, 1987)
Contents: Friends of Alice Wheeldon; Rebel networks in the First World War. *Friends of Alice Wheeldon* was also published, (London: Pluto, 1986), with the text of the author's play of the same name first performed at the Rotherham Arts Centre in March 1980. All the Wheeldon family were involved in left-wing politics and anti-war campaigning. By 1916 the Wheeldons were sheltering conscientious objectors and being helped to smuggle them out to Ireland or the USA. As a result of these activities the Wheeldons were subjected to close surveillance by the intelligence services which in early 1917 intercepted a parcel of poison which had been sent to Alice by her sister Winfred. This gave the authorities a pretext to take action. Alice was charged, along with others (including her sisters Harriet and Winifred) with conspiring to use this poison (to be loaded and fired in darts) to assassinate the prime minister, David Lloyd George, together with the prominent Labour Party war supporter, Arthur Henderson, and other unspecified persons. Alice claimed that the poison was to be used to kill guard dogs at concentration camps where conscientious objectors were being held, in order to help them to escape. She was sentenced to ten years' penal servitude but only served a short period of her sentence, being released from goal in December 1918. She subsequently died in the post-war influenza epidemic, on 21 February 1919.

Sellers, L. *Shot in the Tower: The Story of the Spies Executed in the Tower of London during the First World War* (London: Leo Cooper, 1997)

Thomson, Sir B. H. *My Experiences at Scotland Yard* (Garden City, New York: Doubleday, 1923)
Thomson was appointed assistant commissioner of the Metropolitan Police and head of the CID at New Scotland Yard in

1913.

— *Queer People* (London: Hodder & Stoughton, 1922)

— *The Scene Changes* (London: Collins, 1939)

Thurlow, R. *The Secret State: British Internal Security in the Twentieth Century* (Oxford: Blackwell, 1994, repr. 1995)

Weinberger, B. *Keeping the Peace? Policing Strikes, 1906-1926* (New York: Berg, 1991)

West, N. *MI5: British Security Service Operations 1909-1945* (London: Bodley Head, 1981; repr London, Triad Granada, 1983)

— *MI6: British Secret Intelligence Operations, 1909-45* (London: Weidenfeld & Nicolson, 1983; repr. London: Panther, 1985)

Wigham, E. *Strikes and the Government, 1893-1981*, 2nd edn (London: Macmillan, 1982)

Wrigley, C. J. 'The First World War and State Intervention in Industrial Relations', in *A History of British Industrial Relations, 1914-1939*, edited by C. Wrigley, new edn (Aldershot: Gregg Revivals, 1993)
Facsimile reprint of edn originally published as *A History of British Industrial Relations*, Vol 2: 1914-1939, Brighton: Harvester, 1987

Articles

Boghardt, T. 'A German Spy? New Evidence on Baron Louis von Horst', *Journal of Intelligence History*, 1 (2001)
In relation to the arrest by Scotland Yard detectives (in August 1914) of the German-American businessman, Baron Louis von Horst, on a charge of spying for the German government, this article reveals that new documentary evidence shows that the charge was unjust and that Sir Basil Thomson, director of the Special Branch, ruthlessly exploited the arrest and detention of the baron (who spent the rest of the war in detention camps) as a means of advancing his own career.

Desmarais, R. 'Lloyd George and the Development of the British Government's Strike Breaking Organization', *International Review of Social History*, 20 (1975), 1-15

Englander, D. 'Military Intelligence and the Defence of the Realm: The Surveillance of Soldiers and Civilians in Britain during the First World War', *Bulletin of the Society for the Study of Labour History*, 52 (1987), 23-32

Hiley, N. P. 'Counter Espionage and Security in Great Britain during the First World War', *English Historical Review*, 101 (1986), 635-70

— 'Entering the Lists: MI5's Great Spy Round-up of August 1914', *Intelligence and National Security* 21 (2006), 46-76.
This article reveals that recently-opened records indicate that the famous success long attributed to MI5's round-up of spies in August 1914, and the resulting crippling of the German intelligence network at the beginning of the war, was based on a total fabrication.

— 'Internal Security in Wartime: the Rise and Fall of PMS 2, 1915-1917', *British Security in Wartime*, 1 (1986), 395-415
This article traces the brief organizational life of a British World War I counterintelligence unit, first called the Ministry of Munitions Labour Intelligence Division (MMLI) and renamed Parliamentary Military Security Department, No. 2 Section (P.M.S.2) in June 1916.

— 'The Strategic Origins of Room 40', *Intelligence and National Security*, 2 (1987), 245-73

Hiley, N. P. and J. Putowski 'A Postscript on PMS2', *Intelligence and National Security*, 3 (1988), 325-31

Mór-O'Brien, A. 'Patriotism on Trial: The Strike of the South Wales Miners, July 1915', *Welsh History Review*, 12 (1984)

4.1.4 Censorship

4.1.4.1 General

As was the case with all the governments of the belligerent nations, controlling public opinion as a means of maintaining national unity in time of war became an important feature of the British government's strategy to achieve victory. Improvements in literacy and the development of the popular press meant that opinions expressed in newspapers and magazines had the potential to influence a far larger audience. Well aware of this, the British government developed a system of censorship which included among its principal objectives that of ensuring that what was written did not undermine the nation's war effort or its relations with its allies and neutral countries. It sought to achieve this in a number of ways the most obvious of which was to prevent the publication of information (e.g. troop movements, etc) that might be useful to the enemy, but it ultimately went far beyond this purely military censorship, becoming increasingly involved as the war progressed in censorship methods of a distinctly political nature. With the waning of the early patriotic euphoria as the years passed by without any major victories to report, the government became acutely aware of the need to sustain the morale of the British people and to prevent them from being adversely affected by anti-war propaganda. It therefore set up an apparatus of domestic censorship that aimed not only at controlling the information which journalists received and what they wrote but also at suppressing the literature of anti-war protest from whatever quarter it emerged.

By the summer of 1915 most of the anti-war organisations were producing an output of literature which was of sufficient concern to the government[79] to prompt it to mount its first systematic campaign against these organisations and their literature. Police raids on anti-war organisations began to take place as, for example, when the police on 18 August 1915 invaded the offices of the Independent Labour Party and the National Labour Press (which printed for both the Independent Labour Party and the UDC) and seized 7,000 copies of 19 different pamphlets. From February 1916 onwards guidance on how to deal with anti-war literature began to be sent regularly by the War Office to the Authorised Competent Military Authorities (ACMAs) and by the Home Office to Chief Constables, and police raids were mounted on the basis of lists of prohibited material[80]. In the winter of 1916/17 signs that opposition to the war and support for a negotiated peace was growing prompted the government to decide in October 1917, among other actions for dealing with this problem, to get the head of the Special Branch, Basil Thomson, to investigate all the organisations producing pacifist propaganda. Thomson's report, the conclusions of which were based on police raids authorised by Thomson on the presses or offices of thirteen pacifist and so-called revolutionary organisations[81], convinced the Home Secretary, Sir George Cave that he would be justified in introducing DORA 27C for regulating every leaflet, pamphlet or circular relating to the present war or the making of peace – the most draconian of all the weapons of censorship employed during the war to stifle anti-war literature. Although this regulation was amended it was still sufficiently powerful to enable the police to maintain the number of their raids, already previously greatly increased, on the premises of suspected organizations and individuals. Police raids, however, primarily had the effect of disrupting the distribution of suspect literature, but few bodies involved in publishing it were suppressed and then only as a temporary expedient as was the case, for example, with the suppression of *Britannia*, the suffragette paper, in 1915 and of the socialist paper *Forward*[82] in Glasgow the following year. Even the *Labour Leader*, the most important of all the pacifist newspapers, managed to continue appearing throughout the war in spite of its frequent confrontations with the authorities.

Censorship was applied internationally as well as domestically, the government being concerned to prevent public opinion in allied and neutral countries from being influenced by unfavourable comment on Britain and the Empire. It was greatly assisted in this object by being able to make Germany's communications with the

---

[79] The government had even more cause for concern after the introduction of conscription which led to the opponents of war accelerating their output of posters, pamphlets, and leaflets.

[80] By early summer of 1916 fifteen circulars had been sent out to local police forces, listing 'Hostile Pamphlets' which had already been condemned by the Courts. Supplementary to these, the Special Branch produced their own list of leaflets, the legality of which, however, having not been previously tested in the Courts, had to be tested via a summons subsequent to any police raid related to them.

[81] The 13 organisations included the UDC, FoR, NCCL, NCF, and the Peace Negotiations Committee.

[82] For first-hand accounts of the seizure of *Forward* in Glasgow, see Emanuel Shinwell's *Conflict without Malice* (1955) and David Kirkwood's *My Life of Revolt* (1935).

outside world (particularly with the USA before its entry into the war) extremely difficult by cutting communication cables, and by maintaining, generally, a close watch throughout the war on telegraphy and wireless communication (the War Office, for example, controlled the flow of information and visual images entering and leaving Britain through its work in the cable, postal, and cinema censorship offices).

- **Bibliographies**

Young, K. and R. D. Lawrence. *Bibliography on Censorship and Propaganda* (Eugene, Oregon: University of Oregon, 1928)

- **Autobiographies, Biographies, Diaries**

Brownrigg D. E. R. *Indiscretions of the Naval Censor* (London: Cassell, 1920)

Callwell, Sir C. E. *The Experience of a Dug-Out*, 1914-1918 (London: Constable, 1920)
The author was director of military operations and intelligence, War Office, 1914-16

Charteris, J. *At G.H.Q.: A Record of Service at G.H.Q. during the Great War, 1914-1918* (London: Cassell, 1931)
Until his replacement in January 1918 Charteris was Haig's major source of battlefield intelligence.

Clarke, T. *Northcliffe in History: An Intimate Study of Press Power* (London : Hutchinson, 1950)

Montague, C. E. *Disenchantment* (London: Chatto & Windus, 1922; repr. London: Macgibbon & Kee, 1968)
His memoir of the war, *Disenchantment*, charts the transition in Montague from believer in censorship to hater of censorship

Riddell, G. A., Baron Riddell. *Lord Riddell's War Diary, 1914-1918* (London: Nicholson and Watson, 1933)
The author was chairman of the *News of the World* from 1903-1934.

— *The Riddell Diaries, 1908-1923*, edited and with an introduction by J. M. McEwen (London: Athlone Press, 1986)

- **Books**

Andrew C. and D. Dilks, eds. *The Missing Dimension: Governments and Intelligence Communities in the Twentieth Century* (London: Macmillan, 1984)

Angell, N. *The Press and the Organisation of Society*, rev edn (Cambridge: G. Fraser, Minority Press, 1933)
Originally published London: Labour Pub. Co., 1922.

Beaverbrook, W. M. A., 1st Baron. *Men and Power 1917-1918* (London: Hutchinson, 1956; repr. London: Collins, 1966)

— *Politicians and the Press* (London: Hutchinson, 1926)

Daniel, F. W. *The Field Censor Systems of the Armies of the British Empire, 1914-1918: Unit Allocations* (Burnham on Crouch: Forces Postal History Society , 1984)

Entwistle, C. R. and A. Baker. *A Catalogue of Indian Censorship, 1914-1920* (Perth: Chavril Press, 1994)

Gould, M. H. *British Naval Post and Censor Marks of the First World War*, rev. edn (Burnham on Crouch: Postal History 2000 on behalf of the Forces Postal History Society, 1998)

— *British Naval Post and Censor Marks of the First World War*, supplement [cumulative] 2 (Burnham on Crouch: Postal History 2000 on behalf of the Forces Postal History Society, 2003)

Great Britain. War Office *The Inadvertent Disclosure of Military Information* (London: HMSO?, 1916)

— *Memorandum on Censorship*, Cd. 7670 (London: HMSO?, 1915)

— *Memorandum on the Censorship, 1914-16*, Cd. 7679 (London: HMSO?, 1917)

Hooper, D. *Official Secrets: The Use and Abuse of the Act* (London: Secker & Warburg, 1987)

Lee, J. F. *Blacklead and Whitewash: A Side-Show of the Great War.* (Karachi: G. A. Holdaway, 1923)
On the Indian Censorship

The Mails as a German War Weapon: Memorandum on the Censorship of Mails Carried by Neutral Ships (London: Eyre and Spottiswoode, 1916)

Mark, G. *British Censorship of Civil Mails during World War I, 1914-1919* (Bristol: Stuart Rossiter Trust Fund, 2000)

Martin J. J. and F. L. Walton *West African Censorship: World War I And II: Covering Ascension, Cameroon, Gambia, Gold Coast, Nigeria, St Helena, Sierra Leone and Togo* (Henley: West Africa Study Circle, 1993)

Nicholson, S. *The Censorship of British Drama, 1900-1968*, 4 vols (Exeter: Exeter University Press, 2003-2012), I: *1900-1932* (2003)
This first volume of an analysis of British theatre censorship covering the years from 1900 until 1968, based on previously undocumented material in the Lord Chamberlain's Correspondence archives, deals with the period before 1932 and provides an insight into the day-to-day operation of the system of theatre censorship together with the principles, policies and practice associated with it in the particular period under examination.

Robertson, J. C. *The British Board of Film Censors: Film Censorship in Britain, 1896-1950* (Beckenham, Kent: Croom Helm, 1985)

— *The Hidden Cinema: British Film Censorship in Action, 1913-75*, 2nd rev. edn (London: Routledge, 1993)

Rose, T. *Aspects of Political Censorship, 1914-1918* (Hull: Hull University Press, 1995)

Shepherd, A. *The Postal Censorship in Barbados during the First and Second World Wars* (Manorbier: British West Indies Study Circle, 1984)

Silber, J C. *The Invisible Weapons* (London: Hutchinson, 1932)
The story of a German secret service agent who was employed by the British Postal censorship during the war.

Sloss, R. *An American's View of the British Mail Censorship* (London: W. Speaight & Sons, 1916)

Stuart, Sir C. *Secrets of Crewe House: The Story of a Famous Campaign* (London: Hodder & Stoughton, 1920)

Towle, P. 'The Debate on Wartime Censorship in Britain, 1902-1914', in *War and Society: A Yearbook of Military History*, edited by B. Bond and I. Roy, Vol 1 (London: Croom Helm, 1975)

Williams, D. G. T. *Not in the Public Interest: The Problem of Security in Democracy* (London: Hutchinson, 1965)

- **Articles**

Brotherstone, T. 'The Suppression of the *Forward*', *Scottish Labour History Society Journal*, (May 1969)

Drisceoil, D. O. 'Keeping Disloyalty within Bounds? British Media Control in Ireland, 1914-19' *Irish Historical Studies*, 149 (2012), 52-69

Hopkin, D. 'Domestic censorship in the First World War', *Journal of Contemporary History*, 5 (1970), 151-169

Koch, T. W. 'British Censorship and Enemy Publications', *Library Journal*, 42 (1917), 697-705

McLean, I. S. 'The Ministry of Munitions, the Clyde Workers' Committee, and the Suppression of the *Forward*: An Alternative View', *Scottish Labour History Society Journal*, (December 1972)

Walsh, M. 'No Peace For The Wicked: A Censored Painter [C. R. W. Nevinson] of the Great War ', *Index on Censorship*, 32; Issue 3 (2003), 21-29

- **Theses**

Gassert, I. L. 'Collaborators and Dissidents: Aspects of British Literary Publishing in the First World War, 1914-1919' (unpublished doctoral thesis, University of Oxford, 2001)

Schneider, E. F. 'What Britons Were Told About the War in the Trenches, 1914-1918' (unpublished doctoral thesis, University of Oxford, 1997)

- **Contemporary Material**

Bennett, A. 'The Public and the Censor', *Harper's Weekly*, 59 (1914), 508-10
Doubts about the wisdom of the Allies keeping the public in the dark about the war.

Cecil, R., Viscount Cecil of Chelwood. *Why Mail Censorship is Vital to Britain: An Interview with the Rt. Hon. Lord Robert Cecil, Minister of Blockade* (London: Truscott, 1916)

'British Censorship of the United States', *Independent*, 82 (1915), 230

'The Censorship and its Effects', *Quarterly Review*, 446 (1916), 148-163

Censorship and Trade (London: Eyre & Spottiswoode, 1916)

Dillon, J. *The Censorship and the War. Remarkable Speech by John Dillon: What is the Policy of the Government as Regards the Censorship?* From the Official Report, Vol. 90, No. 8, of the Parliamentary Debates, 20th February, 1917 (London: National Council for Civil Liberties, 1917)

Harrison, A. 'Gott Strafe all Intellect', *English Review*, 24 (1917), 470-73

Lequeux, W. T. *Britian's Deadly Peril. Are We Told the Truth?* (London: S. Paul & Co.,1915)

Montague, C E. 'Would Truth or Lies Cost More?', *Nineteenth Century*, 90 (1921), 27-34

Pollard, A. F. 'Rumour and Historical Science in Time of War', *Contemporary Review*, 107 (1915), 321-30

'Prohibited Post Cards and Photographs', *The Broad Arrow*, 95 (1915), 488

'Recruiting and the Censorship', *Quarterly Review*, 442 (1914), 130-158

Russell, B. A. W., 3rd Earl Russell. 'Freedom of Speech in England', *School and Society*, 4 (1916), 637-38

— 'Individual Liberty and Public Control', *Atlantic Monthly*, 120 (1917), 112-120

Ryan, J. A. 'Freedom of Speech in War-Time', *Catholic World*, 106 (1918), 577-88

'Safeguarding Our Minds', *The Nation*, 107 (1918), 795
Critical of censorship of books soldiers were permitted to read.

Sloss, R. *An American's View of the British Mail Censorship* (London: Speaight, 1916)

Wood, E. F. 'The British Censorship', *Saturday Evening Post*, 189 (April 28 1917), 5-7, 101-02

— 'The British Censorship', *Saturday Evening Post*, 189 (May 5 1917), 18-19, 105-06

4.1.4.2 News Reporting

A Press Bureau was set up on 5th August 1914 under the directorship of F. E. Smith[83] and with a staff largely comprising military officers. Its main function was to exert two forms of control in relation to matters concerning the war, one over the information journalists received and the other over what they wrote. In the case of controlling the information which journalists received it exercised strict censorship of press cables, subjected press material posted from overseas to postal censorship, and initially kept journalists away from the battlefront, forcing them to rely on government briefings. In the case of controlling what journalists wrote the situation was somewhat different as they were not subject to compulsory censorship but expected to engage in voluntary self censorship. Although not compulsorily required to do so, newspaper editors were invited to submit to the Press Bureau articles likely to be sensitive and had to bear in mind that if they (or whoever else was responsible) did publish such material without prior clearance from the Bureau they were liable to prosecution under one of the DORA regulations[84]. Furthermore, even if an article was passed by the Bureau it might still be liable to prosecution by the Home Office. In addition to the task of overseeing the censorship of press cables and articles submitted voluntarily to them, the Directors of the Press Bureau were responsible for passing on to the press almost any information, ranging from warnings to briefings, that other Government departments wanted conveyed. They did this by producing confidential letters, D notices (designed to warn editors about topics to be avoided), instructions, and telephone messages and circulating them to the editors of all the London-based and national daily papers and journals, the major regional dailies (e.g. the *Manchester Guardian* and the *Yorkshire Post*), all the provincial weekly and evening papers, and the Irish Press.

When the war began the army's attitude to correspondents appointed by their newspapers to cover the western front was suspicious and obstructive[85]. Until May 1915 reporters were banned from the front and newspapers had to depend on communiqués from Colonel Sir Ernest Swinton whose reports, subject to censorship at G.H.Q and personal approval by Lord Kitchener, aimed to 'tell as much of the truth as was compatible with safety, to guard against depression and pessimism, and to check unwarranted optimism which might lead to a relaxation of effort'. The attitude of the High Command, however, began to change as it gradually realized that it could be advantageous to have the press on its side and, with the introduction of a system of accredited war correspondents in 1915, the army abandoned its negative attitude to the press and developed a good working relationship with both journalists and newspaper magnates.

The war correspondents mostly collaborated with the military censors, not only providing a sanitised picture of the army at the front and ensuring that no information that might be of use to the enemy was reported, but also by providing stories of heroism and glory, glossing over major setbacks, and shielding the High Command from criticism of its conduct of the war. The acquiescent way in which they allowed themselves to report the news was one of the reasons why Arthur Ponsonby was prompted to write: "there was no more discreditable period in the history of journalism than the four years of the Great War" (*Falsehood in Wartime*, 1928). Some of them defended the role they played as war correspondents both at the time and after the war – a reflection perhaps of their unease with it. Sir Philip Gibbs was quite frank about it when he wrote in 1923: "We identified ourselves absolutely with the Armies in the field ... We wiped out of our minds all thought of personal scoops and all temptation to write one word which would make the task of officers and men more difficult or dangerous. There was no need of censorship of our dispatches. We were our own censors" (*Adventures In Journalism*, 1923).

Although a system of censorships of considerable severity was exercised under DORA, as was especially apparent in the ruthless way in which openly subversive publications of the revolutionary left were handled, the press in general enjoyed a considerable amount of freedom (except in relation to Russia - see below).

---

[83] The first Director, F.E. Smith, appointed on 5 August 1914, was succeeded at the end of September 1914 by Sir Stanley Buckmaster and by the summer of 1915 by a joint Directorate consisting of Sir Frank Swettenham and Sir Edward Cook both of whom continued in office until April 1919.

[84] Penalties that could be incurred under DORA against papers that did not conform could be severe. A notable example of such severity was the two-week suppression of the *Globe* following its publication in November 1915 of stories that Kitchener was being forced to resign.

[85] This attitude, derived from a traditional suspicion of press reporters, was exacerbated by the famous Amiens dispatch written by two of the very small number of correspondents on the Western Front at the beginning of the war. This dispatch, with a headline of 'Broken British Regiments Battling Against Odds', provided a graphic description of British troops, exhausted and depleted, in retreat. Voluntarily submitted for censorship and passed by F. E. Smith, the Director of the Press Bureau, it was published by *The Times* on August 30th, 1914. F. E. Smith passed it for publication because he believed it would inculcate a sense of urgency; he even made additions to it designed not only to increase awareness of the urgency of the situation but also to boost recruiting.

Newspapers were prevented from printing pictures of British dead and wounded but they were allowed to publish official figures of British deaths and casualties, the national and local press giving the latter statistics wide currency, particularly the local press which published casualty lists throughout the war. Mass circulation newspapers were able to get away with criticisms of the government as was notably exemplified early in the war by the Northcliffe press attack on the government over the 'shell scandal'. The local press, through the information it was able to obtain via its closer, more personal links to the soldiers of local regiments, was frequently able to provide articles with an uncensored local focus, describing the battlefront in a realistic fashion in contrast to the sanitized war reports of the national dailies.

Throughout the war prosecutions of newspapers were rare. This can be attributed partly to the effectiveness of the Press Bureau and the heavy penalties which could be imposed through DORA but perhaps rather more to the willingness of the national newspapers to co-operate with the government on the task of maintaining the nation's morale. Most of their editors were happy to acquiesce in a good deal of self-censorship, avoiding negative material and publishing morale-boosting stories. This was the main reason for the press's resentment of the system of official censorship to which it was subject throughout the war, but particularly in its early stages. With its willingness for the most part to be supportive it felt that it should be trusted to use its common sense without the threat of censorship which, in its view, hampered[86] its ability to make patriotic contributions to the war effort. Relations between press and Government did, however, gradually improve, aided no doubt by the willingness of the official war correspondents to fall into line and by the Press Bureau (under Cook and Swettenham) slowly becoming more accommodating towards journalists, but the key factor in this improvement was the government's eventual realization that journalists could perform a valuable propaganda function. For this reason there was a gradual shift in emphasis from controlling the press to courting it as was evident, for instance, from the Government's practice of rewarding[87] influential press figures with important appointments and honours, and journalists with minor posts in the Press Bureau and exclusive access to military sources.

The Government, however, was always keen to maintain a tight rein on news from Russia. From the earliest days of the war the Press Bureau and its controllers took a special interest in closely monitoring news from or about Russia. Their interference with the supply of news from Russia was until 1917 designed to ensure that nothing was written to undermine the rapport with Russia and its efforts on the battlefield. After the October Revolution this interference took a different direction. Calls for peace emanating from Russia gave the British government increasing cause for concern and after the Bolsheviks took power in 1917 this concern escalated into an obsession with the dangers posed by a party which, by virtue of its condemnation of capitalism, was a threat to the status quo. Following the Bolshevik revolution and until the end of the war all news from Russia, unless positively hostile to the Bolsheviks, became subject to intense scrutiny. It was, furthermore, felt necessary to manipulate news from Russia in such a way as to ensure not only that the events in Russia did not arouse the sympathy of the reading public, but also, by placing such an unfavourable construction on them, that the launching of a direct military attack by the Allies on the Bolsheviks would be acceptable to public opinion. This object was achieved by cutting, delaying, or suppressing all news coming out of Russia considered incompatible with this policy. It is for this reason that news from correspondents in Russia like Michael Farbman (Special Correspondent of the *Manchester Guardian* for a few weeks in the summer of 1917), Arthur Ransome (*Daily News*) and Philips Price (*Manchester Guardian*) met with such harsh treatment. All their attempts, for instance, to present a balanced view of events in Russia, facts about Allied meddling in the internal affairs of Russia[88], or views criticising the negative attitude of the Allies to Russia and the Bolsheviks were subject to severe censorship. In contrast other correspondents in Russia had no difficulty getting their articles printed without any restriction so

---

[86] The press was inclined to regard the management of the Press Bureau, as muddled, its way of operating confused, and its decisions unjust; it was also irritated by the hostile attitude of the Government and the service departments in the early stages of the war, and by the scarcity of 'hard news' caused by the censorship.

[87] Appointments of this nature included those of Sir George Riddell, proprietor of the *News of the World*, as a government adviser and of Northcliffe, Beaverbrook, and Rothermere to the Cabinet. In relation to honours, as well as the conferment of several press knighthoods, Alfred Harmsworth became a Viscount (Northcliffe) in 1917; William Aitken, who acquired a controlling interest in the *Daily Express* in 1916, was made a baronet (Beaverbrook) in the same year; Waldorf Astor, owner of the *Observer*, became a Viscount (Astor) in 1917; Sir George Riddell received a peerage (Riddell) in 1918; Robert Donald, editor of the *Chronicle* was offered a baronetcy, but refused it.

[88] Meddling related, for example, to Japanese military intervention on Russian soil, the activities of the Czechs in Siberia, and Allied complicity in the civil war in south eastern Russia.

long as they conformed to the Government's line on Russia[89].

- **Autobiographies, Biographies, Reminiscences**

Charteris, J. *At G.H.Q.: A Record of Service at G.H.Q. during the Great War, 1914-1918* (London: Cassell, 1931)
Until his replacement in January 1918 Charteris was Haig's major source of battlefield intelligence. Tried early in the war, unsuccessfully, to persuade the military authorities to permit journalists to visit the front and report on conditions for themselves rather than having to accept unsatisfactory coverage provided by 'official eye-witnesses'.

Gibbs, Sir P. *Adventures In Journalism* (London: Heinemann, 1923)
The author was a war correspondent in the Great War.

— *Realities of War*, new and revised edn (London: Hutchinson, 1929)

Jones, Sir R. *A Life in Reuters* (London: Hodder & Stoughton, 1951)

Price, M. P. *My Reminiscences of the Russian Revolution* (London: Allen & Unwin, 1921; repr; Westport, Conn.: Hyperion press, 1981)

— *My Three Revolutions* (London: Allen & Unwin, 1969)

Ransome, A. *The Autobiography of Arthur Ransome* (London: Cape, 1976; repr. London: Century, 1985)

Repington, C. à Court. *The First World War, 1914-1918*, 2 vols (Aldershot: Gregg Revivals in association with Department of War Studies, King's College, London, 1991)
Facsimile of edition published London: Constable, 1920 under the title *The First World War, 1914-1918: Personal Experiences*. Obsessive secrecy (e.g. sinking of the battleship *Audacious* on 27 October 1914 was kept secret for the entire war) convinced some journalists, in particular *The Times* military correspondent, Charles Repington, that censorship was 'a cloak to cover all political, naval, and military mistakes' and that journalists had a duty to expose them. But most reporters patiently tolerated restrictions.

— *Vestigia* (London: Constable, 1919)

Steed, H. W. *Through Thirty Years 1892-1922: A Personal Narrative*, 2 vols (London: William Heinemann, 1924)
Vol. 2 especially contains valuable materials on both propaganda and censorship. Steed was head of the foreign department of *The Times*, 1914-1919.

- **Books**

Bell, E. P. *The British Censorship: An Examination of the Institution and of the General Position of American Correspondents in London, From The Point of View of One of their Number*: An address before the American Luncheon Club, Savoy Hotel, London, November 19, 1915 (London: Fisher Unwin, 1915)

Berry, W. E., Viscount Camrose. *British Newspapers and their Controllers* (London: Cassell, 1947)

Cook, Sir E. T. *The Press in War-Time, With Some Account of the Official Press Bureau*: an essay [ed. by A.M. Cook] (London: Macmillan, 1920)
About both censorship and propaganda. Sir Edward Cook had charge of the British censorship during the world war. This book describes use and difficulties of censorship as well as its fallacies.

Crozier, E. *American Reporters on the Western Front, 1914-1918* (New York: Oxford University Press, 1959)
Comprehensive account of the work of American correspondents and of the immense difficulties they faced and sometimes

---

[89] *The Times, Morning Post, Daily Telegraph,* and the *Daily Mail* (the tabloid paper with the largest circulation), who all had their own correspondents in Russia to the end of 1917 (the *Morning Post's* correspondent, Victor Marsden, stayed on until at least May 1918) were among the papers which were allowed to print a great deal of news from Russia because on the whole, especially from the spring of 1918 onwards, they tended to reflect the establishment view of Russia. This is understandable as the proprietors and editors of all four papers were in broad agreement with the government line. Before warning letters from the Press Bureau were issued in May and June of 1918 they were even able to print views and speculations about Japanese intervention; in contrast the *Manchester Guardian* was prevented from printing reports from its correspondent about Japanese's manoeuvring in the build-up to intervention, or about the activities of the Czechs in Siberia.

overcame, with the censors.

Farrar, M. J. *News From the Front: War Correspondents on the Western Front 1914-1918* (Stroud: Sutton Publishing Ltd., 1998)

Gibbs, Sir P. *Now It Can Be Told* (New York: Harper, 1921)

Grieves, K. 'War Correspondents and Conducting Officers on the Western Front, 1915', in *Facing Armageddon; The First World War Experienced*, ed. by H. Cecil and P. H. Liddle (London: Leo Cooper, 1996)

Knightley, P. *The First Casualty: The War Correspondent as Hero, Propagandist and Myth Maker from the Crimea to Iraq* (London: Deutsch, 2003)

Lequeux, W. T. *Britian's Deadly Peril. Are We Told the Truth?* (London: S. Paul & Co.,1915)

Lovelace, C. J. 'British Press Censorship during the First World War', in *Newspaper History from the Seventeenth Century to the Present Day*, edited by G. Boyce, J. Curran and P. Wingate (London: Constable, 1978)

Lytton, N. *The Press and the General Staff* (London: Collins, 1920)

Margach, J. *The Abuse of Power: The War Between Downing Street and the Media from Lloyd George to Callaghan* (London: W. H. Allen, 1978)

Palmer, A. 'The History of the D Notice Committee', in *The Missing Dimension: Governments and Intelligence Communities in the Twentieth Century*, edited by C. Andrew and D. Dilks (London: Macmillan, 1984)

Read, D. *The Power of News: The History of Reuters*, 2nd edn (Oxford: Oxford University Press, 1999)

Riddell, G. A., Baron Riddell. *Censorship* [The British Press Censorship], in *Encyclopaedia Britannica*, 13th edn, 32 vols (London, New York: Encyclopædia Britannica, 1926)
Article is in vol 1 (pp 560-2) of the supplementary volumes of the 13th edn and is a very slightly updated version of his account in the 12th edn, Vol 30 (1922), pp 591-5.

Rose, T. 'Philips Price and the Russian Revolution' (unpublished doctoral thesis, University of Hull, 1988)

Salmon, L. M. *The Newspaper and Authority* (New York: Oxford Press, 1923)

Swinton, Sir E. D. *Eyewitness: Being Personal Reminiscences of Certain Phases of the Great War including the Genesis of the Tank* (London: Hodder & Stoughton, 1932)
Swinton, an army officer and writer, was appointed to GHQ in France on 7 September 1914 to write articles on the operations and battle progress of the Army on the Western front – a task he performed from 1914 to 1915. These reports were first censored in France before being personally vetted by Kitchener and released to the press under the headline of 'Eyewitness'.

- **Articles**

Callwell, Sir C. E. 'The Press Censorship', *Nineteenth Century*, 85 (1919), 1132-45

Cobb, F. I. 'The Press and Public Opinion', *New Republic*, 21 (1919), 144

Headlam, C. 'Censorship of the Press', *Quarterly Review*, 234 (1920), pp. 132-146
Review of war-time censorship in England, with special reference to books of Brownrigg and Cook.

Hiley, N. '"Lord Kitchener Resigns": The Suppression of the Globe in 1915', *Journal of Newspaper and Periodical History*, 8 (1992), 27-41

McEwen, J. M. '"Brass-Hats" and the British Press during the First World War', *Canadian Journal of History*, 18 (1988), 43-67

Riddell, G. A., Baron Riddell. 'The Relations of the Press with the Army in the Field', *Royal United Service Institution Journal*, 66 (1921), 385-397

- **Theses**

Schneider, E. F. 'What Britons Were Told About the War in the Trenches, 1914-1918' (unpublished doctoral thesis, University of Oxford, 1997)

- **Some Contemporary Views**

Baldwin, E. F. 'The English Press', *Outlook*, 108 (1914), 669-72

'The Blue Pencil', *New Statesman*, 6 (1915), 57-59

Cook, Sir E. T. *The Press Censorship: Interview Given by Sir Edward Cook to the Associated Press* (London: Burrup, Mathieson And Sprague, Ltd.,, 1916)

'The Duty of a Newapaper', *Spectator*, 115 (1915), 649
Defence of freedom of the press

'The Government and the Press', *Spectator*, 120 (1918), 197

Harrison, A. 'The Lion In Blinkers', *English Review*, 19 (1915.), 204-215

— 'Off with the Blinkers, *English Review*, 21 (1915), 317-23

'The Liberty of Thought and Discussion', *Economist*, 81 (1915), 767

MacDonald, W. 'The Press and the Censorship in England and France', *Nation*, 10 (1917), 287-89

'The Press and the Public', *Economist*, 81 (1915), 926-7

'The Press Censorship', *Economist*, 79 (1914), 909-910

'Press Control In War Time', *Nation*, 17 (1914), 568-569, 607-608, 637, 639

'The Prime Minister and the Press', *Nation*, 24 (1918), 41-2

'The Responsibility of the Press', *English Review*, 21 (1915), 113-123

Turner, E. R. 'Censorship and False News', *Nation*, 99 (1914), 280

Stewart, H. L. 'Freedom of Speech in War Time', *Nation*, 105 (1917), 219-220

'War and a Free Press, *Outlook*, 116 (1917), 56-7

'War and the Press, *Spectator*, 113 (1914), 222-3

4.2 Propaganda

4.2.1 General

One of the features of the Great War was the use made of the techniques of propaganda which, with the great expansion of the means of communication resulting from developments in technology in the nineteenth and early twentieth century, were able to be employed on a far wider scale in a major war than they had ever been before.

The British government was well aware of the importance of propaganda as a means of dispelling the doubts of those who at the beginning of the war needed convincing of the validity of Britain's cause, but was initially content to leave the task of producing this type of propaganda largely to various unofficial organizations, newspapers and magazines, and private individuals already spontaneously and enthusiastically undertaking it. As the war dragged on for a far longer period than people had been led to expect, the government saw that the range of propaganda on the home front would have to be expanded to include the task of maintaining the support and morale of the nation and that it would have to take a far more active role in the achievement of this. In contrast, it was conscious from the outset that it was of great importance to engage actively in propaganda overseas where it saw its prime objectives as being to convince France and Russia that it was taking its full share of the fighting (not just leaving them to bear the brunt of it), to dilute the effectiveness of the German propaganda campaign in neutral counties (particularly in the USA), and to establish a good rapport with the USA (not simply in the hope of getting it to come in on the side of the Allies, but also to ensure that the Allies were able to benefit from that country's immense manufacturing and financial resources). In spite of the paramount concern to project the right sort image of Britain in allied and neutral countries, undermining morale in enemy countries was not neglected. In this area pioneering work was done by the army's intelligence services who, through their perception of the sort of information which could be usefully disseminated in countries to encourage unrest or desertion, helped to shape the development of propaganda on the military fronts and ultimately on the civilian fronts as well.

In whatever form of communication (print, poster, photograph, moving film, or speech) it was employed the propaganda of all the belligerent nations was slanted with the object of presenting their actions and the cause for which they were fighting in a favourable light and of doing the exact opposite in relation to their opponents. To achieve this object the content of the propaganda could be strictly factual (e.g. the cinema film of the first British tank), or entirely invented (e.g. the stories of the Canadian soldier crucified by the Germans, and of the German 'corpse factory'), or a mixture of fact and fiction (e.g. Germany's alleged atrocities as presented in the official style of the Bryce report[90]).

All the belligerents in the Great War made use of atrocity propaganda (**see section 4.2.1.1**) with two main objects in mind, one being to stir up hatred against the enemy and the other to win the support of neutral nations, especially of the United States, for their cause. Stories of rape, torture, mutilation, desecration, and gross bestiality generally were the sort of themes which were commonly employed in the atrocity propaganda of all the belligerents in order to present the enemy in the worst possible light. Britain and her Allies distributed large quantities of atrocity material in a particularly aggressive and sustained campaign. The Germans were no less active and their atrocity stories were just as extravagant and as unsubstantiated by 'facts' as those of their opponents but for various reasons (see **section 4.2.6** on the **Effects of Propaganda**) they did not achieve the same impact. So concerned were the Germans about the impact of Allied atrocity propaganda that they published an entire 'White Book' devoted to denying that German troops had been guilty of committing atrocities. Many ordinary Germans were also disturbed by Allied atrocity propaganda. The Hamburg scholar, Aby Warburg, for instance, was so upset by the reports of the atrocities which Germany was accused of committing that he spent much of the war collecting evidence from newspapers to refute the charges that were made in these reports (Gombrich, A. H. *Aby Warburg: An Intellectual Biography*, 2nd edn (Oxford: Phaidon, 1986, p. 206)

A list of the sort of material the British employed in their atrocity campaign is provided within the **section 4.2.5.2 (Printed Propaganda Material)** in the sub-section **Books and Pamphlets: Atrocities**.

Bibliographies

Lasswell, H. D. and others, ed. *Propaganda and Promotional Activities: An Annotated Bibliography* (Minneapolis: University of Minnesota Press, 1935; repr. Chicago: Chicago University Press, 1969)

Lutz, R. H. 'Studies of World War Propaganda, 1914-33', *Journal of Modern History*, 5 (1933), 496-516

Wanderscheck, H. *Bibliographie zur englischen Propaganda im Weltkrieg*, Bibliographische Vierteljahrshefte der Weltkriegsbücherei, Heft 7 (Stuttgart: Weltkriegsbücherei, 1935)

---

[90] Lasswell particularly has the Bryce report in mind when he points out in his *Propaganda Technique in World War I* that "an excellent device which was used by the British to lend weight to their stories of German atrocities was to constitute a commission of men with international reputation for truthfulness to collect evidence and deliver findings".

Young, K. and R. D. Lawrence. *Bibliography on Censorship and Propaganda* (Eugene, Oregon: University of Oregon, 1928)

Books

August, T. G. *The Selling of the Empire: British and French Imperialist Propaganda, 1890-1940* (Westport, Conn.: Greenwood Press, 1985)

Black, J. B. *Organising the Propaganda Instrument: The British Experience* (The Hague: Martinus Nijhoff, 1975)

Bruntz, G. B. *Allied Propaganda and the Collapse of the German Empire in 1918*, Hoover War Library Publications, 13 (Stanford: Stanford University Press, 1938; repr. New York: Arno Press, 1972)

Buitenhuis, P. *The Great War of Words: British, American, and Canadian Propaganda and Fiction, 1914-1933* (Vancouver: University of British Columbia Press, 1987; repr. London: Batsford, 1989)
The 1989 reprint published in London was entitled, *The Great War of Words: Literature as Propaganda 1914-18 and After*.

Carruthers, S. L. *The Media at War: Communication and Conflict in the Twentieth Century* (Basingstoke: Macmillan, 2000)

Connors, M. F. *Dealing in Hate: The Development of Anti-German Propaganda.* (London: Britons Publishing Company, 1966; repr. Torrance, Ca.: Institute for Historical Review, 1990)

Cummings, H. R. 'Propaganda', in *Encyclopaedia Britannica*, 13th edn, vol.3 (London: Britannica Publishers, 1926)

Daugherty, W. E. and M. Janowitz. *A Psychological Warfare Casebook* (Baltimore: Johns Hopkins University Press, 1958; repr. Ann Arbor: UMI books on demand, 1998)

Haste, C. *Keep the Home Fires Burning: Propaganda in the First World War* (London: Allen Lane, 1977)

Katz, D., and others, eds. *Public Opinion and Propaganda: A Book of Readings* edited for the Society for the Psychological Study of Social Issues by D. Katz, D. Cartwright, S. Eldersveld, A. McClung Lee (New York: Holt, Rinehart and Winston, 1954)

Lasswell, H. D. *Propaganda Technique in World War I*, new edn (Cambridge, Mass.: M.I.T., 1971)
Original edition published under the title, *Propaganda Technique in the World War*, London: Kegan Paul, 1927.

Lee, H. O. *British Propaganda in the First World War* (London: Imperial War Museum, 1937)
Unpublished Foreign Office account.

MacKenzie, A. J. *Propaganda Boom* (London: Right Book Club, 1938)

MacKenzie, J. M. *Propaganda and Empire: The Manipulation of British Public Opinion, 1880-1960*, new edn (Manchester: Manchester University Press, 1986)

Messinger, G. S. *British Propaganda and the State in the First World War* (Manchester: Manchester University Press, 1992)

Milne, L. *Laughter and War: Humorous-Satirical Magazines in Britain, France, Germany and Russia 1914-1918* (Newcastle upon Tyne: Cambridge Scholars Publishing, 2016)
By means of an examination of the pages of the patriotic humorous-satirical magazines of four countries, *Punch* in the UK, *Le Rire* (France), *Simplicissimus* (Germany), and *Novy Satirikon* (Russia), the author of this book shows how humour made an important contribution to the propaganda campaign in those countries.

Mitchell, P. C. 'Propaganda', in *Encyclopaedia Britannica*, 12th edn, vol.32 (London: Encyclopaedia Britannica, 1922)

— *Report on the Propaganda Library in the Intelligence Division of the War Office and Appendices*, 3 vols (London: HMSO, 1917)
Appendices: I. *Propaganda Chiefly Relating to Nationalities*. II. *Germany and America*.

Muscovici, S. *The Age of the Crowd: A Historical Treatise on Mass Psychology*, translated by J. C. Whitehouse (Cambridge: Cambridge University Press, 1985)

Paddock, T. R. E., ed. *World War I and Propaganda* (Leiden; Boston: Brill, 2014)

Ponsonby, A., Baron. *Falsehood in Wartime: Propaganda Lies of the First World War*, 2nd edn (London: George Allen & Unwin, 1928)
Originally published London: Allen & Unwin, 1928, under the title, *Falsehood in Wartime, Containing an Assortment of Lies Circulated throughout the Nations during the Great War*.

Roetter, C. *Psychological Warfare* (London: Batsford, 1974)

Rogerson, S. *Propaganda in the Next War* (London: G. Bles, 1938: repr. New York, Arno Press, 1972)

Sanders, M. L. and P. M. Taylor *British Propaganda during the First World War, 1914-1918* (London: Macmillan, 1982)

Squires, J. D. *British Propaganda at Home and in The United States from 1914 to 1917* (Cambridge: Harvard University Press, 1935)

Steed, A.. 'British Propaganda and the First World War', in *War, Culture and the Media: Representation of the Military in 20th Century Britain*, edited by I. Stewart and S. L. Carruthers (Trowbridge: Flicks Books, 1996)

Steed, H. W. *The Fifth Arm* (London: Constable, 1940)
Study of propaganda in time of war.

— 'Propaganda', in *Encyclopaedia Britannica*, 14th edn, vol 18 (London: Britannica Publishers, 1929)

Taylor, P. M *British Propaganda in the 20th Century: Selling Democracy* (Edinburgh: Edinburgh University Press, 1999)

— *Munitions of the Mind: A History of Propaganda from the Ancient World to the Present Day*, 3rd edn (Manchester University Press, 2003)

Thimme, H. *Weltkrieg ohne Waffen: Die Propaganda der Westmächte gegen Deutschland, ihre Wirkung und ihre Abwehr* (Stuttgart und Berlin : Cotta, 1932)

Welch, D. *Propaganda: Power and Persuasion* (London: British Library, 2013)
Published to accompany an exhibition held at the British Library, London, 17 May - 17 Sept. 2013.

Welch. D., ed. *Propaganda, Power and Persuasion from World War I to Wikileaks* (London: I.B. Tauris, 2014)
A new paperback edn was published by I. B. Tauris in 2015)

Welch, D. and J. Fox, eds. *Justifying War: Propaganda, Politics and the Modern Age* (Basingstoke : Palgrave Macmillan, c2012)
Based on papers presented at the conference on 'Justifying war: propaganda, politics and the modern age' held in Kent, 2007.

Theses

Peil, M. C. 'Some aspects of British Propaganda during the World War, 1914-1918' (unpublished master's thesis, Marquette University, Milwaukee, Wisconsin, 1942)

Articles

Aston, Sir G. 'Propaganda and the Father of it', *Cornhill Magazine*, n.s. 48 (1920), 233-241

Doty, B. '"As a Mass, a Phenomenon so Hideous": Crowd Psychology, Impressionism, and Ford Madox Ford's Propaganda', *Journal of War and Culture Studies*, 6 (2013), 169-182

Dutton, P. '"Geschäft über Alles": Notes on Some Medallions Inspired by the Sinking of The Lusitania', *Imperial War Museum Review*, 1 (1986)

Englander, D. 'People at War: France, Britain, and Germany, 1914-18 and 1939-45', *European History Quarterly*, 18 (1988), 229-238

Gilmour, T. L. 'Government and Propaganda', *Nineteenth Century*, 85 (1919), 148-58

Grande, J. 'Propagandist Warfare', *Spectator*, 123 (1919), 365-6

'Government propaganda', *The Nation*, 108 (1919), 313

Harker, R. 'Propaganda: Power and Persuasion. The British Library', *Public Historian*, 35 (2013), 103-107
Review of the exhibition, *Propaganda: Power and Persuasion*, held at the British Library, London, 17 May-17 Sept. 2013 (Jude England, Curator; Ian Cooke, Co-Curator) and of the work with the same title by David Welch (q.v) published by the British Library to accompany the exhibition.

Lauterpacht, H. 'Revolutionary Propaganda by Governments', *Transactions of the Grotius Society*, 13 (1928), 143-64

Leikauf, R. 'Justifying War: Propaganda, Politics and the Modern Age', *Historical Journal Of Film Radio And Television*, 33 (2013), 330-332

Lutz, R. H. 'Studies of World War Propaganda, 1914-33', *Journal of Modern History*, 5 (1933), 496-516

Marquis, A. G. 'Words as Weapons. Propaganda in Britain and Germany during the First World War', *Journal of Contemporary History*, 13 (1978), 467-498

Martin, N. '"Fighting a Philosophy": The Figure of Nietzsche in British Propaganda of the First World War', *Modern Language Review*, 98 (2003), 367-380

Nicholson, I. 'An Aspect of British Official Wartime Propaganda', *Cornhill Magazine*, 70 (1931), 593-606

Sanders, M. L. 'Wellington House and British Propaganda during the First World War', *Historical Journal*, 18 (1975), 119-146

Strachan, H. 'John Buchan and the First World War: Fact into Fiction', *War in History*, 16 (2009), 298-324
An exploration of the the ways in which Buchan, a man of affairs, historian, and propagandist as well as a novelist, exploited the inside knowledge of the facts about the war (derived from his government activities) to write his fictions about it both during the war and after it. Also includes a consideration of Buchan's thoughts about the war's conduct and the function of propaganda within it.

Tylee, C. M. '"Munitions of the Mind": Travel Writing, Imperial Discourse and Great War Propaganda by Mrs. Humphry Ward', *English Literature in Transition, 1880-1920*, 39 (1996), 171-192

Wright, D. G. 'The Great War, Government Propaganda and English "Men Of Letters", 1914-16', *Literature and History*, 7 (1978), 70-100

4.2.1.1 Atrocity Propaganda

A brief selection of works which are relevant to the subject of atrocity propaganda is listed below:

Official Publications

Great Britain. Committee of Inquiry into Alleged German Outrages. *Report of the Committee on Alleged German Outrages Appointed by His Britannic Majesty's Government and Presided over by the Right Hon. Viscount Bryce*, Cmnd 7894 (London: HMSO, 1915)

— *The Evidence and Documents Laid Before The Committee on Alleged German Outrages*, Cmnd 7895 (London: HMSO, 1915)
Appendix to the separately published *Report of the Committee on Alleged German Outrages* (q.v.)

Books

Coles, A. *Slaughter at Sea: The Truth Behind a Naval War Crime* (London: Hale, 1986)
This book is about the incident which took place in 1915 when the Q-ship *Baralong*, disguised as a US merchant ship, discarded its camouflage on encountering the U-boat, U27, and not only sank the unsuspecting German vessel but also, allegedly, murdered some of is survivors in cold blood. Germany saw the incident, which caused a huge furore on the international diplomatic front, as highly useful for propaganda purposes.

Felstead, S. T. *Edith Cavell: The Crime that Shook the World*, written from the dossier of the German Secret Police and the personal narratives of survivors by S. Theodore Felstead (London: Newnes, 1940)

Ponsonby, A., Baron. *Falsehood in Wartime: Propaganda Lies of the First World War*, 2nd edn (Sudbury: Bloomfield Books, 1991)
Originally published London: Allen & Unwin, 1928, under the title, *Falsehood in Wartime, Containing an Assortment of Lies Circulated throughout the Nations during the Great War*

Hoehling, A. A. *Edith Cavell* (London: Cassell, 1958)
Originally published as *The Whisper of Eternity*, New York: Yoseloff, 1957.

Horne, J. N. and A. Kramer. *German Atrocities, 1914: A History of Denial* (New Haven, CT: Yale University Press, 2001)

— 'War between Soldiers and Enemy Civilians, 1914-1915', in *Great War, Total War: Combat and Mobilization on the Western Front, 1914-1918*, edited by R. Chickering and S. Forster (Cambridge: Cambridge University Press, 2000)

Read, S. M. *Atrocity Propaganda, 1914-1919* (New Haven: Yale University Press, 1941; repr. New York, Arno Press, 1972)

Rubinstein, S. *German Atrocity or British Propaganda?: The Seventieth Anniversary of a Scandal - German Corpse Utilization Establishments in the First World War* (Jerusalem: Acadamon, 1989)

Articles

Gullace, N. F. 'Sexual Violence and Family Honor: British Propaganda and International Law during the First World War', *American Historical Review*, 102 (1997), 714-747

Horne, J. N. 'German Atrocities 1914: Fact, Fantasy or Fabrication?', *History Today*, 51 (2001), 47-53

Horne, J. N. and A. Kramer. 'German "Atrocities" and Franco-German Opinion, 1914: The Evidence of German Soldiers' Diaries', *Journal of Modern History*, 66 (1994), 4-32

Moore, A. 'Monuments Men and Martyred Towns: The Arras Belfry by Fernand Sabatté', *Journal of Military History*, 79 (2015), 1047-1058
"*The Arras Belfry*, an oil painting by the French artist Fernand Sabatté, is held at the National Gallery of Ireland in Dublin. It depicts the destruction of the town's late medieval belfry by German artillery in 1914 and is part of a genre of First World War propaganda imagery known as the "martyred towns" series … Artist Sabatté was a French army officer based in Arras in Northern France where he was in charge of salvaging artworks from medieval churches and town halls destroyed in the fighting". [Abstract from the internet]

Neander, J. and R. Martin. 'Media and Propaganda: The Northcliffe Press and the Corpse Factory Story of World War I', *Global Media Journal*, 3 (2010), 67-82

Wilson, T. 'Lord Bryce's Investigation into Alleged German Atrocities in Belgium, 1914-15', *Journal of Contemporary History*, 14 (1979), 369-83

4.2.2 Organisation of Official British Propaganda

Official British propaganda was primarily organized during the war within five main bodies, the War Propaganda Bureau at Wellington House, 1914-1916; the Department of Information, 1917; the National War Aims Committee (NWAC), 1917-1918; and the Ministry of Information together with the Department of Enemy Propaganda at Crewe House, 1918. For details relating to the National War Aims Committee see **section 4.2.3.2**; for details relating to the other four bodies see the general preamble to the **section 4.2.4.1**.

One of the most important works in English on the development of British propaganda in the Great War is by Sanders and Taylor (*British Propaganda during the First World War, 1914-1918*) which, as the authors say in the preface, "concentrates more on propaganda abroad than that performed on the home front" ... "because of Cate Haste's recent examination of domestic propaganda in the First World War, *Keep the Home Fires Burning* (1977)". An important point they make in the preface to their work is that in relation to the historiography of the subject there has been undue concentration on propaganda in the final year of the war and a neglect of its operation in the previous wartime years. This was to a large extent due to the exaggerated significance given to the role of Northcliffe's Department of Enemy Propaganda at Crewe House by "prominent enemy personalities" and the publication of such works as vol. 21 of *The Times History and Encyclopaedia of the War* (1919), Ludendorff's *My War Memories* (1919), Sir Campbell Stuart's *Secrets of Crewe House* (1920), Henry Wickham Steed's *Through Thirty Years* (1924), and Hitler's *Mein Kampf* (1925-27)[91]. Sanders and Taylor feel that the latter works contribute to an impression "that very little work was done before 1918 to undermine the will of the enemy to continue the struggle" and that works like Lasswell's *Propaganda Technique in World War I* (1927), Sidney Rogerson's *Propaganda in the Next War* (1938), and Beaverbrook's *Men and Power 1917-1918* (1956), all of them also displaying a lack of appreciation of the earlier work on propaganda, have tended to sustain this impression[92]. Furthermore, they consider that some more modern studies including Doreen Collins' *Aspects of British Politics, 1904-19* (1965), Marjorie Ogilvy Webb's *The Government Explains: A Study of the Information Services* (1965) and Sir Fife Clark's *The Central Office of Information* (1970) have even tended to go so far as to treat the propaganda work of the earlier years of the war "as some sort of chaotic prelude to the order brought to the conduct of British propaganda by Lord Beaverbrook", leaving the overall impression "that British propaganda during the years 1914-17 was ill-organised due to a series of ad hoc arrangements which resulted in inefficiency, wastage of material, duplication of effort and slowness to exploit propaganda opportunities" and that "in short, three years of comparative failure are said to have been followed by one year of spectacular success". In contrast Sanders and Taylor take the view that the successes claimed for British propaganda in the final year of the war were the result of the cumulative effect of the important work developed in the previous war years by a number of other bodies, including especially Wellington House.

Autobiographies, Biographies

Cockerill, Sir G. *What Fools We Were: A Survey of Recent History and a Discussion of Post-War Problems, With Reminiscences of the Author's Part in Public Life* (London: Hutchinson, 1944)

Hitler, A. *Mein Kampf*, with an introduction by D. Cameron Watt; translated by Ralph Manheim (London: Pimlico, 1998)
First published München: Zentralverlag der NSDAP, 1925-1927, in two volumes.

Ludendorff, E. von. *My War Memories, 1914-18*, 2 vols (London: Hutchinson, 1919)

---

[91] A more modern study, Michael Balfour's *Propaganda in War, 1939-45* (1979), does not subscribe to this view of the significance of the work of Crewe House.

[92] Sanders and Taylor have exonerated from this criticism J. D. Squires, *British Propaganda at Home and in the United States from 1914 to 1917* (1935), which provided a good deal, although by no means a comprehensive account, of early British propaganda activities; Peterson's *Propaganda for War: The Campaign against American Neutrality, 1914-17* (1939), which draws attention to the "potency of British propaganda during the American period of neutrality"; and Brigadier-General Cockerill's *What Fools We Were* (1944) which recalls the significance of an important propaganda branch of the War Office both in an early stage and the final year of the war (see also the reference to Cockerill within the preamble to **4.2.4.1 (Overseas Front: General)**.

Masterman, L. *C. F. G. Masterman: A Biography* (London: Nicholson and Watson, 1939; repr. London: Cass, 1968)

Pound, R. and G. Harmsworth. *Northcliffe* (London: Cassell, 1959)

Steed, H. W. *Through Thirty Years 1892-1922: A Personal Narrative*, 2 vols (London: Heinemann, 1924)

Books

Balfour, M. *Propaganda in War, 1939-45: Organisations, Policies and Publics in Britain and Germany* (London: Routledge, 1979)
Contains a view of British propaganda in the First World war. Opening chapter is entitled 'The Demythologising of Crewe House'.

Beaverbrook, W. M. A., 1st Baron. *Men and Power 1917-1918* (London: Hutchinson, 1956; repr. London: Collins, 1966)

Clark, Sir. F. *The Central Office of Information* (London: Allen & Unwin, 1970)

Collins, D. *Aspects of British Politics, 1904-1919* (Oxford: Pergamon Press, 1965)

Haste, C. *Keep the Home Fires Burning: Propaganda in the First World War* (London: Allen & Unwin, 1977)

Lasswell, H. D. *Propaganda Technique in World War I*, new edn (Cambridge, Mass.: M.I.T., 1971)
Original edition published under the title, *Propaganda Technique in the World War*, London: Kegan Paul, 1927.

Mitchell, Sir P. C. *Report on the Propaganda Library in the Intelligence Division of the War Office and Appendices*, 3 vols (London: HMSO, 1917)
Appendix I. Propaganda Chiefly Relating to Nationalities. Appendix II. Germany and America.

Ogilvy-Webb, M. *The Government Explains: A Study of the Information Services* (London: Allen & Unwin, 1965)
A Report of the Royal Institute of Public Administration.

Peterson, H. C. *Propaganda for War: The Campaign against American Neutrality, 1914-1917* (Norman, Oklahoma: Prew, 1939; repr. Port Washington, NY: Kennikat Press, 1968)

Rogerson, S. *Propaganda in the Next War* (London: G. Bles, 1938: repr. New York, Arno Press, 1972)

Sanders, M. L. and P. M. Taylor *British Propaganda during the First World War, 1914-1918* (London: Macmillan, 1982)

Stuart, Sir C. *Secrets of Crewe House: The Story of a Famous Campaign* (London: Hodder & Stoughton, 1920)

Squires, J. D. *British Propaganda at Home and in the United States from 1914 To 1917* (Cambridge: Harvard University Press, 1935)

Times History and Encyclopaedia of the War, 22 vols (London: The Times, 1914-1921), XXI, Chapter CCCXIV: 'British Propaganda in Enemy Countries' (1919)

Articles

Messinger, G. S. 'An Inheritance Worth Remembering: The British Approach to Official Propaganda during the First World War', *Historical Journal of Film, Radio and Television*, 13 (1993), 117-127

Sanders, M. L. 'British Film Propaganda in Russia, 1916-1918', *Historical Journal of Film, Radio And Television*, 3 (1983), 117-129

—— 'Wellington House and British Propaganda during the First World War', *Historical Journal*, 18 (1975), 119-146

4.2.3 Home Front

4.2.3.1 General

On the home front propaganda was required early on to convince doubters of the justice of Britain's involvement in the struggle and to stimulate recruitment to the armed forces. As the war dragged on it was needed to help maintain popular support for the war. It also took the form of appeals consisting of calls for nursing volunteers, and for women to work in munitions factories and the land army; of exhortations to restrict food consumption and avoid waste; and of producing posters and advertisements urging Britons to buy war bonds and to contribute to a vast array of war related charities. Three major campaigns to promote War Savings Certificates were launched by the government in November 1914, June 1915 and January 1917, utilizing all the tools of mass propaganda, including posters, advertisements, rallies and film.

While the Government quickly saw the need to counteract Germany's attempt to influence international (particularly United States) opinion against the Entente Powers by setting up the War Propaganda Bureau at Wellington House on 5th September 1914, it was some time before it consciously developed an official propaganda policy for the home front. The mobilization of opinion behind the war effort was initially left mostly to the voluntary activities of individuals (e.g. well-intentioned in the case of the Oxford historians who produced the famous Oxford Pamphlets[93] and unscrupulously populist in the case of Horatio Bottomley[94]) and a wide assortment of groups - some already in existence (e.g. the Cobden Club and the Victoria League), some newly-formed early in the war (e.g. the United Workers, the Fight for Right Movement[95], the British Empire Union and the Atlantic Union), and some semi-official [the Parliamentary Recruiting Committee (PRC) and the Central Committee for National Patriotic Organizations (CCNPO)]. Some attempt to co-ordinate these voluntary activities was made by the CCNPO. All these efforts were, however, not sufficiently effective to cope with the growing war-weariness and dissent among sections of the population that had become significant by mid-1917. As a result the Government came to realize that it would have to take some positive action which it eventually carried out by establishing in June 1917 the National War Aims Committee (NWAC) to provide home propaganda with more systematic and coherent direction.

Until the introduction of conscription in January 1916 domestic propaganda was focused on the task of stimulating recruitment to the armed forces. In this respect the most important organisation during the first 18 months of the war was the Parliamentary Recruiting Committee (PRC) which was established at the beginning of the war as an all-party organisation led jointly by the three party leaders, Asquith, Bonar Law and Henderson operating under the auspices of the War Office. Its function was to coordinate the activities of the various bodies, official and unofficial, involved in the national recruitment campaign, and as such it was really a political body rather than a department of the Government set up specifically to develop a wide-ranging system of propaganda, as was the case with Wellington House.

The most influential of the voluntary patriotic organisations was the CCPNO which was set up in August 1914 as a coordinating body for patriotic activities and run by H. C. Cust and G. W. Prothero, with Asquith as President and Balfour and the Earl of Rosebery as vice-presidents. Its aims were described as educational but they were in practice geared to propaganda. As well as aiming to co-ordinate the efforts of other voluntary organisations with similar patriotic purposes, it sought to set up its own network of Local Secretaries, Committees, and Helpers enlisted in the task of explaining 'with clearness and with relentless reiteration the true causes, necessities and justification of the War, together with the vital reasons which compel England to fight to

---

[93] A complete list of the 87 titles is given in G. W. Prothero's *A Select Analytical List of Books concerning the Great War* (London: HMSO, 1923).

[94] Bottomley's approach throughout the war was one of extreme chauvinistic patriotism which he expressed with vitriolic aggression via his editorship of *John Bull* (founded by him in 1906) and his speeches at the numerous meetings he addressed up and down the country in the role he assumed as an unofficial recruiter.

[95] The Fight for Right Movement, for which Sir Hubert Parry set Blake's 'Jerusalem' as a rallying hymn in their campaign for the continuation of the war, was founded by Sir Francis Edward Younghusband in 1916. The aims of the Movement were "to brace the spirit of the nation that the people of Great Britain, knowing that they are fighting for the best interests of humanity, may refuse any temptation, however insidious, to conclude a premature peace, and may accept with cheerfulness all the sacrifices necessary to bring the war to a satisfactory conclusion".

the very end' (p. 6 of the Central Committee for National Patriotic Organizations (CCNPO). *Report*, 1916). Meetings, lectures, and the widespread distribution of propagandistic literature were among the chief methods of getting the message across. In addition to the literature it produced itself, the CCPNO was the means of distributing for home consumption hundreds of thousands of instructive publications, such as the Government White paper, *Great Britain and the European Crisis*, Viscount Bryce's *Report* and *Evidence and Documents* of the Committee on Alleged German Outrages; the Parliamentary Recruiting Committee (PRC)'s abbreviated edition of the latter *Report*; the various pamphlets on the war of the Oxford University Press and of the Victoria League; and *The Times* edition of Samuel Harden Church's pamphlet *The American Verdict on the War: A Reply to the Appeal to the Civilized World of 93 German Professors*. In July 1917 CCPNO's work, complete with its local network, was absorbed by NWAC, the first official agency to work on propaganda for the home front.

Bibliographies

Central Committee for National Patriotic Organizations (CCNPO). *Catalogue of War Publications Comprising Works Published to June, 1916*, compiled by G. W. Prothero ... with the assistance of A. J. Philip (London: J. Murray, 1917)

Autobiographies, Biographies, Memoirs

Felstead, S. T. *Horatio Bottomley: A Biography of an Outstanding Personality* (London: J. Murray, 1936)

Field, E. *Advertising: The Forgotten Years* (London: Benn, 1959)

Hyman, A. *The Rise and Fall of Horatio Bottomley* (London: Cassell, 1972)

Swinton, Sir E. D. *Eyewitness: Being Personal Reminiscences of Certain Phases of the Great War Including the Genesis of the Tank* (London: Hodder & Stoughton, 1932)
Swinton freely admits in his book, that some of his articles (released to the press under the headline of 'Eyewitness') were used especially for propaganda purposes against the enemy and to keep the Home Front fully supportive of military operations in France.

Books

Central Committee for National Patriotic Organizations (CCNPO). *Report* (London: Central Committee for National Patriotic Organizations, 1916)

Clark, L.. '"Civilians Entrenched": The British Home Front and the Attitudes to the First World War, 1914-18', in *War, Culture and the Media: Representation of the Military in 20th Century Britain*, edited by I. Stewart and S. L. Carruthers (Trowbridge: Flicks Books, 1996)

Clarke, B. *How The Progress of the War Was Chronicled by Pen and Camera* (London: Amalgamated Press, 1919)

The Fight for Right Movement (London: J. Miles & Co., 1916?)
Consists of list of officials, rules and objects of the Movement.

For the Right, essays & addresses of members of the 'Fight for Right Movement.' (London: Fisher Unwin, 1916)

Haste, C. *Keep the Home Fires Burning: Propaganda in the First World War* (London: Allen & Unwin, 1977)

Messinger, G. S. *British Propaganda and the State in the First World War* (Manchester: Manchester University Press, 1992)

Millman, B. *Managing Domestic Dissent in First World War Britain* (London: Cass, 2000)

Monger, D. *Patriotism and Propaganda in First World War Britain: The National War Aims Committee and Civilian Morale* (Liverpool: Liverpool University Press, 2012)

— 'Transcending the Nation: Domestic Propaganda and Supranational Patriotism in Britain, 1917-18', in *World War I and Propaganda*, edited by T. R. E. Paddock (Leiden; Boston: Brill, 2014)

Osborne, J. M. *The Voluntary Recruiting Movement in Britain, 1914-1916* (New York: Garland, 1982)

Sanders, M. L. and P. M. Taylor. *British Propaganda during the First World War, 1914-1918* (London: Macmillan, 1982)

Squires, J. D. *British Propaganda at Home and in the United States from 1914 To 1917* (Cambridge: Harvard University Press, 1935)

Williams, B. *Raising and Recruiting the New Armies* (London: Constable, 1918)

Williams, J. *The Other Battleground: The Home Fronts, Britain, France and Germany, 1914-1918* (Chicago: Henry Regnery, 1972)

Articles

Bliven, B. 'Selling the War to the Working Man', *Printer's Ink*, 102 (1918), 69

— 'What British Advertisers have Learned in War Time', *Printer's Ink*, 104 (1918), 3-6, 110-17

Burton, P. 'Things Advertising Can Do in War War-Time', *Printer's Ink*, 99 (1917), 28-31

Douglas, R. 'Voluntary Enlistment in the First World War And The Work of the Parliamentary Recruiting Committee [PRC]', *Journal of Modern History*, 42 (1970), 564-85

Dutton, P. 'Moving Images? The Parliamentary Recruiting Committee (PRC)'s Poster Campaign, 1914-1916', *Imperial War Museum Review*, 4 (1989), 43-58

Hiley, N. P. '"Kitchener Wants You" and "Daddy, What Did You Do in the War?": The Myth of British Recruiting Posters', *Imperial War Museum Review*, 11 (1997), 40-58

— 'Sir Hedley Le Bas and the Origins of Domestic Propaganda in Britain, 1914-1917', *Journal of Advertising History*, 10 (1987), 30-46

Kennedy, P. M. 'Imperial Cable Communications and Strategy, 1870-1914', *English Historical Review*, 86 (1971), 725-52

Monger, D. 'Familiarity Breeds Consent? Patriotic Rituals in British First World War Propaganda', *Twentieth Century British History*, 26 (2015), 501-528

Romer, J. I. 'How Can We Overcome the Government's Antagonism to Advertising', *Printer's Ink*, 98 (1917), 46-57

Russell, T. 'Advertisement Stimulated by the War', *Printer's Ink*, 98 (1917), 25-28

— 'British Advertisers Give Space to the War Loan', *Printer's Ink*, 102 (1918), 57-65

— 'The British Government's Use of Advertising in the War', *Printer's Ink*, 1915 (92) 37-45

4.2.3.2 National War Aims Committee (NWAC)

As the war lengthened and the strain on the British people began to tell (as was evident in the escalation of industrial unrest and of the peace movement towards the end of the war) the Government became increasingly concerned about the possibility of losing the nation's support for the war. Its reaction was to set up the NWAC with the specific task of galvanizing the population into believing in the need for a clear-cut victory and for its total commitment, particularly on the part of British industry[96], to achieve this object. For carrying out this task

---

[96] Many of NWAC's pamphlets made a direct appeal to the British working classes.

the NWAC (working closely with the Ministry of Information) employed traditional methods such as distributing pamphlets[97], leaflets and pictorial propaganda such as posters and postcards. As well as this it organised large numbers of rallies and meetings in the manner of an electoral campaign (3192 meetings were arranged from August through to October in 1917). All these efforts were concentrated in areas where morale was most suspect.

In spite of its name, spelling out British war aims did not initially feature among the NWAC's objectives because of the government being wary about make public pronouncements about them. In this respect the government's hand was eventually forced by a combination of circumstances which included the publication of Woodrow Wilson's views on ending the war, the Bolshevik action in discrediting the war aims of the Allies by publishing their secret treaties, and the agreement within the Labour Party in December 1917 on a joint statement of war aims. As a result the government felt obliged to be more transparent about British war aims, and with Lloyd George himself on 5 January 1918 taking the lead by spelling them out publicly as a means of maintaining the support of the nation, particularly the working class, for the war, the NWAC from then on included war aims in its propaganda.

Books

Monger, D. *Patriotism and Propaganda in First World War Britain: The National War Aims Committee and Civilian Morale* (Liverpool: Liverpool University Press 2012)

Articles

Monger, D. 'Nothing Special?: Propaganda and Women's Roles in Late First World War Britain, *Women's History Review*, 23 (2014), 518-542
"This article explores women's roles as subjects, objects and producers of National War Aims Committee propaganda in Britain during 1917–18" (extract from an abstract on the internet)

Contemporary Material

A selection of the sort of pamphlets which the NWAC published appears below. The items listed were all published by the NWAC in London and most of them were also published in Edinburgh by John Menzies & Co.

Appleton, W. A. *America's United Effort*, Searchlights, 6 (London: National War Aims Committee 1918)

Asquith, H. H. *Asquith's Message: International Partnership*, Message series, 4 (London: National War Aims Committee, 1918)
"Speech by the Rt. Hon. H.H. Asquith, in proposing the health of President Wilson, at a dinner to American officers, National Liberal Club, London, July 10, 1918" - verso t.-p.

Balfour, A. J., Earl of Balfour. *Balfour's Message: The Obstacles to Peace* Message series, 5 (London: National War Aims Committee, 1918)
"Substance of a speech delivered by the Rt. Hon. A. J. Balfour ... in the House of Commons, August 8, 1918" - verso t.-p.

Chesterton, G. K. *The So-Called Belgium Bargain*, Searchlights, 22 (London: National War Aims Committee, 1918)
'Reprinted from "The Illustrated London News"' - p.[4]

Churchill, Sir W. *The Munitions Miracle*, British Efforts Series, 1 (London: National War Aims Committee, 1918)
Speech delivered in the House of Commons, April 25, 1918.

Curzon, G. N., Marquis of Curzon. *The British Lion's Share*, Searchlights, 27 (London: National War Aims Committee, 1918)
Caption title: "From a speech in Gray's Inn Hall, July 29, 1918" - p.[4]

Fosdick, H. E. *The Challenge of the Present Crisis*, Searchlights, 17 (London ; Edinburgh: National War Aims Committee, 1918)
Caption title: "Extracted from the volume by H. E. Fosdick, published by the Student Christian Movement".

---

[97] Including utilising for this purpose material produced for foreign audiences by Wellington House.

Gardiner, A. G. *The Blast of Truth*, Searchlights, 13 (London: National War Aims Committee, 1918)

Gerard, J. W. *When Germany Will Break*, Searchlights, 9 (London: National War Aims, 1918)
Caption title: "From 'Face to Face with Kaiserism' (Hodder & Stoughton)" - p.[4]

The German Peace (London: National War Aims Committee, 1917)

Great Britain. Committee on the Treatment by the Enemy of British Prisoners of War. *Prisoners of Prussia: Official Report on the Treatment of British Prisoners by the Enemy during 1918* (London: National War Aims Committee, 1918)

A Letter to a Countryman, Searchlights, 20 (London: National War Aims Committee, 1918)

Leverhulme, W. H. L., Viscount. *One or the Other*, Searchlights, 14 (London: National War Aims Committee, 1918)
Caption title, pp.[2-3]: *Liberty or Enslavement? Lord Leverhulme's Question.* "Extracted from an interview in the Daily Chronicle"

Lloyd George, D. *Britain and France Call*, Searchlights, 1 (London: National War Aims Committee, 1918)
Caption title, pp.[2-3]: *Britain and France Call to their Peoples.* Contents: [I]. *Britain. Mr Lloyd George's Appeal.* [II]. *M. Clemenceau's Appeal.*

— *The British Navy's Part: The Prime Minister's Tribute*, Searchlights, 24 (London: National War Aims Committee, 1918)
Caption title: "Speech by Mr. Lloyd George in the House of Commons, August 7, 1918" - p.[4]

— *Lloyd George's Message: Looking Forward*, Substance of a speech delivered by the Prime Minister at Manchester, September 12, 1918, Message series, 6 (London: National War Aims Committee, 1918)

McCurdy, C. A. *Guilty!: Prince Lichnowsky's Disclosures* (London: National War Aims Committee, 1918)
"Most of the extracts quoted in this pamphlet are from the *Times* translation of the original version published by Vorwärts." - verso t.-p. "The complete text of Prince Lichnowsky's disclosures ... is published under the title of *'My mission to London, 1912-1914'*." - verso t.-p.

Our Real War Aim, by a socialist, Searchlights, 15 (London: National War Aims Committee, 1918)

Robertson, J. M. *The Pacifist Blind Spot*, Searchlights, 23 (London: National War Aims Committee, 1918)
"From the 'Daily Chronicle'" - p.[4]

Roesemeier, H. *A German Speaks: An Open Letter*, Searchlights, 3 (London: National War Aims Committee, 1918)
Caption title, pp.[2-3]: *A German Speaks to British Labour.*

Russell, G. W. E. *Confessions of an Ex-Pacifist*, Searchlights, 25 (London: National War Aims Committee, 1918)
Caption title: "Reprinted from 'The Daily Express'".

Smuts, J. C. *Smuts' Message: The World Awakened*, Message series, 2 (London: National War Aims Committee, 1918)
"Speech delivered ... at the Clothworkers' Company's Hall, April 3, 1918" - verso t.-p.

Those Secret Treaties, Searchlights, 11 (London: National War Aims Committee, 1918)
Caption title, pp.[2-3]: *The Truth about the Secret Treaties.*

Tillett, B. *My Message to Labour*, Searchlights, 7 (London: National War Aims Committee, 1918)
Caption title pp.[2-3]: *Ben Tillett's Message to British Labour.*

Wilson, W. *Our Two Duties*, Searchlights, 8 (London: Edinburgh: National War Aims Committee, 1918)
Caption title, pp.[2-3]: *President Wilson Winning the War.*

— *Why Are We Enlisted?: President Wilson's Answer*, Searchlights, 26 (London: National War Aims Committee,

1918)

— *Wilson's Message: The Conditions of Peace*, Message series, 3 (London: National War Aims Committee, 1918)"
On the occasion of President Wilson's presence at Washington's tomb, Mount Vernon, on Independence Day, July 4, 1918.

A World Peace: President Wilson's Programme, National War Aims Committee publications, 34 (London: National War Aims Committee, 1918)

4.2.4 Overseas Front

4.2.4.1 General

At the beginning of the war the British government's approach to propaganda was primarily determined by the need to counter the German propaganda campaign in neutral countries, particularly the USA, and, as the war progressed, by the need to reassure its allies that Britain was pulling its weight in the combined efforts to defeat the Central Powers. When the war entered its final phase there was a switch in the focus of British propaganda to concerns about preserving Allied unity in relation to war aims and peace terms.

With no propaganda agencies in existence at the outbreak of war the government quickly established a Wartime Propaganda Bureau in Wellington House and also two other bodies, the Neutral Press Committee and the Foreign Office News Department. The work of the War Propaganda Bureau[98], headed by Charles Masterman was mainly directed at foreign targets, including the Allied nations and neutral countries, especially (until 1917) the United States; it rapidly developed into the most active of all the early propaganda departments, arranging for the production and overseas dissemination of books, pamphlets and periodicals as well as photographs, lantern slides and picture postcards. The Neutral Press Committee essentially concerned itself under the direction of G. H. Mair, a recently retired assistant editor of the *Daily Chronicle*, with analyzing the neutral press, promoting the interchange of news between English and foreign newspapers, the promotion of English newspaper sales in foreign countries, the postal distribution of propaganda articles, and, eventually, the inauguration of a wireless news service. The News Department of the Foreign Office concerned itself particularly with the dissemination of news abroad making use of overseas consular and diplomatic missions to which it supplied daily news telegrams and other material, with instructions to make use of them as was considered appropriate in the prevailing local conditions; it also endeavoured to act as a co-ordinating centre providing advice, information and material to other bodies interested in the mechanics of propaganda.

This initial organisational structure of propaganda underwent a considerable number of changes during the course of the war[99]. By 1916 a number of Government departments other than the Foreign Office were taking an increasingly active interest in propaganda work and as the numbers of them grew problems of overlapping, duplication of effort and a general lack of co-ordination, exacerbated by inter-departmental jealousies[100] were undermining the effectiveness of the system of propaganda that had been established. In an attempt to remedy this situation a conference[101] of all the interested parties was held on 26 January 1916. This resulted in a reorganization which, with the Neutral Press Committee absorbed in the Foreign Office News Department and Wellington House brought under the direct control of the Foreign Office, placed the system of propaganda decisively under the aegis of the Foreign Office and Lord Newton as its nominal head.

In spite of the improvements resulting from this reorganisation inter-departmental disagreements persisted and the Foreign Office's direction was subjected to a great deal of criticism, particularly by the War Office. This

---

[98] The work of this body, begun in September 1914, was largely conducted in secret; even parliament did not know about it. At around the time of the establishment of this body in Wellington House there were also in development a number of voluntary amateur organisations and individuals engaged in their own style of propaganda which occasionally resulted in tensions with Wellington House because it conflicted with the propaganda policies established there by Masterman.

[99] A diagrammatic representation of these changes can be found in Appendices 1-6 of Sanders, M. L. and P. M. Taylor *British Propaganda during the First World War, 1914-1918* (London: Macmillan, 1982).

[100] Particularly evident were the jealousies between the Foreign Office and the War Office, the latter department formalizing its particular interest in propaganda by creating in February 1916 its own special propaganda and censorship division known as MI7.

[101] Attended by representatives from the Home Office, the Foreign Office, the War Office, the Admiralty, the Board of Trade, the Colonial Office, the Press Bureau, the Neutral Press Committee and Wellington House.

unsatisfactory situation prompted Lloyd George on January 1st 1917 to invite Robert Donald, editor of the *Daily Chronicle*, to head an enquiry into the system of propaganda. On the basis of the report which resulted from this enquiry responsibility for propaganda was given to a new department of state, the Department of Information, which was housed in the Foreign Office and initially headed by John Buchan but later by Sir Edward Carson. This reorganisation, suffering from constant criticism, not least of which was the irritation within some departments about the Foreign Office's overwhelming influence, fared no better than its predecessor and at the end of 1917 Robert Donald was once again called on by Lloyd George to investigate the system of propaganda. Donald's recommendation in the report he produced was to strengthen the existing machinery. Lloyd George, however, went beyond this by instituting changes which were far more radical. They involved not only disbanding the Department of Information and establishing in its place a Ministry of Information with general responsibility for propaganda at home and abroad under the direction of Lord Beaverbrook, but also, in addition, creating, independent of the Ministry of Information, the Enemy Propaganda Department at Crewe House under the direction of Lord Northcliffe. Under these new arrangements, which included the News Department of the Foreign Office effectively becoming the news division of the Ministry of Information, the Foreign Office was virtually deprived of any remaining control of propaganda[102].

Until the final year of the war the style of propaganda directed at opinion in allied and neutral countries in this period was very much influenced by the Foreign Office, which believed in the idea of targeting the mass of foreign peoples indirectly via the opinion-makers, such as journalists, publicists and politicians, 'the principle being that that it is better to influence those who can influence others than to attempt a direct appeal to the mass of the population'. Hence news issued by the News Department of the Foreign Office was aimed at leading personalities in foreign societies. Wellington House adopted the same approach in its distribution of propagandistic literature[103]. Both the Foreign Office and Wellington House also placed great emphasis on obscuring the fact that they were trying to influence foreign opinion by propaganda. The sort of news and views they supplied to influential people was provided in such a way that the recipients were not really aware that it was designed to enable them to acquaint themselves (and potentially through them to influence others) with the merits of the British case or the extent of Britain's commitment to the allied effort. Between 1914 and 1917 every effort was made to ensure that the style of overseas propaganda was not only restrained in character but also cautious in approach.

This approach did not lend itself to the launching of a major psychological offensive aimed directly at the enemy's people. Nevertheless, such an offensive did gradually develop. At an early stage in the war there was some implementation of the idea of employing the Royal Flying Corps to scatter literature over the enemy lines for the purpose of undermining the morale of German soldiers. By March 1915 the War Office's Directorate of Special Intelligence (MI17), under the supervision of General Cockerill, was not only preparing their own propaganda material for aerial distribution but also undertaking to distribute similar material produced by the French, and continued to be involved in the distribution of such material in military zones even after an official government department to handle propaganda in enemy countries had been set up in 1918. The War Office, in liaison with Wellington House[104] and the Foreign Office, also employed the intelligence functions of M17 to smuggle propaganda material (designed to undermine German morale) into enemy countries via secret service agents operating in neutral countries adjacent to Germany. These agents also gathered information about Germany's military and civilian affairs and also seem to have been involved in the task of attempting to foster and promote revolutionary elements within Germany and the Austro-Hungarian Empire. Yet, in spite of all these earlier activities, psychological warfare operations did not get systematically and effectively focused on Germany and the Austro-Hungarian Empire until Lloyd George established an enemy propaganda department in Crewe House specifically designed to 'reveal to the enemy the hopelessness of their cause and the certainty of Allied victory'.

The establishment of a propaganda department in Crewe House was symptomatic of the complete change which took place in the character of official British propaganda abroad in the period from the winter of 1917 to the

---

[102] The Foreign Office was, however, able to retain the intelligence division of the old Department of Information and reconstitute it as its Political Intelligence Division.

[103] Extreme care was taken to disguise the source of all the material that was distributed in order to preserve the credibility of the views expressed, a factor which was of particular importance in the most vital of neutral countries, the United States of America.

[104] Northcliffe later acknowledged the debt due to S. A. Guest who, operating from Wellington House, was a key figure in directing Britain's campaign in enemy countries in this period.

end of the war. By that time, especially as it was no longer necessary to concern itself with the problem of wooing the USA once that country had joined the allied cause in early 1917, Britain was in a position to be less cautious in its overseas propaganda policy and to replace it with one of greater aggression that was designed to break down the morale of the Central Powers' soldiers and civilians by using direct techniques of mass persuasion. Lloyd George recognised this and, concluding that this more aggressive policy of propaganda pursued with determination could provide a significant additional method of solving the stalemate on the Western front, took the bold step of establishing two new state departments, the Ministry of Information and the Enemy Propaganda Department dedicated to using direct techniques of mass persuasion with, appropriately, in view of the radical change of policy, the press barons, Beaverbrook and Northcliffe in charge rather than the Foreign Office.

Autobiographies, Biographies, Memoirs

Buchanan, Sir G. W. *My Mission to Russia and other Diplomatic Memories*, 2 vols (London: Cassell, 1923; repr. in 1 vol, New York: Arno Press, 1970)

Charteris, J. *At G.H.Q.: A Record of Service at G.H.Q. during the Great War, 1914-1918* (London: Cassell, 1931)

Cockerill, Sir G. *What Fools We Were: A Survey of Recent History and a Discussion of Post-War Problems, With Reminiscences of the Author's Part in Public Life* (London: Hutchinson, 1944)

Gregory, J. D. *On the Edge of Diplomacy: Rambles and Reflections, 1902-28* (London: Hutchinson, 1928)

Ludendorff, E. von. *My War Memories, 1914-18*, 2 vols. (London: Hutchinson, 1919)

Masterman, L. *C. F. G. Masterman: A Biography* (London: Nicholson and Watson, 1939; repr. London: Cass, 1968)
In this biography the author, Masterman's wife, makes the point: 'By far the greatest difficulties in the early years of the war were the absence of any obvious Allied victories to set off the overrunning of Belgium and the evacuation of the Dardanelles. The increasing invisible pressure of the blockade by the fleet was the kind of thing not so easy to "feature".'

Mitchell, Sir P. C. *My Fill of Days* (London: Faber, 1937)
The author was a distinguished zoologist who served in British intelligence during the Great War in MI7 and was involved in the activities of Crewe House.

Newton, T. W. L., 2nd Baron. *Retrospection* (London: Murray, 1941)
Newton was head of the Foreign Office News Department between 1916 and 1918.

Pound, R. *Arnold Bennett: A Biography* (London: Heinemann, 1952)

Pound, R. and H. Harmsworth. *Northcliffe* (London: Cassell, 1959)

Roby, K. E. *A Writer at War: Arnold Bennett, 1914-1918* (Baton Rouge, Louisiana: University of Louisiana Press, 1973)

Rodd, J. R., Baron Rennell. *Social and Diplomatic Memories*, 3 vols (London: Edward Arnold, 1922-1925), III, *1902-1919* (1925)

Seymour, C. *The Intimate Papers of Colonel House Arranged as a Narrative*, 4 vols (London: Benn, 1926-1928)

Smith, J. A. *John Buchan* (London: Hart-Davis, 1965; repr. Oxford: Oxford University Press, 1985)

Steed, H. W. *Through Thirty Years 1892-1922: A Personal Narrative*, 2 vols (London: Heinemann, 1924)

Taylor, H. A. *Robert Donald: Being the Authorized Biography of Sir Robert Donald ... Journalist, Editor and Friend of Statesman* (London: Stanley Paul, 1934)

Books

Balfour, M. *Propaganda in War, 1939-45: Organisations, Policies and Publics in Britain and Germany* (London: Routledge, 1979)
Contains a view of British propaganda in the First World war. Opening chapter is entitled 'The Demythologising of Crewe House'.

Buchanan, A. R. 'European Propaganda and American Public Opinion 1914-1917" (unpublished doctoral thesis, Stanford University, 1935)

Bruntz, G. B. *Allied Propaganda and the Collapse of the German Empire in 1918*, Hoover War Library Publications, 13 (Stanford: Stanford University Press, 1938; repr. New York: Arno Press, 1972)

Calder, K. J. *Britain and the Origins of the New Europe, 1914-18* (Cambridge: Cambridge University Press, 1976)

Cornwall, J. M. 'The Undermining of Austria-Hungary: The Allied Propaganda Campaign of 1918 against the Austro-Hungarian Army on the Italian Front' (unpublished doctoral thesis, University of Leeds, 1988)

— *The Undermining of Austria-Hungary: The Battle for Hearts and Minds* (Basingstoke: Macmillan, 2000)

Hanak, H. *Great Britain and Austria-Hungary during the First World War: A Study in the Formation of Public Opinion* (London: Oxford University Press, 1962)

Lichnowsky, K. M., Fürst von. *My Mission to London: Revelations of the Last German Ambassador in England*, with a preface by Gilbert Murray (London: Cassell, 1918)

Lutz, R. H., ed. *Fall of the German Empire 1914-18*, 2 vols. (Stanford: Stanford University Press, 1932; repr. New York: Octagon Books, 1969)

May, A. J. *The Passing of the Habsburg Monarchy, 1914-18*, 2 vols (Philadelphia: University of Pennyslvania, 1966)

Mitchell, Sir P. C. *Report on the Propaganda Library in the Intelligence Division of the War Office and Appendices*, 3 vols (London: HMSO, 1917)
Appendix I. Propaganda Chiefly Relating to Nationalities. Appendix II. Germany and America

Morris, J. *Distribution of Propaganda by Air, 1914-1918* (London: Lee Richards, 2001)
Originally published in 1920 by the Public Record Office [?]

Sanders, M. L. 'Official British Propaganda in Allied and Neutral Countries during the First World War with particular reference to Organisation and Methods' (unpublished master's thesis, 1972)

Sanders, M. L. and P. M. Taylor. *British Propaganda during the First World War, 1914-1918* (London: Macmillan, 1982)

Seton-Watson, H. and C. Seton-Watson. *The Making of the New Europe: R. W. Seton-Watson and the Last Years of Austria-Hungary* (London: Methuen, 1981)

Squires, J. D. *British Propaganda at Home and in The United States from 1914 To 1917* (Cambridge: Harvard University Press, 1935)

Steed, H. W. *The Fifth Arm* (London: Constable, 1940)

Stuart, Sir C. *Secrets of Crewe House: The Story of a Famous Campaign.* (London: Hodder & Stoughton, 1920)

Taylor, P. M. 'The Projection of Britain: British Overseas Publicity and Propaganda, 1914-1939, with particular reference to the Work of the News Department of the Foreign Office' (unpublished doctoral thesis, University of Leeds, 1978)

— 'Publicity and Diplomacy: The Impact of the First World War upon Foreign Office Attitudes towards the Press', in *Retreat from Power: Studies in Britain's Foreign Policy of the Twentieth Century*, edited by D. Dilks, 2 vols (London: Macmillan, 1981), I: *1906-1939*

Times History of the War, 22 vols (London: The Times, 1914-1921), XXI, Chapter CCCXIV: 'British Propaganda in Enemy Countries' (1919)

Valiani, L. *The End of Austria-Hungary* (London: Secker & Warburg, 1973)

Williams, L. N. and M. Williams. *Forged Stamps of two World Wars: The Postal Forgeries and Propaganda Issues of the Belligerents, 1914-1918, 1939-1945* (London: The Authors, 1954)

— *The 'Propaganda' Forgeries: A History and Description of the Austrian, Bavarian and German Stamps Counterfeited by Order of the British Government during the Great War, 1914-1918* (London: David Field, 1938)

Young, H. F. *Prince Lichnowsky and the Great War* (Athens, Georgia: University of Georgia Press, 1977)

Articles

Bar-Yosef, E. 'The Last Crusade? British Propaganda and the Palestine Campaign, 1917-18', *Journal of Contemporary History*, 36 (2001), 87-110

Neilson, K. '"Joy Rides"? British Intelligence and Propaganda in Russia, 1914-1917', *Historical Journal*, 24 (1981), 885-906

Nicholson, I. 'An Aspect of British Official Wartime Propaganda', *Cornhill Magazine*, 70 (1931), 593-606

Occleshaw, M. E. '"The Stab in the Back" - Myth or Reality?', *Journal of the Royal United Services Institute for Defence Studies*, 120 (1985), 49-54

Robbs, P. H. 'The Great War: Leaflet Evaluation', *Psywar Society Bulletin*, 8 (1959), 10-12

Sanders, M. L. 'British Film Propaganda in Russia, 1916-1918', *Historical Journal of Film, Radio and Television*, 3 (1983), 117-129

— 'Wellington House and British Propaganda during the First World War', *Historical Journal*, 18 (1975), 119-146

Street, C. J. C. 'Propaganda Behind the Lines', *Cornhill Magazine*, 47 (1919), 488-99

— 'Propaganda Behind the Lines', *Cornhill Magazine*, 48 (1919), 490-95

Taylor, P.M. 'The Foreign Office and British Propaganda during The First World War', *Historical Journal*, 23 (1980), 875-98

— 'Propagandists at War: Working for the Secret War Propaganda Bureau at Wellington House', *Gunfire: A Journal of First World War History*, 34 (1995), 14-25

Walpole, H. 'Denis Garstin and the Russian Revolution: A Brief Word in Memory', *Slavonic and East European Review*, 17 (1939), 587-605
Contains extracts from Garstin's notes and correspondence during his stay in Russia on the staff of the British Mission of Propaganda in Petrograd, 1917-1918.

Warman, R. 'The Erosion of Foreign Office Influence in the Making of Foreign Policy, 1916-18', *Historical Journal*, 15 (1972), 113-59

Archival Material

1st Report of the Work of Wellington House, 7 June 1915 (Public Record Office, INF 4/5)

2nd Report of the Work of Wellington House, February , 1916 (Public Record Office, INF 4/5)

3rd Report of the Work of Wellington House, September 1916 (Public Record Office, FO 371/2837)

Donald, R. *Report on Propaganda Arrangements, 9 January 1917* (Public Record Office, INF 4/4B)

—— *Inquiry into the Extent and Efficiency of Propaganda: Reports on Various Branches of Propaganda Work and Recommendations, 4 December 1917* (Public Record Office, INF 4/4B)

Great Britain. Foreign Office. *Schedule of Wellington House Literature* (London: HMSO, 1918)
A copy of this comprehensive list of Wellington House's printed publications, can be found in the Imperial War Museum's Department of Documents (IWM, 79/492).

Lee, H. O. *British Propaganda During the Great War, 1914-1918* (Public Record Office, INF 4/4A)
The 'official' history written shortly after the war but before the papers relating to First World War propaganda were destroyed in 1920.

Contemporary Propaganda Material

A selection representative of the whole range of themes covered in the printed propaganda materials produced in books and pamphlets during the war for overseas (including American) consumption is provided in section **4.2.5.2 (Printed Propaganda Material)**

4.2.4.2 Courting America; Anglo-American Relations

When war broke out in 1914 Britain and Germany became engaged in an intense propaganda battle to win American sympathy. This became particularly important to Britain as it became increasingly dependent on American finance and supplies as the war developed – a situation that made British propagandists determined to ensure that, if the USA did decide to enter the war, it would do so on the side of the Allies.

The British propaganda campaign to win the support of the USA at the start of the war was directed from Wellington House by the War Propaganda Bureau, the establishment of which was largely motivated by the dangers posed by the activities of German propagandists in the United States. To deal with this threat Masterman, the head of the Bureau, created a special branch, headed by Sir Gilbert Parker, which was given the task of countering German propaganda and creating in the USA an adverse image of the Central Powers as tyrannical, ambitious for world domination, and totally lacking in the democratic ideals shared by Britain, France, and the USA, but doing all this with a style of propaganda which would not offend the Americans. The main method that was employed to achieve these objectives up to 1917 was for Wellington House to instigate and control a flow of propaganda materials to the USA among both an educated elite (lawyers, doctors, businessmen, politicians, scientists, academics and teachers) and various leading institutions, newspapers and libraries. The material that was distributed was characterised by a scholarly style, and every effort was made to obscure the fact that it had originated from an official source. For example, Gilbert Parker, the person through whom a great deal of this material was circulated in the USA, obscured the fact that he was an official working for a government propaganda body by giving the impression, in the personal letter he always enclosed in the material he distributed, that he was acting as a private individual.

As well as countering the German propaganda campaign in the USA in this discreet and cautious manner, Britain had to deal with the problem of Americans who were unhappy with British policy on blockade, neutrals, and censorship or who were generally inclined to be suspicious of Britain and her allies. Support for the allied cause and, later, for the USA's entry into the war, was on the whole to be found among American intellectuals but there were also intellectuals like Richard Bourne who deplored this. A particular worry for Britain was the press of W. R. Hearst, who for most of the war, especially before 1917, made extensive use of his newspapers to counteract pro-British propaganda but, as this made these newspapers very unpopular with many Americans, the impact of this adverse press was somewhat diluted. Furthermore, Hearst himself came under attack from his opponents[105] who accused him of disloyalty to his country by his giving support to Germany and opposing the USA getting involved in the war.

With the entry of the USA into the war on 6 April 1917 the work of Gilbert Parker, who retired at the end of

---

[105] One of these opponents was J. M. Beck, who in 1917 criticised Hearst in a speech which was published subsequently as *The Enemy Within our Gates*).

1917, and of Professor Macneile Dixon, who succeeded him, was continued in a new British Bureau of Information (BBI)[106] which was set up in New York on 16 May 1917 (with Geoffrey Butler as its head) to supervise propaganda in America and improve the supply of information to the press. The changed status of the USA from neutral to belligerent and the establishment of the BBI marked the beginning of a gradual departure from the early emphasis upon an academic style of propaganda, aimed in covert fashion at an elite audience, to methods more akin to a campaign geared to overt mass persuasion. For the rest of the war the methods employed were more open and broader in scope, far greater use being made of the use of photographs, paintings and cartoons[107], bazaars[108], the press and the cinema[109] for propaganda purposes, although propaganda material in the form of pamphlets continued to be circulated. Nevertheless, in spite of the critical reports in 1917 by Pomeroy Burton[110] on the previous style of propaganda in the USA, and Northcliffe's efforts while heading a British War Mission in the USA[111] to make it more aggressive, British propagandists in the USA generally continued to operate with a reasonable amount of caution, an approach no doubt influenced by Foreign Office policy and their disapproval of Northcliffe's indiscreet and often controversial dealings with the American press.

The progress of the propaganda campaign to win American support became very closely linked to the secret British intelligence activities which were developed to monitor both the internal conditions of the USA and the changing moods of American public opinion. Two of the most significant figures operating in this way were Captain (later Admiral) Guy Gaunt (head of naval intelligence in the USA)[112] and William Wiseman (head of military intelligence in the USA)[113] who played leading roles in the area of naval and military intelligence. Gaunt's organisation received invaluable information from Admiral Sir Reginald Hall (Director of Naval Intelligence) and the code breakers of Room 40 who were able to supply vital information to British propagandists This information enabled them not only to identify and counteract the work of the German propagandists but also to subject German agents in the USA to a public exposure which was particularly damaging to the promotion of the German cause. Counter espionage was an essential feature of the work of both Gaunt and Wiseman. This was an area in which they both derived considerable benefit from the services of Emmanuel Voska, through whose involvement with an organisation known as the Bohemian National Alliance they were able to achieve and maintain contact with a wide variety of agents and information sources throughout the USA.

After the BBI became the centre of propaganda organisation in the USA Gaunt and Wiseman retained their links to the propaganda set-up, as now organised by the BBI, through Arthur Willert[114] who became the special representative of Geoffrey Butler (Head of the BBI) as the work of the Bureau[115] began to expand.. By this time, as well as his intelligence activities, Wiseman had become involved as liaison officer between Arthur

---

[106] The BBI, which was made directly responsible to the American section of the Department of Information, was rechristened the British Pictorial Service on 24 July 1918.

[107] As well as promoting exhibitions of photographs and paintings the British arranged a personal tour by Raemaekers to the United States in June 1917 that greatly stimulated the circulation of his cartoons.

[108] Collections of war trophies were exhibited as part of a series of Allied bazaars.

[109] The showing of the film *The Tanks of Ancre* in the United States and the preceding press and poster campaign mounted to publicise it is an example of the use made of the cinema.

[110] Pomeroy Burton, a former news editor of *Pulitzer's World* and currently serving as general manager of Northcliffe's newspaper empire, was sent to the United States by Lloyd George (after being persuaded by Northcliffe) to assess the existing propaganda situation there and to report to John Buchan, Head of the Department of Information.

[111] Northcliffe succeeded Balfour as head of the British War Mission in the USA at the end of May 1917.

[112] The British Ambassador, Cecil Spring-Rice, used Gaunt as a liaison officer with Colonel House, the President's personal adviser, for a brief period.

[113] Wiseman was assisted by Norman Thwaites.

[114] During the war Willert was a Washington correspondent of *The Times* in which capacity he became interested and involved in Britain's propaganda activities in the USA (as, for example, undertaking on behalf of the British ambassador tasks such as helping to distribute propaganda material in America).

[115] Branch offices were also opened in Chicago and San Francisco, employing a total of 96 officials.

Balfour, Head of the British War Mission in the USA, and Colonel House (the President's personal adviser). Acting in a liaison capacity between the American and British Governments was a role in which he became increasingly involved, ultimately perhaps achieving more influence with the American administration than any other British official working in the USA.

Once the USA had entered the war as an associated power on the side of the Allies the focus of the aims of British propaganda underwent changes. Some of the main goals were now seen as that of bringing home to the American people the realities of modern warfare, persuading them of the need for urgent and active co-operation in the Allied war effort, and ensuring that they were not distracted by talks of peace. With these goals in mind British propagandists sought to re-emphasise the extent of Britain's contribution to the war effort and to prevent any dilution of American commitment to the war by countering pacifist propaganda. Their task of keeping the American nation fully committed to the Allied war effort was greatly assisted by George Creel who, as chairman of the Committee on Public Information which was established by act of the US Congress on 14 April 1917, devoted a huge amount of effort to the task of mobilising American public opinion.

The British propaganda campaign in the USA benefited from a number of invaluable advantages such as Britain's linguistic and cultural affinity with the USA, Germany being placed at a disadvantage from the start by the indignation of many Americans over the German invasion of Belgium, Britain's control of a significant proportion of the communication channels between Europe and North America[116], the powerful financial and business stake the USA had in the Allies by virtue of the huge expansion of USA's trade with Britain and France resulting from the war, the skilfulness of British intelligence operations in the USA, and the clumsy nature of Germany's propaganda in contrast to the subtle nature of Britain's. Above all British propaganda up to 1917 enjoyed valuable opportunities to exploit a number of events which could cast doubt on the morality of Germany's conduct as, for example, the German invasion of Belgium, the execution of Nurse Cavell and Captain Fryatt[117], the bombing of Britain's civilian population from the air, the use of unrestricted submarine warfare (the USA was particularly outraged by the sinking of the *Lusitania*) and the Zimmermann telegram[118]. Being frequently forced on the back foot in this way Germany was severely handicapped in its attempts to present the justice of its cause, a situation which was not helped by its inability to make the most of the propaganda opportunities that came its way; it was, for example, not able exploit the controversial British blockade in as effective a way as the British exploited Germany's campaign of unrestricted submarine warfare and it was only slightly more successful in capitalizing on Britain's Irish problems.

Autobiographies, Biographies, Diaries, Memoirs

Adams, J. C. *Seated with the Mighty: A Biography of Sir Gilbert Parker* (Ottawa: Borealis Press, 1979)

Bernstorff, J. H., Graf von. *The Memoirs of Count Bernstorff*, translated by E. Sutton (London: Heinemann, 1936)

— *My Three Years in America* (London: Skeffington, 1920)

Bryan, W. J. and M. B. Bryan. *The Memoirs of William Jennings Bryan*, by himself and his wife, Mary Baird Bryan (Philadelphia: United Publishers of America, 1925; repr. in 2 vols, Port Washington; London: Kennikat Press, 1971)

---

[116] This was significantly aided by the British ship *Telconia* cutting the cable links between Germany and the USA at the beginning of the war. This provided Britain from the outset with an important advantage in the propaganda battle with Germany for gaining the support of the USA.

[117] On 28 March 1915 Captain Charles Fryatt, a British merchant captain, attempted - but failed - to ram and sink a German submarine, *U-33*. Fryatt was officially rewarded by the British government for his actions. The Germans charged him with being a franc-tireur - a charge that carried the death sentence. The German and British governments engaged in a war of words over his case. Britain argued that Fryatt had been acting in self-defence, while Germany maintained that Fryatt's action in attempting to ram *U-33* was undertaken without provocation. Fryatt was tried and convicted by a German court and executed on 27 July 1916. The case achieved widespread notoriety in Britain where Captain Fryatt's name and face was everywhere celebrated in newspapers, magazines and even bookmarks..

[118] On 16 January 1917, German Foreign Minister Zimmermann sent the German Minister in Mexico an enciphered message with a proposal to be presented to the Mexican government. Zimmermann's proposal was for a German-Mexican alliance, with the reward for Mexico being the prospect of her recovery of the territory lost in the Mexican-American War. British intelligence intercepted and deciphered the message, and turned it over to the Americans on 24 February. Publication of the message raised considerable anger in the United States, and increased popular support for the U.S. declaration of war a few weeks later.

The War Years

William Jennings Bryan (1860-1925), three times unsuccessful as the Democratic party's candidate for presidential election (in 1896, 1900 and 1908), served as President Wilson's Secretary of State following Wilson's presidential victory in 1912. Bryan adopted and stuck to a policy of strict U.S. neutrality, supported by Wilson. He eventually fell out with Wilson because he believed (wrongly) that Wilson, by the way he handled the situation arising from the sinking of the Lusitania, was moving towards a declaration of war with Germany. As a result Bryan resigned in June 1915.

Dumba, C. *Memoirs of a Diplomat*, translated by I. F. D. Moore (London: Allen & Unwin, 1933)
Dumba, who was the Austro-Hungarian Ambassador to the USA until 1915, includes in his Memoirs impressions of the importance of British propaganda in influencing the USA decision to enter the war on the side of the Allies.

Gaunt, Sir G. *The Yield of the Years: A Story of Adventure Afloat and Ashore*, by Admiral Sir Guy Grant, naval attaché and chief of the British intelligence service in the United States, 1914-1918 (London: Hutchinson, 1940)

Hendrick, B. J. *The Life and Letters of Walter H. Page*, 3 vols (London: Heinemann, 1922-1925)
Page was the American ambassador in London during the war.

Houston, D. F. *Eight Years with Wilson's Cabinet, 1913 to 1920*, with a personal estimate of the President, 2 vols (Garden City, N.Y.: Doubleday, Page & Company, 1926)
Houston was Secretary of the U.S. Department of Agriculture during Wilson's presidency.

Lansing, R. *War Memoirs of Robert Lansing, Secretary of State* (London: Rich & Cowan, 1935)
Robert Lansing (1864-1928) served as US Secretary of State from 1915-20 in President Woodrow Wilson's administration, replacing William Jennings Bryan who resigned in protest at Wilson's allegedly hawkish approach to US neutrality in 1915.

Link, A. S. *Wilson*, 5 vols (Princeton: Princeton University Press, 1947-1965)
Contents: Vol 1. *The Road to the White House*; Vol 2. *The New Freedom*; Vol 3. *The Struggle for Neutrality, 1914-1915*; Vol 4. *Confusions and Crisis, 1915-1916*; Vol 5. *Campaigns for Progressivism and Peace, 1916-1917*.

Seymour, C. *The Intimate Papers of Colonel House arranged as a Narrative*, 4 vols (London: Benn, 1926-1928)

Spring-Rice, Sir C. A. *The Letters and Friendships of Sir Cecil Spring-Rice: A Record*, edited by Stephen Gwynn, 2 vols (London: Constable, 1929)
Spring-Rice was ambassador at Washington, 1913-1918. Acted as a conciliatory influence between Great Britain and the United States during the First World War. His tact contributed to the USA deciding to join the Allies

Strachey, J. St. Loe. *The River of Life* (London: Hodder & Stoughton, 1924)
Diary account of his work in securing close relations between governments of Britain and America and the war correspondents in early years of war. Strachey was an influential editor of *The Spectator* for a number of years.

Swanberg, W. A. *Citizen Hearst: A Biography of William Randolph Hearst* (New York: Scribner's, 1961; repr. New York: Collier Books, Macmillan Publishing Co., 1986)

Thwaites, N. G. *Velvet and Vinegar* (London: Grayson & Grayson, 1932)

Voska, E. V. and W. Irwin. *Spy and Counter-Spy: The Autobiography of a Master-Spy* [The reminiscences of E. V. Voska set down by Will Irwin.] (New York: Harrap, 1941)
Voska ran a Czechoslovak-based counterintelligence organization in the United States prior to the U.S. entry into World War I. He placed his organization at the disposal of British intelligence, and after 1915 cooperated with the FBI as well.

Whitlock, B. *The Letters and Journal of Brand Whitlock*, chosen and edited with a biographical introduction by Allan Nevins, 2 vols (New York; London: D. Appleton-Century,1936)
Brand Whitlock (1869-1934) served as U.S. Ambassador to Belgium during World War I.

Willert, Sir A. *Washington and Other Memories* (Boston: Houghton Mifflin, 1972)

Books

Arnett, A. M. *Claude Kitchin and the Wilson War Policies* (Boston, Mass.: Little, Brown, 1937)
Claude Kitchin represented North Carolina in the U.S. House of Representatives during the early 20th century and served as Speaker of the House during the First World War. He was a consistent anti-militarist and opposed major planks of the

administration's preparedness policy, especially the expansion of the army and navy. In 1915, he co-authored an anti-preparedness pamphlet with William Jennings Bryan. He condemned both German submarine warfare and the British blockade as twin violations of American rights and opposed Wilson's call for war in April 1917. Once war was declared, however, he supported most of Wilson's war measures.

Bailey, T. A. *The Policy of the United States toward the Neutrals, 1917-1918* (Baltimore: The Johns Hopkins Press, 1942; repr. Gloucester, Mass: P. Smith, 1966)

Baker, N. D. *Why We Went to War* (New York: Published by Harper for Council on Foreign Relations, 1936)

Bennett, S. H. and C. F. Howlett, eds. *Antiwar Dissent and Peace Activism in World War I America: A Documentary Reader* (Lincoln: University of Nebraska Press, 2014)

Boghardt, T. *The Zimmermann Telegram: Intelligence, Diplomacy, and America's Entry into World War I* (Annapolis, Md.: Naval Institute Press, 2012)

Bourne, R. S. *War and the Intellectuals: Collected Essays, 1915-1919*, edited, with introduction by Carl Resek (New York: Harper & Row, 1964; repr. New York: Hackett, 1999)
Included in this work is the essay entitled 'War and the Intellectuals' (first published in a magazine, *The Seven Arts*, in 1917) in which Randolph Bourne (whose writing on politics, culture, and literature made him one of the most influential American intellectuals of the twentieth century) bitterly criticises those who supported American entry into the Great War.

Burk, K. M. *Britain, America, and the Sinews of War, 1914-1918* (London: Allen & Unwin, 1985)

— 'British War Missions to the United States, 1914-1918' (unpublished doctoral thesis, Oxford University, 1976)

Campbell, C. W. *Reel America and World War I: A Comprehensive Filmography and History of Motion Pictures in the United States, 1914-1920* (Jefferson, N.C.: McFarland, 1985)

Carlisle, R. P. *Sovereignty at Sea: U.S. Merchant Ships and American Entry into World War I* (Gainesville: University Press of Florida, 2009)

Child, C. J. *The German-Americans in Politics, 1914-1917* (Madison: University of Wisconsin Press, 1939)

Controvich, J. T. *The United States in World War I: A Bibliographic Guide* (Lanham, Md.: Scarecrow Press, 2012)

Coogan, J. W. *The End of Neutrality: The United States, Britain and Maritime Rights, 1899–1915* (Ithaca, NY: Cornell University Press, 1981)

Creel, G. *How We Advertised America* (New York: Harper & Brothers, 1920; repr. New York: Arno Press, 1972)

Daniels, J. *The Wilson Era: Years of Peace: 1910-1917* (Chapel Hill: The University of North Carolina Press, 1944)

— *The Wilson Era: Years of War and After, 1917-1923* (Chapel Hill: University of North Carolina Press, 1946)

Dobson, A. P. *Anglo-American Relations in the Twentieth Century: Of Friendship, Conflict, and the Rise and Decline of Superpowers* (London: Routledge, 2005)

Doerries, R. R. *Imperial Challenge: Ambassador Count Bernstorff and German-American Relations, 1908-1917*, translated by C. D. Shannon (Chapel Hill: University of North Carolina Press, 1989)

Dopperen, R. van and Graham, C. C. *Shooting the Great War: Albert Dawson and the American Correspondent Film Company, 1914–1918* (Charleston, SC: Create Space, 2013)
For the purpose of influencing public opinion in the United States German officials mounted a secret film campaign based on the establishment there of the American Correspondent Film Company For this covert operation photographer Albert K. Dawson was used as a front man and sent to Europe to cover the war in the trenches with his camera. This book describes his life and work as a war photographer and includes information about his films and the way his pictures were used by the German government for foreign propaganda.

Esterquest, R. T. 'War Literature and Libraries: The Role of the American Library in Promoting Interest in and Support of the European War, 1914-1918' (unpublished master's thesis, University of Illinois, 1940)

Floyd, R. *Abandoning American Neutrality: Woodrow Wilson and the Beginning of the Great War, August 1914-December 1915* (Basingstoke: Palgrave Macmillan, 2013)

Fowler, W. B. *British-American Relations 1917-1918: The Role of Sir William Wiseman.* (Princeton: Princeton University Press, 1969)

Fulwider, C. R. *German Propaganda and U.S. Neutrality in World War I* (Columbia, Missouri: University of Missouri Press, 2016)

Friedman, W. F., and C. J. Mendelsohn. *The Zimmermann Telegram of January 16, 1917 and its Cryptographic Background*, prepared under the direction of the Chief Signal Officer by William F. Friedman and Charles J. Mendelsohn (Laguna Hills, CA: Aegean Park Press, 1976; repr. 1994)
Originally published, Washington(D.C.): U.S. Government Printing Office, 1938. Barbara Tuchman was unable to gain access to this study for the first edition of her book, *The Zimmermann Telegram*, and amended her account in a later edition after the 1965 declassification of Friedman and Mendelsohn's work.

Gelber, L. M. *The Rise of Anglo-American Friendship: A Study in World Politics, 1898-1906* (London; New York: Oxford University Press, 1938; repr. Hamden, Conn: Archon Books, 1966)

Grattan, C. H. *Why We Fought* (New York: Vanguard Press, 1929)
An account of the events leading up to the entry of the USA into the First World War.

Hale, W. B. *American Rights and British Pretensions on the Seas: The Facts and the Documents, Official and Other, Bearing Upon the Present Attitude of Great Britain Towards the Commerce of the United States* (New York: McBride, 1915)

— *The Exportation of Arms and Munitions of War: Should the United States Government Allow It or Forbid It?* (New York: Organization of American Women for Strict Neutrality, 1915)

Heindel, R. H. *The American Impact on Great Britain, 1898-1914: A Study of the United States in World History* (Philadelphia: Pennsylvania University Press, 1940; repr. New York: Octagon Books, 1968)

Houston, D. F. *Why We Went to War. I. Submarine Warfare. II. Prussian Militarism* (Washington, D.C., 1918)
Houston (1866-1940) served President Woodrow Wilson as United States Secretary of Agriculture from 1913 to 1920.

Jones, J. P. and P. M. Hollister. *The German Secret Service in America* (Boston: Small, Maynard, 1918)

Katz, F. *The Secret War in Mexico: Europe, the United States, and the Mexican Revolution* (Chicago: University of Chicago Press, 1981)

Kennedy, R. A. *The Will to Believe: Woodrow Wilson, World War I and America's Strategy for Peace and Security* (Kent, Ohio: Kent State University Press, 2009)

Koester, F. *The Lies of the Allies: A Remarkable Collection of Facts, Proofs and Documents of How England, the Anglo-Maniacs and the "Big Dailies" Humbug the American People, First Instalment, 1914-1915* (New York: Issues and Events, 1916)

Landau, H. *The Enemy Within: The Inside Story of German Sabotage in America* (New York: Putnam's, 1937)
Landau headed the Military Division of the British secret service in Holland from 1916. The first part of this book is a brief history of German sabotage and intelligence activities both before and after the U.S. entry into the war.

May, E. R. *The World War and American Isolation, 1914-17* (Cambridge, Mass.: Harvard University Press, 1959; repr. 1966)

McMaster, J. B. *The United States in the World War, 1914-1918* (New York: Appleton, 1918; repr. 1929)

Millis, W. *Road to War: America, 1914-1917* (London: Faber, 1935; repr. New York: Fertig, 1970)

Mitchell, Sir P. C. *Report on the Propaganda Library in the Intelligence Division of the War Office and Appendices*, 3 vols (London: HMSO, 1917)
Appendix I. Propaganda Chiefly Relating to Nationalities. Appendix II. Germany and America.

Morison, S. 'Personality and Diplomacy in Anglo-American Relations, 1917', in *Essays Presented to Sir Lewis Namier*, edited by R. Pares and A. J. P. Taylor (London: Macmillan: 1956; repr. Freeport, NY: Books for Libraries Press, 1971)

Morrissey, A. M. *The American Defense of Neutral Rights, 1914-1917* (Cambridge, Mass.: Harvard University Press, 1939)

Mugridge, I. *The View From Xanadu: William Randolph Hearst and United States Foreign Policy* (Montreal: McGill-Queen's University Press, 1995)

Murray, G. *Great Britain's Sea Policy: A Reply to an American Critic*, reprinted from "The Atlantic Monthly" (London: T. Fisher Unwin, 1917)

Nägler, J. 'Pandora's Box: Propaganda and War Hysteria in the United States during the First World War', paper delivered to the conference on total war ('How Total Was the Great War? Germany, France, Great Britain, and the United States, 1914-1918') held at Schloß Münchenwiler, Bern, October 9-12, 1996

The New Cambridge History of American Foreign Relations, 4 vols (Cambridge: Cambridge University Press, 2013), III: *The Globalizing of America, 1913-1945*, by Akira Iriye

Northcliffe, A. C., Viscount. *Lord Northcliffe's War Book*, with chapters on America at War; being a revised and enlarged edition of "At the war" (New York: Doran, 1917)

Paxson, F. L. *American Democracy and the World War*, 3 vols (Boston: Houghton Miffin, 1936-48; repr. New York: Cooper Square, 1966)
Vol.1: *Pre-War Years, 1913-17*; Vol.2: *America at War, 1917-18*; Vol.3: *Postwar Years, Normalcy, 1918-23*.

Peterson, H. C. *Propaganda for War: The Campaign against American Neutrality, 1914-1917* (Norman, Oklahoma: Prew, 1939; repr. Port Washington, NY: Kennikat Press, 1968)

Pierce, R. N. *Lord Northcliffe: Trans-Atlantic Influences*, Journalism Monographs, 40 (Lexington, Kentucky: Association for Education in Journalism, 1975)
This work begins with a review of the popular press in England and concentrates in the rest of the work on a biographical outline of Lord Northcliffe's career, in which his influence by and on American journalism at the beginning of the twentieth century is emphasised.

Rappaport, A. *The British Press and Wilsonian Neutrality* (Stanford, Calif.: Stanford University Press, 1951)

Rosenberg, E. *Spreading the American Dream: American Economic and Cultural Expansion, 1890-1945* (New York: Hill and Wang, 1982)

Savage, C., ed. *Policy of the United States toward Maritime Commerce in War*, 2 vols (Washington: United States Government Printing Office, 1934-1936; repr. New York; Kraus, 1969)
Contents: Vol 1: 1776-1914 (1934); Vol 2: 1914-1918, with documents (1936).

Schieber, C. E. *The Transformation of American Sentiments toward Germany, 1870-1914* (New York: Russell & Russell, 1973)

Scott, J. B. *A Survey of International Relations between the United States and Germany, August 1, 1914-April 6, 1917*, based on official documents (New York; London: Oxford University Press, 1917)

Seymour, S. *American Diplomacy during the World War* (Baltimore: Johns Hopkins Press, 1934; repr. Wesport, Conn.: Greenwood Press, 1975)

—— *American Neutrality, 1914-1917: Essays on the Causes of American Intervention in the World War* (London: H. Milford, Oxford University Press, 1935)

Spencer, S. R. *Decision for War, 1917: The Laconia Sinking and the Zimmermann Telegram as Key Factors in the Public Reaction against Germany* (Rindge, N.H.: R. R. Smith, 1953)

Sprott, M. E. 'A Survey of British Wartime Propaganda in the U.S.A. issued by Wellington House' (unpublished master's thesis, Stanford University, 1921)

Squires, J. D. *British Propaganda at Home and in The United States from 1914 To 1917* (Cambridge: Harvard University Press, 1935)

Tansill, C. C. *America Goes to War* (Boston: Little, Brown, 1938; repr. Gloucester, Mass.: Peter Smith, 1963)
On the events leading to the intervention of the U.S.A. in the European War, 1914-1919.

Thompson, J. A. *Reformers and War: American Progressive Publicists and the First World War* (Cambridge: Cambridge University Press, 1987)

Tuchman, B. *The Zimmermann Telegram* (London: Constable, 1958; repr. London: Phoenix, 2001)
Tuchman amended her original account in the later reprint after the 1965 declassification of Friedman and Mendelsohn's work, *The Zimmermann Telegram of January 16, 1917 and its Cryptographic Background* (see record above).

Viereck, G. S. *Spreading Germs of Hate*, with a foreword by Colonel Edward M. House (New York: Liveright, 1930)

—— *The Strangest Friendship in History: Woodrow Wilson and Colonel House* (London: Duckworth, 1933)

Ward, A. J. *Ireland and Anglo-American Relations, 1899-1921* (London: Weidenfeld & Nicolson, 1969)

Wiegand, W. A. *An Active Instrument for Propaganda: The American Public Library During World War I* (New York: Greenwood, 1989)

Willert, Sir A. *The Road to Safety: A Study in Anglo-American Relations* (London: Verschoyle, 1952)
During the war Willert was a Washington correspondent of *The Times* in which capacity he became interested and involved in Britain's propaganda activities in the USA (as, for example, undertaking on behalf of the British ambassador tasks such as helping to distribute propaganda material in America).

Wilson, W. *The Public Papers of Woodrow Wilson*, edited by Ray Stannard Baker and William E. Dodd, authorized edn, 6 vols (New York: Harper, 1925-27; repr. New York: Kraus, 1970)
Contents: Vols 1-2: *College and State: Educational, Literary and Political Papers* (1875-1913); Vols 3-4: *The New Democracy: Presidential Messages, Addresses and other Papers* (1913-1917); Vols 5-6: *War and Peace: Presidential Messages, Addresses, and Public Papers* (1917-1924).

Winkler, J. R. *Nexus: Strategic Communications and American Security in World War I* (Cambridge, Mass.: Harvard University Press, 2008)

Woodward, D. R. *America and World War I: A Selected Annotated Bibliography of English-Language Sources* (London: Routledge, 2007)

Articles

Bailey, T. A. 'The United States and the Blacklist During the Great War', *Journal of Modern History*, 6 (1934), 14-36

—— 'World War Analogues of the Trent Affair', *American Historical Review*, 38 (1933), 286-290

Engelbrecht, H C. 'How War Propaganda Won', *World Tomorrow*, 10 (1927), 159-62
Reviews British propaganda against the Germans in the USA. Deals with activities of Sir Gilbert Parker, Lord Northcliffe and others. Relates some atrocity stories.

Fenton, B. 'Telegram that Brought US into Great War is Found', *Daily Telegraph* (London), 17 Oct. 2005
This article reveals the discovery by the official historian of GCHQ of an original typescript of the deciphered Zimmerman Telegram that is believed to be the actual telegram shown to the American ambassador in London in 1917.

Foster, H S 'How America Became Belligerent: A Quantitative Study of War News, 1914-17', *American Journal of Sociology*, 40 (1935), 464-475

Freeman, P. 'The Zimmermann Telegram Revisited: A Reconciliation of the Primary Sources', *Cryptologia* 30 (2006), 98-150.
A critical examination of the primary sources on the transmission, interception and decryption of the Zimmermann Telegram.

Fulwider, C. R. 'Film Propaganda and Kultur: The German Dilemma, 1914-1917', *Film and History*, 45:2 (2015), 4-12

Hachey, T. E. 'British War Propaganda and American Catholics In 1918', *Catholic Historical Review*, 61 (1975), 48-66

Kernek, S. 'Distractions of Peace During War: The Lloyd George Government's Reactions to Woodrow Wilson, December 1916-November 1918' *Transactions of the American Philosophical Society*, New Series, 65 (1975), 5-114

Lockhart, J. B. 'Sir William Wiseman, Bart: Agent of Influence', *Journal of the Royal United Services Institute for Defence Studies*, 134 (1989), 63-67

Millis, W. 'Hearst', *Atlantic Monthly*, 148 (1931), 696-705
The efforts of the Hearst press to discount the flood of propaganda from England, especially before 1917, made these newspapers very unpopular with many Americans.

Parker, Sir G.. 'The United States and the War', *Harper's Monthly Magazine*, 136 (1918), 523-31

Peifer, D. 'The Sinking of the Lusitania, Wilson's Response, and Paths Not Taken: Historical Revisionism, the Nye Committee, and the Ghost of William Jennings Bryan', *Journal of Military History*, 79 (2015), 1025-1046

Spence, R. B. 'Englishmen in New York: The SIS American Station, 1915-21', *Intelligence and National Security* 19 (2004), 511-537.
Spence provides a survey of the organization, personnel and the operations of the Secret Information Service's New York station during the First World War and the years immediately following. Includes the story of Sir William Wiseman and the men who served with and under him.

— 'Secret Agent 666: Aleister Crowley and British Intelligence in America, 1914-1918,' *International Journal of Intelligence and Counterintelligence* 13 (2000), 359-371
Crowley wrote virulent anti-British/anti-Allied writings in U.S. publications during World War I, but Spence is of the opinion that Crowley was actually working for British intelligence.

Spindler, A. 'Der britische Propagandafeldzug gegen die amerikanische Neutralität 1914-1917' *Berliner Monatshefte*, 17 (1939), 929-43

Thompson, J. L. '"To-Tell-The-People-of-America-the-Truth": Lord Northcliffe in the USA; Unofficial British Propaganda, June-November 1917', *Journal of Contemporary History*, 34 (1999), 243-262

Troy, T. F. 'The Gaunt-Wiseman Affair: British Intelligence in New York in 1915, *International Journal of Intelligence and Counterintelligence* 16 (2003), 442-461
The author looks at issues, including Gaunt's later animosity toward Wiseman, surrounding Wiseman's eventual replacement of Gaunt as the most influential British agent in the United States in the World War I period.

Murphy, D. M. and J. F. White. 'Propaganda: Can a Word Decide a War?', *US Army War College Quarterly: Parameters*, 37:3 (2007), 15-27

Macdonald, K. 'The First Cyborg', *History Today*, 66:5 (2016), 31-36
"Created from the bodies of war-wounded soldiers for an unnamed emperor, the first modern cyborg, Soldier 241, appears in a one-act play, *Blood and Iron*, published in the *Strand Magazine* in October 1917 **[see record below]**. Like the invention of the robot three years later in 1920, the cyborg was a product of modern warfare. It was also a rare anti-war statement, challenging British law as, to prevent war continuing, Soldier 241 kills his commanding officer at the end. … New research reveals that its remarkable anti-war message, delivered just after the entry of the United States into the First World War, is a reflection of public anguish. Huge numbers of men were returning from the Western Front with permanent, debilitating injuries and the public were getting nervous about the speed of unstoppable wartime scientific advances: chlorine gas in 1915, the tank in 1916 and unrestricted submarine warfare in 1917… it would seem that the *Strand* actively encouraged an anti-German presentation of this play – a common line to take in wartime – to avoid a legal charge [under DORA] of the play's anti-war message causing 'disaffection'.". [Quotation extracted from Macdonald's article]

Sheehan, P. P. and R. H. Davis. 'Blood and Iron: A play in One Act, by Porley Poore Sheehan and Robt. H. Davis. Illustrated by Steven Spurrin ', *Strand Magazine*, 54 (1917), 359-365 (October 1917)
" … Blood and Iron was first published in August 1917 in the US fiction Periodical, McClure's Magazine, under the title 'Efficiency'. It is probable that Sheehan and Davis sold the play to the Strand Magazine in the UK after (and possibly because) it had been bought for US publication in McClure's … The Strand commissioned the British war artist Steven Spurrier to illustrate the play with anti-German propaganda". [Quotation extracted from Macdonald's article, 'The First Cyborg' **(see record above)**]

Whelpley, J. D. 'America and the U33.', *Fortnightly Review*, (1916), 871-878
On 28 March 1915 Captain Charles Fryatt, a British merchant captain, attempted - but failed - to ram and sink a German submarine, *U-33*. Fryatt was officially rewarded by the British government for his actions. The Germans charged him with being a franc-tireur - a charge that carried the death sentence. The German and British governments engaged in a war of words over his case. Britain argued that Fryatt had been acting in self-defence, while Germany maintained that Fryatt's action in attempting to ram *U-33* was undertaken without provocation. Fryatt was tried and convicted by a German court and executed on 27 July 1916. The case achieved widespread notoriety in Britain where Captain Fryatt's name and face was everywhere celebrated in newspapers, magazines and even bookmarks.

— 'Anglo-American Relations', *Fortnightly Review*, (1916), 691-697

— 'The Courting of America', *Contemporary Review*, 102 (1914), 682-689

— 'President Wilson's Pro-Ally Propaganda', *Fortnightly Review* (1917)

Wiegand, W. A. 'British Propaganda in American Public-Libraries, 1914-1917', *Journal of Library History, Philosophy and Comparative Librarianship*, 18 (1983), 237-254

4.2.4.3 British Propaganda Material Distributed in the USA

According to Professor Lutz in his *Studies of World War Propaganda* (*Journal of Modern History*, 5 (1933), p.511) P. C. Mitchell[119] viewed the subject-matter of British propaganda distributed in the USA as consisting of the following divisions:

"First, the militarist ideal in German life with its contempt for arbitration and its malice aforethought toward neutral Belgium. Second, the war policies of imperial Germany and a comparison of these 'damnable practices' (atrocities, deportation of workers, submarine warfare, etc.) with Allied methods. Third, a comparison of British colonial methods with German methods. Fourth, the idealistic war aims of the Allies in contrast with the German motives for opposing the new world-order. Fifth, Great Britain's friendship for the United States described in the phrase 'hands across the sea'."

What this analysis does not reflect are the propaganda efforts which were made to take account of important sections of the US population (such as the Irish, the Jews and the Catholics); to deal with controversial issues (such as the British blockade, Britain's Irish problems); and to combat premature peace moves and the subversive influence of Bolshevik pacifist propaganda in the later stages of the war.

---

[119] P. C. Mitchell, a distinguished zoologist who served in British intelligence in MI7 during the Great War, produced a three-volume report on propaganda in 1917 (*Report on the Propaganda Library in the Intelligence Division of the War Office and Appendices*).

A bibliography of a large proportion of the propaganda material used to influence American opinion can be seen in a *'A Checklist of British Propaganda Sent to the United States Between 1914 and 1917'* (see **Appendix 2**) which Squires produced as an Appendix to his work, *British Propaganda at Home and in the United States* (q.v.). This checklist, however, as Squires points out in this appendix, 'represents only materials sent over by Wellington House under the direction of Sir Gilbert Parker or of Professor Macneile Dixon' and does not include the propaganda materials dispatched after the entry of the USA into the war on April 6 1917. Materials sent to the the USA after the latter date mostly emanated from the National War Aims Committee (NWAC). Much of NWAC's anti-pacifist material and material emphasizing the commitment of British workers to total victory, for example, was not only produced for domestic consumption but was also sent to the USA.

4.2.4.4 The United States Contribution to the Propaganda Campaign

As soon as the United States entered the war on the side of the Allied Powers in 1917 it set up the Committee on Public Information (consisting of the Secretaries of State, the Army, and the Navy) which became the focal point of a vast campaign of propaganda aimed primarily at mobilising the efforts and public opinion of its own people in support of the USA's involvement in the war. The enlistment of artists, advertisers, poets, historians, photographers, educators, and actors, the production of films, posters, books and pamphlets, the purchase of advertisements in newspapers, the employment of businessmen, preachers, and professors to address meetings throughout the whole country, were among the chief means by which the propaganda campaign, under the direction of George Creel, was conducted.

Before the emergence of the Committee on Public Information (CPI) established propaganda on an official, organized footing there was no lack of individual Americans in the USA (and also abroad, e.g. Henry James and Edith Wharton) unofficially writing sympathetically about the Allies or unfavourably about Germany (see the contemporary American publications cited among the items listed in **section 4.2.5.2 (Printed Propaganda Material)** in the sub-section **Books and Pamphlets: American Attitudes**. After the establishment of the CPI considerable numbers of other American writers were persuaded to help with the production of official propaganda. In his book, *How We Advertised America*, Creel claimed that the CPI "gathered together the leading novelists, essayists, and publicists of the land, and these men and women, without payment worked faithfully in the production of brilliant, comprehensive articles that went to the press as syndicated features". Samuel Hopkins Adams, Booth Tarkington, Mary Roberts Rinehart, Herbert Quick, Gertrude Atherton, Robert Herrick, Wilbur Daniel Steele, Ida Tarbell, Rex Beach, Virginia Boyle and William Allen White were among the writers who were drawn into this work with varying degrees of success. Strangely, Creel seemed chary of sponsoring propaganda efforts in purely fictional form as, for example, was the case in his rejection of help for the publication of the propagandistic novels of Upton Sinclair *(Jimmie Higgins)* and Booth Tarkington *(Ramsey Milholland)*.

One of the most effective supporters of the British propaganda efforts in the United States was Theodore Roosevelt, who enthusiastically joined the group of writers in the United States who wrote on the side of the Allies. The war had hardly begun before he was writing in this vein in a series of newspaper articles that were collected in January 1915 under the title, *America and the World War*. He had no sympathy with Woodrow Wilson's reluctance to get involved in the European war and strove strenuously to arouse the United States to action against German aggression, aligning himself on the side of interventionism in a constant round of speeches, articles, and letter-writing.

The American film industry also contributed to the propaganda campaign. The cinema played an important role during the war, first in the debate for and against intervention; later as a propaganda tool. Up until the end of 1916, prominent film-makers attempted to persuade Americans to support President Wilson's non-intervention policy with a number of influential pro-neutrality films. However, as the war intensified, with American civilians becoming victims of German attacks with increasing frequency, the pressure for the USA to enter the war on the side of the Allies grew to the point where the USA felt justified in declaring war on Germany (on 6 April, 1917). As this pressure grew American film makers generally ceased to support neutrality and became favourable to the view of those who advocated preparedness in the event of a war. After the declaration of war the films that were released included many hundreds that were aimed at criticizing pacifists, encouraging enlistment, exposing spies and attacking slackers. As in Europe, the cinema became closely associated with the war effort, virtually assuming the role of an official participant in the propaganda campaign that was developed by the Creel Committee on Public Information.

The War Years

Autobiographies, Biographies, Letters

Atherton, G. *Adventures of a Novelist* (London: Cape, 1932)

Blankenhorn, H. *Adventures in Propaganda: Letters from an Intelligence Officer in France* (Boston: Houghton Mifflin, 1919)
Blankenhorn, with a group of six intelligence officers, was sent by the USA to France to establish relations with the propaganda organisations of France, Britain and Italy and assemble the machinery for a propaganda drive over the enemy lines during the autumn of 1918.

Creel, G. *Rebel at Large: Recollections of Fifty Crowded Years* (New York: Putnam's, 1947)

Dell, F. *Upton Sinclair: A Study in Social Protest* (New York: Doran, 1927)

Edel, L. *Henry James*, 5 vols (London: Rupert Hart-Davis, 1953-1972), V: *The Master, 1901-1916* (1972)

Lewis, R. W. B. *Edith Wharton: A Biography* (New York; Harper and Row, 1975)

Roosevelt, T. *The Letters of Theodore Roosevelt*, selected and edited by E. E. Morison [and others], 8 vols (Cambridge, Mass: Harvard University Press, 1951-1954), VIII: *The Days of Armageddon, 1914-1919* (1954)

Schickel, R. *D.W. Griffith: An American Life* (London: Simon & Schuster, 1984; New York: Limelight Editions, 1996)

Wharton, E. *A Backward Glance* (New York: Appleton-Century, 1934)

Whitehouse, V. B. *A Year as a Government Agent*, by Vira B. Whitehouse (Mrs. Norman de R. Whitehouse), Director for Switzerland of the Committee on Public Information in 1918 (New York; London: Harper, 1920)
Memoirs of the author's year as the United States government's propaganda representative in Switzerland during the war.

Wister, O. *Roosevelt: The Story of a Friendship, 1880-1919* (New York: Macmillan, 1930)
Wister was the author of *The Pentecost of Calamity* (1916), a book on Germany and the European war in which Wister was as opposed to American neutrality and supportive of intervention on behalf of the Allies as his friend Theodore Roosevelt (see also article by J. Mason below on Owen Wister).

Woodress, J. L. *Booth Tarkington: Gentleman from Indiana* (Philadelphia: Lippincott, 1955)

Books

Abrams, R. H. *Preachers Present Arms: The Role of the American Church in World Wars I and II* ... revised edn (Scottsdale, Pa: Herald Press, 1969)

Blakey, G. T. *Historians on the Homefront: American Propagandists for the Great War* (Lexington: University Press of Kentucky, 1970)

Breen, W. J. *Uncle Sam at Home: Civilian Mobilization, Wartime Federalism, and the Council of National Defense, 1917-1919* (Westport, Conn.: Greenwood Press, 1984)

Buitenhuis, P. *The Great War of Words: British, American, and Canadian Propaganda and Fiction, 1914-1933* (Vancouver: University of British Columbia Press, 1987; repr. London: Batsford, 1989)
The 1989 reprint published in London was entitled, *The Great War of Words: Literature As Propaganda 1914-18 And After*

Campbell, C. W. *Reel America and World War I: A Comprehensive Filmography and History of Motion Pictures in the United States, 1914-1920* (Jefferson, N.C.: McFarland, 1985)

Castellan, J. W., and others. *American Cinematographers in the Great War, 1914-1918*, by James W. Castellan, Ron van Dopperren, and Cooper C. Graham (New Barnet: John Libbey Publishing Ltd., 2014)

Creel, G. *How We Advertised America* (New York: Harper & Brothers, 1920; repr. New York: Arno Press, 1972)

Cooperman, S. *World War I and the American Novel* (Baltimore, MD; Johns Hopkins University Press, 1967)

DeBauche, L. M. 'The United States Film Industry and World War One', in *The First World War and Popular Cinema, 1914 to the Present*, edited by M. Paris (Edinburgh: Edinburgh University Press, 1999)

Fleming, T. *The Illusion of Victory: America in World War I* (New York: Basic Books, 2003)

Hutchinson, H. *The War That Used Up Words: American Writers and the First World War* (New Haven; London: Yale University Press, 2015)
"In this provocative study, Hazel Hutchison takes a fresh look at the roles of American writers in helping to shape national opinion and policy during the First World War. From the war's opening salvos in Europe, American writers recognized the impact the war would have on their society and sought out new strategies to express their horror, support, or resignation. By focusing on the writings of Henry James, Edith Wharton, Grace Fallow Norton, Mary Borden, Ellen La Motte, E. E. Cummings, and John Dos Passos, Hutchison examines what it means to be a writer in wartime, particularly in the midst of a conflict characterized by censorship and propaganda. Drawing on original letters and manuscripts, some never before seen by researchers, this book explores how the essays, poetry, and novels of these seven literary figures influenced America's public view of events, from August 1914 through the Paris Peace Conference of 1919, and ultimately set the literary agenda for later, more celebrated texts about the war". [Summary of book provided by the publisher]

Isenberg, M. I. *War on Film: The American Cinema and World War 1, 1914-1941* (Rutherford, NJ: Fairleigh Dickinson University Press, 1980)

Jacobs, L. *The Rise of the American Film: A Critical History* (New York: Teachers College Press, 1967; repr. 1974)

Mock, J. R. and C. Larson. *Words that Won the War: The Story of the Committee on Public Information, 1917-1919* (Princeton, NJ: Princeton University Press, 1939)

Mould, D. H. *American Newsfilm, 1914-1919: The Underexposed War* (New York: Garland, 1983)

Quinn, P. J. *The Conning of America: The Great War and American Popular Literature* (Amsterdam: Rodopi, 2001)

Schaffer, R. *America in the Great War: The Rise of the War-Welfare State* (New York: Oxford University Press, 1991)

Spears, J. *Hollywood: The Golden Era* (London: Yoseloff, 1971)
Contains a chapter entitled 'The Movies of World War I'

Vaughan, S. *Holding Fast the Inner Lines: Democracy, Nationalism, and the Committee on Public Information* (Chapel Hill, NC: University of North Carolina Press, 1980)

Ward, L. W. *The Motion Picture Goes to War: The U.S. Government's Film Effort during World War I* (Ann Arbor: University of Michigan Research Press, 1985)

Wiegand, W. A. *An Active Instrument for Propaganda: The American Public Library During World War I* (New York: Greenwood, 1989)

Articles

Buitenhuis, P. 'Upton Sinclair and the Socialist Response to World War I', *Canadian Review of American Studies*, Summer (1983), 121-30

Lyons, T. J 'Hollywood and World War 1 1914-1918', *Journal of Popular Film*, 1 (1972), 15-30

Mason, J. 'Owen Wister and World War 1: Appeal for Pentecost', *The Pennsylvania Magazine of History and Biography*, 101 (1977), 89-102

Merritt, R. 'D. W. Griffith Directs the Great War: The Making of *Hearts of the World*', *Quarterly Review of Film Studies*, 6 (1981), 45-65

Peet, C. 'Hollywood at War, 1915-1918', *Esquire*, September (1936), 60

Film Documentary

The Moving Picture Boys in the Great War (1975)
Made in the USA. Directed by Larry Ward. This documentary was about the USA in the period just before and during the First World War. In the section on the latter period it shows how movies did much to sway the attitudes of Americans away from peace and neutrality towards support for the war once their country had entered into it. The narrator is the famous newspaper man, Lowell Thomas.

4.2.5 The Media

4.2.5.1 General

Although TV and radio were not available to them in the Great War, propagandists were nevertheless able for their purposes to make use of a wide range of communications media employing print (such as newspapers, magazines, pamphlets, and leaflets) or visual art (such as posters, cartoons, picture postcards, photographs, film, and lantern slides). Advances in technology and organizational techniques and a public which had become a great deal more literate by 1914 enabled a far more efficient use to be made of the various types of media available to influence mass opinion. The use of film in the cinema for the purpose of conveying information of a propagandistic nature was a particularly important innovation as the cinema was by the end of the war attracting audiences of millions. Of all the different types of media capable of influencing public opinion the newspaper and the cinema probably had the greatest individual impacts because of their ability to reach the widest possible audience. To what extent public opinion was influenced by the various media to which it was exposed has been a matter of considerable debate.

Books

Buitenhuis, P. *The Great War of Words: British, American, and Canadian Propaganda and Fiction, 1914-1933* (Vancouver: University of British Columbia Press, 1987; repr. London: Batsford, 1989)
The 1989 reprint published in London was entitled, *The Great War of Words: Literature As Propaganda 1914-18 And After*.

Carke, B. *How The Progress of the War was Chronicled by Pen and Camera* (London: Amalgamated Press, 1919)

Carruthers, S. L. *The Media At War: Communication and Conflict in the Twentieth Century* (Basingstoke: Macmillan, 2000)

Connelly, M. and D. Welch., eds. *War and the Media: Reportage and Propaganda, 1900-2003* (London: Tauris, 2005)

Hiley, N. P. 'The News Media and British Propaganda, 1914-1918', in *Les Sociétes Européenes et la Guerre de 1914-1918*: actes du colloque organisé à Nanterre et à Amiens du 8 au 11 Décembre 1988, publié sous la direction de Jean-Jacques Becker et Stéphane Audoin-Rouzeau (Nanterre: Université de Nanterre, 1990)

Hudson, M. and J. Stanier. *War and the Media*, rev. paperback edn (Stroud: Sutton, 1999)

Pronay, N. 'The News Media at War' in *Propaganda, Politics and Film 1918-45*, ed. by N. Pronay and D. W. Spring (London: Macmillan, 1982)

Articles

Herrick, R. 'The Paper War', *Dial*, 66. (1919), 113-114

Marquis, A. G. 'Words as Weapons. Propaganda in Britain and Germany during the First World War', *Journal of Contemporary History*, 13 (1978), 467-498

Robbs, P. H. 'The Great War: Leaflet Evaluation', *Psywar Society Bulletin*, 8 (1959), 10-12

Smith, A. 'The Pankhursts and the War: Suffrage Magazines and First World War Propaganda', *Women's History*

Review, 12 (2003), 103-118

Wright, D. G. 'The Great War, Government Propaganda and English "Men Of Letters", 1914-16', *Literature and History*, 7 (1978), 70-100

4.2.5.2 Printed Propaganda Material

Books and Pamphlets

A constant stream of printed materials of a propagandistic nature produced for both home and overseas consumption flowed throughout the war from official, semi-official, and unofficial organisations.

In the case of Wellington House, for long the focal point of overseas propaganda during the war, the use of such materials, particularly the pamphlet, represented the main method of propaganda employed in the first half of the war. Among the various type of material in which Wellington House was involved were pamphlets and books written by private individuals of international repute, official publications such as the Bryce Report on German atrocities in Belgium, official white papers, ministerial speeches, messages from the King, and various documentary publications relating to the origins of the war produced by most of the belligerent countries. Use was made of private shipping companies to transport the material in bulk to targeted destinations from where it was the practice to break it up into smaller quantities which were distributed by foreign agents to voluntary patriotic organisations and Anglophile societies, overseas Clubs and patriotic leagues. Diplomatic and consular representatives serving overseas were frequently able to help with the distribution by arranging for pamphlet material to be placed in libraries, station waiting rooms, barber shops and doctors' surgeries where they might be picked up and read. Voluntary organisations in England also helped to distribute pamphlets through their own private mailing lists. By utilising the distribution networks of voluntary organisations and the shipping companies and by making every effort to disguise the official origin of the material distributed Wellington House was able to achieve a high degree of secrecy for its operations and avoid the mistake of causing offence by too blatant a style of propaganda as happened in the case of the methods employed by Germany.

On the home front propaganda was served by a number of organisations - voluntary, semi-official, and official - and all of them employed the pamphlet as one means of disseminating domestic propaganda. Unlike Wellington House the official bodies involved in domestic propaganda, the Parliamentary Recruiting Committee (PRC) and the National War Aims Committee (NWAC), were able to act openly on behalf of the government. The literature they produced could be distributed without restriction via means such as bookshops[120], libraries, and personal contacts or via articles in the press subsequently reprinted as pamphlets. The PRC reached a large number of people through its householders' returns committee which posted material designed to promote recruitment to every household listed in the Parliamentary Register.

During the early stages of the war it was important for British propagandists to show that the enemy, by deliberately launching an unprovoked attack on neighbouring nations, was to blame for the outbreak of war. Germany's violation of Belgian neutrality and its flouting of international law[121] provided the British government with the opportunity to argue a case for its moral justification for entering the war. For the next four years, official British propagandists endeavoured to sustain this occupation of the moral high ground by maintaining a constant flow of pamphlets vilifying the enemy. The vilification of the enemy was especially directed at Germany which was attacked by the propagandists via a number of themes such as those which employed as their targets the Kaiser, German philosophy, attitudes and religion, Prussian militarism, the characteristics of Germany's rule, her use of submarines and zeppelins, the atrocities she had committed, her war aims, and the nature of her peace proposals.

British propagandists did not always feel that they could take the offensive. Some of their propaganda was of a defensive or semi-defensive nature. In the early stages of the war, before British forces became engaged on the continent to the massive extent that the French and Russian armies were[122], strenuous efforts were made to

---

[120] Distribution was aided by commercial concerns - the booksellers W.H. Smith were 'good enough to undertake gratuitously a very extensive distribution through their large organization extending all over the Kingdom'.

[121] Germany subsequently admitted that it had knowingly flouted international law.

[122] It was not until 1916, at the Somme, that the British could undertake a major offensive alone.

prevent this from becoming a matter of concern to the Allies by stressing the magnitude of the overall British war effort[123] as a way of assuring them of Britain's total commitment to the war.

Handling the effects of Britain's blockade policy on neutral countries was a particularly difficult problem and great pains were taken by Britain in its endeavours to justify British activities on the high seas, such as the searching of neutral ships and the seizing of those carrying contraband. Ireland was another area of sensitivity, especially in 1916, following the Easter Rising and the execution of Sir Roger Casement, events which were particularly important to explain satisfactorily to the American people because of their large Irish immigrant population. There was also a concern about the attitudes, particularly those of the USA, to the British Empire and British imperialism. Every effort was made to foster a favourable impression of British imperialism by demonstrating the unity within the British Empire and countering the attempts of the Germans to impair such an impression[124].

The NWAC was established in 1917 with the specific task of galvanizing the home population into believing in the need for a clear-cut victory and for its total commitment, particularly on the part of British industry, to the task of achieving achieve this object. Among the methods for carrying out this task was the traditional one of distributing pamphlets and leaflets on relevant themes. NWAC publications, which also made use of material originally produced by Wellington House for foreign audiences, were, however, more varied in their themes than those sponsored by the voluntary, semi-official, and official propaganda organizations operating early in the war. Included among this NWAC material were pamphlets on ethical issues, cartoons by Raemaekers, and pamphlets by Allied journalists and writers about England. There were fewer pamphlets vilifying Germany, a reflection perhaps of the entry of the USA into the war and the reduced need, therefore, to win the battle for neutral opinion, but there was an increase in the number of pamphlets relating to British war efforts. There were a number of new themes including German anti-semitism and anti-catholicism, and Germany's intentions if she won the war. Ironically, however, in view of its name, war aims did not figure prominently in NWAC pamphlets at first and it was not until Lloyd George's war aims speech in January 1918 that this became a major propaganda theme. As the war entered its final phase the focus of British propaganda switched to concerns with preserving Allied unity in relation to war aims and peace terms.

Representative examples of some of the main themes on which propagandists wrote are provided below. Most of these examples represent material commissioned and distributed by Wellington House (the major source of such publications for most of the war) and NWAC, but also included are examples representative of the publications of the Parliamentary Recruiting Committee (PRC) and the Central Committee for National Patriotic Organizations (CCNPO) and of unofficial voluntary groups such as the Oxford historians (who produced the famous Oxford Pamphlets), the Cobden Club, the Victoria League, the Fight for Right Movement, the Council of Loyal British Subjects of British, Austrian, and Hungarian Birth, and the Overseas-Club.

A *Schedule of Wellington House Literature* (1918), which is a comprehensive list of Wellington House's printed publications, can be found in the Imperial War Museum's Department of Documents (IWM, 79/492)

- **American Attitudes** (see also section **4.2.4.4 The United States Contribution to the Propaganda Campaign**)

A number of Americans of their own accord produced favourable propaganda material, good use of which was made by Wellington House by their promotion of its wide distribution. There also developed an official policy of commissioning whenever possible neutral, and preferably American, writers such as Morton Prince (e.g his *The Psychology of the Kaiser*), to produce material for pamphlets relating to such issues as the violation of the Belgian neutrality, the British contribution to the Allied war effort and other propaganda subjects. The production by Americans of propaganda favourable to the Allied cause was particularly fostered and aided by the use made of the Foreign Office's News Department to supply news, views, and facilities to American journalists with a view to enabling them to write their own articles, books and pamphlets rather than providing them with ready made and obvious propaganda.

---

[123] By stressing the extent of her contribution in relation not only to her armed services (particularly those of the British Navy) but also to her financial expenditure and industrial efforts, especially in the production of munitions.

[124] The German propagandists tried to inflict such damage by, for example, stressing the significance of the nationalist movement in India and disparaging British rule there as corrupt.

Among the considerable number of Americans unofficially writing sympathetically about the Allies or unfavourably about Germany were several novelists. Novelists writing in this vein were, for example, well-known writers like Upton Sinclair (e.g. his novel, *Jimmie Higgins*) and Booth Tarkington (e.g. his novel, *Ramsey Milholland*). As well as publishing the writings of Americans who were pro-Allied or hostile towards Germany some American publishers were quite happy to promote the pro-British propaganda of English writers as was the case, for example, with the publication of Ian Hay's *Getting Together* and Mrs. Humphrey Ward's *England's Effort* and *Towards the Goal* (see records below).

There were also Americans living abroad who were quite happy to express their pro-Allied views. In this respect the novelists Edith Wharton (e.g. her *Fighting France*, and *The Book of the Homeless*) and Henry James (e.g. his *Within the Rim, and other Essays, 1914-1915*) were particularly influential, the latter writer especially so because of his reputation both in Europe and America.

Atherton, G. F. H. *Life in the War Zone* (New York: New York Times for the benefit of Le Bienêtre du Blessé, Société Franco-Americaine pour nos Combattants, 1916)
Based on a series of propaganda articles the author wrote for the *New York Times*.

Barstow, G. E. *Shall Democracy Endure - in the United States?* (Barstow, Texas: Privately Printed, 1916)
Chides the USA for not emerging from its isolationist shell by coming out against Germany and joining the Allied cause.

Beck J. M. *America and the Allies*, address given by James M. Beck at a meeting of the [Society of] Pilgrims, on Wednesday, July 5th, 1916, at the Savoy Hotel, London (London: Jordan-Gaskell Ltd., 1916)
Beck was at that time a US Congressman. With the encouragement of Gilbert Parker, the Society of Pilgrims rolled out the red carpet for Beck when he visited England in 1916.

Beck, J. M. *The Case of Edith Cavell: A Study of the Rights of Non-Combatants* (New York; London: Putnam's, 1916)
A reply to the German Foreign Office which, as Beck writes, had "in its official apology for the crime, issued over the signature of Herr Doctor Albert Zimmermann, Under Secretary of Foreign Affairs" expressed surprise "that the shooting of an Englishwoman and the condemnation of several women in Brussels for treason have caused a sensation". Reprinted from the *New York Times* in nearly every language of the civilized nations and over a million copies of it were published.

— *The Enemy Within our Gates. An address, Delivered by James M. Beck, at Carnegie Hall, November 2, 1917 to Protest against the Spirit of Disloyalty* (New York: American Defense Society, 1917)
A criticism of William Randolph Hearst.

— *The Evidence in the Case: A Discussion of the Moral Responsibility for the War of 1914, as Disclosed by the Diplomatic Records of England, Germany, Russia, France, and Belgium*, rev. edn., with additional material (New York; London: Putnam's, 1915)
Reprint of Beck's article in the *New York Times* of October 25th, 1915.

— *The War and Humanity: A Further Discussion of the Ethics of the World War and the Attitude and Duty of the United States* (New York; London: G.P. Putnam's Sons, 1916)

Bigelow, P. *An American's Opinion of British Colonial Policy* (London: Darling, 1915)
Reprinted from from the *New York Times*.

Church, S. H. *The American Verdict on the War: A Reply to the Appeal to the Civilized World of 93 German Professors* (Baltimore: Norman, Remington, Co., 1915)
Also published London: The Times Publishing Co., 1915.

Clarke, G. H. *Why The United States of America Entered the War* (New York; London: Hodder & Stoughton, 1917)
Clarke was a Professor in the University of Tennessee. Includes the address which President Wilson delivered at a joint session of the two Houses of Congress on April 2nd, 1917.

Hay, I., pseud. [i.e. John Hay Beith]. *Getting Together* (Boston: Doubleday, Page & Co., 1917)
Essays on the attitude of the United States of America towards Great Britain in the European War. Also published London: Hodder & Stoughton, 1917.

James, H. *England at War: An Essay; The Question of the Mind* (London: Central Committee for National Patriotic Organisations , [1914]).

— *Within the Rim, and other Essays, 1914-1915* (London: Collins, 1918; repr. Freeport (N.Y.): Books for Libraries, 1968)
The titles of the essays are as follows: *Within the Rim* (previously published in the *Fortnightly Review*, August 1917); *Refugees in Chelsea* (previously published in the *Times Literary Supplement*, March 23, 1916); *The American Volunteer Motor-Ambulance Corps in France* (previously issued as a pamphlet in 1914); *France* (previously published in 1915 by Macmillan in *The Book of France*, edited by Winifred Stephens); *The Long Wards* (previously published in 1916 by Macmillan in *The Book of the Homeless*, edited by Edith Wharton).

Johnson, D. W. *My German Correspondence Concerning Germany's Responsibility for the War and for the Method of its Conduct*: being a letter from a German professor together with a reply and foreword (New York: George H. Doran Co., 1917)

— *Plain Words from America: A Letter to a German Professor* (London; New York: Hodder & Stoughton, 1917)
"Appeared in the *Revue de Paris* of September, 1916" – Publisher's note. The American edition of *Plain Words from America* has title *My German Correspondence* (George H. Doran Co., N.Y., 1917) and contains also *The Letter from a German Professor*.

Page, W. H. *The Union of Two Great Peoples* (London; New York: Hodder & Stoughton, 1917)
A speech delivered by W. H. Page (while American ambassador to England) at Plymouth on August 4th, 1917.

Philosophus. *War: What is England Doing?* by Philosophus (an English ranchman in New Mexico, U.S.) (London: J. Truscott, 1916)
"This pamphlet was originally written on a ranch in New Mexico, and published at Las Vegas, New Mexico, by the Optic publishing company" [quotation from Introduction to the work]. It achieved extensive circulation in the USA through the efforts of Sir Gilbert Parker (who also provided the Introduction for it) as a result of its being sent to him, unsolicited, by a friend of the author together with a sum of money to defray the cost of its printing and distribution.

Prince, M. *The American Versus the German View of the War.* (London: Fisher Unwin, 1915)
Originally appeared as two articles written for the *Boston Post* February 7 and 14, 1915

— *The Psychology of the Kaiser: Study of his Sentiments and his Obsessions* (Boston: R. C. Badger, 1915)
Also published, London: Fisher Unwin, 1915

Roosevelt, T. *America and the World War* (New York: Scribner's, 1915)
"Substantially reproduced from articles contributed to the Wheeler syndicate and also to the *Outlook*, the *Independent*, and *Everybody's*." - foreword pp. x-xi. Also published, London: John Murray, 1915.

Sinclair, U. *Jimmie Higgins: A Story* (London: Hutchinson, 1918)
Also published New York: Boni and Liveright, 1919.

Sixty American Opinions on the War. [Edited by S. R. H. and J. F. M.] (London: T. Fisher Unwin, 1915)
A compilation of extracts from books and articles, private letters and letters to newspapers written by Americans prominent in the arts, universities, politics, business, and journalism, generally expressing sympathy for the Allies via opinions ranging from wanting the United States to enter the war immediately on the side of the Allies to advocating neutrality but holding Germany responsible for beginning the war and destroying Belgium. The collection, publication, and distribution of these extracts was covertly instigated by Wellington House. The editors of the compilation were Samuel Robertson Honey and James Fullerton Muirhead who were both born in Britain but became American citizens.

Stephens, W. *The Book of France: In Aid of the French Parliamentary Committee's Fund for the Relief of the Invaded Departments* (London: Macmillan, 1915)

Tarkington, N. B. *Ramsey Milholland* (London: Hutchinson, 1919)
Written in early 1918. Before its publication in book form this novel was turned down by *Collier's* because it was considered too propagandistic but was later published by the *Saturday Evening Post*, a journal that was eager throughout the war to publish pro-Allied material. Also published, Garden City, New York : Doubleday, Page & Co., 1919.

Tatlock, J. S. P. *Why America Fights Germany* (Washington, D.C.: Committee on Public Information, 1918)

Walker, J. B. *America Fallen! The Sequel to the European War: The Germans Sack New York.* (New York: Dodd,

Mead & Co., 1915)
Also published London: Putnam's, 1915.

Ward, Mrs Humphrey [i.e. Mary Augusta Ward] *England's Effort: Six Letters to an American Friend* (New York: Scribner's, 1916)
Her two propaganda works, *England's* Effort and *Towards the Goal* are in the form of letters to Theodore Roosevelt, a personal friend. Also published London, Smith, Elder, 1916.

— *Towards the Goal: A Woman's Letters from the Front* (New York: Scribner's, 1917)
Also published London: John Murray, 1917.

Wharton, E. *Fighting France, From Dunkerque to Belfort* (New York: Appleton-Century, 1915)
Also published London: Macmillan, 1915.

Wharton, E., ed. *The Book of the Homeless* (New York: Scribner's 1916)
A literary anthology containing contributions solicited and published by Edith Wharton for the purpose of raising funds for the hostels and charity organisations involved in the relief of refugees from Belgium and Flanders. The contributions are mostly anti-German. Also published London: Macmillan, 1915.

White, J. W. *America's Arraignment of Germany.* [Concerning the causes of the Great War] (London: Harrap, 1915)
White was a Professor at the University of Pennsylvania.

Wister, O. *The Pentecost of Calamity* (New York, London: Macmillan, 1916)
In this book on Germany and the European war Wister became as opposed to American neutrality and supportive of intervention on behalf of the Allies as his friend Theodore Roosevelt. An earlier text published in the *Saturday Evening Post* (vol 188, July 3 1915) was much more restrained in its criticism of the American administration's policy of neutrality; it was as a result of the influence of his friend Theodore Roosevelt that Wister made some additions to the proofs of his book which made it far more critical of that policy. This book was widely distributed and made a considerable impression. A large part of this distribution and consequent success was through the initiative of Wellington House.

- **Atrocities**

Among the range of subjects treated in the corpus of atrocity propaganda were those relating to the 'rape' of Belgium, deportations, massacres, destruction of places of worship and works of art, ill-treatment of prisoners, mistreatment of natives in East Africa, and, in a somewhat different category, the use of poison gas, unrestricted submarine warfare, and war waged on civilians via Zeppelin raids and the shelling of the English coast. Occasionally atrocities were totally fabricated, such as the rumours which circulated in 1917 about German corpse conversion factories. Germany itself provided much of the raw material for British propaganda by actions which lent themselves to propagandistic attacks (e.g. the coining of the Lusitania medal[125], the nature of its submarine warfare, the attacks on civilian targets, and frequent misjudgement of international reaction as in the cases of the sinking of the *Lusitania* and the executions of Edith Cavell and Captain Fryatt).

One of the NWAC's most successful productions was the 'German Crimes' calendar on which was depicted an enemy atrocity for each month of the year with the actual date of each 'crime against humanity' circled in red. The calendar featured 'crimes' relating to Belgium (the arrest and imprisonment of Cardinal Mercier; the burning of Louvain; the execution of nurse Edith Cavell; and the deportations of Belgian and French workers), U-Boat activities (including the sinking of the *Lusitania* and the *Ancona*, the torpedoing of British hospital ships and the execution of Captain Fryatt, a merchant navy officer who had tried to ram a German submarine), attacks on civilians (the bombardment of Scarborough, Zeppelin raids) and the Turkish massacre of Armenians at Bitlis (German guilt by association).

Archer, W. *The Pirate's Progress: A Short History of the U-Boat* (London: Chatto & Windus, 1918)

Aston, Sir G. G. *The Triangle of Terror in Belgium,* (London: John Murray, 1918)

---

[125] The medal was designed by Karl Goetz as a justification of the sinking of the Lusitania. In conjunction with the 300,000 copies of the medal that were struck and distributed on the instructions of Captain Reginald Hall, RN, Britain's Director of Naval Intelligence, British propagandists were, by representing it an unfavourable and misleading way, able to exploit it with considerable success as part of their anti-German propaganda campaign.

The War Years

Bedier, C. M. J. *How Germany Seeks to Justify Her Atrocities* (Paris: Colin, 1915)

British Civilian Prisoners in German East Africa: A Report by the Government Committee on the Treatment by the Enemy of British Prisoners of War (London: Printed by Messrs. Alabaster, Passmore & Sons, Ltd., 1918)

A Corpse-Conversion Factory: A Peep Behind the German Lines (London: Darling, 1917)

The Death of Edith Cavell (London: Daily News and Leader, 1915)

Frightfulness in Retreat (London: Hodder & Stoughton, 1917)
An account of the devastation caused by the German Army in the retreat from the Somme, with translations of the Proceedings in the Frence Senate, March 31, 1917, and of the official report of the French Commission.

Great Britain. Committee of Inquiry into Alleged German Outrages. *Report of the Committee on Alleged German Outrages Appointed by His Britannic Majesty's Government and Presided over by the Right Hon. Viscount Bryce*, Cmnd 7894 (London: HMSO, 1915)

— *The Evidence and Documents Laid Before the Committee on Alleged German Outrages*, Cmnd 7895 (London: HMSO, 1915)
Appendix to the separately published *Report of the Committee on Alleged German Outrages* (q.v.)

Great Britain. Committee on the Treatment by the Enemy of British Prisoners of War. *The Horrors of Wittenberg: Official Report to the British Government*, by Sir R. Younger (Chairman) (London: Pearson, 1916)
Report of the Committee on the conditions in Wittenberg Camp.

The Horrors of Louvain, by an eyewitness (London: Sunday Times, 1916)

Hurd, A. *Murder at Sea* (London: Fisher Unwin, 1916)
About the sinking of civilian ships by German U-boats.

Maclean, F. *Towards Extermination: Germany's Treatment of the African Native* (St. Albans: Campfield Press, 1918)

Microbe-Culture at Bukarest: Discoveries at the German Legation, from the Rumanian Official Documents. (London: Hodder & Stoughton, 1917)

Morgan, J. H. *A Dishonoured Army: German Atrocities in France* (London: Spottiswoode, 1915)
Reprinted from *Nineteenth Century*, June 1915

— *Germany's Dishonoured Army: Additional Records of German Atrocities in France* (London: Parliamentary Recruiting Committee, 1915)

The Murder of Captain Fryatt (London: Hodder & Stoughton, 1916)

Toynbee, A. J. *Armenian Atrocities: The Murder of a Nation*, with a speech delivered by Lord Bryce in the House of Lords (London: Hodder & Stoughton, 1915)

— *The Murderous Tyranny of the Turks: Joint Note of the Allied Governments in Answer to President Wilson* (London: Hodder & Stoughton, 1917)
In this book Toynbee is referring to the Allies's response of January 11th 1917 to President Wilson's note "to all the belligerent governments", calling "upon both parties to state in the full light of day the aims they have set themselves in prosecuting the War".

The War on Hospital Ships, from the narratives of eye-witnesses (London: T. Fisher Unwin, Ltd., 1917)

Whitlock, B. *The Deportations: Statement by the American Minister to Belgium* (Brand Whitlock) (London: Fisher Unwin, 1917)
Report of the United States Legation to Belgium. Brand Whitlock served as U.S. Ambassador to Belgium during World War I.

Wilson, H. W. *Convicted out of Her Own Mouth: The Record of German Crimes*, repr. from the *National Review*, 1917

(London: Hodder & Stoughton, 1917)

- **Blockade**

Britain's blockade policy inevitably involved controversial actions such as the searching of neutral ships, and the seizing of those carrying contraband. Such actions ran the risk of alienating neutral countries, for which reason Britain did everything within its power to justify them (particularly in relation to the USA).

Balfour, A. J., Earl of Balfour. *The British Blockade* (London: Darling, 1915)

Cecil, R., 1st Viscount Cecil of Chelwood. *Black List and Blockade: Interview with the Rt. Hon. Lord Robert Cecil in Reply to the Swedish Prime Minister* (London: Eyre & Spottiswoode, 1916)

De Chair, Sir D. R. S. *How the British Blockade Works: An Interview with Rear-Admiral Sir Dudley de Chair* (London: Causton, 1916)
Interview by Henry Suydam, London correspondent of the *Brooklyn Eagle*.

Grey, E., 1st Viscount Grey of Fallodon. *Great Britain's Measures against German Trade: A Speech Delivered by the Rt. Hon. Sir E. Grey, Secretary of State for Foreign Affairs, in the House of Commons, on the 26th January 1916* (London: Hodder & Stoughton, 1916)

Headlam, J. W. *The Starvation of Germany* (London: Hodder Stoughton, 1917)
Justification of the British blockade against protestations by the German chancellor.

Hume-Williams, W. E. *International Law and the Blockade.* (London: Causton, 1916)
Reprinted from the *New York Herald*.

Low, A. M.. *The Law of Blockade.* (London: Causton, 1916)
Reprinted from the *New York Herald*.

Milner, A., Viscount. *Cotton Contraband* (London: Darling & Son, 1915)
An interview between Lord Milner and the London correspondent of the *New York Times* published in the *New York Times*, August 22, 1915, under the title of *Justifies Making Cotton Contraband*.

Sprigg, W. S.. *The British Blockade: What it Means, How it Works* (London: Dibblee, 1917)
Reprinted from *Pearson's Magazine*.

- **British Attitudes**

The pamphlets below are selected examples of pamphlets indicative of the support for the war in all walks of British life. These type of pamphlets were produced for the purpose of creating a favourable impression not only on the home front and among Britain's allies but also among neutral nations.

Appleton, W. A. *The Workers' Resolve* (London: Fisher Unwin, 1917)
An interview with W.A. Appleton by Joseph W. Grigg of the *New York World*.

Bryce, J. W., Viscount Bryce of Dechmont. *The Attitude of Great Britain in the Present War* (London: Macmillan, 1916)

Caine, H. *Our Girls: Their Work for the War* (London: Hutchinson, 1916)

Cohn, A. *Some Aspects of the War As Viewed by Naturalized British Subjects* (London: Council of Loyal British Subjects of British, Austrian, and Hungarian Birth, 1916)

Crooks, W. *The British Workman Defends His Home* (London: Whitwell Press, 1917)

Hard, W. *How the English Take the War* (London: Hodder & Stoughton, 1917)
Reprinted from the *Metropolitan*, New York.

Law, A. B. *"A United Nation": A Speech on the War*, delivered in London on December 14th, 1914, by the Rt. Hon A. Bonar Law, M.P. (London: Parliamentary Recruiting Committee, 1914)

Seddon, J. A. *Why British Labour Supports the War* (London: Gill, 1917)

Walker, J. *Parsons and War, and Other Essays in Wartime* (Bradford: Reformers' Bookshop, 1917)

Wile, F. W. *Explaining the Britishers: The Story of the British Empire's Mighty Effort in Liberty's Cause*. Written by an American for American soldiers and sailors (London: Heinemann, 1918)

- **British War Effort**

A considerable amount of the propaganda in this field was aimed at neutral nations with the USA particularly being selected as a target. Squires in his work, *British Propaganda at Home and in The United States from 1914 To 1917*, cites the pamphlets listed below by Fisher, Philosophus, Noyes, Parker, and Revelstoke together with the anonymous pamphlets, *What is Great Britain doing?* and *How Long Will It Last?* as examples of propaganda circulated in the USA for the purpose of conveying "in popular and non-technical form the real immensity of Britain's war effort, and to give the American public the impression that no puny nation was engaged in the struggle with Germany, but a vigorous giant with whom association and partnership would be at once a satisfaction and an accomplishment".

British propagandists also came to realize that it was necessary to impress the Allies as well as neutral nations with the extent of Britain's war effort, in view of the doubts about it that had occasionally been raised in the French and Russian press during the first half of the war. It was for this reason that Wellington House widened its brief to include allies as well as neutral countries as a target for its propaganda operations.

Addison, C. A., Viscount. *British Workshops and the War* (London: Fisher Unwin, 1917)
A speech delivered in the House of Commons on June 28, 1917

Anderson, J. and G. Bruce. *Flying, Submarining, and Mine-Sweeping.* (London: 1916)
Pamphlet composed of four articles, two by Jane Anderson, *Looping the Loop over London*, and *The Submarine At Work* (the former published in the *Daily Mail* and the *New York Tribune*, the latter in *the Daily Mail* and the *New York Sun*) and two by Gordon Bruce, *The Flying Corps* and *Mine Sweeping*, which were published in the *New York Tribune* and many newspapers in Great Britain.

Balfour, A. J., Earl of Balfour. *The Navy and the War: (August, 1914, to August, 1915)* (London: Darling, 1915)
Consists of a letter from Mr. Balfour to Mr. Tuohy of the *New York World*, in response to a derogatory communication from Count Ersnt zu Reventlow (one of the principal propagandists of the Berlin "Marineamt") about the British naval fleet and its activities.

Blood and Treasure: Facts and Figures of Britain's Effort, 1914-17 (London: Hayman, Christy & Lilly, 1918)

Buchan, J., 1st Baron Tweedsmuir. *The Battle of the Somme*, 2 vols (London: Nelson, 1916-1917)

Churchill, Sir W. *The Munitions Miracle* (London: National War Aims Committee, 1917)
Speech delivered in the House of Commons, April 25 1918. Published as No. 1 of the National War Aims Committee's *British Effort Series*.

Cook, Sir E. T. and Villiers M. E., eds. *Britain's Part in the War* (London: Victoria League, 1917)

Davies, E. F. *The Finances of Great Britain and Germany* (London: Fisher Unwin, 1916)

Dixon, W. M.. *The British Navy at War* (London: Heinemann, 1917)

Fisher, H. A. L. *The British Share in the War* (London: Nelson, 1915)

Masterman, C. F. G. *The Triumph of the Fleet* (London: Darling, 1915)
Reprinted from the London journal, *Nation*.

Noyes, A. *What is England Doing?* (London: Burrup, Mathieson & Sprague, 1916)

Parker, Sir G. *Is England Apathetic?: A Reply* (London: Darling, 1915)
Originally published in the *New York Times* on the first anniversary of the declaration of war.

Philosophus. *War: What is England Doing?* by Philosophus (an English ranchman in New Mexico, U.S.) (London: J. Truscott, 1916)

Revelstoke, J. B., 2nd Baron. *British Staying Power: Lord Revelstoke's Views. Anglo-American Sympathies.* Interview given to the United Press of America (London: Causton, 1916)

- **The Empire**

One of the main objects of the propaganda in this area was to demonstrate the idea that all the constituent parts of the British Empire were unified in the common cause of defeating the enemy. At a time when Irish and Indian nationalism seemed to be posing a serious threat to imperial integrity there developed an awareness of the need to bolster the image of the Empire, as was evident, for example, when the British Empire Union was created in 1915 'to inculcate a greater interest in and knowledge of the Empire' (an object which it sought to achieve by fostering the teaching of imperial history in schools and encouraging the celebrations of Empire Day on a more widespread scale). Furthermore, as Lasswell pointed out in his study, *Propaganda Technique in the World War*: 'in order to illustrate the unity of the Empire a number of profusely illustrated volumes[126] were put out, showing the history of British beneficence and the degree of Empire co-operation at the front in order to illustrate the unity of the Empire and the contribution of colonial troops'. This propaganda was considerably aided by popular writers who published adventures novels in which the war was linked to imperial themes of loyalty to the King and Empire (e.g. see Mundy, Kipling below)

Imperial themes enabled propagandists to compensate for the stalemate on the Western Front by giving them the opportunity to highlight more positive aspects of the war (as, for example, Britain's naval superiority and the victories in Africa) and to replace the bleakness of the Western Front with images of 'colourful' peoples and 'exotic' locations.

Basu, B. N. *Why India is Heart and Soul with Great Britain* (London: Macmillan, 1914)

Bean, C. E. W., ed. *The Anzac Book*. Written and illustrated in Gallipoli by the men of Anzac (London: Cassell, 1916)

Beaverbrook, W. M. A., 1st Baron. *Canada in Flanders: The Official Story of the Canadian Expeditionary Force*. With a preface by the Rt. Hon. A. Bonar Law ... and an introduction by the Rt. Hon. Sir R. Borden, 3 vols (London: Hodder & Stoughton, 1916-1918)
Vol. 3 by Charles D.G. Roberts.

Bhownaggree, Sir M. M. *The Verdict of India* (London: Hodder & Stoughton, 1916)

Bevan, E. *Brothers All: The War and the Race Question* (London: Oxford University Press, 1914)
The imperial war effort is seen as symbolizing Christian unity.

Borden, Sir R. L. and J. C. Smuts. *The Voice of the Dominions: Addresses by Sir Robert Borden ... and Lt.-Gen. J. C. Smuts* (London: Empire Parliamentary Association, 1917)
Published in the Empire Parliamentary Association's series, *The Empire at War*.

Canada in Khaki. A tribute to the officers and men now serving in the Canadian Expeditionary Force, 3 vols (London: Published for the Canadian War Records Office by Pictorial Newspaper Co., 1917-19)

Clarke, G. S. 1st Baron Sydenham. *India and the War* (London: Hodder & Stoughton, 1915)

Hardinge, C., Baron Hardinge of Penshurst. *Loyal India: An Interview with Lord Hardinge of Penshurst, ex-Viceroy and Governor-General of India*, by the London correspondent of the *New York Times* (London: Hodder & Stoughton,

---

[126] Such as *India and the War*, and literary anthologies like *The Anzac Book*, *Canada in Khaki* and *Indian Ink*.

1916)

Indian Ink, being splashes from various pens in aid of the Imperial Indian War Fund, edited by Everard Digby [and subsequently C. H. Turner] (Calcutta: Thacker, Spink, 1914-17)
Contains war anecdotes, stories, rhymes, cartoons, etc. relating mainly to the Indian contribution to the war. Published each year in various editions.

Kipling, R. *The Eyes of Asia* (Garden City, N.Y: Doubleday, Page, 1918)
Fiction. "A series of letters purporting to be written by an East Indian officer wounded in France to his relatives at home" [*New York Times Book Review*, Oct. 20, 1918].

Muir, J. R. B. *The Character of the British Empire* (London: Constable, 1917)

Mundy, T. *King of the Khyber Rifles* (Indianapolis: Bobbs-Merrill, 1916; repr. London: Constable, 1916)
Fiction

Poynder, J. P. D., Baron Islington. *Some Facts About India: Interviews with Lord Islington during November, 1916*, by Robert Sloss (London: Burrup, Mathieson & Sprague, 1917)

Sinha, Sir S. P. *The Future of India: Presidential Address to the Indian National Congress* (London: Truscott, 1916)

- **Germany**

The vilification of Germany (in some cases presented in a purely satirical fashion) encompassed a variety of propaganda targets such as atrocities, the Kaiser, German philosophy, attitudes and religion, Prussian militarism, the characteristics of Germany's rule, her use of submarines and zeppelins, her war aims, and the nature of her peace proposals. The considerable number of pamphlets which examined German philosophies were usually produced with the object of showing how the warlike emphasis traceable within them had the effect of paving the way for the war.

Archer, W. *The Villain of the World Tragedy: A Letter to Professor Ulrich v. Wilamowitz Möllendorf* [in reply to his War Addresses] (London: Fisher Unwin, 1916)

Barker, Sir E. *Nietzsche and Treitschke: The Worship of Power in Modern Germany*, Oxford Pamphlets, 20 (Oxford: Oxford University Press, 1914)

Benson, F. L. *Deutschland über Allah* (London: Hodder & Stoughton, 1917)
One of "a series of vigorously written pamphlets" representative of some of the wartime publications for which the *Overseas-Club* was "responsible" ([quotes from J. D. Squires, *British Propaganda at Home and in the United States from 1914 To 1917*, p. 18].

Boulger, D. C. *England's Arch-Enemy*, a collection of essays forming an indictment of German policy during the last sixteen years (London: The author, 1914)

Central Committee For National Patriotic Organisations. *The German Hymn of Hate*, Central Committee leaflet, 112 (London: Thomas and Page (printers), n.d.)

Cook, Sir T. A. *The Mark of the Beast* (London: John Murray, 1917)

Dawson, W. H. *The German Danger and the Working Man* (London: The Central Committee for National Patriotic Organisations, n.d.)

French, Sir. J. *The Germans and the Small Nations: An Interview with Lord French*, by E. P Bell (London: Keliher, 1917)

Germany and the Prussian Spirit (London: Macmillan, 1914)
Reprinted from the special war number of the *Round Table*, Sept. 1914.

Gray, A. *The True Pastime: Some Observations on the German Attitude towards War* (London: Methuen, 1915)

Harrison, A. T. *The Kaiser's War* (George Alien & Unwin, 1914)

Hope, A. *Militarism: German and British* (London: Darling, 1915)
Hope's reply to two articles in the Washington post of Dec. 19 and 20, 1914 in which the author of them disparagingly argues that "there is no distinction to be made between German and British militarism".

Köedt, P. *English and German Culture* (London: Cobden Club, 1915)
"The Cobden Club … put forth several bulletins purporting to show that England deserved victory since her cultural superiority was obviously above that of Germany" [quote from J. D. Squires, *British Propaganda at Home and in the United States from 1914 To 1917*, p. 18]. Squires cites the publication by Köedt as a sample of one of these.

Lucas, E. V. *In Gentlest Germany*, by Hun Svedend. Translated from the Svengalese by E. V. Lucas. With 45 illustrations and 1 map by George Morrow (London: Lane, 1915)
A skit on *With the German Armies in the West* by Sven Hedin.

— *Swollen-headed William: Painful Stories and Funny Pictures after the German!* Text adapted by E. V. Lucas; drawings adapted by G. Morrow (London: Methuen, 1914)
A satire upon the Kaiser William II based on H. Hoffmann's *Struwwelpeter*.

Sheehan, P. P. and R. H. Davis. 'Blood and Iron: A play in One Act, by Porley Poore Sheehan and Robt. H. Davis. Illustrated by Steven Spurrin ', *Strand Magazine*, 54 (1917), 359-365 (October 1917)
" … Blood and Iron was first published in August 1917 in the US fiction Periodical, McClure's Magazine, under the title 'Efficiency'. It is probable that Sheehan and Davis sold the play to the Strand Magazine in the UK after (and possibly because) it had been bought for US publication in McClure's … it would seem that the *Strand* actively encouraged an anti-German presentation of this play – a common line to take in wartime – to avoid a legal charge [under DORA] of the play's anti-war message causing 'disaffection' … [by commissioning] the British war artist Steven Spurrier to illustrate the play with anti-German propaganda". [Quotation extracted from Macdonald's article, 'The First Cyborg', *History Today*, 66:5 (2016), 31-36 **(q.v. in section 4.2.4.2.)**]

Younghusband, Sir F. E. *For the Right: Essays and Addresses by members of the "Fight for right Movement"*, with a preface by Sir Francis Younghusband (London: T. F. Unwin, [1916])
"The series of addresses at King's college, University of London, which are here reprinted, were organized by the Fight for right movement." - Pref.

- **Ireland**

Owing to the USA's large Irish immigrant population it was recognised that the subject of Ireland was a particularly sensitive area requiring a very careful approach, especially after the Easter Rising and the execution of Sir Roger Casement. While no doubt Wellington House was accordingly very concerned to prevent this problem from becoming internationally damaging, it did nevertheless allow the publication of pamphlets that were semi-critical of Britain's handling of Ireland as long as their conclusions were on balance favourable to Britain (see the asterisked items listed blow). Every effort was also made, of course, to publish material that presented relations between Britain and Ireland in a favourable light.

England, Germany and the Irish Question, by an English Catholic (London: Hodder & Stoughton, 1917) *

Kerr, S. P. *What The Irish Regiments Have Done*, with a diary of a visit to the Front by John E. Redmond, M.P (London: Fisher Unwin, 1916)

Lavery, F., comp. *Irish Heroes in War*, foreword by John E. Redmond, M.P. (London: Everett, 1917)
Also includes *The Irish in Great Britain*, by T. P. O'Connor M.P.; *The Tyneside Irish Brigade*, by Joseph Keating.

Law, H. A. *Why is Ireland at War?* (London: Maunsel, 1915) *
A 2nd edition was published in Dublin by Maunsel in 1916.

Macdonagh, M. *The Irish at the Front 1916*, with an introduction by John Redmond (London: Hodder & Stoughton, 1916)

— *The Irish on the Somme*: being the second series of "The Irish at the Front", by Michael MacDonagh, with an introduction by John Redmond (London: Hodder & Stoughton, 1917)

Redmond, J. *Ireland and the War*, extracts from speeches made in the House of Commons and in Ireland since the outbreak of the war, by J. E. Redmond, M.P., Chairman, Irish Parliamentary Party (Dublin: Sealy, Bryers & Walker, 1915)

— *The Voice of Ireland*, being an interview with John Redmond, M.P., and some messages from representative Irishmen Regarding the Sinn Fein Rebellion (London: Nelson, 1916)

Rolleston, T. W. *Ireland and Poland: A Comparison* (London: T. Fisher Unwin, 1917)

- **Moral Justification**

During the early stages of the war it was important for British propagandists to show that the enemy, as a result of deliberately flouting international law by launching an unprovoked attack on France and in the process violating Belgian neutrality, was to blame for the outbreak of war. This provided the British government with the opportunity to argue a case for its moral justification for entering the war. For the rest of the war, official British propagandists made every effort to sustain this occupation of the moral high ground.

Aston, Sir G. *The Triangle of Terror in Belgium* (London: Murray, 1918)

Bryce, J. W., Viscount Bryce of Dechmont. *The Last Phase in Belgium*. Statement by Viscount Bryce, on the Belgian deportations, made in reply to a letter from the representative of the New York "Tribune" (London: Speaight, 1917)

Cook, Sir E. T. *Britain and the Small Nations: Her Principles and Her Policy*, Victoria League Leaflets, 5 (London: Printed for the Victoria League by Wyman & Sons, [1915?])

— *How Britain Strove For Peace: A Record of Anglo-German Negotiations 1898-1914*, told from authoritative sources (London: Macmillan, 1914)

Davignon, H. *Belgium and Germany*. Texts and documents preceded by a foreword by Henri Davignon (London: Nelson, 1915)

Destrée, J. *Belgium and the Principle of Nationality*; translated by H. Clay. (London: Council for the Study of International Relations, 1916)

Germany Condemned by her own Ambassador (London: National War Aims Committee, 1918)

Grondys, L. H. *The Germans in Belgium: Experiences of a Neutral* (London: Heinemann, 1915)

Gwatkin, H. M. *Britain's Case against Germany: A Letter to a Neutral*, by the late Rev. H. M. Gwatkin (London: 1917)
Reply to a letter written to the author by a Swedish clergyman. Reprinted from the *Nation*, October 14th, 1916.

Lichnowsky, K. M., Fürst von. *My Mission to London: Revelations of the Last German Ambassador in England*, with a preface by Gilbert Murray (London: Cassell, 1918)

Massingham, H. W. *Why We Came to Help Belgium* (London: Harrison, 1914)
Reprinted from the *Nation*, 3rd October, 1914.

Mears, E. G. *The Destruction of Belgium: Germany's Confession and Avoidance* (A reply to the German White Book on the conduct of the German troops in Belgium.) (London: Heinemann, 1916)

Murray, G. *How Can War Ever Be Right?*, Oxford Pamphlets 1914-1915, 18 (London: Oxford University Press, 1914)
In this pamphlet, which he wrote for the Oxford series, Murray, although a former neutralist, supports Britain's entry into the war because, in spite of the fact that he was able to 'sympathize with every step' of the pacifist argument, he was not able to acquiesce in what seemed to be the acceptance of evil. It was 'a cardinal fact that in some cases it was better to fight

and be broken than to yield peacefully'. The mere act of resisting to death could be 'in itself a victory'.

Struycken, A. A. H. *The German White Book on the War In Belgium: A Commentary.* (London: Nelson, 1915)

Tillett, B. *Who was Responsible for the War and Why?* (London: Whitwell, 1917)

- **Neutrals**

One of the major aims of British propaganda was to engage the sympathy of neutral countries, particularly of the USA (see also section 4.2.4.2 on Anglo-American Relations; Courting America). Many of the pamphlets listed in the other sub-sections dealing with propaganda themes were written for this purpose. Examples of pamphlets dealing with neutrals and neutrality generally are listed below.

Archer, W. *Colour-Blind Neutrality: An Open Letter to Doctor George Brandes* (London: Hodder & Stoughton, 1916)

— *To Neutral Peace-Lovers: A Plea for Patience* (London: Causton, 1916)

Bryce, J. W., Viscount Bryce of Dechmont. *Neutral Nations and the War* (London: Macmillan, 1914)

Gregory, C. N. *Neutrality and Arms Shipments* (London: Darling, 1915)
Reprinted from the *New York Herald.*

Headlam, J. W. *The Truth about England Exposed in a Letter to a Neutral.* (London: Nelson, 1915)

A List of Neutral Ships Sunk by the Germans from August 8, 1914 to April 26, 1917 (London: Alabastor, Passmore & Sons 1917)

Scott, L. and A. Shaw. *Great Britain and Neutral Commerce* (London: Darling, 1915)
Contents: Part I: *Great Britain and the Right of Search*; Part II: *The British Blockade of Germany.*

- **Peace**

The question of ending the war by means of a negotiated peace was raised from time to time throughout the war especially among those elements in the population who were opposed to the war; it was also raised internationally by President Wilson. Later on in the war pressure for a negotiated peace became more pronounced as the population began to show signs of war weariness, and the Bolshevik's call for peace and President Wilson's efforts in this respect began to exert some influence. Taking the line of Lloyd George's unwillingness to countenance any proposal for peace that was not based on total victory, British propagandists endeavoured to support this by, for example, countering the efforts of those campaigning for peace, galvanizing the British people into a commitment to Lloyd George's concept of a 'knock-out blow' and a 'fight to a finish', and discrediting Germany's offers of peace.

Balfour, A. J., Earl. of Balfour. *Balfour's Message: Obstacles to Peace* (London: National War Aims Committee, 1917)
"Substance of a speech delivered by the Rt. Hon. A.J. Balfour ... in the House of Commons, August 8, 1918" (verso t.-p.)

Goschen, Sir W. E. *The One Condition of Peace.* (London: Truscott, 1916)

Gosling, H. *Peace: How to Get and Keep It* (London: Cassell, 1917)

Headlam, J. W. *The Peace Terms of the Allies* (London: Clay, 1917)

Leverhulme, W. H. L., Viscount. *Negotiate Now?: A Business Man's Answer.* An interview with Lord Leverhulme, by Harold Begbie (London: National War Aims Committee, 1917)
Reprinted from the *Daily Chronicle*. Argued that a compromise peace was bound to prove unsatisfactory, given the nature of the German leadership and its determination to hold on to territorial gains.

Robertson, J. M. *The German Idea of Peace Terms.* (London: Hodder & Stoughton, 1917)

Sanders, W. S. *Germany's Two Voices* (London: Darling, 1917)

— *Those German Peace Offers* (London: W. H. Smith & Sons, 1917)

Tillett, B. *My Message to Labour* (London: National War Aims Committee, 1918)

- **War Aims**

Although Asquith made some speeches in the early days of the war (see pamphlets related to them cited below) that included an indication of Britain's war aims his allusion to them was expressed in general rather than detailed terms. Subsequently, there were no further official public declarations of war aims (because of the government's reluctance to be publicly transparent about their details) until Lloyd George felt under pressure to provide the British people with a clear indication of what they were, as he did in his speech at a conference of trade unionists on 5 January 1918 (see pamphlet related to it cited below). There was, however, an Allied response to President Wilson's request at the end of 1916 that the belligerents should state their war aims, and in the course of the war British propagandists such as Headlam, Namier, and Toynbee wrote pamphlets (whether or not with Foreign Office approval is unclear) which anticipated elements of official policy on war aims.

Asquith, H. H., 1st Earl of Oxford and Asquith. *The War: Its Causes and Its Message*. Speeches delivered by the Prime Minister, August-October 1914 (London: Methuen, 1914)

— *What Britain Is Fighting For: A Reply to the German Chancellor*. A speech by the Rt. Hon. H.H. Asquith … on the 10th April, 1916 (London: Daily Chronicle, 1916)

Barker, E. *The Submerged Nationalities of the German Empire* (London: Darling, 1915)

The Case of The Allies: Being the Replies to President Wilson, and Mr. Balfour's Despatch (London: Hayman, Christy & Lilly, 1917)

Great Britain. National War Aims Committee (NWAC). *Our United War Aims: Summary of the Prime Minister's Declaration. … January 5th, 1918* (London: National War Aims Committee, 1918)
National War Aims Committee publications, no.33.

Grey, E., 1st Viscount Grey of Fallodon. *A League of Nations* (London: W.H. Smith & Son, 1918)
Reprinted from the pamphlet published by the Oxford University Press. Issued by the National War Aims Committee.

Headlam, J. W. *The Dead Lands of Europe* (London: Hodder & Stoughton, 1917)

Lloyd George, D. *British War Aims: Statement by the Prime Minister ... On January 5, 1918* (London: Hayman, Christy & Lilly for His Majesty's Stationery Office, 1918)
'This Statement was delivered to a meeting of the Representatives of Labour called to consider the question of further efforts for the prosecution of the war. "When the Government" said Mr. Lloyd George, "invite organized Labour in this Country to assist them to maintain the might of their Armies in the field, its representatives are entitled to ask that any misgivings and doubts which any of them may have about the purpose to which this precious strength is to be applied should be definitely cleared, and what is true of Organised Labour is equally true of all citizens in this Country without regard to grade or avocation." [Preamble quoted from the pamphlet].

Namier, L. B. *Danzig: Poland's Outlet to the Sea* (London: Spottiswoode, 1917)

— *Germany and Eastern Europe* (London: Duckworth, 1915)

National War Aims Committee (NWAC). *Aims and Effort of the War: Britain's Case after Four Years* (London: The Committee, 1918)

Pincombe, W. J. *A Plain Talk to the People of Britain: Britain, Belgium and the Small Nations*. Based upon Sir Edward Cook's pamphlet 'Britain and the Small Nations' (London: Victoria League, 1914)

A World Peace: President Wilson's Programme (London: National War Aims Committee, 1918)
National War Aims Committee publications, no. 34.

Newspapers, Journals and Magazines

For propaganda purposes newspapers, magazines and journals had the advantage over the pamphlets and books produced by organisations like CCNPO, PRC or NWAC that they could reach a far wider audience through regular and extensive circulation. Listed below is a selection of the media of this type which generally lent itself to propaganda in support of the war and the government.

The tone of this propaganda could descend to the base and obscene, as was particularly the case with many of the writings of Horatio Bottomley. Throughout the war Bottomley expressed his patriotism in an extremely aggressive and chauvinistic fashion via his editorship of *John Bull* (founded by him in 1906).

Newspapers

Much of the propaganda work on behalf of the British war effort was performed voluntarily by newspapers (like those listed below), which, though subject to considerable official constraints, were, in fact, able to enjoy a great deal of freedom to print what they liked as long as they did not divulge sensitive military information, undermine public morale, or 'discourage recruiting'. All the major national newspapers were patriotic and happy to conform. Even those newspapers which had originally opposed Britain entering into the war came to accept it once it had been declared and, after the German invasion of Belgium some of those newspapers switched to a clearly belligerent stance. The 'popular' press tended to go even further, allowing its pages to be a vehicle for the expression of propaganda in its most squalid form.

Because of its much smaller circulation the local press could not have the same propagandistic impact as the national press. By contrast, in fact, the local press, through the information it was able to obtain via its closer, more personal links to the soldiers of local regiments, was frequently able to provide articles with an uncensored local focus, describing the battlefront in a realistic fashion unlike the sanitized war reports that the national dailies tended to produce.

- **Morning Dailies**

    Daily Chronicle
    Daily Express
    Daily Graphic
    Daily Mail
    Daily Mirror
    Daily Sketch
    Daily Telegraph
    Manchester Guardian
    Morning Post
    The Times

- **Evening Dailies**

    Evening Standard
    Evening News
    Evening Post
    Globe
    Pall Mall Gazette
    Westminster Gazette

- **Weeklies**

    Lloyd's Weekly News
    News of the World
    Observer
    People
    Reynolds News

Sunday Pictorial
Sunday Times
Weekly Dispatch

Weekly and Monthly Journals

John Bull
Nation
National Review
New Statesman
New Witness
Punch
Spectator

Magazines

A variety of weekly and monthly magazines (many of them specifically war-related), to accommodate the pockets of all classes of society were published: penny magazines for the working class, more expensive magazines for upper-class and middle-class consumption. A brief selection of the innumerable magazines that were published is listed below. They invariably struck a patriotic or jingoistic note in their contents. Even juvenile magazines became vehicles for patriotic propaganda. In boy's magazines like the *Boy's Own* and *Young England* the war was depicted as exciting, heroic adventure while in magazines directed at girls like the *Girl's Own Paper* and *Girl Guides' Gazette* it was presented as something to be stoically endured or to become actively involved in by carrying out patriotic work such as knitting socks for the troops or canning food.

Blighty
The Boy's Own
The Family Journal
Field
Fragments from France
Girl's Friend
Girl Guides' Gazette
Girl's Own Paper
Graphic
Khaki
Pluck
The Sphere
The War Budget
The War Pictorial
Woman's World
Young England

Magazines for Overseas Consumption

Although Wellington House was responsible for the distribution overseas of a great many pamphlets it realized that they represented the sort of publication that only reached a limited readership. For this reason it sought to reach a wider readership overseas in a number of additional ways such as circulating information to the correspondents of foreign newspapers, promoting the sale of British newspapers abroad, and producing illustrated magazines that were printed in various languages so that they could be distributed for popular consumption in regions around the world. Examples of the latter magazines were *America Latina* (aimed at Spanish-speaking parts of South America), *O Espelho* (published in Portuguese and distributed in Brazil), *Hesperia* (for Greek populations), *Al Hakikat* (with translations in Arabic, Persian, Turkish and Hindustani, mainly for consumption in Middle Eastern countries), and *Cheng Pao* (for distribution in China); for distribution in the Asian subcontinent *Warta Yang Tulus* (in Malay), *Satya Vani* (in Bengali, Hindi, Gujerati and Tamil), and *Jangi Akhbar* (in Hindi and Urdu for the united provinces of India, and in Gurumkhi for the Sikhs) were published. Some of these magazines, mostly published fortnightly or monthly, benefited from being produced in the format and on the presses of the *Illustrated London News*. The most noteworthy of them, launched in 1916, was the extremely popular *War Pictorial*, which had a circulation of 500,000 a month by the end of that year and 700,000 a year later. It could be read in a wide variety of countries as its various editions were published in 10 different languages, including English, French, Dutch, Spanish, Portuguese, Italian, Russian, Greek, Danish, Swedish and German.

Advertising

Advertising constituted another useful tool of propaganda, being employed in assisting with appeals to the British people in areas such as recruitment (of women as nurses, munitions and land army workers as well as of men for the armed services), encouraging the public to buy war bonds and contribute to war-related charities, and exhorting them to restrict food consumption and to avoid waste The three major campaigns to promote War Savings Certificates that were launched by the government in November 1914, June 1915 and January 1917 were all given publicity through advertisements as well as the other tools of mass propaganda, such as posters, rallies and film.

- **Books**

Opie, R. *The 1910's Scrapbook: The Decade of the Great War* (London : New Cavendish Books, 2000)

Rickards, M. and M. Moody. *The First World War: Ephemera, Mementoes, Documents* (London: Jupiter, 1975)
Based on an exhibition of the collection of the Imperial War Museum [IWM], London, 1970.

- **Articles**

Bliven, B. 'Selling the War to the Working Man', *Printer's Ink*, 102 (1918), 69

— 'What British Advertisers have Learned in War Time', *Printer's Ink*, 104 (1918), 3-6, 110-17

Burton, P. 'Things Advertising Can Do in War War-Time', *Printer's Ink*, 99 (1917), 28-31

Hiley, N. P. 'Sir Hedley Le Bas and the Origins of Domestic Propaganda in Britain, 1914-1917', *Journal of Advertising History*, 10 (1987), 30-46

Romer, J. I. 'How Can We Overcome the Government's Antagonism to Advertising', *Printer's Ink*, 98 (1917), 46-57

Russell, T. 'Advertisement Stimulated by the War', *Printer's Ink*, 98 (1917), 25-28

— 'Advertising That Raises $5,000,000 a Week in War Money', *Printer's Ink*, (1917), 43-45

— 'British Advertisers Give Space to the War Loan', *Printer's Ink*, 102 (1918), 57-65

— 'The British Government's Use of Advertising in the War', *Printer's Ink*, 1915 (92), 37-4

4.2.5.3 Visual Propaganda

The Cinema

One of the most powerful, forms of illustrated propaganda employed during the war was the cinema film. It possessed the advantage that it could be seen by a large proportion of the population (by 1916 there was a weekly attendance of 20 million people watching movies) as was not the case with much of the written material that was published. Despite the potentially invaluable role that the movies could play in the area of propaganda Britain was slower to exploit it than Germany and France.

It was in the area of government sponsored and official propaganda that the British film industry made its most powerful and interesting impact. One of the main catalysts for the development of this propaganda arose out of the organisation of the aid provided by existing companies involved in cinema newsreel production and distribution. Initially the military authorities were extremely hostile to cameramen filming in the war zone and subjected their work to frustrating obstruction, providing them with little assistance and making it difficult for them to obtain permission to visit the front. Towards the end of 1915, however, the military authorities relented and a body known as the Cinematograph Trade Topical Committee (which consisted of the chief firms in cinema newsreel production and distribution, i.e. Barker, B. & C., Éclair, Gaumont, Jury, Kineto, and the Tropical Film Company) were able to negotiate with them for the provision of facilities to send cameramen to the Front, agreeing to pay a royalty on the films so obtained to military charities. As a result the first official British cinematographers were sent to France (Geoffrey Malins and another operator, E. G. Tong were among those sent to France immediately) and a system of official war film production gradually developed. By 1916 cinematographers were being despatched to all fronts and the material they filmed and sent home was being made into both newsreels and longer films, which were distributed through Jury's renting system. Later the official view was that the best means of distributing their war footage and communicating news of the war to cinema audiences would be through the regular output of an official newsreel. This led ultimately in November 1917 to the establishment of an official newsreel, *War Office Official Topical Budget*, with exclusive access to film taken by British official cameramen on the Western and other Fronts. This became the main regular outlet for official war film to the end of the war, becoming progressively more successful commercially as a propaganda tool and audience attraction. In February 1918 it changed its name to *Pictorial News (Official)*, and the following month came under the control of the new Ministry of Information, headed by Lord Beaverbrook. It continued to February 1919, when it was purchased by the newspaper proprietor Edward Hulton, and eventually reverted to its old name of *Topical Budget*.

The films that emerged over this whole period of the development of official film production covered all aspects of wartime activity including life on the home front (particularly scenes of recruiting, anti-German protests, military exercises, and women workers), the Western Front and other war zones (particularly the Middle East), naval and air operations, training and the life of troops (including troops from the various Allied countries), particular battles, and Royal visits and tours of inspection in various theatres of war. Particularly memorable in this phase of official production were the films of three 'big battle' pictures (*The Battle of the Somme*, *The Battle of Ancre and the Advance of the Tanks*, and *The Battle of Arras*) made between summer 1916 and spring 1917 by British official cameramen. The most famous of these was *The Battle of the Somme* a five-reel film shot in July 1916 and shown in August. It was received by the public with great enthusiasm, a response which encouraged the belief that it would greatly help to raise morale at home and stimulate greater efforts among the industrial workers.

The lifting of the restrictions on cinematographers by the War Office in 1915 provided Masterman with the opportunity to go ahead with Wellington House's own plans for propaganda films which he did by forming a Cinema Committee in August 1915 with the brief to organise the production and distribution of films suitable for propaganda purposes in allied and neutral countries. Its first and most noteworthy achievement as a piece of British cinema propaganda was *Britain Prepared* which was constructed out of films about the army, navy and the munitions firms of Vickers and Maxim and launched late in December 1915. With a length of 15,000 feet and a running time of around three hours, it achieved great success and worldwide distribution on a commercial basis. It was received favourably among neutrals (including the most important of the neutrals, the USA, where Charles Urban was active in its distribution) and especially among the allies, who were able to derive from it the reassurance that Britain was making a fully committed contribution to the war effort. In the latter respect effective use of it was made in Russia thanks to the efforts of Captain (later Lieut.-Colonel) A.C. Bromhead who, as leader of a British film propaganda mission to Russia in 1916-17, not only arranged an official showing of the film for the Tsar, his Chiefs of Staff, and the Petrograd Press in January 1916 but also introduced it and answered questions about it at public showings for various other Russian audiences. For this work he was awarded the CBE. The showing of films of this type abroad probably had a far greater impact there than any other form of propaganda media.

Film propaganda was also employed effectively by other official and semi-official bodies[127] and particularly by Government Departments, such as the Ministries of Food, Labour, National Service, Pensions, and Munitions, and other official bodies such as the India Office, National War Savings Committee, Women's Land Army and Board of Agriculture. One of the most popular forms of film, made for many of the Service Ministries, was the film tag, a short film, taking about two minutes to show, and embodying, usually in story form, some useful moral such as 'Save Coal' or 'Buy War Loans'; it was attached to newsreels and aimed at home audiences. The National War Savings Committee was among the first agencies to utilize motion pictures for war propaganda. It produced numerous short films encouraging both thrift and the purchase of national war saving certificates (e.g. *Stand by the Men Who Stood by You* and *Her Savings Saved*, both using actors to dramatize the message, the former,

---

[127] In 1915, for example, the semi-official body, the Parliamentary Recruiting Committee, commissioned the London Film Company to produce the recruiting film, *You!*.

however, also employing cartoon and newsreel with the acted appeal for people to buy war savings certificates) and in 1916 it commissioned the Gaumont Film Co to make *For the Empire* as part of that year's war loans drive. Other official ventures into the realm of propaganda films of a dramatised nature included productions like *Everybody's Business* (on the theme of food conservation featuring popular actors like Gerald du Maurier) and *Mrs John Bull Prepared* (dramatising the importance of women's contribution to the war effort), but the greatest success in the dramatic film genre of propaganda was *Hearts of the World*[128] made under British auspices by D. W. Griffith, the outstanding American director of the time. The British government provided no funding but gave Griffith free use of its soldiers, training camps and weapons for the staging of many of its scenes.

A list of a selection of the type of official film mentioned above is provided below under the heading, **Official and Government Sponsored Films**

There were also a considerable number of factual films that were not official but produced independently by the film trade, particularly in the early part of the war, to cater for the public interest in the war. Although unofficial, these films had the effect of assisting in the propaganda process. A selection of these sort of films is provided below under the heading of **Unofficial Factual Films**

- **Autobiographies, Biographies, Memoirs**

Brunel, A. *Nice Work: The Story of Thirty Years in British Film Production* (London: Forbes Robertson, 1948)
Brunel, a leading film director, was a member of Masterman's official film department from the beginning of the war.

Pearson, G. *Flashback: The Autobiography of a British Film-Maker* (London: Allen & Unwin, 1957)

Schickel, R. *D .W. Griffith: An American Life* (London: Simon & Schuster,1984; New York: Limelight Editions, 1996)

Urban, C. *A Yank in Britain: The Lost Memoirs of Charles Urban, Film Pioneer*, edited by Luke McKernan (Hastings: The Projection Box, 1999)

- **Books**

Aitken, I. W. 'John Grierson and the Origins, Ideals and Development of the British Documentary Film Movement 1914-1936' (unpublished doctoral thesis, Polytechnic of Central London, 1988)

Badsey, S. D. *British Official Film in the First World War*, typescript in the Imperial War Museum [IWM] Film Archive

— *British Official Photography in the First World War*, typescript in the Imperial War Museum Film Archive

Barsam, R. M. *Nonfiction Film: A Critical History*, revised and expanded (Bloomington: Indiana University Press, 1992)

Bawden, L-A. *The Oxford Companion to Film* (London: Oxford University Press 1976)

Dopperen, R. van and Graham, C. C. *Shooting the Great War: Albert Dawson and the American Correspondent Film Company, 1914–1918* (Charleston, SC: Create Space, 2013)
For the purpose of influencing public opinion in the United States German officials mounted a secret film campaign based on the establishment there of the American Correspondent Film Company. For this covert operation photographer Albert K. Dawson was used as a front man and sent to Europe to cover the war in the trenches with his camera. This book describes his life and work as a war photographer and includes information about his films and the way his pictures were used by the German government for foreign propaganda.

Faulkner, W. S. 'The Kinema in 1918: Its Increasing Value in Propaganda', in *Daily Mail Yearbook* (London: Associated Newspapers Groups, 1919)

---

[128] In the production of war films in Germany there were more dramas ('field-grey' romances and adventure movies) than documentaries. In striking contrast, war dramas of this sort were rarely produced in the British film industry. In this respect *Hearts of the World* (1916), which was made under British auspices, was exceptional.

Hammond, M. 'Education or Entertainment: Public and Private Interpretations of the Battle of the Somme (1916)', in *Beyond Grierson: Studies in the British Non-Fiction Film*, edited by Alan Burton (Bath: Flicks Books, 1999)

Johnston, W. *Memo on the Movies: War Propaganda, 1914-39* (Norman: Oklahoma Co-operative Books, 1939)

Lovell, A. and J. Hillier. *Studies in Documentary* (London: Secker & Warburg for the British Film Institute, 1972)

Low, R. *The History of the British Film*, 7 vols (London: Allen & Unwin, 1948-1985; repr. London: Routledge, 1997), III: *1914-1918* (1948; repr. 1997)

Malins, G. H. *How I Filmed the War: A Record of the Extraordinary Experiences of the Man Who Filmed The Great Somme Battles*, etc, edited by Low Warren (London: Herbert Jenkens, 1920; repr. London: Imperial War Museum, 1993)

Reeves, N. A. 'Official British Film Propaganda during the First World War' (unpublished doctoral thesis, King's College, London, 1981)

— *Official British Film Propaganda during the First World War* (London: Croom Helm, 1986)

— 'Official British Film Propaganda', in *The First World War and Popular Cinema, 1914 to the Present*, edited by M. Paris (Edinburgh: Edinburgh University Press, 1999)

— *The Power of Film Propaganda: Myth or Reality?* (London: Cassell, 1999; repr. 2003)

— 'Through the Eye of the Camera: Contemporary Cinema Audiences and their "Experience" of War in the Film, Battle of the Somme', in *Facing Armageddon: The First World War Experienced*, ed. by H. Cecil and P. H. Liddle (London, Leo Cooper, 1996)

Sussex, E. *The Rise and Fall of British Documentary: The Story of the Film Movement Founded by John Grierson* (Berkeley: University of California Press, 1975)

- **Articles**

Badsey, S. D, 'Battle of The Somme: British War-Propaganda', *Historical Journal of Film Radio And Television*, 3 (1983), 99-115

Bottomore, S. 'Charles Urban: Pioneering The Non-Fiction Film in Britain and America, 1897-1925' *Historical Journal of Film Radio And Television*, 34 (2014), 276-278

Dutton, P. '"More Vivid than the Written Word" Ellis Ashmead-Bartlett's film, With the Dardanelles Expedition (1915)', *Historical Journal of Film Radio And Television*.,24 (2004), 205-222 [For information relating to this film see Byrnes, P. *Gallipoli on Film* in the section **4.3.2.1 of Part 4: Remembering the War**]

Hammo.nd, M. 'The Men who came Back: Recognition and Anonymity in the Roll of Honour Films of the Great War', *Scope: Online Journal of Film Studies, University of Nottingham*, December (2000)

Hiley, N. P. '"The British Army Film", "You!", and "For The Empire": Reconstructed Propaganda Films, 1914-1916', *Historical Journal of Film, Radio and Television*, 5 (1985), 165-187

McKernan, L. 'Propaganda, Patriotism and Profit: Charles Urban and British Official War Films in America during the First World', *Film History*, 14 (2002) 369-389

— 'The Supreme Moment of the War: "General Allenby's Entry into Jerusalem"', *Historical Journal of Film, Radio and Television*, 13 (1993), 169 - 180

Messinger, G. S. 'An Inheritance Worth Remembering: The British Approach to Official Propaganda during the First World War', *Historical Journal of Film Radio and Television*, 13 (1993), 117-127

Reeves, N. A. 'Cinema, Spectatorship and Propaganda: "Battle Of The Somme" (1916) and its Contemporary Audience', *Historical Journal of Film Radio and Television*, 17 (1997), 5-28

— 'Film Propaganda and its Audience: The Example of Britain's Official Films during the First World War', *Journal of Contemporary History*, 18 (1983), 463-494
Among the statistics provided in this article Reeves points out that as receipts declined in 1917-18 films were shown in areas without cinemas using 'cinemotors', which brought weekly audiences for war documentaries up to 163,000.

— 'The Power of Film Propaganda: Myth or Reality?', *Historical Journal of Film Radio and Television*, 13 (1993), 181-201

— '"The Real Thing at Last": The Battle of the Somme and the Domestic Cinema Audience in the Autumn of 1916', *The Historian*, 51 (1996), 4-8

Robinson, D. 'The Old Lie', *Sight and Sound.*, 31 (1962), 201-4

Sanders, M. L. 'British Film Propaganda in Russia, 1916-1918', *Historical Journal of Film, Radio and Television*, 3 (1983), 117-129

Seton, M. 'War', *Sight and Sound*, 6 (1937), 18, 182-185

Smith, J. M. 'Hearts of the World', *The Silent Picture*, Spring (1971), 6-9

Smither, R '"A Wonderful Idea of The Fighting": The Question of Fakes in "The Battle of the Somme"', *Historical Journal of Film, Radio and Television*, 13 (1993), 149-168

Spears, J. 'World War I on the Screen', *Films in Review*, 17 (1966), 274-292

Taylor, P. M. 'Introduction: Britain and the Cinema In World War I', *Historical Journal of Film, Radio and Television*, 13 (1993), 115-116

- **Official and Government Sponsored Films**

The main source of official and government sponsored propaganda was of a factual nature as manifested in newsreels and feature films designed to help raise morale at home and to create a favourable impression abroad among both allies and neutrals. This was done by providing cinema audiences with films relating to topics such as battles, naval operations, royal visits to the troops, food production, women's role in the war and a variety of other aspects generally demonstrating the war efforts of the British Empire and her Allies.

A considerable number of these factual films gave prominence to fighting in the Middle East (e.g. *General Allenby Enters into Jerusalem, With the Australians in Palestine, With The Forces on the Palestine Front, The New Crusaders, With the Forces in Mesopotamia*). Unlike the Western Front, where trench warfare was static and associated with the slaughter of soldiers on a massive scale, regions like the Middle East lent themselves to filming in a far more ideal environment, affording exotic locations, a variety of 'picturesque' troops, a war of movement and the opportunity to dramatize the imperial spirit. There was no more dramatic illustration of this than the adventurous campaigns of T. E. Lawrence who became the famous 'Lawrence of Arabia', the image of romantic heroism the British public were unable to extract from the depressing stalemate and mass destruction which characterized the Western Front.

Effective use was made of imperial themes. *Sons of the Empire* demonstrated imperial brotherhood; *Canadians on the Western Front, New Zealand Troops in France* emphasised dominion loyalty; *With The Indian Troops at the Front* and *A South African Native Labour Contingent* stressed the devotion of the colonised people of Asia and Africa to the mother country; *A Chinese Labour Contingent* and *An Egyptian Labour Contingent* drew attention to the mix of races involved in the defence of the Empire.

Newsreels and films related to the home front presented patriotic images of civilian life in time of war (e.g. *Day in the Life of a Munition Worker* and *Woolwich Arsenal and its Workers*) but as well as this were often designed as appeals to audiences to help the war effort by, for instance, buying war bonds (e.g. *War Savings Certificates: How To Buy Them, How To Use Them*) or conserving food (e.g. *Fighting the U-Boats in a London Back Garden*).

There were two films, *Sons of the Empire* and *Our Empire's Fight for Freedom* which stand out as being nearer in their style than any of the other films to the documentary as it is known today. *Sons of the Empire* relates to the winter of 1916-1917 in France and covers the preparations for the spring offensive, the fall of Bapaume, the Navy after Jutland, the arrival of transports in France, aerial photography, preparations for battle and the aftermath. *Our Empire's Fight for Freedom* deals with the first two years of the war in a coverage of the declaration of war and its beginning, workers at home, the navy, and the great offensive and after. These filmed stories, connected together largely by the use of titles, painted a broader canvas than usual and in the case of *Our Empire's Fight for Freedom* were accompanied by means of very long titles which provided a political, social and military background with the inclusion of quotations and speeches.

Some of the official or government-sponsored propagandistic films were presented in fictional form (e.g. *Mrs John Bull Prepared, Everybody's Business*), but none of them produced such a successful impact as D. W. Griffith's *Hearts of the World*.

By 1918 some 700 films had been made with a total negative length of half a million feet. Special editions with captions in foreign languages enabled them to be carried to many countries.

A selection of official and government-sponsored films is provided below:

Battle of Arras [alternatively *The German Retreat and the Battle of Arras*] (1917)
Battle of Ancre and the Advance of the Tanks] (1917)
Battle of the Somme (1916)
Britain Prepared (1915)
British Naval Activities after the Great British Victory of Jutland (1918)
British Submarines in the Mediterranean (1917)
British Troops on the Italian Front (1918)
British Women in Khaki (1918)
Canadians on the Western Front (1917)
A Chinese Labour Contingent (1917)
A Day in the Life of a Munition Worker (1917)
The Empire's Shield (1918)
An Egyptian Labour Contingent (1917)
Everybody's Business (1917)
Fighting the U-Boats in a London Back Garden (1918)
For the Empire (1916)
General Allenby Enters into Jerusalem (1918)
German Retreat to St Quentin (1917)
Hearts of the World (1918)
Her Savings Saved (1918)
His Majesty's Visit to His Grand Fleet (1917)
His Royal Highness the Prince of Wales with the Guards in the Front Line (1916)
The King and Queen of England Visit the Battlefields of France (1917)
The King's Visit to the Fleet (1917)
The King Visits his Armies in the Great Advance (1917)
The Life of a WAAC (1918)
Liveliness on the British Front (1916)
A Machine Gun School at the Front (1916)
The New Crusaders: With The Forces on the Palestine Front (1918)
Our Naval Air Power (1918)
Mrs John Bull Prepared (1918)
The New Zealand Troops in France (1917)
Our Naval Air Power (1918)
The Royal Visit to the Battlefields of France (1917)
Sons of our Empire (1917)
A South African Native Labour Contingent (1917)

The South African Forces in France (1917)
Stand by the Men Who Stood by You (1917)
The US Destroyers in British Waters (1917)
War Savings Certificates: How To Buy Them: How To Use Then (1917)
The Way of a Ship on the Sea (1918)
With Lord Kitchener in France (1916)
With our Territorials at the Front (1916)
With the Australians in Palestine (1918)
With the Australian Forces in France (1917)
With the British Troops in Macedonia (1916)
With the Canadians on the Western Front (1917)
With the Empire's Fighters (1916)
With the Forces in Mesopotamia (1918)
With The Indian Troops at the Front (1916)
With the Irish at the Front (1916)
With Lord Kitchener In France (1915)
With Britain's Monster Guns in Action (1916)
With the Royal Field Artillery in Action (1916)
With the Royal Flying Corps (1917)
The Women's Land Army (1917)
Woolwich Arsenal and its Workers (1918)
The Work of the Red Cross (1917)
You! (1916)

- **Unofficial Factual Films**

There were a number of unofficial films, particularly in the early days of the war, primarily designed to satisfy public interest in the war but also having a propagandistic effect (see selection listed below) These were mostly factual war films of a topical nature about such subjects as the Allies and their enemies, activities on the British home front, and the British Army and Navy in operation. A few of these films approached the subject of the war in a somewhat different way as, for instance, through a representation of the events leading up to and immediately following the outbreak of war in the case of Samuelson's *The Great European War* (produced by George Pearson) and through biographies of contemporary heroes in the case of Samuelson's *The Life of Lord Roberts* (produced by George Pearson), the Windsor Film Company's *The Life of Lord Kitchener* (produced and written by Rex Wilson), and Ideal's *The Man Who Saved the British Empire* (produced by Maurice Elvey)

Backbone of England (Captain Kettle, 1914)
Britain's New Army (Kineto, 1915)
Called to the Front (Regent, 1914)
A Day with the Territorials in the Field (Clarendon, 1914)
Germany's Army and Navy (Kineto, 1914)
Fighting the German Air Raiders (Palmer, 1916)
The Life of Lord Kitchener (Windsor, 1918)
The Life of Lord Roberts (Samuelson, 1914)
Lord Kitchener's New Army (Dreadnought, 1914)
The Man Who Saved the British Empire (Ideal, 1918)
Men of the Moment (Hepworth, 1914)
Training our Volunteer Constables (Clarendon, 1914)
A Week with the King (Holmfirth, 1917)
What We are Fighting For (Kineto, 1918)
With the British Forces (Kineto, 1914)
With the Fighting Forces of Europe (Kinemacolor, 1914)

The Illustrative Arts

General

Many illustrated periodicals existed before the war and during the war they were augmented by a number that were created specifically to cover the conflict (such as the *Illustrated War News*, *War Illustrated*, etc). These periodicals required a constant supply of images to fill their pages and by the time the war broke out advances in photography and the ability to reproduce photographs in periodicals meant that photographs were becoming an increasingly important source of this supply. Early in the war the military authorities strongly discouraged the taking of photographs in the war zones although some photographers, including servicemen on campaign who often managed to produce some effective amateur photographs, did manage to get their photographs published. Later on in 1916, when the military authorities began employing official photographers[129], the taking and supply of war photographs came under strict and organised control. Some manipulation of war photographs for propaganda purposes occurred as, for example, in such cases as the posing of war scenes (e.g. smartly turned out soldiers in unnaturally tidy trenches), re-touching photographs to eliminate any of their depressing elements, producing simulations of 'live' actions (e.g. depicting troops 'going over the top' with photographs that were not taken on the actual battlefield but elsewhere in non-combat situations as, for example, in reserve lines), and making use of old, often pre-war, photographs that were made (by giving them erroneous captions or by simply leaving it to implication) to give a favourable impression of the allied troops, or conversely an unfavourable impression of German troops, on active service. Nevertheless, Britain was far less guilty than France and Germany of such manipulation of photographs, a result no doubt of British official policy being influenced by Wellington House's concept of broadcasting only 'the propaganda of fact'.

It had been common practice from the mid-19th century for a number of periodicals such as the *Illustrated London News* and *The Graphic* to illustrate military themes with battle-scenes and similar images drawn by competent illustrators. In spite of the development of photography this practice continued in the Great War, throughout which war-illustrators were employed to provide images of combat that could be published and viewed by the general public. At the beginning of the war some of these images were provided by artists who were also war correspondents in their own right (e.g. Frederic Villiers and H. C. Sepping-Wright both of whom covered the earlier campaigns on the Western Front, the latter also covering campaigns on the Eastern Front). The illustrative work of these artist-correspondents was eventually taken over by photography which by the early years of the war had reached the stage of development where it could be used effectively as a substitute. Nevertheless, home-based war-illustrators continued to be employed throughout the war. Propaganda was implicit in many of the illustrations they produced. Their images are of heroism, of desperate hand-to-hand fights, with casualties unblemished by disfiguring wounds – the sort of unrealistic depiction of battle characteristic of the Victorian period and continued in the Great War so as to prevent the public from being exposed to the potentially morale-sapping effect of the true horrors of war.

The Government scheme to make use of the work of officially appointed war artists and photographers was in a different category. With the potential value of their work for propaganda purposes in mind, these artists were deliberately sent to the various fronts with official blessing to record their impressions of the war in paintings, drawings, and photographs that could be made available to the public [see also **Part 3, section 3.2 (Art)**].

While official war photographs lent themselves to wide distribution, the work of the official war artists, accessible to the public mainly through exhibitions, necessarily reached a limited audience. In contrast was the type of illustrative work of a directly patriotic nature which was distributed on a massive scale through its use in cartoons and illustrated texts, on posters and advertisements, picture postcards, games, puzzles, jigsaws, tins, mugs, cigarette cards, souvenirs, the covers of books, magazines, and sheet music; in short, on virtually every conceivable object (there are numerous examples in Opie's *The 1910's Scrapbook: The Decade of the Great War* cited below). The picture postcard was a particularly heavily used medium for the expression of patriotic sentiment through its depiction of such subjects as battle-scenes, war leaders, and patriotic cartoons. Illustrations from magazines and picture postcards were very popular with soldiers at the front and were universally used to decorate billets and dug-outs.

- **Catalogues**

Catalogue of British Official War Photographs in Colour (London: Grafton Galleries, 1918)
Catalogue of an exhibition held at the Grafton Galleries, London, 4 Mar. - 27 Apr. 1918. "Under the direction of the Ministry of Information. For the benefit of War Charities." - cover. The poster advertising this exhibition was entitled *First Grand Exhibition of British Battle Photographs in Colour*. Both the catalogue and the poster are held in the Imperial War Museum. Exhibitions of these photographs were also held in other locations (see following two records)

---

[129] Britain's employment of an average of 16 officially appointed war photographers, a number considerably less than Germany and France employed, is perhaps an indication that Britain did not set as much store on the value of photographs as propaganda.

Catalogue of British Official War Photographs in Colour (London: British War Photographs, 1918)
Catalogue of an exhibition held at the Peoples Palace, Mile End Road, London, May 6th to June 15th, 1918.

Catalogue of British Official War Photographs in Colour (Brighton: Public Art Galleries, 1918)
Catalogue of an exhibition held at the Brighton Public Art Galleries, 29 July - 17 Aug. 1918.

Onslow's (London). *An Important Collection of Bruce Bairnsfather Cartoons and Collectables, Books, Ephemera, Photographs, Pictures and Prints of the Great War and Second World War, Transport Collectors Items and Posters* [Onslow's Sale Catalogue for 31 March, 1999] (London: Onslow's 1999)

- **Books**

Carmichael, J. *First World War Photographers* (London: Routledge, 1989)

Demm, E. 'The Battle of the Cartoonists: German, French and English Caricatures in World War I', in *France and Germany in an Age of Crisis, 1900-60: Studies in Memory of Charles Bloch*, edited by H. Shamir (Leiden: E. J. Brill, 1990)

Harries, M. and S. Harries. *The War Artists: British Official War Art of the Twentieth Century* (London: Michael Joseph in association with the Imperial War Museum and Tate Gallery, 1983)

Holt, T. and V. Holt. *Till the Boys Come Home: The Picture Postcards of the First World War* (London: Macdonald and Jane's, 1977)

Malvern, S. B. 'Art, Propaganda and Patronage: An History of the Employment of British War Artists, 1916-1919' (unpublished doctoral thesis, University of Reading, 1981)

Opie, R. *The 1910's Scrapbook: The Decade of the Great War* (London: New Cavendish Books, 2000)

Tippett, M. *Art at the Service of War: Canada, Art, and the Great War* (Toronto: University of Toronto Press, 1984)
Includes a discussion of some of the British government propaganda department's use of artists to depict the war.

- **Articles**

Biernoff, S. and J. Tynan. 'Making and Remaking the Civilian Soldier: The World War I Photographs of Horace Nicholls', *Journal of War and Culture Studies*, 5 (2012), 277-293
In this article it is argued that Horace Nicholls' photographs of wartime army recruitment and post-war facial reconstruction represent a response to the brief from Wellington House to record the war effort on the home front that is colured by his artistic aspirations and his love of a good story (seeming to result in an uneasy combination lying between photojournalism, propaganda and record keeping).

Demm, E. 'Propaganda and Caricature in the First World War', *Journal of Contemporary History*, 28 (1993), 163-92

Gilman, S. 'Images Beyond History: Photographs of the Western Front', *History Today*, 51 (2001), 12-19

Posters

In the early 20th century when there was no radio, television or internet, the most publicly visible advertising medium other than the cinema was the poster, an already established means of conveying information to the public by the time the war began.

The heyday of the poster during the war occurred in its early years when it was heavily used as a propaganda tool to encourage men to volunteer for armed service[130]. In May 1916 the publications sub-department of the Parliamentary Recruiting Committee (PRC) calculated that it had printed in the region of 2.5 million copies of

---

[130] With only a small professional army and no policy of conscription at the begining of the war the poster was one of the means used to recruit the large numbers of volunteers needed for the armed forces.

164 different posters of this sort in various shapes and sizes[131]. Even after the principal period of voluntary recruiting ended with the introduction of conscription in May 1916 the poster continued to be extensively employed in relation to war issues. In the last two years of the war its use was particularly motivated by a perception of the need to combat the war weariness which was becoming apparent in the civilian population. For this reason there developed a predominant use of the poster for the purpose of encouraging continued support for government policy, usually by drawing attention to the heroic nature and resolution of Britain's fighting forces and by vilifying the behaviour of the enemy. As well as these uses in relation to the war, the poster was also produced with the object of providing specific information about matters like aircraft identification, food, and war loans, urging wartime economy, and stimulating enrolment in, for example, women's war work and national service.

These posters were designed to convey a simple written statement often in combination with visual imagery. Some of them were translated into Welsh and other minority languages. Their distribution varied; they were often reproduced in newspapers and displayed in shop windows, taxi cabs, trams and railway carriages, banks, public libraries, political clubs and anywhere the public might congregate in large numbers. They were also circulated throughout the Empire and frequently further afield in other parts of the world where their display was the result of private initiative as well as official enterprise.

- **Books**

Aulich, J. *War Posters: Weapons of Mass Communication* (London: Thames & Hudson, 2007)

Aulich, J. and J. Hewitt. *Seduction or Instruction?: First World War Posters in Britain and Europe* (Manchester: Manchester University Press, 2007)

Fairman E. R. *Doomed Youth: The Poetry and the Pity of the First World War*, an exhibition organized by Elisabeth Fairman (New Haven: Yale Center for British Art, 1999)
All the posters in the exhibition (held at the Yale Center for British Art, June 22-September 26, 1999) are from the War Poster Collection, Manuscripts and Archives, Yale University.

Fit Men Wanted: Original Posters from the Home Front, with a foreword by Nigel Steel (London: Thames & Hudson in association with the Imperial War Museum, 2012)
Reproductions of the best (and most forgotten after their initial use) of the Imperial War Museum's collection of over 30,000 British Government wartime posters and proclamations, mostly from the First and Second World Wars.

Gallo, M. *The Poster in History* (New York: American Heritage, 1974; repr. New York: Norton, 2001)

Great Britain. Department of Recruiting for Ireland, Dublin. *Recruiting Posters*, 3 vols (Dublin: Department of Recruiting for Ireland, 1914-1918)

Hadley, F. and M. Pegler. *Posters of the Great War* (London; Pen & Sword, 2013)
Published in Association with Historial de la Grande Guerre, Peronne, France.

Hardie, M. and A. K. Sabin, eds. *War Posters, Issued by Belligerent and Neutral Nations, 1914-1919* (London: Black, 1920)

Hillier, B. *Posters* (London: Weidenfeld & Nicolson, 1969)

Hutchinson, H. *The Poster: An Illustrated History since 1860* (London: Studio Vista, 1968)

James, P., ed. *Picture This: World War I Posters and Visual Culture* (Lincoln, Neb: University of Nebraska Press, 2009)

Metzl, E. *The Poster: Its History and its Art* (New York: Watson-Guptill Publications 1963)

Perry, P. '(Dis)ordering Signs: An Inquiry into British Recruitment Posters of the First World War' (unpublished

---

[131] Among the stream of recruitment posters that were produced was the most famous of them all, *Your Country Wants You!*, featuring Lord Kitchener.

masters thesis, University of Southampton, 1995)

— 'Propaganda Posters: Women and the Great War' (unpublished postgraduate diploma thesis, University of Southampton, 1994)

Rickards, M. *Posters of the First World War*, selected and reviewed by Maurice Rickards (London: Evelyn, Adams & Mackay, 1968)

— *The Rise and Fall of the Poster* (London: David and Charles, 1971)

What Did You Do in the War, Daddy?: A Visual History of Propaganda Posters, introduction by Peter Stanley (Melbourne: Oxford University Press, 1983)

- **Articles**

Curtis, B. 'Posters as Visual Propaganda in the Great War', *The Block*, 2 (1980), 50

Dutton, P. 'Moving Images? The Parliamentary Recruiting Committee [PRC]'s Poster Campaign, 1914-1916', *Imperial War Museum Review*, no. 4 (1989), 43-58

Steel, N. 'The Power of Words', *Despatches* (The Magazine of the Friends of the Imperial War Museum), No. 15 (2012), 42-43
An examination by Nigel Steel, IWM's Principal Historian, of the proclamation posters used in both World Wars.

- **Catalogues and Collections**

Chenault, L. *Battlelines: World War 1 Posters from the Bowman Gray Collection* (Chapel Hill: Rare Book Collection, Wilson Library, University of North Carolina, 1988)

Crawford, A., ed. *Posters of World War I and World War II in the George C. Marshall Research Foundation* (Charlottesville, Virginia: University Press of Virginia, 1979)

Darracott, J. and B. Loftus, eds. *The First World War in Posters from the Imperial War Museum* [IWM], 2nd edn (London: Imperial War Museum, 1981)

Great Britain. His Majesty's Stationery Office. *Catalogue of War Literature Issued By H.M. Government, 1914-1919*, including recruiting, war savings and other pictorial posters, and the more interesting of the numerous publications bearing upon the war, some of which have not previously been offered for sale (London: H.M.S.O., 1921)
Contents: A. Pictorial posters. B. Art reproductions. C. Books.

Harper, P. *War, Revolution and Peace: Propaganda Posters from the Hoover Institution* [Hoover Institution on War, Revolution and Peace] *Archives, 1914-1945*. An exhibition organized by Paula Harper and Marcia Cohn Growdon. Catalogue by Paula Harper (Stanford, Calif.: Hoover Institution, 1971)

Paret, P, and others. *Persuasive Images: Posters of War and Revolution from the Hoover Institution* [Hoover Institution on War, Revolution And Peace] *Archives*. [Compiled by] Peter Paret, Beth Irwin Lewis and Paul Paret (Princeton: Princeton University Press, 1992)

Rudolph G. A. *War posters from 1914 through 1918 in the Archives of the University of Nebraska* (Lincoln: University of Nebraska, 1990)

Wartime Posters: 30 Postcards in Full Colour (Norwich: Jarrold, 1999)

- **Contemporary Posters**

A brief selection of examples of the numerous posters that were produced during the war years are described below:

"AT THE FRONT! Every fit Briton should join our brave men at the Front. ENLIST NOW." (PRC Recruiting Poster, 84, 1915)
Showing a gun team coming into action under fire.

'BRITONS / [image of Kitchener pointing] / "WANTS YOU" / Join your Country's Army! / GOD SAVE THE KING / Reproduction by permission of London Opinion' (London: Printed by the Victoria House Printing Co, 1914)
Showing below the top caption, "BRITONS", a facial picture of Field Marshal Lord Kitchener with his arm and fingers pointing at the viewer, followed underneath by the caption, "WANTS YOU", etc. The poster was designed by Alfred Leete. A similar poster depicting Kitchener with his arm and fingers pointing at the viewer simply used the words "YOUR COUNTRY NEEDS YOU".

"Daddy, what did YOU do in the Great War?" (PRC Recruiting Poster, 79)
Showing a boy on the floor playing and a girl sitting in her father's lap.

"DON'T WASTE BREAD! / SAVE TWO THICK SLICES / EVERY DAY, and / Defeat the 'U'Boat (Ministry of Food poster, n.d.)
Showing a woman cutting bread with a ship ramming a U-Boat in the background.

"THE EMPIRE NEEDS MEN! / THE OVERSEAS STATES / All answer the call./ Helped by the YOUNG LIONS / The OLD LION defies his Foes. ENLIST NOW." (PRC Recruiting Poster, 79, 1915)
Showing a lion with his cubs.

"MORE AEROPLANES ARE NEEDED/ WOMEN COME AND HELP!/FREE TRAINING AND MAINTENANCE ALLOWANCE/Apply at Once" (Ministry of Munitions recruitment poster, 1918)
Showing aeroplanes in the sky and on the ground with a woman worker waving towards them.

"PUBLIC WARNING / The public are advised to familiarise themselves with the appearances of British and German Airships and Aeroplanes, so that they may not be alarmed by British aircraft, and may take shelter if German aircraft appear …" (London: Printed Under The Authority Of His Majesty's Stationery Office, by Sir Joseph Causton And Sons, Limited, 1915)
Text is followed by 24 silhouetted depictions of British and German airships and aircraft.

"PUT IT INTO / NATIONAL / WAR BONDS." (National War Savings Committee, 66)
Showing a smiling helmeted soldier.

"RED CROSS OR IRON CROSS? / WOUNDED AND A PRISONER / OUR SOLDIER CRIES FOR WATER. / THE GERMAN "SISTER" / POURS IT ON THE GROUND BEFORE HIS EYES. / THERE IS NO WOMAN IN BRITAIN / WHO WOULD DO IT. / THERE IS NO WOMAN IN BRITAIN / WHO WILL FORGET IT. (London: Dangerfield Printing Co., Ltd., n.d.)
Showing a German nurse, mockingly pouring a glass of water on to the ground before a thirsty, wounded British soldier lying on a stretcher. Two German officers stand, sneering, background right.

"WHO'S ABSENT? Is It You?". (PRC Recruiting Poster 125)
Showing at the top the caption, "WHO'S ABSENT?", with a broken line of soldiers in the central background and an illustration, dominating the central foreground, of John Bull, his arm and fingers pointing at the viewer, with the caption below "Is it you?".

"WOMEN OF BRITAIN / SAY - / "GO!" (PRC Recruiting Poster, 75, 1915)
Showing a mother, daughter and young son watching soldiers marching off to war.

"Write a Cheque / TO DAY / for / NATIONAL WAR BONDS" (National War Savings Committee, 1918)
Showing a picture of an inkwell with a pen in it.

Cartoons

Cartoonists made a valuable contribution to British propaganda. This was particularly true of Louis Raemaekers, whose cartoons, representative of the passionately held anti-German feelings of a neutral by nationality, were particularly ideal for distribution by British propagandists in neutral countries, especially the USA. In contrast to the bitter cartoons of Raemaekers, the work of many British cartoonists such as Bert Thomas, William Heath Robinson, and Bruce Bairnsfather, and those who contributed cartoons to newspapers and magazines such as *Punch*, was essentially humorous in character but nevertheless just as effective as propaganda, certainly for a British audience.

Of the British cartoonists of the Great War Bruce Bairnsfather had the greatest impact, achieving massive popularity both with civilians and the armed forces, but particularly with British soldiers for whom his humour had a special appeal.. Out of his first contributions to *The Bystander* evolved a whole industry, resulting in the reproduction of Bairnsfather characters and scenes in souvenirs (e.g. jigsaws, mascot dolls) and ceramics (e.g mugs) as well as the publications of his famous series, *Fragments from France*. His character 'Old Bill, the 'old contemptible' with his stolid but indomitable nature expressed by Bairnsfather through the themes of his cartoons (whether flooded trenches, filthy dugouts, the monotony of eating the perennial bully beef and plum jam, or sheer war-weariness, all jocularly depicted), were the result of personal experience to which soldiers could directly relate. It is small wonder that his potential as a booster of morale came to be officially recognised as was evident when, after a period serving as a soldier on the Western front, he was sent out on government sponsored drawing missions.

Animated cartoon films were also made in Britain and utilised for propaganda purposes. Many of these attacked Germany and the Kaiser in a satirical style, having more in common with the broad humorous milieu of the comic strip and postcard than the style of much official propaganda of the time which often simply aimed to vilify the 'evil hun'. In their portrayal of the Kaiser, in particular, these animations demonstrated the power of ridicule for propaganda purposes. The cartoonists who were prominent in this field during the war include Dudley Buxton (*The Devil's Little Joke*, 1917), Harry Furniss (e.g. *Peace and War Pencillings*, 1914) stained glass painter Anson Dyer (e.g. *Old King Cole*, 1917, and jointly with Dudley Buxton, *John Bull's Animated Sketchbook*, 1915), E. H. Mills (*The Romance of David Lloyd George*, 1917), fairytale illustrator Lancelot Speed (*Sea Dreams*, 1914), and magazine illustrator George Studdy (e.g. *Studdy's War Studies*, 1914). Interestingly, some of the cartoons of Bruce Bairnsfather and Louis Raemaekers were utilised by Film Booking Offices (a renting firm) to make and distribute animated films although these were not specially drawn by the original artists for the screen but were simply well-known examples of their work "redrawn" by another artist.

- **Archives**

British Cartoon Archive, University of Kent [http://www.cartoons.ac.uk]
The *British Cartoon Archive* is located in Canterbury at the University of Kent's Templeman Library. It has a library, archive, gallery, and is a registered museum dedicated to the history of British cartooning over the last two hundred years. It holds more than 130,000 original editorial, socio-political, and pocket cartoons, supported by large collections of comic strips, newspaper cuttings, books and magazines. The collection of original artwork dates back to 1904 and includes work by W.K.Hasleden, Will Dyson, Strube, David Low, Vicky, Emmwood, Michael Cummings, Ralph Steadman, Mel Calman, Nicholas Garland, Chris Riddell, Carl Giles, Martin Rowson, and Steve Bell, amongst many others. The main priority of the Archive is to catalogue the cartoon images thereby making them accessible to researchers via the computer database.

- **Books**

Allen, T. *The Cartoons of Louis Raemaekers, 1914-1918* (York: Holgate, 1999)

Bryant, M. *World War I in Cartoons* (London: Grub Street, 2006)

Douglas, R. *The Great War, 1914-1918: The Cartoonist's Vision* (London: Routledge, 1995)

Gifford, D. 'Anson Dyer', in *The World Encyclopaedia of Cartoons*, edited by M. Horn (New York: Chelsea House, 1980)

— *British Animated Films, 1895-1985: A Filmography* (Jefferson, North Carolina: McFarland, 1987)

Holt, T. and V. Holt *In Search of the Better 'Ole: A Biography of Captain Bruce Bairnsfather including a Listing of His Works and Collectables*, updated edn (Barnsley, Leo Cooper, 2001)

Price, R. and G. Geoffrey. *A History of Punch* (London: Collins, 1957)

- **Articles**

Demm, E. 'Propaganda and Caricature in the First World War', *Journal of Contemporary History*, 28 (1993), 163-92

Huxley, D. 'Kidding the Kaiser: British Propaganda Animation, 1914–1919', *Early Popular Visual Culture*, 4 (2006), 307–320

Purseigle, P. 'Mirroring Societies at War: Pictorial Humour in the British and French Popular Press during the First World War', *Journal of European Studies*, 31 (2001), 289-328

Ward, P. 'British Animated Propaganda Cartoons of the First World War: Issues of Topicality', *Animation Journal*, 11 (2003), 64-83

— 'Distribution and Trade Press Strategies for British Animated Propaganda Cartoons of the First World War Era', *Historical Journal of Film, Radio and Television*, 25, (2005), 189-201

- **Contemporary Cartoons**

A selection of the cartoons that were published during the war:

Bairnsfather, B. *Bullets and Billets* (London: Richards, 1916)

— *'The Bystander's 'Fragments from France'* (London: The Bystander, 1916)

— *A Few Fragments from His Life*, collected by a friend with some critical chapters by Vivian Carter (London: Hodder and Stoughton, 1916)

The Book of William: With Apologies to Edward Lear (London: Frederick Warne & Co., 1914?)
Parody of Edward Lear's *The Book of Nonsense* lampooning Kaiser Wilhelm II.

Dyson W. H. *Kultur-Cartoons*, with a Foreword by H. G. Wells (London: Stanley Paul, 1915)

— *War Cartoons*, with descriptive letterpress by Arnold Bennett [and others] (London: Hodder and Stoughton, 1917)

Haselden, W. K. *Daily Mirror Reflections in War Times*, 9 vols (London: Daily Mirror, 1916-1918)

— *The Sad Adventures of Big and Little Willie during the First Six Months of the Great War August 1914 - January 1915*, as portrayed by W. K. Haselden in "The Daily Mirror" (London: Chatto & Windus, 1915)

Kato, S. *A History of the War in Sixty-One Cartoons* (London: "Shimpo", 1914)

Leete, A. *The Bosch Book* (London: Duckworth, 1916)

Moreland, A. *The History of the Hun* (London: Palmer and Hayward, 1917)

Punch Cartoons of the Great War (New York: Doran, 1915)

Raemaekers L. *Cartoons* (London: Hodder and Stoughton, 1915)

— *Raemaeker's Cartoon History of the War*, edited by J. M. Allison (New York: Century, 1918)

— *Catalogue of an Exhibition of War Cartoons* (London: Fine Art Society, 1915)

— *The Great War: A Neutral's Indictment*. Cartoons, with an appreciation by H. P. Robinson and descriptive notes by various writers, 3 vols (London: Fine Art Society, 1916-1919)

— *The "Land and Water" Edition of Raemaekers' Cartoons*, 2 vols (London: "Land & Water", 1916-1917)
Includes descriptive articles by Sir Herbert Warren, G.K. Chesterton, the Dean of St. Paul's, Father Bernard Vaughan, Eden Phillpotts, Hilaire Belloc, Sir Sidney Lee, Edmund Gosse, John Buchan, Boyd Cable, and others.

Robinson, B. *Cartoons on the War* (London: Dent, 1915)
These cartoons by Boardman Robinson were originally published in the *New York Tribune* and *Harper's Weekly*.

Robinson. W. H. *The Saintly Hun: A Book of German Virtues* (London: Duckworth, 1917)

— *Some 'Frightful' War Pictures* (London: Duckworth, 1916)

Thomas, B. and others. *One Hundred Cartoons from 'London Opinion'* (London: London Opinion, 1918)

Poy, pseud. *Poy's War Cartoons from the 'Evening News'*, with an introduction by W. MacCartney (London: Simpkin, Marshall, 1915)

Sullivan, E. *The Kaiser's Garland* (London: Heinemann, 1915)

The Worries of Willhelm: A Collection of Humorous and Satirical War Cartoons from the pages of 'The Passing Show' (London: Odhams, 1915)

The following records represent a selection of recently published collections containing cartoons produced in the Great War:

Holt, T. and V. Holt, comps. *The Best of Fragments from France*, by Bruce Bairnsfather; compiled and edited by Tonie & Valmai Holt (Cheltenham: Phin, 1978; repr. Sandwick: Holt, 1998)

Marsay, M., comp. *The Bairnsfather Omnibus*, written and illustrated by Bruce Bairnsfather; compiled and edited by Mark Marsay (Scarborough: Great Northern Publishing, 2000)
Originally published in London by Grant Richards in 2 vols, entitled *Bullets and Billets*, 1916 and *From Mud to Mufti*, 1919.

— *The 2nd Bairnsfather Omnibus*, written and illustrated by Bruce Bairnsfather; with additional texts by William A. Mutch, Vivian Carter and A.J. Dawson (Scarborough: Great Northern, 2000)
Contents: *The Bairnsfather Case*, originally published: New York, Putnam's, 1920; *Fragments from His Life*, originally published: London, Hodder & Stoughton, 1916; *Somme Battle Stories*, originally published: London, Hodder & Stoughton, 1916.

Onslow's (London). *An Important Collection of Bruce Bairnsfather Cartoons and Collectables, Books, Ephemera, Photographs, Pictures and Prints of the Great War and Second World War, Transport Collectors Items and Posters* [Onslow's Sale Catalogue for 31 March, 1999] (London: Onslow's 1999)

Robinson. W. H. *Heath Robinson at War* (London: Methuen, 1942; repr. London: Duckworth, 1978)
Contents: Some *'Frightful' War Pictures*, originally published: London: Duckworth, 1915; *Hunlikely!*, originally published: London : Duckworth, 1916; Fly papers originally published: London: Duckworth, 1921.

- **Contemporary Animated Film Cartoons**

A selection of animated film cartoons produced during the war:

The Devil's Little Joke (Kine Komedy Kartoons, Broadwest Co., 1917)

The Exploits of the "Emden" (Kineto, 1915)

French's Contemptible Little Army (Neptune, 1914)

John Bull's Animated Sketchbook ("Cartoon Company", 1915)
Sponsored and distributed by the renting firm of Ruffell's.

The Jutland Battle (Kineto, 1916)

Peace and War Pencillings (Furniss Films, 1914)

The Romance of Lloyd George (Kine Komedy Kartoons, Broadwest Co., 1917)

Sea Dreams (Neptune, 1915)

Studdy's War Studies, 3 parts (Gaumont, 1914-1915)

Tank Cartoons (Kineto, 1916)

4.2.6   Effects of Propaganda

One of the major objects of British propaganda was to get neutral opinion (particularly that of the USA) on the side of the Allies. The vigorous campaign that Britain waged in this respect was considerably aided by being able to exploit a number of the acts carried out by the Germans, such as the brutality of the unprovoked invasion of Belgium, the execution of Nurse Cavell and Captain Fryatt, the introduction of the use of poison gas on the battlefield, the bombing of Britain's civilian population from the sea and the air, the use of unrestricted submarine warfare, and the Zimmermann telegram. Germany's own propaganda campaign was severely handicapped by these acts and although it had the opportunity to hit back by drawing attention to potentially damaging acts on the Allied side, such as Britain's controversial use of blockade and its ruthless handling of the Easter rebellion in Ireland, it was only able to exploit them with limited success. In comparison, Britain made more effective use of the propaganda opportunities with which it was presented. Germany found itself constantly on the back foot because of the unscrupulous way it waged the war and the offence it gave by undermining the traditional notion of the clear distinction between combatants and civilians[132] with, for instance, its attacks on non-military vessels and its bombardment of civilian targets in Britain by warship, airship, and aeroplane. The British propaganda campaign made the most of this. While it is difficult to assess how far British propaganda (and Allied propaganda generally) succeeded in swaying neutral opinion it is clear that it caused Germany a great deal of concern judging by the strenuous efforts it made to counteract it. The German Central Bureau for Foreign Service, for instance, produced an entire 'White Book' devoted to refuting the allegations that atrocities[133] had been committed by German troops.

During the period when the USA remained neutral Britain was particularly concerned to have public opinion in that country on its side and to counteract the propaganda campaign which Germany had launched in the USA from the very outset of the war. Britain's propaganda campaign there was subtly and competently conducted and avoided the defects of its German counterpart. Its effectiveness as a means of bringing the USA into the war on the side of the Allies, however, needs to be seen in relation to a number of other factors. Politically, linguistically, culturally, and economically Americans had far more in common with the British than the Germans. This was always likely to predispose the USA in the Allies' favour as much as the use of such propaganda as the horror stories of the Bryce Report or accounts of the sinking of the *Lusitania*. In fact such propaganda, although it did help to enlist American sympathy for the Allies' cause, failed to bring that country into the war at an early stage. When the USA did enter the war in 1917 it was because the German authorities, deciding to resume its submarine campaign, had sunk American merchant ships (in spite of clear warnings from the USA about the consequences of such actions) and, furthermore, had been found guilty of attempting to stir up the Mexican people to commit hostile acts against the USA (the Zimmerman telegram).

A great deal of the propaganda involving the Home Front was initially not directly organised by the Government but produced voluntarily via autonomous organizations **(see Part 3, section 4.2.3.1)**, private individuals, and newspapers and it was not until the formation of the National War Aims Committee (NWAC) in 1917 that the Government became wholeheartedly engaged in the task of influencing domestic opinion. It

---

[132] No country, in practice, was totally of the view that there could be no distinction between combatants and non-combatants or that it was admissible to wage war upon women and children. All countries continued to believe that some sort of limit ought to be set. Germany met with considerable criticism by waging war in a manner, not once but on a series of occasions, which neutrals considered to go beyond the limits that were acceptable.

[133] Many ordinary Germans were also disturbed by the atrocity reports. The Hamburg scholar, Aby Warburg, for instance, was so upset by these reports that he spent much of the war collecting evidence from newspapers to refute the charges that were made in these reports; this task became an obsession with him (Gombrich, A. H. *Aby Warburg: An Intellectual Biography*, 2nd edn (Oxford: Phaidon, 1986, p. 206).

seems inconceivable that the vast outpouring of printed and visual propaganda from these various sources did not help considerably with the Government's task of convincing the nation of the justice of its involvement in the war, recruiting the large numbers required for the armed forces, mines and factories, and generally sustaining public support for the war. It must surely have been the case that quite a large proportion of the British public, which had become a great deal more literate by 1914, was reading some of the large number of propagandistic books and pamphlets[134] and many (by virtue of the their mass circulation and cheapness) of the newspaper articles that were produced; it was certainly the case that the British people were going in their millions to the cinema where they saw not only conventional drama but also films and newsreels of a propagandistic nature. Measuring the effect of all these influences is, however, problematical. The enormous influx of volunteers to the armed forces at the beginning of the war was by no means simply the result of recruitment propaganda; there were a wide variety of other factors involved in their motivation to join up **(see Part 3, section 4.5.1.2)** and recruitment propaganda (including such examples as Alfred Leete's famous poster 'Kitchener Wants You' and the film *You*) failed, after the initial surge of enthusiasm had waned, to arrest the decline in recruitment that ultimately led to the need to introduce conscription. Propaganda appeals to get women into the factories and on the land tended to fare better, helped no doubt by the opportunity that many women were glad to grasp to change their life-style. The cinema, with its mass audiences, was the ideal vehicle for propaganda but the British use of it was not always entirely successful. Certainly the film *For the Empire*[135] was a box office success and Beaverbrook is said to have claimed, according to A. J. P. Taylor in his biography of him[136], that the newsreels he had produced as the Minister for Information were 'the decisive factor in maintaining the moral [sic] of the people during the black days of the early summer of 1918'. The recruiting film *You!*, however, was a commercial failure. Although, in contrast, *The Battle of the Somme*, the most famous British war film produced in the war, was a huge commercial success[137] it nevertheless received quite a lot of criticism in Britain (and even more abroad, particularly in the USA) – a reason perhaps for doubting its value as propaganda. The newspaper press, from the publishers and editors to the reporters[138], mostly played its part in the task of sustaining public support for the war, aiming to avoid printing anything that might undermine morale and often achieving this by being economical with the truth. The novelist John Buchan, who was an important figure in British propaganda during the war, attributed great importance to the role of the newspaper press when he said in 1917: 'So far as Britain is concerned the war could not have been fought for one month without its newspapers'[139]. This is perhaps a somewhat exaggerated view of the influence of the press on a nation that was for the most part inclined to be patriotic and in little need of persuasion. Soldiers at the front did not seem to be particularly impressed by the reporting in the Northcliffe press papers like the *Daily Mail* that were sold at the entrances to their communication trenches, tending to be resentful[140] and even bitter[141] about their often unrealistic accounts of what was happening at the front; they preferred to produce and read their own trench newspapers (around half of which were edited by other ranks) rather than a propagandistic British newspaper.

The reputation for success accorded to British propaganda in the aftermath of the war was due to a considerable extent to the influence attributed to it by people like Ludendorff (*My War Memories*), Hindenburg (*Out of My Life*),

---

[134] The Oxford *Red Book* sold some 46,000 copies; by January 1915 300,000 copies of the famous Oxford pamphlets on the war, priced between 1 and 4 pence, had been sold. Books such as John Masefield's account of the Somme, *The Old Front Line*, Arnold Bennett's *Statement of the British Case* and Gilbert Murray's *Foreign Policy of Sir Edward Grey* also sold well. In the last year of the war it has been estimated that the National War Aims Committee reached over a million readers with its huge output of publications.

[135] It has been calculated that the film *For the Empire* could have been seen by as many as 9 million people by the end of December 1916.

[136] Taylor, A. J. P *Beaverbrook* (London: Hamilton, 1972).

[137] *The Battle of the Somme* had by October 1916 been booked by over 2,000 cinemas across the country and grossed around £30,000.

[138] The war correspondents mostly collaborated with the military censors, not only providing a sanitised picture of the army at the front and ensuring that no information that might be of use to the enemy was reported, but also by providing stories of heroism and glory, glossing over major setbacks, and shielding the High Command from criticism of its conduct of the war..

[139] Quoted in Gebele, H. *Die Probleme von Krieg und Frieden in Grossbritannien während des Ersten Weltkriegs* (1987).

[140] For example, the style of dishonest war reporting that was released to the press under the headline of 'Eyewitness' was ridiculed by soldiers at the font as 'Eyewash'.

[141] For example, Siegfried Sassoon's hatred of the 'yellow-pressmen' in his poem *Fight to the Finish*.

and Hitler (*Mein Kampf*)[142] [see also note appended to Bruntz, *Allied propaganda and the Collapse of the German Empire in 1918* in the section on **Books** below]. These tributes were especially related to the British propaganda operations of Crewe House in the last year of the war. Furthermore, the article, 'British Propaganda in Enemy Countries' published in vol. 21, 1919, of *The Times History and Encyclopaedia of the War*, and the many memoirs which appeared after the war by former participants in British propaganda operations, such as Campbell Stuart, E. T. Cook, Douglas Brownrigg, and Wickham Steed, all served to perpetuate this reputation for success. Northcliffe had little doubt of the value of British propaganda, claiming that 'good propaganda had probably saved a year of war, and this meant the saving of thousands of millions of money and probably at least a million lives'[143], nor did Steed, who felt justified in claiming for Crewe House's propaganda campaign that it was responsible 'not for the actual break-up, but for very materially accelerating the break-up of Austria'; and Roderick Jones[144] clearly felt that through his work for Reuters and Britain's Department of Information and later for her Ministry of Information he had made a significant contribution to Britain's propaganda. In contrast, Germany came to feel that their propaganda had failed to realise the sort of impact achieved by Britain[145].

Whatever conclusions can be drawn about the value of British propaganda in the Great War the fact remains that propaganda, by itself, does not win wars; in the final analysis it is the persistence of the will of a nation to win that is the decisive factor. Propaganda (particularly if it can feed on military achievements) can help to sustain this will but, ultimately, sustaining it depends on the resilience of the civilian population and the state of the morale of its fighting forces. British civilians endured hardships but never on the scale suffered in Germany in terms of the scarcity of food and other domestic necessities that Germany's deteriorating economy was causing by the end of 1915 and rendering even worse in the ensuing years; by the winter of 1916 to 1917, with malnutrition rife, German civilians were losing faith in the state's promise of a victorious peace as the reward for their extreme hardship and increased war efforts, and their morale was steadily breaking down. Towards the end of the war this situation began to cause German soldiers at the front serious concern[146] and was an important factor in the crumbling of their morale and the desertions[147] which occurred. In contrast, British soldiers (mostly oblivious to propaganda and sometimes critical of it) remained stubbornly and stoically committed to fighting the war to the bitter end and, with morale mostly intact, were able in the final year of the war to play an important part in the major offensive which led to victory.

In the aftermath of the Great War British propaganda came in for considerable vilification[148] which was

---

[142] Ludendorff, Hindenburg, and Hitler were also leading exponents of the 'stab-in-the-back' notion that it was the undermining of German morale by traiterous civilians within the home front and not failure of the army on the battlefield which had caused Germany to lose the war.

[143] *The Times*, 31 October 1917.

[144] During the war Jones was managing director of Reuters. Alongside the Agent-Reuter service he ran an official service for Britain's Department of Information and later for her Ministry of Information, of which he for a time became its full-time director of propaganda.

[145] This feeling is exemplified in the following two quotations (which also bear witness to the important influence which Roderick Jones exerted via the Reuters organisation during the war):

'Reuter rules the market, not Wolff; London makes foreign opinion not Berlin. We Germans have remained, despite all our exertions as regards impressing foreign opinion, the same bunglers we always were ... Where Reuters indulges in rapid and skilful swordplay, we bring up our heavy artillery' (Roche, P. *Vossiche Zeitung*, 15 August 1917).

'More powerful than the English fleet, more dangerous than the English army, are Reuters and the English news-propaganda' (A tribute from a German official in July 1918 quoted in Sanders and Taylor's *British Propaganda during the First World War, 1914-1918*).

[146] One result of the concern of German soldiers about the condition of people at home was the formation of Soldiers' Councils which redistributed army food stocks among German people suffering near-starvation. See also G. D. Feldman's review of of Bessel's *Germany After the First World War* (1993) in the **Articles** section below.

[147] Arising out of War Office interrogations of German prisoners, there had developed by the end of the war an assumption that desertions in the German army were considerably influenced by the propaganda literature that was distributed among its troops. The validity of this assumption, however, has been cast into some doubt in recent times. It has been found, for instance, that in investigations of prisoners in relation to the psychology of desertion during the Second World War, it could not be proved beyond all reasonable doubt that their possession of propaganda literature had directly influenced them to desert (see, for instance, Shils, E. A. and M. Janowitz. 'Cohesion and Disintegration in the Wehrmacht in World War II', *Public Opinion Quarterly*, 12 (1948), 280-315).

[148] It cannot be denied that a good deal of British propaganda was based on falsehood and distortion. Furthermore, some of it was of an

exacerbated by the publication of books such as Arthur Ponsonby's *Falsehood in Wartime*, C. E. Montague's *Disenchantment*, Robert Graves's *Goodbye to All That*, Richard Aldington's *Death of a Hero*, and a whole host of post-war memoirs and novels, especially in the late twenties, which expressed the feelings of public resentment about the lies and manipulation that had occurred during the war. By the end of the war hostility, particularly in parliamentary circles, to the government's propaganda organisation was clearly apparent and, in spite of the efforts of Beaverbrook and other senior officials to preserve it into peacetime, it was swiftly wound up as the as soon as the war ended. Dislike of the sort of propaganda that had developed in the Great War lingered among the British people and became so deeply entrenched that they found it difficult to distinguish truth from propaganda as, for instance, when in the Second World War they were initially disinclined to believe government statements about the Nazi treatment of the Jews. In Germany Hitler was so impressed by what he regarded as the success of British propaganda in the Great War that he was determined to emulate it with his own style of Nazi propaganda which he brought into full operation in the inter-war years with the appointment of Goebbels in 1933 as Minister for Popular Enlightenment and Propaganda in his first government. It is largely as a result of Nazi propaganda that the word propaganda has continued to be equated with 'lies', 'deceit', and brainwashing.

Autobiographies, Biographies, Memoirs

Gombrich, A. H. *Aby Warburg: An Intellectual Biography*, 2nd edn (Oxford: Phaidon, 1986)
See note 133. The personal library of the Hamburg scholar Aby Warburg (1866-1929) was the basis of the research institute which in its expanded form became known as the Warburg Institute and was incorporated in 1944 as a member-Institute of the University of London's School of Advanced Study.

Hindenburg, P. von. *Out of my Life*, translated by F. A. Holt (London: Cassell, 1920)
Translation, from the German, of "Aus meinen Leben". An abridged edition of this translation, edited and introduced by Charles Messenger, was published under the title of *The Great War*, London: Greenhill, 2006

Ludendorff, E. von. *My War Memories, 1914-18*, 2 vols. (London: Hutchinson, 1919)

Jones, Sir R., *A Life In Reuters* (London: Hodder & Stoughton, 1951)

Masterman, L. *C. F. G. Masterman: A Biography* (London: Nicholson and Watson, 1939; repr. London: Cass, 1968)

Books

Beaverbrook, W. M. A., 1st Baron. *Men and Power 1917-1918* (London: Hutchinson, 1956; repr. London: Collins, 1966)

Bessel, R. *Germany After the First World War* (Oxford: Clarendon Press, 1993)
See review of his book by G. D. Feldman in the **Articles** section below.

— 'Mobilisation and Demobilisation in Germany, 1916-1919', in *State, Society, and Mobilisation in Europe during the First World War*, edited by J. Horne (Cambridge: Cambridge University Press, 1997, repr. 2002)

Bruntz, G. B. *Allied Propaganda and the Collapse of the German Empire in 1918*, Hoover War Library Publications, 13 (Stanford: Stanford University Press, 1938; repr. New York: Arno Press, 1972)
Judging by the behaviour of some German soldiers and sailors in November 1918, it seems possible to infer that it was the Bolsheviks who achieved more in influencing German opinion than the propaganda of the allies (p. 147).

Davis, B. 'Society United Against the State: The Case of World War I Berlin', paper presented at a conference

---

especially malicious nature as was particularly the case, for example, with a writer like Horatio Bottomley. Nevertheless, there was also a very considerable amount of British propaganda which did not descend to this level. There was, for instance, nothing unscrupulous and despicable about the type of propaganda represented in the series of 'battle' films (like those, for instance, relating to the Somme, Ancre, Arras, St. Quentin, and Allenby's entry into Jerusalem) and the cartoons of Bairnsfather (famous for his 'Old Bill'); nor could a charge about the conduct of its operations be brought against Wellington House which, as one of the chief sources of overseas propaganda for a great deal of the war, was very much influenced by its director, C. F. G. Masterman, who, though his insistence on objectivity, was generally able to restrain the tone of the propaganda it produced.

on "Mobilizing for 'Total' War. Society and the State in Europe, 1914-1918," Trinity College, Dublin, June 1993

Fraser, L. M. *Germany between two Wars: A Study of Propaganda and War-Guilt* (London: Oxford University Press, 1944)

Fuller, J. G. *Troop Morale and Popular Culture in the British and Dominion Armies, 1914-1918* (Oxford: Clarendon Press, 1990)

Gebele, H. *Die Probleme von Krieg und Frieden in Grossbritannien wahrend des Ersten Weltkriegs: Regierung, Parteien und offentliche Meinung in der Auseinandersetzung uber Kriegs- und Friedensziele* (Frankfurt am Main; New York: P. Lang, 1987)
Includes numerous citations and documents in English.

Hadamovsky, E. *Propaganda and National Power* (New York: Arno Press, 1954; repr. 1972)
Translation of the author's *Propaganda und nationale Macht: Die Organisation der offentlichen Meinung für die nationale Politik*, Oldenburg: G. Stalling, 1933. In this book the author says of the war that 'The German people were not beaten on the battlefield, but were defeated in the war of words'

Hansen, F. *The Unrepentent Northcliffe: A Reply to the London 'Times' of October 19, 1920* (Hamburg: Overseas Publishing Co., 1921)
In this open letter to Northcliffe Hansen expresses the animosity shared by many of his fellow Germans after the war towards Norhtcliffe for the poisonous and sensational nature of the propaganda he directed at Germany and her soldiers in the last stages of the war.

Hitler, A. *Mein Kampf*, with an introduction by D. Cameron Watt; translated by Ralph Manheim (London: Pimlico, 1998)
First published München: Zentralverlag der NSDAP, 1925-1927, in two volumes.

Jackson, A. 'Germany, the Home Front: Blockade, Government and Revolution', in *Facing Armageddon: The First World War Experienced*, ed. by H. Cecil and P. H. Liddle (London: Leo Cooper, 1996)

Knightley, P. *The First Casualty: The War Correspondent as Hero, Propagandist and Myth Maker from the Crimea to Kosovo*, rev. edn with a new introduction by John Pilger (London: Prion, 2000)
On December 28, 1917, at a breakfast to which he had invited C. P. Scott of the Manchester Guardian, Lloyd George confided to the newspaperman: " I listened last night, at a dinner given to Philip Gibbs on his return from the front, to the most impressive and moving description from him of what the war in the West really means, that I have heard. Even an audience of hardened politicians and journalists was strongly affected. If people really knew, the war would be stopped tomorrow. But, of course, they don't – and can't know. The correspondents don't write and the censorship would not pass the truth" [quotation from the book]. A new edn of the book with the title *The First Casualty: The War Correspondent as Hero, Propagandist and Myth-Maker from the Crimea to Iraq* was published in 2003 by Andre Deutsch.

Kocka, J. *Facing Total War: German Society, 1914-18*, translated from the German by Barbara Weinberger. (Leamington Spa: Berg, 1984)
Translation of *Klassengesellschaft im Krieg: deutsche Sozialgeschichte, 1914-1918*, Göttingen: Vandenhoeck & Ruprecht, 1978.

Lasswell, H. D. *Propaganda Technique in World War I*, new edn (Cambridge, Mass.: M.I.T., 1971)
Original edition published under the title, *Propaganda Technique in the World War*, London: Kegan Paul, 1927.

Lutz, R. H., ed. *Fall of the German Empire 1914-18*, 2 vols. (Stanford: Stanford University Press, 1932; repr. New York: Octagon Books, 1969)

Offer, A. *The First World War: An Agrarian Interpretation* (Oxford: Clarendon Press, 1989; repr. 1991)

Pound, R. and G. Harmsworth. *Northcliffe* (London: Cassell, 1959)

Sanders, M. L. and P. M. Taylor *British Propaganda during the First World War, 1914-1918* (London: Macmillan, 1982)

Shils, E. A. and M. Janowitz. 'Cohesion and Disintegration in the Wehrmacht in World War II', in *Public Opinion and Propaganda*: a book of readings edited for the Society for the Psychological Study of Social Issues by D. Katz,

D. Cartwright, S. Eldersveld, A. McClung Lee (New York: Holt, Rinehart and Winston, 1954)
Reprint of the article by Shils and Janowitz in *Public Opinion Quarterly*, 12 (1948), 280-315 (q.v.). The authors make the point that in investigations of prisoners in relation to the psychology of desertion during the Second World War it could not be proved beyond all reasonable doubt that the possession of propaganda literature had directly influenced them to desert. This casts into doubt the validity of an assumption, arising out of War Office interrogation of German prisoners at the end of the First World War, that desertions in the German army in that war were considerably influenced by the propaganda literature that was distributed among its troops.

Squires, J. D. *British Propaganda at Home and in the United States from 1914 To 1917* (Cambridge: Harvard University Press, 1935)
"There will, of course, never be any agreement on the percentage of influence which British propaganda had in bringing about the decision of April 6, 1917. It was not *the* cause for American entrance into the World War. But that it was a cause, and a powerful one, it seems impossible for the historian to deny" [quotation from the book on p.81].

Stuart, Sir C. *Secrets of Crewe House: The Story of a Famous Campaign* (London: Hodder & Stoughton, 1920)

Thimme, H. *Weltkrieg ohne Waffen: die Propaganda der Westmächte gegen Deutschland, ihre Wirkung und ihre Abwehr* (Stuttgart und Berlin : Cotta, 1932)
In this book Thimme argues that the success of Entente propaganda on the German front lay not only in the sound psychological basis of its appeal, and its exploitation of the differences of opinion in Germany and of certain attackable aspects of German political philosophy, but also in the failure of Germany either to react in time to the danger posed by enemy propaganda or to devise effective ways of countering it. [Information based on the review of Thimme's book by Eloise Ellery in *American Historical Review*, 38 (1933), 559-560].

Welch, D. *Germany, Propaganda, and Total War: The Sins of Omission* (London: Athlone, 2000)
The author does not view the moral collapse of Germany solely in terms of a failure to get its propaganda across but rather as a failure of the military establishment and the Kaiser not only to provide this propaganda with effective support but also to see the importance of the use of public opinion to create an effective bond between leadership and the people.

Winter, J. M. *The Great War and the British People* (London: Macmillan, 1985)

Articles

Deist, W. 'The Military Collapse of the German Empire: The Reality Behind the Stab-in-the-Back Myth; translated by E. J. Feuchtwanger', *War in History*, 3 (1996), 186–207

Ellery, E. "'Weltkrieg ohne Waffen: die Propaganda der Westmächte gegen Deutschland, ihre Wirkung und ihre Abwehr', by Hans Thimme", *American Historical Review*, 38 (1933), 559-560

Feldman, G. D. 'Germany After the First World War, by Richard Bessel', *Journal of Social History*, 28 (1995), 909-911
One of the points brought out in this review is that German soldiers, "well-fed at the front", were, when on leave, frequently demoralised by witnessing and experiencing the poor conditions which their families had to endure and bitter about the failure of the government to care for them.

Hiley, N. P. '"Kitchener Wants You" and "Daddy, What Did You Do in the War?": The Myth of British Recruiting Posters', *Imperial War Museum Review*, 11 (1997), 40-58

Howard, N. P. 'The Social and Political Consequences of the Allied Food Blockade of Germany, 1918-1919', *German History*, 11 (1993), 161-88

Lutz, R. H. 'Studies of World War Propaganda, 1914-33', *Journal of Modern History*, 5 (1933), 496-516

Marquis, A. G. 'Words as Weapons. Propaganda in Britain and Germany during the First World War', *Journal of Contemporary History*, 13 (1978), 467-498

Shils, E. A. and M. Janowitz. 'Cohesion and Disintegration in the Wehrmacht in World War II', *Public Opinion Quarterly*, 12 (1948), 280-315

Watson, A. 'Stabbed at the Front', *History Today*, 58 (2008), 21-7

The author counters the myth that the German army only lost the war because it had been 'Stabbed in the Back' by defeatists and revolutionaries on the Home Front with a review of the evidence that it had simply lost the will to go on fighting.

Wright, D. G. 'The Great War, Government Propaganda and English "Men Of Letters", 1914-16', *Literature and History*, 7 (1978), 70-100

4.3 War Aims and Strategy

4.3.1 War Aims

Shortly after war had been declared Asquith made in the House of Commons a speech in which he included a general indication of Britain's war aims and later in the year (on 9 December 1914), in a speech he delivered at the Guildhall, he clearly singled out the reconstitution of Belgium as Britain's basic war aim. These speeches and their manipulation by propagandists, were calculated to influence the public into believing that Britain's entry into the war had been for the just purpose of liberating Belgium and that Germany had to be totally defeated to ensure that the situation resulting from her aggression could never be repeated again. The government was happy for the British people to continue to have this simple view of Britain's war aims as it was reluctant for the public to have a more detailed knowledge of them especially, as with the passage of time, they became more complicated and opaque as a result of Britain's involvement in secret and controversial diplomacy[149].

After Asquith's speeches in the early days of the war there were, therefore, no further official public declarations of war aims until Lloyd George felt obliged to make one in his speech at a conference of trade unionists on 5 January 1918. In the intervening years war aims were discussed internally by politicians and service chiefs and views about war aims were also publicly aired by various propagandists. Internal official discussions ranged fundamentally over aims to restore Belgium to its former state, dismantle the German Navy[150], deprive Germany permanently of the colonies which Britain had captured from them in the early days of the war[151], remove the economic threat considered by the Allies to be posed by Germany[152], destroy 'Prussian militarism'[153], and punish Germany for flouting international law and precipitating war in Europe. In August 1916 Asquith asked various leading figures for their ideas on British war aims. Their response, encapsulated in a *Memorandum on War Aims*, showed that there was general agreement on France regaining Alsace-Lorraine, Belgium being restored, and Poland at least becoming autonomous but no desire for extensive annexation of German territory. On the advisability of imposing the economic measures proposed at the Paris Conference of 1916 for weakening Germany's trading position permanently British experts were divided. Another discussion of British war aims, carried out in the Spring 1917 by Committee meetings of the Imperial War Cabinet, produced two reports from the Co-Chairmen, Curzon and Milner. From Milner's report emerged the suggestion that only small reparations should be demanded and an argument against the idea of applying the anti-German economic measures proposed at the Paris Conference of 1916. Curzon's report, which was adopted by the Cabinet, advocated the restoration of Belgium and Serbia; the settlement of the questions of Poland and Alsace-Lorraine on the basis of the wishes of the inhabitants and the need for a lasting peace; and the removal of colonies from Germany, and of Palestine and Mesopotamia from Turkey.

Within official circles soldiers and government ministers were not always in accord in their approach to war aims. The basic aim of the soldiers was simply to inflict such a crushing defeat on Germany that it would cease

---

[149] This secret diplomacy involved the government's agreement to some territorial and other ambitions, both on the part of Britain and those of her allies, that were incompatible with the moral tone and idealism it had adopted with the British people and not something which it would have wished to reveal publicly.

[150] For politicians of both parties and for service chiefs this continued to be considered as a central aim.

[151] The Admiralty took the view that the restoration of Germanys colonies would pose a strategic threat. Few, however, thought that there were economic gains to be obtained from retaining them.

[152] At the Allied Economic Conference in Paris in June 1916 the Allies agreed on measures designed to reduce the competitive strength of German trading. There was divided opinion among the British about whether this policy was advisable.

[153] It was believed by many that this aim could only be achieved as a result of total victory enabling the Allies to dictate the terms of peace and avoid a peace based on compromise.

to have the capability to launch acts of aggression in the future. In contrast, the aim of some ministers was considerably more ambitious; they wanted not only to defeat Germany militarily but also to press for a radical transformation of Germany after the war along the lines of a democratization of her society and institutions. These were by no means the only differences on the question of war aims. Throughout the war views on the subject were frequently liable to be extended or refined. Among the public a number of alternative and often conflicting views on Britain's war aims developed. Broad views about aims were divided between the need on the one hand for a total victory and on the other hand for a negotiated peace based on compromise; the former views found favour with most people. Some people felt that the an attempt should be made to eliminate the threat of war in the future by means of some sort of league of nations through which this object could be achieved. The notion of an international organisation, encapsulated in the phrase 'League of Nations' which seems to have been first coined by Lowes Dickinson, attracted most Liberal newspapers, well-known figures like H. G. Wells and Grey, and a variety of people, including those who were opposed to the war as well those who strongly believed in the need to defeat Germany. Views about the implementation of a League of Nations, however, met with disagreement on the question of whether or not it could only be established after a peace obtained by victory over Germany. Among the anti-war protagonists the views which carried the most weight came from the members of Union of Democratic Control who, wanting to prevent a repetition of the diplomatic mistakes which had, in their opinion, led to the war, believed that this could be achieved by focusing on the two basic aims of ending the war by negotiation and, in its aftermath, establishing an international structure for peace based on open diplomacy.

Lloyd George was in no doubt about Britain's primary war aim which was summed up in his 'a fight to the finish – to a knock-out', a slogan he proclaimed in July 1916 that represented his opposition to any proposal for a peace that was not based on total victory. In the latter half of 1917, however, he saw the necessity of acquainting the public with something more than war aims encapsulated in simple slogans. By that time he was confronted by a number of pressures which included Woodrow Wilson's views on ending the war, the Bolshevik action in discrediting the war aims of the Allies by publishing their secret treaties, and the agreement by the Labour Party in December 1917 on a joint statement of war aims[154]. These pressures convinced him of the need to provide a more detailed statement of British war aims and to give them a public expression in order to rally the support of the nation, particularly the working class members of it. He did this in a speech delivered at a conference of trade unionists on 5 January 1918. In his speech he emphasised that Britain was intent not on the destruction or democratization of Germany but on working towards a number of constructive ends which included the restoration of Belgium, the return of Alsace-Lorraine to France, self-determination for other conquered countries, reparations to the victims of German oppression, and the establishment of an international organization to arbitrate disputes and control arms. This was the fullest statement of British war aims made publicly during the war. It is of some significance that it was very similar to the war aims adopted in the previous month by the TUC/Labour Party joint committee and was made in a speech delivered to an audience of trade unionists - an indication that Lloyd George was motivated more by a desire to rally the nation and particularly the working class to his side than to represent a true reflection of what was in the minds of the members of the cabinet committees involved in producing a list of war aims.

Autobiographies, Biographies, Memoirs

Adams, R. J. Q. *Bonar Law* (London: John Murray, 1999)

Armstrong, H. C. *Grey Steel (J. C. Smuts): A Study in Arrogance* (Harmondsworth: Penguin 1939)

Blake, R. *The Unknown Prime Minister: The Life and Times of Andrew Bonar Law, 1858-1923* (London: Eyre and Spottiswoode, 1955)

Esher, R. B. B., 2nd Viscount. *Journals and Letters of Reginald, Viscount Esher*, edited by M. V. Brett and O. S. B. Brett, 4 vols (London: Nicholson and Watson, 1934-38), III: *1910-1915* (1934) and IV: *1916-1930* (1938) edited by Oliver S. B. Brett, Viscount Esher.

---

[154] This Memorandum on War Aims was drafted mainly by MacDonald and, not surprisingly, therefore, was very similar to the programme which the UDC had been advocating since the beginning of the war. Like the latter programme it repudiated secret diplomacy, emphasised the need for reconciliation with Germany, and was generally favourable to the idea of a peace based on a formula of no Annexations and Idemnities as had been suggested in Lenin's peace decree of November 1917.

"During the First World War, Esher served in France liaising informally between French and British generals. He spoke excellent French and perhaps because his mother was French he understood the French better than most. He also reported to his cabinet and court friends on the problems of the British staff officers. His role was not well defined and inspired the jealousy of the British ambassador. There had been similar protests in the newspapers about his 'irresponsible' influence before the war. While some distrusted him, others confided in him as a useful conduit to those in high office. Kitchener, Haig, Asquith, Balfour, Stamfordham, and George V regarded him as contributing to the war effort." [Quotation extracted from William M. Kuhn, W. M. 'Brett, Reginald Baliol, second Viscount Esher (1852–1930)', *Oxford Dictionary of National Biography*, Oxford University Press, 2004; online edn, Jan 2008 [http://www.oxforddnb.com/view/article/32055, accessed 14 Nov 2013].

Gilbert, M. *The Challenge of War: Winston Churchill, 1914-1916* (London: Minerva, 1990)
Originally published as *Winston S. Churchill*, by R. S. Churchill and M. Gilbert, vol 3, 1914-1916, London, Heinemann, 1971.

— *World In Torment: Winston S. Churchill, 1916-1922* (London: Minerva, 1995)
Originally published as *Winston S. Churchill*, by R. S. Churchill and M. Gilbert, vol 4, 1916-1922, London, Heinemann, 1975.

Gilmour, D. *Curzon* (London: John Murray, 1994; repr. 2003)

Gollin, A. M. *Proconsul in Politics: A Study of Lord Milner in Opposition and in Power* (London: A. Blond, 1964)

Grey, E., 1st Viscount Grey of Fallodon. *Twenty-five years, 1892-1916*, 2 vols (London: Hodder & Stoughton, 1925)

Hancock, W. K. *Smuts*, 2 vols (Cambridge: Cambridge University Press, 1962-1968), I: *The Sanguine Years, 1870-1919* (1962)
Smuts drafted Lloyd George's speech on British war aims in January 1918, in which he denounced the capitalist exploitation of colonial territories and proclaimed the relevance of self-determination to the German colonies, and which became embodied in Woodrow Wilson's 'fourteen points'.

Lloyd George, D. *War Memoirs*. 2nd edn, 2 vols (London: Odhams, 1942)

Koss, S. E. *Asquith* (London: Hamilton, 1976; repr. 1985)

Newton, T. W. L., 2nd Baron. *Lord Lansdowne: A Biography* (London: Macmillan, 1929)

Tomes, J. *Balfour and Foreign Policy: The Intellectual Thought of a Conservative Statesman* (Cambridge: Cambridge University Press, 1997)

Books

Bunselmeyer, R. E. *The Cost of the War, 1914-1919: British Economic War Aims and the Origins of Reparation* (Hamden, Conn.: Archon Books, 1975)

— 'The Cost of the War; British Plans For the Post-War Economic Treatment of Germany, 1914-1918' (unpublished doctoral thesis, Yale University, 1968)

Calder, K. J. *Britain and the Origins of the New Europe, 1914-1918* (Cambridge: Cambridge University Press, 1976)

Cassar, G. H. *Lloyd George at War 1916-1918* (London: Anthem Press, 2009; repr. 2011)

Cornwall, J. M. *The Undermining of Austria-Hungary: The Battle for Hearts and Minds* (Basingstoke: Macmillan, 2000)

Davis, R.O. 'British Policy and Opinion on War Aims and Peace Proposals, 1914-1918"(unpublished doctoral thesis, Duke University, 1958)

— 'Lloyd George: Leader or Led in British War Aims, 1916-1918', in *Power, Public Opinion and Diplomacy*: essays in honour of Eber Malcolm Carroll by his former students, edited by L. P. Wallace and W. C. Askew (London: Cambridge University Press, 1959)

Dehne, P. A. *On the Far Western Front: Britain's First World War in South America* (Manchester: Manchester

University Press, 2009)

Dunn, S. and T. G. Fraser, eds. *Europe and Ethnicity: The First World War and Contemporary Ethnic Conflict* (London: Routledge, 1996)

Dutton, D. *Politics of Diplomacy: Britain and France in the Balkans in the First World War* (London: Tauris, 1997)

Ekstein-Frankl, M. G. 'The Development of British War Aims, August 1914-March 1915' (unpublished doctoral thesis, University of London, 1969)

Fest, W. *Peace or Partition: The Habsburg Monarchy and British Policy, 1914-1918* (London: Prior, 1978)

French, D. *British Strategy and War Aims, 1914-1916* (London: Allen and Unwin, 1986)

Friedman, I. *British Pan-Arab Policy, 1915-1922: A Critical Appraisal* (New Brunswick: Transaction Publishers, 2010)

Gooch, J. 'Soldiers, Strategy and War Aims in Britain, 1914-18', in *War Aims and Strategic Policy in the Great War, 1914-1918*, edited by B. Hunt and A. Preston (London: Croom Helm, 1977)

— 'The Weary Titan: Strategy and Policy in Great Britain, 1890-1918', in *The Making of Strategy: Rulers, States, and War*, edited by W. Murray, M. Knox, A. Bernstein (Cambridge: Cambridge University Press, 1994)

Guinn, P. *British Strategy and Politics, 1914-1918* (Oxford: Clarendon Press, 1965)

Hanak, H. *Great Britain and Austria-Hungary during the 1st World War: A Study in the Formation of Public Opinion* (London: Oxford University Press, 1962)

Hankey, M. P. A., Baron Hankey. *The Supreme Command, 1914-1918*, 2 vols (London: Allen & Unwin, 1961)

Hinsley, F. H., ed. *British Foreign Policy under Sir Edward Grey* (Cambridge: Cambridge University Press, 1977)
Contains valuable material on economic policy-making and the blockade.

Hunt, B. and A. Preston, eds. *War Aims and Strategic Policy in the Great War, 1914-1918* (London: Croom Helm, 1977)

Jaffe, L. S. *The Decision to Disarm Germany: British Policy Towards Postwar German Disarmament, 1914-1919* (London: Allen & Unwin, 1985)

Kennedy, P. M. 'Strategy versus Finance in Twentieth Century Britain', in *Strategy and Diplomacy 1870-1945*, eight studies by Paul Kennedy (London: Fontana, 1983; repr. 1993)

Miller, R., ed. *Britain, Palestine and Empire: The Mandate Years* (Farnham: Ashgate Publishing Ltd, 2010)

Millman, B. *Pessimism and British War Policy, 1916-1918* (London: Frank Cass, 2001)

Neilson, K. *Strategy and Supply: The Anglo-Russian Alliance, 1914-17* (London: Allen & Unwin, 1984)

Nelson, H. I. *Land and Power: British and Allied Policy on Germany's Frontiers, 1916-19* (London: Routledge, 1963)

Porter, B. 'Britain and the Middle East in the Great War', in *Home Fires and Foreign Fields, British Social and Military Experience in the Great War*, ed. by P. H. Liddle (Manchester: Manchester University Press, 1985)

Rothwell, V. H. *British War Aims and Peace Diplomacy, 1914-18* (Oxford: Clarendon Press, 1971)

Schneer, J. *The Balfour Declaration: The Origins of the Arab-Israeli Conflict* (London: Bloomsbury, 2011)

Scott, J. B. *Official Statements of War Aims and Peace Proposals, Dec. 1916-Nov. 1918*, prepared under the supervision of J. B. Scott (Washington: Carnegie Edowment for International Peace, Division of International Law, 1921)

Stein, L. J. *The Balfour Declaration* (London: Valentine, Mitchell, 1961)

Taylor, A. J. P. 'The War Aims of the Allies in the First World War', in *Essays Presented to Sir Lewis Namier*, edited by R. Pares and A. J. P. Taylor (London: Macmillan, 1956; repr. Freeport, NY: Books for Libraries Press, 1971)

— 'The War Aims of the Allies in the First World War', in *Politics in Wartime and other Essays*, by A. J. P Taylor (London: H. Hamilton, 1964)

Articles

Callcott, W. R. 'The Last War Aim: British Opinion and the Decision for Czechoslovak Independence, 1914-1919', *Historical Journal*, 27 (1984), 979-89

Fest, W. B. 'British War Aims and German Peace Feelers During the First World War (December 1916-November 1918)', *Historical Journal*, 15 (1972), 285-308

French, D. 'The Origins of the Dardanelles Campaign Reconsidered', *History*, 68 (1983), 210-224

Galbraith, J. S. 'British War Aims in World War I: A Commentary on "Statesmanship"', *Journal of Imperial and Commonwealth History*, 13 (1984), 25-45

Gilbert, B. 'Pacifist to Interventionist: David Lloyd George in 1911 and 1914; Was Belgium An Issue?', *Historical Journal*, 28 (1985)

Hanak, H. H. 'British Opinion About the Dissolution of The Habsburg Monarchy and Independence for the Czechs and Slovaks, 1914 to 1918', *Bulletin of the Institute of Historical Research*, 33 (1960), 129-32

— 'The Government, the Foreign Office and Austria-Hungary, 1914-18', *Slavonic and East European Review*, 47 (1969), 161-97

Hay, W. A. 'A Problem Postponed: Britain and the Future of Austria-Hungary, 1914-18', *Diplomacy and Statecraft*, 13 (2002), 57-80

Kernek, S. 'Distractions of Peace During War: The Lloyd George Government's Reactions to Woodrow Wilson, December 1916-November 1918', *Transactions of the American Philosophical Society*, n.s. 65 (1975), 1-117

McDermott, J. 'Total War and the Merchant State; Aspects of British Economic Warfare against Germany, 1914-16', *Canadian Journal of History*, 21 (1986), 61-76

Millman, B. 'A Counsel of Despair: British Strategy and War Aims, 1917-18', *Journal of Contemporary History*, 36 (2001), 241-270

Morgan, K. O. 'Lloyd George and Germany', *Historical Journal*, 39 (1996), 755-766

Peterson, J. E. 'Southwest Arabia and the British during World War I', *Journal of South African and Middle Eastern Studies*, 2 (1979), 18-37

Reinharz, J. 'The Balfour Declaration and its Maker: A Reassessment', *Journal of Modern History*, 64 (1992), 455-99

Rodman, B-S. 'Britain Debates Justice: An Analysis of the Reparations Issue of 1918', *Journal of British Studies*, 8 (1968), 140-54

Rothwell, V. H. 'Mesopotamia in British War Aims, 1914-18', *Historical Journal*, 13 (1970), 273-94

Schwarz, B. 'Divided Attention: Britain's Perception of a German Threat to her Eastern Position in 1918', *Journal of Contemporary History*, 28 (1993), 103-22

Stevenson, D. 'The Failure of Peace by Negotiation in 1917', *Historical Journal*, 34, (1991), 65-86

Vereté, M. 'The Balfour Declaration and its Makers', *Middle Eastern Studies*, 6 (1970), 48–75

Woodward, D. R. 'The Origins and Intent of David Lloyd George's January 5 "War Aims" Speech', *The Historian* (Wiley Online Library), 34 (1971), 22-39

Yearwood, P. '"On the Safe and Right Lines": The Lloyd George Government and the Origins of the League of Nations, 1916–1918', *Historical Journal*, 32 (1989), 131-155
This article covers such matters as the coalition government's attitude to the concept of establishing a league of nations, the incorporation of ideas for a 'league of nations to insure peace and justice' as an important plank in President Wilson's peace initiative, the joint endorsement of the creation of such a body by the *Entente* in response to Wilson's initiative, and the explanation by A. J. Balfour, the foreign secretary, that, as a condition of durable peace, 'behind international law, and behind all treaty arrangements for preventing or limiting hostilities, some form of international sanction should be devised which would give pause to the hardiest aggressor'.

Contemporary Material

Official public statements about war aims were rare but there were a considerable number of non-governmental views on war aims expressed in the publications of individuals or organizations like the Union of Democratic Control and the Labour Party. Some of the individual publicists worked for government propaganda departments but their publications would have appeared to the public to have been independently, rather than officially, produced. Some of these publications were not even officially representative of government policy, in fact on occasions went beyond it as happened, for example, in the case of Namier's *Danzig: Poland's Outlet to the Sea* and his *Germany and Eastern Europe*, and of Headlam's *The Dead Lands of Europe*. In the latter publications of Namier and Headlam, both officials working at Wellington House (War Propaganda Bureau), the case was argued for aims on which the British government had yet to establish any firm policy. Whether or not the Foreign Office approved or encouraged such works is unclear but, whatever its attitude, it would have felt secure in the knowledge that they were unlikely to be traced to a government source because of the close secrecy which was observed in the distribution of propaganda material from Wellington House.

Angell, N. *The Political Conditions of Allied Success: Plea for Protective Union of Democracies* (London: Putnam, 1918)

— *War Aims: The Need for a Parliament of the Allies* (London: Headley, 1918?)

Armstrong, G. G. *Our Ultimate Aim in the War* (London: Allen & Unwin, 1916)

Asquith, H. H., 1st Earl of Oxford and Asquith. *The War: Its Causes and Its Message: Speeches Delivered by the Prime Minister August-October 1914* (London: Methuen & Co., 1914)

— *What Britain Is Fighting For: A Reply to the German Chancellor*, A Speech by … H. H. Asquith … on 10th April, 1916 (London: Daily Chronicle, 1916)

Bryce, J. W., Viscount Bryce of Dechmont. *The Attitude of Great Britain in the Present War* (London: Macmillan, 1916)

— *The War of Democracy: The Allies' Statement: Chapters on the Fundamental Significance of the Struggle for a New Europe* (New York: Doubleday, 1917)

Clutton-Brock, A. *Are We To Punish Germany If We Can?*, Papers for Wartime, Series 3, no. 32 (London: Oxford University Press, 1915)

Great Britain. Foreign Office. *The Case of the Allies: Being the Replies to President Wilson, and Mr. Balfour's Dispatch* (London: Hayman, Christy & Lilly, Ltd., 1917)

— *Note from the Russian Provisional Government and the British Reply respecting the Allied War Aims*, Cd 8587 (London: HMSO, 1917)

Headlam, J. W. *The Dead Lands of Europe* (London: Hodder & Stoughton, 1917)
Headlam envisages the dismemberment of the Dual Monarchy.

— *The Peace Terms of the Allies* (London: Clay, 1917)

Henderson, A. *The Aims of Labour* (London: Headley, 1917)
Contains the Labour Party's *Memorandum on War Aims* in Appendix 1.

Lansdowne, H. C. K. Petty-Fitzmaurice., 5th Marquis of Lansdowne. '[Letter Calling for Belligerents to Present their War Aims and Consider the Possibilities of a Negotiated Peace]', *Daily Telegraph*, 29 November, 1917

Lloyd George, D. *British War Aims: Statement by the Prime Minister ... on January 5, 1918* (London: HMSO, 1918)
"This statement was delivered to a meeting of the Representatives of Labour called to consider the question of further efforts for the prosecution of the war.". –cover title.

— *When Will the War End* (London: Alabaster, Passmore & Son,1917)
Lloyd George's speech in Glasgow on 29 June 1917.

McCurdy, C. A. *A Clean Peace: The War Aims of British Labour: Complete Text of the Official War Aims Memorandum of the Interalllied Labour and Socialist Conference held in London, February 23 1918* (London: Smith, 1918)

Namier, L. B. *Danzig – Poland's Outlet to the Sea* (London: Spottiswoode, 1917)
Namier argues that the reconstitution of Poland after the war should include the port of Danzig. This pamphlet was reprinted from *The Nineteenth Century and After*, February 1917.

— *Germany and Eastern Europe* (London: Duckworth, 1915)
Namier argues for the dissolution of the Austro-Hungarian Empire and the reconstruction of the Near East on the basis of nationalistic principles.

The War Aims of the British People: An Historic Manifesto; Complete Text of the Official War Aims Memorandum adopted by the Joint Conference of the Labour Party and the Parliamentary Committee of the Trade Union Congress on December 28, 1917, with an introduction by Charles A. McCurdy, M.P. (London: Hodder & Stoughton, 1918)
See also Henderson, *The Aims of Labour*, cited above.

4.3.2 Strategy

Up to 1914 Britain's traditional approach to wars abroad had been based on the concept that Britain could conduct them successfully with the use of minimal land forces rather than mass armies because of the operational advantage she derived from possessing the backup of undisputed maritime supremacy. At the outset of the war the Government (including Reginald McKenna, Chancellor of the Exchequer, and Walter Runciman, President of the Board of Trade) believed that this 'navalist' strategy could continue to work on the assumption that all that was needed to win the war (which was anticipated to be of short duration) was on the one hand to support the Allies on the continent with financial credit and raw materials and a small professional army, the BEF, and on the other hand to employ Britain's naval supremacy to blockade Germany, destroy her ocean trade, and divest her of her colonies. This was the strategy of 'limited liability' or 'business as usual' (with the government intervening as little as possible and only on an ad hoc basis), described by General Robertson early in the war as a policy 'to find out what is the smallest amount of money and smallest number of men with which we may hope, some day, to win the war, or rather not to lose it' (quoted in Beckett's *The Great War, 1914-1918* on p.110). In this the way the Government hoped to get away with the minimum of state intervention and a minor military presence on the continent leaving France and Russia to carry out the bulk of the fighting there. This proved however, to be unrealisable. The Government was forced eventually to accept the view of Lord Kitchener who, on his appointment as Secretary of State in the early months of the war, made it quite clear that he thought the war would last far longer than everyone else had anticipated and that victory could only be achieved by Britain sending troops to the Continent in far larger numbers than had ever been previously envisaged. Furthermore it soon became evident that France and Russia were far from content to shoulder the bulk of the fighting, with minimal troop support from Britain.

Once Britain had reluctantly accepted that she would have to support her allies by providing troops on a massive scale her military strategy for the rest of the war became subject to a conflict between the 'westerners', who believed that complete victory could only achieved by defeating the German Army on the Western Front because it was the major theatre of operations, and the 'easterners', who believed that the only way to break the stalemate on the Western Front was to divert the enemy's attention from it by attacking her vulnerable flanks in the Balkans and the Middle East. Lloyd George strongly favoured the 'easterner' view (as did notably also Churchill and Bonar Law) and after he became prime Minister in 1916 this brought him into continuous conflict over strategy with the chief protagonists of the 'westerners' policy, Robertson and Haig, until the spring of 1918. To a considerable extent the 'easterners' got their way as is evident from the campaigns that were fought in Gallipoli, at Salonika, in Palestine, and on the Mesopotamian Front but those military operations were never sufficient (particularly after the failure of the Gallipoli operation and the disasters on the Mesopotamian Front) to convince Robertson and Haig that the strategy the 'easterners' represented was feasible. Robertson and Haig remained hostile to the switching of resources to 'sideshows', maintaining their belief that the maximum amount of manpower should be focussed on the Western Front where a policy of 'offensive attrition' should be employed as a mean of gradually wearing out the resistance of the German Army until the point was reached where it could be engaged and decisively defeated in a final major offensive. This policy was based firmly on the idea that the crucial area of operation was the Western Front and that the war could only be concluded by a decisive victory there. In the spring of 1918 Lloyd George himself became convinced of the vital importance of the Western Front when the German army launched there a massive offensive that seemed likely to result in a colossal defeat of the Allied forces. From that point on Lloyd George, seeing not only that it was imperative to avert defeat on the Western Front but also that a major victory there was the key to ending the war, acquiesced in the withdrawal of troops from his favoured 'sideshows' to reinforce the Allies on the Western Front and did everything within his power to make sure that Haig was provided with all the manpower, shells, and equipment he required to make a final, decisive impact on the battlefield.

One of the innovatory features of the war was the emergence of the aeroplane as a military weapon and the realisation by some that it had the potential to become a valuable element in the strategy for waging a war (see also preamble to section **4.5.3** on the **Air Force**). During the war the aeroplane (and the airship in some cases) was used for a number of purposes including reconnaissance, detecting and attacking enemy ships and submarines in home waters, and defending Britain from German aerial attacks but it was quite late in the war before its use in a more aggressive strategic role began to be considered. Partly triggered by the Gotha bombing raids on Britain between 27 May and 7 July 1917, thought began to be given to the idea of a long-range air-offensive against Germany not simply as reprisals for the latter raids but as a means of weakening the enemy by carrying out mass bombing raids on industrial and military targets behind their lines. Aerial actions carried out in this way were masterminded by Major General Trenchard, Britain's most convinced advocate of strategic bombing but even he had to admit that their impact was insignificant.

Autobiographies, Biographies, Memoirs, Diaries

Arthur, Sir G. *The Life of Lord Kitchener*, 3 vols (London: Macmillan, 1920)

Barr, J. *Setting the Desert On Fire: T. E. Lawrence and Britain's Secret War in Arabia, 1916–1918* (London: Bloomsbury, 2006)

Ash, B. *The Lost Dictator: A Biography of Field Marshall Sir Henry Wilson* (London: Cassell, 1968)

Blake, R. N. W., ed. *The Private Papers of Douglas Haig, 1914-19: Being Selections from the Private Diary and Correspondence of Field Marshall Earl Haig of Bemersyde* (London: Eyre & Spottiswoode, 1952)

Boyle, A. *Trenchard: Man of Vision* (London: Collins, 1962)

Cassar, G. H. *Kitchener: Architect of Victory* (London: Kimber, 1977)

Cregier, D. M. 'McKenna, Reginald (1863–1943)', *Oxford Dictionary of National Biography*, Oxford University Press, 2004; online edn, Jan 2011 [http://www.oxforddnb.com/view/article/34744, accessed 16 Nov 2013]
McKenna favoured the 'Business as usual' approach and, as a 'navalist, was not in accord with the view of Lloyd George and the War Office that victory could be achieved by bolstering the war efforts of France and Russia with the presence of a

large British army on the battlefield, being firmly of the opinion that it was by means of the British naval blockade that Germany would be defeated. [Information extracted from the above item in the online Oxford DNB].

Callwell, C. E. *Field Marshall Sir Henry Wilson: His Life and Diaries*, 2 vols (London: Cassell, 1927)

Charteris, J. *At G.H.Q.: A Record of Service at G.H.Q. during the Great War, 1914-1918* (London: Cassell, 1931)

Farr, M. *Reginald McKenna, 1863-1943: A Life* (London: Frank Cass, 2004)

Hancock, W. K. *Smuts*, 2 vols (Cambridge: Cambridge University Press, 1962-1968), I: *The Sanguine Years, 1870-1919* (1962)
Smuts represented the Union of South Africa in the meetings in London in 1917 of the Imperial War Conference and the Imperial War Cabinet. As a member subsequently of the British cabinet he played an important role in advising on military strategy and establishing the independent organisation of the RAF.

Hough, R. A. *Former Naval Person: Churchill and the Wars at Sea* (London: Weidenfeld & Nicolson, 1985; repr, 1987)

Mackay, R. F. *Fisher of Kilverstone* (Oxford: Clarendon Press, 1973)

Magnus, P. *Kitchener: Portrait of an Imperialist* (London: John Murray, 1958; repr. Harmondsworth: Penguin, 1968)

Patterson, A. T. *Jellicoe: A Biography* (London: Macmillan, 1969)

Pugh, M. 'Runciman, Walter, first Viscount Runciman of Doxford (1870–1949)', *Oxford Dictionary of National Biography*, Oxford University Press, 2004
Online edn, Jan 2011 [http://www.oxforddnb.com/view/article/35868, accessed 9 Jan 2014]
Runciman (Liberal MP for Dewsbury, 1902-1918) reluctantly acquiesced in Britain's decision to involve itself in the war in the hope that her role in it would be mostly a naval one and state intervention in the conduct of it would be minimal. He soon realised that this 'business as usual' type of approach would not be feasible and as President of the Board of Trade (a post to which he was appointed in August 1914 and held until December 1916) he felt it necessary, for example, to arrange for his department to take over the building of merchant ships and, when confronted with the problem of rising food prices and food shortages, to adopt measures to discourage people from hoarding, to ban the export of certain items of food, and to limit price rises by importing meat and wheat supplies for sale domestically. [Information extracted from above item in online Oxford DNB]

Robertson, Sir W. R. *From Private to Field-Marshal* (London: Constable, 1921)
Robertson was appointed Chief of the Imperial General Staff on 23rd December, 1915.

— *Soldiers and Statesman* (London: Cassell, 1926; repr. London: Gregg Revivals, 1991)
In this work Robertson gives a generally even-handed account of the formulation of British wartime policy and strategy.

Woodward, D. R. *Field Marshal Sir William Robertson, Chief of the Imperial General Staff in the Great War* (Westport, Conn.: Praeger, 1998)

— *Lloyd George and the Generals* (London: Associated University Presses, 1983)

Books

Biddle, T. D. *Rhetoric and Reality in Air Warfare: The Evolution of British and American Ideas about Strategic Bombing, 1914-1945* (Princeton, N.J.: Princeton University Press, 2002)

Billing, N. P. *Air War: How to Wage It* (London: Gale & Polden, 1916)

Brooks, S. *Bomber: Strategic Air Power in Twentieth Century Conflict* (London: Imperial War Museum, 1983)

Cassar, G. H. *Kitchener's War: British Strategy from 1914 to 1916* (Washington, D.C.: Brassey's, 2004)

Cooper, M. *The Birth of Independent Air Power: British Policy in the First World War* London: Allen & Unwin, 1986)

Corbett, J. S. *Some Principles of Maritime Strategy* (London: Longman Green, 1911; repr. London: Brassey's Defence Publishing, 1988)

Dehne, P. A. *On the Far Western Front: Britain's First World War in South America* (Manchester: Manchester University Press, 2009)

Dockrill, M. and D. French, eds. *Strategy and Intelligence: British Policy during the First World War* (London: Hambledon, 1996)

Freedman, L., and others, eds. *War Strategy and International Politics: Essays in Honour of Sir Michael Howard*, edited by Lawrence Freedman, Paul Hayes, and Robert O'Neill (Oxford: Oxford University Press 1992)

French, D. *British Economic and Strategic Planning 1905-1915* (London: Allen & Unwin, 1982; repr. London: Routledge, 2006)

— '"A One-Man Show?" Civil-Military Relations during the First World War', in *Government and the Armed Forces in Britain 1856-1990*, edited by Paul Smith (London: Hambledon Press, 1996)

— *The Strategy of the Lloyd George Coalition, 1916-18* (Oxford: Oxford University Press, 1995)

— 'Who Knew What and When? The French Army Mutinies and the British Decision to Launch the Third Battle of Ypres', in *War Strategy and International Politics: Essays in Honour of Sir Michael Howard*, edited by Lawrence Freedman, Paul Hayes, and Robert O'Neill (Oxford: Oxford University Press 1992)

Gooch, J. *The Plans of War: The General Staff and British Military Strategy c. 1900-1916* (London: Routledge, 1974)

Hankey, M. P. A., Baron Hankey. *The Supreme Command, 1914-1918*, 2 vols (London: Allen & Unwin, 1961)

Horne, J. and A. Kramer. 'War between Soldiers and Enemy Civilians, 1914-1915', in *Great War, Total War: Combat and Mobilization on the Western Front, 1914-1918*, edited by R. Chickering and S. Forster (Cambridge: Cambridge University, 2000)

Howard, M. E. 'British Grand Strategy in World War I', in *Grand Strategies in War and Peace*, edited by Paul Kennedy (New Haven: Yale University Press, 1991)

— *The British Way in Warfare: A Reappraisal* (London: Jonathan Cape, 1975)

— *The Continental Commitment: The Dilemma of British Defence Policy in the Era of the Two World Wars* (London: Maurice Temple Smith, 1972; repr. London: Ashfield, 1989)

— *Studies in War and Peace* (London: Maurice Temple Smith, 1970; repr. Aldershot: Gregg Revivals, 1991)

Hughes, M. *Allenby and British Strategy in the Middle East, 1917-1919* (London: Cass, 1999)

Joynson-Hicks, William, 1st Viscount Brentford. *The Command of the Air, or, Prophecies Fulfilled*, being speeches delivered in the House of Commons. (London: Nisbet, 1916)

Jones, N. *The Origins of Strategic Bombing: A Study of the Development of British Air Strategic Thought and Practice up to 1918* (London: Kimber, 1973)

Kennedy, G., ed. *Imperial Defence: The Old World Order, 1856-1956* (London: Routledge, 2008)

Kennedy, P. M. 'Britain in the First World War', in *Military Effectiveness*, edited by A. R. Millett and W. Murray, 3 vols (London: Unwin Hyman, 1987-1988), I: *The First World War* (1987)

— *The Rise and Fall of British Naval Mastery* (London: Allen Lane, 1976; repr. London: Penguin, 1991)

Kennett, L. B. *A History of Strategic Bombing* (New York: Scribner, 1982)

Lambert, N. A. *Planning Armageddon: British Economic Warfare and the First World War* (Cambridge, Mass.: Harvard University Press, 2012)

Liddell Hart, B. H. *The British Way in Warfare*, new edn, revised and enlarged (Harmondsworth: Penguin 1942)

Neilson, K. *Strategy and Supply: The Anglo-Russian Alliance, 1914-17* (London : Allen & Unwin, 1984)

Neilson, K. and G. Kennedy, eds. *The British Way in Warfare: Power and the International System, 1856-1956.* Essays in Honour of David French (Farnham: Ashgate, 2010)

Pattee, P. G. *At War in Distant Waters. British Colonial Defence in the Great War* (Barnsley: Seaforth Publishing, 2014)

Peden, G. C. *Arms, Economics and British Strategy: From Dreadnoughts to Hydrogen Bombs* (Cambridge: Cambridge University Press, 2007)

Philpott, W. J. *Anglo-French Relations and Strategy on the Western Front, 1914-18* (Basingstoke: Macmillan in association with King's College London, 1996)

Powers, B. D. *Strategy Without Slide Rule: British Air Strategy, 1914-1939* (London: Croom Helm, 1976)

Prete, R.A. *Strategy and Command: The Anglo-French Coalition on the Western Front, 1914* (Montreal: McGill-Queen's University Press, 2009)

Robertson, Sir W. R. 'Paper Submitted to the War Committee by the Chief of the Imperial General Staff, 31 March 1916', in *Military Operations, France and Belgium, 1916*, compiled by J. E. Edmonds, 2 vols + 2 vols. of appendices and maps and 1 case of maps, History of the Great War Based on Official Documents (London: Macmillan, 1932-38)
Robertson's paper is in Appendix 4 of this work. A reprint of the entire work was published by the Battery Press, Nashville, TN. in 1991-96.

Satia, P. *Spies in Arabia: The Great War and the Cultural Foundations of Britain's Covert Empire in the Middle East* (Oxford: Oxford University Press, 2008)

Schurman, D. M. *The Education of a Navy: The Development of British Naval Strategic Thought, 1867-1914* (Chicago: Chicago University Press, 1965; repr. Malabar, Fla; Robert E. Krieger, 1984))

Simkins, P. 'Kitchener and the Expansion of the Army', in *Politicians and Defence: Studies in the Formulation of British Defence Policy, 1846-1970*, edited by I. F. W. Beckett and J. Gooch (Manchester: Manchester University Press, 1981)

Siney, M. C. *The Allied Blockade of Germany, 1914-1916* (Ann Arbor, Michigan: 1957)

— 'The Allied Blockade Committee and the Inter-Allied Trade Committee: The Machinery of Economic Warfare, 1917-18', in *Studies in International History*, essays presented to W.N. Medlicott (London: Longmans, 1967)

Smith, M. 'The Tactical and Strategic Application of Air Power on the Western Front', in *Home Fires and Foreign Fields, British Social and Military Experience in the Great War*, ed. by P. H. Liddle (Manchester: Manchester University Press, 1985)

Strachan, H. 'The British Way in Warfare', in *The Oxford History of the British Army*, new edn, general editor, David Chandler, associate editor, Ian Beckett. (Oxford: Oxford University Press, 1996; repr 2003)
Previous edn published as *The Oxford Illustrated History of the British Army*, 1994.

Townshend, C. *Desert Hell: The British Invasion of Mesopotamia* (Cambridge, Mass.: Belknap Press of Harvard University Press, 2011)

Originally published as: When God Made Hell: The British Invasion of Mesopotamia and the Creation of Iraq, 1914-1921, London: Faber, 2010.

Turner, J. 'Lloyd George, the War Cabinet, and High Politics', in *Passchendaele in Perspective: The Third Battle of Ypres*, edited by P. H. Liddle (London: Lee Cooper, 1997)

Vincent, C. P. *The Politics of Hunger: The Allied Blockade of Germany, 1915-1919* (Athens, Ohio: Ohio University Press, 1985)

Williams, G. K. 'Statistics and Strategic Bombardment: Operations and Records of the British Long-Range Bombing Force during World War I and their Implications for the Development of the Post-War Royal Air Force, 1917-1923' (unpublished doctoral thesis, University of Oxford, 1989)

Williams, R. 'Lord Kitchener and the Battle of Loos: French Politics and British Strategy in the Summer of 1915', in *War Strategy and International Politics: Essays in Honour of Sir Michael Howard*, edited by Lawrence Freedman, Paul Hayes, and Robert O'Neill (Oxford: Oxford University Press 1992)

Wilson, T. and R. Prior. 'British Decision-Making, 1917: Lloyd George, the Generals and Passchendaele', in *Facing Armageddon: The First World War Experienced*, ed. by H. Cecil and P. H. Liddle (London: Leo Cooper, 1996)

Wise, S. 'The Royal Air Force and the Origins of Strategic Bombing', in *Man at War: Politics, Technology and Innovation in the Twentieth Century*, edited by Timothy Travers and Christon Archer (Chicago: Precedent Publishing, 1982)

Woodward, D. R. *Lloyd George and the Generals* (London: Associated University Presses, 1983)

Articles

Cooper, M. 'The Development of Air Policy and Doctrine on the Western Front', *Aerospace Historian*, 28 (1981), 38-51

— 'British Flying Operations on the Western Front, July 1917: A Case Study of Trenchard's Offensive Policy in Action, *Cross and Cockade*, 23 (1982), 354-70

Cox, M. E. 'Hunger Games, or How the Allied Blockade in the First World War Deprived German Children of Nutrition, and Allied Food Aid Subsequently Saved Them', *Economic History Review*, 68 (2015) 600-631

Dehne, P. 'The Ministry of Blockade during the First World War and the Demise of Free Trade', *Twentieth Century British History*, 27:3 (2016), 333-356

Dutton, D. 'The "Robertson Dictatorship" and the Balkan Campaign in 1916', *Journal of Strategic Studies*, 9 (1986), 64-78

Freedman, L. 'Alliance and the British Way in Warfare', *Review of International Studies*, 21 (1995), 145-158

French, D. 'The Dardanelles, Mecca and Kut: Prestige as a Factor in British Eastern Strategy, 1914-16', *War and Society*, 5 (1987), 45-61

— 'The Meaning of Attrition', *English Historical Review*, 103 (1988), 385-405

— 'The Origins of the Dardanelles Campaign Reconsidered', *History*, 68 (1983), 210-224

Greenhalgh, E. 'David Lloyd George, Georges Clemenceau, and the 1918 Manpower Crisis', *Historical Journal*, 50 (2007), 397-422

Kennedy, P. M. 'Imperial Cable Communications and Strategy, 1870-1914', *English Historical Review*, 86 (1971), 725-52

Liddell Hart, B. H. 'Economic Pressure or Continental Victories', *Journal of the Royal United Services Institute for Defence Studies*, 76 (1931), 486-510

Maiolo, J. and T. Insall. 'Sir Basil Zaharoff and Sir Vincent Caillard as Instruments of British Policy towards Greece and the Ottoman Empire during the Asquith and Lloyd George Administrations, 1915-8', *International History Review*, 34 (2012), 819-839

"The notorious arms trader Sir Basil Zaharoff is remembered as the archetypal 'merchant of death'. During the First World War he is alleged to have exercised a malign influence over statesmen in London and Paris. Recently released Foreign Office files now allow us to document Zaharoff's wartime activities on behalf of the British government as an agent of influence in the Levant. The new sources reveal that Sir Vincent H.P. Caillard, the financial director of the arms-maker Vickers, played a key role in making Zaharoff's services available to prime ministers Asquith and Lloyd George. While Zaharoff has often been portrayed as a sinister force, manipulating statesmen into pursuing his financial and political interests, the reality was the reverse. Zaharoff was a convenient tool of two prime ministers rather than a powerful political manipulator in his own right." [Abstract on the internet]

Martin, C. 'The Complexity of Strategy: '"Jackie"' Fisher and the Trouble with Submarines', *Journal of Military History*, 75 (2011), 441-470

McDermott, J. 'Total War and the Merchant State; Aspects of British Economic Warfare against Germany, 1914-16', *Canadian Journal of History*, 21 (1986), 61-76

Millman, B. 'A Counsel of Despair: British Strategy and War Aims, 1917-18', *Journal of Contemporary History*, 36 (2001), 241-270

— 'Sir Henry Wilson's Mischief: Field Marshal Sir Henry Wilson's Rise to Power, 1917-18', *Journal of Canadian History*, 30 (19950, 467-86

Morrow, J. 'Aviation Technology and Strategic Air Power in World War I: The English, French and Italian Experiences', *Revue Internationale d'Histoire Militaire*, 63(1985), 89-98

Neilson, K. 'Kitchener: A Reputation Refurbished', *Canadian Journal of History*, 15 (1980), 207-227

Philpott, W. J. 'Kitchener and the 29th Division: A Study in Anglo-French Strategic Relations, 1914-15', *Journal of Strategic Studies*, 16 (1993), 375-407

— 'The Great Landing: Haig's Plan to Invade Belgium from the Sea in 1917', *Imperial War Museum Review*, 10 (1995), 84-9

— 'The Strategic Ideas of Sir John French', *Journal of Strategic Studies*, 12 (1989), 458-478

Strachan, H. 'The Battle of the Somme and British Strategy', *Journal of Strategic Studies*, 21 (1998), 79-95

— 'The British Way in Warfare Revisited', *Historical Journal*, 26 (1983), 447-61

Wise, S. F. 'The Strategic Use of Air Power in the Context of the Evolution of the Air Weapon in the First World War', in ICMH (International Commission of Military History), *Acta 10*, 225-40

Woodward, D. R. 'Britain in a Continental War: The Civil-Military Debate over the Strategical Direction of the Great War of 1914-1918', *Albion*, 12 (1980), 37-65

— 'Did Lloyd George Starve the British Army of Men prior to the German Offensive of 21 March 1918?', *Historical Journal*, 27 (1984), 241-52

Varnava, A. 'Imperialism First, the War Second: The British, an Armenian Legion, and Deliberations on Where to Attack the Ottoman Empire, November 1914-April 1915', *Historical Research* (Oxford), 87 (2014), 533-555

4.4 Intelligence, Espionage

Spying and gathering intelligence to gain an advantage over an enemy, or perceived enemy, had long been employed as auxiliary tools of warfare. Both Britain and Germany were involved in spying on each other's countries before the war began and a number of spies were caught and arrested in both countries as result of the operations of their espionage and counter-espionage organisations. In Britain the foundation of official organisations of this sort was laid before the war when the War Office and the Admiralty in 1909 agreed jointly to establish a 'Secret Service Bureau' to coordinate intelligence work (with the aim particularly to combat Germany's espionage operations in the United Kingdom). By 1914 this intelligence organisation had become divided into two sections - MI5, (the Security Service) responsible for internal security and domestic counterintelligence activities in Britain, and MI6 (the Secret Intelligence Service) responsible for gathering intelligence abroad on Britain's potential enemies – and these were in active operation throughout the Great War.

Spying during the war proved to be an extremely dangerous occupation. A considerable number of spies from both sides were apprehended and executed. An Allied female spy, Gabrielle Petit, for example, was captured and executed by the Germans in 1916 after having been recruited by Ernest Wallinger of the British GHQ in France and sent into Belgium to report on enemy troop movements. Britain also executed spies, the first of whom was Carl Hans Lody, a junior Lieutenant in the German naval reserve who was sent to England almost immediately after the outbreak of war to spy on the Royal Navy and the Naval Dockyards. Of the 31 German agents who were apprehended in Britain 12 were executed; the rest were either given a sentence of death that was commuted to penal servitude, imprisoned, or discharged.

In the course of the war intelligence gathering underwent considerable development as a result of the advances which had been made in the area of wireless telegraphy, the telephone and radio. As was the case in other countries Britain began to make considerable use of these advances in relation to intelligence gathering. It continued to utilise human resources (obtaining intelligence, for instance, from trench raids, the capture of documents such as paybooks, and the interrogation of prisoners, and also from the espionage agent networks which it had set up in other countries) but it increasingly as well made use of the intelligence gathered from signals communicated by wireless telegraphy, telephone or radio. Communication by the latter means involved sending messages in encrypted code to render them secure. Britain had considerable success in breaking enemy codes as was demonstrated, for example, by the work of the Admiralty's Room 40 which played a major intelligence role by deciphering German naval codes; it was also this group which, in January of 1917, intercepted the Zimmermann telegram[155], one of the greatest successes of British cryptographers during the war.

Bibliographies

Clark, J. R. *The Literature of Intelligence: A Bibliography of Materials, with Essays, Reviews, and Comments* [http://intellit.muskingum.edu/index.html]

Autobiographies, Biographies, Memoirs, Diaries

Capstick, P. H. *Warrior: The Legend of Colonel Richard Meinertzhagen* (New York: St. Martin's, 1997)
Richard Meinertzhagen served as a British intelligence officer in the Middle East and North Africa in World War I.

Ewing, A. W. *The Man of Room 40: The Life of Sir Alfred Ewing* (London: Hutchinson, 1939)
Sir Alfred Ewing supervised the deciphering of German wireless messages, 1914-17.

Gaunt, Sir G. *The Yield of the Years: A Story of Adventure Afloat and Ashore*, by Admiral Sir Guy Grant, naval attaché and chief of the British intelligence service in the United States, 1914-1918 (London: Hutchinson, 1940)

James, W. M. *The Eyes of the Navy: A Biographical Study of Admiral Sir Reginald Hall* (London: Methuen, 1956)

— *The Code Breakers of Room 40: The Story of Admiral Sir Reginald Hall, Genius of British Counterintelligence* (New York: St. Martin's Press, 1956)

---

[155] The telegram, offering United States territory to Mexico in return for joining the German cause, sent by German Foreign Minister, Arthur Zimmermann, to Johann Bernstorff (German ambassador in Washington, D.C.) who, at Zimmermann's request, forwarded it to the German ambassador in Mexico, Heinrich von Eckardt.

The War Years

Judd, A. *The Quest for C: Mansfield Cumming and the Founding of the Secret Service* (London: HarperCollins, 2000)

King, M. *Secrets in a Dead Fish: The Spying Game in the First World War* (Oxford: Bodleian Library 2014)

Lockhart, Sir R. B. *Memoirs of a British Agent*, introduction, epilogue and notes by Robin Bruce Lockhart (London: Folio Society, 2003)
Originally published London: Putnam, 1932 (2nd edn 1934) under the title, *Memoirs of a British Agent: Being an Account of the Author's Early Life in Many Lands and of his Official Mission to Moscow in 1918*
Lockhart was acting consul-general in Moscow from 1914-17 and in 1918 headed a special mission to Russia where in that year his activities led to his imprisonment and subsequently his release in exchange for Maxim Litvinov[156].

Schaepdrijver, S. de. *Gabrielle Petit: The Death and Life of a Female Spy in the First World War* (London: Bloomsbury Academic, 2015)

Voska, E. V. and W. Irwin. *Spy and Counter-Spy: The Autobiography of a Master-Spy* [The reminiscences of E. V. Voska set down by Will Irwin.] (New York: Harrap, 1941)
Voska ran a Czechoslovak-based counterintelligence organization in the United States prior to the U.S. entry into World War I. He placed his organization at the disposal of British intelligence, and after 1915 cooperated with the FBI as well.

Winstone, H. V. F. *Gertrude* Bell, rev. edn (London: Barzan, 2004)
The author tells the story of a "most remarkable upper-class, privileged, eccentric Victorian lady." She was "the first women officer in British military intelligence," serving in the Arab Bureau, headquartered in Cairo, during World War I.

Young, K, ed. *The Diaries of Sir Robert Bruce Lockhart*, 2 vols (London: Macmillan, 1973-80), I: *1915-38* (1980)
See also Lockhart's *Memoirs of a British Agent*.

Books

Andrew, C. M. *The Defence of the Realm: The Authorized History of MI5* (London: Allen Lane, 2009)

— 'The Mobilization of British Intelligence in the two World Wars', in *Mobilization for Total War: The Canadian, American and British Experience 1914-1918, 1939-1945*, edited by N. F. Dreisziger (Waterloo, Ontario: Wilfried Laurier University Press, 1981)
Papers of the 7th Military History Symposium of the Royal Military College of Canada.

— *Secret Service: The Making of the British Intelligence Community* (London: Heinemann, 1985)

Aston, Sir G. G. *Secret Service* (London: Faber & Faber, 1930)

Bailey, F. M. *Mission to Tashkent* (Oxford: Oxford University Press, 1992)
This book is about Bailey's activities in Russian Central Asia in the period immediately after Russia had dropped out of .Naval Institute Press, 2012)

Brook-Shepard, G. *Iron Maze: The Western Secret Services and the Bolsheviks* (London: Macmillan, 1998)
A retelling, with new material, of the Lockhart plot and associated events. This work presents the story of the secret war waged by Western intelligence against the Bolsheviks in Russia from 1917.

Cook, A. *Ace of Spies: The True Story of Sidney Reilly* (Stroud: Tempus, 2004)
This is a reissue with updated information, especially concerning forensic details following Reilly's execution in a Russian park in 1925, of the biography Cook first published in 2002 under the title, *On His Majesty's Secret Service, Sydney Reilly Codename St1*.

Everitt, N. *British Secret Service during the Great War* (London: Hutchinson,1920)

Ferris, J. R. "'Airbandit": C^3I and Strategic Air Defence during the First Battle of Britain, 1915-1918', in *Strategy*

---

[156] After the October Revolution of 1917, Litvinov was appointed by Vladimir Lenin as the Soviet government's representative in Britain. In 1918, Litvinov was arrested by the British government and held until exchanged for Lockhart, who had been imprisoned in Russia.

and Intelligence: British Policy during the First World War, edited by Michael Dockrill and David French (London: Hambledon, 1996)

— '"FORTITUDE" in Context: The Evolution of British Military Deception in Two World Wars, 1914-1945', in *Paradoxes of Strategic Intelligence: Essays in Honour of Michael I. Handel*, edited by Richard K. Betts and Thomas G. Mahnken (London: Cass, 2003)

Ferris, J. R., ed. *The British Army and Signals Intelligence during the First World War* (London: Alan Sutton for Army Records Society, 1992)

Grant, R. M. *U-Boat Hunters: Codebreakers, Divers and the Defeat of the U-Boats, 1914-1918* (Penzance: Periscope, 2003)

— *U-Boat Intelligence, 1914-1918: Admiralty Intelligence Division and the Defeat of the U-boats 1914-18* (Penzance: Periscope, 2002)
Originally published London: Putnam, 1969.

Hill, G. A. *Go Spy the Land: Being the Adventures of I.K. 8 of the British Secret Service* (London: Cassell, 1932)
An account of Hill's secret service work in Russia during World War I.

Jeffery, K. *MI6: The History of the Secret Intelligence Service 1909-1949* (London: Bloomsbury, 2011)

Landau, H. *All's Fair: The Story of the British Secret Service Behind the German Lines* (New York: Putnam's, 1934)
Landau headed the Military Division of the British secret service in Holland from 1916, running networks in France and Belgium. The "largest and considered the most successful" network was named the White Lady. This book and the one cited below are the memoirs of "a field intelligence officer."

— *Secrets of the White Lady* (New York: Putnam's, 1935)

McMahon, P. *British Spies and Irish Rebels: British Intelligence and Ireland, 1916-1945* (Woodbridge: Boydell Press, 2008)

Mohs, P. A. *Military Intelligence and the Arab Revolt: The First Modern Intelligence War* (London: Routledge, 2008)
In relation to the development of Britain's strategy for the Arab Revolt during the First World War the author analyses the way intelligence was used and exploited, and in the process provides an examination of what T. E. Lawrence achieved as an intelligence officer and guerrilla leader.

Morgan, J. *The Secrets of Rue St. Roch: Intelligence Operations Behind Enemy Lines in the First World War* (London: Allen Lane, 2004)
Based on Janet Morgan's research on an archive of correspondence and documents related to the work of Captain George Bruce (later 7th Baron Balfour of Burleigh) who was involved in the recruitment and organisation of agents from "an unmarked office" on Rue St. Roch in Paris from 1917. Ignoring orders, Captain Bruce retained all documents relating to this operation and from them the author has in this book produced a comprehensive account of a First World War espionage operation from conception to completion.

Morton, J. *Spies of the First World War: Under Cover for King and Kaiser* (London: National Archives, 2010)
Contents: PART ONE: 1. The early spy novels and Germans in England; 2. The formation of MI5 and MI6. 3. Pre-First World War German spies in England and abroad; 4. Pre-First World War British and other spies abroad; PART TWO: 5. German spies; 6. The spy-masters, English, French and German; 7. Codes and codebreakers; PART THREE: 8. Shot in the tower 1914-1916; 9. The spy survivors; 10. Women spies; 11. German spies in Europe, America and India during the war; 12. After the war was over.

Occleshaw, M. E. *Armour Against Fate: British Military Intelligence in the First World War* (London: Columbus, 1988)

— *Dances in Deep Shadow: Britain's Clandestine War in Russia* (London: Constable & Robinson, 2006)
The author "suggests that the role of allied intelligence services, particularly Britain's" in the intervention in Russia at the end of World War I "was far greater than heretofore acknowledged".

Oliver, D. *Airborne Espionage: International Special Duties Operations in the World Wars* (Stroud: Sutton, 2005)

Plotke, A. J. *Imperial Spies Invade Russia: The British Intelligence Interventions, 1918* (Westport, Conn, and London: Greenwood Press, 1993)
The book hinges on War Office Military Intelligence and the Dunsterville mission dispatched to the Caucasus to engage in covert operations.

Popplewell, R. J. 'British Intelligence in Mesopotamia 1914-16', in *Intelligence and Military Operations*, edited by Michael I. Handel (London: Cass, 1990)

Satia, P. *Spies in Arabia: The Great War and the Cultural Foundations of Britain's Covert Empire in the Middle East* (Oxford: Oxford University Press, 2008)

Seligmann, M. S. *Spies in Uniform: British Military and Naval Intelligence on the Eve of the First World War* (Oxford: Oxford University Press, 2006)
The focus of the book is on "the military and naval attachés in Berlin between 1900 and 1914". A useful insight into Anglo-German relations, pre-World War I intelligence, and the role of service attachés in the intelligence gathering process.

Seligmann, M. S., ed. *Naval Intelligence from Germany: The Reports of the British Naval Attachés in Berlin, 1906-1914* (Aldershot: Ashgate for the Navy Records Society, 2007)
Useful collection of primary documents meant to provide insight into British thinking about Germany and its navy during the Anglo-German naval arms race before the Great War. On topics, such as the enlargement of the German battle fleet, the aims of Admiral von Tirpitz and German naval development, it examines the reports of the last four officers to hold the post of naval attaché in Berlin before the outbreak of war in 1914.

Sheffy, Y. *British Intelligence in the Palestine Campaign, 1914-1918* (London: Frank Cass, 1998)
In relation to the campaign in the desert against the Ottoman Empire on the Egyptian and Palestinian fronts the author examines the development, operations and contribution of British Military Intelligence and shows the relationship between intelligence gathering and battle-field performance.

— 'Institutionalized Deception and Perception Reinforcement: Allenby's Campaigns in Palestine', in *Intelligence and Military Operations*, edited by Michael I. Handel (London: Cass, 1990)
In a comparison of Allenby's use of deception prior to the Battle of Gaza and in the Megiddo Campaign Sheffy notes Allenby's distinctive approach to the planning of the deception and its implementation in terms of the staff work involved.

Smith, M. *Six: A History of Britain's Secret Intelligence Service; Part 1: Murder and Mayhem 1909-1939* (London: BiteBack, 2010)

Teague-Jones, R. *The Spy Who Disappeared: Diary of a Secret Mission to Russian Central Asia in 1918*, introduction and epilogue by Peter Hopkirk (London: Gollancz, 1990)
Before he died Reginald Teague-Jones, who had previously assumed the name of Ronald Sinclair for fear of Russian retribution for his clandestine activities in Russia, published this diary in which he recounts his secret mission to Baku where he organized and sustained the resistance to the Turkish and Bolshevik efforts to establish control of the vital railway which linked Turkey and Russia to Afghanistan.

Thomas, M. *Empires of Intelligence: Security Services and Colonial Disorder after 1914* (Berkeley: University of California Press, 2008)

Verrier, A. *Agents of Empire: Anglo-Zionist Intelligence Operations, 1915-1919; Brigadier Walter Gribbon, Aaron Aaronsohn and the NILI Ring* (London: Brassey's, 1995)
In this work Verrier makes use of Walter Gribbon's private papers and Aaron Aaronsohn's diaries for the purpose of providing an account of a collaboration which led to the development of an intelligence operation which helped General Allenby to destroy the Turkish Army in the Levant, an event which laid the foundations for a Zionist state in the Middle East.

West, N. *MI6: British Secret Intelligence Operations, 1909-45* (London: Weidenfeld & Nicolson, 1983)

Articles

Beach, J. 'British Intelligence and German Tanks, 1916-1918', *War in History*, 14 (2007), 454-475

— '"Intelligent Civilians in Uniform": The British Expeditionary Force's Intelligence Corps Officers, 1914-1918', *War and Society*, 27, Issue 1 (2008), 1-22

— 'Origins of the Special Intelligence Relationship: Anglo-American Intelligence Co-operation on the Western Front, 1917-18', *Intelligence and National Security*, 22, (2007), 229-249

Crossland, J. 'British Spies in Plot to Save Tsar', *Sunday Times* (London), 15 Oct. 2006
"A newly discovered ... diary of Captain Stephen Alley, second in command of the British intelligence mission in Petrograd - now St Petersburg - shows he positioned four undercover agents ready to extract ... the deposed Tsar Nicholas II and the Russian imperial family from the House of Special Purpose [in Ekaterinburg] where they were held [and later executed]". [Quotation extracted from the *Sunday Times* online abstract of the above article at http://www.thesundaytimes.co.uk/sto/news/uk_news/article158934.ece]. The diary, which was found accidentally by Alley's descendants in a trunk of his papers, was featured in a TV programme about Queen Victoria's grandchildren, a documentary that was shown in December 2006.[157]

Debo, R. K. 'Lockhart Plot or Dzerzhinski Plot', *Journal of Modern History*, 43 (1971), 413-439

Ewing, A. W. 'Some Special War Work, Part 1', *Cryptologia* 4 (1980), 193-203
This article and the following article deal with Sir Alfred Ewing's work in Room 40 and the solution of the German diplomatic ciphers in World War I.

— 'Some Special War Work, Part 2', *Cryptologia* 5 (1981), 33-39

Ferris, J. R. 'The British Army and Signals Intelligence in the Field during the First World War', *Intelligence and National Security* 3 (1988), 23-48

French, D. 'Watching the Allies: British Intelligence and the French Mutinies of 1917', *Intelligence and National Security* 6 (1991), 573-592
In this article it is pointed out that Britain's decision to engage in the Flanders offensive (Third Ypres) was to a crucial extent influenced by British concerns about France's state of political volatility and the deterioration of her national morale, of which the mutinies in the French Army were a symptom.

Friedman, H. A. 'British Espionage Forgeries of the First World War', *American Philatelist*, (1973)
During the course of the war, the British counterfeited eight stamps of three enemy nations. These were the 5, 10 and 25 heller stamps of Austria, the 5, 10 and 15-pfennig stamps of Bavaria, and the 10 and 15-pfennig stamps of Germany. It is assumed that these stamps were forged to be used to mail pro-Allied propaganda behind enemy lines.

— 'A WWI British Forgery', *International Banknote Society Journal*, 25 (1986)
The British forged the banknotes of Germany, Turkey, and German East Africa. These could have been produced to hurt the enemy economy, or to be used by agents behind enemy lines to pay for their every day expenses.

Gill, D. W. J. 'Research Note. Harry Pirie-Gordon: Historical Research, Journalism and Intelligence Gathering in the Eastern Mediterranean (1908-18)', *Intelligence and National Security* 21 (2006), 1045-1059
Pirie-Gordon was part of the British intelligence community in both world wars.

Heffernan, M. 'Geography, Cartography and Military Intelligence: The Royal Geographical Society and the First World War', *Transactions of the Institute of British Geographers*, n.s. 21 (1996), 504-533

Hiley, N. 'The Failure of British Espionage Against Germany 1907-1914', *Historical Journal* 26 (1983), 866-881

Jones, R.V. 'Alfred Ewing and Room 40', *Notes and Records of the Royal Society of London*, 34 1979), 65-90

Kahn, David. 'Edward Bell and His Zimmermann Telegram Memorandum, *Intelligence and National Security* 14 (1999), 143-159
Kahn provides biographic details on the U.S. diplomat who liaised with British intelligence in London with regard to the Zimmermann Telegram. Included are two memoranda by Bell and one by Nigel de Grey (a member of the Naval Intelligence Division Room 40 codebreaking section) who assisted with the decrypting of the telegram.

---

[157] Shown on TV (Channel 4) under the title *Three Kings at War* on 14 December 2006.

Kennedy, G. 'Intelligence and the Blockade, 1914-17: A Study in Administration, Friction and Command', *Intelligence and National Security*, 22 (2007), 699-721
One of the points made in this article is that for the handling of the key elements of the blockade strategy those responsible for implementing it were able to rely on the constant flow of accurate and timely information derived from a highly sophisticated and wide-ranging intelligence assessment operation.

Larsen, D. 'Spying on Your Friends: Breaking American Codes in the First World War', *The Fountain* (Trinity College Cambridge), Issue 19 (2014), 4-5
Describes the code-breaking activities of the naval group known as Room 40 and a lesser known army orgaganization called MI1(b). Dwells particularly on the activities of MI1(b) in its breaking of the diplomatic codes of the United States.

Lockhart, J. B. 'Sir William Wiseman, Bart: Agent of Influence', *Journal of the Royal United Services Institute for Defence Studies*, 134 (1989), 63-67

Long, J. W. 'Plot and Counter-plot in Revolutionary Russia: Chronicling the Bruce Lockhart Conspiracy, 1918', *Intelligence and National Security*, 10 (1995), 122-143

Neilson, K. '"Joy Rides"? British Intelligence and Propaganda in Russia, 1914-1917', *Historical Journal*, 24 (1981), 885-906

Popplewell, R. J. 'British Intelligence in Mesopotamia 1914-16', *Intelligence and National Security*, 5 (1990), 139-172

Sheffy, Y. 'British Intelligence and the Middle East, 1900-1918: How Much Do We Know?', *Intelligence and National Security*, 17 (2002), 33-52

Siegel, J. 'British Intelligence on the Russian Revolution and Civil War: A Breach at the Source, *Intelligence and National Security*, 10 (1995), 468-485
In this review of the disputes between and around Robert Bruce Lockhart, Britain's representative in Russia after January 1918, and General Alfred Knox, the former British military attaché in Petrograd, the conclusion is reached that, ultimately, the thinking of the policy-makers wrestling with questions of intervention was dominated by domestic political and economic concerns, and that events and conditions in Russia were not the determinants in the formulation of British policy.

Spence, R. B. 'Englishmen in New York: The SIS American Station, 1915-21', *Intelligence and National Security*, 19 (2004), 511-537.
This article surveys the organization, personnel and operations of the Secret Intelligence Service's New York station during the Great War and its immediate aftermath. A large part of the survey is about Sir William Wiseman and the men who served with and under him.

— 'Secret Agent 666: Aleister Crowley and British Intelligence in America, 1914-1918,' *International Journal of Intelligence and Counterintelligence*, 13 (2000), 359-371
Spence believes that Crowley was working for British intelligence in spite of his anti-British and anti-Allied writings in U.S. publications during the First World War.

Troy, T. F. 'The Gaunt-Wiseman Affair: British Intelligence in New York in 1915, *International Journal of Intelligence and Counterintelligence*, 16 (2003), 442-461
Analyses the background, including Gaunt's falling out with Wiseman, to Wiseman's eventual replacement of Gaunt as the most important British agent in the United States during the First World War.

Williams, L. N. and M. Williams. *Forged Stamps of two World Wars: The Postal Forgeries and Propaganda Issues of the Belligerents, 1914-1918, 1939-1945* (London: The Authors, 1954)

— *The 'Propaganda' Forgeries: A History and Description of the Austrian, Bavarian and German Stamps Counterfeited by Order of the British Government during the Great War, 1914-1918* (London: David Field, 1938)

Winkler, J. R. 'Information Warfare in World War I', *Journal of Military History*, 73 (2009), 845-868

4.5 The Armed Forces

4.5.1 The Army

4.5.1.1 General

The Great War was fought in many quarters of the world, by sailors and airman as well as soldiers, but our perception of it is inevitably dominated by the trench warfare on the Western Front and the huge loss of life it involved.

Britain entered the war with a small regular army, reserves, and territorials amounting in all to some quarter of a million men. This was the army which Haldane had reorganised in the pre-war years in the belief that the nature of any future war was likely to be fast, mobile and of short duration and involve limited British commitment on the continent. By Christmas 1914 the open war of movement which the generals had expected and for which they had planned had failed to materialise. Instead from 1914 to 1918 they were confronted by the problems of the static battle style represented by trench warfare and the possibility of a far longer war than they had ever expected. For this style of warfare the BEF which had been sent to France at the beginning of the war was inadequate. Kitchener was soon calling for 100,000 volunteers to fight in a long, drawn out war (in his first estimation, lasting at least three years). Through recruitment of volunteers, and subsequently conscripts, the army had in fact grown to nearly 6 million men by November 1918 in comparison to its pre-war size of less than 250,000. The vast majority of these men fought the enemy over the trenches of the Western Front for the remainder of the war, sustaining the huge losses that were the inevitable result of exposing massed formations of assault troops to the devastating firepower of greatly improved weaponry.

The role of new technology and equipment in the fighting on the Western Front became increasingly important as the war wore on. Apart from the developments that increased the effectiveness of firepower, gas was brought into use as a weapon (its first use by the British was at Loos in 1915) and by the summer of 1916 tanks were being employed in offensive operations. Gas, however, never had a decisive effect and tanks, vulnerable and unreliable[158], never reached a stage of development to enable them to have the sort of impact they achieved in the Second World War. Aeroplanes played a more significant role on the Western Front where, apart from their use for defence against enemy air attacks, were also used for spotting targets, directing artillery fire, and keeping a look-out for enemy troop concentrations.

Ultimate success on the Western Front depended crucially on an army having an adequate and constant supply of soldiers, munitions, and equipment (including the products of the latest technology) and on their generals being able to make the most effective use of them with operational methods and tactics able to overcome the problems of trench warfare. By July of 1918 all these ingredients for success had come together for the British army, and Haig was finally able to mount a major offensive capable of resulting in a decisive victory.

Bibliographies

Van Hartesveldt, F. R. *The Battles of the British Expeditionary Forces, 1914-1915: Historiography and Annotated Bibliography* (Westport, Conn.: Praeger, 2005)

White, A. S. A., comp. *A Bibliography of Regimental Histories of the British Army*; with addendum (Dallington: Naval and Military Press, 1992)
Originally published by the Society for Army Historical Research in conjunction with the Army Museums Ogilby Trust, 1965.

Books

Ascoli, D. *The Mons Star: The British Expeditionary Force, 1914* (London: Harrap, 1981; repr. Edinburgh: Birlinn, 2001)

Ashworth, T. *Trench Warfare, 1914-18: The Let and Let Live System* (London: Macmillan, 1980; repr. London: Pan, 2000)

---

[158] Tanks did, however, make an important contribution during the first day of the Battle of Cambrai (20 November 1917) but they suffered heavy losses. Tanks, deployed on the basis of plans carefully prepared and coordinated with the infantry, were also engaged in the attacks which began to break up the German positions during the British offensive in July and August 1918.

The War Years

Barrie, A. *War Underground* (London: Frederick Muller, 1962; repr. Staplehurst: Spellmount, 2000)
An account of the tunnellers' trench warfare in World War 1914-1918.

Beckett, I. F. W. 'The British Army, 1914-1918: The Illusion of Change', in *Britain and the First World War*, ed. by J. Turner (London: Routledge, 1988)

Beckett, I. F. W. and K. Simpson, eds. *A Nation in Arms: A Social Study of the British Army in the First World War* (Manchester: Manchester University Press, 1985; repr. London: Donovan, 1990)

Bet-El, I. R. *Conscripts: Forgotten Men of the Great War*, new paperback edn (Stroud: Sutton, 2003)

Bidwell, S. and D. Graham. *Fire-Power: The British Army, Weapons and Theories of War, 1904-1945* (Barnsley: Pen & Sword, 2004)

Bond, B. *The Victorian Army and the Staff College, 1854-1914* (London: Eyre Methuen, 1972)

Bond, B., and others, eds. *Look To Your Front: Studies in the First World War* by the British Commission for Military History, edited by B. Bond [and others] (Staplehurst: Spellmount, 1999)
Papers by noted authorities on the Great War presented to the British Commission for Military History during a commemorative seminar of the 80th anniversary of the Battle of the Somme.

Bourne, S. *Black Poppies: Britain's Black Community and the Great War* (Stroud: The History Press, 2014)

Brown, I. M. *British Logistics on the Western Front, 1914-1919* (Westport, Connecticut: Praeger, 1998)

Brown, M. *Tommy Goes to War*, with additional research by Shirley Seaton, new edn (Stroud: Tempus, 1978; repr. 1999)

Brown, M. and S. Seaton. *The Christmas Truce: The Western Front, December 1914*, rev. and expanded edn (Basingstoke: Papermac, 1994; repr. London: Pan 2001)

Chandler, D. G. and I. F. W. Beckett, eds. *The Oxford History of the British Army*, new edn (Oxford: Oxford University Press, 1996; repr 2003)
Previous edn published as *The Oxford Illustrated History of the British Army*, 1994.

Chappell, M. *The British Army in World War I*, 3 vols (Oxford: Osprey, 2003-2005)

Connelly, M. *Steady the Buffs!: A Regiment, a Region and the Great War*, Oxford Scholarship Online (Oxford: Oxford University Press, 2006)

Costello, R. *Black Tommies: British Soldiers of African Descent in the First World War* (Liverpool: Liverpool University Press, 2015)

Crocker, T. B. *The Christmas Truce: Myth, Memory, and the First World War* (Lexington, Kentucky: University Press of Kentucky, 2015)

Ellis, J. *Eye-Deep in Hell: Trench Warfare in World War I* (London: Croom Helm, 1976; repr. London: Penguin, 2002)

Emsley, C. *Soldier, Sailor, Beggarman, Thief: Crime and the British Armed Services since 1914* (Oxford: Oxford University Press, 2013)
Focusing particularly on the First and Second World Wars, this work investigates criminal offending by members of the British armed forces both during and immediately after these wars.

Ferris, J. R. '"FORTITUDE" in Context: The Evolution of British Military Deception in Two World Wars, 1914-1945', in *Paradoxes of Strategic Intelligence: Essays in Honor of Michael I. Handel*, edited by Richard K. Betts and Thomas G. Mahnken (London: Cass, 2003)

Ferris, J. R., ed. *The British Army and Signals Intelligence during the First World War* (London: Alan Sutton for Army

Records Society, 1992)

Fletcher, D. *Landships: British Tanks in the First World War* (London: HMSO, 1984)

Fletcher, D., ed. *Tanks and Trenches: First-Hand Accounts of Trench Warfare in the First World War* (Phoenix Mill: Alan Sutton, 1994)

Forty, G. and A. Forty. *Bovington Tanks* (Wincanto: Wincanto Press, 1988)

Graham, D. 'Sans Doctrine: British Army Tactics in the First World War', in *Men at War: Politics, Technology, and Innovation in the Twentieth Century*, edited by T. Travers and C. Archer (Chicago: Precedent, 1982)

Green, H. *The British Army in the First World War: The Regulars, the Territorials and Kitchener's Army*; with some of the campaigns into which they fitted (London: Clowes 1968)

Grieves, K. 'The Transportation Mission to GHQ', *Look To Your Front: Studies in the First World War* by the British Commission for Military History, edited by B. Bond [and others] (Staplehurst: Spellmount, 1999)

Griffith, P. *Battle Tactics of the Western Front: The British Army's Art of Attack, 1916-18* (New Haven: Yale University Press, 1994)

Griffith, P., ed. *British Fighting Methods in the Great War* (London: Cass, 1996)

Harris, J. P. *Men, Ideas, and Tanks: British Military Thought and Armoured Forces, 1903-1939* (Manchester: Manchester University Press, 1995)

Hart, P. *Voices from the Front: An Oral History of the Great War* (London: Profile Books 2015)

Hughes, C. 'The New Armies', in *A Nation in Arms: A Social Study of the British Army in the First World War*, ed. by I. Beckett and K. Simpson (Manchester: Manchester University Press, 1985; repr. London: Donovan, 1990)

Hutchison, G. S. *Machine Guns: Their History and Tactical Employment (being also a History of the Machine Gun Corps, 1916-1922)* (London: Macmillan, 1938)

Hynes, S. *The Soldier's Tale: Bearing Witness To Modern War* (London: Pimlico, 1998)

Keegan, J. *The Face of Battle* (London: Cape, 1976; repr. London: Pimlico, 1995)

Liddell Hart, B. H. *The Tanks: The History of the Royal Tank Regiment and its Predecessors, Heavy Branch Machine-Gun Corps, Tank Corps and Royal Tank Corps, 1914-1945*, 2 vols (London: Cassell, 1959), I, *1914-1939* (1959)
The first volume includes a history of the development of tanks during the First World War.

Lytton, N. *The Press and the General Staff* (London: Collins, 1920)

Mallinson. A. *1914: Fight the Good Fight: Britain, the Army and the Coming of the First World War* (London: Bantam Press, 2013)

Marble, S. *British Artillery on the Western Front in the First World War: "The Infantry Cannot Do With A Gun Less"* (Farnham:: Ashgate 2013}

Mason, T. and E. Riedi. *Sport and the Military: The British Armed Forces, 1880–1960* (Cambridge: Cambridge University Press, 2010)

Messenger, C. *Call To Arms: The British Army 1914-1918* (London: Cassell Military, 2006)

Mitchell, F. *Tank Warfare: The Story of the Tanks of the Great War* (London: T. Nelson, 1933; repr. Stevenage: Spa with Tom Donovan Pub., 1987)

Morton-Jack, G. *The Indian Army on the Western Front: India's Expeditionary Force to France and Belgium in the First World War* (Cambridge: Cambridge Univ. Press, 2013)

Moynihan, M., ed. *Black Bread and Barbed Wire: Prisoners of the First World War* London: Leo Cooper, 1978)

Nicholson, W. N. *Behind the Lines: An Account of Administrative Staffwork in the British Army 1914-18* (London: Cape, 1939)

Occleshaw, M. E. *Armour Against Fate: British Military Intelligence in the First World War* (London: Columbus, 1988)

Pegler, M. *British Tommy* (Oxford: Osprey Publishing Ltd, 1996)

Prete, R.A. *Strategy and Command: The Anglo-French Coalition on the Western Front, 1914* (Montreal: McGill-Queen's University Press, 2009)

Roy, K. *The Indian Army in the Two World Wars* (Boston: Brill, 2012)

Seal, G. *The Soldiers' Press: Trench Journals in the First World War* (Basingstoke: Palgrave Macmillan, 2013)

Shephard, B. *A War of Nerves: Soldiers and Psychiatrists 1914-1994* (London: Cape, 2000; repr. London: Pimlico, 2002)

Simkins, P. 'Soldiers and Civilians: Billeting in Britain and France', in *A Nation in Arms: A Social Study of the British Army in the First World War*, ed. by I. Beckett and K. Simpson (Manchester: Manchester University Press, 1985; repr. London: Donovan, 1990)

Simpson, K. 'The British Soldier on the Western Front', in *Home Fires and Foreign Fields, British Social and Military Experience in The Great War*, ed. by P. H. Liddle (Manchester: Manchester University Press, 1985)

— *The Old Contemptibles: A Photographic History of the British Expeditionary Force, August – December, 1914* (London: Allen & Unwin, 1981)

Smithers, A. J. *A New Excalibur: The Development of the Tank, 1909-1939* (London: Leo Cooper and Secker and Warburg, 1986)

Snape, M. *God and the British Soldier* (Christianity and Society in the Modern World) (London: Routledge, 2005)

Spiers, E. M. *Haldane: An Army Reformer* (Edinburgh: Edinburgh University Press, 1980)

— 'The Regular Army in 1914', in *Home Fires and Foreign Fields, British Social and Military Experience in The Great War*, ed. by P. H. Liddle (Manchester: Manchester University Press, 1985)

— 'The Scottish Soldier at War', in *Facing Armageddon: the First World War Experienced*, ed. by H. Cecil and P. H. Liddle (London: Leo Cooper, 1996)

Travers, T. *The Killing Ground: The British Army, the Western Front and the Emergence of War, 1900–1918* (London, Allen and Unwin, 1987)

Tynan, J. *British Army Uniform and the First World War: Men in Khaki* (Houndmills: Palgrave Macmillan 2013)

Winter, D. *Death's Men: Soldiers of the Great War* (London: Allen Lane, 1978)

Winter, J. 'The Army and Society: The Demographic Context', in *A Nation in Arms: A Social Study of the British Army in the First World War*, ed. by I. Beckett and K. Simpson (Manchester: Manchester University Press, 1985; repr. London: Donovan, 1990)

Yockelson, M. A. *Borrowed Soldiers: Americans under British Command, 1918* (Norman: University of Oklahoma

Press 2008?)

Articles

Ashworth, T. 'The Sociology of Trench Warfare, 1914-18', *British Journal of Sociology*, 19 (1968), 407-23

Bessel, R. and D. Englander. 'Up From the Trenches: Some Recent Writing on the Soldiers of The Great War', *European Studies Review*, 11(1981), 387-95

Boff, J. 'Combined Arms during the Hundred Days Campaign, August-November 1918', *War in History*, 17 (2010), 459-478

Carrington, C. E. 'Kitchener's Army; the Somme and After', *Journal of the Royal United Services Institute for Defence Studies*, 123 (1978), 15-20

Constantine, S. '"If an inhabitant attacks, wounds or kills a soldier, the whole village will be destroyed". Communication and Rehearsal in Soldiers' Phrasebooks 1914-1918', *Journal of War and Culture Studies*, 6 (2013), 154-168

Englander, D. and J. Osborne. 'Jack, Tommy, and Henry Dubb: The Armed Forces and the Working Class', *Historical Journal*, 21 (1978), 593-621

Feltman, B. K. 'Tolerance As a Crime? The British Treatment of German Prisoners of War on the Western Front, 1914-1918', *War in History*, 17 (2010), 435-458

French, D. 'The Military Background to the Shell Crisis of 1915', *Journal of Strategic Studies*, 2 (1979), 192-205

Harris, P. and S. Marble. "The "Step-by-Step" Approach: British Military Thought and Operational Method on the Western Front, 1915-1917', *War in History*, 15 (2008), 17-42

Jack, G. M. 'The Indian Army on the Western Front, 1914-1915: A Portrait of Collaboration', *War in History*, 13 (2006), 329-362

Jenkinson, J. '"All in the Same Uniform?" The Participation of Black Colonial Residents in the British Armed Forces in the First World War', *Journal of Imperial and Commonwealth History*, 40, (2012), 207-230

Merrick, P. 'Horses for the Great War', *Local Historian*, 44:3 (2014), 221-242

Perry, N. 'Maintaining Regimental Identity in the Great War: The Case of the Irish Infantry Regiments', *Stand to!: The Journal of the Western Front Association*, 52 (1998), 5-11

Phillips, C. 'Not Your Typical Soldier, Not Your Typical Service: Sir Francis Dent and the First World War', *Historian* (Historical Association), 122 (2014), 28-31

Phillips, G. 'Black Beauties of the Western Front', *History Today*, 62, Issue 1 (2012), 5-6
About the horses and mules employed by the British army during the First World War

Riddell, G. A., Baron Riddell. 'The Relations of the Press with the Army in the Field', *Royal United Service Institution Journal*, 66 (1921), 385-397

Ugolini, L. 'War-stained: British Combatants and Uniforms, 1914-18', *War and Society* (Duntroon Australia), 33 (2014), 155-171

4.5.1.2 Recruitment

Based on pre-war plans (masterminded by Haldane), which had tended to envisage a future war of six months' duration, Britain had available at the outset of the war in the region of 250,000 men distributed between a small regular army, reserves and territorials (the latter being a separate volunteer unit intended primarily for home defence but permitted to volunteer for overseas service). In the absence of conscription, Kitchener's initial call on 7 August 1914 (based on his view of a war lasting at least 3 years) was for 100,000 volunteers. There was a huge response (but by no means uniform either regionally or locally) and "by the end of 1914, slightly over one million men had enlisted" in the New Armies (Dewey, P. E. 'Military Recruiting and the British Labour Force During the First World War', *Historical Journal*, 27 (1984), p. 199), with workers in finance and commerce, the professions and entertainment volunteering with greater readiness than industrial, transport, manufacturing, and agricultural workers. It was some time before the New Armies were trained and ready for combat but the BEF, consisting of regular army soldiers and reservists, augmented by Territorial units which had volunteered for service overseas, were shipped to France almost immediately after the war had begun.

The reason why such huge numbers of people volunteered to join up at the beginning of the war has been attributed to a variety of influences such as patriotism, recruitment drives, newspaper publicity, propaganda posters, pressure from peer-groups (e.g. Pals' Battalions) and employers, the scorn accorded to those not in uniform, boredom, opportunities for employment or better wages. Whatever the influence, there existed an underlying assumption by a large part of the population that the war would be short and not particularly dangerous.

By 1915 the far fewer numbers of people volunteering for the New Armies were inadequate for coping with the massive demand for military manpower occasioned by the nature of trench warfare on the Western Front. Government schemes (e.g. the Derby Scheme) and recruitment campaigns failed to produce the numbers of men required and on 5 January 1916 conscription was introduced. Its introduction, however, was met with difficulties which reduced the numbers conscripted; large numbers of men had to be exempted because they were engaged in other war work and others had to be rejected on medical or racial grounds. Conscientious objection also reduced the number of conscripts, but by an insignificant amount as only 16,500 claims for exemption were made on those grounds (see **Part 3, preamble to section 2.11.2** on **Conscription and Conscience**). The War Office estimated that a total of almost five million (4,970,000) men had entered the army by the time of the armistice on 11 November 1918 and a breakdown of this figure indicates that just over 50% of this number had been conscripted (War Office. *Statistics of the Military Effort of the British Empire during the Great War, 1914-1920, 1922*, pp. 363-4).

The attempt to introduce conscription in Ireland in 1918 met with such strong opposition in that country that the Government abandoned it. Nevertheless, over 200,000 Irishmen from North and South volunteered for service in the British Army in the course of the war, joining up at a rate which was broadly comparable to that of Great Britain as a whole.

As a result of the expansion of the army and the high rate of casualties suffered at the officer level after the war had begun it became necessary to meet the shortfall with a substantial addition to the complement of 18,497 pre-war regular and reserve officers available in August 1914. Some of this shortfall was met by the 'Officer Training Corps', which were operating in 120 public schools and 20 universities by the beginning of the war, but these organisations were incapable of providing the numbers of officers required. Promoting officers from the ranks to fill the gaps became a necessity as the casualty rate of officers from the conventional background of the upper classes grew, a situation which resulted in an army with a much larger number of officers from a lower-middle-class background and a considerable change, therefore, in the class structure at the officer level.

In spite of the fact that in the early days of the war large numbers of working men were volunteering of their own accord, recruitment drives were carried out in all quarters of the country with the working-class as their main target (not surprisingly in view of the fact that it represented 70 % of the population). Much of this recruiting of working men was carried out unofficially by employers who played on feelings of patriotism or offered inducements, and sometimes even had recourse to threats, in their efforts to recruit volunteers. It is hardly surprising that this sometimes caused resentment particularly in rural communities where agricultural workers were often subject to the aggressively enthusiastic efforts of their landed class employers to get them to volunteer. As the war dragged on into a second year volunteers from the working-class population dwindled significantly. Conscription had to be brought in (Military Service Act of 1916) but many thousands tried to avoid being conscripted (e.g. by bribing civilian clerks to remove their files from recruiting offices), an indication perhaps that the initial patriotic enthusiasm was waning. The introduction of conscription caused considerable controversy, particularly in relation to the resentment aroused by the operations of the tribunals that were established to make decisions on applications for exemption from military service. Nevertheless, support for the war by the working class remained solid for the most part and its overall attitude throughout the war was in tune with the generally patriotic sentiments of the nation.

Biographies

Churchill, R. F. E. S. *Lord Derby, 'King of Lancashire': The Official Life of Edward, Seventeenth Earl of Derby, 1865-1948* (London: Heinemann, 1959)
Lord Derby was particularly associated in the First World War with the recruiting drive.

Books

Allinson, A. *The Bantams: The Untold Story of World War I* (London: Howard Baker,1981)

Beckett, I. F. W. *The Amateur Military Tradition, 1558-1945* (Manchester: Manchester University Press, 1991)

— 'The British Army, 1914-1918: The Illusion of Change', in *Britain and the First World War*, ed. by J. Turner (London: Routledge, 1988)

— 'The Nation in Arms, 1914-1918', in *A Nation in Arms; A Social Study of the British Army in the First World War*, ed. by I. Beckett and K. Simpson (Manchester: Manchester University Press,1985; repr. London: Donovan, 1990)

— 'The Territorial Force', in *A Nation in Arms; A Social Study of the British Army in the First World War*, ed. by I. Beckett and K. Simpson (Manchester: Manchester University Press,1985; repr. London: Donovan, 1990)

Bowman, T. 'The Irish Recruiting and Anti-Recruiting Campaigns, 1914-1918', in *Propaganda: Political Rhetoric and Identity, 1300-2000*, edited by Bertrand Taithe and Tim Thornton (Stroud: Sutton, 1999)

Kernahan, C. *The Experience of a Recruiting Officer* (London: Hodder & Stoughton, 1915)

Great Britain. War Office. *Statistics of the Military Effort of the British Empire during the Great War, 1914-1920* (London: HMSO, 1922)
Facsimile reprint published London: London Stamp Exchange, 1992.

Grieves, K. R. *The Politics of Manpower, 1914-1918* (Manchester: Manchester University Press, 1988)

— 'The Recruiting Margin: Debates on Manpower during the Third Battle of Ypres', in *Passchendaele in Perspective: The Third Battle of Ypres*, edited by P. H. Liddle (London : Lee Cooper, 1997)

Howie, D. and J. Howie. 'Irish Recruiting and the Home Rule Crisis of August-September 1914', in *Strategy and Intelligence: British Policy during the First World War*, edited by M. Dockrill and D. French (London: Hambledon Press, 1996)

Hughes, C. 'The New Armies', in *A Nation in Arms: A Social Study of the British Army in the First World War*, ed. by I. Beckett and K. Simpson (Manchester: Manchester University Press,1985; repr. London: Donovan, 1990)

Liddle, P. H. 'The Territorial Force in the Great War', in *Home Fires and Foreign Fields, British Social and Military Experience in The Great War*, ed. by P. H. Liddle (Manchester: Manchester University Press, 1985)

Killingray, D. 'All the King's Men: Blacks in the British Army in the First World War', in *Under the Imperial Carpet: Essays in Black History, 1780-1950*, edited by R. Lotz and I. Pegg (Crawley: Rabbit Press, 1986)

Osborne, J. M. *The Voluntary Recruiting Movement in Britain, 1914-1916* (London: Garland, 1982)

Robertson, I. 'Fighting and Bleeding for the Land: The Scottish Highlands and the Great War', in *Scotland and the Great War*, edited by Catriona M. M. Macdonald and Elaine W. McFarland (East Linton: Tuckwell, 1998)

Simkins, P. 'Kitchener and the Expansion of the Army', in *Politicians and Defence: Studies in the Formulation of British Defence Policy, 1846-1970*, edited by I. F.W. Beckett and J. Gooch (Manchester: Manchester University Press,

1981)

— *Kitchener's Army: The Raising of Britain's New Armies, 1914-1916*, (Manchester: Manchester University Press, 1988; repr. Barnsley: Pen & Sword, 2007)

Simpson, K. 'The Officers', in *A Nation in Arms: A Social Study of the British Army in the First World War*, ed. by I. Beckett and K. Simpson (Manchester: Manchester University Press, 1985; repr. London: Donovan, 1990)

Spiers, E. 'The Scottish Soldier at War', in *Facing Armageddon: The First World War Experienced*, ed. by H. Cecil and P. H. Liddle (London: Leo Cooper, 1996)

— 'The Regular Army', in *A Nation in Arms: A Social Study of the British Army in the First World War*, ed. by I. Beckett and K. Simpson (Manchester: Manchester University Press, 1985; repr. London: Donovan, 1990)

Thomson, M. 'Status, Manpower and Mental Fitness: Mental Deficiency in the First World War', in *War, Medicine and Modernity*, edited by R. Cooter, M. Harrison and S. Sturdy (Stroud: Sutton, 1998; repr. 1999)

Urquhart, G. 'Negotiations for War: Highland Identity under Fire', in *War: Identities in Conflict 1300-2000*, edited by Bertrand Taithe & Tim Thornton (Stroud : Sutton, 1998)

Wallace, E. *Kitchener's Army and the Territorial Forces: The Full Story of a Great Achievement* (London: Newnes, 1915)

Watson, A. *Enduring the Great War: Combat, Morale and Collapse in the German and British Armies, 1914–1918* (Cambridge: Cambridge University Press, 2009)
In an examination and comparison of the motivation, morale and endurance of German and British soldiers confronted by the horrific nature of the warfare in which they were engaged the author provides an explanation of why the ability of British soldiers to cope with it outlasted that of their opponents.

Williams, B. *Raising and Training the New Armies* (London: Constable, 1918)

Articles

Beckett, I. F. W. 'Aspects of a Nation in Arms: Britain's Volunteer Training Corps in the Great War', *Revue Interntionale d'Histoire Militaire*, 63 (1985), 27-39

— 'The Real Unknown Army: British Conscripts, 1916-1919', *The Great War*, 2 (1989), 4-13

Bowman, T. 'Composing Divisions: The Recruitment of Ulster and National Volunteers into the British Army in 1914', *Causeway*, 2/1 (1995), 24-29

Callan, P. 'British Recruitment in Ireland', *Revue Internationale d'Histoire Militaire*, 63 (1985), 41-50

— 'Recruiting for the British Army in Ireland during the First World War', *Irish Sword*, 17 (1987), 442-56

Denman, T. 'The Catholic Irish Soldier in the First World War: The Racial Environment,' *Irish Historical Studies*, 27 (1991), 352-65

Dewey, P. E. 'Military Recruiting and the British Labour Force During the First World War', *Historical Journal*, 27 (1984), 192-223

Douglas, R. 'Voluntary Enlistment in the First World War and the Work of the Parliamentary Recruiting Committee [PRC]', *Journal of Modern History*, 42 (1970), 564-85

Fitzpatrick, D. 'The Logic of Collective Sacrifice: Ireland and the British Army, 1914-1918', *Historical Journal*, 38 (1995), 1017-30

Grieves, K. R. '"Lowther's Lambs": Rural Paternalism and Voluntary Recruitment in the First World War', *Rural History*, 4 (1993), 55-75

Johnson, M. 'The Liberal War Committee and the Liberal Advocacy of Conscription in Britain, 1914-1916', *Historical Journal*, 51 (2008), 399-420

Killingray, D. 'Race and Rank in the British Army in the Twentieth Century', *Ethnic and Racial Studies*, 10 (1987), 276-90

McConnel, J. 'Recruiting Sergeants for John Bull? Irish Nationalist MPs and Enlistment during the Early Months of the Great War', *War In History*, 14 (2007), 408-428

Phillips, G. 'Dai Bach Y Soldiwr: Welsh Soldiers in the British Army, 1914-1918', *Llafur*, 6 (1993), 94-105

Pollins, H. 'Jews in the British Army in the First World War, *Jewish Journal of Sociology*, 37 (1995), 100-11

Winter, J. 'Britain's Lost Generation of the First World War', *Population Studies*, 31 (1977), 449-66

— 'Military Fitness and Civilian Health in Britain during the First World War', *Journal of Contemporary History*, 15 (1980), 211-44

4.5.1.3 Morale and Discipline

The Army attached great importance to morale and devoted a considerable amount of effort to the task of trying to maintain it at a high level by, for example, providing regular leave, and keeping soldiers occupied between tours of frontline service with recreation and entertainment[159]. A visit to a concert party provided by an entertainment troupe particularly helped to cheer up troops in their rest periods behind the immediate front. With every army division eventually possessing its own entertainment troupe this sort of entertainment became widely available to the troops. Regimental bands were also valued for their potential to boost morale and were sent out to the front from the regimental depots in England. There were not, however, sufficient numbers of these bands, and in the areas of the front where they were not available the Army encouraged the efforts of soldiers to form new bands with the instruments and musicians that could be found among their ranks.

The British Tommy was not without grumbles about his life in the trenches; he could, for instance, get resentful about the comparative safety which staff officers enjoyed. He sometimes went well beyond grumbling, committing serious acts of indiscipline, such as absence without leave, disobedience and insubordination, desertion in the face of the enemy and even crimes such as murder and rape. A considerable number of Courts Martial for trying individual offences of such a nature had to be carried out throughout the war but having to deal with collective indiscipline of a mutinous nature was rare. Mutinies did take place but they were more like strike protests on trade union lines about matters such as living conditions and rates of pay[160] and not really about an unwillingness to continue fighting. There was inevitably some erosion of morale as the war ground on but it was never in any real danger of reaching a point of major crisis. Whatever disillusionment the average British soldier may have experienced by the end of the war it never escalated to the stage where he refused to go on fighting.

Shell shock and its affects (see also **Part 3, section 4.6.5** on **Medicine**) were ill understood in the early stages of the war and some acceptance of them as a valid reason for a soldier being declared unfit to return to the front line, or as mitigating factor in relation to his being charged with cowardice in the face of the enemy, was only gradually achieved in the course of the war.

Although there were signs of greater public awareness of homosexuality and openness of discussion about it during the war the attitude of the Army on the subject remained one of total intolerance and lack of understanding. The Army stuck to its own code of morality which it ruthlessly enforced. Between 1914 and 1919 22 officers and 270 soldiers were court-martialled for homosexual acts in the British Army.

---

[159] Officers organized seaside excursions to Dunkirk or Boulogne, horse races, football, and cricket matches, concert parties and films. For the showing of films the army maintained its own cinemas for frontline troops.

[160] For example, mass meetings of some units of the 25th Division took place in 1916 to protest against poor billets. Much more serious was the mutiny at Etaples in 1917, involving soldiers of the 51st Highland Division, the Northumberland Fusiliers and Australians, but this occurred largely as a result of the Military Police shooting dead a regular army corporal.

The War Years

Books

Allison, W. and J. Fairley. *The Monocled Mutineer* (London: Quartet Books, 1978)

Babington, A. *For The Sake of Example: Capital Courts Martial, 1914-1920*, revised edn (London: Leo Cooper, 1993)

Baynes, J. *Morale: A Study of Men And Courage, the Second Scottish Rifles at The Battle of Neuve Chapelle, 1915* (London: Cassell, 1967, reprinted. London: Leo Cooper, 1987)

Bowman, T. 'The Discipline and Morale of the BEF in France and Flanders, 1914-1918, with particular reference to Irish Units' (unpublished doctoral thesis, University of Luton, 1999)

— *Irish Regiments in the Great War: Discipline and Morale* (Manchester: Manchester University Press, 2003)

Brown, E. D. 'Between Cowardice and Insanity: Shell Shock and the Legitimation of the Neuroses in Great Britain' in *Science, Technology and the Military*, edited by E. Mendelsohn [and others] (Boston: Kluwer Academic Publishers, 1989)

Corns, C., and J. Hughes-Wilson. *Blindfold and Alone: British Military Executions in the Great War.* (London: Cassell & Co, 2001)

Cooter, R. 'Malingering in Modernity: Psychological Scripts and Adversarial Encounters during the First World War', in *War, Medicine and Modernity*, edited by R. Cooter, M. Harrison and S. Sturdy (Stroud: Sutton, 1998; repr. 1999)

Dallas, G. and D. Gill. *The Unknown Army: Mutinies in the British Army in World War I* (London: Verso, 1985)

Englander, D. 'Discipline and Morale in the British Army', in *State, Society, and Mobilisation in Europe during the First World War*, edited by J. Horne (Cambridge: Cambridge University Press, 1997, repr. 2002)

Fuller, J. G. *Troop Morale and Popular Culture in the British and Dominion Armies, 1914-1918* (Oxford: Clarendon Press, 1990)
This book brings out the point that, in spite of enduring terrible conditions in the trenches and witnessing the slaughter of their comrades on a massive scale, the morale of the front-line soldiers remained intact and that this "as much as the strategy of their commanders" was a crucial factor in the outcome of the Great War.

Gibson, C. *Behind the Front: British Soldiers and French Civilians, 1914-1918* (Cambridge: Cambridge University Press, 2014)

Hallett, C. E. *Containing Trauma: Nursing Work in the First World War* (Manchester: Manchester University Press, 2009)

Kellett, A. *Combat Motivation: The Behaviour of Soldiers in Battle* (Londo: Kluwer-Nijhoff, 1982)

Killick, A. *Mutiny! The Story of the Calais Mutiny, 1918* (Brighton: Spark, 1968)

Leed, E. J. *No Man's Land: Combat and Identity In World War I* (Cambridge: Cambridge University Press, 1979; repr. 1981)

Lynch, P. J. 'The Exploitation of Courage: Psychiatric Care in the British Army, 1914-1918' (unpublished master's thesis, University College, London 1977)

Mackenzie, S. P. *Politics and Military Morale: Current Affairs and Citizenship Education in the British Army, 1914-50* (Oxford: Oxford University Press, 1990)

Moore, W. *The Thin Yellow Line* (London: Leo Cooper, 1974; repr. Ware: Wordsworth Editions, 1999)

Moran, C. M. W., Baron. *The Anatomy of Courage*, 2nd edn (London: Constable, 1966, repr. New York: Avery, 1988)

Oram, G. *Death Sentences Passed by Military Courts of the British Army, 1914-1924*, rev. edn (London: Francis Boutle, 2005)

— *Military Executions during World War I* (Basingstoke: Palgrave Macmillan, 2003)

— *Worthless Men: Race, Eugenics, and the Death Penalty in the British Army during the First World War* (London: Francis Boutle, 1998)

Peaty, J. 'Capital Courts-Martial during the Great War', in *Look To Your Front: Studies in the First World War*, edited by B. Bond [and others] (Staplehurst: Spellmount, 1999)

— 'Haig and Military Discipline', in *Haig: A Reappraisal 70 Years On*, edited by B. Bond and N. Cave (London: Cooper, 1999)

Putkowski, J. and J. Sykes. *Shot at Dawn: Executions in World War One by Authority of the British Army Act*, new and revised edn (London: Leo Cooper, 1992)

Reid, F. *Broken Men: Shell Shock, Treatment and Recovery in Britain, 1914-1930* (London: Continuum, 2010)

Scott, P. 'Law and Orders; Discipline and Morale in the British Armies in France, 1917', in *Passchendaele in Perspective: The Third Battle of Ypres*, edited by P. H. Liddle (London: Cooper, 1997)

Sellers, L. *Death for Desertion: The Story of the Court Martial and Execution of Temporary Sub-Lieutenant Arthur Leopold Arthur Dyett, Nelson Battalion, 63rd (RN) Division, during the First World War* (Barnsley: Leo Cooper, 2003)

Sheffield, G. D. 'Officer-Man Relations, Discipline and Morale in the British Army in the Great War', in *Facing Armageddon: The First World War Experienced*, ed. by H. Cecil and P. H. Liddle (London: Leo Cooper, 1996)

— 'Officer-Man Relations, Morale and Discipline in the British Army, 1902-22' (unpublished doctoral thesis, University of London 1994)

— 'The Operational Role of British Military Police on the Western Front, 1914-1918', in *British Fighting Methods in the Great War*, edited by P. Griffith (London: Cass, 1996)

Simpson, K. 'Dr James Dunn and Shell-Shock', in *Facing Armageddon: The First World War Experienced*, ed. by H. Cecil and P. H. Liddle (London: Cooper, 1996)

Waite, H., comp. *How to Keep "Fit": or, The Soldiers' Guide to Health in War and Peace*, war edn (London: Gale & Polden Ltd., 1915)
First published in 1900.

Watson, A. *Enduring the Great War: Combat, Morale and Collapse in the German and British Armies, 1914-1918* (Cambridge: Cambridge University Press, 2008)

Wilson, J. B.. 'The Morale and Discipline of the B.E.F., 1914-1918' (unpublished master's thesis, University of New Brunswick, 1978)

Articles

Bogacz, T. 'War Neuroses and Cultural Change in England, 1914-22: The Work of the War Office Committee of Enquiry into "Shell Shock"', *Journal of Contemporary History*, 24 (1989), 227-56

Dallas, G. and D. Gill. 'Mutiny at Etaples Base in 1917', *Past and Present*, 69 (1975), 88-112

Egan, D. 'The Swansea Conference of the British Council of Soldiers' and Workers' Delegates, July 1917', *Llafur*, 1 (1975), 162-87

Fletcher, A. 'Between the Lines: First World War Correspondence', *History Today*, 5, Issue 11 (2009), 45-51
A consideration of what soldiers' letters home reveal about their inner lives. By helping to make life in the trenches more bearable these letters provided siome emotional solace and contributed to the maintenance of morale.

Gibson, K. C. 'Sex and Soldiering in France and Flanders: The British Expeditionary Force along the Western Front, 1914–1918', *The International History Review*, 23 (2001), 535–79

Hanna, E. 'Putting the Moral into Morale: YMCA Cinemas on the Western Front, 1914–1918', *Historical Journal of Film, Radio and Television*, 35 (2015), 615-630

Harrison, M. 'The British Army and the Problem of Venereal Disease in France and Egypt during the First World War', *Medical History*, 39 (1995), 133-58

Jones, E. 'The Psychology of Killing: The Combat Experience of British Soldiers during the First World War', *Journal of Contemporary History*, 41:2 (2006), 229–246

Laugesen, A. 'Forgetting Their Troubles for a While: Australian Soldiers' Experiences of Cinema during the First World War', *Historical Journal of Film, Radio and Television*, 35 (2015), 596-614

Mackenzie, S. P. 'Morale and the Cause: The Campaign to Shape the Outlook of Soldiers of the BEF, 1914-1918', *Canadian Journal of History*, 25 (1990), 215-31

Simpson, K. 'Dr Dunn and Battle Stress: The Experiences of a Regimental Medical Officer of 2nd Royal Welch Fusiliers, 1915-1918', *The Great War*, 3 (1991), 76-86

Strachan, H. 'Training, Morale, and Modern War', *Journal of Contemporary History*, 41 (2006), 211-227

Watson, A. 'Self-Deception and Survival: Mental Coping Strategies on the Western Front, 1914-18', *Journal of Contemporary History*, 41 (2006), 247-268
This article examines the resilience displayed by German and British soldiers during the war in terms of a focus on the personal psychology which enabled them to cope with such success with the dangers and horrors of trench warfare and to sustain their combat motivation.

Watson, A. and P. Porter, 'Bereaved and Aggrieved: Combat Motivation and the Ideology of Sacrifice in the First World War', *Historical Research*, 83 (2010), 146–64

Wessely, S. 'Twentieth-Century Theories on Combat Motivation and Breakdown', *Journal of Contemporary History*, 41 (2006), 268-286

4.5.1.4 Attitudes

In any consideration of the Great War one of the questions which comes to mind is why, with no major victories to boost their morale, were millions of British soldiers, whether members of the regular Army, volunteers, or conscripts, willing to carry on fighting in the front-line trenches of the Western front where they had to endure appalling living conditions, interminable shelling, the endless sight of slaughtered comrades, and the constant possibility (even probability) of being killed, maimed or permanently disabled. Answers to this question have been made in relation to a multiplicity of disparate factors such as the temporary relief afforded by alternation of spells in the front-lines with periods in the rest areas behind the lines, the effectiveness of military discipline, regimental pride, the bonding in camaraderie and loyalty of groups sharing common dangers, the influence on some soldiers of their civilian background of working class solidarity, the nature of the leadership provided by officers brought up in the traditions and values of the public school, the influence of religion, or just simply patriotism; in the case of some soldiers the motivation may have lain in the fact that the war engendered a feeling of excitement, a sense of purpose, a thirst for revenge, a hatred of the enemy, or even a pleasure in killing. Whichever of these factors had an influence on the British soldier, one or other of them, or a combinat.ion of them, seem to have contributed to his steadfast determination to stick it out, come what may.

The enthusiasm of soldiers on the Western Front at the beginning of the war inevitably waned as they became worn down by the inescapable horrors of trench warfare. The early mood, however, did not give way to total disillusionment even in the most devastating periods of the war. Soldiers came to adopt a stoical attitude, doggedly resigning themselves to the situation, often with sardonic humour[161], and insulating themselves against the miserable conditions[162] in which they existed by making their daily existence as bearable as possible by preoccupying themselves with their creature comforts, food, drink, warmth, and links with home. As a further antidote to the discomfort and danger of their stints in the front-line trenches and to the monotony of their daily chores in their periods behind the front line, soldiers contrived to make the most of their off-duty leisure moments in a number of ways as, for instance, engaging in sporting activities, enjoying wine or a beer and a sing-song in the local estaminet, playing an instrument in an improvised band, participating in troop theatricals[163], and listening to, or simply recollecting[164], the songs they had heard on their visit to the theatre or musical hall when they were on leave at home. These aspects of the attitudes of the front-line soldier are in contrast to the idea of his descent into disillusionment and despair that can be derived from the poems of Graves, Sassoon, Owen and some other soldier-poets, and from the works of those war novelists who wrote in disillusioned fashion in the aftermath of the war. It can be regarded as misleading to see these 'protest' writers, most of whom were officers from an educated background, as typical of the soldiers who fought on the Western Front during the Great War.

British soldiers had an attitude to the war which differed in many respects from that prevailing among civilians on the home front. From their first-hand acquaintance with the horrific nature of modern warfare soldiers tended to see the war in a more critical, ironic, and fatalistic light than civilians. Few of the frontline troops were possessed of the virulently anti-German feelings displayed by many civilians, and tended rather to have sympathy for the sufferings of their counterparts in German trenches that were seen as no different from their own. They could get resentful about such matters as profiteering on the home front, the rabid jingoism and lack of understanding of the true nature of trench warfare evinced by some civilians, and the dishonesty of reporting by war correspondents. They tended to become bored by recruiting songs written by civilians and to amuse themselves by sardonically changing the words of many of the patriotic songs when they sang them in the trenches or on marches. The irreverence and bawdiness of the parodies of popular songs (and even of hymns) and of the lyrics that soldiers made up themselves were a source of relief and humour that were representative of the songs soldiers preferred to sing. The other songs that were very popular among soldiers were those of a nostalgic and sentimental nature (e.g. *It's a Long Way to Tipperary, Take me Back to Dear Old Blighty, The Roses of Picardy*), a reflection of another side to the nature of the front-line soldier[165].

The attitudes of soldiers are particularly well reflected in the hundreds of different trench papers and magazines written and edited by members of a particular infantry battalion or artillery battery and usually published on a monthly basis, the printing being done by the troops themselves on abandoned French presses or on Army equipment or via agents in Paris or London. The best known of the trench journals was *The Wipers Times*; others included *The Dud, The Dump, The Growler, The Shell Hole Advance,* and *The Dead Horse Corner Gazette*. These papers presented a view of the war which ranged from the sardonic humour and irreverence displayed in soldier's songs and the cartoons of Bairnsfather to the stark realism associated with soldier-poets like Sassoon

---

[161] This characteristic was immortalized by 'Old Bill', the cartoon character created by Bruce Bairnsfather satirizing Army life and mocking the heroic image of war. This was the best known object of humour among soldiers.

[162] An infantryman did not spend all his time in the front line; his time alternated between the frontline and the rear 'rest areas' where the conditions, although not entirely restful because of the chores which had to be carried out there (e.g. digging, repairing, loading and unloading), were a great deal more pleasant than they were in the frontline and frequently enlivened by concerts and other leisure activities.

[163] Most army divisions sponsored troop theatricals which staged productions reminiscent of the musical-hall. For these theatricals soldiers wrote and performed comic songs and skits about mothers-in-law or fat ladies bathing at the seaside, satirical songs about Army life (e.g. making light of unbearable conditions, poking fun at those in authority, lampooning pompous, overbearing officers), and sentimental ballads.

[164] Recollection would no doubt have been helped by the pin-ups of glamorous stars of the theatre and the music hall that soldiers pinned on the walls of their billets.

[165] In her introduction to Max Arthur's *When this Bloody War is Over: Soldiers' Songs of the First World War* Lyn Macdonald alludes to "the lighter side, which was so important to the soldiers themselves" and sees this in the following way: "The music, the laughter, and above all the songs of the Great War have been described as 'a protest of life against death', but perhaps they merely represent the ascendency of the human spirit over the cruel inhumanity of the war itself".

and Owen. They parodied civilian newspapers, including in their columns, all written in a mocking style[166], letters to the editor, advice columns, fashion news, poetry and prose and 'in jokes' only understandable to the frontline soldier. Trench journalism also served as a vehicle for expressing, usually by means of satire or humour, grievances such as the ignorance of civilians and politicians, the incompetence of the War Office, and the bad food and miserable conditions of trench life.

The jaded, albeit frequently humorous, view of the war portrayed in the trench newspapers is in complete contrast to the unrealistic way the war was presented in most of the home front press, but the sort of disillusionment it represented was related neither to pacifism nor defeatism. Soldiers may have become angry with the patriotic excesses on the home front but this did not affect their determination to see the war through to the bitter end. In spite of the weary and irreverent note struck by soldiers in the trench papers, this determination remains clearly apparent in their ballads and writings in these papers.

Books

Arthur, M. *When This Bloody War is Over: Soldiers Songs of the First World War*. Introduction by Lyn Macdonald (London: Judy Piatkus Ltd., 2001)

Beaver, P. *The Wipers Times*: A Complete Facsimile of the Famous World War One Trench Newspaper, Incorporating the 'New Church Times', the 'Kemmel Times', the 'Somme Times', the 'B.E.F. Times', and the 'Better Times'. Introduction, notes and glossary by Patrick Beaver; foreword by Henry Williamson (London: P. Davies, 1973; repr. London: Papermac, 1988)

Brophy, J. and E. Partridge. *The Long Trail: What the British Soldier Sang and Said in the Great War of 1914-18*, revised edn (London: Sphere, 1969)
Previous edn published as *Songs and Slang of the British Soldier, 1914-18*, London: Deutsch, 1931.

Duffett, R. *The Stomach for Fighting: Food and the Soldiers of the Great War* (Manchester: Manchester University Press 2012

Fuller, J. G. *Troop Morale and Popular Culture in the British and Dominion Armies, 1914-1918* (Oxford: Clarendon Press, 1990)

Gibson, C. *Behind the Front: British Soldiers and French Civilians, 1914-1918* (Cambridge: Cambridge University Press, 2014)

Ivelaw-Chapman, J. *The Riddles of Wipers: An Appreciation of the Wipers Times, A Journal of the Trenches* (London: Cooper, 1997)

McCartney, H. B. *Citizen Soldiers: The Liverpool Territorials in the First World War* (Cambridge: Cambridge University Press, 2005)
Uses diaries, letters and memoirs as well as other official sources to access the thoughts and feelings of the soldier at war.

Merridale, C., ed. *Culture and Combat Motivation* (London: Sage, 2006)
Special issue of *Journal of Contemporary History*, vol. 41, no.2, April 2006

Murdoch, B. *Fighting Songs and Warring Word: Popular Lyrics of two World Wars* (London: Routledge, 1990)

Palmer, R. *What a Lovely War: British Soldiers' Songs from the Boer War to the Present Day*. Foreword by Lyn Macdonald (London: M. Joseph, 1990)

Postcards from the Trenches: Images of the First World War. Introduction by Andrew Roberts (Oxford: Bodleian Library, 2008)
The postcards have the effect of portraying the range of the human experience and behaviour, from the sombre to the light-hearted and humorous, of the soldiers who fought in the subterranean world of the trenches.

---

[166] The trench papers took a particular delight in pillorying the bombastic reportage of war correspondents or civilian writers like Horatio Bottomley and Hilaire Belloc.

Roper, M. *The Secret Battle: Emotional Survival in the Great War* (Manchester: Manchester University Press, 2010)

Schweitzer, R, *The Cross and the Trenches: Religious Faith and Doubt among British and American Great War Soldiers* (Westport, CN: Praeger, 2003)

Seal, G. *The Soldiers' Press: Trench Journals in the First World War* (Basingstoke: Palgrave Macmillan, 2013)

Walsh, C. *Mud, Songs and Blighty: A Scrapbook of the First World War* (London: Hutchinson, 1975)

Wilson, R. J.. *Landscapes of the Western Front: Materiality during the Great War* (London: Routledge, 2011)

Articles

Bourke, J. 'The Emotions in War: Fear and the British and American Military, 1914-45', *Historical Research* (Oxford), 74 (2001), 314-330

Brown, M. '"Somewhere in France"', *History Today*, 56, Issue 7 (2006), 22-24
In welcoming a new publication of the collected numbers of The Wipers Times, Malcolm Brown wonders why we find the idea of humour in the trenches so shocking

Duffett, R. 'Beyond the Ration: Sharing and Scrounging on the Western Front', *Twentieth Century British History*, 22, (2011), 453-473

Feltman, B. K. 'Tolerance As a Crime? The British Treatment of German Prisoners of War on the Western Front, 1914-1918', *War in History*, 17 (2010), 435-458

Fletcher, A. 'Between the Lines: First World War Correspondence', *History Today*, 5, Issue 11 (2009), 45-51
A consideration of what soldiers' letters home reveal about their inner lives. By helping to make life in the trenches more bearable these letters provided siome emotional solace and contributed to the maintenance of morale.

Jones, E. 'The Psychology of Killing: The Combat Experience of British Soldiers during the First World War', *Journal of Contemporary History*, 41 (2006), 229-246

Munslow, A. 'Landscapes of the Western Front: Materiality during the Great War', *Rethinking History*, Special Issue: Historical Justice, 18, (2014), 304-308

Nordlund, A. '"Done My Bit": British Soldiers, the 1918 Armistice, and Understanding the First World War', *Journal of Military History*, 81 (2017), 425-446

Roper, M. 'Nostalgia as an Emotional Experience in the Great War', *Historical Journal*, 54 (2011), 421-452

Schweitzer, R. 'The Cross and the Trenches: Religious Faith and Doubt among Some British Soldiers on the Western Front', *War and Society*, 16 (1998), 33-58

Taylor, M. 'The "Open Exhaust" and Some Other Trench Journals of the First World War', *Imperial War Museum Review*, 5 (1990)

Watson, A. and P. Porter. 'Bereaved and Aggrieved: Combat Motivation and the Ideology of Sacrifice in the First World War', *Historical Research*, 83 (2010), 146-164

Wilson, R. 'The Burial of the Dead: The British Army on the Western Front, 1914-18', *War and Society* (Duntroon Australia), 31 (2012), 22-41
An examination of the development of a 'war culture' within the British Army in relation to the response of soldiers to death and burial on the Western Front.

4.5.1.5 Battle Fronts and Campaigns

The Western Front

Ball, T. 'When This Bloody War is Over: The Northumberland Fusiliers in 1918', *Journal of the Society for Army Historical Research*, 91 (2013), 24-59

Barton, P. *Passchendaele* (London: Constable, in association with the Imperial War Museum, 2007)

Barton, P. and others. *Beneath Flanders Fields: The Tunneller's War, 1914-18*, by Peter Barton, Peter Doyle and Johan Vanderwalle (Staplehurst: Spellmount, 2004; repr. in paperback 2006)

Bechthold, M. 'Command, Leadership, and Doctrine on the Great War Battlefield: The Australian, British, and Canadian Experience at the Battle of Arras, May 1917', *War and Society*, 32 (2013), 116-137

Beckett, I. F. W. *Ypres: The First Battle, 1914* (Harlow: Pearson Education, 2004)

Blair, D. *The Battle of Bellicourt Tunnel: Tommies, Diggers and Doughboys on the Hindenburg Line, 1918* (London: Frontline Books, 2011)

Boff. J. 'Combined Arms during the Hundred Days Campaign, August-November 1918', *War in History*, 17 (2010), 459-478

— *Winning and Losing on the Western Front: The British Third Army and the Defeat of Germany in 1918* (Cambridge: Cambridge University Press, 2012)
An examination of how the opposing armies fought during the 'Hundred Days' campaign and an assessment of how far the British Army's application of adaptation to the changing nature of modern warfare provided the basis for this army's part in the Allied victory.

Bond, B. ed. *Liddell Hart's Western Front: Impressions of the Battle of the Somme*, with war letters, diary and occasional notes written on active service in France and Flanders 1915 and 1916, limited edn (Brighton: Tom Donovan, 2010)

Brown, M., ed. *Imperial War Museum [IWM] Book of the Western Front* (London: Pan, 2001)
Diaries and letters of ordinary soldiers

Cassar G. H. *Trial by Gas: The British Army at the Second Battle of Ypres* (Washington, D.C.: Potomac Books 2014)

Clayton, A. *Martin-Leake: Double VC* (London: Leo Cooper 1994)

Corrigan, G. *Sepoys in the Trenches: The Indian Corps on the Western Front, 1914-15* (Staplehurst: Spellmount, 1999)

Dixon, J. *Magnificent but not War: The Battle for Ypres, 1915* (Barnsley: Leo Cooper, 2003)

Doherty, S. and T. Donovan. *The Indian Corps on the Western Front: A Handbook and Battlefield Guide* (Brighton: Tom Donovan Editions, 2014)

Doyle, Sir A. C. *The British Campaigns in Europe, 1914-1918* (London: Geoffrey Bles, 1928)
"The main part of this book has appeared as British campaigns in France and Flanders [*The British Campaign in France and Flanders 1914-1918*, 6 vols, London: Hodder & Stoughton, 1916-20]. It has now been enlarged so as to include the Italian and Salonican campaigns."--Pref

Duffy, C. *Through German Eyes: The British and the Somme* (London: Weidenfeld and Nicolson, 2006)

Edmonds, Sir J. E. and others, comps. *Military Operations: France and Belgium, 1914-1918*, 14 vols [+ box of maps & appendices] (London: Macmillan, 1922-1949)
Contents: Vol.1 1914: Mons, the retreat to the Seine, the Marne and the Aisne; vol.2 1914: Antwerp, La Bassée, Armentières, Messines and Ypres; vol.3 Winter 1914-5: Battle of Neuve Chapelle, Battle of Ypres; vol.4 1915: Battles of Aubers Ridge, Festubert, and Loos; vol.5 1916: Sir Douglas Haig's command to 1st July, Battle of the Somme; vol.6 1916: 2nd July 1916 to end of Battles of the Somme; vol.7 1917: German retreat to the Hindenurg Line and the Battles of Arras; vol.8 1917: 7 June-10 November, Messines and Third Ypres (Passchendaele); vol.9 1917: Battle of Cambrai; vol.10 1918: German March offensive and its preliminaries; vol.11 1918: March-April, continuation of German offensives; vol.12 1918: May-July German diversion offensives and first Allied counter-offensive; vol.13 1918: 8 August-26 September, Franco-British offensive; vol.14 1918: 26 September-11, November advance to victory. [In the series *History of the Great War Based*

on Official Documents by direction of the Historical Section of the Committee of Imperial Defence. Editions vary. The Naval and Military Press published reprints of the volumes in the 1990's].

Farrar-Hockley, Sir A. H. *Death of an Army* (London: Barker, 1967; repr. Ware, Herts.: Wordsworth Editions, 1998)
About the first battle of Ypres.

— *The Somme* (London: Batsford, 1964; repr. London: Pan, 1983)

Foley, R. 'Verdun: The Killing Field', *History Today*, 66: 9 (2016), 30-38

Foulkes, C. H. *Gas: The Story of the Special Brigade* (Edinburgh: Blackwood, 1934)

Hallett, C. E. 'Saving Lives on the Front Line', *History Today*, 67:7 (2017), 24
The significance of the work of military nurses at Passchendaele.

Harris, P. and S. Marble. 'The "Step-by-Step"' Approach: British Military Thought and Operational Method on the Western Front, 1915-1917', *War in History*, 15 (2008), 17-42

Hart, P. *1918: A Very British Victory* (London: Weidenfeld & Nicolson, 2008)

— *Voices from the Front: An Oral History of the Great War* (London: Profile Books 2015)

Herwig, H. H. *The Marne, 1914: The Opening of World War I and the Battle that Changed the World* (New York: Random House, 2009; repr. in paperback 2011)

Horne, A. *The Price of Glory: Verdun 1916* (London: Macmillan, 1962; repr. London : Penguin, 1993)

Hudson, R. 'Ypres Cloth Hall Bombarded, *History Today*, 65, Issue 1 (2015), 36-37
An examination of a 1915 photograph of the medieval Cloth Hall in the Belgian city of Ypres following heavy German shelling, together with details of the Ypres battles and a brief history of the Cloth Hall and Ypres.

Hughes, C. *Mametz: Lloyd George's 'Welsh Army' at the Battle of the Somme*, [new edn] (Norwich: Gliddon Books, 1990)
Previous edition: Gerrards Cross: Orion, 1982

Jankowski, P. *Verdun: The Longest Battle of the Great War* (Oxford: Oxford University Press, 2013)

Keegan, J. *The Face of Battle* (London: Cape, 1976; repr. London: Pimlico, 1995)
Reassessment of three battles, Agincourt, Waterloo and the Somme.

Liddle, P. H., ed. *Passchendaele in Perspective: The Third Battle of Ypres* (London: Cooper, 1997)

Lloyd, N. *Hundred Days: The Campaign that Ended World War I* (New York: Basic Books 2014)

— 'The Imperial Triumph of Amiens', *History Today*, 64, Issue 5 (2014), 72
Nick Lloyd revisits John Terraine's ground-breaking 1958 article on the decisive, though neglected, Allied victory at Amiens in 1918

Mace, M. and J. Grehan. *Slaughter on the Somme, 1 July 1916: The Complete War Diaries of the British Army's Worst Day* (London: Pen & Sword, 2013)
In this work are gathered together, for the first time ever, all the War Diary entries for those battalions that were enagaged in the battle on that day.

Marble, S. .*British Artillery on the Western Front in the First World War: 'The Infantry Cannot Do With A Gun Less"* (Farnham:: Ashgate 2013)

Mayhew, E. *Wounded: A New History of the Western Front in World War I* (Oxford: Oxford University Press 2013)

The War Years

Middlebrook, M. *The First Day on the Somme* (London: Allen Lane, 1971; repr. London: Leo Cooper, 2003)

— *The Kaiser's Battle, 21 March 1918: The First Day of the German Spring Offensive* (London : Allen Lane, 1978; repr. London: Penguin, 2000)

Montgomery, Sir A. A. *The Story of the Fourth Army in the Battle of the Hundred Days, August 8th to November 11th, 1918* (London: Hodder & Stoughton, 1920)

Moore, W. *See How They Run: British Retreat of 1918* (London: Leo Cooper, 1970; repr. London: Sphere, 1975)

Morton-Jack, G. *The Indian Army on the Western Front: India's Expeditionary Force to France and Belgium in the First World War* (Cambridge: Cambridge Univ. Press, 2013)

Mosier, J. *Verdun: The Lost History of the Most Important Battle of World War I, 1914-1918* (New York: Penguin Group, 2013)

Neiberg, M. S. *The Second Battle of the Marne* (Bloomington: Indiana University Press, 2008)

Neillands, R. *The Death of Glory: The Western Front, 1915* (London: John Murray, 2006)

Passingham, I. *Pillars of Fire: The Battle of Messines Ridge, June 1917* (Stroud: Sutton, 1998; repr. 2004)

Philpott, W. J. *Anglo-French Relations and Strategy on the Western Front, 1914-18* (Basingstoke: Macmillan in association with King's College London, 1996)

— *Three Armies on the Somme: The First Battle of the Twentieth Century* (New York: Vintage, 2011)
Originally published in Great Britain as *Bloody victory: The Sacrifice on the Somme and the Making of the Twentieth Century* by Little, Brown, an imprint of Little, Brown Book Group, London, in 2009, and subsequently published in hardcover in the United States in different form by Alfred A. Knopf, a division of Random House, Inc., New York, in 2010.

Prete, R.A. *Strategy and Command: The Anglo-French Coalition on the Western Front, 1914* (Montreal: McGill-Queen's University Press, 2009)

Prior, R. and T. Wilson. *Passchendaele: The Untold Story*, 2nd edn (New Haven: Yale University Press, 2002)

— *The Somme* (New Haven: Yale University Press, 2005)

Rogerson, S. *Twelve Days*, with a foreword by B. H. Liddell Hart (London: Arthur Baker, 1933)
A personal record of twelve days on the Somme in 1916 while Rogerson was serving as a subaltern with the 2nd Battalion of the West Yorkshire Regiment. Reprinted London: Greenhill, 2006 under the title, *Twelve Days on the Somme: A Memoir of the Trenches, 1916*, with a new preface and introduction.

Sharpe, A. 'The Battle of Neuve Chappelle & the Indian Corps, Andrew Sharpe describes a neglected 1915 battle over the "most dismal, swampy and disgusting region of the British Front"', *History Today*, 65, Number 8 (2015), 46-50

Sheffield, G. D. *The Somme* (London: Cassell, 2003)

Sheffield, G. D., ed. *War on the Western Front: In the Trenches of World War I* (Oxford: Osprey, 2007)

Simkins, P. and D. Gibbon. *Chronicles of the Great War: The Western Front, 1914-1918* (London: Bramley Books, 1997)
Originally published as *World War 1: The Western Front*, Godalming: CLB International, 1991.

Smither, R., ed. *The Battles of the Somme and Ancre* (London: Imperial War Museum, 1993)

Smithers, A. J. *Cambrai: The First Great Tank Battle, 1917* (London: Leo Cooper, 1992)

Spears, Sir E. L. *Liaison: A Narrative of the Great Retreat*, new edn (London: Cassell, 2000)

Originally published London: Heinemann, 1930.

— *Prelude to Victory* (London: Cape, 1939)

Stevenson, D. *With Our Backs to the Wall: Victory and Defeat in 1918* (London: Allen Lane, 2011; repr. London: Penguin, 2012)

Terraine, J. *Mons: The Retreat to Victory* (London: Batsford, 1960; repr. Ware: Wordsworth Editions, 2002)

— *The Road to Passchendaele, The Flanders Offensive of 1917: A Study in Inevitability* [compiled by] John Terraine (London: Cooper; 1977, repr.1984)

— *The Western Front, 1914-1918* (London: Hutchinson, 1964; repr. Barnsley: Pen and Sword, 2003)
A selection of John Terraine's articles which tend to support Haig and the 'westerners'.

Turner, P. W. and R. H. Haigh. *Not for Glory* (London: Maxwell, 1969)
Based on the experiences of Gilbert Hall on the Western Front, 1914-1918.

Van Hartesveldt, F. R. *The Battles of the British Expeditionary Forces, 1914-1915: Historiography and Annotated Bibliography* (Westport, Conn.: Praeger, 2005)

Walker, J. *The Blood Tub: General Gough and the Battle of Bullecourt, 1917* (Staplehurst: Spellmount, 1998, repr. 2000)

Ward, C. *Living on the Western Front: Annals and Stories, 1914-1919* (London; New York: Bloomsbury Academic 2013)

Whittaker, W. and G. Whittaker. *Somewhere in France: A Tommy's Guide to Life on the Western Front* (Stroud: Amberley Publishing, 2014)
By means of the letters of William Whittaker, a soldier in the Great War, and family anecdotes Geoffrey Whittaker, his son, re-creates the world of the Tommy in the trenches.

Williams, H. N. *Sir Douglas Haig's Great Push: The Battle of the Somme*, a popular, pictorial and authoritative work on one of the great battles in history, illustrated by about 700 wonderful official photographs and cinematograph films and other authentic pictures, by arrangement with the War Office (London: Hutchinson, 1917)
A narrative and photographic history. The photographs were taken from the film made at the time and shown to the British public.

Williamson, W. *A Tommy at Ypres: Walter's War*, the diary and letters of Walter Williamson Williamson compiled by Doreen Priddey (Stroud: Amberley 2013)
Originally published: 2011

Wolff, L. *In Flanders Fields: The 1917 Campaign* (New York: Viking, 1958; repr. London: Penguin, 2001)

Woollcombe, R. *The First Tank Battle: Cambrai, 1917* (London: Arthur Barker, 1967)

Italian Front

Cassar, G. H. *The Forgotten Front: The British Campaign in Italy 1917-1918* (London: Hambledon, 1998)

Dalton, E. H. J. H., Baron. *With British Guns in Italy: A Tribute to Italian Achievement* (London: Methuen, 1919)

Dillon, J. *"Allies are a Tiresome Lot": The British Army in Italy in the First World War* (Solihull: Helion & Company, 2015)

Edmonds, Sir J. E. and H. R. Davies, comps. *Military Operations: Italy, 1915-1919* (London: HMSO, 1949; repr. in facsimile London: Imperial War Museum, 1991)
In the series *History of the Great War Based on Official Documents* by direction of the Historical Section of the Committee of Imperial Defence.

Gladden, E. N. *Across the Piave: A Personal Account of the British Forces in Italy, 1917-1919* (London: HMSO, 1971)

Low, Sir S. *Italy in the War* (London: Longmans, 1916)

Thompson, M. *The White War: Life and Death on the Italian Front 1915-1919* (London: Faber, 2009)

Lucas, E. V. *Outposts of Mercy: The Record of a Visit in November and December, 1916, to the Various Units of the British Red Cross in Italy* (London: Methuen, 1917)

Wilks, J. and E. Wilks. *The British Army in Italy, 1917-1918* (Barnsley: Cooper, 1998)

Macedonian Front

Cumberland, T. D., ed. *9th Battalion, King's Own Royal Lancaster Regiment in Macedonia, March 1918 to October 1918.* From the war diary of Captain Cumberland RAMC with additional details from the official battalion war diary, edited by P. Donnelly (Lancaster: King's Own Royal Regiment Museum, 2000)

DiNardo, R. L. *Invasion: The Conquest of Serbia, 1915* (Santa Barbara, California: Praeger, 2015)

Donnelly, P. *The King's Own Royal Lancaster Regiment, Macedonian Front in World War One: A Brief Record of the Actions of the 2nd and 9th Battalions in the Salonikan Campaign 1915-1919* (Lancaster: King's Own Royal Regiment Museum, 1999)

Falls, C. B., comp. *Military Operations: Macedonia, From the Outbreak of War to the Spring of 1917*, 2 vols (London: HMSO, 1933-1935)
In the series History of the Great War Based on Official Documents by direction of the Historical Section of the Committee of Imperial Defence.

Hall, R. C. *Balkan Breakthrough: The Battle of Dobro Pole 1918* (Bloomington: Indiana University Press, 2010)

Harfield, D. H. B. *A Diary of the Balkan Front World War 1: 22nd November 1915 to 16th October 1919* (London: Tessa Harfield, 2003)

Lyon, J. B. *Serbia and the Balkan Front, 1914: The Outbreak of the Great War* (New York: Bloomsbury Academic, 2015)

Packer, C. *Return to Salonika* (London: Cassell, 1964)

Palmer, A. W. *The Gardeners of Salonika* (London: Deutsch, 1965)

Wakefield, A. and S. Moody. *Under the Devil's Eye: Britain's Forgotten Army at Salonika, 1915-1918* (Stroud: Sutton, 2004)

Gallipoli Expedition

Bean, C. E. W. *Bean's Gallipoli: The Diaries of Australia's Official War Correspondent*, edited and annotated by Kevin Fewster, 3rd edn (Crows Nest, N.S.W.: Allen & Unwin, 2007)
Previous edn published as *Frontline Gallipoli: C.E.W. Bean, Diaries from the Trenches*, Sydney: Allen & Unwin, 1990.

Bridge, C. 'Australia's Gallipoli, 1915: Myths And Realities', *Historian*, 125 (2015), 34-37

Bush, E. W. *Gallipoli* (London: Allen & Unwin, 1975)

Clews, T. *Churchill's Dilemma: The Real Story behind the Origins of the 1915 Dardanelles Campaign* (Santa Barbara: ABC-CLIO, 2010)

Crawley, C. *Climax at Gallipoli: The Failure of the August Offensive* (Norman: University of Oklahoma Press 2014)

Dutton, P. '"More Vivid than the Written Word" Ellis Ashmead-Bartlett's film, With the Dardanelles Expedition (1915)', *Historical Journal of Film Radio And Television*, 24 (2004), 205-222 [For information relating to this film see Byrnes, P. *Gallipoli on Film* in the section **4.3.2.1 of Part 4: Remembering the War**]

Emden, R. van and S. Chambers. *Gallipoli: The Dardanelles Disaster in Soldiers' Words and Photographs* (London: Bloomsbury 2015)

Erickson, E. J. *Gallipoli: Command under Fire* (Oxford: Osprey Publishing, 2015)

— *Gallipoli: The Ottoman Campaign* (Barnsley: Pen & Sword Military, 2010)

— *Gallipoli and the Middle East, 1914-1918: From the Dardanelles to Mesopotamia* (London: Amber Books, 2008)

Hamilton, Sir I. *Gallipoli Diary*, 2 vols (London: Arnold, 1920)

Hamilton, I. B. M. *The Happy Warrior: A Life of General Sir Ian Hamilton* (London: Cassell, 1966)

Hart, P. *Gallipoli* (London: Profile Books 2013)

Haythornthwaite, P. J. *Gallipoli 1915: Frontal Assault on Turkey* (Oxford: Osprey, 1991; repr. Westport, Conn: Praeger, 2004)

Hickey, M. *Gallipoli* (London: John Murray, 1995; repr. 1998)

James, R. R.. *Gallipoli* (London: Batsford, 1965; repr. London: Pimlico, 1999)

Liddle, P. H. The Dardanelles Gallipoli Campaign: Concept and Execution', in *Home Fires and Foreign Fields, British Social and Military Experience in the Great War*, ed. by P. H. Liddle (Manchester: Manchester University Press, 1985)

— *Men of Gallipoli: The Dardanelles and Gallipoli Experience, August 1914 to January 1916* (London: Allen Lane, 1976; repr. Newton Abbot: David & Charles, 1988)

Macleod, J. *Gallipoli*, Great Battles (Oxford: Oxford University Press 2015)

— *Reconsidering Gallipoli* (Manchester: Manchester University Press 2004)

Macleod, J., ed. *Gallipoli: Making History* (London: F. Cass 2004)

Moorhead, A. *Gallipoli*, new edn (London: New English Library, 1968)
Originally published London: Hamilton, 1956

Oglander, C. F. A. *Military Operations: Gallipoli*, 2 vols (London: H.M.S.O., 1929-1932; repr. London: Imperial War Museum, in association with The Battery Press, Nashville, 1992)
In the series *History of the Great War Based on Official Documents* by direction of the Historical Section of the Committee of Imperial Defence.

Prior, R. *Gallipoli: The End of the Myth* (New Haven, Conn.; London: Yale University Press, 2010)

Ruddeno, V. *Gallipoli: Attack from the Sea* (Sydney: University of New South Wales Press, 2008)

Steel, N. and P. Hart. *Defeat at Gallipoli* (London: Macmillan, 1994; repr. London: Pan, 2002)

Stanley, P. *Die in Battle, Do Not Despair: The Indians on Gallipoli, 1915* (Solihull: Helion 2015)

Van Hartesveldt, F. W. *The Dardanelles Campaign: Historiography and Annotated Bibliography* (Westport, Conn.; London: Greenwood Press, 1997)

The War Years

The Middle East and Palestinian Front

Allen, J. J. *T. E. Lawrence and the Red Sea Patrol: The Royal Navy's Role in Creating the Legend* (London: Pen & Sword Military, 2015)

Allenby, E. H. H., 1st Viscount. *Allenby in Palestine: The Middle East Correspondence of Field Marshal Viscount Allenby, June 1917-October 1919*, edited and selected by Matthew Hughes (Stroud: Sutton, 2004)

Bar-Yosef, E. 'The Last Crusade? British Propaganda and the Palestine Campaign, 1917-18', *Journal of Contemporary History*, 36 (2001), 87-110

Brown, M. *T. E. Lawrence* (London: British Library 2003)

Bruce, A. P. C. *The Last Crusade: The Palestine Campaign in the First World War* (London: Murray, 2002; repr. 2003)

Bullock, D. L. *Allenby's War: The Palestine-Arabian Campaigns, 1916-1918* (London: Blandford, 1988)

Erickson, E. J. *Palestine: The Ottoman Campaigns of 1914—1918* (Barnsley: Pen & Sword Military, 2016)

Falls, C. B. *Armageddon, 1918* (London: Weidenfeld & Nicolson, 1964)
Another edition was published, Philadelphia, University of Pennsylvania Press, 2003, under the title, *Armageddon, 1918: The Final Palestinian Campaign of World War I*.

Faulkner, N. *Lawrence of Arabia's War: The Arabs, the British, and the Remaking of the Middle East in WWI* (New Haven, CT: Yale University Press, 1916)

Ford, R. *Eden to Armageddon: World War I in the Middle East* (London: Weidenfeld & Nicolson, 2009)

Gardner, R. B. Allenby (London: Cassell, 1965)

Grainger, J. D. *The Battle for Palestine, 1917* (Woodbridge, UK; Rochester, NY: Boydell Press, 2006)

Hughes, M. *Allenby and British Strategy in the Middle East, 1917-1919* (London: Cass, 1999)

Hyde, H. M. *Solitary in the Ranks: Lawrence of Arabia as Airman and Private Soldier* (London: Constable 1977)
Altghough this biography is mostly about T. E. Lawrence's life as a low-ranking member of the R.A.F. from 1922 to 1935, shortly before his death in a motorcycle accident, it does also feature his organisation during the Great War of the Arab revolt against the Turks.

Kitchen, J. E. The *British Imperial Army in the Middle East: Morale and Military Identity in the Sinai and Palestine Campaigns, 1916-1918* (London: Bloomsbury, 2014)

Lawrence, T. E. *Revolt In The Desert* (Ware: Wordsworth Editions, 1997)
Originally published: London: Cape, 1927. "Abridged version of Seven Pillars of Wisdom." – cover.

— *Secret Dispatches from Arabia*, and other writings by T. E. Lawrence. Foreword by A. W. Lawrence; edited and introduced by Malcolm Brown. (London: Bellew, 1991)
A collection of Lawrence's wartime reports during the Arab Revolt.

— *Seven Pillars of Wisdom: A Triumph*. The complete 1922 text, 2nd edn (Fordingbridge: Castle Hill Press, 2003)
"... edited by Jeremy Wilson, assisted by Richard Westwood, from the manuscript in the Bodleian Library and T. E. Lawrence's annotated copy of the 1922 Oxford Times printing. It was first published [in 3 vols] by Castle Hill Press in 1997 .... For this new edition the text was revised by Jeremy and Nicole Wilson ..." -- verso of t.p.

Mack, J. E. *A Prince of Disorder: The Life of T. E. Lawrence* (London: Weidenfeld & Nicolson, 1976; repr. Cambridge, Mass.: Harvard University Press, 1998)

MacMunn, Sir G. F. and C. Falls, comps. *Military Operations: Egypt and Palestine*, 2 vols (in 3) London: HMSO,

1928-30)
In the series *History of the Great War Based on Official Documents* by direction of the Historical Section of the Committee of Imperial Defence

Maude, R. and D. Maude. *The Servant, The General and Armageddon* (Oxford: Ronald, 1998)
The "General" is Allenby.

Mohs, P. A. *Military Intelligence and the Arab Revolt: The First Modern Intelligence War* (London: Routledge, 2008)
In relation to the development of Britain's strategy for the Arab Revolt during the First World War the author analyses the way intelligence was used and exploited, and in the process provides an examination of what T. E. Lawrence achieved as an intelligence officer and guerrilla leader.

Rogan, E. *The Fall of the Ottomans: The Great War in the Middle East, 1914-1920* (London: Allen Lane, 2015)

Sheffy, Y. *British Intelligence in the Palestine Campaign, 1914-1918* (London: Frank Cass, 1998)
In relation to the campaign in the desert against the Ottoman Empire on the Egyptian and Palestinian fronts the author examines the development, operations and contribution of British Military Intelligence and shows the relationship between intelligence gathering and battle-field performance.

— 'Chemical Warfare and the Palestine Campaign, 1916-1918', *Journal of Military History*, 73 (2009), 803-844

— 'Institutionalized Deception and Perception Reinforcement: Allenby's Campaigns in Palestine', in *Intelligence and Military Operations*, edited by Michael I. Handel (London: Cass, 1990)
In a comparison of Allenby's use of deception prior to the Battle of Gaza and in the Megiddo Campaign Sheffy notes Allenby's distinctive approach to the planning of the deception and its implementation in terms of the staff work involved.

Ulrichsen, K. C. *The First World War in the Middle East* (London: Hurst, 2014)

Wavell, A. P., Earl Wavell. *Allenby: A Study in Greatness*, 2 vols (London: Harrap, 1940-1943)

— *The Palestine Campaigns*, 3rd edn (London: Constable, 1941)

Woodfin, E. C. *Camp and Combat on the Sinai and Palestine Front: The Experience of the British Empire Soldier, 1916-1918* (Houndmills, Basingstoke,: Palgrave Macmillan, 2012)

Woodward, D. R. *Hell in the Holy Land: World War I in the Middle East* (Lexington, Ky.: The University Press of Kentucky, 2006)

Mesopotamian Front

Barker, A. J. *The Neglected War: Mesopotamia, 1914-1918* (London: Faber, 1967)

— *Townshend of Kut: A Biography of Major-General Sir Charles Townshend* (London: Cassell., 1967)

Berridge, W. J. and Sattar al-Aboody, 'The Battle of Sha'iba, 1915: Ottomanism, British Imperialism and Shia Religious Activism during the Mesopotamian Campaign', *Journal of Imperial and Commonwealth History*, VOL 45 (2017), 630-651

Callwell, Sir C. E. *The Life of Sir Stanley Maude* (London: Constable, 1920)

Gardner, N. *The Siege of Kut-al-Amara: At War in Mesopotamia 1915-1916* (Bloomington: Indiana University Press, 2014)

Goold, D. 'Lord Hardinge and the Mesopotamia Expedition and Inquiry, 1914–1917', *Historical Journal*, 19 (1976), 919–45

Moberly, F. J., comp. *Military Operations: The Campaign In Mesopotamia 1914-1818*, 4 vols (London: HMSO, 1923-27)
In the series *History of the Great War Based on Official Documents* by direction of the Historical Section of the Committee of

Imperial Defence.

Popplewell, R. J. 'British Intelligence in Mesopotamia 1914-16', in *Intelligence and Military Operations*, ed. by Michael I. Handel (London: Cass, 1990)

Townshend, C. *Desert Hell: The British Invasion of Mesopotamia* (Cambridge, Mass.: Belknap Press of Harvard University Press, 2011)
Originally published as: *When God Made Hell: The British Invasion of Mesopotamia and the Creation of Iraq, 1914-1921*, London : Faber, 2010.

Transcaucasian Front

Dunsterville, L. C. *The Adventures of Dunsterforce* (London: Arnold, 1920; repr. 1932)

Ellis, C. H. *The Transcaspian Episode: 1918-1919* (London: Hutchinson, 1963)
About he British 'intervention' in Transcaspia

Colonial and other Campaigns and Expeditions

Abbott, P. *Armies in East Africa 1914-18* (Oxford: Osprey, 2002)

Anderson, R. *The Forgotten Front: The East African Campaign, 1914-1918* (Stroud: Tempus, 2004)

Burdick, C. B. *The Japanese Siege of Tsingtau: World War I in Asia* (Hamden, Conn: Archon Books, 1976)

Farwell, B. *The Great War in Africa, 1914-1918* (Harmondsworth: Viking, 1987)

Gardner, R. B. *German East: The Story of the First World War in East Africa* (London: Cassell, 1963)

Hordern, C., comp. *Military Operations: East Africa. Vol.1: August 1914 - September 1916.* Compiled by C. Hordern; founded on a draft by H. Fitz M. Stacke (London: HMSO, 1941; repr. Nashville: Battery Press, in association with the Imperial War Museum, Department of Printed Books, 1990)
In the series *History of the Great War Based on Official Documents* by direction of the Historical Section of the Committee of Imperial Defence.

Hoyt, E. P. *The Fall of Tsingtao* (London: Arthur Barker, 1975)

Moberly, F. J., comp. *Military Operations: Togoland and the Cameroons, 1914-1916* (London: HMSO, 1931)
In the series *History of the Great War Based on Official Documents* by direction of the Historical Section of the Committee of Imperial Defence.

Strachan, H. *The First World War in Africa* (Oxford: Oxford University Press, 2004)
Originally published in Vol 1 of Strachan's *The First World War*, Oxford: Oxford University Press, 2001

Young, F. B. *Marching on Tanga: With General Smuts in East Africa* (London: Collins, 1917; repr. Gloucester: Alan Sutton, 1984)

4.5.1.6 Personal Reminiscences

The following selection of works are representative of the personal experiences expressed in the books, diaries, letters, and journals written by soldiers during the war (some of which were not published until after the war had ended). A selection of works representative of personal experiences viewed in retrospect (i.e. written after the war) will be found in the section **4.2.2 of Part 4 (Remembering the War)**

Alexander, H. M. *On Two Fronts: Being the Adventures of an Indian Mule Corps in France and Gallipoli* (London: Heinemann, 1917)

Attwell, L. *Laurence Attwell's Letters from the Front*. Edited by W. A. Attwell (London: Pen & Sword, 2005)
Attwell was in the Prince of Wales Own, Civil Service Rifles.

Waging War

Bell, D. H. *A Soldier's Diary of the Great War*, with an introduction by Henry Williamson (London: Faber, 1929)
Henry Williamson edited this diary and served with the author in 1914 in the 1st London Rifle Brigade. Later Bell was commissioned into the 1st Queen's Own Cameron Highlanders.

Bolwell, F. A. *With a Reservist in France: A Personal Account of all the Engagements in Which the 1st Division 1st Corps Took Part ...* (London: Routledge, 1917)
Bolwell was a regular reservist in 1914 recalled to the colours with the 1st Loyal North Lancashire Regiment, and this book is an account of his service with the BEF in the first six months of the war.

Borton, A. C. *My Warrior Sons: The Borton Family Diary, 1914-1918*, edited by G. Slater (London: Peter Davies, 1973)
An abridgement of a 9 vol diary kept by A. C. Borton, which includes transcriptions of letters written by various members of the Borton family and friends.

Corbett-Smith, A. *Retreat from Mons, by One Who Shared In It* (London: Cassell, 1916)

Dunham, F. *The Long Carry: The Journal of Stretcher Bearer Frank Dunham, 1916-1918*, edited by R. H. Haigh and P. W. Turner; with a foreword by Correlli Barnett (London: Pergamon, 1970)

Fielding, R. *War Letters to a Wife: France and Flanders, 1915-1919* (London: Medici Society, 1929)

Fitzwilliam, J. *Letters from a Gunner, 1914-1918* (Privately printed, 1935)

Gillilands H. G. *My German Prisons: Being The Experience of an Officer during Two-And-A-Half Years as a Prisoner of War* (London: Hodder & Stoughton, 1918)

Glubb, J. *Into Battle: A Soldier's Diary of the Great War* (London: Cassell, 1978)

Greenwell, G *An Infant in Arms: War Letters of a Company Officer, 1914-1918* (London: Dickson & Thompson, 1935; repr. London: Allen & Unwin, 1972)

Hankey, D. *A Student in Arms* (London: Melrose, 1916)
Mixes fact with fiction

Houseman, L., ed. *War Letters of Fallen Englishmen* (London: Gollancz, 1930; Philadelphia, Pa.: Pine St. Books, 2002)
A selection of letters written by soldiers, sailors and airmen who were killed during the war.

Hulse, E. H. W. *Letters Written from the English Front in France between September 1914 and March 1915* (Privately printed, 1916)

Jack, J. L. *General Jack's Diary 1914-1918: The Trench Diary of Brigadier-General J. L. Jack, D.S.O*, edited by John Terraine (London: Eyre & Spottiswoode, 1964; repr. London: Cassell, 2000)

Kernahan, C. *The Experience of a Recruiting Officer* (London: Hodder & Stoughton, 1915)

Laffin, J., ed *Letters From The Front, 1914-1918* (London: Dent, 1973)

Leonard, P. *The Fighting Padre: Letters from the Trenches, 1915-1918, of Pat Leonard ...* edited by John Leonard and Philip Leonard-Johnson (Barnsley: Pen & Sword Military, 2010)

Liveing, E. G. D. *Attack: An Infantry Subaltern's Impressions of July 1st 1916* (London: Heinemann, 1918)

Martin, A. A. *A Surgeon in Khaki* (London: Arnold, 1915)

Maultsaid, J. A. B. *Star Shell Reflections, 1914-1916: The Great War Diaries of Jim Maultsaid*, [edited by] B. A. McClune (London: Pen & Sword, 2015)

Moynihan, M., ed. *Greater Love - Letters Home, 1914-1918* (London: W. H. Allen, 1980)

Read, H. E. 'A War Diary, 1915-18', in *The Contrary Experience: Autobiographies*, by Herbert Read (London: Faber, 1963)

Redmond, W. *Trench Pictures From France* (London: Melrose, 1917)

Roe, E. *Diary of an Old Contemptible: Private Edward Roe, East Lancashire Regiment, from Mons to Baghdad, 1914-1919*, edited by P. Downham (Barnsley: Pen & Sword Military, 2004)

Sansom, A. J. *Letters from France: June 1915-July 1917*, edited by his wife Ivy Sansom (London: Melrose, 1921)

Simpkin, A. *Despatch Rider on the Western Front, 1915-18: The Diary of Sergeant Albert Simpkin MM*, edited by David Venner (London: Pen & Sword, 2015)

Smith, L. *Drawing Fire: The Diary of a Great War Soldier and Artist* (London: Collins, 2009)
Len Smith, enlisting as an infantryman in the City of London Regiment on 22 September 1914, saw action in a number of battles, including those at Loos and Vimy Ridge, and during his life in the trenches kept a journal of his thoughts, together with colour sketches of the people and places he had encountered, on scraps of paper which he managed to smuggle home at the end of the war. One of the uses made of his drawing skills in the course of the war was to gather and record intelligence on German army positions that could be used to help plan military strategy, an undertaking which involved him in great personal risk.

Spicer, L. D. *Letters from France, 1915-1918* (London: Robert York, 1979)

Tapert, A. *Despatches from the Heart: An Anthology of Letters from the Front during the First and Second World Wars* (London: Hamilton in association with the Imperial War Museum, 1984)

Vaughan, E.C. *Some Desperate Glory: The Diary of a Young Officer, 1917* (London: Warne, 1981; repr. London: Papermac, 1994)

West, A. G. *The Diary of a Dead Officer: Being the Posthumous Papers of Arthur Graeme West* (London: The Herald, 1918)
A facsimile reprint of this work with a new introduction by Dominic Hibberd was published in 1991 by the Imperial War Museum (IWM), Department of Printed Books'.

4.5.2 The Navy

Britain's past naval glories and her pre-war naval arms race with Germany[167] had led the Royal Navy and the British people to expect that the war would produce a decisive naval battle on the heroic lines of Trafalgar. Such a battle did not take place, much to the disappointment of the Royal Navy[168], and, ever after, this absence of a dramatic naval victory has tended to create a negative impression of Britain's naval performance in the Great War. Nevertheless, the Navy, contributed valuably in a number of less dramatic ways to the ultimate victory of the Allies. Although early in the war Admiral von Spee raided ships on Allied trade routes all over the southern hemisphere and destroyed a squadron of the Royal Navy at Coronel on 1 November 1914, these German naval successes were short-lived. By December 1916 the Royal Navy had eliminated most of the German ships and squadrons (including von Spee's[169]) which were operating in isolation from their main High Seas Fleet in the early stages of the war. Further raids by German surface ships over 1916 to 1917 had little impact and the Royal Navy remained in almost complete control of the global seas, the main danger being posed by German submarine operations.

---

[167] Admiral Fisher, the architect of British pre-war naval policy, which included the commissioning of the Dreadnought, contributed to the international arms race with his blatantly belligerent attitude to the German Navy.

[168] This disappointment is frequently evident in the memoirs of those who served in the Royal Navy in the Great War, and blame for it has tended to be placed, unjustifiably in the view of some historians, on the defensive nature of the strategy pursued by Admiral Jellicoe in his leadership of the Grand Fleet, an approach contrasting in the popular imagination to the more aggressive style of Admiral Beatty, his eventual successor.

[169] Admiral von Spee was defeated by a British fleet at the Falkland Islands in December 1914 and was himself among the 2,200 German sailors killed during this battle.

While Britain's Grand Fleet was largely kept in home waters to keep the German High Seas Fleet tied up, other elements of the Royal Navy operated effectively in other quarters of the world by, for instance, using its submarines to attack German trade in the Baltic and carry out highly successful attacks on enemy shipping behind the Turkish lines in the Sea of Marmora, assisting in the invasion and conquest of German colonies in Africa, and supporting the advance of the British Army up the Tigris with a flotilla of gunboats in the Mesopotamian campaign. Although it was unsuccessful in its attempts on its own to unlock the Turkish stranglehold on the Dardanelles it, nevertheless organized, covered and supplied the landings of British troops in that region and subsequently evacuated the entire invasion force there with impressive efficiency. As well as these contributions to Britain's overseas military campaigns the Royal Navy provided in home waters effective support of the military operations on the Western Front as exemplified by its invaluable help at a crucial early stage of the war in securing important Channel ports through its bombardment of the advancing German Army but, above all, by the role it played throughout the war, by means of the work of the Dover Patrol, in protecting the ships crossing the Channel with the enormous volume of supplies and men required on the Western Front.

One of the most important elements of the Royal Navy's strategy was to keep the greater part of the Grand Fleet always together in home waters in superior numbers to prevent Germany's High Seas Fleet from breaking out into home and global waters and enabling Germany to make use of it to influence the course of the war. To counter this, Germany's naval strategy was to avoid a major battle with the whole might of the Grand Fleet until its High Seas Fleet was in a position to engage it on level terms in respect of numbers, a situation it aimed to achieve by means of diversionary tactics[170] designed to reduce the size of the Grand Fleet by luring ships away from it and destroying them individually or in small groups. Ships of the German High Seas Fleet remained sporadically active in the North Sea right up to the end of the war carrying out raids, laying mines, and shelling towns on the East Coast of England (see below *Bombardment: The Day the East Coast Bled*, by M. Marsay). As it turned out, however, the only major naval battle that took place was at Jutland[171] where the High Seas Fleet engaged the Grand Fleet with fewer losses of men and ships than those sustained by its opponent[172]. The battle could be claimed by Germany as a victory of a sort, at least morally, but in spite of this the Grand Fleet still had a considerable numerical superiority which continued to render it highly risky for the High Seas Fleet to challenge it for the command of the sea in a pitched battle. Instead, Germany chose to erode the effect of the Royal Navy's command of the seas by concentrating its strategy on the use of submarines to attack merchant ships carrying supplies to the Allies. This strategy might well have succeeded (especially when the number of merchant ships sunk reached critical proportions after Germany's switch to unrestricted submarine warfare in 1917 and the failure of a number of methods, including the use of Q ships, employed to combat it) had it not been for the reduction of merchant shipping losses achieved as a result of the Navy's eventual adoption of the convoy system and the addition to the arsenal of anti-submarine weaponry of technological innovations, such as the hydrophone, depth charge and mine barrage[173].

The bottling up of the German High Seas Fleet in its home ports and the resulting limitation of its operations in home waters constituted a blockade which was designed not only as a defensive move to prevent the German

---

[170] These tactics included shelling the British coastal towns of Norwich, Lowestoft, Yarmouth and Lincoln in the hope that the Grand Fleet would be lured into responding by deploying some of its ships into waters where they could be destroyed by German ships lying in wait.

[171] The first British ships to meet the German fleet at Jutland were led by Admiral Beatty's fast battle cruisers as a prelude to Admiral Jellicoe arriving on the scene and joining in the battle. Handicapped by their thin armour the four British battle cruisers of Beatty's squadron that engaged the enemy's fleet suffered terrible losses. *Lion* was badly damaged, and *Indefatigable*, *Queen Mary* and *Invincible* were sunk with the loss of most of their crews. Admiral Jellicoe's performance in the battle has been viewed by some as too cautious (as, for instance, in relation to his breaking off pursuit of the ships of Admiral Scheer at the height of the action because of his concern about the danger of a torpedo attack). Jellicoe and the analyses of the Battle of Jutland continue to be a subject of considerable controversy but the fact remains that, although suffering considerable losses of ships, Jellicoe emerged from the battle with a Grand Fleet still numerically and in a number of other respects stronger than the High Sea Fleet which, although it escaped to harbour with fewer losses, was not for the rest of the war in a position to pose a significant threat.

[172] The British lost 14 ships totalling 111,000 tons in comparison with German losses of 11 ships of 62,000 tons but, while the Grand Fleet was ready to put to sea again almost immediately after the battle, the High Seas Fleet had sustained damage to its ships which returned to harbour that would require several weeks of repair work before they could become operational again.

[173] Of immense importance was the contribution to the war effort of the merchant marine which continued to transport the food and raw materials required by the Allies throughout the war in spite of appalling losses of men and ships until the convoy system was adopted.

High Seas Fleet having a damaging impact on the course of the war but also as an offensive operation to cut off important supplies by sea to Germany and her allies. The latter commercial blockade was carried out in an increasingly aggressive manner as the war progressed with German merchant shipping being seized or forced into internment and Britain leading the way in imposing increasingly severe restrictions on trading by neutrals with the enemy[174]. The main element of this blockade was carried out in the area of the North Sea but it was also carried out on a world-wide scale with the Royal Navy combining with Allied naval forces to blockade the Syrian coast, Greece (while it was a German ally), Bulgaria, the Straits both of Otranto and the Dardanelles, and to guard the entrances to the Mediterranean at Gibraltar and Suez. The commercial blockade did not of itself affect the German economy to the crippling extent that Britain had envisaged. This was partly due to Germany's self-sufficiency, and the availability to it of the raw materials and food that continued to be supplied from the domestic production of northern neutrals not affected by the blockade, and eventually also of the oil and grain that could be supplied from Romania after the collapse of that country in 1916. Although factors like these helped to protect Germany from some of the damaging effects of the blockade, the additional pressure exerted by the blockade on its war economy can be numbered among the important elements which contributed to the situation where Germany's ability to sustain the amount of the food, manpower, and industrial resources required to wage the war effectively was steadily eroded.

By the time of the armistice on 11 November 1918, some 470,000 men had entered the Navy (War Office. *Statistics of the Military Effort of the British Empire during the Great War, 1914-1920*, 1922, p. 363). A curious feature of the the Navy's contribution to the war effort was the formation at the beginning of the war of a number of naval infantry brigades, comprising over 20,000 mobilised naval reservists for whom places in ships could not initially be found. These brigades saw service in the attempted defence of Antwerp soon after the outbreak of war and subsequently served in the Gallipoli campaign and on the Western Front, but by 1916 most of the men in these brigades who had experienced previous sea service had been transferred to the Royal Navy, and on 29 April 1916 those men remaining were officially renamed the 63rd (Royal Naval) Division and brought under the control of the War Office. Fighting with great distinction and success this Royal Naval Division remained in existence until the end of the war when it was disbanded.

Autobiographies, Biographies

Aspinall-Oglander, C. F. *Roger Keyes: Being the Biography of Admiral of the Fleet Lord Keyes of Zeebrugge and Dover* (London: Hogarth Press, 1951)

Beatty, C. R. L. *Our Admiral: A Biography of Admiral of the Fleet Earl Beatty* (London: W. H. Allen, 1980)

Chalmers, W. S. *The Life and Letters of David, Earl Beatty* (London: Hodder and Stoughton, 1951)

Hough, R. A. *Former Naval Person: Churchill and the Wars at Sea* (London: Weidenfeld & Nicolson, 1985; repr, 1987)

Mackay, R. F. *Fisher of Kilverstone* (Oxford: Clarendon Press, 1973)

Patterson, A. T. *Jellicoe: A Biography* (London: Macmillan, 1969)

Roskill, S. W. *Admiral of the Fleet Earl Beatty, The Last Naval Hero: An Intimate Biography* (London: Collins, 1980)

Diaries, Memoirs, Personal Accounts, Letters

Bartlett, C. P. O. *In the Teeth of the Wind: The Story of a Naval Pilot on the Western Front 1916-1918*, edited by his son, Nick Bartlett, new rev. edn (London: Leo Cooper, 1994)
Previous edn published as *Bomber Pilot, 1916-1918*, London: Allan, 1974.

Brandon, B. *The Silent Service: Diary of an Old Sailor* (Bognor Regis: New Horizon, 1978)

Brocklebank, H. C. R. *Tenth Cruiser Squadron Northern Patrol: From The Diaries and Letters of Captain H. C. R. Brocklebank, CBE, Royal Navy, July 1914-August 1917* (Dorchester: [Joan Brocklebank], 1974)

---

[174] Britain had an even freer rein to tighten its restrictions after the USA, hitherto frequently critical as a neutral of Britain's interpretation of the international rules of blockade, had entered the war on the side of the Allies.

Denham, H. M. *Dardanelles: A Midshipman's Diary 1915-16* (London: Murray, 1981)

Dixon, T. B. *The Enemy Fought Splendidly: Being the 1914-1915 Diary of the Battle of the Falklands and its Aftermath* (Poole, Dorset: Blandford Press, 1983)

Fawcett, H. W. and G. W. W. Hooper. *The Fighting at Jutland: The Personal Experiences of Sixty Officers and Men of the British Fleet* (London: Chatham, 2001)
Originally published: Glasgow: MacLure, MacDonald, 1921.

Fisher, J. A., Baron Fisher of Kilverstone. *Fear God and Dread Nought: The Correspondence of Admiral of the Fleet Lord Fisher of Kilverstone*. Selected and edited by Arthur J. Marder, 3 vols (London: Jonathan Cape, 1952-59)

— *The Papers of Admiral Sir John Fisher*, 2 vols (London: Navy Records Society, 1960-64)

Hayward, V. *HMS Tiger at Bay: A Sailor's Memoir 1914-18* (London: Kimber, 1977)

Keyes, R. J. B., Baron Keyes. *The Keyes Papers: Selections from the Private and Official Correspondence of Admiral of the Fleet Baron Keyes of Zeebrugge*, edited by Paul G. Halpern, 3 vols (London: Allen & Unwin, 1972-1981), II: *1914-1918*

— *The Naval Memoirs of Admiral of the Fleet Sir Roger Keyes*, 2 vols (London: T. Butterworth, 1934-1935)
Contents: Vol. 1. The Narrow Seas to the Dardanelles, 1910-1915; Vol 2. Scapa Flow.

Rosher, H. *In the Royal Naval Air Service: Being the Letters of the Late Harold Rosher to his Family*, with an introduction by Arnold Bennett (London: Greenhill, 1986)
Facsim of edn published: London: Chatto & Windus, 1916.

Young, F. *With the Battlecruisers* (London: Cassell, 1921; repr. Edinburgh: Birlinn, 2002)
Originally published: London : Cassell, 1921.

Books

Abbatiello, J. J. *Anti-Submarine Warfare in World War I: British Naval Aviation and the Defeat of the U-Boats* (London: Routledge, 2006)

— *British Naval Aviation and the Anti-Submarine Campaign, 1917-18* (unpublished doctoral thesis, University of London)

Allen, J. J. *T. E. Lawrence and the Red Sea Patrol: The Royal Navy's Role in Creating the Legend* (London: Pen & Sword Military, 2015

Barnett, C. *The Swordbearers: Supreme Command in the First World War* (London: Eyre & Spottiswoode, 1963; repr. London: Cassell, 2001)
Includes a study of Admiral Sir John Jellicoe.

Beesly, P. *Room 40: British Naval Intelligence, 1914-18* (London: Hamilton, 1982)
Room 40 was the office of British Naval Intelligence during the Great War.

Bell, A. C. *A History of The Blockade of Germany and of the Countries Associated with her in the Great War, Austria-Hungary, Bulgaria, and Turkey, 1914-1918* (London: HMSO, 1937; repr. 1961)
In the series *History of the Great War Based on Official Documents* by direction of the Historical Section of the Committee of Imperial Defence.

Ben-Yehuda, N. *Atrocity, Deviance, and Submarine Warfare: Norms and Practices during the World Wars* (Ann Arbor: The University of Michigan Press, 2013)

Bennett, G. M. *The Battle of Jutland* (London: Batsford, 1964; repr. Ware: Wordsworth, 1999)

The War Years

— *Coronel and the Falklands* (London: Batsford, 1962; repr. Edinburgh: Birlinn, 2000)

— *Naval battles of the First World War* (London: Pan, 1974; repr. 1983)

Black. N. *The British Naval Staff in the First World War* (Woodbridge, Suffolk: Boydell Press, 2009)

Burt, R. A. *British Cruisers in World War One* (Poole: Arms and Armour, 1987)

— *British Destroyers in World War One* (London: Arms & Armour, 1986)

Butler, D. A.. *Distant Victory: The Battle of Jutland and the Allied Triumph in the First World War* (Westport, Conn.: Praeger, 2006)

Campbell, N. J. M. *Jutland: An Analysis of the Fighting* (London: Conway Maritime, 1986; repr. 1998)

Carr, W. G. *By Guess and by God: The Story of the British Submarines in the War* (London: Hutchinson, 1930)

Coles, A. *Slaughter at Sea: The Truth Behind a Naval War Crime* (London: Hale, 1986)
This book is about the incident which took place in 1915 when the Q-ship *Baralong*, disguised as a US merchant ship, discarded its camouflage on encountering the U-boat, U27, and not only sank the unsuspecting German vessel but also, allegedly, murdered some of is survivors in cold blood. Germany saw the incident, which caused a huge furore on the international diplomatic front, as highly useful for propaganda purposes.

Conley, M. *From Jack Tar to Union Jack: Representing Naval Manhood in the British Empire* (Manchester; Manchester University Press, 2009)

Cook, G. *Silent Marauders* (London: Hart-Davis MacGibbon, 1976)

Corbett, Sir. J. S. *Naval Operations*, 5 vols (London: Longmans, 1920-31)
Contents: Vol 1. To the Battle of the Falklands, December 1914; Vol 2. From the Battle of the Falklands to the entry of Italy into the war in May 1915; Vol 3. The Dardanelles campaign; Vol 4. June 1916 to April 1917; Vol 5. From April to the end of the war. Vol.4-5 by Henry Newbolt. Vols 1-3 were published in a new edition by Longmans between 1938 and 1940 and reprinted by the Imperial War Museum, 1995-1997. In the series *History of the Great War Based on Official Documents* by direction of the Historical Section of the Committee of Imperial Defence.

Cumming, A. J. *Battle for Britain: Interservice Rivalry between the Royal Air Force and the Royal Navy, 1909-40* (Annapolis, Maryland: Naval Institute Press, 2015)

Davies, W. *The Sea and the Sand: The Story of H.M.S. Tara and the Western Desert Force* (Caernarfon: Gwynedd Archives and Museums Service, 1988)

Davison, R. L. *The Challenges of Command: The Royal Navy's Executive Branch Officers, 1880-1919* (Farnham: Ashgate, 2011)

Dawson, L. *Flotillas: A Hard-Lying Story*, with a foreword by Admiral of the Fleet Sir Roger Keyes, bart. (London: Rich & Cowan Ltd, 1933)
"The career of a naval officer in the service from the time of joining it until the conclusion of the war."—Pref.

Dorling, H. T. ("Tafrail", pseud.). *Swept Channels: Being An Account of the Work of the Minesweepers in the Great War* (London: Hodder & Stoughton, 1935)

Everitt, D. *K Boats: Steam-Powered Submarines in World War I* (Shrewsbury: Airlife, 1999)
Originally published as The K Boats: A Dramatic First Report on the Navy's most Calamitous Submarines (London: Harrap, 1963)

Friedman, N. *Fighting the Great War at Sea: Strategy, Tactics, and Technology* (Barnsley: Seaforth Publishing, 2014)

Fryer, C. *The Royal Navy on the Danube* (New York: Columbia University Press, 1988)

Gardiner, I. *The Flatpack Bombers: The Royal Navy and the Zeppelin Menace* (London: Pen & Sword Military, 2009)

Goldrick, J. *Before Jutland: The Naval War in Northern European Waters, August 1914 - February 1915* (Annapolis, Maryland: Naval Institute Press 2015)

— *The King's Ships were at Sea: The War in the North Sea, August 1914-February 1915* (Annapolis, MD: Naval Institute Press, 1984)

Gordon, A. *The Rules of the Game: Jutland and British Naval Command* (London: J. Murray, 2000)

Grainger, J. D. *The Maritime Blockade of Germany in the Great War: The Northern Patrol, 1914-1918*, Navy Records Society Publications 145 (Aldershot: Ashgate, 2003)

Grant, R. M. *U-Boat Hunters: Codebreakers, Divers and the Defeat of the U-Boats, 1914-1918* (Annapolis, MD: Naval Institute Press, 2003)

— *U-Boat Intelligence, 1914-1918: Admiralty Intelligence Division and the Defeat of the U-boats 1914-18* (Penzance: Periscope, 2002)
Originally published London: Putnam, 1969

— *U-boats Destroyed: The Effect of Anti-submarine Warfare 1914-1918* (London: Putnam, 1964; repr. Penzance: Periscope, 2002)

Gray, E. A. *British Submarines in the Great War: A Damned Un-English Weapon* (London: Leo Cooper, 2001)
Originally published as *A Damned Un-English Weapon* by Charles Schribner's Sons, 1971.

— *The Killing Time: The U-Boat War 1914-18* (London: Seely, Service and Co., 1972)

Great Britain. Admiralty. *British Vessels Lost At Sea 1914-18* (Cambridge: Stephens, 1977)
A reprint of the original official publications, *Navy Losses* and *Merchant Shipping (Losses)*, which were first published in August 1919 by HMSO, London.

Great Britain. War Office. *Statistics of the Military Effort of the British Empire during the Great War, 1914-1920* (London: HMSO, 1922)
Facsimile reprint published London: London Stamp Exchange, 1992.

Halpern, P. G. *A Naval History of World War 1* (London: UCL Press, 1994)

— *The Naval War in the Mediterranean, 1914-1918* (London: Allen & Unwin, 1987)

Halpern, P. G., ed. *The Royal Navy in the Mediterranean, 1915-1918* (Aldershot: Temple Smith for the Navy Records Society, 1987)

Hampshire, A. C. *The Blockaders* (London: Kimber, 1980)

Hargrave, J. *The Suvla Bay Landing* (London: Macdonald, 1964)

Hough, R. A. *The Great War at Sea 1914-1918* (Oxford: Oxford University Press, 1983; repr. Edinburgh: Birlinn, 2000)

Hoyt, E. P. *Disaster at the Dardanelles, 1915* (London: Barker, 1976)

Humphreys, R. S. *The Dover Patrol, 1914-1918* (Stroud: Sutton, 1998)

Hurd, Sir A. *The Merchant Navy*, 3 vols (London: J. Murray, 1921-1929)
In the series *History of the Great War Based on Official Documents* by direction of the Historical Section of the Committee of Imperial Defence.

Jellicoe, J. R., 1st Earl Jellicoe. *The Crisis of the Naval War* (London: Cassell, 1920)

—— *The Grand Fleet, 1914-1916: Its Creation, Development and Work* (London : Cassell, 1919)

Jerrold, D. *The Royal Naval Division*, with an introduction by the Right Hon. Winston S. Churchill (Uckfield: Naval & Military Press, 1995)
Originally published London : Hutchinson & Co., 1923.

Kennedy, P. M. *The Rise and Fall of British Naval Mastery* (London: Allen & Unwin, 1976; repr. London: Penguin, 2004)

Lake, D. *The Zeebrugge and Ostend Raids 1918* (Barnsley: Leo Cooper, 2002)

Lambert, N. *The Submarine Service, 1900-1918* (Aldershot: Ashgate for the Navy Records Society, 2001)

Leyland, J. *The Achievement of the British Navy in the World-War*, 2nd edn, rev. (London: Hodder: Stoughton, 1918)

Liddle, P. H. *The Sailor's War, 1918-1918* (Poole: Blandford, 1985)

Marder, A. J. *From the Dardanelles to Oran: Studies of the Royal Navy in War and Peace, 1915-1940* (London: Oxford University Press, 1974)

—— *From the Dreadnought to Scapa Flow: The Royal Navy in the Fisher Era, 1904-1919*, 5 vols (London: Oxford University Press, 1961-1970)
Contents: Vol 1. The Road to War, 1904-1914, 1961; Vol 2. The War Years: To the Eve of Jutland, 1914-1916, 1965; Vol 3. Jutland and After (May 1916-Dec. 1916), 2nd edn, 1978 (originally published 1966); Vol 4. 1917: Year of Crisis, 1969; Vol 5. Victory and Aftermath, 1970.

Marsay, M. *Bombardment: The Day the East Coast Bled* (Scarborough: Great Northern Publishing, 1999)
Additional sub-title: 'Accounts of the German naval raids on Scarborough and Whitby on Wednesday, 16th December 1914: (with details of the raid on the Hartlepools) and the German submarine attack on Scarborough on Tuesday, 4th September 1917'.

Massie, R. K. *Castles of Steel: Britain, Germany and the Winning of the Great War at Sea* (New York: Random House, 2003; repr. London: Pimlico, 2005)

Miles, G. *Superior Force: The Conspiracy Behind the Escape of Goeben and Breslau* (Hull: University of Hull Press, 1996)

Osborne, E.W. *Britain's Economic Blockade of Germany 1914-1919* (London: Frank Cass, 2004)

Parker, J. *The Silent Service: The Inside Story of the Royal Navy's Submarine Heroes* (London: Headline, 2001; repr. 2002)

Pattee, P. G. *At War in Distant Waters. British Colonial Defence in the Great War* (Barnsley: Seaforth Publishing, 2014)

Philpott, M *Air and Sea Power in World War I: Combat Experience in the Royal Flying Corps and the Royal Navy* (London: I.B. Tauris, 2012)

Pitt, B. *Zeebrugge: Eleven VCs Before Breakfast* (London: Cassell Military, 2003)
Originally published: as *Zeebrugge, St George's Day, 1918* (London: Cassell, 1958)

Poolman, K. *Armed Merchant Cruisers* (London: Cooper in association with Secker & Warburg, 1985)

Ranft, B. 'The Royal Navy and the War at Sea', in *Britain and the First World War*, edited by J. Turner (London: Routledge, 1988)

Ranft, B., ed. *Technical Change and British Naval Policy, 1860-1939* (London: Hodder & Stoughton, 1977)

Redford, D. and P. D. Grove. *The Royal Navy : A History since 1900* (London: I.B. Tauris 2014)

Ritchie, C. I. A. *Q-Ships* (Lavenham: Dalton, 1985)

Robbins, G. *The Aircraft Carrier Story, 1908-1945* (London: Arms & Armour, 2001)

Rose, L. A. *Power at Sea*, 3 vols (Columbia: University of Missouri Press, 2007), III: *The Age of Navalism, 1890-1918*

Roskill, S. W. *Churchill and the Admirals* (London: Collins, 1977)

Roskill, S. W., ed. *Documents Relating to the Naval Air Service* (London: Navy Records Society, 1969), I: *1908-1918* (1969)

Rossano, G. L. and T. Wildenberg. *Striking the Hornets Nest: Naval Aviation and the Origins of Strategic Bombing in World War I* (Annapolis, Maryland: Naval Institute Press, 2015)

Schurman, D. M. *The Education of a Navy: The Development of British Naval Thought, 1867-1914* (Chicago: University of Chicago Press, 1965; repr. Malabar, Fla.: R.E. Krieger Pub. Co., 1984)

Shankland, P. *The Phantom Flotilla: The Story of the Naval Africa Expedition, 1915-16* (London: Collins, 1968)

Shankland, P. and A. Hunter. *Dardanelles Patrol* (London: Collins, 1964; repr. London: Granada, 1983)

Simpson, C. *Anglo-American Naval Relations 1917-1919* (Aldershot: Published by Scolar for the Navy Records Society, 1991)

— *The Ship that Hunted Itself* (Harmondsworth: Penguin 1979)
On the operations of the British and German armed merchant cruisers 'Carmania' and 'Cap Trafalgar' in 1914.

Siney, M. C. *The Allied Blockade of Germany, 1914-1916* (Ann Arbor, Michigan: University of Michigan Press 1957; repr. Westport, Conn. : Greenwood Press, 1973)

Sondhaus, L. *The Great War at Sea: A Naval History of the First World War* (Cambridge: Cambridge University Press, 2014)

Sumida, J. T. *In Defence of Naval Supremacy: Finance, Technology and British Naval Policy, 1889-1914*, new edn (London: Routledge, 1993)

Swales, R. *Nelson at War, 1914-1918: The History of Nelson Battalion* (London: Pen & Sword Maritime, 2004)
The battalion was part of the Royal Naval Air Service which was formed in September 1914 from Royal marines and naval reservists surplus to sea-going requirements. The RNAS battalions were named after famous admirals.

Tennent, A. J. *British Merchant Ships Sunk by U Boats in the 1914-1918 War* (Newport, Gwent: Starling Press, 1990)

Terraine, J. *Business in Great Waters: The U-Boat Wars, 1916-1945* (London: Cooper, 1989; repr. London: Wordsworth Editions, 1999)

Thomas, R. D. and B. Patterson. *Dreadnoughts in Camera: Building the Super Dreadnoughts, 1905-20* (Stroud: Sutton, 1998; repr. 2000)

Thompson, J. *The Imperial War Museum [IWM] Book of the War at Sea 1914-1918* (London: Sidgwick & Jackson in association with The Imperial War Museum, 2005)

Till, G. 'Brothers in Arms: The British Army and Navy at the Dardanelles', in *Facing Armageddon: The First World War Experienced*, ed. by H. Cecil and P. H. Liddle (London: Leo Cooper, 1996)

— *The Development of British Naval Thinking: Essays in Memory of Bryan Ranft* (London: Routledge, 2006)

— 'Passchendaele: The Maritime Perspective', in *Passchendaele in Perspective: The Third Battle of Ypres*, edited by P. H. Liddle (London: Leo Cooper, 1997)

Towle, P. 'The Evaluation of the Experience of the Russo-Japanese War', in *Technical Change and British Naval Policy, 1860-1939*, edited by B. Ranft (London: Hodder & Stoughton, 1977)

Turner, F. R. *The Mystery Towers of World War One: An Attempt by the Royal Navy to Blockade the English Channel in 1918* (Gravesend: F.R. Turner, 1994)

Warner, P. *The Zeebrugge Raid* (London: W. Kimber, 1978)

White, C. 'The Navy and the Naval War Considered', in *Home Fires and Foreign Fields, British Social and Military Experience in the Great War*, ed. by P. H. Liddle (Manchester: Manchester University Press, 1985)

Wilson, M. *Baltic Assignment: British Submariners in Russia 1914-1919* (London: Leo Cooper in association with Secker & Warburg, 1985)

— *Destination Dardenelles* (London: Cooper, 1988)

Articles

Bullen, J. 'The Royal Navy and Air Power: The Projected Torpedo-Bomber Attack on the High Seas Fleet at Wilhelmshaven in 1918', *Imperial War Museum Review*, 2 (1987), 71-7

Halpern, P. 'Jutland: A Battle in One Dimension', *U.S. Naval Institute Proceedings*, 132 (2006), 56-61

Hiley, N. P. 'The Strategic Origins of Room 40', *Intelligence and National Security*, 2 (1987), 245-73
Room 40 was the office of British Naval Intelligence during World War I.

Hines, J. 'Sins of Omission and Commission: A Reassessment of the Role of Intelligence in the Battle of Jutland', *Journal of Military History* 72 (2008), 1117-1153

Martin, C. 'The Complexity of Strategy: "Jackie"' Fisher and the Trouble with Submarines', *Journal of Military History*, 75 (2011), 441-470

Roskill, R. 'The Dismissal of Admiral Jellicoe', *Journal of Contemporary History*, 1 (1966), 69–93

Santoni, A. 'The First Ultra Secret: The British Cryptanalysis of the Naval Operations of the First World War', *Revue Internationale d'Histoire Militaire*, 63 (1985), 99-110

Sumida, J. T. 'British Capital Ship Design and Fire Control in the Dreadnought Era: Sir John Fisher, Arthur Hungerford Pollen, and the Battle Cruiser', *Journal of Modern History*, 51(1979, 205-30

— 'British Naval and Operational Logistics, 1914-18', *Journal of Military History*, 57 (1993), 447-80

Towle, P. 'The Effect of the Russo-Japanese War on British Naval Policy', *Mariner's Mirror*, 60 (1974), 383-94

4.5.3 The Air Force

On the outbreak of war Britain had two air arms in existence, the Army's Royal Flying Corps (which was created in 1912 out of the Air Battalion, Royal Engineers, an army kite-balloon unit) and the Royal Naval Air Service. Their role initially was largely in the areas of defence and reconnaissance, the RFC being used on the Western Front for spotting targets, directing artillery fire, and keeping a look-out for enemy troop concentrations, and the RNAS, which had airships as well as aeroplanes operating from coastal stations, being used to detect enemy ships and submarines in home waters and to defend Britain from German aerial attacks (the latter task was taken over by the RFC in February 1916).

As the aeroplane design and weaponry became more sophisticated the RFC and the RNAS were increasingly employed for more aggressive purposes. The RFC became involved in offensive reconnaissance and tactical bombing missions (General Trenchard's policy of sending air patrols deep behind enemy lines) and the implementation in 1917 and 1918 of new techniques of close ground support for the army requiring low level attacks on German ground forces and batteries.

The adoption by the RNAS of a more aggressive role took the form initially of light bombing missions in support of the retreat to Dunkirk at the beginning of the war, followed subsequently by long-range operations as, for example, its bombing of air sheds in Alsace and the Rhineland (the attack on Düsseldorf and Cologne constituting the first genuine strategic bombing mission on a military target). The RNAS also provided effective additional protection for convoys after Germany accelerated its submarine campaign in 1917; organized in the 'Spider's Web' patrol system and equipped with depth charges and radio, its seaplanes, flying boats and airships made a valuable contribution to the restriction of U-boat operation in home waters and sank several U-boats.

Some of the aircraft of the RNAS flew from warships and vessels converted to aircraft carriers. The old cruiser *Hermes*, commissioned in 1913 with a downward-sloping take-off deck fitted to it, was the Royal Navy's first seaplane carrier but was sunk by a torpedo early in October 1914, and in December 1914 the converted collier *Ark Royal* became operational as the first British ship to be specifically completed as a seaplane carrier. Seaplanes (mostly winched in and out of the water unless the carrying vessel had a particularly long flight deck) and from late 1916 wheeled seaborne aircraft, were mainly used for reconnaissance but were sometimes used for offensive purposes. The performance of seaplanes was generally poor and for most of the war wheeled seaborne aircraft, although capable of being launched from a short flight deck, suffered from the problem of landing back on the carrier. Some improvements in this respect were, however, being made as evidenced by the conversion after 1916 of the liner *Argus* to a carrier with efficient take-off and landing facilities and by the laying down in 1917 of a new HMS *Hermes*, the first vessel designed from the outset as an aircraft carrier, but neither saw service in the war as the *Argus*, although entering service in October 1918, was still undergoing trials at the time of the Armistice and HMS *Hermes* was not put into commission until 1923. Although the use of aircraft carriers was making gradual progress during the war they were, like tanks and manned aircraft, nowhere near the level of development that would make them so effective in future wars.

As the significance and potential of air power became clearer there developed a debate about its use and the best way to organize it. Sykes believed that the trench deadlock could be solved by rendering the German field army inoperable by means of air attacks on its centres of supply. There were those who felt that separate air wings for the Army and the Navy represented wasteful duplication of training and supply. There were also public demands, following Gotha bombing raids on English cities between 27 May and 7 July 1917, for reprisals focused on a long-range air-offensive against Germany. It was against this background of debate that Smuts was appointed by the War Cabinet in 1917 to investigate not only defence against air raids but also the much wider matter of the organization and direction of Britain's air forces and their operations. The major result of this investigation was the formation of the Air Ministry and the merger of the RFC and the RNAS into the RAF in April 1918. This was followed by the establishment in June 1918 of the Independent Air Force (that is, a force independent of military or naval operations) under Major-General Trenchard as a strategic bombing arm of the RAF to carry out mass raids on industrial and military targets deep inside enemy territory. The IAF achieved little. It dropped 543 tons of bombs in some 242 raids on Germany during which 109 of its bombers went missing and 243 were wrecked. Although the raids resulted in 1170 German casualties (797 dead and 380 wounded) and an estimated 15 million marks' worth of damage, the tonnage of bombs dropped was too small to have any real impact. Trenchard himself thought it was a 'gigantic waste of effort and personnel'.

Although RFC units were concentrated on the Western Front some of its units also flew in support of army operations on all the other battlefronts except Gallipoli, performing an important role on the Mesopotamian and Palestinian Fronts (but making little impact in Africa), and were also employed from late 1917 on the Italian Front where they played a part in the decisive battle of Piave in June 1918. The RNAS also contributed some support to overseas operations, playing a small part in the Dardenalles campaign of 1915-1916, carrying out photo-reconnaissance for the Gallipoli landings, and sinking two Turkish vessels with torpedoes launched from Short 184 seaplanes.

At the start of the war the public's perception of air warfare was very much influenced by the press and propaganda depicting pilots as heroes engaged in a glamorous and chivalrous contest in the sky. In reality the war in the air proved to be as unromantic, attritional, and wasteful of life as the war on the ground. The contest in the air and the winning of air superiority became not so much a matter of the skills and courage of individual pilots and the exploits of 'aces' as a matter of a combatant nation being able to produce aircraft in the quantity and of the technical quality (in terms of speed, manoeuvrability, and weaponry) required to outstrip the enemy's capability in all these respects[175]. As a result there was a huge increase in the number of aeroplanes manufactured and of pilots required to fly them. The number of pilots killed or wounded and of aircraft shot down inevitably escalated. Britain's increasingly aggressive air strategy resulted in particularly heavy air losses. On the Western Front 141 pilots were killed or went missing during the battle of the Somme and between June 1917 and November 1917 the RFC were losing some 200 pilots a month (this rate of loss mounting until the end of the war and reaching its peak in September 1918, when in that month 235 aircraft were shot down). During this period a pilot in the front line was considered lucky if he survived more than a few weeks. Losses were, however, by no means all due to combat. In fact, of the total estimated number of 14166 pilots killed between 1914 and 1918, 8000 died in training and 6166 were killed in action.

Bibliographies

Smith, M. J. *World War I in the Air: A Bibliography and Chronology* (Metuchen, N.J.: Scarecrow Press, 1977)

Autobiographies, Biographies and Memoirs

Armstrong, H. C. *Grey Steel: J. C. Smuts, A Study in Arrogance* (London: A. Barker, 1937)
Smuts played an important role in advising on military strategy and establishing the independent organisation of the RAF.

Ash, E.   *Sir Frederick Sykes and the Air Revolution, 1912-1918* (London: Frank Cass, 1999)

Bartlett, C. P. O. *Bomber Pilot, 1916-1918*, edited by Chaz Bowyer (Allan, 1974)

Boyle, A. *Trenchard: Man of Vision* (London: Collins, 1962)

Charlton, L. E. O. *Charlton: An Autobiography* (Harmondsworth: Penguin Books, 1938)
Originally published London; Faber, 1931

— *More Charlton* (London: Longmans, 1940)
Charlton saw active service as a high-ranking officer in the RFC throughout the war, reaching the rank of substantive lieutenant-colonel and temporary brigadier-general in the RAF when it it was formed in 1918. Took command of an RFC brigade in France on 18 October 1917; his squadrons supported the British Fifth Army during the 'disaster' of the German advance in March 1918 and the Fourth Army in its 'triumphant progress' before Armistice Day. Honoured with CMG in 1916 and CB in 1919. Also received the French Légion d'Honneur.

Grinnell-Milne, D. *Wind in the Wires* (London: Hurst & Blackett, 1933; repr. London: Grub Street, 2014)
Memoir of a British pilot about his experiences of flying in the First World War

Havard, C. W. H. *The Trenchard Touch* (Chichester: Countrywise Press, 2000)

Smith, A. *Mick Mannock, Fighter Pilot: Myth, Life and Politics* (Basingstoke: Macmillan, 2001)

Sykes, F. H. *From Many Angles: An Autobiography* (London: Harrap, 1942)

Diaries, Letters

Archer, W. D. *Death in the Air: The War Diary and Photographs of a Flying Corps Pilot* (London: Greenhill, 1985)
Facsimile of edn published: London: Heinemann, 1933.

Lee, A. S. G. *No Parachute: A Fighter Pilot in World War I; Letters Written in 1917* (London: Jarrolds, 1968)

---

[175] In terms of technical quality Germany tended to have the edge (although the balance in this respect between the opposing nations fluctuated throughout the war) but by mid 1918 the numerical balance had swung overwhelmingly towards the Allies (helped by the entry of the USA into the war and the expansion of the British aero-industry after 1916 (until which year Britain had been heavily dependent on French production for aeroplanes).

Rennles, K. *Independent Force: The War Diary of the Daylight Bomber Squadrons of the Independent Air Force, 6 June-11 November 1918* (London: Grub Street, 2002)

Rosher, H. *In the Royal Naval Air Service: Being the Letters of the Late Harold Rosher to his Family*, with an introduction by Arnold Bennett (London: Greenhill, 1986)
Facsimile of edn published: London : Chatto & Windus, 1916.

Wortley, R. S. *Letters from a Flying Officer* (London: Milford, 1928; repr. Gloucester: Sutton, 1982)

Books

Abbatiello, J. J. *Anti-Submarine Warfare in World War I: British Naval Aviation and the Defeat of the U-Boats* (London: Routledge, 2006)

— 'British Naval Aviation and the Anti-Submarine Campaign, 1917-18' (unpublished doctoral thesis, University of London)

Abbott, P. *The British Airship at War, 1914-1918* (Lavenham: Terence Dalton, 1989)

Ash, E. *Sir Frederick Sykes and the Air Revolution, 1912-1918* (London: Cass, 1999)

Baring, M. *Flying Corps Headquarters 1914-1918*, new edn (London: Buchan & Enright, 1985)
Originally published: London: Bell, 1920

Barker, R. *A Brief History of the Royal Flying Corps in World War I* (London: Robinson, 2002)
Originally published as: *The Royal Flying Corps in France*, London: Constable, 1995.

Bennett, L. *Gunning for the Red Baron* (College Station, Texas: Texas A and M University Press, 2006)

Bickers, R. T. *The First Great Air War* (London: Hodder & Stoughton, 1988)

Biddle, T. D. *Rhetoric and Reality in Air Warfare: The Evolution of British and American Ideas about Strategic Bombing, 1914-1945* (Princeton, N.J.: Princeton University Press, 2002)

Brooks, S. *Bomber: Strategic Air Power in Twentieth Century Conflict* (London: Imperial War Museum, 1983)

Buckley, J. *Air Power in the Age of Total War* (London: UCL Press, 1998)

Chamier, J. A. *The Birth of the Royal Air Force: The Early History and Experiences of the Flying Services* (London: Pitman, 1943)

Charlton, L. E. O. *War from the Air: Past, Present, Future* (London: Thomas Nelson 1935)
"This book is based on a course of lectures, delivered at Trinity College, Cambridge, in the Michaelmas term of [1934]".

Cole, C., ed. *Royal Air Force, 1918* (London: Kimber, 1968)

— *Royal Flying Corps, 1915-1916* (London: Kimber 1969)

Cole, C. and E. F. Cheeseman. *The Air Defence of Britain, 1914-1918* (London: Putnam, 1984)

Cooper, M. *The Birth of Independent Air Power: British Policy in the First World War* (London: Allen & Unwin, 1986)

Cormack, A. *British Air Forces, 1914-18*, 2 vols (Oxford: Osprey Military, 2000-2001)

Cumming, A. J. *Battle for Britain: Interservice Rivalry between the Royal Air Force and the Royal Navy, 1909-40* (Annapolis, Maryland: Naval Institute Press, 2015)

Dye, P. *The Bridge to Airpower: Logistics Support for the Royal Flying Corps Operations on the Western Front, 1914—1918* (Annapolis, Maryland: Naval Institute Press ,2015)

Eyck, F. 'The Royal Air Force and the Origins of Strategic Bombing', in *Men at War: Politics, Technology, and Innovation in the Twentieth Century*, edited by Timothy Travers and Christon Archer (Chicago: Precedent, 1982; repr. New Brunswick (U.S.A.): Transaction Publishers, 2011)

Ferris, J. '"Airbandit": C31 and Strategic Air Defence during the First Battle of Britain', in *Strategy and Intelligence: British Policy During the First World War*, ed. by M. Dockrill and D. French (London: Hambledon, 1986)

Franks, N. L. R. *Sopwith Camel Aces of World War I* (Oxford: Osprey, 2003)

— *Sopwith Triplane Aces of World War 1* (Oxford: Osprey, 2004)

Fredette, R. H. *The First Battle of Britain, 1917-1918, and The Birth of the Royal Air Force* (London: Cassell, 1966)

— The Sky On Fire: The First Battle of Britain, 1917-1918 and The Birth of the Royal Air Force (Washington, D.C.: Smithsonian Institution Press, 1991)

Gollin, A. 'A Flawed Strategy: Early British Air Defence Arrangements', in *The Great War, 1914-18: Essays on the Military, Political and Social History of the First World War*, edited by R. J. Q. Adams (Basingstoke: Macmillan in association with King's College London, 1990)

— *The Impact of Air Power on the British People and their Government, 1909-14* (London: Macmillan in association with King's College, London, 1989)

Gordon, T. C. *Early Flying in Orkney: Seaplanes in World War One* (Kirkwall: BBC Radio Orkney, 1985)

Great Britain. Air Ministry. *Synopsis of British Air Effort during the War*, presented by Parliament by command of His Majesty April 1919, Cmd 100 (London: HMSO, 1919)

Greenhous, B. 'Aircraft versus Armour: Cambrai to Yom Kippur', in *Men at War: Politics, Technology, and Innovation in the Twentieth Century*, edited by Timothy Travers and Christon Archer (Chicago: Precedent, 1982; repr. New Brunswick (U.S.A.): Transaction Publishers, 2011)

Henshaw, T. *The Sky Their Battlefield: Air Fighting and the Complete List of Allied Air Casualties from Enemy Action in the First War: British, Commonwealth and United States Air Services 1914 To 1918* (London: Grub Street, 1995)

Joynson-Hicks, W., 1st Viscount Brentford. *The Command of the Air, or, Prophecies Fulfilled*, being speeches delivered in the House of Commons. (London: Nisbet, 1916)

Hyde A. P. *The First Blitz: The German Air Campaign Against Britain 1917-1918* (Barnsley: Leo Cooper, 2002)

Jones H. A. *Over the Balkans and South Russia, 1917-1919: Being the History of No. 47 Squadron, Royal Air Force* (London: E. Arnold, 1923; repr. Elstree: Greenhill, 1987)

Jones, N. *The Origins of Strategic Bombing: A Study of the Development of British Air Strategic Thought and Practice up to 1918* (London: Kimber, 1973)

Kennett, L. B. *The First Air War, 1914-1918* (New York: Free Press, 1991)

— *A History of Strategic Bombing* (New York: Scribner, 1982)

Lewis, G. H. *Wings over the Somme, 1916-1918*, edited by Chaz Bowyer, new edn (Wrexham: Bridge Books, 1994)

Liddle, P. H. *The Airman's War, 1914-1918* (Poole: Blandford, 1987)

London, P. *U-boat Hunters: Cornwall's Air War, 1916-1919* (Truro: Dyllansow Truran, 1999)

Macmillan, N. *Offensive Patrol: The Story of the RNAS, RFC and RAF in Italy, 1917-18* (London: Jarrold, 1973)

Mckenna, M. C. 'The Development of Air Raid Precautions in World War I', in *Men at War: Politics, Technology and Innovation in the Twentieth Century*, edited by T. Travers and C. Archer (Chicago: Precedent, 1982; repr. New Brunswick (U.S.A.): Transaction Publishers, 2011)

Mead, P. *The Eye in the Air: History of Air Observation and Reconnaissance for the Army 1785-1945* (London: HMSO, 1983)

Morris, J. *German Air Raids on Britain 1914-1918* (London: Sampson Low, 1925; repr. London: History Press Ltd, 2007)

— *Distribution of Propaganda by Air, 1914-1918* (London: Lee Richards, 2001)
Originally published in 1920 by the Public Record Office [?]

Mowthorpe, C. *Battlebags: British Airships of the First World War, An Illustrated History* (Stroud: Sutton, 1995)

Norris, G. *The Royal Flying Corps: A History* (London: F. Muller, 1965)

O'Connor, M. *Airfields and Airmen: Arras* (London: Wharncliffe Books, 2004)

— *Airfields and Airmen: Cambrai* (Barnsley: Leo Cooper, 2003)

— *Airfields and Airmen: Somme* (London: Leo Cooper, 2002)

— *Airfields and Airmen: Ypres* (London: Leo Cooper, 2001)

Oliver, D. *Airborne Espionage: International Special Duties Operations in the World Wars* (Stroud: Sutton, 2005)

Paris, M. J. *Winged Warfare: The Literature and Theory of Aerial Warfare in Britain, 1859-1917* (Manchester: Manchester University Press, 1992)

Philpott, M *Air and Sea Power in World War I: Combat Experience in the Royal Flying Corps and the Royal Navy* (London: I.B. Tauris, 2012)

Pisano, D. *Legend, Memory and the Great War in the Air* (Seattle: University of Washington Press, 1992)

Platt, B. '"Terrorizing the Fortress of London"? German Bombings, Public Pressure, and the Creation of the British Home Defense System in World War I', A thesis presented in partial fulfilment of the requirements for the degree Master of Arts in History (unpublished masters thesis, Terre Haute, Indiana State University, 2010) [http://hdl.handle.net/10484/959]

Raleigh, Sir W. A. *The War In The Air: Being The Story of the Part Played in the Great War by the Royal Air Force*, 6 vols (London, HMSO, 1922-37; repr. Uckfield: Naval and Military Press, 2002)
Vols. 2-6 and Appendices by H. A. Jones
In the series *History of the Great War Based on Official Documents* by direction of the Historical Section of the Committee of Imperial Defence.

Rimmell, R. *Zeppelin!: A Battle for Air Supremacy in World War I* (London: Conway Maritime Press, 1984)

— *The Royal Flying Corps in World War One* (London: Arms & Armour, 1985)

Robbins, G. *The Aircraft Carrier Story, 1908-1945* (London: Arms & Armour, 2001)

Rossano, G. L. and T. Wildenberg. *Striking the Hornets Nest: Naval Aviation and the Origins of Strategic Bombing in World War I* (Annapolis, Maryland: Naval Institute Press, 2015)

Sheffield, G. D. and P. Gray, eds. *Changing War: The British Army, the Hundred Days Campaign and the Birth of the Royal Air Force, 1918* (London: Bloomsbury, 2013)

Shores, C. F., and others. *Above the Trenches: A Complete Record of the Fighter Aces and Units of the British Empire Air Forces 1915-1920*, by C. Shores, N. Franks and R. Guest (London: Grub Street, 1990)

— *Above the Trenches*, Supplement (London: Grub Street, 1996)

Simkins, P. *Air Fighting 1914-18: The Struggle for Air Superiority over the Western Front* (London: Imperial War Museum, 1978)

Smith, M. 'The Tactical and Strategic Application of Air Power on the Western Front', in *Home Fires and Foreign Fields, British Social and Military Experience in the Great War*, ed. by P. H. Liddle (Manchester: Manchester University Press, 1985)

Steel, N. and P. Hart. *Tumult in the Clouds: The British Experience of the War in the Air 1914-1918* (London: Hodder & Stoughton, 1997).

Sykes, Sir F. *Aviation in Peace and War* (London; Arnold, 1922)
"First written and delivered as the Lees-Knowles lectures at Cambridge university…1921."-Introd.

Townsend, P. B. *Eye in the Sky 1918: Recollections of a World War One Pilot on Artillery and Infantry Co-operation Duties* (Knaresborough: [P.B. Townsend], 1986)

Whitehouse, A. *The Zeppelin Fighters*, new edn (London: New English Library, 1978)

Williams, G. *Wings over Westgate: The Story of a Front Line Naval Air Station during World War 1* (Maidstone: Kent County Library, 1985)

Williams, G. K. *Biplanes and Bombsights: British Bombing in World War I* (Maxell Air Force Base, Ala.: Air University Press, 1999)

— 'Statistics and Strategic Bombardment: Operations and Records of the British Long-Range Bombing Force during World War I and their Implications for the Development of the Post-War Royal Air Force, 1917-1923' (unpublished doctoral thesis, University of Oxford, 1989)

Winter, D. *The First of the Few: Fighter Pilots of the First World War* (London: Allen Lane, 1982)

Wise, S. F. 'The Royal Air Force and the Origins of Strategic Bombing', in *Men at War: Politics, Technology, and Innovation in the Twentieth Century*, edited by Timothy Travers and Christon Archer (Chicago: Precedent, 1982; repr. New Brunswick (U.S.A.): Transaction Publishers, 2011)

Wohl, R. *A Passion for Wings: Aviation and the Western Imagination, 1908 to 1918* (New Haven: Yale University Press, 1994)

Articles

Collins, M. 'A Technocratic Vision of Empire: Lord Montagu and the Origins of British Air Power', *Journal of Imperial and Commonwealth History*, 45 (2017), 652-671

Cooper, M. 'The Development of Air Policy and Doctrine on the Western Front', *Aerospace Historian*, 28 (1981), 38-51

— 'British Flying Operations on the Western Front, July 1917: A Case Study of Trenchard's Offensive Policy in Action', *Cross and Cockade*, 23 (1982), 354-70

Holman, B. 'The Shadow of the Airliner: Commercial Bombers and the Rhetorical Destruction of Britain, 1917-35', *Twentieth Century British History*, 24, (2013), 495-517

Morrow, J. 'Aviation Technology and Strategic Air Power in World War I: The English, French and Italian Experiences', *Revue Internationale d'Histoire Militaire*, 63 (1985), 89-98

Sweetman, J. 'Crucial Months for Survival: The Royal Air Force, 1918-19', *Journal of Contemporary History*, 19 (1984), 529-547

—— 'The Smuts Report of 1917: Merely Political Window Dressing?', *Journal of Strategic Studies*, 4 (1981), 152-74

Wise, S. F. 'The Strategic Use of Air Power in the Context of the Evolution of the Air Weapon in the First World War', in ICMH (International Commission of Military History), *Acta 10*, 225-40

4.6 Science and Technology

4.6.1 General

In the early years of the war complaints in the press about the neglect of science and pleas from many quarters (including, not surprisingly, a strong lobby of leading scientists) for educational reforms which would provide science with a more significant role in education were indicative of the feeling shared by many that an elite educational system which was heavily biased towards the classics had left the British in a weak position to engage in a war of a highly technological nature. Yet science and technology had by no means, however, been entirely neglected before the war; in the areas of the armed services, industry, civil research and education significant developments had taken place and central government had been sponsoring research into an increasingly diverse range of areas. The war, however, had the effect of raising science and technology to a new level of awareness among the British people, particularly by the state. The government itself soon recognized that science and technology and expertise in these fields would play an important role in the war. Great numbers of scientists[176] were mobilized to assist in the war effort, and their utilization by the government for war purposes lent itself to a great acceleration of the pace of scientific and technological development.

The war also had the effect of significantly increasing the interest of people generally in science and technology, the potential applications of which gripped the public imagination to an extent it had never done before. This manifested itself in a number of ways. People began to believe that scientists might be able to come up with some new ways of trying to break the seemingly insurmountable deadlock on the Western Front. Newspapers and magazine began to expand their coverage of items related to science and technology to cater for the public's increasing interest in weaponry, tanks, and airplanes. When the Munitions Inventions Department was set up it was flooded with suggestions from the public, many of them of a bizarre nature from people with an interest in scientific gadgetry bordering on the obsessive (to which the cartoonist, Heath Robinson, drew humorous attention). This wartime fascination with gadgetry is also reflected in some popular war novels in which scientific and technical devices are woven into their plots (as, for example, in Arthur Benjamin Reeve's *The War Terror: Further Adventures with Craig Kennedy, Scientific Detective*, and Guy Thorne's *The Secret Sea-Plane*, both published in 1915)

The accelerated expansion of science and technology during the war was applauded by some contemporaries but others viewed it in terms of the dangers it posed for the future. The *Report of the British Association* for 1916 contains an account of an address, in which Professor G. C. Henderson, speaking to the Chemical Section of the British Association at its meeting on 8th September, 1916, argues that the war had aroused the British nation from 'its state of apathy towards science' to a realization that its future prosperity was 'ultimately dependent on the progress of science'. While some of his contemporaries shared this optimistic view, others were less sanguine and were filled with concern about the potentially destructive capability of modern science. In a speech made in 1916 Sir William Osler, a professor of medicine at Oxford, expressed the view that modern science 'has made slaughter possible on a scale never dreamt of before, and it has enormously increased man's capacity to maim and disable his fellow man'. Osler was by no mean alone in feeling that science and technology could no longer be viewed solely as a means to beneficial progress. The views of those who felt this way were aptly reflected in Sigmund Freud's *Reflections upon War and Death* (1915) in which it was argued that the war 'tarnished the lofty impartiality of our science, it revealed our instincts in all their nakedness and let loose the evil spirits within us which we thought had been tamed for ever by centuries of continuous education by the noblest minds'. During the war H. G. Wells hoped that the horrifying results of the use of weapons capable of destruction on a scale

---

[176] Geologists (e.g. planning of trench systems and tunnels), physicists (e.g. design of acoustic devices), biologists (development of disinfectants), chemists (manufacture of high explosive and gas), geographers (e.g. construction of artillery maps), psychologists (e.g. treatment of shell shock) are examples of some of the scientists whose expertise was called on.

never previously witnessed would actually deter nations from resorting to war in the future but in the inter-war years he felt unable to hold on to this hope.

It is in the area of armaments, tactics, and innovative technology that the Great War is particularly distinguishable from any of the wars which preceded it. The methods of warfare underwent revolutionary changes. Not only did trench warfare take the place of a war of movement, but the nature of warfare was fundamentally changed by the exploitation of science and technology. In the course of the war the applications of the new technology of the years prior to 1914 (such as telephones, bicycles, motorised vehicles, wireless telegraphy, aircraft, submarines, and more powerful weapons of destruction) and of other inventions developed during the war years (such as radio, poison gas, the tank, depth charges, gun- and bomb-sights, high explosives, underwater detection, armoured cars, flame-throwers, and synchronised machine guns in aeroplanes) were all brought into play. Much of the new technology, however, was developed and exploited too slowly or appeared too late in the war to have a major impact for either side. Its real significance lay in the future.

Autobiographies, Biographies, Letters

Caroe, G. M. *William Henry Bragg, 1862-1942: Man and Scientist* (Cambridge: Cambridge University Press, 1978)
Bragg became a member of the Admiralty Board of Invention and Research for whom he worked on underwater acoustics for the purpose of submarine detection from 1914-18.

Douglas, C. G. 'Haldane, John Scott (1860-1936)', *Obituary Notices of Fellows of the Royal Society*, 2 (1936–8), 115–39

Eve, A. S. *Rutherford: Being The Life and Letters of the Rt Hon. Lord Rutherford, O.M.* (Cambridge: Cambridge University Press, 1939)

Heilbron, J. L. *H. G. J. Moseley: The Life and Letters of an English Physicist, 1887-1915* (Berkeley: University of California Press, 1974)

Strutt, R. J., Baron Rayleigh. *The Life of Sir J. J. Thomson* (Cambridge: Cambridge University Press, 1942)

Sturdy, S. 'Haldane, John Scott (1860–1936)', *Oxford Dictionary of National Biography*, Oxford University Press, 2004 [http://www.oxforddnb.com/view/article/33642, accessed 19 Nov 2013]
" … In April 1915 he [Haldane] was asked by Kitchener to advise the War Office on the development of defensive and retaliatory measures against the German's use of gas as a chemical weapon. He went on to work on the design of respirators, and subsequently on the medical aspects of war-gas poisoning, and did much to demonstrate the value of oxygen for treating gassed soldiers … " [Quotation extracted from above item in online Oxford DNB]

Thomson, Sir J. J. *Recollections and Reflections* (London: G. Bell, 1936)
Thomson was one of the members of the Board for Invention and Research during the First World War and presided over the government commission of 1916 to inquire into the position of science in education.

Wilson, D. *Rutherford: Simple Genius* (London: Hodder & Stoughton, 1983)
Professor of Physics at Manchester from 1907. During the war Rutherford acted as consultant to the Admiralty board of invention and research on anti-submarine warfare, leading the way in submarine detection, in which W. H. Bragg and A.S. Eve were also notably engaged during the war. Cavendish professor of experimental physics, Cambridge, 1919-37.

Books

Aubin, D. and C. Goldstein, eds. *The War of Guns and Mathematics: Mathematical Practices and Communities in France and its Western Allies around World War I* (Providence, Rhode Island: American Mathematical Society, 2014)

Bond, A. R. *Inventions of the Great War* (New York: Century, 1920; repr. Read Books, 2009)

Burk, K., ed. *War and the State: The Transformation of British Government 1914-1919* (London: Allen & Unwin, 1982)

Cardwell, D. S. L. *The Organization of Science in England*, rev. edn (London: Heinemann, 1957)

Bynum, W. F. ed. *Companion Encyclopaedia of the History of Medicine* (London: Routledge, 1993)

Edgerton, D. E. H.. 'British Scientific Intellectuals and the Relations of Science, Technology and War', in *National Military Establishments and the Advancement of Science and Technology*, Studies in 20th Century History, edited by Paul Forman and Josê M. Sânchez-Ron (Dordrecht; London: Kluwer Academic, 1996)

— 'Science and War', in *Companion to the History of Modern Science*, edited by R. C. Olby [and others] (London: Routledge, 1990; repr. 1996)

Ellis, J. *The Social History of the Machine Gun* (London: Croom Helm, 1975)

Hartcup, G. *The War of Invention: Scientific Developments, 1914-1918* (London: Brassey's Defence, 1988)

Kloot, W. van der. *Great Scientists Wage the Great War: The First War of Science, 1914-1918* (Stroud: Fonthill, 2014)

McKenna, M. C. 'The Development of Air Raid Precautions in Britain during the First World War', in *Men at War: Politics, Technology, and Innovation in the Twentieth Century*, edited by T. Travers and C. Archer (Chicago: Precedent, 1982)

MacLeod, R. M. and E. K. MacLeod. 'The Social Relations of Science and Technology, 1914-1939', in *Fontana Economic History of Europe*, edited by C. Cipolla, 6 vols in 9 (London: Collins/Fontana, 1972-78), V: *The Twentieth Century*, part 1 (1976)

Osler, Sir W. 'The Old Humanities and the New Science', in A *Way of Life and Selected Writings of Sir William Osler*, ed. G. L. Keynes (New York: Dover, 1958)
'The Old Humanities and the New Science' was an address delivered by Osler to the Classical Association at Oxford in May, 1919, about eight months before his death. In this address Osler takes the gloomy view that the Great War has demonstrated man's unwillingness to use the forces Science puts at his disposal in the service of life.

— *Science and War: An Address Delivered at the University of Leeds Medical School in October, 1915* (Oxford: Clarendon Press, 1915)
Although Osler indicates in this address that he is able to see the beneficial effects of science at the service of war, as exemplified by the advances made in the care of the wounded and sick and in the prevention of epidemics among soldiers, he is emotionally horrified by the fact that science has increased man's capacity to wreak mass destruction of human beings by air, land, and sea to an horrific level.

Pearton, M. *The Knowledgeable State: Diplomacy, War and Technology Since 1830* (London: Burnett Books, 1982)

Pick, D. *War Machine: The Rationalization of Slaughter in the Modern Age* (New Haven: Yale University Press, 1993)

Rieger, B. *Technology and the Culture of Modernity in Britain and Germany, 1890-1945* (Cambridge: Cambridge University Press, 2005; repr. 2009)

Rose, H. and S. Rose. *Science and Society* (Harmondsworth: Penguin, 1969)

Travers, T. and C. Archer, eds. *Men at War: Politics, Technology, and Innovation in the Twentieth Century*, edited by Timothy Travers and Christon Archer (Chicago: Precedent, 1982; repr. New Brunswick (U.S.A.): Transaction Publishers, 2011)

Vernon, K. 'Science and Technology', in *The First World War in British History*, edited by S. Constantine (London: Edward Arnold, 1995)

Winter, J. M, ed. *War and Economic Development* (Cambridge: Cambridge University Press, 1975)

Articles

Cardwell, D. S. L. 'Science in World War I', *Proceedings of the Royal Society of London*, 342 (1975), 447-56

Fara, P. 'A Social Laboratory: The First World War Provided Unprecedented Opportunities for Scientists, Especially Women', *History Today*, 64 (2014), 43

Juniper, D. 'The First World War and Radio Development', *History Today*, 54; Issue 5 (2004), 32-41

Kevles, D. J. 'Into Hostile Camps: The Reorganisation of International Science in World War One, *Isis*, 62 (1971), 47-60

MacLeod, R. M. 'The Chemists Go to War: The Mobilization of Civilian Chemists and the British War Effort', *Annals of Science*, 50 (1993), 455-81

4.6.2 The Armed Forces

Galvanised by the need to try and produce some new ways of breaking the stalemate in which the war had become bogged down, the Admiralty, the War Office and the Ministry of Munitions set up a number of inventions and research departments[177]. All this activity produced results in areas of development such as radio technology, poison gas, the tank, anti-aircraft ballistics, the Stokes mortar (developed by the Trench Warfare Department), the small box respirator, depth charges, gun- and bomb-sights, high explosives, underwater detection of submarines, aircraft carriers, and aircraft design. The combined effect of these efforts was, however, incapable of altering the course of the war. The advances made and the innovations introduced were numerous but some of the most important of them were unable to be fully exploited either because of insufficient development (e.g. radio technology) or because they came on stream too late to be of use (e.g. sonar). Above all, the advances represented by the tank, manned aircraft, and the aircraft carrier had still not reached the point where they could have a major impact on the outcome of the war; the devastating potential of these advances lay in the future. In the end, in a war that continued to be fought by all the belligerents on largely traditional lines (albeit with far deadlier weaponry), it was Britain's industrial capacity to maintain a flow of manpower, munitions and equipment to the battlefronts in the massive quantities[178] required rather than scientific and technological sophistication that contributed most to the ultimate victory over Germany.

Books

Edgerton, D. E. H. *England and the Aeroplane: An Essay on a Militant and Technological Nation* (Basingstoke: Macmillan, 1991)

Gusewelle, J. K. 'Science and the Admiralty during World War I: The Case of the Board of Invention and Research', in *Naval Warfare in the Twentieth Century, 1900-1945. Essays in Honour of Arthur Marder*, edited by G. Jordan (London: Croom Helm, 1977)

Haber, L. F. *The Poisonous Cloud: Chemical Warfare in the First World War* (Oxford: Clarendon Press, 1986)

Harris, J. P. *Men, Ideas and Tanks: British Military Thought and Armoured Forces, 1903-1939* (Manchester: Manchester University Press, 1995)

Lyon, H. 'The Relationships between The Admiralty and Private Industry in the Development of Warships', in *Technical Change and British Naval Policy, 1860-1939*, edited by B. Ranft (London: Hodder and Stoughton, 1977)

McNeill, W. H. *The Pursuit of Power: Technology, Armed Force, and Society Since A.D.1000* (Oxford: Blackwell, 1983)

Palazzo, A. *Seeking Victory on the Western Front: The British Army and Chemical Warfare in World War I* (Lincoln: University of Nebraska Press, 2000)

Ranft, B., ed. *Technical Change and British Naval Policy, 1860-1939* (London: Hodder and Stoughton, 1977)

---

[177] The three main invention departments were the Munitions Inventions Department, the Royal Navy's Board of Invention and Research, and the Air Inventions Committee.

[178] It was not the sophistication of aircraft, tanks, and weaponry but their availability on the Western Front in larger numbers than ever before in coordination with mass concentrations of artillery and infantry that helped to produce the offensive that finally wore down the resistance of the Germany army in 1918.

Richter, D. *Chemical Soldiers: British Gas Warfare in World War One* (London: Leo Cooper, 1992)

Spiers, E. M. *Chemical Warfare* (Basingstoke: Macmillan, 1986

Terraine, J. *White Heat: The New Warfare 1914-18* (London: Sidgwick & Jackson, 1982; repr. London: Cooper, 1992)

Travers, T. 'Future Warfare: H. G. Wells and British Military Theory, 1895-1916', in *War and Society: A Yearbook of Military History*, edited by B. Bond and I. Roy, Vol 1 (London: Croom Helm, 1975)

— *How the War Was Won: Command and Technology in the British Army on the Western Front, 1917-18* (London: Routledge, 1992)

— *The Killing Ground* (London: Allen & Unwin, 1987)

Articles

Griffin, N. J. 'Scientific Management and the Direction of Britain's Military Labour Establishment during World War I', *Military Affairs*, 42 (1978), 197-201

Macleod, R. M. and E. K. Andrews. 'Scientific Advice in the War at Sea, 1915-1917: The Board of Invention and Research', *Journal of Contemporary History*, 6 (1971), 3-40

Pattison, M. 'Scientists, Inventors, and the Military in Britain, 1915-19: The Munitions Inventions Department', *Social Studies of Science*, 13 (1983), 521-68

Sheffy, Y. 'Chemical Warfare and the Palestine Campaign, 1916-1918', *Journal of Military History*, 73 (2009), 803-844

Trumpener, U. 'The Road to Ypres: the Beginnings of Gas Warfare in World War I', *Journal of Modern History*, 47 (1975), 460–80

4.6.3 Industry

When the war started Britain was faced with an acute shortage of scientific products such as organic chemicals, dyestuffs, optical glass, magnetos and other electrical equipment due to heavy reliance in pre-war years on their supply from Germany. Although this situation can be seen as the result of neglect by the government and British industry of scientific research and technical education, the armed services and industry in Britain had in fact been engaged to a considerable extent in scientific research and development from at least the turn of the century, and the government had been sponsoring research from the late nineteenth century as well as attempting to improve scientific and technical education. Britain did, therefore, have an infrastructure on which it could build and within two years of the outbreak of war it had made good from its own factories the original shortage of war materials and was, moreover, able to maintain a supply of them until the end of the war in the volume required to meet unprecedented demands. The part played by the Ministry of Munitions in this was crucial. It was through this Ministry's coordination and sponsorship of the scientific and technical research carried out by university, industrial, and government laboratories, military experimental establishments and private workshops, allied to the mass production techniques and scientific management developed in British industry, that Britain was so successful in maintaining a supply of products to British forces (and to a considerable extent to her Allies as well) in the quantity and technological sophistication required.

Books

Baker, W. J. *A History of the Marconi Company* (London: Methuen, 1970)

Burn, D. *The Economic History of Steelmaking, 1867-1939: A Study in Competition* (Cambridge: Cambridge University Press, 1961)

Great Britain. Ministry of Munitions. *History of the Ministry of Munitions*, 12 vols (London: HMSO, 1920-22) Contents: Vol. 1. Industrial mobilisation, 1914-1915; Vol. 2. General organisation for munitions supply; Vol. 3. Finance and contracts; Vol. 4. The supply and control of labour, 1915-1916; Vol. 5. Wages and welfare; Vol. 6. Man power and dilution; Vol. 7. The control of materials; Vol. 8. Control of industrial capacity and equipment; Vol. 9. Review of munitions supply; Vol. 10-12. The supply of munitions.

Hogg, O. F. G. *The Royal Arsenal: Its Background, Origin and Subsequent History*, 2 vols (London: Oxford University Press, 1963)

Liebenau, J., ed. *The Challenge of New Technology: Innovation in British Business Since 1850* (Aldershot: Gower Press, 1987)

Little, C. R. *The Development of the Labour Process in Capitalist Societies: A Comparative Study of the Transformation of Work Organization in Britain, Japan and the USA* (London: Heinemann Educational, 1982; repr. Aldershot: Gower, 1986)

Lyon, H. 'The Relationships between the Admiralty and Private Industry in the Development of Warships', in *Technical Change and British Naval Policy, 1860-1939*, edited by B. Ranft (London: Hodder & Stoughton, 1977)

Pattison, M. 'Scientists, Government and Invention: The Experience of the Invention Boards, 1915-1918', in *Home Fires and Foreign Fields, British Social and Military Experience in the Great War*, ed. by P. H. Liddle (Manchester: Manchester University Press, 1985)

Reader, W. *Imperial Chemical Industries: A History*, 2 vols (London: Oxford University Press, 1970-75), I: *The Forerunners, 1870-1926* (1970)

Sanderson, M. *The Universities and British Industry, 1850-1970* (London: Routledge and Kegan Paul, 1972)

Saul, S. B. 'Research and Development in British Industry from the end of the Nineteenth Century to the 1960s', in *The Search for Wealth and Stability: Essays in Economic and Social History presented to M. W. Flinn*, edited by T. C. Smout (London: Macmillan, 1979)

William, T. I. *A History of the British Gas Industry* (Oxford: Oxford University Press, 1981)

Wrigley, C. 'The Ministry of Munitions: An Innovatory Department', in *War and the State: The Transformation of British Government 1914-1919*, edited by K. Burk (London: Allen & Unwin, 1982)

Young, P. *Power of Speech: A History of Standard Telephones and Cables, 1883-1983* (London: Allen & Unwin, 1983)

Articles

Coleman, D. C. and C. MacLeod. 'Attitudes to New Techniques: British Businessmen, 1800-1950', *Economic History Review*, 39 (1986), 588-611

Edgerton, D. E. H. 'Science and Technology in British Business History', *Business History*, 29 (1987), 84-103

Edgerton, D. E. H. and S. M. Horrocks. 'British Industrial Research and Development Before 1945', *Economic History Review*, 47 (1994), 213-38

MacLeod, R. M. 'The "Arsenal" in the Strand: Australian Chemists and the British Munitions Effort 1916-1919', *Annals of Science*, 46 (1989), 45-67

Reinharz, J. 'Science in the Service of Politics: The Case of Chaim Weizmann during the First World War', *English Historical Review*, 100 (1985), 573-603

Sanderson, M. 'The English Civic Universities and the "Industrial Spirit", 1870-1914', *Historical Research*, 61 (1988), 90-104

— 'The Professor as Industrial Consultant – Oliver Arnold', *Economic History Review*, 32, (1978), 585-600

Trebilcock, R. C. '"A Special Relationship": Government, Rearmament, and the Cordite Firms', *Economic History Review*, 19 (1966), 364-79

— '"Spin-Off" in British Economic History: Armaments and Industry, 1760-1914', *Economic History Review*, 22 (1969), 474-90

4.6.4 Role of the State

The Government, by promoting science and technology through its sponsoring of new scientific research, creation of the Department of Scientific and Industrial Research (DSIR)[179], and support and coordination of British industry through the Ministry of Munitions, clearly demonstrated that it had come to accept the responsibility of the state to fund science properly and to develop a coherent science policy.

The development of a more positive and constructive attitude to science and technology and the recognition of the value of science and scientists in a modern society did not occur immediately the war began. In the area of science and technology the Government, as was the case in other fields of occupational skill, failed at first to make full use of the expertise available. Initially it did not try to stop scientists being recruited into the forces and made little effort to take advantage of scientific advice even when a body like the Royal Society offered its services. The classic example of the Government's lack of foresight with regard to science in the early stages of the war can be seen in the recruitment and death at Gallipoli of H. G. J. Moseley, one of the most promising physicists of his generation. By 1915, however, the Government, by then acutely aware of the shortage of scientific expertise and personnel and the serious handicap of having placed such heavy reliance in the past on Germany for the supply of scientific products, had begun to address these problems and subsequently made systematic and coherent use of the country's scientific potential.

Scientific and technical education fared less well. There was little practical expansion during the war of the attempts at improvement that had taken place in this area in the late nineteenth century and in the years preceding the war[180]. On the outbreak of war, all such plans were suspended until, with the formation of the Coalition Government in 1916, the state began considering the matter of post-war reconstruction. This resulted in Christopher Addison devising a wide-ranging scheme for education, industrial training and research, the appointment of the Thompson Committee to enquire into the place of science in the educational system, and H. A. L Fisher, an eminent academic, being placed in charge of the Board of Education where he began working on a new Education Act. Not much was achieved by these initiatives. Fisher's Education Act (the most significant feature of which was the concept of the day continuation school to enable school leavers to receive extra education while working full time) was primarily a continuation of pre-war developments. The Thompson Committee's recommendations failed to have much influence until the mid-1920's. However, the part of Addison's scheme covering industrial research was taken up by the DSIR.

Before the war, scientists had experienced decidedly low status with poor pay and few career prospects. The war had the effect of elevating the public perception of science and boosting the status and remuneration of the scientific community. The scientists achieved this enhanced status by willingly placing themselves at the service of the government for war purposes. This was symbolized from the outset of the war when the Royal Society convened a War Committee 'to organize assistance to the Government in conducting or suggesting scientific investigations in relation to the war'. As a result of the recognition of the importance of the contribution that scientists could make to the war effort their status, pay and career prospects and the number of jobs available to them in government and industry had improved significantly by the end of the war.

Autobiographies, Biographies, Diaries

Addison, C. A., Viscount. *Four and a Half Years: A Personal Diary from June 1914 to January 1919*, 2 vols (London:

---

[179] The DSIR – a reorganisation in December 1916 of the Advisory Council for Science which the Government created in August of that year – acted as a clearing house for research problems and a channel for liaison with university laboratories where academic scientists adapted themselves with considerable success to war research, especially at 'red brick' universities such as Birmingham, Bristol, Leeds and Manchester.

[180] In the years before the war schemes to expand the system of secondary and technical education that had been initiated in the 1902 Act began to be considered by the Board of Education.

Hutchinson, 1934)

Ashby, E. and M. Anderson. *Portrait of Haldane at Work on Education* (London: Macmillan, 1974)
Biography of Richard Burdon Haldane, 1st Viscount Haldane, 1856-1928.

Fisher, H. A. L. *An Unfinished Autobiography* (London: Oxford University Press, 1940)
In December 1916 Lloyd George invited Fisher to join his newly formed coalition government as president of the Board of Education.

Matthew, H. C. G. 'Haldane, Richard Burdon, Viscount Haldane (1856–1928)', *Oxford Dictionary of National Biography*, Oxford University Press, 2004; online edn, Jan 2011
[http://www.oxforddnb.com/view/article/33643, accessed 19 Nov 2013]
"Haldane ... chaired the education sub-committee of Asquith's reconstruction committee in 1916, and on 12 July 1916 made in the Lords 'perhaps the greatest education speech in his career", advocating a progressive and co-ordinated approach to educational reform ... Haldane was not offered a post when Lloyd George formed his coalition government in December 1916, but he continued to be active at the fringes of the government, particularly striking up a constructive relationship with H. A. L. Fisher, president of the Board of Education. He advised Fisher during the preparation of the Education Act of 1918 ..." [Quotation extracted from above item in online Oxford DNB]

Sommer, D. *Haldane of Cloan: His Life and Times* (London: Allen & Unwin, 1960)

Books

Alter, P. *The Reluctant Patron: Science and the State in Britain, 1850-1920* (Oxford: Berg, 1987)

Andrews, L. *The Education Act, 1918* (London: Routledge, 1976)

Argles, M. *South Kensington to Robbins: An Account of English Technical and Scientific Education Since 1851* (London: Longmans, 1964)

Austoker, J. and L. Bryder, eds. *Historical Perspectives on the Role of the MRC: Essays in the History of the Medical Research Council of the United Kingdom and its Predecessor, the Medical Research Committee, 1913-1953* (Oxford: Oxford University Press, 1989)

Committee to Enquire into the Position of Natural Science in the Educational System of Great Britain, Cd. 9011 (London: HMSO, 1918)

Cruickshank, A. D. 'Government, Industry and Scientific Research: Twenty years of the Department of Scientific and Industrial Research [DSIR] – 1915-35' (unpublished B.Litt thesis, Wadham College, University of Oxford)

Medical Research Council. *First Annual Report, 1914-1915* (London: HMSO, 1915)

Pattison, M. 'The Munitions Inventions Department: A Case Study in the State Management of Military Science' (unpublished doctoral thesis, Teeside Polytechnic, 1981)

— 'Scientists, Government and Invention', in *Home Fires and Foreign Fields, British Social and Military Experience in the Great War*, ed. by P. H. Liddle (Manchester: Manchester University Press, 1985)

Report of the Privy Council for Scientific and Industrial Research, 1915-16, Cd. 8336 (London: HMSO, 1916)

Scheme for the Organisation and Development of the Department of Scientific and Industrial Research [DSIR] Cd. 8005 (London: HMSO, 1915)

Sherrington, G. *English Education, Social Change and War 1911-20* (Manchester: Manchester University Press, 1981)

Summerfield, P. and E. J. Evans, eds. *Technical Education and the State Since 1850* (Manchester: Manchester University Press, 1990)

Thompson, A. L. *Half A Century of Medical Research*, 2 vols (London: HMSO, 1973-1975)
Contents: Vol.1. *Origins and Policy of the Medical Research Council (UK)*, 1973; Vol.2. *The Programme of the Medical Research Council (UK)*, 1975, later published London: Medical Research Council, 1987.

Varcoe, I. *Organizing for Science In Britain: A Case Study* (London: Oxford University Press, 1974)

Articles

Dean, D. W. 'H. A. L. Fisher, Reconstruction and the Development of the 1918 Education Act', *British Journal of Educational Studies*, 18 (1970), 259-76

Haber, L. F. 'Government Intervention at the Frontiers of Science: British Dyestuff and Synthetic Organic Chemicals, 1914-1939, *Minerva*, 11 (1973), 79-94

Holmes, C. J. 'Science and the Farmer: The Development of the Agricultural and Advisory Service, in England and Wales, 1900-1939', *Agricultural History Review*, 36 (1988), 77-86

Jenkins, E. W. 'The Board of Education and the Reconstruction Committee, 1916-1918', *Journal of Education Administration and History*, 5 (1973), 42-51

— 'The Thompson Committee and Board of Education, 1916-1922,' *British Journal of Educational Studies*, 21 (1973), 76-87

Macleod, R. M. and E. K. Andrews. 'The Origins of the DSIR: Reflections on Ideas and Men, 1914-16', *Public Administration*, 48 (1970), 23-48

MacLeod, R. M. and K. MacLeod. 'The Contradictions of Professionalisation: Scientists, Trade Unionism and the First World War, *Social Studies of Science*, 9 (1979), 1-32

Varcoe, I. 'Scientists, Government and Organized Research: The Early History of the DSIR, 1914-1916', *Minerva*, 8 (1970), 192-217

4.6.5 Medicine

The war acted as a stimulus to medical research and the development of new medical techniques and skills. Advances in x-ray technology, pharmacology, neurosurgery, orthopaedics, prosthetics, psychiatry, blood transfusion, and antisepsis, the invention of plastic surgery, and pioneering research into heart disease among soldiers (a condition known as 'soldier's heart') were a direct response to the need to alleviate the devastating effects of frontline battles and bombardment (shell-shock, mutilation, loss of limbs, bone fractures, septic wounds, gas gangrene) and of exposure to numerous health hazards (trench fever, enteric fever, nephritis, malaria, dysentery and typhus). Physiologists were also involved in helping to devise defensive measures against gas warfare which, ironically, they themselves were also involved in developing. The success of the medical research and advances in the Great War is reflected in the fact that it was the first war where more soldiers died from battle injuries than from disease or infection and where the wounded had a greater chance of surviving than dying as a result of their wounds.

The psychological, neurological, and physiological effects of prolonged combat in a war fought with weapons of destruction of unprecedented power, particularly in relation to incessant bombardment from heavy artillery, was ill understood in the early stages of the war and often discounted as a reason for unfitness to return to the front line or as mitigating factor in relation to a charge of cowardice in the face of the enemy. As the war progressed medical understanding of these effects improved and attitudes towards the mental and physical breakdowns suffered by members of the armed forces became more sympathetic.

The Times History and Encyclopaedia of the War (q.v.) concluded that 'medicine and surgery were reborn on the fields of France and Flanders'. Certainly there was a massive increase in resources and activity in hospital beds, surgery and medical specialisation. A huge number of doctors participated in the war; within the UK half of its 22,000 doctors were mobilised. The war also saw an unprecedented rise in international cooperation and the first emergence of America on the world stage as the leader of medical research. This was the first European war in which the medical services made a real difference in terms of a reduced death toll, and in which their ability to conserve manpower may well have had some impact on the outcome.

Autobiographies, Biographies, Diaries, Letters

Cushing, H. *From a Surgeon's Journal, 1915-18* (London: Constable, 1936)

Deardon, H. *Medicine and Duty: A War Diary* (London: Heinemann, 1928)

Dunn, J. C. *The War the Infantry Knew, 1914-1919* (London: Jane's, 1987; repr. London: Abacus, 1994)
Captain J. C. Dunn was a temporary officer in the RAMC and served as Regimental Officer to the Second Battalion, the Royal Welsh Fusiliers between November 1915 and May 1918.

Herringham, Sir W. M. *A Physician in France* (London: Arnold, 1919)

Martin, A. A. *A Surgeon in Khaki* (London: Arnold, 1915)

Owens, H. *A Doctor on the Western Front; The Diary of Henry Owens*, edited by John Hutton (London: Pen & Sword, 2013)

Rutherford, N. J. C. *Memories of an Army Surgeon* (London: Stanley Paul, 1939)

Slobodin, R. *W. H. R. Rivers: Pioneer Anthropologist, Psychiatrist of "The Ghost Road"*, rev. edn (Stroud: Sutton, 1997)
Originally published: New York: Columbia University Press, 1978. (See also below *The Regeneration Trilogy*, by Pat Barker, a set of novels in which Rivers appears as one of the characters).

Willcox, P. H. A. *The Detective-Physician: The Life and Work of Sir William Willcox* (London: Heinemann Medical, 1970)

Books

Ash, E. *The Problem of Nervous Breakdown* (London: Mills and Boon, 1919)

Austroker, J. and L. Bryder, eds. *Historical Perspectives on the Role of the MRC: Essays in the History of the Medical Research Council of the United Kingdom and its Predecessor, the Medical Research Committee, 1913-1953* (Oxford: Oxford University Press, 1989)

Bamji, A. 'Facial Surgery: The Patient's Experience', in *Facing Armageddon: The First World War Experienced*, ed. by H. Cecil and P. H. Liddle (London, Leo Cooper, 1996)

Barker, P. *The Regeneration Trilogy* (London: Viking 1996)
Contents: *Regeneration, The Eye in the Door, The Ghost Road*, novels which were originally published separately (i.e. *Regeneration*, London: Viking, 1991; *The Eye in the Door*, London: Viking, 1993; *The Ghost Road*, London: Viking, 1995). Dr W. H. R. Rivers FRS (1864-1922), the distinguished neurologist and social anthropologist who served in the First World War as a Captain in the RAMC and treated both Siegfried Sassoon and Wilfred Owen at Craiglockhart War Hospital during that period, appears as a character in this trilogy of novels.

Bergen, L. van. *Before My Helpless Sight: Suffering, Dying and Military Medicine on the Western Front* (Farnham: Ashgate, 2009)
Translation of book originally published in Dutch as: *Zacht en eervol : lijden ensterven in een Grote Oorlog*. Antwerp, 1999.

Bosanquet, N. 'Health Systems in Khaki: The British and American Medical Experience', in *Facing Armageddon: The First World War Experienced*, ed. by H. Cecil and P. H. Liddle (London, Leo Cooper, 1996)

Bourke, J. *Dismembering the Male: Men's Bodies, Britain, and the Great War* (London: Reaktion Books, 1996)

—— 'The Experience of Medicine in Wartime', in *Medicine in the Twentieth Century*, edited by Roger Cooter and John Pickstone (Abingdon: Marston, 2000)

Brock, C. *British Women Surgeons and Their Patients, 1860–1918* (Cambridge: Cambridge University Press, 2017)

Brown, E. D. 'Between Cowardice and Insanity: Shell Shock and the Legitimation of the Neuroses in Great Britain' in *Science, Technology and the Military*, edited by E. Mendelsohn [and others] (Boston: Kluwer Academic Publishers, 1989)

Bryder, L. 'Public Health Research and the MRC', in *Historical Perspectives on the Role of the MRC. Essays in the History of the Medical Research Council of the United Kingdom and its Predecessor, the Medical Research Committee, 1913-1953*, edited by J. Austoker and L. Bryder (Oxford: Oxford University Press, 1989)

Buckley, S. 'The Failure To Resolve the Problem of Venereal Disease Among The Troops in Britain during World War One', in *War and Society*, edited by B. Bond and I. Roy, vol 2 (London: Croom Helm, 1977)

Cantor, D. and E. Ramsden, eds. *Stress, Shock, and Adaptation in the Twentieth Century* (Suffolk: Boydell & Brewer 2014)

Carden-Coyne, A. *The Politics of Wounds: Military Patients and Medical Power in the First World War* (Oxford: Oxford University Press 2014)

Cohen, D. 'The War Come Home: Disabled Veterans in Great Britain and Germany' (unpublished doctoral thesis, University of California, Berkeley, 1996)

Cooter, R. 'Malingering in Modernity: Psychological Scripts and Adversarial Encounters during the First World War', in *War, Medicine and Modernity*, edited by R. Cooter, M. Harrison and S. Sturdy (Stroud: Sutton, 1998; repr. 1999)

— 'War and Modern Medicine', in *Companion Encyclopaedia of the History of Medicine*, edited by W. F. Bynum and Roy Porter, 2 vols (London: Routledge, 1993)

Cooter, R., and others, eds. *War, Medicine and Modernity* (Stroud: Sutton, 1998; repr. 1999)

Fenton, N. *Shell Shock and its Aftermath* (London: Henry Kimpton, 1926)

Great Britain. War Office. Committee on "Shell-Shock." *Report of the War Office Committee of Enquiry into "Shell-Shock" (Cmd. 1734)*, featuring a new historical essay on shell shock by Anthony Richards (London: Imperial War Museum, 2004)
Report originally published London: HMSO, 1922.

Hall, L. '"War always brings it on": War, STDs, the Military and the Civilian Population in Britain, 1850–1950', in *Medicine and Modern Warfare*, edited by Roger Cooter, Mark Harrison and Steve Sturdy (Amsterdam; Atlanta, GA: Rodopi, 1999)

Hallett, C. E. *Containing Trauma: Nursing Work in the First World War* (Manchester: Manchester University Press, 2009)

Harrison, M. 'The Fight Against Disease in the Mesopotamia Campaign', in *Facing Armageddon: The First World War Experienced*, ed. by H. Cecil and P. H. Liddle (London, Leo Cooper, 1996)

— *The Medical War: British Military Medicine in the First World* (Oxford: Oxford University Press, 2010)

Herrick, C. 'Of War and Wounds: The Propaganda, Politics and Experience of Medicine in World War I' (Unpublished doctoral thesis, University of Manchester, 1996)

Howell, J. D. '"Soldier's Heart": The Redefinition of Heart Disease and Speciality Formation in Early Twentieth Century Great Britain', in *War, Medicine and Modernity*, edited by R. Cooter, M. Harrison and S. Sturdy (Stroud: Sutton, 1998; repr. 1999)

Hutchinson, W. *The Doctor in War* (London: Cassell, 1919)

Leese, P. *Shell Shock: Traumatic Neurosis and the British Soldiers of the First World War* (Basingstoke: Palgrave Macmillan, 2002)

— 'A Social and Cultural History of Shellshock, with particular reference to the Experience of British Soldiers during and after the Great War' (unpublished doctoral thesis, Open University, 1989)

Linden, S. *They Called it Shell Shock: Combat Stress in the First World War* (Solihull: Helion, 2017)

Lovegrove, P. *Not Least in the Crusade: A Short History of the Royal Army Medical Corps* (Aldershot: Gale & Polden, 1951)

Lynch, P. J. 'The Exploitation of Courage: Psychiatric Care in the British Army, 1914-1918' (unpublished master's thesis, University College, London, 1977)

McGann, S., and others. *A Voice for Nurses: A History of the Royal College of Nursing, 1916-90*, by Susan McGann, Anne Crowther, Rona Dougall (Manchester: Manchester University Press, 2009)

Macpherson, Sir W. G. *Medical Services: General History*, 4 vols (London: HMSO 1921-1924)
Contents: Vol. 1. Medical services in the United Kingdom; in British garrisons overseas; and during operations against Tsingtau, in Togoland, the Cameroons, and South-West Africa; Vol. 2. The medical services on the Western Front, and during the operations in France and Belgium in 1914 and 1915; Vol. 3. Medical services during the operations on the Western Front in 1916, 1917 and 1918; in Italy; and in Egypt and Palestine; Vol. 4 (by Sir W.G. Macpherson and T. J. Mitchell). Medical services during the operations on the Gallipoli Peninsula; in Macedonia; in Mesopotamia and north-west Persia; in East Africa; in the Aden Protectorate, and in North Russia. Ambulance transport during the war. [In the series *History of the Great War Based on Official Documents* by direction of the Historical Section of the Committee of Imperial Defence].

Macpherson, Sir W. G., and others, ed. *Medical Services: Diseases of the War*, 2 vols (London: HMSO, 1922-23)
In the series *History of the Great War Based on Official Documents* by direction of the Historical Section of the Committee of Imperial Defence.

— *Medical Services: Hygiene of the War*, 2 vols (London: H.M.S.O., 1923)
In the series *History of the Great War Based on Official Documents* by direction of the Historical Section of the Committee of Imperial Defence.

Mayhew, E. *Wounded: A New History of the Western Front in World War I* (Oxford: Oxford University Press 2013)

Medical Research Council. *First Annual Report, 1914-1915* (London: HMSO, 1915)

Merskey, H. 'Shell Shock', in *150 Years of British Psychiatry, 1841-1991'*, edited by G. E. Berrios and H. Freeman, 2 vols (London: Gaskell : Athlone, 1991)
Volume 2 (1991) published by Athlone and reprinted by this publisher in 1996.

Mitchell, T. J. and G. M. Smith. *Medical Services: Casualties and Medical Statistics of the Great War* (London: HMSO, 1931)
In the series *History of the Great War Based on Official Documents* by direction of the Historical Section of the Committee of Imperial Defence.

Mott, F. W. *War Neuroses and Shell Shock* (London: Hodder & Stoughton, 1919)

Noon, G. 'The Treatment of Casualties in the Great War', in *British Fighting Methods in the Great War*, edited by P. Griffith (London: Cass, 1996)

Reid, F. *Broken Men: Shell Shock, Treatment and Recovery in Britain, 1914-1930* (London, Continuum, 2010)

Rivers, W. H. R. *Conflict and Dream* (London: Kegan Paul, 1923; repr. London: Routledge, 1999)

Shephard, B. *A War of Nerves: Soldiers and Psychiatrists 1914-1994*, (London: Cape, 2000; repr. London: Pimlico, 2002)

Showalter, E. *The Female Malady: Women, Madness, and Culture in England, 1830-1980* (London : Virago, 1987)

— 'Rivers and Sassoon: The Inscription of Male Gender Anxieties' in *Behind The Lines: Gender and the Two World Wars*, edited by M. R. Higonnet [and others] (New Haven: Yale University Press, 1987)

Simpson, K. 'Dr James Dunn and Shell-Shock', in *Facing Armageddon: The First World War Experienced*, ed. by H. Cecil and P. H. Liddle (London: Cooper, 1996)

Stone, M. 'Shell Shock and the Psychologists', in *The Anatomy of Madness: Essays in the History of Psychiatry*, edited by W. T. Bynum, R. Porter and M. Shepherd, 3 vols (London: Tavistock Publications, 1985; repr. London; Routledge, 2004), II: *Institutions and Society* (2004)

Sturdy, S. 'War as Experiment: Physiology, Innovation and Administration in Britain, 1914-1918: The Case of Chemical Warfare', in *War, Medicine and Modernity*, edited by R. Cooter, M. Harrison and S. Sturdy (Stroud: Sutton, 1998; repr. 1999)

Thompson, A. L. *Half a Century of Medical Research*, 2 vols (London: HMSO, 1973-1975)
Contents: Vol.1. *Origins and Policy of the Medical Research Council (UK)*, 1973; Vol.2. *The Programme of the Medical Research Council (UK)*, 1975, later published London: Medical Research Council, 1987.

Thomson, M. 'Status, Manpower and Mental Fitness: Mental Deficiency in the First World War', in *War, Medicine and Modernity*, edited by R. Cooter, M. Harrison and S. Sturdy (Stroud: Sutton, 1998; repr. 1999)

Times History and Encyclopaedia of the War, 22 vols (London: The Times., 1914-1921), IV, Chapter LXVI: Medical Work in the Field and at Home (1915); XIV, Chapter CCXVIII: The Army Medical Services and the New Medicine (1918)

Whitehead, I. R. *Doctors in the Great War* (London: L. Cooper, 1999)

— 'Medical Officers and the British Army During the First World War' (unpublished doctoral thesis, University of Leeds, 1993)

— 'Not a Doctor's Work?: The Role of the British Regimental Medical Officers in the Field', in *Facing Armageddon: The First World War Experienced*, ed. by H. Cecil and P. H. Liddle (London: Cooper, 1996)

— 'Third Ypres - Casualties and British Medical Services: An Evaluation', in *Passchendaele in Perspective: The Third Battle of Ypres*, edited by P. H. Liddle (London: Lee Cooper, 1997)

Yealland, L. R. *Hysterical Disorders of Warfare* (London : Macmillan, 1918)

Articles

Barger, A. C., and others. 'Walter B. Cannon and the Mystery of Shock: A Study of Anglo-American Co-operation in World War I', *Medical History*, 35 (1991), 217–49

Beardsley, E. H., 'Allied Against Sin: American and British Responses to Venereal Disease in World War I', *Medical History*, 20 (1976), 189–202

Bennett, J. D. C. 'Medical Advances Consequent to the Great War, 1914-18', *Journal of the Royal Society of Medicine*, 83 (1990), 738-42

Birley, J. 'A Lecture on the Psychology of Courage', *Lancet*, 21 (1923)

Bogacz, T. 'War Neuroses and Cultural Change in England, 1914-22: The Work of the War Office Committee of Enquiry into "Shell Shock"', *Journal of Contemporary History*, 24 (1989), 227-56

Bourke, J. 'Effeminacy, Ethnicity and the End of Trauma: The Sufferings of "Shell-Shocked" Men in Great

Britain and Ireland, 1914-39', *Journal of Contemporary History*, 35.1, Special Issue: Shell-Shock (2000), 57-69

— 'The Emotions in War: Fear and the British and American military, 1914-45', *Historical Research* (Oxford), 74 (2001), 314-330

Brosnan, M. 'Saving Lives: Frontline Medicine in a Century of Conflict', *Despatches* (The Magazine of the Friends of the Imperial War Museum), No. 15 (2012), 12-16
The author provides an insight into an exhibition which explores war and medicine from the First World War to the conflict in Afghanistan. This exhibition was mounted at IWM North in March 2012 and ran until 1 September 2013.

Bryder, L. 'The First World War: Healthy or Hungry?,' *History Workshop Journal*, 24 (1987), 141–57

Burton-Fanning, F. W. 'Neurasthenia in Soldiers of the Home Forces', *Lancet*, (1917)

Cooter, R. 'Medicine and the Goodness of War', *Canadian Bulletin of Medical History*, 12 (1990), 147–59

Dean, E. 'War and Psychiatry', *History of Psychiatry*, 4 (1993), 61-82

Feudtner, C. 'Minds the Dead have Ravished: Shell Shock, History, and the Ecology of Disease-Systems', *History of Science*, 31(1993), 377-420

Haller, J. S. 'Treatment of Infected Wounds during the Great War, 1914-1918, *Southern Medical Journal*, 85 (1992), 305-13

Harrison, M. 'The British Army and the Problem of Venereal Disease in France and Egypt during the First World War', *Medical History*, 39 (1995) 133-58

—'Medicine and the Culture of Command: The Case of Malaria Control in the British Army during the Two World Wars', *Medical History*, 40 (1996), 437–52

— 'Medicine and the Management of Modern Warfare', *History of Science*, 34 (1996), 379-410

'Incidence of Mental Disease Directly Due to War', *The Lancet* (23 October 1915)

Hartley, P. 'Change Me: Facial Injuries in the First World War', *History Today*, 58, Issue 3 (2008), 70-71

Humphries, M. O. and K. Kurchinski. 'Rest, Relax and Get Well: A Re-Conceptualisation of Great War Shell Shock Treatment', *War and Society* (Duntroon Australia), 27, Issue 2 (2008), 89-110

Koven, S. 'Remembering and Dismemberment: Crippled Children, Wounded Soldiers, and the Great War in Great Britain', *American Historical Review*, 99 (1994), 1167–1202

Macmillan, A. '1917: Queries Regarding The Royal Army Medical Corps and its Predecessors', *Journal of the Society for Army Historical Research*, 90, NUMB 362 (2012), 125

Reid, F. Distinguishing between Shell-shocked Veterans and Pauper Lunatics: The Ex-Services' Welfare Society and Mentally Wounded Veterans after the Great War', *War in History*, 14 (2007), 347-371

Rivers, W. H. R. 'The Representation of War Experience', *Lancet* (2 February 1918)

Simpson, D. 'Brain Wounds in the First World War: Lessons from the Steel Thunderstorms', *War and Society* (Duntroon Australia) 23 (2005), 53-58

Simpson, K. 'Dr. Dunn and Battle Stress: The Experiences of a Regimental Medical Officer of 2nd Royal Welch Fusiliers, 1915-18', *The Great War*, 3 (1991), 76-86

Sturdy, S. and R. Cooter. 'Science, Scientific Management, and the Transformation of Medicine in Britain c. 1870-1950', *History of Science*, 36, (1998), 114

Talbott, J. E. 'Soldiers, Psychiatrists, and Combat Trauma', *Journal of Interdisciplinary History*, 27 (1997), 437-454

Tomkins, S. M. 'Palminate or Permanganate: The Venereal Prophylaxis Debate in Britain, 1916-1926', *Medical History*, 37 (1993), 382–98

Towers, B. 'Health Education Policy 1916–1926: Venereal Disease and the Prophylaxis Dilemma', *Medical History*, 24 (1980), 70–87

'War Shock in the Civilian', *The Lancet* (4 March 1916)

Wiltshire, H. 'A Contribution to the Etiology of Shell Shock', *The Lancet* (17 June 1916)

Winter, J. 'Military Fitness and Civilian Health in Britain during the First World War', *Journal of Contemporary History*, 15 (1980), 211-44

5. Legacies

5.1 General

Interpretations of the impact of the war on Britain has inspired a wide-ranging debate among many writers. Some of the more general works which have been engaged in this debate or have touched on it are listed below. Works in relation to such specific topics as the effects of the war on the involvement of the state, on the economy, on social structure, on the political landscape, and on the status of women will be found **in Part 3, sections 5.2, 5.3, 5.4, and 5.5**

Books

Aubin, D. and C. Goldstein, eds. *The War of Guns and Mathematics: Mathematical Practices and Communities in France and its Western Allies around World War I* (Providence, Rhode Island: American Mathematical Society, 2014)

Barham. P. *Forgotten Lunatics of the Great War* (New Haven: Yale University Press, 2004)
A history of the thousands of rank-and-file servicemen who were psychiatric casualties, and put into lunatic asylums.

Beckett, I. F. W. *The Making of the First World War* (New Haven, Conn.; London: Yale University Press 2012)
This global perspective of the Great War provides a revision and expansion of our perception of the legacy of the war.

Carnegie Endowment for International Peace. *Economic and Social History of the Great War*, British Series, 24 vols (Oxford: University Press, 1919-34)

Cabanes, B. *The Great War and the Origins of Humanitarianism, 1918-1924* (Cambridge: Cambridge University Press, 2013)

Carnevali, F. and J-M. Strange, eds. *Twentieth-Century Britain: Economic, Cultural and Social Change*, 2nd edn (Harlow: Pearson Longman, 2007)
Rev. edn of: *Twentieth-Century Britain: Economic, Cultural and Social Change*, edited by Paul Johnson. London: Longman, 1994.

Cohen, D. The War Come Home: Disabled Veterans in Britain and Germany, 1914-1939 (Berkeley: University of California Press, 2001)

Cohrs, P. O. *The Unfinished Peace after World War I: America, Britain, and the Stabilisation of Europe, 1919-1932* (Cambridge: Cambridge University Press, 2006)

Crouthamel, J. and P. Leese, eds. *Psychological Trauma and the Legacies of the First World War* (Switzerland: Palgrave Macmillan, 2017)

Feltman, B. K. *The Stigma of Surrender: German Prisoners, British Captors, and Manhood in the Great War and Beyond*

(Chapel Hill: University of North Carolina Press, 2015)

Grayzel, S. R. '"A promise of Terror to Come": Air Power and the Destruction of Cties in British Imagination and Experience, 1908-39', in *Cities into Battlefields: Metropolitan Scenarios, Experiences and Commemorations of Total War*, edited by S. Goebel, and D. Keene (Farnham: Ashgate, 2011)

Grogan, S. *Shell Shocked Britain: The First World War's Legacy for Britain's Mental Health* (London: Pen & Sword, 2014)

Hendley, M. C. *Organized Patriotism and the Crucible of War: Popular Imperialism in Britain, 1914-1932* (Montréal, Québec: McGill-Queen's University Press, 2012)
In this book's comparison of how three major patriotic organizations founded between 1901 and 1902 (the National Service League, the League of the Empire, and the Victoria League) fared during the war the author shows that the National Service League, with its strongly masculinist and militaristic character, failed to flourish in wartime whereas the League of the Empire and the Victoria League, strongly female in their membership and with aims and concepts related to education and hospitality, family, home and kinship, prospered not only during the war but beyond into the 1920's. The author sees this as an indication of how the traumatic nature of the Great War produced a fundamental reshaping of popular patriotism and imperialism that is evident to the author in his comparison of the post-war histories of the above organizations. This book affords an insight into women's roles in Britain during the height of popular imperialism.

Hirst, F. W. *The Consequences of the War to Great Britain* (London: Oxford University Press, 1934; repr. New York: Greenwood Press, 1968)

Holman, B. *The Next War in the Air: Britain's Fear of the Bomber, 1908-1941* (Farnham: Ashgate Publishing Limited 2014)

Hynes, S. *A War Imagined: The First World War and English Culture* (London: Bodley Head, 1990; repr. London: imlico, 1992)

Jalland, P. *Death in War and Peace: A History of Loss and Grief in England, 1914-1970* (Oxford: Oxford University Press, 2010)

Johnson, P., ed. *Twentieth-Century Britain: Economic, Cultural and Social Change* (London: Longman, 1994)

Kent, S. K. *Aftershocks: Politics and Trauma in Britain, 1918-1931* (Basingstoke: Palgrave Macmillan, 2008)

Kettenacker, L. and T. Riotte, eds. *The Legacies of Two World Wars: European Societies in the Twentieth Century* (New York: Berghahn Books, 2011)

Keynes, J. M. *The Economic Consequences of the Peace, The Collected Writings of John Maynard Keynes*, vol 2 (London: Macmillan; St. Martin's Press, for the Royal Economic Society, 1971)

Lawrence, J. 'The First World War and its Aftermath', in *Twentieth-Century Britain: Economic, Cultural and Social Change*, edited by Paul Johnson (London: Longman, 1994)

Lentin, A. *General Smuts, South Africa: The Peace Conferences of 1919-23 and their Aftermath* (London: Haus Publishing 2010)

Marwick, A. *The Deluge: British Society and the First World War*, 2nd edn (Basingstoke: Macmillan Education, 1991)

— *The Explosion of British Society, 1914-1962* (London: Pan, 1963)

— *Britain in the Century of Total War: War, Peace and Social Change* (London: Bodley Head, 1968)

Marwick, A. ed. *Total War and Social Change* (Basingstoke: Macmillan, 1988)

Middlemass, K. *Politics in Industrial Society: The Experience of the British System since 1911* (London: Deutsch, 1980)

Milward, A. S. *The Economic Effects of the two World Wars upon Britain* (London: Macmillan, 1970)

Mulligan, W. *The Great War for Peace* (New Haven, CT: Yale University Press, 2014)
In this book the author refutes the view that the Great War and its immediate aftermath had a disastrous effect on the rest of the 20th century and takes the unconventional line that the first two decades of the century - and the Great War in particular - played an important role in assisting the development of a peaceful new order on a global scale.

Nicolson, J. *The Great Silence: 1918-1920: Living in the Shadow of the Great War* (London: John Murray, 2009)
The author provides her view of British society in the changed world with which it was faced in the immediate aftermath of the Great War.

Pedersen, S. *The Guardians: The League of Nations and the Crisis of Empire* (Oxford: Oxford University Press, 2015)

Pope. R. *War and Society in Britain, 1899-1948* (London: Longman, 1991)

Reynolds, D. *The Long Shadow: The Great War and the Twentieth Century* (London: Simon & Schuster, 2013

Seldon, A. and D. Walsh. *Public Schools and the Great War: The Generation Lost* (Barnsley: Pen & Sword Military 2013)

Sharp, A., ed. *Consequences of the Peace, The Versailles Settlement: Aftermath and Legacy 1919-2010* (London: Haus, 2015)

Titmus, R. M. *Essays on 'The Welfare State'* (London: Allen & Unwin,1958)

Turner, J., ed. *Britain and the First World War* (London; Unwin Hyman, 1988)

Wall, R. and J. M. Winter, eds. *The Upheaval of War: Family, Work and Welfare in Europe, 1914-18* (Cambridge: Cambridge University Press, 1988; repr. 2005)

Whittle, E. Y. 'British casualties on the Western Front 1914-1918 and their influence on the military conduct of the Second World War' (unpublished doctoral thesis, University of Leicester, 1991)
In this thesis Whittle argues against the assertion which is often made that the memory of British army casualties in the Great War influenced the way the army fought in the Second World War.

Winter, J. M., ed. *The Legacy of the Great War: Ninety Years On* (Columbia: Kansas City, Mo.: University of Missouri Press; National World War I Museum, 2009)

Articles

Biernoff, S. and J. Tynan. 'Making and Remaking the Civilian Soldier: The World War I Photographs of Horace Nicholls', *Journal of War and Culture Studies*, 5 (2012), 277-293
In this article it is argued that Horace Nicholls' photographs of wartime army recruitment and post-war facial reconstruction represent a response to the brief from Wellington House to record the war effort on the home front that is colured by his artistic aspirations and his love of a good story (seeming to result in an uneasy combination lying between photojournalism, propaganda and record keeping.

Cox, M. E. 'Hunger Games, or How the Allied Blockade in the First World War Deprived German Children of Nutrition, and Allied Food Aid Subsequently Saved Them', *Economic History Review*, 68 (2015) 600-631

Davis, B. 'Experience, Identity, and Memory: The Legacy of World War I', *Journal of Modern History*, 75 (2003), 111-131
Review article

Feu, J. du 'Factors Influencing Rehabilitation of British Soldiers After World War I', *Historia Medicinae*, 2, Issue 1, E10 (21 December 2009)
"World War I led to large numbers of formerly healthy young men returning to Britain with various disabilities, ranging from 'shell-shock' to paraplegia. This article explains the factors that affected the rehabilitation of these men. Areas to be mentioned include: aspects of treatment, state and charity provision for the war wounded, functional restoration, pension allocation, training and employment. The impact each of these factors had on rehabilitation of the war wounded will be discussed". [Abstract]

Grayzel, S. R. 'Defence Against the Indefensible: The Gas Mask, the State and British Culture during and after the First World War', *Twentieth Century British History*, 25 (2014), 418-434

Janes, D. 'Eminent Victorians, Bloomsbury Queerness and John Maynard Keynes' The Economic Consequences of the Peace (1919)', *Literature and History*, 23 (2014), 19-32

Mantin, M. 'Coalmining and the National Scheme for Disabled Ex-Servicemen after the First World War', *Social History*, 41:2 (2016), 155-170

Markham, B. 'The Challenge to 'Informal' Empire: Argentina, Chile and British Policy-Makers in the Immediate Aftermath of the First World War', *Journal of Imperial and Commonwealth History*, 45 (2017), 449-474

Marwick, A. 'The Impact of the First World War on British Society', *Journal of Contemporary History*, 3 (1968), 51-63

Pugh, M. 'A Nationalism Born of the Great War', *History Today*, 64, Issue 7 (2014), 6-7
This article relates to the impact of the war on Scottish society.

Rubery, M. 'From Shell Shock to Shellac: The Great War, Blindness, and Britain's Talking Book Library, *Twentieth Century British History*, 26:1 (2015), 1-25

Stuart, J. T. 'The Question of Human Progress in Britain after the Great War,' *British Scholar*, 1 (2008), 53-78

Wild, J. '"A Merciful, Heaven-Sent Release"?: The Clerk and The First World War in British Literary Culture', *Cultural And Social History*, 4 (2007), 73-94
An exploration of the experience of the Great War by the large number of British office workers who enlisted in the armed forces and the effect which, it is argued, this had on shaping a more democratic postwar society as was evidenced by the figure of the fictional clerk that emerges in British literature after 1918.

Witt, S. 'International Mind Alcoves: The Carnegie Endowment for International Peace, Libraries, and the Struggle for Global Public Opinion, 1917–54', *Library & Information History*, 30 (2014), 273-290

5.2 Social Conditions, Social Structure

During the course of the war the British class structure (to the limited extent to which it is possible to define it in terms of upper, middle and lower classes) underwent some modifications. In 1914 the upper class consisted of a landed élite and those who had become wealthy in the business and commercial world, with the former group possessing the dominant political influence; by the end of the war the balance that this represented had shifted from the landed to the business group. This was not simply because many of the old landed élite had been badly hit by wartime taxation and the losses of their sons and relatives[181] on the battlefield but because the wealthiest and most astute among them had, like members of the upper class who were already well-off in the commercial and financial world, seen the opportunities for moving into the area of business growth and investment that the war offered and been successful in grasping them. Within the middle class the war produced an increase in their numbers resulting from an expansion of the professions, the civil service (civil servants and clerical administrators), the managerial groups, and the employment of women. The working class emerged from the war with a rise in its overall standard of living and with an influence and stature enhanced by its contributions through military service and munitions work.

Members of all classes drew together patriotically in the common cause of supporting the nation in the crisis of war but this did not result in a significant change in class attitudes in spite of the exposure of the nation to such wartime slogans of class solidarity as 'equality of sacrifice', 'the comradeship of the trenches' and 'all classes

---

[181] In a comparison of the huge losses of life among the different classes involved in military operations, officers (particularly from the junior officers recruited from the universities, public schools, and from the upper and middle classes generally) suffered proportionately more dead than other ranks in relation to the numbers who served in each of these two broad categories. These figures provide a sort of statistical justification for the post-war notion of a 'lost generation' as applied to the losses of 'elites', of whom the members of the landed aristocracy constituted a considerable proportion.

standing together'. Grumbles among working-class people about such matters as the high prices and shortages of food could elicit an unsympathetic response from the upper classes who could also be quite ready to attribute war production problems to the slackness or drunkenness of factory workers. Feelings of dissatisfactions sometimes occurred among working-class people about such matters as the disproportionate share of the burden of war they thought they were shouldering in comparison with that of their social superiors, and the large sums of money some businessmen were making out of the war. Some members of the middle class, unhappy with the unaccustomed hardship they were suffering in the war, became inclined to compare their lot with the benefits that capitalist 'profiteers' and trade unionist workers seemed to be enjoying. Some contemporary writers, often for propaganda purposes, liked to recount stories of women of all classes mixing on the workshop floor as an example of the disappearance of social barriers between them[182]. This was not really the case. Most of the women working on the workshop floor were working-class and, to the limited extent that upper or middle class women were involved in factories, their job was most likely to be supervisory. There was a similar differentiation of role in the trenches where officers were primarily drawn from the upper classes, although this situation had changed by the end of the war as a result of the necessity of replacing the huge numbers of them who were killed with soldiers promoted from the other ranks. It is because of the latter dilution of the traditional officer-class together with the bond that developed between men of all classes exposed to the shared horrors of trench warfare that the rigid class-bound structure of the Army was perhaps less pronounced by the end of the war. Generally, however, Britain emerged from the war as class conscious as ever.

Many of the hopes arising during the war for major post-war social, economic and political change were not realized in the aftermath of the war. The majority of the women who had taken the opportunity to engage in wartime employment soon left it, and, though some of them had been granted the right to vote, many of the traditional gender inequalities continued to exist. In industry pre-war practices were restored once the war had ended, thwarting hopes that the development of wartime cooperation between the government, employers and trade unions would continue. For all the discussion of post-war reconstruction which took place during the war and the expectations to which it gave rise, everyday life for many in the early 1920's, although not, of course, for the bereaved and the disabled, would not have seemed so very different from what it was like just before the war. Nevertheless some aspects of life had changed. The rise in the overall standard of living of the working class during the war had, in the opinion of some contemporary commentators, given it greater self-confidence and a less deferential attitude. The keeping of servants in middle-class households declined during the war and was steadily becoming less of a feature of the middle class. The war had perhaps generated greater openness about sexual matters and there were signs of a lessening of the restraints on women's lives. For a number of reasons, of which the undue fervour and bigotry displayed by some clerics during the war can be counted as one, the Church and religion had lost some of its power and influence. In general, British society seemed to be less inhibited and to be emerging from its Victorian and Edwardian shackles.

The works in this section facilitate an assessment of the impacts of the war on the various classes, focusing on such specific areas as employment, wages, occupations and consumers' expenditure and the broader areas of wealth and poverty in British society.

Books

Abrams, M. *The Condition of the English People, 1911-1945*, a study prepared for the Fabian Society (London: Gollancz, 1945)

Bensusan, S. L. *Latter Day Rural England* (London: Ernest Benn, 1928)

Bowley, Sir A. L. *The Change in the Distribution of the National Income, 1880-1913* (Oxford: Clarendon Press, 1920)

— *The Nature and Purpose of the Measurement of Social Phenomena*, 2nd edn (London: P. S. King & Son, 1915)

— *The Division of the Product of Industry: An Analysis of National Income before the War* (Oxford: Clarendon Press, 1919)

---

[182] L. K. Yates, for instance, wrote in his book, *The Woman's Part: A Record of Munitions Work* (1918) that: 'Even in the early days of the advent of women in the munition shops, I have seen working together, side by side, the daughter of an Earl, a shop keeper's widow, a graduate from Girton, a domestic servant, and a young woman from a lonely farm in Rhodesia, whose husband had joined the colours. Social status, so stiff a barrier in this country in pre-war days, was forgotten in the factory, as in the trenches, and they were all working together as happily as the members of a united family'.

— *Some Economic Consequences of the Great War* (London: 1930)

— *Three Studies on the National Income*: Being *The Division of the Product of Industry*, by A. L. Bowley; *The Change in the Distribution of the National Income 1880-1913*, by A. L. Bowley; *The National Income, 1924*, by A. L. Bowley and Sir Josiah Stamp (London: London School of Economics, 1938)
This work is a reprint of *The Division of the Product of Industry: An Analysis of National Income before the War*, by A. L. Bowley, Oxford: Clarendon Press, 1919; *The Change in the Distribution of the National Income, 1880-1913* by A. L. Bowley, Oxford: Clarendon Press, 1920; and *The National Income, 1924: A Comparative Study of the Income of the United Kingdom in 1911 and 1924*, by A. L. Bowley and Sir J. Stamp published Oxford: Clarendon Press, 1927.

Bowley, Sir A. L. and A. R. Burnett-Hurst. *Livelihood and Poverty: A Study in the Economic Conditions of Working-Class Households in Northampton, Warrington, Stanley and Reading* (London: G. Bell, 1915; repr. London: Routledge/Thoemmes, 1997)

Bowley, Sir A. L. and M. Hogg. *Has Poverty Diminished?*, a sequel to *Livelihood and Poverty* [by A. L. Bowley and A. R. Burnett-Hurst] (London: P. S. King & Son, 1925; repr. New York: Garland, 1985)

Bowley, Sir A. L. and Sir J. Stamp. *The National Income, 1924: A Comparative Study of the Income of the United Kingdom in 1911 and 1924* (Oxford: Clarendon Press, 1927)

Cannandine, D. *The Decline and Fall of the British Aristocracy* (New Haven: Yale University Press, 1990)

Carr-Saunders, A. M. and D. C. Jones. *A Survey of the Social Structure of England and Wales* (London: Oxford University Press, 1927)
The third edition of this work (Oxford: Clarendon Press, 1958) was published under the title *A Survey of Social Conditions in England and Wales*.

Cole, G. *Trade Unionism and Munitions* (Oxford: Clarendon Press, 1923)

Dewey, P. E. 'Nutrition and Living Standards in Wartime Britain', in *The Upheaval of War: Work and Welfare in Europe, 1914-1918*, edited by R. Wall and J. Winter (Cambridge: Cambridge University Press, 1988)

Feinstein, C. H. 'Changes in the Distribution of the National Income in the United Kingdom since 1860', in *The Distribution of National Income*, edited by J. Marchal and B. Ducros (London: Macmillan, 1968)

Gibbs, P. *More that Must be Told* (London: Harper, 1921)
Has a chapter, 'The Social Revolution in English Life'.

Gleason, A. *What the Workers Want: A Study of British Labor* (New York: Harcourt, Brace and Howe, 1920; repr. New York: Garland, 1985)
Published in the series, *English Workers and the Coming of the Welfare State, 1918-1945*.

Guttsman, W. L. *The British Political Elite* (London: Macgibbon & Kee, 1963; repr. 1968)

Guttsman, W. L., ed. *The English Ruling Class*, edited and introduced by W. L. Guttsman (London: Weidenfeld & Nicolson, 1969)

Halsey, A. H. and J. Webb, ed. *Twentieth-Century British Social Trends*, edited by A. H. Halsey with Josephine Webb (Basingstoke: Macmillan, 2000)
Rev. (i.e. 3rd) edn. of *Trends in British Society Since 1900: A Guide to the Changing Social Structure of Britain*, published London: Macmillan, 1972.

Hatton, T. J. 'Unemployment and the Labour Market, 1870-1939', in *The Cambridge Economic History of Modern Britain*, edited by R. Floud and P. Johnson, 3 vols (Cambridge: Cambridge University Press, 2004), II: *Economic Maturity, 1860-1939* (2004)

Hobsbawm, E. J. *Labouring Men: Studies in the History of Labour* (London: Weidenfeld and Nicolson, 1964; repr. 1974)

— 'The Making of the Working Class', in *Worlds of Labour: Further Studies in the History of Labour*, by E. J. Hobsbawm (London: Weidenfeld and Nicolson, 1984)

Hutt, A. *The Post-War History of the British Working Class* (London: Gollancz, 1937)

Johnson, P. *Saving and Spending: The Working-Class Economy in Britain, 1870-1939* (Oxford: Clarendon Press, 1985)

Jones, D. C. *Social Survey of Merseyside*, 3 vols. (Liverpool: Liverpool University Press, 1934)

Jones, H. *Health and Society in Twentieth Century Britain* (London: Longman, 1994)
The book has the following chapters: 1. Introduction: a Picture of health; 2. The Race for health: Edwardian Britain; 3. Fighting fit? 1914-1918; 4. Poverty and the public health: the inter-war years; 5. The people's health: 1939-45; 6. Hidden from view: 1945-68; 7. Open sores: the late 1960's to early 1990's; 8. Inequalities in health experience: the debate.

Kimball, C. C. 'The Ex-Service Movement in England and Wales, 1916–1930' (unpublished doctoral thesis, Stanford University, 1990)

Lee, J. M. *Social Leaders and Public Persons: A Study of County Government in Cheshire since 1888* (Oxford: Clarendon Press, 1963)

Marsh, D. C. *Changing Social Structure of England and Wales, 1871-1961*, revised edn (London: Routledge and Kegan Paul, 1965; repr. 1998)
Rev. edn. of *The Changing Social Structure of England and Wales, 1871-1951*. London : Routledge, 1958

Masterman, C. F. G. *England after War: A Study* (London: Hodder & Stoughton, 1923)

— *The Condition of England* (London: Methuen, 1909)
A reset edition was published by Methuen in 1960.

Mitchison, R. *British Population Change since 1860* (London: Macmillan, 1977)

Money, Sir L. G. C. *Riches and Poverty*, rev. and enl. edn (London: Methuen, 1913)
Originally published by Methuen in 1905.

Peel, D. C. ["Mrs. C. S. Peel"]. *How We Lived Then: A Sketch of Social and Domestic Life in England during the War* (London: John Lane, 1929)

Perkin, H. *The Rise of Professional Society: England Since 1880* (London: Routledge, 1989)

Prest, A. R. and A. A. Adam. *Consumers' Expenditure in the United Kingdom, 1900-1919* (Cambridge: Cambridge University Press, 1954)

Reid, A. 'The Impact of the First World War on British Workers', in *The Upheaval of War: Work and Welfare in Europe, 1914-1918*, edited by R. Wall and J. Winter (Cambridge: Cambridge University Press, 1988)

Reeves, M. P. *Round About a Pound a Week* (London: Virago, 1979; repr. 1999)
Facsimile. of publication: London: G. Bell, 1913.

Roberts, R. *The Classic Slum: Salford Life in the First Quarter of the Century* (London: Penguin, 1971)

Routh, G. *Occupation and Pay in Great Britain, 1906-79*, 2nd edn (London: Macmillan, 1980)
Previous edn published as: Occupation and pay in Great Britain 1906-60. London : Cambridge University Press, 1965.

Rubinstein, W. D. *Men of Property: The Very Wealthy in Britain since the Industrial Revolution*, 2nd edn rev. (London: Social Affairs Unit, 2006)
Previously published: London: Croom Helm, 1981.

Runciman, W. G. *Relative Deprivation and Social Justice: A Study of Attitudes to Social Inequality in Twentieth Century*

England, new edn (Aldershot: Gregg Revivals, 1993)

Sherington, G. *English Education, Social Change and War 1911-20* (Manchester: Manchester University Press, 1981)

Smith, H. L., ed. *New Survey of London Life and Labour*, 8 vols (London: P. S. King & Son, 1930-35)
Contents: Vol. 1. Forty years of change; Vol. 2. London industries, 1; Vol. 3. Survey of social conditions, 1: The Eastern area (text); Vol. 4. Maps; Vol. 5. London industries, 2; Vol. 6. Survey of social conditions, 2: The Western area (text); Vol. 7. Maps 2; Vol. 8. London industries 3; Vol. 9. Life and leisure
The survey (which was undertaken by the London School of Economics and Political Science and directed by Sir H. L. Smith) was made with special reference to the changes since the publication of Charles Booth's *Life and Labour of the People in London* in 17 vols (London: Macmillan, 1902-1904).

Thompson, F. M. L. *English Landed Society in the Nineteenth Century* (London: Routledge: 1963; repr., 1971)

Waites, B. *A Class Society at War: England 1914-1918* (Leamington Spa: Berg, 1987)

Webb, S. and A. Freeman. *Great Britain after the War* (London: Allen & Unwin, 1916)
Sub-title: *Being Facts and Figures, Quotations and Queries, Suggestions and Forecasts, Designed to Help Individual Inquirers and Study Circles in Considering What Will Happen After War with regard to Trade, Employment, Wages, Prices, Trade Unionism, Co-operation, Women's Labour, Foreign Commerce, The Railways, The Coal Supply, Education, Taxation, Etc*. Includes the prediction of a more egalitarian society brought about through state intervention in the lives of the poor.

Whiteside, N. 'The British Population at War', in *Britain and the First World War*, ed. by J. Turner (London: Routledge, 1988)

Articles

Abrams, P. 'The Failure of Social Reform, 1918-1920', *Past and Present*, 24 (1963), 43-64

Allen, J. E. 'Some Changes in the Distribution of the National Income during the War', *Journal of the Royal Statistical Society*, 83 (1920), 86-126

Boswell, J. and J. Bruce. 'Patriots or Profiteers?: British Businessmen and the First World War', *Journal of European Economic History*, 11 (1982), 423-45

Bryder, L. 'The First World War: Healthy or Hungry?', *History Workshop Journal*, 24 (1987), 141–57

Dewey, P. E. 'British Farming Profits and Government Policy during the First World War', *Economic History Review*, n.s. 37 (1984), 373-90

Englander, D. and J. Osborne. 'Jack, Tommy, and Henry Dubb; The Armed Forces and the Working Class', *Historical Journal*, 21 (1978), 593-621

Grayzel, S. R. 'Defence Against the Indefensible: The Gas Mask, the State and British Culture during and after the First World War', *Twentieth Century British History*, 25 (2014), 418-434

Guttsman, W. L. 'Aristocracy and the Middle Class in the British Political Elite 1886-1916: A Study of Formative Influences and of the Attitude to Politics', *British Journal of Sociology*, 5 (1954), 12-32

— 'The Changing Social Structure of the British Political Élite, 1886-1935', *British Journal of Sociology*, 2 (1951), 122-134

Koven, S. 'Remembering and Dismemberment: Crippled Children, Wounded Soldiers, and the Great War in Great Britain', *American Historical Review*, 99 (1994), 1167–1202

Melling, J. '"Non-Commissioned Officers": British Employers and their Supervisory Workers, 1880-1920', *Social History*, 5 (1980), 183-221

Sheffield, G. D. 'The Effect of the Great War on Class Relations in Britain: The Career of Major Christopher

Stone DSO MC', *War and Society*, 7 (1989), 87-105

Waites, B. 'The Effect of the First World War on Class and Status in England, 1919-20', *Journal of Contemporary History*, 11 (1976), 27-48

Whiteside, N. 'Industrial Welfare and Labour Regulation in Britain at the Time of the First World War', *International Review of Social History*, 25 (1980), 307-331

Whiting, R. 'Taxation and the Working Class, 1915-24', *Historical Journal*, 33 (1990), 895-916

Winter, J. M. 'The Impact of the First World War on Civilian Health in Britain', *Economic History Review*, 30 (1977), 487-507

5.3 The State

The controls[183] introduced by the state during the war affected practically every aspect of the life of its citizens but they did not represent a conscious policy for the development of a permanent policy of state intervention; they were introduced in piecemeal fashion as ad hoc solutions to the social and economic problems that emerged as a result of having to wage a war on an unprecedented scale. The wartime intervention of the state was motivated by expediency rather than ideology. Once the war had ended there was little enthusiasm for a continuation of this sort of intervention and as a result most of the apparatus of wartime state control was dismantled. The reconstructionist ideas[184] that prevailed in the last years of the war fared little better. These ideas had found expression in the large programme of reconstruction planned in the Ministry of Reconstruction after that body was set up in July 1917 (see last paragraph in the preamble to **Part 3, section 2.4: Labour, Industrial Relations**). Addison and his colleagues in this Ministry not only tackled the social remit given to them by Lloyd George's undertaking to create a 'land fit for heroes' but also developed an ambitious economic agenda which reflected their desire to see the wartime improvements in business organization and industrial efficiency resulting from government intervention prolonged after the war as an integral part of peacetime reconstruction. Much of the post-war social, economic and political change they desired failed to materialize in the immediate post war years[185]. In the area of social policy, however, the war did strengthen a growing acknowledgment (already apparent in measures of state welfare provision in Britain before 1914) of the fact that the government alone had sufficient resources to cope with the nature and magnitude of many social problems. It was for this reason that during the war the decision was taken in major areas of social policy that the government should depart from the practice of subsidising voluntary charitable agencies traditionally responsible for provision of essential services and instead provide these services directly itself. This alteration in the relationship between central government and voluntary agencies and the notion (in spite of many people in the aftermath of the war wanting a diminution of state intervention) that the state should take a more proactive role in social policies became a permanent feature of post-war Britain.

As a result of the war the machinery of government was radically overhauled. The establishment in 1916 of a Cabinet Secretariat, the rationalisation of the home civil service immediately after the war, the retention of new specialist departments (such as the Ministries of Health and Labour), the clarification of the formal relationship between central and local government as represented by the 1919 Local Government Act, were the sort of changes resulting from the war that cumulatively produced, at a central and local level, the evolution of an administrative structure geared to serving the needs of a modern, industrial society. For the latter purpose Britain was aided by a radical change in the attitude to public expenditure of which the traditional view about its proper level was abandoned during the war. As an example of this, public expenditure by 1918 had been allowed to rise to the unprecedented level of 48% of GDP (with the basic rate of income tax increasing from 6p

---

[183] Among these controls were rent control, food rationing, and the nationalization of strategically important industries, all representing striking departures from pre-war habits. Sidney Webb was characteristically disposed to see these developments as harbingers of a new collectivist Britain, which he sketched in a *New Statesman* series, 'The Rebuilding of the State', in the Spring of 1917.

[184] In the words of a War Cabinet report of 1917 reconstruction was 'not so much a question of rebuilding society as it was before the war, but of moulding a better world out of the social and economic conditions which have come into being during the war', a statement no doubt worded with a view to inspiring soldiers and workers at a time when news from the fighting front was doing little to lift morale.

[185] However, the recasting of Unemployment Insurance in 1920 and 1921 and the Housing Act of 1919, which made possible the building between 1919 and 1921 of 70,000 houses a year, did represent some limited success.

in the pound in 1914 to 30p in the pound in 1918). This departure from the severe fiscal constraints which had inhibited the expansion of the Edwardian state was not temporary. There was no return to the attitude to public expenditure that prevailed in the pre-war years.

The outbreak of war initially halted plans to bring forward new legislation to expand the system of secondary and technical education that had been initiated in the 1902 Act. Later, in the climate of state enthusiasm for reconstruction prevalent in the last years of the war, H. A. L Fisher began work in 1917 on new education legislation that led in March 1918 to the introduction of an Education Act mainly designed to produce greater secondary education provision. The economic difficulties that prevailed in the immediate post-war years prevented this legislation from achieving its main objectives. The numbers of free places at secondary schools remained limited; the idea of continuation classes designed for those between the ages of 14 and 18 was not implemented, and there was no acceptance of the principal of universal secondary education.

Books

Alter, P. *The Reluctant Patron: Science and the State in Britain, 1850-1920* (Oxford: Berg, 1987)

Bowley, M. *Housing and the State*, 1919-1944 (London: Allen & Unwin, 1945; repr. New York: Garland, 1985)

Burk, K.. 'The Treasury: From Impotence to Power', in *War and the State: The Transformation of British Government 1914-1919*, edited by K. Burk (London: Allen & Unwin, 1982)

Burk, K., ed. *War and the State: The Transformation of British Government 1914-1919* (London: Allen & Unwin, 1982)

Cline, P. 'Eric Geddes and the "Experiment" with Businessmen in Government, 1915-22', in *Essays in Anti-Labour History: Responses to the Rise of Labour in Britain*, edited by K. D. Brown (London: Macmillan, 1974)

— 'Winding Down the War Economy: British Plans for Peacetime Recovery, 1916-19, in *War and the State: The Transformation of British Government 1914-1919*, edited by K. Burk (London: Allen & Unwin, 1982)

Cronin, J. E. 'The Crisis of State and Society in Britain, 1917-22', in *Strikes, Wars and Revolutions in an International Perspective: Strike Waves in the Late Nineteenth and Early Twentieth Centuries*, edited by L. H. Haimson and C. Tilly (Cambridge: Cambridge University Press, 1989)

— *The Politics of State Expansion: War, State, and Society in Twentieth-Century Britain* (London: Routledge, 1991)

Davidson, R. and R. Lowe. 'Bureaucracy and Innovation in British Welfare Policy, 1870-1945', in *The Emergence of the Welfare State in Britain and Germany, 1850-1950*, edited by W. J. Mommsen in collaboration with Wolfgang Mock (London: Croom Helm on behalf of the German Historical Institute, 1981)

Finlayson, G. *Citizen, State and Social Welfare in Britain, 1830–1990* (Oxford: Clarendon Press, 1994)

French, D. 'The Rise and Fall of Business as Usual', in *War and the State: The Transformation of British Government, 1914-1919*, ed. by K. Burk (London: Allen & Unwin, 1982)

Garton Foundation. *Memorandum on the Industrial Situation after the War* ... Privately circulated among employers, representatives of labour, and public men of all parties, May-September, 1916. Now published as revised in the light of criticisms and suggestions received, October, 1916 (London: Harrison, 1916)

Gladstone, D., ed. *Before Beveridge: Welfare before the Welfare State*, Choice in Welfare, 47 (London: Institute of Economic Affairs, Health and Welfare Unit, 1999)

Great Britain. Ministry of Reconstruction. *The Aims of Reconstruction*, Reconstruction Problems 1(London: HMSO, 1918)

— *Housing in England and Wales*: Memorandum by the Advisory Housing Panel of the Ministry of Reconstruction on the Emergency Problem, Cd. 9087 (London: HMSO, 1918)

— *Report of the Machinery of Government Committee*, Cd. 9230 (London: HMSO, 1918) Committee chaired by Viscount Haldane of Cloan.

Grieves, K. *Sir Eric Geddes: Business and Government in War and Peace* (Manchester: Manchester University Press, 1989)

Harris, J. 'Political Thought and the Welfare State 1870-1940: An intellectual framework for British Social Policy', in *Before Beveridge: Welfare before the Welfare State*, edited by David Gladstone, Choice in Welfare, 47 (London: Institute of Economic Affairs, Health and Welfare Unit, 1999)

— 'Society and the State in Twentieth Century Britain', in *Cambridge Social History of Britain*, 3 vols (Cambridge: Cambridge University Press, 1990), III: *Social Agencies and Institutions* (1990)

Hurwitz, S. J. *State Intervention in Great Britain: A Study of Economic Control and Social Response, 1914-1919* (New York: Columbia University Press, 1949; repr. London: Cass, 1968)

Johnson, P. B. *Land Fit for Heroes: The Planning of British Reconstruction, 1916-1919* (Chicago: University of Chicago Press, 1968)

Lowe, R. *Adjusting to Democracy: The Role of the Ministry of Labour in British Politics, 1916-1939* (Oxford: Clarendon Press, 1986)

— 'Government', in *The First World War in British History*, edited by S. Constantine, M. W. Kirby and M. B. Rose (London: Edward Arnold, 1995)

— 'The Demand for a Ministry of Labour: Its Establishment and Initial Role' (unpublished doctoral thesis, University of London, 1975)

— 'The Ministry of Labour, 1916-19: A Still Small Voice?', in *War and the State: The Transformation of British Government, 1914-1919*, ed. by K. Burk (London: Allen & Unwin, 1982)

McLeod, R. M. *Government and Expertise in Britain: Specialists, Administrators and Professionals, 1860-1919* (Cambridge: Cambridge University Press, 1988)

Mommsen, W. J., ed. *The Emergence of the Welfare State in Britain and Germany, 1850-1950*, edited by W. J. Mommsen in collaboration with Wolfgang Mock (London: Croom Helm on behalf of the German Historical Institute, 1981)

Orbach, L. F. *Homes for Heroes: A Study of the Evolution of British Public Housing, 1915-21* (London: Seeley, 1977)

Roseveare, H. *The Treasury: The Evolution of a British Institution* (London: Allen & Unwin, 1969)

Royal Commission on Housing in Scotland. *Report of the Royal Commission on the Housing of the Industrial Population of Scotland Rural and Urban*, Cd. 8731 (Edinburgh: HMSO, 1917)

Rubin, G. R. *War, Law and Labour: The Munitions Acts, State Regulation and the Unions, 1915-1921* (Oxford: Clarendon Press, 1987)

Sherington, G. *English Education, Social Change and War 1911-20* (Manchester: Manchester University Press, 1981)

Swenarton, M. *Homes Fit for Heroes: The Politics and Architecture of Early State Housing in Britain* (London: Heinemann, 1981)

Tawney, R. H. 'The Abolition of Economic Controls, 1918-1921', in *History and Society*, essays by R. H. Tawney edited and with an introduction by J. M. Winter (London: Routledge, & Kegan Paul, 1978)

Thane, P. 'Government and Society in England and Wales, 1750-1914', in *Cambridge Social History of Britain*, 3 vols (Cambridge: Cambridge University Press, 1990), III: *Social Agencies and Institutions* (1990)

Tolliday, S. and J. Zeitlin, eds. *Shop Floor Bargaining and the State: Historical and Comparative Perspectives* (Cambridge: Cambridge University Press, 1985)

Turner, J. 'Cabinets, Committees and Secretariats: The Higher Direction of the War', in *War and the State: The Transformation of British Government, 1914-1919*, ed. by K. Burk (London: Allen & Unwin, 1982)

— '"Experts" and Interests: David Lloyd George and the Dilemma of the Expanding State, 1906-1919', in *Government and Expertise in Britain: Specialists, Administrators and Professionals, 1860-1919*, edited by R. M. McLeod (Cambridge: Cambridge University Press, 1988)

Wickwar, H and M. Wickwar. *The Social Services: A Historical Survey* (London: Cobden-Sanderson, 1936)
A revised edition was published: London: Bodley Head, 1949.

Wrigley, C. J. *David Lloyd George and the British Labour Movement: Peace and War* (Hassocks: Harvester, 1976; repr. London: Gregg Revivals, 1992)
This work includes as a major subject the development of the state's role in industrial relations during the first world war, focussing on the key role of David Lloyd George.

— 'The First World War and the State Intervention in Industrial Relations', in *A History of British Industrial Relations*, edited by Chris Wrigley, 2 vols (Brighton: Harvester, 1982-1987), II: 1914-1939 (Brighton: Harvester, 1987; repr. Aldershot: Gregg Revivals, 1993)

— 'The Ministry of Munitions: An Innovatory Department', in *War and the State: The Transformation of British Government, 1914-1919*, ed. by K. Burk (London: Allen & Unwin, 1982)

— 'The State and the Challenge of Labour in Britain, 1917-20', in *Challenges of Labour: Central and Western Europe, 1917-20*, edited by Chris Wrigley (London: Routledge, 1993)

Articles

Abrams, P. 'The Failure of Social Reform, 1918-1920', *Past and Present*, 24 (1963), 43-64

Cline, P. 'Reopening the Case of the Lloyd George Coalition and the Post War Economic Transition, 1918-1919', *Journal of British Studies*, 10 (1971), 162-175

Daunton, M. J. 'How to Pay for the War: State, Society and Taxation in Britain, 1917-24', *English Historical Review*, 111 (1996), 883-919
The issue of war time finance and its implications for the post-war period is explored in this article.

Dewey, P. E. 'British Farming Profits and Government Policy during the First World War', *Economic History Review*, n.s. 37 (1984), 373-90

Dowie, J. '1919-20 is in Need of Attention', *Economic History Review*, 28 (1975), 429-450

Harris, B. 'The Demographic Impact of the First World War: An Anthropometric Perspective', *Social History of Medicine*, 6 (1993), 343–66.

Harris, J. 'Political Thought and the Welfare State, 1870-1940: An Intellectual Framework for British Social Policy', *Past and Present*, 135 (1992), 116-41

Lowe, R. 'The Erosion of State Intervention in Britain, 1917-24', *Economic History Review*, 31 (1978), 270-86

— 'The Failure of Consensus in Britain: The National Industrial Conference, 1919-1921', *Historical Journal*, 21 (1978), 649-75

McDermott, J. '"A Needless Sacrifice": British Businessmen and Business as Usual in the First World War', *Albion*, 21 (1989), 263-82

McDonald, A. 'The Geddes Committee and the Formulation of Public Expenditure Policy, 1921-22', *Historical Journal*, 32 (1989), 643-74

Offer, J. 'Idealism Versus Non-Idealism: New Light on Social Policy and Voluntary Action in Britain Since 1880', *Voluntas: International Journal of Voluntary and Nonprofit Organizations*, 14 (2003), 227-240
In this paper the author examines and categorises ideas and practices of voluntary action in Britain in the period from the 1880's to the 1990's.

Rubin, G. R. 'Law as a Bargaining Weapon: British Labour and the Restoration of Pre-War Practices Act 1919', *Historical Journal*, 32 (1989), 925-945

Tawney, R. H. 'The Abolition of Economic Controls, 1918-1921', *Economic History*, 13 (1943), 1-30

Trentmann, F. 'The Transformation of Fiscal Reform: Reciprocity, Modernization, and the Fiscal Debate within the Business Community in Early Twentieth Century Britain', *Historical Journal*, 39 (1996), 1005-1048

Turner, J. 'State Purchase of the Liquor Trade in the Firsts World War', *Historical Journal*, 23 (1980), 589-615

Whiteside, N. 'Industrial Welfare and Labour Regulation in Britain at the Time of the First World War', *International Review of Social History*, 25 (1980)

— 'Welfare Legislation and the Unions during the First World War', *Historical Journal*, 23 (1980), 857-74

Whiting, R. Taxation and the Working Class, 1915-24', *Historical Journal*, 33 (1990), 895-916

5.4 Politics

The First World War led to a fundamental realignment of British politics. The Liberal Party suffered a major setback from which it never fully recovered. In contrast, the Liberal Party's competitors reached the end of the war with their positions improved. The Conservative Party, in which the balance was gravitating from a landed élite to an élite of businessmen, did especially well out of the war, profiting from the split of the Liberal Party and emerging from the general election of 1918 with by far the largest number of MPs. The Labour Party reached the end of the war reorganized and revitalized and no longer, as it was in beginning of the war, little more than a trade union pressure group dependent on the patronage of the Liberal Party; it also fared quite well in the 1918 election as a result of which it achieved a modest increase in the number of its MPs, in contrast to the Liberal Party which emerged from that election with a substantially reduced number of MPs. The additional number of seats with which the Labour Party began the post-war era was not, however, sufficiently significant (except in comparison with the losses of seats suffered by the Liberal Party) and it was not until 1922 that it reached the real point of breakthrough in terms of seats. Nevertheless the stage had been set for the replacement in the post-war era of a two-party by a three-party system with the Conservatives dominant and Labour gradually taking over from the Liberals as the main parliamentary party of opposition. To what extent the war played a part in these political developments, particularly in relation to the decline in Liberal electoral support, remains a subject of considerable debate.

Books

Ball, S. *Portrait of a Party: The Conservative Party in Britain 1918-1945* (Oxford: Oxford University Press 2013)

Bentley, M. *The Liberal Mind, 1914–1929* (Cambridge: Cambridge University Press, 1977)

Clarke, P. *Lancashire and the New Liberalism* (Cambridge: Cambridge University Press, 1971; repr . Aldershot: Gregg Revivals, 1993)

Craig, F. W. S., ed. *British Electoral Facts, 1885-1975*, 3rd edn (London: Macmillan, 1976)

The War Years

Fawcett, M. G., Dame. *The Women's Victory - And After: Personal Reminiscences, 1911-1918* (London: Sidgwick & Jackson, 1920; repr. London: British Library, 1987)

Gottlieb, J. V. and R. Toye, eds. *The Aftermath of Suffrage: Women, Gender, and Politics in Britain, 1918-1945* (Basingstoke: Palgrave Macmillan, 2013)

Guttsman, W. L. *The British Political Elite* (London: Macgibbon & Kee, 1963; repr. 1968)

Hinton, R. *Labour and Socialism: A History of the British Labour Movement, 1867-1974* (Brighton: Wheatsheaf, 1983)

Holton, S. S. *Feminism and Democracy: Women's Suffrage and Reform Politics in Britain, 1900–1918* (Cambridge: Cambridge University Press, 1986; repr 2002)

Lawrence, J. and M. Taylor, eds.. *Party, State and Society: Electoral Behaviour in Britain since 1820* (Aldershot: Scolar Press, 1997)

Lee, J. M. *Social Leaders and Public Persons: A Study of County Government in Cheshire since 1888* (Oxford: Clarendon Press, 1963)

Lenman, B. P. *The Eclipse of Parliament: Appearance and Reality in British Politics since 1914* (London: Edward Arnold, 1992)

McCrillis, N. *The British Conservative Party in the Age of Universal Suffrage: Popular Conservatism, 1918-1929* (Columbus: Ohio State University Press, 1998)

McKibbin, R. I. *The Evolution of the Labour Party, 1910-1924* (Oxford: Clarendon Press, 1974; repr.1991)

Miliband, R. *Parliamentary Socialism: A Study in the Politics of Labour*, 2nd edn (London: Merlin Press, 1972)

Pugh, M. *Electoral Reform in War and Peace, 1906-18* (London: Routledge & Kegan Paul, 1978)

— *The Making of Modern British Politics, 1867-1939*, 2nd edn (Oxford: Blackwell, 1993; repr. 1996)

— *Women and the Women's Movement in Britain, 1914-1999*, 2nd edn (Basingstoke: Macmillan, 2000)
Rev. edn of: *Women and the Women's Movement in Britain*, 1914-1959.

— *Women's Suffrage in Britain, 1867-1928* (London: Historical Association, 1980)

Searle, G. R. *The Liberal Party: Triumph and Disintegration,, 1869-1929*, 2nd edn (Basingstoke: Palgrave, 2001)

Stubbs, J. O. 'The Impact of the Great War on the Conservative Party', in *The Politics of Reappraisal*, ed. by G. Peele and C. Cook (London: Macmillan, 1975)

Tanner, D. *Political Change and the Labour Party, 1900-1918* (Cambridge: Cambridge University Press, 1990)

Taylor, A. J .P. *Politics in Wartime and Other Essays* (London: Hamilton, 1964)

Thorpe, A. 'Labour Leaders and the Liberals, 1906-24', [paper read at the] conference on the Liberal Party, 1906-24, University of Rouen, France, January 2011

Thompson, F. M. L. *English Landed Society in the Nineteenth Century* (London: Routledge, 1963; repr., 1971)

Turner, J. *British Politics and the Great War: Coalition and Conflict, 1915-1918* (New Haven, Conn.: Yale University Press, 1992)

— 'The Labour Vote and the Franchise after 1918: An Investigation of the English Evidence', in *History and Computing II*. 2nd Annual conference; selected papers edited by Peter Denley, Stefan Fogelvik and Charles Harvey (Manchester: Manchester University Press, 1989)

—— 'The Politics of Organised Business in the First World War', in *Businessmen and Politics: Studies of Business Activity in British Politics, 1900-1945*, edited by John Turner (London: Heinemann, 1984)

Vellacott, J. *Pacifists, Patriots and the Vote: The Erosion of Democratic Suffragism in Britain during the First World War* (Basingstoke: Palgrave Macmillan, 2007)

Williamson, W. 'The Conservative Party, 1900-1939: From Crisis to Ascendancy', in *A Companion to Early Twentieth-Century Britain*, edited by Chris Wrigley (Oxford: Blackwell, 2003; repr. Oxford: Wiley-Blackwell, 2009)

Wilson, T. *The Downfall of the Liberal Party, 1914-1935* (London: Collins, 1966)

Winter, J. M. *Socialism and the Challenge of War: Ideas and Politics in Britain, 1912-18* (London: Routledge & Kegan Paul, 1974; repr. Aldershot: Gregg Revivals, 1993)

Wrigley, C. J. 'The Impact of the First World War on the British Labour Movement', in *Strategy and Intelligence: British Policy During the First World War*, ed. By M. Dockrill and D. French (London: Hambledon, 1986)

Articles

Adams, T. 'Labour and the First World War: Economy, Politics and the Erosion of Local Peculiarity?', *Journal of Regional and Local Studies*, 10 (1990), 23-47

Barker, R. 'Political Myth; Ramsay MacDonald and the Labour Party', *History*, 61 (1976), 46-56
Minimises the importance of the commitment to socialism in the famous Clause 4 of the Labour Party's new constitution of 1918.

Berger, S. 'The Decline of Liberalism and the Rise of Labour: The Regional Approach', *Parliamentary History*, 12 (1993), 84-92

Binard, F. '"The Injustice of the Woman's Vote": Opposition to Female Suffrage after World War I', *Womens History Review*, (2014), 381-400
Special Issue: Feminism and Feminists after Suffrage.

Blewett, N. 'The Franchise in the United Kingdom 1885-1918', *Past and Present*, 32 (1965), 34-43

Childs, M. 'Labour Grows Up: The Electoral System, Political Generations and British Politics, 1890-1929', *Twentieth Century British History*, 6 (1995), 123-144

Close, D. 'The Collapse of Resistance to Democracy: Conservatives, Adult Suffrage and Second Chamber Reform 1911-1928', *Historical Journal*, 20 (1977), 893-918

David, E. I. 'The Liberal Party Divided 1916-18', *Historical Journal*, 13 (1970), 509-32

Hart, M. 'The Liberals, the War and the Franchise', *English Historical Review*, 97 (1982), 820-32

Kent, K. 'The Politics of Sexual Difference: World War I and the Demise of British Feminism', *Journal of British Studies*, 27 (1988), 232-253

Lawrence, J. 'The Transformation of British Public Politics After the First World War', *Past and Present*, 190 (2006), 185-216

McEwen, J. M. 'The Coupon Election of 1918 and the Unionist Members of Parliament', *Journal of Modern History*, 34 (1962), 294-306

Matthew, H. C. G., and others. 'The Franchise Factor and the Rise of the Labour Party', by H. C. G. Matthew, R. I. McKibbin and J. A. Kay, *English Historical Review*, 91 (1976), 723-53

Pugh, M. 'Politicians and the Women's Vote, 1914-1918', *History*, 69 (1974), 358-74

— 'The Rise of Labour and the Political Culture of Conservatism, 1890-1945', *History*, 87 (2002), 514-537

Rolfe, D. 'Origins of Mr. Speaker's Conference during the First World War', *History*, 64 (1979), 36-46

Tanner, D. 'The Parliamentary Electoral System, the "Fourth" Reform Act, and the Rise of Labour in England and Wales', *Bulletin of the Institute of Historical Research*, 56 (1983), 205-219

— 'Elections, Statistics, and the Rise of the Labour Party, 1906-1931', *Historical Journal*, 34 (1991), 893-908

Ward, P. 'Women of Britain Say Go: Women's Patriotism in the First World War', *Twentieth Century British History*, 12 (2001), 23-45
The author examines the patriotic activities of some aristocratic and middle-class women in Great War and notes that these had repercussions on postwar politics

Wilson, T. 'The Coupon and the British Election of 1918', *Journal of Modern History*, 36 (1964), 28-42

Winter, J. M. 'Arthur Henderson, the Russian Revolution and the Reconstruction of the Labour Party', *Historical Journal*, 15 (1972), 753-773

5.5 Gender, Sex and Sexuality

During the war there was a loosening of sexual constraints. Chaperoning in polite society declined, courtship became less formal, hemlines shortened, women smoking in public, frequenting public houses, or making use of cosmetics became less frowned on, sex outside marriage increased. Many women enjoyed a great deal more freedom and independence and in many cases were involved in jobs hitherto only performed by men. Subjects such as illegitimacy, venereal disease and homosexuality, hitherto regarded as taboo, were discussed in public in a franker fashion, and depictions of homosexuality, almost totally absent in pre-war novels, also began to feature in such works as Rose Allatini's *Despised and Rejected* (1918), Violet Tweedale's *The Heart of a Woman* (1917), D. H. Lawrence's *The Rainbow* (1915), and Christobel Marshall's *Hungerheart* (1915, written under the masculine pseudonym Christopher St John)[186].

Such signs of changes in British society did not, however, lead immediately to a comprehensive transformation of social attitudes in the post-war years. While there was more visibility of homosexuality during the war and signs of greater public tolerance and understanding towards it, traditional prejudices remained strong (even at times hysterical[187]) and in the Army 22 officers and 270 soldiers were court-martialled for homosexual acts between 1914 and 1919. The war did not lead to a major breakthrough in either the public or the official attitude to homosexuality. In the case of what women gained from the war opinion has been divided. Until recently, there was a tendency to emphasise the notion of women emerging from the war with their role in society and their perception of it fundamentally changed by their war experience[188]. This notion, however, has been the subject of some doubt among recent feminist scholars, who have been inclined to view the aftermath of the war in terms of the persistence of traditional gender ideology[189] and the reversion of women to their role in society and the public perception of it as it was in the years preceding the war. This is borne out by what happened

---

[186] Allatini's *Despised and Rejected* and D. H. Lawrence's *The Rainbow*, however, encountered severe official hostility. Allatini's book was suppressed under DORA as a threat to the war effort and Lawrence's was banned for its alleged obscenity (over 1000 copies of the novel were burned by the examining magistrate's order).

[187] See references to homosexuality in **Part 3, section 2.12** on **War Hysteria**).

[188] Some contemporary observers believed that many women emerged from the war with attitudes of greater self-confidence and independence. Such attitudes are difficult to assess but, if factory magazines published by women munitions workers and commemorative histories written by women engaged as military auxiliaries are anything to go by, it is not unreasonable to believe that many women who had an active experience of the war felt that they had contributed significantly to the role and status of women.

[189] During the war women received a great deal of praise for their work as nurses, munitions workers, and military auxiliaries, much of which was voiced in exaggerated patriotic press accounts, but concealed behind this praise there remained a hard core of male prejudice against the way the increasing employment of young women was giving them a more independent attitude and freer existence. It is this sort of prejudice which was behind the wartime propaganda which sought to emphasise the traditional notion of women's role in society.

once the war was over. For most women who had been engaged in war work in traditionally male jobs it was 'Back to Home and Duty', mostly willingly but in some cases as a result of government compulsion[190]. There was a renewed emphasis on motherhood and the domestic ideal. The traditional notion of the place of women in the home remained largely intact.

Nevertheless there were some wartime gains for women which were not nullified by a resurgence of the domestic ideal and a conservative backlash. Most of the large numbers of women who were recruited as clerical workers to meet the wartime expansion of activity in the areas of banking, finance, and commerce kept their jobs after the war, unlike the majority of the women who had been drafted into other areas of work, such as industry and transport. In 1918, women's contributions to the war effort were acknowledged by granting them the vote, though initially only women over 30 were enfranchised in order to ensure that men remained a majority of voters. This restriction was not removed until 1928. Parliament also passed the Sex Disqualification Removal Act, which opened the Civil Service and professions to women at the end of the war. Another important gain was the lifting in 1920 of Oxford University's restriction on women taking its degrees.

It was also evident that, despite the reversion generally to the traditional notion of women in the role of motherhood and domesticity, women seemed to be more in control of their fertility in the post war years, judging by the average number of children .borne by women in the 1920's (i.e. 2.4 children in comparison with the average of 3.5 in the decade before the war). This may well have been helped by the publication of such works as the Women's Cooperative Guild's *Maternity* (1917) or Marie Stopes's *Married Love* (1918) that were designed to make the public aware of the consequences of women bearing children too often, and to erode traditional opposition to birth control. The efforts of these women to raise public consciousness of these issues were aided during the war by the spread of contraceptive knowledge among women in factories, shops, and offices and the increased use of condoms by soldiers as a way of preventing the spread of venereal disease

The British people during the war became less inhibited and stifled by the straitjacket of Victorian and Edwardian social influences but this release from them did not lead to their complete disappearance in Britain's post-war society. It is true that in the 1920's (the Roaring Twenties) the bohemian and extravagant behaviour of youth of the upper classes, people of the theatre world, and 'the flapper' resulted in considerable publicity in the contemporary press but these groups only reflect a part of the social culture of the time. For the majority of people the traditional values associated with marriage[191], family and the place of women in the home remained largely sacrosanct and the nation's moral stance continued to be reflected in obscenity laws[192] and a film censorship applied as rigorously as ever. British society still had a long way to go before it could be described as truly 'permissive'.

Books

Adams, M. C. C. *The Great Adventure: Male Desire and the Coming of World War I* (Bloomington: Indiana University Press, 1990)

Alberti, J. *Beyond Suffrage: Feminists in War and Peace, 1914-1928* (London: Macmillan, 1989)

Andrews, I. and M. A. Hobbs. *The Economic Effects of the War upon Women and Children in Great Britain* (New York: Oxford University Press, 1918)

Beauman, N. "'It is not the Place of Women to Talk of Mud": Some Responses of British Women Novelists to

---

[190] The Restoration of Pre-War Practices Bill forcibly deprived a considerable number of women of their factory jobs. Not all women willingly accepted this. In 1918 a number of them marched on Westminster to demand their jobs back.

[191] There was some loosening of some aspects of marriage and the family in the later inter-war years with the modification of the Church of England's stance on birth control in 1930 and the occurrence of some liberalization of the divorce laws in 1937 but this produced little change in that period to traditional attitudes to the institution of marriage.

[192] In the years after the war there were a considerable number of prosecutions for obscenity as, for instance, the trial in 1928 involving Radclyffe Hall's *The Well of Loneliness* that led to the novel being banned. The Attorney General described it as "propaganda for the practice which has long been known as Lesbianism ... it is corrupting and obscene and its publication is a misdemeanour". For similar sorts of reasons related to sex, books like James Joyce's *Ulysses* and D. H. Lawrence's *Lady Chatterley's Lover* were banned in Britain in the 1920's and had to be published abroad to escape prosecution.

World War I', in *Women and World War I: The Written Response*, edited by D. Goldman (Basingstoke: Macmillan, 1993)

Beddoe, D. *Back to Home and Duty: Women Between the Wars 1918-1939* (London: Pandora, 1989)

Bland, L. *Modern Women on Trial: Sexual Transgression in the Age of the Flapper* (Manchester: Manchester University Press, 2013)

Bourke, J. *Dismembering the Male: Men's Bodies, Britain, and the Great War* (London: Reaktion Books, 1996)

Braybon, C. G. 'Attitudes To Working Women In British Industry 1914-1920' (unpublished master's thesis, University of Sussex, 1977)

Braybon, C. G. and P. Summerfield. *Out of the Cage: Women's Experiences in two World Wars* (London: Pandora, 1987)

Brittain, V. *Lady into Woman: A History of Women from Victoria to Elizabeth II* (London: Andrew Dakers, 1953)

Brophy, J. and C. Smart, eds. *Women in Law: Explorations in Law, Family and Sexuality* (London: Routledge, 1985)

Browne, F. W. S. *Sexual Variety and Variability among Women and their Bearing upon Social Reconstruction* (London: Printed for the British Society for the Study of Sex Psychology by C. W. Beaumont, 1917)
"This paper was read at a meeting of the B.S.S.P., on October 14th, 1915. A few additions have since been made." - p. [2]

Carden-Coyne, A., ed. *Gender and Conflict since 1914: Historical and Interdisciplinary Perspectives* (Basingstoke: Palgrave Macmillan, 2012)

Collins, M. *Modern Love: An Intimate History of Men and Women in Britain, 1900–2000* (London: Atlantic, 2003)

Condell, D. and J. Liddiard, comps. *Working for Victory?: Images of Women in the First World War, 1914-18* (London: Routledge, 1987; repr. 1991)
Includes a selection of contemporary photos which, with extended captions and accompanying text illustrations, demonstrate the roles played by women during the Great War.

Cooke, M. and A. Woollacott, eds. *Gendering War Talk* (Princeton: Princeton University Press, 1993)
In relation to whether perceptions of the roles men and women play in war have been altered by warfare in the 20th century, this collection of essays (written during and immediately after a ten-week school held at Dartmouth College during the spring of 1990) surveys gender experiences in various conflicts and demonstrates the way in which these experiences have been described in literature, film, history and philosophy.

Cooper, H. M., and others, eds. *Arms and the Woman: War, Gender, and Literary Representation* (Chapel Hill: University of North Carolina Press, 1989)

Culleton, C. A. *Working-Class Culture, Women and Britain, 1914-1921* (Basingstoke: Macmillan, 2000)

Das, S. *Touch and Intimacy in First World War Literature* (Cambridge: Cambridge University Press, 2005)

Doan, L. *Disturbing Practices: History, Sexuality, and Women's Experience of Modern War* (Chicago: The University of Chicago Press, 2013)

Ellis, H. H. *The Erotic Rights of Women, and the Objects of Marriage: Two Essays* (London: British Society for the Study of Sex Psychology, 1918)

— *Essays in Wartime*, 1st series (London: Constable, 1916)

— 'Eugenics in Relation to War', in *The Philosophy of Conflict and Other Essays in Wartime*, by Havelock Ellis, 2nd series (London: Constable, 1919; repr. Freeport, N.Y.: Books for Libraries Press, 1970)

— *The Philosophy of Conflict and Other Essays in Wartime*, 2nd series (London: Constable, 1919; repr. Freeport, N.Y.:

Books for Libraries Press, 1970)
Contents: Europe; Civilization; On a certain kind of war; "Væ victoribus."; The origin of war; The philosophy of conflict; Élle Faure; The star in the East; Luther; Herbert Spencer; Eugenics in relation to the war; Birth control and eugenics; War and the sex problem; The unmarried mother; The mind of woman; "Equal pay for equal work."; The politics of women; Psycho-analysis in relation to sex; The drink programme of the future; Rodó; Mr. Conrad's world; The human Baudelaire; A friend of Casanova's; Cowley; Index. See also First Series which had the title *Essays in Wartime* (see record above).

Enloe, C. *Does Khaki Become You?: The Militarization of Women's Lives* (London: Pluto, 1983; repr. London: Pandora, 1988)

— *Maneuvers: The International Politics of Militarizing Women's Lives* (Berkeley, California: University of California Press, 2000)

Fell, S. S. and I. Sharp, eds. *The Women's Movement in Wartime: International Perspectives, 1914-1919* (London: Palgrave Macmillan, 2007)

Fussell, P. *The Great War and Modern Memory*, new edn (Oxford: Oxford University Press, 2000)

Gilbert, S. M. and S. Gubar. *No Man's Land: The Place of the Woman Writer in the Twentieth Century*, 3 vols (New Haven: Yale University Press, 1988-1994), II: *Sexchanges* (1989)

Gottlieb, J. V. and R. Toye, eds. *The Aftermath of Suffrage: Women, Gender, and Politics in Britain, 1918-1945* (Basingstoke: Palgrave Macmillan, 2013)

Grayzel, S. R. *Women and the First World War* (Harlow; Longman, 2002)

— '"The Mothers of our Soldiers' Children": Motherhood, Immorality and the War Baby Scandal, 1914-18', in *Maternal Instincts: Visions of Motherhood and Sexuality in Britain, 1875-1925*, edited by C. Nelson and A. S. Holmes (Basingstoke: Macmillan, 1997)

— *Women's Identities at War: Gender, Motherhood, and Politics in Britain and France during the First World War* (Chapel Hill: University of North Carolina Press, 1999)

Gullace, N. *The Blood of Our Sons: Men, Women and the Renegotiation of British Citizenship during the Great War* (New York: Palgrave Macmillian, 2000)

Hall, L. *Hidden Anxieties: Male Sexuality, 1900-1950* (London: Polity Press, 1991)

Haste, C. *Rules of Desire: Sex in Britain, World War 1 to the Present* (London: Chatto and Windus, 1992; repr. London: Vintage, 2002)

Hendley, M. C. *Organized Patriotism and the Crucible of War: Popular Imperialism in Britain, 1914-1932* (Montréal, Québec: McGill-Queen's University Press, 2012)
In this book's comparison of how three major patriotic organizations founded between 1901 and 1902 (the National Service League, the League of the Empire, and the Victoria League) fared during the war the author shows that the National Service League, with its strongly masculinist and militaristic character, failed to flourish in wartime whereas the League of the Empire and the Victoria League, strongly female in their membership and with aims and concepts related to education and hospitality, family, home and kinship, prospered not only during the war but beyond into the 1920's. The author sees this as an indication of how the traumatic nature of the Great War produced a fundamental reshaping of popular patriotism and imperialism that is evident to the author in his comparison of the post-war histories of the above organizations. This book affords an insight into women's roles in Britain during the height of popular imperialism.

Higonnet, M. R., and others, eds. *Behind The Lines: Gender and the Two World Wars* `(New Haven: Yale University Press, 1987)
Essays analyze the two world wars in respect to gender politics and reassesses the differences between men and women in relation to war.

Hirschfeld, M. *The Sexual History of the World War* (New York: The Panurge Press, 1934)

Hoare, P. *Wilde's Last Stand: Decadence, Conspiracy and the First World War* (London: Duckworth, 1997)
As well as portraying the darker side of wartime society, (e.g. transvestites in the trenches, drug clubs in London, and what the author discerns as the seeds of post-war British fascism) the author also uses original documents and archives to provide a history of the sensational libel trial that followed the publication of the article, 'The Cult of the Clitoris' which was published in *The Vigilante* in April 1918.

Kent, S. 'Gender Reconstruction after the First World War', in *British Feminism in the Twentieth Century*, edited by H. L. Smith (Aldershot: Elgar, 1990)

— *Making Peace: The Reconstruction of Gender in Interwar Britain* (Princeton, N.J.: Princeton University Press, 1993)

Koureas, G. *Memory, Masculinity and National Identity in British Visual Culture, 1914-1930: A Study of 'Unconquerable Manhood'* (London: Ashgate, 2007)

Leed, E. J. *No Man's Land: Combat and Identity In World War I* (Cambridge: Cambridge University Press, 1979; repr. 1981)

Longenbach, J. 'The Women and Men of 1914', in *Arms and the Woman: War, Gender, and Literary Representation*, edited by H. M. Cooper and others (Chapel Hill: University of North Carolina Press, 1989)

Melman, B., ed. *Borderlines: Gender and Identities in War and Peace, 1870-1930* (London: Routledge, 1998)
Placing the Great War in the context of the years 1870-1939 this work surveys women's and men's experiences of global modern war, revolution and social disintegration, and, in the process, through the inclusion of a number of different nations within the survey (Great Britain, France, Germany, the United States, Russia, Turkey, Greece, Egypt, Palestine and West Africa) some current interpretations of the gendered experience of war (especially that of women) and its relation to national identity are challenged.

Nelson, C. and A. S. Holmes, eds. *Maternal Instincts: Visions of Motherhood and Sexuality in Britain, 1875-1925* (Basingstoke: Macmillan, 1997)

Nicholson, V. *Singled Out: How Two Million Women Survived Without Men after the First World War* (London: Viking, 2007)
In this work the author draws attention to the plight of a generation of young women who, finding themselves in the situation of a post-war society in which there was a significant shortage of men available for marriage, were faced with the prospect of having to fend for themselves.

Ouditt, S. A. *Fighting Forces, Writing Women: Identity and Ideology in the First World War* (London: Routledge, 1994)
A memorial volume for the fiftieth anniversary of the Armistice

Pugh, M. *Women and the Women's Movement in Britain, 1914-1999*, 2nd edn (Basingstoke: Macmillan, 2000)
Rev. edn of: *Women and the Women's Movement in Britain, 1914-1959*.

— *Women's Suffrage in Britain, 1867-1928* (London: Historical Association, 1980)

Rowbotham, S. *Hidden from History: 300 Years of Women's Oppression and the Fight Against It* (London: Pluto Press, 1973)

Sauerteig, L. 'Sex, Medicine and Morality during the First World War', in *War, Medicine and Modernity*, edited by R. Cooter, M. Harrison and S. Sturdy (Stroud: Sutton, 1998; repr. 1999)

Scharlieb, M. A. D. (Mary Ann Dacomb Bird), Dame. *The Hidden Scourge* [i.e. venereal disease with a foreword by the Right Rev. the Lord Bishop of London (London: C. A. Pearson Ltd., 1916)

Smith, A. *Discourses Surrounding British Widows of the First World War* (London: Bloomsbury Academic, 2013)

Stopes, M. C. *Married Love: A New Contribution to the Solution of Sex Difficulties* (London: Pelican Press, 1918)

— 'The Race', in *Gold in the Wood; The Race: Two New Plays of Life* (London: A. C. Fifield, 1918)

— *Radiant Motherhood* (London: Putnam's, 1920)

Taylor, M., ed. *Lads: Love Poetry of the Trenches* (London: Constable, 1989; repr. London, Duckbacks, 2002)

Thom, D. 'Women and Work in Wartime Britain', in *The Upheaval of War: Work and Welfare in Europe, 1914-18*, edited by Richard Wall and Jay Winter (Cambridge: Cambridge University Press, 1988)

Trotter, D. 'Lesbians before Lesbianism: Sexual Identity in Early Twentieth Century British Fiction', in *Borderlines: Gender and Identities in War and Peace, 1870-1930*, edited by B. Melman (London: Routledge, 1998)

Tylee, C. *The Great War and Women's Consciousness: Images of Militarism and Womanhood in Women's Writings, 1914-64* (Basingstoke: Macmillan, 1990)

Vellacott, J. *Pacifists, Patriots and the Vote: The Erosion of Democratic Suffragism in Britain During The First World War* (Basingstoke: Palgrave Macmillan, 2007)

Weeks, J. *Coming Out: Homosexual Politics in Britain from the Nineteenth Century to the Present*, rev. and updated edn (Lonond: Quartet Books, 1990)

— *Sex, Politics and Society: The Regulation of Sexuality since 1800*, 2nd edn (London: Longman, 1989)

Wheelwright, J. *Amazons and Military Maids: Women Who Dressed as Men in the Pursuit of Life, Liberty and Happiness*, new edn (London: Pandora, 1994)

Woollacot, A. 'Sisters and Brothers in Arms; Family, Class, and Gendering in World War 1 Britain', in *Gendering War Talk*; ed. by M. Cooke and A. Woollacott (Princeton: Princeton University Press, 1993)

Articles

Bibbings, L. 'Images of Manliness: The Portrayal of Soldiers and Conscientious Objectors in the Great War', *Social and Legal Studies*, 12:3 (2003), 335-58

Binard, F. '"The Injustice of the Woman's Vote": Opposition to Female Suffrage after World War I', *Womens History Review*, 2014), 381-400
Special Issue: Feminism and Feminists after Suffrage

Bourke, J. "Masculinity, Men's Bodies and the Great War", *History Today*, 46 (1996), 8-11

Bruley, S. '"The Love of an Unknown Soldier": A Story of Mystery, Myth and Masculinity in World War I', *Contemporary British History*, 19 (2005), 459-479
An anonymous book published in 1918, purporting to be the diary of a dead junior army officer on the Western Front in the Great War, is the focus of this article in which Sue Bruley provides a solution to the mystery of the authorship of this book and, in the process, not only examines questions of masculinity at this time and its connections with contemporary ideologies of gender, race and empire, but also explores, through one particular writer, the complexities of the factors involved in most soldiers supporting the war.

Gilbert, S. 'Soldier's Heart: Literary Men, Literary Women, and the Great War', *Signs*, 8 (1983), 422-50

Gottlieb, J. V. '"The Women's Movement Took the Wrong Turning": British Feminists, Pacifism And the Politics of Appeasement', *Womens History Review*, 23 (2014), 441-462
Special Issue: Feminism and Feminists after Suffrage.

Gullace, N. 'White Feathers, and Wounded Men: Female Patriotism and the Memory of the Great War', *Journal of British Studies*, 36 (1997), 178-206

Harrison, M. 'The British Army and the Problem of Venereal Disease', *Medical History*, 39 (1995) 133-58

Jensen, K. 'War, Transnationalism and Medical Women's Activism: The Medical Women's International Association and the Women's Foundation for Health in the aftermath of the First World War', *Women's History Review*, 26 (2017), 213-228

Kent, K. 'The Politics of Sexual Difference: World War I and the Demise of British Feminism', *Journal of British Studies*, 27 (1988), 232-253

McCarthy, H. 'Pacifism and Feminism in the Great War', *History Today*, 65, Issue 4 (2015), 4

Pedersen, S. 'Gender, Welfare, and Citizenship in Britain during the Great War, *American Historical Review*, 95 (1990), 993-1006

Roper, R. 'Between Manliness and Masculinity': The "War Generation" and the Psychology of Fear in Britain, 1914-1950', *Journal of British Studies*, 44 (2005), 343-62

Surridge, K. T. 'More Than a Great Poster: Lord Kitchener and the Image of the Military Hero', *Historical Research*, 74 (2001), 298-313

Tylee, C. M. 'Maleness Run Riot - The Great War and Women's Resistance to Militarism', *Women Studies International Forum*, 2 (1988), 199-210

Vellacott, J. 'Feminist Consciousness and the First World War', *History Workshop Journal*, 23 (1987), 81-101

Watson, J. 'Khaki Girls, VADs and Tommy's Sisters: Gender and Class in First World War Britain', *International History Review*, 19, (1997), 32-51

Woollacott. A. 'Khaki Fever and its Control: Gender, Class, Age and Sexual Morality on the British Homefront in the First World War', *Journal of Contemporary History*, 29 (1994), 325-34

PART 4: REMEMBERING THE WAR

1. General

In the interwar years there was largely a common desire to honour the heroism and sacrifices which had brought victory in a war which most people felt, or wanted to feel, had been fought in a just cause. This was particularly reflected in the erection of war memorials and the annual observance of Remembrance Day. This attitude to the war was not shared by everyone and by the late 1920's and early 1930's there were a considerable number of people who had come to the depressing conclusion that the sacrifices made in the Great War had been in vain and that Britain had failed to grasp the opportunity to build constructively on the victory which had been achieved in that war[193]. Their memory of the war, conditioned no doubt by the sight of the maimed and disabled ex-servicemen who had survived, had become imprinted with its slaughter, horror and human suffering. They were remembering it too from the point of view of their belief that the war was responsible for crippling economic damage to the nation and decimation of a whole generation (the 'Lost Generation'[194]), a belief, which gave rise to the feeling at the time that the Great War was responsible for Britain sliding into a decline in terms of both human and economic resources.

Many people by the 1930's, particularly those who looked back on the Great War as futile and responsible for all that had gone wrong in its aftermath, dreaded the possibility of another war and passionately believed that Britain should do everything within its power to avoid this happening. They wanted to avoid the kind of huge military casualties that Britain had sustained in the Great War[195] and were particularly fearful of the potentially massive destruction (well publicised by the RAF and some politicians, especially Churchill, and graphically brought home to cinema audiences in 1936 in the film, *Things to Come*) that aerial bombing could cause in Britain in any future war. In this climate of fear, pacifists and disarmers flourished and not only was there no inclination to listen to those who advocated re-armament (a large scale programme of re-armament was not in fact launched until well into 1936) but British foreign policy also became hampered by a desire to preserve peace at all costs.

Books

Adams, R. J. Q. *British Politics and Foreign Policy in the Age of Appeasement, 1935–39* (London: Macmillan, 1993)

The Ashgate Companion to Heritage and Identity, edited by Brian Graham and Peter Howard (Aldershot: Ashgate, 2008)

Barham. P. *Forgotten Lunatics of the Great War* (New Haven: Yale University Press, 2004)
A history of the thousands of rank-and-file servicemen who were psychiatric casualties, and put into lunatic asylums.

Baxter, R. *Guilty Women* [Short accounts of women who have played a prominent part in causing the second World War.] (London: Quality Press Ltd, 1941)
See also a reference to this book in Hucker, D. 'Review of Julie Gottlieb's book *"Guilty Women", Foreign Policy, and Appeasement in Inter-War Britain'*, (Institute of Historical Research review no. 1959)

Black, J. *The Great War and the Making of the Modern World* (London: Continuum, 2011)

---

[193] The development of this disillusioned way of remembering the Great War was aided to a significant extent by a number of writers of the best-selling memoirs and novels about life on the Western front produced between 1928 and 1931. The disenchantment expressed by these writers (e.g. Blunden, Sassoon, Aldington, and Graves) had a profound effect on the minds of many British people (especially the middle class reading public) and helped to create a jaundiced memory of the Great War in the inter-war years that still persists to-day in spite of recent revisionist histories and other types of writing which have viewed the Great War in a different light.

[194] The notion of 'The Lost Generation', especially in relation to the numbers killed on the Western Front, was most applicable to the upper ruling classes which suffered a much higher proportionate loss than the nation as a whole because of the large numbers of that class who served as officers and were killed.

[195] The massive slaughter of soldiers at the Battle of the Somme is still indelibly stamped on popular modern consciousness of the Great War.

Bushaway, B. 'The Obligation of Remembrance or the Remembrance of Obligation: Society and the Memory of World War', in *The Great World War 1914-45*, edited by J. Bourne, P. H. Liddle and I. R. Whitehead, 2 vols (London: HarperCollins, 2000-2001), II: *The Peoples' Experience* (2001)

Calder, A. *Disasters and Heroes: On War, Memory and Representation* (Cardiff: University of Wales Press, 2004)

Carden-Coyne, A., ed. *Gender and Conflict since 1914: Historical and Interdisciplinary Perspectives* (Basingstoke: Palgrave Macmillan, 2012)

Cato [pseud.] *Guilty Men* (London: Gollancz, 1940)
Guilty Men was a British polemical book, written under the pseudonym "Cato" by three journalists: Michael Foot (a future Leader of the Labour Party), Frank Owen (a former Liberal MP), and Peter Howard (a Conservative), attacking 15 public figures for their responsibility for Britain being so ill-prepared to enter the war against Germany. [See also a reference to this book in Hucker, D. 'Review of Julie Gottlieb's book *"Guilty Women", Foreign Policy, and Appeasement in Inter-War Britain'*, (Institute of Historical Research review no. 1959)]

Crocker, T. B. *The Christmas Truce: Myth, Memory, and the First World War* (Lexington, Kentucky: University Press of Kentucky, 2015)

Crouthamel, J. and P. Leese, eds. *Psychological Trauma and the Legacies of the First World War* (Switzerland: Palgrave Macmillan, 2017)

Dyer, G. *The Missing of the Somme* (London: Penguin, 1994)

Eksteins, M. *Rites of Spring: The Great War and the Birth of the Modern Age* (London: Papermac, 2000)

Emsley, C. *Soldier, Sailor, Beggarman, Thief: Crime and the British Armed Services since 1914* (Oxford: Oxford University Press, 2013)
Focusing particularly on the First and Second World Wars, this work investigates criminal offending by members of the British armed forces both during and immediately after these wars.

Fabiansson, N. 'The Internet and the War: The Impact on the Making and Meaning of Great War History', in *Matters of Conflict: Material Culture, Memory and the First World War*, edited by N. J. Saunders (London: Routledge, 2004)

Ferguson, N., ed *Virtual History: Alternatives and Counterfactuals* (London: Picador, 1997; repr. London: Penguin, 2011)
Contains a chapter by Niall Ferguson entitled 'Kaiser's European Union': what if Britain had "stood aside" in August 1914?

Frantzen, A. J. *Bloody Good. Chivalry, Sacrifice, and the Great War* (Chicago, Ill: University of Chicago Press, 2004)

Goebel, S. *The Great War and Medieval Memory: War, Remembrance and Medievalism in Britain and Germany, 1914-1940*, Studies in the Social and Cultural History of Modern Warfare, 23 (Cambridge: Cambridge University Press, 2007)
A comparative study of the cultural impact of the Great War on British and German societies in the first half of the twentieth century.

Gottlieb, J. *'Guilty Women', Foreign Policy, and Appeasement in Inter-War Britain* (London: Palgrave Macmillan, 2015)

Grayzel, S. R. '"A promise of Terror to Come": Air Power and the Destruction of Cties in British Imagination and Experience, 1908-39', in *Cities into Battlefields: Metropolitan Scenarios, Experiences and Commemorations of Total War*, edited by S. Goebel, and D. Keene (Farnham: Ashgate, 2011)

Grogan, S. *Shell Shocked Britain: The First World War's Legacy for Britain's Mental Health* (London: Pen & Sword, 2014)

Halbwachs, M. *On Collective Memory*, edited, translated, and with an introduction by L. A. Coser (Chicago: University of Chicago Press, 1992)

General

Holman, B. *The Next War in the Air: Britain's Fear of the Bomber, 1908-1941* (Farnham: Ashgate Publishing Limited 2014)

Hucker, D. 'Review of [Julie Gottlieb's book] *"Guilty Women", Foreign Policy, and Appeasement in Inter-War Britain*', (*Reviews in History* (Institute of Historical Research), review no. 1959 (9 November 2016)

Hüppauf, . B. 'War and Death: The Experience of the First World War', in *Essays on Mortality*, edited by M. Crouch and B. Hüppauf (Sydney: University of New South Wales, 1985)

Jalland, P. *Death in War and Peace: A History of Loss and Grief in England, 1914-1970* (Oxford: Oxford University Press, 2010)

Keynes, J. M. *The Economic Consequences of the Peace*, The Collected Writings of John Maynard Keynes, vol 2 (London: Macmillan; St. Martin's Press, for the Royal Economic Society, 1971)

Lentin, A. *General Smuts, South Africa: The Peace Conferences of 1919-23 and their Aftermath* (London: Haus Publishing 2010)

Lynch, C. 'A Matter of Controversy: The Peace Movement and British Arms Policy in the Interwar Period', in *Arms Limitation and Disarmament: Restraints on War, 1899-1939*, edited by B. McKercher (Westport, Conn.: Praeger, 1992)

Mosse, G. *Fallen Soldiers: Reshaping the Memory of the World Wars* (Oxford: Oxford University Press, 1990)

A Part of History: Aspects of the British Experience of the First World War, introduced by Michael Howard (London: Continuum, 2009)
As well as considering various aspects of the British experience of the war as they have been featured in the historiographical trends of recent years, this work also provides a prediction of how historians will research them and write about them in the future, when the last survivors of the Great War have gone and first-hand experience of the war can no longer be called on.

Pound, R. *The Lost Generation* (London: Constable, 1964)

Seldon, A. and D. Walsh. *Public Schools and the Great War: The Generation Lost* (Barnsley: Pen & Sword Military 2013)

Smith, A. *Discourses Surrounding British Widows of the First World War* (London: Bloomsbury Academic, 2013)

Tate, T. and K. Kennedy, eds. *The Silent Morning: Culture and Memory after the Armistice* (Manchester: Manchester University Press, 2013)

Taylor, D. *Memory, Narrative and the Great War: Rifleman Patrick MacGill and the Construction of Wartime Experience* (Liverpool Liverpool University Press 2013)

Todman, D. *The Great War: Myth and Memory* (London: Hambledon & London, 2005)

Tombs, R. and E. Chabal. *Britain and France in Two World Wars: Truth, Myth and Memory* (London: Bloomsbury Publishing, 2013)

Vance, J. F. W. *Death So Noble: Memory, Meaning, and the First World War* (Vancouver: UBC Press, 1997)
This work explores the many ways in which Canadians remembered and celebrated their involvement in the Great War and how their memories afforded them not only understanding and consolation but also hope that the war would result in the emergence of a new sense of national identity.

Watson, J. S. K. *Fighting Different Wars: Experience, Memory, and the First World War in Britain* (Cambridge: Cambridge University Press, 2004)

Williams, D. *Media, Memory and the First World War* (Montreal; Ithaca, NY: McGill-Queen's University Press, 2009)

Wilson, K., ed. *Forging the Collective Memory: Government and International Historians through two World Wars* (Providence: Berghahn Books, 1996)

Winter, J. M. 'Communities in Mourning', in *Authority, Identity and the Social History of the Great War*, edited by F. Coetzee and M. Coetzee-Shevin (Providence, USA: Berghan Books, 1995)

— *Dreams of Peace and Freedom: Utopian Moments in the Twentieth Century* (London: Yale University Press, 2006)

— *Remembering War: The Great War between Memory and History in the Twentieth Century* (London: Yale University Press, 2006)

— *Sites of Memory, Sites of Mourning: The Great War in European Cultural History* (Cambridge: Cambridge University Press, 1995).

Winter, J. M., ed. *The Legacy of the Great War: Ninety Years On* (Columbia: Kansas City, Mo.: University of Missouri Press; National World War I Museum, 2009)

Winter, J. M. and A. Prost. *The Great War in History: Debates and Controversies, 1914 to the Present*, Studies in the Social and Cultural History of Modern Warfare, 21 (Cambridge: Cambridge University Press, 2005)

Winter, J. M. and E. Sivan. *War and Remembrance in the Twentieth Century*, Studies In the Social and Cultural History of Modern Warfare, 5 (Cambridge: Cambridge University Press, 1999)

Wohl, R. *The Generation of 1914* (London: Weidenfeld & Nicolson, 1980)

Articles

Beaumont, J. 'Lives of the First World War, Sponsored by the Imperial War Museums in Partnership with Findmypast', *Public Historian*, 39:2 (2017), 108-110
"There is an ongoing debate about the causes of the boom in the memory of war over the past four decades. However, it seems clear that, whatever it origins, this phenomenon is sustained by a symbiotic relationship between governments and their agencies intent on promoting nationalistic narratives of the past and individuals seeking to position their personal and family histories within these wider narratives. *Lives of the First World War* is an exemplar of such interaction. Sponsored by the British Imperial War museum (IWM), in collaboration with a genealogical website, Findmypast, this website [https://livesofthefirstworldwar.org/] aims to engage the public in researching the personal stories of nearly eight million men and women who "made a contribution" to the First World War." [Abstract on the internet]

Bourke, J. 'Introduction "Remembering" War', *Journal of Contemporary History*, 39.4 Special Issue: Collective Memory (2004), 473-485

Carr, R. 'Conservative Veteran M.P.s and the Lost Generation Narrative after the First World War', *Historical Research* (Oxford) 85 (2012), 284-305
"Using veterans of the First World War who became Conservative party M.P.s after 1918, this article re-examines the way the conflict was interpreted in post-1918 Britain. Pointing to the substantial numbers of men who fulfilled the above criteria (and how they used the conflict to reach such office) it illustrates one way in which the war was already being used as a significant political device before the more famous authors like Robert Graves began to bend the event to their narrative will from 1929. This had two important consequences: the Conservative party was given a greater 'national' appeal by proxy; and a somewhat simplified account of the war experience began to be forwarded, albeit not without some contestation and contradiction, earlier than we might think." [Abstract from the internet]

Cooper, S. 'Taking Sides on the Great War', *History Today*, 64 (2014), 19-23
An historiographical survey of the debate among British historians over the last hundred years.

Davis, B. 'Experience, Identity, and Memory: The Legacy of World War I', *Journal of Modern History*, 75 (2003), 111-131
Review article

England, P. 'Remembering the First World War: Touched From a Distance', *History Today*, 61, Issue 11 (2011), 3

General

The author considers the ways we remember and how historians may write about the Great War with the passing of the last veterans of it..

Fletcher, A. 'Patriotism, the Great War and the Decline of Victorian Manliness', *History*, 99, (2014), 40-72

Francis, M. 'Attending to Ghosts: Some Reflections on the Disavowals of British Great War Historiography', *Twentieth Century British History*, 25 (2014), 347-367

Goebel, S. 'Intersecting Memories: War and Remembrance in Twentieth-Century Europe', *Historical Journal*, 44 (2001), 853-858

Hastings, M. and Ferguson, N. 'Was it Worth It?, *Radio Times*, 22-28 February (2014), 14-19
The authors present their opposite views on the case for Britain entering the Great War.

Heathorn, S. 'The Mnemonic Turn in the Cultural Historiography of Britain's Great War', *Historical Journal*, 48 (2005), 1103-1124

IWM (Imperial War Museums) Friends. 'First World War Centenary Special Edition', *Despatches*, Number 18 (2014)

Irish, T. 'Fractured Families: Educated Elites in Britain and France and the Challenge of the Great War', *Historical Journal*, 57, (2014), 509-530

Janes, D. 'Eminent Victorians, Bloomsbury Queerness and John Maynard Keynes' The Economic Consequences of the Peace (1919)', *Literature and History*, 23 (2014), 19-32

Monaghan, S. 'Whose Country, Whose Soldiers, Whose Responsibility? First World War Ex-Servicemen and the Development of the Irish Free State, 1923-1939', *Contemporary European History*, 23(2014), 75-94

Moriarty, C. 'The Material Culture of Great War Remembrance', *Journal of Contemporary History*, 4 (1999), 653-662

Mosse, G. L. 'Two World Wars and the Myth of the War Experience', *Journal of Contemporary History*, 21 (1986), 491-513

Neilson, K. 'Orme Sargent, Appeasement and British Policy in Europe, 1933–39', *20th Century British History*, 21 (2010), 1-28

Peifer, D. C. 'The Past in the Present: Passion, Politics, and the Historical Profession in the German and British Pardon Campaigns', *Journal of Military History*, 71 (2007), 1107-1132

Quinn, B., and others. 'First World War: How Countries Across Europe Will Mark Centenary', *The Guardian*, Thursday 16 January 2014
[http://www.theguardian.com/world/2014/jan/16/first-world-war-europe-centenary]

Reid, F. 'Distinguishing between Shell-shocked Veterans and Pauper Lunatics: The Ex-Services' Welfare Society and Mentally Wounded Veterans after the Great War', *War in History*, 14 (2007), 347-371

Roper, M. 'Re-Remembering the Soldier Hero: The Psychic and Social Construction of Memory in Personal Narratives of the Great War', *History Workshop Journal*, 50 (2000), 181-204

Sheffield, G. 'The Centenary of the First World War: An Unpopular View', *Historian* (Historical Association), 122 (2014), 20-27
"Unpopular as it undoubtedly is to say so, between 1914 and 1918 Britain fought a defensive, just war" (the concluding sentence of the article).

— 'The Great War was a Just War', *History Today*, 63, Issue 8 (2013), 6
Gary Sheffield argues that Britain was right to take up arms against Germany in 1914.

Spinney, L. 'Monuments to Catastrophe', *History Today*, 67:4 (2017), 72

About the Spanish flu pandemic of 1918, in an examination by the author of our shared memory of that and earlier tragedies.

Wark, W. K. 'Review article: Appeasement Revisited', *International History Review*, 17 (1995), 545-562

Wilson, R. 'Memory and Trauma: Narrating the Western Front 1914-1918', *Rethinking History*, 13:2 (2009) 251-267

Winter, J. M. 'Catastrophe and Culture: Recent Trends in the Historiography of the First World War', *Journal of Modern History*, 64 (1992), 525-32

2. Memorialisation and Commemoration

2.1 General

During the Great War many nations experienced huge losses of life. As well as the individual responses offamilies mourning the loss of relatives, there were also local and national responses. Most cities in the countries involved in the conflict erected memorials, and the memorials in smaller villages and towns often listed the names of each local soldier who had been killed. Massive monuments commemorating thousands of dead with no identified war grave, such as the Menin Gate at Ypres and the Thiepval memorial on the Somme, were also constructed.

After the war there was an increasing number of sponsored as well as individual pilgrimages to the cemeteries and battlefields in Europe – a practice which is still prevalent in present times. Numerous guides to the cemeteries and battlefields have been produced in recent yearsNumerous websites were inaugurated in 2014 to commemorate the centenary of the First World War (see below under the sub-heading **Websites** in the section headed **Britain and Ireland)**

Books

Ashplant, T. G. 'War Commemoration in Western Europe: Changing Meanings, Divisive Loyalties, Unheard Voices', in *Commemorating War: The Politics of Memory*, edited by T. G. Ashplant [and others] (NewBrunswick, N.J.: Transaction Publishers, 2004)

Ashplant, T. G. and others, eds. *Commemorating War: The Politics of Memory*, edited by Timothy G. Ashplant, Graham Dawson, and Michael Roper, 1st paperback edn (London: Transaction Publishers, 2004)
Originally published under the title, *The Politics of War Memory and Commemoration*, London: Routledge, 2000.

Ashworth, G. J. 'The Memorialization of Violence and Tragedy: Human Trauma as Heritage', in *The Ashgate Companion to Heritage and Identity*, edited by Brian Graham and Peter Howard (Aldershot: Ashgate, 2008)

Borg, A. *War Memorials from Antiquity to the Present* (London: Leo Cooper, 1991)
Bostyn, F. *Passchendaele 1917: The Story of the Fallen and Tyne Cot Cemetery* (Barneley: Pen & Sword Military, 2007)

Coombs, R. *Before Endeavours Fade: A Guide to the Battlefields of the First World War*, by Rose B. Coombs [completely revised by Karel Margry], 12th rev. edn (Old Harlow: Battle of Britain International Ltd., 2006)
First published in 1976

Curl, J. S. *A Celebration of Death: An Introduction to Some of the Buildings, Monuments, and Settings of Funerary Architecture in the Western European Tradition* (London: Constable, 1980)

Davies, J. 'War Memorials', in *The Sociology of Death*, edited by D. Clark (Oxford: Blackwell, 1993)

Frantzen, A. J. *Bloody Good: Chivalry, Sacrifice, and the Great War* (Chicago: University of Chicago Press, 2004)

Garfield, J. The Fallen: A Photographic Journey through the War Cemeteries and Memorials of the Great War,

Memorialisation and Commemoration

1914-1918 (London: Leo Cooper, 1990) Goebel, S and D. Keene, eds. *Cities into Battlefields: Metropolitan Scenarios, Experiences, and Commemorations of Total War* (Farnham: Ashgate, 2011)
In an analysis of the global impact of military conflict on metropolises in the era of the First and Second World Wars this work explores the way in which cities were transformed into battlefields as a result of the blurring of the the boundaries between home and front.

Gough, P. 'Commemoration of War', in *The Ashgate Companion to Heritage and Identity*, edited by Brian Graham and Peter Howard (Aldershot: Ashgate, 2008)

Harris, J. and G. Stamp. *Silent Cities 1914-1919: An Exhibition of the Memorial and Cemetery Architecture of the Great War* [organized by John Harris and Gavin Stamp]. (London: Royal Institute of British Architects, 1977)
The exhibition 'Silent Cities' was first mounted at the Heinz Gallery of the Royal Institute of British Architects from November 9th to December 22nd 1977.

Hurst, S. C. *The Silent Cities: An Illustrated Guide to the War Cemeteries and Memorials to the 'Missing' in France and Flanders, 1914-1918* (London: Methuen, 1929; repr. London: Naval & Military Press, 1993)

Jones, N. H. *The War Walk: A Journey along the Western Front* (London: Robert Hale, 1983; repr. London: Cassell, 2004)

Laqueur, T. 'Memory and Naming in the Great War', in *Commemorations: The Politics of National Identity*, edited by J. Gillis (Princeton: Princeton University Press, 1994)

Laffin, J. *Battlefield Archaeology* (London: I. Allan, 1987)

Richardson, M. 'A Changing Meaning for Armistice Day', in *At the Eleventh Hour: Reflections, Hopes and Anxieties at the Closing of the Great War, 1918*, edited by P. Liddle and H. Cecil (Barnsley: Leo Cooper, 1998)

McIntyre, C. *Monuments of War: How to Read a War Memorial* (London: Robert Hale, 1990)

Robertshaw, A. and D. Kenyon. *Digging the Trenches: The Archaeology of the Western Front* (Barnsley: Pen & Sword Military, 2008)

Saunders, N. J. 'Apprehending Memory: Material Culture and War, 1919-39', in *The Great World War 1914-45*, edited by J. Bourne, P. H. Liddle and I. R. Whitehead, 2 vols (London: HarperCollins, 2000-2001), II: *The Peoples' Experience* (2001)

— *Trench Art*, 2nd edn (Barnsley: Pen & Sword Military, 2011)

Saunders, N. J., ed. *Matters of Conflict: Material Culture, Memory and the First World War* (London: Routledge, 2004)

Saunders, N. J. and P. Cornish. *Contested Objects: Material Memories of the Great War* (Abingdon: Routledge, 2009)

Scates, B. *Return to Gallipoli: Walking the Battlefields of the Great War* (Cambridge: Cambridge University Press, 2006)

Stamp, G. *The Memorial to the Missing of the Somme*, new edn (London: Profile Books, 2007)

Walter, T. 'War Grave Pilgrimage', in *Pilgrimage in Popular Culture*, by I. Reader and T. Walter (London: Macmillan, 1993)

Winter, J. 'Forms of Kinship and Remembrance in the Aftermath of the Great War', in *War and Remembrance in the Twentieth Century*, edited by J. Winter and E. Sivan (Cambridge: Cambridge University Press, 2000)

— 'Rites of Remembrance', *BBC History Magazine*, 1.7 (2000), 22-25

Wittman, L. *The Tomb of the Unknown Soldier: Modern Mourning, and the Reinvention of the Mystical Body* (Toronto; Buffalo University of Toronto Press, 2011

Articles

Goebel, S. 'Beyond Discourse? Bodies and Memories of Two World Wars', *Journal of Contemporary History*, 42 (2007), 377-386
Review article.

— 'Intersecting Memories: War and Remembrance in Twentieth-Century Europe', *Historical Journal*, 44 (2001), 853-858

Knight, L. 'In Memoriam', *Ancestors* (February 2004), 28-31

Lethaby, W. R. 'Memorials of the Fallen: Sacrifice or Service?', *Hibbert Journal*, 17 (1918-19), 621-25

Lucas, J. 'Memorials are Made of These', *Weekend Telegraph*, 7 November 1998, 12

McIntyre, C. 'War Memorials: A Magnificent Primary Source', *Family Tree Magazine*, 9.1 (1992), 16

— 'War Memorials: A Neglected Primary Source?', *Local History Magazine*, 52 (1995), 7-9

Moriarty, C. 'The Absent Dead and Figurative First World War Memorials', *Transactions of the Ancient Monuments Society*, 39 (1995), 7-40

— 'Christian Iconography and First World War Memorials, *Imperial War Museum Review*, 6 (1991), 63-74

— 'The Material Culture of Great War Remembrance', *Journal of Contemporary History*, 34 (1999), 653-62

Switzer, C. '"Letters of Imperishable Gold": The Role of Lists of Names in the Experience and Commemoration of the Great War', *Local Historian*, 38.3 (2008), 205-215

Tarlow, S. 'An Archaeology of Remembering: Death, Bereavement and the First World War', *Cambridge Archaeological Journal*, 7.1 (1997), 105-21

Wright, S. 'My Favourite History Place: Tyne Cot Cemetery, near Ypres', *Historian* (Historical Association), 122 (2014), 42

2.2 Britain and Ireland

The creation of war cemeteries, cenotaphs, and other local and national war memorials[196], the production of medals, commemorative plaques and honour scrolls, the distribution of poppies sold by the British Legion for use in wreaths and lapel buttons on the occasion of Remembrance Day, the organization of pilgrimages to war cemeteries and battlefields abroad, the foundation of local and national war museums (especially the Imperial War Museum [IWM]), and recourse to spiritualism [see also **section 2.8 (Church and Religion)** in **Part 3 (Waging War)**] were among the numerous ways in which the memory of the war, particularly of the dead, was perpetuated. One of the most interesting privately inspired acts of commemoration was the building of the Sandham Memorial Chapel[197] which was designed to house the paintings on the theme of the war that Stanley Spencer was commissioned to paint.

---

[196] There is a United Kingdom Inventory of War Memorials at http://www.ukniwm.org.uk/

[197] Louis and Mary Behrend, a wealthy couple, commissioned the architect, Lionel Pearson, to design the chapel and Stanley Spencer to produce the paintings to adorn its interior. It was built at Burghclere in Hampshire (previously in Berkshire) and dedicated by the Bishop of Guildford in March 1927 as the Oratory of All Souls. It later became known as the Sandham Memorial Chapel – in memory of Mary Behrend's brother, Lieutenant Henry Willoughby Sandham who died in Macedonia during the Great War – and was given to the National Trust in 1947. Each of the nineteen canvases with which Spencer decorated the interior walls of the chapel is dedicated to the same theme, the experience of war. Although there is no single narrative thread, there is a progression around the chapel, and the focus is on the painting on the large east wall.

The commissioning of the Tomb of the Unknown Warrior and the Cenotaph, which both became accessible to the public in 1920, represented Britain's most important act of national commemoration. Within a week of the burial of the Unknown Warrior in Westminster Abbey nearly one million people came to pay homage at the Tomb and over 400,000 people visited the Cenotaph during the first three days after it was unveiled. The ceremony at the Cenotaph subsequently became the focal point of commemoration in Britain each year. Over the years this annual ritual and all the local annual ceremonies that take place around the country have attracted a considerable amount of controversy, arising mainly from an aversion to them from pacifists, from those with bitter experience of war, and from those who have regarded the ceremonies as a hypocritical and chauvinistic glorification of the dead. Generally, however, these ceremonies were, and still are, treated with reverence by the public, perhaps even more so in the 21st century now that they include a commemoration of the lives which are lost in current wars and fresh in the minds of the public.

Another important act of commemoration was the establishment in 1960 of the Commonwealth War Graves Commission (CWGC) with the principal function of marking, recording and maintaining the graves and places of commemoration of Commonwealth of Nations military service members who died in the two World Wars. This body evolved out of the Imperial War Graves Commission (IMWGC) which was established on 21 May 1917 with the remit to build and maintain the cemeteries and memorials for those who fell in the First World War. The leading figure in the establishment of the IMWGC was Fabian Ware who had gone to France with the British Red Cross Society, and set up the Graves Registration Unit in 1915. During the First World War the decision was taken that no bodies were to be repatriated to Great Britain and that the graves, wherever situated, would be provided with standard headstones and designs reflecting the principle of equality in death. In due course the remit of the IMWGC was extended to the Second World War and, to reflect this, its name was changed in 1960 to 'Commonwealth War Graves Commission'. More information about the latter organisation can be found on the Commonwealth War Graves Commission website at www.cwgc.org

The Imperial War Museum (IWM) plays a particularly important part in preserving the memory of the Great War. In 1917 the Cabinet decided that a National War Museum should be set up to collect and display material relating to the Great War, which was then still being fought. The interest taken by the Dominion governments led to the museum being given the title of Imperial War Museum. It was formally established by Act of Parliament in 1920 and a governing Board of Trustees appointed. The Museum was opened in the Crystal Palace by King George V on 9 June 1920. From 1924 to 1935 it was housed in two galleries adjoining the former Imperial Institute, South Kensington. On 7 July 1936 the Duke of York, shortly to become King George VI, reopened the Museum in its present home in Southwark. At the outset of the Second World War the Museum's terms of reference were enlarged to cover both world wars and they were again extended in 1953 to include all military operations in which Britain or the Commonwealth have been involved since August 1914. In a recent profile the Museum is described on its website as "unique in its coverage of conflicts, especially those involving Britain and the Commonwealth, from the First World War to the present day".

Books

Archer, G. *The Glorious Dead: Figurative Sculpture of British First World War Memorials* (Norwich: Frontier, 2009)

Ashley, P. *Lest We Forget: War Memorials* (Swindon: English Heritage, 2004)

Baker, T. *Sutton-on-Sea Remembers: A Tribute to Those Whose Names are on the Village War Memorial* (Brinkhill: Corner House Books, 2006)

Barr, N. *The Lion and the Poppy: British Veterans, Politics and Society, 1921-1939* (Westport, Connecticut: Greenwood Press, 2005)

Boorman, D. *At the Going Down of the Sun: British First World War Memorials*, 2nd edn (York: Sessions, 1988)

Bushaway, B. 'Name Upon Name: The Great War and Remembrance', in *Myths of the English*, edited by R. Porter (Cambridge: Polity Press, 1992)

Cannadine, D 'War and Death, Grief and Mourning in Modern Britain', in *Mirrors of Mortality: Studies in the Social History of Death*, edited by J. Whaley (London: Europa, 1981)

Charman, T. 'A Museum of Man's Greatest Lunatic Folly: The Imperial War Museum [IWM] and its Commemoration of the Great War, 1917-2008', in *A Part of History: Aspects of the British Experience of the First World War*, introduced by Michael Howard (London: Continuum, 2009)

Connelly, M. *The Great War, Memory and Ritual: Commemoration in the City and East London, 1916-1939* (London: Boydell, 2002)

Cornish, P. The *First World War Galleries* (London: Imperial War Museum, 2014)
See also article below by James Taylor entiled 'New First World War Galleries'. The contents of the book by Cornish reflect the themes of these new (IWM London) galleries, i.e. 1. Hope and Glory; 2. Shock; 3. Your Country Needs You; 4. Deadlock; 5. World War; 6. Feeding the Front; 7. Total War; 8. At All Costs; 9. Life at the Front; 10. Machines Against Men; 11. Breaking Down; 12. Seizing Victory; 13. War Without End

Cookstown's War Dead, 1914-1918; 1939-1945, compiled and edited by Cookstown District Council in conjunction with The Friends of the Somme Mid Ulster Branch (Cookstown: Cookstown District Council, 2007)

Donaldson, P. *Ritual and Remembrance: The Memorialisation of the Great War in East Kent* (Cambridge: Cambridge Scholars Press, 2006)

Gaffney, A. *Aftermath: Remembering the Great War in Wales* (Cardiff: University of Wales Press, 1998; repr. 2000)

Gibson, E. and K. Ward, eds. *Courage Remembered: The Story Behind the Construction and Maintenance of the Commonwealth's Military Cemeteries and Memorials of the Wars of 1914-1918 and 1939-19*45 (London: HMSO, 1989)

Goodman, A. *The Street Memorials of St Albans Abbey Parish* (St Albans: St Albans and Hertfordshire Architectural Society, 1987)

Grayson, R. S. and F. McGarry, eds. *Remembering 1916: The Easter Rising, the Somme and the Politics of Ireland* (Cambridge: Cambridge University Press 2016)

Gregory, A, *The Silence of Memory: Armistice Day, 1919-1946* (Oxford: Berg, 1994)

Hazelgrove, J. *Spiritualism and British Society between the Wars* (Manchester: Manchester University Press, 2000)

Heathorn, S. *Haig and Kitchener in Twentieth-Century Britain: Remembrance, Representation and Appropriation* (Farnham: Ashgate, 2013)

Hughes, P. R. *Campden. 1914-1918* (Campden: Campden District Branch of Gloucestershire Family History Society, 2008)

Hussey, C. *The Life of Sir Edward Lutyens* (London: Antique Collectors' Club, 1984)
Reprint of *Country Life* 1953 Special edn.

Jamet, C. 'Oxford and Cambridge College War Memorials' (unpublished master's thesis, University of Cambridge, 1993)

Johnson, N. C. *Ireland, the Great War, and the Geography of Remembrance* (Cambridge: Cambridge University Press, 2003)

Kavanagh, G. *Museums and the First World War: A Social History* (London: Leicester University Press, 1994)

King, A. 'Acts and Monuments: National Celebrations in Britain from the Napoleonic to the Great War', in *Government and Institutions in the Post-1832 United Kingdom*, edited by A. O'Day (Lewiston, New York: Edwin Mellen Press, 1995)

— *Memorials of the Great War in Britain: The Symbolism and Politics of Remembrance* (Oxford: Berg, 1998).

Koureas, G. *Memory, Masculinity and National Identity in British Visual Culture, 1914-1930: A Study of 'Unconquerable*

Manhood' (London: Ashgate, 2007)

Leitch, M. *What Happened to Joe? Immingham's War Dead Remembered* (Immingham: WEA, 1995)

Leonard, J. *The Culture of Commemoration: The Culture of War Commemoration* (Dublin: Cultures of Ireland, 1996)

Lloyd, D. W. *Battlefield Tourism:. Pilgrimage and the Commemoration of the Great War in Britain, Australia and Canada 1919-1939* (Oxford: Berg, 1998)

Longworth, P. *The Unending Vigil: The History of the Commonwealth War Graves Commission*, 2nd edn (Barnsley: Leo Cooper, 1985)

Lutyens: The Work of the English Architect Sir Edwin Lutyens (1869-1944) (London: Arts Council of Great Britain, 1981)
Catalogue of an exhibition at the Hayward Gallery, London, 18 November 1981 - 31 January 1982 organized by Janet Holt.

Malvern, S. '"For King and Country": Frampton's Edith Cavell 1915-1920 and the Writing of Gender in Memorials to the Great War', in *Sculpture and the Pursuit of the Modern Ideal in Britain, c.1880-1930*, edited by David Getsy (Aldershot: Ashgate, 2004)

Moriarty, C. 'Private Grief and Public Remembrance: British First World War Memorials', in *War and Memory in the Twentieth Century*, edited by M. Evans and K. Lunn (Oxford: Berg; 1997)

Oliver, N. *Not Forgotten* (London: Hodder & Stoughton, 2005)

Potts, M. and J. Bratherton. *Dear Mrs Jones: The Great War Dead of Nantwich and Crewe* (Nantwich: Wonderworks Design Studio, 2001)

Quinlan, M. *British War Memorials* (Hertford: Authors Online, 2005)

— *Remembrance* (Hertford: Authors Online, 2005)

Sheldon, C. W. *'Roll of Honour': The Story of the Hundreds of Leek Men who fell in the First World War* (Leek: Three Counties Publishing, 2001)

Skelton, T. and G. Gliddon. *Lutyens and the Great War* (London: Frances Lincoln, 2008)

Stamp, G. *The Memorial to the Missing of the Somme*, new edn (London: Profile Books, 2007)

Summers, J. *Remembered: The History of the Commonwealth War Graves Commission*, photography by Brian Harris (London: Merrell, 2007)

Switzer, C. *Unionists and Great War Commemoration in the North of Ireland, 1914-1939: People, Places and Politics* (Dublin: Irish Academic Press, 2007)

Tiller, K. *Remembrance and Community: War Memorials and Local History* (Somersal Herbert: British Association for Local History 2013)

Westlake, R. *First World War Grave and Memorials in Gwent*, 2 vols (Barnsley: Wharncliffe Books, 2001)

— *Remembering the Great War in Gloucestershire and Herefordshire* (Studley: Brewin Books, 2002)

Wootton, G. *The Official History of the British Legion* (London: Macdonald & Evans, 1956)

Whittick, A. *War Memorials* (London: Country Life, 1946)

Articles

Bartlett, J. and K. M. Ellis. 'Remembering the Dead in Northop', *Journal of Contemporary History*, (1999), 231-42

Beaupré, D. and A. Watkinson. 'A Study of the Great War Canadians Commemorated in the United Kingdom', *Bulletin of the Western Front Association*, 90 (June/July 2011), 17-20

Beddard, R. 'Modern Monuments: A Quartet of the [National] Trust's 20th-century Buildings' [including Sandham Memorial Chapel, Burghclere]', *History Today*, 45 (1995), 56

Bourke, J. 'Heroes and Hoaxes: The Unknown Warrior, Kitchener, and "Missing Men" in the 1920s', *War and Society*, 13.2 (1995), 41-63

Brown, J. 'Recording War Memorials in Northumberland', *Local Historian*, 26:4 (1996), 209-222

Campbell, S. 'UK Heritage: Entering Spencer's World at War', *Daily Telegraph* (1 November, 2008)
"To mark the 90th anniversary of the armistice, Sophie Campbell visits the Sandham Memorial Chapel, adorned by Stanley Spencer's amazing paintings" [sub-title of the *Daily Telegraph* article].

Carmichael, J. 'Olive Edis: Imperial War Museum [IWM] Photographer in France and Belgium, March, 1919', *Imperial War Museum Review*, 4 (1989)[198]

Connelly, M. 'The Ypres League and the Commemoration of the Ypres Salient, 1914-1940', *War In History*, 16 (2009), 51-76

Curtis, P. 'The Whitehall Cenotaph: An Accidental Monument', *Imperial War Museum Review*, 9 (1994), 31-41

Durey, M. 'The Great Trust: Mrs Edith Ash's Campaign of Remembrance, 1916-1954', *History* 96 (2011), 260-279

Dutton, P. 'The Dead Man's Penny: A History of the Next of Kin Memorial Plaque', *Imperial War Museum Review*, 3 (1988), 60-8

Goebel, S. 'Re-Membered and Re-Mobilized: The "Sleeping Dead" in Interwar Germany and Britain', *Journal of Contemporary History*, 39.4 Special Issue: Collective Memory (2004), 487-501

Greenberg, A. 'Lutyens's Cenotaph', *Journal of Architectural Historians*, 48 (1989), 5-23

Grieves, K. Grieves, K. 'C. E. Montague and the Making of *Disenchantment*, 1914-1921', *War in History*, 4 (1997), 35-59

— 'C. E. Montague, Manchester and the Remembrance of War, 1918-1925', *Bulletin of the John Rylands University Library of Manchester*, 77 (1995), 85-104

— 'Commemorating the Fallen: War Memorial Debates in Four Sussex Villages after the Armistice', *The Poppy and the Owl*, no. 24 (November 1998)

— 'Commemorating the Fallen: The Lord Lieutenant's Soldier Sons in the First World War and the Making of the Memorial Chapel at St. Barnabas Church, Ranmore', *Surrey History*, 6 (2000), 107-124

— 'Common Meeting Places and the Brightening of Rural Life: Local Debates on Village Halls in Sussex after the First World War', *Rural History*, 10 (1999), 171-192

---

[198] " ... In 1918 the Imperial War Museum commissioned her [Olive Edis] to record war work by the British women's services in France and Flanders. As the only official woman photographer, and with a specially designed uniform, she travelled 2000 wintry miles in March 1919, testing her stamina, ingenuity, and three cameras to the limit, and brought back unique and poignant pictures. Many are still in the museum's collection with the diary that she kept. One shows six WAACs at Étaples in 1919, tending rows of war graves bearing temporary numbered wooden crosses, a bleak, snow-covered and wooded hill in the background ... " [Extracted from Shirley Neale, 'Edis, (Mary) Olive (1876–1955)', *Oxford Dictionary of National Biography*, Oxford University Press, 2004 (online edn)]

Memorialisation and Commemoration

— 'Investigating Local War Memorial Committees: Demobilised Soldiers, the Bereaved and Expressions of Local Pride in Sussex Villages, 1918-1921', *Local Historian*, 30.1 (2000), 39-58

— 'Rural Parish Churches and the Bereaved in Sussex after the First World War', *Sussex Archaeological Collections*, 139 (2001), 203-214

Gullace, N. 'Memory, Memorials, and the Postwar Literary Experience: Traditional Values and the Legacy of World War I', *Twentieth Century British History*, 10 (1999), 235-13

Heathorn, S. 'A "Matter for Artists, and Not for Soldiers"? The Cultural Politics of the Earl Haig National Memorial, 1928-1937', *Journal of British Studies*, 44 (2005), 536-61

Heffernan, M. 'For Ever England: The Western Front and the Politics of Remembrance in Britain', *Ecumene*, 2.3 (1995), 293-323

Hewitt, N. 'Permanence in a Changing World', *Despatches: The Bulletin of the Friends of the Imperial War Museum* [IWM] (December 2001), 13-15
Related to the launching of the UK National Inventory of War Memorials in November 2001 at the Imperial War Museum.

Hewitt, N. 'Return of the Fallen', *History Today*, 59, Issue 9 (2009), 3
Changing attitudes towards commemorating Britain's war dead.

Homberger, E. 'The Story of the Cenotaph', *The Times Literary Supplement*, 12 (1976), 1429-30

Horne, J. 'Ireland at the Somme: A Tale of Two Divisions', *History Today*, 57, Issue 4 (2007), 12-19
The author considers why the heroic efforts of the two Irish divisions, the 16th (Irish) and the 36th (Ulster) on the Western Front in 1916, have been represented so differently in terms of the inividual monuments which were erected to commemorate them

Inglis, K.S. 'The Homecoming: The War Memorial Movement in Cambridge, England', *Journal of Contemporary History*, 27 (1992), 583-605

Kavanagh, G. 'Museum as Memorial: The Origins of the Imperial War Museum [IWM]', *Journal of Contemporary History*, 23 (1988), 77-97

Keating, A. 'Remembrance Today: Poppies, Grief and Heroism', *Contemporary British History*, 28, (2014), 117-119

Kitching, P. 'Out and About: First World War Memorials in the Heart of London', *Historian* (Historical Association), 122 (2014), 44-47

Knight, L. and N. Hewitt. 'War Memorials and Local History: The UK National Inventory of War Memorials', *Local Historian*, 31.4 (2001), 221-229

Malone, C. 'The Art of Remembrance: The Arts and Crafts Movement and the Commemoration of the British War Dead, 1916-1920', *Contemporary British History*, 26 (2012), 1-23

Mansell, J. G. 'Musical Modernity and Contested Commemoration at the Festival of Remembrance, 1923-1927', *Historical Journal*, 52 (2009), 433-454

Mansfield, N. 'Class Conflict and Village War Memorials, 1914-24', *Rural History*, 6 (1995), 67-87

Moriarty, C. 'The National Inventory of War Memorials', *Local Historian*, 20:3 (1990), 123-125

Newman, S. 'The Gallipoli Memorial, Eltham', *The Historian*, 71 (2001), 29-34

Robinson, H. 'Remembering War in the Midst of Conflict: First World War Commemorations in the Northern Irish Troubles', *Twentieth Century British History*, 21 (2010), 80-101
Following the outbreak of the Troubles tthere has been a tendency in Northern Ireland for the commemorations of the world wars to be associated with the Protestant and unionist community, with Catholics often alienated or choosing not to

be involved. This tendency.has grown stronger with the result that these commeorations have become increasingly rowdy and loyalist and much less clearly linked with war remembrance

Skipwith, P. 'Gilbert Ledward and the Guards' Division Memorial', *Apollo*, 127 (1988), 22–6

Sokoloff, S. 'Researching "The Fallen" in Local Histories of the Great War', *Local Historian*, 46:4 (2016), 336-340

Stephens, J. '"The Ghosts of Menin Gate": Art, Architecture and Commemoration', *Journal of Contemporary History*, 44 (2009), 7-26
This article relates both to the gate, designed by the architect Reginald Blomfield in 1922 to commemorate the 56,000 British Empire soldiers lost in the battles of the Ypres Salient, and to the picture, *Menin Gate at Midnight* (painted by the Australian artist and soldier, William Longstaff, in 1927) showing the gate in the context of a landscape inhabited by ghostly soldiers.

Taylor, J. 'New First World War Galleries', *Despatches* (The Magazine of the Friends of the Imperial War Museum), no. 18 (2014), 14-19
In this articles James Taylor, IWM's Head of Research and Information, provides a description of the background and contents of IWM London's new First World War galleries which were opened to the public on 19 July 2014 after the completion of a project involving over four years of planning and research. A book by Paul Cornish entitled 'The First World War Galleries' (q.v.) was published to accompany the completion of the project.

Todman, D. '"Sans Peur et Sans Raproche": The Retirement, Death and Mourning of Sir Douglas Haig, 1918-1928', *Journal of Military History*, 67 (2003), 1083-1106

Westlake, R. 'Remembering the Great War in London: 31 May 2006', *Firestep: The Magazine of the London Branch of the Western Front Association*, 8.1 (2007), 31-39

Websites

North East War Memorials Project. [http://www.newmp.org.uk/index.php]
"The NEWP is intended to assist members of the public, Local and Family History Groups, Military Historians, Schools and individuals to learn about and research their local War Memorials and record the results. It aims to record every War Memorial located between the River Tweed and River Tees" [extracted from website introduction]. Under the sub-section, 'Resources', there is a bibliography which covers works on monuments, war graves and cemeteries, war memorials and rolls of honours, and war memorial artists, both generally and also by specific regions and towns around the world - mostly related to the two World Wars. Although the bibliography is to a certain extent global in its approach its emphasis is on Great Britain.

Numerous websites were inaugurated from 2014 to commemorate the centenary of the First World War. Among them were:

Baker, C. *The Long, Long Trail* [http://1914-1918.net/]
"A truly vast resource based on decades of research, the *Long, Long Trail* provides a detailed account of the structure, organization and regulations which shaped the British Army, the battles across the globe in which it fought, and a comprehensive guide to genealogists and researchers on how best to find and interpret the official records generated during the conflict. In addition, the website provides transcripts of items such as the despatches written by successive commanders-in-chief of the British Expeditionary Force, Sir John French and Sir Douglas Haig, an impressive – but by no means comprehensive – selection of campaign maps digitised from various sources, and a colossal and knowledgeable forum boasting over 44,000 members. For anyone requiring further information on any aspect of the British Army in the First World War, the website is unsurpassed in terms of the quantity and quality of information available". [Quotations extracted from Philips, C. Review of *First World War Digital Resources*, q.v.]

BBC. History. *World War One* [http://www.bbc.co.uk/ww1]
"The BBC has … enlisted the support of senior academics, alongside the more instantly recognisable faces of journalists and presenters …. Linked to the iPlayer service, and utilizing a combination of audio, visual and textual resources, the BBC have created a website with a broad range of materials aimed at both the relative novice and the more informed viewer … The centrepiece, a series of articles under the banner of *World War I at Home* … concentrates upon the presentation of 'local stories from a global conflict'". [Quotations extracted from Philips, C. Review of *First World War Digital Resources*, q.v.]

— *World War One at Home* [http://www.bbc.co.uk/programmes/p01nhwgx]

Memorialisation and Commemoration

The BBC has partnered with Imperial War Museums and the Arts and Humanities Research Council. to produce this growing collection of stories that show how WW1 affected the people and places of the UK and Ireland.

— *WW1 Interactive Guide* [http://www.bbc.co.uk/history/0/ww1/25768752]
Presented by historians (such as Gary Sheffield), television presenters (Gareth Malone, Matt Baker) and BBC journalists (Kate Adie, Rory Cellan-Jones).

BBC. Media Centre. *The BBC Announces its Four-Year World War One Centenary Season*, 16 October, 2013
[http://www.bbc.co.uk/mediacentre/latestnews/2013/world-war-one-centenary.html]
The BBC's announcement on 16 October, 2013, of its plans to mark the First World War Centenary with a project designed to feature "four years of programming and events spanning 2014-2018 – echoing the timeframe of the war".

— *Marking the Centenary of World War One across the BBC*, 4 February, 2014
[http://www.bbc.co.uk/mediacentre/mediapacks/ww1/]
The website provides an introduction and also affords links to information provided under the following headings: Documentaries, Historical Debate, Commemoration, Arts & Music, Drama, Across the UK, Digital & Online, Children's & Schools, Special Editions

Exeter University. *First World War in the Classroom* [http://ww1intheclassroom.exeter.ac.uk/]
Presents "the findings of an AHRC[Arts and Humanities Research Council] - funded project led by Catriona Pennell, which examined the links between education and the manner in which the war was both perceived and commemorated". [Quotation extracted from Philips, C. Review of *First World War Digital Resources*, q.v.]

Gateways to the First World War [http://www.gatewaysfww.org.uk]
"Staff from the [University of Kent's] School of History are involved in a major project funded by the Arts and Humanities Research Council (AHRC). The Gateways to the First World War public engagement centre was launched in May 2014 with the aim of encouraging and supporting public interest in the centenary of the First World War through a range of events, activities, advice and expertise.
Led by the School of History's Professor Mark Connelly, Gateways to the First World War is a collaborative project involving leading First World War researchers Dr Brad Beaven (Portsmouth), Dr Helen Brooks (Kent), Professor Alison Fell (Leeds), Dr Emma Hanna (Greenwich), Dr Lucy Noakes (Brighton) and Dr Dan Todman (Queen Mary, London). The centre was launched in May 2014 and the team is working on a wide range of community activities commemorating the centenary across the UK" [extract from the website's introduction].

'The Great War and the Moving Image' (joint conference of the University of Kent and the University of Southampton, held in Canterbury, 15–16 April 1916) under the auspices of the AHRC-funded 'Gateways to the First World War' project [see www.kent.ac.uk/ww1/].

Imperial War Museum. *First World War Centenary Partnership*.
[http://www.iwm.org.uk/corporate/projects-partnerships/first-world-war-centenary-partnership]
"The First World War Centenary Programme is a vibrant global programme of cultural events, exhibitions and activities, and online resources that connect current and future generations with the lives, stories and impact of the First World War. The programme is presented by the First World War Centenary Partnership, a network of local, regional, national and international cultural and educational organisations, led by IWM". [IWM's description of the website]

Imperial war Museum. *Lives of the First World War* [https://livesofthefirstworldwar.org/]
The focal point of the IWM's contribution to the WW1 centenary is the *Lives of the First World War* project which aims aims to create a "permanent digital memorial to more than eight million men and women from across Britain and the Commonwealth" before the end of the centenary. "This innovative, interactive platform will bring material from museums, libraries, archives and family collections from across the world together in one place, inspiring people of all ages to explore, reveal and share the life stories of those who served in uniform and worked on the home front". [The quotations are extracted fro IWM's description of the websiste]

United Kingdom. Government. *First World War Centenary*, 2014 [https://www.gov.uk/government/topical-events/first-world-war-centenary]
Announcement of plans led by the Department for Culture, Media & Sport (and also involving the Ministry of Defence, Department for Education, Department for Communities and Local Government and Foreign & Commonwealth Office), working alongside partners including Imperial War Museums, Heritage Lottery Fund and the Commonwealth War Graves Commission, "to build a commemoration fitting of this significant milestone in world history"

3. The Military Post-Mortem

British command and generalship in the Great War has been the subject of voluminous debate and controversy ever since that war began. During the war itself the civilian debate about it tended to be uncritical, because of the effects of a combination of propaganda, the attitude of the bulk of war correspondents who, like Philip Gibbs, chose to describe the performance of the High Command on the Western front in a favourable light, and the ability of censorship to stifle the outspoken criticism of writers like Charles Repington (the military correspondent of *The Times* at beginning of the war). Even Liddell Hart, who was to be far more critical in hispost-war writings, was full of praise for the British High Command and staff in 1916. British histories such as Conan Doyle's *The British Campaign in Flanders* and John Buchan's *Nelson's History of the* War (both works started in the war and completed after it), tended to be on the whole uncritical of the High Command and to have the same sort of traditional, patriotic, and even romantic characteristics of the popular war fiction and memoirs produced during the war.

After the war the situation changed. A post mortem inevitably followed and one of its features was the generation of persistent and bitter debates over the reputations of Kitchener, Lloyd George and the senior Western Front commanders, including French, Smith-Dorrien, Gough and above all, Haig. This particularly found expression in biographies, memoirs, and other historical works in which the authors took one side or another of the debate and, in the case of some memoirs, were motivated by the desire for personal vindication. Dewar and Boraston's *Sir Douglas Haig's Command* (1922) is an example of a work biased towards representing British generalship and staff work in a blatantly favourable light while works such as Fuller's *Generalship, Its Diseases and their Cure* (1933), Gibbs' *Realities of War* (1920), Liddell Hart's *The Real War* (1930) and Cruttwell's *A History of the Great War* (1934) were intent on analysing it in a more critical way, and even the series of official histories, edited chiefly by Sir J. E. Edmonds, were by no means devoid of criticism, albeit expressed obliquely rather than overtly. J. C. Fuller was particularly strident in his criticism, while Cruttwell, although voicing criticism in his *History of the Great War*, generally displayed greater balance and objectivity than either Fuller or Liddell Hart. It was also evident from his *War Books: A Critical Guide* (1930) that Cyril Falls was another writer who did not take the same line as Fuller and Liddell Hart as became clearer in the moderate, balanced view of British generalship he took in his *The First World War* published in 1960. It was, however, the positively critical view of British generals and generalship taken in Churchill's *The World Crisis* (first published between 1923 and 1929), Liddell Hart's *The Real War* (first published in 1930), and Lloyd George's *War Memoirs* (first published between 1933 and 1936), and the focus in these books on the personalities of the senior commanders as a means of analyzing the military conduct of the war, that exerted the most profound influence on the direction taken by studies on the war in the years to come (in spite of the efforts of historians like Cyril Falls in *War Books*, 1930, and Douglas Jerrold in *The Lie about the War*, to present a more balanced and objective view via their appraisal of the war literature that had been published). In particular the resurgence of public interest in the Great War in the 1960's tended to revive the personality-driven controversies on the performance of British generals and generalship and set the scene for the decade of debunking which in the world of print was heralded by Leon Wolff's *In Flanders Fields* (first published in Britain in 1959), notoriously exemplified by Alan Clark in his *Donkeys* (first published in 1961), but subsequently moderated by a number of historians who, eschewing the prevailing fashion for debunking, presented a more positive, revisionist viewpoint on the subject. John Terraine's efforts in this respect were among the earliest in the period after the Second World War and they were later built on by a host of other historians including Tim Travers, Dominick Graham, David French, Trevor Wilson, Robin Prior, Brian Bond, John Bourne, Ian Beckett, Peter Simkins, Stephen Badsey, John Lee and Nigel Cave.

The musical drama, *Oh! What a Lovely War* (first performed on the stage in 1963 and later filmed in 1969), took debunking to the extremes, powerfully helping to lay the foundations with other forms of 1960's debunking for a mythology portraying British officers generally as brainless members of the upper class and, in particular, pillorying generals as incompetent and insensitive, callously sending their men off to be butchered while they lived it up in chateaux behind the lines. These views, encapsulated with brilliantly comical effect in Thacker, T. *British Culture and the First World War: Experience, Representation and Memory* (London: Bloomsbury Academic, 2014) (1989), have continued to maintain their grip on popular opinion about the Great War in spite of a number of military historians who have recently expressed more objective and balanced opinions. This grip is being loosened by the stimulus of the vastly expanded range of documentary and other sources now available as, for example, in the collections at the Imperial War Museum (IWM) and in numerous local and regimental museums, and as a result of the release from 1968 onwards of a great deal of previously inaccessible material in the Public Record Office (now known as the National Archives). With the availability of a greater range of resources a number of military historians have grasped the opportunity to divert the focus from the controversial debate on the performance of senior British generals and the notion of them as 'butchers and bunglers' to a closer, dispassionate examination of the structure of command and control that is leading, it is to be hoped, to a military reassessment of the Great War in less emotional and polemical terms.

Bibliographies

Van Hartesveldt, F. R. *The Battles of the British Expeditionary Forces, 1914-1915: Historiography and Annotated Bibliography* (Westport, Conn.: Praeger, 2005)

Autobiographies, Biographies, Diaries, Letters

Arthur, Sir G. *The Life of Lord Kitchener*, 3 vols (London: Macmillan, 1920)

Ash, B. *The Lost Dictator: A Biography of Field-Marshal Sir Henry Wilson* (London: Cassell, 1968)

Ballard, C. *Smith-Dorrien* (London: Constable, 1931)

Barrow, Sir. G. *The Life of General Sir Charles Carmichael Monro* (London: Hutchinson, 1931)

Bayne, J. *Far From a Donkey: The Life of General Sir Ivor Maxse* (London: Brassey's, 1995)

Birdwood, W. R., 1st Baron Birdwood of Anzac and Totnes. *In My Time: Recollections and Anecdotes* (London: Skeffington, 1946)

— *Khaki and Gown*, an autobiography by Field Marshal Lord Birdwood, with a foreword by the Rt. Hon. Winston Churchill (London: Ward Lock & Co., 1941)

Bonham-Carter, V. *Soldier True: The Life and Times of Field-Marshal Sir William Robertson* (London: Muller, 1963)

Callwell, Sir C. E. *Experiences of a Dug-Out, 1914-1918* (London: Constable, 1920)
Sir Charles Calwell served as Director of Military Operations and Intelligence, War Office 1914-16. Performed liaison duties with Allies 1916-1918. Major-General and KCB 1917.

— *Field-Marshall Sir Henry Wilson ... His Life And Diaries*, 2 vols (London: Cassell, 1927)

Cassar, G. H. *Kitchener: Architect of Victory* (London: Kimber, 1977)

Chapman-Huston, D. and O. Rutter. *General Sir John Cowans: The Quartermaster-General of the Great War*, 2 vols (London: Hutchinson, 1924)

Charteris, J. *Field-Marshall Earl Haig* (London: Cassell, 1929)

Collier, B. *Brasshat: A Biography of Field-Marshal Sir Henry Wilson* (London: Secker & Warburg, 1961)

Cooper, A. D., Viscount Norwich. *Haig*, 2 vols (London: Faber, 1935-1936)

Crowley, P. *Loyal to Empire: The life of General Sir Charles Monro, 1860-1929* (Stroud: The History Press, 2016)

Crozier, F. P. *A Brass Hat in No Man's Land* (London: Cape 1930; repr. Norwich: Gliddon, 1989)
Crozier was an experienced professional soldier who in 1914 joined the Royal Irish Fusiliers with the rank of Captain. During the next five years he won the D.S.O., C.M.G., C.B., Croix de Guerre with palm, was mentioned seven times in despatches, and ended the war as a Brigadier-General.

DeGroot, G. J. *Douglas Haig, 1861-1928* (London: Unwin Hyman, 1988)

Esher, R. B. B., 2nd Viscount. *The Tragedy of Lord Kitchener* (London: Murray, 1921)

Farr, D. *Silent General: Horne of the First Army: A Biography of Haig's Trusted Great War Comrade-in-Arms* (Solihull: Helion, 2007)

Farrar-Hockley, A. *Goughie: The Life of General Sir Hubert Gough* (London: Hart Davis MacGibbon, 1975)

French, J. D. P, 1st Earl of Ypres. *1914*, 2nd edn (London : Constable, 1919)

— *The Despatches of Lord French*: Mons, the Marne, the Aisne, Flanders, Neuve Chapelle, the Second Battle of Ypres, Loos, Hohenzollern Redoubt, and a complete list of the officers and men mentioned (London: Chapman & Hall, 1917)

Gardner, R. B. *Allenby* (London: Cassell, 1965)

Germains, V. W. *The Truth About Kitchener* (London: Lane, 1925)

Gough, Sir. H. *Soldiering On* (London: Arthur Barker, 1954)

Haig, D., Earl Haig. *The Private Papers of Douglas Haig, 1914-19: Being Selections from the Private Diary and Correspondence of Field Marshall Earl Haig of Bemersyde*, edited by Robert Blake (London: Eyre & Spottiswoode, 1952)

Harington, Sir C. *Plumer of Messines* (London: Murray, 1935)

— *Tim Harington Looks Back* (London: Murray, 1941)
Sir Charles Harington, known as Tim, served as Major-General, general staff, under General Plumer, 1916-18.

Headlam, Sir. C. M. *The Military Papers of Lieutenant-Colonel Sir Cuthbert Headlam 1910-1942*, edited by Jim Beach, Publications of the Army Records Society, 30 (Brimscombe Port: History Press, 2010)
Cuthbert Headlam joined the Bedfordshire Yeomanry in 1910 and went with them to France in 1915. After moving across to the General Staff and reaching the rank of Lieutenant-Colonel he served in a variety of mainly intelligence posts before becoming the British Expeditionary Force's principal doctrine writer. He became a Conservative politician after the First World War and also edited the *Army Quarterly* until 1942.. His letters and diary entries provide an informative insight into the British Army in in a time of war.

Holmes, R. *The Little Field-Marshal: Sir John French* (London: Cape, 1981)

Lawrence, J. *Imperial Warrior: The Life and Times of Field-Marshal Viscount Allenby* 1861-1936 (London: Weidenfeld and Nicolson, 1993)

Lee, J. 'William Birdwood: Fourth Army 1918; Fifth Army 1918', in *Haig's Generals*, edited by I. F. W. Beckett and S. J. Corvi (London: Leo Cooper, 2006)

Lloyd George, D. *War Memoirs*. 2nd edn, 2 vols (London: Odhams, 1942)
Originally published in 6 vols: London: Nicholson & Watson, 1933-36.

Macready, Sir. G. N. *Annals of an Active Life*, 2 vols (London: Hutchinson, 1924)
Macready served as GOC, Belfast, 1914; Adjutant-General, British Expeditionary Force, 1914-16; Adjutant-General to the forces 1916-18.

Magnus, P. *Kitchener: Portrait of an Imperialist* (London: John Murray, 1958; repr. Harmondsworth: Penguin, 1968)

Maurice, Sir F. B., ed. *The Life of General Lord Rawlinson of Trent: From His Journals and Letters* (London: Cassell, 1928)
Rawlinson commanded IV Corps, 1914-15; in temporary command of 1st Army, 1915; Lieutenant-General in command of Fourth Army, 1916; General 1917; representative in Supreme War Council 1918; commanded Fifth Army, which he reconstituted as Fourth, 1918.

Mead, G. *The Good Soldier: A Biography of Douglas Haig* (London: Atlantic Books, 2007)

Nash, N. S. *Chitral Charlie: The Rise and Fall of Major General Charles Townshend* (London: Pen & Sword, 2010)
This biography provides an objective examination of Townshend's controversial conduct (after a series of brilliant victories at Kurma, Amara and Kut, and his ill-judged advance on Baghdad) during and after the siege of Kut where he had been forced to retreat and endure a humiliating surrender, and an assessment of whether his fall from favour and popularity was justified. Townshend became known as 'Chitral Charlie' as a result of the skill and judgement he displayed when he was in command of the besieged garrison fort at Chitral in 1895.

Powell. G. *Plumer, the Soldier's General: A Biography of Field-Marshal Viscount Plumer of Messines* (London: Cooper, 1990)

Reid, W. *Architect of Victory: Douglas Haig* (Edinburgh: Birlinn, 2006)

Robertson, Sir W. R. *From Private to Field-Marshal* (London: Constable, 1921)

— *The Military Correspondence of Field-Marshal Sir William Robertson, Chief of the Imperial General Staff, December 1915-February 1918*, edited by David R. Woodward (London: Bodley Head for the Army Records Society, 1989)

— *Soldiers and Statesman, 1914-1918*, 2 vols (London: Cassell, 1926; repr. Aldershot: Gregg Revivals in association with Department of War Studies, King's College London, 1991)

Savage, L. *Allenby of Armageddon: A Record of the Career and Campaigns of Field-Marshal Viscount Allenby*, with a preface by the Right Honourable David Lloyd George (London: Hodder and Stoughton, 1925)

Seely, J. E. B., 1st Baron Mottistone. *Adventure* (London: Heinemann, 1930)
Seely commanded Canadian Cavalry Brigade in France, 1914-18.

— *Fear, and Be Slain: Adventures by Land, Sea and Air* (London: Hodder & Stoughton, 1931)

Smith-Dorrien, Sir H. L. *Memories of Forty-Eight Years' Service* (London: Murray, 1925)

Smithers, A. J. *The Man Who Disobeyed: Sir Horace Smith-Dorrien and his Enemies* (London: Leo Cooper, 1970)

Stewart, W. F. *The Embattled General: Sir Richard Turner and the First World War* (Montreal: McGill-Queen's University Press 2015)

Syk, A., ed. *The Military Papers of Lieutenant-General Frederick Stanley Maude, 1914-1917* (Stroud: History Press for the Army Records Society, 2012)

Terraine, J. *Douglas Haig: The Educated Soldier* (London: Hutchinson, 1963; repr. London: Cassell, 2000)

Trythall, A. J. *'Boney' Fuller: The Intellectual General* (London: Cassell, 1977)

Wavell, A. P., Earl Wavell. *Allenby: A Study in Greatness*, 2 vols (London: Harrap, 1940-1943)

Willliams, J. *Byng of Vimy: General and Governor General* (London: Leo Cooper, 1983; repr, 1992)

Wooward, D. R. *Field Marshall Sir William Robertson* (London: Praeger, 1998)

Books

Badsey, S. *The British Army in Battle and its Image, 1914-18* (London: Continuum, 2009)

— *Doctrine and Reform in the British Cavalry, 1880-1918*, Birmingham Studies in First World War History (Aldershot: Ashgate, 2008)

Beach, J. *Haig's Intelligence GHQ and the German Army, 1916-1918* (Cambridge: Cambridge University Press 2013)

Beckett, I. F. W. 'Frocks and Brasshats', in *The First World War and British Military History*, edited by B. Bond (Oxford: Clarendon, 1991)

— 'Hubert Gough, Neill Malcolm, and Command on the Western Front', in *Look To Your Front: Studies in the First World War* by the British Commission for Military History, edited by B. Bond [and others] (Staplehurst: Spellmount, 1999)
Cautiously favourable portrait of Gough.

Beckett, I. F. W. and S. J. Corvi. *Haig's Generals* (London: Leo Cooper, 2006)
Allenby, Byng, Birdwood, Gough, Horne, Monro, Plumer, Rawlinson and Smith-Dorrien are included in this assessment of Douglas Haig's army commanders on the Western Front in relation to their careers and characters, performance in command, relationship with their subordinates and with Haig himself, and of the methods they employed to find a solution to the problem of war on the Western Front.

Boff. J. *Winning and Losing on the Western Front: The British Third Army and the Defeat of Germany in 1918* (Cambridge: Cambridge University Press, 2012)
An examination of how the opposing armies fought during the 'Hundred Days' campaign and an assessment of how far the British Army's application of adaptation to the changing nature of modern warfare provided the basis for this army's part in the Allied victory.

Bond, B. *The Unquiet Western Front: Britain's Role in Literature and History* (Cambridge: Cambridge University Press, 2002)

Bond, B., ed. *The First World War and British Military History* (Oxford: Clarendon Press, 1991)

Bond, B. and N. Cave, eds. *Haig: A Reappraisal 70 Years On* (London: Cooper, 1999)

Bourne, J. 'The BEF's Generals on 29 September, 1918: An Empirical Portrait with Some British and Australians Comparisons', in *1918: Defining Victory*, proceedings of the Chief of Army's History Conference held at the National Convention Centre, Canberra, 29 September 1998, edited by P. Dennis and J. Grey (Canberra: Army History Unit, Dept. of Defence, 1999)

Brown, I. M. *British Logistics on the Western Front, 1914-1919* (London: Praeger, 1998)
In this examination of the evolution of the British Expeditionary Force's (BEF's) logistic and administrative infrastructure in France and its impact on operations the author challenges the popular notion of bungling, incompetent generals by demonstrating the professional manner in which they tackled the administrative and logistic problems which arose from the enormous expansion of the BEF and its artillery-dominated style of warfare.

Churchill, Sir W. *The Fighting Line: Two Speeches on the Army delivered in the House of Commons on May 23rd and May 31st, 1916* (London: Macmillan, 1916)

— *The World Crisis*, 3rd edn, 6 vols (London: Butterworth, 1931)
Vol 1, 1911-1914; Vol 2, 1915: Vols 3-4, 1916-1918; Vol 5, The Aftermath; Vol 6, The Eastern Front.

Clark, A. *Donkeys* (London: Hutchinson, 1961; repr. London: Pimlico, 1991)
A study of the Western Front in 1915, this book is a crushing indictment of incompetent generalship. The author explores the truth of the observation that British troops were "lions led by donkeys" and shows how the huge losses that were sustained almost completely destroyed the old professional army. In a review of the 1991 reprint of the book provided by Kirkus UK it is described as "a book that helped set the tone for the sceptical 60's: an attack on the British high command in France in 1915, which in the author's view destroyed by incompetence what was left of the British Expeditionary Force of August 1914 (half of whom, as he might have mentioned, had become casualties before that Christmas). An immoderate statement of a moderately strong case …" (see also annotations accompanying Sheffield's *Forgotten Victory* and Sheffield and Todman's *Command and Control on the Western Front* as examples of differing and more moderate views).

Corrigan, G. *Mud, Blood and Poppycock: Britain and the First World War* (London: Cassell, 2003)
In this work Gordon Corrigan refutes the popular view of incompetent, bungling generals treating their soldiers as cannon fodder, as exemplified by the 'Blackadder' TV series and Alan Clark's *The Donkeys*, and concentrates instead on the way the British Army was able to develop an approach to trench warfare that ultimately enabled it to achieve the military breakthrough that ended the war.

Cruttwell, C. R. M. F. *A History of the Great War, 1914-1918* (Oxford: Clarendon Press, 1934)

The Military Post-Mortem

Davies, F. and G. Maddocks. *Bloody Red Tabs: General Officer Casualties of the Great War 1914-1918* (London: Cooper, 1995)
In an examination of the origin and perpetuation of the myth that most senior British officers of the First World War had spent their time in safety far behind the front lines the authors show, through the biographies of over 200 officers who held the rank of Brigadier-General or above who were killed or wounded during the war, that this myth was at odds with the real facts.

Dennis, P. and J. Grey, eds. *1917: Tactics, Training and Technology; the 2007 Chief of Army Military History Conference* ([Loftus, N.S.W.?]: Australian Military History Publications 2007)

Dewar, G. A. B. and J. H. Boraston. *Sir Douglas Haig's Command, December 19, 1915, to November 11, 1918*, by George A. B. Dewar, assisted by J. H. Boraston, 2 vols (London: Constable, 1922)

Dixon, N. F. *On the Psychology of Military Incompetence* (London: Cape, 1976)
In this survey of military inefficiency over a period of 100 years that includes the campaigns of the Great War, there is an examination of the social psychology of military organizations, including case studies of individual commanders, that reveal a pattern in the causes of military disasters.

Erickson, E. J. *Gallipoli: Command under Fire* (Oxford: Osprey Publishing, 2015)

Farrar-Hockley, A. 'Sir Hubert Gough and the German Breakthrough, 1918', in *Fallen Stars*, edited by Brian Bond (London: Brassey's, 1991)

French, E. G. F. *French Replies to Haig* (London: Hutchinson, 1936)
In this work the author refutes the accusations made in the diaries of Earl Haig against the Earl of Ypres [John French] during the time he was Commander-in-Chief at the beginning Great War.

Fuller, J. F. C. *Generalship, its Diseases and their Cure: A Study of the Personal Factor in Command* (London: Faber, 1933)

Gibbs, Sir P. *Realities of War*, new and revised edn (London: Hutchinson, 1929)
Basically an attack on Haig and GHQ

Gough, Sir. H. *The Fifth Army* (London: Hutchinson, 1931)
Gough's defence of his record in the First World War, ghosted by the novelist Bernard Newman. Gough also extracted the chapters on 1918 and published them separately as *The March Retreat*, London: Cassell, 1934.

— *The March Retreat* (London: Cassell. 1934)
On the operations of the Fifth Army in the spring of 1918.

Graham, D. *Against Odds: Reflections on the Experiences of the British Army, 1914-45* (Basingstoke: Macmillan, 1998)
In this work which provides a comparison of the performance of the British Army in the two world wars, the author takes the view that the source of failure in the Great War was that Sir Douglas Haig was unable either to adopt operations which were appropriate for the strategy he had chosen or to develop tactics suitable for the implementation of these operations.

— 'Sans Doctrine: British Army Tactics in the First World War', in *Men at War: Politics, Technology, and Innovation in the Twentieth Century*, edited by Timothy Travers and Christon Archer (Chicago: Precedent, 1982; repr. New Brunswick (U.S.A.): Transaction Publishers, 2011)

Green, A. *Writing the Great War: Sir James Edmonds and the Official History 1915-1948* (London: Cass, 2003)

Griffith, P., ed. *British Fighting Methods in the Great War* (London: Cass, 1996)
In this collection of essays which focus on tactical issues in relation to the war on the Western Front, it is shown that the British high command achieved more success in the realm of tactics than is usually assumed.

Harris, J. P. *Douglas Haig and the First World War*, [new edn] (Cambridge: Cambridge University Press, 2009)

Heathorn, S. J. *Haig and Kitchener in Twentieth-Century Britain: Remembrance, Representation and Appropriation.* (Farnham: Ashgate, 2013)

Hodgkinson, P. E. *British Infantry Commanders in the First World War* (Farnham: Ashgate Publishing Limited, 2015)

Jerrold, D. *The Lie About the War: A Note on Some Contemporary War Books* (London: Faber, 1930)

Laffin, J. *British Butchers and Bunglers of World War One* (Stroud: Sutton, 1988)
In this analysis of the British generals' leadership during the Great War John Laffin emphatically lays the blame for the catastrophic reverses and huge loss of life in the campaigns on the Western front on the incompetence and callousness of the generals who commanded the armies. (See also annotations accompanying Sheffield's *Forgotten Victory* and Sheffield and Todman's *Command and Control on the Western Front* as examples of differing and more moderate views).

Liddell Hart, B. H. *The Real War 1914-1918* (London: Faber, 1930)
An enlarged edition of *The Real War, 1914-1918* was published in 1934 by Faber as *A History of the World War 1914-1918*, and a larger format edition of it published by Cassell in 1970 as *History of the First World War* was reprinted by Papermac (Basingstoke) in 1992 and 1997.

— *Through the Fog of War* (London: Faber, 1938)
Includes some critical comments about many senior British commanders, reflecting Liddell Hart's change from uncritical admiration of them as a young subaltern in 1915.

Macphail, Sir A. *Three Persons* (London: Murray, 1929)
Includes a study of Sir Henry Wilson, with special reference to his *Life and Diaries*.

Mallinson, A. *Too Important for the Generals: Losing and Winning the First World War* (London: Bantam, 2016)

Marble, S. *British Artillery on the Western Front in the First World War: "The Infantry Cannot Do With A Gun Less"* (Farnham:: Ashgate 2013}

Marshall-Cornwall, Sir J. H. *Haig as Military Commander* (London: Batsford, 1973)

Maurice, Sir F. *Intrigues of the War*, startling revelations hidden until 1922; important military secrets now disclosed (London: Printed by Loxley Bros., 1922)
Reprinted from the Westminster Gazette.

— *The Maurice Case: From the Papers of Major-General Sir Frederick Maurice*, edited by Nancy Maurice (London: Cooper, 1972)
Also reproduces Sir Frederick Maurice's *Intrigues of the War*

Morris, R. *Haig: The General's Progress* (London: Robson, 1982)

Mosier, J. *The Myth of the Great War: A New Military History of World War 1* (London: Profile, 2001)

Neillands, R. *The Great War Generals on the Western Front, 1914-18* (London: Robinson, 1998)

Nicholson, W. N. *Behind the Lines: An Account of Administrative Staffwork in the British Army 1914-18* (London: Cape, 1939; repr. Stevenage: Strong Oak, 1989)

Philpott, W. J. *Anglo-French Relations and Strategy on the Western Front, 1914-18* (Basingstoke: Macmillan in association with King's College London, 1996)

Pois, R. A. and P. Langer. *Command Failure in War: Psychology and Leadership* (Bloomington, Ind.: Indiana University Pres, 2004)
See chapter 7: Conventional Historical Explanations: The British Military in World War I

Prete, R.A. *Strategy and Command: The Anglo-French Coalition on the Western Front, 1914* (Montreal: McGill-Queen's University Press, 2009)

Prior, R. *Churchill's 'The World Crisis' as History* (London: Croom Helm, 1983)

Prior, R. and T. Wilson. *Command on the Western Front: The Military Career of Sir Henry Rawlinson, 1914-1918*

(Oxford: Blackwell, 1992)
In this work the authors use the contents of the diary in which Rawlinson recorded his views on tactics and day-to-day events of the battlefield as the basis for studying the tactics of the time (in relation, for example, to night attacks, poison gas, the introduction of the tank, hurricane bombardment and creeping barrages).

Robbins, S. *British Generalship during the Great War: The Military Career of Sir Henry Horne (1861-1929)* (Farnham: Ashgate Publishing Ltd, 2010)

Royle, T. *The Kitchener Enigma* (London: Joseph, 1985)

Sheffield, G. D. 'An Army Commander on the Somme: Hubert Gough', in *Command and Control on the Western Front: The British Army's Experience, 1914-1918*, edited by G. Sheffield and D. Todman (Statplehurst: Spellmount, 2004)
Unfavourable view of Gough.

— *Forgotten Victory: The First World War, Myths And Realities* (London: Headline, 2001)
While not underestimating the tragic loss of so many soldiers or glossing over the disasters on the battlefield Gary Sheffield seeks in this work to dispel many of the myths about the Great War, arguing in particular that the British army, although often disparaged as 'lions led by donkeys', developed in the course of the war into such an effective fighting force that it was ultimately able to bring the war to an end in 1918 with a series of highly impressive victories.

Sheffield, G. D., ed. *Leadership and Command: The Anglo-American Military Experience Since 1861*, rev. edn (London: Brassey's, 2002)

Sheffield, G. D. and P. Gray, eds. *Changing War: The British Army, the Hundred Days Campaign and the Birth of the Royal Air Force, 1918* (London: Bloomsbury, 2013)

Sheffield, G. D. and D. Todman, eds. *Command and Control on the Western Front: The British Army's Experience, 1914-1918* (Statplehurst: Spellmount, 2004)
This collection of studies by a number of established historians and younger scholars, covering all aspects of command at all levels on the Western Front, provides a view of a British army which was not as inflexible and incompetent as it has frequently been described (and disparagingly portrayed by the phrase 'lions led by donkeys') but which was, in fact, capable of developing in the course of the war to a stage of military effectiveness which enabled it to win the series of decisive victories in 1918 that ended the war.

Simkins, P. 'Co-Stars or Supporting Cast? British Divisions in the "Hundred Days", 1918', in *British Fighting Methods in the Great War*, edited by P. Griffith (London: Cass, 1996)

— 'For Better or Worse: Sir Henry Rawlinson and His Allies in 1916 and 1918', in *Leadership as Conflict 1914-1918*, edited by M. Hughes and M. Seligman (Barnsley: Leo Cooper, 2000)

Simpson, A. *Directing Operations: British Corps Command on the Western Front 1914-18* (Staplehurst: Spellmount, 2005)

Sixsmith, E. K. G. *British Generalship in the Twentieth Century* (London: Arms and Armour Press, 1970)

Smith-Dorrien, Sir H. L. *The Judgement of History: Sir Horace Smith-Dorrien, Lord French and 1914*, incorporating General Smith-Dorrien's statement with regard to Lord French's book *1914*, with an introductory essay by Ian F. W. Beckett (London: T. Donovan, 1993)

Stevenson, D. *With Our Backs to the Wall: Victory and Defeat in 1918* (London: Allen Lane, 2011; repr. London: Penguin, 2012)

Stevenson, R. C. *To Win the Battle: The 1st Australian Division in the Great War, 1914-1918* (Cambridge: Cambridge University Press, 2013)

Stewart, I. and S. L. Carruthers, eds. *War, Culture and the Media: Representation of the Military in 20th Century Britain* (Trowbridge: Flicks Books, 1996)
Includes among its chapters: British propaganda and the First World War, by Andrew Steed; "Civilians entrenched": the British home front and the attitudes to the First World War, 1914-18, by Lloyd Clark; "Oh! What a futile war":

representations of the Western Front in modern British media and popular culture, by G.D. Sheffield; Presenting arms: portrayals of war and the military in British cinema, by Ian Stewart; Cultural myths and realities: the British Army, war, and Empire as portrayed on film, 1900-90, by Edmund J. Yorke.

Strachan, H. 'Liddell Hart, Cruttwell and Falls', in *The First World War and British Military History*, edited by B. Bond (Oxford: Clarendon, 1991)

Terraine, J. 'British Military Leadership in the First World War', in *Home Fires and Foreign Fields, British Social and Military Experience in the Great War*, ed. by P. H. Liddle (Manchester: Manchester University Press, 1985)

— *The Smoke and the Fire: Myths and Anti-Myths of War, 1861-1945* (London: Sidgwick & Jackson, 1980; repr. London: Cooper, 1992)

— *The Western Front, 1914-1918* (London: Hutchinson, 1964; repr. Barnsley: Pen and Sword, 2003)
A selection of John Terraine's articles which tend to support Haig and the 'westerners'.

— *To Win a War: 1918 the Year of Victory* (London: Sidgwick and Jackson, 1978; repr. London: Cassell, 2000)

Travers, T. *How the War was Won: Command and Technology in the British Army on the Western Front, 1917-18* (London: Routledge, 1992; repr. Barnsley: Pen & Sword Military Classics, 2005)

— *The Killing Ground: The British Army, the Western Front and the Emergence of Modern Warfare, 1900-1918* (London: Allen & Unwin, 1987)
In this work Travers takes the view that the ideas, tactics and strategies developed by the British high command on the Western front were conditioned by pre-war social and military attitudes and that as a result of this it never quite managed entirely to adapt itself to the new technological warfare.

Trythall, A. J. 'Fuller and the Tanks', in *Home Fires and Foreign Fields, British Social and Military Experience in the Great War*, ed. by P. H. Liddle (Manchester: Manchester University Press, 1985)

Wiest, A. A. 'Haig, Gough and Passchendaele', in *Leadership And Command: The Anglo-American Military Experience Since 1861*, edited by G. D. Sheffield, rev. edn (London: Brassey's, 2002)

— *Haig: The Evolution of a Commander* (Dulles, Va.: Potomac Books, 2005)
Contents: The Great Haig Debate; The military education of Douglas Haig; A corps commander rises to prominence; Commander of the BEF; The death of a generation? - The Battle of the Somme; Battles in the mud - The Year of Passchendaele; 1918 - the year of victory; Conclusion.

Winter, D. *Haig's Command: A Reassessment* (London: Viking, 1991; repr. London: Penguin, 2001)

Woodward, D. *Lloyd George and the Generals* (London: Associated University Presses, 1983; repr. London: Cass, 2004)

Theses

Snowden, K. L. 'British 21st Infantry Division on the Western Front, 1914-1918: A Case Study in Tactical Evolution' (unpublished M.Phil thesis, University of Birmingham, School of Historical Studies, 2001)

Articles

Anderson, H. 'Lord Horne as Army Commander', *Journal of the Royal Artillery*, 56 (1930), 407-18

The Army Quarterly, 1920 -
In the inter-war years the pages of this journal were dominated by articles and book reviews about the First World War and its impact on the army. It provides an invaluable insight into post-war military opinion and debates about controversial issues.

Barnett, C. 'A Military Historian's View of the Great War', *Essays by Divers Hands*, 36 (1970), 1-18

— 'Of Horrors and Scapegoats: Ending World War I Legends', *Encounter*, 50 (1978), 66-74

Bechthold, M. 'Command, Leadership, and Doctrine on the Great War Battlefield: The Australian, British, and Canadian Experience at the Battle of Arras, May 1917', *War and Society*, 32 (2013), 116-137

Beckett, I. 'The Military Historian and the Popular Image of the Western Front, 1914-1918', *The Historian*, 53 (1997), 11-14
In this review of recent revisionist works on the Western Front Ian Beckett bemoans the part teachers have played in helping to foster the popular and persistent image of the Great War represented by the literary legacy of poets like Siegfried Sassoon, Wilfred Owen and Robert Graves (who are representative of only a small fraction of the huge number of soldiers who fought in the war), and applauds the strong criticism by Robin Prior and Trevor Wilson of Paul Fussell's way of interpreting the war in his still influential book, *The Great War and Modern Memory*.

Casey, G. 'General Sir Herbert Plumer and "Passchendaele": A Reassessment', *Firestep*, 5.2 (2004), 40-60

DeGroot, G. J. 'Educated Soldier or Cavalry Officer?: Contradictions in the Pre-1914 Career of Douglas Haig', *War and Society*, 4 (1986), 51-69

Delaney, D.E. 'Mentoring the Canadian Corps: Imperial Officers and the Canadian Expeditionary Force, 1914-1918', *Journal of Military History*, 77 (2013), 931-954
The highly effective Canadian Corps of 1918, commanded and staffed almost entirely by Canadian officers, was the product of the help provided between 1914-1918 by the British Army which sent scores of officers to Canadian formations to make up key command and staff deficiencies in the Canadian Expeditionary Force and to train selected officers to take their places.

French, D. 'Sir Douglas Haig's Reputation, 1918-1928: A Note', *Historical Journal*, 28 (1985), 953-60

Greenhalgh, E. 'General Ferdinand Foch and Unified Allied Command in 1918', *Journal of Military History*, 79 (2015), 997-1024

— 'Myth and Memory: Sir Douglas Haig and the Imposition of Allied Unified Command in March 1918', *Journal of Military History*, 68 (2004), 771-820

Hall, B.N. 'Technological Adaptation in a Global Conflict: The British Army and Communications beyond the Western Front, 1914-1918', *Journal of Military History*, 78 (2014), 37-72

Harris, P. and S. Marble. 'The "Step-by-Step"' Approach: British Military Thought and Operational Method on the Western Front, 1915-1917', *War in History*, 15 (2008), 17-42

Lawrence, A. 'Was Stalemate on the Western Front the Fault of the Generals?', *History Review*, 53 (2005), 48-50

Lloyd, N. 'The Imperial Triumph of Amiens', *History Today*, 64, Issue 5 (2014), 72
Nick Lloyd revisits John Terraine's ground-breaking 1958 article on the decisive, though neglected, Allied victory at Amiens in 1918.

— '"With Faith and Without Fear": Sir Douglas Haig's Command of First Army During 1915', *Journal of Military History*, 71 (2007), 1051-1076

Mallinson, A. 'The Permanent Stain of the Somme', *History Today*, 66:11(2016), 72
Allan Mallinson takes issue with Gary Sheffield's reading of the Somme as a bloody but worthwhile battle.

Meriwether, J. L. 'Leaving Kitchener's Shadow: Frances Aylmer Maxwell, a Modern Warrior', *Archives* (Journal of the British Records Association), 30, Issue 112 (2005), 60-72

Millman, B. 'Henry Wilson's Mischief: Field Marshall Sir Henry Wilson's Rise to Power 1917-18', *Canadian Journal of History*, 30 (1995), 467-486

Neilson, K. 'Kitchener: A Reputation Refurbished', *Canadian Journal of History*, 15 (1980), 207-227

Travers, T. 'A Particular Style of Command: Haig and GHQ', *Journal of Strategic Studies*, 10 (1987), 363-76

Wilkinson, R. 'Lloyd George and the Generals', *History Review*, 61 (2008), 31-36
About the fractious relations between Lloyd George and the generals during the Great War

Wilson, T. 'The Killing Ground: The British Army, the Western Front, and the Emergence of Modern Warfare' [Review by: Trevor Wilson], *International History Review*, 10 (1988), 488-490

Woodward, D. 'Did Lloyd George Starve the British Army of Men Prior to the German Offensive of 21 March 1918', *Historical Journal*, 27 (1984), 241-252

4. Cultural Impacts

In his book *A War Imagined* Samuel Hynes uses the phrase 'Myth of the War' which he sees as "a tale that confirms a set of attitudes, an idea, of what the war was and what it meant" that he summarises as follows: " … a generation of innocent men, their heads full of high abstractions like Honour, Glory, and England, went off to war to make the world safe for democracy. They were slaughtered in stupid battles planned by stupid generals. Those who survived were shocked, disillusioned and embittered by their war experience, and saw that their real enemies were not Germans, but the old men at home who had lied to them. They rejected their values of the society that had sent them to war, and in doing so separated their own generation from the past and their cultural inheritance" (pp. ix-x)

As Hynes points out, this Myth of the War has featured in histories of the war, novels, memoirs, poems, plays, paintings and films and "was given its fullest definition around the end of the Twenties, when the great war memoirs and novels, and the first full edition of the poems of Wilfred Owen were published" (p. x). To this day it still exerts a powerful influence on the public imagination in spite of the efforts of some historians to dispel some aspects of the myth and present a more balanced, historical view of the war as opposed to one approached predominantly through its literary legacy. John Terraine's efforts to present a more balanced view were among the earliest in the period after the Second World War and they were later built on by a host of other historians including Tim Travers, Dominick Graham, David French, Trevor Wilson, Robin Prior, Brian Bond, John Bourne, Ian Beckett, Peter Simkins, Stephen Badsey, John Lee and Nigel Cave.

The literary legacy was, and still is, powerfully influenced by Paul Fussell's *The Great War and Modern Memory* about which Brian Bond wrote in his *The Unique Western Front*: "By popularising an approach to the war through literature and cultural artefacts Fussell has contributed greatly to what one scholar has termed the emergence of 'Two Western Fronts'"[the term was coined by Stephen Badsey in an article, 'Blackadder Goes Forth and the "Two Western Fronts" Debate', which he contributed to *Television and History*, edited by Graham Roberts and Philip M. Taylor (Luton: University of Luton Press, 2001)]. Fussell's book received a particularly hostile reception from Robin Prior and Trevor Wilson ('Paul Fussell at War', *War in History*, 1 (1994), 63-80).

4.1 General

Books

Hynes, S. *A War Imagined: The First World War and English Culture*, new edn (London: Pimlico, 1992)

Meyer, J., ed. *British Popular Culture and the First World War* (Leiden; Boston: Brill, 2008)

Smith, M. 'The War and British Culture', in *The First World War in British History*, edited by S. Constantine, M. W. Kirby and M. B. Rose (London: Edward Arnold, 1995)

— 'Representations of the First World War in British Popular Culture' (unpublished doctoral thesis, University of Cambridge, 2003)

Stewart, I. and S. L. Carruthers, eds. *War, Culture and the Media: Representation of the Military in 20th Century Britain* (Trowbridge: Flicks Books, 1996)
Includes: The influence of the media on recent British military operations, by Stephen Badsey; British propaganda and the First World War, by Andrew Steed; "Civilians entrenched": the British home front and the attitudes to the First World War, 1914-18, by Lloyd Clark; "Oh! What a futile war": representations of the Western Front in modern British media and popular culture, by G. D. Sheffield; Presenting arms: portrayals of war and the military in British cinema, by Ian Stewart; Cultural myths and realities: the British Army, war, and Empire as portrayed on film, 1900-90, by E. J. Yorke; Reporting terrorism: the British state and the media, 1919-94, by Susan L. Carruthers; Media misperceptions of Saddam Hussein's army, by Sean McKnight; From Morse to modem: developments in transmission technologies and their impact upon the military-media relationship, by John Allen; The meanings of war-toys and war-games, by Jonathan Bignell; Postmodernism and military history, by Nigel de Lee

Thacker, T. *British Culture and the First World War: Experience, Representation and Memory* (London: Bloomsbury Academic, 2014)

Watson, J. S. K. *Fighting Different Wars: Experience, Memory, and the First World War in Britain* (Cambridge: Cambridge University Press, 2004)

Articles

Heathorn, S. 'The Mnemonic Turn in the Cultural Historiography of Britain's Great War', *Historical Journal*, 48 (2005), 1103-1124

4.2 Literature

There was a steady stream of books on the Great War in the inter-war years which in the late 1920's and 1930's was characterised by a wave of literature which can be termed 'anti-war' as applied to writers who, distancing themselves from those who wrote about the war in popular heroic and romantic terms, portrayed the war on the basis of stark, sometimes brutal, realism, stripping it of its idealism, emphasising its horrors, and condemning it as futile. Among the works written in this vein of disenchantment were Blunden's *Undertones of War*, Graves's *Goodbye to All That*, Sassoon's *The Complete Memoirs of George Sherston*, Remarque's *All Quiet on the Western Front*, Aldington's *Death of a Hero* and Sheriff's play, *Journey's End*. Public attitudes to the Great War were considerably influenced by the latter works. The translation of Remarque's *All Quiet on the Western Front*, published in Britain in 1929, and Sheriff's play, *Journey's End*, first performed in London in the same year, had a particularly sensational impact on contemporaries and to this day, like the other works mentioned in this paragraph, still exert a powerful influence on the way people view the Great War.

These 'anti-war' writers, were by no means, however, without their opponents in the inter-war years. Opposition to them came from so many quarters (which included war historians, senior army officers, and some literary critics) that the term 'War Book Controversy' began to be used among contemporary journalists to describe the battle of views about war literature. Two well-known examples of this opposition came from Cyril Falls and Douglas Jerrold, who in works they published in 1930 (C. B. Falls, *War Books: An Annotated Bibliography of Books about the Great War* and D. Jerrold, *The Lie About the War: A Note on Some Contemporary War Books*) deplored the manner in which some war literature demeaned patriotic virtues, brutalised the soldier's experience and dwelt on the more squalid aspects of the war. There were also soldiers like Charles Carrington who did not subscribe to the disenchanted view of the war. Carrington, writing under the pseudonym of Charles Edmonds, made this quite clear in an epilogue to his *Subaltern's War* (see entry below for this work under **Edmonds** in **Part 4, section 4.2.2.1**). There were a considerable number of other soldiers who did not write in an 'anti-war' vein in their memoirs and letters, many of them being able to write about their war experience in positive terms such as feelings of pride or its uplifting effects on the rest of their lives. To Guy Chapman (author of a *A Passionate Prodigality*), a well-known example of a soldier who wrote about his experience in the latter positive vein, could be added a host of other authors (not only officers like Vivian de Sola Pinto, Harold Macmillan, Lord Reith, Graham Greenwell, and P. J. Campbell but also other ranks like Norman Gladden, George Coppard and Frank Dunham) who recalled their war service in a similarly positive way.

In spite of the views of such writers as Falls and Jerrold and soldiers such as Carrington and Chapman the 'anti-war' strand in the literature of the Great War continued and, after the hiatus of the Second World War, was resuscitated and boosted in the 1960's onwards as a result of the publication of books such as Alan Clark's *The Donkeys* (1961) and Joan Littlewood's play *Oh! What a Lovely War* (1963), the reprinting of works such as

Graves's *Goodbye to All That* and Aldington's *Death of a Hero*, and the prominence given in anthologies and discussions about war poetry to the verse of poets like Wilfred Owen and Siegfried Sassoon.

The flow of books on the Great War slowed to a trickle during the Second World War and its immediate aftermath but resumed in the 1960's. This resumption occurred as a result of a resurgence of public interest in the Great War that publishers and authors saw as an opportunity to resurrect a popular market for books on that war, particularly as its 50th anniversaries would fall between 1964 and 1968.

4.2.1 General

Bibliographies

Falls, C. B. *War Books: An Annotated Bibliography of Books about the Great War*, with a new introduction and additional entries by R. J. Wyatt, new edn (London: Greenhill Books, 1989)
Previous edn published as: *War Books: A Critical Guide*, London : P. Davies, 1930

Lengel, E. G. *World War I Memories: An Annotated Bibliography of Personal Accounts Published in English Since 1919* (Oxford: Scarecrow Press, 2004)

Ouditt, S. *Women Writers of the First World War: An Annotated Bibliography* (London: Routledge, 2000)

Schuleter, P. and J. Schuleter, eds. *An Encyclopedia of British Women Writers*, rev. and expanded edn (New Brunswick, N. J.; London: Rutgers University Press, 1998)
Contains nearly 400 biographical entries for British women writers from the eighteenth century to the present. Each entry includes a list of the author's primary works and a bibliography of critical sources. Entries are signed and a list of contributors is provided. The detailed index is cross-referenced for pseudonyms or variant names used by an author.

Collections

Brophy, J., ed. *The Soldier's War: A Prose Anthology* (London: Dent, 1929)

Cardinal, A., and others, eds. *Women's Writing on the First World War*, edited by Agnès Cardinal, Dorothy Goldman, and Judith Hattaway (Oxford: Oxford University Press, 1999)

Higonnet, M. R. *Lines of Fire: Women Writers of World War I* (New York: Plume, 1999)

Critical Studies

- **Books**

Barlow, A. *Great War in British Literature* (Cambridge: Cambridge University Press, 2000)

Bergonzi, B. *Heroes' Twilight: A Study of the Literature of the Great War*, 3rd edn (Manchester: Carcanet, 1996)

Bond, B. 'British "Anti-War" Writers and their Critics', in *Facing Armageddon: The First World War Experienced*, ed. by H. Cecil and P. H. Liddle (London: Leo Cooper, 1996)

— *The Unquiet Western Front: Britain's Role in Literature and History* (Cambridge: Cambridge University Press, 2002)

Booth, A. *Postcards from the Trenches: Negotiating The Space Between Modernism and the First World War* (New York: Oxford University Press, 1996)

Buitenhuis, P. *The Great War of Words: British, American, and Canadian Propaganda and Fiction, 1914-1933* (Vancouver: University of British Columbia Press, 1987; repr. London: Batsford, 1989)
The 1989 reprint published in London was entitled, *The Great War of Words: Literature as Propaganda 1914-18 And After*.

Cooper, H. M., and others, eds. *Arms and the Woman: War, Gender, and Literary Representation* (Chapel Hill: University of North Carolina Press, 1989)

Coroneos, C. 'Flies and Violets in Katherine Mansfield', in *Women's Fiction and the Great War*, edited by S. Raitt and T. Tate (Oxford: Clarendon Press, 1997)

Das, S. *Touch and Intimacy in First World War Literature* (Cambridge: Cambridge University Press, 2005)

Field, F. *British and French Writers of the First World War: Comparative Studies in Cultural History* (Cambridge: Cambridge University press, 1991)

Fussell, P. *The Great War and Modern Memory*, new edn (Oxford: Oxford University Press, 2000)

Gilbert, S. M. 'Soldier's Heart: Literary Men, Literary Women and the Great War', in *Behind the Lines: Gender and the Two World Wars*, Workshop on Women and War; papers edited by Margaret Randolph Higonnet ... [et al.] (New Haven: Yale University Press, 1987)

Gilbert, S. M. and S. Gubar. *No Man's Land: The Place of the Woman Writer in the Twentieth Century*, 3 vols (New Haven: Yale University Press, 1988-1994)
Contents: Vol 1: *The War of the Words*; Vol 2: *Sexchanges*; Vol 3: *Letters from the Front*.

Goldman, D, ed. *Women and World War I: The Written Response* (Basingstoke: Macmillan, 1993)

Greicus, M. S. *Prose Writers of World War 1* (London: Longmans, 1973)

Jerrold, D. *The Lie About the War: A Note on Some Contemporary War Books* (London: Faber, 1930)

Jeffery, K. 'Irish Prose Writers of the First World War', in *Modern Irish Writers and the Wars*, ed. by K. Devine (Gerrards Cross: Colin Smythe, 1998)

Kimber, G. and others, eds.. *Katherine Mansfield and World War One*, edited by Gerri Kimber, Todd Martin, Delia da Sousa Correa, Isobel Maddison and Alice Kelly (Edinburgh: Edinburgh University Press, 2014)

Klein, Y. M. *Beyond the Home Front: Women's Autobiographical Writing of the two World Wars* (New York: New York University Press, 1997)

Longenbach, J. 'The Women and Men of 1914', in *Arms and the Woman: War, Gender, and Literary Representation*, edited by H. M. Cooper and others (Chapel Hill: University of North Carolina Press, 1989)

Miles, P. and M. Smith. *Cinema, Literature and Society: Elite and Mass Culture in Interwar Britain*, Croom Helm Studies on Film, Television and the Media (London: Croom Helm, 1987)

Münz, P. *Contrary Experiences: Attitudes to the German Enemy in English Great War Literature* (Marburg: Tectum, 2004)

Onions, J. *English Fiction and Drama of the Great War, 1918-39* (Basingstoke: Macmillan, 1990)

Ouditt, S A. 'Fighting Forces/Female Identity: Women Writers of the First World War' (unpublished doctoral thesis, University of Leicester, 1992)

— *Fighting Forces, Writing Women: Identity and Ideology in the First World War* (London: Routledge, 1994)

— 'Tommy's Sisters: The Representation of Working Women's Experience', in *Facing Armageddon: The First World War Experienced*, ed. by H. Cecil and P. H. Liddle (London: Leo Cooper, 1996)

Potter, J. *Boys in Khaki, Girls in Print: Women's Literary Responses to the Great War 1914—1918* (Oxford: Clarendon, 2005)

— 'A Great Purifier: The Great War in Women's Romances and Memoirs', in *Women's Fiction and the Great War*, edited by S. Raitt and T. Tate (Oxford: Clarendon Press, 1997)

Raitt, S. '"Contagious Ecstasy": May Sinclair's War Journals', in *Women's Fiction and the Great War*, edited by S. Raitt and T. Tate (Oxford: Clarendon Press, 1997)

Roucoux, M., ed. *English Literature of the Great War Revisited*, Proceedings of the Symposium on the British Literature of the First World War, University of Picardy, 1986 (Picardie: Presses de l'UFR, 1987)

Rutherford, A. *The Literature of War: Studies in Heroic Virtue*, 2nd (rev.) edn (Basingstoke: Macmillan, 1978; repr. 1989)

Rydstrand, H. 'Ordinary Discordance: Katherine Mansfield and the First World War', in *Katherine Mansfield and World War One*, edited by Gerri Kimber, Todd Martin, Delia da Sousa Correa, Isobel Maddison and Alice Kelly (Edinburgh: Edinburgh University Press, 2014)

Sherry, V. B. *The Great War and the Language of Modernism* (Oxford: Oxford University Press, 2003)

Sherry, V. B., ed. *Cambridge Companion to the Literature of the First World War* (Cambridge: Cambridge University Press, 2005)

Silver, S. 'History Not Yet Written: Writing the First World War in Britain 1914-1935' (Unpublished Master's Thesis, Brandeis University Department of History, 2010)
"Despite the level of interest in the First World *War*, little writing exits about the early histories of the *war* published in Britain during the *inter-war* period. The historians who do discuss this literature propose either a divide between the histories of the 1920s and 1930s, representing a shift to a tragic narrative influenced by fiction about the *war*, or lump together all of the *inter-war* histories as sharing similar characteristics. This study expands on the debate by exploring twenty-eight general, non-fiction historical texts about the *war* aimed at popular consumption published in Britain between 1914 and 1935, and analyzes four elements of their depictions of the *war*: the origins, casualties, outcome, and any over-arching meaning that they present. It argues that there are three distinct *inter-war* periods of writing on the *war*: 1914 to 1920, 1922 to 1927, and 1928 to 1935, with each period characterized by changes in these four elements. The most profound change is between the First Period (1914 to 1920) and the Second Period (1920 to 1927) during which we see a dramatic rise to prominence of impersonal, structural causes for the *war*, over-arching meanings of the *war* as a tragedy, and a heightened iv emphasis on the horrors of the *war*. Over the entire *inter-war* period, we see the narrowing of authors' over-arching meanings of the *war* down to two: the *war* as a tragedy, or the *war* as a costly national victory. This study is an addition to the historiography of the First World *War*, and will contribute to future research on the topic." [Abstact at http://hdl.handle.net/10192/23858)

Small, H. 'Mrs Humphrey Ward and the First Casualty of War', in *Women's Fiction and the Great War*, edited by S. Raitt and T. Tate (Oxford: Clarendon Press, 1997)

Smith, A. K. *The Second Battlefield: Women, Modernism and the First World War* (Manchester: Manchester University Press, 2000)

Tate, T. *Modernism, History and the First World War* (Manchester: Manchester University Press, 1998)

Taylor, D. *Memory, Narrative and the Great War: Rifleman Patrick MacGill and the Construction of Wartime Experience* (Liverpool Liverpool University Press 2013)

Tylee, C. *The Great War and Women's Consciousness: Images of Militarism and Womanhood in Women's Writings, 1914-64* (Basingstoke: Macmillan, 1990)
Contents: The heroic pageantry of war - journalism, women war-correspondents 1914-16, and the ideology of war (Mildred Aldrich, May Sinclair, Mrs St Clair Stobart); mental flannel - a woman's diary 1913-16 - propaganda and the construction of consciousness (Vera Brittain); "The Magic of Adventure" - the Western Front and women's tales about the war zone, 1915-16 (May Cannan, Katherine Mansfield, Ellen La Motte, Mary Borden); "despised and rejected" - censorship and women's pacifist novels of the First World War, 1916-18 (Mary Hamilton, Rose Macaulay, Rose Allatini); best-sellers – women's best-selling novels, 1918-28 (May Sinclair, Cicely Hamilton, Rebecca West, Virginia Woolf, Radclyffe Hall); memoirs of a generation – women's autobiographies and fictionalized war memoirs, 1929-33 (Enid Bagnold, Mary Borden, Evadne Price, Sylvia Pankhurst, Vera Brittain); "Old Unhappy, Far-off Things" – women's elegies, 1932-60 (Hilda Doolittle, Pamela Hinkson, Antonia White). Conclusion: "Forbidden Zone" - the Great War and women's myths. Appendices: dates of significant women writers and their war-writings; extracts from "The Defence of the Realm Act [DORA], 1914".

Waller, P. *Writers, Readers and Reputations: Literary Life in Britain 1870-1918* (Oxford: Oxford University Press, 2006)

Cultural Impacts

- **Articles**

Barnett, C. 'A Military Historian's View of the Great War', *Essays by Divers Hands*, 36 (1970), 1-18

— 'Of Horrors and Scapegoats: Ending World War I Legends', *Encounter*, 50 (1978), 66-74

Burnett, G. 'A Poetics out of War: H. D.'s Responses to the First World War', *Agenda*, 25 (1988), 54-63

Cullen, S. M. '"The Land of My Dreams": The Gendered Utopian Dreams and Disenchantment of British literary Ex-Combatants of the Great War', *Cultural And Social History*, 8 (2011), 195 - 211

— 'Oxford's Literary War: Oxford University's Servicemen and the Great War', *Historian* (Historical Association), 110 (2011), 12-17

Doty, B. '"As a Mass, a Phenomenon so Hideous": Crowd Psychology, Impressionism, and Ford Madox Ford's Propaganda', *Journal of War and Culture Studies*, 6 (2013), 169-182

Eksteins, M. 'History or Histrionics: Recent Writing on the Great War', *Canadian Journal of History*, 20 (985), 393-403

— 'War, Memory, And Politics - The Fate of the Film "All Quiet On The Western Front"', *Central European History*, 13 (1980), 60-62

Fox, F. 'These Scandalous War Books and Plays', *National Review*, no.568 (June 1930), 192-200

Galer, G. 'Myths of the Western Front', *Global Society*, (2004), 175 –195
In this paper there is an exploratory examination of the ways in which myths have developed from the experiences of those who fought on the Western Front in 1914-1918 and of the role literature has played, and continues to play, in the creation, dissemination and perpetuation of these myths.

Grieves, K. 'Nelson's History of the War: John Buchan as a Contemporary Military Historian 1915-22', *Journal of Contemporary History*, 28:3 (1993), 533-551

Howard, M. 'Military Experience in European Literature', *Essays by Divers Hands*, n.s. 41, (1980), 29-39

Paris, M. 'A Different View of the Trenches: Juvenile Fiction and Popular Perceptions of the First World War', *War Studies Journal*, 3.1 (1997), 32-46

Pittock, M. 'Max Plowman and the Literature of the First World War', *Cambridge Quarterly*, 33 (2004), 217-243
In this article the author considers the case of Max Plowman's court-martial for refusing to return to the Front and his Memoir, *A Subaltern on the Somme*, and shows how they can throw light on the partly parallel case of Siegfried Sassoon's protest of 1917 and give rise to a reassessment of the accepted account of the literature of the First World War.

Schoentjes, P. 'War: "A Railway Running Across a Picturesque Mountain Scene". Images of Nature in the Literature of the Great War', *Journal of War and Culture Studies*, 6 (2013), 141-153

Scutts, J. 'Contemporary Approaches to the Literature of the First World War: A Critical Survey', *Literature Compass*, 3.4 (2006), 914–23

Simons, J. 'The Times Broadsheets: A Canon for the Front', *Literature and History*, 11:2 (2002) 39-51
A critical analysis of contents of *The Times* broadsheets issued in 1915, and 1943-1946. An offprint of this paper is held at http://www.iwm.org.uk/collections/item/publication/121012

Strachan, H. 'John Buchan and the First World War: Fact into Fiction', *War in History*, 16 (2009), 298-324
An exploration of the the ways in which Buchan, a man of affairs, historian, and propagandist as well as a novelist, exploited the inside knowledge of the facts about the war (derived from his government activities) to write his fictions about it both during the war and after it. Also includes a consideration of Buchan's thoughts about the war's conduct and the function of propaganda within it.

Taylor, D. 'From Fighting the War to Writing the War: From Glory to Guilt?', *Contemporary British History*, 23 (2009), 293-313
About Patrick MacGill, the Irish journalist, poet and novelist, known as "The Navvy Poe" because he had worked as a navvy before he began writing, During the Great War he joined the London Irish Rifles and was wounded at the Battle of Loos in 1915, subsequent to which he served in Military Intelligence between 1916 and the Armistice in 1918. His wartime experiences provided inspiration for his autobiographical novels, *The Amateur Army* (1915) and *The Great Push* (1916). His post-war novel *Fear!*, published in 1921 is an early example of disillusionment with the war by an individual whose perceptions of the Great War as expressed in his writing while seving as a soldier changed dramatically in what he wrote after the war had ended..

Tylee, C. M. '"Munitions of the Mind": Travel Writing, Imperial Discourse and Great War Propaganda by Mrs. Humphry Ward', *English Literature in Transition, 1880-1920*, 39 (1996), 171-192

Vance, J. F. 'The Soldier as Novelist: Literature, History, and the Great War'. *Canadian Literature* 179 (2003), 22-37

Wild, J. '"A Merciful, Heaven-Sent Release"?: The Clerk and the First World War in British Literary Culture', *Cultural And Social History*, 4 (2007), 73-94
An exploration of the experience of the Great War by the large number of British office workers who enlisted in the armed forces and the effect which, it is argued, this had on shaping a more democratic postwar society as was evidenced by the figure of the fictional clerk that emerges in British literature after 1918.

4.2.2 Personal Reminiscences, Autobiographical Works

A number of people who had lived through the Great War subsequently produced works of personal reminiscence or of an autobiographical or semi-autobiographical nature. The selection of these works in the following sections all contain some allusion to the war and in many cases are devoted entirely to a recollection of that period in the life of the author.

Also included in this section are a selection of diaries and collections of letters that were written during the war but not published until after it had ended.

Works relating to senior ranking soldiers who held commands during the war will be found in **section 3 (The Military Post-Mortem) of Part 4.**

4.2.2.1 Inter War Years

Most of the works in this section were produced solely as a means of recounting the author's experiences and attitudes during the years of the Great War and provide an idea of the sort of books related to the war that people were reading in the inter-war years, particularly in the late 1920's and early 1930's when a dramatic renaissance of interest in the war was manifested by the flood of books published on the subject. The selection below includes Blunden's *Undertones of War*, Graves's *Goodbye to All That*, and Sassoon's *The Complete Memoirs of George Sherston* (fictional but strongly autobiographical), all of which had a particularly strong impact on the public mind.

Andrews, Sir W. L. *Haunting Years: The Commentaries of a War Territorial* (London: Hutchinson, 1930)

Archer, W. D. *Death in the Air: The War Diary and Photographs of a Flying Corps Pilot* (London : Heinemann, 1933)
Reprinted London: Greenhill, 1985

Asquith, M., Countess of Oxford and Asquith. *Autobiography*, 2 vols (London: Thornton Butterworth, 1920-22)
Lady Emma Alice Margaret Asquith (generally known as Margot) was the sixth daughter of Sir Charles Tennant. Married Herbert Henry Asquith (Prime Minister and Liberal Leader) as his second wife, 1894.

Barr, J. C. *Home Service: The Recollections of a Commanding Officer serving in Great Britain during the War 1914-1919* (Paisley: Alexander Gardner, 1920)

Blunden, E. *Undertones of War* (London: Richard Cobden Sanderson, 1928)

Cultural Impacts

In this autobiography Edmund Blunden records his experiences as an infantry subaltern in France and Flanders in two parts, the first part being a prose narrative concerned with the events of everyday life in France (including his observations of the heroism and despair of his fellow officers), the second part consisting of poems illustrating the various aspects of the experiences recounted in the first part.

Borden, M. *The Forbidden Zone: A Nurse's Impressions of the First World War* (London: Heinemann, 1929)

Brittain, V. *Testament of Youth: An Autobiographical Study of the Years 1900-1925* (London: Victor Gollancz, 1933)

Carstairs, C. *A Generation Missing*, with a foreword by Osbert Sitwell (London: Heinemann, 1930)
A memoir of the Great War by an American art dealer who served in the war in the Grenadier Guards of the British Army.

Chapman, G. *A Passionate Prodigality: Fragments of Autobiography* (London: Nicholson & Watson, 1933)

Chapman, G., ed. *Vain Glory: A Miscellany of the Great War, 1914-1918*, written by those who fought in it on each side and on all fronts (London: Cassell, 1937)

Courtney, C., Baroness Courtney of Penwith. *Extracts from a Diary during the War* (London: Printed for private circulation, 1927)
Kate Courtney, a suffragist and peace campaigner, became Lady Courtney of Penwith on the elevation of her husband Leonard Courtney, Liberal MP and woman's suffrage campaigner, to the peerage in 1906. She persisted with her pacifism throughout the war. In the pre-war period to 1914 she was honorary secretary of the National Union of Women's Suffrage Societies (NUWSS).

Crutchlow, W. *Tale of an Old Soldier* (London: Robert Hale, 1937)

Cushing, H. *From a Surgeon's Journal, 1915-18* (London: Constable, 1936)

Deardon, H. *Medicine and Duty: A War Diary* (London: Heinemann, 1928)

Douie, C. *The Weary Road: Recollections of a Subaltern of Infantry* (London: Murray, 1929)

Dunn, J. C. *The War the Infantry Knew, 1914-1919*, a chronicle of service in France and Belgium with the Second Battalion His Majesty's Twenty-Third Foot, the Royal Welch Fusiliers; founded on personal records, recollections and reflections, assembled, edited and partly written by one of their Medical Officers [i.e. J. C. Dunn] (London: P. S. King & Sons, 1938)
Reprinted by London publishers, Cardinal (1987 and 1989), Jane's (1987) and Abacus (1994). Captain J. C. Dunn was a temporary officer in the RAMC and served as Regimental Officer to the Second Battalion, the Royal Welsh Fusiliers between November 1915 and May 1918. This work can be seen as contradicting to a certain extent the views expressed in the accounts of service published in the 1920's by Siegfried Sassoon and Robert Graves, both officers in the regiment featured in this compilation of the diaries, letters, and recollections related to it that were published in 1938.

Edmonds, C. (pseud of C. E. Carrington). *A Subaltern's War: Being a Memoir of the Great War from the Point of View of a Romantic Young Man*, with candid accounts of two particular battles, written shortly after they occurred, and an essay on militarism (London: Peter Davies, 1929)
In an epilogue to this work Carrington wrote "a legend has grown up, propagated not by soldiers but by journalists, that these men who went gaily to fight in the mood of Rupert Brooke and Julian Grenfell, lost their faith amid the horrors of the trenches and returned in a mood of anger and despair. To calculate the effect of mental and bodily suffering, not on a man but on a whole generation of men, may seem an impossible task, but it can at least be affirmed that the legend of disenchantment is false".

Fawcett, H. W. and G. W. W. Hooper. *The Fighting at Jutland: The Personal Experiences of Sixty Officers and Men of the British Fleet* (Glasgow: MacLure, MacDonald, 1921)
Reprinted London: Chatham, 2001.

Fawcett, M. G., Dame. *The Women's Victory - And After: Personal Reminiscences, 1911-1918* (London: Sidgwick & Jackson, 1920; repr. London: British Library, 1987)
Millicent Fawcett was a leader of the women's suffrage movement. President of the National Union of Women's Suffrage Societies (NUWSS) during the war. Fiercely anti-pacifist and a wholehearted supporter of Britain's war effort.

Four Years on the Western Front, by a Rifleman [Aubrey Smith]: *Being the Experiences of a Ranker in the London Rifle Brigade, 4th, 3rd and 56th Divisions* (London: Odhams, 1922)
Facsimile of 1922 edition was published Uckfield: Naval & Military Press, 2001.

Forbes, A. S. B., Lady. *Memories and Base Details* (London: Hutchinson, 1921)
Lady Angela Forbes was a wartime catering organizer, opening canteens, run with voluntary staff, for soldiers both in England and France. Her British Soldiers' Buffets were commonly known as angelinas.

Fraser-Tytler, N. *Field Guns in France, 1915-1918* (London: Hutchinson, 1929)
New edn of the author's *With Lancashire Lads and Field Guns in France* (Manchester: Manchester University Press, 1922).

Fuller, J. F. C. *Memoirs of an Unconventional Soldier* (London: Nicholson and Watson, 1936)

Graham, S. *A Private in the Guards* (London: Macmillan, 1919)

Graves, R. *Goodbye to All That* (London: Jonathan Cape, 1929)

Greenwell, G. H. *An Infant in Arms: War Letters of a Company Officer, 1914-1918*, with an introduction and note by John Terraine (London: Lovat Dickson & Thompson, 1935)

Grey, E., 1st Viscount Grey of Fallodon. *Twenty-Five years 1892-1916*, 2 vols. (London: Hodder & Stoughton, 1925)

Griffith, W. *Up to Mametz* (London: Faber, 1931)

Hanbury-Sparrow, A. *The Land-Locked Lake* (London: Arthur Barker, 1932)
Impressions of active service in the Great War

Herringham, Sir W. M. *A Physician in France* (London: Arnold, 1919)

Hutchison, G. S. *Footslogger*, by Graham Seton [pseud. of Lieutenant-Colonel G. S. Hutchison] (London: Hutchinson, 1931)

Jenkin, A. *A Tank Driver's Experiences: or, Incidents in a Soldier's Life* (London: Stock, 1922)

Jones, I. *An Air Fighter's Scrapbook* (London: Nicolson & Watson, 1938)

Jünger, E. *The Storm of Steel: From the Diary of a German Storm-Troop Officer on the Western Front* ... with an introduction by R. H. Mottram (London : Chatto & Windus, 1929)
"Translated from the original text [*In Stahlgewittern* published in 1920] ... by Basil Creighton."

Kelly, Sir D. V. *39 Months with the "Tigers" (the 110th Infantry Brigade), 1915-1918* (London: Benn, 1930)

Keyes, R. J. B., Baron Keyes. *The Naval Memoirs of Admiral of the Fleet Sir Roger Keyes*, 2 vols (London: T. Butterworth, 1934-1935)
Contents: Vol. 1. The Narrow Seas to the Dardanelles, 1910-1915 (1934); Vol 2. Scapa Flow to the Dover Straits, 1916-1918 (1935.).

Lawrence, T. E. *Revolt In The Desert* (London: Cape, 1927)
"Abridged version of *Seven Pillars of Wisdom*."– cover.

— *Seven Pillars of Wisdom: A Triumph* (London: Jonathan Cape, 1926)

Lewis, C. *Sagittarius Rising*, (London: Peter Davies, 1936)
A personal account by a British airman of the air fighting that took place in the Great War.

Lewis, P. W. *Blasting and Bombardiering* (London: Eyre & Spottiswoode, 1937)
Wyndham Lewis served as a second lieutenant in the Royal Artillery during the Great War.

Cultural Impacts

Lloyd, R. A. *A Trooper in the 'Tins'* (London: Hurst and Blacklett, 1938)

Lucy, J. F. *There's a Devil in the Drum* (London: Faber & Faber, 1938; repr. Uckfield: Naval & Military Press, 1993)

Montague, C. E. *Disenchantment* (London: Chatto & Windus, 1922)[199]
The author was a journalist who initially served in the Great War as a grenadier-sergeant, rising to lieutenant and then captain of intelligence in 1915.

Peel, D. C. ["Mrs. C. S. Peel"]. *Life's Enchanted Cup: An Autobiography (1872-1933)* (London: John Lane, 1933)
Constance Peel was involved in a number of activities in aid of the war effort, organizing a Soldiers' and Sailors' Wives Club in Lambeth, working as a speaker for the United Workers' Association and the National War Savings Association, co-directing the women's service for the Ministry of Food during the period of voluntary food rationing (March 1917–March 1918) and touring the country to address meetings on the promotion of the economical use of food.

Pethick-Lawrence, E., Baronesss Pethick-Lawrence. *My Part in a Changing World* (London: Gollancz, 1938)
The author was a women's rights activist and pacifist. Treasurer of the Women's International League for Peace and Freedom, 1915-22. Co-editor of *Votes for Women* (London: The Reformer's Press, 1907-1918). Attended the international women's peace conference at The Hague in 1915. Highly critical of the terms of the Versailles peace settlement.

Plowman, M. *A Subaltern on the Somme* (London: Dent, 1927)

Pollard, A. O. *Fire Eater: The Memoirs of a V.C.* (London: Hutchinson, 1932)

Richards, F. *Old Soldiers Never Die* (London: Faber, 1933)

Rogerson, S. *Twelve Days*, with a foreword by B. H. Liddell Hart (London: Arthur Baker, 1933)
A personal record of twelve days on the Somme in 1916 while serving as a subaltern with the 2nd Battalion of the West Yorkshire Regiment.

Rutherford, N. J. C. *Memories of an Army Surgeon* (London: Stanley Paul, 1939)

Sassoon, S. *The Complete Memoirs of George Sherston* (London: Faber & Faber, 1937)
Contains *Memoirs of a Fox-Hunting Man*, originally published London: Faber & Gwyer,1928; *Memoirs of an Infantry Officer*, originally published London: Faber & Faber, 1931; *Sherston's Progress*, originally published London: Faber & Faber, 1936.

Severn M. *The Gambardier: Giving some Account of the Heavy and Siege Artillery in France 1914-1918* (London: Benn, 1930)

Scrivenor J. B. *Brigade Signals* (London: Blackwell, 1932)
Experiences of a brigade signalling officer in the Great War.

Shaw, B. *What I Really Wrote About the War* (London: Constable, 1930)
Contents: Before the war; Common sense about the war; The hard case of Belgium; Nonsense about neutrality; The case against Germany; The humours of patriotic indignation; Early war reputations; Compulsory soldiering; The conscientious objectors; Joy riding at the front; Cataclysm; Peace conference hints; Post-war controversy; The Washington conference; Burning the candle at both ends; The League of nations; Appendix.

Strange, L. A. *Recollections of an Airman* (London: John Hamilton, 1933)

Swanwick, H. M. *I Have Been Young* (London: Victor Gollancz, 1935)
Throughout the war the author lent her support to the campaign for a negotiated peace and the future creation of an organization devoted to maintaining international peace.

Tilsey, W. V. *Other Ranks*, with an introduction by Edmund Blunden (London: Cobden-Sanderson, 1931)

Vivian, A. P. G. *The Phantom Brigade: or, The Contemptible Adventures* (London: Benn, 1930)

---

[199] This work is an early example of the disillusioned view of the war that became prominent in many of the novels that were published in the late 1920's and 1930's.

Voigt, F. A. *Combed Out* (London: Swarthmore Press, 1920)
"A record of the Great War as seen by a private soldier in the British army."—Author's note.

Wade, A. *The War of the Guns: Western Front 1917 and 1918*, with an introduction by Edmund Blunden (London: Batsford, 1936)
Reprinted under the title *Gunner on the Western Front*, 1959.

Wortley, R. S. *Letters from a Flying Officer* (London: Milford, 1928)
Reprinted Gloucester: Sutton, 1982

Young, F. *With the Battlecruisers* (London: Cassell, 1921)
Reprinted Edinburgh: Birlinn, 2002.

4.2.2.2 Post 2nd World War

Many of the works listed below are specifically related to the Great War and directly reflect the renewed interest in individual experiences of that war that occurred in the 60's and beyond. In the case of the works like those of Dungan, Vansittart, Macdonald, Holmes, Gold, Cross and Arthur these individual experiences are expressed through the accounts of eyewitnesses and survivors woven into the narrative.

In this section are also included reminiscences of three British servicemen who had lived through the Great War and survived until the first decade of the 21st century (i.e. Allingham and Patch who both died in 2109, and Choules who died in 2011).

A number of the works listed below originally appeared in the inter-war years and were presumably reprinted by publishers in the belief that there would be a ready market for them in the climate of renewed interest in the Great War.

Allingham, H. *Kitchener's Last Volunteer: The Life of Henry Allingham, the Oldest Surviving Veteran of the Great War*, by Henry Allingham, with Dennis Goodwin (London: Mainstream Publishing, 2008)
Allingham enlisted with the Royal Naval Air Service in 1915 and trained as an Air Mechanic, in which capacity he saw action on land, sea and in the air. He transferred to the Royal Air Force when the RNAS and the RFC were merged on 1 April 1918.

Appleton, E.. *A Nurse at the Front: The First World War Diaries of Sister Edith Appleton*, edited by R. Cowen, War Diaries (London: Simon and Schuster, 2013)

Archer, W. D. *Death in the Air: The War Diary and Photographs of a Flying Corps Pilot* (London: Greenhill, 1985)
Facsimile of edn published: London : Heinemann, 1933

Arthur, M. *Forgotten Voices of the Great War*, new edn (London: Ebury, 2006)
Published in association with the Imperial War Museum

— *The Road Home: The Aftermath of the Great War Told by the Men and Women Who Survived It* (London: Phoenix, 2010)

Asquith, Lady C. *Diaries, 1915-1918*, with a foreword by L. P. Hartley (London: Hutchinson, 1968; repr. London: Century, 1987)
Lady Cynthia Asquith, daughter of the 11th Earl of Wemyss, was the wife of Herbert ('Beb') Asquith, the second son of Herbert Henry Asquith (Prime Minister from 1908-1916) by the latter's first wife Helen (died 1891). " … Her diaries provide a dynamic portrait of aristocratic life during the war; side by side with trivia about hair-styles and dinner parties are simple and moving entries about the deaths of many of the young men with whom she had grown up, including two of her brothers … " [quotation extracted from Raymond N. MacKenzie, 'Asquith , Lady Cynthia Mary Evelyn (1887–1960)', *Oxford Dictionary of National Biography*, Oxford University Press, 2004; online edn, Jan 2011 accessed 7 Nov 2013].

Asquith, M., Countess of Oxford and Asquith. *The Autobiography of Margot Asquith*, edited by Mark Bonham-Carter (London: Eyre & Spottiswoode, 1962; repr. London: Weidenfeld & Nicolson, 1995)
Originally published in 2 vols, London: Thornton Butterworth, 1920-1922. The author, Lady Emma Alice Margaret Asquith (generally known as Margot), was the sixth daughter of Sir Charles Tennant. Married Herbert Henry Asquith

Cultural Impacts

(Prime Minister, 1908-16) as his second wife, 1894.

Bagnold, E. *A Diary without Dates* (London: W. Heinemann, 1918; repr. London : Virago, 1978)
In this work the author wrote of her hospital experiences in the Great War as a nurse (a job from which she was dismissed for writing critically of the hospital administration, and as a result subsequently became a driver in France for the remainder of the war years). She wrote of her driving experiences in her novel *The Happy Foreigner* (see below in **Part 4, section 4.2.3.2**).

Barrett, D. *Men of Letters* (Basingstoke: AA Publishing,, 2014)
The author uses the personal stories, letters and diary entries of the men who joined the Post Office Rifles to produce an account which highlights the important role of the mail in relation to the ordinary lives of people during the war.

Bartlett, C. P. O. *In the Teeth of the Wind: The Story of a Naval Pilot on the Western Front 1916-1918*, edited by his son, Nick Bartlett, new rev. edn (London: Leo Cooper, 1994)
Previous edn published as *Bomber Pilot, 1916-1918*, London: Allan, 1974.

Begg, R. C. *Surgery on Trestles: A Saga of Suffering and Triumph* (London: Jarrold, 1967)
A memoir of surgery under field conditions in Mesopotamia.

Behrend, A. *As from Kemmel Hill: An Adjutant in France and Flanders, 1917 and 1918* (London: Eyre and Spottiswoode, 1963)

— *Make me a Soldier* (London: Eyre and Spottiswoode, 1961)
A memoir by a temporary territorial officer serving with the 4th East Lancashire Regiment at Gallipoli.

Best, K. *A Chaplain at Gallipoli: The Great War Diaries of Kenneth Best*, edited by G. Roynon, War Diaries (London: Simon & Schuster in association with the Imperial War Museum, 2011

Bland, L. and K. Rowold, eds. *Reconsidering Women's History: Twenty Years of the Women's History Network*, edited by Lucy Bland and Katharina Rowold (Abingdon, Oxon: Routledge, 2015)
Includes a chapter entitled 'Peg's War: A Story Told Through Letters' by Charmian Cannon. [See also below Cannon, C. 'Peg's War: A Story Told Through Letters', *Women's History Review*, 22:4 (2013), 591-606]

Blunden, E. *Undertones of War* (London: Penguin, 2000)
Originally published London: Richard Cobden Sanderson, 1928. In this autobiography Edmund Blunden records his experiences as an infantry subaltern in France and Flanders in two parts, the first part being a prose narrative concerned with the events of everyday life in France (including his observations of the heroism and despair of his fellow officers), the second part consisting of poems illustrating the various aspects of the experiences recounted in the first part.

Bond, B. ed. *Liddell Hart's Western Front: Impressions of the Battle of the Somme*, with war letters, diary and occasional notes written on active service in France and Flanders 1915 and 1916, limited edn (Brighton: Tom Donovan, 2010)

Bondfield, M. G. *A Life's Work* (London: Hutchinson, 1949)
As an ILP [Independent Labour Party] administrative committee member (1913–21) Bondfield criticized the government's war policies. Helped Mary Macarthur (with whom she established the National Federation of Women Workers in 1906) to organize and protect women involved in war work. In 1915 she resumed full-time union work as the NFWW's organizing secretary.

Borden, M. *The Forbidden Zone: A Nurse's Impressions of the First World War* (London: Hesperus Press, 2008)
A paperback reprint of the author's *The Forbidden Zone* published London: Heinemann, 1929.

Brandon, B. *The Silent Service: Diary of an Old Sailor* (Bognor Regis: New Horizon, 1978)

Brittain, V. *Chronicle of Youth: War Diary 1913-1917*, ed. by Alan Bishop and Terry Smart (London: Gollancz, 1981; repr. London: Phoenix, 2002)
Vera Brittain's *Testament of Youth* was based on this diary.

— *Testament of Youth: An Autobiographical Study of the Years 1900-1925*, with a new introduction by Mark Bostridge and a preface by Shirley Williams (London: Virago Press, 2004)
Originally published: London: Victor Gollancz, 1933. First published by Virago Press in 1978.

Brocklebank, H. C. R. *Tenth Cruiser Squadron Northern Patrol: From the Diaries and Letters of Captain H. C. R. Brocklebank, CBE, Royal Navy, July 1914-August 1917* (Dorchester: [Joan Brocklebank], 1974)

Buckle, H. *A Tommy's Sketchbook: Writings and Drawings from the Trenches*, edited by David Read (Stroud: The History Press, 2012)

Campbell, P. J. *The Ebb and Flow of Battle* (London: Hamilton, 1977; repr. Oxford: Oxford University Press, 1979)

— *In the Cannon's Mouth* (London: Hamilton, 1979, repr. 1986)
Reprint includes *The Ebb and Flow of Battle* (q.v.)

Cannon, C. 'Peg's War: A Story Told Through Letters', *Women's History Review*, 22:4 (2013), 591-606

Carrington, C. E. *Soldier from the Wars Returning* (London: Hutrchinson, 1965; repr. Aldershot: Gregg Revivals, 1991)
Partly based on *A Subaltern's War*, which Charles Carrington had written in 1929 under the pseudonym Charles Edmonds.

Carstairs, C. *A Generation Missing*, with a foreword by Osbert Sitwell (Stevenage: Strong Oak Press with Tom Donovan Publishing, 1989)
A memoir of the Great War by an American art dealer who served in the war in the Grenadier Guards of the British Army. First Published: London: Heinemann, 1930.

Carter, V. B., Baroness Asquith of Yarnbury. *Champion Redoubtable: The Diaries and Letters of Lady Violet Bonham Carter, 1914-1945*, edited by Mark Pottle (London: Weidenfeld and Nicolson, 1998)
Violet Bonham Carter, the only daughter of H. H. Asquith, kept a diary from the age of 18. Supported her father on political platforms, 1905-1918. Inside British politics and upper class social life from the outbreak of the first world war to the end of the second, she wrote revealingly about what she saw in her diaries and letters.

Chapman, G. *A Passionate Prodigality: Fragments of Autobiography*, 2nd edn (London: McGibbon & Kee, 1965; repr. London, Buchan & Enright, 1985)
Originally published: London : Nicholson & Watson, 1933.

Chapman, G., ed. *Vain Glory: A Miscellany of the Great War, 1914-1918*, written by those who fought in it on each side and on all fronts, 2nd edn (London: Cassell, 1968)
Originally published: London: Cassell, 1937.

Chapman, S. *Home in Time for Breakfast: A First World War Diary* (London: Athena, 2007)

Choules, C. *The Last of the Last: The Final Survivor of the First World War* (Edinburgh: Mainstream, 2010)
Choules began training to join the Royal Navy in April 1915 at the age of 14 and after the completion of his training joined the Royal Navy's Grand Fleet in 1917.

Cloete, S. *A Victorian Son* (London: Collins, 1972)
Memoir of a young middle-class man commissioned as a temporary officer in the 9th King's Own Light Infantry.

Clouting, B. *Tickled to Death to Go: Memoirs of a Cavalryman in the First World War*, edited by R. van Emden (Tonbridge: Spellmount, 1996)

Collins, N. *Last Man Standing: The Memoirs of a Seaforth Highlander during the Great War*, edited by R. van Emden (Barnsley: Leo Cooper, 2002)

Cooper, Lady D., Viscountess Norwich. *Autobiography* (Wilton, Salisbury: M. Russell, 1979)
Contents: *The Rainbow Comes and Goes*. Originally published, London: Hart Davis, 1958; *The Light Of Common Day*. Originally published, London: Hart Davis, 1959; *Trumpets from the Steep*. Originally published, London: Hart Davis, 1960.
The author's assumed father was Henry John Brinsley Manners, later the 8th Duke of Rutland. She gained some notoriety in pre 1914 years as a member of the 'corrupt coterie', a group of young English aristocrats and intellectuals of the 1910's. When the First World War came in 1914 she performed service as a nurse at Guy's and at the hospital established by her parents in their London house in Arlington Street.. She married Duff Cooper, later 1st Viscount Norwich, in 1919.

Cultural Impacts

Coppard, G. *With a Machine Gun to Cambrai: The Tale of a Young Tommy in Kitchener's Army, 1914-1918*, revised and enlarged edn (London: Imperial War Museum, 1980; repr. London Cassell, 1999)

Craster, J. M. *'Fifteen Rounds a Minute': The Grenadiers at War, August to December, 1914* (London: Macmillan, 1976)

Crewdson, R., ed. *Dorothea's War: The Diary of a First World War Nurse* (London: Weidenfeld & Nicolson 2013)

Cross, R. *In Memoriam: Remembering the Great War* (London: Ebury Press, 2008)
An illustrated book published to complement an exhibition mounted by the Imperial War Museum (IWM) to commemorate the 90th anniversary of the end of the Great War. Using letters, diary entries, photographs, eye-witness accounts, and archive material published for the first time Robin Cross presents a narrative of the war through the personal stories of its heroes.

Crowdy, T. and S. Bagin, eds. *Donald Dean VC: Memoirs of a Volunteer and Territorial from two World Wars* (London: Pen & Sword, 2010)

Denham, H. M. *Dardanelles: A Midshipman's Diary 1915-16* (London: Murray, 1981)

Dixon, T. B. *The Enemy Fought Splendidly: Being the 1914-1915 Diary of the Battle of the Falklands and its Aftermath* (Poole, Dorset: Blandford Press, 1983)

Dolden, A. S. *Cannon Fodder: An Infantryman's Life on the Western Front , 1914-1918* (London: Blandford Press, 1980)

Dungan, M. *Irish Voices from the Great War* (Dublin: Irish Academic Press, 1995)
Drawing on diaries, letters, literary works and oral accounts of soldiers, this account tells some of the personal stories of the participation of Irishmen - Unionist and Nationalist - in the Great War.

Dunham, F. *The Long Carry: The Journal of Stretcher Bearer Frank Dunham, 1916-1918*, edited by R. H. Haigh and P. W. Turner; with a foreword by Correlli Barnett (London: Pergamon, 1970)

Dunn, J. C. *The War the Infantry Knew, 1914-1919*, a chronicle of service in France and Belgium with the Second Battalion His Majesty's Twenty-Third Foot, the Royal Welch Fusiliers; founded on personal records, recollections and reflections, assembled, edited and partly written by one of their Medical Officers [i.e. J. C. Dunn] (London: Cardinal, 1987; repr London: Abacus, 1994)
Reprinted by London publishers, Cardinal (1987 and 1989), Jane's (1987) and Abacus (1994). Captain J. C. Dunn was a temporary officer in the RAMC and served as Regimental Officer to the Second Battalion, the Royal Welsh Fusiliers between November 1915 and May 1918. This work can be seen to a certain extent as contradicting the views expressed in the accounts of service published in the 1920's by Siegfried Sassoon and Robert Graves, both officers in the regiment featured in this compilation of the diaries, letters, and recollections related to it that were published in 1938.

Eberle, V. F. *Sapper Venture* (London: Pitman, 1973)

Eden, A. *Another World, 1897-1917* (London: Allen Lane, 1976)
During the First World War, Anthony Eden (Prime Minister, 1955-57) served with the 21st (Yeoman Rifles) Battalion of the King's Royal Rifle Corps, and reached the rank of captain. He received a Military Cross, and at the age of twenty-one became the youngest brigade-major in the British Army.

Emden, R. *Boy Soldiers of the Great War* (London: Headline, 2005)
Drawing on personal testimonies, as well as diaries and letters, the author recounts the stories of Britain's young boys (some as young as thirteen) who enlisted in the Great War.

— *Britain's Last Tommies: Final Memories from Soldiers of the 1914-18 War in their own Words* (Barnsley: Pen & Sword Military, 2005)

Fawcett, H. W. and G. W. W. Hooper. *The Fighting at Jutland: The Personal Experiences of Sixty Officers and Men of the British Fleet* (London: Chatham, 2001)
Originally published: Glasgow: MacLure, MacDonald, 1921.

Fawcett, M. G., Dame. *The Women's Victory - And After: Personal Reminiscences, 1911-1918* (London: Sidgwick & Jackson, 1920; repr. London: British Library, 1987)
A leader of the women's suffrage movement. President of the National Union of Women's Suffrage Societies (NUWSS) during the war. Fiercely anti-pacifist and a wholehearted supporter of Britain's war effort.

Furse, K. S., Dame. *Hearts and Pomegranates: The Story of Forty-Five years, 1875-1920* (London: Peter Davies, 1940)
The author organized the VAD Department in London 1914-17 and became Commandant-in-Chief in 1916 when a joint committee was set up to co-ordinate the VAD work of the British Red Cross Society and the order of St John of Jerusalem. From 1917-19 she was director, with the equivalent rank of rear-admiral, of a new organization, the Women's Royal Naval Service (WRNS).

Gladden, N. *Across the Piave: A Personal Account of the British Forces in Italy, 1917-1919* (London: HMSO, 1971)

—— *The Somme, 1916: A Personal Account* (London: Kimber, 1974)

—— *Ypres, 1917: A Personal Account* (London: Kimber, 1967)

Gold, M. *Wartime is Your Time. Women's Lives in World War: Women's Image in Magazines Compared with the Reality of their Wartime Lives* (Edgeware: Hytheway, 1996)
Includes interviews with women who recalled their experiences in factories, and hospitals, and wherever they aided the war effort.

Graves, R. *Goodbye to All That: An Autobiography*, edited, with a biographical essay and annotations, by Richard Perceval Graves (Oxford: Berghahn Books, 1995)
One of the several post-2nd world war reprints and editions of the work originally published by Jonathan Cape in 1929. The author fought in the Great War as an officer in the Royal Welch Fusiliers. Following Siegfried Sassoon's public anti-war statement in 1917 Graves, fearing that this action could result in his friend facing a court martial, managed to persuade the military authorities to believe that Sassoon was suffering from shell shock, and to treat him accordingly.

Greenwell, G. H. *An Infant in Arms: War Letters of a Company Officer, 1914-1918*, with an introduction and note by John Terraine (London: The Penguin Press, 1972)
Originally published London: Lovat Dickson & Thompson, 1935.

Grinnell-Milne, D. *Wind in the Wires* (London: Hurst & Blackett, 1933; repr. London: Grub Street, 2014)
Memoir of a British pilot about his experiences of flying in the First World War

Groom, W. H. A. *Poor Bloody Infantry* (London: Kimber, 1976)

Hamilton, P. *Three Years or the Duration: The Memoirs of a Munitions Worker, 1914-1918* (London: Peter Owen, 1978)

Harrison, M. C. C. and H. A. Cartwright. *Within Four Walls: A Classic of Escape* (London: Pen & Sword Military, 2015)

Hayward, V. *HMS Tiger at Bay: A Sailor's Memoir 1914-18* (London: Kimber, 1977)

Hiscock, E. *The Bells of Hell Go Ting-A-Ling-A-Ling: An Autobiographical Fragment without Maps* (London: Arlington, 1976)
The author served in the Royal Regiment of Fusiliers during the Great War

Holmes, R. *Tommy: The British Soldier on the Western Front, 1914-1918* (London: HarperCollins, 2004)
The experiences of British soldiers who fought in the trenches are recounted through the letters, diaries and poems they wrote, expressing their thoughts and fears about being part of the war.

Jones, I. *An Air Fighter's Scrapbook* (London: Greenhill, 1990)
Originally published, London: Nicolson & Watson, 1938.

Jünger, E. *The Storm of Steel*, translated by Michael Hofmann (London: Allen Lane 2003)
The original text of this work (*In Stahlgewittern* published in 1920) was first translated in 1929 by Basil Creighton.

Cultural Impacts

Lamin, B. *Letters from the Trenches: A Soldier of the Great War* (London: Michael O'Mara, 2009; repr. 2013)

Lawrence, M. *Fourteen to Forty-Eight: A Diary in Verse* (London: Robert Hale, 1949)

Lawrence, T. E. *Revolt In The Desert* (Ware: Wordsworth Editions, 1997)
Originally published: London: Cape, 1927. "Abridged version of *Seven Pillars of Wisdom*." – cover.

— *Seven Pillars of Wisdom: A Triumph*. The complete 1922 text, 2nd ed (Fordingbridge : Castle Hill Press, 2003)
"... edited by Jeremy Wilson, assisted by Richard Westwood, from the manuscript in the Bodleian Library and T. E. Lawrence's annotated copy of the 1922 Oxford Times printing. It was first published [in 3 vols] by Castle Hill Press in 1997.... For this new edition the text was revised by Jeremy and Nicole Wilson ..." -- verso of t.p.

Lee, A. S. G. *No Parachute: A Fighter Pilot In World War I; Letters Written in 1917* (London: Jarrolds, 1968)

Levine, J. *Forgotten Voices of the Somme: The Most Devastating Battle of the Great War in the Words of Those Who Were There* (London: Ebury Press, 2008)
An oral history featuring contributions from soldiers of differing backgrounds, ranks and roles, many of them previously unpublished.

Levine J, ed. *Forgotten Voices of the Somme: The Most Devastating Battle of the Great War in the Words of those Who Survived*, [compiled and edited by] Joshua Levine. (London : Ebury Press 2008)

Lewis, C. *Sagittarius Rising*, 3rd edn (London: Greenhill, 1993; repr. 2003)
Originally published London: Peter Davies, 1936. A personal account by a British airman of the air fighting that took place in the Great War.

Lewis, P. W. *Blasting and Bombardiering: Autobiography (1914-1926)*, with a new introduction by Catherine Wallace (London: Imperial War Museum, 1992)
First published London: Eyre & Spottiswoode, 1937, Wyndham Lewis served as a second lieutenant in the Royal Artillery during the Great War.

Liddell Hart, Sir B. H. *The Memoirs of Captain Liddell Hart*, 2 vols (London: Cassell, 1965)

Liddle, P. H. *Captured Memories, 1900-1918; Across the Threshold of War* (London: Pen & Sword, 2010)
This work by Peter Liddle, a pioneer in the recording of memories of personal experience in the Great War and in the social background of those who lived through those years, has for its main focus the Great War and, in this respect, ranges over a multiplicity of areas and lives as, for instance, from the battles of the Western, Gallipoli, Mesopotamian and East African fronts to the naval battle of Jutland, from the work of nurses, the exploits of Victoria Cross award winners and a fighter pilot ace, the experiences of people whose distinction was to come later in their lives (like Harold Macmillan, Henry Moore, Gordon Jacob, Emanuel Shinwell, Barnes Wallis and Victor Silvester) to the ordeal of the first conscientious objector to be court-martialled and sentenced to death before commutation of his sentence.

Livingstone, T. C. *Tommy's War: A First World War Diary 1913-1918* (London: HarperPress, 2008)

Lynch, E. P. F. *Somme Mud: The War Experiences of an Infantryman in France 1916-1919*, edited by W. Davies (London: Doubleday, 2008)

MacDonald, L. *1914: The Days of Hope* (London : Joseph, 1987)

— *1915: The Death of Innocence* (London: Headline, 1993; repr. Baltimore: Johns Hopkins University Press, 2000)

— *The Roses of No Man's Land* (Basingstoke: Macmillan, 1980)

— *Somme* (London: Joseph, 1983; repr. London: Penguin, 1993)

— *They Called It Passchendaele: The Story of Ypres and the Men Who Fought in It* (London: Joseph, 1978; repr. London: Papermac, 1990)

— *To the Last Man: Spring 1918* (London: Viking, 1998)

Mace, M. and J. Grehan. *Slaughter on the Somme, 1 July 1916: The Complete War Diaries of the British Army's Worst Day* (London: Pen & Sword, 2013)
In this work are gathered together, for the first time ever, all the War Diary entries for those battalions that were enagaged in the battle on that day.

Machin, T., ed. "Coward's War": The Diaries of Private George H. Coward, Somerset Light Infantry and Royal Engineers; an "Old Contemptible's" View of the Great War (Leicester: Matador, 2006)

MacKenzie, R. N. 'Asquith, Lady Cynthia Mary Evelyn (1887–1960)', *Oxford Dictionary of National Biography*, Oxford University Press, 2004; online edn, Jan 2011) [http://www.oxforddnb.com/view/article/30480, accessed 7 Nov 2013]

Macmillan, H. *Winds of Change, 1914-1939* (London: Macmillan, 1966)
Macmillan (Prime Minister, 1957-1963) served with distinction as a captain in the Grenadier Guards during the war, and was wounded on three occasions.

Mellersh, H. E. L. *Schoolboy into War* (London: Kimber, 1978)

Montague, C. E. *Disenchantment* (London: Macgibbon & Kee, 1968)
Originally published, London: Chatto & Windus, 1922. The author was a journalist who initially served in the Great War as a grenadier-sergeant, rising to lieutenant and then captain of intelligence in 1915.

Moore, C. *Trench Fever* (London: Abacus 2013)
The author tracres the war-time experiences of his grandfather, Private Walter Butterworth of the Fifth Battalion, the Leicestershire Regiment, by following the three year march of the latter regiment through France and Flanders. Originally published: London: Little, Brown, 1998

Moynihan, M., ed. *Greater Love - Letters Home, 1914-1918* (London: W.H. Allen, 1980)

Owens, H. *A Doctor on the Western Front; The Diary of Henry Owens*, edited by John Hutton (London: Pen & Sword, 2013)

Panichas, G. A, ed. *Promise of Greatness: The War of 1914-1918* (London: Cassell, 1968)
A Memorial Volume for the Fiftieth Anniversary of the Armistice

Patch, H. *The Last Fighting Tommy: The Life of Harry Patch, the Oldest Surviving Veteran of the Trenches*, Harry Patch with Richard van Emden (London: Bloomsbury, 2007)
Patch was conscripted as a private into the Duke of Cornwall's Light Infantry in October 1916, serving in a machine gun section.

Pethick-Lawrence, E., Baronesss Pethick-Lawrence. *My Part in a Changing World* (Westport, Conn.: Hyperion Press, 1976)
Originally published, London: Gollancz, 1938. The author was a women's rights activist and pacifist. Treasurer of the Women's International League for Peace and Freedom, 1915-22. Co-editor of *Votes for Women* (London: The Reformer's Press, 1907-1918). Attended the international women's peace conference at The Hague in 1915. Highly critical of the terms of the Versailles peace settlement.

Pinto, V. de Sola. *The City that Shone: An Autobiography, 1895-1922* (London: Hutchinson, 1969)

Read, H. *Annals of Innocence and Experience*, revised and enlarged edn (London: Faber, 1946)
First published in 1940. Includes *The Innocent Eye* and *In Retreat*. The author served with the Green Howards in France in the Great War, reaching the rank of Captain. He was awarded the Military Cross and the Distinguished Service Order.

— *The Contrary Experience* (London: Faber, 1963)
Contents: *The Innocent Eye*; *A War Diary, 1915-18*; *The Falcon and the Dove*; *A Dearth of Wild Flowers*.

Reith, J. C. W., Baron Reith. *Into the Wind* (London: Hodder & Stoughton, 1949)

Richards, F. *Old Soldiers Never Die*, annotated by H. J. Krijnen and D. E. Langley (Peterborough: Krijnen and Langley, 2004)

Originally published London: Faber, 1933. Another reprint of the 1933 edn was published: Uckfield: Naval & Military Press, 2010.

Rogerson, S. *Twelve Days on the Somme: A Memoir of the Trenches* (London: Greenhill, 2006)
Originally published: London: Arthur Baker, 1933, under the title *Twelve Days*. A personal record of twelve days on the Somme in 1916 while serving as a subaltern with the 2nd Battalion of the West Yorkshire Regiment

Ronayne, I. ed. *Amateur Gunners: The Great War Adventures, Letters and Observations of Alexander Douglas Thorburn* (Barnsley: Pen & Sword Military, 2014)

Rosher, H. *In the Royal Naval Air Service: Being the Letters of the Late Harold Rosher to his Family*, with an introduction by Arnold Bennett (London: Greenhill, 1986)
Facsimile of edn published: London: Chatto & Windus, 1916.

Sassoon, S. *The Complete Memoirs of George Sherston*, 3 vols (London: Folio Society, 1993)
Contains *Memoirs of a Fox-Hunting Man,* originally published London: Faber & Faber, 1928; *Memoirs of an Infantry Officer,* originally published London: Faber & Faber, 1931; *Sherston's Progress,* originally published London: Faber & Faber, 1936. Sassoon served as an officer in the 3rd Battalion (Special Reserve), Royal Welch Fusiliers. Received an MC in 1916.

Scrimgeour, A. C. S. *Scrimgeour's Scribbling Diary: The Truly Astonishing Wartime Diary and Letters of an Edwardian Gentleman, Naval Officer, Boy and Son*, compiled by Richard Hallam and Mark Beynon (London: Conway, 2008)
The diaries include the author's experiences as a naval officer in the Great War up to 1916 when he was killed in the Battle of Jutland

Shevin-Coetzee, M and F. Coetzee. *Commitment and Sacrifice: Personal Diaries from the Great War* (New York, NY : Oxford University Press 2015)

Skirth, R. *The Reluctant Tommy*, edited by Duncan Barrett (London: Macmillan, 2010)
The focus of this memoir is Ronald Skirth's reaction to an experience on the Western front that so disturbed him that he became utterly opposed to war, vowing that he would never again help to take a human life, a vow to which he remained true.

Slack, C. M. *Grandfather's Adventures in the Great War, 1914-1918* (London: Arthur Stockwell, 1977)
An account of the author's service in the 4th East Yorkshire Regiment.

Staniforth, J. H. M. *At War with the 16th Irish Division 1914-1918: The Staniforth* [John Hamilton Maxwell Staniforth] *Letters*, edited by Richard S. Grayson (Barnsley: Pen & Sword Military in association with the Imperial War Museum, 2012)

Strange, L. A. *Recollections of an Airman* (London: Greenhill, 1989)
Facsimile of edition originally published, London: John Hamilton, 1933

Tustin, H. W. *Escaping from the Kaiser: The Dramatic Experiences of a Tommy POW* (Barnsley: Pen & Sword Military, 2014)

Vansittart, P. *Voices from the Great War* (London: Cape, 1981; repr. London, Pimlico, 1998)
In this anthology of 'voices' letters from the trenches are juxtaposed with music-hall songs, and the words of poets, politicians, and various contemporaries (including Sigmund Freud, Osip Mandelstam, Lloyd George, Bertrand Russell, Isaac Rosenberg, Siegfried Sassoon, Vera Brittain).

Wade, A. *Gunner on the Western Front* (London: Batsford, 1959)
Originally published, London: Batsford, 1936 under the title, *The War of the Guns*

Wadsworth, J. *Letters from the Trenches: The First World War by Those Who Were There* (London: Pen & Sword Military, 2014)
The author uses the letters to reveal the human side of the First World War (people's thoughts and feelings) in relation to all social classes and groups – from officers to other ranks, service women to conscientious objectors

Webb, B. P. *Diaries, 1912-1924*, edited by M. I. Cole (London: Longmans, 1952)

—*The Diary of Beatrice Webb*, edited by N. and J. Mackenzie, 4 vols (London: Virago, published in association with the London School of Economics and Political Science, 1982-1985), III: *'The Power to Alter Things', 1905-1924*(1984)
This diary presents a unique record of the time when Beatrice Webb and her husband, Sidney were at the centre of British left-wing intellectual and political life. An abridged version of this work by Lynn Knight, entitled *The Diaries of Beatrice Webb*, was published in 2000 by Virago in association with The London School of Economics and Political Science.

Weir, N. A. C. *Mud and Bodies: The War Diaries and Letters of Captain N. A. C. Weir, 1914-1920*, edited by Saul David (Barnsley: Frontline Books, 2013)
Although Neil Weir died in 1967 it was not until 2009 that his grandson, Mike Burns, discovered his diary among boxes he had been left. Mike Burns worked closely with Saul David and Frontline Books in the publication of this book.

Whittaker, W. and G. Whittaker. *Somewhere in France: A Tommy's Guide to Life on the Western Front* (Stroud: Amberley Publishing, 2014)
By means of the letters of William Whittaker, a soldier in the Great War, and family anecdotes Geoffrey Whittaker, his son, re-creates the world of the Tommy in the trenches.

Williamson, W. *A Tommy at Ypres: Walter's War, the diary and letters of Walter Williamson Williamson* compiled by Doreen Priddey (Stroud: Amberley 2013)
Originally published: 2011

Wortley, R. S. *Letters from a Flying Officer* (Gloucester: Sutton, 1982)
Originally published London: Milford, 1928

Young, F. *With the Battlecruisers* (London: Cassell, 1921; repr. Edinburgh: Birlinn, 2002)
Originally published London: Cassell, 1921.

4.2.3 Fiction

4.2.3.1 General

After a spate of war novels in 1919 that were mostly jingoistic and celebratory of patriotic sacrifice there was a decline in their numbers during the following years that continued until 1928, although during this interval three bestsellers were published (Wilfrid Ewart's *Way of Revelation*, 1921; Robert Keable's *Simon Called Peter*, 1921; and Ernest Raymond's *Tell England*, 1922), and writers like Virginia Woolf (in *Mrs Dalloway*, 1925, *Jacob's Room*, 1922, and *To the Lighthouse*,1927), Aldous Huxley (in *Antic Hay*, 1923), and D. H. Lawrence (in a long digressive chapter entitled 'The Nightmare' in *Kangaroo*, 1923) were contributing their reflections on the war or reactions to it. This interval was followed in the late 1920's and into the 1930's by a resurgence of the war novel which, in contrast to most of the previous publications of this sort, was dominated by writers who were intent on presenting a starkly disillusioned view of the war (epitomized by Remarque's *All Quiet on the Western Front* which was published in Britain in 1929 and became one of the best-sellers of all time). Nevertheless, there was still a considerable readership for the idealistic and romantic novels about the war that had been, and were still being, published, but awareness of this tends to be obscured by the prominence given to the dominance in the late 1920's and early 1930's of the 'anti-war' novel.

Around 1938 to 1939 the flow of war novels had dried up and in the ensuing years of the 2nd World War and its aftermath public interest was inevitably deflected away from the Great War. It was not until the 1960's and beyond that there was a general revival, indeed an explosion, of interest in the Great War. This manifested itself in a number of ways among which was the resurrection of the Great War as the theme of some of the novels which were published.

A large number of British novelists have written about the Great War but very few of them have been regarded as having outstanding qualities as war writers. Among the literary critics of Great War fiction there appears to be some agreement that a list of the novelists who possessed such qualities should include Siegfried Sassoon for his *The Complete Memoirs of George Sherston*, Richard Aldington for his *Death of a Hero*, V. M. Yeates for his *Winged Victory*, Ford Madox Ford for his *'Tietjens Tetralogy'*, Frederic Manning for *The Middle Parts of Fortune*, and Henry Williamson for his *The Chronicle of Ancient Sunlight*, five of the 15 volumes of which are a retrospective look at his experience of the Great War.

Bibliographies

Cecil, H. 'The Literary Legacy of the War: The Post-War British Novel – A Select Bibliography', in *Home Fires and Foreign Fields, British Social and Military Experience in the Great War*, ed. by P. H. Liddle (Manchester: Manchester University Press, 1985)

Falls, C. B. *War Books: An Annotated Bibliography of Books about the Great War*, with a new introduction and additional entries by R. J. Wyatt, new edn (London: Greenhill Books, 1989)
Previous edn published as: *War Books: A Critical Guide*, London: P. Davies, 1930.

Hager, P. and D. Taylor. *The Novels of World War 1: An Annotated Bibliography* (New York: Garland Publishing, 1981)

Critical Studies

- **Books**

Barlow, A. *Great War in British Literature* (Cambridge: Cambridge University Press, 2000)

Bergonzi, B. *Heroes' Twilight: A Study of the Literature of the Great War*, 3rd edn (Manchester: Carcanet, 1996)

Bracco, R. M. *Merchants of Hope: British Middlebrow Writers and the First World War, 1919-1939* (Oxford: Berg, 1992)

Buitenhuis, P. *The Great War of Words: British, American, and Canadian Propaganda and Fiction, 1914-1933* (Vancouver: University of British Columbia Press, 1987; repr. London: Batsford, 1989)
The 1989 reprint published in London was entitled, *The Great War of Words: Literature as Propaganda 1914-18 And After*.

Cecil, H. 'British War Novelists', in *Facing Armageddon: The First World War Experienced*, ed. by H. Cecil and P. H. Liddle (London: Leo Cooper, 1996)

Cecil, H., ed. *The Flower of Battle: British Fiction Writers of the First World War* (London: Secker & Warburg, 1995)

Cohen, D. R. *Remapping the Home Front: Locating Citizenship in British Women's Great War Fiction* (Boston: Northeastern University Press, 2002)

Greicus, M. S. *Prose Writers of World War 1* (London: Longmans, 1973)

Hulme, M. 'Woolf at War: Selected Aspects of Virginia Woolf's Representation of the Great War in *Jacob's Room, Mrs Dalloway, To the Lighthouse* and *The Years* (unpublished master's thesis, University of Birmingham, 2001)

Jeffery, K. 'Irish Prose Writers of the First World War', in *Modern Irish Writers and the Wars*, ed. by K. Devine (Gerrards Cross: Colin Smythe, 1998)

Hussey, M., ed. *Virginia Woolf and War: Fiction, Reality and Myth* (Syracuse, N.Y.: Syracuse University Press, 1991)

Klein, H., ed. *The First World War in Fiction: A Collection of Critical Essays* (London: Macmillan, 1976)

Levenback, K. L. *Virginia Woolf and the Great War* (Syracuse, N.Y.: Syracuse University Press, 1999)

MacCallum-Stewart, E. *The Cause of Nowadays and the End of History: First World War Historical Fiction*, Working Papers on the Web [http://extra.shu.ac.uk/wpw/historicising/MacCallum-Stewart.htm]

Mallett, P., ed. *Kipling Considered* (Basingstoke: Macmillan, 1989)

Morrow, P. D. *Katherine Mansfield's Fiction* (Bowling Green, Ohio: Bowling Green State University Popular Press, 1993)

Orel, H. *Popular Fiction in England, 1914-1918* (London: Harvester Wheatsheaf, 1992)

Parfitt, G. *Fiction of the First World War: A Study* (London: Faber and Faber, 1988)

Raitt, S. and T. Tate, eds. *Women's Fiction and the Great War* (Oxford: Clarendon Press, 1997)

Rollyson, C. E. *The Literary Legacy of Rebecca West* (London: International Scholars Publications, 1998)

Trotter, D. *The English Novel in History, 1895-1920* (London: Routledge, 1993)

— 'Lesbians before Lesbianism: Sexual Identity in Early Twentieth Century British Fiction', in *Borderlines: Gender and Identities in War and Peace, 1870-1930*, edited by B. Melman (London: Routledge, 1998)

- **Articles**

Firchow, P. E. 'Kipling's "Mary Postgate": The Barbarians and the Critics', *Etudes Anglaises*, 29 (1976), 27-39

Howard, M. 'Military Experience in Literature', *Essays by Divers Hands*, n.s. 41, (1980), 29-39

Meyer, E. 'Ford's War and (Post) Modern Memory: *Parade's End* and National Allegory', *Criticism*, 32 (1990), 81-99

Biographical Material

Carr, J. D. *The Life of Sir Arthur Conan Doyle*, 2nd edn (New York: Carroll & Graf, 2003)

Carrington, C. E. *Rudyard Kipling: His Life and Work*, new edn (Harmondsworth: Penguin in association with Macmillan, 1986)
Originally published: London: Macmillan, 1955.

Delany, P. *D. H. Lawrence's Nightmare: The Writer And His Circle during the Years of the Great War* (Hassocks: Harvester Press, 1979)

Drabble, M. *Arnold Bennett: A Biography* (London: Weidenfeld & Nicolson, 1974; repr. Harmondsworth: Penguin, 1985)

Gindin, J. *John Galsworthy's Life and Art: An Alien's Fortress* (Basingstoke: Macmillan, 1987)

Hart-Davis, R. *Hugh Walpole: A Biography* (London: Macmillan, 1952; repr. London: Hamilton, 1985)

Hunt, V. *The Flurried Years* (London: Hurst & Blackett, 1926)

Lawrence, D. H. *The Letters of D. H. Lawrence*, edited by James T. Boulton, 8 vols (Cambridge: Cambridge University Press, 1979-2000)
Vol. 1. September 1901-May 1913; Vol. 2. June 1913-October 1916 edited by George J. Zytaruk and James T. Boulton; Vol. 3. October 1916-June 1921 edited by James T. Boulton and Andrew Robertson; Vol. 4. June 1921-March 1924 edited by Warren Roberts, James T. Boulton, and Elizabeth Mansfield; Vol. 5. March 1924-March 1927 edited by James T. Boulton and Lindeth Vasey; Vol. 6. March 1927-November 1928 edited by James T. Boulton and Margaret H. Boulton, with Gerald M. Lacy; Vol. 7. November 1928-February 1930 edited by Keith Sagar and James T. Boulton; Vol. 8. Previously uncollected letters, general index edited and compiled by James T. Boulton.

Lee, H. *Virginia Woolf* (London: Chatto & Windus, 1996)

Mansfield, K. *The Collected Letters of Katherine Mansfield*, edited by Vincent O'Sullivan and Margaret Scott, 4 vols (Oxford: Clarendon Press, 1984-1996)
Vol. 1. 1903-1917; Vol. 2. 1918-1919; Vol. 3. 1919-1920; Vol. 4. 1920-1921.

— *Journal of Katherine Mansfield*, [selected and edited by John Middleton Murry] (London: Persephone Books, 2006)

Originally published: London: Constable, 1927

— *The Scrapbook of Katherine Mansfield*, edited by J. M. M. [John Middleton Murry] (London: Constable, 1939)

Marrot, H. V. *The Life and Letters of John Galsworthy* (London: Heinemann, 1935)

Pearson, H. *Conan Doyle: His Life and Art* (London: Methuen, 1943; repr. London: Macdonald and Jane's, 1977)

Roby, K. E. *A Writer at War: Arnold Bennett, 1914-1918* (Baton Rouge, Louisiana: University of Louisiana Press, 1973)

Rollyson, C. *Rebecca West: A Saga of the Century* (London; Hodder & Stoughton, 1995)

Saunders, M. *Ford Madox Ford: A Dual Life*, 2 vols. (Oxford: Oxford University Press, 1996.)
Contents: Vol. 1. The world before the war; Vol. 2. The after-war world.

— 'Sinclair, Mary Amelia St Clair (1863–1946)', *Oxford Dictionary of National Biography*, Oxford University Press, Sept 2004; online edn, Jan 2007 [http://www.oxforddnb.com/view/article/37966, accessed 13 Jan 2014]
Soon after the war began Mary Sinclair joined Dr Hector Munro's volunteer ambulance corps in a multi-functional capacity "acting as secretary, treasurer, banker, financial supporter, and publicist" [Extract from above item in online Oxford DNB]

Smith, J. B. A. *John Buchan: A Biography* (London: Hart-Davis, 1965; repr. London: Oxford University Press, 1985)

Spender, S. 'D. H. Lawrence, England and the War', in *D. H. Lawrence: Novelist, Poet, Prophet*, ed. by S. Spender (London: Weidenfeld & Nicolson, 1973)

Tomalin, C. *Katherine Mansfield: A Secret Life* (London: Viking, 1987)

Trevelyan, J. P. *The Life of Mrs. Humphry Ward* (London: Constable, 1923)

West, A. *H. G. Wells: Aspects of Life* (London: Hutchinson, 1984)

Whitelaw, L. *The Life and Rebellious Times of Cicely Hamilton, Actress, Writer, Suffragist* (London: Women's Press, 1990)
During the First World War Hamilton served with the Scottish women's ambulance unit and as an administrator in a military hospital outside Paris and from 1917 to 1919 she was a member of a repertory company organized by her friend Lena Ashwell which provided wartime entertainment for the troops.

Wilson, A. *The Strange Ride of Rudyard Kipling: His Life and Works* (London: Secker and Warburg, 1977; repr. London: Pimlico, 1994)

Woolf, V. *The Diary of Virginia Woolf*, introduced by Quentin Bell; edited by Anne Olivier Bell, 5 vols. (London: Hogarth Press, 1977–84)
Contents: Vol. 1. 1915-1919; Vol. 2. 1920-1924; Vol. 3. 1925-1930; Vol. 4. 1931-1935; Vol. 5. 1936-1941. Vols. 2-5 edited by Anne Olivier Bell assisted by Andrew McNeillie.

— *Letters of Virginia Woolf*, editor Nigel Nicolson; assistant editor Joanne Trautmann, 6 vols (London: Hogarth Press, 1975-1980)
Contents: Vol. 1. The flight of the mind, 1888-1912; Vol. 2. The question of things happening, 1912-1922; Vol. 3. A change of perspective, 1923-1928; Vol. 4. A reflection of the other person, 1929-1931; Vol. 5. The sickle side of the moon, 1932-1935; Vol. 6. Leave the letters till we're dead.

Zilboorg, C. *Richard Aldington and H.D.: Their Lives in Letters, 1918-61*, edited with an introduction and commentary by Caroline Zilboorg, new collected edn (Manchester: Manchester University Press, 2003)

Anthologies

Tate, T., ed. *Women, Men and the Great War: An Anthology of Stories* (Manchester: Manchester University Press,

1995)

In this anthology of short stories of the Greta War from 25 classic writers Gertrude Stein, Virginia Woolf and Katherine Mansfield are among the women writers whose works occupy half the work. "These stories focus on the divisions the war created between men and women, and create an impression of the depth of its impact on British society and of how many ghosts it left behind" [quotation by Pat Barker from back cover of book].

The fiction listed below is a selection (almost all British and published in the inter-war and post 2nd World war years) which recall the Great War in some way.

4.2.3.2 Inter-War Years

War novels of this period do not lend themselves to a simple division into patriotic and anti-patriotic, disillusioned writing. The distinction is often blurred. The novels could, for example, be both patriotic and also highly critical of the purposes and management of the war. Nevertheless, the fiction of the inter war years tends to be remembered particularly for the publication of a number of novels in which a disenchanted view of the war is clearly dominant The most famous of these novels were Aldington's *Death of a Hero* (1929), Remarque's *All Quiet on the Western Front* (1929), and Sassoon's *Memoirs of an Infantry Officer* (1931); they are still well known today. Examples of other novels that took a disillusioned view at this time were Williamson's *Patriot's Progress* (1930), Bertram's *The Sword Falls* (1929), Harrison's *Generals Die in Bed* (1930), O'Flaherty's *The Return of the Brute* (1929), Acland's *All Else is Folly* (1929), Blake's *The Path of Glory* (1929), Ford's *No Enemy* (1929, although it was actually written in 1919), Gristwood's *The Somme* (1927), Gurner's *Pass Guard at Ypres* (1929), Thompson's *In Araby Orion* (1930) and *These Men Thy Friends* (1927), Tomlinson's *All Our Yesterdays* (1930), Yeates's *Winged Victory* (1934), Bennett's *Lord Raingo* (1929), Galsworthy's *The Burning Spear* (1919), Kipling's *Debits and Credits* (1927), and Wells's *Bulpington of Blup* (1932). In the case of Arnold Bennett, John Galsworthy, Rudyard Kipling, Ford Madox Ford, and H.G. Wells their expression of disenchantment is in complete contrast to the attitude which had motivated them to be willingly and actively involved in Britain's propaganda campaign during the war, a reflection perhaps of their unease after the war with their wartime propagandistic contributions.

The prominence which has been given by many writers on the Great War to the impact of war novels of disenchantment (particularly the most famous of them) in the inter war years obscures the multifarious nature of the war novels which were published. There were humorous satires (e.g. Mann's *Grope Carries On*, 1932; Smiths's *Not So Quiet*, 1930), thriller fiction (e.g. MacDonald's *Patrol*, 1927; Hope's *Beaumaroy Home from the War*, 1919), spy novels (e.g. Hueffer's *Cousins German*, 1930), school stories in a war setting (Pocock's *Knight's Gambit*, 1929), romances (e.g. Asquith's *Roon*, 1929), animal stories (e.g. Goodchild and Mottram's, *'Old Sport'*, 1919), and even fantasies (e.g. Deehan's *The Just Steward*, 1922). The Western Front was, inevitably, the most obvious backdrop for novelists writing about the war but as well as that they embraced many other regions and themes such as the Arabs in Palestine (e.g. Hankey's *Battles in the Smoke*, 1931), Serbia (e.g. Graham's *Balkan Monastery*), Russia (e.g. Walpole's *The Dark Forest*, first published in 1916 but reissued in the inter-war years), South Africa (e.g. Greene's *Tug of War*), Ireland (e.g. Hinkson's *The Ladies Road*, 1932), Gallipoli (e.g. Blake's *The Path of Glory*, 1929), the French Army (e.g. Cobb's *Paths of Glory*, 1935), the Home Front (e.g. Waytemore's *The Profiteer*, 1932), the Eastern Mediterranean (e.g. McFee's *Command*, 1922), the North Sea (e.g. Logan's *Dress of the Day*, 1930), the air (e.g. Johns' *"Biggles" of the Camel Squadron*, 1934), prisoner-of-war camps in Germany (Purcell's *The Other Side of No-Man's Land*, 1929), the Friend's Ambulance Brigade (Stapledon's *Last Men in London*, 1932).

Many of the above writers simply wanted to entertain but a number of writers were motivated in a different way. Some set out to examine particular social and political problems and their solution (Gibbs's *Back to Life*, 1920, *The Middle of the Road*, 1923; Onions's *Peace in our Time*; Deane's *The Victors*, 1925; Herbert's *The Secret Battle*, 1919); some concerned themselves with the social effects of the war (e.g. Ford's 'Tietjens Tetralogy', 1924-1928; Mottram's *Spanish Farm Trilogy*, 1927; Blake's *The Valiant Heart*, 1939) or its psychological effects in terms of war neuroses (e.g. H.D.'s *Kora and Ka*, 1934). John Brophy (*The World Went Mad*, 1934) tried to fit the war into the history of the times; Robert Briffault used his novels *Europa* (1936) and *Europa in Limbo* (1937) to convey marxist interpretations of the war; some tackled feminist issues (e.g Brittain's *Honourable Estate*, 1936) and even the more controversial area of gay issues (e.g. Hall's *Well of Loneliness*, 1928 and *Miss Ogilvy Finds Herself*, 1934). Some, although frequently critical of the High Command, were mainly concerned to present their impressions of the war as realistically and accurately as possible (e.g. Benstead's *Retreat*, 1930; Blaker's *Medal Withour Bar*, 1930; Manning's *Her Privates We*, 1930; Hodson's *Grey Dawn, Red Night* (1929); some wrote novels which are expressions of patriotism and British values (e.g. Deeping's *No Hero-This*, 1936, *Sorrell and Son*, 1925; Morton's *The Barber of Putney*, 1919; Raymond's *The Jesting Army*, 1930, *Tell England*, 1922; Thompson's *Lament for Adonis*, 1932); and some focused on the effects of the war on personal development (e.g. Ewart's *Way of Revelation*, 1921; Frankau's *Peter Jackson, Cigar Merchant*, 1920; Hutchinson's *If Winter Comes*, 1921, *One Increasing Purpose*, 1925; Ingram's *Out of Darkness*, 1927; Keable's *Simon Called Peter*; Miller's *The Natural Man*, 1924; Stapledon's *Last Men in London*, 1932).

It was mainly in the late 1920's and the early 1930's that a large number of novels that took an 'anti-war', disillusioned view began to appear and to capture the public imagination. In spite of readers being exposed to this flood of 'anti-war' literature, effusively patriotic novels such as Ernest Raymond's *Tell England* and A.S.M. Hutchinson's *If Winter Comes* continued to be popular, and the success of Herbert Asquith's *Young Orland* (1927) and *Roon* (1929) demonstrated that a delicate and poetical handling of the war theme could still command the public's appreciation. Moreover, there were a considerable number of books that were published after 1929 that did not subscribe to the prevailing fashion for viewing the war in a disenchanted light (e.g. Deeping's *No Hero-This*, 1936; Ernest Raymond's *The Jesting Army*, 1930; Edward Thompson's *Lament for Adonis*, 1932; C. S. Forester's *Brown on Resolution*, 1929; Leslie Robert's *When the Gods Laughed*, 1930). Nevertheless, there still remains a tendency to regard the novels published during the late 1920's and early 1930's on the theme of the war as dominated by disillusionment.

The following list is a representative selection of the sort of fiction that was published:

Acland, P. *All Else Is Folly: A Tale of War and Passion*, with a note by way of preface by Ford Madox Ford (London: Constable, 1929)

Aldington, R. *Death of a Hero* (London: Chatto & Windus, 1929)

Asquith, H. *Young Orland* (London: Hutchinson, 1927)

Bagnold, E. *The Happy Foreigner* (London: W. Heinemann, 1920)
This novel encompasses the author's experiences as a driver in France during the war years.

Barbusse, H. *Under Fire: The Story of a Squad*, translated by Fitzwater Wray (London: J. M. Dent, 1917; repr. 1926)
First published in French (with the title, *Le Feu*) in 1916. There were several other reprints of this translation in the inter-war years.

Bennett, A. *Lord Raingo* (London: Cassell, 1926)

Benstead, C. R. *Retreat: A Story of 1918* (London: Methuen, 1930)

Bertram, A. *The Sword Falls* (London: Allen & Unwin, 1929)

Blake, G. *The Path of Glory* (London: Constable, 1929)

— *The Valiant Heart* (London: Collins, 1939)

Blaker, R. *Medal Without Bar* (London: Hodder & Stoughton, 1930)

Briffault, R. *Europa: A Novel of the Days of Ignorance* (London: Robert Hale, 1936)

— *Europa in Limbo* (London: Robert Hale, 1937)
Sequel to *Europa: A Novel of the Days of Ignorance*.

Brittain, V. *Honourable Estate: A Novel of Transition* (London: Gollancz, 1936)

Deane, P. *The Victors* (London: Constable, 1925)

Deeping, W. *No Hero-This* (London: Cassell, 1936)
This writer made a large fortune as the author of sentimental fiction and, like Ernest Raymond, owed his reputation to his appeal to patriotic gratitude after the war.

— *Sorrell and Son* (London: Cassell, 1925)

Ewart, W. *Way of Revelation:: A Novel of Five Years* (London: Putnam's, 1921)

Ford, F. M. (Joseph Leopold Ford Hermann Madox Hueffer). *No Enemy: A Tale of Reconstruction* (New York: The Macaulay Co., 1929)
The author wrote this in 1919 and had to wait ten years before he could find a publisher - in the USA.

— *Some Do Not* (London: Duckworth, 1924)
First vol. of the 'Tietjens' tetralogy.

— *No More Parades* (London: Duckworth, 1925)
Second vol. of the 'Tietjens' tetralogy.

— *A Man Could Stand Up* (London: Duckworth, 1926)
Third vol. of the 'Tietjens' tetralogy.

— *The Last Post* (London: Duckworth, 1928)
Final volume of the 'Tietjens' tetralogy.

Frankau, G. *Peter Jackson, Cigar Merchant: A Romance of Married Life* (London: Hutchinson, 1920)
Begun in 1917.

H.D. [Hilda Doolittle]. *Kora and Ka* (Dijon: Privately printed for the author's friends, 1934)

Hall, R *Miss Ogilvy Finds Herself* (London: Heinemann, 1934)

— *The Well of Loneliness* (New York: Sun Dial Press, 1928)

Hamilton, C. M. *William: An Englishman* (London: Skeffington & Son, 1919)
A novel about the harrowing effect of the First World War on William, a socialist clerk, and Griselda, a suffragette.

Harrison, C. Y. *Generals Die in Bed: A Novel from the Trenches* (London: Noel Douglas, 1930)

Galsworthy, J. *The Burning Spear: Being The Experiences of Mr. John Lavender in Time of War*, recorded by A. R. P-M. (London: Chatto & Windus, 1919; repr. London: Heinemann, 1925)
Published in 1919 under a pseudonym and reprinted in 1925 under his own name.

Gibbs, P. *Back to Life* (London: Heinemann, 1920)

— *The Middle of the Road* (London: Hutchinson, 1923)

Gristwood, A. D. *The Somme, including also The Coward*, with a preface by H. G. Wells (London: Jonathan Cape, 1927)

Gurner, S. R. K. *Pass Guard at Ypres* (London: Dent, 1929)

Herbert, A. P. *The Secret Battle*, with an introduction by Winston S. Churchill (London: Methuen, 1919)

Hueffer, O. M. *Cousins German* (London: Ernest Benn, 1930)

Hutchinson, A. S. M. *If Winter Comes* (London: Hodder & Stoughton, 1921)

— *One Increasing Purpose* (London: Hodder & Stoughton, 1925)

Huxley, A. *Antic Hay* (London: Chatto & Windus, 1923)
Can be seen as a reflection of the disillusionment of many of the post-war intellectual generation in England in the aftermath of the Great War.

Ingram, K. *Out of Darkness; A Drama of Flanders* (London: Chatto & Windus, 1927)

Keable, R. *Simon Called Peter* (London: Constable, 1921)

Kipling, R. *Debits and Credits* (London: Macmillan, 1927)
Includes the short stories, 'The Gardener', 'The Janeites', 'The Madonna of the Trenches'. The realism, compassion, and sadness expressed in these war stories is quite different from the exultant patriotism of the fiction, verse and propaganda he wrote during the war.

Lawrence, D. H. *Kangaroo* (London: Martin Secker, 1923)
See chapter entitled 'The Nightmare' for his thoughts on the war. An edition, edited by Bruce Steele, published by Cambridge University Press in 1994 is among the latest reprints of this novel.

Logan, W. B. *Dress of the Day: War-And-After Reminiscences of the British Navy* (London: A. E. Marriott, 1930)

Miller, P. *The Natural Man* (London: G. Richard, 1924)

MacDonald, P. *Patrol* (London: Collins, 1927)
A film entitled *Lost Patrol*, 1929 (see below in **section 4.3.2.2**) was based on this novel.

MacGill, P. *Fear!* (London : Herbert Jenkins 1921)

Mann, F. O. *Grope Carries On: Being the Further Adventures of Albert Grope during the Great War* (London: Faber, 1932)

Manning, F. *Her Privates We*, by Private 19022 [pseud.] (London: Peter Davies, 1930)
Originally published anonymously as *The Middle Parts of Fortune: Somme and Ancre, 1916*, 2 vols (London: Piazza Press, 1929). The version published in 1930 was under the title *Her Privates We*.

Mansfield, K. 'The Fly', in *The Dove's Nest and other Stories* (London: Constable, 1923)
The 'Fly' first appeared in the *Nation and Athenaeum* in March 1922. *The Fly* can be interpreted as a personal reaction to the tragedy of the Great War. Her brother was killed in that war.

Morton, J. B. *The Barber of Putney* (London: P. Allan, 1919)

Mottram, R. H. *Spanish Farm Trilogy* (London: Chatto & Windus, 1927)
An edition, in one volume, of *The Spanish Farm*; *Sixty-Four, Ninety-four!*; and *The Crime at Vanderlynden's*. "Between these three novels now appear for the first time in book form three connecting pieces: D'Archeville, The winner and The stranger." – frontispiece.

O'Flaherty, L. *The Return of the Brute* (London: Mandrake Press, 1929)

Onions, O., pseud. [i.e. George Oliver] *Peace in Our Time* (London: Chapman & Hall, 1923)

Raymond, E. *The Jesting Army* (London; Cassell, 1930)

— *Tell England: A Study in a Generation* (London: Cassell, 1922)
This patriotic novel made a major impact in the inter-war years.

Remarque, E. M. *All Quiet on the Western Front*, translated by A. W. Wheen (London: Putnam, 1929)

Sassoon, S. *The Complete Memoirs of George Sherston* (London: Faber, 1937)
Contains *Memoirs of a Fox-Hunting Man*, originally published London: Faber & Faber, 1928; *Memoirs of an Infantry Officer*, originally published London: Faber & Faber, 1931; *Sherston's Progress*, originally published London: Faber & Faber, 1936.

Sherriff, R. C. and V. Bartlett. *Journey's End: A Novel* (London: Gollancz, 1930)

Smith, H. Z., pseud. [i.e. Evadne Price]. *Not So Quiet: Stepdaughters of War* (London: A. E. Marriot, 1930; repr;. New York: Feminist Press, 1989)

Stapledon, O. *Last Men in London* (London: Methuen, 1932)

Thompson, E. J. *In Araby Orion* (London: Ernest Benn, 1930)

— *Lament for Adonis* (London: Ernest Benn, 1932)

— *These Men Thy Friends* (London: Knopf, 1927)

Tomlinson, H. M. *All Our Yesterdays* (London: Heinemann, 1930)

Walpole, H. *Dark Forest* (London: Nelson, 1916; repr. 1919, 1924; repr. London: Macmillan, 1923, 1926, 1934, 1937)

Wells, H. G. *Bulpington of Blup: Adventures, Poses, Stresses, Conflicts, and Disaster in a Contemporary Brain* (London: Hutchinson, 1932)

Williamson, H. *Patriot's Progress: Being the Vicissitudes of Pte. John Bullock*, related by Henry Williamson and drawn by William Kermode (London: Bles, 1930)

Woolf, V. *Mrs Dalloway* (London: L. & V. Woolf at the Hogarth Press, 1925)
The Oxford University Press edition of 2008, edited with an introduction and notes by David Bradshaw, is among the latest reprints of this novel.

— *Jacob's Room* (London: L. & V. Woolf at the Hogarth Press, 1922)
The Oxford University Press edition of 2008, edited with an introduction and notes by Kate Flint., is among the latest reprints of this novel.

— *To the Lighthouse* (London: L. & V. Woolf, 1927)
The Oxford University Press edition of 2008, edited with an introduction and notes by David Bradshaw, is among the latest reprints of this novel.

— *The Years* (London: L. & V. Woolf at the Hogarth Press, 1937)
The Oxford University Press edition of 2009, edited with an introduction by Hermione Lee., is among the latest reprints of this novel.

Yeates, V. M. *Winged Victory* (London: Cape, 1934)

4.2.3.3 Post 2nd World War

After the Second World War it was the most recent world war that was most likely to be uppermost in the mind of those who chose to write a war novel. There was, however, a major revival of general interest in the Great War in the 1960's and beyond. This produced a climate in which a number of publishers increasingly took the opportunity to reprint some of the more marketable war novels which had appeared in the inter-war years (as, for example, those asterisked in the list below). At the same time the Great War as a theme or backdrop began to return in some of the contemporary novels that were published and continued to be employed by novelists right into the 21st century.

In the post Second World War years many authors who have written novels which relate in some way to the Great War have tended to focus on the Western Front although occasionally other war zones are featured, even obscure sideshows as was the case with William Boyd who wrote about the campaign in German East Africa in an *Ice Cream War* (1982). But it is the war in France and Flanders (particularly images of the slaughter on the first day of the Somme campaign) which has continued to have a special fascination for novelists as is evident, for instance, in novels such as *Covenant with Death* (1961) by John Harris, *Strange Meeting* (1971) by Susan Hill, and *Birdsong* (1993) by Sebastian Faulks, all of which feature the battle of the Somme. *Birdsong* became a bestseller, as did Pat Barker's *The Regeneration Trilogy* (1996) - an indication of the fascination that the war has continued to evoke.

The following list is a representative selection of the Great War fiction published after the Second World War:

Cultural Impacts

*Aldington, R. *Death of a Hero* (London: Hogarth, 1984)
One of several reprints of this novel published in Britain after the Second World War. First published, London: Chatto & Windus, 1929.

Allatini, R. *Despised and Rejected* (London: Daniel, 1918; repr. London: Gay Men's Press, 1988)
Written under the pseudonym of A. T. Fitzroy. DORA (the Defence of the Realm Act) was employed to suppress this work on the grounds that it was "likely to prejudice the recruiting, training, and discipline of persons in his Majesty's Forces". It remained out of print until 1988, when it was reissued by the Gay Men's Press.

*Barbusse, H. *Under Fire*, translated by Robin Buss, with an introduction by Jay Winter (London: Penguin, 2003)
First published in French (with the title, *Le Feu*) in 1916. It was first translated into English in 1917 by Fitzwater Wray (London: J.M. Dent, 1917) and reprinted several times before this new translation was published.

Barker, P. *The Regeneration Trilogy* (London: Viking, 1996; repr. London: Penguin, 1998)
Contents: *Regeneration* (originally published by Viking in 1991), *The Eye in the Door* (originally published by Viking in 1993), *The Ghost Road* (originally published by Viking in 1995).

Barry, S. *A Long Long Way* (London: Faber, 2005)

Boyd, W. *An Ice Cream War* (London: Hamish Hamilton, 1982; repr. London: Penguin 1997)

*Brittain, V. *Honourable Estate: A Novel of Transition* (London: Virago, 2000)
First published, London: Gollancz, 1936.

Burgess, A. *The Wanting Seed* (London: Heiemann, 1962; repr. Feltham: Hamlyn, 1983)
"Anthony Burgess was born during the Great War; he would have been too young to remember it, but in this novel *The Wanting Seed* ["a dystopian futurological fantasy"] he makes a vivid, caricatural reproduction of it". [Quotation, including the quotation within square brackets, from *Heroes' Twilight* by Bernard Bergonzi, p. 202]

Cloete, S. *How Young They Died* (London: Collins, 1969)

Colegate, I. *The Shooting Party* (London: Hamish Hamilton, 1980; repr. Harmondsworth, 1982))
Although this novel is set in 1913 and does not mention the Great War until its final pages it provides the atmosphere of an Edwardian society on the brink of being plunged into the Great War. A film based on the book, directed by Alan Bridges, was made in 1985.

*Deeping, W. *Sorrell and Son* (Harmondsworth, Penguin, 1984)
First published, London; Cassell, 1925.

Eldridge, J. *The Trenches: A First World War Soldier, 1914-1918* (London : Scholastic, 2008)
Fiction aimed at 8 to 12 year-olds

Elton, B. *The First Casualty* (London: Bantam, 2005)

*Ewart, W. *Way of Revelation: A Novel of Five Years* (Gloucester: Sutton, 1986)
First published, London: Putnam's, 1921

Fallas, C. *Saint Mary's Village: Through the eyes of an Unknown Soldier who Lived On* (London: Hodder & Stoughton, 1954)

Faulks, S. *Birdsong* (London: Hutchinson, 1993; repr. London: Vintage, 2005)

Fitzroy, A. T., pseud. [i.e. Rose Laure Allatini, afterwards Scott]. *Despised and Rejected* (London : GMP, 1988)
Originally published, London: Daniel, 1918, but DORA (the Defence of the Realm Act) was employed to suppress it on the grounds that it was a threat to the war effort.

*Ford, F. M. (Joseph Leopold Ford Hermann Madox Hueffer). *No Enemy: A Tale of Reconstruction* (Manchester: Carcanet, 2002)
First published, New York: The Macaulay Co., 1929.

— *Parade's End* (Harmondsworth: Penguin, 1982; repr 2002)
Contents: *Some Do Not*; *No More Parades*; *A Man Could Stand Up*; *The Last Post*. Originally published separately by Duckworth from 1924 to 1928.

*Frankau, G. *Peter Jackson, Cigar Merchant: A Romance of Married Life* (London: Brown, Watson, 1958)
First published, London: Hutchinson, 1920.

Fullerton, A. *Flight to Mons* (London: Little, Brown, 2003; London: Time Warner, 2004)

H.D. [Hilda Doolittle]. *Bide Me to Live* (New York: Grove Press, 1960; repr. London: Virago, 1983)
Written and revised during the late 1930's and 1940's but not published until 1960.

— *Kora and Ka: With Mira-Mare*, introduction by Robert Spoo (New York: New Directions, 1996)
Originally printed privately in 1934 for the author's friends by Imprimerie Darantière at Dijon. Also reprinted in *That Kind of Woman: Stories from the Left Bank and Beyond*, edited by Bronte Adams and Trudi Tate (London: Virago, 1991).

*Hamilton, C. M. *William: An Englishman*, with a new preface by Nicola Beauman (London: Persephone Books, 1999)
First published London: Skeffington & Son, 1919. A novel about the harrowing effect of the First World War on William, a socialist clerk, and Griselda, a suffragette.

Harris, J. *Covenant with Death* (London: Hutchinson, 1961; repr. 1973)

*Harrison, C. Y. *Generals Die in Bed: A Novel from the Trenches* (London Definitions, 2004)
First published, London: Noel Douglas, 1930

*Herbert, A. P. *The Secret Battle*, with a preface by Winston. S. Churchill and an introduction by John Terraine (Oxford: Oxford University Press, 1982)
First published, London: Methuen, 1919.

Hill, S. *Strange Meeting* (London: Hamish Hamilton, 1971; repr. Harlow: Longman, 1984)
The reprint has a specially written introduction by the author.

*Hutchinson, A. S. M. *If Winter Comes* (London: Morley-Baker, 1968)
First published, London: Hodder & Stoughton, 1921.

*Huxley, A. *Antic Hay* (London: Vintage 2004)
Can be seen as a reflection of the disillusionment of many of the post-war intellectual generation in England in the aftermath of the Great War. Originally published London: Chatto & Windus, 1923.

*Kipling, R. *Debits and Credits* (London: House of Stratus, 2003)
Includes the short stories, 'The Gardener', 'The Janeites', 'The Madonna of the Trenches'. The realism, compassion, and sadness expressed in these war stories is quite different from the exultant patriotism of the fiction, verse and propaganda he wrote during the war. First published, London: Macmillan, 1927.

*Manning, F. *Her Privates We*, with an introduction by William Boyd (London: Serpent's Tail, 1999)
Originally published anonymously as *The Middle Parts of Fortune: Somme and Ancre, 1916*, 2 vols (London: Piazza Press, 1929). A version of this was published in 1930 by Peter Davies under the title *Her Privates We*, several reprints of which were published after the Second World War.

*Mansfield, K. 'The Fly', in *The Dove's Nest and other Stories* (London: Century Hutchinson, 1988)
The 'Fly' first appeared in the *Nation and Athenaeum* in March 1922 and was published in *The Dove's Nest and other Stories*: London: Constable, 1923. *The Fly* can be interpreted as a personal reaction to the tragedy of the Great War. Her brother was killed in that war.

*Mottram, R. H. *Spanish Farm Trilogy, 1914-1918* (Harmondsworth: Penguin 1979)
Contains *The Spanish Farm*; *Sixty-Four; Ninety-four!*; and *The Crime at Vanderlynden's* which were originally published separately by Chatto & Windus from 1924 to 1926.

*O'Flaherty, L. *The Return of the Brute* (Dublin: Wolfhound, 1998)

First published, London: Mandrake Press, 1929.

*Raymond, E. *Tell England: A Study in a Generation* (London: Cassell, 1973)
First published, London: Cassell, 1922.

*Remarque, E. M. *All Quiet on the Western Front*. [Translated by Brian Murdoch] (London: Vintage, 2005)
One of the several post 2nd World War reprints of a translation from the German that was originally published in Britain in 1929 (translated then by A. Wheen).

Robinson, D. *Goshawk Squadron* (London: Heinemann, 1971; repr. London, Robinson, 2005)

— *Hornet's Sting* (London: Cassell, 2001)

— *War Story* (London: Cassell, 1987; repr. 2001)

*Sassoon, S. *The Complete Memoirs of George Sherston*, 3 vols (London: Folio Society, 1993)
Contains: *Memoirs of a Fox-Hunting Man*, originally published London: Faber & Faber, 1928; *Memoirs of an Infantry Officer*, originally published London: Faber & Faber, 1931; *Sherston's Progress*, originally published London: Faber & Faber, 1936. All 3 books were first published in one vol, London: Faber 1937.

*Smith, H. Z., pseud. [i.e. Evadne Price]. *Not So Quiet: Stepdaughters of War* (London: Virago, 1988)
First published London: A. E. Marriot, 1930.

*Stapledon, O. *Last Men in London* (London: Magnum Books, 1978)
First published, London: Methuen, 1932.

Wilding, V. *Road to War: A First World War Girl's Diary 1916-1917* (London : Scholastic, 2008)
Fiction aimed at 8 to 12 year-olds.

Williamson, H. *Patriot's Progress: Being the Vicissitudes of Pte. John Bullock*, related by Henry Williamson and drawn by William Kermode, new edn (Stroud: Sutton, 2004)
Previous edition: London: Macdonald and Co, 1968. Originally published London: Bles, 1930).

— *How Dear is Life*, A Chronicle of Ancient Sunlight, 4 (London: Macdonald, 1954; repr. 1984)

— *A Fox under my Cloak*, A Chronicle of Ancient Sunlight, 5 (London: Macdonald, 1955; repr. Stroud, Sutton 1996)

— The *Golden Virgin*, A Chronicle of Ancient Sunlight, 6 (London: Macdonald, 1957; repr. Stroud: Sutton, 1996)

— *Love and the Loveless: A Soldier's Tale*, A Chronicle of Ancient Sunlight, 7 (London: Macdonald, 1958; repr. Stroud: Sutton, 1997)

— *A Test to Destruction*, A Chronicle of Ancient Sunlight, 8 (London: Macdonald, 1960; repr. Stroud: Sutton, 1997)

*Yeates, V. M. *Winged Victory* (London: Buchan & Enright, 1985)
First published: London: Cape, 1934.

Young, L. *My Dear, I Wanted to Tell You* (London: HarperCollins, 2011)
A novel in which the author encapsulates the effect of the Great War on those left behind as well as on those who fight.

— *The Heroes' Welcome* (London: The Borough Press, 2014)
In this sequel to the above novel the author evokes the trauma and hopes of families in the aftermath of the Great War

4.2.4 Poetry

Since the early 1920's, Great War literature has undergone two major revivals of interest. The first, at the end of the 1920's was dominated by prose (represented by the publication of a spate of war novels and memoirs) rather than poetry. Poems on aspects of the Great War continued to be published after the war but the output of 'war' poetry generally dwindled in the early twenties[200], and the flood of 'war books' at the end of that decade included only one anthology of war poetry (Brereton's *An Anthology of War Poems*, 1930). Rupert Brooke's poetry, however, remained popular (by 1930 his *Collected Poems* had sold 300,000 copies) but the verse of poets such as Isaac Rosenberg and Wlfred Owen was little known in 1930 (although collections of Rosenberg's poems had been published in 1922 and Owen's in 1920). The second revival of interest in Great War literature arrived in the 1960's and this time it was poetry rather than prose which led the way. The latter period witnessed the beginning of the full acceptance of the poetry of the Great War as a coherent literary and academic subject, with Denis Welland's publication in 1960 of the first critical study of Wilfred Owen paving the way for the development in the ensuing years of a significant body of works on the poetry of the Great War, encompassing studies of poets, works of criticism and biography, anthologies, and editions of the verse of individual poets. Great prominence was, and still is, given to the verse of a small number of poets such as Wilfred Owen, Siegfried Sassoon, Rupert Brooke, Isaac Rosenberg, Charles Sorley, and Ivor Gurney, in spite of the efforts in recent years of some anthologists and literary critics to include in their anthologies and critical works a wider range of poets (especially those who are less well-known) in order to provide a more representative picture of Great War poetry.

Archives

The First World War Poetry Digital Archive (http://www.oucs.ox.ac.uk/ww1lit/)
"The name of the site is … something of a misnomer. Although poems (and links to archival collections) from the likes of Owen, Sassoon, Graves and Jones are available, only ten poets and authors are featured, leading to the omission of significant names like Brooke, McCrae and the hugely popular John Oxenham. What the site does provide is a remarkable collection of publications from the war itself, including digitised copies of the Craiglockheart Hospital journal *The Hydra*, and links to the university's sister project, the *Great War Archive*. Now linked to the *Europeana* project [q.v.] … the archive contains over 6,500 items contributed by members of the public in 2008. As a result, the vast majority of material provided relates to British soldiers, the most of whom have little to no relationship with the poets showcased on the main site. With the final project report for the poetry digital archive having been written in January 2010, and the focus upon contributing to the larger *Europeana* project, it would appear that the archive is now effectively closed for entries and will not be further expanded". [Quotation extracted from Philips, C. Review of *First World War Digital Resources*, q.v.]

Bibliographies

Birmingham Public Libraries. Reference Department. *Catalogue of the War Poetry Collection* (Birmingham: Printed for the donor by the Birmingham Printers Ltd, 1921)
The catalogue was presented by an Anonymous Donor in Memory of Private William John Billington, 2/24 London Regiment (Queen's), formerly of 2/2 South Midland Field Ambulance, who fell in Palestine, March 9th, 1918.

Reilly, C. *English Poetry of the First World War: A Bibliography* (London: Prior, 1978)

Critical Studies

- **Books**

Adcock, A. St. John. *For Remembrance: Soldier Poets who have Fallen in the War* (London: Hodder & Stoughton, 1918; repr. 1920)

Barlow, A., ed. *Six Poets of the Great War* (Cambridge: Cambridge University Press, 1995)

Bergonzi, B. *Heroes' Twilight: A Study of the Literature of The Great War*, 3rd edn (Manchester: Carcanet, 1996)
Of the poets who wrote during the Great War Bergonzi includes chapters on Brooke, Grenfell, and Sorley; on Graves, Blunden, and Read; on Thomas and Gurney; on Sassoon; and on Rosenberg and Owen. The chapter on Graves, Blunden and Read includes a brief consideration of Gibson, Binyon, Johnson, Watson, Nichols, Ford, Aldington, Manning, and West.

---

[200] In contrast to the unprecedented popularity of such poetry during the Great War.

Cultural Impacts

Blunden, E. *War Poets, 1914-1918* (London: Longmans, Green for the British Council and the National Book League, 1958; repr, 1969)

Bomberg, D. *Poems and Drawings from the First World War* (London: Gillian Jason Gallery, 1992)
Includes essay by Richard Cork entitled 'Bomberg's war poetry'.

Brearton, F. *The Great War in Irish Poetry: W. B. Yeats to Michael Longley* (Oxford: Oxford University Press, 2000)

Caesar, A. *Taking it Like a Man: Suffering, Sexuality and the War Poets* (Manchester: Manchester University Press, 1993)

Campbell, P. *Siegfried Sassoon: A Study of the War Poetry* (Jefferson, NC: McFarland, 1999)

Carter, D. N. G. *Robert Graves: The Lasting Poetic Achievement* (Basingstoke: Macmillan, 1989)

Crawford, F. D. *British Poets of the Great War* (London: Associated University Presses, 1988)

Dilworth, T. *Reading David Jones* (Cardiff: University of Wales Press, 2008)

— *The Shape of Meaning in the Poetry of David Jones* (Toronto: Toronto University Press, 1988)

Featherstone, S., ed. *War Poetry: An Introductory Reader* (London: Routledge, 1995)

Gates, N. T. *Poetry of Richard Aldington: A Critical Evaluation and an Anthology of Uncollected Poems* (University Park: Pennsylvania State University Press, 1975)

Giddings, R. *The War Poets* (London: Bloomsbury, 1988; repr. 1990)

Hibberd, D. *Owen the Poet* (London: Macmillan, 1988)

— 'Who were the war poets, anyway?', in *English Literature of the Great War Revisited*, Proceedings of the Symposium on the British Literature of the First World War, University of Picardy, 1986, ed. by M. Roucoux (Picardie: Presses de l'UFR, 1987)

Hughes, C. A. *David Jones: The Man Who Was on the Field: 'In Parenthesis' as Straight Reporting* (Manchester: David Jones Society, 1979)

Johnson, T. *A Critical Introduction to the Poetry of Thomas Hardy* (London: Macmillan, 1991)

Johnston, J. H. *English Poetry of the First World War: A Study in the Evolution of Lyric and Narrative Form* (London; Oxford University Press, 1964)
Contents: I. Foreground and background; II. The early poets: Rupert Brooke, Julian Grenfell, Robert Nichols, Charles Sorley; III. Realism and satire: Siegfried Sassoon; IV. Undertones: Edmund Blunden; V. Poetry and pity: Wilfred Owen; VI. Poetry and pity: Isaac Rosenberg; VII. The "higher reality": Herbert Read; VIII. The heroic vision: David Jones.

Kerr, D. *Wilfred Owen's Voices: Language and Community* (Oxford: Clarendon Presss, 1993)

Kirkham, M. *The Poetry of Robert Graves* (London: Athlone Press, 1969)

Lane, A. E. *An Adequate Response: The War Poetry of Wilfred Owen* (Detroit: Wayne State University Press, 1972)

Lehmann, J. *The English Poets of the First World War* (London: Thames & Hudson, 1981)

Lilly, M. *Gay Men's Literature in the Twentieth Century* (Basingstoke: Macmillan, 1993)
Includes a chapter entitled 'The Love Poetry of World War I'.

Marsland, E. A. *The Nation's Cause: French, English and German Poetry of the First World War* (London: Routledge, 1991)

Motion, A. *The Poetry of Edward Thomas* (London: Hogarth, 1980)

Sola Pinto, V. de. *Crisis in English poetry, 1880-1940*, 5th edn (London: Hutchinson, 1967)

Spear, H. D. *Remembering, We Forget: A Background Study to the Poetry of the First World War* (London: Davis-Poynter, 1979)

Stephen, M. *The Price of Pity: Poetry, History and Myth in the Great War* (London: Cooper, 1996)

Swinnerton, F. *The Georgian Literary Scene, 1910-1935: A Panorama* (London: Hutchinson, 1935)
Includes a chapter on war poetry entitled 'The War-Time Afflatus, 1914-1918'.

Thorpe, M. *Siegfried Sassoon: A Critical Study* (London: Oxford University Pres, 1966)

Vandiver, E. *Stand in the Trench, Achilles: Classical Receptions in British Poetry of the Great War* (Oxford: Oxford University Press, 2010; repr. in paperback 2013)

Welland, D. S. R. *Wilfred Owen: A Critical Study* (London: Chatto & Windus, 1960)

- **Articles**

Bogacz, T. 'A Tyranny of Words: Language, Poetry and Anti-Modernism in England in the First World War', *Journal of Modern History*, 58 (1986), 643-68

Brock, C. 'War and Poetry', *Times Literary Supplement*, (October 8, 1914)

Brophy. J. D. 'The War Poetry of Wilfred Owen and Osbert Sitwell: An Instructive Contrast', *Modern Language Studies*, 1:2 (1971) 22-29

Taylor, M. '"You smug-faced crowds": Poetry and the Home Front in the First World War', *Imperial War Museum Review*, 3 (1988), 87-96

Biographies, Letters, Diaries

Boden, A. *F. W. Harvey: Soldier, Poet* (Stroud: Alan Sutton, 1988)

Cannan, M. W. *The Tears of War: The Love Story of a Young Poet and a War Hero*, edited by C. Fyfe (Upaven: Cavalier, 2000)
The poignant story of the poet May Cannan and her fiancé Bevil Quiller-Couch told through her poetry, with passages from her autobiography and letters from Bevil and his father, interspersed with official war diary extracts.

Brooke, R. *The Letters of Rupert Brooke*, edited by Geoffrey Keynes (London: Faber, 1968)

Campbell, C. and R. Green. *Can't Shoot a Man with a Cold: Lt. E. Alan Mackintosh MC 1893-1917, Poet of the Highland Division* (Glendaruel: Argyll Publishing, 2004)

Cohen, J. *Journey to the Trenches: The Life of Isaac Rosenberg* (London: Robson Books, 1975)

Cooke, W. *Edward Thomas: A Critical Biography* (London: Faber, 1970)

Curtayne, A. *Francis Ledwidge: A Life of the Poet, 1887-1917* (Dublin: New Island Books, 1998)

Doyle, C. *Richard Aldington: A Biography* (Basingstoke: Macmillan, 1989)

Farjeon, E. *Edward Thomas: The Last Four Years*, with a foreword by P. J. Kavanagh and an introduction by Anne Harvey (Stroud: Sutton, 1997)

Foster, R. F. *W. B. Yeats: A Life*, 2 vols (Oxford: Oxford University Press, 1997-2003)

Cultural Impacts

Contents: Vol.1: *The Apprentice Image, 1865-1914* (1997); Vol. 2: *The Arch-Poet, 1915-1939* (2003)

Graves, R. *In Broken Images: Selected Letters of Robert Graves, 1914-1946*, edited by Paul O'Prey (London: Hutchinson, 1982)

— *Between Moon and Moon: Selected letters of Robert Graves, 1946-1972*, edited by Paul O'Prey (London: Hutchinson, 1984)

Graves, R. P. *Robert Graves*, 2 vols (London: Weidenfeld & Nicolson, 1986-1990)
Vol 1. *The Assault Heroic, 1896-1926* (1986). Vol 2. *The Years with Laura, 1926-1940* (1990)

Grundy, M. *A Fiery Glow in the Darkness: Woodbine Willie – Padre and Poet* (Worcester: Osborne Books, 1997)

Gurney, I. *Collected Letters*, edited by R. K. Thornton (Ashington: Mid Northumberland Arts Group, 1991)

— *War Letters*, a selection edited by R. K. Thornton (Ashington: Mid Northumberland Arts Group, 1983)

Hassell, C. *Rupert Brooke: A Biography* (London: Faber, 1972)

Hibberd, D. *Wilfred Owen: A New Biography* (London: Weidenfeld & Nicolson, 2002)

— *Wilfred Owen: The Last Year, 1917-1918* (London: Constable, 1992)

Hurd, M. *The Ordeal of Ivor Gurney* (Oxford: Oxford University Press, 1978)

Jones, N. H. *Rupert Brooke: Life, Death and Myth* (London: R. Cohen, 1999)

King, J. *The Last Modern: A Life of Herbert Read* (London: Weidenfeld & Nicolson, 1990)

Liddiard, J. *Isaac Rosenberg: The Half-Used Life* (London: Gollancz, 1975)

Lucas, J. *Ivor Gurney* (Tavistock: Northcote House, 2001)

McPhail, H. *Wilfred Owen: Poet and Soldier* (London: Gliddon Books, 1993)

McPhail, H. and P. Guest. *Edmund Blunden* (London: Pen & Sword Books, 1999)

Miles, J. and D. Shiel. *David Jones: The Maker Unmade* (Bridgend: Seren, 1996)

Mosley, N. *Julian Grenfell: His Life and the Times of his Death, 1888-1915* (London: Weidenfeld & Nicolson, 1976; repr. with a new preface by the author, London: Persephone, 2000)

Owen, H. *Journey from Obscurity*, 3 vols (Oxford: Oxford University Press, 1963-65)

Owen, W. *Collected Letters*, edited by Harold Owen and John Bell (London: Oxford University Press, 1967)

— *Selected Letters*, edited by J. Bell, 2nd edn (Oxford: Oxford University Press, 1998)

Read, H. *Annals of Innocence and Experience*, revised and enlarged edn (London: Faber, 1946; repr. New York: Haskell House, 1982)
First published in 1940. Includes *The Innocent Eye* and *In Retreat*.

Sassoon, S. *Diaries,*, edited by Rupert Hart-Davis, 3 vols (London: Faber, 1981-1985)
Contents: Vol. 1. 1915-18 (1983); Vol. 2. 1920-22 (1981); Vol. 3. 1923-25 (1985).

Sorley, C. H. *The Collected Letters of Charles Hamilton Sorley*, edited by J. M. Wilson (London: Cecil Woolf, 1990)

— *Poems and Selected Letters*, edited by H. D. Spear (Dundee: Blackness Press, 1978)

Seymour-Smith, M. *Robert Graves: His Life and Works*, revised and extended edn (London: Bloomsbury, 1995)

Stallworthy, J. *Wilfred Owen: A Biography*, new edn (Oxford: Oxford University Press, 1998)

Swann, T. B. *The Ungirt Runner: Charles Hamilton Sorley, Poet of World War I* (Hamden, Conn.: Archon Books, 1965)

Thomas, E. *The Diary of Edward Thomas: 1 Jan-8 Apr 1917*, with an introduction by Roland Gant (Andoversford: Whittington Press, 1977)

— *Edward Thomas: Selected Letters*, edited by R. G. Thomas (Oxford: Oxford University Press, 1996)

Thomas, R. G. *Edward Thomas*, rev. edn (Cardiff: University of Wales Press, 1993)

Townsend, F. *The Laureate of Gloucestershire: The Life and Work of F. W. Harvey, 1888-1957* (Bristol: Redcliffe, 1988)

Webb, B. *Edmund Blunden: A Biography* (New Haven: Yale University Press, 1990)

Williams, M. *Wilfred Owen* (Bridgend: Seren, 1993)

Wilson, J. M. *Charles Hamilton Sorley: A Biography* (London: Cecil Woolf, 1985)

— *Siegfried Sassoon: The Making of a War Poet: A Biography (1886-1918)* (London: Duckworth, 1998; repr. London: Duckbacks, 2002)

— *Siegfried Sassoon: The Journey from the Trenches: A Biography (1918-1967)* (London: Duckworth, 2004)

Zilboorg, C. *Richard Aldington and H.D.: Their Lives in Letters, 1918-61*, edited with an introduction and commentary by Caroline Zilboorg, new collected edn (Manchester: Manchester University Press, 2003)

Anthologies

Many anthologists of Great War poetry have selected their material, not necessarily with literary merit or other considerations in mind, but often with a view to reflecting particular attitudes to the war[201]. In the case of anthologies published during the Great War and in its immediate aftermath this gave rise to a representation of a mythology of 'heroism' and the 'just war'[202]; in the case of later anthologies, especially those compiled in the 1960's, it gave rise to the mythology which can be described as 'anti-war' in the sense of its focus on the horrors and futility of the war, and the anguish and suffering it generated, with anthologists often arranging the poems they have selected in a manner which is calculated to give the impression that the attitudes of the poets were expressive of a progression from idealism, to realism, disillusionment, and protest[203]. This has helped to give rise to a myth which, in spite of the efforts of some anthologists (e.g. Dominic Hibberd, John Onions, Martin Stephen, Catherine Reilly) to provide a more balanced and representative view of Great War poetry, tends to persist in the public mind and to continue to influence modern perceptions of the Great War.

The works recorded below represent a selection of anthologies published in the years after the Great War to the present day:

---

[201] A reflection which can be seen as the result of a two-way process of anthologists influencing, and being influenced by, contemporary attitudes to the war.

[202] In the immediate aftermath of the war Lloyd's anthology, *The Paths of Glory*, does not entirely fit into this category. Lloyd sees the poetry he has selected as expressive of an ambivalence which was 'to curse the horror and banefulness of war, and yet to be constantly idealising it (implicitly at least), and lauding its ennobling influence, and the courage and heroism it invokes'. The title and theme of Trotter's *Valour and Vision* (1920) were more typical, being arranged to tell a tale of heroic events leading up to 'that great October which brought the long-sought victory'.

[203] As, for example, Parsons's *Men Who Marched Away* which is divided into sections such as 'Visions of Glory', 'The Bitter Truth', 'No More Jokes', 'The Pity of War.

Balcon, J. *The Pity of War: Poems of The First World War*, selected with an introduction by Jill Balcon; preface by Edward Carpenter; calligraphy by Rosemary Grossman; illustrations by Barrington Barber (London: Shepherd-Walwyn, 1985)

Black, E. L., ed. *1914-18 in Poetry: An Anthology*, selected and edited by E. L. Black (London: University of London Press, 1970)

Brereton, F., comp. *An Anthology of War Poems*, compiled by Frederick Brereton; introduction by Edmund Blunden (London: Collins, 1930)

Clarke, G. H., ed. *A Treasury of War Poetry: British and American Poems of The World War, 1914-1919* (London: Hodder & Stoughton, 1919)

Davison, E., ed. *Cambridge Poets 1914-1920: An Anthology* (Cambridge: W. Heffer, 1920)

Duffy, C. A., ed. *1914: Poetry Remembers* (London: Faber, 2013)
This anthology to mark the centenary of the First World War in 2014 was the result of the Poet Laureate, Carol Ann Duffy, engaging the most eminent poets of the present to choose the writing from the Great War that had the most profound impact on them and also commissioning them to write a poem of their own encapsulating their response to the war.

Fuller, S, ed. *The Poetry of War, 1914-1989* (Harlow: Longman, 1990)

Gardner, B. *Up the Line to Death: The War Poets 1914-1918*, an anthology selected and arranged by Brian Gardner (London: Methuen, 1986)

Georgian Poetry, edited by Sir Edward H. Marsh, 5 vols (London: The Poetry Bookshop, 1915-1922)
Contents: Vol 1. 1911-1912 ; Vol 2. 1913-1915; Vol 3. 1916-1917; Vol 4. 1918-1919; Vol 5. 1920-1922. In these anthologies the poems of the following writers were featured: Gordon Bottomley, Rupert Brooke, William H. Davies, Walter de la Mare, John Drinkwater, James Elroy Flecker, Wilfrid Wilson Gibson, Ralph Hodgson, D. H. Lawrence, Francis Ledwidge, John Masefield, Harold Monro, James Stephens, Lascelles Abercrombie, Herbert Asquith, Maurice Baring, John Freeman, Robert Graves, Robert Nichols, Isaac Rosenberg, Siegfried Sassoon, J. C. Squire, W. J. Turner, Francis Brett Young, Thomas Moult, J. D. C Pellow, Edward Shanks, Fredegond Shove.

Hamilton, J., ed. *From Gallipoli to Gaza* (East Roseville, NSW: Simon & Schuster, 2003)

Hibberd, D. and J. Onions, eds. *Poetry of the Great War: An Anthology* (London: Macmillan, 1986)

— *The Winter of the World: Poems of the First World War* (London: Constable, 2007; repr. 2008)

Hussey, M. P. *Poetry of the First World War: An Anthology*, selected and edited by Maurice Hussey (London: Longmans, 1967; repr. 1979)

Lloyd, B.. ed. *The Paths of Glory: A Collection of Poetry Written During the War, 1914-1919* (London: Allen and Unwin, 1919)

Martin, C. *War Poems*, 2nd edn (London: Collins, 2004)

Motion, A. *First World War Poems* (London: Faber & Faber, 2003)

Nichols, R. M. B. *Anthology of War Poetry: 1914-1918*, assembled by Robert Nichols (London: Nicholson & Watson, 1943)

Noakes, V. *Voices of Silence: The Alternative Book of First World War Poetry*, compiled by Vivien Noakes (Stroud: Sutton, 2006)

O'Prey, P. *First World War Poems from the Front* (London: Imperial War Museum 2014)

Parsons, I. M. *Men Who Marched Away: Poems of the First World War* (London: Chatto & Windus, 1965; repr.

London: Hogarth, 1987)

Poems from Punch, 1909-1920, [selected and] with an introduction by W. B. Drayton Henderson (London: Macmillan, 1922)

Powell, A., ed. *A Deep Cry: A Literary Pilgrimage to the Battlefields and Cemeteries of First World War British Soldier-Poets Killed in Northern France and Flanders*, edited and introduced by Anne Powell (Aberporth: Palladour, 1993; repr. Stroud: Sutton, 1998)
For each of 66 published British poets killed in Flanders this book, which is arranged by date of death, provides a short story of his life and death, including an account of the battle in which he died, together with his poems, letters and diaries.

Reilly, C., ed. *Scars Upon My Heart: Women's Poetry and Verse of the First World War* (London: Virago, 1981)

Roberts, D. *Minds at War: Essential Poetry of the First World War in Context* (Burgess Hill: Saxon Books, 1996)

Silkin, J., ed. *The Penguin Book of First World War Poetry*, 2nd edn revised with new material (London: Penguin, 1996)

Stallworthy, J. *Anthem for Doomed Youth: Twelve Soldier Poets of the First World War* (London: Constable in association with the Imperial War Museum, 2002)

Stallworthy, J, comp. *The Oxford Book of War Poetry*, new edn (Oxford: Oxford University Press, 1984)

Stephen, M., ed. *Never Such Innocence: A New Anthology of Great War Verse* (London: Buchan & Enright, 1988)
Reprinted as *'Never Such Innocence': Poems of the First World War*, London: Dent, 1993.

Taylor, M. *Lads: Love Poetry of the Trenches* (London: Constable, 1989; repr. London: Duckbacks, 2002)
The introductory essay discusses the friendships intensified under fire and the strong homo-erotic element characterising the poetry of Siegfried Sassoon, Wilfred Owen and others.

Trotter, J., ed. *Vision and Valour; Poems of the War, 1914-1918*, arranged and edited by Jacqueline T. Trotter. (London: Longmans, 1920)
"The intention is to present the poet as the historian, and to illustrate the different aspects and phases of the war by contemporary poetry."--Pref. note.

Wheels: An Anthology of Verse, Cycle [1]-6 (Oxford: Blackwell, 1916-1921)
Includes contributions by O. Sitwell, A. Huxley, S. Sitwell, A. James, I. Tree, S. Vines, E. Sitwell, E. W. Tennant, H. Rootham, A. V. L. de Guevara, N. Cunard. 3rd-6th cycles edited by Edith Sitwell. Cycle 5 published: London: Leonard Parsons, 1920; Cycle 6 published: London: C. W. Daniel, 1921.

Works of Individual Poets

This section lists a selection of poetical works which have been published since the Great War and contain war poems written during or after that war. As well as the collections of some of the best known soldier-poets who fought in the First World War (Richard Aldington, Edmund Blunden, Rupert Brooke, Robert Graves, Ivor Gurney, Wilfred Owen, Herbert Read, Isaac Rosenberg, Siegfried Sassoon, Charles Hamilton Sorley, Edward Thomas, and Francis Ledwidge) the works listed below also include collections of a sample of other poets whose works include some poems in which the Great War was directly or indirectly recalled. Some of these poems (as exemplified by the poets asterisked below) were written after the Second World War and are symptomatic of the continued fascination of the British people, even though the latter war would have been freshest in their memory, with the Great War. In this section is also listed David Jones's *In Parenthesis* which was written as a combination of prose and free verse.

Aldington, R. *The Complete Poems of Richard Aldington* (London: Wingate, 1948)

— *Images of War: A Book of Poems* (London: George Allen & Unwin Ltd., 1919)
Richard Aldington, better known as a novelist than as a poet, was nevertheless a prolific poet who wrote a good many poems on active service, collected in *Images of War*.

Cultural Impacts

— *An Imagist at War: The Complete War Poems of Richard Aldington*, selected with an introduction and notes by Michael Copp (London: Associated University Presses, 2002)

Alington, C.A. *Eton Lyrics* (London: Clement Ingleby, 1925)

Barnes, L. *Youth at Arms* (London: Davies, 1933)

Blunden, E. *The Shepherd and other Poems of Peace and War* (London: Cobden-Sanderson, 1922)

— *Masks of Time: A New Collection of Poems Principally Meditative* (London: Beaumont Press, 1925)
'Includes the poems, 'Pillbox' (1925), 'Come On, My Lucky Lads' (1925), 'In Senlis Once' (1925).

— *Undertones of War* (Chicago: Chicago University Press, 2007)
Originally published, London: Cobden-Sanderson, 1928. Includes a selection of Blunden's war poems. A Penguin edition (Harmondsworth) was published in 2000.

— *Poems, 1914-1930* (London: Cobden-Sanderson, 1930)
'Includes the poem, 'Premature Rejoicing' (1930).

Borden, M. *The Forbidden Zone: A Nurse's Impressions of the First World War* (London: Hesperus, 2008)
Includes poems. Originally published, London: William Heinemann, 1929 under the title *The Forbidden Zone*.

Bridges, R. S. *October and other Poems: With Occasional Verses on the War* (London: Heinemann, 1920)

Brittain, V. *Poems of the War and After* (London: Gollancz, 1934)

Bowman, A. A. *Sonnets from a Prison Camp* (London: John Lane The Bodley Head, 1919)

Box, W. *Forty Poems* (London: Chester & Long, 1944)
Rear jacket blurbs by Siegfried Sassoon and Walter de la Mare.

Brooke, R. *The Poetical Works of Ruper Brooke*, edited by Geoffrey Keynes (London: Faber, 1970)

— *Rupert Brooke: The Collected Poems*, with a memoir by Edward Marsh; introduction by Gavin Ewart (London: Papermac, 1992)
First published: London: Sidgwick & Jackson, 1918.

Cannan, M. W. *The Splendid Days* (Oxford: Blackwell, 1919)

— *The Tears of War: The Love Story of a Young Poet and a War Hero, May Cannan, Bevil Quiller-Couch*, edited by C. Fyfe (Upaven: Cavalier, 2000)
The poignant story of the poet May Cannan and her fiancé Bevil Quiller-Couch told through her poetry, with passages from her autobiography and letters from Bevil and his father, interspersed with official war diary extracts.

Carstairs, C. *My Window Sill* (London: William Heinemann, 1930)

Chesterton, G. K. *The Ballad of St. Barbara, and other Verses* (London: Palmer, 1922)
Includes the poem, 'Elegy in a Country Churchyard' (1922)

Cranmer, E. P. *To the Living Dead and Other Poems* (London: C.W. Daniel, 1920)

De Stein, Sir E. *The Poets in Picardy* (London: Murray, 1919)
"The rhymes contained in this volume were all jotted down in France during 1916, 1917 and 1918, either in the trenches, in billets, or ... purlieus of staff offices." A few are reprinted from "The Times," "Punch" and "The Bystander"--Pref.

Dobell, E. *A Bunch of Cotswold Grasses* (London: Arthur H. Stockwell, 1919)
Includes the poems, 'Pluck', 'Gramophone Tunes' and 'Night Duty'.

*Enright, D. J. *The Terrible Shears: Scenes from a Twenties Childhood* (London: Chatto & Windus, 1973)
Includes the poem, 'A Grand Night'.

Eliot, T. S. *Collected Poems, 1909-1962*, new edn (London: Faber, 2002)
Includes *The Wasteland* and *The Hollow Men*, two poems exemplifying the post Great War literary expressions of disillusionment.

Farjeon, E. *First and Second Love: Sonnets* (London: Oxford University Press, 1959)
Includes the poem, 'Easter Monday'.

Frankau, G. *The Poetical Works of Gilbert Frankau*, 2 vols (London: Chatto & Windus, 1923)
Vol. 1: 1901-1916; Vol. 2: 1916-1920.

Fyson, G. F. *The Survivors, and other Poems* (London: Erskine Macdonald, 1919)

Gibson, W. W. *Collected Poems, 1905-1925* (London: Macmillan, 1926)

Golding, L. *Sorrow of War: Poems* (London: Methuen, 1919)

Graves, R. *Collected Poems* (London: Cassell, 1975)

— *Poems about War* (London: Cassell, 1988)

Gurney, I. *Collected Poems of Ivor Gurney*, edited with an introduction by P. J. Kavanagh, revised and corrected edn (Manchester: Fyfield, 2004)
Previous edition published by Oxford University Press, 1982.

— *War's Embers and other Verses* (London: Sidgwick and Jackson, 1919)

Hardy, T. *The Variorum Edition of the Complete Poems of Thomas Hardy*, edited by James Gibson (Basingstoke: Macmillan, 1979)
A section, *War Poems*, including those related to the Great War, is on pages 86-99.

Harvey, F. W. *Comrades in Captivity* (London: Sidgwick & Jackson, 1920)

Head, H. *Destroyers, and Other Verses* (London: Humphrey Milford, 1919)

*Heaney, S. *Wintering Out* (London: Faber, 1972; repr. 1980)
Includes the poem 'Veteran's Dream'.

Heywood, R. *The Greater Love: Poems of Remembrance* (London: Elkin Matthews, 1919)

Hogben, J. *The Highways of Hades: War Verses*, with some Prose (Edinburgh: Oliver & Boyd, 1919)

*Hughes, T. *New Selected Poems 1957-1994* (London: Faber, 1995)
Includes the poems, 'The Last of the 1st/5th Lancashire Fusiliers (A Souvenir of the Gallipoli Landings)', 'Six Young Men'.

Jones, D. *In Parenthesis* (London: Faber, 1937; repr. 2010)

Kennedy, G.A. S. *The Unutterable Beauty: The Collected Poetry of G. A. Studdert Kennedy* ('Woodbine Willie') (London: Diggory Press, 2006)
Originally published, London: Hodder & Stoughton, 1927.

Kerr, R. W. *War Daubs: Poems* (London: John Lane The Bodley Head, 1919)

Kipling, R. *The Complete Verse*, rev edn (London: Kylie Cathie Ltd., 2002)
Includes the poems, 'Gethsemane' (1919), 'Epitaphs of the War' (1919).

*Larkin, P. *Collected Poems*, edited with an introduction by Anthony Thwaite (London: Marvell, 1988)
Includes the poem, 'MCMXIV' (1960)

Ledwidge, F. *The Complete Poems of Francis Ledwidge*, edited by Alice Curtayne, new edn (Dublin; Poolbeg Press,

1998)

*Longley, M. *Selected Poems* (London: Cape, 1998)
Includes the poems ''Wounds', 'The War Poets' and 'In Memoriam'.

Macaulay, R. *Three Days* (London: Constable, 1919)
Includes the poems 'Picnic' and 'The Shadow'.

MacColl, D. S. *Bull and other War Verses* (London: Constable, 1919)

MacDiarmid, H. [pseudonym of C. M. Grieve]. *Hugh MacDiarmid: Selected Poems*, edited with an introduction by D. Craig and J. Manson (London: Penguin, 1970)
Includes the poem, 'Another Epitaph on an Army of Mercenaries' (1935) [Plainly a response to A. E. Housmans's 'Epitaph on an Army of Mercenaries']. MacDiarmid's poem first appeared in his *Second Hymn to Lenin and other Poems*, published London: Stanley Knott, 1935.

Macdonald, N. *War-Time Nursery Rhymes: Dedicated to DORA* (London: George Routledge, 1919)

*Maxwell, G. *The Breakage* (London: Faber, 1998)
Includes the poem 'My Grandfather at the Pool'.

Mew, C. *Collected Poems and Prose*, edited and with an introduction by Val Warner (London: Virago in association with Carcanet, 1982)
Includes the poems, 'The Cenotaph, September 1919', 'May 1915', 'June 1915'.

Meynell, A. C. *Poems*, complete edn (London: Burns Oates and Washbourne, 1940)
Includes the poems, 'Lord I Owe Thee a death', ' Summer in England, 1914'

Miles, P. *The Victory March and other Poems* (London: Arthur H. Stockwell, 1920)

Milne, A. A. *The Sunny Side* (London: Snowbooks, 2005)
Originally published: London: Methuen, 1921. Sketches and verse, chiefly reprinted from *Punch*. Contains most of his war verse.

*Muldoon, P. *New Selected Poems, 1968-1994* (London: Faber, 1996)
Includes the poem 'Truce'.

Noyes, A. *Selected Verse: Including 'A Victory Dance' and other Poems Old and New* (Edinburgh: W. Blackwood, 1921)

Oman, C. *The Menin Road and other Poems* (London: Hodder & Stoughton, 1919)

Owen, W. *Poems*, with an introduction by Siegfried Sassoon (London: Chatto & Windus, 1920)

— *The Poems*, edited by Edmund Blunden (London: Chatto & Windus, 1931)

— *The Complete Poems and Fragments*, edited by Jon Stallworthy, 2 vols (London: Chatto & Windus, 1983)

— *The Poems of Wilfred Owen*, edited by Jon Stallworthy (London: Chatto & Windus, 1990)

— *War Poems*, edited by Jon Stallworthy (London: Chatto & Windus, 1994)

Oxenham, J. *"All Clear!": A Book of Verse Commemorative of the Great Peace* (London: Methuen, 1919)

Peterson, J. *Roads and Ditches* (Lerwick: T. & J. Manson, 1920)

*Porter, P. *Once Bitten, Twice Bitten* (London: Scorpion Press, 1961)
Includes the poem, 'Somme and Flanders'.

Poulten, W. C. *The Bukshee Ration and other War-time Sketches* (The Souvenir Book of the Royal Naval Division) (London: Morland Press, 1919)

Powell, S. W. *One-Way Street and other Poems* (London: Harrap, 1934)
Includes the poem, 'Gallipoli'.

Read, Sir H. E. *Collected Poems* (London: Sinclair-Stevenson, 1992)

— *The End of a War* (London: Faber, 1933)

— *Naked Warriors* (London: Art & Letters, 1919)

Rickword, E. *Behind the Eyes* (London: Sidgwick & Jackson, 1921)

— *Collected Poems* (London: Bodley Head 1947; repr, Manchester: Carcanet, 1991)
Includes the poems, 'Moonrise over Battlefield' (1921), 'Trench Poets' (1921), 'War and Peace' (1921).

Rosenberg, I. *The Collected Works of Isaac Rosenberg: Poetry, Prose, Letters, Paintings and Drawings*, with a foreword by Siegfried Sassoon; edited with an introduction and notes by Ian Parsons (London: Chatto & Windus, 1984)

Sassoon, S. *Collected Poems, 1908-56* (London: Faber, 1961)

— *Picture-Show* (Cambridge: Cambridge University Press, 1919)
Includes the poem, 'Everyone Sang' (written 1919).

— *War Poems*, edited by Rupert Hart-Davis (London: Faber, 1983)

*Scannell, V. *Collected Poems, 1950-93* (London: Robson, 1993)
Includes the poem, 'The Great War'.

Shanks, E. *Poems, 1912-32* (London: Macmillan, 1933)
Includes the poem, 'The Halt', 'Armistice Day, 1921'

Sitwell, O. *Argonaut and Juggernaut* (London: Chatto & Windus, 1919; repr. London: Duckworth, 1927)
Includes the poem, 'The Next War (November 1918)'.

Sorley, C. *Collected Poems*, edited by J. M. Wilson (London: Cecil Woolf, 1985; repr. 1995)

— *Poems and Selected Letters*, edited by H. D. Spear (Dundee: Blackness Press, 1978)

Stuart, M. *Poems* (London: Heinemann, 1922)
Includes the poem, 'Forgotten Dead, I Salute You'.

Thomas, E. *Collected Poems*, edited by Walter de la Mare (London: Faber, 1949)

— *Selected Poems*, edited by R. G. Thomas (London: Faber, 1964)

— *Collected Poems of Edward Thomas*, edited by R. G. Thomas (Oxford: Oxford University Press, 1981)

Vickridge, A. *The Sea Gazer* (London: Erskine Macdonald, 1919)

Waring, J. *The Unknown Warrior* (London: Arthur H. Stockwell, 1922)

Williams, E. C. *Clouds and the Sun* (London: George Allen & Unwin, 1919)

Willis, G. *Any Soldier to His Son* (London: George Allen & Unwin, 1919)

Wilson, E. E. *Comrades of the Mist and Other Rhymes of the Grand Fleet* (New York: George Sulley, 1919)

Wilson, T. P. C. *Magpies in Picardy* (London: The Poetry Bookshop, 1919)

Yeats, W. B. *Collected Poems*, Picador Classics (London: Pan in association with Macmillan, 1990)
Includes 'An Irish Airman Foresees his Death' (1919).

4.2.5 Drama

With the war over 'war plays' ceased to dominate the stage as they had done between 1914 and 1918 but the Great War as a central theme by no means entirely disappeared from the plays staged in Britain in the inter-war and post second world war years, as can be seen from the selection of productions listed below. The play which particularly captured the public imagination in the inter-war years was Sherriff's *Journey's End*. When it was first produced in 1929 it was an immediate success and ran for two years. No other play on the theme of the Great War had such a powerful impact on the British public until the production of the Theatre Workshop's *Oh! What a Lovely War*, a musical entertainment which was first performed at Stratford East on 19 March 1963 and staged many times since with great commercial success. It was well received by most reviewers, few of whom seem to have been particularly concerned by its blatant anti-military bias or historical distortions. A film adaptation of it directed by Richard Attenborough that was released in 1969 made a world-wide impression, aided no doubt by its all-star cast, and became the version which has tended to linger in the public memory.

Books

Barker, C. and M. B. Gale, eds. *British Theatre between the Wars, 1918-1939* (Cambridge: Cambridge University Press, 2008)

Baylis, L. and C. Hamilton. *The Old Vic* (London: Cape, 1926)

Chisholm, C. *Repertory: An Outline of the Modern Theatre Movement; Production, Plays, Management* (London: P. Davies, 1934)

Ervine, St John, *The Theatre in My Time* (London: Rich & Cowan, 1933)

Fordham, J. 'Theatres of Resistance: Gender, Class and the First World War in Plays by Sheila Rowbotham and Chris Hannan; International Essays 1914-1999', in *Women: The First World War and the Dramatic Imagination*, edited by C. M. Tylee (Lewiston: Mellen, 2000)

Gibbs, A. M. *Heartbreak House: Preludes of Apocalypse* (New York: Twayne, 1994)

Hartnoll, P. *A Concise History of the Theatre* (Norwich: Thames & Hudson, 1968)

Holroyd, M. *Bernard Shaw*, 5 vols (London: Chatto & Windus, 1988-1992), III: *1918-1950* (1991)

Hudson, L. *The English Stage 1850-1950* (London: Harrap, 1951)

Hunt, H. H. *The Revels History of Drama in English* (London: Methuen, 1978)

Kosok, H. 'The First World War in Irish Drama', in *Modern War on Stage and Screen*, edited by W. Görtschacher and H. Klein (Lewiston, NY: Mellen, 1997)

— *The Theatre of War: The First World War in British and Irish Drama* (London: Palgrave Macmillan, 2007)
In this work more than two hundred plays related to the Great War, written, published and/or performed in Britain and Ireland between 1909 and 1998, are examined in terms of the five major aspects of subject matter, technique, attitude, reception and evaluation.

Macqueen-Pope, W. J. *Ghosts and Greasepaint* (London: Hale, 1951)

Nicholson, S. *The Censorship of British Drama, 1900-1968*, 4 vols (Exeter: Exeter University Press, 2003-2012)

Nicoll, A. *British Drama* (London: Harrap, 1925)

— *English Drama 1900-1930* (Cambridge: Cambridge University Press, 1973)

Rowell, G. and A. Jackson. *The Repertory Movement: A History of Regional Theatre in Britain* (Cambridge: Cambridge University Press, 1984)

Sanderson, M. *From Irving to Olivier* (London: Athlone, 1984)

Short, E. *Sixty Years of Theatre* (London: Eyre & Spottiswoode, 1951)

Taylor, G. *History of the Amateur Theatre* (Melksham: Venton, 1976)

Trewin, J. C. 'The Great War and the Theater', *in Modern British Dramatists, 1900-45*, edited by S. Weintraub, 2 vols (Detroit, Mich.: Gale Research Co., 1982)
Vol. 10 in the series 'Dictionary of Literary Biography' published by Gale.

Tylee, C. M., ed. *Women: The First World War and the Dramatic Imagination*, edited by C. M. Tylee (Lewiston, NY: Mellen, 2000)

Tylee, C. M., and others, eds. *War plays by Women: An International Anthology*, edited by Claire M. Tylee with Elaine Turner and Agnès Cardinal (London: Routledge, 1999)

Weintraub, S. *Bernard Shaw, 1914-1918: Journey to Heartbreak* (London; Routledge, 1973)
Originally published as, *Journey To Heartbreak: The Crucible Years of Bernard Shaw*, New York, Weybright and Talley, 1971.

Articles

Fowle, T. C. 'Journey's End: Another View', *Cornhill Magazine*, (August 1929), 171-3

Fox, F. 'These Scandalous War Books and Plays', *National Review*, no.568 (June 1930), 192-200

Kosok, H. 'Ireland, Yeats and World War I', *Yeats Studies*, 29 (1998), 3-19

—— 'Two Irish Perspectives on World War I: Bernard Shaw and Sean O'Casey', *Journal of Bernard Shaw Studies*, 4 (1999), 1-25

Martelli, G. A. '"Journey's End": A War Play and the Younger Generation', *Cornhill Magazine*, (June 1929), 740-2

Productions

A variety of approaches are evident in the way the 'war theme' was handled in the plays that have been produced since the Great War ended. Among the themes which playwrights have explored were **the serviceman's battlefront experience**[204] [e.g. Hamilton's *The Child in Flanders* (1919); Berkeley's *French Leave*[205] (1920) and *The White Chateau* (1927); Wall's *Havoc* (1923); Griffith,'s *Tunnel Trench* (1925); Sherriff's *Journey's End* (1928); Bairnsfather and Eliot's *The Better 'Ole* (1929); Hodson's *Red Night* (1930); MacGill's *Suspense* (1930); Williams's, *One Goes Alone* (1934); Box's *Angels of War* (1935); Dennis Johnston's *The Scythe and the Sunset* (1958); Wilson's *Hamp* (1964); Home's *A Christmas Truce* (1989); Bill Murphy's *Absent Comrades* (1997)]; **the home-front dimension to the war** [e.g. Shaw's *Heartbreak House* (1920); Barrie's *Barbara's Wedding* (1927); Harvey's *The Last Enemy* (1929); Rowbotham's *Friends of Alice Wheeldon* (1980); Whelan's *The Accrington Pals* (1981); MacDonald's *Not About Heroes* (1982); Hannan's *Elizabeth Gordon Quinn* (1985)]; **the returned soldier** [e.g. Maugham's *Home and Beauty* (1919) and *The Unknown* (1920); Dane's *A Bill of Divorcement* (1921); Galsworthy's *Windows* (1922)

---

[204] Plays about battle fronts were dominated by scenes portraying soldiers in the northern sector of the Western Front. The war at sea [e.g. King-Hall's *B.J. One* (1930)] and the war in the air [e.g. Williams's *One Goes Alone* (1934)] were the subjects of very few plays. There were also few plays employing the subject of servicemen who had been captured and detained in POW camps [e.g. Ackerley's *The Prisoners of War* (1925), Gregory's *Prisoners of War* (1934)].

[205] Berkeley's *French Leave* (1920) is an example of a play which treats the subject in a comical manner. Other examples in a similar vein are Bairnsfather and Eliot's *The Better 'Ole* (1929), Hoffe's *The Faithful Heart* (1921), McEvoys's *The Likes of Her* (1923). Judging by the fact that these were all box-office successes, it seems that the comedy approach was what the theatre-going public wanted at the time.

and *The Sun* (1922); McEvoy's *The Likes of Her* (1923); Millar's *Thunder in the Air* (1928); Temple's *The Widow's Cruise* (1926); Van Druten's *The Return of the Soldier* (1928) and *Flowers of the Forest* (1934); Coward's *Post Mortem* (1931)]; **the relation of the war to Ireland** [e.g Robinson's *The Big House* (1926); O'Casey's *The Plough and the Stars* (1926) and *The Silver Tassie* (1928); Yeats's *The Dreaming of the Bones* (1931); Plunkett's *The Risen People* (1958); Gallivan's *Decision at Easter* (1959); Shaws' *O'Flaherty V.C.* (1966); McCabe's *Pull Down a Horseman* (1966) and *Gale Day* (1979); Rudkin's *Cries from Casement as His Bones Are Brought to Dublin* (1974); D'Arcy and Arden's *The Non-Stop Connolly Show* (1975); Trevor's *Scenes from an Album* (1981); McGuinness's *Observe the Sons of Ulster Marching Towards the Somme* (1985); Reid's *My Name, Shall I Tell You My Name* (1989); Tom Murphy's *The Patriot Game* (1991); Mac Mathúna's *The Winter Thief/ Gadai Gear na Geamh-Oiche* (1992); Jennifer Johnston's *How Many Miles to Babylon?* (1993); Barry's *The Steward of Christendom* (1995); Brian Ervine's *Somme Day Mourning* (1994); McCartney's *Heritage* (1998)]; **the post-war situation (in terms of after effects and consequences)** [e.g. Brighouse's *Once a Hero* (1922); Pinero's *The Enchanted Cottage* (1922); Zangwill's *We Moderns* (1924); Maugham's *The Sacred Flame* (1928); Thomson's *War Memorial* (1929); Sylvaine's *The Road of Poplars* (1930); Mackenzie's *Musical Chairs* (1931) and *For Services Rendered* (1932); Chetham-Strode's *Sometimes Even Now* (1933); Daviot's *The Laughing Woman* (1934); Hims's *The Breakfast Soldiers* (1996)]; **the likelihood of another war**[206] [e.g. St. John Ervine's *Progress* (1922); Hamilton's *The Old Adam* (1924); Corrie's *And So to War* (1936); Auden and Isherwood's *On the Frontier* (1938)]

Apart from the above type of 'war plays' there were some which were produced as vehicles of **intellectual debate about the war** [e.g. Munro's *The Rumour* (1922); Shaw's *The Gospel of the Brothers Barnabas* (1922); Nichols and Browne's, *Wings over Europe* (1928); Pilcher's *The Searcher* (1930); Fernald's *To-Morrow* (1931); Stoppard's *Travesties* (1974)]; some which employed a **broad canvas, portraying the war experience panoramically through the three stages of soldiers departing from home, of fighting at the front, and of returning to the world of civilian life after the was over** [e.g. Monkhouse's *The Conquering Hero* (1924); O'Casey's *The Silver Tassie* (1929); Coward's *Cavalcade* (1931); Bryden's *The Big Picnic* (1994)]; some in which **the Great War is approached obliquely [e.g.** Rattigan's *The Winslow Boy* (1946); Fry's *A Sleep of Prisoners* (1951)]; and a few, in which the playwrights, although evidently having the Great War theme in mind, have linked it to **locations which are historically or geographically remote, or simply fantastic** [e.g. Grant's *The Last War* (1936); Theatre Workshop's *Oh What a Lovely War* (1963)]

An alphabetical listing by playwright of the selection of 'war plays' mentioned above is provided below. Information about a play's first production is given in parentheses. Where no production details are given it is likely that the play has remained unperformed or that a performance of it has never been recorded. Included are some one-act plays which are marked with a **hash**. For a number of the records a bibliographical note is given about the publication of the play.

Ackerley, J. R. *The Prisoners of War* (London: Playhouse, 1925)
J.R. Ackerley, *The Prisoners of War: A Play in Three Acts* (London: Chatto & Windus, 1925)

Auden, W .H. and C. Isherwood. *On the Frontier* (Cambridge: Arts Theatre, 1938)
W. H. Auden and Christopher Isherwood, *On the Frontier: A Melodrama in Three Acts*, in: *Plays and Other Dramatic Writings by W. H. Auden*, The Complete Works of W. H. Auden, vol 1 (Princeton UP, 1988), 357-418

Bairnsfather, B. and A. Eliot. *The Better 'Ole* (London: Regent, 1929)
First produced London, Oxford Theatre, 1917. Filmed by Warner Brothers in 1926

Barrie, J. M. *Barbara's Wedding* (London: Savoy, 1927)
J. M. Barrie, *Barbara's Wedding*, in: *The Plays of J. M. Barrie* (London: Hodder & Stoughton, rev. edn. 1942), 1167-82

Barry, S. *White Woman Street* (London: Bush Theatre, 1992)
Sebastian Barry, *The Only True History of Lizzie Finn, The Steward of Christendom, White Woman Street* (London: Methuen, 1995), 135-81

— *The Steward of Christendom* (London: Royal Court Upstairs, 1995)
Sebastian Barry, *The Only True History of Lizzie Finn, The Steward of Christendom, White Woman Street* (London: Methuen, 1995), 67-133

---

[206] A theme related to fears and speculations about the future that were derived from the pessimistic view that the Great War had not turned out to be 'the war to end all wars'.

Berkeley, R. *French Leave* (London: Globe, 1920)
Reginald Berkeley, *French Leave: A Light Comedy in Three Acts* (London: French, 1921)

— *The White Chateau* (BBC, 1925; London: Everyman Theatre: 1927)
Reginald Berkeley, *The White Chateau*, in: J. W. Marriott (ed.), *Great Modern British Plays* (London: Harrap, 1929), 807-58

Box, M. *Angels of War* (1935)
First produced by Mrs Worthington's Daughters on UK tour, 1981
Muriel Box, *Angels of War: A Play in Three Acts*, in: *Five New Full-Length Plays for All-Women Casts* (London: Lovat Dickson & Thompson, 1935),7-74; also in: Claire M. Tylee (ed.), *War Plays by Women: An International Anthology* (London, New York: Routledge, 1999), 115-39

Brighouse, H. *Once a Hero* (Southend: Ambassadors, 1922)
Harold Brighouse, *Once a Hero: A Comedy in One Act* (London: Gowans & Gray, 1922)

Bryden, B. *The Big Picnic* (Govan, Glasgow: Harland & Wolff Engine Shed, 1994)

Chetham-Strode, W. *Sometimes Even Now* (London: Embassy, 1933)
W. Chetham-Strode, *Sometimes Even Now: A Play in Three Acts*, in: *Famous Plays of 1933* (London: Gollancz, 1933), 369-464

Corrie, J. *And So to War* (London: Old Vic, 1936)
Produced in the Finals of the British Drama League Community Theatre Festival.
Joe Corrie, *And So to War: A Satirical Comedy*, in: William Armstrong (ed.), *8 New One-Act Plays of 1936* (London: Lovat Dickson, 1936), 167-96

Coward, N. *Cavalcade* (London: Drury Lane 1931)
Noël Coward, *Cavalcade*, in: Noel Coward, *Plays: Three* (London: Eyre Methuen, 1979), 125-99

— *Post Mortem* (1931)
First produced by British soldiers at POW camp, Eichstatt, Germany, 1944; first professional production BBC 2, 1968.
Noël Coward, *Post Mortem*, in Noël Coward, *Plays: Two* (London: Eyre Methuen, 1979), 277-361

Dane, C. [Winifred Ashton] *A Bill of Divorcement* (London: St. Martin's, 1921)
Clemence Dane, *A Bill of Divorcement*, in: J. W. Marriott (ed.), *Great Modern British Plays* (London: Harrap, 1929), 645-95

D'Arcy, M. and J. Arden, *The Non-Stop Connolly Show* (Dublin: Liberty Hall, 1975; London: Almost Free Theatre, 1976)

Daviot, G. [Elizabeth Mackintosh] *The Laughing Woman* (London: New Theatre, 1934)
Gordon Daviot, *The Laughing Woman: A Play*, in: *Famous Plays of 1933-34* (London: Gollancz, 1934), 369-471

Ervine, B. *Somme Day Mourning* (Belfast: Shankill Community Theatre Company, 1994)

Ervine, St. John. *Progress* (London: Little Theatre, 1922)

Fernald, C. B. *To-Morrow* (London: Arts Theatre, 1931)
C. B. Fernald, *To-Morrow: A Play: In Three Acts of Drama and an Epilogue of Discovery* (London: Benn, 1928)

Fry, C. *A Sleep of Prisoners* (Oxford: University Church, and London: St. Thomas's Church, Regent Street, 1951)
Christopher Fry, *A Sleep of Prisoners*, in: Christopher Fry, *Plays* (London: Oxford UP, 1971), 1-57

Gallivan, G. P. *Decision at Easter* (Dublin: Gate, 1959)
G.P. Gallivan, *Decision at Easter: A Play in Three Acts* (Dublin: Progress House, 1960)

Galsworthy, J. *Windows* (London: Royal Court, 1922)
John Galsworthy, *Windows*, in: *The Plays of John Galsworthy* (London: Duckworth, 1929), 687-736

— # *The Sun* (Liverpool: Playhouse, 1922)
John Galsworthy, *The Sun*, in: *The Plays of John Galsworthy* (London: Duckworth, 1929), 963-9

Grant, N. *The Last War* (London: Old Vic, 1936)
Performed in the Finals of the British Drama League Community Theatre Festival, London, Old Vic, 1936.
Neil Grant, *The Last War: A Fantasy in One Act*, in: William Armstrong (ed.), *8 New One-Act Plays of 1936* (London: Lovat Dickson, 1936),197-222

Griffith, H. *Tunnel Trench* (London: Repertory Players at Prince's Theatre, 1925)
Hubert Griffith, *Tunnel Trench: A Play in Three Acts and Seven Scenes* (London: Alien & Unwin, 1924)

Hamilton, C. *The Child in Flanders* (Bethnal Green: Excelsior Hall, 1919)
Cicely Hamilton, *The Child in Flanders: A Nativity Play in a Prologue, Five Tableaux, and an Epilogue*, in: J. W. Marriott (ed.), *One-Act Plays of To-day: Second Series* (London: Harrap, 1925), 237-67

— *The Old Adam* (Birmingham: Repertory Theatre [under the title *The Human Factor*], 1924; London: Kingsway Theatre, 1925)
Cicely Hamilton, *The Old Adam: A Fantastic Comedy* (Oxford: Blackwell,1926)

Hannan, C. *Elizabeth Gordon Quinn* (Edinburgh: Traverse Theatre, 1985)
Chris Hannan, *Elizabeth Gordon Quinn: A Serious Melodrama*, in: Alasdair Cameron (ed.), *Scot-Free: New Scottish Plays* (London: Nick Hern Books, 1990), 105-46

Harvey, F. *The Last Enemy* (London: Fortune Theatre, 1929)
Frank Harvey, *The Last Enemy: A Play in Three Acts and Seven Scenes* (London: Allen & Unwin, 1930)

Hims, K. *The Breakfast Soldiers* (Manchester: Contact Theatre, and London: Finborough Theatre, 1996)

Hodson, J. L. *Red Night* (Huddersfield: Huddersfield Thespians, 1930)
James Lansdale Hodson, *Red Night: A War Play in a Prologue and Four Acts* (London: Gollancz, 1930)

Hoffe, M. *The Faithful Heart* (London: Comedy Theatre, 1921)
Monckton Hoffe, *The Faithful Heart: An Original Play* (London: Heinemann, 1922)

Home, W. D. *A Christmas Truce* (Basingstoke: Horseshoe Theatre Company, Haymarket Theatre, 1989)
William Douglas Home, *A Christmas Truce: A Play* (London: French, 1990)

Johnston, D. *The Scythe and the Sunset* (Dublin: Abbey, 1958)
Denis Johnston, *The Scythe and the Sunset: A Play in Three Acts*, in: *The Dramatic Works of Denis Johnston*, vol. 1 (Gerrards Cross: Smythe, 1977), 83-166

Johnston, J. *How Many Miles to Babylon? A Play in Two Acts* (Belfast: Lyric: 1993)
An adaptation of Jennifer Johnston's novel, *How Many Miles to Babylon?*, firsts published London: Hamish Hamilton, 1974.

King-Hall, S. *B.J. One* (London: Globe, 1930)
Stephen King-Hall, *Three Plays and a Plaything* (London: Nicholson & Watson, 1933), 167-254

McCabe, E. *Pull Down a Horseman* (Dublin: Eblana Theatre, 1966)
Eugene McCabe, *Pull Down a Horseman / Gale Day* (Dublin: Gallery Books, 1979), 9-34

— *Gale Day* (Dublin: Peacock Theatre, 1979)
Eugene McCabe, *Pull Down a Horseman / Gale Day* (Dublin: Gallery Books, 1979), 35-70

McCartney, N. *Heritage* (Edinburgh, Traverse Theatre, 1998)

MacDonald, S. *Not About Heroes* (Edinburgh: Netherbow Theatre, 1982; Glasgow: Tron Theatre, 1982; London: King's Head, 1983)
Stephen MacDonald, *Not About Heroes: The Friendship of Siegfried Sassoon and Wilfred Owen* (London: Faber, 1983)

McEvoy, C. *The Likes of Her* (Battersea: Town Hall, and London: St. Martin's, 1923)
Charles McEvoy, *The Likes of Her*, in: J.W. Marriott (ed.), *Great Modern British Plays* (London: Harrap, 1929), 859-902

MacGill, P. *Suspense* (London, Duke of York's, 1930)
Patrick MacGill, *Suspense: A Play in Three Acts* (London: Jenkins, 1930)

McGuinness, F. *Observe the Sons of Ulster Marching Towards the Somme* (Dublin: Peacock, 1985)
Frank McGuinness, *Observe the Sons of Ulster Marching Towards the Somme* (London: Faber, 1986)

Mackenzie, R. *Musical Chairs* (London: Arts Theatre Club, 1931)
Ronald Mackenzie, *Musical Chairs: A Play in Three Acts*, in: *Famous Plays of 1932* (London: Gollancz, 1932), 9-88; and in: *Plays of a Half-Decade* (London, Southampton: Camelot Press, 1933), 859-926

Mac Mathúna, S. *The Winter Thief/Gadai Gear na Geamh-Oiche* (Dublin: Peacock, 1992)

Maugham, W. S. *Home and Beauty* (London: Playhouse, and New York, Booth Theatre [under the title *Too Many Husbands*], 1919)
W. Somerset Maugham, *Home and Beauty: A Farce in Three Acts*, in: Maugham, *Plays*, vol. 3 (London: Heinemann, 1932), 225-324

— *The Unknown* (London,: Aldwych, 1920)
W. Somerset Maugham, *The Unknown: A Play in Three Acts*, in: Maugham, *Plays*, vol 6 (London: Heinemann, 1934), 1-89

— *The Sacred Flame* (Washington: Belasco Theatre, and New York: Henry Miller Theatre, 1928; London: Playhouse, 1929)
W. Somerset Maugham, *The Sacred Flame: A Play in Three Acts*, in: Maugham, *Plays*, vol. 5 (London: Heinemann, 1934), 221-319

— *For Services Rendered* (London, Globe, 1932)
W. Somerset Maugham, *For Services Rendered: A Play in Three Acts*, in: Maugham, Plays, vol 6 (London: Heinemann, 1934), 91-181

Millar, R. *Thunder in the Air* (London: Duke of York's, 1928)
Robins Millar, *Thunder in the Air: A Play in Three Acts* (London, New York: French, 1928)

Monkhouse, A. *The Conquering Hero* (Leeds: Albert Hall, and London: Aldwych, 1924)
Allan Monkhouse, *The Conquering Hero: A Play in Four Acts*, Contemporary British Dramatists II (London: Ernest Benn, 1923)

Morpurgo, M. *War Horse*, by Michael Morpurgo, adapted by Nick Stafford (London: National Theatre, 2009)
Michael Morpurgo, *War Horse*, by M. Morpurgo, adapted by N. Stafford (Oxford: Oxford University Press, 2009)

Munro, C. K. [C. W. K. McMullan], *The Rumour* (London: Globe, 1922)
C. K. Munro, *The Rumour: A Play in Four Acts*. Stage Version (London: Collins, 1927)

Murphy, B. *Absent Comrades: A One-Act Play* (Dublin: Focus Theatre, 1997)

Murphy, T. *The Patriot Game* (Dublin: Peacock, 1991
Tom Murphy, *The Patriot Game*, in: Murphy, *Plays: One* (London: Methuen, 1992), 92-142

Nichols, R. and M. Browne, *Wings over Europe* (New York: Martin Beck Theatre, 1928)
Robert Nichols and Maurice Browne, *Wings over Europe*, in: Burns Mantle (ed.), *The Best Plays of 1928-29 and the Year Book of the Drama in America* (New York: Dodd, Mead, 1929), 88-119

O'Casey, S. *The Plough and the Stars* (Dublin: Abbey, 1926; London: Fortune: 1926)
Sean O'Casey, *The Plough and the Stars: A Tragedy in Four Acts*, in: O'Casey, *Collected Plays*, vol 1 (London: Macmillan, 1949), 159-261

— *The Silver Tassie* (London: Apollo Theatre, 1929)
Sean O'Casey, *The Silver Tassie: A Tragi-Comedy in Four Acts*, in: O'Casey, *Collected Plays*, vol 2 (London: Macmillan, 1949), 1-111

Pilcher, V. *The Searcher* (London: Grafton Theatre, 1930)
Velona Pilcher, *The Searcher: A War Play*. Reading Version (London: Heinemann, 1929)

Pinero, A. W. *The Enchanted Cottage* (London: Duke of York's, 1922)

Cultural Impacts

Arthur Pinero, *The Enchanted Cottage: A Fable in Three Acts* (London: Heinemann, 1922)

Plunkett, J. *The Risen People* (Dublin: Abbey, 1958)
James Plunkett, *The Risen People* (Dublin: Irish Writers' Co-operative, 1978)

Rattigan, T. *The Winslow Boy* (London: Lyric, 1946)
Terence Rattigan, *The Winslow Boy*, in: Rattigan, *Plays: One* (London: Methuen, 1981), 81-178

Reid, C. *My Name, Shall I Tell You My Name* (Dublin: Theatre Festival, 1989, and London: Young Vic, 1990)
First performed by BBC Radio 4 1988. Christina Reid, *My Name, Shall I Tell You My Name* in: Claire M. Tylee (ed.) *War Plays by Women: An International Anthology* (London, New York: Routledge, 1999), 213-22

Robinson, L. *The Big House* (Dublin: Abbey, 1926)
Lennox Robinson, *The Big House: Four Scenes in Its Life*, in: Christopher Murray (ed.), *Selected Plays of Lennox Robinson*, Irish Drama Selections, 1 (Gerrards Cross: Smythe, 1982), 137-98

Rowbotham, S. *Friends of Alice Wheeldon* (Rotherham: Arts Centre, 1980)
Sheila Rowbotham, *Friends of Alice Wheeldon* (London: Pluto Press, 1986), 109-206

Rudkin, D. *Cries from Casement as His Bones Are Brought to Dublin* (London: Royal Shakespeare Company, 1974)
First performed as a BBC radio play, 1973. David Rudkin, *Cries from Casement as His Bones Are Brought to Dublin* (London: British Broadcasting Corporation, 1974)

Shaw, G. B. *Heartbreak House* (New York: Garrick, 1920; London: Court Theatre, 1921)
George Bernard Shaw, *Heartbreak House: A Fantasia in the Russian Manner on English Themes*, in: *The Complete Plays of Bernard Shaw* (London: Hamlyn,1965), 758-802

— # *The Gospel of the Brothers Barnabas* [Part II of *Back to Methuselah*] (New York: Garrick Theatre, 1922)
George Bernard Shaw, *The Gospel of the Brothers Barnabas*, in: *The Complete Plays of Bernard Shaw* (London: Hamlyn, 1965), 869-91

— *O'Flaherty V.C.* (Treizennes, Belgium: Officers of the 40th Squadron R.F.C., 1917; London: Mermaid Theatre, 1966)
George Bernard Shaw, *O'Flaherty V.C.: A Recruiting Pamphlet*, in: *The Complete Plays of Bernard Shaw* (London: Hamlyn, 1965) and also in *Heartbreak House, Great Catherine, and Playlets of the War* (London: Constable, 1925). Contents of the latter work include *O'Flaherty VC, The Inca of Perusalem, Augustus Does His Bit, Annajanska.*

Sherriff, R. C., *Journey's End* (London: Apollo, 1928; London: Savoy, 1929)
R.C. Sherriff, *Journey's End: A Play in Three Acts*, in: *Famous Plays of Today* (London: Gollancz, 1929), 10-136

Stoppard, T. *Travesties* (London: Aldwych, 1974)
Tom Stoppard, *Travesties* (London: Faber, 1975)

Sylvaine, V. *The Road of Poplars* (Liverpool: Playhouse, and London: Coliseum, 1930)
Vernon Sylvaine, *The Road of Poplars*, in: Constance M. Martin (ed.), *Fifty One-Act Plays* (London: Gollancz, 1934), 313-46

Temple, J. *The Widow's Cruise* (London: Ambassadors', 1926)
Joan Temple, *The Widow's Cruise: A Comedy in Three Acts*, Contemporary British Dramatists, vol 41 (London: Benn, 1926)

Theatre Workshop and C. Chilton. *Oh! What a Lovely War* (London: Theatre Royal Stratford, 1963; London: Wyndham's, 1963)
A published version by Methuen appeared in 1965, later revised as *Oh! What a Lovely War*, [A Stage Musical] by Theatre Workshop, Charles Chilton, Gerry Raffles and the members of the original cast; military adviser, Raymond Fletcher. Rev. and restored to the original version by Joan Littlewood (London: Methuen, 2000). A film version (Director: Richard Attenborough; Screenplay: Len Deighton) was distributed by British Paramount Pictures in 1969.

Thomson, D. C. *War Memorial* (Edinburgh: The Hall, 1929)
David Cleghorn Thomson, *War Memorial: A Parochial Satire in One Act*, Scottish National Plays Series no. 4 (Glasgow: Wilson, 1930)

Trevelyan, H. B. [Guy Bolton], *The Dark Angel* (London: Everyman, 1925)

H. B. Trevelyan, *The Dark Angel: A Play of Yesterday and To-day* (London: Benn, 1928)

Trevor, W. *Scenes from an Album* (Dublin: Abbey, 1981)
William Trevor, *Scenes from an Album,* New Irish Plays (Dublin: Co-op Books, 1981)

Van Druten, J. *The Return of the Soldier* (London: Playhouse, 1928)
John van Druten, *The Return of the Soldier: A Play in Three Acts* (London: Gollancz, 1928)

— *Flowers of the Forest* (London: Whitehall Theatre, 1934)
John van Druten, *Flowers of the Forest: A Play in Three Acts*, in: *Famous Plays of 1934-5* (London: Gollancz, 1935), 463-569

Wall, H. *Havoc* (London: Regent Theatre, 1923; London: Haymarket, 1924)
A. L. Muir and Harry Wall, *Havoc* (London: Readers Library Publishing Co., 1926) was a novel based on the play.

Whelan, P. *The Accrington Pals* (London: The Warehouse, 1981)
Peter Whelan, *The Accrington Pals: A Play* (London: Methuen, 1982)

Whitby, N. *To the Green Fields Beyond* (London: Donmar Warehouse, 2000)
Nick Whitby, *To the Green Fields Beyond* (London: Faber, 2000)

Williams, Edward, *One Goes Alone* (1934)
Edward Williams, *One Goes Alone*, in: Geoffrey Whitworth (ed.), *Twelve One-Act Plays* (London: Sidgwick & Jackson, 1934), 183-206

Wilson, J. *Hamp* (Newcastle: Theatre Royal, and Edinburgh: Lyceum, 1964)
John Wilson, *Hamp: A Play in Three Acts*, based on an episode from the novel *Return to the Wood* by J. L. Hodson (London, New York: Evans, 1966) [filmed as *King and Country*, 1964, see below in Part 4, **section 4.3.2.2: 2nd World War and After**].

Yeats, W. B. *The Dreaming of the Bones* (Dublin: Abbey, 1931)
W. B. Yeats, *The Dreaming of the Bones*, in: *The Collected Plays of W. B. Yeats* (London: Macmillan, 1960), 431-45

Zangwill, I. *We Moderns* (New York, Gaiety: 1924; London: New Theatre and Fortune Theatre, 1925)
Israel Zangwill, *We Moderns: A Post-War Comedy in Three Movements (Allegro, Andante, Adagio)* (London: Heinemann, 1926)

4.3 Film Making

4.3.1 General

In contrast to Samuel Hynes, who in *A War Imagined* suggests that that it is through literature that the Great War has been 'imagined' and the popular memory of the Great War developed, it has been suggested by some that from at least the mid-1920's, if not before, the popular memory was due as much, if not more, to the influence of the filmic image. It is undoubtedly true that films about the Great War have the capability to reach a far wider public than the printed word, not only through projection in cinemas, but through subsequent re-release, through television screenings, the video cassette, and the DVD. The accessibility of film to a mass audience potentially gives it an advantage over the written word for influencing a popular view of the war, and for those generations who know little about the war the cinema or television screen might well provide their dominant impression of it.

Autobiographies, Biographies, Memoirs

Balcon, M. *Michael Balcon Presents ... A Lifetime of Films* (London: Hutchinson, 1969)

Boyne, S. Emmet Dalton: Somme Soldier, Irish General, Film Pioneer (Sallins, Co. Kildare: Merrion Press, 2015)
From 1923 he worked in Ireland and the U.S. in film production. In 1958 he founded Irish Ardmore Studios in Bray. His company helped produce films such as *The Blue Max*, *The Spy Who Came in from the Cold* and *The Lion in Winter*, all of which were filmed in Ireland.

Brown, S. 'Barker, Will (1867-1951)', in *Reference Guide to British and Irish Film Directors* (British Film Institute) [http://www.screenonline.org.uk/people/id/519480/]

Brownlow, K. *David Lean: A Biography* (London: Cassell, 1996)

Brunel, A. *Nice Work: The Story of Thirty Years in British Film Production* (London: Forbes Robertson, 1949)

Gifford, D. 'The Early Memoirs of Maurice Elvey', *Griffithiana*, 60–61 (Oct 1997), 77–124

Hepworth, C. *Came the Dawn: Memories of a Film Pioneer* (London: Phoenix House, 1951)

McKernan, L. 'Samuelson, George Berthold (1889–1947)', *Oxford Dictionary of National Biography*, Oxford University Press, 2004; online edn, Jan 2011

Minney, R. J. *'Puffin' Asquith: A Biography of the Hon. Anthony Asquith, Aesthete, Aristocrat, Prime Minister's Son and Film Maker* (London: Frewin, 1973)

Pearson, G. *Flashback: The Autobiography of a British Film-Maker* (London: Allen & Unwin, 1957)

Wood, L. *The Commercial Imperative in the British Film Industry: Maurice Elvey, a Case Study* (London: British Film Institute, 1987)

Books

Aitken, I. W. 'John Grierson and the Origins, Ideals and Development of the British Documentary Film Movement 1914-1936' (unpublished doctoral thesis, Polytechnic of Central London, 1988)

Barsam, R. M. *Nonfiction Film: A Critical History*, revised and expanded (Bloomington: Indiana University Press, 1992)

Bawden, L-A. *The Oxford Companion to Film* (London: Oxford University Press 1976)

Butler, I. *The War Film* (London: Tantivy Press, 1974)

Commission on Educational and Cultural Films. *The Film in National Life: Being the Report of an Enquiry Conducted by the Commission on Educational and Cultural Films into the Service which the Cinematograph may Render to Education and Social Progress* [Chairman: Sir Benjamin Gott] (London: Allen & Unwin, 1932)

Cook, D. A. *A History of Narrative Film*, 4th edn (New York: Norton, 2004)

Dibbetts, K. and B. Hogenkamp, eds. *Film and the First World War* (Amsterdam: Amsterdam University Press, 1995)

Furhammer, L. and F. Isakkson. *Politics and Film*, translated by K. French (London: Studio Vista, 1971)

Hardy, F., ed. *Grierson on Documentary*, rev. edn (London: Faber, 1966)

Jeavons, C. *A Pictorial History of War Films* (London: Hamlyn, 1974)

Johnston, W. *Memo on the Movies: War Propaganda, 1914-39* (Norman: Oklahoma Co-operative Books, 1939)

Landy, M., ed. *The Historical Film: History and Memory in Media* (London: Athlone 2001)

Lovell, A. and J. Hillier. *Studies in Documentary* (London: Secker & Warburg for the British Film Insitute, 1972)

Low, R. *The History of the British Film*, 7 vols (London: Allen & Unwin, 1948-1985; repr. London: Routledge, 1997)
Contents: Vol.1 1896-1906; vol.2 1906-1914; vol.3 1914-1918; vol.4 1918-1929; vol.5 1929-1939: Documentary and

educational films of the 1930's; vol.6 1929-1939: Films of comment and persuasion of the 1930's; vol.7 1929-1939: Film making in 1930's Britain.

Paris, M. *Images of War and British Youth, 1850-1992* (London: Reaktion Books, 1999)

Pronay, N. and D. W. Spring, eds. *Propaganda, Politics and Film, 1918-1945* (London: Macmillan, 1982)

Richards, J. *Visions of Yesterday* (London: Routledge, 1973)

Robertson, J. C. *The British Board of Film Censors: Film Censorship in Britain, 1896-1950* (Beckenham: Croom Helm, 1985)

Sheffield, G. D. 'Oh! What A Futile War!: Representations of the Western Front in Modern British Media and Popular Culture', in *War, Culture and the Media: Representations of the Military in 20th Century Britain*, edited by I. Stewart and S. L. Carruthers (Trowbridge: Flicks Books, 1996) Short, K. R. M., ed. *Feature Films as History* (London: Croom Helm, 1981)

Smith, P. ed. *The Historian and Film* (Cambridge: Cambridge University Press, 1976)

Stewart, I. 'Presenting Arms: Portrayals of War and the Military in British Cinema', in *War, Culture and the Media: Representation of the Military in 20th Century Britain*, edited by I. Stewart and S. L. Carruthers (Trowbridge: Flicks Books, 1996)

Sussex, E. *The Rise and Fall of British Documentary: The Story of the Film Movement founded by John Grierson* (Berkeley: University of California Press, 1975)

Virilio, P. *War and the Cinema: The Logistics of Perception*, translated by Patrick Camiller (London: Verso, 1989)

Yorke, E. J. 'Cultural Myths and Realities: The British Army, War, and Empire as Portrayed on Film, 1900-90', in *War, Culture and the Media: Representation of the Military in 20th Century Britain*, edited by I. Stewart and S. L. Carruthers (Trowbridge: Flicks Books, 1996)

Articles

Graham, C. C. and R. van Dopperen. 'Roger Casement on Screen: The Background Story on an Historical Film Opportunity, 1915–1916', *Historical Journal of Film, Radio and Television*, 36 (2016), 493-508

4.3.2 The Cinema

4.3.2.1 General

In the inter-war years the cinema enjoyed great popularity, particularly with the working-class, as a place for relaxation and entertainment. Films from Hollywood found a good market in Britain because they were better and cheaper than those produced locally. Nevertheless, in spite of this competition and a recession in the British industry in the years immediately following the war (up to the mid 1920's), films continued to be produced in Britain, and throughout the inter-war period a considerable number of them, as in other countries, were about the Great War or in some way related to it. During this period British film-makers had generally been reluctant to portray that war in the critical, disenchanted way in which it tended to be portrayed after the Second World War. The interpretation of the war years 1914-1918, seen negatively in terms of the horrors of trench warfare, bungling generals, 'Tommies' as cannon-fodder, and futility in general, did not begin to capture the public imagination fully until the 1960's when a flood of histories, novels, poetry, documentaries and films came on stream to mark the fiftieth anniversary of the conflict.

Books

Aldgate, A. and J. Richards. *Best of British: Cinema and Society from 1930 to the Present*, new edn (London: Tauris, 2002)

Cultural Impacts

Armes, R. *A Critical History of the British Cinema* (London: Secker & Warburg, 1978)

Barr, C., ed. *All Our Yesterdays: 90 Years of British Cinema* (London: British Film Institute, 1986)

Bawden, L-A. *The Oxford Companion to Film* (London: Oxford University Press 1976)

Berry, D. and S. Horrocks, eds. *David Lloyd George: The Movie Mystery* (Cardiff: University of Wales Press, 1998)
This work is about the film biography which was made and completed in 1918 with the co-operation of David Lloyd George but never released because of an allegation that the film company's executives were of German origin. It was long thought that the film had been lost or destroyed but in 1994 it was found amongst material supplied by Viscount Tenby (Lloyd George's grandson) and restored. The critical guide to the film that this work provides is accompanied by a number of illustrations which include frame enlargements from the film, photographs of Lloyd George, and reproductions of trade advertisements.

Brownlow, K. *The War, the West and the Wilderness* (London: Secker & Warburg, 1979)

Burton, A. and L. Porter, eds. *Scene-Stealing: Sources for British Cinema Before 1930* (Trowbridge: Flicks Books, 2003)

Cook, D. A. *A History of Narrative Film*, 4th edn (New York: Norton, 2004)

Curran, J. and V. Porter, eds. *British Cinema History* (London: Weidenfeld and Nicolson, 1983)
d
Field, A. *Picture Palace: A Social History of the Cinema* (London: Gentry Books, 1974)

Fitzsimmons, L. and S. Street, eds. *Moving Performance: British Stage and Screen 1890's-1920's* (Trowbridge: Flicks Books, 2000)

Halliwell's Film, DVD and Video Guide (London: HarperCollins Entertainment, 2004-)

Hammond, M and M. Williams, eds. *British Silent Cinema and the Great War* (Houndmills, Basingstoke: Palgrave Macmillan, 2011)
This book examines the response of the British cinema industry to the Great War in the years of the conflict and the way it helped to shape the war's memory through the 1910's and 1920's."

Higson, A, ed. *Young and Innocent?: The Cinema in Britain 1896-1930*, Exeter Studies in Film History (Exeter: University of Exeter Press, 2002)

Low, R. *The History of the British Film*, 7 vols (London: Allen & Unwin, 1948-1985; repr. London: Routledge, 1997)
Contents: Vol.1 1896-1906; vol.2 1906-1914; vol.3 1914-1918; vol.4 1918-1929; vol.5 1929-1939: Documentary and educational films of the 1930's; vol.6 1929-1939: Films of comment and persuasion of the 1930's; vol.7 1929-1939: Film making in 1930's Britain.

Kelly, K. *Cinema and the Great War* (London: Routledge, 1997)

Manvell, R., ed. *The International Encyclopedia of Film* (London: Joseph, 1972)

Miles, P. and M. Smith. *Cinema, Literature and Society: Elite and Mass Culture in Interwar Britain*, Croom Helm Studies on Film, Television and the Media (London: Croom Helm, 1987)

Napper, L. *British Cinema and Middlebrow Culture in the Interwar Years*, Exeter Studies in Film History (Exeter: University of Exeter Press, 2009)

— 'British Cinema and the Middlebrow', in *British Cinema, Past and Present*, edited by Justine Ashby and Andrew Higson (Routledge: London, 2000)

Paget, P. "Remembrance Play: 'Oh! What a Lovely War' and History", in *Acts of War: The Representation of Military Conflict on the British Stage and Television since 1945*, edited by Tony Howard and John Stokes (Aldershot: Scolar Press, 1996)

Paris, M. 'Enduring Heroes: British Feature Films and the First World War', in *The First World War and Popular Cinema, 1914 to the Present*, edited by M. Paris (Edinburgh: Edinburgh University Press, 1999)

Paris, M., ed. *The First World War and Popular Cinema, 1914 to the Present* (Edinburgh: Edinburgh University Press, 1999)

Quinlan, D. *The Illustrated Guide to Film Directors* (London: Batsford, 1991)
The author provides an assessment of the work of over 500 of the most influential directors and film-makers in the history of cinema, together with a full biography and filmography for each of them and the inclusion of photographs of the directors at work and scenes from the films they directed.

Richards, J. *The Age of the Dream-Palace: Cinema and Society in Britain 1930-1939* (London: Routledge, 1984)

— *Films and British National Identity: From Dickens to "Dad's Army"* (Manchester: Manchester University Press, 1997)

Ryall, T. *Britain and the American Cinema* (London: Sage Publications, 2001)

Sedgwick, J. *Popular Filmgoing in 1930's Britain: A Choice of Pleasures*, Exeter Studies in Film History (Exeter: University of Exeter Press, 2000)

Sexton, J. *Alternative Film Culture in Interwar Britain*, Exeter Studies in Film History (Exeter: University of Exeter Press, 2008)

Stewart, I. 'Presenting Arms: Portrayals of War and the Military in British Cinema', in *War, Culture and the Media: Representation of the Military in 20th Century Britain*, edited by I. Stewart and S. L. Carruthers (Trowbridge: Flicks Books, 1996)

Articles

Barber, D. 'Lawrence of Arabia (1962): A Dying Empire's Cri de Coeur', *Film and History*, 47:1 (2017), 28-45

'Bryher' [Winifred Ellerman]. 'The War from Three Angles', *Close Up*, 1 (1927), 19
Review of the film *Mons* (1926)

— 'The War from Three More Angles', *Close Up*, 1 (1927), 45
Review of *The Battles of Coronel and Falkland Islands* (1927).

Byrnes, P. 'Gallipoli on Film' (Australia's Audiovisual Heritage Online)
http://aso.gov.au/titles/collections/gallipoli-on-film/

Eksteins, M. 'War, Memory, And Politics - The Fate of the Film "All Quiet On The Western Front"', *Central European History*, 13 (1980), 60-62

h, L, and others. '"Snapshots": Local Cinema Cultures in the Great War', by L. Engelen, L. DeBauche, and M. Hammond, *Historical Journal of Film, Radio and Television*, 35 (2015), 631-655

Everson, W. 'Journey's End', *Films in Review*, 26.1 (1975), 31-5

Hanna, E. 'Putting the Moral into Morale: YMCA Cinemas on the Western Front, 1914–1918', *Historical Journal of Film, Radio and Television*, 35 (2015), 615-630

Harrison, R. 'Writing History on the Page and Screen: Mediating Conflict through Britain's First World War Ambulance Trains', *Historical Journal of Film, Radio and Television*, 35 (2015), 559-578

Heathorn, S. '"A Great Grey Dawn for the Empire": Great War Conspiracy Theory, the British State and the "Kitchener Film" (1921-1926)', *War and Society* (Duntroon Australia), 26, Issue 2 (2007), 51-72
"This article considers the political and commercial manipulation of interwar conspiracy theories about Field Marshal Earl

Kitchener's death in 1916, by focusing on a five-year struggle between a film-promoter and the Home Office over a filmic counter-narrative to the official story of Kitchener's demise. The use of Kitchener's iconic status by competing interests in the immediate postwar era was tied to concrete political anxieties and fears about the collapse of the rhetoric of the 'equality of sacrifice' in a period of perceived social and economic crisis. Ultimately, the state's success in suppressing 'the Kitchener film' set an important precedent for unofficial state political censorship of film in 1920s Britain". [Abstact from the internet]

Hockenhull, S. 'Everybody's Business: Film, Food and Victory in the First World War', *Historical Journal of Film, Radio and Television*, 35 (2015), 579-595

Isenberg, T. 'An Ambiguous Pacifism: A Retrospective on World War 1 Films, 1930-1938', *Journal of Popular Culture*, 4 (1975), 98-115

Kelly, A. 'Trench Footnotes', *Sight and Sound*, 7.12 (1997), 25

Laugesen, A. 'Forgetting Their Troubles for a While: Australian Soldiers' Experiences of Cinema during the First World War', *Historical Journal of Film, Radio and Television*, 35 (2015), 596-614

Richards, J. 'The British Board of Film Censors and Content Control in the 1930's: Foreign Affairs', *Historical Journal of Film, Radio and Television*, 2 (1982), 39-48

Richards, J. and J. Hulbert. 'Censorship in Action: The Case of Lawrence of Arabia', *Journal of Contemporary History*, 19.1 (1984), 153-69

Robertson, J. C. '*Dawn* (1928): Edith Cavell and Anglo-German Relations', *Historical Journal of Film, Radio and Television*, 4.1 (1984), 15-28

Smith, A. and M. Hammond. 'The Great War and the Moving Image', *Historical Journal of Film, Radio and Television*, 35 (2015), 553-558

Winter, J. 'Film and the Matrix of Memory', *American Historical Review*, 106 (2001), 857-864

4.3.2.2 Film Productions

The selection of films listed in the following sections relate to British film productions in which the Great War was featured. As well as the latter war films cinema-goers in Britain would also have been able to see films of this sort emanating from other countries particularly the United States which, as the dominant player and competitor in the film industry, was producing and exporting films like *The Four Horsemen of the Apocalypse* (Rex Ingram, 1921), *The Big Parade* (King Vidor, 1925), *What Price Glory* (Raoul Walsh, 1926; John Ford, 1952), *Wings* (William Wellman, 1927), *All Quiet on the Western Front* (Lewis Milestone, 1930), *Hell's Angels* (Howard Hughes, 1930), *The Dawn Patrol* (Howard Hawks, 1930; Edmund Goulding, 1938), *A Farewell to Arms* (Frank Borzage, 1932: Charles Vidor, 1957), *Paths of Glory* (Stanley Kubrick, 1957), *The Blue Max* (John Guillermin, 1966), *Johnny Got his Gun* (Dalton Trumbo, 1971).

- **Inter War Years**

After their almost complete disappearance from the screen in the immediate aftermath of the war, films involving the Great War or in some way related to it began to re-emerge in the 1920's and from then on throughout the inter-war period British film-makers frequently returned to the theme.

Generally the bulk of the film output consisted of **documentary-drama reconstructions** (e.g. *The Battle of Jutland*, 1921; *Zeebrugge*, 1924: *Ypres*, 1925; *Mons: The Story of the Immortal Retreat*, 1926; *The Somme*, 1927: *'Q' Ships*, 1928), **films which portrayed the war in traditional, patriotic and romantic terms** (e.g. *Comradeship*, 1919; *Mademoiselle from Armentières*, 1926; *Roses of Picardy*, 1926; *The Poppies of Flanders*, 1927; *The Guns of Loos*, 1928; *The Burgomaster of Stilemonde*, 1929), or **films which aimed to treat the war as straightforward adventure**, (e.g. *The W Plan*, 1930; *I Was a Spy*, 1933; *Forever England* (1935); *Secret Agent* (1936); *The Spy in Black* (1939). There were a few films in the 1930's which were of **an anti-war or pacifist nature** (e.g. *Thunder in the Air, 1934; Jubilee*, 1935; *Hell Unlimited*, 1936; *The Tunnel*, 1935; *Things to Come*, 1936); they were certainly not typical of the British film output of the inter-war years and were far outweighed by the more popular patriotic, romantic, or adventure type of war film.. Yet even in the latter films it is sometimes possible to sense the occasional note of disenchantment[207], a sign perhaps that there was a certain ambiguity in the attitude of some film-makers to the Great War and that they were not always willing to make films that conformed totally to the predominant desire of most people to remember the war in terms of heroism and patriotism.

The Battle of Jutland (1921)
Directed by H. Bruce Woolfe

Blighty (1927)
Directed by Adrian Brunel

The Burgomaster of Stillemonde (1929)
Directed by George J. Banfield

Comradeship (1919)
Directed by Maurice Elvey

Dark Journey (1937)
Directed by Victor Saville

Dawn (1928)
Directed by Herbert Wilcox who remade the story for RKO in 1939 as *Nurse Edith Cavell*

'East Lynne' on the Western Front (1931)
Directed by George Pearson

Forever England (1935)
Directed by Walter Forde. Originally titled *Brown on Resolution*

The Guns of Loos (1928)
Directed by Sinclair Hill

Hell Unlimited (1936)
Directed by Helen Biggar, Norman McLaren. Uses puppets, diagrams, animation and live action to present an anti-war message for use by peace organisations. The film (a short) was made as a protest against profits in armaments during a period when fascism was growing throughout Europe.

I Was a Spy (1933)
Directed by Victor Saville

Journey's End (1930)
UK/USA co-production. Directed by James Whale. Based on R.C. Sherriff's famous play.

Jubilee (1935)
Contrasts the 1935 Silver Jubilee celebrations in East London (c.25.5.35) with working class poverty and national progress towards war. Produced by the North London Film Society.

The Lost Patrol (1929)
Directed by Arthur Maude

Mademoiselle from Armentières (1926)
Directed by Maurice Elvey

Mons (1926)
Directed by Walter Summers

The Poppies of Flanders (1927)
Directed by Walter Summers

---

[207] In some of these films a mood of disenchantment is quite pronounced (e.g. *Réveille*, 1924; *Journey's End*, 1930; *Tell England* (1931).

Cultural Impacts

Q-Ships (1928)
Directed by Geoffrey Barkas and Michael Barringer. The story of Captain Lieutenant Stockmar and the unrestricted German submarine warfare of the Great War is the subject of this dramatised account of real events.

Réveille (1924)
A story of the hectic, forced gaiety of the year 1918, and the disillusion which comes to many at the end of the War. Directed by George Pearson

Roses of Picardy (1926)
Directed by Maurice Elvey

Secret Agent (1936)
Directed by Alfred Hitchcock. Based on the novel *Ashenden* by W. Somerset Maugham.

The Somme (1927)
Directed by M.A. Wetherell

The Spy in Black (1939)
Directed by Michael Powell

Suspense (1930)
Directed by Walter Summers

Tell England (1931)
Directed by Anthony Asquith and Geoffrey Barkas

Things to Come (1936)
Directed by William Cameron Menzies. This sci-fi movie shows the horrors of war and the price of progress predicted by a film made in 1936 looking at a world heading towards World War II. Scripted by H. G. Wells from his novel. An anti-war film no doubt influenced by the memory of the Great War.

Thunder in the Air (1934)
Directed by Hans Nieter. A story of a son who goes off to the war. His mother is reminded of his father who joined up to fight in the Great War. Partly dramatised propaganda film attacking the armaments industry and pleading for international peace.

The Tunnel (1935)
Directed by Maurice Elvey. Although it is never satisfactorily explained how, it is argued throughout this sci-fi film that the joint project of Britain and America to build a trans-Atlantic tunnel will result in increased commerce, the easing of international tensions and the prevention of future wars. To quote Lloyd, one of the projects financiers featured in the film, the tunnel means "world peace through the union of the English-speaking peoples".

Victory (1928)
Directed by M. A. Wetherell

W Plan (1930)
Directed by Victor Saville

Ypres (1925)
Directed by Walter Summers

Zeebrugge (1924)
Directed by A. V. Bramble and H. Bruce Woolfe

- **2nd World War and After**

While there are some references to the Great War (in relation to its futility) that can be found in *The Dawn Guard* (1941) and The *Gentle Sex* (1943), British cinema films about war were almost totally concerned with the Second World War both during the progress of that war and in the years after it had ended. The only films directly related to the Great War that appeared in the 1950's were *The African Queen* (1951) and *The Diary of an Unknown Soldier* (1959). Strangely, the revival of public interest in the Great War, which began in the 1960's with a flood of books of every description (military histories, personal reminiscences, war poetry, etc) and the BBC's massive 26 part history of the Great War (1964), and which has continued to the present day, failed to create a significant impact on the British cinema film industry. Only three cinema films dealing with the war (i.e. *Lawrence of Arabia*, 1962; *King and Country*, 1964; *Oh, What a Lovely War!*, 1969) were made during the entire decade of the 1960's when the revival of public interest in the Great War was at its height. After that there was a long gap during which only *Aces High* (1976) and *Zeppelin* (1971) were made. Subsequently there was an even longer gap; it was not until 1997 that British cinema film-makers returned to the Great War with *Regeneration* (1997) and *The Trench* (1999). It was in the field of British TV where the revived interest in the Great War had its greatest impact both through its drama and its documentaries.

Aces High (1976)
Directed by Jack Gold. "Based on R.C.Sheriff's play 'Journey's End' with additional material from 'Saggitarius Rising' by Cecil Lewis". [British Film Institute note]

The African Queen (1951)
Directed by John Huston. British/USA production. This film, set in Africa during the Great War, features the sister of a missionary and a heavy-drinking engineer, who escape from the Germans down a river in an old boat and, on a lake at the river's end, succeed in blowing up a German gun-boat with improvised torpedoes.

The Dawn Guard (1941)
Diected by Roy Boulting. (See note about this film in the preamble to this section above).

The Diary of an Unknown Soldier (1959)
Directed by Peter Watkins. Amateur film about the reactions of a young soldier to battle in the First World War.

The Gentle Sex (1943)
Directed by Leslie Howard. Direction completed by Maurice Elvey. (See note about this film in the preamble to this section above).

King and Country (1964)
Directed by Joseph Losey. A film about an army private in the Great War accused of desertion during battle.

Lawrence of Arabia (1962)
Directed by David Lean. A dramatised version of the phase of T.E. Lawrence's life during the Great War when as a young intelligence officer in the Middle East he became involved in the Arab revolt against the Turks, organising an Arab guerrilla army which he used to harass the Turks with raids, train-wrecking and camel attacks and, eventually, to help General Allenby to achieve the victories which ultimately enabled him to inflict the final decisive defeat on the Turks in 1918.

The Life Story of David Lloyd George (1918; 'premiered' 1996)
Made in 1918 by the Ideal Film Company, it was mysteriously suppressed before its release and disappeared for seventy six years before rediscovery by the Wales Film and Television Archive (now the National Screen and Sound Archive of Wales). There followed a painstaking two-year restoration, leading to the film's 'premiere' in Cardiff in 1996, and other screenings in Britain and around the world (see also *David Lloyd George: The Movie Mystery*, edited by D. Berry and S. Horrocks, cited above in **section 4.3.2.1: Books**).

Oh! What a Lovely War (1969)
Directed by Richard Attenborough. Based on the Joan Littlewood/Theatre Workshop musical play which was adapted from the radio feature 'The Long, Long Trail' by Charles Chilton, this film version was presented as an anti-war satirical entertainment with songs, entirely set on the Brighton Pier.

Regeneration (1997)
Directed by Gillies MacKinnon. British/Canadian film based on the novel *Regeneration* by Pat Barker. The film features the fictional representation in Pat Barker's novel of the real-life event of the psychiatric treatment of Siegfried Sassoon and Wilfred Own by Dr William Rivers at Craiglockhart army hospital in Scotland in 1917.

The Trench (1999)
Directed by William Boyd. British/French production. This film employs a handful of characters, including the 17-year-old Billy, who only joins up to be near his older brother Eddie, to portray the build-up to the Battle of the Somme as experienced in the trenches.

Zeppelin (1971)
Directed by Étienne Périer. A story of espionage during the Great War involving the use by Germany of a Zeppelin to carry out a commando-type raid on Balcoven Castle in Scotland for the purpose of stealing numerous British historical documents, including the Magna Carta, secretly hidden there for security reasons.

4.3.3 Television

4.3.3.1 General

After the Second World War the memory of the Great War was brought back to millions of viewers through the medium of British television, mainly by means of documentaries although television drama also played an important part.

In British television's documentary history of the Great War the important landmark was the launching in 1964 of the biggest documentary series ever made for British television – *The Great War* (in 26 parts) – to commemorate the 50th anniversary of the Great War. Its immediate popularity can be measured by the fact that the first showing of each episode was watched by an average of 8 million viewers who could hardly have failed to be struck particularly by the horrific nature of trench warfare and the huge losses of life that were so graphically screened. The series seemed to serve mainly to confirm the negative, 'gloom and doom', interpretation of the war years 1914-1918 - its horrors, carnage, military incompetence, tragic waste of life, and futility – that were characteristic of many of the popular histories, poetry and other works that were also published to mark the fiftieth anniversary of the conflict and that have helped to mould the popular perception of the Great War which still persists. Subsequent British television documentaries (e.g. *1914-1918: The Great War and the Shaping of the 20th Century*, 1997, and *The Western Front*, 1999) have tended to reinforce the latter perception, failing to take sufficient account of the work of the academic revisionists who have sought to challenge the myths surrounding the Great War and to produce a more balanced interpretation of it. There have, however, been attempts to adopt a modified approach in some television documentaries on aspects of the Great War as was the case, for example, with the 'Timewatch' presentation in 1996 of *Haig: The Unknown Soldier* which sought to produce a portrait of the frequently maligned and little understood military figure with balance and fairness. Although in the area of television drama there were a number of productions related to the Great War, the ones that continue to stand out, particularly in the public mind, are *Oh! What a Lovely War* (cinema version) and *Blackadder Goes Forth* (both frequently repeated), which portray in satirical fashion (comically farcical as well in the case of *Blackadder*) a futile war fought by long-suffering soldiers led by incompetent generals who callously send off their men to be massacred on the killing fields of the Western Front. The latter productions (particularly *Blackadder Goes Forth*), together with some of the television documentaries mentioned above and listed below, have powerfully contributed to the development of a popular perception of the Great War which has made the task even harder for those historians who have tried to counter it by presenting a more balanced view of that war.

Books

Dillon, R. *History on British Television: Constructing Nation, Nationality and Collective Memory* (Manchester: Manchester University Press, 2010)

Hanna, E. *The Great War on the Small Screen: Representing the First World War in Contemporary Britain* (Edinburgh: Edinburgh University Press, 2009)

— 'Representations of the Battle of the Somme in British Television Documentaries', in *Televising History: The Past on the Small Screen*, edited by Erin Bell & Ann Gray (London: Palgrave Macmillan, 2010)

Theses

Mahoney, E. L. 'The Great War on the Small Screen: A Cultural History of The First World War on British Television, 1964-2005' (doctoral thesis, University of Kent, Canterbury, 2006)
Not a definitive survey of every British television documentary about the First World War, but an analysis of the most significant series and single programmes.

Articles

Badsey, S. 'The Great War Since The Great War', *Historical Journal of Film Radio And Television*, 22 (2002), 37-46

Burke, W. 'The Great War on the Small Screen: Representing the First World War in Contemporary Britain', *Historical Journal of Film Radio and Television*, 31(2011), 113-115

Downing, T. 'The Great War: Television Revisited', *History Today*, 52 (2002), 3-4
About BBC Television's 1964 series *The Great War*.

—— 'History on TV', *History Today*, 64, Issue 6 (2014), 18-20
Taylor Downing looks at the making in 1964 (for the newly launched BBC2) of the pioneering television series on the Great War that marked the 50th anniversary of this war and revolutionised the history documentary.

Gardiner, J. 'Variations on a Theme of Elgar: Ken Russell, the Great War, and the Television 'life' of a composer', *Historical Journal of Film Radio and Television*, 23 (2003), 195-210

Hanna, E. 'Reality-Experiential History Documentaries: *The Trench* (BBC, 2002) and Britain's Modern Memory of the Frist World War', *Historical Journal of Film, Radio and Television*, 27 (2007), 531-547

—— 'A Small Screen Alternative to Stone and Bronze: "The Great War" (BBC, 1964)' *European Journal of Cultural Studies*, 10 (2007), 89-111

Kuehl, J. 'The Great War on DD Video', *Historical Journal of Film Radio and Television*, 23 (2003), 285-287

Lewis, J. and H. Strachan. 'Filming the First World War', *History Today*, 53, Issue 10 (2003), 20-29

Ramsden, J. A. 'The Great War: The Making of the Series', *Historical Journal of Film, Radio, and Television*, 22 (2002), 7-19
About BBC Television's 1964 series *The Great War*.

Thomson, D. 'Parade's End: Ford Madox Ford's Masterpiece Comes to the Screen', *New Republic*, 244, January 27 (2013), 64-65

Todman, D. 'The Reception of The Great War in the 1960s', *Historical Journal of Film Radio And Television*, 22 (2002), 29-36
The author examines the reception of the TV series *The Great War* by its original audience in 1964–1965

Websites

BBC. Media Centre. *The BBC Announces its Four-Year World War One Centenary Season*, 16 October, 2013 [http://www.bbc.co.uk/mediacentre/latestnews/2013/world-war-one-centenary.html]
The BBC's announcement on 16 October, 2013, of its plans to mark the First World War Centenary with a project designed to feature "four years of programming and events spanning 2014-2018 – echoing the timeframe of the war".

—— *Marking the Centenary of World War One across the BBC*, 4 February, 2014
[http://www.bbc.co.uk/mediacentre/mediapacks/ww1/]
The website provides an introduction and also affords links to information provided under the following headings: Documentaries, Historical Debate, Commemoration, Arts & Music, Drama, Across the UK, Digital & Online, Children's & Schools, Special Editions. A great deal of this information is related to programmes that will be shown on TV.

4.3.3.2 Documentaries

1914: The War Revolution (BBC, 2003)
Directed by Paul Bradshaw. "Documentary [in the Timewatch series] examining how the whole nature of warfare changed after the first few months of the First World War, moving from initial traditional cavalry skirmishes between the German and British troops to trench warfare and stalemates that lasted the rest of the War. Looks at the reasons for this". [British Film Institute synopsis]

Cultural Impacts

1914-1918: The Great War and the Shaping of the 20th Century. (BBC, 1997)
Television Series narrated by Dame Judi Dench. Executive Producer: Blaine Baggett, Series Historian: Jay Winter. A co-production of the KCET/BBC in association with the Imperial War Museum (IWM). A web site (http://www.pbs.org/greatwar) and a book by Jay Winter and Blaine Baggett, both with the same title, are companions to the TV series.

1916 The Irish Rebellion (BBC, 2016)
A three-part documentary series broadcast worldwide in 2016. Narrated by Liam Neeson, the documentary was the initiative of the Keough-Naughton Institute for Irish Studies at the University of Notre Dame. It was broadcast on BBC 4 on 28 March 2016.

Aces Falling (BBC, 2009)
"Edward Mannock VC and James McCudden VC rose from modest backgrounds to become two of Britain's greatest fighter aces in World War One. As their number of victories grew, so did their chances of dying in flames. 'Timewatch' tells the story of their battle to survive against the odds, and of the 90-year-old mystery surrounding the death of one of them". [Note by series editor John Farren]

The Crucified Soldier (Channel 4, 2002, 2005)
Directed by Jonathan Dent. In the TV series *Secret History*. "An investigation into the story from the First World War that began to spread from April 1915 that a Canadian soldier had been found crucified at St. Julien, near Ypres in Belgium. The story caused outrage and fuelled the image of the German army committing atrocities. Later claims by Germany that the story was purely Allied propaganda were upheld, but this film offers new evidence to support the story and even puts a name to the soldier". [British Film Institute synopsis]

Battle of the Somme (BBC, 1976)
Produced by Malcolm Brown. "Programme for the 60th anniversary of the Battle of the Somme, in which Leo McKern walks the fields of Picardy and retells the story of the battle, with the letters, diaries and memories of men who took part". [British Film Institute synopsis]

The First World War (Channel 4, 2003)
10 part series narrated and produced by Jonathan Lewis. Based on the book of the same name by Professor Huw Strachan

Gallipoli: The First D Day (BBC, 2003)
Directed by John-Hayes Fisher. This documentary re-examines the Great War British landings in Gallipoli in 1915, an event which led to a disaster which resulted in 250,000 Allied casualties and an ignominious withdrawal.

A Game of Ghosts (BBC, 1991)
Directed by Stephen Walker in the series, *Everyman*. This documentary is about four survivors of the Battle of the Somme talking about their experiences and emotions related to it and the distress, which includes feelings of guilt at surviving killed comrades, that they continue to suffer even after so many years since the battle took place

The Great War (BBC, 1964, 2003-2004)
BBC's 26 part series on the history of the 1914-1918 War, in collaboration with the Imperial War Museum (IWM), CBC (Canadian Broadcasting Company) and ABC (Australian Broadcasting Company), to commemorate the fiftieth anniversary of the outbreak of the Great War. Series producer, Tony Essex Series narrator, Sir Michael Redgrave. 21 of the episodes were scripted by Correlli Barnett (7) and John Terraine. (14). A new edition of Correlli Barnett's book, *The Great War* (text first published by the Park Lane Press in 1979), was published to accompany the re-transmission in 2003-04 on BBC2 of the television series broadcast in 1964.

Haig: The Unknown Soldier (BBC, 1996)
Produced by Helen Bettinson. In the series, *Timewatch*. In this documentary the reputation of Field Marshall Douglas Haig is explored in the light of a new perspective on the man, with veterans of the Somme as well as historians giving their views.

Journey To Hell (BBC, 2004)
Directed by Catrine Clay, this looked at war poet Wilfred Owen.

Last Day of WW1 (BBC, 2008)
Directed by John Hayes-Fisher, this film - presented by Michael Palin - looked at the last day, and last casualties of the Great War.

"Lions Led by Donkeys" – The Battle of the Somme (Channel 4, 1985, 1988)
Directed by B. A. Duffy. In this documentary survivors of the Battle of the Somme in 1916 discuss their experiences.

My Family At War (BBC, 2008)
This four part series was specially commissioned for the 90th Anniversary of the Armistice, and took eight celebrities back to the battlefields in search of their ancestors who fought and died: these included Kate Silverton, Rolf Harris, Kirsty Wark and Dan Snow.

Peace in No Man's Land (BBC, 1981)
This documentary looks at the Christmas truce of 1914 as remembered by three soldiers (Graham Williams, Leslie Walkinton, and Albert Moren) who actually experienced it.

Shot at Dawn (Channel 4, 1998)
The cases of some of those British and Commonwealth servicemen who were executed for 'military offences' during the Great War are examined in this documentary.

The Somme (Channel 4, 2005)
Directed by Carl Hindmarch. This drama-documentary, recounting the events of the 1st July 1916 and the Battle of the Somme on the Western Front during the First World War, is told through the letters and journals of soldiers who were there.

The Trench (BBC, 2002)
3 part series recreating life in a First World War trench; directed by Dominic Ozanne.

Veterans: The Last Survivors of the Great War (BBC, 1998)
2 part documentary (produced by Steve Humphries) in which veterans of World War One recall life at the front.

The Western Front (BBC, 1999)
Series of six documentary films in which Richard Holmes examines how the First World War was fought in trenches, forts and bunkers. Series producer, Mark Fielder. Brian Bond, taking the view in his *The Unquiet Western Front*, that "the BBC book of the series differs markedly from the TV script, and, in scholarly terms is far superior" and that it has "a sensitive text that displays up-to-date knowledge and a judicious handling of controversial issues", considers it to be "a pity that many more viewers will have watched the series on TV than will buy and carefully read the book".

What Sank the Britannic (Channel 5, 2005)
Directed by Tom Gorham. In the series *Ocean's Greatest Wrecks*. A documentary which investsigates the sinking of the *Britannic*, a hospital ship which was evacuating casualties when it was sunk in the Mediterranean off Greece in 1916 – an investigation involving a diving expedition which provided the opportunity to study the wreck further and add to pre-existing theories about what happened and why the ship sank so quickly.

World War I in Colour (Channel 5, 2003)
6 part series about the First World War using original black and white footage colourised by computer technology. Narrated by Kenneth Branagh. Executive Producers: Simon Berthon, Philip Nugus. A booklet was published to accompany the series

Ypres: The Forgotten Battlefield, Meet the Ancestors Special (BBC2, 2001)
Directed by John-Hayes Fisher. A programme about a local Belgian archaeology group, known as The Diggers, who for several years worked on the site of the trenches established in April 1915 on the former front at Boesinghe, north of Ypres, through which over a period of two years regulars from 4th Division, territorials from 49th (West Riding) Division, Kitchener's men from 14th (Light) Division and the Guards all passed, until the trenches were finally captured, during the Battle of Passchendaele, on 31st July 1917, by elements of 38th (Welsh) Division.
[http://battlefields1418.50megs.com/forgotten_battlefield.htm]

4.3.3.3 Drama

Aces High (BBC, 1981, 1983, 1985; Tyne Tees Television, 1986; Granada, 1987; Border Television, 1987; Central Independent Television, 1987; Yorkshire Television, 1987; LWT, 1988; TSW, 1988; Thames, 1992; Channel Four, 1996, 1998, 1999, 2000, 2002, 2004; ITV, 2005, 2008, 2009)
TV transmission of the British cinema film production released in 1976, directed by Jack Gold. Based on R.C.Sheriff's play *Journey's End* with additional material from *Sagittarius Rising* by Cecil Lewis.

The African Queen (BBC, 1962, 1982, 1984, 1986, 1988, 1990, 1991, 1993; Channel 4, 1998, 2000)
Directed by John Huston. British/USA production. This film, set in Africa during the Great War, features the sister of a

Cultural Impacts

missionary and a heavy-drinking engineer, who escape from the Germans down a river in an old boat and, on a lake at the river's end, succeed in blowing up a German gun-boat with improvised torpedoes.

All the King's Men (BBC, 1999)
Directed by Julian Jarrold. Feature-length drama about the mystery of Sandringham Company (commanded by Captain Frank Beck, their estate manager) which disappeared in action at Gallipoli in 1915.

The Anzacs (BBC, 1987)
BBC's transmission of the 5-part Australian TV mini series produced in 1985, tracing the experiences of a group of Australians in WWI.

Ashenden (BBC, 1991)
Directed by Christopher Morahan. Four-part drama about a writer recruited into espionage work by British intelligence during the First World War. Based on the writings of Somerset Maugham

Blackadder Goes Forth (BBC, 1989)
Comedy series set during the Great War, featuring the Blackadder character who featured in various other series.

The Blue Max (ITV, 1988; Channel 4, 1995; LWT, 2000; BBC, 2004, 2006)
TV transmission of the American film production released in 1966, directed by John Guillermin, about a man in the German Flying Corps achieving his coveted aim of winning the Blue max, the most prestigious award to airmen, but being subsequntly killed as a result of his enemies sending him out in a faulty plane.

Britannic (ITV, 2000, 2005; Channel 5, 2005, 2006, 2007, 2008, 2009)
Directed by Brian Trenchard-Smith. War drama about the sinking of the *Titanic's* sister ship during the Great War, involving a British agent falling in love with a spy while on a mission aboard the *Britannic*.

The Dawn Patrol (Channel 4, 1984, 1998, 1999, 2001)
TV transmission of the American film production released in 1938, directed by Edmund Goulding, about the dilemma in the Great War of Royal Flying Corps squadron commanders confronted with the problem of reconciling heartless orders from headquarters with the welfare of their pilots.

Farewell to Arms (BBC, 1966, 1973, 1999, 2001, 2002)
Three-part dramatisation of Ernest Hemingway's 1929 novel.

Gallipoli (Thames Television, 1985; BBC, 1998; Channel 5, 2004, 2005)
TV transmission of the Australian film production released in 1981, directed by Peter Weir, about the friendship of two Australian youths from different social backgrounds, followed from their enlistment in the army at the same time during the Great War to their ending up together on the same stretch of beach at Gallipoli.

A Horseman Riding By (BBC, 1978)
13-part dramatisation of novel set in a small Devon valley, spanning the first two decades of the 20th century. Parts 7-12 cover the Great War period, 1914-1918.

How Many Miles to Babylon ? (BBC, 1982)
Drama by Derek Mahon, adapted from a novel by Jennifer Johnston, about Alexander Moore and Jerry Crowe, childhood friends from different social backgrounds who, joining up in 1914, are posted to the same Army unit where they remain close friends (in spite of Alexander having become an officer whereas Jerry was a private) until Jerry is court-martialed for desertion, and Alexander is put in charge of the firing squad.

King and Country (BBC, 1975, 1979: Channel Four, 1992)
TV transmission of the British film production released in 1964, directed by Joseph Lose, about, an army private in the Great War accused of desertion during battle and the court-martial case which resulted from this.

Lawrence of Arabia (ITV, 1975, 1977, 1982, 1990, 1998, 2000; Channel 4, 2001, 2004)
TV transmission of the British film production released in 1962, directed by David Lean, of a dramatised version of a the phase of T.E. Lawrence's life during the Great War when as a young intelligence officer in the Middle East he became involved in the Arab revolt against the Turks, organising an Arab guerrilla army which he used to harass the Turks with raids, train-wrecking and camel attacks and, eventually, to help General Allenby to achieve the victories which ultimatelyenabled him to inflict the final decisive defeat on the Turks in 1918.

Mad Jack (BBC, 1970, 1971)
Directed by Jack Gold. In the series, *The Wednesday Play*. This drama deals with the life of Siegfried Sassoon and his protest about the war.

The Monocled Mutineer (BBC, 1986)
Directed by Jim O'Brien. Adapted from a book by John Fairley and William Allison. This drama scripted by Alan Bleasdale is about the life of Percy Topliss who led a mutiny in an Army training camp in France during the Great War.

My Boy Jack (ITV, 2007)
Directed by Brian Kirk. This is a recreation of the true story of how the poet Rudyard Kipling used his influence during the Great War to get his 17-year-old son Jack a commission with the Irish Guards, despite the boy's severe myopia, and how his parents spent many years searching for him after he was reported missing in action during the Battle of Loos.

Oh! What a Lovely War (Channel 4, 1988; BBC, 1992; Sky Movies Cinema 2, 2005)
TV transmission of the joint Amercan/British film production released in 1969, directed by Richard Attenborough. Based on the Joan Littlewood/Theatre Workshop musical play which was adapted from the radio feature 'The Long, Long Trail' by Charles Chilton, this film version was presented as an anti-war satirical entertainment with songs, entirely set on the Brighton Pier.

Parade's End (BBC, 2012)
TV adaptation of Ford Madox Fords's 'Tietjens' tetralogy (i.e. *Some Do Not, No More Parades, A Man Could Stand Up, The Last Post*)

Paths of Glory (BBC, 1981, 1985, 1989, 1992; Sky Movies, 1995; Channel 4, 1998, 2000)
TV transmission of the American film production released in 1957, directed by Stanley Kubrick, and based on the novel *Paths of Glory* by Humphrey Cobb. This drama, set in 1916, is about the failure of an attack on a German strong-point ordered by a French general without any regard for the numbers of lives that would be lost, and, in the wake of this failure, the subsequent court-martial for cowardice of three men, picked at random as an example to the rest of the soldiers and sentenced to death, in spite of all their colonel can do to save them.

Regeneration (BBC, 1999, 2004, 2005)
TV transmission of the British/Canadian film production released in 1997, directed by Gillies MacKinnon and based on the novel *Regeneration* by Pat Barker. The film features the fictional representation in Pat Barker's novel of the real-life event of the psychiatric treatment of Siegfried Sassoon and Wilfred Own by Dr William Rivers at Craiglockhart army hospital in Scotland in 1917.

Shoulder to Shoulder (BBC, 1974)
Series of 6 plays dramatising the struggle fought between 1895 and 1918 by British women to gain the right to vote, focusing in particular on the determining role played by the Pankhurst family. The 6 parts were: *Sylvia Pankhurst* (directed by Waris Hussein), *Outrage* (directed by Moira Armstrong), *Christabel Pankhurst* (directed by Moira Armstrong), *Lady Constance Lytton* (directed by Waris Hussein), *Annie Kenney* (directed by Waris Hussein), *The Pankhursts* (directed by Waris Hussein). A joint British/USA production.

Testament of Youth (BBC, 1979, 1992)
Five-part serialisation of Vera Brittain's autobiography, depicting her life between 1913 and 1918. Vera Brittain's world falls to pieces around her as, one by one, the young men of her circle are caught up in the Great War.

The Trench (Sky Movies Screen 1, 2001; BBC, 2003; FilmFour, 2004; Channel 4, 2005; BBC, 2007)
TV transmission of the British/French film production released in 1999, directed by William Boyd. This film employs a handful of characters, including the 17-year-old Billy, who only joins up to be near his older brother Eddie, to portray the build-up to the Battle of the Somme as experienced in the trenches.

Zeppelin (LWT, 1979; ITV, 1981; LWT, 1983; BBC, 1986, 1992, 1998, 1999, 2003, 2005)
TV transmission of the British film production released in 1971, directed by Etienne Périer. A story of espionage during the Great War involving the use by Germany of a Zeppelin to carry out a commando-type raid on Balcoven Castle in Scotland for the purpose of stealing numerous British historical documents, including the Magna Carta, secretly hidden there for security reasons.

4.4 Art

In art the memory of the war was to a large extent evoked for the public in the architectural designs and sculptures associated with war memorials (see also the various sub-sections of **section 2 [Memorialisation and Commemoration]** of **Part 4: Remembering the War**) and in the paintings produced in the aftermath of the war. Many of the latter paintings had been officially commissioned at the end of the war via the War Artists Advisory Committee set up by the Department of Information under the British War Memorials programme in 1918. Remembrance was also perpetuated in Galleries and Museums with exhibitions of paintings and photographs related to the war.

Autobiographies, Biographies

Arnold, B. *Orpen: Mirror to an Age* (London: Cape, 1981)

Behrend, C. *Stanley Spencer at Burghclere: Stanley Spencer 1891-1959* (London: Macdonald, 1965)

Brangwyn, R. *Brangwyn* (London: Kimber, 1978)

Buckle, R. *Jacob Epstein* (London: Faber, 1963)

Carline, R. *Stanley Spencer at War* (London: Faber, 1978)

Clements, K. *Henry Lamb: The Artist and his Friends* (Bristol: Redcliffe, 1985)

Cork, R. *David Bomberg* (New Haven; London: Yale University Press, 1987)

Epstein, J. *Epstein: An Autobiography*, rev. and extended edition (London: Hutton Press, 1955)
Originally published, London: Michael Joseph, 1940, under the title *Let there be Sculpture: An Autobiography*.

Jenkins, D. F. *Paul Nash: The Elements*, with essays by David Boyd Haycock and Simon Grant; Paul Nash photographs printed by Rod Tidnam (London: Scala, 2010)
Published to accompany the exhibition held 10 Feb. - 9 May 2010 at the Dulwich Picture Gallery, London. This book examines the career of Paul Nash, official war artist and one of the great pioneers of British Modernism.

Konody, P. G. and S. Dark *Sir William Orpen: Artist and Man* (London: Seeley, 1932)

Lewis, P. W. *Blasting and Bombardiering*, rev. edn (London: Calder, 1982)
Originally published London: Eyre & Spottiswood, 1937; rev. and issued as a 2nd edn.: London: Calder and Boyars, 1967.

MacDougall, S. *Mark Gertler* (London: John Murray, 2002)

Moriarty, C. *The Sculpture of Gilbert Ledward* (Aldershot: The Henry Moore Foundation in association with Lund Humphries, 2003)

Mount, C. M. *John Singer Sargent: A Biography* (London: Cresset Press, 1957)

Nash, P. *Outline: An Autobiography* (London: Columbus, 1988)
Originally published, London Faber, 1949, under the title *Outline: An autobiography and Other Writings*.

Nevinson, C. R. W. *Paint and Prejudice* (London: Methuen, 1937)

Olson, S. *John Singer Sargent: His Portrait* (London: Barrie & Jenkins, 1986)

Orpen, Sir W. *An Onlooker in France* (London: Williams & Norgate, 1921)

Pople, K. *Stanley Spencer: A Biography* (London: HarperCollins, 1991)

Walsh, M. J. K. *C. R. W. Nevinson: This Cult of Violence* (New Haven: Yale University Press, 2002)

Catalogues

Bell, K. *Stanley Spencer: A Complete Catalogue of the Paintings* (London: Phaidon in association with Christie's and the Henry Moore Foundation, 1992)

British War Art of the 20th Century: The Official War Artists Record of the two World Wars (London: Mindata, 1982)

Imperial War Museum [IWM]. *A Concise Catalogue of Paintings, Drawings and Sculpture of the First World War 1914-1918*, 2nd edn (London: Imperial War Museum, 1963)
Catalogue of an exhibition held in 1963.

— *Oil Paintings in Public Ownership in the Imperial War Museum*, A. Ellis, director; S. Roe, editor; A. Johnson, photography (London: The Public Catalogue Foundation, 2006)

Books

Black, J. 'Blessing a Holy War?: The Church of England, First World War Memorial Sculpture and the Rituals of Commemoration' in *Art, Religion, Ritual*, edited by Peter Martyn and Piotr Paszkiewicz, in collaboration with Francis Ames-Lewis (Warsaw: Institute of Art, Polish Academy, 2003)
Proceedings of the Fifth Joint Conference of Art Historians from Britain and Poland, Warsaw, 7th-9th June 2000.

— 'First World War Memorial Sculpture in Scotland', *in Memory and Memorials: The Commemorative Century*, edited by William Kidd and Brian Murdoch (Aldershot: Ashgate, 2004)

— *The Sculpture of Eric Kennington* (Much Hadham: Henry Moore Foundation in association with Lund Humphries, 2002)

— 'Thanks for the Memory: War Memorials, Spectatorship and the Trajectories of Commemoration c. 1919-2001', in *Matters of Conflict: Material Culture, Memory and the First World War*, edited by Nicholas Saunders (London: Routledge, 2004)

— 'Who Dies if England Live?: Masculinity, the Problematics of Englishness and the Image of the Ordinary British Soldier in British War Art c.1915-28', in *Relocating Britishness: Studies in Popular Culture*, edited by Steven Caunce, Ewa Maziorska, Susan Sydney-Smith and John K. Walton (Manchester: Manchester University Press, 2004)

Compton, A. *The Sculpture of Charles Sargeant Jagger* (Aldershot: Henry Moore Foundation in association with Lund Humphries, 2004)

Corbett, D. P., ed. *Wyndham Lewis and the Art of Modern War* (Cambridge: Cambridge University Press, 1998)

Cork, R. *A Bitter Truth: Avant-Garde Art and the Great War* (New Haven and London: Yale University Press in association with Barbican Art Gallery, 1994)
This book was in effect a catalogue of an exhibition organised by Richard Cork and held at the Altes Museum, Berlin in June 1994 and the Barbican Art Gallery, London, from 28 September - 11 December 1994.

— *Vorticism and Abstract Art in the First Machine Age*, 2 vols (London: G. Fraser, 1976)
Contents: Vol 1. Origins and Development; Vol. 2. Synthesis and Decline.

Ford, M. R. D. *Art and War: Twentieth Century Warfare as depicted by War Artists* (London: Headline in association with the Imperial War Museum, 1990)

Fox, J. *British Art and the First World War, 1914-1924* (Cambridge: Cambridge University Press, 2015)

Gough, P. '"An Epic of Mud": Artistic Interpretations of Third Ypres', in *Passchendaele in Perspective: The Third Battle of Ypres*, edited by P. H. Liddle (London: Leo Cooper, 1997)

— '"A War of the Imagination": The Experience of the British Artist', in *The Great World War 1914-45*, edited by J. Bourne, P. H. Liddle and I. R. Whitehead, 2 vols (London: HarperCollins, 2000-2001), II: *The Peoples' Experience*, 2001
Vol.2. has spine cover title: *Who won? Who lost?*

Cultural Impacts

Harries, S. and M. Harries. *The War Artists: British Official War Art of the Twentieth Century* (London: Joseph in association with the Imperial War Museum and the Tate Gallery, 1983)

Harrison, C. *English Art and Modernism, 1900–1939*, 2nd edn (New Haven: Yale University Press for the Paul Mellon Centre for Studies in British Art, 1994)

Hynes, S. *A War Imagined: The First World War and English Culture*, new edn (London: Pimlico, 1992)

Malvern, S. 'For King and Country: Frampton's Edith Cavell 1915-1920 and the Writing of Gender in Memorials to the Great War', in *Sculpture and the Pursuit of the Modern Ideal in Britain, c.1880-1930*, edited by David Getsy (Aldershot: Ashgate, 2004)

— *Modern Art, Britain and the Great War: Witnessing, Testimony and Remembrance* (London: Yale University Press, 2004)
Contents: Art, propaganda and persuasion at Wellington House; Realism, representation and censorship; Making history: the British War Memorials Committee; Modern art, modern war and the impossible project of history painting; Post-War modernisms: William Roberts, David Bomberg, Wyndham Lewis and C.R.W. Nevinson; Redeeming the War: 'Englishness' and remembrance.

McEnroe, N. and others, eds. *The Hospital in the Oatfield: The Art of Nursing in the First World War*, edited by Natasha McEnroe and Tig Thomas; editorial consultant: Christine E. Hallett (London: Florence Nightingale Museum, 2014)
"This book accompanies the exhibition 'The hospital in the oatfield' displayed in the Florence Nightingale Museum in 2014 as art of the First World War centenary, and curated by Natasha McEnroe and Holly Carter-Chappell." [Quotation from the front cover flyleaf]. **See also** the article below by Natasha McEnroe ('The Duchess and the Soldier', *History Today*, 64 (2014), 4-5) and the item entitled *The Hospital in the Oatfield: The Art of Nursing in the First World War* in the section below headed **Exhibitions.**

Moriarty, C. *The Sculpture of Gilbert Ledward* (Aldershot: The Henry Moore Foundation in association with Lund Humphries, 2003)
Ledward served in the Great War as a lieutenant with the Royal Garrison Artillery. In 1918 he was seconded to the Ministry of Information as an official war artist. Later he became a sought after sculptor of war memorials. His best-known work is the Guards Division memorial in St James's Park, London (1926). For the Imperial War Graves Commission he sculpted two great lions for the Memorial to the Missing, Ploegsteert, Belgium.

Nevinson, C. R. W. *The Great War, Fourth Year*, with an essay by J. E Crawford Flitch (London: G. Richards, 1918)

Roberts, W. *Paintings, 1917–1958* (London: Canale, 1960)

Robinson, D. *Stanley Spencer: Visions from a Berkshire Village* (Oxford: Phaidon, 1979)

Rothenstein, J. *British Artists and the War* (London: P. Davies, 1931)

Silber, E. *The Sculpture of Epstein: With a Complete Catalogue* (London: Phaidon Press, 1986)

Sillars, S. *Art and Survival in First World War Britain* (Basingstoke: Macmillan, 1987)

Slocombe, R. *Art from the First World War*, with an introductory essay by R. Tolson (London: Imperial War Museum,)

Stamp, G. *The Memorial to the Missing of the Somme* (London: Profile Books, 2006)
This book about the Edwin Lutyens Memorial to the Missing of the Somme (bearing the names of 73,000 soldiers whose bodies were never found) at Thiepval in Northern France provides an account of its origins, an examination of it in architectural terms, and a consideration of its significance in the world of to-day.

Viney, N. *Images of Wartime: British Art and Artists of World War I* (Newton Abbot: David & Charles, 1991)
Catalogue of an IWM exhibition in 1991. This selection of paintings from the Imperial War Museum [IWM]'s collection features the work of almost 70 artists who either officially or unofficially produced paintings related to the war and is accompanied by a text which considers the artists in the context of their times, examining particularly the motivation of

propaganda which lay behind the government's involvement in the commissioning of much of their work.

Wees, W. C. *Vorticism and the English Avant-Garde* (Manchester: Manchester University Press, 1972)

Wilcox, D. J. *The London Group, the Artists and their Works* (London: Scolar Press, 1995)

Articles

Black, J. 'The Bite of War's Reality: Charles Sargeant Jagger's Great Western Railway War Memorial for Paddington Station (1921-22)', *Firestep: The Magazine of the Western Front Association*, 4 (2003), 29-49

— 'The Real Thing?: Eric Kennington's 24th Infantry Division Memorial in Battersea Park', *The Burlington Magazine*, 145 (2003), 854-859

— 'The Legions Who Have Suffered: The War Memorials of Eric Kennington c.1921-1954', *Sculpture Journal* 11 (2004), 81-99

Doherty, C. 'The War Art of C. R. Nevinson', *Imperial War Museum Review*, 8 (1993), 48-62

'The Edith Cavell Memorial: The Unveiling of the Statue', *The British Journal of Nursing*, (1920), 189-90

Harrington, P. 'Early Paintings of the Great War', *Imperial War Museum Review*, 7 (1992), 47

Jones, N. 'At Arms, At Easels: Winston Churchill and Adolf Hitler', *History Today*, 64, Issue 5 (2014), 4-5
Nigel Jones compares two artists, Churchill and Hitler, of the Western Front.

Malvern, S. '"War As It Is": The Art of Muirhead Bone, C. R. W. Nevinson and Paul Nash, 1916-1917', *Art History*, 9 (1986) 487-515

McEnroe, N. 'The Duchess and the Soldier', *History Today*, 64 (2014), 4-5
This article is about the ten oil paintings by Victor Tardieu (1870-1937) which depict the tented field hospital established and run by Millicent, Duchess of Sutherland, at Bourbourg, twelve miles south-west of Dunkirk, during the summer of 1915. Tardieu served there as an auxiliary with the Duchess of Sutherland for several months and subsequently joined the American Ambulance Field Service, during which time he was commissioned to produce war posters used to generate funds from the American public. The ten paintings were given to the Duchess by the artist and have descended through the Sutherland family. They have now been acquired by the Florence Nightingale Museum, which exhibited them to honour the work of the Duchess of Sutherland and her nurses in the First World War from March 14th to October 26th, 2014 [https://www.florence-nightingale.co.uk/resources/the-hospital-in-the-oatfield/?v=79cba1185463] The image accompanying the McEnroe's article [Oil on panel. 8.5 x 10.75 inches. Signed, inscribed and dated, 'Bourbourg Aout 1915'. Dedicated to Millicent, Duchess of Sutherland (1867-1955)] was one of the ten paintings being exhibited.

Penny, N. 'English Sculpture and the First World War', *Oxford Art Journal*, 4 (1981), 36-42

Slocombe, R. 'The Human Tragedy of the First World War', *Despatches* (The Magazine of the Friends of the Imperial War Museum), 2, No. 13 (2011), 36-38
An article by Richard Slocombe, Senior Curator at Imperial War Museum London, about C. R. W. Nevinson's *Paths of Glory*

Stephens, J. '"The Ghosts of Menin Gate": Art, Architecture and Commemoration', *Journal of Contemporary History*, 44 (2009), 7-26
This article relates both to the gate, designed by the architect Reginald Blomfield in 1922 to commemorate the 56,000 British Empire soldiers lost in the battles of the Ypres Salient, and to the picture, *Menin Gate at Midnight* (painted by the Australian artist and soldier William Longstaff in 1927) showing the gate in the context of a landscape inhabited by ghostly soldiers.

'To Charge Nothing for Cavell Statue', *New York Times*, 2 November 1915

Walsh, M. 'No Peace For The Wicked: A Censored Painter [C. R. W. Nevinson] of the Great War ', *Index on Censorship*, 32; Issue 3 (2003), 21-29

Cultural Impacts

Theses

Black, J. A. A. '"Neither Beasts nor Gods but Men": Constructions of Masculinity and the Image of the Ordinary British Soldier or "Tommy" in The First World War Art of C. R. W. Nevinson, (1889-1946); Eric Henri Kennington (1888-1960) and Charles Sargeant Jagger (1885-1934)' (unpublished doctoral thesis, University of London, 2003)

Chaney, S. 'How Far Can First World War Art and the War Artists Scheme be Seen as Important in the Creation of the Imperial War Museum [IWM] in 1917-20?' (unpublished master's thesis, London University [Courtauld Institute of Art], 2002)

Frith, L. 'C. R. W. Nevinson and Art during the First World War' (unpublished master's thesis, Sheffield University, 1994)

Jezzard, A. 'The Sculptor Sir George Frampton' (unpublished doctoral thesis, University of Leeds, 1997)

Malvern, S. 'Art, Propaganda and Patronage: An History of the Employment of British War Artists, 1916-1919' (unpublished doctoral thesis, University of Reading, 1981)

Pitkin, A. 'The Critical Reception of Academic Military Art in Britain in the First World War' (unpublished master's thesis, London University [Courtauld Institute of Art], 1999)

Websites

Art from Different Fronts of World War One, by Roger Tolson (BBC History Trails: Wars and Conflict: Art and War: Art from the Frontline in World War One)
[http://www.bbc.co.uk/history/trail/wars_conflict/art/art_frontline_gal.shtml]
Works created by eye witness artists examined by Imperial War Museum's Head of Art, Roger Tolson.

Art of the First World War
[http://www.memorial-caen.fr/10EVENT/EXPO1418/gb/visite.html]
110 paintings from international collections to commemorate the 80th Anniversary of the end of the First World War. Under the patronage of UNESCO.

Imperial War Museum (IWM). *Concise Art Collection* [http://www.vads.ac.uk/collections/IWM.html]
Result of collaboration between VADS (Visual Arts Data Service) with the Documentation Manager of the Imperial War Museum Art Collection to develop a fully searchable on-line database of the Museum's concise Art Collection (which includes coverage of the work of the war artists).

Imperial War Museum (IWM). *The Fatal Salient*
[http://www.iwm.org.uk/upload/package/45/FatalSalient/index.htm]
Online exhibition about Harold Sandys Williiamson.

Millicent, Duchess of Sutherland Ambulance. [This item can be accessed in the menu for the website at:
[http://westfrontassoc.mtcdevserver.com/the-great-war/great-war-on-land/casualties-medcal/2383-millicent-duchess-of-sutherland-ambulance.html#sthash.YH7TUS6g.dpbs]
See also Article above by McEnroe and the Exhibition below entitled *The Hospital in the Oatfield* for further information related to the Duchess of Sutherland.

Vortex (University of the West of England, School of Creative Arts)
[http://www.vortex.uwe.ac.uk/index.htm]
This site provides essays, catalogues and other writing related to the representation of war and peace in the twentieth and twenty-first century with the aim of exploring "the monumental language of remembrance and commemoration, and the relationship between memorial landscapes and national identity".

War Memorials Trust. *Bibliography* [http://www.warmemorials.org/bibliography]
Provides the details of a selection of books related to war memorials, remembrance and commemoration.

Paintings

Remembering the War

The items selected below are examples of works in which memories of the war are evoked. Most of this selection represents examples of works (indicated with a + sign) which were officially commissioned[208]. A notable exception was the work of Stanley Spencer in the Sandham Memorial Chapel in Burghclere, Hampshire. His series of frescoes there were commissioned by Louis and Mary Behrend.

The works selected below are all from the period 1919-1939 but the influence of the Great War continued to be evident in some of the works of post 2nd world war artists as can be seen from a perusal of *Vortex* (http://www.vortex.uwe.ac.uk/index.htm)

The asterisked items below are held in the Imperial War Museum (IWM).

Bomberg, D. *Sappers at Work: A Canadian Tunneling Company*, second version (1919) [National Gallery of Canada, Ottawa]+
Oil painting on canvas.

Brangwyn, F. *A Tank in Action* (1925–6) [National Museum and Gallery of Wales, Cardiff]
Tempera on canvas.

Butler, Lady E. (née Thompson). *In Retreat from Mons: The Royal Horse Guards* (1920) [Durban Art Gallery]

Carline, R. *Gaza Seen from the Air, over British Lines on Ali Muntar Hill looking towards the Sea* (1919)*
Oil painting on canvas. In March 1920 Sydney and Richard Carline held an exhibition of their war paintings. Later, Sydney Carline went on to illustrate T. E. Lawrence's *Revolt in the Desert*.

Carline, S. W. *The Destruction of the Turkish Transport in the Gorge of the Wadi Fara, Palestine* (1920)*+
Oil painting on canvas.

Dodd, F. *Interrogation* (1919)*+
Tempera painting on canvas.

Gill, C. U. *Evening after a Push* (1919)*+
Oil painting on canvas. Gill served in France from 1915-1918. He was recruited as an official war artist in the last year of the war and all his paintings on the war were completed after the Armistice.

Hill, A. K. G. *Interior of a Dugout at Gavrelle* (1927)*
Oil painting on canvas. Hill was an Official War Artist on the Western Front from 1917-1919.

— *Fraternity* (1920)*
Oil painting on canvas.

— *Ruins between Burnafay Wood and Maricourt* (1918)*+
Oil painting on canvas.

Lamb, H. *Irish Troops in the Judaen Hills Surprised by a Turkish Bombardment* (1919)*+
Oil painting on canvas.

Lavery, J. *Army Post Office 3, Boulogne* (1919)*+
Oil painting on canvas.

— *The Cemetery, Etaples* (1919)* +
Oil painting on canvas.

---

[208] "The Department of Art [Imperial War Museum] holds the majority of works commissioned under the official war artists scheme set up by the Government during the First World War. Begun in 1916 mainly for propaganda purposes, the scheme eventually aimed much higher; at the creation of a record and a memorial to the Great War through paintings commissioned from the best and, on occasion, the most avant-garde, British artists of the day. These included Percy Wyndham Lewis, Paul Nash, CRW Nevinson, John Singer Sargent, Stanley Spencer and Sir William Orpen." (Extract from Imperial War Museum website)

Cultural Impacts

Lewis, P. W. *A Battery Shelled* (1919)* +
Oil painting on canvas.

Meninsky, B. *The Arrival of a Leave Train, Victoria Station, 1918* (1919)*
Oil painting on canvas.

Nash, P. *The Menin Road* (1919)*+
Oil painting on canvas.

Nevinson, C. R. W. *The Harvest of Battle* (1919)*+
Oil painting on canvas.

— *The Unending Cult of Human Sacrifice* (c. 1934)*
Oil painting on canvas.

Orpen, Sir W. *A Peace Conference at the Quai D'Orsay* (1919)*+
Oil painting on canvas.

— *The Signing of the Peace in the Hall of Mirrors, Versailles, 28 June 1919* (1919)*+
Oil painting on canvas.

— *To the Unknown British Soldier in France* (1921-1928)
Oil painting on canvas. The original painting depicted the draped coffin flanked by two ghostly figures of soldiers standing guard. There was such an outcry when it was exhibited in 1919 that Orpen was forced to paint out the soldiers.

Sargent, J. S. *Gassed* (1919)*+
Oil painting on canvas (seven feet high by twenty feet long). In mid 1918 Singer was commissioned to execute a painting for memorial purposes. This was arranged through both a formal invitation by the British War Memorials Committee, and a personal letter sent by Lloyd George. Following a visit to the Western Front with Henry Tonks in July 1918 he composed several studies for the subject he had chosen (i.e. soldiers blinded by gas being led in lines back to the hospital tents and the dressing stations) in preparation for the large canvas *Gassed* which was completed in 1919.

— *General Officers of World War I* (1922) [National Portrait Gallery]
Oil painting on canvas. This is one of the portraits commissioned by the financier Sir Abraham Bailey to commemorate the role of the army, the navy and politicians in bringing the First World War to a close. Sargent, who initially declined the commission, began work on the military group portrait on his return from America in August 1920.

Spencer, S. *The Resurrection of the Soldiers* (1928-29) [East wall of Sandham Memorial Chapel, Burghclere, Hampshire]
After the war Stanley Spencer was commissioned to paint decorative murals for the Sandham Memorial Chapel (see note 197) in Burghclere, Hampshire (1926-32). The cycle of scenes from everyday military life culminates in the altarpiece, *The Resurrection of the Soldiers*.

— *Travoys Arriving with Wounded at a Dressing Station at Smol, Macedonia, September 1916* (1919)*+
Oil painting on canvas.

Wyllie, H. *Artillery Observations: BE2C Machines over Hooge Ranging British Guns by Means of Wireless Trelegraphy, 1915* (1920)*
Oil painting on canvas.

— *Night Bombers Getting Off from Trezennes Aerodrome, 1917* (1920)*+
Oil painting on canvas.

Wyllie, W. L. *Destruction of the German Raider 'Leopard' by 'HMS Achilles' and 'HMS Dundee'* (1920)*
Oil painting on canvas

— *Loss of 'HMS Pathfinder', 5 September 1914* (1920)*
Oil painting on canvas

War Memorial Sculptures

Typically the public memorials erected after the war consisted of a list of hundreds, often thousands, of names of the dead of all ranks. There were also war memorials commissioned for erection in public places that incorporated, or consisted solely of, a figure or figures representative of the war's victims or participants. The listing below, with the exception of Jagger's *No-Man's Land* and Epstein's *The Risen Christ*, is a brief selection of some of the sculptors who produced works of the latter sort.

Epstein, Sir J. *The Risen Christ* (1917-1919)[209] [National Galleries of Scotland. Gallery of Modern Art]
Sculpture, bronze.

Frampton, Sir G. *Monument to Edith Cavell* (1920)
Granite and marble, St Martin's Place, London.

Jagger, C. S. *Monument of the Royal Artillery Regiment* (1925)
Stone and bronze, Hyde Park Corner, London.

— *No-Man's Land* (1919-1920) [Tate Collection]
Bronze relief. This work of Charles Jagger, who served with the army and was twice wounded, is a memorial relief depicting a 'listening post' (employed on the Western front in the Great War) that in the original plaster had appended to it a verse which was suppressed in the bronze because of uncertainty about whether or not the artist intended it to be ironic.

— *Great Western Railway War Memorial* (1922)
Incorporates a bronze figure by Charles Jagger. The stonework was designed by the architect Thomas S. Tait. Located at Paddington Station, London.

Kennington, E. *Memorial to the 24th Infantry Division* (1924)
Portland stone. Consists of the figures of three infantry soldiers with helmets, rifles and full kit, with a serpent at their feet, standing upon a three part columnar base. The figure to the left was modelled on the poet and writer Robert Graves. The memorial commemorates over 10,000 men who had been killed or listed as 'missing presumed dead' whilst serving with the 24th Infantry Division; it was unveiled on 4 October 1924 in an opening ceremony performed by Field Marshall Plumer and the Bishop of Southwark. Located in Battersea Park.

Ledward, G. *The Guards Memorial*, (1926)
The memorial is of portland stone and features five bronze figures of guardsmen all standing "at ease". Located in St James Park.

Mackenzie, T. *The Home Coming* (1922)
Bronze monument to the men of Cambridge who fought in the Great War. Located at the roundabout near the railway station in Cambridge.

Smith. G. H. T. *Bronze Reliefs* (1930)
Decorating the Cenotaph (architect: Lionel Baily Budden) in front of St George's Hall, Liverpool

Wood, D. *'David', Memorial of the Machine Gun Corps* (1925)
Bronze, Hyde Park Corner, London.

Exhibitions

The exhibitions listed below are related to mostly British artists who produced some works, either during the war or after, that recall the First World War in some fashion.

Black, J. *The Graphic Art of Eric Kennington* (London: College Art Collections, University College, London, 2001)
Exhibition catalogue to accompany the exhibition held at the Strang Print Room, University College, London, 3 October-14

---

[209] "The Risen Christ' began as a portrait of Epstein's friend, the composer Bernard van Dieren. It was begun in 1917 when van Dieren was ill, and Epstein wanted to make a mask of him looking 'spiritual and worn with suffering'. After making a mask from clay, the piece then developed into the figure of Christ. Work was temporarily put on hold when Epstein was enlisted in 1917 but continued a year later. The artist considered the figure to be an anti-war statement and declared that he would ideally like it to be remodelled and made hundreds of feet high as a 'mighty symbolic warning to all lands". [Caption of NGS Online Collection]

Cultural Impacts

December 2001.

Birmingham Museums & Art Gallery. *Art of the First World War from the Imperial War Museum* [IWM], *London: "Women: Mothers, Workers and Politicians, 1910-1920"* (Birmingham: Birmingham City Museum and Art Gallery 1992)
Catalogue of two exhibitions held concurrently at Birmingham Museums and Art Gallery, 27 February - 4 May 1992.

Blond Fine Art Ltd. *Ernest Procter: Drawings from the Trenches. Also Prints and Drawings from the First World War.* Catalogue for the Exhibition at Blond Fine Art, September 18 - October 11, 1980 (London: Blond Fine Art Ltd, 1980)

Bomberg, D. *David Bomberg 1890-1957: Centenary Exhibition, Works on Paper* (London: Gillian Jason Gallery, 1990)
Catalogue of an exhibition held at Gillian Jason Gallery, London, 28 November 1990 - 11 January 1991 and Plymouth City Museum and Art Gallery, 26 January - 10 March 1991. Text by Richard Cork.

— *Poems and Drawings from the First World War* (London: Gillian Jason Gallery, 1992)
Catalogue related to an exhibition entitled *David Bomberg Drawings, 1914-1919* held in London at the Gillian Jason Gallery in 1992. Includes essay by Richard Cork: 'Bomberg's war poetry'.

Brangwyn, Sir F. *Frank Brangwyn Centenary* (Cardiff: National Museum of Wales; Welsh Arts Council, 1967)
Catalogue of an exhibition organized jointly by the National Museum of Wales and the Welsh Arts Council to celebrate the 100th anniversary of the birth of Sir Frank Brangwyn. Exhibition held at the National Museum of Wales, 17 June - 16 July, 1967; National Library of Wales, Aberystwyth, 29 July - 26 August, 1967; Pembrokeshire County Museum, Haverfordwest, 9 - 30 Sept., 1967; Glynn Vivian Gallery, Swansea, 7 - 28 Oct., 1967; and Bangor Art Gallery, 25 Nov. - 16 Dec., 1967.

Canada House. *The Art of War 1914-18, 1939-45: An Exhibition of Paintings and Drawings by Canadian and British Artists produced during the two Great Wars* (London: Canadian Commission, 1994)
Catalogue of an exhibition held at Canada House, London 19 May-19 August 1994.; text by Laura Brandon.

Carline, S. W. and R. C. Carline. *The East: Egypt, Palestine, Mesopotamia, Persia, India,* [a catalogue of an exhibition of] a series of paintings, and drawings by Sydney W. and Richard Carline, March 1920 (London: William Marchant & Co., The Goupil Gallery, 1920)
This was an exhibition of their war paintings.

Compton, A., ed. *Charles Sargeant Jagger: War and Peace Sculpture* (London: Imperial War Museum, 1985)
Published on the occasion of the centenary exhibition 1885-1985, Imperial War Museum, 1 May - 29 September, 1985.

Cork, R. *A Bitter Truth: Avant-Garde Art and the Great War* (New Haven and London: Yale University Press in association with Barbican Art Gallery, 1994)
This book was in effect a catalogue of an exhibition organised by Richard Cork and held at the Altes Museum, Berlin in June 1994 and the Barbican Art Gallery, London, from 28 September - 11 December 1994.

— *David Bomberg* (London: Tate Gallery, 1988)
Catalogue of an exhibition held at the Tate Gallery 17 February - 8 May 1988.

— *David Bomberg 1890-1957: Centenary Exhibition, Works on Paper* (London: Gillian Jason Gallery, 1990)
Catalogue of an exhibition held at Gillian Jason Gallery, London, 28 November 1990 - 11 January 1991 and Plymouth City Museum and Art Gallery, 26 January - 10 March 1991. Text by Richard Cork.

— *Poems and Drawings from the First World War* (London: Gillian Jason Gallery, 1992)
Catalogue related to an exhibition entitled *David Bomberg Drawings, 1914-1919* held in London at the Gillian Jason Gallery in 1992. Includes essay by Richard Cork: 'Bomberg's war poetry'.

— *Vorticism and its Allies* (London: Arts Council of Great Britain, 1974)
Catalogue of an exhibition organised by Richard Cork in collaboration with the Arts Council of Great Britain, held at the Hayward Gallery, London, 27 March - 2 June 1974. Catalogue prepared by Richard Cork.

C. R .W. Nevinson, The Twentieth Century (London: Merrell Holberton in association with the Imperial War Museum, 1999)

Published to accompany the exhibition at the Imperial War Museum [IWM], London, Oct. 28, 1999 - Jan. 30, 2000 and the Yale Center for British Art, New Haven, Feb. 25 - May 7, 2000. Partial contents: *Utterly Tired of Chaos: The Life of C.R.W. Nevinson*, by Richard Ingleby ; *A Curious, Cold Intensity: C. R. W. Nevinson as a War Artist, 1914-1918*, by Jonathan Black; *The Rising City: Urban Themes in the Art and Writings of C. R. W. Nevinson*, by David Cohen; *C. R. W. Nevinson as a Printmaker*, by Gordon Cooke.

Cumming, R. *Artists At War, 1914-1918: Paintings and Drawings by Muirhead Bone, James McBey, Francis Dodd, William Orpen, Eric Kennington, Paul Nash and C.R.W. Nevinson* (Cambridge: Kettle's Yard Gallery, 1974)
Catalogue of an exhibition held at Kettle's Yard Gallery, Cambridge, 19 October -15 November 1974.

Edwards, P., and others. *Wyndham Lewis: Art and War* (London: Wyndham Lewis Memorial Trust in association with Lund Humphries, 1992)
Catalogue of an exhibition held June 25 to October 11, 1992, at the Imperial War Museum, London.

Fairclough, O., and others, eds. *Art in Exile: Flanders, Wales and the First World War* (Cardiff: National Museums & Galleries of Wales, 2002)
This catalogue was published in conjunction with the exhibition *Art in Exile: Flanders, Wales and the First World War* at the National Museums & Galleries of Wales in Cardiff (22 June - 15 September 2002).

Gresty, H. *C. R. W. Nevinson, 1889–1946: Retrospective Exhibition of Paintings, Drawings and Prints* (Cambridge: Kettle's Yard Gallery, 1988)
Catalogue of the touring exhibition shown first at Kettle's Yard, Cambridge, 10 September - 30 October 1988. Exhibition selected by Elizabeth Knowles and organised by Hilary Gresty.

Hildred, A. *C. R. W. Nevinson, War Paintings, 1914-1918* (Sheffield: Graves Art Gallery, 1972)
Catalogue, compiled by Anne Hildred, of an exhibition held at the Graves Art Gallery, Sheffield, 9th Sept. - 8th Oct. 1972

The Hospital in the Oatfield: The Art of Nursing in the First World War, New Exhibition to Honour Nurses in the First World War, 13th March – 26th October 2014.
[https://www.florence-nightingale.co.uk/resources/the-hospital-in-the-oatfield/?v=79cba1185463]
"The Florence Nightingale Museum will mark the centenary of the First World War with a special exhibition honouring the inspirational work of nurses in war-torn France. The exhibition centres on a series of remarkable paintings by Victor Tardieu of the field hospital run by the Society beauty, Millicent, Duchess of Sutherland. The exhibition explores the crucial role played by women in the battlefields of France and Belgium and shows the incredible innovation displayed by nurses under challenging and dangerous conditions". [The Museum's description of the exhibition]

Imperial War Museum [IWM]. *The Nation's War Paintings and other Records* (London: The Royal Academy of Arts, 1919)
2nd edition of catalogue of exhibition held 12 Dec. 1919 - 7 Feb. 1920, Royal Academy of Arts, London.

Imperial War Museum North. *Witness: Highlights of First World War Art*, an exhibition at Imperial War Museum North, 4 February 2006 - 23 April 2006 [http://www.iwm.org.uk/upload/pdf/Witness.pdf]
An online review of this exhibition with the title *Witness: Art of the First World War at IWM* was produced by Richard Moss on 14 February 2006 on the Culture24 website:
http://www.culture24.org.uk/history+%2526+heritage/war+%2526+conflict/world+war+one/art34159

Loftus, B. *Richard and Sydney Carline: An Exhibition of Their Paintings, Drawings and Watercolours executed for the Official War Artist Scheme during and after the First World War*, [held] 4 July - 9 September 1973 [at the Imperial War Museum] (London: Imperial War Museum, 1973)

Manchester Art Gallery. *The Nation's War Paintings from the Imperial War Museum* [Manchester: City of Manchester Art Gallery, 1920]
Catalogue of an exhibition held at the City of Manchester Art Gallery, March - April, 1920. "Consists of a selection of works from those recently on view in the Galleries of the Royal Academy in Burlington House" – preface.

— *Paintings and Drawings of the First World War*, (Manchester: City Art Gallery, 1964)
Catalogue of an exhibition held at the Manchester City Art Gallery, 18th September - 11th October 1964 , text by C. M. Mount.

Mark Gertler: A New Perspective (London: Ben Uri Gallery, 2002)
Catalogue of an exhibition held at the Ben Uri Gallery, the London Jewish Museum of Art, 30 September - 1 December, 2002. Includes an essay by Sarah MacDougall, a short text by the artist's son Luke Gertler, and texts by David J. Glasser

and Peter Gross.

Metropole Arts Centre. *The War Artists*. Memorial exhibition, New Metropole Arts Centre, The Leas, Folkestone, Aug 4th - Sept 18th (Folkestone: The Gallery, 1964)
Exhibition catalogue. Foreword by Sir Kenneth Clark.

— *The War Artists: A Selection of Oils, Watercolours and Drawings on Loan from the Imperial War Museum* (Folkestone: Arts Centre, 1979)
Catalogue of an exhibition held at the Arts Centre, New Metropole, Folkestone, 9 June - 8 July 1979.

Nash, P. and C. R. W. Nevinson. *Nash and Nevinson in War and Peace: The Graphic Work, 1914–20* (London: Ernest Brown & Phillips, 1977)
Catalogue of an exhibition by Paul Nash and Christopher Richard Wynne held by the Leicester Galleries at the Alpine Club Gallery, London, October 31 - November 19, 1977.

Nevinson, C. R. W. *C. R. W. Nevinson: The Great War and After* (London: Maclean Gallery, 1980)
Catalogue of an exhibition held at the Maclean Gallery, 6 February - 4 March 1980

Newcastle upon Tyne Polytechnic Art Gallery. *Artists and the Great War: An Exhibition of Pictures from the Collections of the Imperial War Museum [IWM]* (Newcastle upon Tyne: Newcastle upon Tyne Polytechnic Art Gallery, 1979)
Catalogue of an exhibition held 23 April - 18 May 1979 at Newcastle upon Tyne Polytechnic Art Gallery.

Nottingham University Art Gallery. *Base Details: British Artists of the First World War* (Nottingham: Nottingham University Art Gallery, 1972)
Catalogue of an exhibition held at Nottingham University Art Gallery, as part of the 'Nottingham Festival: University Summer Exhibition', from the 8th to the 23 July, 1972.

Parkin, M. *The Appalling Loss: An Exhibition of 1914-18 War Artists* (London: Michael Parkin Fine Art Ltd., 1973)
Exhibition held at the Parkin Gallery, 8 June - 14 July, 1973

Scottish National Gallery of Modern Art. *We Are Making a New World: Artists in the 1914-18 War; Paintings, Sculpture, Prints and Photographs from the Imperial War Museum, London* (Edinburgh: Scottish National Gallery of Modern Art, 1974)
Catalogue of an exhibition held at the Scottish National Gallery of Modern Art, Edinburgh, 12 Oct. - 10 Nov. 1974; Aberdeen Art Gallery and Museum, Aberdeen, 16 Nov.- 7 Dec. 1974; Dundee City Museum and Art Gallery, Dundee, 14 Dec. 1974 - 4 Jan. 1975.

Silber, E. and others. *Jacob Epstein: Sculpture and Drawings* (Leeds: Maney in association with the Henry Moore Centre for the Study of Sculpture, 1989)
Catalogue of an exhibition held a the Henry Moore Centre for the Study of Sculpture, Leeds City Art Galleries, 16 April – 21 June 1987 and the Whitechapel Art Gallery, London, 3 July - 13 September, 1987.

Spencer, Sir S. *Stanley in Macedonia*. [Catalogue of] an exhibition during the Cookham Festival 1971, 26 May to 6 June, at the Sir Stanley Spencer Memorial Gallery, Cookham (Cookham-on-Thames: Stanley Spencer Gallery, 1971)

Truth and Memory: British Art of the First World War. An exhibition held at the Imperial War Museum London from December 2014 to 8 March 2015

Verdi, R. *Apocalypse Then: Graphic Art and the Great War* (Birmingham: Barber Institute of Fine Arts, 2001)
Catalogue of an exhibition held at the Barber Institute of Fine Arts, Birmingham from 11 May - 11 November 2001.

Wadsworth, B. *Edward Wadsworth, 1889-1949* (Bradford: Bradford Art Galleries and Museums, 1989)
Catalogue of an exhibition to celebrate the centenary of his birth: Cartwright Hall, Bradford, 12 October 1989 - 14 January 1990; Camden Arts Centre, 14 March 1990 - 22 April 1990.

Yale, B. and M. Houlihan. *No Man's Land: Paintings of the Battlefields of the First World War*, by Brian Yale; historical perspective by Michael Houlihan (Wolverhampton: Wolverhampton Art Gallery, 1984)
Exhibition catalogue.

4.5 Music

Several classical works (see under **Compositions** below) written in the inter-war years by composers who had lived through the Great War reflected the emotions which their memory of that war had generated. In the case of Bliss[210] (who served throughout the war, initially in the Royal Fusiliers, 1914-17, and from 1917 to 1919 in the Grenadier Guards) and Vaughan Williams (who, in his early forties, served in the RAMC[211] in Northern France as an ambulance driver) these emotions resulted from their first-hand experience of the slaughter on the Western Front. Other composers who had lived through the war years as non-combatants also reacted emotionally in some sort of manner. The music of Frank Bridge[212], for example, was inspired by his pacifist convictions and memory of friends and colleagues who had been killed in action. John Foulds, Havergal Brian[213], Arnold Bax, Frederick Delius, Gustav Holst, Edward Elgar, and Benjamin Britten are examples of other non-combatants who reacted to the Great War in some of their music (see below under **Compositions**). In the music of Arnold Bax the memory of the war is primarily related to his feelings about the Easter Rising of 1916 and the subsequent execution of its leaders, some of whom he knew personally. In his *Cello Concerto* Elgar seems to be distancing himself from the mostly patriotic and propagandistic music he wrote during the war and expressing a lament not only for those who had died but also for a world he felt had vanished with the war.

Even after the Second World War the memory of the Great War was still being evoked in classical music. In 1961 Benjamin Britten, a lifelong pacifist, wrote his *War Requiem*[214]. Although in this work (dedicated to four friends who had been killed in the Second World War) he expresses the futility and senselessness of war generally he also had the Great War in mind when he placed texts from the traditional *Mass for the Dead* alongside some verse of Wilfred Owen, the Great War poet who was killed one week before the Armistice. In 2008 The Imperial War Museum (IWM) marked the 90th anniversary of the Armistice with a programme of exhibitions and events across its five branches. As part of its programme the Imperial War Museum (IWM), in association with the Royal Philharmonic Society, offered composition and music students a chance to mark this historic anniversary in a competition to write a piece of music for string quartet on the theme of '*In Memoriam*'. Five finalists (Benjamin Cox, Edward Nesbit, Richard Norris, Robert Peate and Duncan Ward) were chosen and their pieces were professionally recorded by the Solaris Quartet, the recordings becoming part of the Imperial War Museum's *In Memoriam: Remembering the Great War* exhibition (30 September 2008 to 6 September, 2009 at the Imperial War Museum in London) A panel of judges picked one overall winning piece for which the composer (Benjamin Cox) was awarded a prize of £500. After the exhibition closed in September 2009, all five pieces of music were placed in the Museum's digital Sound Archive where they can be accessed and listened to by the public at the Museum and online.

Autobiographies, Biographies

Anderson, R. *Elgar* (London: Dent, 1993)
/
Beecham, Sir. T. *Frederick Delius*, revised edn (London: Severn House, 1975)
Contains a discography compiled by Malcolm Walker.

---

[210] "… the death of his brother Kennard in action had a long-lasting effect on him, and the futility of war was engraved on his personality. Its deepest musical expression is the choral symphony *Morning Heroes* (1930); but it also surfaces in sudden shifts in his music to threatening, malevolent moods, for example in the interlude 'Through the Valley of the Shadow of Death' in *Meditations on a Theme by John Blow* (1955)…" [Extracted from Andrew Burn, 'Bliss, Sir Arthur Edward Drummond (1891–1975)', *Oxford Dictionary of National Biography*, Oxford University Press, Sept 2004; online edn, Oct 2009].

[211] Like many veterans he rarely referred to his wartime experiences in later years, but the harrowing scenes encountered daily in the RAMC undoubtedly left deep psychological scars, some of which are hinted at in his later music.

[212] The First World War had a deep influence on Bridge's life and music. A pacifist himself (and in any case too old to be involved in the fighting) he was much affected by the death on the battlefield of many of his friends and colleagues, including Thomas Morris, first violinist in the English String Quartet, and his fellow composer Ernest Farrar, to whose memory Bridge later dedicated his *Piano Sonata* (1921-24).

[213] He joined the army as a volunteer but saw no service before he was invalided out with a hand injury in 1915.

[214] Composed in 1961 in response to the commission he received in relation to the reconsecration of Coventry Cathedral.

Bliss, Sir A. E. D. *As I Remember*, 2nd rev. and enl. edn (London: Thames Publishing, 1989)

Bray, T. *Frank Bridge: A Life in Brief* (2004-13)
[http://www.trevor-bray-music-research.co.uk/Bridge%20LinB/introduction.html]

Carpenter, H. *Benjamin Britten: A Biography* (London: Faber, 1992)

Day, J. *Vaughan Williams*, 3rd edn (Oxford: Oxford University Press, 1998)

Eastaugh, E. *Havergal Brian: The Making of a Composer* (London: Harrap, 1976)

Foreman, L. *Bax: A Composer and His Times*, 3rd edn (Woodbridge: Boydell & Brewer, 2007)

Holst, I. *Gustav Holst: A Biography*, 2nd edn (Oxford: Oxford University Press, 1969)

Kennedy, M. *Portrait of Elgar*, 3rd edn (Oxford: Clarendon Press, 2004)

MacDonald, M. *John Foulds and his Music* (London: Kahn & Averill, 1989)

McVeagh, E. E. *Edward Elgar: His Life and Music*, edited by Diana M. McVeagh (London: J. M. Dent, 1955)

Moore, J. N. *Edward Elgar: A Creative Life* (Oxford: Oxford University Press, 1984)

Nettel, R. *Havergal Brian and His Music*, with a catalogue of his music by Lewis Foreman (London: Dobson, 1976)

Payne, A. *Frank Bridge: Radical and Conservative*, rev. edn (London: Thames Publishing 1999)

Short, M. *Gustav Holst: The Man and His Music* (Oxford: Oxford University Press, 1990)

Vaughan Williams, U. *R. V. W.: A Biography of Ralph Vaughan Williams* (London: Oxford University Press, 1964)

Books

Carley, L. ed.. *Frederick Delius: Music, Art and Literature* (Aldershot, Hants: Ashgate, 1998)

Cooke, M. ed. *The Cambridge Companion to Benjamin Britten* (Cambridge: Cambridge University Press, 1999)

Evans, P. *The Music of Benjamin Britten*, rev. edn (Oxford: Clarendon Press, 1996)

Holst, I. *The Music of Gustav Holst*, 2nd edn (London: Oxford University Press, 1968)

— *The Music of Gustav Holst and Holst's Music Reconsidered* (London: Oxford University Press, 1968)
This work consists of a 3rd rev. edn (slightly shortened version) of *The Music of Gustav Holst*, followed by a new work in which Imogen Holst brings her long experience of editing and performing the music to bear on certain aspects not discussed in the earlier book.

Hughes, M. and R. A. Stradling. *The English Musical Renaissance, 1860-1940: Constructing a National Music*, 2nd edn (Manchester: Manchester University Press, 2001)

Monk, R. ed. *Edward Elgar: Music and Literature* (Aldershot: Scolar Press, 1993)

Redwood, C. ed. *A Delius Companion*, rev. edn (London: J. Calder, 1980)

— *An Elgar Companion* (Ashbourne: Moorland Publishing, 1983)

Watkins, G. *Proof through the Night: Music and the Great War* (Berkeley: University of California Press, 2002)

Articles

Mansell, J. G. 'Musical Modernity and Contested Commemoration at the Festival of Remembrance, 1923-1927', *Historical Journal*, 52 (2009), 433-454

Saylor, E. '"It's Not Lambkins Frisking At All": English Pastoral Music and the Great War', *Musical Quarterly*, 91 (2008), 39-59

Compositions

Bax, Sir A. E. T. *First Symphony* (1921-22)
The stormy first and gloomy second symphonies have been regarded as Bax's mature reflections on the war, albeit perhaps in the context of the Easter Rising of 1916 which inspired him to compose *In Memoriam* [see **section 3.4.3** of **Part 3 (The War Years)**] under **Contemporary Compositions**) in the same year.

— *Second Symphony* (1924-26)
A particularly dark work, with an almost apocalyptic climax in the finale, followed by a sense of utter desolation. At one point it alludes to *In Memoriam* of 1916.

Bliss, Sir A. E. D. *Meditations on a Theme by John Blow* (1955)
Includes an interlude 'Through the Valley of the Shadow of Death' which is regarded as an example of *Bliss*'s musical expression of the deeply traumatic effect on him of his experience of the Great War.

— *Morning Heroes* (1930)
One of the most deeply personal of Bliss's works, this choral symphony (a production of which was performed at the Norwich Festival in 1930) was written as a tribute to those who died in the Great War.

Brian, W. H. *The Tigers* (1930)
Satirical anti-war opera which opens with a quasi-naturalistic depiction of a bank holiday carnival at the beginning of the Great War and proceeds to chronicle the misadventures of an enlisted regiment training on the home front.

Bridge, F. *Oration* (1930)
All Bridge's convictions and emotions about the Great War were enshrined in the *Oration* for solo cello and orchestra. Bridge apparently changed the title from *Concerto Elegiaco* to *Oration* because he wanted to make clear that it was an outcry against the futility of war.

— *Piano Sonata* (1921–24)
Bridge wrote this work in memory of his fellow composer Ernest Farrar who was killed in action in the Great War.

Britten, E. B. *War Requiem* (1961)
Britten's lifelong pacifist and anti-militarist attitude is evident in a number of his compositions but particularly in his *War Requiem* where he very clearly expresses his feelings about the futility and senselessness of war by placing texts from the traditional Latin *Mass for the Dead* alongside the bitter poetry of Wilfred Owen[215].

Cox, B. *In Memoriam* (2008)
Winner of the Imperial War Museum's 'In Memoriam' music competition (see note about it in the introductory preamble above).

Delius, F. *Requiem* (1916)
Between 1913 and 1916 Delius composed his *Requiem*, dedicated 'to the memory of all young Artists fallen in the war'. It was not performed until 1922.

Elgar, Sir E. W. *Cello Concerto* (1919)
The concerto seems like a personal requiem for a world that Elgar felt had vanished with the war. It was written in 1919, and when listening to it one seems to hear an elegy for those who died in the Great War.

---

[215] On the frontispiece of the score, Britten quotes Owen: "My subject is War, and the pity of War. The Poetry is in the pity . . . All a poet can do today is warn".

Cultural Impacts

Foulds, J. H. *The World Requiem* (1919-1921)
Composed in memory of the war dead of all nations. It was recommended for national performance by the committee of the British Music Society and adopted by the British Legion as the musical component of the Armistice Night commemorations. Performed annually at the Royal Albert Hall during 1923–6 by a chorus and orchestra conducted by Foulds, it became a constituent part of the first Festivals of Remembrance in Britain.

Holst, G. *Ode to Death* (1919)
After the war Gustav Holst composed *Ode to Death* on lines of a poem by Walt Whitman. Whitman's poem commemorated the death of Lincoln, but Holst more probably had in mind the waste and futility of the Great War, then just ended.

Nesbit, E. *Each Slow Dusk* (2008)
Finalist in the Imperial War Museum's In Memoriam music competition (see note about it in introduction above).

Norris, R. *In Memoriam* (2008)
Finalist in the Imperial War Museum's In Memoriam music competition (see note about it in introduction above).

Peate, R. *In Memoriam* (2008)
Finalist in the Imperial War Museum's In Memoriam music competition (see note about it in introduction above).

Vaughan Williams, R. *Pastoral Symphony* (Symphony no. 3) (1921)
The *Pastoral Symphony*, ideas for which had begun to form as early as 1916, when Vaughan Williams was in France with the Royal Army Medical Corps[216], was written as a result of his experiences during the war and has been likened to a 'war requiem' without words. Reminders of the war are clearly evident in the work as, for example, in the evocation of an out-of-tune 'bugle call' for a natural trumpet in the slow movement and the sudden inclusion in the last movement of the off-stage vocal line which is like a lament for the dead. While it is atmospheric of the bleak war ridden landscape of France it also evokes the English landscape[217] and reflects a sense of peace after the harrowing effects of war

Ward, D. *Eugene Cruft's Radio* (2008)
Finalist in the IWM's In Memoriam music competition (see note about it in introduction above)

---

[216] To his future wife, Ursula, he confided in 1939: "It's not really lambkins frisking at all, as most people take for granted... It's really wartime music - a great deal of it incubated when I used to go up night after night with the ambulance wagon at Écoivres and we went up a steep hill and there was a wonderful Corot-like landscape in the sunset".

[217] Vaughan Williams wrote that he composed the music to convey 'the song of the soldier far from home and thinking of a landscape he loves'.

Part 5: APPENDICES

1. Research Aids

The main aim of this appendix is to help people who want to pursue their interest in the Great War in greater depth to find their way around the sort of bibliographical, reference, and other sources which could be useful for this purpose and that are likely to be accessible via any of the academic and major public reference libraries they are able to use or that they can access from their home over the internet.

1.1 Bibliographical Tools

1.1.1 Library Catalogues

Apart from the catalogues of the major 'national libraries' of the world, such as the British Library and the Library of Congress, there are a large range of catalogues of other types of libraries, such as university, public, and special libraries. Apart from providing information about where particular books can be found they are useful for obtaining accurate verification of the bibliographical details of books. Nowadays, most of these libraries have catalogues which are freely accessible on the internet. There are also online catalogues like *Copac* (see below) which are particularly useful to the researcher as an aid to discovering the whereabouts of particular books in a whole range of major academic, special and national libraries in the United Kingdom and Ireland; for the national libraries of Europe *The European Library* (see below) serves a similar purpose.

The following entries represent a selection of web sites giving access to important catalogues:

British Library Catalogues [https://www.bl.uk/catalogues-and-collections]
This website provides access to the main British Library catalogues.

CONUL [http://www.conul.ie/]
CONUL is a consortium of Ireland's main research libraries. Its mission is to develop and improve the library and information services of the CONUL members through the exchange of experience and the organisation of cooperative activities.

Copac [https://copac.jisc.ac.uk/]
A union catalogue, providing free access to the merged online catalogues of many major University, Specialist and National libraries in the UK and Ireland, including the British Library. Summaries are provided for some of the items recorded.

Inform25 [https://www.search25.ac.uk/]
A union catalogue of the libraries within the M25 Consortium, a collaborative organisation that works to improve library and information services within the M25 region and across the East and Southeast.

International Institute of Social History [http://www.iisg.nl]
This site outlines the collections available from the International Institute of Social History (IISH). There is an on-line catalogue, which can be searched through a web or telnet interface, providing records of material (including books, periodicals, posters, photographs and archives) which are held at the International Institute of Social History, the Netherlands Economics History Archive and the Dutch Press Museum. The site also has an index of archives which provides descriptions of all the archive collections of the IISH. These are provided as alphabetical lists of Dutch, non-Dutch and all archives. The site also provides links to HTML and SGML inventories of these collections. It is possible to search these archival collections. Other features of the site include descriptions, lists and databases of collections, details of recent acquisitions and links to digitized collections. The site has a virtual information desk and details of microfilms of IISH collections.

Library of Congress [https://www.loc.gov/]
The Library of Congress is the U.S.A.'s oldest federal cultural institution, and it serves as the research arm of Congress. It is also the largest library in the world, with more than 126 million items on approximately 530 miles of bookshelves. The collections include nearly 19 million books, 2.6 million recordings, 12 million photographs, 4.8 million maps, and 56 million

manuscripts.

London Library [http://www.londonlibrary.co.uk/]
The London Library's Online Catalogue currently contains details of all books and periodicals acquired since 1950, with earlier material being added daily as part of the Retrospective Cataloguing Project. For full coverage of pre-1950 acquisitions it is necessary to consult the printed catalogues [i.e. *Catalogue*, 2 vols covering accessions to 1913 [And] *Supplements* 1-3, covering accessions, 1913-1953 [And] *Subject Index*, 4 vols, covering accessions, 1909-1953].

RASCAL (Research and Special Collections Available Locally) [http://www.rascal.ac.uk/]
RASCAL is an electronic gateway to research resources in Ireland. You can use this web-site to search and browse information about the wide range of research and special collections held in libraries, museums and archives across the region. The Directory consists of comprehensive descriptions of collections available to researchers in the Humanities and Social Sciences recording details of content, location, format, and access. Links to institutions' on-line catalogues and other digital resources are provided where appropriate.

Women's Library [http://www.lse.ac.uk/Library/Collections/Collection-highlights/The-Womens-Library]
The Women's Library is a cultural centre, housing the most extensive collection of women's history in the UK. The Women's Library has an online catalogue, Millennium, for most published materials, and also has a brief archives guide for its archival collections. A full range of finding aids for other parts of the collection are available in the Reading Room.

1.1.2 Book Trade Catalogues

Nowadays most booksellers and publishers have websites where searchable listings of the books they have on sale can be found. Quite often the items listed are annotated with a review or product description. With the exception of *Amazon*, which, among other activities, is a bookseller comprehensively covering all subjects, the selection below is a list of some of the publishers in the UK specialising in war and military history.

Amazon [http://www.amazon.co.uk/]

Brassey's Defence Publishers [https://openlibrary.org/publishers/Brassey's_Defence_Publishers /]

Frank Cass Publishers [http://www.frankcass.com/] opens as [https://www.routledge.com/strategicstudies]

Helion and Co. Ltd [http://www.helion.co.uk/]

Leo Cooper Ltd (see Pen and Sword)

Naval and Military Press [http://www.naval-military-press.com/]

Osprey Publishing [http://www.ospreypublishing.com/]

Pen and Sword [http://www.pen-and-sword.co.uk/]
Born out of the Leo Cooper Ltd imprint and its backlist [http://isbndb.com/d/publisher/leo_cooper_ltd.html]

1.1.3 Bibliographies

The following items represent a selection of printed and online bibliographies, some general, some in the broad area of History, and in the case of items listed below under **Printed Services** mostly in the specialized area of the Great War.

1.1.3.1 Printed Services

Bayliss, G. *Bibliographic Guide to the two World Wars: An Annotated Survey of English-Language Reference Materials* (London: Bowker, 1977)

British Museum. Department of Printed Books. *A Subject Index of Books Relating to the European War 1914-1918*, acquired by the British Museum, 1914-1920 (London: Printed by order of the Trustees, 1922)
Available online at http://openlibrary.org/authors/OL18620A/British_Museum._Dept._of_Printed_Books

Appendix 1

Bulkley, M. E. *Bibliographical Survey of Contemporary Sources for the Economic and Social History of the War* (Oxford: Clarendon Press, 1922)
Contains British publications, with a few American and foreign books included. Arranged under subjects, with author and subject index.

Enser, A.G. S. *A Subject Bibliography of the First World War*, 2nd edn (Aldershot: Gower, 1990)

Falls, C. B. *War Books: An Annotated Bibliography of Books about the Great War*, with a new introduction and additional entries by R. J. Wyatt, new edn (London: Greenhill Books, 1989)
Previous edn published as: *War Books: A Critical Guide*, London: P. Davies, 1930.

Grieves, K. 'Britain at War, 1914-1918', *The Historian*, 27 (1990), 10-12
A brief critical survey of a selection of works related to Britain and the Great War.

Hanham, H. J. *Bibliography of British History, 1851-1914* (Oxford: Clarendon Press, 1976)

Higham, R. D. S., ed. *A Guide to the Sources of British Military History*; sponsored by the Conference of British Studies (London: Routledge & Kegan Paul, 1972)

Jordan, G., ed. *British Military History: A Supplement to Robin Higham's "Guide to the Sources"* (New York: Garland, 1988)

Lange, F. W. T and W. T. Berry. *Books on the Great War: An Annotated Bibliography of Literature issued during the European Conflict*, with a preface by R.A. Peddie, 4 vols (London: Grafton, 1915-1916)

Noffsinger, J. P. *World War I Aviation: A Bibliography of Books in English, French, German, and Italian*, with a price list supplement, rev. edn (London: Scarecrow Press, 1997)

Prothero, G. W. *Catalogue of War Publications Comprising Works Published to June 1916* (London: Murray, 1917)

— *Select Analytical List of Books Concerning the Great War* (London: HMSO, 1923)

Robbins, K., ed. *A Bibliography of British History, 1914-1989* (Oxford: Clarendon Press, 1996)

Simpson, K. 'An Annotated Bibliography of the British Army, 1914-1918', in *A Nation in Arms: A Social Study of the British Army in the First World War*, ed. by I. Beckett and K. Simpson (Manchester: Manchester University Press, 1985; repr. London: Donovan, 1990)

Smith, M. J. *World War I in the Air: A Bibliography and Chronology* (Metuchen, N.J.: Scarecrow Press, 1977)

1.1.3.2 Online Services

Bibliography of British and Irish History
An authoritative guide to what has been written about British and Irish history from the Roman period to the present day. Previously known as the *Royal Historical Society Bibliography*; now published under the new title as a partnership between the Royal Historical Society, the Institute of Historical Research and Brepols Publishers. Includes records from partner projects: *London's Past Online* and *Irish History Online*. Subscriptions are available to institutions and individuals. Accessible via http://www.brepolis.net/

British National Bibliography (http://www.bl.uk/bibliographic/natbib.html)
The national bibliography (operating since 1950) records the publishing activity of the United Kingdom and the Republic of Ireland via a system of legal deposit (i.e. UK and Irish publishers are obliged by law to send a copy of all new publications, including serial titles, to the Legal Deposit Office of the British Library). Traditionally limited primarily to printed publications it has more recently been extended to include electronic publications following the extension of legal deposit to this class of material in 2003. The BNB also contains details of forthcoming books. Under the Cataloguing-in-Publication Programme (CIP) information on new titles appears up to 16 weeks ahead of the announced publication date. Advance information on well over 50,000 titles each year is provided in this way.

History Guide (Netzwerk Internetressourcen Geschichte (Network Subject Gateways History)

[http://www.historyguide.de]
The *History Guide* is a subject gateway to scholarly relevant websites in history maintained in cooperation with Netzwerk Internetressourcen Geschichte (Network Subject Gateways History).

History On-Line (https://www.history.ac.uk/history-online/)
History On-Line is a section of the Institute of Historical Research (IHR) website. It provides information about and for historians. It publishes details of university lecturers in the UK and the Republic of Ireland (Teachers), current and past historical research (Theses), digital history projects (Projects), new books and journals from a range of leading publishers (Books, Journals) and sources of funding available for researchers (Grants). The database also provides details of history libraries and collections and digital research tools for historians. It currently holds more than **75,000 records**, and new material is added regularly..

Irish History Online (http://www.irishhistoryonline.ie/)
An authoritative guide (in progress) to what has been written about Irish history from earliest times to the present. It was established in association with the *Royal Historical Society Bibliography of British and Irish History* (of which it is now the Irish component) and *London's Past Online*. Includes articles from journals, both national and local history journals, and collective volumes. Searches can be made by author, by subject, by publication details, or by period covered.

London's Past Online: A Bibliography of London History
This bibliography has now been incorporated into the subscription-only *Bibliography of British and Irish History* (q.v.)

Royal Historical Society Bibliography (http://www.royalhistoricalsociety.org/respubs.php)
From 1 January 2010 this bibliographical service operated under a new name - *Bibliography of British and Irish History* (see record above) – and as partnership between the Royal Historical Society, the Institute of Historical Research and Brepols Publishers.

1.1.4 Theses

Information about this sort of material is provided by comprehensive indexes (e.g. *Dissertation Abstracts* and *Index to Theses*) or guides which provide links to the relevant resources which are available (e.g. British Library's *EthOS: e-theses online service*). At a more specialised or local level the Institute of Historical Research (via *History Online*) and some universities have on their websites sections on completed theses and theses in progress. Some periodicals in specialised areas such as history, etc, also occasionally include a section listing theses.

British Library. *EthOS: e-theses online service* [https://ethos.bl.uk/About.do /]

Dissertation Abstracts
(https://www.proquest.com/products-services/dissertations/Dissertations-Abstract-International.html)
The largest single repository of graduate dissertations and theses. Includes 4 million works – grows by 130K each year. International scope – deposits from universities in 88 countries.

EthOS (Electronic Theses Online Service) [http://ethos.bl.uk]
The EthOS e-theses service is delivered by the British Library on behalf of Higher Education under a shared service arrangement. For further information about this service see next entry.

— EthOS Toolkit [http://ethostoolkit.cranfield.ac.uk/tiki-index.php]
"EThOS aims to enable end-users to access the full text of electronically stored UK theses, in secure format, via a single Web interface. The toolkit shows how theses produced by students at your institution can be accessed, via EThOS, from the British Library or from your institutional (or consortium) repository." [Extract from website introduction]

History Online [http://www.history.ac.uk/history-online/theses]
The online information about UK theses completed and theses in progress in the area of history has been provided from information supplied by university registrars, secretaries of faculty boards and heads of departments. A published printed version of this information is provided in *Historical Research for Higher Degrees in the UK* which is issued each year in May. Retrospective volumes of this publication covering theses completed from 1901 onwards are available.

ProQuest Dissertations and Theses – UK and Ireland [https://capitadiscovery.co.uk/port/items/506518]
This database is the most comprehensive available record of theses accepted for higher degrees by universities in the United Kingdom and Ireland, since 1716. It includes bibliographic listings for content for 1950-1986 and abstracts for content since 1986. Access is via personal or institutional subscription. This particular website relates to the University of

Appendix 1

Portsmouth's Library's holding of the database. Several other UK university libraries also have this database.

1.1.5 Newspapers

1.1.5.1 Directories

Tercentenary Handlist of English and Welsh Newspapers, Magazines and Reviews, 1620-1920 (London: The Times, 1920)

Newspaper Press Directory, 1846-
Known under this title[218] for many years, eventually becoming briefly known as *Benn's Press Directory* but ultimately as *Benn's Media Directory incorporating Benn's Press Directory*. The press directory covers UK newspapers and the press overseas.

UlrichsWeb Global Serials Directory [http://www.ulrichsweb.com/ulrichsweb/faqs.asp]
The authoritative online source of bibliographic and publisher information on more than 300,000 periodicals of all types - academic and scholarly journals, Open Access publications, peer-reviewed titles, popular magazines, newspapers, newsletters, and more from around the world. Detailed bibliographic records provide data such as print and electronic ISSN, title, publisher, online availability, subject area, language, abstracting and indexing coverage, list prices, searchable tables of contents, and full-text reviews. Access via personal or corporate subscription. Also available in a printed version which can be consulted in many major libraries.

Willings Press Guide, 1874-
Main sequence of this UK directory covers newspapers, periodicals and annuals in one alphabetic order and also includes substantial sections recording overseas newspapers and periodicals

1.1.5.2 Catalogues of Holdings

The British Library Newspaper Library Catalogue
[https://www.bl.uk/subjects/news-media]
The British Library's major collections of **British and overseas newspapers** (also including popular magazines, trade papers and comics) can be searched via the above web address. Printed versions of the newspaper catalogue (i.e. *Catalogue of the Newspaper Library, Colindale*, compiled by P. E. Allen, 8 vols, London: British Library, 1975, and *The British Library Newspaper Library Catalogue Supplement*, 2 vols, London: British Library,1995) can also be consulted in some major libraries. [See also *The British Newspaper Archive* in section 1.1.5.3 below]

HOSNILL XVII: A Handlist of Selected Newspaper Holdings, National, Regional and Foreign, in London Public Libraries, 17th edn (Croydon: Croydon Libraries, Museums and Arts, Reference and Information Service, 2000)

1.1.5.3 Indexes to Articles

The British Newspaper Archive [http://www.britishnewspaperarchive.co.uk/]
"The British Newspaper Archive is a partnership between the British Library and BrightSolid online publishing to digitise up to 40 million newspaper pages from the British Library's vast collection over the next 10 years. All searching is free on this site but it costs to view images in the viewer ... There are both Subscription and Credit Packages available to best suit your needs. If you do not have a valid package you will be asked to register with a valid email address and then purchase a Package before being able to view images." [extract from website introduction]

The Guardian Digital Archive [https://www.theguardian.com/gnm-archive]
This archive will eventually contain the digital reproduction of every page, article and advert published in the *Guardian* (since 1821) and the *Observer* (since 1791 – the oldest Sunday paper in the world). As a result it is possible to search, browse, save and print articles and adverts from the *Digital Archive*. Searching is free of charge. However, if the full text or a print out of material is required it is necessary to subscribe to a timed access pass (24 hours, three days or a month). During the purchased time subscribers are free to search and print as much as they like – there are no restrictions on downloads.

The Illustrated London News Historical Archive, 1842-2003
[https://www.gale.com/intl/c/illustrated-london-news-historical-archive]
The *Illustrated London News Historical Archive* gives students and researchers unprecedented online access to the entire run of the *ILN* from its first publication on 14 May 1842 to its last in 2003. Each page has been digitally reproduced in full colour

---

[218] Originally published by C. Mitchell under whose name it was formerly known.

and every article and caption is full-text searchable with hit-term highlighting and links to corresponding illustrations. Facsimiles of articles and illustrations can be viewed, printed and saved either individually or in the context of the page in which they appear. Wherever possible Special Numbers covering special events such as coronations or royal funerals have been included. Researchers who are members of an institution which takes out an institutional subscription to the archive will be able to gain free access to it.

The Sunday Times Digital Archive, 1822-2016 [https://www.gale.com/intl/c/sunday-times-digital-archive]
Researchers who are members of an institution which takes out an institutional subscription to the archive will be able to gain free access to it.

The Times Literary Supplement Historical Archive, 1902-2013 [https://www.gale.com/intl/c/the-times-literary-supplement-historical-archive]
Researchers can access this online archive as an individual and purchase a 48 hr or 7 day pass. Researchers who are members of an institution which has taken out an institutional subscription to the archive will be able to gain free access to it.

The Times Literary Supplement Index: 1902-1939, 2 vols (Reading: Newspaper Archive Developments Ltd., 1978)

— *1940-1980*, 3 vols (Reading: Research Publications Ltd., 1982)

— *1981-1985*, 2 vols (Reading: Research Publications Ltd., 1986)

The Times Digital Archive, 1785-2012 [https://www.gale.com/intl/c/the-times-digital-archive]
Full-text image online archive of every page published by *The Times* (London) from 1785-2006. The text within the images is fully searchable at the article level. Users can easily search news articles, obituaries, advertising and classifieds - virtually everything that appeared in the newspaper. Results are displayed at the article level and subscribers may view the article - or the full page upon which it appeared. Includes 8 million articles spanning 200 years. Available free in a number of public libraries. Also available free to members of some academic institutions.

1.1.6 Periodicals

1.1.6.1 Abstracting and Indexing Services

The task of tracking down articles in periodicals is well served by the following **on-line** bibliographical services. All of them provide the facility to view or, if desired, to download, the full text of articles directly or via online links. A number of them are only accessible to individuals via institutions which have purchased site licences for their use.

BHI: British Humanities Index [http://www.proquest.co.uk/en-UK/catalogs/databases/detail/bhi-set-c.shtml]
An international abstracting and indexing tool for research in the humanities, BHI indexes over 370 internationally respected humanities journals and weekly magazines published in the UK and other English speaking countries, as well as quality newspapers published in the UK. Regular monthly updates ensure subscribers can retrieve the latest material on a wide range of arts and humanities subjects, aided by a completely interactive thesaurus and the capability to link to electronic full text of many journal articles. Accessible to members of some public libraries, academic institutions, and corporate bodies.

British Library Direct [https://ondemand.bl.uk/onDemand/home]
A searchable database of over 20,000 journals (covering most subjects, languages and places of publication - around 9 million records) from which full texts of items can be purchased. Purchasers can choose the delivery time and the format which best suit their needs.

Historical Abstracts [https://www.ebsco.com/products/research-databases/historical-abstracts]
Originated with ABC-Clio's database (see record below entitled *Historical Abstracts: Bibliography of the World's Historical Literature,* Santa Barbara, California: ABC-Clio, 1955-2007) and was subsequently taken over by EBSCO which makes it available as an online subscription database restricted to institutions with a site license to it. The latter database provides abstracts of scholarly literature on the history of the world from 1450 to the present (excluding North America[219]) published

---

[219] This area is covered by the EBSCO's online database *America: History and Life* (restricted to institutions with a site license for it). This provides an Index and abstracts of literature covering the history and culture of the United States and Canada, from prehistory to the present. For further details see: http://www.ebscohost.com/thisTopic.php?marketID=1&topicID=838

Appendix 1

since 1955. Over 20,000 new abstracts and citations to journal articles, books, and dissertations are added to the database annually.

Humanities and Social Sciences Index Retrospective: 1907-1984 [https://www.ebsco.com/products/research-databases/humanities-social-sciences-index-retrospective-1907-1984]
Accessible only to members of some public libraries and academic institutions. This database indexes 747 periodicals; some 800,000 articles, including books reviews. It provides online coverage of these printed indexes:
International Index: 18 volumes, 1907 - March 1965
Social Sciences & Humanities Index: 9 volumes April 1965 – March 1974
Humanities Index: 10 volumes: April 1974 – March 1984

Ingenta Connect [http://www.ingentaconnect.com/]
IngentaConnect offers free searching online of one of the most comprehensive collections of academic and professional research articles, books, monographs, reports, statistics - some 4 million articles from 11,000 publications. Provides abstracts. Full texts can be downloaded via subscription or pay-per-view.

JSTOR [http://www.jstor.org]
Offers a high quality, interdisciplinary archive to support scholarship and teaching. It includes archives of over one thousand leading academic journals across the humanities, social sciences, and sciences, as well as select monographs and other materials valuable for academic work. The entire corpus is full-text searchable, offers search term highlighting, includes high-quality images, and is interlinked by millions of citations and references. Accessible to members of some public libraries, academic institutions, and corporate bodies.

Project Muse [http://muse.jhu.edu/]
Currently, *Project Muse* provides full-text access to current content from over 400 titles in the humanities and social sciences representative of nearly 100 not-for-profit publishers, under an agreement with the Johns Hopkins University Press. Most of the journals are available online from 1995 or 1996 onwards (the earliest date back to 1993), and new publications are added to the database each year, The site provides a sophisticated search engine and allows browsing by title and subject area. Electronic journal articles feature hypertext links, variable-size illustrations, and full bibliographical details.

Social Sciences Index Retrospective: 1907-1983 [https://www.ebscohost.com/archives/atla-monographs/social-sciences-index-retrospective]
Accessible only to members of some public libraries and academic institutions. This database indexes some 1,000,000 articles, including book reviews. It provides online coverage of these indexes:
International Index: 18 volumes, 1907 - March 1965
Social Sciences & Humanities Index: 9 volumes April 1965 – March 1974
Social Sciences Index: 9 volumes April 1974 – March 1983

Web of Knowledge [http://wok.mimas.ac.uk/about]
Provides a single route of access to Thomson Reuters's products subscribed to by an individual institution. It includes *Web of Science*; *Journal Citation Reports*; *Current Contents Connect*; *Derwent Innovations Index* and many others. This platform provides a unique way of searching, including the ability to perform an 'All Database' search on the content of multiple searchable products. One of its products, **Web of Science**, includes among its databases *Social Sciences Citation Index* (1970-) and *Arts and Humanities Citation Index* (1975-) which between them cover the full range of subjects in their fields. Coverage is updated weekly. Where the original publication has an abstract, these have been included in the records from 1992 in the case of *Social Sciences Citation Index* and from 2000 in the case of *Arts and Humanities Citation Index*. Includes a linkage service which links between WOK resources and electronic full text.

Zetoc: Electronic Table of Contents [http://zetoc.mimas.ac.uk/]
Zetoc currently (April 2012) provides access to the British Library's Electronic Table of Contents of around 28,000 current journals and 45 million article citations and conference papers. The database covers 1993 to the present, and is updated on a daily basis. It includes an email alerting service, to enable researchers to keep up-to-date with relevant new articles and papers. From July 2009 some Zetoc records included abstracts. Inclusion of the abstract data is with agreement between the British Library and the publisher. Not all new article data will have abstracts included but the number is expected to increase as further agreements are reached. The abstracts when present are found on the 'Full record' page. Zetoc is free to use for members of JISC (Joint Information Services Committee)-sponsored UK higher and further education institutions and research councils.

Recourse can also be made to the following selection of indexes all of which are printed versions of items included among the online databases cited above. These printed indexes can be found in some major public and academic libraries.

British Humanities Index, 1962-
An international abstracting and indexing tool (a continuation in part of Subject Index to Periodicals – see record below) covering the arts, literature, cinema, economics, history, current affairs, popular science, religion, music, and architecture. Continuation of Humanities items of Subject Index to Periodicals (see record below). Available both as a quarterly print publication and also on the web (see online version above under *BHI: British Humanities Index* .

Historical Abstracts: Bibliography of the World's Historical Literature (Santa Barbara, California: ABC-Clio, 1955-2007)
Provided a coverage of abstracts and citations to journal articles, books, and dissertations initially of the whole world, but from 1965 USA and Canada were removed and included in *America: History and Life*. In 2007 *Historical Abstracts*[220] was taken over by EBSCO and made available on the web (see additional entry above under *Historical Abstracts*).

Humanities Index, 1974-
Continuation of Humanities items of *Social Sciences and Humanities Index* (q.v.)

International Index to Periodicals, 1920-1965
Continuation of *Readers Guide to Periodical Literature, Supplements* (q.v.)

Readers Guide to Periodical Literature, Supplements 1907-1915, 1916-1919
Continued as *International Index to Periodicals* (q.v.)

Social Sciences and Humanities Index, 1965-1974
Continuation of *International Index to Periodicals* (q.v.)

Social Sciences Index, 1974-
Continuation of social sciences items of *Social Sciences and Humanities Index* (q.v.)

Subject Index to Periodicals, 1915-1961
Part of it was continued as *British Humanities Index* (q.v.)

1.1.6.2 Periodicals Containing Reviews and Bibliographic Information

Many periodicals have a section which is devoted to reviews or bibliographic information provided in the form of annotated or unannotated lists of books, periodical articles and other material. In some periodicals both reviews and bibliographic information are included. The reviews which are featured are usually of individual items selected in arbitrary fashion from the published literature of the subject field in which the periodical specializes. There are, however, some periodicals which provide a type of review which attempts to summarize the literature on a particular subject systematically and critically. This sort of bibliographic review is very often presented as an article or as a commentary on the year's work.

A selection of some periodicals providing bibliographical and reviewing services of use to a person researching on historical subjects are listed below.

American Historical Review (American Historical Association)
Book reviews. Classified lists of current books, articles, documents in all fields of history.

Annual Bulletin of Historical Literature (Historical Association)
The *Annual Bulletin of Historical Literature* (*ABHL*) is a unique publication, providing a selective and critical analysis of new historical books, journals and journal articles. Epoch by epoch and area by area, *ABHL* provides an indispensable guide to recent work by established and emerging scholars from around the world. Reviews, all written by acknowledged experts and extensively cross referenced, place new works in the context of ongoing and emerging debates.

Economic History Review (Economic History Society)
The *Economic History Review* aims at broad coverage of themes of economic and social change, including the intellectual, political and cultural implications of these changes. The extensive book review section in each issue provides a guide to the latest literature on economic and social history in the British Isles and throughout the rest of the world. Each volume also contains **Essays in Bibliography and Criticism** which are designed to bring readers up to date with the latest writings on a particular country and topical themes in economic and social history.

---

[220] *America History and Life* was also taken over by EBSCO.

Appendix 1

English Historical Review (Oxford University Press)
Book reviews. "Short Notices". July issue contains a classified section of periodical articles appearing during the previous year.

Historical Journal (Cambridge University Press)
The *Historical Journal* publishes papers on all aspects of British, European, and world history since the fifteenth century. The best contemporary scholarship is represented. Contributions come from all parts of the world. The journal aims to publish some thirty-five articles and communications each year and to review recent historical literature, mainly in the form of historiographical reviews and review articles. The journal provides a forum for younger scholars making a distinguished debut as well as publishing the work of historians of established reputation.

Historical Journal of Film, Radio And Television
Includes book reviews and review essays, historical documents, annual listings of dissertations and archival materials, reviews of films, radio and television programmes of historical or educational importance.

Historische Zeitschrift (Oldenbourg Wissenschaftsverlag GmbH)
Book reviews. Brief notices of books and periodical articles. Lists of recent books.

History (Historical Association)
First published in 1912 *History* has been a leader in its field ever since. It is unique in its range and variety, packing its pages with stimulating articles, extensive book reviews, and editorial notes. *History* balances its broad chronological coverage with a wide geographical spread of articles featuring contributions from social, political, cultural, economic and ecclesiastical historians. An integral part of each issue is the review section giving critical reviews of the latest scholarship.

History Reviews
A tri-annual publication, published March, September and December each year, in print and online at www.historytoday.com. Back issues are available in print and online. The online archival database starts at 1995. The online *History Reviews* archive is part of the online *History Today* archive - it is not a separate online product.

History Today (The Educational Archive of Articles, News and Study for Teachers, Students and Enthusiasts), 1951- [http://www.historytoday.com/]
A monthly periodical available in print and online. Provides the facility to purchase a print subscription or an online subscription or a combined print and online package. Accessible in some institutions via a corporate subscription. Back issues are available in print and online. The online archival database includes back issues of *History Today* (at present going back to 1970), *History Reviews* (going back to 1995; see record above), and a Book Reviews archive.

International History Review
The *International History Review* is the only English-language quarterly devoted entirely to the history of international relations. An international journal on international history, the *Review* publishes articles, notes with documents, bibliographies, and reviews, on everything that affected, or was affected by, the relations between all states, throughout the world, throughout history. Diplomacy, trade, warfare, revolution, imperialism, cultures, social structures, mentalités, communications, and systems are some of the subjects studied from the ancient world to the Gulf Wars.

International Review of Social History (International Institute of Social History)
Provides review essays, book reviews, abstracts, and bibliography containing brief summaries of more than 350 new books annually.

Journal of British Studies (The North American Conference on British Studies)
JBS publishes research articles and thematic review essays by an array of international authors in history, literature, and allied disciplines in the humanities and social sciences. Contributors cover fields that include social history, religion, economics, law, demographics, and gender and cultural studies. *JBS* also explores the changing character and significance of British culture in Britain itself and in areas of the world previously contained within the ambit of the British Empire ranging chronologically from the Middle Ages to the present.

Journal of Contemporary History (Sage Publications Ltd)
From 2008 it has included reviews of individual books, in addition to review articles covering a range of books within the compass of a single critical essay.

Journal of Economic History (Economic History Association)
Devoted to the multidisciplinary study of history and economics, and is of interest not only to economic historians but to social and demographic historians, as well as economists in general. It has an extensive book review section which keeps

readers informed about the latest work in economic history and related fields.

Journal of Military History (Society for Military History)
The quarterly journal of the Society for Military History includes book reviews, documents of note, a list of recent articles dealing with military history published by other journals, an annual list of doctoral dissertations in military history.

Journal of Modern History
Book reviews. Bibliographical articles. Select bibliography of current books. Covers history since 1500

Reviews in History (Institute of Historical Research)[http://www.history.ac.uk/reviews]
Launched in 1996, this e-journal of the Institute of Historical Research publishes reviews and reappraisals of significant work in all fields of historical interest.

The Times Literary Supplement
Includes reviews and annotated lists of 'Books Received'. There are printed indexes of this publication covering issues from 1902 to 1985 [see entries related to these items in **section 1.1.5.3** (**Newspapers: Indexes to Articles**) of Appendix 1]. There is also recorded in **section 1.1.5.3** an online facsimile edition of the complete run of the *TLS* from 1902-2006, with full-text searching and additional annual updates scheduled. The latter archive, *The Times Literary Supplement Historical Archive, 1902-2013* (see https://www.gale.com/intl/c/the-times-literary-supplement-historical-archive) is only accessible to individuals via institutions which have purchased a site licences for its use.

Women's History Review (Routledge) [https://www.tandfonline.com/toc/rwhr20/current]
A major international journal whose aim is to provide a forum for the publication of new scholarly articles in the field of women's history. The time span covered by the journal includes the 19th, 20th and 21st centuries as well as earlier times. The journal seeks to publish contributions from a range of disciplines (for example, women's studies, history, sociology, cultural studies, literature, political science, anthropology, philosophy and media studies) that further feminist knowledge and debate about women and/or gender relations in history. A substantial Book Reviews section is normally included in each issue.

1.1.6.3 Union Lists and Directories

Most academic libraries and major public reference libraries provide a list of the periodicals they hold that can be individually accessed through their online catalogues. To avoid having to search individual catalogues to discover where a particular periodical is held, there are available union lists of periodicals designed to list the periodicals held in a particular region or country and to indicate the actual holdings of the libraries which have them in stock. In some cases these union lists cover a federation of libraries in a particular institution (e.g. the *Cambridge Union List of Serials* and *University of London Union List of Serials*). Some of the most useful union lists covering the UK are listed below:

The British Union-Catalogue of Periodicals: A Record of the Periodicals of the World from the Seventeenth Century to the present Day, in British Libraries, 4 vols (London: Butterworths Scientific Publications, 1955-58)
Supplements extend the coverage to 1980.

Cambridge. University. *List of serials available in Cambridge University Library and other libraries connected with the University* [http://linux02.lib.cam.ac.uk/~cjs2/serials.html]
The *Cambridge Union List of Serials* contains well over 100,000 current and non-current serial titles held in Cambridge University Library and in the 100 contributing libraries.

Inform25 [https://www.search25.ac.uk/]
A union catalogue of the libraries within the M25 Consortium, a collaborative organisation that works to improve library and information services within the M25 region and across the East and Southeast.

JISC Guides [https://www.jisc.ac.uk/guides]
A membership organisation, providing digital solutions for UK education and research. Futher details about the work of JISC can be found at https://www.jisc.ac.uk/

Suncat [http://www.suncat.ac.uk/]
A free union catalogue service enabling researchers, librarians and others to locate serials held in libraries throughout the UK. The Catalogue contains information on both print and electronic serials, including journals, periodicals, newspapers, newsletters, magazines, annual reports and other publications of a continuing nature. Currently contains serials' information from over 60 UK research libraries, including the British Library and the National Libraries of Scotland and

Appendix 1

Wales. New libraries continue to be added to the catalogue on a regular basis.

The periodical holdings of libraries can also be discovered by using the following general online catalogue:

Copac [https://copac.jisc.ac.uk/]
A union catalogue, providing free access to the merged online catalogues of many major University, Specialist and National libraries in the UK and Ireland, including the British Library. Summaries are provided for some of the items recorded.

The titles of periodicals (and a great deal of other information about them) which are published around the world can be obtained from the following online directory:

UlrichsWeb Global Serials Directory [http://www.ulrichsweb.com/ulrichsweb/faqs.asp]
The authoritative online source of bibliographic and publisher information on more than 300,000 periodicals of all types - academic and scholarly journals, Open Access publications, peer-reviewed titles, popular magazines, newspapers, newsletters, and more from around the world. Detailed bibliographic records provide data such as print and electronic ISSN, title, publisher, online availability, subject area, language, abstracting and indexing coverage, list prices, searchable tables of contents, and full-text reviews. Access via personal or corporate subscription. Also available in a printed version which can be consulted in many major libraries.

1.2 Archives and Special Collections

1.2.1 Guides and Aids

AIM25 [http://www.aim25.ac.uk/]
A major project to provide electronic access to collection level descriptions of the archives of over one hundred higher education institutions, learned societies, cultural organisations and livery companies within the greater London area. This work is in progress - new data is being added regularly.

AM Adam Matthew: Primary Sources for Teaching and Research
[https://www.amdigital.co.uk/]
Adam Matthew is a digital publisher of unique primary source collections from archives around the world.

Archives Hub [https://archiveshub.jisc.ac.uk/]
A national gateway to descriptions of archives in UK universities and colleges.

Badsey, S. "'The IWM series': A Guide to the Imperial War Museum Collection of Archive Film of the First World War', *Historical Journal of Film, Radio and Television*, 13 (1993), 203 - 214

Bettey, J. H. ed. *English Historical Documents, 1906 to 1939*, a selection edited by J. H. Bettey (London: Routledge, 1967)

British Film Institute [http://www.bfi.org.uk/]
Provides information on British and international film and television titles - as well as people, music groups, organisations and events dating back to the beginning of film production. The BFI - through its library and archive - has been documenting information on film and television productions since it was established in 1933. Much of this information is now freely searchable through the Film & TV Database. Details of television programmes broadcast in the UK have been selectively added to the database since the 1960's and information about earlier broadcasts is being added retrospectively. Information about the BFI National Archive is provided below under the section headed **Collections.**

— *Screenonline: The Definitive Guide to Britain's Film and TV History* [http://www.screenonline.org.uk/index.html]

British History Online [https://www.british-history.ac.uk/catalogue]
Digital library containing some of the core printed primary and secondary sources for the medieval and modern history of the British Isles. Created by he Institute of Historical Research and the History of Parliament Trust.

British National Archives, Government Publications Sectional List, 24 (London: H. M. S. O., 1991)

Beckett, I. F. W. *The First World War: The Essential Guide to Sources in the UK National Archives* (Kew: Public

Record Office, 2002)

Burton, A. and L. Porter, eds. *Scene-Stealing: Sources for British Cinema Before 1930* (Trowbridge: Flicks Books, 2003)

European History Primary Sources (WWW Virtual Library) [http://primary-sources.eui.eu/]
European History Primary Sources (EHPS) is a joint initiative of the Library and the Department of History and Civilisation of the European University Institute. The purpose of the portal is to provide historians with an easily searchable index of websites that offer online access to primary sources on the history of Europe. EHPS is updated continuously.

Foster, J. and J. Sheppard, eds. *British Archives: A Guide to Archive Resources in the United Kingdom* (Basingstoke: Palgrave, 2002)

Greenhalgh, E. 'The Archival Sources for a Study of Franco-British Relations During the First World War', *Archives* (Journal of the British Records Association), 27, Issue 107 (2002), 148-172

Haig, M., comp. *Women Film-Makers of the Silent Era: The Holdings of the National Film and Television Archive* (London: British Film Institute, 1996)

Hall, H. *British Archives and the Sources for the History of the World War* (Oxford: H. Milford, Oxford University Press, 1925)

Higson, A., ed. *Young and Innocent: The Cinema in Britain 1896-1930* (Exeter: University of Exeter Press, 2002)
This contains an excellent section on Bibliographical and Archival Resources compiled by Stephen Bottomore (for the period before the First World War) and Jon Burrows (from the First World War to the coming of the second) and a bibliography for British cinema before 1930 compiled by Andrew Higson, Michael Williams and Jo-Anne Blanco.

MASC25 (Mapping Access to Special Collections in the London Region) [http://www.ucl.ac.uk/ls/masc25]
An online resource guide to printed special collections in libraries within the M25 Consortium, a collaborative organisation that works to improve library and information services within the M25 region and across the East and Southeast. In the case of special collections containing both printed and manuscript material, *MASC25* provides a description of the printed elements, and a reference to a complementary description of the manuscript material where appropriate, most commonly via a link to the holding institution's web pages, to AIM25 (see record above), or the Archives Hub (see record above).

Mayer, S. L. and W. J. Koenig. *The Two World Wars: A Guide to the Manuscript Collections in the United Kingdom* (London: Bowker, 1976)

National Archives Project [http://www.nationalarchives.gov.uk/pathways/firstworldwar/about.htm]
Based on 'The First World War: Sources for History', a National Archives project, in partnership with the Imperial War Museum (IWM), with external funding from the New Opportunities Fund, and presented as an exhibition which makes available an online selection of unique and richly varied source material on the First World War, set in its historical context. The exhibition draws on historical documents, film and sound available in Britain's National Archives and one of its leading museums [i.e. the Imperial War Museum (IWM)]. It starts from, but is not limited to, a British perspective on the war, and also aims to create a wider understanding of the global nature of the conflict and the profound consequences that resulted from it – consequences which, in areas such as the Balkans and Palestine, are still being felt.

The National Archives [http://www.nationalarchives.gov.uk/]
Provides a gateway to record repositories in the United Kingdom and also for institutions elsewhere in the world which have substantial collections of manuscripts noted under the indexes to the National Register of Archives.

The National Register of Archives [https://media.nationalarchives.gov.uk/index.php/the-national-register-of-archives]
The indexes to the UK National Register of Archives (NRA) are maintained by the Historical Manuscripts Commission. The NRA contains information on the nature and location of manuscripts and historical records that relate to British history. The Historical Manuscripts Commission is not itself a repository and the NRA does not hold any manuscripts or historical records.

Primary Sources on the Web
[http://www.ala.org/rusa/sections/history/resources/primarysources]. Part of the History section of the Reference and User Services Association (A Division of the American Library Association). The aim of this brief guide to making use of online primary sources is to provide students and researchers with information that will assist them in the task of evaluating the internet sources and the quality of primary materials that can be found when surfing online

Appendix 1

RASCAL (Research and Special Collections Available Locally) [http://www.rascal.ac.uk/]
An electronic gateway to research resources in the Humanities and Social Sciences in Ireland. You can use this web-site to search and browse information about the wide range of research and special collections held in libraries, museums and archives across the region. Links to institutions' on-line catalogues and other digital resources are provided where appropriate.

Scottish Archive Network [https://www.scan.org.uk/]
Provides descriptions of special collections held in Scottish libraries, museums and archives, and collections about Scottish topics held elsewhere. The records provide links to digital collections and online finding aids such as catalogues where available.

Smither, R., ed. *Imperial War Museum* [IWM] *Film Catalogue*, introduction by Stephen Badsey, vol 1- (Trowbridge: Flicks, 1994-), I: *The First World War Archive*.

1.2.2 Collections

British Film Institute National Archive [http://www.bfi.org.uk/archive-collections]
Clicking on the above web address affords online access to the BFI National Archive which is one of the world's greatest collections of film and television. The majority of the collection is British material but it also features internationally significant holdings from around the world. Also collected are films which feature key British actors and the work of British directors. There is a wealth of material of every genre from silent newsreels to CinemaScope epics, from home movies to avant-garde experiments, from classic documentaries to vintage television, from advertisements to 3-D films, soap opera to football. The archive contains more than 50,000 fiction films, over 100,000 non-fiction titles and around 625,000 television programmes.

Cambridge. University. Churchill College. Churchill Archives Centre [http://www.chu.cam.ac.uk/archives]
The Churchill Archives Centre in Churchill College, Cambridge, was purpose-built in 1974 to house Sir Winston Churchill's papers – some 3000 boxes of letters and documents ranging from his first childhood letters, to his great war-time speeches and writings which earned him the Nobel Prize for Literature. The Churchill Papers served as the inspiration and the starting-point for a larger endeavour – the creation of a wide-ranging archive of the Churchill era and after, covering those fields of public life in which Sir Winston played a personal role or took a personal interest. Today it holds the collections of papers of some 570 important figures, including politicians, statesmen, scientists, public servants, diplomats, soldiers, sailors and airmen, and the number is still increasing.

Cambridge. University Library. War Reserve Collection [http://www.ampltd.co.uk/digital_guides/f.aspx]
A series of microfilms were made of the rare and unique sources relating to the First World War (ephemera, and a large number of minor periodicals and pamphlets) contained in this collection. A Description, Contents and Digital Guide relating to this major microfilm project can be found at the above website address of Adam Matthew Publicatuions by clicking on *Digital Guides* and searching under the headings FIRST WORLD WAR: A DOCUMENTARY RECORD.

Hull. University. Brynmor Jones Library. Union of Democratic Control
[http://www.hullhistorycentre.org.uk/research/research-guides/democratic-control.aspx]
One of the major collections of these archives is that of the Union of Democratic Control. The UDC Collection contains minutes (of the General Council, Executive Committee and sub-committees), accounts (particularly relating to the sale of publications), subject and correspondence files, press cuttings, photocopies, and numerous copies of UDC publications (books, pamphlets and leaflets), including some original drafts and typescripts. The collection covers the whole peiod of its history, including the important formative and turbulent years of the Great War, 1914-1918.

Leeds. University. Edward Boyle Library. Liddle Collection
[https://library.leeds.ac.uk/special-collections/collection/723]
The Liddle Collection was founded over thirty years ago to collect and preserve first-hand individual experiences of the First World War. The archive includes original letters and diaries, official and personal papers, photographs, newspapers and artwork, as well as written and tape-recorded recollections. Material is arranged within 30 sections, according to nature of service or geographical area, and these are listed in a Summary Guide. This guide also contains subject indexes to uncatalogued material where appropriate. A further section is devoted to material relating to the Second World War. There are both general and specific search options for the 1914-1918 and 1939-1945 Catalogues, and guidance notes are available from the .Search pages. The First World War catalogue contains 4300 records. The Second World War catalogue contains 488 records.

London. Imperial War Museum (IWM) [http://www.iwm.org.uk]
Web site of the Imperial War Museum, based in London. This immense online presentation includes details of the

Museum's unique coverage of the twentieth century conflicts, especially involving Britain and the Commonwealth (from the First World War to the Gulf War and the present day). Online search access to the IWM's collections can be obtained via http://collections.iwm.org.uk/.

London. University. King's College. Liddell Hart Centre for Military Archives
[http://www.kingscollections.org/catalogues/lhcma/]
The Centre holds the private papers of over 500 senior defence personnel who held office in the 20th century. Individual collections range in size from a single file to the 1000 boxes of Capt Sir Basil Liddell Hart's papers. For the holdings of the Centre which relate to the First World War an introductory research guide can be consulted.

National Archives [http://www.nationalarchives.gov.uk/]
The National Archives is the UK government's official archive, containing almost 1,000 years of history, with records ranging from parchment and paper scrolls through to digital files and archived websites. It brings together the Public Record Office, Historical Manuscripts Commission, the Office of Public Sector Information and Her Majesty's Stationery Office.

Public Record Office of Northern Ireland [https://www.nidirect.gov.uk/proni/]
The Public Record Office of Northern Ireland (PRONI) is the official archive for Northern Ireland. It aims to identify and preserve records of historical, social and cultural importance and make them available for the information, education and enjoyment of the public. PRONI is the official place of deposit for public records in Northern Ireland. In addition, it collects a wide range of archives from private sources. PRONI also advises on and promotes best practice in archive and records management to ensure that today's records will be available for future generations. Located in Belfast, PRONI is a government organisation founded in 1923 (shortly after the partition of Ireland). It now operates as part of the Department of Culture, Arts and Leisure within the Northern Ireland Civil Service.

The World War 1 Document Archive [http://wwi.lib.byu.edu/index.php/Main_Page]
This archive is international in focus and intended to present in one location primary documents concerning the Great War. This archive has been assembled by volunteers of the World War I Military History List (WWI-L).

1.3   Research Centres

Bill Douglas Cinema Museum. [http://humanities.exeter.ac.uk/film/billdouglascentre/]
The Bill Douglas Museum, located in the University of Exeter Library, is a museum and research centre which houses one of Britain's largest public collections of books, prints, artefacts and ephemera relating to the history and prehistory of cinema.

Centre for First World War Studies (University of Birmingham) [http://www.greatwar.co.uk/organizations/centre-ww1-studies.htm]
The Centre is part of the Departments of Medieval and Modern History at the University of Birmingham and was launched on 11 November 2002. Its aim is to provide an intellectual and social focus for the University of Birmingham's community of staff and graduate students and for lay persons interested in one of the seminal historical events of the modern world. The Centre also includes an outstanding group of 'external' Members who have contributed much to the recent flowering of scholarship on the Great War. The Centre's website includes, and provides links to, a considerable amount of research material relating to the Great War and for a time published a journal (*Journal of the Centre for First World Studies*).

Centre for the Study of War, Propaganda and Society (University of Kent)
[http://www.kent.ac.uk/history/centres/war-propaganda-and-society/index.html]
Established at the University of Kent in 1994. The Centre is conducting a number of research projects among which are British propaganda in WWI and WWII, The First World War in children's fiction 1914-1939. The Centre is also compiling a detailed archival and bibliographical database of propaganda material in the twentieth century.

Centre for War Studies (Trinity College, Dublin) [http://www.tcd.ie/warstudies]
The Centre for War Studies was established in February 2008 to promote the study of the origins, nature and consequences of war in history and in the contemporary world. It draws on the existing interests of staff in the School of Histories and Humanities [of Trinity College, Dublin] with convergence on three periods in particular: the Thirty Years war and the wars in Britain and Ireland in the 17th century; the Revolutionary and Napoleonic Wars, 1792-1815; and the era of the two world wars, 1914-45, with special emphasis on the First World War. While the cultural history of war is a special strength of the Centre, the study of all aspects of war – from military operations to politics, society and the economy – is supported.

Institute of Historical Research [http://www.history.ac.uk/about]
Founded in 1921 by A. F. Pollard, the Institute of Historical Research is an important resource and meeting-place for

Appendix 1

scholars from all over the world. It offers a wide range of services both onsite and remotely which promote and facilitate excellence in historical research, teaching and scholarship in the UK, by means of its library, seminars, conferences, fellowships, training, consultancy, Continuing Professional Development and publications (both electronic and in printed form). The IHR web site provides information about all of these activities, and offers access to a wide range of electronic resources, from electronic journals to directories of historical research in UK universities, from catalogues of web sites for history to high quality learning and teaching material. It also acts as a bulletin board for the history profession in the UK, with information about conferences and events held throughout the country. The Institute also houses three research centres of national distinction:

Victoria County History (http://www.victoriacountyhistory.ac.uk/NationalSite/Home/Main),

Centre for Metropolitan History (http://www.history.ac.uk/cmh/about),

Centre for Contemporary British History (https://www.history.ac.uk/makinghistory/resources/articles/ccbh.html).

1.4 Reference Tools

Sometimes there is a need for quick, factual or digested information; sometimes it is a comprehensive or specialised guide to resources for researchers that is required. For these purposes there are various types of reference works. A selection of these are recorded in the sub-sections below:

1.4.1 Guides

Craver, K. W. *Using Internet Primary Sources to Teach Critical Thinking Skills in History* (Westport, Conn.: Greenwood Press, 1999)

The New Walford Guide to Reference Resources, editor-in-chief, Ray Lester, 3 vols (London: Facet Publishing, 2005-2009)
Contents: Vol 1. Science, Technology and Medicine; Vol 2. The Social Sciences; Vol 3. Arts, Humanities and General Reference. First published in 1959 as *Walford's Guide to Reference Material* which achieved international recognition as a leading bibliographic tool. *The New Walford* is a new, radically different Guide which provides an expertly chosen selection of key, quality resources - accessible via the web and in print - across all areas of knowledge in broad subject groupings. It includes a detailed topic index, and each subject grouping has a short introductory essay, highlighting the distinctive features of its reference resources. Each resource is given a succinct description, leading the busy user straight to its key features. The focus is on resources that are most likely to be found and used within public, government, education or business information services.

Reagan, P. D. *History and the Internet: A Guide* (Boston: McGraw-Hill, 2002)

Trinkle, D. A. and S. A. Merriman, eds. *The European History Highway: A Guide to Internet Resources* (Armonk, N.Y.: M.E. Sharpe, 2002)

1.4.2 Companions

Arnold-Baker, C. *The Companion to British History* (Tunbridge Wells: Longcross Press, 1996)

Cannon, J., ed. *The Oxford Companion to British History* (Oxford: Oxford University Press, 1997)

The First World War A-Z: From Assassination to Zeppelin - Everything You Need To Know (London: Imperial War Museum, 2014)

Gardiner, J. and N. Wenborn, eds. *The History Today Companion to British History* (London: Collins and Brown, 1995)

Haythornthwaite, P. J. *The World War One Source Book* (London: BCA, 1992)

The Hutchinson History Reference Suite
A CD-ROM covering topics such as world events, ideas and trends from pre-history to modern times. Useful for students and general users, this disc provides a one-stop reference source for any historical question. A selective search facility

enables searching by whatever theme is relevant to a researcher's historical studies across all 6 of its constituent parts[221].

Nicolson, C. *The Longman Companion to the First World War: Europe 1914-1918* (Harlow: Longman, 2001)

Panton, K. J. and K. A. Cowland. *Historical Dictionary of the United Kingdom*, 2 vols, European Historical Dictionaries, 17 (London: Scarecrow Press, 1998)

Pope, S. and E-A. Wheal. *The Macmillan Dictionary of The First World War* (London: Macmillan, 1997)

1.4.3 Encyclopaedias and Encyclopaedic Works

As well as providing specific items of information, an article in an encyclopaedia can provide a valuable starting point in the study of a particular subject and, if a bibliography is appended to it, it can, in addition, be useful as a guide to sources of further information. The *Encyclopaedia Britannica* stands out in this respect and retains its reputation as the most trusted scholarly source of encyclopaedic information.

Brill's Encyclopedia of the First World War, edited by Gerhard Hirschfeld, Gerd Krumeich, Irina Renz; in cooperation with Markus Pohlmann, rev. edn, 2 vols (Leiden; Boston: Brill, 2012)

Britannica Online [http://www.britannica.com/]
Provides complete text of *Encyclopaedia Britannica* with search capabilities, related links, and multimedia enhancements. Full text for subscribers only. Some public libraries provide free online access to *Britannica Online Library Edition*.

Encyclopaedia Britannica 2007, 32 vols (London: Encyclopaedia Britannica (UK) Ltd, 2007)
A limited revised edition of 500 sets was released in 2010. It was announced in 2012 that after 244 years the reference book firm Encyclopaedia Britannica had decided to stop publishing its famous and weighty 32-volume print edition

Information Please [http://www.infoplease.com/]
Includes an edition of *Columbia Encyclopedia* (accessible by clicking on the 'Encyclopedia' box.)

Oxford Reference Online [http://www.oxfordreference.com/]
An extensive selection of dictionaries, encyclopaedias and other reference works covering many subjects. Many public libraries provide free online access to it for their members.

Spartacus Educational. [https://spartacus-educational.com/]
Encyclopaedic entries covering a variety of historical topics (such as British History, WW1, etc) usually include a narrative, illustrations and primary sources. The text within each entry is hypertexted to other relevant pages in the encyclopaedia. In this way it is possible to research individual people and events in great detail. The sources are also hypertexted so that the student is able to find out about the writer, artist, newspaper, organization, etc., that produced the material.

Tucker, S. C. and P. M. Roberts, eds. *The Encyclopedia of World War I: A Political, Social, and Military History*, 5 vols (Santa Barbara, Calif.: ABC-CLIO, 2005)

Wikipedia [http://en.wikipedia.org/wiki/Main_Page]
A free encyclopaedia with millions of articles contributed collaboratively (by largely anonymous Internet volunteers who write without pay using Wiki software) in dozens of languages. Anyone with Internet access can write and make changes to Wikipedia articles (except in certain cases where editing is restricted to prevent disruption and/or vandalism).

World Book Encyclopedia, 22 vols (Chicago, Ill.; London: World Book inc., 2011)
An encyclopaedia, published in the United States since 1917, designed especially to meet the needs of elementary, junior high, and senior high school students. It is accessed via an alphabetical arrangement of articles, cross-references. and a comprehensive index. A revised edition is published each year. Since 1998, in addition to the print and CD-ROM editions of the encyclopaedia, World Book also publishes an online version called *World Book Online*. The online version includes all of the articles contained in the print set as well as several thousand additional articles and the contents of every yearbook

---

[221] The parts are: *The Hutchinson Directory of World History, Hutchinson Concise Chronology of World History, Hutchinson Dictionary of Biography, Hutchinson Dictionary of Ideas, Helicon Book of Days, Hutchinson Directory of History Web Sites.*

Appendix 1

World Book has published since 1922; this online version is accessible via: www.worldbookonline.com/wb/Login?ed=wb.

1.4.4 Biographical Dictionaries

For obtaining biographical information about British people the *Dictionary of National Biography*, and the *Oxford Dictionary of National Biography* represent a collection of reference works among those listed below likely to be of the greatest use. The rest of the selection below are international in scope.

Chambers Biographical Dictionary
The printed CBD, published since 1897, is regularly revised and updated. Its 9th edition (2007) contains over 20,000 entries. It has been regarded as one of the most comprehensive and authoritative single-volume biographical dictionaries available since it was first published in 1897. Full cross-referencing allows the reader to explore beyond the individual - thus not only answering a specific enquiry about one person, but leading to information on their contemporaries or the people they influenced - and thousands of suggestions for further reading direct the reader to key works on or by the person in question. *Chambers Biographical Dictionary* (1997 edition with amendments), together with the *Chambers 21st Century Dictionary* and the *Chambers Thesaurus* can also be consulted online free at: http://chambers.co.uk/

Concise Dictionary of National Biography
Part I, epitome of the DNB from earliest times to 1900, published in 1903; Part 2, epitome of the supplements to the DNB, 1901–70, published 1982. A consolidated three-volume edition of the *Concise DNB* providing the epitomes of the DNB and its supplements from the earliest times to 1985 was published in 1992. The *Concise DNB* acts both as an index to the DNB and its supplements and also as an independent reference tool as it gives shortened versions of the much longer articles of the DNB.

Dictionary of National Biography
The main work (designed to include only deceased persons and to cover noteworthy people of Great Britain and the colonies from the earliest times) was published between 1885 and 1901 and augmented by supplements published at intervals up to 1996 (covering people who had died between 1885 and 1900, or who had been overlooked in the original alphabetical sequence, and people who had died in the 20th century up to 31 December 1990). Updated and extended by the *Oxford Dictionary of National Biography* (q.v.)

Herwig, H. H. and N. M. Heyman. *Biographical Dictionary of World War 1* (London: Greenwood, 1982)

The Hutchinson Dictionary of Biography
This work is a constituent part of the CD-ROM, *The Hutchinson History Reference Suite* [see entry above under **section 1.4.2 (Reference Tools: Companions) of Appendix 1**].

Oxford Dictionary of National Biography [http://www.oxforddnb.com/]
A collection of specially written biographies, which describe the lives of people who shaped the history of the British Isles and beyond from the 4th century BC to the 21st century. Published in print and online in 2004, it is extended with three annual updates (each January, May and October), adding new biographies from the Romans to the 21st century. It replaces and extends the original Victorian DNB by providing re-written biographies of all subjects included in the latter DNB and adding biographies of new subjects from all periods. The original Victorian DNB entries on the rewritten subjects can be accessed separately through a link to the "DNB Archive". Some public libraries and academic institutions provide free online access to this work for their members.

Merriam-Webster's Biographical Dictionary
Webster's Biographical Dictionary, which included living personages as well as those who had died, was first published in 1943. Various editions have been published since then. The edition cited above (i.e. *Merriam-Webster's Biographical Dictionary*), first published in 1995, now only lists people who are no longer living and provides brief lives of more than 30,000 men and women – "the famous, the not-so-famous, and the downright obscure" - who lived during the past 5000 years.

Who Was Who
An historical archive going back to 1897, which includes the entries of over 100,000 people, now deceased, who were included in previous editions of *Who's Who*. The online edition of *Who Was Who* contains links to the *Oxford Dictionary of National Biography* (q.v.) available to subscribers to both resources. *Who's Who*, published annually since 1849 by A & C Black, contains over 33,000 short autobiographies, continually updated, of living noteworthy and influential individuals, from all walks of life, worldwide. Some public libraries provide free online access to *Who's Who*, *Who Was Who*, and the *Oxford Dictionary of National Biography* for their members.

1.4.5 Atlases

Banks, A. *A Military Atlas of the First World War. A Map History of the War of 1914-18 on Land, at Sea and in the Air.* Commentary by Alan Palmer (London: Leo Cooper, 1989; repr. London, Pen & Sword, 2002)
Banks' 250 maps present both broad general surveys of political and military strategy and closely detailed treatments of individual campaigns and engagements. These are supplemented by comprehensive analyses of military strengths and command structures and illustrations of important guns, tanks, ships, airplanes and personal weapons.

Gilbert, M *The Routledge Atlas of the First World War*, 3rd edn (London: Routledge, 2008)
"A series of maps which illustrate the military, social, political and economic aspects of the war. This new edition contains an entirely new section depicting the visual remembrance of the war; and a fascinating visitors guide to the memorials that commemorate the tragedy of the Somme".

Hughes, M. and W. J. Philpott, eds. *The Palgrave Concise Historical Atlas of the First World War* (New York: Palgrave Macmillan, 2004)
Drawing on recent scholarship the editors present fifty maps, accompanied by supporting text and statistical tables, that provide a survey of the main battles and political features of the war.

Livesey, A. *The Viking Atlas of World War I* (London: Viking, 1994)
The maps and text of this atlas cover the development of all the major campaigns and theatres of the Great War (in China, Africa, the Middle East and the Balkans, as well as the Eastern, Western and Italian fronts, with special attention paid to the impact of the war on the British and French colonial empires) and also encompasses the broader implications of the war: changes in civilian attitudes, the role of pacifists, the changing status of women and the social, political and economic effects of the war.

1.4.6 Web Directories

The items selected below are a brief selection of directories of websites:

Best of History Websites [http://besthistorysites.net/]
An award-winning portal that contains annotated links to over 1000 history web sites

History Guide (Netzwerk Internetressourcen Geschichte (Network Subject Gateways History))
The *History Guide* [https://www.sub.uni-goettingen.de/en/humanities-and-theology/history/history-guide/] is a subject gateway to scholarly relevant websites in history maintained in cooperation with Netzwerk Internetressourcen Geschichte (Network Subject Gateways History).

The Hutchinson Directory of History Web Sites
This work [which is a constituent part of the CD-ROM, *The Hutchinson History Reference Suite* - see entry for it above under **section 1.4.2 (Reference Tools: Companions) of Appendix 1**] provides access to web sites of special interest to the historian and history student.

Robert Teeter's Web Site: Generalities [http://www.interleaves.org/~rteeter/gen.html]
A guide to a wide range of material including reference sources, bibliographies and indexes.

Spartacus Educational. [https://spartacus-educational.com/]
Encyclopaedic entries covering a variety of historical topics (such as British History, WW1, etc) usually include a narrative, illustrations and primary sources. The text within each entry is hypertexted to other relevant pages in the encyclopaedia. In this way it is possible to research individual people and events in great detail. The sources are also hypertexted so that the student is able to find out about the writer, artist, newspaper, organization, etc., that produced the material.

The World Wide Web Virtual Library: WWW-VL History Central Catalogue [http://vlib.iue.it/history/index.html]
This is the central catalogue for the WWW-VL network of indexes to Historical materials on-line. There is a UK section entitled *WWW-VL: HISTORY of the United Kingdom* at: http://vlib.iue.it/history/europe/uk/uk.html

1.5 Great War Websites

Listed below is a selection of the vast number of websites devoted entirely or mostly to the Great War (**see also** below for a review of Great War digital resources by C. Phillips, and a number of other sites above included in

Appendix 1

Part 4 (**Remembering the War**), under the sub-heading of **Websites** in the sub-section 2.2: **British Aspects** of Section 2.: **Memorialisation and Commemoration**)

1914-1918: The Great War and the Shaping of the 20th Century [http://www.pbs.org/greatwar]
The companion website for the 1996 TV series (a KCET/BBC co-production in association with the IWM (Imperial War Museum) and book with the same title. The website is a comprehensive multimedia exploration of the history and effects of World War 1. An interactive timeline lets you examine the events leading up to and during the war, as well as its aftermath. Other features include an interactive gallery of maps and locations; interviews from respected World War 1 historians covering a variety of topics; synopses; and programme excerpts from each of the eight television episodes. There is also a list of related web sites and research materials. Includes numerous images and maps. See also https://en.wikipedia.org/wiki/The_Great_War_and_the_Shaping_of_the_20th_Century

1914-1918-online. International Encyclopedia of the First World War [http://www.1914-1918-online.net/]
This website of a three-year international joint research project which is aiming to develop and make available a multi-perspective, public-access English-language virtual reference work on the Great War is planned to be released in the centenary year of that war in 2014.

British Association For Local History. *Local History and the First World War*
[http://www.balh.org.uk/education/local-history-and-the-first-world-war]

British Library. *World War One* [http://www.bl.uk/world-war-one]
"Supported by over 500 historical sources from across Europe, this resource examines key themes in the history of World War One. Explore a wealth of original source material, over 50 newly-commissioned articles written by historians, teachers' notes and more to discover how war affected people on different sides of the conflict".[Britiah Library's description of the website]

Documents of World War I [http://www.mtholyoke.edu/acad/intrel/ww1.htm]
A link from the home page of Vincent Ferraro, the Ruth C. Lawson Professor of International Politics, Mount Holyoke College [http://www.mtholyoke.edu/acad/intrel/feros-pg.htm]

Encyclopaedia of the First World War (Spartacus Educational)
[https://spartacus-educational.com/FWW.htm]
A comprehensive encyclopaedia of the First World War. Each entry contains a narrative, illustrations and primary sources. The text within each entry is hypertexted to other relevant pages in the encyclopedia. In this way it is possible to research individual people and events in great detail. The sources are also hypertexted so the student is able to find out about the writer, artist, newspaper, organization, etc., that produced the material. So far there are sections on: Chronology, Outbreak of War, Allied Armed Forces, Central Powers, Important Battles, Technology, Political Leaders, British Home Front, Military Leaders, Trench War, The Soldiers, Major Offensives, War at Sea, War in the Air, War Artists, War Literature, War Heroes, Women at War, Organisations, Strategies & Tactics, Weapons & Machines, Inventors and the War, Theatres of War and War Statistics.

Europeana, 1914-1918 [http://www.europeana1914-1918.eu/en]
"Launched in January 2014, the website contains material from 20 European countries divided into broad categories (remembrance, propaganda, aerial warfare, etc.) and searchable by the resource type … In addition to official documents, the site also aims to digitise personal papers and memorabilia held by the families of servicemen via a series of family history roadshows held in 17 nations across Europe". [Quotations extracted from Philips, C. Review of *First World War Digital Resources*, q.v.] **See also** *The First World War Poetry Digital Archive* in Part 4 (**Remembering the War**), under the sub-heading of **Archives** in section **4.2.4: Poetry.**

Firstworldwar.com (A multimedia history of World War One) [http://www.firstworldwar.com/index.htm]
Site editor's note: "The purpose of this website is to provide a summary overview of the First World War. Necessarily a long-term undertaking - and approaching ten years in the making - a significant amount of material remains to be covered. Whole aspects of the conflict are light on material at present - rest assured, this is not deliberate: in time the intent is that it should all find its place on the site. A word of caution however; this is by no means an academic website. It is authored as spare time permits and is geared towards a general rather than scholarly readership. Given this, it is not recommended that this site be used for academic reference purposes for school or university papers. This does not so much indicate a concerning lack of authorial confidence in the accuracy of site content as an acknowledgement that material on the site has not been submitted for formal peer review."

The Great War in a Different Light [http://www.greatwardifferent.com/]
The idea behind this website is to provide a view of the Great War based on the news articles, magazines and books that

people of that period read and the photos and illustrations they saw in the media of the time.

A Guide to WW1 Battlefields and History of the First World War [http://www.greatwar.co.uk/]

The Heritage of the Great War [http://greatwar.nl/]
Extract from introduction: "This website is dedicated to the events and consequences of World War One. We put some emphasis on unorthodox and thought-provoking points of view. We are averse to historicism and military fetishism. And we show *people* rather than strategic plans or statistics. To this end this website features one of the most extensive and explicit WW-1 photo collections on the Internet."

International Society for First World Studies [http://www.firstworldwarstudies.org/]
"Provides a location for those with a more recognisably academic approach to the war. Created in 2001 by Jenny Macleod and Pierre Purseigle, the society [International Society for First World Srudies] is an international network which organizes or sponsors conferences, seminars and workshops, and is responsible for the publication of a journal, *First World War Studies*, and a series of edited volumes based on conference proceedings". The reviewer also points out that the society provides "one essential resource for researchers both new and experienced, a colossal – and expanding – collaborative bibliography of reference materials associated with the First World War … in a multitude of languages.". [Quotations extracted from Philips, C. Review of *First World War Digital Resources*, q.v.]

Paths of Memory Project [http://arch.oucs.ox.ac.uk/detail/103907/index.html/]
Paths of Memory is the website of this multinational project focusing on the First and Second World Wars and the Spanish Civil War, and the effects of these conflicts on Europe. It is also a meditation on memory, how different nations remember and celebrate a common past. Each section explores the themes of Military Operations, the Home Front and the War Effort, Occupation, and Liberation. Each war has a very good description, accompanied by illustrations and maps. A place index, also grouped according to the three major wars discussed, allows a different approach to the rich material on the site. For each place selected from the alphabetical list, a detailed text comprising the related events and peoples is offered. The site is available in English, French, German, Italian and Spanish. The partner institutions are: Le Mémorial de Caen (France); Haus der Geschichte der Bundesrepublik Deutschland (Bonn, Germany); D-Day Museum Portsmouth; Centre Guerres et Sociétés Contemporaines (Bruxelles, Belgium); Museo de la Paz (Gernika-Luma, Spain); Istituto per i Beni Culturali (Bologne, Italy).

Phillips, C. 'Review of First World War Digital Resources', *Reviews in History* (Institute of Hisorical Research), review no. 1626 (July 2014)

Scaled Scenarios (Historical media of WW1)
[https://www.birmingham.ac.uk/research/activity/warstudies/links/ww1-links.aspx]
This website contains original historical media from the period of World War 1 (1914-1918) including soldiers' letters and post cards, civilian letters, official documents, business letters and documents. Also included are original photographs and snapshots of the war.

A Short Bibliography of Great War Books
[http://web.archive.org/web/20080807154609/http://www.greatwardifferent.com/Great_War/Bibliography/Bibliography_01.htm]

Trenches on the Web: An Internet History of the Great War [http://www.worldwar1.com/]
This website, designed as an evolving project with new material added on a continuing basis, provides information on the people, places, and events involved in the history of the Great War

Appendix 2

2. Propaganda Materials Sent to the USA

The entries and preamble below represent an exact reproduction of what was recorded in the Check List provided by J. D. Squires in the Appendix to his work, *British Propaganda at Home and in the United States from 1914-1917* published in 1935.

A CHECK LIST OF BRITISH PROPAGANDA SENT TO THE UNITED STATES BETWEEN 1914 AND 1917

The following bibliography of British propaganda materials sent to the United States between 1914 and 1917 is, it is believed, fairly complete. It represents, however, only materials sent over by Wellington House under the direction of Sir Gilbert Parker or of Professor W. Macneile Dixon. In a few cases when there is doubt as to whether these gentlemen were responsible for certain titles, this fact is indicated by # prefixed to such titles. The materials are classified under two heads: (a) official documents published by the British government; (b) other publications sponsored by Wellington House. Reprints of certain official British documents and official documents from other countries are listed under (b) alphabetically by title.

British Official Documents

Parliamentary Papers. Documents respecting the Negotiations Preceding the War published by the Russian Government. Miscellaneous No. 11. (1914) Command 7626.

Parliamentary Papers. Diplomatic Correspondence respecting the War published by the Belgian Government. Miscellaneous No. 12 (1914) Command 7627.

Parliamentary Papers. Despatch from His Majesty's Ambassador at Constantinople Summarising Events Leading up to Rupture of Relations with Turkey, and Reply Thereto. Miscellaneous No. 14 (1914) Command 7716.

Parliamentary Papers. Diplomatic correspondence respecting the War published by the French Government. Miscellaneous No. 15 (1914) Command 7717.

Parliamentary Papers. Correspondence between His Majesty's Government and the United States Ambassador respecting the Treatment of German Prisoners of War and Interned Civilians in the United Kingdom. Miscellaneous No. 5 (1915) Command 7815.

Parliamentary Papers. Correspondence between His Majesty's Government and the United States Government respecting the Rights of Belligerents. Miscellaneous No. 6 (1915) Command 7816.

Parliamentary Papers. Correspondence between His Majesty's Government and the United States Ambassador respecting the Treatment of Prisoners of War and Interned Civilians in the United Kingdom and Germany Respectively. Miscellaneous No. 7 (1915) Command 7817.

Parliamentary Papers. Collected Diplomatic Documents relating to the Outbreak of the European War. Command 7860. London, 1915.

Parliamentary Papers. Correspondence relative to the Alleged Ill-Treatment of German Subjects Captured in the Cameroons. European War. Command 7974. London, 1915

Parliamentary Papers. Correspondence with the United States Ambassador respecting the Execution of Miss Cavell at Brussels. Miscellaneous No. 17 (1915) Command 8013.

Parliamentary Papers. Report of a Formal Investigation into the circumstances attending the foundering on 28th March of the

Propaganda Materials Sent to the USA

British Steamship "Falaba" of Liverpool, in or near Latitude 51° 30' N., Longitude 6° S6' W., whereby loss of life ensued. Shipping Casualties (Loss of the Steamship "Falaba"). Command 8021. London, 1915.

Parliamentary Papers. Report of a Formal Investigation into the circumstances attending the foundering on 7th May, 1915, of the British Steamship "Lusitania" of Liverpool, after bring torpedoed off the Old Head of Kinsale, Ireland. Shipping Casualties (Loss of the Steamship "Lusitania"). Command 8022. London, 1915.

Parliamentary Papers. Correspondence with the United States Ambassador respecting the Treatment of British Prisoners of War and Interned Civilians in Germany. Miscellaneous No. 19 (1915) Command 8108.

Parliamentary Papers. Correspondence with the United States Ambassador respecting the Safety of Alien Enemies Repatriated from India on the S.S. "Golconda". Miscellaneous No. 4 (1916) Command 8163.

Parliamentary Papers. Selection from Papers Found in the Possession of Captain von Papen, Late German Military Attaché at Washington, Falmouth, January 2 and 3, 1916. Miscellaneous No. 6 (1916) Command 8174.

Parliamentary Papers. Further Correspondence with the United States Ambassador respecting the Safety of Alien Enemies Repatriated from India on the S.S. "Golconda". Miscellaneous No. 8 (1916) Command 8178.

Parliamentary Papers. Memorandum Presented by His Majesty's Government and the French Government to Neutral Governments regarding the Examination of Parcels and Letter Mails. Miscellaneous No. 9 (1916) Command 8223.

Parliamentary Papers. Report by the Government Committee on the Treatment by the Enemy of British Prisoners of War regarding the Conditions Obtaining at Wittenberg Camp during the Typhus Epidemic of 1915. Miscellaneous No. 10 (1916) Command 8224.

Parliamentary Papers. Sworn Statement by Horst von der Goltz, alias Bridgeman Taylor. Miscellaneous No. 13 (1916) Command 8232.

Parliamentary Papers. Further Correspondence between His Majesty's Government and the United States Government respecting the Rights of Belligerents. Miscellaneous No. 14 (1916) Command 8233.

Parliamentary Papers. Further Correspondence between His Majesty's Government and the United States Government respecting the Rights of Belligerents. Miscellaneous No. 15 (1916) Command 8234.

Parliamentary Papers. Further Correspondence with the United States Ambassador respecting the Treatment of British Prisoners of War and Interned Civilians in Germany. Miscellaneous No. 16 (1916) Command 8235.

Parliamentary Papers. Report by Doctor A. E. Taylor on the Conditions of Diet and Nutrition in the Internment Camp at Ruhleben received through the United States Ambassador. Miscellaneous No. 18 (1916) Command 8259.

Parliamentary Papers. Correspondence respecting the Employment of British and German Prisoners of War in Poland and France Respectively. Miscellaneous No. 19 (1916) Command 8260.

Parliamentary Papers. Further Correspondence respecting the Conditions of Diet and Nutrition in the Internment Camp at Ruhleben. Miscellaneous No. 21 (1916) Command 8262.

Parliamentary Papers. Recommendations of the Economic Conference of the Allies held at Paris on June 14, 15, 16 and 17, 1916. Command 8271. London, 1916.

Parliamentary Papers. Note Addressed by His Majesty's Government to Neutral Representatives in London respecting The Withdrawal of the Declaration of London Orders in Council. Miscellaneous No. 22 (1916) Command 8293

Parliamentary Papers. Note Addressed to the United. States Ambassador regarding the Examination of Parcels and Letter Mails. Miscellaneous No. 23 (1916) Command 8294

Parliamentary Papers. Correspondence with the United States Ambassador regarding the Relief of Allied Territories in the Occupation of the Enemy. Miscellaneous No. 24 (1916) Command 8295

Appendix 2

Parliamentary Papers. Further Correspondence respecting the Conditions of Diet and Nutrition in the Internment Camp at Ruhleben and the Proposed Release of Interned Civilians. Miscellaneous No. 25 (1916) Command 8296.

Parliamentary Papers. Further Correspondence with the United States Ambassador respecting the Treatment of British Prisoners of War and Interned Civilians in Germany. Miscellaneous No. 26 (1916) Command 8297

Parliamentary Papers. Collective Note addressed to the Greek Government by the French, British, and Russian Ministers and the Reply of the Greek Government. Miscellaneous No. 27 (1916) Command 8298

Parliamentary Papers. Papers relating to German Atrocities, and Breaches of the Rules of War, in Africa. European War. Command 8306. London, 1916

Parliamentary Papers. Correspondence with the Swedish Minister on the object of the Detention by the Swedish Government of the British Transit Mail to Russia as a Reprisal For the Search of Parcels Mail by His Majesty's Government. Miscellaneous No. 28 (1916) Command 8322

Parliamentary Papers. Reports of Visits of Inspection made by Officials of the United States Embassy to Various Interment camps in United Kingdom. Miscellaneous No. 30 (1916) Command 8324.

Parliamentary Papers. The Treatment of Armenians in the Ottoman Empire 1915-1916. Documents Presented to Viscount Grey of Fallodon, Secretary of State for Foreign Affairs, by Viscount Bryce. With a. Preface by Viscount Bryce. Miscellaneous No. 31 (1916) Command 8336.

Parliamentary Papers. Correspondence respecting the Relief of Allied Territories in the Occupation of the Enemy. Miscellaneous No. 32 (1916) Command 8348

Parliamentary Papers. *Report en the Typhus Epidemic of Gardelegen by the Government Committee on the Treatment of the Enemy of British Prisoners of War during the Spring and Summer of 1915.* Miscellaneous No. 34 (1916) Command 8351

Parliamentary Papers. Further Correspondence respecting the proposed Release of Civilians Interned in the British and German Empires. Miscellaneous No. 35 (1916) Command 8352.

Parliamentary Papers. Further Correspondence with the United States Ambassador respecting the "Trading with the Enemy (Extension of Powers) Act, 1915". Miscellaneous No. 36 (1916) Command 8353.

Parliamentary Papers. Correspondence with the Belgian Minister respecting the Deportation of Belgians to Germany and the Forced Labour Imposed upon Them by the German Authorities. Miscellaneous No. 37 (1916) Command 8404.

Parliamentary Papers. Further Correspondence respecting the Proposed Release of Civilians Interned in the British and German Empires. Miscellaneous No. 1 (1917) Command 8437.

Parliamentary Papers. Memorandum Addressed by the French and British Governments to the United States Government regarding the Examination of Parcels and Letter Mails. Miscellaneous No. 2 (1917) Command 8438.

Parliamentary Papers. Despatch to His Majesty's Ambassador at Washington, respecting the Allied Note of January 10, 1917. Miscellaneous No. 3 (1917) Command 8489.

Parliamentary Papers. Further Correspondence with the United States Ambassador respecting the Treatment of British Prisoners of War and Interned Civilians in Germany. Miscellaneous No. 7 (1917) Command 8477.

Parliamentary Papers. Reports on the Treatment by the Germans of British Prisoners and Natives in German East Africa. Miscellaneous No. 13 (1917) Command 8689

Parliamentary Papers. Correspondence with the German Government regarding the Alleged Misuse of British Hospital Ships. Miscellaneous No. 16 (1917) Command 8692.

Parliamentary Papers. Correspondence respecting the Transit Traffic across Holland of Materials Susceptible of Employment as Military Supplies. Miscellaneous No. 17 (1917) Command 8693.

Other Publications

#Addis, Sir Charles. *The Means of War Finance.* London, 1916.

Addison, Christopher. *British Workshops and the War.* London, 1917.

Addison, Christopher. *The Manufacture of Munitions.* London, 1916.

Les Allemands à Lille et dans le Nord de la France. Paris, 1916.

Les Allemands destructeurs de Cathedrales et de Tresors du passé. Paris, 1915.

Anderson, Jane and Gordon Bruce. *Flying, Submarining, and Mine-Sweeping.* London, 1916.

Anderson, R. Wherry. *The Romance of Air-Fighting.* London, 1917.

Appleton, W. A. *The Workers' Resolve.* London, 1917.

Archer, William. *Colour-Blind Neutrality.* London, 1916

Archer, William. *A Plea for Patience.* London, 1916.

Archer, William. *The Pirate's Progress. A Short History of the U-Boat.* London, 1918.

Archer, William. *Shirking the Issue.* London, 1917.

Archer, William. *Six of One and Half-A-Dozen of the Other.* London, 1917.

Archer, William. *The Villain of the World Tragedy.* London, 1916.

Ashley, W. J. *Germany's Food Supply.* London, 1916.

Ashley, W. J. *The War and its Economic Aspects.* Oxford Pamphlet No.4. Oxford, 1914.

Asquith, H. H. *A Call to Arms.* London, 1914.

Asquith, H. H. *A Free Future for the World.* London, 1916.

Asquith, H. H. *Italy Our Ally.* London, 1916.

Asquith, H. H. *The War Its Causes and Its Message.* London, 1914.

Asquith, H. H. *What Britain is Fighting For.* London, 1916.

Asquith, H. H. *Where Do We Stand Today?* London, 1915.

Bainbridge, Oliver. *England's Arch-Enemy The Kaiser.* London, 1915.

Balfour, Arthur J. *The British Blockade.* London, 1915.

Balfour, Arthur J. *The Freedom of the Seas.* London, 1916.

Balfour, Arthur J. *The Navy and the War.* London, 1915.

Barker, Ernest. *The Submerged Nationalities of the German Empire.* London, 1915.

Appendix 2

Barrés, Maurice. *The Soul of France.* London, 1915.

Bavier, André de. *Chivalrous England.* London, 1916.

Beck, James M. *America and the Allies.* London, 1916.

Beck, James M and Charles W. Eliot. *America's View of Germany's case.* London, 1914.

Beck, James M. *The Evidence in the Case.* London and New York, 1915.

Bedier, Joseph. *How Germany Seeks to Justify her Atrocities.* Paris, 1915.

Bell, Sir Hugh. *On The Division of the Product of Industry.* London, 1916.

#Belloc, Hilaire. *The Second Year of the War.* London, 1916.

#Benson, F. L. *Deutschland über Allah.* London, 1917.

#Bevan, Edwyn. *Brothers All: The War and the Race Question.* Oxford, 1915.

Bhownaggree, Mancherjee. *The Verdict of India.* London, 1916.

Blatchford, Robert. *The War that Was Foretold.* London, 1915.

Borsa, Mario. *England and her Critics.* London, 1917.

Brockway, A. F., Baron Brockway. *Is Britain blameless?* London, 1915.

Bryce, Viscount James W. *The Attitude of Great Britain in the Present War.* London, 1916.

#Bryce, Viscount James W. *The Presidential Address to the British Academy, June 30, 1915.* Oxford, 1915.

Buchan, John. *The Battle of Jutland.* London, 1916.

Buchan, John. *The Battle of the Somme.* London, 1917

Bury, J. B. *Germany and Slavonic Civilisation.* London, 1917.

Butler, Geoffrey G. *International law and Autocracy.* London, 1917.

Buxton, T. F. V. *Slavery in Europe.* London, 1917.

Cammaerts, Emile. *Through the Iron Bars.* London, 1917.

Cammaerts, Emile. *To the Men Behind the Armies.* London, 1917.

Carson, Sir Edward. *The War on German Submarines.* London, 1917.

The Case of the Allies. Being the Replies to President Wilson, and Mr. Balfour's Despatch. London, 1917.

Cecil, Lord Robert. *Black List and Blockade.* London, 1916.

Cecil, Lord Robert. *Why Mail Censorship is Vital to Britain.* London, 1916.

Church, Samuel Harden. *The American Verdict on the War.* New York and London, 1914.

#Cohn, August. *Some Aspects of the War as Viewed By Naturalized British Subjects.* London, 1916.

Propaganda Materials Sent to the USA

Cook, Sir Edward. *Britain and Turkey: The Causes of the Rupture.* London, 1914.

Cook, Sir Edward. *Britain's Part in the War.* London, 1916.

Cook, Sir Edward. *How Britain Strove for Peace.* London, 1914.

Cook, Sir Edward. *The Press Censorship.* London, 1914.

Cook, Sir Edward. *Why Britain Is at War.* London, 1914.

Corbett, Julian. *The League of Peace and a Free Sea.* London, 1917.

Corbett, Julian. *The Spectre of Navalism.* London, 1915.

The Crimes Of Germany. An Illustrated Synopsis. London, 1916.

Cromer, Earl of. *Germania contra Mundum.* London, 1915.

Crooks, Will. *The British Workman Defends His Home.* London, 1917.

Curzon, Earl of Kedleston. *Germany's Move and Britain's Answer.* London, 1916.

Davies, E. F. *The Finances of Great Britain and Germany.* London, 1916.

De Chair, Sir Dudley. *How the British Blockade Works.* London, 1916.

The Deportation of Women and Girls from Lille. London, 1916.

Dixon, W. Macneile. *The British Navy at War.* London and New York, 1917.

Dixon, W. Macneile. *The Fleets Behind the Fleet.* New York, 1917.

Documents Diplomatiques 1914 La Guerre Européenne. Paris, 1915.

Donald, Robert. *Trade Control in War.* London, 1916.

Donald-Smith, Helen. *War Distress and War Help.* London, 1916.

Durkheim, Emile. *Germany Above All.* Paris, 1915.

Durkheim, Emile and E. Denis. *Qui a voulu la guerre?* Paris, 1915.

Ericson, Carl. *Some Swedish Reflections.* London, 1916.

Evidence and Documents Laid Before the Committee on Alleged German Outrages, presided over by the Right Hon. Viscount Bryce. London, 1915.

Fisher, H A L. *The British Share in the War.* London, 1915.

French, Sir John. *The Germans and the Small Nations.* London, 1917.

German Atrocities in France. A Translation of the Official Report of the French Commission. London, 1915.

The German Note of December 12, 1916 and the Reply of the Allies. London, 1917.

Gibbs, Philip. *The Germans on the Somme.* London, 1917.

Goschen, Sir Edward. *The One Condition of Peace.* London, 1916.

Appendix 2

Gosling, Harry. *Peace: How To Get And Keep It*. New York and London, 1917.

Gray, Alexander. *The True Pastime: the German Attitude Towards War*. London, 1915.

Great Britain and the European Crisis. London, 1914.

Grey, Sir Edward. *Great Britain's Measures against German Trade*. London, 1916.

Grey, Sir Edward. *Why Britain is in the War*. London, 1916.

Grey, Sir Edward. *A Free Europe*. London, 1916.

Gwatkin, H M. *Britain's Case against Germany*. London, 1916.

Hardinge, Lord of Penshurst. *Loyal India*. London, 1916.

#Harrison, Frederic. *The Meaning of the War*. London, 1914.

Hauser, Henri. *Economic Germany*. London, 1915.

Headlam, J. W. *Belgium and Greece*. London, 1917.

Headlam, J. W. *England, Germany and Europe*. London, 1914.

Headlam, J. W. *The History of Twelve Days*. London, 1915.

Headlam, J. W. *The Peace Terms of the Allies*. London, 1917.

Headlam, J. W. *The Starvation of Germany*. London, 1917.

Higgins, A. Pearce. *Defensively-Armed Merchant Ships and Submarine Warfare*. London, 1917.

Hill, G. F. *The Commemorative Medal in the Service of Germany*. London, 1917.

Hope, Anthony. *Militarism German and British*. London, 1915.

Hope, Anthony. *Why Italy is with the Allies*. London, 1917.

How Long Will It Last? Reprinted from the New York *Tribune* of the 3rd May, 1916. London, 1916.

Hume-Williams, W E. *International Law and the Blockade*. London, 1916.

Hurd, Archibald. *If the British Fleet Had Not Moved!* London, 1915.

Hurd, Archibald. *If There Were No Navies!* London, 1916.

Hurd, Archibald. *An Incident of War*. London, 1916.

Hurd, Archibald. *Murder at Sea*. London, 1916.

Hurd, Archibald. *Naval Prospects in 1917*. London, 1917.

Hurd, Archibald. *Submarines and Zeppelins*. London, 1916.

Islington, Sir Charles. *Some Facts About India*. London, 1917.

Jacks, L P. *An Interim Religion*. London, 1916

Propaganda Materials Sent to the USA

Johnson, Douglas W. *Plain Words From America.* London, 1917.

Jonescu, M. Take. *The Policy of National Instinct.* London, 1916.

Judicial Committee of the Privy Council. Report on the "Zamora". London, 1916.

#Koedt, Peschke. *English and German Culture.* London, 1915.

Lavisse, E. and Ch. Andler. *German Theory and Practice of War.* London, 1915.

#Law, A. Bonar. *A Speech on the War, December 14, 1914.* London, 1915.

Leeper, A. W. A. *The Justice of Rumania's Cause.* London, 1917.

A List of Neutral Ships Sunk by the Germans. From August 8, 1914 to April 26, 1917. London, 1917.

Lloyd George, David. *Peace Proposals and the Attitude of the Allies.* London, 1916.

Lloyd George, David. *Why The Allies Will Win.* London, 1916.

Low, A. Maurice. *The Law of Blockade.* London, 1916.

Mackail, J. W. *Russia's Gift to the World.* London, 1915.

Masterman, C. F. G. *After Twelve Months of War.* London, 1915.

Masterman, C. F. G. *The Triumph of the Fleet.* London, 1915.

Mears, E. Grimwood. *The Destruction of Belgium.* London, 1916.

Memorandum of the Belgian Government on the Deportations Ordered by the German Government. London, 1917.

Memorandum on the Censorship. The Mails as a German War Weapon. London, 1916.

Mendonça, Henrique Lopes de. *Moral Aspects of the European war.* London, 1917.

Mercier, Cardinal. *An Appeal to Truth.* London, 1915.

Mercier, Cardinal. *For Our Soldiers.* London, 1916.

Mills, J. Saxon. *The Gathering of the Clans.* London, 1916.

Milner, Viscount. *Cotton Contraband.* London, 1915.

Montague, Edwin. *The Means of Victory.* London, 1916.

Morgan, J. H. *A Dishonored Army: German Atrocities In France.* Reprinted from June 1915 *Nineteenth Century.* London, 1915.

Morison, J. L. *Modern British Foreign Policy.* Kingston, 1915.

Muir, Ramsey. *The Character of the British Empire.* London, 1917

Muir, Ramsey. *The Freedom of the Seas.* London, 1917.

Muir, Ramsey. *Great Britain's Case.* London, 1914.

Appendix 2

Murray, Gilbert. *The Foreign Policy of Sir Edward Grey.* Oxford, 1914.

Murray, Gilbert. *Great Britain's Sea Policy.* London, 1917.

Murray, Gilbert. *The United States and the War.* London, 1916.

Namier, Lewis B. *The Case of Bohemia.* London, 1917.

Namier, Lewis B. *The Czecho-Slovaks.* London, 1917.

Niepage, Martin. *The Horrors of Aleppo.* London, 1916.

Northomb, Pierre. *La Belgique Martyre.* Paris, 1915.

Noyes, Alfred. *What is England Doing?* London, 1916.

An Open Letter to the German Professors. London, 1915.

#Osler, Sir William. *Science and War.* Oxford, 1915.

Page, Walter Hines. *The Union of Two Great Peoples.* London, 1917.

Parfit, Canon J. T. *Mesopotamia: The Key to the Future.* London, 1917.

Parker, Sir Gilbert. *Is England Apathetic?* London, 1915.

Parker, Sir Gilbert. *Two years of War.* London, 1916.

Parker, Sir Gilbert. *The United States and This War.* London, 1915.

Parker, Sir Gilbert. *What Is The Matter with England?* London, 1915

"Philosophus". *What is England Doing?* London, 1916.

Picton, Harold. *Is It to Be Hate?* London , 1917.

Prothero, G. W. *A Lasting Peace.* London, 1917.

Raleigh, Sir Walter. *The War of Ideas.* London, 1917.

The Reception of Wounded Prisoner Soldiers of Great Britain in Switzerland. London, 1916

Redmond, John. *Mr. Redmond's Visit to the Front.* London, 1915.

Redmond, John. *Strong Words from Mr. Redmond.* London, 1916.

Redmond, John. *The Voice of Ireland.* London, 1916

Reiss, R. A. *How Austria-Hungary Wages War in Serbia.* Paris, 1915.

Report of the Committee on Alleged German Outrages, presided over by the Right Hon. Viscount Bryce. London, 1915

Revelstoke, Sir George. *British Staying Power.* London, 1916.

Robertson, J. M. *Britain versus Germany.* London, 1917.

Robertson, J. M. *The German Idea of Peace Terms.* London, 1917.

Propaganda Materials Sent to the USA

Robertson, J. M. *German Truth and a Matter of Fact.* London, 1917.

Rolleston, T. W. *Ireland and Poland.* London, 1917.

#Rose, J. Holland. *German Misrepresentations.* London, 1916.

Russia and Her Allies. Extract From The Verbatim Report of the Imperial Duma. IV Session. 16th Sitting. London, 1917.

Sadler, M. E. *Modern Germany and the Modern World.* London, 1914.

Sargant, E. B and Marie Sargant. *The Country's Call: A Short Selection of Patriotic Verse.* London, 1914

Scraps of Paper. German Proclamations in Belgium and in France. London, 1916.

The Second Belgian Grey Book. London, 1915.

Siriha, S. P. *The Future of India.* London, 1916.

Smuts, J. C. *The British Commonwealth of Nations.* London, 1917.

Some American Opinions on the Indian Empire. London, 1915.

Sprigg, W. Stanhope. *The British Blockade.* London, 1916.

Stanley, Arthur. *Mercy-Workers of the War.* London, 1916.

Struycken, A. A. H. *The German White Book on the War in Belgium: A Commentary.* London, 1915.

Supplement to the London Gazette. London, 1914-1917, *passim.*

Supplement to Punch October 14, 1914. London, 1914.

Symposium. *After Two Years.* London, 1916.

Symposium. *Belgian Independence Day.* London, 1916.

Symposium of Spanish Writers. *To Belgium.* 1916.

Thompson, Alex M. *Prussia's Devilish Creed.* London, 1915.

Toynbee, Arnold J. *The Belgian Deportations.* London, 1917.

Toynbee, Arnold J. *The Destruction of Poland.* London, 1916.

Toynbee, Arnold J. *The German Terror in France.* London, 1917.

Toynbee, Arnold J. *"The Murderous Tyranny of the Turks".* London, 1917.

Toynbee, Arnold J. *Turkey a Past and a Future.* London, 1917.

Treatment of Prisoners of War in England and Germany during the First Eight Months of the War. London, 1915.

Turkish Prisoners in Egypt: A Report by the Delegates of the International Committee of the Red Cross. London, 1917.

"Vedette". *Britain and Armageddon.* London, 1914.

The Violation of Belgian Neutrality. London, 1915.

Vogel, J. P. *The British Administration in India.* London, 1915.

Weiss, Andre. *La Violation de la neutralité belge et luxembourgeoise par l'Allemagne.* Paris, 1915.

What is Great Britain Doing? Reprinted from the Philadelphia *North American* May 5, 1916. London, 1916.

Wilson, H. W. *Convicted Out of Her Own Mouth.* London, 1917.

Wise, Bernhard R. *The Freedom of the Seas.* London, 1915.

Withers, Hartley. *War and Self Denial.* London, 1915.

Wood, Thomas M. and Arthur Henderson. *British Finance and Prussian Militarism.* London, 1917.

#Younghusband, Francis. *The Fight for Right.* London, 1916.

Anonymous

Bernhardi Converted. London, 1915.

Britain's Financial Effort. London, 1917.

Britain Transformed. London, 1916.

The Care of the Dead. London, 1916.

Censorship And Trade. London, 1916.

The Commercial Future of Baghdad. London, 1917.

The Condition of the Belgian Workmen now Refugees in England. London, 1917.

Frightfulness in Retreat. London, 1917.

Germany and the Prussian Spirit. London, 1914.

The Horrors of Louvain. London, 1916.

The Horrors of Wittenberg. London, 1916.

The Jutland Battle By Two Who Took Part in It. London, 1916.

The King of Hedjaz and Arab Independence. London, 1917.

The Murder of Captain Fryatt. London, 1916.

The New German Empire. London, 1917.

The Ottoman Domination. London, 1917.

Poland Under the Germans. London, 1916.

The Sentinels of the Seas. London, 1915.

The Straight Path and the Crooked. London, 1916.

Propaganda Materials Sent to the USA

Their Crimes. London, 1917.

Through Swamp and Forest. London, 1916.

The War on Hospital Ships. London, 1917.

.The World's Largest Loan. London, 1917.

Appendix 3

3. Artists Active during the Great War

Although the years 1914-1918 were dominated by official war art **(see Part 3 in section 3.2 on Art)** the period was not devoid of works which bore no relation to the war as can be seen, for example, in the works selected below:

Bone, Sir. M. *Piccadilly Circus* (1915) [Mildred Lane Kemper Art Museum, Washington University]
Drypoint on paper.

— *San Frediano in Castello, Florence* (1915) [Fine Arts Museums of San Francisco]
Drypoint on paper.

Dodd, F. *In the Park* (1916) [Tate Collection]
Oil painting on canvas.

Epstein, Sir J. *Doves* (1914-15) [Tate Collection]
Sculpture, Greek marble.

— *Portrait of Iris Beerbohm Tree* (1915) [Tate Collection]
Sculpture, Bronze. Iris Beerbohm Tree (1897–1968) was a poet and actress who posed for many artists including Vanessa Bell and Duncan Grant.

Gertler, M. *The Tea Pot* (1918) [Tate Collection]
Oil painting on canvas.

Gilman, H. *Mrs. Mounter at the Breakfast Table* (exhibited 1917) [Tate Collection]
Oil painting on canvas'

Grant, D. *Vanessa Bell Painting* (1915)[National Galleries of Scotland. Scottish National Gallery of Modern Art]
British painter and designer Vanessa Bell was the older sister of Virginia Woolf and like Duncan Grant was a member of Bloomsbury Group. Vanessa Bell lived with Grant from 1916 and gave birth to their daughter in 1918.

— *Interior* at *Gordon Square* (1916) {Tate Collection]
Oil painting on wood. Duncan Grant, like other artists in the Bloomsbury Group, painted their friends engaged in such activities as painting, reading or writing, as well as the objects and furnishings (often home-made) in their rooms. This painting shows the view between the front and back rooms on the first floor of 46 Gordon Square in London, where Grant lived for a time with Vanessa Bell.

John, A. E. *Galway* (1916 and 1920) [Tate Collection]
Oil painting on canvas. With the painting of this mural work (a triptych), the largest he ever produced, Augustus John hoped to make 'a vast picture synthesizing all that's fine and characteristic in Galway City – a grand marshalling of the elements'.

— *The Orange Jacket* (circa 1916) [Tate Collection]
Oil painting on canvas

— *Rachel* (1917) [Tate Collection]
Oil painting on canvas

— *Washing Day* (circa 1915) [Tate Collection]
Oil painting on wood

Sickert, W. R. *Belvedere, Bath* (circa 1917) [Tate Collection]
Oil painting on canvas

— *The Little Tea Party: Nina Hamnett and Roald Kristian* (1915-16) [Tate Collection]
Oil painting on canvas

— *The New Bedford* (1915-1916) [Tate Collection]
Oil painting on canvas

Spencer, Sir S. *Mending Cowls, Cookham* (1915) [Tate Collection]
Oil painting on canvas

— *Swan Upping at Cookham* (1915-19) [Tate Collection]
Oil painting on canvas. The completion of this work, which was delayed by Spencer's involvement in the First World War., presented him with difficulties when he returned to it because of his feeling, as he expressed it, that 'it is not proper or sensible to expect to paint after such experience'. [Tate display caption]

Wadsworth, E. *Abstract Composition* (1915) [Tate Collection]
Gouache, pen and pencil on paper. This Vorticist composition "with its sharp diagonal lines converging towards a 'nodal point' exemplifies Pound's definition of the Vortex as 'absorbing all that is around it in a violent whirling - a violent central engulfing' ... Other artists associated with Vorticism included William Roberts, Henri Gaudier-Brzeska, C. R. W. Nevinson David Bomberg, and Wyndham Lewis ... Lewis's attempts to revive the movement in 1919 came to nothing". [Information extracted from Tate display caption]

— *The Open Window* (circa 1915) [Tate Collection]
Woodcut on paper. Most of Wadsworth's surviving Vorticist works are woodcuts, which he continued to make throughout the war.

— *The Port* (circa 1915) [Tate Collection]
Woodcut on paper. This print resembles the illustrations Wadsworth produced for the Vorticists' magazine *Blast*.

Appendix 4

4. Sassoon's Public Protest (1917)

While convalescing in England in 1917 from a wound he had received at the front Sassoon prepared, with the encouragement and assistance of Bertrand Russell, a statement of strong protest about the war (see text below) to his commanding officer. Copies were printed and distributed to influential people and to the press. It was published in the *Bradford Pioneer* on July 27 1917, read in the House of Commons on July 30, and printed the next day in *The Times*. He was saved from being court-martialled for this public protest by his friend and fellow-officer Robert Graves who pleaded that Sassoon was mentally ill. As a result of this plea and of its influence on the Medical Board convened to consider Sassoon's mental state he was sent to Craiglockhart Hospital and treated for shell shock under the care of W. H. R. Rivers. A novel woven around these historical events was written by Pat Barker under the title of *Regeneration*, first published by Viking in 1991.

Finished with the War: A Soldier's Declaration (1917)

"I am making this statement as an act of wilful defiance of military authority because I believe that the war is being deliberately prolonged by those who have the power to end it. I am a soldier, convinced that I am acting on behalf of soldiers.

I believe that the war upon which I entered as a war of defence and liberation has now become a war of aggression and conquest. I believe that the purposes for which I and my fellow soldiers entered upon this war should have been so clearly stated as to have made it impossible to change them and that had this been done the objects which actuated us would now be attainable by negotiation.

I have seen and endured the sufferings of the troops and I can no longer be a party to prolonging these sufferings for ends which I believe to be evil and unjust. I am not protesting against the conduct of the war, but against the political errors and insincerities for which the fighting men are being sacrificed.

On behalf of those who are suffering now, I make this protest against the deception which is being practised upon them; also I believe it may help to destroy the callous complacency with which the majority of those at home regard the continuance of agonies which they do not share and which they have not enough imagination to realise".

S. Sassoon
July 1917

In early 1918 Sassoon, a courageous soldier with a Military Cross to his name (although during the period of his public protest he had thrown the ribbon of his MC into the Mersey), left Craiglockhart and after a brief spell of duty in Palestine rejoined his battalion in France, alongside his fellow soldiers, where, in spite of his misgivings about the war, he had really always wanted to be.

INDEX

The following pages provide a list of keywords on which the bibliography can be searched. This list is not comprehensive; it is representative of a selection of the people and organizations referred to in the bibliography, interspersed with a number of the subjects covered that are included for the purpose of providing a supplement to the list of subjects contained in the <u>Contents</u> pages.

Addison, Christopher, 1st Viscount Addison (1869-1951), 72, 208, 262, 357, 373, 513
advertisements, 231, 251, 278, 502
air raids, 151, 152, 157, 196, 345
Aldington, Richard (1892-1962), 173, 174, 176, 177, 289, 387, 413, 414, 430, 433, 434, 435, 439, 442, 443, 444, 446, 448, 449
Allatini, Rose (c.1890-1980), 147, 167, 380, 416, 439
Allen, Reginald Clifford, Baron Allen of Hurtwood (1889-1939), 124, 128
Allenby, Edmund Henry Hyman, 1st Viscount Allenby (1861-1936), 158, 274, 275, 276, 289, 301, 308, 332, 333, 404, 405, 406
Amazon, viii, 491
Amery, Leopold Stennett, (1873-1955), 85
Angell, Sir Norman (1872-1967), 22, 26, 29, 45, 65, 127, 128, 130, 131, 133, 134, 136, 138, 140, 142, 143, 216, 297
appeasement, 385, 387, 388, 389, 391, 392
Armistice Day, 346, 393, 396, 452
Asche, Oscar (1871-1936), 187, 188, 196
Ashwell, Lena Margaret (1872-1957), 186, 196, 197, 198, 433
Asquith, Anthony (1902-1968), 461, 467
Asquith, Herbert Henry, 1st Earl of Oxford and Asquith (1864-1945), 55, 84, 85, 87, 92, 93, 99, 231, 234, 268, 292, 513
Asquith, Lady Cynthia Mary Evelyn (1887-1960), 111, 112, 422
Asquith, Margot, Countess of Oxford and Asquith (1964-1945), 70, 112
atrocities, 61, 134, 147, 163, 224, 250, 255, 259, 264, 286
Baden-Powell, Robert Stephenson Smyth, 1st Baron (1857-1941), 44
Bagnold, Enid (1889-1981), 112, 416, 423, 435
Bairnsfather, Charles Bruce (1888-1959), 169, 170, 171, 201, 202, 283, 284, 285, 289, 323, 454, 455
Balcon, Michael (1896-1977), 460
Balfour, Arthur James ,1st Earl of Balfour (1848-1930), 12, 70, 86, 89, 231, 234, 242, 243, 261, 262, 267, 268, 294, 296, 297, 307, 513, 514
Barbour, Mary (1875–1958), 80
Barker, Dame Lilian Charlotte (1874-1955), 114
Barker, Sir Ernest (1874-1960), 60, 65, 136
Barnes, George Nicoll (1859-1940), 68, 72, 78, 85

Barrie, Sir James Matthew (1860-1937), 58, 169, 170, 171, 174, 183, 197, 202, 312, 454, 455, 475
Bax, Sir Arnold Edward Trevor (1883-1953), 60, 190, 191, 486, 487, 488
Baylis, Lilian Mary (1874-1937), 168, 169, 197, 453
Beatty, David, 1st Earl Beatty (1871-1936), 336, 337, 338
Beaverbrook, William Maxwell Aitken, 1st Baron, 86, 88, 89, 92, 94, 95, 96, 156, 159, 216, 229, 230, 237, 238, 263, 272, 287, 289
Beecham, Sir Thomas (1879-1961), 185, 189, 190, 191, 486
Bell, Gertrude Margaret Lowthian (1868-1926), 306
Bennett, Arnold (1867-1931), 58, 79, 156, 167, 182, 183, 218, 238, 432, 433, 434, 435
Benson, Sir Francis Robert (1858-1939), 168
Beresford, Charles William De la Poer Beresford, Baron (1846-1919), 70, 147, 148
Bernstorff, Johann Heinrich, Graf von (1862-1939), 243, 245
Bertie, Francis Levison, 1st Viscount Bertie of Thame (1844-1919), 33
Bevin, Ernest (1881-1951), 72, 73, 76
Billing, Noel Pemberton (1881-1948), 147, 148, 300
birth control, 381
Bliss, Sir Arthur Edward Drummond (1891-1975), 190, 192, 486, 487, 488
blockade, 39, 59, 63, 134, 206, 218, 238, 241, 243, 245, 250, 256, 261, 267, 286, 290, 291, 295, 298, 300, 302, 303, 310, 337, 339, 341, 342, 343, 344, 367, 513, 514, 515, 516, 517, 519
Bloomsbury Group, 68, 69, 162, 194, 522
Bondfield, Margaret Grace (1873-1953), 112, 114, 123, 423
Bone, Sir Muirhead (1876-1953), 155, 156, 157, 161, 162, 478, 484, 522
Borden, Mary (1886-1968), 112, 174, 416
Bottomley, Horatio William (1860-1933), 94, 146, 148, 231, 232, 269, 289, 324, 447
Boy Scouts, 44
Bragg, William Henry (1862-1942), 61, 63, 352
Brailsford, Henry Noel (1873-1958), 131, 133, 134, 136, 139, 143, 146
Brangwyn, Sir Frank (1867-1956), 161, 162, 475, 480, 483
Brian, Havergal (1876-1972), 190, 486, 487

INDEX

Bridge, Frank (1879-1941), 190, 191, 192, 486
British Bureau of Information (BBI), 242
British Empire Union, 146, 148, 149, 150, 231, 263
British Neutrality Committee, 30, 62, 135
British Socialist Party, 78, 79, 85
British War Memorials Committee, 155, 160, 477, 481
British Workers' League, 77
Brittain, Vera Mary (1893-1970), 18, 57, 112, 113, 114, 140, 174, 181, 382, 416, 419, 423, 429, 434, 435, 439, 449, 474
Britten, Edward Benjamin, Baron Britten of Aldeburgh (1913-1976), 486, 487, 488
Brockway, Archibald Fenner, Baron Brockway (1888-1988), 80, 94, 123, 124, 139, 140, 211, 212, 514
Brooke, Rupert Chawner (1887-1915), 16, 57, 158, 173, 174, 177, 419, 442, 443, 444, 445, 447, 448, 449
Brownrigg, Sir Douglas Egremont (1867-1939), 216, 222, 288
Brunel, Adrian (1892-1958), 273, 461, 466
Bryan, William Jennings (1860-1925), 199, 201, 243, 244, 245
Bryce Group, 61
Bryce, James, Viscount Bryce (1838-1922), 61, 65, 133, 134, 135, 136, 137, 140, 141, 147, 157, 158, 224, 228, 229, 232, 255, 260, 261, 266, 267, 286, 297, 512, 514, 515, 518
Buchan, John, 1st Baron Tweedsmuir (1875-1940), 147, 163, 165, 183, 237, 238, 242, 262, 285, 287, 402, 417, 433, 514
Buchanan, Sir George William (1854-1924), 33, 238
Burns, John Elliot (1858-1943), 84, 87
Burton, Sir Pomeroy (1869-1947), 242
Butler, Lady Elizabeth, (1846-1933), 156, 158, 480
Buxton, Charles Roden (1875-1942), 127, 131, 133, 139, 140, 145, 146
Caine, Sir Hall (1853-1931), 58, 110, 121, 182, 183, 203, 261
Callwell, Sir Charles Edward (1859-1928), 216, 222, 300, 333, 403
Cambrai, 54, 311, 326, 328, 329, 348, 349, 425
Cambridge Magazine, 60, 140
Cannan, May Wedderburn (1893-1973), 174, 181, 416, 444, 449
Cardus, Sir Neville (1889-1975), 190, 196
Carrington, Charles Edmund (1897-1990), 18, 315, 413, 419, 424, 432
Carson, Edward Henry, Baron Carson (1854-1935), 86, 103, 104, 237, 514
Carter, Violet Bonham, Baroness Asquith of Yarnbury (1887-1969), 86, 113, 424
cartoons, 161, 162, 199, 201, 242, 254, 256, 264, 278, 283, 284, 289, 323
Casement, Roger David (1864-1916), 86, 103, 104, 105, 107, 256, 265, 455, 459
Cave, George, Viscount Cave (1856-1928), 87, 215

Cecil, Robert., 1st Viscount Cecil of Chelwood (1864-1958), 133, 134, 135, 218, 261
cemeteries, 392, 394, 395
Cenotaph, 395, 398, 399, 451, 482
censorship, 94, 123, 157, 168, 170, 171, 210, 211, 212, 215, 216, 217, 218, 219, 220, 221, 222, 236, 290, 381, 402, 416, 477
Central Committee for National Patriotic Organisations (CCNPO), 231, 232, 256, 258, 264, 265, 269
Chamberlain, Joseph (1836-1914), 42
Chamberlain, Sir Austen (1863-1937), 86
Chaplin, Charlie (1889-1977), 194, 200, 202, 205
Chapman, Guy (1889-1972), 413, 419, 424
Charteris, John (1877-1946), 216, 221, 403
Chesterton, Cecil (1879-1918), 79, 81, 82
Chesterton, Gilbert Keith (1874-1936), 58, 174, 177, 180, 183, 234, 285, 449
Christmas Truce, 312, 388, 454, 457
Church of England, 99, 101, 381, 476
Churchill, Sir Winston Spencer (1874-1965), 13, 23, 46, 51, 54, 86, 87, 92, 234, 262, 294, 299, 300, 338, 342, 343, 387, 402, 403, 406, 408, 436, 440, 502
cinema, 184, 193, 194, 198, 199, 200, 201, 202, 216, 224, 242, 251, 254, 271, 272, 275, 279, 287, 322, 387, 460, 462, 464, 465, 467, 469, 501, 503
Clifford, John (1836-1923), 100
Clyde Workers' Committee, 73, 74, 79, 80, 217
Clynes, John Robert (1869-1949), 72, 73
Cobden Club, 256
Coborn, Charles (1852-1945), 197
Cochran, Sir Charles Blake (1872-1951), 187, 197
Cockerill, Sir George Kynaston (1867-1957), 229, 237, 238
Cole, George Douglas Howard (1889-1950), 74, 79
Collins, Michael (1890-1922), 104
comics, 15, 20. *See also* humour
Committee on Public Information (CPI), 251
Connolly, James (1886-1916), 104, 105, 109
conscientious objectors, 47, 68, 94, 100, 114, 123, 124, 125, 128, 141, 153, 211, 212, 213, 385, 421, 429
conscription, 55, 68, 79, 80, 103, 104, 111, 112, 123, 124, 127, 128, 141, 185, 196, 206, 211, 215, 231, 279, 280, 287, 316
Conservative Party, 40, 84, 89, 90, 91, 93, 377, 378, 379
Cooper, Lady Diana, Viscountess Norwich (1892-1986), 70, 113, 424
Cooper, Selina (1864–1946), 114
Copac, 490, 500
Coulton, George Gordon (1858-1947), 65, 131, 142
Council of Loyal British Subjects, 256, 261
Cowans, Sir John Steven (1862-1921), 403
Creel, George, (1876-1953), 243, 245, 251, 252
Croft, Henry Page, 1st Baron Croft (1881-1947), 85, 86, 88, 92, 146

INDEX

Crowe, Sir Eyre (1864-1925), 33, 36
Cumming, Sir Mansfield (1859-1923), 306
Curzon, George Nathaniel, Marquess Curzon of Keddlestone (1859-1925), 70, 234, 292, 294, 515
Dalton, Emmet (1898-1978), 104
Dardanelles, 35, 40, 161, 238, 274, 296, 303, 330, 331, 337, 338, 339, 340, 341, 342, 343, 420, 425
Davis, Henry William Carless (1874-1928), 63, 64, 65
Dawson, Albert Knox (1885-1967), 245, 273
Dawson, Geoffrey (1874-1944), 96
Dean, Basil (1888-1978), 197, 198
Defence of the Realm Act (DORA), 122, 139, 140, 147, 164, 167, 211, 212, 219, 220, 380, 416, 439, 451
Delius, Frederick (1862-1934), 190, 192, 486, 488
Department of Information, 183, 229, 237, 242, 288, 475
Department of Scientific and Industrial Research (DSIR), 357, 358, 359
Derby, Edward George Villiers Stanley, 17th Earl of (1865-1948), 316, 317
Despard, Charlotte (1844-1939), 115
Docker, Dudley, 1862-1944, 208
Donald, Sir Robert (1860-1933), 237, 238, 241
Doyle, Sir Arthur Conan (1859-1930), 58, 77, 100, 101, 102, 165, 174, 177, 180, 183, 326, 402, 432, 433
drink, 71, 193, 206, 323, 383
Drinkwater, John (1882-1937), 169, 171, 172, 174, 177, 180, 447
Dual Monarchy, 21, 237, 298
Dumba, Constantin (1856-1947), 244
Easter Rising, 103, 104, 105, 106, 107, 108, 109, 191, 256, 265, 486, 488
Elcho, Lady Mary (1862-1937), 70
Elgar, Sir Edward William (1857-1934), 185, 190, 191, 192, 384, 486, 487, 488
Eliot, Thomas Stearns (1888-1965), 450
Entente Cordiale, 34, 35
Epstein, Sir Jacob (1880-1959), 155, 156, 157, 158, 161, 475, 477, 482, 485, 522
Ervine, St. John Greer (1883-1971), 109, 453, 455, 456
Esher, Reginald Baliol Brett, 2nd Viscount (1852-1930), 39, 293, 403
espionage, 18, 118, 150, 213, 214, 304, 309. *See also* spies and spying
Ewing, Sir Alfred (1855-1935), 305, 309
Fawcett, Dame Millicent (1847-1929), 111, 113, 114, 115, 118, 126, 378, 419, 425, 426
Fellowship of Reconciliation, 123, 126, 128, 130, 211
Fielding, Lady Dorothie (1889-1935), 114
Fight for Right Movement,, 231, 256
film, 146, 199, 201, 202, 224, 231, 242, 251, 254, 271, 272, 273, 287, 329, 381, 382, 387, 437, 453, 459, 460, 462, 464, 465, 467, 468, 471, 472, 473, 474, 500, 501, 502
First Aid Nursing Yeomanry, 110, 117
Fisher, Herbert Albert Laurens (1856-1940), 58, 61, 62, 65, 134, 140, 262, 357, 359, 374, 515
Fisher, John Arbuthnot, 1st Baron Fisher of Kilverstsone (1841-1920), 32, 33, 41, 158, 300, 339, 344
food, 71, 72, 115, 171, 174, 206, 208, 231, 270, 273, 275, 276, 280, 288, 323, 324, 337, 338, 369, 373, 421, 465
Forbes, Lady Angela (1876-1960), 113, 420
Ford, Ford Madox (1873-1939), 60, 164, 167, 174, 177, 182, 183, 430, 432, 433, 434, 436, 439, 442
Foulds, John Herbert (1880-1939), 487, 489
French, John Denton Pinkstone, 1st Earl of Ypres (1852-1925), 264, 285, 304, 402, 404
Fuller, John Frederick Charles (1878-1966), 402, 405, 407, 410, 420
Furse, Dame Katharine (1875-1952), 114, 426
Fussell, Paul, 16, 383, 411, 412, 415
Fyfe, Henry Hamilton (1869-1951), 90, 95
Gallacher, William (1881-1965), 73, 79, 80
Gallipoli, 49, 59, 62, 100, 161, 163, 175, 183, 184, 263, 274, 299, 330, 331, 334, 338, 345, 357, 362, 393, 399, 407, 423, 427, 434, 447, 450, 452, 464, 471, 473
Galsworthy, John (1867-1933), 58, 155, 167, 170, 171, 172, 180, 182, 183, 194, 432, 433, 434, 436, 454, 456
Garnett, David (1892-1981), 68
Garvin, James Louis (1868-1947), 94, 97, 98
Geddes, Sir Eric Campbell (1875-1937), 208, 210, 374, 375, 377
George V (1865-1936), 148, 294, 395
Gertler, Mark (1891-1939), 155, 156, 158, 475, 484, 522
Gollancz, Sir Victor (1893-1967), 191, 197
Gooch, George Peabody (1873-1968), 22, 31, 33, 39, 61, 64, 65, 92, 137, 139, 140, 143, 295, 301, 302, 317
Goschen, Sir William Edward (1847-1924), 33, 267, 515
Gough, Sir Hubert de la Poer (1870-1963), 329, 402, 404, 406, 407, 409, 410
Graves, Robert (1895-1985), 18, 173, 174, 177, 178, 197, 289, 323, 387, 411, 413, 414, 418, 420, 426, 442, 443, 445, 446, 447, 448, 450, 524
Greet, Sir Philip Barling Ben (1857-1936), 169
Grenfell, Julian Henry Francis (1888-1915), 57, 70, 178, 419, 442, 443, 445
Grey, Sir Edward, Viscount Grey of Fallodon (1875-1953), 33, 34, 35, 36, 37, 54, 61, 66, 87, 88, 129, 137, 141, 142, 261, 268, 293, 294, 295, 420, 512, 516, 518
Griffith, David Llewelyn Wark (1875-1948), 199, 201, 202, 203, 252, 253, 273

INDEX

Gurney, Ivor (1890-1937), 173, 174, 177, 178, 190, 192, 442, 445, 448, 450
Gwynne, Howell Arthur (1865-1950), 95, 98
Gwynne-Vaughan, Dame Helen Charlotte Isabella (1879-1967), 114
Haig, Douglas, 1st Earl Haig (1861-1928), 94, 157, 158, 160, 161, 216, 221, 299, 304, 311, 321, 326, 329, 399, 400, 402, 403, 404, 405, 406, 407, 408, 410, 411, 412, 469, 471, 501
Haldane, John Scott (1860-1936), 61, 352
Haldane, Richard Burdon, Viscount Haldane (1856-1928), 33, 43, 87, 148, 311, 314, 315, 358, 375
Hall, Sir William Reginald (1870-1943), 242, 305
Hamilton, Mary Agnes (1884-1966), 80, 114, 128, 139, 167
Hankey, Maurice Pascal Alers, 1st Baron Hankey (1877-1963), 295, 301, 335, 434
Hardie, James Keir (1856-1915), 30, 73, 79, 80, 81, 125, 141
Hardinge, Charles, Baron Hardinge of Penshurst (1858-1844), 33, 37, 263, 333, 516
Hardinge, Sir Arthur Henry (1859-1933), 34
Hardy, Thomas (1840-1928), 58, 162, 168, 169, 173, 174, 177, 180, 183, 184, 443, 450, 461
Harington, Sir Charles (1872-1940), 404
Harvey, Frederick William (1888-1957), 178, 444, 446, 450
Harvey, Sir John Martin (1863-1944), 168
Hearst, William Randolph (1863-1951), 241, 244, 247, 249, 257
Henderson, Arthur (1863-1935), 30, 45, 54, 72, 74, 77, 79, 80, 81, 83, 85, 87, 89, 92, 93, 123, 136, 139, 141, 142, 213, 231, 298, 380, 520
Henson, Leslie Lincoln (1891-1957), 102, 197
Hepworth, Cecil Milton (1874-1953), 199, 200, 202, 203, 204, 205, 277, 461
Hirst, Francis Wrigley (1873-1953), 94, 95, 128, 366
Hobhouse, Emily (1860-1926), 126, 127, 131
Hobhouse, Leonard Trelawney (1864-1929), 62
Hobson, John Atkinson (1858-1940), 62, 131, 133, 135, 136, 139, 141, 143, 146
Hodge, John (1855-1937), 73
Holst, Gustav Theodore (1874-1934), 190, 191, 192, 486, 487, 489
homosexuality, 147, 149, 212, 319, 380, 385
Horne, Henry Sinclair, Baron Horne (1861-1929), 404, 406, 410
Horniman, Annie Elizabet Fredericka (1860-1937), 169
housing, 373, 491
humour, 17, 154, 163, 188, 194, 196, 201, 283, 323, 325. *See also* comics; trench jounalism
Huxley, Aldous Leonard (1894-1963), 69, 176, 430, 436, 448
Hyndman, Henry Mayers (1842-1921), 78, 79, 80, 83
Imperial War Museum, 46, 157, 195, 271, 273, 281, 326, 336, 343, 394, 395, 396, 398, 399, 402, 425, 471, 476, 477, 479, 480, 483, 484, 485, 486, 489, 500, 501, 502, 503, 508
Independent Labour Party, 78, 80, 81, 82, 83, 84, 85, 89, 90, 91, 92, 93, 126, 127, 128, 131, 135, 139, 140, 141, 211
Industrial Relations, 13, 71, 73, 74, 75, 76, 210, 214, 376
Inglis, Elsie Maud (1864-1917), 114, 399
internment, 20, 52, 147, 338
Ireland, John Nicholson (1879-1962), 190, 191, 193
Irish Rebellion, 107, 108, 109, 471
James, Henry (1843-1916), 70, 251, 252, 257, 258
Jellicoe, John Rushworth, 1st Earl Jellicoe (1859-1935), 158, 300, 337, 338, 339, 341, 344
John Bull, 94, 148, 194, 204, 231, 269, 270, 273, 276, 282, 283, 285, 438, 441
Jones, Sir Roderick (1877-1962), 95, 288
Joynson-Hicks, William, 1st Viscount Brentford (1856-1932), 147, 148, 301, 348
Jutland, 276, 285, 337, 339, 340, 341, 342, 344, 419, 425, 427, 429, 465, 466, 514, 520
Kaiser (i.e. William II (1859-1941), German Emperor (1888-1918), 102, 188, 189, 212, 255, 256, 265, 283, 284
Kennington, Eric (1888-1960), 155, 156, 157, 159, 161, 162, 476, 478, 479, 482, 484
King, Gladys Lilian (1884-1970), 120
Kipling, Rudyard (1865-1936), 58, 107, 164, 174, 177, 180, 183, 184, 185, 190, 263, 264, 431, 432, 433, 434, 437, 440, 450
Knoblauch, Edward (1874-1945), 169, 170, 172
Labour Party, 54, 55, 71, 72, 73, 74, 78, 79, 80, 82, 83, 84, 85, 89, 90, 91, 92, 93, 112, 114, 123, 124, 125, 126, 133, 135, 139, 141, 142, 211, 213, 215, 234, 293, 297, 298, 377, 378, 379, 380, 423
Lane, Lupino (1892-1959), 197, 202, 203
Lang, (William) Cosmo Gordon, Baron Lang of Lambeth (1864–1945), 100
Lansbury, George (1859-1940), 30, 81, 123, 124, 128, 129
Lansdowne, Henry Charles Keith Petty-Fitzmaurice, 5th Marquis of Lansdowne (1845-1927), 36, 87, 126, 129, 131, 132, 294, 298
Lansing, Robert, (1864-1928), 244
Lauder, Sir Harry (1870-1950), 189, 197
Law, Andrew Bonar (1858-1923), 84, 85, 92, 231, 293, 299, 517
Lawrence, David Herbert (1885-1930), 69, 128, 141, 162, 167, 176, 182, 380, 430, 432, 433, 437, 447
Lawrence, Thomas Edward (1888-1935), 275, 299, 332, 420, 427, 465, 468, 473, 480
League of Free Nations Association, 133, 138
League of Nations, 60, 65, 68, 116, 122, 129, 133, 134, 135, 136, 137, 138, 142, 143, 146, 268, 293
League of Nations Society, 62, 133, 137, 138
League of Nations Union, 133, 138
Lean, David (1908-1991), 461, 468, 473

INDEX

Ledward, Gilbert (1888-1960), 156, 400, 475, 477, 482
Ledwige, Francis (1891-1917), 104, 178
Lee, Vernon, pseud. [i.e. Violet Paget] (1856-1935), 128, 131, 139, 140
Lewis, Percy Wyndham (1882-1957), 154, 155, 156, 157, 159, 168, 171, 420, 427, 459, 475, 476, 477, 480, 481, 484
Liberal Party, 78, 84, 90, 91, 92, 93, 109, 127, 129, 142, 377, 378, 379
Liddell Hart, Sir Basil Henry (1895-1970), 18, 302, 304, 313, 402, 408, 410, 421, 427, 503
Lloyd George, David, 1st Earl Lloyd-George of Dwyfor (1863-1945), 30, 31, 36, 46, 54, 55, 61, 62, 76, 84, 85, 86, 87, 88, 90, 92, 93, 95, 99, 109, 112, 121, 123, 125, 128, 134, 136, 156, 160, 207, 208, 209, 210, 213, 214, 222, 234, 235, 237, 238, 242, 249, 256, 267, 268, 283, 286, 292, 293, 294, 296, 297, 298, 299, 300, 301, 303, 304, 327, 358, 373, 376, 402, 404, 405, 410, 412, 429, 463, 468, 481, 517
Lloyd, Marie (1870-1922), 196
Loraine, Robert (1876-1935), 197
Ludendorff, Erich von (1865-1937), 229, 238, 287, 289
Lupino, Stanley (1894-1942), 197
Lusitania, HMS, 147, 192, 203, 227, 243, 244, 259, 286, 511
Lutyens, Edwin (1869-1944), 396, 397, 398, 477
Macdonald, James Ramsay (1866-1937), 45, 55, 73, 78, 79, 81, 85, 86, 87, 91, 92, 128, 138, 140, 141, 379
Maclean, John (1879-1923), 79, 80, 81
Macmillan, Harold (1894-1986), 413, 427, 428
Macready, Sir Gordon Nevil (1891-1956), 404
Manners, Lady Diana. *See* Cooper, Lady Diana, Viscountess Norwich (1892-1986)
Manning, Frederic (1882-1935), 178, 430, 434, 437, 440, 442
Mansfield, Katherine (1888-1923), 69, 415, 416, 431, 432, 433, 434, 437, 440
Marne, 326, 327, 328, 404
Marshall, Catherine Elizabeth (1880–1961), 116, 117, 121, 123, 124, 127, 129, 132
Mary, queen consort of George V (1867-1953), 115, 158
masculinity, 12, 17, 44, 166, 384, 385, 386, 396, 476, 479
Massingham, Henry William (1860-1924), 30, 93, 95, 123, 266
Masterman, Charles Frederick Gurney (1874-1927), 58, 65, 157, 159, 161, 183, 230, 236, 238, 241, 262, 272, 273, 289, 371, 517
Maxse, Sir Ivor (1862-1958), 403
Maxton, James (1885-1946), 72, 80, 81
Maxwell, Sir John Grenfell (1859-1929), 104
McKenna, Reginald (1863-1943), 86, 298, 300
medicine, 60, 351, 359
Meinertzhagen, Richard Henry (1878-1967), 305
memorials, 18, 155, 161, 387, 392, 394, 395, 475, 477, 479, 482, 507
Military Service Tribunals, 50, 125, 126
Milner, Alfred, Viscount Milner (1854-1925), 54, 77, 85, 87, 92, 261, 292, 294, 517
Ministry of Food, 115, 190, 208, 282, 421
Ministry of Information, 95, 155, 183, 229, 234, 237, 238, 272, 278, 288, 477
Ministry of Munitions, 74, 78, 208, 209, 210, 212, 214, 217, 282, 354, 355, 356, 357, 376
Mitchell, Hannah Maria (1872-1956), 115
Mitchell, Sir Peter Chalmers (1864-1945), 225, 230, 238, 239, 247
Monro, Sir Charles Carmichael (1860-1920), 403, 406
Montagu, John Walter Edward Scott, 2nd Baron Montagu of Beaulieu (1866-1929), 350
Montague, Charles Edward (1867-1928), 55, 161, 216, 218, 289, 398, 421, 428, 517
morale, 59, 93, 105, 168, 171, 174, 185, 215, 220, 224, 234, 237, 238, 269, 272, 275, 288, 319, 320, 321, 322, 464
Morel, Edmund Dene (1873-1924), 122, 138, 139, 140, 143, 144, 145, 146, 212
Morgan, John Pierpoint (1837-1913), 50
Morley, John, Viscount Morley of Blackburn (1838-1923), 55, 84, 87
Morrell, Lady Ottoline Violet Anne (1873-1938), 68
Moseley, Henry Gwyn Jeffreys (1887-1915), 59, 62, 352, 357
Muir, Ramsay (1872-1941), 65, 66, 517
Muirhead, John Henry (1855-1940), 65, 66
Munitions Inventions Department, 351, 354, 355, 358
Murphy, John Thomas (1888-1966), 72, 73, 75
museums, 18, 153, 194, 394, 402, 501, 502
music halls, 184, 195
Namier, Sir Lewis Bernstein (1888-1960), 59, 62, 66, 247, 268, 296, 297, 298, 518
Nash, John (1893-1977), 156
Nash, Paul (1889-1946), 155, 156, 157, 159, 161, 475, 478, 481, 484, 485
Nathan, Sir Matthew (1862-1939), 105
National Council Against Conscription, 211
National Council for Civil Liberties, 211
National Democratic Party, 77, 85
National Party, 85, 92, 146, 150
National Service League, 44
National Socialist Party, 78, 79, 85
National Union of Women's Suffrage Societies (NUWSS), 111, 113, 114, 116, 118, 126, 127, 128, 419, 426
National War Aims Committee (NWAC), 229, 231, 232, 233, 234, 251, 255, 256, 259, 268, 269, 286
Neutrality, 9, 16, 28, 30, 36, 62, 98, 127, 135, 230, 244, 245, 246, 247, 248, 267

INDEX

Nevinson, Christopher Richard Wynne (1889-1946), 155, 156, 157, 160, 161, 475, 477, 478, 479, 480, 481, 483, 484, 485, 523

Newbolt, Sir Henry John (1862-1938), 58, 180, 183, 184, 185, 340

Newton, Thomas Wodehouse Legh, 2nd Baron (1857-1942), 87, 129, 236, 238, 294

No Conscription Fellowship (NCF), 115, 123, 124, 126, 128, 129, 141, 211, 215

Noel-Buxton, Noel Edward Buxton, 1st Baron (1869-1948), 33, 127, 142

Northcliffe, Alfred Harmsworth, Viscount (1865-1922), 94, 95, 96, 97, 98, 99, 133, 137, 230, 237, 238, 242, 247, 248, 249, 287, 290

Novello, Ivor (1893-1951), 185, 186, 187, 188, 189, 197

nurses, 110, 114, 116, 118, 119, 162, 327, 362, 380, 449

Oman, Sir Charles William Chadwick (1860-1946), 22, 59, 62

Osler, Sir William (1849-1919), 60, 66, 351, 353, 518

Overseas-Club, 256, 264

Owen, Wilfred (1893-1918), 16, 58, 173, 174, 177, 323, 360, 411, 412, 414, 442, 443, 444, 445, 446, 448, 451, 457, 471, 486, 488

Oxenham, John (1852-1941), 174, 181, 451

pacifism, 21, 29, 113, 126, 127, 128, 324, 419

Page, Walter Hines (1855-1918), 244, 258, 518

Parker, Sir Gilbert (1862-1932), 58, 184, 241, 243, 248, 251, 257, 258, 262, 263, 510, 518

Parliamentary Recruiting Committee (PRC), 57, 231, 232, 233, 255, 256, 269, 279, 281, 282, 318

Parsons, Sir Charles Algernon (1854-1931), 60, 62

Passchendaele, 119, 209, 303, 317, 321, 326, 327, 328, 329, 344, 363, 392, 410, 411, 427, 472, 476

peace movement, 30, 99, 126, 127, 233

Pearse, Padraic (1879-1916), 103, 104, 107, 192

Pearson, George (1875-1973), 199, 202, 203, 204, 273, 466, 467

Peel, Dorothy Constance ["Mrs. C. S. Peel"] (1872-1934), 51, 115, 195, 371, 421

Pethick-Lawrence, Emmeline, Baronesss Pethick-Lawrence (1867-1954), 115, 129, 421, 428

Pethick-Lawrence, Frederick William, Baron Pethick-Lawrence (1871-1961), 123, 139, 140, 141

photography, 276, 278, 397, 476

Pinero, Sir Arthur Wing (1855-1934), 58, 169, 171, 172, 204, 455, 458, 459

Plumer, Herbert Charles Onslow, 1st Viscount Plumer (1857-1932), 404, 405, 406, 411

poison gas, 259, 286, 352, 354, 409

Ponsonby, Arthur, 1st Baron Ponsonby of Shulbrede (1871-1946), 94, 133, 138, 141, 144, 145, 146, 219, 226, 228, 289

Pope, Jessie (1868-1941), 111, 174, 181, 182

Pound, Ezra (1885-1972), 154

Press Bureau, 59, 62, 94, 211, 219, 220, 221, 236

Price, Morgan Philips (1885-1973), 139, 220

Prisoners, 16, 17, 20, 52, 235, 260, 314, 315, 325, 365, 454, 455, 456, 510, 511, 512, 519

promiscuity, 120

psychiatry, 359

Queen Mary's Army Auxiliary Corps, 114

Quiller-Couch, Sir Arthur Thomas (1863-1944), 58, 60, 67

Raemaekers, Louis (1869-1956), 161, 162, 242, 256, 282, 283, 284, 285

Randall, Harry (1860-1932), 197

Ransome, Arthur Mitchell (1884-1967), 220, 221

rationing, 115, 206, 208, 373, 421

Rawlinson, Sir Henry Seymour, Baron Rawlinson (1864-1925), 404, 406, 408, 409

Read, Sir Herbert Edward (1893-1968), 173, 174, 336, 428, 442, 443, 445, 448, 452

recruitment, 108, 111, 231, 255, 280, 282, 287, 311, 316, 357

Red Cross, 60, 63, 99, 110, 114, 160, 167, 180, 277, 330, 395, 426, 519

Redmond, John Edward (1856-1918), 103, 104, 109, 265, 518

Redmond, William Hoey Kearney (1861-1917), 104, 163, 336

rehabilitation, 157, 367

Repington, Charles à Court (1858-1925), 95, 221, 402

Reuters, 95, 98, 221, 222, 288

Rhondda, David Alfred Thomas, Viscount Rhondda (1856-1918), 208

Riddell, George Allardice, Baron Riddell (1865-1934), 95, 99, 216, 222, 223, 315

Rivers, William Halse Rivers (1864-1922), 360, 362, 363, 364, 524

Roberston, Sir William Robert (1860-1933), 298, 300, 302, 303, 403, 405

Robey, Sir George Edward (1869-1954), 187, 189, 196, 197, 202

Rodd, James Rennell, Baron Rennell (1858-1941), 22, 238

Roosevelt, Theodore (1858-1919), 251, 252, 258, 259

Rose, John Holland (1855-1942), 65, 67, 519

Rosenberg, Isaac (1890-1918), 173, 174, 177, 179, 429, 442, 443, 444, 445, 447, 448, 452

Rothermere, Harold Sidney Harmsworth, 1st Viscount (1868-1940), 98

Rowntree, Arnold Stephenson (1872-1951), 129, 139, 142

Royal Air Force, 111, 114, 303, 347, 348, 349, 350

Royal Flying Corps, 237, 277, 344, 347, 349

Royal Naval Air Service, 163, 339, 343, 344, 347, 429

Royden, Maude (1876-1956), 102, 112, 113, 127, 128, 131

530

INDEX

Runciman, Walter, 1st Viscount Runciman of Doxford (1870–1949), 88, 298, 300, 371
Russell, Bertrand, 3rd Earl Russell (1872-1970), 54, 58, 60, 61, 62, 63, 65, 67, 68, 69, 122, 124, 127, 129, 130, 132, 134, 139, 141, 144, 212, 429, 524
Russian Revolution, 73, 74, 84, 85, 93, 143, 221, 222, 240, 310, 380
Rutherford, Ernest, Baron Rutherford of Nelson (1871-1937), 59, 61, 63, 352
Sargent, John Singer (1856-1925), 156, 157, 160, 475, 480, 481
Sassoon, Siegfried (1886-1967), 60, 173, 174, 175, 177, 179, 196, 287, 323, 360, 363, 387, 411, 413, 414, 418, 421, 426, 429, 430, 434, 437, 441, 442, 443, 444, 445, 446, 447, 448, 449, 452, 457, 524
Schlieffen Plan, 28, 29
scientists, 59, 60, 62, 64, 67, 351, 357, 502
Scott, Charles Prestwich (1846-1932), 55, 88, 93, 95, 96
Scottish Labour Party, 81
Seely, John Edward Bernard, 1st Baron Mottistone (1868-1947), 405
Shakespeare, William (c.1564-1616), 67, 168, 170, 173, 196
Shaw, George Bernard (1856-1950), 58, 66, 69, 79, 133, 162, 168, 169, 170, 171, 172, 173, 182, 185, 191, 196, 421, 453, 454, 455, 459
shell-shock, 319, 320, 321, 351, 359, 361, 362, 363, 365, 426, 524
Sherriff, Robert Cedric (1896-1975), 18, 437, 453, 454, 459, 466
Shinwell, Emanuel (1884-1986), 80, 81, 215, 427
Sinclair, May (1863-1946), 58, 121, 163, 167, 182, 416
Sinclair, Upton (1878-1968), 251, 253, 257, 258
Sinn Fein, 107, 110, 266
Sitwell, Sir Francis Osbert Sacheverell, 5th Baronet (1892-1969), 174, 175, 176, 179, 419, 424, 444, 448, 452
Smillie, Robert (1857-1940), 81
Smith, Arthur Lionel (1850-1924), 63, 68
Smith, Frederick Edwin, 1st Earl of Birkenhead (1872-1930), 86, 219
Smith-Dorrien, Sir Horace Lockwood (1858-1930), 402, 403, 405, 406, 409
Smuts, Jan Christian (1870-1950), 85, 137, 144, 235, 263, 294, 300, 334, 345, 346, 351, 519
Snowden, Philip, Viscount Snowden (1864-1937), 78, 81, 85, 88, 131, 141
Socialist Labour Party, 85
Somme, 47, 88, 96, 104, 106, 107, 109, 125, 161, 162, 178, 184, 190
Sorley, Charles Hamilton (1895-1915), 173, 174, 177, 179, 442, 443, 445, 446, 448, 452
Souls, 55, 56, 70, 71
Spencer, Sir Stanley (1891-1959), 156, 394, 398, 475, 477, 480, 481, 485, 523
Spender, John Alfred (1862-1942), 55, 88, 91, 95, 96, 433
spies and spying, 118, 147, 149, 150, 162, 164, 201, 211, 212, 213, 214, 244, 251, 305, 306, 307, 308, 434, 465, 467, 473. *See also* espionage
spiritualism, 394
sport, 193
Spring-Rice, Sir Cecil Arthur (1859-1918), 244
Stanford, Sir Charles Villiers (1852-1924), 185, 190, 191, 193
state intervention, 372, 373
Steed, Henry Wickham (1871-1956), 96, 221, 226, 229, 230, 238, 239, 288
Stopes, Marie (1880-1958), 182, 381, 384
Strachey, John St. Loe (1860-1927), 96, 97, 244
Strachey, Lytton (1880-1932), 68, 69, 128, 141
strikes, 71, 79, 170
submarines, 61, 63, 211, 243, 245, 250, 259, 286, 336, 337, 341, 342, 345, 352. *See also* U-Boats
suffrage, 113, 115, 116, 127, 128, 139, 141, 419, 426
suffragettes, 111
Swanwick, Helena Maria (1864-1939), 116, 117, 126, 129, 130, 139, 142, 144, 421
Swinton, Sir Ernest Dunlop (1868-1951), 219, 222, 232
Sykes, Sir Frederick Hugh (1877-1954), 345, 346, 347, 350
Tarkington, Booth (1869-1946), 251, 252, 257, 258
Tawney, Richard Henry (1880-1962), 63, 79, 80, 81, 144, 207, 375, 377
television, 13, 15, 118, 279, 460, 469, 471, 498, 500, 502, 508
theatre, 41, 168, 170, 184, 185, 187, 193, 195, 196, 198, 217, 299, 323, 381, 454
Thomas, Philip Edward (1878-1917), 173, 174, 176, 179, 444, 446, 448, 452
Thomas, Sir William Beach (1868-1957), 96
Thomson, Sir Basil Home (1861-1939), 149, 212, 213, 214, 215
Thomson, Sir Joseph John (1856-1940), 63, 67, 352
Thwaites, Norman Graham (1872-1956), 242, 244
Tomb of the Unknown Warrior, 395
Townshend, Sir Charles Vere Ferrers (1861-1924), 333, 405
Toynbee, Arnold Joseph (1889-1975), 11, 59, 62, 63, 65, 68, 260, 268, 519
trade unions, 111, 115, 369
Tree, Sir Herbert Beerbohm (1852-1917), 70, 168, 169, 173, 522
trench journalism, 324
trench warfare, 174, 275, 311, 312, 316, 323, 352, 369, 462, 469
Trenchard, Hugh Montague, 1st Viscount Trenchard (1873-1956), 299, 303, 345, 346, 350
Turner, Sir Richard (1871-1967), 405
U-Boats, 183, 259, 282, 307, 341, 343, 513. *See also* submarines
Ulster Volunteer Force, 103, 104, 108

INDEX

Union of Democratic Control, 60, 61, 62, 63, 65, 79, 85, 89, 116, 122, 126, 127, 128, 129, 130, 131, 132, 133, 134, 135, 136, 138, 140, 141, 142, 143, 144, 145, 146, 211, 215, 293, 297, 502

Urban, Charles (1867-1942), 272, 273, 274

Vaughan Williams, Ralph (1872-1958), 190, 486, 489

venereal disease, 322, 361, 363, 364, 365, 385

Verdun, 327, 328

Victoria League, 56, 67, 68, 117, 231, 232, 256, 262, 266, 268, 366, 383

Voluntary Aid Detachment (VAD), 110, 117, 121

Voska, Emmanuel Viktor (1875-1960), 242, 244, 306

Wadsworth, Edward Alexander (1889-1949), 154, 155, 485, 523

Walpole, Sir Hugh (1884-1941), 167, 240, 432, 434, 438

war artists, 155, 156, 157, 278, 480

War Emergency Workers' National Committee, 71, 73, 77, 79, 81, 82

War Graves Commission, 395, 397, 477

War Propaganda Bureau. *See* Wellington House

Warburg, Aby (1866-1929), 224, 286, 289

Ward, Humphry, Mrs (1851-1920), 164, 182, 184, 257, 259, 433

Webb, Beatrice Potter (1858-1943), 71, 80, 81, 116, 429

Webb, Sidney James, 1st Baron Passfield (1859-1947), 71, 79, 142, 372

Wellington House, 58, 65, 155, 156, 183, 227, 229, 231, 234, 236, 237, 240, 241, 248, 251, 255, 256, 258, 259, 262, 265, 270, 272, 278, 289, 297, 477, 510

Wells, Herbert George (1866-1946), 58, 70, 79, 95, 133, 134, 137, 167, 182, 183, 194, 284, 293, 351, 355, 433, 434, 436, 438, 467

West, Rebecca, Dame (pseud. of Cicely Isabel Fairfield (1892-1983), 164, 416, 432, 433, 442

Wharton, Edith (1862-1937), 70, 251, 252, 257, 258, 259

Wheatley, John (1869-1930), 80

Wheeldon family, 86, 125, 213

Wheeldon, Alice (1866-1919), 123, 125, 213, 459

Whitlock, Brand (1869-1934), 244, 260

Wilde, Oscar (1854-1900), 70, 147, 149, 202, 203, 204, 384

Willcox, Sir William Henry (1870-1941), 360

Willert, Sir Arthur (b. 1882), 242, 244, 248

Williamson, Henry (1895-1977), 324, 335, 430, 434, 438, 441

Wilson, Sir Henry Hughes (1864-1922), 299, 304, 403, 408, 411

Wilson, Woodrow (1856-1924), 16, 18, 90, 128, 130, 131, 135, 138, 139, 235, 244, 248, 249, 251, 294, 296

Wiseman, Sir William (b. 1885), 242, 246, 249, 310

Wister, Owen (1860-1938), 252, 253, 259

Women Police, 117, 119, 120

Women's Army Auxiliary Corps, 111, 114, 117

Women's International League for Peace and Freedom, 115, 116, 121, 126, 129, 131, 142, 211, 421, 428

Women's Peace Crusade, 114, 126, 128, 140

Women's Royal Air Force (WRAF), 111, 114

Women's Social and Political Union (WSPU), 111, 112, 115, 118

Wood, Sir Henry Joseph (1869-1944), 185, 189, 191

Woolf, Leonard Sidney (1880-1969), 68, 69, 133, 134, 135, 137, 138, 139, 142, 146

Woolf, Virginia (1882-1941), 69, 113, 416, 430, 431, 432, 434, 438, 522

Wylie, William Evelyn (1881-1964), 105

Yeats, William Butler (1865-1939), 443, 444, 453, 454, 455, 460

Zangwill, Israel (1864-1926), 58, 139, 170, 183, 455, 460

zeppelins, 151, 153, 255, 264, 516

www.ingramcontent.com/pod-product-compliance
Lightning Source LLC
Chambersburg PA
CBHW081421300426
44108CB00016BA/2275